# Frommer's®

# Japan

## 8th Edition

### by Beth Reiber

### with Janie Spencer

Here's what the critics say about Frommer's:

"Amazingly easy to use. Very portable, very complete."

—*Booklist*

"Detailed, accurate, and easy-to-read information for all price ranges."
—*Glamour Magazine*

"Hotel information is close to encyclopedic."

—*Des Moines Sunday Register*

"Frommer's Guides have a way of giving you a real feel for a place."
—*Knight Ridder Newspapers*

WILEY
Wiley Publishing, Inc.

Published by:

## Wiley Publishing, Inc.

111 River St.
Hoboken, NJ 07030-5774

ISBN-13: 978-0-471-76391-8

ISBN-10: 0-471-76391-8

Editor: Christina Summers
Production Editor: Katie Robinson
Cartographer: Roberta Stockwell
Photo Editor: Richard Fox
Production by Wiley Indianapolis Composition Services

Front cover photo: Yamanashi: Mount Fuji and Churei Tower, cherry blossoms in bloom. Back cover photo: Schoolgirl writing with paintbrush.

For information on our other products and services or to obtain technical support, please contact our Customer Care Department within the U.S. at 800/762-2974, outside the U.S. at 317/572-3993 or fax 317/572-4002.

Wiley also publishes its books in a variety of electronic formats. Some content that appears in print may not be available in electronic formats.

Manufactured in the United States of America

5   4   3   2

# Contents

# List of Maps

*To my parents, who, while I was growing up in Kansas, always encouraged me to look farther than my own backyard.*

—Beth Reiber

*To Amanda, who helped me see a whole new Japan through a child's eye.*

—Janie Spencer

## Acknowledgments

We would like to thank some fine and very special people, without whose generous assistance and advice this book would not be possible. A special arigatoo goes to Naoto Aoyama, Marian Goldberg, Yoko Takano, Yumicie D'Avout, Satomi Sugiyama, and Yoko Tanaka of the Japan National Tourist Organization for their years of support and hard work. We would also like to thank the following for their regional expertise and the assistance they extended to us during our travels: Shizue Ishibashi of the Hokkaido Tourist Association; Sigenori Iwai of Noboribetsu; Toru Ishizawa and Jun Miura of the Akita Prefectural Tourist Federation; Masashi Kakuta and Kerianne Panos of Aomori Prefecture; Keiko Miki and Yoshihiko Nakagawa of Osaka City; Rie Tokura of Kyoto City; Yuichi Fukushima, Mutsko Itadani and Sayaka Bessho of the Okayama Prefectural Tourist Federation; Hirono Satoshi and Matsuo Shuichiro of the Shimane Prefectural Tourism Federation; Matthew Sleath of Matsue City; Masako Okibe and Keigo Sakomoto of the Hiroshima Prefectural Government; Manabu Kitsukawa and Rie Degawa of Takamatsu City; Yoriyuki Mizuno of the Benesse Art Site Naoshima; Kazuki Shiratori, Chizu Takeuchi, Hisashi Harada and Naomi Matsuda of the Ehime Prefectural Tourist Federation; Makoto Omiya of the Fukuoka Prefecture Tourist Assocation; Tomoko Matsuo and Yukiko Hisata of the Nagasaki Prefectural Tourist Federation; Mitsuo Matsuoka of the Kumamoto Prefectural Government; Satsuki Watanabe and Masaya Tojo of the Kagoshima Prefectural Tourist Federation; and Shu Nagatomo of the Miyazaki Prefectural Government. We'd also like to express our gratitude to Naoko Koizumi, Mariko Minami, Yoshiro Ushida, Stephan Pearlman and Naomi Ichikawa, Yoshi Owaki and Skip Cronin, Mutsuko Akesaka, Aki Yoshida, Jun Oda, and Mary Frances Fagan kindnesses too numerous to list. Debbie Howard gets kudos for her moral support, not to mention her years as a partner in crime researching Tokyo's nightlife, while Junko Matsuda gets a huge thanks for her tireless fact-checking skills and valuable knowledge of Tokyo. A very special thanks goes to our children—Matthias, Johannes, and Amanda—for putting up with our absences for as long as they can remember.

—Beth Reiber and Janie Spencer

## An Invitation to the Reader

In researching this book, we discovered many wonderful places—hotels, restaurants, shops, and more. We're sure you'll find others. Please tell us about them, so we can share the information with your fellow travelers in upcoming editions. If you were disappointed with a recommendation, we'd love to know that, too. Please write to:

*Frommer's Japan,* 8th Edition
Wiley Publishing, Inc. • 111 River St. • Hoboken, NJ 07030-5774

## An Additional Note

Please be advised that travel information is subject to change at any time—and this is especially true of prices. We therefore suggest that you write or call ahead for confirmation when making your travel plans. The authors, editors, and publisher cannot be held responsible for the experiences of readers while traveling. Your safety is important to us, however, so we encourage you to stay alert and be aware of your surroundings. Keep a close eye on cameras, purses, and wallets, all favorite targets of thieves and pickpockets.

## About the Authors

Long before she could read, **Beth Reiber** spent hours pouring over her grandparents' latest *National Geographic* magazines. After living several years in Germany as a freelance travel writer writing for major U.S. newspapers and in Tokyo as editor of *Far East Traveler*, she authored several Frommer's guides, including *Frommer's Tokyo* and *Frommer's Hong Kong.* She also contributes to several Frommer's guides, including *Frommer's Europe by Rail, Frommer's China,* and *Frommer's USA.* When not on the road, she resides in Lawrence, Kansas, with her two sons, a dog, and a cat.

**Janie Spencer** spent 7 years in Japan working for *Kyodo News Service* and *Tokyo Journal,* as well as freelancing for many Asian-based magazines including *Discovery* and *Far East Traveler.* She now lives near Paris with her husband and daughter.

## Frommer's Star Ratings, Icons & Abbreviations

Every hotel, restaurant, and attraction listing in this guide has been ranked for quality, value, service, amenities, and special features using a **star-rating system.** In country, state, and regional guides, we also rate towns and regions to help you narrow down your choices and budget your time accordingly. Hotels and restaurants are rated on a scale of zero (recommended) to three stars (exceptional). Attractions, shopping, nightlife, towns, and regions are rated according to the following scale: zero stars (recommended), one star (highly recommended), two stars (very highly recommended), and three stars (must-see).

In addition to the star-rating system, we also use **seven feature icons** that point you to the great deals, in-the-know advice, and unique experiences that separate travelers from tourists. Throughout the book, look for:

| Finds | Special finds—those places only insiders know about |
| Fun Fact | Fun facts—details that make travelers more informed and their trips more fun |
| Kids | Best bets for kids and advice for the whole family |
| Moments | Special moments—those experiences that memories are made of |
| Overrated | Places or experiences not worth your time or money |
| Tips | Insider tips—great ways to save time and money |
| Value | Great values—where to get the best deals |

The following **abbreviations** are used for credit cards:

| AE | American Express | DISC | Discover | V | Visa |
| DC | Diners Club | MC | MasterCard | | |

## Frommers.com

Now that you have the guidebook to a great trip, visit our website at **www.frommers.com** for travel information on more than 3,000 destinations. With features updated regularly, we give you instant access to the most current trip-planning information available. At Frommers.com, you'll also find the best prices on airfares, accommodations, and car rentals—and you can even book travel online through our travel booking partners. At Frommers.com, you'll also find the following:

- Online updates to our most popular guidebooks
- Vacation sweepstakes and contest giveaways
- Newsletter highlighting the hottest travel trends
- Online travel message boards with featured travel discussions

# What's New in Japan

**THE 21ST-CENTURY TRAVELER** Since Japan uses a different system for **mobile phones** that is incompatible with GSM or the U.S. system, most international visitors must rent cellphones for travel in Japan. You can, however, now use your **mobile phone number** in Japan by using Vodafone or NTT DoCoMo's 3G (3rd generation) service areas. Simply bring your own SIM card and insert it into a rental phone or your own 3G handset. For more information, contact your mobile phone service provider, Vodafone (www.vodafone-rental.jp/eng/index.html), or NTT (http://roaming.nttdocomo.co.jp/index.html).

**GETTING AROUND JAPAN** The Japan Railways (JR) Group, which operates most trains in Japan including the Shinkansen bullet train, has regrettably **suspended** its free online seat-reservation service at **www.world.eki-net.com**. A new online reservation system may be revived in the future; check www.japanrail.com for updates.

**ACCOMMODATIONS Toyoko Inn** (www.toyoko-inn.com), a domestic chain of business hotels, has raised the bar on cheap accommodations (and forced other chains to update their facilities) by offering lobby computers with free Internet access, free domestic calls from lobby phones, free movie channels (often in English), and free Japanese breakfast. More than 100 Toyoko Inns are spread throughout Japan, mostly in handy locations like downtown or next to major train stations.

**FAST FACTS** In many cities, such as Tokyo, Osaka, and Sapporo, there are **nonsmoking ordinances** that ban smoking on sidewalks but allow it in designated areas, usually near train stations. Many restaurants nowadays have nonsmoking sections, though bars do not. Most hotels have designated nonsmoking floors, except for some business hotels and Japanese-style inns.

Hotels and restaurants have long added a 5% **government tax** to their published prices, which, together with a 10% to 15% service charge in the more expensive establishments, can add up to real sticker shock when it comes time to pay the bill. A new law now requires hotels and restaurants to include the tax in their published rates. However, some smaller ma-and-pa operations have yet to comply, especially when it comes to outdated English-language menus. Service charge is still extra, as is a local hotel tax in Tokyo.

**TOKYO The Tourist Information Center (TIC)** has extended its hours. At the airport, the TIC in both terminals is now open from 8am to 8pm daily. The downtown TIC, in Yurakucho, is now open daily 9am to 5pm.

Several subway and train lines now have **women-only compartments** on their busiest routes, available weekdays until 9:30am.

**KYOTO** Although there's a **Kyoto City Tourist Information Office** on the second floor of Kyoto Station, it's for Japanese only. Foreign visitors are shunted to

the roomier but less convenient **Kyoto Tourist Information** on the ninth floor of Isetan department store in Kyoto Station (© **075/344-3300;** open daily 10am–6pm, closed the second and fourth Tues of every month), which can prove quite a challenge if you're toting luggage and battling shoppers for space in the crowded elevators. On the plus side, you can make reservations here for inexpensive lodging throughout Japan free of charge.

Two Kyoto landmark hotels have closed. The **Kyoto Park Hotel** has closed for several years due to a complete overhaul, while the **Ladies' Hotel Chorakukan** has closed its hotel operation forever to make way as a wedding venue. (Its restaurant and coffee shop remain open.)

**THE REST OF WESTERN HONSHU Nagoya** Japan's newest international airport, formally known as the Central Japan International Airport but dubbed **Centrair** (www.centrair.jp/en), is a sleek facility with hotels, shopping (including Japan's largest duty-free store), and even a hot-spring bath. Trains connect to Nagoya Station, with Shinkansen service onward, in 40 minutes.

In **Kanazawa**, the new **21st Century Museum of Contemporary Art** (© **076/ 220-2800;** www.kanazawa21.jp), located near famed Kenrokuen Garden, is a striking circular building with sunlit galleries and darkened rooms that display art from the past 15 years, concentrating on Japanese artists born after 1965 and contemporary works from around the world.

Many prefectures and cities in Japan offer so-called Welcome Cards to international visitors, which provide discounts to various attractions and establishments. **Matsue** goes one step further by doing away with the card and allowing international visitors to simply show their passports to receive 50% discounts on admission prices at major attractions around town.

A **new boat service,** provided by Aqua Net Hiroshima (© **082/240-5955**), operates from Motoyasu-bashi Bridge near downtown **Hiroshima** directly to Miyajima island in 45 minutes, with five departures daily (except during winter months). Note, however, that service is suspended in inclement weather and when the tide is low.

**KYUSHU** Japan's first new national museum to open in 100 years made its debut in nearby Daizafu in 2005. The **Kyushu National Museum** (© **092/918-2807;** www.kyuhaku.jp) explores Japan's cultural heritage and Kyushu's role in international exchange through the centuries.

Thanks to the new Kyushu Shinkansen that rolled into town a couple of years ago, connecting **Kagoshima** to Fukuoka in 2 hours and 11 minutes, Kagoshima's revamped Kagoshima Chuo Station (formerly called Nishi Kagoshima Station) includes Amu Plaza, a shopping and dining complex that provides more options in what was once a culinary wasteland. More dining options are available at Dolphin Port, a new shopping and dining complex just a few minutes' walk from the Sakurajima ferry pier and aquarium. Similar changes can be expected in Kumamoto when Shinkansen service is extended to that city in 2011.

Hot-spring baths that employ lots of natural woods and take advantage of scenic views are the rage nowadays. The trend is especially in evidence at the Sheraton Grande Ocean Resort's new **Shosenkyu** deluxe hot-spring spa (© **0985/ 21-1133**), nestled in a pine forest with both indoor and outdoor baths.

In **Beppu,** Suginoi Palace, with one of Japan's most famous hot-spring baths, has closed its hangarlike facility and replaced it with sophisticated baths that take advantage of a hillside perch with great views toward the sea, including outdoor baths with headrests so you can recline as you gaze upon the view.

# The Best of Japan

**H**ardly a day goes by that you don't hear something about Japan, whether the subject is trade, travel, cuisine, the arts, or Japanese imports ranging from Sony and Toyota to karaoke and anime. Yet Japan remains something of an enigma to people in the Western world. What best describes this Asian nation? Is it the giant producer of cars, computers, and a whole array of sleek electronic goods that compete favorably with the best in the West? Or is it still the land of the geisha and bonsai, the punctilious tea ceremony, and the delicate art of flower arrangement? Has it become, in its outlook and popular culture, a country more Western than Asian? Or has it retained its unique ancient traditions while forging a central place in the modern industrialized world?

In fact, Japan is an intricate blend of East and West. Its cities may look Westernized—often disappointingly so—but beyond first impressions there's very little about this Asian nation that could lull you into thinking you're in the West. Yet Japan also differs greatly from its Asian neighbors. Although it borrowed much from China in its early development, including Buddhism and its writing system, the island nation remained steadfastly isolated from the rest of the world throughout much of its history, usually deliberately so. Until World War II, it had never been successfully invaded; and for more than 200 years, while the West was stirring with the awakenings of democracy and industrialism, Japan completely closed its doors to the outside world and remained a tightly structured feudalistic society with almost no outside influence.

It's been only some 140 years since Japanese opened their doors, embracing Western products wholeheartedly, yet at the same time altering them and making them unquestionably their own. Thus, that modern high-rise may look Western, but it may contain a rustic-looking restaurant with open charcoal grills, corporate offices, a pachinko parlor, a high-tech bar with views of Mount Fuji, a McDonald's, an acupuncture clinic, a computer showroom, and a rooftop shrine. Your pizza may come with octopus, beer gardens are likely to be fitted with Astroturf, and "parsley" refers to unmarried women older than 25 (because parsley is what's left on a plate). City police patrol on bicycles, garbage collectors attack their job with the vigor of a well-trained army, and white-gloved elevator operators, working in some of the world's swankiest department stores, bow and thank you as you exit.

Because of this unique synthesis of East and West into a culture that is distinctly Japanese, Japan is not easy for Westerners to comprehend. Discovering it is like peeling an onion—you uncover one layer only to discover more layers underneath. Thus, no matter how long you stay in Japan, you never stop learning something new about it—and to me that constant discovery is one of the most fascinating aspects of being here.

## 1 The Best Travel Experiences

Long ago, Japanese ranked the three best of almost every natural wonder and attraction in their country: the three best gardens, the three best scenic spots, the three best waterfalls, even the three best bridges. But choosing the "best" of anything is inherently subjective, and decades—even centuries—have passed since some of the original "three best" were so designated. Still, lists can be useful for establishing priorities. To help you get the most out of your stay, I've compiled this list of what I consider the best Japan has to offer based on years of traveling through the country. From the weird to the wonderful, the profound to the profane, the obvious to the obscure, these recommendations should fire your imagination and launch you toward discoveries of your own.

- **Making a Pilgrimage to a Temple or Shrine:** From mountaintop shrines to neighborhood temples, Japan's religious structures rank among the nation's most popular attractions. Usually devoted to a particular deity, they're visited for specific reasons: Shopkeepers call on Fushimi-Inari Shrine outside Kyoto, dedicated to the goddess of rice and therefore prosperity, while couples wishing for a happy marriage head to Kyoto's Jishu Shrine, a shrine to the deity of love. Shrines and temples are also the sites for most of Japan's major festivals. See chapter 2, the regional chapters, and "The Best Temples & Shrines" section, below, for more on Japan's temples and shrines.

- **Taking a Communal Hot-Spring Bath:** No other people on earth bathe as enthusiastically, as frequently, and for such duration as Japanese. Their many hot-spring resorts—thought to cure all sorts of ailments as well as simply make you feel good—range

from hangarlike affairs to outdoor baths with views of the countryside. No matter what the setup, you'll soon warm to the ritual of soaping up, rinsing off, and then soaking in near-scalding waters. Hot-spring spas are located almost everywhere in Japan, from Kyushu to Hokkaido; see regional chapters for more information.

- **Participating in a Festival:** With Shintoism and Buddhism as its major religions, and temples and shrines virtually everywhere, Japan has multiple festivals every week. These celebrations, which range from huge processions of wheeled floats to those featuring horseback archery and ladder-top acrobatics, can be lots of fun; you may want to plan your trip around one. See the "Japan Calendar of Events" in chapter 2 for a list of some of the most popular festivals.

- **Dining on Japanese Food:** There's more to Japanese cuisine than sushi, and part of what makes travel here so fascinating is the variety of national and regional dishes. Every prefecture, it seems, has its own style of noodles, its special vegetables, and its delicacies. If money is no object, order kaiseki, a complete meal of visual and culinary finesse. See the "Tips on Dining, Japanese Style" section of chapter 2, the "Where to Dine" sections in the regional chapters, and "The Best Culinary Experiences," later in this chapter, for more on Japanese food.

- **Viewing the Cherry Blossoms:** Nothing symbolizes the coming of spring so vividly to Japanese as the appearance of the cherry blossoms—and nothing so amazes visitors as the way Japanese gather under the blossoms to celebrate the season with

food, drink, dance, and karaoke. See the "Japan Calendar of Events" in chapter 2 for cherry blossom details.

- **Riding the Shinkansen Bullet Train:** Asia's fastest train whips you across the countryside at more than 290km (180 miles) an hour as you relax, see the country's rural countryside, and dine on boxed meals filled with local specialties of the area through which you're speeding. See "Getting Around Japan" in chapter 2 for more.

- **Staying in a Ryokan:** Japan's legendary service reigns supreme in a top-class ryokan, a traditional Japanese inn. Staying in one is the height of both luxury and simplicity: You'll bathe in a Japanese tub, feast your eyes on lovely views (usually a Japanese garden) past shoji screens, dine like a king in your own room, and sleep on a futon. See "Tips on Accommodations" in chapter 2 and the "Where to Stay" sections in the regional chapters for more on ryokan.

- **Shopping in a Department Store:** Japan's department stores are among the best in the world, offering everything from food to designer clothing to electronics to kimono and traditional crafts. Service also is among the best in the world: If you arrive when the store opens, staff will be lined up at the front door to bow as you enter. See the "Shopping" sections throughout this book.

- **Attending a Kabuki Play:** Based on universal themes and designed to appeal to the masses, Kabuki plays are extravaganzas of theatrical displays, costumes, and scenes—but mostly they're just plain fun. See

"Cultural Snapshots: Japanese Arts in a Nutshell" in appendix A and the Kabuki section of "Tokyo After Dark" in chapter 5.

- **Strolling Through Tokyo's Nightlife District:** Every major city in Japan has its own nightlife district, but probably none is more famous, more wicked, or more varied than Tokyo's Kabuki-cho in Shinjuku, which offers everything from hole-in-the-wall bars to strip joints, discos, and gay clubs. See "Tokyo After Dark" in chapter 5.

- **Seeing Mount Fuji:** It may not seem like much of an accomplishment to see Japan's most famous and tallest mountain, visible from 161km (100 miles) away. But the truth is, it's hardly ever visible except during the winter months and rare occasions when the air is clear. Catching your first glimpse of the giant peak is truly breathtaking and something you'll never forget, whether you see it from aboard the Shinkansen, from a Tokyo skyscraper, or from a nearby national park. If you want to climb it, be prepared for a group experience— 600,000 people climb Mount Fuji every year. See "Climbing Japan's Most Famous Mountain: Mount Fuji" in chapter 6 for more information.

- **Spending a Few Days in Kyoto:** If you see only one city in Japan, Kyoto should be it. Japan's capital from 794 to 1868, Kyoto is one of Japan's finest ancient cities, boasting some of the country's best temples, Japanese-style inns, traditional restaurants, shops, and gardens. See chapter 8 for extensive information on the city.

## 2 The Best Temples & Shrines

- **Sensoji Temple** (Tokyo): The capital's oldest temple is also its liveliest.

Throngs of visitors and stalls selling both traditional and kitschy items

lend it a festival-like atmosphere. This is the most important temple to see in Tokyo. See p. 176.

- **Meiji Jingu Shrine** (Tokyo): Tokyo's most venerable and refined Shinto shrine honors the Emperor Meiji and his empress with simple yet dignified architecture surrounded by a dense forest. This is a great refuge in the heart of the city. See p. 173.
- **Kotokuin Temple** (Kamakura): This temple is home to the Great Buddha, Japan's second-largest bronze image, which was cast in the 13th century and sits outdoors against a magnificent wooded backdrop. The Buddha's face has a wonderful expression of contentment, serenity, and compassion. See p. 224.
- **Hase Kannon Temple** (Kamakura): Although this temple is famous for its 9m-tall (30-ft.) Kannon of Mercy, the largest wooden image in Japan, it's most memorable for its thousands of small statues of Jizo, the guardian deity of children, donated by parents of miscarried, stillborn, or aborted children. It's a rather haunting vision. See p. 224.
- **Toshogu Shrine** (Nikko): Dedicated to Japan's most powerful shogun, Tokugawa Ieyasu, this shrine is the nation's most elaborate and opulent, made with 2.4 million sheets of gold leaf. It's set in a forest of cedar. See p. 227.
- **Kiyomizu Temple** (Kyoto): One of Japan's best-known temples with a structure imitated by lesser temples around the country, Kiyomizu commands an exalted spot on a steep hill with a sweeping view over Kyoto. The pathway leading to the shrine is lined with pottery and souvenir shops, and the temple grounds have open-air pavilions where you can drink beer or eat noodles. Don't neglect the smaller **Jishu Shrine** on its grounds—it's dedicated to the god of love. See p. 318.
- **Sanjusangendo Hall** (Kyoto): Japan's longest wooden building contains the spectacular sight of more than 1,000 life-size wood-carved statues, row upon row of the thousand-handed Kannon of Mercy. See p. 319.
- **Kinkakuji (Temple of the Golden Pavilion)** (Kyoto): Constructed in the 14th century as a shogun's retirement villa, this three-story pavilion shimmers in gold leaf and is topped with a bronze phoenix; it's a beautiful sight when the sun shines and the sky's blue. See p. 319.
- **Todaiji Temple** (Nara): Japan's largest bronze Buddha sits in the largest wooden structure in the world, making it the top attraction in this former capital. While not as impressive as the Great Buddha's dramatic outdoor stage in Kamakura (see above), the sheer size of Todaiji Temple and its Buddha make this a sight not to be missed if you're in the Kansai area. See p. 340.
- **Horyuji Temple** (Nara): Despite the fact that Todaiji Temple with its Great Buddha (see above) gets all the glory, true seekers of Buddhist art and history head to the sacred grounds of Horyuji Temple with its treasures and ancient buildings. See p. 341.
- **Ise Grand Shrines** (Ise): Although there's not much to see, these shrines are the most venerated Shinto shrines in all of Japan, and pilgrims have been flocking here for centuries. Amazingly, the Inner Shrine, which contains the Sacred Mirror, is razed and reconstructed on a new site every 20 years according to strict rules governing purification in the Shinto religion. Follow the age-old route of former pilgrims after you visit the shrines, and stop for a meal in the nearby Okage Yokocho District. See p. 359.

- **Itsukushima Shrine** (Miyajima): The huge red *torii* (the traditional entry gate of a shrine) standing in the waters of the Seto Inland Sea is one of the most photographed landmarks in Japan and signals the approach to this shrine. Built over the tidal flats on a gem of an island called Miyajima, it's considered one of Japan's most scenic spots. At night, the shrine is illuminated. See p. 460.

- **Kotohiragu Shrine** (Kotohira, on Shikoku): One of Japan's oldest and most popular shrines beckons at the top of 785 granite steps on the Yashima Plateau with great views of the Seto Inland Sea, but for most Japanese, it's the "I made it!" that counts. See p. 468.

- **Dazaifu Tenmangu Shrine** (Fukuoka): Established in 905 to deify the god of scholarship, this immensely popular shrine has a festive atmosphere and is popular with students wishing to pass school exams. The road leading to the shrine is lined with souvenir and craft shops; the new Kyushu National Museum is an escalator ride away. See p. 489.

## 3 The Best Gardens

- **Hama Rikyu Garden** (Tokyo): Considered by some to be the best garden in Tokyo, this peaceful oasis has origins stretching back 300 years when it served as a retreat for a former feudal lord and as duck-hunting grounds for the Tokugawa shogun. Surrounded by water on three sides, it contains a tidal pool, moon-viewing pavilions, and teahouses. See p. 181.

- **Sankeien Garden** (Yokohama): Historic villas, tea arbors, a farmhouse, a pagoda, and other authentic buildings, all set in a century-old landscaped garden with ponds and streams, make this one of the most interesting and picturesque gardens in Japan. See p. 239.

- **Ryoanji Temple** (Kyoto): Japan's most famous Zen rock garden, laid out at the end of the 15th century, consists of moss-covered boulders and raked pebbles enclosed by an earthen wall. It is said that it's impossible to see all 15 rocks from any vantage point; see if you can. Come early in the morning for some peaceful meditation. See p. 320.

- **Katsura Imperial Villa** (Kyoto): Designed by Japan's most famous gardener, Kobori Enshu, the garden surrounding this imperial villa is, in my view, Japan's most beautiful. A "strolling garden," its view changes with every step but is always complete, perfectly balanced, and in harmony. It's well worth the extra effort involved to see it. See p. 330.

- **Saihoji** (Kyoto): Popularly known as the Moss Temple, Saihoji is Japan's most famous moss garden, with more than 100 varieties spread throughout the grounds, giving off an iridescent glow. It's especially beautiful after a rainfall. See p. 331.

- **Kenrokuen Garden** (Kanazawa): Considered by some to be Japan's grandest landscape garden (and rated one of the "three best"), Kenrokuen is also one of the largest. The garden took 150 years to complete and consists of ponds, streams, rocks, mounds, trees, grassy expanses, and footpaths. Best of all, no tall buildings detract from the views. After Katsura (see above), this is my top choice. See p. 368.

- **Koko-en** (Himeji): It isn't old (it was laid out in 1992), but this is a wonderful surprise package of nine small

gardens, each one different but typical of gardens during the Edo Period, which lasted from 1603 to 1867. Upon seeing what can be accomplished with skill and money in little more than a decade, some gardeners may turn green with envy. See p. 419.

- **Korakuen Garden** (Okayama): Rated one of Japan's three most beautiful gardens, Korakuen was completed in 1700 and incorporates the surrounding hills and Okayama Castle into its design. It's definitely worth a visit if you're in the vicinity, though personally, I like Kenrokuen (see above) more. See p. 423.

- **Ritsurin Park** (Takamatsu): Dating from the 17th century, this former private retreat of the ruling Matsudaira clan is an exquisite strolling garden that incorporates Mount Shiun in its landscaping and boasts 1,600 pine trees and 350 cherry trees. Stop for tea in the Feudal-Era teahouse and contemplate the view at leisure. See p. 467.

- **Sengan'en** (Kagoshima): Laid out more than 300 years ago by the Shimazu clan, this summer retreat with a 25-room villa was known for its poem-composing parties, held beside a rivulet that still exists. After touring the garden and villa, be sure to visit the nearby museum with relics belonging to the Shimadzu family. This garden is one of my favorites. See p. 525.

## 4 The Best Castles, Palaces & Villas

- **Matsumoto Castle** (Matsumoto): Popularly known as the Crow Castle due to its black color, this small castle boasts the oldest **keep** *(donjon)* in Japan (more than 400 years old). A moon-viewing room was added in 1635, and exhibited inside the castle is a superb collection of Japanese matchlocks and samurai armor dating from the mid–16th century through the Edo Period. Volunteer guides stand ready for personal tours. See p. 258.

- **Kyoto Imperial Palace** (Kyoto): Home to Japan's imperial family from the 14th century to the 19th century, this palace is praised for its Heian design and graceful garden. Good news for travelers: Guided tours of the palace are free. See p. 315.

- **Nijo Castle** (Kyoto): One of the few castles built by the mighty Tokugawa shogunate as a residence rather than for defense, Nijo Castle is where the shogun stayed whenever he was in Kyoto. It's famous for its creaking floorboards that warned of enemy intruders. The castle is considered the quintessence of Momoyama architecture. See p. 283.

- **Katsura Imperial Villa** (Kyoto): Built in the 1600s by a brother of the emperor, this villa and garden are considered to be among the best—if not the best—in traditional architecture and landscape gardening. More than anyplace else, the villa illustrates the life of refinement enjoyed by 17th-century nobility, when leisurely pursuits included such activities as moon viewing. See p. 330.

- **Osaka Castle** (Osaka): Although just a reproduction of what was once the mightiest castle in the land, Osaka Castle still impresses with its sheer size. Inside you'll find a high-tech museum detailing the life and times of Toyotomi Hideyoshi, the warrior general who built the castle. See p. 385.

- **Himeji Castle** (Himeji): Said to resemble a white heron poised in flight over the plains, this is quite

simply Japan's most beautiful castle. With its extensive gates, moats, turrets, and maze of passageways, it has survived virtually intact since feudal times. If you see only one castle in Japan, make it this one. See p. 418.

- **Matsue Castle** (Matsue): This 17th-century castle is one of Japan's few remaining original castles (not a reconstruction). It features a five-story donjon with samurai gear and artifacts belonging to the ruling Matsudaira clan. See p. 438.

- **Matsuyama Castle** (Matsuyama): Occupying a hill above the city, this is also one of the few original castles left in Japan. It boasts good views over Matsuyama from its three-story donjon as well as a collection of armor and swords of the Matsudaira clan. See p. 475.

- **Kumamoto Castle** (Kumamoto): Although a ferroconcrete reconstruction not nearly as huge as the original, this massive castle is still an impressive sight, especially at night when it's illuminated. It's famous for its curved walls, which made invasion virtually impossible. The interior houses a museum with palanquins, armor, swords, and other artifacts of the former ruling clans. See p. 514.

- **Tamozawa Imperial Villa** (Nikko): Comprised of a 1632 villa and an 1899 expansion, this 106-room villa was the home of a prince who later became emperor. You can learn about traditional Japanese architectural details and lifestyles of the aristocracy on self-guided tours, and unlike Japan's other imperial villas, it does not require a reservation. See p. 232.

## 5 The Best Museums

- **Tokyo National Museum** (Tokyo): Even professed museumphobes should make a point of visiting the National Museum, the largest repository of Japanese arts in the world. Lacquerware, china, kimono, samurai armor, swords, woodblock prints, religious art, and more are on display, making this the best place in Japan to view Japanese antiques and decorative objects. If you visit only one museum in Japan, this should be the one. See p. 177.

- **Edo-Tokyo Museum** (Tokyo): Housed in a high-tech modern building, this ambitious museum chronicles the fascinating and somewhat tumultuous history of Tokyo (known as Edo during the Feudal Era) with models, replicas, artifacts, and dioramas. See p. 172.

- **Hakone Open-Air Museum** (Chokoku-no-Mori, Hakone): Beautifully landscaped grounds and

spectacular scenery showcase approximately 700 20th-century sculptures, from Giacomo and Rodin to Henry Moore. Here, too, is the Picasso Pavilion, housing 200 of the artist's works. See p. 246.

- **Japan Ukiyo-e Museum** (Matsumoto): One of the best woodblock-print museums in Japan, this museum displays the largest collection of prints in the world on a rotating basis. A must-see in Matsumoto. See p. 259.

- **Hida Minzoku Mura Folk Village** (Takayama): Picturesquely situated around a pond with flowers, more than 30 shingled and thatched farmhouses—many transported from the surrounding Japan Alps—are filled with farm implements and objects of daily life, providing fascinating insight into the life and times of the extended families that once inhabited them. See p. 268.

- **Inro Museum** (Takayama): Of Takayama's many specialty museums, this one is my favorite: It houses Japan's largest collection of small containers *(inro)* with toggles *(netsuke)* that were once standard accessories of the kimono. You could spend hours looking at these miniature works of art. See p. 270.

- **Museum Meiji Mura** (Nagoya): This open-air architectural museum is an absolute treasure with more than 60 original buildings and structures dating from the Meiji Period situated on 100 beautifully landscaped hectares (250 acres) on the shore of a lake. Western-style homes, churches, a Kabuki theater, a bathhouse, a prison, a brewery, and much more are open for viewing and filled with furniture and household items. Mail a postcard from an authentic post office, buy candy from an old candy store, and drink tea in the lobby of the original Imperial Hotel, which was designed by Frank Lloyd Wright. See p. 352.

- **Ishikawa Prefectural Museum for Traditional Products and Crafts** (Kanazawa): Kanazawa is famous for its handcrafted items, including gold leaf, umbrellas, stringed instruments, Buddhist altars, pottery, and more. English-language explanations, a detailed pamphlet, and an audio guide explain how they're made. See p. 369.

- **Disaster Reduction and Human Renovation Institution** (Kobe): You can't tell by its name, but this excellent museum is devoted to Kobe's 1995 earthquake, with films, dioramas, and exhibits detailing the city's destruction and rebirth. See p. 405.

- **Ohara Museum of Art** (Kurashiki): Founded in 1930, this museum just keeps getting better, with works by both Western and Japanese greats spread throughout several buildings. Its location in the picturesque Kurashiki historic district is a bonus. See p. 431.

- **Adachi Museum** (Matsue): This museum near Matsue combines two of my passions—art and gardens—making it a winner. Japanese modern art is the focus indoors, while the perfectly landscaped garden—one of Japan's best—comes into view through framed windows, making it part of the art in a very surreal way. See p. 442.

- **Louis C. Tiffany Museum and Gardens** (Matsue): This, one of the world's best collections of Tiffany paintings, furniture, ceramics, stained-glass windows, and jewelry, will take your breath away—and make you wonder how much insurance the museum pays in this earthquake-prone land. See p. 440.

- **Peace Memorial Museum** (Hiroshima): Japan's most thought-provoking museum contains exhibits examining Hiroshima's militaristic past, the events leading up to the explosion of the world's first atomic bomb, the city's terrible destruction, and its active antinuclear movement. See p. 450.

- **Fukuoka Asian Art Museum** (Fukuoka): This fascinating museum is devoted to contemporary and modern art from around Asia, including the Philippines, Indonesia, Malaysia, Thailand, China, Korea, and India. See p. 488.

- **Benesse Art Site Naoshima** (Takamatsu): This is not a single museum, but rather an island in the Seto Inland Sea that's devoted to cutting-edge art, with two museums (both designed by Tadao Ando) and interactive art installations in traditional Japanese buildings. There's no other place in Japan quite like this. See p. 470.

## 6 The Best National Parks

- **Nikko National Park:** This 80,000-hectare (200,000-acre) national park centers on the sumptuous Toshogu Shrine with its mausoleum for Tokugawa Ieyasu, majestic cedars, and lakeside resorts. See p. 228.

- **Fuji-Hakone-Izu National Park:** Boasting magnificent Mount Fuji at its core, this popular weekend getaway beckons vacationing Tokyoites with its many hot-spring spas, stunning close-up views of Mount Fuji, sparkling lakes, historic attractions relating to the famous Feudal-Era Tokaido Highway, and coastal areas of Izu Peninsula. One of the best ways to see Hakone is via a circular route that involves travel on a two-car mountain streetcar, a cable car, a ropeway, and a boat; the delightful journey offers wonderful scenery and interesting sights along the way. See p. 242.

- **Japan Alps National Park:** Encompassing Honshu's most impressive mountain ranges and the site of the 1998 Winter Olympics, this national park offers skiing as well as unique villages worth a visit in their own right. See p. 256.

- **Ise-Shima National Park:** Boasting a rugged seascape of capes, inlets, and islets, this park is the birthplace of cultivated pearls. It's famous for its bays dotted with pearl-cultivating oyster rafts, its female divers, a pearl museum, plus a top-notch aquarium and the Ise Grand Shrines, Japan's most venerable shrines. Two theme parks are also located here. See p. 358.

- **Seto-Naikai (Inland Sea) National Park:** Covering 650 sq. km (251 sq. miles) of water, islands, islets, and coastline, this sea park stretches from Kobe in the east to Beppu in the west. It's studded with numerous islands of all sizes, the most famous of which is Miyajima, home of the Itsukushima Shrine. Cruises ply the waters of the Seto Inland Sea, as do regular ferries sailing between Honshu, Shikoku, and Kyushu. The adventuresome can even cycle across the Seto Inland Sea via the Shimanami Kaido route linking Honshu with Shikoku (see "The Best Outdoor Adventures," below). See p. 452.

- **Unzen-Amakusa National Park:** At western Kyushu's high-altitude national park, you can climb Mount Fugen (1,229m/4,462 ft. above sea level), relax in a hot-spring bath, and take a walk through the Hells, the park's extrasteamy sulfur springs. See p. 508.

- **Towada-Hachimantai National Park:** Tohoku's most popular park beckons with scenic lakes, rustic hot-spring spas, hiking, and skiing. See p. 553.

- **Shikotsu-Toya National Park:** This 987-sq.-km (381-sq.-mile) park in eastern Hokkaido encompasses lakes, volcanoes, and famous hot-spring resorts like Noboribetsu. See p. 591.

- **Daisetsuzan National Park:** The largest of Japan's 28 national parks—and some say Hokkaido's most beautiful—Daisetsuzan boasts three volcanic chains, fir- and birch-covered hillsides, the impressive Sounkyo Gorge, and plenty of skiing and hiking opportunities. See p. 596.

- **Akan National Park:** Popular for hiking, skiing, canoeing, and fishing, Akan National Park in Hokkaido is characterized by dense forests of subarctic primeval trees and caldera lakes, the most famous of which are Kussharo, one of Japan's largest mountain lakes, and Mashu, considered one of Japan's least-spoiled lakes and one of the world's clearest. See p. 600.

## 7 The Best of Old Japan

- **Splurging on a Night in a Ryokan:** If you can afford to, splurge on at least 1 night in one of the country's best ryokan, where the service is impeccable, the kaiseki meals are out of this world, and glorious views outside your tatami room are of miniature landscaped gardens. You'll be pampered in a manner befitting an emperor—many of the nation's oldest ryokan were indeed born to serve members of the imperial court and feudal lords as they traveled Japan's highways. See "Tips on Accommodations" in chapter 2; the "Where to Stay" sections in the regional chapters; and "The Best Traditional Ryokan," below.

- **Attending a Sumo Match:** There's nothing quite like watching two monstrous sumo wrestlers square off, bluff, and grapple as they attempt to throw each other on the ground or out of the ring. Matches are great cultural events, but even if you can't attend one, you can them on TV during one of six annual 15-day tournaments. For more information, see "Spectator Sports" in chapter 5 and "Sumo" in appendix A.

- **Strolling through a Japanese Garden:** Most of Japan's famous gardens are relics of the Edo Period, when the shogun, *daimyo* feudal lords, imperial family, and even samurai and Buddhist priests developed private gardens for their own viewing pleasure. Each step in a strolling garden brings a new view to die for. Refer to "The Best Gardens," earlier in this chapter, and the "Attractions" sections in the regional chapters to see which are heaven on earth.

- **Participating in Zazen Meditation in a Buddhist Temple:** Zazen, or sitting meditation, is practiced by Zen Buddhists as a form of spiritual training and by laypeople as a way to relieve stress and clear the mind. Several temples in Japan are willing to take in foreigners for zazen sessions. See the "Five Unforgettable Ways to Immerse Yourself in Japanese Culture" section in chapter 5 and the "Here & Zazen: Buddhism in Japan" box on p. 609.

- **Attending a Traditional Tea Ceremony:** Developed in the 16th century as a means to achieve inner harmony with nature, the highly ritualized ceremony is carried out in teahouses throughout the country, including those set in Japan's many parks and gardens. Several Tokyo hotels offer English-language instruction in the tea ceremony. See p. 179.

- **Getting a Shiatsu Massage:** Shiatsu, or pressure-point massage, is available in virtually all first-class accommodations in Japan and at most moderately priced ones as well. After a hard day of work or sightseeing, nothing beats a relaxing massage in the privacy of your room.

- **Relaxing at a Hot-Spring Resort:** No country in the world boasts more natural hot springs than Japan, which has 19,500 different springs. Hot-spring spas are found in virtually all regions of the country and feature everything from hot-sand baths to open-air baths. See the regional chapters for more information.

- **Spending a Day in Asakusa (Tokyo):** Asakusa is the best place to experience Tokyo's old downtown, with its popular Sensoji Temple, Nakamise shopping lane with crafts and kitsch, and casual traditional restaurants. As in days of yore, arrive by boat on the Sumida River. See chapter 5.

- **Exploring Kyoto's Higashiyama-ku District:** Kyoto's eastern sector is a lovely combination of wooded hills, temples, shrines, museums, shops, and traditional restaurants, making it one of the best neighborhoods in Japan for a stroll. See "A Stroll through Higashiyama-ku" in chapter 8.

- **Visiting Kyoto's Gion District:** Japan's most famous geisha houses may be off-limits to anyone without a proper introduction, but an early-evening stroll through this enclave of wooden homes and plain facades is like a journey back in time. You might even catch a glimpse of an elaborately made-up apprentice *(maiko)* on her way to an appointment or hear strains of a *shamisen* (a traditional three-stringed Japanese instrument) played behind closed doors. See chapter 8.

- **Watching Cormorant Fishing:** Every night in summer, wooden boats gaily decorated with paper lanterns will take you out on rivers outside Kyoto and Nagoya for an up-close look at cormorant fishing. The birds, maneuvered by fishermen in traditional garb, have tight collars around their necks to prevent them from swallowing their catch. Drinking and dining on board contribute to the festive air. See p. 281 and 352.

- **Walking to Kobo Daishi's Mausoleum on Mount Koya:** Ever since the 9th century, when Buddhist leader Kobo Daishi was laid to rest at Okunoin on Mount Koya, his faithful followers have followed him to their graves—and now tomb after tomb line a 1.6km (1-mile) pathway to Daishi's mausoleum. Cypress trees, moss-covered stone lanterns, and thousands upon thousands of tombs make this the most impressive graveyard stroll in Japan, especially at night. See "Exploring Mount Koya" in chapter 9.

## 8 The Best of Modern Japan

- **Attending a Baseball Game** (Tokyo): After sumo, baseball is Japan's most popular spectator sport. Watching a game with a stadium full of avid fans can be quite fun and can shed new light on America's favorite pastime. See the "For It's Ichi, Ni, San Strikes You're Out . . ." box on p. 198 and the "Take Me Out to the Ballgame" box on p. 490.

- **Visiting Tsukiji Fish Market** (Tokyo): One of the largest wholesale fish markets in the world, this indoor market bustles with activity from about 3am on as frozen tuna is unloaded from boats, auctions are held, and vendors sell octopus, fish, squid, and everything else from the sea that's edible to the city's restaurants. Be sure to bring your camera. See p. 178.

- **Seeing Tokyo from the TMG:** On the 45th floor of the Tokyo Metropolitan Government Office (TMG), designed by well-known architect Kenzo Tange, an observatory offers a bird's-eye view of Shinjuku's cluster of skyscrapers, the never-ending metropolis and, on fine winter days, Mount Fuji. Best of all, it's free. See p. 187.

- **Hanging Out in Harajuku** (Tokyo): Nothing beats Sunday in Harajuku, where you can begin the day leisurely with brunch and then stroll the promenade of Omote Sando Dori, shop the area's many boutiques, take in a museum or two and perhaps a flea market, and then relax over drinks at a sidewalk cafe and watch the never-ending parade of humanity. See "A Stroll through Harajuku & Aoyama" in chapter 5.

- **Shopping for Japanese Designer Clothes** (Tokyo): Japanese designer clothing is often outrageous, occasionally practical, but mostly just fun. Department stores and designer boutiques in Aoyama are the places to try on the styles if you have both the money and the figure for them. See "Shopping" in chapter 5.

- **Spending an Evening in an Entertainment District:** A spin through one of Japan's famous nightlife districts, such as **Shinjuku** or **Roppongi** in Tokyo or **Dotombori** in Osaka, is a colorful way to rub elbows with the natives as you explore narrow streets with their whirls of neon, tiny hole-in-the-wall bars and restaurants, and all-night amusement spots. See "Tokyo After Dark" in chapter 5 and "Osaka After Dark" in chapter 9.

- **Seeing Fish Eye-to-Eye in an Aquarium** (Nagoya, Toba, Osaka, Kagoshima, Beppu): Because Japan is surrounded by sea, it's no surprise that it has more than its fair share of aquariums. Several have made splashy debuts in the past decade with innovative displays that put you eye-to-eye with the creatures of the deep. My favorite is the one in Osaka. See p. 350, 362, 387, 526, and 549.

## 9 The Best Outdoor Adventures

- **Climbing Mount Fuji:** Okay, so climbing Japan's tallest—3,716m high (12,388 ft.)—and most famous mountain is not the solitary, athletic pursuit you may have envisioned—but with 600,000 people climbing it annually, it's a great, culturally enriching group activity. The most recent trend is to climb through the night with a flashlight and then cheer the sunrise from the top of the mountain. See "Climbing Japan's Most Famous Mountain: Mount Fuji" in chapter 6.

- **Hiking the Nakasendo Highway** (Japan Alps): Back in the days of the shogun, feudal lords were required to return to Edo (now Tokyo) every other year, traveling designated highways. Nakasendo was one of these highways, and an 8km (5-mile) stretch through a valley still exists between the old post towns of **Magome** and **Tsumago.** It's a beautiful walk, and the towns are historic relics. See p. 264.

- **Skiing in Honshu & Hokkaido:** Host of two winter Olympics (in Sapporo in 1972 and Nagano in 1998) and riddled with mountain chains, Japan is a great destination for skiing, the most popular winter sport in the country. The Japan Alps in Central Honshu and the mountains of Tohoku and Hokkaido are popular destinations. See chapters 7, 12, and 13.

  If you'd rather leave the planning to someone else, join a trip sponsored by the **Shinyi Ski Club;** contact Julia Nolet (© **03/3423-8858**) from 10am to 10pm Tokyo time; fax 03/3423-8859; jnworwor@gol.com.

- **Cycling** (Matsuyama and Hiroshima): Hard to believe, but you can bike between Shikoku and Hiroshima Prefecture via the 80km (50-mile) Shimanami Kaido route, which actually comprises seven bridges and six islands in the Seto Inland Sea. A well-maintained, dedicated biking path makes cycling one of Japan's best outdoor activities. See "Cycling the Shimanami Kaido" in chapter 10 and "Exploring Sights of the Seto Inland Sea" in chapter 9.

- **Shooting the Kumagawa Rapids** (Kumamoto): You can glide down one of Japan's most rapid rivers in a long, traditional wooden boat,

powered by men with poles. See "Shooting the Kumagawa Rapids" under "Kumamoto" in chapter 10.

- **Fishing:** Most foreigners laugh when they see Japanese fishing spots—a stocked pool in the middle of Tokyo or a cement-banked river, lined elbow to elbow with fishermen. For more sporting conditions, head to Lake Akan in Hokkaido's **Akan National Park,** where you can fish for rainbow trout or white spotted char. See "Akanko Spa & Akan National Park" in chapter 13.

## 10 The Best Traditional Ryokan

- **Hiiragiya Ryokan** (Kyoto; ✆ 075/221-1136): If ever there was an example of the quintessential ryokan, Hiiragiya is it. Located in the heart of old Kyoto, it's the ultimate in tatami luxury: a dignified enclave of polished woods and rooms with antique furnishings overlooking private gardens. Six generations of the same family have provided impeccable service and hospitality here since 1861. See p. 293.
- **Tawaraya** (Kyoto; ✆ 075/211-5566): This venerable inn has been owned and operated by the same family since it opened in the first decade of the 1700s; it's now in its 11th generation of innkeepers. Located in old Kyoto, its guest list reads like a who's who of visitors to Japan, including Leonard Bernstein, the king of Sweden, Alfred Hitchcock, and Saul Bellow. See p. 294.
- **Ryokan Kurashiki** (Kurashiki; ✆ 086/422-0730): Located right beside the willow-lined canal of Kurashiki's famous historic district, this ryokan occupies an old mansion and three 250-year-old antiques-filled warehouses. It's a great place to explore as you wander the corridors and peek into nooks and crannies, admiring all the antiques. See p. 433.
- **Iwaso Ryokan** (Miyajima; ✆ 0829/44-2233): The setting here is as romantic as any you'll find in Japan. If you can afford it, stay in one of the ryokan's 80-year-old cottages, where you'll have a view of maples and a gurgling brook on one of Japan's most scenic and famous islands. If staying here doesn't make you feel like a samurai or a geisha, nothing will. See p. 462.
- **Hakusuikan Ryokan** (Ibusuki; ✆ 0993/22-3131): I'm usually partial to historic Japanese inns, but this sprawling complex right on the coast, with manicured lawns dotted by pine trees, offers an assortment of accommodations (the oldest building is 45 years old), along with one of the best hot-spring spas I've ever seen, modeled after a public bath of the Edo Era. See p. 534.
- **Kannawaen** (Beppu; ✆ 0977/66-2111): This century-old ryokan spreads through lush and carefully tended gardens. Its tatami rooms with shoji screens look out onto hot springs, bamboo, streams, bonsai, stone lanterns, and flowers. It's the perfect place to escape the crowds and relax in the traditional bathhouse or the open-air hot springs. See p. 550.

## 11 The Best Western-Style Hotels

- **Park Hyatt Tokyo** (Tokyo; ✆ 800/233-1234 in the U.S. and Canada): Occupying the 39th to 52nd floors of a skyscraper designed by Kenzo Tange, this might well be the most gorgeous and sophisticated hotel in

all of Japan, if not the world. Offering unparalleled views of the city, one of Tokyo's hottest restaurants, rooms you could live in, and legendary service, it's a must for anyone who can afford it (no wonder it was the hotel featured in *Lost in Translation*). See p. 121.

- **Four Seasons Hotel Tokyo at Chin-zan-So** (Tokyo; ✆ **800/332-3442**): Surrounded by a lush, 7-hectare (17-acre) garden, this top-rated hotel is a wonderful respite in one of the world's most crowded cities, with its impeccable service and a terrific spa and health club free for hotel guests. See p. 123.
- **Nikko Kanaya Hotel** (Nikko; ✆ **0288/54-0001**): Dating from the 19th century, this rambling, old-fashioned hotel combines the rustic charm of a European country lodge with design elements of old Japan— and it's just a 15-minute walk from Toshogu Shrine. See p. 232.
- **The Fujiya Hotel** (Hakone; ✆ **0460/2-2211**): Established in 1878 and nestled on a wooded hillside, the Fujiya is one of Japan's oldest, grandest, and most majestic Western-style hotels. Resembling a Japanese ryokan from the outside, it boasts a comfortable interior of detailed woodwork, old-fashioned antiques-filled guest rooms, and a delightful 1930s dining hall. It also offers indoor/outdoor pools, extensive landscaping, and hot-spring baths. A stay here makes you feel like you've traveled not just to Hakone but to another century. See p. 249.
- **Kawana Hotel** (Ito; ✆ **0557/45-1111**): Built in 1936 to resemble an English country estate, this relaxed yet refined hotel boasts large, manicured

lawns that slope to the sea, and two famous 18-hole golf courses. It's a great getaway from Tokyo. See p. 254.
- **The Westin Miyako** (Kyoto; ✆ **800/WESTIN-1** in the U.S. and Canada): First built in 1890 but completely remodeled, this smartly appointed hotel sprawls across more than 6.4 hectares (16 acres) of hilltop on the eastern edge of town near many famous temples. Good views, a satellite check-in counter at Kyoto Station, free shuttle service to the hotel, indoor/outdoor swimming pools, a children's play room, a tea-ceremony room, and a Japanese garden make this a winner. There's even an annex with Japanese-style rooms as well. See p. 299.
- **Nara Hotel** (Nara; ✆ **0742/26-3300**): From far away, this 1909 building just a short walk from Nara Park resembles a palace. Rooms in the main building have high ceilings, antique light fixtures, and old-fashioned decor. See p. 343.
- **The Ritz-Carlton, Osaka** (Osaka; ✆ **800/241-3333** in the U.S. and Canada): This chain's first venture in Japan has the company's trademark antiques, artwork, and intimate public spaces, as well as such pluses as free access to its fitness center and large, well-appointed rooms. It's not far from Osaka Station. See p. 389.
- **Unzen Kanko Hotel** (Unzen; ✆ **0957/73-3263**): This rustic mountain lodge of ivy-covered wood and stone was built in 1935 to cater to foreigners in search of Mount Unzen's cooler climate. It offers a casual and relaxed atmosphere, hot-spring baths, and comfortable, old-fashioned rooms not far from the Hells. See p. 511.

## 12 The Best Affordable Japanese-Style Places to Stay

- **Homeikan** (Tokyo; ✆ **03/3811-1181**): Although it's a bit far from

Tokyo's main attractions, this is my top pick for an affordable, authentic

Japanese inn. Rooms do not have private bathrooms, but pluses include a Japanese garden, nice public baths, and detailed tatami rooms adorned with traditional architectural features. Meals (optional) are served in your room. Another great plus: The owner speaks English. See p. 138.

- **Ryokan Fujioto** (Tsumago; © 0264/ 57-3009): This 100-year-old inn is nestled back from the main street of Tsumago, a delightful village on the Edo-Era Nakasendo Highway. Meals feature local specialties. The owner speaks English; his daughter volunteers to guide visitors for free (you can request her services when making reservations). See p. 266.

- **Antique Inn Sumiyoshi** (Takayama; © 0577/32-0228): Located in the heart of Takayama on the banks of the Miyagawa River, this 90-year-old former silkworm factory features an open-hearth fireplace *(irori)* in the high-ceilinged communal room, antiques and painted screens throughout, and simple but delightfully old-fashioned tatami rooms overlooking the river. See p. 272.

- **Minshuku in Shirakawago's Ogimachi:** Nestled in a narrow valley of the Japan Alps, Ogimachi is a small village of paddies, flowers, irrigation canals, and 200-year-old thatched farmhouses, about two dozen of which offer simple tatami accommodations and meals featuring local

cuisine. This is a great, inexpensive escape. See p. 277.

- **Matsubaya Ryokan** (Kyoto; © 075/ 351-3727): Opened in 1885 and owned and managed by friendly Mrs. Hayabashi, the fifth generation of innkeepers, this wooden ryokan has rooms with balconies facing a miniature inner courtyard, and rooms facing a tiny enclosed garden. See p. 292.

- **Temple Accommodations on Mount Koya:** If your vision of Japan includes temples, towering cypress trees, shaven-headed monks, and religious chanting at the crack of dawn, head for the religious sanctuary atop Mount Koya, where some 50 Buddhist temples offer tatami accommodations—some with garden views—and two vegetarian meals a day. See "The Temples of Mount Koya" in chapter 9.

- **Miyajima Morinoyado** (Miyajima; © 0829/44-0430): This public people's lodge on picturesque Miyajima island is modern yet traditional and would easily cost four times as much if it were privately owned. See p. 462.

- **Tsuru-no-yu Onsen** (Nyuto Onsen; © 0187/46-2139): This rustic inn, with a history stretching back to the Edo Period, thatched-roof building, and outdoor hot-spring baths, is as close as you can get to time travel. To really save money, opt for the self-cooking wing and prepare your own meals. See p. 567.

## 13 The Best Culinary Experiences

- **Experiencing a Kaiseki Feast:** The ultimate in Japanese cuisine, *kaiseki* is a feast for the senses and the spirit. Consisting of a variety of exquisitely prepared and arranged dishes, a kaiseki meal is a multicourse event to be savored slowly. Both the ingredients and the dishes they comprise are chosen with great care to complement

the season. There are hundreds of exceptional kaiseki restaurants in Japan, from old-world traditional to sleek modern; A standout is **Kagetsu** in Nagasaki. Traditional ryokan also serve kaiseki. See p. 505 as well as "Tips on Dining, Japanese Style" in chapter 2.

- **Spending an Evening in a Robatayaki:** Harking back to the olden days when Japanese cooked over an open fireplace, a *robatayaki* is a convivial place for a meal and drinks. One of the most famous is **Inakaya** in Tokyo, where diners sit at a counter; on the other side are two cooks, grills, and mountains of food. You'll love the drama of this place. See p. 164 as well as "Tips on Dining, Japanese Style" in chapter 2.

- **Dining on Western Food in Modern Settings:** Japan has no lack of great Western food, and some of the best places to dine are its first-class hotels. The **New York Grill,** on the 52nd floor of the Park Hyatt in Tokyo, epitomizes the best of the West with its sophisticated setting, great views, great food, and great jazz. See p. 154.

- **Buying Prepared Meals at a Department Store:** The basement floors of department stores are almost always devoted to foodstuffs, including takeout foods. Shopping for your meal is a fun experience: Hawkers yell their wares, samples are set out for you to nibble, and you can choose anything from tempura and sushi to boxed meals. See chapter 5, the regional chapters, and "Tips on Dining, Japanese Style" in chapter 2.

- **Slurping Noodles in a Noodle Shop:** You're supposed to slurp when eating Japanese noodles, which are prepared in almost as many different ways as there are regions. Noodle shops range from stand-up counters to traditional restaurants; one of my favorites is **Raitei** in Kamakura. See p. 227 as well as "Tips on Dining, Japanese Style" in chapter 2 and the "Where to Dine" sections in regional chapters.

- **Rubbing Elbows in a Yakitori-ya:** Yakitori-ya are the pubs of Japan— usually tiny affairs with just a counter, serving up skewered grilled chicken. They're good places to meet the natives and are inexpensive as well. You'll find them in every nightlife district in the country. See the regional chapters and also "Tips on Dining, Japanese Style" in chapter 2.

## 14 The Best Destinations for Serious Shoppers

- **For Everything:** Japanese department stores are microcosms of practically everything Japan produces, from the food halls in the basement to the departments selling clothing, accessories, office supplies, souvenirs, pottery, household goods, and cameras, to rooftop garden centers. What's more, service is great, and purchases are beautifully wrapped. You'll be spoiled for life. See "Shopping" in chapter 5.

- **For Designer Fashions:** Tokyo's **Shibuya District** has the most designer boutiques in town, while **Aoyama** boasts main shops for all the big-name designers, including Issey Miyake and Comme des Garçons. Department stores also carry big-name designers; their annual summer sales are mob scenes. See "Shopping" in chapter 5.

- **For Souvenirs:** Japanese are avid souvenir shoppers when they travel, so souvenirs are sold literally everywhere, even near shrines and temples. **Nakamise Dori,** a pedestrian lane leading to Tokyo's Sensoji Temple, is one of Japan's most colorful places to shop for paper umbrellas, toys, and other souvenirs. The two best places for one-stop memento shopping are the **Oriental Bazaar** (p. 202) in Tokyo and the **Kyoto Handicraft Center** (p. 333), both of which offer several floors of everything from fans to woodblock prints.

- **For Traditional Crafts:** Japan treasures its artisans so highly that it designates the best as National Living Treasures. The two best shops for a varied inventory of traditional crafts, from knives and baskets to lacquerware and ceramics, are the **Japan Traditional Craft Center** in Tokyo and the **Kyoto Craft Center.** Department stores also offer an excellent collection of traditional crafts. See "Shopping" in chapter 5 and "Shopping Kyoto" in chapter 8 as well as p. 202 and 333 respectively.

- **For Antiques & Curios:** Flea markets are great for browsing; you'll see everything from used kimono to Edo-Era teapots for sale. Japan's largest and one of its oldest monthly markets is held the 21st of each month at **Toji Temple** in Kyoto. (A lesser flea market is held there the first Sun of each month.) **Tokyo** also has great weekend markets. See chapters 5 and 8.

- **For Electronics:** Looking for that perfect digital camera, MP3 player, calculator, or rice cooker? Then join everyone else in the country by going to one of the nation's two largest electronics and electrical-appliance districts. In Tokyo, it's **Akihabara,** where open-fronted shops beckon up to 50,000 weekday shoppers with whirring fans, blaring radios, and sales pitches. In Osaka, head to **Den Den Town.** Be sure to comparison-shop and bargain. See "Shopping" in chapters 5 and 9.

- **For Local Specialties:** Many prefecture capitals have a government-owned exhibition hall where local products are displayed for sale. Often called a *kanko bussankan,* the hall may have everything from locally produced pottery to folk toys and foodstuffs. Cities with kanko bussankan include **Kanazawa, Okayama, Matsuyama,** and **Kumamoto.** See chapters 9, 10, and 11.

- **For Porcelain & Pottery:** Porcelain and pottery are produced seemingly everywhere in Japan. Some of the more famous centers include **Nagoya,** home to Noritake, Japan's largest chinaware company; **Kanazawa,** known for its Kutani pottery with its distinctive colorful glaze; **Matsuyama,** famous for its Tobe pottery (white porcelain with cobalt-blue designs); and **Kagoshima,** with its Satsuma pottery, which comes in white (used by the upper class in feudal Japan) and black (used by the common people). See chapters 9, 10, and 11.

# 2

# Planning Your Trip to Japan

This book is designed to guide you through your own discoveries of Japan, however brief or extended your visit may be. From experience, I know that the two biggest concerns for visitors to Japan are the language barrier and the high cost of living. To help alleviate fears about the first, I've provided Japanese symbols for establishments that do not have English-language signs so you can recognize their names (see appendix C), given brief instructions on how to reach most of the places I recommend, made suggestions for ordering in restaurants without English-language menus, and provided prices for everything from subway rides to admission to museums.

As for costs, probably everyone has heard horror stories about Japan's high prices. After the dramatic fall of the dollar against the yen in the 1980s and 1990s, Tokyo and Osaka did indeed become two of the world's most expensive cities, with food and lodging costing as much as in New York or London, maybe more. But since Japan's economic bubble burst in the early 1990s, something happened that would have been unthinkable during the heady spending days of the 1980s—Japanese became bargain-conscious. There are now inexpensive French bistros, secondhand clothing stores, 100-yen shops, and budget hotels.

Still, it's difficult not to suffer an initial shock about Japan's high prices, which will seem especially exorbitant if you insist on living and eating exactly as you do back home. The secret is to live and eat as Japanese do. This book will help you do exactly that, with descriptions of eateries and Japanese-style inns that cater to the native population. By following this book's advice and exercising a little caution on your own, you should be able to cut down on needless expenses and learn even more about Japan in the process. While you may never find Japan cheap, you will find it richly rewarding for all the reasons you chose Japan as a destination in the first place.

Despite the difficulties inherent in visiting any foreign country, I think you'll find Japan very easy to navigate. There are many more signs in English now than there were even just a decade ago. And Japan remains one of the safest countries in the world; in general, you don't have to worry about muggers, pickpockets, or crooks. In fact, I sometimes feel downright coddled in Japan. Everything runs like clockwork: Subway trains are on time, all the public telephones work, and the service—whether in hotels, restaurants, or department stores—ranks among the best in the world. I know if I get truly lost, someone will help me and will probably even go out of his or her way to do so. Japanese are honest and extremely helpful toward foreign visitors. Indeed, it's the people themselves who make traveling in Japan such a delight.

This chapter will help you with the what, when, where, and how of travel to Japan—from what documents you should take with you to how to get around easily and economically.

## 1 The Regions in Brief

Separated from mainland China and Korea by the Sea of Japan, the nation of Japan stretches in an arc about 2,898km (1,800 miles) long from northeast to southwest, yet it is only 403km (250 miles) wide at its broadest point. Japan consists primarily of four main islands— **Honshu, Hokkaido, Shikoku,** and **Kyushu.** Surrounding these large islands are more than 6,000 smaller islands and islets, most of them uninhabited; farther to the south are the **Okinawan islands,** perhaps best known for the fierce fighting that took place there during World War II and for their continued (and controversial) use as an American military base. If you were to superimpose Japan's four main islands onto a map of the United States, they would stretch all the way from Maine down to Florida, which should give you an idea of the diversity of Japan's climate, flora, and scenery— Hokkaido in the north is subarctic, while southern Kyushu is subtropical. Honshu, Japan's most populous island and home to Tokyo, Kyoto, and Osaka, is connected to the other three islands by tunnel or bridge, which means you can travel to all four islands by train.

As much as 70% of Japan consists of **mountains.** They are found on all four main islands and most are volcanic in origin. Altogether, there are some 265 **volcanoes,** more than 30 of them still considered active. Mount Fuji (on Honshu), dormant since 1707, is Japan's highest and most famous volcano, while Mount Aso (on Kyushu) boasts the largest caldera in the world. Because of its volcanic origins, earthquakes have plagued Japan throughout its history. In the 20th century, the two most destructive earthquakes were the 1923 Great Kanto Earthquake, which killed more than 100,000 people in the Tokyo area,

and the 1995 Great Hanshin Earthquake, which claimed more than 6,000 lives in Kobe.

Japan is divided into 47 regional divisions, or **prefectures.** Each prefecture has its own prefectural capital and is comparable to the U.S. state or the British county. Japan's total landmass is slightly smaller than California in area, yet Japan has almost half (43%) the population of the United States. And because three-fourths of Japan is mountainous and therefore uninhabitable, its people are concentrated primarily in only 10% of the country's landmass, with the rest of the area devoted to agriculture. In other words, imagine 43% of the U.S. population living in California—primarily in San Diego County—and you get an idea of how crowded Japan is. For this island nation—isolated physically from the rest of the world; struck repeatedly through the centuries by earthquakes, fires, and typhoons; and possessed of only limited space for harmonious living—geography and topography have played major roles both in determining its development and in shaping its culture, customs, and arts.

## HONSHU

Of the four main islands, Honshu is the largest and most populated. Because it's also the most important historically and culturally, it's where most visitors spend the bulk of their time.

### KANTO DISTRICT

Located in east-central Honshu and comprising metropolitan **Tokyo** and six prefectures, this district is characterized by the Kanto Plain, the largest flatland in Japan. Although development of the district didn't begin in earnest until the establishment of the shogunate government in Edo (present-day Tokyo) in 1603, Tokyo and surrounding giants like

**Yokohama** make this the most densely populated region in Japan.

## KANSAI DISTRICT

Also called the Kinki District and encompassing seven prefectures, this is Japan's most historic region. **Nara** and **Kyoto**—two of Japan's ancient capitals—are here, as are two of Japan's most important port cities, **Kobe** and **Osaka.** With the opening of Kansai International Airport outside Osaka in 1994, many foreign visitors opt to bypass Tokyo altogether in favor of Kansai's many historic spots, including **Mount Koya** with its many temples, **Himeji** with what I consider to be Japan's most beautiful castle, **Ise-Shima National Park** with Japan's most revered Shinto shrine, Nara with its Great Buddha and temples, and, of course, Kyoto, the former capital for more than 1,000 years with so many temples, imperial villas, and gardens that it ranks as Japan's foremost tourist destination.

## CHUBU DISTRICT

The Chubu (Central) District lies between Tokyo and Kyoto and straddles central Honshu from the Pacific Ocean to the Japan Sea, encompassing nine prefectures. **Nagoya,** Japan's fourth-largest city and home to an international airport nicknamed Centrair, is Chubu's most important city and a gateway to its other destinations. The district is marked by great variety—mountain ranges (including the **Japan Alps,** see below), volcanoes (including **Mount Fuji**), large rivers, and coastal regions on both sides of the island. It's popular for skiing and hiking, for quaint mountain villages such as **Takayama,** and for tourist attractions that include the open-air Museum Meiji Mura (near Nagoya), the castle in **Matsumoto,** and Kenrokuen Garden in **Kanazawa,** considered one of Japan's finest.

## THE JAPAN ALPS

Spreading over central Honshu in the Chubu District, the Japan Alps are among Japan's most famous mountain ranges, especially since hosting the 1998 XVIII Winter Olympics in **Nagano. Chubu-Sangaku National Park** (also called the Japan Alps National Park) contains some of the nation's most beautiful mountain scenery, while destinations like **Takayama** and **Shirakawago** provide everything from quaint historic districts to thatched-roof farmhouses.

## ISE-SHIMA

Shima Peninsula, in Mie Prefecture, juts into the Seto Inland Sea and is famous for **Ise-Shima National Park,** noted for its coastal scenery and Ise Jingu Shrines. **Toba,** birthplace of the cultured pearl, is popular for its Mikimoto Pearl Island and the Toba Aquarium. Shima Peninsula also boasts two theme parks, one fashioned after Japan's Warring States Era and the other an amusement park with a Spanish theme.

## CHUGOKU DISTRICT

Honshu's western district has five prefectures and is divided by the Chugoku Mountain Range. Industrial giants such as **Hiroshima** and **Okayama** lead as the major cities, drawing tourists with reconstructed castles, Korakuen Garden, and the sobering Peace Memorial Park in Hiroshima, dedicated to victims of the world's first atomic bomb. **Kurashiki** is a must for its photogenic, historic warehouse district, while **Miyajima,** part of the Seto-Naikai (Inland Sea) National Park, is considered one of Japan's most beautiful islands.

## TOHOKU DISTRICT

Northeastern Honshu, with **Sendai** as its regional center, encompasses six prefectures. Known as the Tohoku District, it isn't nearly as developed as the central and southern districts of Honshu, due in large part to its rugged, mountainous terrain and harsh climate. **Matsushima,** about halfway up the coast between Tokyo and the northern tip of Honshu,

# Japan

0 100 mi
0 100 km

**Kuril Islands**
(Occupied by the Soviet Union in 1945, administered by Russia, claimed by Japan)

Wakkanai

Abashiri

*AKAN NAT'L PARK*

*DAISETSUZAN NAT'L PARK*

Asahigawa

Kushiro

*HOKKAIDO*

Obihiro

Otaru

**Sapporo**

Chitose

Jozankei

Tomakomai

*Erimo saki*

*Lake Toya*

Noboribetsu

*SHIKOTSU-TOYA NAT'L PARK*

*Uchiura-wan*

**Hakodate**

*Tsugaru Strait*

*MUTUSU-WAN*

Hachinohe

Aomori

*Lake Towada*

Hirosaki

*RIKUCHU-KAIGAN NAT'L PARK*

*TOWADA-HACHIMANTEI NAT'L PARK*

Morioka

Akita

Kakunodate

*TOHOKU*

*Sea of Japan*

Sakata

Matsushima

Yamagata

**Sendai**

*HONSHU*

Fukushima

Niigata

*Abukuma*

*Sado Island*

Hitachi

Tokamachi

Nikko

Mito

*Lake Kasumigaura*

*JOSHIN-ETSU NAT'L PARK*

*Shinano*

*KANTO*

**Tokyo**

Takaoka

**Matsumoto**

*Tokyo Bay*

Kanazawa

Yokohama

*Mt. Fuji*

Kamakura

**Takayama**

Hakone

Atami

*Fuji*

Ito

*CHUBU*

*Izu Peninsula*

Shizuoka

Shimoda

*Ibi*

Nagoya

**Kyoto**

*ISE-SHIMA NAT'L PARK*

*Dalsen*

*KANSAI*

Toba

Kobe

Nara

Osaka

**Matsue**

*CHUGOKU*

Himeji

*PACIFIC OCEAN*

Okayama

Takamatsu

Kurashiki

Tokushima

**Hiroshima**

Kochi

*Korea Strait*

Shimonoseki

Matsuyama

*SHIKOKU*

Fukuoka

Beppu

*Tsushima*

*Iki*

*ASO NAT'L PARK*

Sasebo

Kumamoto

*KYUSHU*

**Nagasaki**

Miyazaki

*Sendai*

Kagoshima

Ibusuki

*Tanega*

*East China Sea*

*Yaku*

**RUSSIA**

*Kuril Islands*

**CHINA**

*Hokkaido*

**NORTH KOREA**

*Honshu*

**SOUTH KOREA**

**Tokyo**

*JAPAN*

*Kyushu*

*Ryukyu Islands*

is the district's major tourist destination; with its pine-clad islets dotting the bay, it's considered one of Japan's most scenic spots. **Kakunodate,** located inland, is a former castle town offering preserved samurai houses and, during cherry-blossom season, a stunning show of pink flowers to travelers willing to take a road less traveled. **Towada-Hachimantai National Park,** which extends over three prefectures, boasts scenic lakes, rustic hot-spring spas, hiking, and skiing.

## SHIKOKU

Shikoku, the smallest of the four main islands, is fairly undeveloped and off the beaten path for many foreign visitors. It's famous for its 88 Buddhist temples founded by one of Japan's most interesting historical figures, the Buddhist priest Kukai, known posthumously as Kobo Daishi. Other major attractions are Ritsurin Park in **Takamatsu,** Matsuyama Castle in **Matsuyama,** and **Dogo Spa,** one of Japan's oldest hot-spring spas. For active travelers, the **Shimanami Kaido route** offers 80 scenic km (50 miles) of dedicated biking trails that connect Shikoku with Hiroshima via six islands and a series of bridges in the Seto Inland Sea.

## KYUSHU

The southernmost of the four main islands, Kyushu boasts a mild subtropical climate, active volcanoes, and hot-spring spas. Because it's the closest to Korea and China, Kyushu served as a gateway to the continental mainland throughout much of Japan's history, later becoming the springboard for both traders and Christian missionaries from the West. **Fukuoka,** Kyushu's largest city, serves as the rail gateway from Honshu, dispersing travelers to hot springs in **Beppu, Unzen,** and **Ibusuki** and to such major attractions as Kumamoto Castle in **Kumamoto** and Sengan'en Garden in **Kagoshima. Nagasaki,** victim of the world's second atomic bomb, is one of Japan's most cosmopolitan cities and one of my favorites. In recent years, Kyushu has become a major destination for tourists from Taiwan, Korea, and Hong Kong, who flock to the region's many theme parks, including Ocean Dome in **Miyazaki** and Huis Ten Bosch outside Nagasaki.

## HOKKAIDO

Japan's second-largest island, Hokkaido lies to the north of Honshu and is regarded as the country's last frontier with its wide-open pastures, evergreen forests, mountains, gorges, crystal-clear lakes, and wildlife, much of it preserved in national parks. Originally occupied by the indigenous Ainu, it became colonized by Japanese settlers mostly after the Meiji Restoration in 1868. Today it's home to 5.6 million people, 1.8 million of whom live in **Sapporo.** With a landmass that accounts for 22% of Japan's total area, Hokkaido has the nation's lowest population density: less than 5% of the total population. That, together with the island's cold, severe winters but mild summers and its unspoiled natural beauty, make this island a nature lover's paradise.

## 2 Visitor Information

The **Japan National Tourist Organization (JNTO)** publishes a wealth of free, colorful brochures and maps covering Japan as a whole and various regions of the country. Be sure to get "The Tourist's Language Handbook," a phrase booklet to help foreign visitors communicate with Japanese. Other useful publications available from JNTO include "Directory of Welcome Inns," which lists inexpensive accommodations throughout Japan, with a free reservation system; "Hotels in Japan"; the "Japan Ryokan Guide," which lists 600 Japanese inns; and the "Railway

Timetable," which contains timetables for Shinkansen bullet trains and major train lines throughout Japan. JNTO has offices in the following locations.

In the **United States:** One Rockefeller Plaza, Suite 1250, New York, NY 10020 (© 212/757-5640; visitjapan@jntonyc.org); 515 S. Figueroa, Suite 1470, Los Angeles, CA 90071 (© 213/623-1952; info@jnto-lax.org); and 1 Daniel Burnham Court, Suite 250C, San Francisco, CA 94109 (© 415/292-5686; info@jntosf.org).

In **Canada:** 165 University Ave., Toronto, ON M5H 3B8, Canada (© 416/366-7140; info@jntoyyz.com).

In the **United Kingdom:** Heathcoat House, 20 Savile Row, London W1S 3PR, England (© 020/7734-9638; info@jnto.co.uk).

In **Australia:** Room 1813, Australia Square Tower, 264 George St., Sydney, NSW 2000, Australia (© 02/9251-3024; jntosyd@tokyonet.com.au).

**JNTO ONLINE** Information is available via the Internet at **www.jnto.go.jp** (and at **japantravelinfo.com** for North American travelers; **www.seejapan.co.uk** for British travelers), where you can read up on what's new, view maps of more than 20 major cities, check train and flight schedules and fares around Japan, get the latest weather reports, find links to online hotel reservation companies, and browse through information ranging from reasonable accommodations and hints on budget travel to regional events, museums, and attractions. You can also download regional guides to various cities and destinations throughout Japan by going to www.jnto.go.jp and clicking on *Regional Tourist Guides.*

**THE JNTO IN JAPAN** In Japan, your best bet for general or specific information is at one of JNTO's three excellent **Tourist Information Centers (TICs).** They're located in downtown Tokyo, at Narita Airport outside Tokyo, and at Kansai International Airport outside Osaka (see chapters 4 and 9 for locations and open hours). All distribute leaflets on destinations throughout Japan that are not available at the destinations themselves (though you can download them at JNTO's website). They also provide train, bus, and ferry schedules and leaflets on major attractions and sights—for example, Japanese gardens, hot springs, museums, and art galleries. They also carry information on hotels and ryokan in Japan and will even book inexpensive accommodations for you free of charge.

**LOCAL INFORMATION** You'll also find locally run tourist offices in nearly every city and town throughout Japan, most of them conveniently located at or near the main train station. Look for the logo of a red question mark with the word INFORMATION written below. Although the staff at a particular tourist office may not speak English (many do), they can point you in the direction of your hotel, perhaps provide you with a map in English, and, in many cases, even make hotel bookings for you. Note, however, that they're not equipped to provide you with information on other regions of Japan (for that, go to a TIC). I've included information on local tourist offices throughout this book (see "Visitor Information" in the regional chapters), including how to reach them after you disembark from the train and their open hours.

## 3 Entry Requirements & Customs

### ENTRY REQUIREMENTS
**Americans, Australians,** and **New Zealanders** traveling to Japan as tourists

for a stay of 90 days or less need only a valid passport to gain entry into the country. **Canadians** don't need a visa for

stays of up to 3 months, and **United Kingdom** and **Irish citizens** can stay for up to 6 months without a visa.

*Note:* Only tourists don't need a visa—that is, those in the country for sight-seeing, sports activities, family visits, inspection tours, business meetings, or short study courses. Tourists cannot work in Japan or engage in any remunerative activity including the teaching of English (though some young people ignore the law). No extensions of stay are granted, which means tourists *must* leave the country after 90 days. If you're going to Japan to work or to study for longer than 90 days, you'll need a visa; contact the Japanese embassy or consulate nearest you (see www.jnto.go.jp for a list of addresses).

## CUSTOMS

**WHAT YOU CAN BRING INTO JAPAN**   If you're 20 or older, you can bring duty-free into Japan up to 400 non-Japanese cigarettes or 500 grams of tobacco or 100 cigars; three bottles (760cc each) of alcohol; and 2 ounces of perfume. You can also bring gifts and souvenirs with a total market value of less than ¥200,000 ($1,900).

**WHAT YOU CAN TAKE HOME**   Returning **U.S. citizens** who have been away for at least 48 hours or more are allowed to bring back, once every 30 days, $800 worth of merchandise duty-free including (for those 21 and older) 1 liter of wine or spirits. You'll be charged a flat rate of duty on the next $1,000 worth of purchases. Any dollar amount beyond that is dutiable at whatever rates apply. On mailed gifts, the duty-free limit is $200. Be sure to have your receipts or purchases handy to expedite the declaration process.

With few exceptions, you cannot bring fresh foodstuffs into the United States. For specifics on what you can bring back, download the free pamphlet *Know Before You Go* online at **www.cbp. gov.** (Click on "Travel," then on "Know Before You Go Online Brochure.") Or contact **U.S. Customs & Border Protection** at ✆ 877/287-8867 to request the pamphlet.

For a summary of **Canadian** rules, write for the booklet *I Declare,* issued by the **Canada Border Services Agency** (✆ **800/461-9999** in Canada, or 204/983-3500; www.cbsa-asfc.gc.ca). Canada allows its citizens a C$750 exemption, and you're allowed to bring back duty-free one carton of cigarettes, one can of tobacco, 40 imperial ounces of liquor, and 50 cigars. In addition, you're allowed to mail gifts to Canada valued at less than C$60 a day, provided they're unsolicited and don't contain alcohol or tobacco. *Note:* The $750 exemption can only be used once a year and only after an absence of 7 days.

**U.K.** citizens returning from Japan have a Customs allowance of 200 cigarettes; 50 cigars; 250 grams of smoking tobacco; 2 liters of still table wine; 1 liter of spirits or strong liqueurs (over 22% volume); 2 liters of fortified wine, sparkling wine, or other liqueurs; 60cc (ml) perfume; 250cc (ml) of toilet water; and £145 worth of all other goods, including gifts and souvenirs. People under 17 cannot have the tobacco or alcohol allowance. For more information, contact **HM Customs & Excise** at ✆ **0845/010-9000** (from outside the U.K., ✆ **020/8929-0152**), or consult their website at www.hmce.gov.uk.

The duty-free allowance in **Australia** is A$400 or, for those under 18, A$200. Citizens can bring in 250 cigarettes or 250 grams of loose tobacco, and 1,125 milliliters of alcohol. For more information, call the **Australian Customs Service** at ✆ **1300/363-263,** or log on to www.customs.gov.au.

> ### ⌒Tips **An Important Note**
>
> At all times, foreigners are required to carry either their passports or, for those who have been granted longer stays, their alien registration cards. Passports must also be presented at check-in for all lodgings in Japan. The police generally do not stop foreigners, but if you're caught without the proper identification, you'll be taken to the local police headquarters. Safeguard your passport in an inconspicuous, inaccessible place like a money belt. If you lose it, visit the nearest consulate of your native country as soon as possible for a replacement. Keeping a photocopy of your passport information page will facilitate its replacement.

The duty-free allowance for **New Zealand** is NZ$700. Citizens over 17 can bring in 200 cigarettes, 50 cigars, or 250 grams of tobacco (or a mixture of all three if their combined weight doesn't exceed 250g); plus 4.5 liters of wine and beer, or 1.125 liters of liquor. New Zealand currency does not carry import or export restrictions. For more information, contact **New Zealand Customs,** The Customhouse, 17–21 Whitmore St., Box 2218, Wellington (© **04/473-6099** or 0800/428-786; www.customs.govt.nz).

## 4 Money

**CURRENCY** The currency in Japan is called the *yen,* symbolized by ¥. Coins come in denominations of ¥1, ¥5, ¥10, ¥50, ¥100, and ¥500. Bills come in denominations of ¥1,000, ¥2,000, ¥5,000, and ¥10,000. You'll find that all coins get used (though it's hard to get rid of ¥1 coins), and you'll want to keep plenty of change handy for riding local transportation such as buses or streetcars. Although change machines are virtually everywhere, even on buses where you can change larger coins and ¥1,000 bills, you'll find it faster to have the exact amount on hand.

Although the **conversion rate** varies daily and can fluctuate dramatically, the prices in this book are based on the rate of US$1 to ¥105, or ¥100 to US95¢.

Some people like to arrive in a foreign country with that country's currency already on hand, but I do not find it necessary for Japan. **Narita, Kansai,** and **Nagoya international airports** all have exchange counters for all incoming international flights that offer better exchange rates than what you'd get abroad, as well as ATMs. Change enough money to last several days, since exchanging money is not as convenient in Japan as it is in many other countries.

Personal checks are not used in Japan. Most Japanese pay with either credit cards or cash—and because the country overall has such a low crime rate, you can feel safe walking around with money (though of course you should always exercise caution). The only time you really need to be alert to possible pickpockets in Japan is when you're riding a crowded subway during rush hour or walking in heavily visited areas of Tokyo and other large cities.

In any case, although the bulk of your expenses—hotels, train tickets, major purchases, meals in tourist-oriented restaurants—can be paid for with credit cards, you'll want to bring traveler's checks for those times when you might not have easy access to an ATM for cash withdrawals.

**ATMs**   The best way to get cash away from home is from an ATM (automated teller machine). Most ATMs in Japan, however, accept only cards issued by Japanese banks. Your best bet for obtaining cash, therefore, is at one of 21,000 **post offices** with ATMs that accept foreign bank cards operating on the **Cirrus** (© 800/424-7787; www.mastercard.com) and **PLUS** (© 800/843-7587; www.visa.com) systems. Although major post offices, usually located near main train stations, have long open hours for ATMs (generally 7am–11pm weekdays and 9am–7 or 9pm on weekends), small post offices may have only limited hours for ATMs (depending on the post office, that may be until 6 or 7pm weekdays and until 5pm on weekends). Besides post offices, other places with ATMs that might accept foreign-issued cards include Citibank (which usually accepts both Visa and MasterCard and sometimes American Express as well) and large department stores in major cities. Note that there is no public American Express office in Japan.

Be sure you know your four-digit personal identification number (PIN) and your daily withdrawal limit before leaving home. Also keep in mind that many banks impose a fee every time a card is used at a different bank's ATM, and that fee can be higher for international transactions than for domestic ones. For international withdrawal fees, ask your bank.

In addition to bank cards, credit cards can also be used to get cash advances from an ATM. Keep in mind that credit card companies try to protect themselves from theft by limiting the funds someone can withdraw outside their home country, so call your credit card company before you leave home. And keep in mind that you'll pay interest from the moment of your withdrawal, even if you pay your monthly bills on time.

**CREDIT CARDS**   Credit cards are convenient for obtaining cash (provided you know your four-number PIN), paying for accommodations and meals at expensive restaurants, and making major purchases. They also provide a convenient record of your purchases and generally offer a relatively good exchange rate. Keep in mind, however, that many banks now assess a 1% to 3% transaction fee on *all* charges you incur abroad.

The most readily accepted cards are **MasterCard** (also called Eurocard), **Visa,** and the Japanese credit card **JCB** (Japan Credit Bank); many tourist-oriented facilities also accept **American Express** and **Diners Club.**  Shops and restaurants accepting credit and charge cards will usually post which cards they accept at the door or near the cash register. However, some establishments may be reluctant to accept cards for small purchases and inexpensive meals, so inquire beforehand. In addition, note that the vast majority of Japan's smaller and least-expensive businesses, including many restaurants, noodle shops, fast-food joints, ma-and-pa establishments, and the cheapest accommodations, do not accept credit cards.

**TRAVELER'S CHECKS**   Although traveler's checks are something of an anachronism now that ATMs have come onto the scene, they're still useful for Japan, where ATMs for foreign-issued cards are limited. Traveler's checks have a slight advantage in that they generally fetch a better exchange rate than cash and also offer protection in case of theft. Note, however, that in some very remote areas, even banks won't cash them. Before taking off for small towns, be sure you have enough cash.

You can get traveler's checks before leaving home at almost any bank. Or, you can get traveler's checks by phone for **American Express** (© 800/673-3782),

Visa (© 800/732-1322), and **Master-Card** (© 800/223-9920) in denominations of $20 to $500 or $1,000, plus a 1% to 4% service fee. American Express charges a $15 order fee, plus shipping charges.

All banks in Japan displaying an AUTHORIZED FOREIGN EXCHANGE sign can exchange currency and traveler's checks, with exchange rates usually displayed at the appropriate foreign-exchange counter. **Banks** are generally open Monday through Friday from 9am to 3pm, though business hours for exchanging foreign currency usually don't begin until 10:30 or 11am (be prepared for a long wait; you'll be asked to sit down as your order is processed). If you need to exchange money outside banking hours, inquire at your **hotel.** Likewise, large **department stores** also offer exchange services and are often open until 7:30 or 8pm. Note, however, that hotels and department stores may charge a handling fee, offer a slightly less favorable exchange rate, and require a passport for all transactions.

## The Japanese Yen

**For American Readers**    At this writing $1 = approximately ¥105, or ¥100 = 95¢. This was the rate of exchange used to calculate the dollar values given in this guide (rounded off to the nearest nickel for prices less than $10 and to the nearest dollar for prices more than $10). To roughly figure the price of something in dollars, calculate $9.50 for every ¥1,000. For example, ¥2,000 is $19.

**For British Readers**    At this writing £1 = approximately ¥195, or ¥100 = 51p; this was the rate of exchange used to calculate the pound values in the table below. The euro is worth approximately ¥133.

| ¥ | US$ | UK£ | ¥ | US$ | UK£ |
|---|---|---|---|---|---|
| 10 | 0.10 | 0.05 | 1,500 | 14.25 | 7.69 |
| 25 | 0.24 | 0.13 | 2,000 | 19.00 | 10.26 |
| 50 | 0.48 | 0.26 | 2,500 | 23.75 | 12.82 |
| 75 | 0.71 | 0.38 | 3,000 | 28.50 | 15.38 |
| 100 | 0.95 | 0.51 | 4,000 | 38.00 | 20.51 |
| 200 | 1.90 | 1.03 | 5,000 | 47.50 | 25.64 |
| 300 | 2.85 | 1.54 | 6,000 | 57.00 | 30.77 |
| 400 | 3.80 | 2.05 | 7,000 | 66.50 | 35.90 |
| 500 | 4.75 | 2.56 | 8,000 | 76.00 | 41.03 |
| 600 | 5.70 | 3.08 | 9,000 | 85.50 | 46.15 |
| 700 | 6.65 | 3.59 | 10,000 | 95.00 | 51.28 |
| 800 | 7.60 | 4.10 | 15,000 | 125.00 | 76.92 |
| 900 | 8.55 | 4.62 | 20,000 | 142.505 | 102.57 |
| 1,000 | 9.50 | 5.28 | 25,000 | 237.50 | 128.21 |

*A note on exchange rates:* Since these rates will surely fluctuate, check the rate again when you travel to Japan and use this table only as an approximate guide. For up-to-the-minute currency conversions, check www.xe.com/ucc.

## 5 When to Go

**CLIMATE**  Most of Japan's islands lie in a temperate seasonal wind zone similar to that of the East Coast of the United States, which means there are four distinct seasons. Japanese are very proud of their seasons and place much more emphasis on them than people do in the West. Kimono, dishes and bowls used for kaiseki, and even Noh plays change with the season. Certain foods are eaten during certain times of the year, such as eel in summer and *fugu* (blowfish) in winter. Almost all haiku have seasonal references. The cherry blossom signals the beginning of spring, and most festivals are tied to seasonal rites. Even urban dwellers note the seasons; almost as though on cue, businessmen will change virtually overnight from their winter to summer attire.

Because Japan's four main islands stretch in an arc from northeast to southwest at about the same latitudes as Boston and Atlanta, you can travel in the country at virtually any time of year. Winters in southern Kyushu are mild, while summers in northern Hokkaido are cool. In addition, there's no rainy season in Hokkaido.

**Summer,** which begins in June, is heralded by the rainy season, which lasts from about mid-June to mid-July. Although it doesn't rain every day, it does rain a lot, sometimes quite heavily, and umbrellas are imperative. You'll also be more comfortable in light cottons, though you should bring a light jacket for unexpected cool evenings or air-conditioned rooms. After the rain stops, it turns very hot (in the 80s°F/high 20s°C) and uncomfortably humid throughout the country, with the exception of the northern island of Hokkaido, mountaintop resorts like Hakone, and the Japan Alps.

The period from the end of August through September is **typhoon season,** although most storms stay out at sea and generally vent their fury on land only in thunderstorms.

**Autumn,** which lasts until about November, is one of the best times to travel in Japan. The days are pleasant and slightly cool, and the changing red and scarlet of leaves contrast brilliantly with the deep blue skies. There are also many chrysanthemum shows in Japan at this time, popular maple-viewing spots, and many autumn festivals. Be sure to pack a jacket in autumn.

**Winter,** lasting from December to March, is marked by snow in much of Japan, especially in the mountain ranges where the skiing is superb. Many tourists also flock to hot-spring resorts during this time. The climate is generally dry, and on the Pacific coast the skies are often blue. Tokyo, where the mean winter temperature is about 40°F (4°C), doesn't get much snow, though it can be crisp, cold, and wet. Northern Japan's weather, in Tohoku and Hokkaido, can be quite severe, while southern Japan, especially Kyushu, enjoys generally mild, warm weather. Wherever you are, you'd be wise to bring warm clothing throughout the winter months.

**Spring** arrives with a magnificent fanfare of plum and cherry blossoms in March and April, an exquisite time when all of Japan is ablaze in whites and pinks. The **cherry-blossom season** starts in southern Kyushu toward the end of March and reaches northern Japan about mid-April. The blossoms themselves last only a few days, symbolizing to Japanese the fragile nature of beauty and of life itself. Other flowers also bloom through May or June, including azaleas and irises. During spring, numerous festivals throughout Japan celebrate the rebirth of nature.

## Tokyo's Average Daytime Temperatures & Rainfall

|              | Jan | Feb | Mar | Apr | May | June | July | Aug | Sept | Oct | Nov | Dec |
|--------------|-----|-----|-----|-----|-----|------|------|-----|------|-----|-----|-----|
| Temp. (°F)   | 41  | 45  | 50  | 61  | 69  | 71   | 78   | 81  | 76   | 68  | 57  | 48  |
| Temp. (°C)   | 5   | 7   | 10  | 16  | 21  | 22   | 26   | 27  | 24   | 20  | 14  | 9   |
| Days of Rain | 4.3 | 6.1 | 8.9 | 10  | 9.6 | 12.1 | 10   | 8.2 | 10.9 | 8.9 | 6.4 | 3.8 |

**BUSY SEASONS**  Japanese have a passion for travel, and they all generally travel at the same time, resulting in jam-packed trains and hotels. The worst times of year to travel are around **New Year's,** from December 27 to January 4; **Golden Week,** from April 29 to May 5; and during the **Obon Festival,** about a week in mid-August. Avoid traveling on these dates at all costs, since all long-distance trains, domestic airlines, and most accommodations are booked solid. The weekends before and after these holidays are also likely to be crowded or booked. Exceptions are major cities like Tokyo or Osaka—since the major exodus is back to hometowns or the countryside, metropolises can be downright blissful during major holidays such as Golden Week, especially since most restaurants and museums do not close (privately owned museums are generally closed on public holidays; municipal and national museums that are normally closed on Mon will remain open if it's a public holiday, closing the next day on Tues instead). *Note:* During New Year's, all museums and most restaurants in Japan are closed, often for 3 or 4 days. ATMs are closed January 1 through January 3.

Another busy time is during the **school summer vacation,** from about July 19 or 20 through August. It's best to reserve train seats and book accommodations during this time in advance. In addition, you can expect destinations to be packed during major festivals, so if one of these is high on your list, be sure to make plans well in advance.

**HOLIDAYS**  National holidays are January 1 (New Year's Day), second Monday in January (Coming-of-Age Day), February 11 (National Foundation Day), March 20 or 21 (Vernal Equinox Day), April 29 (Greenery Day; from 2007 it will be called Showa Day, after Emperor Showa), May 3 (Constitution Memorial Day), May 4 (to be called Greenery Day beginning 2007), May 5 (Children's Day), third Monday in July (Maritime Day), third Monday in September (Respect-for-the-Aged Day), September 23 or 24 (Autumn Equinox Day); second Monday in October (Health Sports Day); November 3 (Culture Day), November 23 (Labor Thanksgiving Day); and December 23 (Emperor's Birthday).

When a national holiday falls on a Sunday, the following Monday becomes a holiday. Although government offices and some businesses are closed on public holidays, restaurants and most stores remain open. The exception is during the New Year's celebration, January 1 through January 3, when virtually all restaurants, public and private offices, stores, and even ATMs close; during that time, you'll have to dine in hotels.

All museums close for New Year's for 1 to 4 days, but most major museums remain open for the other holidays. If a public holiday falls on a Monday (when most museums are closed), many museums will remain open but will close instead the following day, Tuesday. Note that privately owned museums, such as art museums or special-interest museums, generally close on public holidays. To

avoid disappointment, be sure to phone ahead if you plan to visit a museum on a holiday or the day following it.

**FESTIVALS** With Shintoism and Buddhism the major religions in Japan, it seems as though there's a festival going on somewhere in the country almost every day, especially in summer. Every major shrine and temple has at least one annual festival. Such festivals are always free, though admission may be charged for special exhibitions such as flower shows. There are also a number of national holidays observed throughout the country with events and festivals, as well as such annual seasonal events as cormorant fishing and cherry-blossom viewing.

The larger, better-known festivals are exciting to attend but do take some advance planning since hotel rooms may be booked 6 months in advance. If you haven't made prior arrangements, you may want to let the following schedule be your guide in avoiding certain cities on certain days.

*A note on festival dates:* If you do plan your trip around a certain festival, be sure to double-check the exact dates with the Japan National Tourist Organization since these dates can change. In Japan, stop by a TIC office in Tokyo or at Narita or Kansai airports for a leaflet called "Calendar Events," which comes out monthly and describes major festivals in Tokyo and the rest of Japan. You can also try calling the local tourist office of the city hosting each festival for more information (see the regional chapters), though staff may not always speak English.

## JAPAN CALENDAR OF EVENTS
### January

**New Year's Day** is the most important national holiday in Japan. Because this is a time when Japanese are with their families and because virtually all businesses, restaurants, museums, and shops close down, it's not a particularly rewarding time of the year for foreign visitors. Best bets are shrines and temples, where Japanese come in their best kimono or dress to pray for good health and happiness in the coming year. January 1.

**Tamaseseri (Ball-Catching Festival),** Hakozakigu Shrine, Fukuoka. The main attraction here is a struggle between two groups of youths who try to capture a sacred wooden ball. The winning team is supposed to have good luck the whole year. January 3.

**Dezomeshiki (New Year's Parade of Firemen),** Odaiba, Tokyo. Agile firemen dressed in traditional costumes prove their worth with acrobatic stunts atop tall bamboo ladders in this parade. January 6.

**Usokae (Bullfinch Exchange Festival),** Dazaifu Temmangu Shrine, outside Fukuoka. The object here is to get hold of the bullfinches made of gilt wood passed from person to person. Given away by priests, they're supposed to bring good luck. January 7.

**Coming-of-Age Day,** a national holiday. This day honors young people who have reached the age of 20, when they can vote and assume other responsibilities. On this day, they visit shrines throughout the country to pray for their future. In Tokyo, the most popular shrine for the occasion is Meiji Shrine near Harajuku Station. Second Monday in January.

**Toka Ebisu Festival,** Imamiya Ebisu Shrine, Osaka. Ebisu is considered the patron saint of business and good fortune, so this is the time when businesspeople pray for a successful year. The highlight of the festival is a parade of women dressed in colorful kimono and

carried through the streets in palanquins (covered litters). January 9 to 11.

**Ame-Ichi (Candy Fair),** Matsumoto. Formerly a salt fair, this lively festival has featured traditional candy for the past century. Second weekend in January.

**Grass Fire Ceremony,** Nara. As evening approaches, Wakakusayama Hill is set ablaze and fireworks are displayed. The celebration marks a time more than 1,000 years ago when a dispute over the boundary of two major temples in Nara was settled peacefully. Second Sunday in January.

**Toshi-ya,** Kyoto. This traditional Japanese archery contest is held in the back corridor of Japan's longest wooden structure, Sanjusangendo Hall. January 15.

**Sounkyo Ice Festival,** Sounkyo Onsen. Ice sculptures, ice slides, frozen waterfalls lit in various colors, and evening fireworks are the highlights of this small-town festival. End of January through March.

## February

**Oyster Festival,** Matsushima. Matsushima is famous for its oysters, and this is the time they're considered to be at their best. Oysters are given out free at booths set up at the seaside park along the bay. First Sunday in February.

**Setsubun (Bean-Throwing Festival),** at leading temples throughout Japan. According to the lunar calendar, this is the last day of winter; people throng to temples to participate in the traditional ceremony of throwing beans to drive away imaginary devils, yelling, "Evil go out, good luck come in." February 3 or 4.

**Lantern Festival,** Kasuga Shrine, Nara. A beautiful sight in which more than 3,000 stone and bronze lanterns are lit. February 3 or 4.

**Snow Festival,** Odori Avenue, Sapporo. This famous 7-day Sapporo festival features huge, elaborate statues and figurines carved in snow and ice. Competitors come from around the world. Early February.

## March

**Omizutori (Water-Drawing Festival),** Todaiji Temple, Nara. This festival includes a solemn evening rite in which young ascetics brandish large burning torches and draw circles of fire. The biggest ceremony takes place on the night of March 12; on the next day, the ceremony of drawing water is held to the accompaniment of ancient Japanese music. March 1 to 14.

**Hinamatsuri (Doll Festival),** observed throughout Japan. It's held in honor of young girls to wish them a future of happiness. In homes where there are girls, dolls dressed in ancient costumes representing the emperor, empress, and dignitaries are set up on a tier of shelves along with miniature household articles. March 3.

**Kasuga Matsuri,** Kasuga Shrine, Nara. This 1,100-year-old festival features traditional costumes and classical dances. March 13.

**Vernal Equinox Day** is a national holiday. Throughout the week, Buddhist temples hold ceremonies to pray for the souls of the departed. March 20 or 21.

**Cherry-Blossom Season (Sakura Matsuri).** This rite of spring begins in late March in Kyushu and Shikoku, travels up Honshu through April, and reaches Hokkaido by the beginning of May; early to mid-April is when the blossoms bloom in Tokyo and Kyoto. Late March to May.

## April

**Kanamara Matsuri,** Kanayama Shrine, Kawasaki (just outside Tokyo). This festival extols the joys of sex and fertility (and more recently raises awareness about AIDS). It features a parade of giant phalluses, some carried by transvestites. You'll definitely get some unusual photographs here. First Sunday in April.

**Buddha's Birthday** (also called Hana Matsuri, or Floral Festival), observed throughout Japan. Ceremonies are held at all Buddhist temples. April 8.

**Kamakura Matsuri,** Tsurugaoka Hachimangu Shrine, Kamakura. This festival honors heroes from the past, including Minamoto Yoritomo, who made Kamakura his shogunate capital back in 1192. Highlights include horseback archery (truly spectacular to watch), a parade of portable shrines, and sacred dances. Second to third Sunday of April.

**Takayama Spring Festival,** Takayama. Supposedly dating from the 15th century, this festival is one of Japan's grandest with a dozen huge, gorgeous floats that are wheeled through the village streets. April 14 and 15.

**Gumonji-do (Firewalking Ceremonies),** Miyajima. Walking on live coals is meant to show devotion and to pray for purification and protection from illness and disaster. Daishoin Temple. April 15 and November 15.

**Yayoi Matsuri,** Futarasan Shrine, Nikko. Yayoi Matsuri features a parade of house-shaped floats embellished with artificial cherry blossoms and paper lanterns. April 16 to 17.

**Golden Week** is a major holiday period throughout Japan, when many Japanese offices and businesses close down and families go on vacation. It's a crowded time to travel; reservations are a must. April 29 to May 5.

## May

**Hakata Dontaku,** Fukuoka. Citizens dressed as deities ride through the streets on horseback to the accompaniment of flutes, drums, and traditional instruments. May 3 and 4.

**Children's Day** is a national holiday honoring all children, especially boys. The most common sight throughout Japan is colorful streamers of carp—which symbolize perseverance and strength, attributes desirable for boys—flying from poles. May 5.

**Takigi Noh Performances,** Kofukuji Temple, Nara. These Noh plays are presented outdoors after dark under the blaze of torches. May 11 and 12.

**Kanda Festival,** Kanda Myojin Shrine, Tokyo. This festival began during the Feudal Era as the only time townsmen could enter the shogun's castle and parade before him; today it features a parade of dozens of portable shrines carried through the district plus a tea ceremony. Held in odd-numbered years on the Saturday and Sunday before May 15.

**Aoi Matsuri (Hollyhock Festival),** Shimogamo and Kamigamo Shrines, Kyoto. This is one of Kyoto's biggest events, a colorful pageant commemorating the days when the imperial procession visited the city's shrines. May 15.

**Kobe Matsuri,** Kobe. This relatively new festival celebrates Kobe's international past with fireworks at Kobe Port, street markets, and a parade on Flower Road with participants wearing native costumes. Mid-May.

**Grand Festival of Toshogu Shrine,** Nikko. Commemorating the day in 1617 when Tokugawa Ieyasu's remains were brought to his mausoleum in Nikko, this festival re-creates that drama with more than 1,000 armor-clad people escorting three

palanquins through the streets. May 17 and 18.

**Sanja Matsuri,** Asakusa Shrine, Tokyo. Tokyo's most celebrated festival features about 100 portable shrines carried through the district on the shoulders of men and women in traditional garb. Friday, Saturday, and Sunday closest to May 18.

**Mifune Matsuri,** Arashiyama, on the Oi River outside Kyoto, is when the days of the Heian Period, when the imperial family used to take pleasure rides on the river, are reenacted. Third Sunday in May.

### June

**Takigi Noh Performances,** Kyoto. Evening performances of Noh are presented on an open-air stage at the Heian Shrine. June 1 and 2.

**Hyakumangoku Matsuri (One Million Goku Festival),** Kanazawa. Celebrating Kanazawa's production of one million *goku* (5.119 bushels) of rice, this extravaganza features folk songs and traditional dancing in the streets, illuminated paper lanterns floating downriver, public tea ceremonies, geisha performances, and—the highlight—a parade that winds through the city in reenactment of Lord Maeda Toshiie's triumphant arrival in Kanazawa on June 14, 1583, with lion dances, ladder-top acrobatics by Kaga firemen, and a torch-lit outdoor Noh performance. June 8 to 14.

**Sanno Festival,** Hie Shrine, Tokyo. This Edo Period festival, one of Tokyo's largest, features the usual portable shrines, transported through the busy streets of the Akasaka District. June 10 to 16.

**Rice-Planting Festival,** Sumiyoshi Shrine, Osaka. In hopes of a successful harvest, young girls in traditional farmers' costumes transplant rice seedlings in the shrine's rice paddy to

the sound of music and traditional songs. June 14.

**Cormorant Fishing,** Nagara River near Gifu, Kiso River in Inuyama (near Nagoya), and Oi River near Kyoto. Visitors board small wooden boats after dark to watch cormorants dive into the water to catch *ayu,* a kind of trout. Generally June to September.

### July

**Ueki Ichi (Potted-Plant Fair),** Fuji Sengen Shrine, Tokyo. Held near Asakusa, this fair displays different kinds of potted plants and bonsai (miniature, dwarfed trees) as well as a miniature Mount Fuji that symbolizes the opening of the official climbing season. July 1.

**Hakata Yamagasa,** Fukuoka. The main event takes place on the 15th, when a giant fleet of floats, topped with elaborate decorations that range from miniature castles to dolls, is paraded through the streets. July 1 to 15.

**Tanabata (Star Festival),** celebrated throughout Japan. According to myth, the two stars Vega and Altair, representing a weaver and a shepherd, are allowed to meet once a year on this day. If the skies are cloudy, however, the celestial pair cannot meet and must wait another year. Celebrations may differ from town to town, but in addition to parades and food/souvenir stalls, look for bamboo branches with colorful strips of paper bearing children's wishes. July 7.

**Hozuki Ichi (Ground-Cherry Pod Fair),** Tokyo. This colorful affair at Sensoji Temple in Asakusa features hundreds of stalls selling ground-cherry pods and colorful wind bells. July 9 and 10.

**Yamakasa,** Fukuoka. Just before the crack of dawn, seven teams dressed in loincloths and happi coats (short, colorful, kimono-like jackets) race

through town, bearing 1-ton floats on their shoulders. In addition, elaborately decorated, 9m-tall (30-ft.) floats designed by Hakata doll masters are on display throughout town. July 15.

**Gion Matsuri,** Kyoto. One of the most famous festivals in Japan, this dates back to the 9th century, when the head priest at Yasaka Shrine organized a procession to ask the gods' assistance in a plague raging in the city. Although celebrations continue throughout the month, the highlight is on the 17th, when more than 30 spectacular wheeled floats wind their way through the city streets to the accompaniment of music and dances. Many visitors plan their trip to Japan around this event. July 16 and 17.

**Maritime Day.** Dedicated to those employed in the marine industry, this national holiday celebrates the importance of the sea in Japan's livelihood. Third Monday in July.

**Kobe Summer Festival,** Kobe. Community groups, including many national and international samba teams, parade through the streets of Sannomiya and Motomachi. This is followed by fireworks displays over Kobe Port along with many staged events throughout the city. July 20.

**Obon Festival.** This national festival commemorates the dead who, according to Buddhist belief, revisit the world during this period. Many Japanese return to their hometowns for the religious rites, especially if a family member has died recently. As one Japanese whose grandmother had died a few months before told me, "I have to go back to my hometown—it's my grandmother's first Obon." Mid-July or mid-August, depending on the area in Japan.

**Tenjin Matsuri,** Temmangu Shrine, Osaka. One of the city's biggest festivals,

this dates from the 10th century when the people of Osaka visited Temmangu Shrine to pray for protection against diseases prevalent during the long, hot summer. They would take pieces of paper cut in the form of human beings and, while the Shinto priest said prayers, would rub the paper over themselves in ritual cleansing. Afterward, the pieces of paper were taken by boat to the mouth of the river and disposed of. Today, events are reenacted with a procession of more than 100 sacred boats making their way downriver, followed by a fireworks display. There's also a parade of some 3,000 people in traditional costume. July 24 and 25.

**Matsuri-Miyazaki Festival,** on the riverside by City Hall, Miyazaki. Miyazaki Prefecture's largest festival attracts more than 300,000 people with its performing arts and stalls selling food and local products. Late July.

**Kangensai Music Festival,** Itsukushima Shrine, Miyajima. There is classical court music and *Bugaku* dancing, and three barges carry portable shrines, priests, and musicians across the bay along with a flotilla of other boats. Because this festival takes place according to the lunar calendar, the actual date changes each year. Late July or early August.

**Hanabi Taikai (Fireworks Display),** Tokyo. This is Tokyo's largest summer celebration, and everyone sits on blankets along the banks of the Sumida River near Asakusa to see the show. It's great fun! Last Saturday of July.

## August

**Oshiro Matsuri,** Himeji. This celebration is famous for its Noh dramas lit by bonfire and performed on a special stage on the Himeji Castle grounds, as well as a procession from the castle

to the city center with participants dressed as feudal lords and ladies in traditional costume. First Friday and Saturday of August.

**Peace Ceremony,** Peace Memorial Park, Hiroshima. This ceremony is held annually in memory of those who died in the atomic bomb blast of August 6, 1945. In the evening, thousands of lit lanterns are set adrift on the Ota River in a plea for world peace. A similar ceremony is held on August 9 in Nagasaki. August 6.

**Tanabata Festival,** Sendai. Sendai holds its Star Festival 1 month later than the rest of Japan. It's the country's largest, and the whole town is decorated with colored paper streamers. August 6 to 8.

**Matsuyama Festival,** Matsuyama. Jubilant festivities include dances, fireworks, a parade, and a night fair. August 11 to 13.

**Takamatsu Festival,** Takamatsu. About 6,000 people participate in a dance procession that threads its way along Chuo Dori Avenue; anyone can join in. There's also a fireworks display. August 12 to 14.

**Toronagashi and Fireworks Display,** Matsushima. A fireworks display is followed by the setting adrift on the bay of about 5,000 small boats with lanterns, which are meant to console the souls of the dead; another 3,000 lanterns are lit on islets in the bay. Evening of August 15.

**Yamaga Lantern Festival**, Kumamoto. Women dressed in *yukata* dance through town with illuminated paper lanterns on their head. August 15 and 16.

**Daimonji Bonfire,** Mount Nyoigadake, Kyoto. A huge bonfire in the shape of the Chinese character *dai*, which means "large," is lit near the peak of the mountain; it's the highlight of the Obon Festival (see July, above). Mid-August.

## September

**Yabusame,** Tsurugaoka Hachimangu Shrine, Kamakura. Archery performed on horseback recalls the days of the samurai. September 16.

## October

**Okunchi Festival,** Suwa Shrine, Nagasaki. This 350-year-old festival, one of Kyushu's best, illustrates the influence of Nagasaki's Chinese population through the centuries. Highlights include a parade of floats and dragon dances. October 7 to 9.

**Marimo Matsuri,** Lake Akan, Hokkaido. This festival is put on by the native Ainu population to celebrate *marimo* (a spherical weed found in Lake Akan) and includes dances. Mid-October.

**Takayama Matsuri (Autumn Festival),** Takayama. As in the festival held here in April, huge floats are paraded through the streets. October 9 and 10.

**Nagoya Festival, Nagoya.** Nagoya's biggest event commemorates three of its heroes—Tokugawa Ieyasu, Toyotomi Hideyoshi, and Oda Nobunaga—in a parade that goes from City Hall to Sakae and includes nine floats with mechanical puppets, marching bands, and a traditional orchestra. Second weekend in October.

**Nada Kenka Matsuri (Roughhouse Festival),** Matsubara Shrine, Himeji. Youths shouldering portable shrines jostle each other as they attempt to show their skill in balancing their heavy burdens. October 14 and 15.

**Doburoku Matsuri Festival,** Ogimachi, Shirakawago. This village festival honors unrefined sake, said to

represent the spirit of god, with a parade, an evening lion dance, and plenty of eating and drinking. October 14 to 19.

**Nikko Toshogu Shrine Festival,** Nikko. A parade of warriors in early-17th-century dress are accompanied by spear-carriers, gun-carriers, flag-bearers, Shinto priests, pages, court musicians, and dancers as they escort a sacred portable shrine. October 17.

**Jidai Matsuri (Festival of the Ages),** Kyoto. Another of Kyoto's grand festivals, this one began in 1894 to commemorate the founding of the city in 794. It features a procession of more than 2,000 people dressed in ancient costumes representing different epochs of Kyoto's 1,200-year history, who march from the Imperial Palace to Heian Shrine. October 22.

### November

**Ohara Matsuri,** Kagoshima. About 15,000 people parade through the town in cotton *yukata,* dancing to the tune of popular local folk songs. A sort of Japanese Mardi Gras, this event attracts several hundred thousand spectators each year. November 2 to 3.

**Daimyo Gyoretsu,** Hakone. The old Tokaido Highway that used to link Kyoto and Tokyo comes alive again with a faithful reproduction of a feudal lord's procession in the olden days. November 3.

**Shichi-go-san (Children's Shrine-Visiting Day),** held throughout Japan. Shichi-go-san literally means "seven-five-three" and refers to children of these ages who are dressed in their kimono best and taken to shrines by their elders to express thanks and pray for their future. In Tokyo, the most popular sites are Asakusa Shrine, Kanda Myojin, and Meiji Shrine. November 15 (or the nearest Sun).

**Tori-no-Ichi (Rake Fair),** Otori Shrine, Tokyo. This fair in Asakusa features stalls selling rakes lavishly decorated with paper and cloth, which are thought to bring good luck and fortune. Based on the lunar calendar, the date changes each year. Mid-November.

### December

**Gishi-sai,** Sengakuji Station, Tokyo. This memorial service honors 47 *ronin* (master-less samurai) who avenged their master's death by killing his rival and parading his head; for their act, all were ordered to commit suicide. Forty-seven men dressed as the ronin travel to Sengakuji Temple (the site of their and their master's burial) with the enemy's head to place on their master's grave. December 14.

**On-Matsuri,** Kasuga Shrine, Nara. This festival features a parade of people dressed as courtiers, retainers, and wrestlers of long ago. Mid-December.

**Hagoita-Ichi (Battledore Fair),** Sensoji Temple, Tokyo. Popular since Japan's feudal days, this Asakusa festival features decorated paddles of all types and sizes. Most have designs of Kabuki actors—images made by pasting together padded silk and brocade—and make great souvenirs and gifts. December 17 to 19.

**New Year's Eve.** At midnight, many temples ring huge bells 108 times to signal the end of the old year and the beginning of the new. Families visit temples and shrines throughout Japan to pray for the coming year. In Tokyo, Meiji Shrine is the place to be for this popular family celebration, as thousands throng to the shrine to usher in the new year at midnight; many of the area coffee shops and restaurants stay open all night, and trains operate the entire night. December 31.

## 6 Travel Insurance

Check your existing insurance policies and credit card coverage before you buy travel insurance. You may already be covered for lost luggage, canceled tickets, or medical expenses. The cost of travel insurance varies widely, depending on the cost and length of your trip, your age, your health, and the type of trip you're taking. You can get estimates from various providers through **InsureMyTrip.com**. Enter your trip cost and dates, your age, and other information for prices from more than a dozen companies.

### TRIP-CANCELLATION INSURANCE

Trip-cancellation insurance helps you get your money back if you have to back out of a trip, if you have to go home early, or if your travel supplier goes bankrupt. Allowed reasons for cancellation can range from sickness to natural disasters to the State Department declaring your destination unsafe for travel. (Insurers usually won't cover vague fears, though, as many travelers discovered who tried to cancel their trips in Oct 2001 because they were wary of flying.) In this unstable world, trip-cancellation insurance is a good buy if you're getting tickets well in advance—who knows what the state of the world, or of your airline, will be in 9 months? Insurance policy details vary, so read the fine print—and especially make sure that your airline is on the list of carriers covered in case of bankruptcy. For information, contact one of the following insurers: **Access America** (✆ 866/807-3982; www.accessamerica.com); **Travel Guard International** (✆ 800/826-4919; www.travelguard.com); **Travel Insured International** (✆ 800/243-3174; www.travelinsured.com); or **Travelex Insurance Services** (✆ 888/457-4602; www.travelex-insurance.com).

### MEDICAL INSURANCE For travel overseas, most health plans (including Medicare and Medicaid) do not provide coverage, and the ones that do often require you to pay for services upfront and reimburse you only after you return home. Even if your plan does cover overseas treatment, most out-of-country hospitals make you pay your bills upfront, and send you a refund only after you've returned home and filed the necessary paperwork with your insurance company. As a safety net, you may want to buy travel medical insurance. Try **MEDEX Assistance** (✆ 410/453-6300; www.medexassist.com) or **Travel Assistance International** (✆ 800/821-2828; www.travelassistance.com).

### LOST-LUGGAGE INSURANCE

While checked baggage on domestic flights is covered up to $2,500 per ticketed passenger, on international flights (including U.S. portions of international trips), baggage is limited to approximately $9.07 per pound, up to approximately $635 per checked bag. If you plan to check items more valuable than the standard liability, see if your valuables are covered by your homeowner's policy, get baggage insurance as part of your comprehensive travel-insurance package, or buy Travel Guard's "BagTrak" product. Don't buy insurance at the airport, as it's usually overpriced. Be sure to pack any valuables or irreplaceable items in your carry-on luggage, as many valuables (including books, money, and electronics) aren't covered by airline policies.

If your luggage is lost, immediately file a lost-luggage claim at the airport, detailing the luggage contents. For most airlines, you must report delayed, damaged, or lost baggage within 4 hours of arrival. The airlines are required to deliver luggage, once found, directly to your house, hotel, or destination free of charge.

## 7 Health & Safety

### STAYING HEALTHY

It's safe to drink tap water and eat to your heart's content everywhere in Japan (pregnant women, however, are advised to avoid eating raw fish or taking hot baths).

You don't need any inoculations to enter Japan. **Prescriptions** can be filled at Japanese pharmacies *only if they're issued by a Japanese doctor.* To avoid hassle, bring more prescription medications than you think you'll need, clearly labeled in their original vials, and be sure to pack them in your carry-on luggage. But to be safe, bring copies of your prescriptions with you, including generic names of medicines in case a local pharmacist is unfamiliar with the brand name. Over-the-counter items are easy to obtain, though name brands are likely to be different from back home, some ingredients allowed elsewhere may be forbidden in Japan, and prices are likely to be higher.

If you suffer from a chronic illness, consult your doctor before your departure. For conditions like epilepsy, diabetes, or heart problems, wear a **Medic-Alert Identification Tag** (© 888/633-4298; www.medicalert.org), which will immediately alert doctors to your condition and give them access to your records through MedicAlert's 24-hour hot line.

In Japan, the local consulate and sometimes even the local tourist office can provide a list of area doctors who speak English. You might also consider asking your hotel concierge to recommend a local doctor—some hotels even have in-house doctors or clinics. If you can't find a doctor who can help you right away, try the emergency room at the local hospital. Many emergency rooms also have walk-in-clinics for cases that are not life-threatening; you may not get immediate attention, but you won't pay the high price of an emergency room visit.

### STAYING SAFE

One of the greatest delights of traveling in Japan is that the country is safe and the people are honest. When a friend of mine forgot her purse in a public restroom in Osaka in 2003, someone turned it in to the police station complete with money, digital camera, and passport. That said, petty crime is on the increase and you should stay alert for pickpockets in congested areas like Narita airport and Tokyo subways. Women should avoid public parks at night. Otherwise, I feel safe walking anywhere in Japan alone, day or night.

## 8 Specialized Travel Resources

### TRAVELERS WITH DISABILITIES

For travelers with disabilities, traveling can be a nightmare in Japan, especially in Tokyo and other large metropolises. City sidewalks can be so jam-packed that getting around on crutches or in a wheelchair is exceedingly difficult. Some subway stations are accessible only by stairs, and although trains have seating for passengers with disabilities—called "Priority Seats" and located in the first and last compartments of the train—subways can be so crowded that there's barely room to move. Moreover, Priority Seats are almost always occupied by commuters—so unless you look visibly handicapped, no one is likely to offer you a seat.

As for accommodations, only 10% of the nation's 8,500 hotels have barrier-free rooms (called a "universal" room in Japan and used primarily by the elderly), mostly in the expensive category. Only a scant 1% of Japanese inns have such rooms. Restaurants can also be difficult to navigate, with raised doorsills, crowded dining areas, and tiny bathrooms. Even

Japanese homes are not very accessible, since the main floor is always raised about a foot above the entrance-hall floor.

When it comes to **facilities for the blind,** however, Japan has a very advanced system. At subway stations and on many major sidewalks in Tokyo, raised dots and lines on the ground guide blind people at intersections and to subway platforms. In some cities, streetlights chime a theme when the signal turns green east-west, and chime another for north-south. Even Japanese yen notes are identified by a slightly raised circle—the ¥1,000 note has one circle in a corner, while the ¥10,000 note has two. And finally, many elevators have floors indicated in Braille, and some hotels identify rooms in Braille.

In any case, a disability shouldn't stop anyone from traveling. There are more resources out there than ever before. You can join the **Society for Accessible Travel and Hospitality** (© 212/447-7284; www.sath.org) for $45 annually, $30 for seniors and students, to gain access to its vast network of connections in the travel industry, including information on travel destinations, travel agents, and tour operators that specialize in travel for those with disabilities.

## GAY & LESBIAN TRAVELERS

While there are many gay and lesbian establishments in Tokyo, the gay community in Japan is not a vocal one, and in any case, information in English is hard to come by. The **International Gay & Lesbian Travel Association** (**IGLTA;** © 800/448-8550; www.iglta.org) is the trade association for the gay and lesbian travel industry and offers an online directory of gay- and lesbian-friendly travel businesses. **Above and Beyond Tours** (© 800/397-2681; www.abovebeyond tours.com) is the exclusive gay and lesbian tour operator for United Airlines.

The following travel guides are available at most travel bookstores and gay and lesbian bookstores, or you can order them from **Giovanni's Room** bookstore, 1145 Pine St., Philadelphia, PA 19107 (© 215/923-2960; www.giovannisroom. com): *Out and About* (© 800/929-2268 or 415/644-8044; www.outand about.com), which offers guidebooks and a newsletter ($20/year, 20 issues) packed with solid information on the global gay and lesbian scene; *Spartacus International Gay Guide* (Bruno Gmünder Verlag; www.spartacusworld.com/gayguide) and *Odysseus: The International Gay Travel Planner* (Odysseus Enterprises Ltd.), both good, annual English-language guidebooks focused on gay men; the *Damron* guides (www.damron.com), with separate, annual books for gay men and lesbians; and *Gay Travel A to Z: The World of Gay & Lesbian Travel Options at Your Fingertips* by Marianne Ferrari (Ferrari International; Box 35575, Phoenix, AZ 85069), a very good gay and lesbian guidebook series.

## SENIOR TRAVEL

More and more attractions are offering **free admission** to seniors over 65 (be sure to have your passport handy). However, discounts may not be posted, so be sure to ask. In addition, visitors to Japan should be aware that there are many stairs to navigate in metropolitan areas, particularly in subway and train stations and even on pedestrian overpasses.

Before leaving home, consider becoming a member of **AARP** (formerly known as the American Association of Retired Persons), 601 E St. NW, Washington, DC 20049 (© 800/424-3410 or 202/434-2277; www.aarp.org), for $13, which brings you a wide range of special benefits, including *AARP: The Magazine* and a monthly newsletter.

If you want something more than the average vacation or guided tour, **Elderhostel** (© 877/426-8056; www. elderhostel.org), arranges study programs

for those 55 and over (and a spouse or companion of any age) in the United States and more than 80 countries around the world, including Japan. On these escorted tours, the days are packed with seminars, lectures, and field trips, and academic experts guide the sightseeing. Most courses last 2 to 4 weeks and may include airfare, accommodations in student dormitories or modest inns, and meals.

## FAMILY TRAVEL

Japanese are very fond of children, which makes traveling in Japan with kids a delight. All social reserve seems to be waived for children. Taking along some small and easy-to-carry gifts (such as colorful stickers) for your kids to give to other children is a great icebreaker. Your children will be pampered and played with and receive presents and lots of attention.

While children may not like such foreign customs as eating raw fish, they will find many other Japanese experiences to their taste. What child could resist taking baths *en famille* and actually getting to splash? If you go to a ryokan, chances are your kids will love wearing *yukata* (cotton kimono). There are many attractions throughout Japan geared just toward kids, including sophisticated theme parks. Tourist spots in Japan almost always have a table or counter with a stamp and ink pad so that visitors can commemorate their trip; you might wish to give your children a small notebook so that they can collect imprints of every attraction they visit.

As for the food, the transition from kid-favorite spaghetti to udon noodles is easy, and udon and soba shops are inexpensive and ubiquitous. In addition, most family-style restaurants, especially those in department stores, offer a special children's meal that often includes a small toy or souvenir. For those real emergencies, Western fast-food places such as McDonald's and Kentucky Fried Chicken are seemingly everywhere in Japan.

Children 6 to 11 years old are generally charged half price for everything from temple admission to train tickets, while children under 6 are often admitted free. If your child under 6 sleeps with you, you generally won't even have to pay for him or her in most hotels and ryokan. However, it's always advisable to ask in advance.

Safety also makes Japan a good destination for families. Still, plan your itinerary with care. To avoid crowds, visit tourist sights on weekdays. Never travel on city transportation during rush hour or on trains during popular public holidays. And remember that with all the stairways and crowded sidewalks, strollers are less practical than baby backpacks.

To locate those accommodations, restaurants, and attractions that are particularly kid-friendly, refer to the "Kids" icon throughout this guide.

You can find good family-oriented vacation advice on the Internet from **Traveling Internationally with Your Kids** (www.travelwithyourkids.com), a comprehensive site offering sound advice for long-distance and international travel with children.

## STUDENT TRAVEL

Students sometimes receive discounts at museums, though occasionally discounts are available only to students enrolled in Japanese schools. Furthermore, discounted prices are often not displayed in English. Your best bet is to bring along an International Student Identity Card (ISIC; see below) together with your university student ID and show them both at museum ticket windows.

Before you leave home, arm yourself with the **International Student Identity Card (ISIC),** which offers substantial savings on entrance fees. It also provides

you with basic health and life insurance and a 24-hour help line. The card is available for $22 from **STA Travel** ((C) **800/781-4040** in North America; statravel.com), the biggest student travel agency in the world.

## 9 Planning Your Trip Online

### SURFING FOR AIRFARES

The "big three" online travel agencies—**Expedia.com, Travelocity.com,** and **Orbitz.com**—sell most of the air tickets bought on the Internet. (Canadian travelers should try expedia.ca and travelocity.ca; U.K. residents can go to expedia.co.uk and opodo.co.uk.). Each has different business deals with the airlines and may offer different fares on the same flights, so it's wise to compare.

Be sure to check **airline websites,** too. Even with major airlines you can often shave a few bucks from a fare by booking directly through the airline website and avoiding a travel agency's transaction fee (even airline phone agents may not know the cheapest online fare). For websites of airlines that fly to and from Japan, go to "Getting There," below. The **Japan National Tourist Organization** provides convenient links to airlines on its website; for a roundup of cheap fares originating in North America, go to JNTO's www.japantravelinfo.com.

### SURFING FOR HOTELS

Shopping online for hotels is generally done one of two ways: by booking through the hotel's own website or through an independent booking agency. These Internet hotel agencies have multiplied in mind-boggling numbers, competing for the business of millions of consumers surfing for accommodations around the world. This competitiveness can be a boon to consumers who have the patience and time to shop and compare online sites for good deals—but shop they must, for prices can vary considerably from site to site. And keep in mind that hotels at the top of a site's listing may

be there for no other reason than that they paid money to get the placement.

**Expedia.com** offers a long list of special deals and "virtual tours" or photos of available rooms so you can see what you're paying for (a feature that helps counter the claims that the best rooms are often held back from bargain websites). **Travelocity.com** posts unvarnished customer reviews and ranks its properties according to the AAA rating system. An excellent free program, **TravelAxe** (www.travelaxe.net), can help you search multiple hotel sites at once, even ones you may never have heard of—and conveniently lists the total price of the room, including the taxes and service charges. Other good sources include **Hotels.com, Asiatravel.com,** and **Asia-hotels.com,** but be sure to compare rates with individual hotel websites to make sure you're getting a good deal.

For Japan-specific websites, some 300 government-approved moderate and higher-priced hotels that are members of the Japan Hotel Association are listed at **www.j-hotel.or.jp/welcome-e.html**. Likewise, high-priced, government-registered members of the Japan Ryokan Association can be found at **www.ryokan.or.jp**. Budget-priced Japanese inns—which do not offer the service or the class of high-priced inns but do offer the experience of sleeping Japanese-style—are listed at **www.jpinn.com**. In addition, some 700 modestly priced accommodations throughout Japan are members of the Welcome Inn Reservations system, all priced at about ¥13,000 ($124) or less for a double (see **www.itcj.jp** for information and bookings). But Japan's largest online hotel reservations company for budget

and moderately priced accommodations is **http://travel.rakuten.co.jp**.

More websites are listed below under "Tips on Accommodations." In any case, it's always a good idea to **get a confirmation number** and **make a printout** of any online bookings.

## 10 The 21st-Century Traveler

### INTERNET ACCESS AWAY FROM HOME

Travelers have any number of ways to check their e-mail and access the Internet on the road, from their own laptops to cybercafes.

### WITHOUT YOUR OWN COMPUTER

Cybercafes are finally catching on in Japan, though they're still nonexistent in small towns. We've listed cybercafes for many destinations when we could find them (see individual chapters), but more may have opened by the time you travel. Ask local tourist offices for locations; or check **www.cybercaptive.com** or **www.cybercafe.com**, though from my experience information on these sites can be outdated. Avoid **hotel business centers** unless you're willing to pay exorbitant rates.

To retrieve your e-mail, ask your **Internet service provider (ISP)** if it has a Web-based interface tied to your existing e-mail account. If it doesn't, use the free **mail2web** service (www.mail2web.com) to view and reply to your home e-mail. For more flexibility, you may want to open a free, Web-based e-mail account with **Yahoo! Mail** (http://mail.yahoo.com). (Microsoft's Hotmail has severe spam problems.) Your home ISP may be able to forward your e-mail to the Web-based account automatically.

### WITH YOUR OWN COMPUTER

Wi-Fi (wireless fidelity), whereby you can get high-speed connection without cable wires, networking hardware, or a phone line is not yet big in Japan, though more hotels may come on board in the next couple years. In the meantime, all upper-end hotels and many moderately priced ones have high-speed dataports; some even have TVs that double as computers.

Major Internet service providers (ISPs) have **local access numbers** around the world, allowing you to go online by simply placing a local call. Check your ISP's website or call its toll-free number and ask how you can use your current account away from home and how much it will cost.

If you're traveling outside the reach of your ISP, the **iPass** network has dial-up numbers in most of the world's countries. You'll have to sign up with an iPass provider, who will then tell you how to set up your computer for Japan. For a list of iPass providers, go to www.ipass.com and click on "Individuals Buy Now." One solid provider is **i2roam** (www.i2roam. com; © **866/811-6209** or 920/235-0475).

Wherever you go, bring a **connection kit** of the right power and phone adapters, a spare phone cord, and a spare Ethernet network cable—or find out whether your hotel supplies them to guests. For Japan's electric requirements, see "Fast Facts: Japan," later in this chapter.

### USING A CELLPHONE

The three letters that define much of the world's **wireless capabilities** are GSM (Global System for Mobiles). Unfortunately, Japan uses a system that is incompatible with GSM. You can, however, use your **own mobile phone number** in Japan using Vodafone or NTT DoCoMo's 3G (3rd generation) service areas. Simply

bring your own SIM card and insert it into a rental phone or your own 3G handset. For more information, contact your mobile phone service provider, Vodafone (www.vodafone-rental.jp/eng/index.html), or NTT (http://roaming.nttdocomo.co.jp/index.html).

Otherwise, your best bet may be to rent a cellphone before leaving home. One well-known rental company is **InTouch USA** (© **800/872-7626;** www.intouchglobal.com), which charges $49 per week for telephone rental in Japan, plus 99¢ per minute for domestic calls and $1.50 per minute for calls to the U.S. (incoming calls are free).

Otherwise, if you're in Japan for only a few days and are staying in an upper-class hotel, most convenient but most expensive is to rent a mobile phone from your hotel. A quick check of several hotels in Tokyo turned up rental fees ranging from ¥520 to ¥1,500 ($4.95–$14) per day (the more expensive the hotel, the more expensive the rental), with placed calls costing an extra ¥250 to ¥330 ($2.40–$3.15) per minute (there is no charge for incoming calls).

Otherwise, Narita, Osaka, and Nagoya international airports offer phone rentals.

Narita, for example, has all the major phone companies, including **Nokia** (© **476/32-7636** in Terminal 1 or **476/34-6666** in Terminal 2) and **Vodafone Global** (© **03/5786-2030** in Terminal 1 or 2). Even the baggage delivery counters in the arrivals hall offer rental phones (check www.narita-airport.or.jp/airport_e/index.html for a list of phone rental companies and locations). Rental prices range from about ¥250 to ¥1,200 ($2.40–$11) per day, depending on the phone and company. If you want to order your phone through the Internet and pick it up upon arrival, try www.vodafone-rental.jp/inbound/eng/index.html or www.pupuru.com.

For extended stays, it's cheaper to purchase a mobile phone. **Tu-Ka,** based mostly in the Kanto (Tokyo) area and **Au** are two major cellphone companies, with outlets seemingly on every corner. You'll have to show proof of residence in Japan (which your hotel should be able to provide). Basic phones start at around ¥4,500 ($43), plus you'll have to purchase special prepaid cards (available at convenience stores) that are good for a limited number of calls within 3 months or so. Many plans are available.

## 11 Getting There

### BY PLANE
Japan has three international airports. Outside Tokyo is **Narita International Airport,** where you'll want to land if your main business is in the capital, in the surrounding region, or at points north or east such as Hokkaido. Another international airport, **Kansai International Airport (KIX)** outside Osaka, is convenient if your destination is Osaka, Kobe, Nara, Kyoto, or western or southern Japan; it is also convenient for domestic air travel within Japan, since most domestic flights out of Tokyo depart from Haneda Airport, necessitating an airport transfer if

you arrive at Tokyo International Airport. In between Narita and Kansai airports is the new **Central Japan International Airport (Centrair),** which offers the advantage of slick airport facilities (including hot-spring baths!) and easy access to Nagoya, the Shinkansen bullet train, Japan Alps, and beyond.

### THE MAJOR CARRIERS
Since the flying time to Tokyo is about 12 hours from Los Angeles and 14 hours from Chicago or New York, you'll want to consider onboard services and even mileage programs (you'll earn lots of

miles on this round-trip) as well as ticket price when choosing your carrier.

**Japan Airlines** (© 800/525-3663; www.japanair.com), is Japan's flagship airline and largest domestic carrier. Offering more international flights to Japan than any other carrier, it's noted for its excellent service, Western and Japanese cuisine, personal video screens even in economy on long-haul flights, and wireless Internet service on flights between Tokyo and New York and between Tokyo and London. JAL flies to Tokyo from Los Angeles, San Francisco, Honolulu, Chicago, and New York, and to Osaka from Los Angeles and Honolulu. JAL also serves other countries worldwide, including flights from London to Tokyo and Osaka and flights from New Zealand and Australia. One advantage to flying JAL is its Yokoso Japan Airpass, which allows passengers flying JAL to Japan to purchase discounted airfares for travel within Japan (see "Getting Around Japan," below, for more information).

Other airlines flying to Japan from North America, Europe, Australia, and New Zealand include:

**Air Canada** (© 888/247-2262; www.aircanada.com) offers flights from Vancouver and Toronto to Tokyo and from Vancouver to Osaka.

**Air New Zealand** (© 0800/737-000 in New Zealand; www.airnewzealand.com) flies from Auckland to Tokyo, Osaka, and Nagoya and from Christchurch to Osaka and Tokyo.

**All Nippon Airways** (© 800/235-9262; www.anaskyweb.com), which has a code-share alliance with United Airlines (you can earn United frequent-flier miles with ANA), offers flights from New York, Washington, D.C., Los Angeles, and San Francisco to Tokyo, Osaka, and Nagoya. It also flies from London and Sydney to Tokyo.

**American Airlines** (© 800/433-7300; www.aa.com) code-shares with Japan Airlines, giving it one of the largest networks from North America to airports throughout Japan (you can also earn American frequent-flier miles with JAL). It offers flights daily from Los Angeles, San Jose, Dallas, Chicago, and New York to Tokyo. It also offers nonstop flights from Dallas to Osaka.

**British Airways** (© 0870 850 9850 in Britain; www.ba.com) flies from London to Tokyo.

**Continental Airlines** (© 800/523-3273; www.continental.com) offers flights daily from Newark and Houston to Tokyo.

**Northwest Airlines** (© 800/447-4747; www.nwa.com), operating across the Pacific longer than any other airline, offers flights to Tokyo from Los Angeles, San Francisco, Seattle, Detroit, New York, Minneapolis–St. Paul, Portland, and Honolulu. It also offers direct flights from Detroit to Osaka and Nagoya.

**Qantas** (© 13-13-13 in Australia; www.qantas.com) flies from Sydney, Melbourne, Perth, and Cairns to Tokyo.

**United Airlines** (© 800/538-2929; www.united.com) has daily flights from San Francisco, Los Angeles, and Chicago to Tokyo. It code-shares with ANA.

### AIRFARES

Because the flight to Japan is such a long one, you may wish to splurge on upgraded service and a roomier seat. JAL's unrestricted round-trip first-class fare with 180-degree reclining seats from New York to Tokyo averages about $15,307, plus tax. JAL's business class restricted round-trip Business Saver fare is about $4,790 plus tax. Even full-fare economy-class tickets run about $5,834, but I doubt many people end up paying full fare.

JAL's Value economy fares run about $900, but you can save even more money with a Super Sale ticket, which carries restrictions. There are three fare seasons: Peak season (summer) is the most expensive, basic season (winter) is the least expensive, and shoulder season is between the other two in price and time. In all three seasons, fares are a little higher on weekends. **JAL**'s advance purchase Super Sale fare in February 2006 with minimum and maximum stay restrictions was $680 for round-trip travel between New York and Tokyo on a weekday.

## FLYING FOR LESS: TIPS FOR GETTING THE BEST AIRFARE

Passengers sharing the same airplane cabin rarely pay the same fare. Here are ways to keep your costs down.

- Passengers who can book their ticket **long in advance** or who **fly midweek** or **at less-trafficked hours** will pay a fraction of the full fare.
- Search **the Internet** for cheap fares (see "Planning Your Trip Online," above).
- Check local newspapers for **promotional specials** or **fare wars,** when airlines lower prices on their most popular routes. You rarely see fare wars offered during peak travel times, but if you can travel in the off season, you may snag a bargain.
- **Consolidators,** also known as bucket shops, are great sources of international tickets. Start by looking in Sunday newspaper travel sections; U.S. travelers should focus on the *New York Times, Los Angeles Times,* and *Miami Herald.* I also like looking at offers from Japanese travel agencies, such as JTB USA (© **800/ 235-3523;** www.jtbusa.com).
- Join **frequent-flier clubs.** Accrue enough miles, and you'll be rewarded with free flights and elite status. You don't need to fly to build frequent-flier miles—**frequent-flier credit cards** can provide thousands of miles in exchange for shopping.

## LONG-HAUL FLIGHTS: HOW TO STAY COMFORTABLE

Long flights can be trying, but with planning you can make an otherwise unpleasant experience almost bearable.

- Your choice of airline and airplane will definitely affect your leg room. Find more details at **www.seatguru. com**, which has extensive details about almost every seat on major U.S. airlines. For international airlines, research firm Skytrax has a list of average seat pitches at **www. airlinequality.com**.
- Emergency exit seats and bulkhead seats typically have the most legroom. Emergency exit seats are usually assigned the day of a flight (to ensure that the seat is filled by someone able-bodied); it's worth getting to the ticket counter early to snag one of these spots for a long flight. Keep in mind that bulkheads are where airlines often put baby bassinets, so you may be sitting next to an infant, plus you have to stow bags in overhead bins.
- To have two seats for yourself in a three-seat row, try for an aisle seat in a center section toward the back of coach. If you're traveling with a companion, book an aisle and a window seat. Middle seats are usually booked last, so chances are good you'll end up with three seats to yourselves. And in the event that a third passenger is assigned the middle seat, he or she will probably be more than happy to trade for a window or an aisle.
- Ask about entertainment options. Many airlines offer seat-back video systems where you get to choose your

## Tips  Coping with Jet Lag

A major consideration for visitors flying to Japan, especially on long flights from North America, is jet lag. Flying west has slightly less effect than flying east, which means you'll have a harder time recovering from your flight from Japan back to North America.

Here are some tips for combating jet lag:

- **Reset your watch** (and your mental clock) to your destination time as soon as you board the plane.
- **Drink lots of water** before, during, and after your flight. Avoid alcohol.
- **Exercise and sleep well** for a few days before your trip.
- If you have trouble sleeping on planes, **fly eastward on morning flights.**
- **Daylight** is the key to resetting your body clock. At the website for **Outside In** (www.bodyclock.com), you can get a customized plan of when to seek and avoid light. Upon reaching Japan, put in a normal day.
- If you need help getting to sleep earlier than you usually would (or staying asleep until morning), some doctors recommend taking either the hormone **melatonin** or the sleeping pill **Ambien**—but not together.

movies or play video games—but only on some of their planes.

- To sleep, avoid the last row of any section or a row in front of an emergency exit, as these seats are the least likely to recline. Avoid seats near highly trafficked toilet areas. Avoid seats in the back of many jets—these can be narrower than those in the rest of coach class. You also may want to reserve a window seat so that you can rest your head and avoid being bumped in the aisle.
- Get up, walk around, and stretch every 60 to 90 minutes to keep your blood flowing. This helps avoid **deep vein thrombosis,** or "economy-class syndrome," a potentially deadly condition that can be caused by sitting in cramped conditions for too long. Other preventative measures include drinking lots of water and avoiding alcohol (see next bullet).

- Drink water before, during, and after your flight to combat the lack of humidity in airplane cabins—which can be drier than the Sahara. Bring a bottle of water on board. Avoid alcohol, which will dehydrate you.

## 12 Escorted & Package Tours

### ESCORTED TOURS

If you're the kind of traveler who doesn't like arranging all the details of a trip, consider joining an escorted tour of Japan. Escorted tours are structured group tours, with a group leader. The price usually includes everything from airfare to hotels, meals, tours, admission costs, and local transportation. Many people derive a certain ease and security from escorted trips; whether made by bus, motorcoach, train, or boat, they let travelers sit back and enjoy their trip without having to spend lots of time worrying about details. You know your costs upfront, and there are few surprises. Escorted tours can take you to the maximum number of sights in the minimum amount of time with the

least amount of hassle—you don't have to sweat over the plotting and planning of a vacation schedule. On the downside, an escorted tour often requires a big deposit upfront, and lodging and dining choices are predetermined. You'll get fewer opportunities for serendipitous interaction with locals. Tours can be jam-packed with activities, leaving little room for individual sightseeing, whim, or adventure—plus they often focus on heavily touristed sites, so you miss out on the lesser-known gems.

Lots of tour companies offer group trips to Japan, including **General Tours** (© 800/221-2216; www.generaltours. com) and **Kintetsu International** (© 800/422-3481; www.kintetsu.com), both of which offer tours to major tourist destinations in Japan. **JTB USA** (© 800/235-3523; www.jtbusa.com) offers tours that may highlight anything from Japanese cuisine to art, while **Esprit Travel** (© 800/377-7481; www.esprit travel.com) specializes in small-group walking trips, hiking trips, and cultural trips that cover such interests as textile arts, Japanese gardens, and the old Tokaido Road. If you want someone else to take care of logistics but don't like group tours, **Artisans of Leisure** (© 800/214-8144; www.artisansof leisure.com) provides luxury tours with private guides that are tailored to your interests. For current information on escorted tours departing North America, including special-interest tours that may cover everything from gardens to Geisha to Frank Lloyd Wright in Japan, go to www.japantravelinfo.com.

## PACKAGE TOURS

Before searching for the lowest airfare, consider booking your flight as part of a travel package. Package tours are not the same as escorted tours. They are simply ways to buy the airfare, accommodations, and other elements of your trip (such as airport transfers and day tours) at the same time and often at discounted prices—kind of like one-stop shopping. Packages are sold in bulk to tour operators, who resell them to the public at a cost that usually undercuts standard rates.

Packages vary widely. Some offer a better class of hotels than others, or offer the same hotels for lower prices or a range of hotel choices at different prices. Flights may be on scheduled airlines; others book charters. Some allow you to add excursions or day trips (at lower prices than you could find yourself).

Travel packages are listed in the travel section of Sunday newspapers. Or check ads in national travel magazines like *Arthur Frommer's Budget Travel Mazazine, Travel & Leisure, National Geographic Traveler,* and *Condé Nast Traveler.*

Companies offering independent packages to Japan include **JTB USA** (© 800/235-3523; www.jtbusa.com), with many more listed at www.japantravel info.com, the North American website for JNTO.

Another great resource is the airlines themselves, which often package their flights with accommodations. **Japan Airlines,** Japan's flagship and largest domestic carrier, operates **JALPAK** (© 800/221-1081; www.jalpak.com) in North America and **Jaltour** (© 020/7462-5577; www. jaltour.co.uk) in Great Britain, with airfare and hotel packages to Japan, plus optional escorted day trips. In 2006 a 7-day, 5-night JAL package to Tokyo and Kyoto, for example, departing from Los Angeles and including tours of Kyoto and Nara, was $1,829 plus tax. **American Airlines** (© 800/949-3556; www.aa.com) offers hotels in Tokyo, Kyoto, Osaka, Nagoya, and other cities that can be combined with its flights.

## 13 Getting Around Japan

Japan has an extensive public transport system, the most convenient segment of which is the nation's excellent rail service. You can also travel by plane (good for long-distance hauls but expensive), bus (the cheapest mode of travel), ferry, and car.

### BY TRAIN

The most efficient way to travel around Japan is by train. Whether you're being whisked through the countryside aboard the famous Shinkansen bullet train or are winding your way up a wooded mountainside in a two-car electric streetcar, trains in Japan are punctual, comfortable, dependable, safe, and clean. All trains except local commuters have washrooms, toilets, and drinking water. Bullet trains even have telephones and carts selling food and drinks. And because train stations are usually located in the heart of the city next to the city bus terminal or a subway station, arriving in a city by train is usually the most convenient method. Furthermore, most train stations in Japan's major cities and resort areas have tourist offices. The staff may not speak English, but the office usually has maps or brochures in English and can point you in the direction of your hotel. Train stations also often have a counter where hotel reservations can be made free of charge. Most of Japan's trains are run by six companies (such as JR East and JR Kyushu) that make up the **Japan Railways (JR) Group,** which operates as many as 27,800 trains daily, including more than 500 Shinkansen bullet trains.

### SHINKANSEN (BULLET TRAIN)

The Shinkansen is probably Japan's best-known train. With a front car that resembles a space rocket, the Shinkansen hurtles along at a maximum speed of 300kmph (187 mph) through the countryside on its own special tracks.

There are five basic Shinkansen routes in Japan. The most widely used line for tourists is the **Tokaido-Sanyo Shinkansen,** which runs from Tokyo and Shinagawa stations west to such cities as Nagoya, Kyoto, Osaka, Kobe, Himeji, Okayama, and Hiroshima, before reaching its final destination in Hakata/Fukuoka on the island of Kyushu. Only *Nozomi Super Express* trains, the fastest and most frequent trains, however, cover the entire 1,175km (729 miles) between Tokyo and Hakata. Since the *Nozomi* is not covered by the Japan Rail Pass (see "Japan Rail Pass," below), most travelers must transfer in Osaka or Okayama if they're traveling the entire line. Trains run so frequently—as often as four times an hour during peak times not including the *Nozomi*—that it's almost like catching the local subway. The **Tohoku Shinkansen Line** runs north from Tokyo and Ueno stations to Sendai,

---

### *Tips* Travel Tip

In the following chapters, to help you reach the hotels, restaurants, and sights recommended in this book, I've included the nearest train or subway station or bus or streetcar information followed by the approximate number of minutes it takes to walk from the station or bus stop to your destination.

Morioka, Kakunodate, and Hachinohe, with branches extending to Shinjo and Akita. The **Joetsu Shinkansen** connects Tokyo and Ueno stations with Niigata on the Japan Sea coast. The **Nagano Shinkansen,** completed in time for the 1998 Winter Olympics, connects Tokyo and Ueno stations with Nagano in the Japan Alps. The newest line is the **Kyushu Shinkansen,** which currently runs between Shin-Yatsuhiro and Kagoshima but will extend all the way from Kagoshima to Hakata by 2011.

Shinkansen running along these lines offer two kinds of service—trains that stop only at major cities (like the *Nozomi* and *Hikari* trains on the Tokaido-Sanyo Line) and trains that make more stops and are therefore slightly slower. If your destination is a smaller city on the Shinkansen line, make sure the train you take stops there. As a plus, information on stops is broadcast in English.

**REGULAR SERVICE** In addition to bullet trains, there are also two types of long-distance trains that operate on regular tracks. The **limited-express trains,** or LEX *(Tokkyu)*, branch off the Shinkansen system and are the fastest after the bullet trains, while the **express trains** *(Kyuko)* are slightly slower and make more stops. Slower still are **rapid express trains** *(Shin-Kaisoku)* and the even slower **rapid trains** *(Kaisoku)*. To serve the everyday needs of Japan's commuting population, **local trains** *(Futsu)* stop at all stations.

There are also privately owned lines that operate from major cities to tourist destinations. **Kintetsu (Kinki Nippon Railway)** lines, for example, are useful for traveling in the Kansai area and to the Ise Shima Peninsula, while **Odakyu** serves Hakone.

**INFORMATION** For the most comprehensive site covering rail travel in Japan, go to **www.japanrail.com**, which also provides links to the websites of all six JR Group companies, gives fares and timetables for long-distance JR trains (including the Shinkansen), displays maps of Tokyo and Shinjuku stations, and contains information on rail passes.

In Japan, stop by the **Tourist Information Center** in downtown Tokyo or at the international airports in Narita or Osaka (see chapters 4 and 9 for locations and open hours) for the invaluable *Railway Timetable,* published annually in English and providing train schedules for the Shinkansen and limited express JR lines. To be on the safe side, I also stop by the train information desk or the tourist information desk as soon as I arrive at a new destination to check on train schedules onward to my next destination.

**TRAIN DISTANCES/TRAVELING TIME** Because Japan is an island nation, many people erroneously believe that the traveling time between destinations is of little concern. However, the country is much longer than most people imagine. Its four main islands, measured from the northeast to the southwest, cover roughly the distance from Maine to Florida. (Thank goodness for the Shinkansen bullet train!) In addition, transportation can be slow in mountainous regions, especially if you're on a local train.

The chart below measures the distances and traveling times from Tokyo to principal Japanese cities. Traveling times do not include the time needed for transferring and are calculated for the fastest trains available, excluding the *Nozomi* Shinkansen. (I have excluded the *Nozomi* because most tourists to Japan use the JR Rail Pass, which is not valid on the *Nozomi*.)

## Train Travel from Tokyo to Principal Cities

| City | Distance (Miles) | Travel Time |
|------|------------------|-------------|
| Beppu* | 763 | 7 hr. |
| Fukuoka (Hakata Station) | 730 | 6 hr. |
| Hakodate* | 549 | 6 hr. 10 min. |
| Hiroshima | 554 | 4 hr. 50 min. |
| Ito | 75 | 1 hr. 45 min. |
| Kagoshima | 927 | 9 hr. |
| Kamakura | 32 | 53 min. |
| Kanazawa* | 386 | 4 hr. 30 min. |
| Kobe (Shin-Kobe Station) | 366 | 3 hr. 20 min. |
| Kumamoto* | 804 | 9 hr. |
| Kyoto | 319 | 2 hr. 36 min. |
| Matsue* | 578 | 5 hr. 45 min. |
| Matsumoto | 146 | 2 hr. 30 min. |
| Matsuyama* | 589 | 7 hr. |
| Miyazaki* | 900 | 11 hr. |
| Nagasaki* | 826 | 8 hr. 30 min. |
| Nagoya | 227 | 1 hr. 55 min. |
| Narita Airport | 49 | 1 hr. |
| Nikko | 93 | 1 hr. 59 min. |
| Okayama | 455 | 3 hr. 52 min. |
| Osaka (Shin-Osaka Station) | 343 | 2 hr. 54 min. |
| Sapporo* | 746 | 10 hr. |
| Takamatsu* | 500 | 5 hr. 10 min. |
| Takayama* | 331 | 4 hr. |
| Toba* | 303 | 3 hr. 40 min. |
| Yokohama | 18 | 30 min. |

*Destination requires a change of trains.

**TRAIN FARES & RESERVATIONS**
Trains are expensive in Japan; ticket prices are based on the type of train (Shinkansen bullet trains are the most expensive), the distance traveled, whether your seat is reserved, and the season, with slightly higher prices (usually a ¥200/$1.65 surcharge) during peak season (Golden Week, July 21–Aug 31, Dec 25–Jan 10, and Mar 21–Apr 5). Children (ages 6–11) pay half fare, while up to two children 5 and younger travel for free with one adult (otherwise the third will pay half fare). I've included train prices from Tokyo for many destinations covered in this book (see individual cities for more information). Unless stated otherwise, prices in this guide are for adults for *nonreserved* seats on the fastest train available during regular season. You can buy JR tickets and obtain information about JR trains traveling throughout Japan at any Japan Railways station (in Tokyo this includes major stations along the Yamanote Line, which loops around Tokyo). If you wish to purchase a ticket using a credit card, go to a Reservation Ticket Office at any major JR station.

No matter which train you ride, be sure to hang onto your ticket—you'll be

## (Tips) Train Travel Tips

Pack lightly, since porters are virtually nonexistent, overhead luggage space is small, and most rail stations have lots of stairs. Your best sources for train schedules are at **www.japanrail.com** or the *Railway Timetable* available at JNTO's **Tourist Information Centers.** For routing information and questions about train times once you've begun your trip, call the Tourist Information Center at ⓒ **03/3201-3331** in Tokyo. You can also call the **JR East Infoline** in Tokyo for information in English (ⓒ **03/3423-0111**) daily from 10am to 6pm; no reservations are accepted by phone, but you can inquire about time schedules, fares, location of reservation offices, lost-and-found offices, and more.

required to give it up at the end of your trip as you exit through the gate.

**Seat Reservations**    You can reserve seats for the Shinkansen, as well as for limited-express and express trains (but not for slower rapid or local trains, which are on a first-come, first-served basis) at any major Japan Railways station in Japan. Reserved seats cost slightly more than unreserved seats (¥510/$4.85 for the Shinkansen). The larger stations have a special reservation counter called **Midori-no Madoguchi (Reservation Ticket Office)** or View Plaza (Travel Service Center), easily recognizable by their green signs with RESERVATION TICKETS written on them. If you're at a JR station with no special reservation office, you can reserve your seats at one of the regular ticket windows. You can also purchase and reserve seats at several travel agents, including the giant **Japan Travel Bureau (JTB),** which has offices all over Japan. It's a good idea to reserve your seats for your entire trip through Japan as soon as you know your itinerary, especially if you'll be traveling during peak times; however, you can only reserve 1 month in advance. If it's not peak season, you'll probably be okay using a more flexible approach to traveling—all trains also have nonreserved cars that fill up on a first-come, first-seated basis. You can also reserve seats on the day of travel up to departure time. I hardly ever reserve

a seat when it's not peak season, preferring instead the flexibility of being able to hop on the next available train (or, sometimes I reserve a seat just before boarding). If you want to sit in the non-smoking car of the Shinkansen bullet train, ask for the *kinensha.*

**Tips for Saving Money**    If your ticket is for travel covering more than 100km (62 miles), you can make as many stopovers en route as you wish as long as you complete your trip within the period of the ticket's validity. Tickets for 100 to 200km (62–124 miles) are valid for 2 days, with 1 day added for each additional 200km. Note, too, that stopovers are granted only if your trip does not originate or end in Tokyo, Yokohama, Osaka, Nagoya, Kyoto, Kobe, Hiroshima, Kitakyushyu, Fukuoka, Sendai, or Sapporo. You can, however, purchase a ticket, say, in Takayama bound for Nagasaki (a total of about 1,860km/1,155 miles), stopping in Kyoto and Hiroshima along the way. In short, you can save money by purchasing tickets for long distances even though you plan to break up your journey.

You can also save money by purchasing a round-trip ticket for long distances. A round-trip by train on distances exceeding 600km (373 miles) one-way costs 20% less than two one-way tickets.

There are also regional tickets good for sightseeing. The **Hakone Free Pass,** for

## *Value*  Japan Rail Pass

You can save quite a bit by purchasing a rail pass, even if you only plan to travel a little. How economical is a Japan Rail Pass? For example, if you were to buy a round-trip reserved-seat ticket on the Shinkansen from Tokyo to Kyoto, it would cost you ¥26,440 ($252), which is almost as much as a week's ordinary rail pass. If you plan to see more than just Tokyo and Kyoto, it pays to use a rail pass, *which you must buy outside Japan* (some regional rail passes, however, described below, can be purchased in Japan if you're a tourist in Japan).

Another advantage to a rail pass is that it offers a 10% discount or more off room rates at 50 JR Hotel Group hotels, including the Hotel Granvia in Kyoto, Okayama, and Hiroshima; the Crowne Plaza Metropolitan in Tokyo; and Hotel Kurashiki, Nara Hotel, JR Kyushu Hotel Fukuoka, JR Kyushu Hotel Kumamoto, JR Kyushu Hotel Nagasaki, ANA Hotel Clement Takamatsu, and many more. A Japan Rail Pass booklet, which comes with your purchase of a rail pass, lists member hotels (or go to www.jrhotelgroup.com).

example, offered by Odakyu railways (www.odakyu-group.co.jp), includes round-trip transportation from Tokyo and unlimited travel in Hakone for a specific number of days. If you don't qualify for a Japan Rail Pass (see below), the **Seishun 18 (Seishun ju-hachi kippu)** is a 5-day rail pass for ¥11,500 ($110) for travel anywhere in Japan so long as you use JR local and rapid trains (that is, no Shinkansen, limited express or express trains), making it a good bet for day excursions in the countryside (see www.jr.east.co.jp/e/pass/index.html). There's also a **Hokkaido Furii Pasu** (www.jrhokkaido.co.jp) valid for 7 days of JR train and bus travel in Hokkaido costing ¥23,750 ($226) for one person or ¥43,220 ($412) for two persons traveling together.

**JAPAN RAIL PASS** The Japan Rail Pass is without a doubt the most convenient and most economical way to travel around Japan. With the rail pass, you don't have to worry about buying individual tickets, and you can reserve your seats on all JR trains for free. The rail pass entitles you to unlimited travel on all JR train lines including the Shinkansen (except the

*Nozomi Super Express*), as well as on most JR buses and the JR ferry to Miyajima.

There are several types of rail passes available; make your decision based on your length of stay in Japan and the cities you intend to visit. You might even find it best to combine several passes to cover your travels in Japan, such as a 1-week standard pass for longer journeys, say, to Kyushu, plus a regional Kansai Area Pass for visiting Kyoto and other destinations in the Kansai area. Information is on passes is available online at www.japan railpass.net and www.japanrail.com.

**The Standard Pass** If you wish to travel throughout Japan, your best bet is to purchase the standard Japan Rail Pass. It's available for ordinary coach class and for the first-class Green Car and is available for travel lasting 1, 2, or 3 weeks. Rates for the ordinary pass, as of January 2006, are ¥28,300 ($269) for 7 days, ¥45,100 ($430) for 14 days, and ¥57,700 ($550) for 21 days. Rates for the Green Car are ¥37,800 ($360), ¥61,200 ($583), and ¥79,600 ($758) respectively. Children (ages 6–12) pay half fare. Personally, I have never traveled first class in Japan and don't consider it necessary. However,

during peak travel times (New Year's, Golden Week, and the Obon season in mid-Aug), you may find it easier to reserve a seat in the first-class Green Car, which you can get by paying a surcharge in addition to showing your ordinary pass.

**Before You Leave Home** The standard Japan Rail Pass is available only to foreigners visiting Japan as tourists and *can be purchased only outside Japan*. It's available from most travel agents (chances are your travel agent sells them), including the **Japan Travel Bureau (JTB;** ✆ **800/ 235-3523;** www.jtbusa.com). If you're flying **Japan Airlines (JAL;** ✆ **800/ 525-3663** in the U.S. and Canada; www.japanair.com) or **All Nippon Airways (ANA;** ✆ **800/235-9262** in the U.S. and Canada; www.anaskyweb.com), you can also purchase a rail pass from them.

Upon purchasing your pass, you'll be issued a voucher (called an **Exchange Order**), which you'll then exchange for the pass itself after you arrive in Japan. Note that once you purchase your Exchange Order, you must exchange it in Japan for the pass itself within 3 months of the date of issue of the Exchange Order. When obtaining your actual pass, you must then specify the date you wish to start using the pass within a 1-month period.

**Once You've Arrived** In Japan, you can exchange your voucher for a Japan Rail Pass at more than 40 JR stations that have Japan Rail Pass exchange offices, at which time you must present your passport and specify the date you wish to begin using the pass; most offices are open daily from 10am to 6 or 7pm, some even longer.

At both Narita Airport (daily 6:30am–9:45pm) and Kansai International Airport (daily 5:30am–11pm), you can pick up Japan Rail Passes at either the Travel Service Center or the Ticket Office. Other Travel Service Centers or Ticket Offices, all located in JR train stations, include those at Tokyo (daily

5:30am–10:45pm), Ueno, Shinjuku, Ikebukuro, and Shibuya stations in Tokyo; Kyoto Station; Shin-Osaka and Osaka stations; and Hiroshima, Sapporo, Nagoya, Okayama, Takamatsu, Matsuyama, Hakata, Nagasaki, Kumamoto, Miyazaki, and Kagoshima Chuo stations. Stations and their open hours are listed in a pamphlet you'll receive with your voucher.

**Regional Passes** In addition to the standard Japan Rail Pass above, there are regional rail passes available for ordinary coach class that are convenient for travel in eastern or western Honshu, Kyushu, or Hokkaido. These passes can be purchased before arriving in Japan from the same vendors that sell the standard pass. They can also *be purchased inside Japan* within the area covered by the pass (for example, the Hokkaido Rail Pass can be purchased either outside of Japan or, in Japan, only in Hokkaido). These regional passes are available *only to foreign visitors* and require that you present your passport to verify your status as a "temporary visitor"; you may also be asked to show your plane ticket. Only one pass per region per visit to Japan is allowed.

If you're arriving by plane at the Kansai Airport outside Osaka and intend to remain in western Honshu, you may wish to opt for one of two different **JR-West Passes** (www.westjr.co.jp), available at Kansai Airport, Osaka JR station, and other locations. The **Kansai Area Pass,** which can be used for travel between Osaka, Kyoto, Kobe, Nara, Himeji, and other destinations in the Kansai area, is available as a 1-day pass for ¥2,000 ($19), 2-day pass for ¥4,000 ($38), 3-day pass for ¥5,000 ($48), or 4-day pass for ¥6,000 ($57). Travel is restricted to JR rapid and local trains (that is, Shinkansen and limited express trains are not included in the pass) and unreserved seating.

The other JR-West Pass available is the **Sanyo Area Pass,** which covers a larger

area, allows travel via Shinkansen (including the superfast *Nozomi)* and JR local trains from Osaka as far as Hakata (in the city of Fukuoka on Kyushu), and includes Hiroshima, Okayama, Kurashiki, Himeji, and Kobe. It's available for 4 days for ¥20,000 ($190) and for 8 days for ¥30,000 ($286). Children pay half price for all passes.

Though not as popular as western Honshu, eastern Honshu also offers its own **JR-East Pass** (www.jreast.co.jp), which includes travel from Tokyo to parts of the Japan Alps and throughout the Tohoku District, including Sendai, Kakunodate, and Aomori via Shinkansen and local JR lines. Passes for travel in ordinary coach cars are available for 5 days for ¥20,000 ($190), 10 days for ¥32,000 ($305); a 4-day flexible pass (which is valid for any 4 consecutive or nonconsecutive days within a month) costs ¥20,000 ($190). Half-fare children's passes and Green Car passes are also available. Passes are available at Narita airport and JR stations in Tokyo, including Tokyo, Shinagawa, and Shinjuku.

If your travels are limited to the island of Kyushu, consider the **JR-Kyushu Rail Pass** (www.jrkyushu.co.jp), valid for 5 days for ¥16,000 ($152) and available for purchase at Hakata, Nagasaki, Kumamoto, Kagoshima Chuo, Miyazaki, and Beppu JR stations. Likewise, there's a **Hokkaido Rail Pass** (www.jrhokkaido. co.jp) valid for 3 days of travel for ¥14,000 ($133) or 5 days for ¥18,000 ($171), sold at Hakodate and Sapporo JR stations.

## BY PLANE

Because it takes the better part of a day and night to travel by train from Tokyo down to southern Kyushu or up to northern Hokkaido, you may find it more convenient to fly at least one stretch of your journey in Japan. You may, for example, fly internationally into Osaka and then onward to Fukuoka on Kyushu, from where you can take a leisurely 2 weeks to travel by train through Kyushu and Honshu before returning to Osaka. I don't, however, advise flying short distances—say, from Tokyo to Osaka—simply because the time spent getting to and from airports is longer and flights are costlier than the time spent traveling by Shinkansen.

Almost all domestic flights from Tokyo leave from the much more conveniently located **Haneda Airport.** If you're already in Tokyo, you can easily reach Haneda Airport via monorail from Hamamatsu-cho Station on the Yamanote Line. If you're arriving on an international flight at Narita Airport, therefore, make sure you know whether a connection to a domestic flight is at Narita or requires a transfer to Haneda Airport via the Airport Limousine Bus (see chapter 4 for details).

Two major domestic airlines are **Japan Airlines (JAL;** ⟨ **0120/25-5971** toll-free in Japan; see "Getting There," earlier in this chapter, for U.S. phone numbers; www.jal.co.jp); and **All Nippon Airways (ANA;** ⟨ **0120/029-222** toll-free in Japan; www.anaskyweb.com). **Japan Asia Airways (JAA;** ⟨ **0120/747-801),** is a smaller company with networks that stretch all the way from Okinawa to northern Hokkaido. Regular fares are generally the same no matter which airline you fly domestically. However, fares change often, with the most expensive fares charged for peak season including New Year's, Golden Week, and summer vacation. However, bargains do exist. Some flights early in the day or late at night may be cheaper than flights during peak time; you can also save by purchasing tickets 7 days in advance and even more by purchasing them 21 days in advance (ask carriers for details). Round-trip tickets provide a slight discount.

Purchasing domestic tickets in advance in connection with your international flight, however, may be the most economical way to go. JAL's "Yokoso (Welcome) Japan" air pass, purchased in conjunction with a JAL flight to Japan and sold only outside Japan, provides discount fares (¥10,000/$95 per flight) for domestic travel to 42 cities in Japan served by JAL and its two subsidiaries, JAL Express and Japan TransOcean Air. Visitors flying other airlines into Japan can take advantage of JAL's "Welcome to Japan Fare," which provides discounts on JAL's domestic flights regardless of which international airline is used to reach Japan. Also sold only outside Japan, it costs ¥12,600 ($120) per flight, with a minimum of two flights required. Note that there are blackout dates for both programs. ANA offers a similar program called Visit Japan Fare, which must be purchased outside Japan, allows you to travel any international carrier to Japan, and costs ¥12,600 ($120) per flight (a minimum of two flights required). Contact JAL or ANA or your travel agent for details.

Otherwise, there are small, regional airlines that generally offer fares that are cheaper than the standard full fare charged by JAL or ANA. These include **Skymark** (© **03/3433-7670** in Tokyo, or 092/736-3131 in Fukuoka), operating out of Fukuoka on the island of Kyushu; **Skynet Asia Airways** (© **0120/737-283** toll-free), connecting Nagasaki, Kumamoto, and Miyazaki on Kyushu with Tokyo; and **Air Do** (© **0120/ 0570-333** toll-free), out of Sapporo on the island of Hokkaido.

It pays, therefore, to shop around. Although it's subject to change, the regular fare for a one-way flight aboard JAL from Tokyo to Kagoshima, for example, is about ¥33,600 ($320) during the regular season, but drops to ¥20,500 ($195) for a 7-day advance purchase of certain

flights. Skynet's regular fare is ¥25,300 ($241) but drops to ¥9,800 ($93) for selected days if bought 2 months in advance. For comparison, a train ticket between the two cities is ¥23,420 ($223) one-way. Where airline fares are provided in this book (see individual city listings), fares are for regular tickets during the regular season. Tickets can be purchased directly through the airline, at **View Plazas** located at major JR train stations, or at a travel agent such as **Japan Travel Bureau (JTB),** which has offices virtually everywhere in Japan.

## BY BUS

Buses often go where trains don't and thus may be the only way for you to get to the more remote areas of Japan, such as Shirakawago in the Japan Alps. In Hokkaido, Tohoku, Kyushu, and other places, buses are used extensively.

Some intercity buses require you to make reservations or purchase your ticket in advance at the ticket counter at the bus terminal. For others (especially local buses), when you board a bus you'll generally find a ticket machine by the entry door. Take a ticket, which is number-coded with a board displayed at the front of the bus. The board shows the various fares, which increase with the distance traveled. You pay your fare when you get off.

In addition to serving the remote areas of the country, **long-distance buses** (called *chokyori basu*) also operate between major cities in Japan and offer the cheapest mode of transportation. Although **Japan Railways** operates almost a dozen bus routes eligible for JR Rail Pass coverage, the majority of buses are run by private companies. Some long-distance buses travel during the night and offer reclining seats and toilets, thus saving passengers the price of a night's lodging. For example, special buses depart from **Tokyo Station's** Yaesu south side every night for

Kyoto (¥8,180/$78), Osaka (¥8,610/$82), and Hiroshima (¥11,600/$110), arriving at those cities' main train stations the next morning. Night buses also depart from **Shinjuku Station**'s new south exit or from the **Shinjuku Highway Bus Terminal** (a 3-min. walk from Shinjuku Station's west exit) bound for Kyoto, Nagoya, Okayama, and beyond. Night buses also travel from these cities in reverse back to Tokyo. Slight discounts are given for round-trip travel completed within 6 to 10 days, depending on the city. There are also day buses traveling between Tokyo and Kyoto or Osaka for ¥6,000 ($50). Long-distance bus tickets can be purchased at View Plazas at major JR stations (for JR buses), at travel agencies such as JTB, or at bus terminals.

For more information on local and long-distance bus service, refer to individual cities covered in this guide or contact the **Tourist Information Center** in Tokyo (see "Visitor Information" in chapter 4).

## BY CAR

With the exception, perhaps, of Izu Peninsula, the Tohoku region, and Hokkaido, driving is not recommended for visitors wishing to tour Japan. Driving is British style (on the left side of the road), which may be hard for those not used to it; traffic can be horrendous; and driving isn't even economical. Not only is gas expensive (about $4.60 a gallon), but all of Japan's expressways charge high tolls—the one-way toll from Tokyo to Kyoto is almost the same price as a ticket to Kyoto on the Shinkansen. And whereas the Shinkansen takes only 3 hours to get to Kyoto, driving takes about 8 hours. In addition, you may encounter few signs in English in remote areas. Driving in cities is even worse: Streets are often hardly wide enough for a rickshaw, let alone a car, and many roads don't have sidewalks so you have to dodge people, bicycles, and telephone poles.

Free parking is hard to find, and garages are expensive. Except in remote areas, it just doesn't make sense to drive.

There are approximately a dozen major car-rental companies in Tokyo alone, with branch offices throughout the city and at the Narita Airport, including **Nippon Rent-A-Car Service** (© 03/3485-7196 for the English Service Desk), **Toyota Rent-A-Car** (© 03/5954-8008 in Tokyo, or 0070-8000-10000 toll-free), **Nissan Rent-A-Car** (© 0120/00-4123), and **Avis** (© 03/6436-6404); these companies also have branches throughout Japan. In almost every city with a JR train station, there is also a **JR Eki Rent-A-Car** office, offering 20% discounts on car rentals booked in conjunction with train tickets; you can reserve these cars at any JR Travel Service Center (located in train stations) anywhere in Japan. Rates vary, but the average cost for 24 hours with unlimited mileage ranges from about ¥8,000 to ¥13,000 ($76–$124) for a subcompact including insurance but not gas; in some tourist areas, such as Hokkaido, rates are more expensive in peak season.

If you do intend to drive in Japan, you'll need either an **international** or a **Japanese driving license.** Remember, cars are driven on the left side of the road, and signs on all major highways are written in both Japanese and English. It is against the law to drink alcohol and drive, and you must wear seat belts at all times. Be sure to purchase a bilingual map, since back roads often have names of towns written in Japanese only. Recommended is the *Shobunsha Road Atlas Japan,* available in bookstores that sell English-language books; it also contains maps of major cities, including Tokyo, Sapporo, Hiroshima, and others.

**BREAKDOWNS/ASSISTANCE** The **Japan Automobile Federation (JAF)** maintains emergency telephone boxes

along Japan's major arteries to assist drivers whose cars have broken down or drivers who need help. Calls from these telephones are free and will connect you to JAF's operation center.

## BY FERRY

Because Japan is an island nation, an extensive ferry network links the string of islands. Although travel by ferry takes longer, it's also cheaper and can be a pleasant, relaxing experience. For example, you can take a ferry from Osaka to Beppu (on Kyushu), with fares starting at ¥7,900 ($75) for the 11-hour trip. Contact the **Tourist Information Center** (see "Visitor Information" in chapter 4) for more details concerning ferries, prices, schedules, and telephone numbers of the various ferry companies.

## 14 Tips on Accommodations

Accommodations available in Japan range from Japanese-style inns to large Western-style hotels, in all price categories. Although you can travel throughout Japan without making reservations beforehand, it's essential to book in advance if you're traveling during peak travel seasons and is recommended at other times (see "When to Go," earlier in this chapter for peak travel times). If you arrive in a town without reservations, most local tourist offices—generally located in or near the main train station—will find accommodations for you at no extra charge. Note that in popular resort areas, most accommodations raise their rates during peak times. Some also charge more on weekends.

*A note on reservations:* When making reservations at Japanese-style accommodations and small business hotels, it's usually best if the call is conducted in Japanese or by fax or e-mail if available, as written English is always easier for most Japanese to understand. First-class hotels, however, always have English-speaking staff.

*A note about taxes:* A 5% consumption tax is included in all hotel rates, including those given in this book. However, upper-end hotels and some moderately priced hotels also add a 10% to 15% service charge to their published rates, while expensive ryokan will add a 10% to 20% service charge (in instances when hotels or ryokan include service charge in their rates, I indicate so in their individual listings). No service charge is levied at business hotels, pensions, and *minshuku* (accommodations in a private home) for the simple reason that no services are provided. In resort areas with hot-spring spas, a spa *(onsen)* tax of ¥150 ($1.45) is added per night. Tokyo levies its own local hotel tax (¥100–¥200/95¢–$1.90 per person per night). Unless otherwise stated, the room rates quoted in this book include consumption tax but not service charge, onsen tax, or local hotel tax.

## JAPANESE-STYLE INNS

Although an overnight stay in a traditional Japanese inn *(ryokan)* can be astoundingly expensive, it's worth the splurge at least once during your stay. Nothing quite conveys the simplicity and beauty—indeed the very atmosphere—of old Japan more than these inns with their gleaming polished wood, tatami floors, rice-paper sliding doors, and meticulously pruned gardens. Personalized service by kimono-clad hostesses and exquisitely prepared kaiseki meals are the trademarks of such inns, some of which are of ancient vintage. Indeed, staying in one is like taking a trip back in time.

If you want to experience a Japanese-style inn but can't afford the prices of a full-service ryokan, a number of alternatives are described below. Although they

don't offer the same personalized service, beautiful setting, or memorable cuisine, they do offer the chance to sleep on a futon in a simple tatami room and, in some cases, eat Japanese meals.

**RYOKAN**   Ryokan developed during the Edo Period, when feudal lords *(daimyo)* were required to travel to and from Edo (present-day Tokyo) every 2 years. They always traveled with a full entourage including members of their family, retainers, and servants. The best ryokan, of course, were reserved for the daimyo and members of the imperial family. Some of these exist today, passed down from generation to generation.

Traditionally, ryokan are small, only one or two stories high, contain about 10 to 30 rooms, and are made of wood with a tile roof. Most guests arrive at their ryokan around 3 or 4pm. The entrance is often through a gate and small garden; upon entering, you're met by a bowing woman in a kimono. Take off your shoes, slide on the proffered plastic slippers, and follow your hostess down the long wooden corridors until you reach the sliding door of your room. After taking off your slippers, step into your tatami room, almost void of furniture except for a low table in the middle of the room, floor cushions, an antique scroll hanging in an alcove *(tokonoma),* and a simple flower arrangement. Best of all is the view past rice-paper sliding screens of a Japanese landscaped garden with bonsai, stone lanterns, and a meandering pond filled with carp. Notice there's no bed in the room.

Almost immediately, your hostess serves you welcoming hot tea and a sweet at your low table so you can sit there for a while, recuperate from your travels, and appreciate the view, the peace, and the solitude. Next comes your hot bath, either in your own room (if you have one) or in the communal bath. Since many ryokan are clustered around onsen, many

offer the additional luxury of bathing in thermal baths, including outdoor baths. (For bathing, be sure to follow the procedure outlined in "Minding Your Ps & Qs," in appendix A—soaping and rinsing *before* getting into the tub.) After bathing and soaking away all tension, aches, and pains, change into your *yukata,* a cotton kimono provided by the ryokan.

When you return to your room, you'll find the maid ready to serve your kaiseki dinner, an elaborate spread that is the highlight of a ryokan stay. It generally consists of locally grown vegetables, raw fish *(sashimi),* grilled or baked fish, tempura, and various regional specialties, all spread out on many tiny plates; the menu is determined by the chef. Admire how each dish is in itself a delicate piece of artwork; it all looks too wonderful to eat, but finally hunger takes over. If you want, you can order sake or beer to accompany your meal (but you'll pay extra for drinks).

After you've finished eating, your maid will return to clear away the dishes and to lay out your bed. The bed is really a futon, a kind of mattress with quilts, and it is laid out on the tatami floor. The next morning, the maid will wake you, put away the futon, and serve a breakfast of fish, pickled vegetables, soup, dried seaweed, rice, and other dishes. Feeling rested, well fed, and pampered, you're then ready to pack your bags and pay your bill. Your hostess sees you off at the front gate, smiling and bowing as you set off for the rest of your travels.

Such is life at a good ryokan. Sadly, however, the number of upper-class ryokan diminishes each year. Unable to compete with more profitable high-rise hotels, many ryokan in Japan have closed down, especially in large cities; very few remain in such cities as Tokyo and Osaka. If you want to stay in a Japanese inn, it's best to do so in Kyoto or at a resort or hot-spring spa.

In addition, although ideally a ryokan is an old wooden structure that once served traveling daimyo or was perhaps the home of a wealthy merchant, many today—especially those in hot-spring resort areas—are actually modern concrete affairs with as many as 100 or more rooms. Meals are served in dining rooms. What they lack in intimacy and personal service, however, is made up for with cheaper prices and such amenities as modern bathing facilities and perhaps a bar and outdoor recreational facilities. Most guest rooms are fitted with a TV, a telephone, a safe for locking up valuables, and a cotton yukata, as well as such amenities as soap, shampoo, a razor, a toothbrush, and toothpaste.

**Rates** in a ryokan are per person rather than per room and include breakfast and dinner. Thus, while rates may seem high, they're actually competitively priced compared to what you'd pay for a hotel room and comparable meals in a restaurant. Although rates can vary from ¥9,000 to an astonishing ¥150,000 ($86–$1,425) per person, the average cost is generally ¥12,000 to ¥20,000 ($114–$190). Even within a single ryokan the rates can vary greatly, depending on the room you choose, the dinner courses you select, and the number of people in your room. If you're paying the highest rate, you can be certain you're getting the best room, the best view of the garden or perhaps even your own private garden, and a much more elaborate meal than lower-paying guests. All the rates for ryokan in this book are based on double occupancy; if there are more than two of you in one room, you can generally count on a slightly lower per-person rate; small children who sleep in the same bed as their parents often receive a discount as well. Although most Japanese would never dream of checking into an exclusive ryokan solo, lone travelers may be able to secure a room if it's not peak season.

Although I heartily recommend you try spending at least 1 night in a ryokan, there are a number of **disadvantages** to this style of accommodation. The most obvious problem is that you may find it uncomfortable sitting on the floor. And because the futon is put away during the day, there's no place to lie down for an afternoon nap or rest, except on the hard, tatami-covered floor. In addition, some of the older ryokan, though quaint, are bitterly cold in the winter and may have only Japanese-style toilets. As for breakfast, you might find it difficult to swallow raw egg, rice, and seaweed in the morning. (I've even been served grilled grasshopper—quite crunchy.) Sometimes you can get a Western-style breakfast if you order it the night before, but more often than not the fried or scrambled eggs will arrive cold, leading you to suspect they were cooked right after you ordered them.

A ryokan is also quite rigid in its **schedule.** You're expected to arrive sometime between 3 and 5pm, take your bath, and then eat at around 6 or 7pm. Breakfast is served early, usually by 8am, and checkout is by 10am. That means you can't sleep in, and because the maid is continually coming in and out, you have a lot less privacy than you would in a hotel.

Another drawback of the ryokan is that some will not take you. They simply do not want to deal with the problems inherent in accepting a foreign guest, including the language barrier and differing customs. I've seen a number of beautiful old ryokan I'd like to include in this book, but I've been turned away at the door. Sadly, I've also lost ryokan that once accepted foreigners but have stopped doing so following unacceptable behavior (such as climbing in the window at midnight). In any case, those recommended in the pages that follow do welcome Westerners.

You should always make a **reservation** if you want to stay in a first-class ryokan (and even in most medium-priced ones), because the chef has to shop for and prepare your meals. The ryokan staff members often do not look kindly upon unannounced strangers turning up on their doorstep (though I did this on a weekday trip to Nikko without any problems at all). You can make a reservation for a ryokan through any travel agency in Japan or by contacting a ryokan directly. You may be required to pay a deposit. For more information on ryokan in Japan, including destinations not covered in this guide, pick up the *Japan Ryokan Guide* at one of the Tourist Information Centers in Japan, which lists some 1,600 members of the **Japan Ryokan Association** (© **03/3231-5310**); or go online at www.ryokan.or.jp.

**JAPANESE INN GROUP**  If you want the experience of staying in a Japanese-style room but cannot afford the extravagance of a ryokan, you might consider staying in one of the participating members of the Japanese Inn Group—a special organization of more than 80 Japanese-style inns and hotels throughout Japan offering inexpensive lodging and catering largely to foreigners. Although you may balk at the idea of staying at a place filled mainly with foreigners, keep in mind that many inexpensive Japanese-style inns are not accustomed to guests from abroad and may be quite reluctant to take you in. I have covered several Japanese Inn Group members in this book over the years and have found the owners for the most part to be an exceptional group of friendly people eager to offer foreigners the chance to experience life on tatami and futons. In many cases, these are good places in which to exchange information with other world travelers, and they are popular with both young people and families.

Although many of the group members call themselves ryokan, they are not ryokan in the true sense of the word, because they do not offer the trademark personalized service nor the beautiful setting common to ryokan. However, they do offer simple tatami rooms that generally come with TVs and air conditioners; most have towels and cotton yukata. Some offer Western-style rooms as well, and/or rooms with private bathrooms. Facilities generally include a coin-operated washer and dryer and a public bath. The average cost of a 1-night stay is about ¥4,000 to ¥7,000 ($38–$67) per person, without meals. Breakfast is usually available if you pay extra; dinner is also sometimes available.

You can view member inns at **www. jpinn.com**. Or, upon your arrival in Tokyo, head to the Tourist Information Center for the free pamphlet called *Japanese Inn Group*. Make reservations directly with the ryokan in which you wish to stay (most have faxes and e-mail). In some cases, you'll be asked to pay a deposit (most accept American Express, MasterCard, and Visa). Many member inns belong to the Welcome Inn Group as well (see "Finding a Hotel or Inn," below), which means you can also make reservations through one of the methods described there.

**MINSHUKU**  Technically, a *minshuku* is inexpensive Japanese-style lodging in a private home—the Japanese version of a bed-and-breakfast. Usually located in tourist areas, rural settings, or small towns, minshuku can range from thatched farmhouses and rickety old wooden buildings to modern concrete structures. Because minshuku are family-run affairs, there's no personal service, which means you're expected to lay out your own futon at night, stow it away in the morning, and tidy up your room. Most also do not supply a towel or

yukata, nor do they have rooms with a private bathroom. There is, however, a public bathroom, and meals, included in the rates, are served in a communal dining room. Since minshuku cater primarily to domestic travelers, they're often excellent places to meet Japanese.

Officially, what differentiates a ryokan from a minshuku is the level of service and corresponding price, but the differences are sometimes very slight. I've stayed in cheap ryokan providing almost no service and in minshuku too large and modern to be considered private homes. The average per-person cost for 1 night in a minshuku is generally ¥7,000 to ¥9,000 ($67–$86), including two meals.

Reservations for minshuku should be made directly with the establishment. Or, contact the **Japan Minshuku Center** (© **03/3216-6558;** www.koyado.net/english.html) for a reservation in one of its 3,000 member minshuku throughout Japan. Accommodations are for a minimum of two people, and a small handling fee of ¥300 to ¥500 ($2.85–$4.75) is charged for each reservation.

**KOKUMIN SHUKUSHA** A *kokumin shukusha* can be translated as a People's Lodge—public lodging found primarily in national parks and resort and vacation areas. Established by the government, there are more than 300 of these facilities throughout Japan. Catering largely to Japanese school groups and families, they offer basic, Japanese-style rooms at an average daily rate of about ¥8,000 ($76) per person, including two meals. Since they're usually full during the summer, peak seasons, holidays, and weekends, reservations are a must and can be made directly at the facility or through a travel agency; many are also in the *Directory of Welcome Inns* (see "Finding a Hotel or Inn," below). The drawback to many of these lodges is that because they're often located in national parks and scenic spots, the best way to reach them is by car.

**SHUKUBO** These are lodgings in a Buddhist temple, similar to inexpensive ryokan, except they're attached to temples and serve vegetarian food. There's usually an early-morning service at 6am, which you're welcome—in some *shukubo,* required—to join. Probably the best place to experience life in a temple is at Mount Koya (see chapter 9). Prices at shukubo generally range from about ¥7,000 to ¥15,000 ($67–$143) per person, including two meals.

## WESTERN-STYLE ACCOMMODATIONS

Western-style lodgings range from luxurious first-class hotels to inexpensive ones catering primarily to Japanese businessmen.

When selecting and reserving your hotel room, contact the hotel directly to inquire about rates, even if a North American toll-free 800 number is provided; sometimes there are special packages, such as weekend or honeymoon packages, that central reservations desks will not be aware of. Special rates are also often available only through the hotel's website. In any case, always ask what kinds of rooms are available. Almost all hotels in Japan offer a wide range of rooms at various prices; room size is the most important factor in pricing. Rooms with views—whether of the sea or a castle—are also generally more expensive, as are rooms on higher floors. In Japan, a **twin room** refers to a room with twin beds, and a **double room** refers to one with a double (or larger) bed; most hotels charge more for a twin room, but others charge more for doubles. Since Japanese couples generally prefer twin beds, doubles are often in short supply, especially in business hotels. A **Hollywood twin** means two twin beds pushed together side by side.

Some of the upper-priced hotels also offer executive floors, which are generally

on the highest floors and offer such perks as a private lounge with separate check-in, more in-room amenities, complimentary breakfast and evening cocktails, extended checkout time, and privileges that can include free use of the health club.

Once you decide on the type of room you want, ask for the best in that category. For example, if you want a standard room, and deluxe rooms start on the 14th floor, ask for a standard on the 13th floor, where you might have a better view than on the 4th floor. In addition, be specific about the kind of room you want, whether it's a nonsmoking room, a room with a view of Mount Fuji, or a room with a dataport for your computer modem.

Be sure to give your approximate time of arrival, especially if it's after 6pm when they might give your room away. Check-in ranges from about 1 or 2pm in first-class hotels to 3 or 4pm for business hotels. Checkout is generally about 10am for business hotels and 11am or noon for upper-range hotels. In any case, it's perfectly acceptable to leave luggage with the front desk or bell captain if you arrive early or want to sightsee after checking out.

**HOTELS**    Both first-class and medium-priced hotels in Japan are known for excellent service and cleanliness. The first-class hotels in the larger cities can compete with the best hotels in the world and offer a **wide range of services,** from health clubs and aesthetic spas with massage services to business centers and top-class restaurants and shopping arcades. Unfortunately, health clubs and swimming pools usually cost extra—anywhere from ¥1,050 to an outrageous ¥5,000 ($10–$48) per single use. In addition, outdoor pools are generally open only in July and August. Rooms in upper-range hotels and many moderate hotels in large cities catering to tourists come with such **standard features** as a minibar, bilingual cable TV with pay movies and English-language channels like CNN or BBC, a

clock, a radio, cotton yukata robe, a hot-water pot and tea (and occasionally coffee, though you usually have to pay extra for it), a hair dryer, and a private bathroom with a tub/shower combination. (Since Japanese are used to soaping down and rinsing off before bathing, it would be rare to find tubs without showers; similarly, showers without tubs are practically non-existent in this nation of bathers.) Most hotels nowadays also have "Washlet" toilets, which are combination toilets and spray bidets with a controllable range of speeds and temperatures. Because they're accustomed to foreigners, most hotels in this category employ an English-speaking staff and offer nonsmoking floors or rooms. Services provided include room service, same-day laundry and dry cleaning, and English-language newspapers (often complimentary) delivered to your room. Note that in medium-range hotels, same-day laundry service is not available Sundays and holidays and you must turn in your laundry by 10am to receive it by 5pm that day.

The most expensive hotels in Japan are in Tokyo and Osaka, where you'll pay at least ¥30,000 ($285) for a double or twin room in a first-class hotel and ¥15,000 to ¥29,000 ($143–$275) for the same in a medium-priced hotel. Outside the major cities, rooms for two people generally range from about ¥18,000 to ¥22,000 ($171–$209) for first-class hotels and ¥12,000 to ¥16,000 ($115–$152) for medium-priced hotels.

Although some internationally known chains have a presence in Japan, including Four Seasons (www.fourseasons.com), Hilton (www.hilton.com), Hyatt (www.hyatt.com), Holiday Inn (www.holiday-inn.com), Marriott (www.Marriott.com), Radisson (www.radisson.com), Ritz-Carlton (www.ritzcarlton.com), and Westin (www.starwood.com/westin/index.html), Japanese chains naturally dominate. ANA (associated with All Nippon

## (Value)  Tips for Saving on Your Hotel Room

Although Japanese hotels have traditionally remained pretty loyal to their published **rack rates,** which are always available at the front desk, the recession has opened possibilities for bargains.

- **Always ask politely whether a room less expensive than the first one mentioned is available.** Since there are usually many categories, ask what the difference is, say, between a standard twin and a superior twin. If there are two of you, ask whether a double or a twin room is cheaper. Ask whether there are corporate discounts. Find out the hotel's policy on children—do children stay free in the room or is there a special rate?
- **Contact the hotel directly.** In addition to calling a hotel's toll-free number, call the hotel directly to see where you can get the best deal.
- **Check the Internet.** If the hotel has a website, check to see whether discounts or special promotions are offered. Some hotels offer discounts exclusively through the Internet.
- **Ask about promotions and special plans.** Hotels frequently offer special "plans," including "Spring Plans," "Ladies' Plans," and even "Shopping Plans" that provide cheaper rates and services.
- **Remember the law of supply and demand.** Resort hotels are more crowded and therefore more expensive on weekends and during peak travel periods such as Golden Week. Discounts, therefore, are often available for midweek and off-season stays.
- **Ask about hotel membership plans.** Some chain business hotels offer hotel memberships with discounts on meals and free stays after a certain number of nights. Others, such as the New Otani, Okura, and the Imperial in Tokyo, allow free use of the hotel swimming pool simply if you become a member at no extra charge. Ask the concierge or front desk.
- **Ask the local tourist office whether there's a Welcome Card.** Several tourist regions around Japan, including Kagawa Prefecture (Shikoku), Fukuoka, Aomori Prefecture (Tohoku District), and Hiroshima, offer a free **Welcome Card** to foreign visitors, providing discounts on room rates in participating hotels. Find out more about Welcome Cards at JNTO's website (www.jnto.go.jp/eng/GJ/BTG/welcome_cards.html).

Airways; www.anahotels.com), New Otani (www1.newotani.co.jp/en), Nikko (associated with Japan Airlines; www.nikkohotels.com), and Prince (www.princehotels.co.jp) are some of the top names.

In addition to the hotel recommendations in this guide, you can also check out the more than 400 members of the Japan Hotel Association listed in the brochure *Hotels in Japan* available from the Tourist Information Centers in Japan or online at www.j-hotel.or.jp/welcome-e.html.

Finally, some 50 hotels that are members of the Japan Railways Group (www.jrhotelgroup.com), almost always located next to major train stations, provide discounts (usually 10%) for holders of the Japan Rail Pass.

**BUSINESS HOTELS** Catering traditionally to traveling Japanese businessmen, a "business hotel" is a no-frills establishment with tiny, sparsely furnished rooms, most of them singles but usually with some twin or double rooms also available. Primarily just places to crash for the night, these rooms usually have everything you need, but in miniature form—minuscule bathroom, tiny bathtub/shower, small bed (or beds), and barely enough space to unpack your bags. If you're a large person, you may have trouble sleeping in a place like this. There are no bellhops, no room service, and sometimes not even a lobby or coffee shop, although usually there are vending machines selling beer, soda, cigarettes, and snacks. Some business hotels do not have nonsmoking rooms, though this is slowly changing. The advantages of staying in business hotels are price—starting as low as ¥6,000 or ¥7,000 ($57 or $66) for a single—and location—usually near major train and subway stations. Check-in is usually not until 3 or 4pm, and checkout is usually at 10am; you can leave your bags at the front desk.

As for business-hotel chains, I'm partial to the Toyoko Inn chain (www.toyoko-inn.com), which boasts more than 100 locations around Japan. Often managed by women, they offer minuscule rooms outfitted with about everything you need, including free Internet access, and have raised the bar in business-hotel amenities by adding lobby computers with free Internet access, free domestic calls from lobby phones, free movie channels (often in English), and free Japanese breakfast. Another chain to look for is Tokyu Hotels (www.tokyuhotels.co.jp), including its budget Tokyu Inns, all with specially designed Ladies Rooms with female-oriented toiletries and amenities.

For a short list of business hotels in Japan, check the Japan City Hotel Association's list at www.jcha.or.jp. Another good site is http://travel.rakuten.co.jp, Japan's largest online hotel reservation company for budget and moderately priced accommodations.

**PENSIONS** Pensions are like minshuku, except that accommodations are Western-style with beds instead of futons, and the two meals served are usually Western. Often managed by a young couple or a young staff, they cater to young Japanese and are most often located in ski resorts and in the countryside, sometimes making access a problem. Averaging 10 guest rooms, many seem especially geared to young Japanese women and are thus done up in rather feminine-looking decor with lots of pinks and flower prints. The average cost is ¥8,000 to ¥10,000 ($76–$95) per person per night, including two meals.

**YOUTH HOSTELS** There are some 350 youth hostels in Japan, most of them privately run and operating in locations ranging from temples to concrete blocks. There's no age limit (though children younger than 4 may not be accepted), and although most of them require a youth hostel membership card from the Japan Youth Hostel Association, they let foreigners stay without one at no extra charge or for ¥600 ($5.70) extra per night (after 6 nights you automatically become a YH member). Youth hostels are reasonable, costing about ¥3,500 ($33) per day including two meals, and can be reserved in advance. However, there are usually quite a few restrictions, such as a 9 or 10pm curfew, a lights-out policy shortly thereafter, an early breakfast time, and closed times through the day, generally from about 10am to 3pm. In addition, rooms generally have many bunk beds or futons, affording little privacy. On the other hand, they're certainly the cheapest accommodations in Japan.

Because youth hostels are often inconveniently located, I have included only a couple in this guide, but if you plan on staying almost exclusively in hostels, pick up a pamphlet called "Youth Hostel Map of Japan," available at the **Tourist Information Centers** in Japan, or check www.jyh.or.jp. For youth hostel membership in the U.S., contact **Hostelling International USA** (© **301/495-1240;** www.hiusa.org). Cards cost $28 for adults, $18 for seniors older than 54, and are free for children younger than 18.

**CAPSULE HOTELS**   Capsule hotels, which became popular in the early 1980s, are used primarily by Japanese businessmen who have spent an evening out drinking and missed the last train home—costing about ¥4,000 to ¥5,000 ($38–$48) per person, a capsule hotel is sometimes cheaper than a taxi to the suburbs. Units are small—no larger than a coffin and consisting of a bed, a private color TV, an alarm clock, and a radio—and are usually stacked two deep in rows down a corridor; the only thing separating you from your probably inebriated neighbor is a curtain. A cotton kimono and a locker are provided, and bathrooms and toilets are communal. Most capsule hotels do not accept women, but those that do have separate facilities.

**INTERNATIONAL VILLAS**   International Villas are such a great deal for foreigners that I want to give them special mention here. These small country inns are financed and maintained by the Okayama prefectural government and are open only to foreigners, although accompanying Japanese guests are welcome. Each villa is small, with a half-dozen or so guest rooms (usually without private bathroom), and is equipped with public bathroom and kitchen facilities. No meals are served, but you can cook your own or visit one of the local restaurants. There are five International Villas, most of them in small villages or rural settings with mostly Western-style twins. An overnight stay is ¥3,000 ($29) per person for nonmembers and ¥2,500 ($24) for members, but membership costs only ¥500 ($4.75) and is available at any villa. For more information, see "Okayama: Gateway to Shikoku," in chapter 9.

**LOVE HOTELS**   Finally, a word about Japan's so-called "love hotels." Usually found close to entertainment districts and along major highways, such hotels do not provide sexual services themselves; rather, they offer rooms for rent by the hour to couples. You'll know that you've wandered into a love-hotel district when you notice hourly rates posted near the front door, though gaudy structures shaped like ocean liners or castles are a dead giveaway. Because many of them have reasonable overnight rates as well, I have friends who, finding themselves out too late and too far from home, have checked into love hotels, solo.

## FINDING A HOTEL OR INN

If you find all my recommendations for a certain city fully booked, or if you're traveling to destinations not covered in this guide, there are several ways to find alternative accommodations. High-end hotels and ryokan can be booked through travel agencies in Japan, including the ubiquitous Japan Travel Bureau.

Websites are also a good bet. Check all the websites mentioned above, as well as those listed in "Planning Your Trip Online," earlier in this chapter.

For budget accommodations, at the top of my list are those that are members of **Welcome Inns,** operated in cooperation with the Japan National Tourist Organization. Some 700 modestly priced accommodations in Japan, including business hotels and Japanese inns, are members of Welcome Inns, with rates ¥8,000 ($76) or less for a single and ¥13,000 ($124) or less for a double. No

fee is charged for the reservation service, though you are asked to guarantee your reservation with a credit card.

In addition to booking rooms via the Internet at www.itcj.jp, you can also book a room by appearing in person at one of the three Tourist Information Centers in Japan—at Narita Airport (in the arrivals lobbies of Terminals 1 and 2); near Yurakucho Station in the heart of Tokyo (see "Visitor Information" in chapter 4); and at Osaka's Kansai International Airport (see "Osaka" in chapter 9). Reservations are accepted at the Narita TIC daily from 9am to 7:30pm; at the Tokyo TIC daily from 9:15 to 11:30am and 1 to 4:45pm; and at the Kansai TIC daily 9am to 8:30. You can also make Welcome Inn reservations at the **Kyoto Tourist Information** on the ninth floor of Isetan department store in Kyoto Station (© **075/344-3300;** daily 10am–6pm,

closed the second and fourth Tues of every month).

Finally, if you arrive at your destination and then discover you need help obtaining accommodations, most major train stations contain a tourist information office or a hotel and ryokan reservation counter where you can inquire about a place to stay. Although policies may differ from office to office, you generally don't have to pay a fee for their services, but you usually do have to pay a percentage of your overnight charge as a deposit. The disadvantage is that you don't see the locale beforehand, and if there's space left at a ryokan even in peak tourist season, there may be a reason for it. Although these offices can be a real lifesaver in a pinch and in most cases may be able to recommend quite reasonable and pleasant places in which to stay, it certainly pays to plan in advance.

## 15 Tips on Dining, Japanese Style

Whenever I leave Japan, it's the food I miss the most. Sure, there are sushi bars and other Japanese specialty restaurants in many major cities around the world, but they don't offer nearly the variety available in Japan (and often they aren't nearly as good). For just as America has more to offer than hamburgers and steaks and England more than fish and chips, Japan has more than just sushi and teppanyaki. For both the gourmet and the uninitiated, Japan is a treasure-trove of culinary surprises.

### JAPANESE CUISINE

Altogether, there are more than a dozen different and distinct types of Japanese cuisine, plus countless regional specialties.

A good deal of what you eat may be completely new to you as well as completely unidentifiable. Sometimes Japanese themselves don't even know what they're eating, so varied and so wide is the range of available edibles. The rule is simply to enjoy.

To Japanese, **presentation** of food is as important as the food itself, and dishes are designed to appeal not only to the palate but to the eye. In contrast to the American way of piling as much food as possible onto a single plate, Japanese use lots of small plates, each arranged artfully with bite-size morsels of food.

Below are explanations of some of the most common types of Japanese cuisine. Generally, only one type of cuisine is served in a given restaurant—for example,

---

_Tips_ **Taxes**

Keep in mind that first-class restaurants will also add a 10% to 15% service charge, as do most hotel restaurants.

only raw seafood is served in a sushi bar, whereas tempura is featured at a tempura counter. There are exceptions to this, especially in regards to raw fish, which is served as an appetizer in many restaurants, and set meals, which contain a variety of dishes. In addition, Japanese restaurants in hotels may offer a great variety, and some Japanese drinking establishments (called *izakaya* or *nomiya*) offer a wide range of foods from soups to sushi to skewered pieces of chicken known as *yakitori.*

For a quick rundown of the various types of Japanese foods and individual dishes, refer to the menu terms in appendix B.

**FUGU** Known as blowfish, pufferfish, or globefish in English, *fugu* is one of the most exotic and adventurous foods in Japan—if it's not prepared properly, it means almost certain death for the consumer. In the past decade or so, some 50 people in Japan have died from fugu poisoning, usually because they tried preparing it at home. The fugu's ovaries and intestines are deadly and must be entirely removed without puncturing them. So why eat fugu if it can kill you? Well, for one thing, it's delicious; for another, fugu chefs are strictly licensed by the government and are greatly skilled in preparing fugu dishes. Ways to order it include raw *(fugu-sashi),* when it's sliced paper-thin and dipped into soy sauce with bitter orange and chives; in a stew *(fugu-chiri)* cooked with vegetables at your table; and as a rice porridge *(fugu-zosui).* The season for fresh fugu is October or November through March, but some restaurants serve it throughout the year.

**KAISEKI** The king of Japanese cuisine, kaiseki is the epitome of delicately and exquisitely arranged food, the ultimate in Japanese aesthetic appeal. It's also among the most expensive meals you can eat and can cost ¥25,000 ($238) or more per person; some restaurants, however, do offer more affordable mini-kaiseki courses. In addition, the better ryokan serve kaiseki, a reason for their high cost. Kaiseki, which is not a specific dish but rather a complete meal, is expensive because much time and skill are involved in preparing each of the many dishes, with the ingredients cooked to preserve natural flavors. Even the plates are chosen with great care to enhance the color, texture, and shape of each piece of food.

Kaiseki cuisine is based on the four seasons, with the selection of ingredients and their presentation dependent on the time of the year. In fact, so strongly does a kaiseki preparation convey the mood of a particular season, the kaiseki gourmet can tell what season it is just by looking at a meal.

A kaiseki meal is usually a lengthy affair with various dishes appearing in set order. First come the appetizer, clear broth, and one uncooked dish. These are followed by boiled, broiled, fried, steamed, heated, and vinegared dishes and finally by another soup, rice, pickled vegetables, and fruit. Although meals vary greatly depending upon the region and what's fresh, common dishes include some type of sashimi, tempura, cooked seasonal fish, and bite-size pieces of various vegetables. Since kaiseki is always a set meal, there's no problem in ordering. Let your budget be your guide.

**KUSHIAGE** Kushiage foods are breaded and deep-fried on skewers and include chicken, beef, seafood, and lots of seasonal vegetables (snow peas, green pepper, gingko nuts, lotus root, and the like). They're served with a slice of lemon and usually a specialty sauce. The result is delicious, and I highly recommend trying it. You'll find it at shops called *kushiage-ya (ya* means "shop"), which are often open only at night, like yakitori-ya. Ordering the set meal is easiest, and what you get is often determined by both the chef and the season.

**OKONOMIYAKI** *Okonomiyaki,* which originated in Osaka after World War II and literally means "as you like it," is often referred to as Japanese pizza. To me, it's more like a pancake to which meat or fish, shredded cabbage, and vegetables are added, topped with Worcestershire sauce. Since it's a popular offering of street vendors, restaurants specializing in this type of cuisine are very reasonably priced. At some places the cook makes it for you, but at other places it's do-it-yourself, which can be quite fun if you're with a group. Fried Chinese noodles and cabbage *(yakisoba)* are also usually on offer at okonomiyaki restaurants.

**RICE** As in other Asian countries, rice has been a Japanese staple for about 2,000 years. In fact, rice is so important to the Japanese diet that *gohan* means both "rice" and "meal." There are no problems here—everyone is familiar with rice. The difference, however, is that in Japan it's quite sticky, making it easier to pick up with chopsticks. It's also just plain white rice—no salt, no butter, no soy sauce (it's thought to be rather uncouth to dump a lot of sauces in your rice). In the old days, not everyone could afford the expensive white kind, which was grown primarily to pay taxes or rent to the feudal lord; the peasants had to be satisfied with a mixture of brown rice, millet, and greens. Today, some Japanese still eat rice three times a day, although they're now just as apt to have bread and coffee for breakfast. Restaurants specializing in organic foods often offer unpolished brown rice *(genmai).*

**ROBATAYAKI** *Robatayaki* refers to restaurants in which seafood and vegetables are cooked over an open charcoal grill. In the olden days, an open fireplace *(robata)* in the middle of an old Japanese house was the center of activity for cooking, eating, socializing, and simply keeping warm. Therefore, today's robatayaki restaurants are like nostalgia trips back into Japan's past and are often decorated in rustic farmhouse style with the staff dressed in traditional clothing. Robatayaki restaurants—mostly open only in the evening—are popular among office workers for both eating and drinking.

There's no special menu in a robatayaki restaurant—rather, it includes just about everything eaten in Japan. The difference is that most of the food will be grilled. Favorites of mine include gingko nuts *(ginnan),* asparagus wrapped in bacon (asparagus bacon), a type of green pepper *(piman),* mushrooms (various kinds), potatoes *(jagabataa),* and just about any kind of fish. You can usually get skewers of beef or chicken as well as a stew of meat and potatoes *(nikujaga).* Since ordering is usually a la carte, you'll just have to look and point.

**SASHIMI & SUSHI** It's estimated that the average Japanese eats 38 kilograms (84 lb.) of seafood a year—that's six times the average American consumption. Although this seafood may be served in any number of ways from grilled to boiled, a great deal of it is eaten raw.

**Sashimi** is simply raw seafood, usually served as an appetizer and eaten alone (that is, without rice). If you've never eaten it, a good choice to start out with is *maguro,* or lean tuna, which doesn't taste fishy at all and is so delicate in texture that it almost melts in your mouth. The way to eat sashimi is to first put pungent green horseradish *(wasabi)* into a small dish of soy sauce and then dip the raw fish in the sauce using your chopsticks.

**Sushi,** which is raw fish with vinegared rice, comes in many varieties. The best known is *nigiri-zushi:* raw fish, seafood, or vegetables placed on top of vinegared rice with just a touch of wasabi. It's also dipped in soy sauce. Use chopsticks or your fingers to eat sushi; remember you're supposed to eat each piece in one bite—quite a mouthful, but about the only way to keep it from falling apart. Another

trick is to turn it upside down when you dip it in the sauce, to keep the rice from crumbling.

Also popular is *maki-zushi,* which consists of seafood, vegetables, or pickles rolled with rice inside a sheet of nori seaweed. *Inari-zushi* is vinegared rice and chopped vegetables inside a pouch of fried tofu bean curd.

Typical sushi includes tuna *(maguro),* flounder *(hirame),* sea bream *(tai),* squid *(ika),* octopus *(tako),* shrimp *(ebi),* sea eel *(anago),* and omelet *(tamago).* Ordering is easy because you usually sit at a counter where you can see all the food in a refrigerated glass case in front of you. You also get to see the sushi chefs at work. The typical meal begins with sashimi and is followed by sushi, but if you don't want to order separately, there are always various set meals or courses *(seto).*

By the way, the least expensive sushi is *chirashi,* which is a selection of fish, seafood, and usually tamago on a large shallow bowl of rice. Because you get more rice, those of you with bigger appetites may want to order chiraishi. Another way to enjoy sushi without spending a fortune is at a *kaiten* sushi shop, in which plates of sushi circulate on a conveyor belt on the counter—customers reach for the dishes they want and pay for the number of dishes they take.

## SHABU-SHABU & SUKIYAKI   Until

about 100 years ago, Japanese could think of nothing so disgusting as eating the flesh of animals (fish was okay). Considered unclean by the Buddhists, meat consumption was banned by the emperor way back in the 7th century. Imagine the horror of Japanese when they discovered that Western "barbarians" ate bloody meat! It wasn't until Emperor Meiji himself announced more than a century ago his intention to eat meat that Japanese accepted the idea. Today, Japanese have become skilled in preparing a number of beef dishes.

**Sukiyaki** is among Japan's best-known beef dishes and is one many Westerners seem to prefer. Whenever I'm invited to a Japanese home, this is the meal most often served. Like fondue, it's cooked at the table.

Sukiyaki is thinly sliced beef cooked in a broth of soy sauce, stock, and sake along with scallions, spinach, mushrooms, tofu, bamboo shoots, and other vegetables. All diners serve themselves from the simmering pot and then dip their morsels into their own bowl of raw egg. You can skip the raw egg if you want (most Westerners do), but it adds to the taste and also cools the food down enough so that it doesn't burn.

**Shabu-shabu** is also prepared at your table and consists of thinly sliced beef cooked in a broth with vegetables in a kind of Japanese fondue. (It's named for the swishing sound the beef supposedly makes when cooking.) The main difference between the two dishes is the broth: Whereas in sukiyaki it consists of stock flavored with soy sauce and sake and is slightly sweet, in shabu-shabu it's relatively clear and has little taste of its own. The pots used are also different.

Using their chopsticks, shabu diners hold pieces of meat in the watery broth until they're cooked. This usually takes only a few seconds. Vegetables are left in longer to swim around until fished out. For dipping, there's either sesame sauce with diced green onions or a more bitter fish stock sauce. Restaurants serving sukiyaki usually serve shabu-shabu as well, and they're usually happy to show you the right way to prepare and eat it.

## SHOJIN RYORI   **Shojin Ryori** is the

ultimate vegetarian meal, created centuries ago to serve the needs of Zen Buddhist priests and pilgrims. Dishes may include *yudofu* (simmered tofu) and an array of local vegetables. Kyoto is the best place to experience this type of cuisine.

**SOBA & UDON NOODLES** Japanese love eating noodles, but I suspect at least part of the fascination stems from the way they eat them—they slurp, sucking in the noodles with gravity-defying speed. What's more, slurping noodles is considered proper etiquette. Fearing it would stick with me forever, however, slurping is a technique I've never quite mastered.

There are many different kinds of noodles, and it seems like almost every region of Japan has its own special style or kind—some are eaten plain, some in combination with other foods such as shrimp tempura, some served hot, some served cold. *Soba,* made from unbleached buckwheat flour and enjoyed for its nutty flavor and high nutritional value, is eaten hot *(kake-soba)* or cold *(zaru-soba).* **Udon** is a thick white wheat noodle originally from Osaka; it's usually served hot. **Somen** is a fine white noodle eaten cold in the summer and dunked in a cold sauce. Establishments serving noodles range from stand-up eateries to more refined noodle restaurants with tatami seating. Regardless of where you eat them, noodles are among the least expensive dishes in Japan.

**TEMPURA** Today a well-known Japanese food, tempura was actually introduced by the Portuguese in the 16th century. Tempura is fish and vegetables coated in a batter of egg, water, and wheat flour and then deep-fried; it's served piping hot. To eat it, dip it in a sauce of soy, fish stock, radish *(daikon),* and grated ginger; in some restaurants, only some salt, powdered green tea, or a lemon wedge is provided as an accompaniment. Various tempura specialties may include eggplant *(nasu),* mushroom *(shiitake),* sweet potato *(satsumaimo),* small green pepper *(shishito),* sliced lotus root *(renkon),* shrimp *(ebi),* squid *(ika),* lemon-mint leaf *(shiso),* and many kinds of fish. Again, the easiest thing to do is to order the set meal, the *teishoku.*

**TEPPANYAKI** A teppanyaki restaurant is a Japanese steakhouse. As in the famous Benihana restaurants in many U.S. cities, the chef slices, dices, and cooks your meal of tenderloin or sirloin steak and vegetables on a smooth hot grill right in front of you—though with much less fanfare than his U.S. counterpart. Because beef is relatively new in Japanese cooking, some people categorize teppanyaki restaurants as "Western." However, I consider this style of cooking and presentation special enough to be referred to as Japanese. Teppanyaki restaurants also tend to be expensive, simply because of the price of beef in Japan, with Kobe beef the most prized.

**TONKATSU** *Tonkatsu* is the Japanese word for "pork cutlet," made by dredging pork in wheat flour, moistening it with egg and water, dipping it in bread crumbs, and deep-frying it in vegetable oil. Since restaurants serving tonkatsu are generally inexpensive, they're popular with office workers and families. The easiest order is the *teishoku,* which usually features either the pork filet *(hirekatsu)* or the pork loin *(rosukatsu).* In any case, your tonkatsu is served on a bed of shredded cabbage, and one or two different sauces will be at your table, a Worcestershire sauce and perhaps a specialty sauce. If you order the teishoku, it will come with rice, miso soup, and pickled vegetables.

**UNAGI** I'll bet that if you eat unagi without knowing what it is, you'll find it very tasty—and you'll probably be very surprised to find out you've just eaten eel. Popular as a health food because of its rich protein and high vitamin A content, eel is supposed to help you fight fatigue during hot summer months but is eaten year-round. Broiled eel *(kabayaki)* is prepared by grilling filet strips over a charcoal fire; the eel is repeatedly dipped in a sweetened barbecue soy sauce while cooking. A favorite way to eat broiled eel

is on top of rice, in which case it's called *unaju* or *unagi donburi*. Do yourself a favor and try it.

**YAKITORI** Yakitori is chunks of chicken or chicken parts basted in a sweet soy sauce and grilled over a charcoal fire on thin skewers. Places that specialize in yakitori (yakitori-ya, often identifiable by a red paper lantern outside the front door) are technically not restaurants but drinking establishments; they usually don't open until 5 or 6pm. Most yakitori-ya are popular with workers as inexpensive places to drink, eat, and be merry.

The cheapest way to dine on yakitori is to order a set course, which will often include various parts of the chicken including the skin, heart, and liver. Since this may not be entirely to your taste, you may wish to order a la carte, which is more expensive but gets you exactly what you want. In addition to chicken, other skewered, charcoaled delicacies are usually offered (called *kushi-yaki*). If you're ordering by the stick, you might want to try chicken breast *(sasami)*, chicken meatballs *(tsukune)*, green peppers *(piman)*, chicken and leeks *(negima)*, mushrooms *(shiitake)*, or gingko nuts *(ginnan)*.

**OTHER CUISINES** During your travels you might also run into these types of Japanese cuisine: **Kamameshi** is a rice casserole served in individual-size cast-iron pots with different toppings that might include seafood, meat, or vegetables. **Donburi** is also a rice dish, topped with tempura, eggs, and meat like chicken or pork. **Nabe,** a stew cooked in an earthenware pot at your table, consists of chicken, sliced beef, pork, or seafood; noodles; and vegetables. **Oden** is a broth with fish cakes, tofu, eggs, and vegetables, served with hot mustard. If a restaurant advertises that it specializes in **Kyodo-Ryori,** it serves local specialties for which the region is famous and is often very rustic in decor. In recent years, restaurants

serving **crossover fusion cuisine**—creative dishes inspired by ingredients from both sides of the Pacific—have popped up in major cities.

Although technically Chinese fast-food restaurants, **ramen shops** are a big part of dining in Japan. Serving what I consider to be generic Chinese noodles, soups, and other dishes, ramen shops can be found everywhere; they're easily recognizable by red signs, flashing lights, and quite often pictures of various dishes displayed right by the front door. Many are stand-up affairs—just a high counter to rest your bowl on. In addition to noodle and vegetable soup *(ramen),* you can also get such things as fried noodles *(yakisoba)* or—my favorite—fried pork dumplings *(gyoza).* What these places lack in atmosphere is made up for in price: Dishes average ¥650 ($6.20), making them some of the cheapest places in Japan for a meal.

## DRINKS

All Japanese restaurants serve complimentary **green tea** with meals. If that's a little too weak, you may want to try **sake,** an alcoholic beverage made from rice and served either hot or cold. It goes well with most forms of Japanese cuisine. Produced since about the 3rd century, sake varies by region, production method, alcoholic content, color, aroma, and taste. Altogether, there are more than 1,800 sake brewers in Japan producing about 10,000 varieties of sake. Miyabi is a prized classic sake; other popular brands are Gekkeikan, Koshinokanbai, Hakutsuru (meaning White Crane), and Ozeki.

Japanese **beer** is also very popular. The biggest sellers are Kirin, Sapporo, Asahi, and Suntory, with each brand offering a bewildering variety of brews. They enjoyed exclusive brewing rights until deregulation in the 1990s opened the gates to competition; now microbreweries are found everywhere in Japan. Businessmen are fond of **whiskey,** which they

usually drink with ice and water. Popular in recent years is **shochu,** an alcoholic beverage usually made from rice but sometimes from wheat, sweet potatoes, or sugar cane. It used to be considered a drink of the lower classes, but sales have increased so much that it's threatening the sake and whiskey businesses. A clear liquid comparable, perhaps, to vodka, it can be consumed straight but is often combined with soda water in a drink called *chuhai.* My personal favorite is *ume-shu,* a plum-flavored shochu. But watch out—the stuff can be deadly. **Wine,** usually available only at restaurants serving Western food, has gained in popularity in recent years, with both domestic and imported brands available. Although **cocktails** are available in discos, hotel lounges, and fancier bars at rather inflated prices, most Japanese stick with beer, sake, or whiskey.

## TIPS ON DINING IN JAPAN
### RESTAURANT ESSENTIALS
**ORDERING**   The biggest problem facing the hungry foreigner in Japan is ordering a meal in a restaurant without an English-language menu. This book alleviates the problem to a large extent by giving some sample dishes and prices for recommended restaurants throughout Japan; we've also noted which restaurants offer English-language menus.

One aid to simplified ordering is the common use of plastic food models in glass display cases either outside or just inside the front door of many restaurants. Sushi, tempura, daily specials, spaghetti—they're all there in mouthwatering plastic replicas along with the corresponding prices. Simply decide what you want and point it out to your waitress.

Unfortunately, not all restaurants in Japan have plastic display cases, especially the more exclusive or traditional ones. In fact, you'd be missing a lot of Japan's best cuisine if you restrict yourself to eating only at places with displays. If there's no display from which to choose, the best thing to do is to look at what people around you are eating and order what looks best. An alternative is to order the *teishoku,* or daily special meal (also called "set course" or simply "course," especially in restaurants serving Western food); these fixed-price meals consist of a main dish and several side dishes, including soup, rice, and Japanese pickles. Although most restaurants have special set courses for dinner as well, lunch is the usual time for the teishoku, generally from 11 or 11:30am to 1:30 or 2pm.

**HOURS**   In larger cities, the usual open hours for restaurants are from about 11am to 10 or 11pm. Of course, some establishments close earlier at 9pm, while others stay open past midnight; the majority close for a few hours in the afternoon (2–5pm). The main thing to remember is that if you're in a big city like Tokyo or Osaka, you'll want to avoid the lunchtime rush, which is from noon to 1pm. In rural areas and small towns, restaurants tend to close early, often by 7:30 or 8pm.

Another thing to keep in mind is that the closing time posted for most restaurants is exactly that—everyone is expected to pay his or her bill and leave. A general rule of thumb is that the last order is taken at least a half-hour before closing time, sometimes an hour or more for kaiseki restaurants. To be on the safe side, therefore, try to arrive at least an hour before closing time so you have time to relax and enjoy your meal.

### ETIQUETTE
**UPON ARRIVAL**   As soon as you're seated in a Japanese restaurant (that is, a restaurant serving Japanese food), you'll be given a wet towel, which will be steaming hot in winter or pleasantly cool in summer. Called an *oshibori,* it's for wiping your hands. In all but the fancy

restaurants, men can get away with wiping their faces as well, but women are not supposed to (I ignore this if it's hot and humid outside). Sadly, some cheaper Japanese restaurants now resort to a paper towel wrapped in plastic, which isn't nearly the same. Oshibori are generally not provided in Western restaurants.

**CHOPSTICKS** The next thing you'll probably be confronted with is chopsticks. The proper way to use a pair is to place the first chopstick between the base of the thumb and the top of the ring finger (this chopstick remains stationary) and the second one between the top of the thumb and the middle and index fingers. (This second chopstick is the one you move to pick up food.)

The best way to learn to use chopsticks is to have a Japanese person show you how. It's not difficult, but if you find it impossible, some restaurants might have a fork as well. How proficiently foreigners handle chopsticks is a matter of great curiosity for Japanese, and they're surprised if you know how to use them; even if you were to live in Japan for 20 years, you would never stop receiving compliments on how talented you are with chopsticks.

**Chopstick Etiquette** If you're taking something from a communal bowl or tray, you're supposed to turn your chopsticks upside down and use the part that hasn't been in your mouth; after transferring the food to your plate, you turn the chopsticks back to their proper position. The exception is shabu-shabu and sukiyaki.

Never stick your chopsticks down vertically into your bowl of rice and leave them there—that is done only when a person has died. Also, don't pass anything from your chopsticks to another person's chopsticks; that's done only to pass the bones of the cremated.

**EATING SOUP & NOODLES** If you're eating soup, you won't use a spoon. Rather, you'll pick up the bowl and drink from it. Use your chopsticks to fish out larger pieces of food. It's considered in good taste to slurp with gusto, especially if you're eating noodles. Noodle shops in Japan are always well orchestrated with slurps and smacks.

**DRINKING** If you're drinking in Japan, the main thing to remember is that you never pour your own glass. Bottles of beer are so large that people often share one. The rule is that in turn, one person pours for everyone else in the group, so be sure to hold up your glass when someone is pouring for you. As the night progresses Japanese get sloppy about this rule. It took me awhile to figure this out, but if no one notices your empty glass, the best thing to do is to pour everyone else a drink so that someone will pour yours. If someone wants to pour you a drink and your glass is full, the proper thing to do is to take a few gulps so that he or she can fill your glass. Because each person is continually filling everyone else's glass, you never know exactly how much you've had to drink, which (depending on how you look at it) is either very good or very bad.

**PAYING THE BILL** If you go out with a group of friends (not as a visiting guest of honor and not with business associates), it's customary to split the dinner bill equally, even if you all ordered different things. Even foreigners living in Japan adopt the practice of splitting the bill; it certainly makes figuring everyone's share easier, especially since **there's no tipping in Japan.** But it can be hard on frugal diners on a budget.

**OTHER TIPS** It's considered bad manners to walk down the street eating or drinking (except at a festival). You'll notice that if a Japanese buys a drink

from a vending machine, he'll stand there, gulp it down, and throw away the container before going on. To the chagrin of their elders, young Japanese sometimes ignore this rule.

## HOW TO EAT WITHOUT SPENDING A FORTUNE

During your first few days in Japan—particularly if you're in Tokyo—money will seem to flow from your pockets like water. In fact, money has a tendency to disappear so quickly that many people become convinced they must have lost some of it somehow. At this point, almost everyone panics (I've seen it happen again and again), but with time they slowly realize that because prices are markedly different here (steeper), a bit of readjustment in thinking and habits is necessary. Coffee, for example, is something of a luxury, and some Japanese are astonished at the thought of drinking four or five cups a day. Here are some tips for getting the most for your yen.

**BREAKFAST**    Buffet breakfasts are popular at Japanese hotels and are often an inexpensive way to eat your fill. Otherwise, coffee shops offer what's called "morning service" until 10 or 11am; it generally consists of a cup of coffee, a small salad, a boiled egg, and the thickest slice of toast you've ever seen for about ¥500 ($4.75). That's a real bargain when you consider that just one cup of coffee can cost ¥250 to ¥500 ($2.40–$4.75). (Except at most hotel breakfast buffets in Japan, there's no such thing as the bottomless cup.) There are many coffee-shop chains in Japan, including Doutour, Pronto, and an ever-expanding Starbucks (500 in Japan at last count).

**SET LUNCHES    Eat your biggest meal at lunch.** Many restaurants serving Japanese food offer a daily set lunch, or *teishoku,* at a fraction of what their set dinners might be. Usually ranging in price from ¥700 to ¥1,500 ($6.65–$14),

they're generally available from 11 or 11:30am to 1:30 or 2pm. A Japanese *teishoku* will often include the main course (such as tempura, grilled fish, or the specialty of the house), soup, pickled vegetables, rice, and tea, while the set menu in a Western-style restaurant (often called set lunch) usually consists of a main dish, salad, bread, and coffee.

**CHEAP EATS**    Inexpensive restaurants can be found in department stores (often one whole floor will be devoted to various kinds of restaurants, most with plastic-food displays), underground shopping arcades, nightlife districts, and in and around train and subway stations. Some of the cheapest establishments for a night out on the town are the countless **yakitori-ya, noodle shops,** and **ramen shops.** For sushi, the cheapest places are those that deliver food via a conveyor belt; you simply reach out and take the plates that look good. **Coffee shops** often offer inexpensive Western food, including sandwiches. Japan also has American **fast-food chains,** such as McDonald's (where Big Macs cost about ¥250/$2.40), Wendy's, and KFC, as well as Japanese chains—Freshness Burger and First Kitchen, among them—that sell hamburgers and french fries.

**Ethnic restaurants,** particularly those serving Indian, Korean, Chinese, Italian, and other cuisines, are plentiful and usually inexpensive. **Hotel restaurants** can also be good bargains for inexpensive set lunches or buffets (called *viking* in Japanese), while inexpensive drinking places are good bets for dinner.

Street-side stalls, called ***yatai,*** are also good sources of inexpensive meals. These restaurants-on-wheels sell a variety of foods, including fish cakes *(oden),* skewered barbecued chicken *(yakitori),* and fried noodles *(yakisoba),* as well as sake and beer. They appear mostly at night, lighted by a single lantern or a string of lights, and most have a counter with

stools as well, protected in winter by a wall of tarp. These can be great, cozy places for rubbing elbows with the locals. Fukuoka, in Kyushu, is famous for its yatai, but you'll find them in many cities, especially in nightlife districts. Sadly, however, traditional pushcarts are being replaced by motorized vans, which do not offer seating.

**PREPARED FOODS** You can save even more money by avoiding restaurants altogether. There are all kinds of prepared foods you can buy; some are even complete meals, perfect for picnics in a park or right in your hotel room.

Perhaps the best known is the **obento,** or box lunch, commonly sold on express trains, on train-station platforms, in food sections of department stores, and at counter windows of tiny shops throughout Japan. In fact, the obento served by vendors on trains and at train stations are an inexpensive way to sample regional cuisine since they often include food typical of the region you're passing through. Costing between ¥800 and ¥1,500

($7.60–$14), the basic obento contains a piece of meat (generally fish or chicken), various side dishes, rice, and pickled vegetables. Sushi boxed lunches are also readily available.

My favorite place to shop for prepared foods is **department stores.** Located in basements, these food and produce sections hark back to Japanese markets of yore, with vendors yelling out their wares and crowds of housewives deciding on the evening's dinner. Different counters specialize in different items—tempura, yakitori, eel, Japanese pickles, cooked fish, sushi (sometimes made by robots!), salads, vegetables, and desserts. Almost the entire spectrum of Japanese cuisine is available, as are numerous samples. There are also counters selling obento box meals. In any case, you can eat for less than ¥1,200 ($11), and there's nothing like milling with Japanese housewives to make you feel like one of the locals. Though not as colorful, **24-hour convenience stores** also sell packaged foods, including sandwiches and obento.

## 16 Packing Tips

The first thing you'll want to do when you're packing is select the smallest bag you can get away with and **pack as lightly as you can.** Storage space is limited on Japan's trains, including the Shinkansen bullet train, business hotels sometimes lack closets, and there are multitudes of stairs and overhead and underground passageways to navigate in virtually every train station in the country.

The most important item is **a good pair of walking shoes,** well broken in. You will probably be walking much more than you do at home. Keep in mind, too, that because you have to remove your shoes to enter Japanese homes, inns, shrines, and temples, you should bring a pair that's easy to slip on and off. And since you may be walking around in

stocking feet, save yourself embarrassment by packing socks and hose without holes.

As for **clothes,** you'll need a coat in winter and very light clothing for the hot and humid summer months. Jackets are necessary for spring and autumn; I've seen it snow in March in Tokyo, and even May can be quite crisp. Japan's top French restaurants often require jackets and ties for men. Although the older generation considers it inappropriate for women to wear dresses without hose or tops without sleeves, I've noticed that the younger generation ignores this, especially in resort areas. Jeans and capris are okay for casual dining and sightseeing, but shorts are uncommon in Japan outside hiking and sports areas.

**Tips** **Help with Heavy Bags**

If your bag becomes a burden but you don't want to mail items home, an alternative is to send a bag onward to your next or last stop by *takkyu-bin,* available at larger hotels, train stations, and convenience stores. Bags reach most destinations in 1 or 2 nights, with the delivery cost of an average-size bag weighing 10 kilograms (22 lb.) ¥1,400 ($13). I love this amazingly efficient service—it's a lifesaver!

Virtually all hotels and Japanese-style inns—save youth hostels and some budget-priced inns—provide towels, soap, washcloths, toothbrushes, toothpaste, shampoo, a cotton kimono (called a *yukata* and not a giveaway), and usually razors. If you run out of something, you'll have no problem finding it in Japan. Most hotels and inns also provide a thermos of hot water or a water heater as well as some tea bags. If you're a coffee addict, you can save money by buying instant coffee and drinking your morning cup in your hotel room. Hair dryers are a standard feature in virtually all rooms with private bathrooms, including business hotels. Because the sun rises early in summer (as early as 4am), you might want to include a pair of eyeshades.

It's also good to carry a supply of **pocket tissues,** which you can pick up at newspaper stands near and in train stations, because some public restrooms do not have toilet paper. It's also a good idea to carry change for local buses (faster than trying to change ¥1,000 notes), a folding umbrella, and a compass for getting your bearings and following directions using local maps. Finally, pack small, inexpensive gifts from home that can be given to those who show unexpected kindness, including candy, postcards, and hometown souvenirs.

## 17 Recommended Books

Japanese publisher **Kodansha International** (www.kodansha-intl.com) has probably published more books on Japan in English—including Japanese-language textbooks—than any other company. Available at major bookstores in Japan, they are also available at www.amazon.com.

**HISTORY** The definitive work of Japan's history through the ages is *Japan: The Story of a Nation* (Alfred A. Knopf, 1991) by Edwin O. Reischauer, a former U.S. ambassador to Japan. Ivan Morris's *The World of the Shining Prince: Court Life in Ancient Japan* (Kodansha, 1994) highlights the golden age of the imperial court through diaries and literature of the Heian Period (794–1192), while

*Everyday Life in Traditional Japan* (Tuttle, 2000) details the daily lives of samurai, farmers, craftsmen, merchants, courtiers, and outcasts during the Edo Period.

For personal accounts of Japan in ages past, there's no better anthology than Donald Keene's *Travelers of a Hundred Ages: The Japanese as Revealed Through 1,000 Years of Diaries* (Holt, 1989). Written by Japanese from all walks of life, the journals provide fascinating insight into the hidden worlds of imperial courts, Buddhist monasteries, isolated country inns, and more. Lafcadio Hearn, a prolific writer about things Japanese, describes life in Japan around the turn of the 20th century in *Writings from Japan* (Penguin, 1985), while Isabella Bird, an

Englishwoman who traveled in Japan in the 1870s, writes a vivid account of rural Japanese life in *Unbeaten Tracks in Japan* (Virago Press Limited, 1984). *Autobiography of a Geisha* (Columbia University Press, 2003), first published in 1957, is Sayo Masuda's account of being sold to a geisha house as a child, working as a geisha at a hot-spring spa, and living under harsh conditions during and after World War II.

**SOCIETY**    Reischauer's *The Japanese Today* (Tuttle, 1993) offers a unique perspective of Japanese society, including historical events that have shaped and influenced Japanese behavior and the role of the individual in Japanese society. A classic description of Japanese and their culture is found in Ruth Benedict's brilliant *The Chrysanthemum and the Sword: Patterns of Japanese Culture* (Houghton Mifflin Co., 1989), first published in the 1940s but reprinted many times since. For a more contemporary approach, read *The Japanese Mind: The Goliath Explained* (Linden Press/ Simon & Schuster, 1983) by Robert C. Christopher, valuable for its insight into Japanese people and the role history has played in developing their psyche. Debunking theories that have long shaped the outside world's views of Japan (many of which are espoused by the books above) is *Japan: A Reinterpretation* (Pantheon, 1997) by former *International Herald Tribune* Tokyo bureau chief Patrick Smith, who gives a spirited reinterpretation of Japan's economic miracle and demise.

For advice on Japanese etiquette, refer to *Etiquette Today: A Guide to Business and Social Customs* (Tuttle, 1994) by James M. Vardaman and Michiko Sasaki Vardaman; it covers everything from bowing and bathing to eating and dining customs, office etiquette, and the complicated art of giving gifts. Business travelers may also want to read *Business Japan: A Practical Guide to Understanding Japanese Business Culture* by Peggy Kenna and Sonra Lacy (NTC Publishing, 1994), which compares American and Japanese business styles, practices, and social customs.

**CULTURE & THE ARTS**    For a cultural overview in one book, see *Introduction to Japanese Culture,* edited by Daniel Sosnoski (Tuttle, 1996), which covers major festivals, the tea ceremony, flower arranging, Kabuki, sumo, Japanese board games, Buddhis, kanji, and much more. Elizabeth Kiritani's *Vanishing Japan: Traditions, Crafts & Culture* (Tuttle, 1995) covers a wide spectrum of traditional Japanese crafts and professions that were once a part of daily life, from potato vendors, shoe shiners, and tatami makers to Japanese umbrellas and handmade paper, many of which are fast disappearing in today's modern Japan.

The Japan Travel Bureau puts out nifty pocket-size illustrated booklets on things Japanese (available in Japan at bookstores with an English-language section, including those recommended in the Tokyo chapter), including *Eating in Japan, Festivals of Japan, Martial Arts & Sports in Japan,* and *Japanese Family & Culture,* which covers everything from marriage in Japan to problems with mothers-in-law and explanations of why Dad gets home so late. My favorite is *Salaryman in Japan* (JTB, 1986), which describes the private and working lives of Japan's army of white-collar workers who receive set salaries.

And while some might argue it's not art, there's no denying the power *manga* (Japanese comics) has over Japanese readers. Although dated, the best primer in manga history and its various genre is Frederik L. Schodt and Tezuka Osamu's *Manga! Manga!: The World of Japanese Comics* (Kodansha, 1988), with a follow-up provided in Schodt's *Dreamland Japan: Writings on Modern Manga* (Stone Bridge Press, 1996).

## CONTEMPORARY CHRONICLES

For contemporary experiences of foreigners in Japan, there's the inimitable Dave Barry, who describes his whirlwind trip to the land of the rising sun in the comical *Dave Barry Does Japan* (Random House, 1992) and solves such puzzling mysteries as why Japanese cars sell successfully (they're made of steel!). A delightful account of Japanese and their customs is given by the irrepressible George Mikes in *The Land of the Rising Yen* (Penguin, 1973); I doubt you'll be able to find the book in the United States, but it's in major bookstores in Japan and would make enjoyable reading during your trip. *Traveler's Tales Guides: Japan* (Traveler's Tales, 1999) relates the firsthand experiences of Dave Barry, Pico Iyer, and other writers who tackle such issues as sand bathing and Washlet toilets. A book seemingly from another era is *Geisha* (Vintage, 2000) by Liza C. Dalby; first published in 1983, it describes her year living as a geisha in Kyoto as part of a research project.

**FICTION**   Whenever I travel in Japan, I especially enjoy reading fictional accounts of the country; they put me more in tune with my surroundings and increase my awareness and perception. The world's first major novel was written by a Japanese woman, Murasaki Shikibu, whose classic, *The Tale of Genji* (Knopf, 1978), dating from the 11th century, describes the aristocratic life of Prince Genji.

In Tokyo bookstores, you'll find whole sections dedicated to English translations of Japan's best-known modern and contemporary authors, including Mishima Yukio, Soseki Natsume, Abe Kobo, Tanizaki Junichiro, and Nobel prize winners Kawabata Yasunari and Oe Kenzaburo. An overview of Japanese classical literature from the earliest times to the mid–19th century is provided in *Anthology of Japanese Literature* (Grove Press, 1988), edited by Donald Keene. Likewise, *The Showa Anthology: Modern Japanese Short Stories* (Kodansha, 1992), edited by Van C. Gessel and Tomone Matsumoto, covers works by Abe Kobe, Mishima Yukio, Kawabata Yasunari, Oe Kenzaburo, and others written between 1929 and 1984, while *Modern Japanese Stories: An Anthology* (Tuttle, 1962), edited by Ivan Morris, introduces short stories by some of Japan's top modern writers, including Mori Ogai, Tanizaki Junichiro, Kawabata Yasunari, and Mishima Yukio.

For novels, you might wish to read Mishima's *The Sea of Fertility* (Knopf), a collection of four separate works, the last of which, *The Decay of the Angel*, was delivered to his publisher on the day of his suicide; or *The Sound of Waves* (Knopf, 1956), about young love in a Japanese fishing village. Other famous works by Japanese authors include Soseki Natsume's first novel, *I am a Cat* (Charles E. Tuttle, 1972), which describes the foibles of upper-middle-class Japanese during the Meiji Era through the eyes of a cat; and his later novel, *Kokoro* (Regnery Gateway Co., 1985), as well as Kawabata Yasunari's *Snow Country* (Knopf, 1956), translated by Edward G. Seidensticker. Although not well known in the West, Enchi Fumiko wrote an absorbing novel about women in an upper-class, late-19th-century family in *The Waiting Years* (Kodansha, 2002), first published in 1957.

Oe Kenzaburo gained international recognition when he became the second Japanese to win the Nobel prize for literature in 1994. In addition to such well-known novels as *A Personal Matter* (Grove Press, 1968), about a man in search of himself after the birth of a handicapped son, and *Hiroshima Notes* (Grove/Atlantic, 1996), with personal accounts of atomic bomb survivors and a moving commentary on the meaning of the Hiroshima

bombing, is one of his latest works, *A Healing Family* (Kodansha, 1996), a collection of essays written over several years dealing primarily with Oe's severely handicapped autistic son, Hikari, who has become a celebrity in his own right as a composer of classical music. Favorite writers of Japan's baby-boom generation include Murakami Ryu, who burst onto the literary scene with *Almost Transparent Blue* (Kodansha, 1977) and later captured the undercurrent of decadent urban life in his best-selling *Coin Locker Babies* (Kodansha, 1995). Murakami Haruki's writings include *Dance Dance Dance* (Kodansha, 1994); *Hard-Boiled Wonderland and the End of the World* (Vintage, 1993); *The Wind-Up Bird Chronicle* (Knopf, 1997), which centers on the massacre of Japanese troops in Mongolia by Soviet soldiers in 1939; *South of the Border, West of the Sun* (Knopf, 1999), the story of a bewildered man in contemporary Tokyo; and *Norwegian Wood* (Vintage, 2000), a coming-of-age story set during the 1969 student movement in Japan. His *After the Quake: Stories* (Knopf, 2002) centers on fictional characters in the months after the 1995 Kobe earthquake. Yoshimoto Banana's first novel, *Kitchen* (Washington Square Press, 1993), about free-spirited young women in contemporary Japan, created a "Bananamania" when first published in Japan in 1988.

For works of fiction about Japan by Western writers, most Westerners are familiar with James Clavell's *Shogun* (Dell, 1975), a fictional account based on the lives of Englishman William Adams and military leader Tokugawa Ieyasu around 1600. The best-selling *Memoirs of a Geisha* (Knopf, 1997), by Arthur Golden and also a movie, is the fictional autobiography of a fisherman's daughter sold to a geisha house, later becoming one of Kyoto's most celebrated geisha of the 1930s.

For fictional yet personal contemporary accounts of what it's like for Westerners living in Japan, entertaining novels include *Ransom* (Vintage, 1985) by Jay McInerney and *Pictures from the Water Trade* (Harper & Row, 1986) by John D. Morley. Pico Iyer taps into the mysterious juxtaposition of the old Japan vs. the new in *The Lady and the Monk: Four Seasons in Kyoto* (Knopf, 1991). *Audrey Hepburn's Neck* (Simon & Schuster, 1996) is Alan Brown's poignant portrait of Japan's mishmash of Western and Japanese culture, as seen through the eyes of a confused young Japanese comic illustrator. Mystery fans should read Sujata Massey's six novels following the adventures of Japanese-American Rei Shimura; Massey's latest, *The Samurai's Daughter* (HarperCollins, 2003), delves into atrocities committed during World War II.

---

## FAST FACTS: Japan

*American Express* There are no American Express customer-service offices in Japan.

*Business Hours* Government offices and private companies are generally open Monday through Friday 9am to 5pm. Banks are open Monday through Friday 9am to 3pm (but usually will not exchange money until 10:30 or 11am, after that day's currency exchange rates come in). Neighborhood post offices are open Monday through Friday 9am to 5pm. Major post offices, however (usually located near major train stations), have longer hours and may be open weekends as well (Some central post offices, such as those in Tokyo and Osaka, are open 24 hr. for mail.)

Department stores are open from about 10 or 11am to 8pm; they sometimes close irregularly (but always the same day of the week). Smaller stores are generally open from 10am to 8pm, closed 1 day a week. Convenience stores such as 7-Eleven are open 24 hours.

Keep in mind that museums, gardens, and attractions stop selling admission tickets at least 30 minutes before the actual closing time. Similarly, restaurants take their last orders at least 30 minutes before the posted closing time (even earlier for kaiseki restaurants).

*Currency*  See "Money," p. 27.

*Drugstores*  Drugstores, called *kusuri-ya,* are found readily in Japan. Note, however, that you cannot have a foreign prescription filled in Japan without first consulting a doctor in Japan, so it's best to bring an adequate supply of important medicines with you. No drugstores in Japan stay open 24 hours. However, convenience stores, open day and night throughout Japan, carry such nonprescription items as aspirin.

*Earthquakes*  Kobe's tragic 1995 earthquake brought attention to the fact that Japan is earthquake-prone, but in reality, most earthquakes are too small to detect. However, in case of an earthquake you can feel, there are a few precautions you should take. If you're indoors, take cover under a doorway or against a wall and do not go outdoors. If you're outdoors, stay away from trees, power lines, and the sides of buildings; if you're surrounded by tall buildings, seek cover in a doorway. Never use elevators during a quake. Other precautions include noting emergency exits wherever you stay; all hotels supply flashlights, usually found attached to your bedside table.

*Electricity*  The electricity throughout Japan is 100 volts AC, but there are two different cycles in use: In Tokyo and in regions northeast of the capital, it's 50 cycles, while in Nagoya, Kyoto, Osaka, and all points to the southwest, it's 60 cycles. Leading hotels in Tokyo often have two outlets, one for 110 volts and one for 220 volts; almost all have hair dryers in the rooms. You can use many American appliances in Japan because the American standard is 110 volts and 60 cycles, but they may run a little slowly. Note, too, that the flat, two-legged prongs used in Japan are the same size and fit as in North America, but three-pronged appliances are not accepted.

*Embassies & Consulates*  Most embassies are located in Tokyo (see "Fast Facts: Tokyo" in chapter 4). There are, however, U.S., British, and Australian consulates in Osaka (see "Osaka" in chapter 9). For the location of other consulates, inquire at the respective embassies.

*Emergencies*  The national emergency numbers are ✆ **110** for **police** and ✆ **119** for **ambulance** and **fire.** You do not need to insert money into public telephones to call these numbers. However, if using a green public telephone, you must push a red button before dialing. If calling from a gray public telephone or one that accepts only prepaid cards, simply lift the receiver and dial. Be sure to speak slowly and precisely.

*Holidays*  See "Japan Calendar of Events," earlier in this chapter.

*Internet Access* Most upper-range hotels in major cities offer in-room high-speed dataports for laptop modems and adapters (few offer wireless connections); some even have TVs that double as computers. Although some hotels provide Internet access free of charge, the majority charge anywhere from ¥500 to ¥1,500 ($4.75–$14) a day. Many hotels offer business centers as well (though hefty fees are charged for Internet use), but more and more business hotels have lobby computers you can use for free or a small fee. Otherwise, most major cities in Japan have Internet cafes where you can check e-mail either by paying a fee or by purchasing a drink or a meal. Check individual city and regional chapters for information on Internet cafes and hotels with Internet access. Finally, Nippon Telegraph & Telephone (NTT) operates public telephones equipped with a modular jack for portable computer hookups, making it possible to scan websites and receive e-mail. Look for gray ISDN telephones—readily available in lobbies of major hotels, airports, and train stations—which have English-language explanations on how to use them and which accept prepaid telephone cards.

*Laundry & Dry Cleaning* All upper- and most medium-range hotels offer laundry and dry-cleaning services (but it's expensive, with a laundered shirt costing about ¥400/$3.80). For same-day service, it's usually necessary to turn in your laundry by 10am; many hotels do not offer laundry service on Sundays and holidays. Budget accommodations sometimes have coin-operated washers and dryers. Otherwise, launderettes are abundant, and many hotel guest rooms have a pull-out laundry line over the tub for hand washables.

*Liquor Laws* The legal drinking age is 20. *Note:* If you intend to drive in Japan, you are not allowed even one drink.

*Lost & Found* Be sure to tell all of your credit card companies the minute you discover your wallet has been lost or stolen, and file a report at the nearest police precinct. Your credit card company or insurer may require a police report number or record of the loss. Most credit card companies have an emergency toll-free number to call if your card is lost or stolen; they may be able to wire you a cash advance immediately or deliver an emergency credit card in a day or two. **Visa's** U.S. emergency number is © 800/847-2911 or 410/581-9994; in Japan it's 00531-11-155. For lost **American Express** cards or traveler's checks, call © 800/221-7282 in the U.S. or 0120/020-120 in Japan. **MasterCard** holders should call © 800/307-7309 or 636/722-7111 in the U.S., or 00531/11-3886 in Japan.

*Luggage & Lockers* Because storage space on Shinkansen bullet trains is limited, travel with the smallest bag you can get away with. Coin-operated lockers are located at all major train stations as well as at most subway stations, but most lockers are generally not large enough to store huge pieces of luggage (and those that are large enough are often taken). Lockers generally cost ¥300 to ¥800 ($2.85–$7.60) depending on the size. Some major stations also have check-in rooms for luggage, though these tend to be rare. If your bag becomes too much to handle, you can have it sent ahead via *takkyubin,* a wonderful and efficient luggage/parcel forwarding service available at upper-range hotels

and all convenience stores in Japan. At Narita and Kansai international airports, delivery service counters will send luggage to your hotel the next day (or vice versa) for about ¥1,700 ($16) for bags up to 20 kilograms (44 lb.).

*Mail* If your hotel cannot mail letters for you, ask the concierge where the nearest post office is. Post offices are easily recognizable by the red logo of a capital T with a horizontal line over it. Mailboxes are bright orange-red. It costs ¥110 ($1.05) to airmail letters weighing up to 25 grams and ¥70 (65¢) to mail postcards to North America and Europe. Domestic mail costs ¥80 (75¢) for letters weighing up to 25 grams and ¥50 (50¢) for postcards. Post offices throughout Japan are also convenient for their ATMs, which accept international bank cards operating on the PLUS and Cirrus systems, as well as MasterCard and Visa.

Although all **post offices** are open Monday through Friday from 9am to 5pm, international post offices (often located close to the central train station) have longer hours, often until 7pm or later on weekdays and with open hours also on weekends (in Tokyo and Osaka, counters are open 24 hr.). If your hotel does not have a shipping service, it is only at these larger post offices that you can mail packages abroad. Conveniently, they sell cardboard boxes in several sizes with the necessary tape. Packages sent via surface mail cannot weigh more than 20 kilograms (about 44 lb.) and take about a month to reach North America, with a package weighing 10 kilograms (about 22 lb.) costing ¥6,750 ($65) to North America. Express packages, which take 3 days to North America and can weigh up to 30 kilograms (66 lb.), cost ¥12,900 ($123) for 10 kilograms (22 lb.). For more information, check the website www.post.japanpost.jp.

*Maps* The Japan National Tourist Organization publishes a free *Tourist Map of Japan* showing the four main islands and the major highway and railway lines, with maps of major cities on the reverse side. Free city maps are available at local tourist offices throughout Japan.

*Measurement* Before the metric system came into use in Japan, the country had its own standards for measuring length and weight. One of these old standards is still common—rooms are still measured by the number of **tatami** straw mats that will fit in them. A six-tatami room, for example, is the size of six tatami mats, with a tatami roughly 3 feet wide and 6 feet long.

*Newspapers & Magazines* Three English-language newspapers are published daily in Japan: the *Japan Times* and the *Daily Yomiuri* (both with weekly supplements from the *Los Angeles Times*, *Washington Post*, and London's *The Times*), as well as the *International Herald Tribune/Asahi Shimbun*. Hotels and major bookstores carry the international editions of such newsmagazines as *Time* and *Newsweek*. You can also read the *Japan Times* online at www.japantimes.co.jp.

*Passports* **For Residents of the United States:** Whether you're applying in person or by mail, you can download passport applications from the U.S. State Department website at http://travel.state.gov. To find your regional passport office, either check the U.S. State Department website or call the National Passport Information Center toll-free number (© **877/487-2778**) for automated information.

**For Residents of Canada:** Passport applications are available at travel agencies or from the central Passport Office, Department of Foreign Affairs and International Trade, Ottawa, ON K1A 0G3 (© **800/567-6868;** www.ppt.gc.ca).

**For Residents of the United Kingdom:** Pick up an application for a standard 10-year passport (5-year passport for children under 16) at your nearest passport office, major post office, or travel agency, or contact the United Kingdom Passport Service (© **0870/521-0410;** www.ukpa.gov.uk).

**For Residents of Ireland:** You can apply for a 10-year passport at the Passport Office, Setanta Centre, Molesworth Street, Dublin 2 (© **01/671-1633;** www. irlgov.ie/iveagh). Those under age 18 and over 65 must apply for a €12 3-year passport. You can also apply at 1A South Mall, Cork (© 021/272-525) or at most main post offices.

**For Residents of Australia:** Pick up an application from your local post office or any branch of Passports Australia, but you must schedule an interview at the passport office to present your application materials. Call the Australian Passport Information Service at © **131-232,** or visit the government website at www.passports.gov.au.

**For Residents of New Zealand:** Pick up a passport application at any New Zealand Passports Office or download it from their website (© **0800/225-050** or 04/474-8100; www.passports.govt.nz).

*Police* The national emergency number for police is © **110.**

*Restrooms* If you need a restroom, your best bets are at train and subway stations (though these tend to be dirty), big hotels, department stores, and fast-food restaurants. Use of restrooms is free in Japan, but since public facilities often do not supply toilet paper, it's a good idea to **carry a packet of tissues.**

To find out whether a stall is empty, knock on the door. If it's occupied, someone will knock back. Similarly, if you're inside a stall and someone knocks, answer with a knock back or else the person will just keep on knocking persistently and try to get in. And don't be surprised if you go into some restrooms and find men's urinals and individual private stalls in the same room. Women are supposed to simply walk right past the urinals without noticing them.

Many toilets in Japan, especially those at train stations and in rural areas, are **Japanese-style:** They're holes in the ground over which you squat facing the end that has a raised hood. Men stand and aim for the hole. Although Japanese lavatories may seem uncomfortable at first, they're quite sanitary because no part of your body touches anything.

Everywhere you go in Japan nowadays you'll encounter **Washlet toilets,** combination toilet/bidets with heated toilet seats and buttons and knobs directing sprays of water of various intensities and temperatures to different body parts. Alas, instructions may be in Japanese only. The voice of experience: Don't stand up until you've figured how to turn the darn spray off.

*Smoking* You must be 20 years old to smoke in Japan. Smoking is banned in most public areas, including train and subway stations and office buildings. In many cities, there are also nonsmoking ordinances that ban smoking on sidewalks but allow it in marked areas, usually near train stations. Many restaurants

nowadays have nonsmoking sections, though bars do not. Most hotels have designated nonsmoking floors, except for some business hotels and Japanese-style inns. If you want to sit in the nonsmoking car of the Shinkansen bullet train, ask for the *kinensha*. During peak travel times, be sure to reserve a seat in the nonsmoking car in advance.

*Taxes* A 5% consumption tax, imposed on goods and services in Japan including hotel rates and restaurant meals, is included in all prices. However, even though hotels and restaurants are required to include the tax in their published rates, you might come across some establishments that have not yet done so (especially on English-language menus that may be several years old). In Tokyo, hotels also levy a separate accommodation tax of ¥100 (95¢) per person per night on rooms costing ¥10,000 to ¥14,999 ($95–$142); rates ¥15,000 and up are taxed at ¥200 ($1.90) per night per person. Some hotels include the local tax in their published rack rates, while others do not. In hot-spring resort areas, a ¥150 ($1.45) onsen tax is added for every night of your stay.

In addition to these taxes, a 10% to 15% **service charge** will be added to your bill in lieu of tipping at most of the fancier restaurants and at moderately priced and upper-end hotels. Business hotels, minshuku, youth hostels, and inexpensive restaurants do not impose a service charge.

As for **shopping**, a 5% consumption tax is also included in the price of most goods. (Some of the smaller vendors are not required to levy tax.) Travelers from abroad, however, are eligible for an exemption on goods taken out of the country, although only the larger department stores and specialty shops seem equipped to deal with the procedures. In any case, most department stores grant a refund on the consumption tax only when the total amount of purchases for the day exceeds ¥10,000 ($95). You can obtain a refund immediately by having a sales clerk fill out a list of your purchases and then presenting the list to the tax-exemption counter of the department store; *you will need to show your passport*. Note that no refunds for consumption tax are given for food, drinks, tobacco, cosmetics, film, and batteries.

*Telephones* **To call Japan:** For dialing Japan, the country code is **81.** In addition, all telephone area codes for all of Japan's cities begin with a zero; Tokyo's area code, for example, is 03, while Osaka's is 06. For other area codes, check the listings for each city in this guide. Use the entire area code only when dialing from outside the area but from within Japan. When calling Japan from abroad, drop the zero in the area code. When calling from the United States, for example, dial 011 for the international access code, 81 for Japan, followed by only 3 for Tokyo (not 03) and 6 (not 06) for Osaka. If you have questions, call the international operator in the country from which you are placing your call.

**Domestic calls:** You can make local, domestic, and international calls from your room in all but the cheapest hotels. It's more economical, however, to use a **public telephone.** Despite the proliferation of cellphones, public telephones are readily available—in telephone booths on the sidewalk, on train platforms, in restaurants and coffee shops, even on bullet trains (but these require a prepaid telephone card; see below). A local call costs ¥10 (10¢) for each minute; a

warning chime will ring to tell you to insert more coins or you'll be discon-nected. I usually insert two or three coins at the start so I won't have to worry about being disconnected; ¥10 coins that aren't used are always returned at the end of the call. Some older models available for public use outside ma-and-pa shops accept only ¥10 coins, but most public phones accept both ¥10 and ¥100 coins. The latter is convenient for long-distance calls but no change is given for unused minutes. All gray, ISDN telephones are equipped for interna-tional calls and have dataports for Internet access.

**Toll-free numbers** in Japan begin with **0120** or **0088**. However, calling a 1-800 number in the U.S. from Japan is not toll-free but costs the same as an interna-tional call.

If you think you'll be making a lot of domestic calls from public telephones and don't want to deal with coins, purchase a magnetic **prepaid telephone card.** These are available in values of ¥1,000 ($9.50) and are sold at vending machines (many of which are located right beside telephones), station kiosks, and convenience stores. Green and gray telephones accept telephone cards. In fact, many nowadays accept only telephone cards; insert the card into the slot. On the gray ISDN telephones, there's a second slot for a second telephone card, which is convenient if the first one is almost used up or if you think you'll be talking a long time. Domestic long-distance calls are 20% to 40% cheaper at night, on weekends, and on national holidays for calls of distances more than 60km (37 miles).

In addition to the common green and gray public phones, NTT also has its own silver and orange IC Card Payphones (found mostly in hotel lobbies) with its own card (sold in adjacent vending machines) which you insert into the phone.

**Mobile Phones:** Of course, you can also avoid public telephones altogether by joining what seems like the rest of the population and using a **mobile phone** *(keitai denwa).* Unfortunately, Japan uses a system that is incompatible with GSM or the U.S. system. Your best bet may be to rent a cellphone before leav-ing home, though there are also many options for phone rental in Japan. See "The 21st-Century Traveler," earlier in this chapter, for more information.

**To make international calls:** There are several ways to make international calls. For a collect call, or to place an operator-assisted call through KDDI, dial the international telephone operator at ⓒ **0051.** From a public telephone, look for a specially marked INTERNATIONAL AND DOMESTIC CARD/COIN TELEPHONE. Although many of the specially marked green or gray telephones, the most common pub-lic telephone, accept both coins and magnetic telephone cards for domestic calls, most do not accept magnetic cards for international calls (due to illegal usage of telephone cards), especially in big cities. You'll therefore either have to use coins, or purchase a special prepaid international telephone card that works like telephone cards issued by U.S. telephone companies. An access num-ber must first be dialed, followed by a secret telephone number and then the number you wish to dial. Such cards are often sold from a vending machine next to telephone booths in hotels or in convenience stores like 7-Eleven or

Lawson. There are numerous such cards (with instructions in English), such as the **Brastel Smart Phonecard** (② **0120/659-543**; www.brastel.com), **Primus' Phonebank** (② **03/5846-3754**; www.primustel.co.jp); and the **KDDI Super World Card** (② **0057**; www.www.kddi.com). Some hotels also have special phones equipped to accept credit cards.

**International rates** vary according to when you call, which telephone company you use, and what type of service you use. Direct-dial service is cheaper than operator-assisted calls and is offered by both international public telephones and by hotels that advertise the service (though remember to ask about the surcharge). The cheapest time to call is between 11pm and 8am Japan time, while the most expensive time is weekdays from 8am to 7pm. From a pay phone, a ¥1,000 ($9.50) call to the United States will allow you to talk 7 minutes and 25 seconds during prime time and 9 minutes and 45 seconds after 11pm.

If you're not using a prepaid card (which has its own set of instructions and access numbers), to make a direct-dial international call you must first dial one of the international access codes—**001** (KDDI), **0041** (Japan Telecom), **0033** (NTT-Com), or **0061** (Japan Telecom IDC)—followed by **010** and then the country code. The country code for the United States and Canada is **1**; for the United Kingdom, it's **44**; for Australia, it's **61**; and for New Zealand, it's **64**. To call the United States, for example, dial an access code such as 001, followed by 010, the country code 1, the area code, and the telephone number. If you're dialing from your hotel room, you must first dial for an outside line, usually 0.

If you wish to be connected with an operator in your home country, you can do so from green international telephones by dialing ② **0039** followed by a three-digit country code. (For the United States, dial **0039-111**.) These calls can be used for collect calls or credit card calls. Some hotels and other public places are equipped with special phones that will link you to your home operator with the push of a button, and there are instructions in English.

If you have a U.S. calling card, ask your phone company for the direct access number from Japan that will link you directly to the United States. If you have AT&T, for example, dial **00539-111** (you can also pay by credit card at this number for calls made to the United States); if you're using MCI, however, it depends on which Japanese company you're using (for KDD, it's **0053-121**).

*Television*  If you enjoy watching television, you've come to the wrong country. Almost nothing is broadcast in English; even foreign films are dubbed in Japanese. However, if your hotel room has what's called a **bilingual television,** you can switch from Japanese to the original language to hear programs and movies in English. Most upper-range hotels offer bilingual TVs, though note that there are very few English-language movies and sitcoms broadcast each week (and most of these are fairly old). In my opinion, a major plus of bilingual TVs is that they allow you to listen to the nightly national news broadcast by NHK at 7 and 10pm. Otherwise, major hotels in larger cities also have cable TV with English-language programs like CNN broadcasts and BBC World as well as in-house pay movies. Note, however, that CNN is sometimes broadcast in Japanese only, particularly in outlying areas. On the other hand, even if you don't understand Japanese, I suggest that you watch TV at least once; maybe you'll catch a samurai series. Commercials are also worth watching.

A word on those **pay video programs** offered by hotels and many resort ryokan: Upper-range hotels usually have a few choices in English, and these are charged automatically to your bill. Most business hotels usually offer only one kind of pay movie—generally "adult entertainment" programs. If you're traveling with children, you'll want to be extremely careful about selecting your TV programs. Many adult video pay channels appear with a simple push of the channel-selector button, and they can be difficult to get rid of. In budget accommodations, you may come across televisions with coin boxes attached to their sides, or, more common nowadays, vending machines offering prepaid cards. These are also for special adult entertainment videos. Now you know.

*Time Zone*   Japan is 9 hours ahead of Greenwich Mean Time, 14 hours ahead of New York, 15 hours ahead of Chicago, and 17 hours ahead of Los Angeles. Since Japan does not go on daylight saving time, subtract 1 hour from the above times in the summer when calling from countries that have daylight saving time such as the United States.

Because Japan is on the other side of the international date line, you lose a day when traveling from the United States to Asia. (If you depart the United States on Tues, you'll arrive on Wed.) Returning to North America, however, you gain a day, which means that you arrive on the same day you left. (In fact, it often happens that you arrive in the states at an earlier hour than you departed from Japan.)

*Tipping*   One of the delights of being in Japan is that there's no tipping—not even to waitresses, taxi drivers, or bellhops. If you try to tip them, they'll probably be confused or embarrassed. Instead, you'll have a 10% to 15% service charge added to your bill at higher-priced hotels and restaurants.

*Water*   The water is safe to drink anywhere in Japan, although some people claim it's too highly chlorinated. Bottled water is also readily available.

# 3

# Suggested Japan Itineraries

Japan, with its rich culture and varied geography, has much to offer the curious visitor, not only in and around the major cities but in many of the outlying regions as well. If you want to see *everything*, you should plan on spending at least a year in Japan. More likely, your time will be limited to a week or two, so you'll have to be selective; this section will help you decide on an itinerary.

If you're in Japan for several weeks, you can fashion a personalized itinerary by combining several of these suggested itineraries, along with recommended routes provided in the chapters for the Japan Alps (chapter 7) and Kyushu (chapter 11). But regardless of what itinerary you plan, I am adamant about one thing: *Kyoto is a must.* In addition to having served as the nation's capital for more than 1,000 years, it has more temples, shrines, and historic sights than any other Japanese city.

## 1 Japan in 1 Week

This trip takes you to Japan's highlights, from fast-paced Tokyo to the quiet temples of Kyoto, along with a couple of other worthwhile destinations. It's designed for first-timers, so if you've already been to Japan and seen all the must-sees, refer to the other itineraries to create your own 1-week itinerary.

### Day ❶: Arrive in Tokyo
After your arrival at Narita Airport, head to your hotel in Tokyo (about a 2-hr. trip). Recuperate from your flight, settle in, and get a feel for the city. Take a walk through a neighborhood close to your hotel and top off the day with a meal in a traditional restaurant. Try to stay up as late as you can to adjust to the new time zone.

### Day ❷: Exploring Tokyo
Because of the difference in time zones, you'll probably be wide awake in the wee hours of the morning, so get up and head for **Tsukiji Fish Market.** After a breakfast of fresh sushi, head to **Hama Rikyu,** one of Tokyo's best Japanese gardens (it opens at 9am), from which you can board a ferry for a cruise up the Sumida River to **Asakusa,** where you can visit **Sensoji Temple** and shop for souvenirs along **Nakamise Dori.** Afterward, see the **Tokyo National Museum,** the world's finest repository of Japanese art and crafts. Toward evening, head to Ginza for a stroll through a department store; if possible, try to attend a **Kabuki** play. See chapter 5.

### Day ❸: Hakone 🕭🕭🕭
Take the train to Hakone Yumoto, gateway to the wonderful **Fuji-Hakone-Izu National Park** (if possible, leave your luggage at Hakone Yumoto Station and travel overnight only with a small bag).

0    200 mi
0    200 km

HOKKAIDO

Sea of
Japan

HONSHU

PACIFIC
OCEAN

Tokyo
Hakone    1-2
Kyoto    3
5-6    4
Hiroshima
7

Korea Strait

SHIKOKU

KYUSHU

❶ Arrive in Tokyo
❷ Tokyo
❸ Hakone
❹ Hakone to Kyoto
5-6 Kyoto
❼ Hiroshima, then
   back to Tokyo to
   depart Japan

Here you can travel through some of Japan's most scenic countryside via a circuitous route that includes a two-car streetcar, a cable car, ropeway, and a boat, while seeing such sights as the wonderful **Hakone Open-Air Museum** and, if you're lucky, the elusive Mount Fuji. Be sure to schedule some time for a dip in a hot-spring bath, and spend the night in **The Fujiya Hotel** (p. 249), one of my favorites in all of Japan, or in a Japanese inn. See chapter 6.

## Day ❹: Hakone to Kyoto

Complete your trip through Hakone, returning afterward to Hakone Yumoto to pick up your luggage and then heading to Odawara, where you can transfer to

the 3-hour Shinkansen bullet train to **Kyoto.** End the day with a stroll through Kyoto's central shopping area, topped with a stroll through the **Pontocho nightlife area.** Spend the night in one of Kyoto's many traditional Japanese-style inns. See chapter 8.

## Day ❺: Exploring Kyoto ✿✿✿

Start the day with a self-guided walk through eastern Kyoto (p. 321), seeing **Sanjusangendo Hall** with its 1,001 wooden statues, **Kiyomizu Temple,** and **Heian Shrine** with its garden, followed by shopping at the **Kyoto Handicraft Center.** If it's summer, spend the evening watching cormorant fishing from a flat-bottom boat in nearby Arashiyama (p. 281).

## Day ❻: Exploring Kyoto 🍁🍁🍁

Visit Kyoto's other main attractions—**Nijo Castle,** former home of the shogun; **Kyoto Imperial Palace; Ryoanji Temple** with its famous Zen rock garden; and the **Golden Pavilion.** In the evening, head for **Gion**, Japan's most famous Geisha quarters, followed by an evening performance at **Gion Corner** with its cultural demonstrations (p. 336).

## Day ❼: Hiroshima 🍁🍁

One hour away by Shinkansen bullet train, Hiroshima is best known for its **Peace Memorial Park** (p. 449), which contains the sobering **Peace Memorial Museum** outlining that fateful day in 1945 when the city became the world's first city destroyed by an atomic bomb. If time permits, see also **Hiroshima Castle** before heading back to Tokyo (p. 451).

## 2  Japan in 2 Weeks

This is something of a whirlwind trip, but it allows you to take in some of the best that Honshu island has to offer. If you have 1 or 2 extra days, you might wish to devote more time to Kyoto or head over to Kyushu (see chapter 11).

## Days ❶ & ❷: Arrive in Tokyo

Hit Tokyo's highlights as outlined above under "Japan in 1 Week."

## Day ❸: More of Tokyo

Visit the **Edo-Tokyo Museum** for a colorful portrayal of the city's tumultuous history, followed by a stroll through **Akihabara,** the country's largest concentration of shops devoted to electronics, with store after store offering the latest computers, digital cameras, cellphones, calculators, and more (p. 205). Next, go to Harajuku to see **Meiji Shrine,** Tokyo's most popular shrine, followed by shopping at **Oriental Bazaar,** great for Japanese souvenirs. End the day with eye-popping views from the 45th-floor observatory in Shinjuku's **Tokyo Metropolitan Government Office,** followed by a stroll through Japan's most notorious and craziest nightlife district, **Kabuki-cho** (p. 213).

## Day ❹: Nikko 🍁🍁🍁

Take a day trip outside of Tokyo. An excellent choice is **Nikko,** famous for its sumptuous mausoleum of Shogun Tokugawa Ieyasu, Japan's most famous shogun, set in a forest of majestic cedars (p. 227).

## Day ❺: Takayama & the Japan Alps 🍁🍁🍁

Early in the morning, take the Shinkansen to Nagoya (about 2 hr.) and then a 3-hour train ride to **Takayama** in the Japan Alps (if you don't have a rail pass, there are also direct buses from Tokyo's Shinjuku Station). Explore the picturesque, narrow streets of this old castle town and its many interesting museums and merchants' homes. Since Takayama has more traditional Japanese inns than hotels, this is the perfect place to experience tatami living, with accommodations available at various price ranges (p. 271).

## Day ❻: Exploring Takayama

To get a feel for the small-town atmosphere, start your day with a stroll through the **Miyagawa Morning Market** (p. 268) on the bank of a river. Of the many small museums in Takayama, most unique is the **Inro Museum,** dedicated to the small, portable medicine cases and their counterweights, worn over kimono sashes (p. 270). Also not to be missed is the **Historical Government House,** the only regional administrative building from the shogun era still in existence (p. 270).

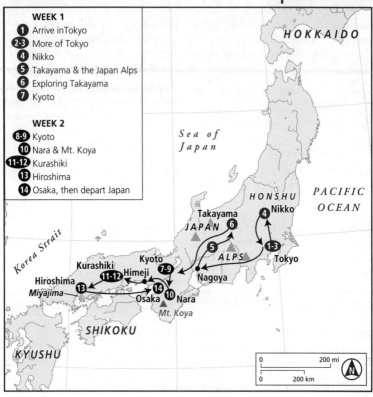

## Japan in 2 Weeks

**WEEK 1**
- ❶ Arrive inTokyo
- ❷-❸ More of Tokyo
- ❹ Nikko
- ❺ Takayama & the Japan Alps
- ❻ Exploring Takayama
- ❼ Kyoto

**WEEK 2**
- ❽-❾ Kyoto
- ❿ Nara & Mt. Koya
- ⓫-⓬ Kurashiki
- ⓭ Hiroshima
- ⓮ Osaka, then depart Japan

### Days ❼, ❽ & ❾: Kyoto 🅐🅐🅐

Spend the next few days in Kyoto as outlined above in "Japan in 1 Week." For more sightseeing ideas, see chapter 8.

### Day ❿: Nara 🅐🅐 & Mount Koya 🅐🅐🅐

Early in the morning, head for **Nara,** an ancient capital even older than Kyoto. Most of Nara's historic buildings and temples, including **Todaiji Temple** with its **Great Buddha,** are enclosed within an expansive park that is also home to free-roaming deer (p. 340). From Nara, take the Kintetsu train to Kintetsu Namba Station in Osaka, transferring there for a train and cable car to **Mount Koya.** Mount Koya is Japan's most sacred religious site,

achingly beautiful with more than 115 Buddhist temples spread through the forests. Spend the night in one of these temples, dining on vegetarian food (p. 416). Be sure to take a nighttime stroll past towering cypress trees and countless tombs and memorial tablets to **Okunoin,** the burial ground of Kobo Daishi, one of Japan's most revered Buddhist priests (p. 414).

### Days ⓫ & ⓬: Kurashiki 🅐🅐🅐

After a vegetarian breakfast and perhaps an early-morning Buddhist service, followed by a daytime stroll to Okunoin (when the atmosphere is completely different), return to Osaka and transfer to a train bound for Kurashiki. En route,

make a stopover in **Himeji** to see **Himeji Castle,** easily the most impressive castle in Japan, and **Koko-en,** a garden composed of nine different styles of gardens typical of the Feudal Era (p. 419). Spend the night in Kurashiki and take an evening stroll along the canal. The next day, take in the sights of Kurashiki, including its many museums like the **Ohara Museum of Art** with its impressive collection of Western masters (p. 431).

### Day ⓭: Hiroshima 🦌🦌
Leave for Hiroshima first thing in the morning (it's about 1 hr. away by Shinkansen). Spend the morning at **Peace Memorial Park** with its sobering memorials and museum that does an impressive job of detailing events before, during, and after the explosion of the atomic bomb (p. 449). Afterward, board a boat for the 45-minute trip to the tiny island of **Miyajima,** considered sacred since ancient times and famous for its **Itsukushima Shrine** (p. 460).

### Day ⓮: Departing Japan
I suggest departing Japan from Osaka's Kansai International Airport (it takes a little less than 2 hr. to reach Shin-Osaka Station, followed by a 45-min. train ride to the airport). Otherwise, you might consider a direct flight to Narita airport. (ANA has an early morning, 1-hr. and 40-min. flight.) Or, if you have more time—or if you just can't leave—head to Kyushu and tack on a few days or more from the suggested sightseeing route in chapter 11.

## 3 Japan for Families

There is no end to family entertainment in Japan. To keep your children's interest and preserve your sanity, this itinerary includes temples, shrines, museums, and castles for culture and a little education, along with a healthy dose of Japanese pop culture, from theme parks to sophisticated game arcades. Of course, you'll want to tailor your itinerary to fit your children's ages and interests; just be sure to schedule a lot of downtime so you don't burn out on sensory overload.

### Day ❶: Arrive in Japan
After your arrival at Osaka's Kansai International Airport, take the train 75 minutes to **Kyoto.** Don't plan anything strenuous the first day, but do walk around to absorb your new environment and to help adjust your time clocks.

### Days ❷ & ❸: Exploring Kyoto 🦌🦌🦌
You'll want to limit yourselves to only the highlights: **Kiyomizu Temple** is one of Kyoto's most famous temples, with plenty of food stalls and activities to keep little ones interested (be sure to have them walk the distance between the two stones at Jishu Shrine; p. 318). **Nijo Castle** is a painless introduction to the world of the shogun (p. 316). And be sure the darlings walk down **Nishiki-Koji Dori** for an up-close look at the octopus, fish, and everything else Japanese eat (p. 315). But probably the biggest hit with children is **Toei Uzumasa Movieland,** an actual working studio for Edo-Era film productions, along with a Ninja show, haunted house, and other attractions (p. 320). In summer, kids would also enjoy watching cormorant fishing from a flat-bottom boat (p. 281).

### Day ❹: Nara 🦌🦌
Although your children may not care that **Nara** is even older than Kyoto and served as the nation's capital for 74 years, they'll be intrigued by **Nara Park,** where deer (considered divine messengers) roam free.

- **1** Arrive in Japan
- **2-3** Exploring Kyoto
- **4** Nara
- **5-6** Okayama Prefecture's International Villas
- **7** Kurashiki
- **8** Hiroshima
- **9** Space World
- **10** Beppu
- **11-12** Osaka

They might also be impressed by the **Great Buddha,** Japan's largest bronze Buddha. See if they can crawl through a tiny passageway behind the Buddha—and supposedly attain enlightenment (p. 340). Back in Kyoto, good evening diversions for older kids include a stroll through **Gion,** where they might catch glimpse of a geisha, and **Gion Corner,** where they'll be exposed to traditional cultural pursuits, including *Bunraku* (Japanese puppetry; p. 336).

### Days **5** & **6**: Okayama Prefecture's International Villas

By now you might need some R & R in a rural setting, where you can take a couple of days to unwind and see something of the countryside. Maintained by Okayama Prefecture and open only to foreigners (and their Japanese guests) at greatly reduced prices, five **International Villas** are located in settings that range from an island in the Seto Inland Sea to a copper-mining town (p. 427).

### Day **7**: Kurashiki ★★★

Most visitors to **Kurashiki** come to see its picturesque historic district, centered on a willow-lined canal lined with black-and-white-mortared former warehouses now housing shops and ryokan. Your kids, however, will probably be more interested in **Tivoli Park,** located right next to the train station and modeled after the Copenhagen original (p. 432).

After a few hours here to get back in the swing of things, either spend the night in Kurashiki or continue on to Hiroshima for the night.

## Day ❽: Hiroshima 🦌🦌 or Space World

If you have teenagers, they're old enough for **Peace Memorial Park,** where they'll learn about the horrors of war, particularly the devastation caused by an atomic bomb (pictures are too graphic, however, for younger children; p. 449). If time permits, **Miyajima** is also a good destination, not only for the ferry ride and the free-roaming deer but also for the trails through the woods, its swimming beaches, and cable car (p. 459).

## Day ❾: Space World

If you can stand another theme park, **Space World,** with the usual roller coasters and amusement rides based on space travel, offers diversions for children of all ages (p. 489). From nearby Kokura Station, it's a 1½-hour train ride to Beppu, the king of hot-spring resorts in Kyushu.

## Day ❿: Beppu 🦌🦌

There's probably no child who wouldn't be fascinated by **The Hells,** a series of thermal wonders ranging from red, bubbling waters to hot springs that house crocodiles (you might not be impressed, but your kids will be; p. 548). They'll also like the wild monkey refuge on **Mount Takasaki** and the nearby **Umitamago**

aquarium (p. 549). But the highlight for everyone will undoubtedly be **Aqua-Beat,** an indoor water park. Your kids will like the splash rides and wave pool; you'll like unwinding in its outdoor hot spring (p. 547).

## Days ⓫ & ⓬: Osaka

It's a 4-hour train trip from Beppu to Osaka (not including a transfer in Kokura). Or, depart Beppu on Day 10 by ferry for an overnight trip to Osaka (at last check, a ferry departed Beppu at 4pm, arriving at Osaka at 8:40pm). There's more than enough in Osaka to keep families entertained, including the **Floating Garden Observatory** with its surreal views (p. 384), **Osaka Castle** (a remake, but impressive nonetheless; p. 385), and **Osaka Aquarium** (bigger and better than Beppu's; p. 387). It's also a trip at **Sega Amusement Theme Park,** the reigning king of amusement arcades. Teenagers will also want to take in **Den Den Town,** Osaka's electronics shopping street, and **America-Mura,** where young Osakans shop for American fashions. But if you want to end your trip with a bang, take your kids to **Universal Studios Japan.** It's almost a carbon copy of its U.S. counterpart, and most attractions are dubbed in Japanese, but do your kids really care? If you can't call it quits, continue on to Tokyo, where there's enough to keep you busy for another week (see chapter 5).

## 4 Northern Japan in 2 Weeks

Tohoku and Hokkaido are usually ignored on a journey through Japan. Though it's true that the country's most significant historic treasures lie in the southern regions, Northern Japan, where the emphasis is on natural wonders and hot-spring spas, offers a more relaxed vacation for repeat travelers who have already seen the country's must-sees.

## Day ❶: Arrive in Tokyo

Spend the night in Tokyo; if you wish to spend a few days in the capital sightseeing, refer to the 1- and 2-week itineraries above.

## Day ❷: Matsushima 🦌

Take the Shinkansen from Tokyo to Sendai (about 2 hr.) and then board a sightseeing boat for a 50-minute trip to **Matsushima,** famous for its scenic

## Northern Japan in 2 Weeks

**WEEK 1**
1. Arrive in Tokyo
2. Matsushima
3-4. Kakundate Castle Town
5. Nyuto Onsen
6. Hakodate
7. Noboribetsu Spa

**WEEK 2**
8-9. Sapporo
10-11. Daisetsuzan National Park
12-13. Akan National Park
14. Back to Tokyo, depart Japan

coastline of pine-studded islets. Visit the venerable **Zuiganji Temple,** northern Japan's most famous Zen temple, **Entsuin Temple** with its nice gardens and restaurant serving Buddhist vegetarian cuisine, and a museum or two (p. 557).

### Day ❸: Kakunodate Castle Town ⚑
Return to Sendai and take the Shinkansen onward to Kakunodate, a small and relatively unspoiled castle town famous for its samurai district and cherry trees. Be sure to see the **Aoyagi Samurai Manor,** a compound of traditional buildings packed with Edo-Period memorabilia (p. 563).

### Days ❹ & ❺: Back in Time at Nyuto Onsen
Backtrack one stop on the Shinkansen to Tazawako and board a bus for **Nyuto**

**Onsen,** a secluded valley of hot springs and rustic inns. It's a good base from which to explore the many wonders of the Towada-Hachimantai National Park, including skiing in winter and hiking and swimming in summer (p. 566). For the ultimate ryokan experience, spend the night in Tsuru-no-yu Onsen, a rustic and remote Japanese inn with outdoor baths (p. 567).

### Day ❻: Hakodate Port Town ⚑
Head north for Hakodate. Wander the **warehouse district** and historic **Motomachi,** a picturesque neighborhood of steep slopes and turn-of-the-20th-century clapboard homes and other buildings, relics of when Hakodate opened as one of Japan's first international ports following 2 centuries of isolation. In the

evening, take a cable car to the top of **Mount Hakodate,** famous for its night view of Hakodate (p. 575).

## Day ❼: Noboribetsu Spa 🐾🐾
Visit Hakodate's **morning market** (famous for its hairy crabs; p. 576) and then depart for **Noboribetsu Onsen,** known for its curative hot-springs. Hike through **Hell Valley** for a view of the bubbling hot water that has made Noboribetsu famous, and then experience its magic at the Daiichi Takimotokan hot-spring baths (p. 591).

## Days ❽ & ❾: Sapporo
Capital of Hokkaido Prefecture and the island's largest city, Sapporo is an easygoing city that's easy to navigate. Highlights include the **Botanic Garden,** the **Sapporo Beer Museum,** and **Nopporo Forest Park,** where you can visit the **Historical Museum of Hokkaido** and see vintage homes and buildings at the **Historical Village of Hokkaido** (p. 584).

## Days ❿ & ⓫: Daisetsuzan National Park 🐾🐾🐾
Depart Sapporo by train to Kamikawa (a 2½-hr. ride), followed by a 30-minute bus ride to the quaint village of **Sounkyo.** It's nestled in **Daisetsuzan National Park,** one of Hokkaido's most spectacular parks. Rent a bike and ride to the pretty Sounkyo Gorge, and then take the cable car to the top of Mount Kurodake for the view or some hiking. Top off the day with a soak in a hot-spring spa (p. 596).

## Days ⓬ & ⓭: Akan National Park 🐾🐾
Depart Sounkyo early in the morning by bus back to Kamikawa and then take the train 2½ hours to Bihoro. There, board a **sightseeing bus** for a 5-hour tour of **Akan National Park** and its natural wonders, ending up at Akanko Spa (p. 600). Take a boat cruise of **Lake Akan,** famous for its *marimo,* a spongelike ball of duckweed, and tour the marimo museum. Visit **Ainu Kotan Village** with its shops and traditional Ainu dancing. Outdoor pursuits include hiking and fishing (including ice fishing in winter; p. 603).

## Day ⓮: Back to Tokyo
From Kushiro Airport (about 1 hr. and 20 min. by bus from Akanko Onsen), planes bring you back to Tokyo's Haneda Airport in about 1½ hours.

# Settling into Tokyo

To the uninitiated, Tokyo may seem like a whirlwind of traffic and people, so confusing that visitors might think they have somehow landed on another planet. Little wonder first-time visitors are almost invariably disappointed. They come expecting an exotic Asian city, but instead they find a city Westernized and modernized to the point of ugliness, much of it a drab concrete jungle of unimaginative buildings clustered so close together that there's hardly room in which to breathe.

Simply stated, Tokyo is a crush of humanity. Its subways are often packed, its sidewalks are crowded, its streets are congested, and its air is filled with noise, pollution, and what can only be called mystery smells. Approximately 12 million people live in its 2,100 sq. km (840 sq. miles), many of them in bedroom towns from which they have to commute to work for an average of 2 to 3 hours every day. No matter where you go in Tokyo, you're never alone. After you've been here for a while, Paris, London, and even New York will seem deserted.

Crowds and urban ugliness, however, are what you'll see only if you don't bother to look beneath the surface. For Tokyo is alluring in its own way, and if you open yourself to it you'll find a city unlike any other in the world, humming with energy and vitality. People rush around here with such purpose, such determination, it's hard not to feel that you're in the midst of something important, that you're witnessing history in the making.

**A LOOK AT THE PAST** Though today the nation's capital, Tokyo is a relative newcomer to the pages of Japanese history. For centuries it was nothing more than a rather unimportant village called Edo, which means simply "mouth of the estuary." In 1603, Edo was catapulted into the limelight when the new shogun, Tokugawa Ieyasu, made the sleepy village the seat of his government. He expanded Edo Castle, making it the largest and most impressive castle in the land, and surrounded it with an ingenious system of moats that radiated from the castle in a great swirl, giving him easy access to the sea and an upper hand in thwarting enemy attack.

The town developed quickly, due largely to the shogun's decree requiring all feudal lords (daimyo) to permanently leave their families in Edo, a shrewd move to thwart insurrection in the provinces. There were as many as 270 daimyo in Japan in the 17th century, all of whom maintained several mansions in Edo, complete with elaborate compounds and expansive gardens. The daimyos' trusted samurai soon accounted for more than half of Edo's population, and the merchant class expanded as well. By 1787 the population had grown to 1.3 million, making Edo—even then—one of the largest cities in the world.

When the Tokugawas were overthrown in 1868, the Japanese emperor was restored to power and moved the capital from Kyoto to Edo, now renamed Tokyo (Eastern Capital). Japan's Feudal Era—and its isolation from the rest of the

world—was over. As the capital city, Tokyo was the hardest hit in this new era of modernization, with fashion, architecture, food, and even people imported from the West. West was best, and things Japanese were forgotten or ignored.

It didn't help that Tokyo was almost totally destroyed twice in the first half of the 20th century: In 1923, a massive earthquake measuring 7.9 on the Richter scale destroyed more than a third of the city and claimed more than 100,000 lives; disaster struck again in 1945, toward the end of World War II when Allied incendiary bombs laid more than half the city to waste and killed another 100,000 people.

**TOKYO TODAY** Perhaps that's why most visitors are disappointed with Tokyo—it has almost nothing of historical importance to match Kyoto or Kamakura. So put your notions of quaint Japan out of your mind and plunge headfirst into the 21st century, because that's what Tokyo is all about. In fact, in the past few years, skyscrapers and new developments have been mushrooming faster than you can say *shiitake,* some of them the most ambitious land projects Japan has ever seen.

As the financial nerve center of Japan, Tokyo has long set the pace for what happens in the rest of Asia. The city is so wired and electric you can feel it in the air. It's the reigning capital of Asian pop art and kitsch, fads, and trends.

But even though the city has a fast-paced, somewhat zany side, it also has a quieter and often overlooked side that makes the city both loveable and livable.

Although formidable at first glance, Tokyo is nothing more than a series of small towns and neighborhoods clustered together, each with its own atmosphere, narrow, winding streets, mom-and-pop shops, fruit stands, and stores. Look for the details, and you'll notice carefully pruned bonsai adorning the sidewalks; old women in kimono shuffling down the streets; traditional wooden houses tucked between massive apartment complexes; everywhere, neatness and order. Peer inside those concrete high-rises, and you're apt to find Japanese restaurants that are perfect replicas of wood-beamed farmhouses side-by-side with cocktail bars that epitomize high-tech avant-garde.

I love Tokyo. Despite its daily frustrations, Tokyo is exhilarating, often exciting, and unceasingly interesting. Best of all, it's one of the world's safest metropolises, with the lowest theft rate of any large city on the planet. Although common sense dictates I avoid public parks after dark when I'm out alone and watch my purse in crowded subways, I otherwise walk without fear anywhere and anytime in Tokyo, day or night. The city's safety is best illustrated by what an American friend living in Tokyo was told when her daughter started first grade in a Japanese school: Parents were to refrain from walking their children to or from school, allowing, instead, the children to walk on their own.

Perhaps the only thing in Tokyo you have to watch out for are those Japanese businessmen who've had too much to drink—reserve thrown off, they might want to practice their English on you.

## 1 Orientation

### ARRIVING
#### BY PLANE

There are two airports serving Tokyo, but most likely you'll arrive at **Narita International Airport,** 65km (40 miles) outside Tokyo. If you're arriving in Tokyo from elsewhere in Japan, your flight will probably land at **Haneda Airport,** used primarily for domestic flights.

**FACILITIES AT NARITA AIRPORT**  Narita International Airport (© **0476/ 34-5000;** www.narita-airport.co.jp/airport_e/index.html) consists of two terminals, Terminal 1 and Terminal 2. Arrival lobbies in both terminals have banks for money exchange open daily 6am to 11pm, as well as ATMs (change money here, as facilities in town are limited), and are connected to all ground transportation to Tokyo.

A **Tourist Information Center (TIC),** managed by the Japan National Tourist Organization, is located in the arrival lobbies of both Terminal 1 (© **0476/30-3383)** and Terminal 2 (© **0476/34-5877).** The TIC offers free maps and pamphlets and can direct you to your hotel or inn. Both are open daily 8am to 8pm; if you don't yet have a hotel room and want one at a modest price, you can make reservations here free of charge until 7:30pm.

If you've purchased a Japan Rail Pass, you can turn in your voucher at one of the **Japan Railways (JR) View Plazas** (Travel Service Centers), located in both Terminal 1 and Terminal 2 and open daily 6:45am to 9:45pm. Other facilities at both terminals include post offices, medical clinics, shower rooms, day rooms for napping, children's playrooms, and coin-operated computers with Internet capabilities (¥100/85¢ for 10 min.).

**GETTING TO TOKYO FROM NARITA AIRPORT**  Jumping into a **taxi** is the easiest way to get to Tokyo, but it's also prohibitively expensive—and may not even be the quickest if you happen to hit rush hour. Expect to spend around ¥25,000 ($238) or more for a 1½- to 2-hour taxi ride from Narita.

**By Bus**  The most popular way to get from Narita to Tokyo is via the **Airport Limousine Bus** (© **03/3665-7220;** www.limousinebus.co.jp), which picks up passengers and their luggage from just outside the arrival lobbies of terminals 1 and 2 and delivers them to downtown hotels. This is the best mode of transportation if you have heavy baggage or are staying at one of the 40 or so major hotels served by the bus. Buses depart for the various hotels generally once an hour, and it can take almost 2 hours to reach a hotel in Shinjuku. Buses also travel to both Tokyo and Shinjuku stations and the **Tokyo City Air Terminal (TCAT)** in downtown Tokyo, with more frequent departures (up to 4 times an hour in peak times). If your hotel is not served by limousine bus, take it to the hotel or station nearest your destination. In addition to taxis, TCAT, Shinjuku Station, and Tokyo Station are also served by public transportation; TCAT is connected to the subway Hanzomon Line via moving walkways and escalators; Shinjuku and Tokyo stations are hubs for subway lines and commuter trains.

Check with the staff at the Airport Limousine Bus counter in the arrival lobbies to inquire which bus stops nearest your hotel, and its departure time. The fare to most destinations is ¥3,000 ($29). Children 6 to 12 are charged half fare; those under 6 ride free.

**By Train**  The quickest way to reach Tokyo is by train, with several options available. Trains depart directly from the airport's two underground stations, called Narita Airport Station (which is in Terminal 1) and Airport Terminal 2 Station.

The JR **Narita Express** (**NEX;** © **03/3423-0111;** www.jreast.co.jp) is the fastest way to reach Tokyo Station, Shinagawa, Shinjuku, and Yokohama, with departures approximately once an hour, or twice an hour during peak hours. The 53-minute trip to Tokyo Station costs ¥2,940 ($28) one-way. Note, however, that if you have a validated JR Rail Pass, you can ride the NEX free (as mentioned above, you must first validate your rail pass at the JR View Plaza, also called the JR Travel Service Center, located in both terminals). *Note:* Seats are sometimes sold out in advance, especially during peak travel times. If you wish to reserve a seat for your return trip to Narita

Airport—and I strongly urge that you do—you can do so here at the NEX counter or at any of Tokyo's major JR stations. Plan to arrive at Narita 2 hours before your plane's departure.

If the NEX is sold out and you're still determined to use your rail pass, you can take the slower **JR Airport Liner,** which will get you to Tokyo Station in 80 minutes. Without a rail pass, this rapid train will cost you ¥1,280 ($12).

An alternative is the privately owned **Keisei Skyliner** train (© **03/3831-0131;** www.keisei.co.jp), which departs directly from both Narita Airport Station (Terminal 1) and Airport Terminal 2 Station and travels to Ueno Station in Tokyo in about 1 hour, with a stop at Nippori Station on the way. You'll find Keisei Skyliner counters in the arrival lobbies of both terminals. Trains depart approximately every 40 minutes between 7:49am and 10pm. The fare from Narita Airport to Ueno Station in Tokyo is ¥1,920 ($18) one-way; early morning and evening fares are cheaper. If you're on a strict budget, you can take one of Keisei's slower limited express trains to Ueno Station, with fares starting at ¥1,000 ($9.50) for the 71-minute trip. At Ueno Station, you can take either the subway or the JR Yamanote Line to other parts of Tokyo. There are also plenty of taxis there.

**GETTING TO HANEDA AIRPORT**    If you're connecting to a domestic flight, you may need to transfer to Haneda Airport. The **Airport Limousine Bus** makes runs between Narita Airport and Haneda Airport that cost ¥3,000 ($29). The trip takes about 75 minutes.

**GETTING FROM HANEDA AIRPORT INTO CENTRAL TOKYO**    If you're arriving by domestic flight at Haneda Airport (© **03/5757-8111**), located near the center of Tokyo, you can take the **Airport Limousine Bus** to Shinjuku Station, Tokyo Station, the Tokyo City Air Terminal (TCAT) in downtown Tokyo, and to hotels in Shinjuku, Ikebukuro, and Akasaka. Fares run from ¥900 to ¥1,200 ($8.55–$11). The locals, however, are more likely to take the **monorail** from Haneda Airport 15 minutes to Hamamatsucho Station (fare: ¥470/$4.45) or the **Keikyu Line** 19 minutes to Shinagawa (fare: ¥400/$3.80). Both Hamamatsucho and Shinagawa connect to the very useful Yamanote Line, which travels to major stations, including Tokyo Station and Shinjuku Station. There is also a Tokyo Tourist Information Center (© **03/ 5757-9345**) in Haneda Airport, open daily 9am to 10pm.

## BY LAND OR SEA

**BY TRAIN**    If you're traveling to Tokyo by the Shinkansen bullet train, you'll probably arrive at either **Tokyo Station** or **Shinagawa Station,** both connected to the rest of the city via JR commuter trains and the subway (avoid Tokyo Station if you can; it's very big and confusing). Trains from northern Japan also stop at Ueno Station.

**BY BUS**    Long-distance bus service from Hiroshima, Nagoya, Osaka, Kyoto, and other major cities delivers passengers to **Tokyo Station,** which is connected to the rest of the city via subway and commuter train. Other bus terminals serving the region outside Tokyo include Shinagawa and Shinjuku stations, both of which are served by the JR Yamanote Line, which loops around the city.

**BY FERRY**    Long-distance ferries arrive in Tokyo at the **Tokyo Ko Ferry Futo (Tokyo Port Ferry Terminal).** From there, you can board a bus for Shinkiba JR Station and catch a train to town.

## VISITOR INFORMATION

The **Tourist Information Center (TIC),** 2–10–1 Yurakucho (℃ **03/3201-3331**), is located on the 10th floor of a rather obscure office building called Kotsu Kaikan Building next to the JR Yurakucho Station (look for its circular top). Assuming you're able to find them, the TIC staff can answer all your questions regarding Tokyo and Japan, can give you a map of the city plus various sightseeing materials, and will even book inexpensive hotels for you around the country, charging no fee for the service. They're courteous and efficient; I cannot recommend them highly enough. Maintained by the Japan National Tourist Organization, the TIC also has information on the rest of Japan, including pamphlets and brochures on major cities and attractions. Be sure to stop here if you plan to visit other destinations, because information in English may not be available at the destination itself. The TIC is open daily from 9am to 5pm. Other TIC offices are located in the arrival lobbies of Terminal 1 and Terminal 2 at Narita Airport, open daily from 8am to 8pm.

Another great source of information is the **Tokyo Tourist Information Center,** operated by the Tokyo Metropolitan Government and located on the first floor of the Tokyo Metropolitan Government (TMG) Building No. 1, 2–8–1 Nishi-Shinjuku (℃ **03/5321-3077;** www.tourism.metro.tokyo.jp; station: Tochomae or Shinjuku); you'll probably want to come here anyway for the TMG's great observation floor. The center dispenses pamphlets, its own city map (which is a great complement to the one issued by JNTO's TIC), and handy one-page detailed maps of various city districts, from Ueno to Roppongi. It's open daily 9:30am to 6:30pm. Other city-run information counters are located at Keisei Ueno Station (℃ **03/3836-3471;** station: Ueno), open daily 9:30am to 6:30pm; and Haneda Airport (℃ **03/5757-9345**), open daily 9am to 10pm.

Finally, another convenient source of information is the **TCVB Tourist Information Center,** 3–2–2 Marunouchi (℃ **03/3287-7024;** www.tcvb.or.jp; station: Hibiya, Nijubashimae, or Yurakucho), operated by the Tokyo Convention & Visitors Bureau. Located just east of the Imperial Palace Outer Garden and dispensing maps, pamphlets, and souvenirs, it's open Monday to Friday 10am to 5pm; Saturday, Sunday, and holidays from 10am to 4pm.

**TOURIST PUBLICATIONS** Be sure to pick up *Calendar Events* at the TIC, a monthly leaflet listing festivals, antiques and crafts fairs, and other events throughout the metropolitan area. Of the many free giveaways available at TIC, restaurants, bars, bookstores, hotels, and other establishments visitors and expats are likely to frequent, best is the weekly *Metropolis* (www.metropolis.japantoday.com), with features on Tokyo, club listings, and restaurant and movie reviews. Look also for the free *JapanZine* (www.japan-zine.com) and *att.Japan*. Weekly entertainment sections on theater, films, and special events are also published in the English-language newspapers, appearing on Friday in the *Japan Times* and on Thursday in the *Daily Yomiuri*.

## CITY LAYOUT

Your most frustrating moments in Tokyo will probably occur when you find that you're totally lost. Maybe it will be in a subway or train station, when all you see are signs in Japanese, or on a street somewhere as you search for a museum, restaurant, or bar. At any rate, accept it here and now: You *will* get lost if you are at all adventurous and strike out on your own. It's inevitable. But take comfort in the fact that Japanese get lost,

# Tokyo at a Glance

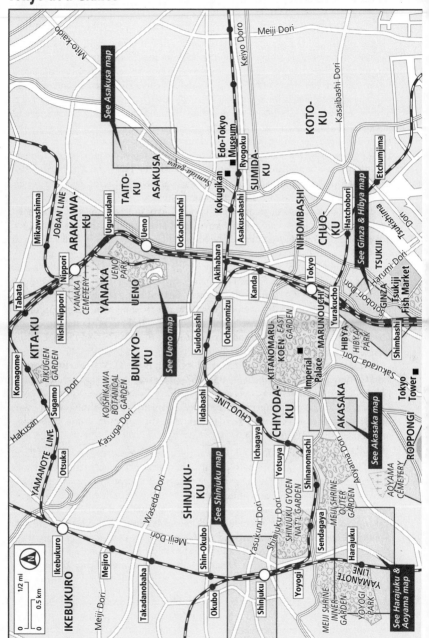

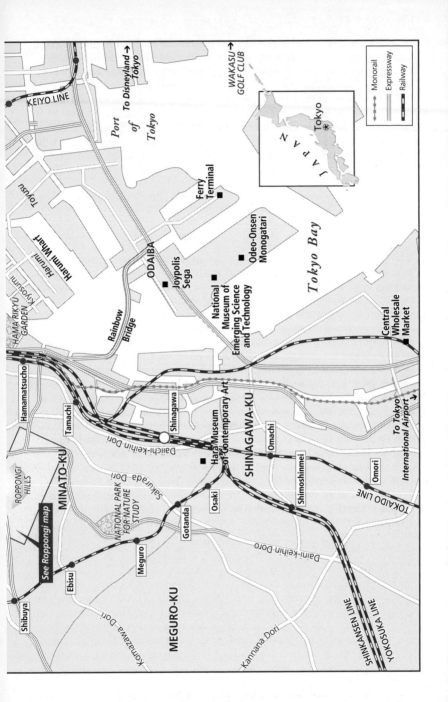

too—even taxi drivers! And don't forget that most of the hotel and restaurant listings in this book have the number of minutes it takes to walk there from the nearest station; if you take note, you'll at least know the radius from the station to your destination. It's wise, too, to always allow extra time to find your way around.

Tokyo, situated at one end of Tokyo Bay and spreading across the Kanto Plain, still retains some of its Edo Period features. If you look at a map, you'll find a large green oasis in the middle of the city, site of the Imperial Palace and its grounds. Surrounding it is the castle moat; a bit farther out are remnants of another circular moat built by the Tokugawa shogun. The JR Yamanote Line forms another loop around the inner city; most of Tokyo's major hotels, nightlife districts, and attractions are near or inside this oblong loop.

For administrative purposes, Tokyo is broken down into **23 wards,** known as *ku.* Its business districts of Marunouchi and Hibiya, for example, are in Chiyoda-ku, while Ginza is part of Chuo-ku (Central Ward). These two ku are the historic hearts of Tokyo, for it was here that the city had its humble beginnings.

**MAIN STREETS & ARTERIES**    One difficulty in finding your way around Tokyo is that hardly any streets are named. Think about what that means—12 million people living in a huge metropolis of nameless streets. Granted, major thoroughfares and some well-known streets in areas like Ginza and Shinjuku received names after World War II at the insistence of American occupation forces, and a few more have been labeled or given nicknames that only the locals know, but for the most part, Tokyo's address system is based on a complicated number scheme that must make the postal worker's job here a nightmare. To make matters worse, most streets in Tokyo zigzag— an arrangement apparently left over from olden days, to confuse potential attacking enemies. Now they confuse Tokyoites and visitors alike.

Among Tokyo's most important named streets are **Meiji Dori,** which follows the loop of the Yamanote Line and runs from Minato-ku in the south through Ebisu, Shibuya, Harajuku, Shinjuku, and Ikebukuro in the north; **Yasukuni Dori** and **Shinjuku Dori,** which cut across the heart of the city from Shinjuku to Chiyoda-ku; and **Sotobori Dori, Chuo Dori, Harumi Dori,** and **Showa Dori,** which pass through Ginza. (*Dori* means avenue or street, as does *michi.*)

Intersections in Tokyo are called a crossing; it seems every district has a famous crossing. **Ginza 4-chome Crossing** is the intersection of Chuo Dori and Harumi Dori. **Roppongi Crossing** is the intersection of Roppongi Dori and Gaien-Higashi Dori.

**ADDRESSES**    Because streets did not have names when Japan's postal system was established, the country has a unique address system. A typical Tokyo address might read 1–11–1 Marunouchi, Chiyoda-ku, which is the address of the Four Seasons Hotel Tokyo at Marunouchi. Chiyoda-ku is the name of the **ward.** Wards are further divided into **districts,** in this case Marunouchi. Marunouchi itself is broken down into **chome** (numbered subsection), here 1-chome. Number 11 refers to a smaller area within the chome—usually an entire block, sometimes larger. Thus, houses on one side of the street will usually have a different middle number than houses on the other side. The last number, in this case 1, refers to the actual building. Although it seems reasonable to assume that next to a number 1 building will be a number 2, that's not always the case; buildings were assigned numbers as they were constructed, not according to location.

Addresses are usually, but not always, posted on buildings beside doors, on telephone poles, and at major intersection traffic lights, but sometimes they are written

in kanji only. One frustrating trend is that new, modern buildings omit posting any address whatsoever on their facades.

**FINDING YOUR WAY AROUND**    If you're traveling by subway or JR train, the first thing you should do upon exiting your compartment is to look for **yellow signs** posted on every platform that tell you which exit to take for particular buildings, attractions, and chome. At Roppongi Station, for example, you'll find yellow sign-boards that tell you which exit to take for Roppongi Hills, which will at least get you pointed in the right direction once you emerge from the station. Stations also have maps of the areas either inside the station or at the exit; these are your best plan of attack when trying to find a particular address.

As you walk around Tokyo, you will also notice **maps** posted beside sidewalks giving a breakdown of the postal number system for the area. The first time I tried to use one, I stopped one Japanese, then another, and asked them to point out on the map where a particular address was. They both studied the map and pointed out the direction. Both turned out to be wrong. Not very encouraging, but if you learn how to read these maps, they're invaluable.

Another invaluable source of information is the numerous **police boxes,** called *koban,* located in every neighborhood throughout the city. Police officers have area maps and are very helpful (helping lost souls seems to occupy much of their time). You should also never hesitate to ask a Japanese the way, but be sure to ask more than one. You'll be amazed at the conflicting directions you'll receive. Apparently, Japanese would rather hazard a guess than impolitely shrug their shoulders and leave you standing there. The best thing to do is ask directions of several Japanese and then follow the majority opinion. You can also duck into a shop and ask someone where a nearby address is, although in my experience employees do not even know the address of their own store. They may, however, have a map of the area.

**MAPS**    Before setting out on your own, arm yourself with a few maps. Maps are so much a part of life in Tokyo that they're often included in shop or restaurant advertisements or brochures, on business cards, and even in private party invitations. Even though I've spent years in Tokyo, I rarely venture forth without a map. The Tourist Information Center issues a *Tourist Map of Tokyo,* which includes a subway map. Better, in my opinion, are the free maps given away by the Tokyo Metropolitan Government, which range from a city map to detailed maps of Tokyo's many districts (such as Shinjuku). Armed with these maps, you should be able to locate at least the general vicinity of every place mentioned in this chapter and the next. Hotels also sometimes distribute their own maps. In short, never pass up a free map.

For a detailed map, head for **Tower Books, Kinokuniya,** or another English-language bookstore (see "Shopping from A to Z" in chapter 5). My own personal favorite is Shobunsha's *Bilingual Map of Tokyo,* listing chome and chome subsections for major areas; the compact folded map can be carried in a purse or backpack. If you plan to write a guidebook, consider Shobunsha's *Map of Central Tokyo,* a compact folding map listing chome and chome subsections for major areas. Or, consider Shobunsha's *Tokyo Metropolitan Atlas,* a book covering all 23 of Tokyo's wards with specific postal maps, as well as greater Tokyo and its vicinity, along with expressway and Tokyo-area road maps, or Kodansha International's *Tokyo City Atlas,* which has both Japanese- and English-language place names, along with rail and subway maps, district maps, and an index to important buildings, museums, and other places of interest.

# TOKYO'S NEIGHBORHOODS IN BRIEF

Taken as a whole, Tokyo seems formidable and unconquerable. It's best, therefore, to think of it as nothing more than a series of villages scrunched together, much like the pieces of a jigsaw puzzle. Holding the pieces together, so to speak, is the **Yamanote Line,** a commuter train loop around central Tokyo that passes through such important stations as Yurakucho, Tokyo, Ueno, Ikebukuro, Shinjuku, Harajuku, Shibuya, and Shinagawa. Since 2001, several districts have witnessed massive redevelopment, including Shinagawa, both sides of Tokyo Station, and Roppongi.

**Hibiya** This is not only the business heart of Tokyo, but its spiritual heart as well. This is where the Tokugawa shogun built his magnificent castle, and was thus the center of old Edo. Today, Hibiya, in Chiyoda-ku Ward, is no less important as the home of the **Imperial Palace,** built on the ruins of Edo Castle and the residence of Japan's 125th emperor. Bordering the palace is the wonderful East Garden, open free to the public.

**Ginza** Ginza is the swankiest and most expensive **shopping area** in all Japan. When the country opened to foreign trade in the 1860s, following 2 centuries of self-imposed seclusion, it was here that Western imports and adopted Western architecture were first displayed. Today, Ginza is where you'll find a multitude of department stores, boutiques, exclusive restaurants, hotels, art galleries, and drinking establishments. On the edge of Ginza is **Kabukiza,** venue for Kabuki productions.

**Tsukiji** Located only two subway stops from Ginza, Tsukiji was born from reclaimed land during the Tokugawa shogunate; its name, in fact, means "reclaimed land." Today it's famous for the **Tsukiji Fish Market,** one of the largest wholesale fish markets in the world. Nearby is the Hama Rikyu Garden, considered by some to be the best garden in Tokyo.

**Akihabara** Tokyo's center for electronic and electrical appliances has more than 600 shops offering a look at the latest in gadgets and gizmos. In recent years, stores dealing in Japanese animation have also set up shop here. A stop on the Yamanote Line, this is a fascinating place for a stroll, even if you aren't interested in buying anything. About a 12-minute walk west is **Kanda,** with many stores specializing in new and used books.

**Asakusa** In the northeastern part of central Tokyo, Asakusa served as the pleasure quarters for old Edo. Today it's known throughout Japan as the site of the famous **Sensoji Temple,** one of Tokyo's top and oldest attractions. It also has a wealth of tiny shops selling traditional Japanese crafts. When Tokyoites talk about old downtown (*shitamachi*), they are referring to the traditional homes and tiny narrow streets of the Asakusa and Ueno areas.

**Ueno** Located just west of Asakusa, on the northern edge of the JR Yamanote Line loop, Ueno is also part of the city's old downtown. Ueno boasts **Ueno Park,** a huge green space comprising a zoo and several acclaimed museums, including the **Tokyo National Museum,** which houses the largest collection of Japanese art and antiquities in the world. Ueno Station serves as a stop for major train lines heading north and eastward, including some lines of the Shinkansen bullet train. Under the train tracks of the JR Yamanote Line loop is a thriving market for food, clothing, and accessories.

**Shinjuku** Originating as a post town in 1698 to serve the needs of feudal lords and their retainers traveling between Edo and the provinces, Shinjuku was hardly touched by the 1923

Great Kanto Earthquake, making it an attractive alternative for businesses wishing to relocate following the destruction. In 1971, Japan's first skyscraper was erected with the opening of the Keio Plaza Hotel in western Shinjuku, setting a dramatic precedent for things to come. Today more than a dozen skyscrapers, including several hotels, dot the Shinjuku skyline, and with the opening of the **Tokyo Metropolitan Government Office (TMG)** in 1991 (with a tourist office and a great observation floor), Shinjuku's transformation into the capital's upstart business district was complete. Eastern Shinjuku is known for its shopping, particularly the huge **Takashimaya Times Square** complex, and for its nightlife, especially in **Kabuki-cho,** a thriving amusement center, and in **Shinjuku 2-chome,** Tokyo's premier gay nightlife district. Separating eastern and western Shinjuku is **Shinjuku Station,** the nation's busiest commuter station and located on the western end of the Yamanote Line loop. An oasis in the middle of Shinjuku madness is Shinjuku Gyoen Park, a beautiful garden for strolling.

**Ikebukuro** Located north of Shinjuku on the Yamanote Line loop, Ikebukuro is the working person's Tokyo, less refined and a bit rougher around the edges. Ikebukuro is where you'll find **Seibu** and **Tobu,** two of the country's largest department stores, as well as the **Japan Traditional Craft Center** with its beautifully crafted traditional items. The **Sunshine City Building,** one of Tokyo's tallest skyscrapers, is home to a huge indoor shopping center.

**Harajuku** The mecca of Tokyo's younger generation, Harajuku swarms throughout the week with teenagers in search of fashion and fun. At its center is **Omotesando Dori,** a fashionable tree-lined avenue flanked by trendy shops, sidewalk cafes, and restaurants. Nearby is **Takeshita Dori,** a narrow pedestrian lane packed with young people looking for the latest in inexpensive clothing and cosmetics. Harajuku is also the home of one of Japan's major attractions, **Meiji Jingu Shrine,** built in 1920 to deify Emperor and Empress Meiji. Another drawing card is the **Oriental Bazaar,** a great shop specializing in products and souvenirs of Japan.

**Aoyama** While Harajuku is for teenyboppers, Aoyama is a yuppified playground and shopping mecca for Tokyo's trendsetters, chic and upscale, and boasting more designer fashion outlets than anywhere else in the city. Located on the eastern end of Omotesando Dori (and an easy walk from Harajuku), Aoyama boasts a number of fine shops and a great array of tempting restaurants.

**Shibuya** Located on the southwestern edge of the Yamanote Line loop, Shibuya serves as a vibrant nightlife and shopping area for the young. More subdued than Shinjuku, more down-to-earth than Harajuku, and less cosmopolitan than Roppongi, it's home to more than a dozen department stores specializing in everything from designer clothing to housewares and CDs. Don't miss the light change at Shibuya Crossing, reportedly Japan's busiest intersection, with its hordes of pedestrians, neon, and five video billboards that have earned it the nickname "Times Square of Tokyo" (and a spot also in the movie *Lost in Translation*).

**Ebisu** One station south of Shibuya on the JR Yamanote Line, Ebisu was a minor player in Tokyo's shopping and nightlife league until the 1995 debut of **Yebisu Garden Place,** a smart-looking complex of apartments, concert halls,

two museums, restaurants, a department store, and a first-class hotel, all connected to Ebisu Station via moving walkway. The vicinity east of Ebisu Station, once a sleepy residential and low-key shopping district, has recently blossomed into a small but thriving nightlife mecca popular with ex-pats who find Roppongi too crass or commercial.

**Roppongi** Tokyo's best-known nightlife district for young Japanese and foreigners, Roppongi has more bars and nightclubs than any other district outside Shinjuku, as well as a multitude of restaurants serving international cuisines. The newest kid on the block, however, is the eye-popping, 11-hectare (28-acre) **Roppongi Hills,** Tokyo's largest urban development housing 230 shops and restaurants, a first-class hotel, a garden, apartments, offices, a cinema complex, and Tokyo's highest art museum, on the 53rd floor of Mori Tower. Astonishingly, Roppongi Hills will be upstaged in 2007, when the massive Tokyo Midtown Project opens (along with a Ritz-Carlton hotel).

**Akasaka** With its several large hotels and small nightlife district, Akasaka caters mostly to businessmen but is otherwise of little interest to tourists. It does, however, boast some good restaurants; in recent years, so many Korean restaurants and establishments have set up shop here that it could be nicknamed "Little Korea."

**Shinagawa** Once an important post station on the old Tokaido Highway, Shinagawa remains an important crossroads due to **Shinagawa Station,** a stop on the Shinkansen bullet train route and on the southern end of the Yamanote Line loop. Home to several major hotels, it has also witnessed a major blossoming of office construction in recent years, making it a serious rival to Shinjuku's business district.

**Odaiba** This is Tokyo's newest district, quite literally—it was constructed from reclaimed land in Tokyo Bay. Connected to the mainland by the **Rainbow Bridge** (famous for its chameleon colors after nightfall), the Yurikamome Line monorail, the Rinkai Line, and a vehicular harbor tunnel, Odaiba is home to a few hotels, Japan's largest convention space, several shopping complexes (including the fancy Venus Fort and the interesting Tokyo Decks with its "Little Hong Kong" and "postwar Japan" themes), the **Museum of Maritime Science,** the **National Museum of Emerging Science and Innovation,** a hot-spring public bath that harkens back to the Edo Era, a monolithic Ferris wheel, and **Megaweb,** a huge multimedia car amusement and exhibition center sponsored by Toyota. For young Japanese, it's one of Tokyo's hottest date spots.

## 2 Getting Around

The first rule of getting around Tokyo: It will always take longer than you think. For short-term visitors, calculating travel times in Tokyo is a tricky business. Taking a taxi is expensive and involves the probability of getting stuck interminably in traffic, with the meter ticking away. Taking the subway is usually more efficient, even though it's more complicated and harder on your feet: Choosing which route to take isn't always clear, and transfers between lines are sometimes quite a hike in themselves. If I'm going from one end of Tokyo to the other by subway, I usually allow anywhere from 30 to 60 minutes, depending on the number of transfers and the walking distance to my final destination. If you don't have to change trains, you can travel from one end of Tokyo to the other in about 30 minutes or less. In any case, travel times to destinations within

each line are posted on platform pillars, along with diagrams showing which train compartments are best for making quick transfers between lines.

Your best bet for getting around Tokyo is to take the subway or Japan Railways (JR) commuter train such as the Yamanote Line to the station nearest your destination. From there you can either walk, using a map and asking directions along the way, or take a taxi.

## BY PUBLIC TRANSPORTATION

If you think you'll be using a combination of public transportation systems in 1 day—subway, JR train, and Toei bus (except double-decker buses)—consider purchasing a **Tokyo Free Kippu,** which, despite its name, costs ¥1,580 ($15) but does allow unlimited travel for 1 day. It's available at all JR stations, JR View Plazas, and most subway stations. Otherwise, tickets you purchase for the subway cannot be used for JR trains, and vice versa.

### BY SUBWAY & JR TRAIN

**BY SUBWAY**    To get around Tokyo on your own, it's imperative to learn how to ride its subways. Fortunately, the Tokyo Metro system (which uses a symbol "M" vaguely reminiscent of MacDonald's famous arches) is efficient, modern, clean, and easy to use, and all station names are written in English. Many cars also post the name of the next station in English on digital signs above their doors or even announce stops in English. Altogether, 12 subway lines crisscross underneath the city, and each line is color-coded. The Ginza Line, for example, is orange, which means all its coaches and signs are orange. If you're transferring to the Ginza Line from another line, just follow the orange signs and circles to the Ginza Line platform. Additionally, each station along the way is assigned a number, so you always know how many stops until you reach your destination. Before boarding, however, make sure the train is going in the right direction; otherwise you'll end up at the opposite end of the city. Tokyo's newest line, the Oedo Line, makes a zigzag loop around the city and is useful for traveling between Roppongi and Shinjuku; be aware, however, that it's buried deep underground and that platforms take a while to reach, despite escalators. And remember, once you reach your destination, look for the yellow signs on station platforms designating which exit to take for major buildings, museums, and addresses. If you're confused about which exit to take, ask someone at the window near the ticket gate. Taking the right exit can make a world of difference, especially in Shinjuku, where there are more than 60 station exits.

**Tickets**    Vending machines at all subway stations sell tickets; fares begin at ¥160 ($1.50) for the shortest distance and increase according to how far you're traveling. Children under 6 ride free; children 6 to 11 pay half fare. Vending machines give change, and most accept ¥1,000, ¥2,000, ¥5,000, and ¥10,000 notes. **To purchase your ticket,** insert money into the vending machine until the fare buttons light up, then push the amount for the ticket you want. Your ticket and change will drop onto a little platform at the bottom of the machine.

**Fares** are posted on a large subway map above the vending machines, but they're generally in Japanese only; major stations also post a smaller map listing fares in English, but you may have to search for it. An alternative is to look at the subway map contained in the "Tourist Map of Tokyo" issued by TIC—it lists stations in both Japanese and English. When you know what the Japanese characters look like, you may be able to locate your station and the corresponding fare. If you still don't know

## *Value* **Saving on Transportation**

If you think you'll be using Tokyo's subway system a lot or simply wish to avoid the hassle of figuring out the fare for individual rides, I strongly urge you to invest in an **Passnet Card,** a prepaid card sold at station vending machines for ¥1,000 ($9.50), ¥3,000 ($29), and ¥5,000 ($48) worth of rides. Insert the card into the automatic ticket gates when you enter and exit the subway wickets; the charge for the ride will be deducted automatically from your card. You can also use your Passnet Card in the vending machine to purchase regular single tickets for someone traveling with you. Since rides on the subway can really add up, you'll find the ¥1,000 Metro Card useful even if you're staying in Tokyo just 3 or 4 days. Alternatively, a **One-day Economy Pass (Kyotsu Ichinichi Josha Ken)** for unlimited rides on all subway lines costs ¥1,000 ($9.50). Although other types of tickets and passes are available, I find them too complicated for short-time visitors.

If you'll be using the JR lines frequently, there's a similar prepaid card called Suica iO Card for ¥2,000 ($19), which includes a ¥500 ($4.75) deposit (the deposit is returned when you turn in the card, but you'll be charged a ¥210/$2 service fee for a refund of any unused portion remaining on the card). It allows you to travel without having to purchase a separate JR ticket each time and is used by placing it on a scanner at the automatic fare gate. Otherwise, there's also a **JR One-Day Tokunai Free Kippu,** which allows unlimited travel on JR trains for 1 day for ¥730 ($6.95).

the fare, just buy a basic-fare ticket for ¥160 ($1.50), When you exit at your destination, look for the **fare adjustment machine;** insert your ticket to find out how much more you owe, or look for a subway employee at the ticket window to tell you how much extra you owe.

In any case, be sure to hang onto your ticket, since you must give it up at the end of your journey.

**Hours**   Most subways run from about 5am to midnight, although the times of the first and last trains depend on the line, the station, and whether it's a weekday or weekend. Schedules are posted in the stations, and throughout most of the day, trains run every 3 to 5 minutes.

Avoid taking the subway during the weekday morning **rush hour,** from 8 to 9am—the stories you've heard about commuters packed into trains like sardines are all true. There are even "platform pushers," men who push people into compartments so that the doors can close. If you want to witness Tokyo at its craziest, go to Shinjuku Station at 8:30am—but go by taxi unless you want to experience the crowding firsthand. Most lines provide women-only compartments weekdays until 9:30am.

**BY TRAIN**   In addition to subway lines, electric commuter trains operated by the **East Japan Railways Company (JR)** run aboveground throughout greater Tokyo. These are also color-coded, with fares beginning at ¥130 ($1.25). Buy your ticket from vending machines just as you would for the subway.

The **Yamanote Line** (green-colored coaches) is the best-known and most convenient JR line. It makes an oblong loop around the city, stopping at 29 stations along

the way. In fact, you may want to take the Yamanote Line and stay on it for a roundup view of Tokyo; the entire trip takes about an hour, passing stations like Shinjuku, Tokyo, Akihabara, Ueno, Harajuku, and Shibuya on the way.

Another convenient JR line is the orange-colored **Chuo Line;** it cuts across Tokyo between Shinjuku and Tokyo stations, with both express (which doesn't make as many stops) and local trains available. The yellow-colored **Sobu Line** runs between Shinjuku and Akihabara and beyond to Chiba. Other JR lines serve outlying districts for the metropolis's commuting public. Since the Yamanote, Chuo, and Sobu lines are rarely identified by their specific names at major stations, look for signs that say JR LINES.

For more information on JR lines and tickets, stop by one of JR's **Information Centers,** including those at Tokyo Station (central and south passages, open daily 9am–6pm), Ueno Station (Park exit, daily 9:30am–6pm), and Shinjuku Station (south and east exits, open daily 10am–7pm). Or, call the JR's English–JR East Infoline at ⓒ **050/2016-1603** daily from 10am to 6pm or check its website at www.jreast.co.jp/e.

**A NOTE ON TRANSFERS**    You can transfer between most subway lines without buying another ticket, and you can transfer between JR train lines on one ticket. However, your ticket or prepaid card does not allow a transfer between Tokyo's two subway companies (Metro and Toei), JR train lines, and private train lines connecting Tokyo with outlying destinations such as Nikko. You usually don't have to worry about this, though, because if you exit through a wicket that keeps your ticket, you'll know you have to buy another one. If the wicket sounds a buzzer, you know you have to pay more at the fare adjustment machine.

The general rule is that if your final destination and fare are posted above the ticket vending machines, you can travel all the way to your destination with only one ticket. But don't worry about this too much—the ticket collector will set you straight if you've miscalculated. *Note:* If you pay too much for your ticket, the portion of the fare that's left unused is not refundable—so, again, the easiest thing to do if in doubt is to buy the cheapest fare.

## BY BUS

Buses are difficult to use in Tokyo because destinations are sometimes written in Japanese only and most bus drivers don't speak English. However, they are sometimes convenient for short distances. If you're feeling adventurous, board the bus at the front and drop the exact fare into the box by the driver. If you don't have the exact fare (usually ¥200/$1.90), slots accept coins or bills; your change will come out below, minus the fare. A signboard at the front of the bus displays the next stop, sometimes in English. When you wish to get off, press one of the buttons on the railing near the door or the seats. You can pick up an excellent Toei bus map showing all major routes at one of the Tokyo Tourist Information Centers operated by the Tokyo Metropolitan Government (see "Visitor Information," earlier in this chapter). Or, check the Toei website at www.kotsu.metro.tokyo.jp.

On Odaiba, there's a rotating free BayShuttle bus operating to area sights from 11am to 8pm daily.

## BY TAXI

Taxis are shamefully expensive in Tokyo. **Fares** start at ¥660 ($6.25) for the first 2km (1¼ miles) and increase ¥80 (75¢) for each additional 274m (904 ft.) or 40 seconds of waiting time. There are also smaller, more compact taxis that start out slightly less at ¥640 ($6.10) for the first 2km (1¼ miles) but then increase ¥80 (75¢) for each

additional 290m (957 ft.). Fares are posted on the back of the front passenger seat. If you're like me, however, you probably won't shop around—you'll just gratefully jump into the first taxi that stops. *Note:* From 11pm to 5am, an extra 30% is added to your fare. Perhaps as an admission of how expensive taxis are, fares can even be paid with a credit card.

With the exception of some major thoroughfares in the downtown area, you can **hail a taxi** from the street or go to a taxi stand or a major hotel. A red light will show above the dashboard if a taxi is free to pick up a passenger; a green light indicates the taxi is occupied. Be sure to stand clear of the back door—it swings open automatically. Likewise, it shuts automatically once you're in. Taxi drivers get upset if you try to manhandle it yourself.

Unless you're going to a well-known landmark or hotel, it's best to **have your destination written out in Japanese,** since most taxi drivers don't speak English. But even that may not help. Tokyo is so complicated that even taxi drivers may not know a certain area, although they do have detailed maps and some even have GPS navigation systems. If a driver doesn't understand where you're going, he may refuse to take you. Otherwise, don't be surprised if he jumps out of the cab to ask for directions at a nearby shop—with the meter ticking.

There are so many taxis cruising Tokyo that one is always around and available—except when you need it most. That is, when it's raining and sometimes just after 1am on weekends, after all subways and trains have stopped. To call a major taxi company for a pickup, try **Nihon Kotsu** (② 03/5755-2151) or **Kokusai** (② 03/3505-6001). Note, however, that only Japanese is spoken, and you'll be required to pay extra (usually not more than ¥500/$4.75) for the pickup. I have rarely telephoned for a taxi—just like in the movies, a taxi usually cruises by just when you raise your hand.

## *FAST FACTS:* Tokyo

If you can't find answers to your questions here, check "Fast Facts: Japan," in chapter 2. If you still can't find an answer, call the **Tourist Information Center** (② 03/3201-3331) daily from 9am to 5pm; the city-run **Tokyo Tourist Information Center** (② 03/5321-3077) daily from 9:30am to 6:30pm; or the **TCVB Tourist Information Center** (② 03/3287-7024) Monday to Friday 10am to 5pm and weekends and holidays 10am to 4pm. If you're staying in a first-class hotel, another valuable resource is the concierge or guest-relations desk; the staff there can tell you how to reach your destination, can answer general questions, and can even make restaurant reservations.

*American Express* There is no public American Express office in Japan.

*Area Code* If you're calling a Tokyo number from outside Tokyo but within Japan, the area code for Tokyo is **03**. For details on calling Tokyo from outside Japan, see "Telephones" in "Fast Facts: Japan" in chapter 2.

*Babysitters* Most major hotels can arrange babysitting services, but expect to pay about ¥5,000 ($48) for 2 hours. Some hotels also have day-care centers for young children. See individual listings or "Family-Friendly Hotels," later in this chapter.

*Business Hours* See "Fast Facts: Japan" in chapter 2.

*Currency Exchange* You can exchange money in major banks throughout Tokyo, often indicated by an English-language sign near the front door. Banks give a slightly better exchange rate for traveler's checks than for cash; *you'll need your passport to exchange traveler's checks.* And be prepared for long waits—apparently the procedure for turning foreign currency into yen is a long one (and they aren't open for currency exchange until around 10:30 or 11am). If you need to exchange money outside banking hours, your best bet is your hotel or a large department store, though exchange rates won't be as favorable (you'll need your passport). At Narita Airport, exchange counters are open from 6am to 11pm and there are also ATMs for major credit and bank cards. It's wise to exchange enough money at the airport to last a few days, since the exchange rate is the same as in town and the process is speedier.

Otherwise, since most bank ATMs in Japan will not accept foreign bank or credit cards, the most convenient ATMs that do are located at post offices, available for Visa, MasterCard, and PLUS and Cirrus cards during regular post office hours. The ATM at the Central Post Office near Tokyo Station (see "Post Offices," below) is open Monday to Friday 7am to 11:55pm, Saturday 5am to 11:55pm, and Sunday and holidays from 5am to 8pm; note, however, that it did not accept my Visa debit card. You can also get cash advances by using your Visa credit card at any Sumitomo Bank and by using your MasterCard at Union Credit (UC) banks and some Sumitomo banks, Citibanks, Mitsubishi-Tokyo banks, and affiliated banks, with branches all over town; you'll have to show your passport for cash advances.

*Dentists & Doctors* Many first-class hotels offer medical facilities or an in-house doctor. Otherwise, your embassy can refer you to English-speaking doctors, specialists, and dentists. In addition, the **AMDA International Medical Information Center** (© 03/5285-8088), available Monday through Friday 9am to 8pm, can provide information on English-speaking staff. The following clinics have some English-speaking staff and are popular with foreigners living in Tokyo: **The International Clinic,** 1–5–9 Azabudai, Minato-ku, within walking distance of Roppongi or Azabu Juban stations (© 03/3582-2646; open Mon–Fri 9am–noon and 2–5pm, Sat 9am–noon; walk-ins only); and **Tokyo Medical & Surgical Clinic,** 32 Mori Building, 3–4–30 Shiba-koen, Minato-ku, near Kamiyacho, Onarimon, or Shiba-koen stations and across from Tokyo Tower (© 03/3436-3028; open Mon–Fri 8:30am–5:30pm, Sat 8:30am–noon; appointments only). At the Tokyo Medical & Surgical Clinic, above, is also the **Tokyo Clinic Dental Office** (© 03/3431-4225; open Mon–Thurs 9am–6pm and Sat 9am–5pm). Just a 3-minute walk away is the **United Dental Office,** 2–3–8 Azabudai, Minato-ku (© 03/5570-4334; uniteddentaloffice.com; Mon–Fri 9am–6pm, Sat 9am–5pm). You can also make appointments to visit doctors at the hospitals listed below.

*Drugstores* There is no 24-hour drugstore in Tokyo, but ubiquitous 24-hour convenience stores such as 7-Eleven, Lawson, and FamilyMart carry things like aspirin. If you're looking for specific pharmaceuticals, a good bet is the **American Pharmacy,** in the basement of the Marunouchi Building, 2–4–1 Marunouchi,

Chiyoda-ku (📞 **03/5220-7716**; open Mon–Fri 9am–9pm, Sat 10am–9pm, and Sun and holidays 10am–8pm), which has many of the same over-the-counter drugs you can find at home (many of them imported from the United States) and can fill American prescriptions—but note that you *must first visit a doctor in Japan* before foreign prescriptions can be filled, so it's best to bring an ample supply of any prescription medication with you.

*Embassies & Consulates* Visa or passport sections of most embassies are open only at certain times during the day, so it's best to call in advance.

- **U.S. Embassy:** 1–10–5 Akasaka, Minato-ku, near Toranomon subway station (📞 **03/3224-5000**; http://japan.usembassy.gov; consular section open Mon–Fri 8:30am–12:30pm and 2–4pm; telephone inquiries accepted Mon–Fri 8:30am–1pm and 2–5:30pm).
- **Canadian Embassy:** 7–3–38 Akasaka, Minato-ku, near Aoyama-Itchome Station (📞 **03/5412-6200**; www.dfait-maeci.gc.ca/asia/country/japan-en.asp; consular section open Mon–Fri 9:30am–noon; embassy open Mon–Fri 9am–5:30pm).
- **British Embassy:** 1 Ichibancho, Chiyoda-ku, near Hanzomon Station (📞 **03/3265-5511**; www.uknow.or.jp; consular section open Mon–Fri 9–11:30am and 2–4pm).
- **Embassy of Ireland:** 5th floor, 2–10–7 Kojimachi, Chiyoda-ku, near Hanzomon Station, exit 4 (📞 **03/3263-0695**; www.embassy-avenue.jp/ireland; Mon–Fri 10am–12:30pm and 2–4pm; telephone inquiries accepted Mon–Fri 9:30am–5:30pm).
- **Australian Embassy:** 2–1–14 Mita, Minato-ku (📞 **03/5232-4111**; www.australia.or.jp; open Mon–Fri 9am–12:30pm and 1:30–5:25pm). A 15-minute walk from Shiba-koen Station; or take a taxi from Kamyacho, Mita, Hamamatsucho, or Tamachi.
- **New Zealand Embassy:** 20–40 Kamiyama-cho, Shibuya-ku, a 15-minute walk from Shibuya Station (📞 **03/3467-2271**; www.nzembassy.com/japan; open Mon–Fri 9am–5:30pm; call for consular hours).

*Emergencies* The national emergency numbers are 📞 **110** for police and 📞 **119** for ambulance and fire. You do not have to insert a coin or telephone card for an emergency number from a public phone. However, if using a green public telephone, it's necessary to push a red button before dialing. If calling from a gray public telephone or one that accepts only prepaid cards, simply lift the receiver and dial. Be sure to speak slowly and precisely.

*Hospitals* In addition to going to these hospitals for an emergency, you can also make appointments at their clinics to see a doctor: **The International Catholic Hospital (Seibo Byoin),** 2–5–1 Naka-Ochiai, Shinjuku-ku, near Meijiro Station on the Yamanote Line (📞 **03/3951-1111**; clinic hours Mon–Sat 8–11am; closed third Sat of each month; walk-ins accepted); **St. Luke's International Hospital (Seiroka Byoin),** 9–1 Akashi-cho, Chuo-ku, near Tsukiji Station on the Hibiya Line (📞 **03/3541-5151**; Mon–Fri 8:30–11am; appointments necessary for some treatments); and the **Japan Red Cross Medical Center (Nihon Sekijujisha Iryo Center),** 4–1–22 Hiroo, Shibuya-ku (📞 **03/3400-1311**; Mon–Fri 8:30–11am; walk-ins only), whose closest subway stations are Roppongi, Hiroo, and Shibuya—from there, you should take a taxi.

*Internet Access* If your hotel doesn't provide Internet access, the best place to set up your temporary office is at the sophisticated **Gran Cyber Café Bagus,** on the 12th floor of the Roi Building, 5–5–1 Roppongi (© 03/5786-2280; station: Roppongi). Open 24 hours, it offers individual cubicles with prices that depend on the chair you select: ¥500 ($4.75) for the first hour for a straight-backed chair, ¥530 ($5.05) for a reclining chair, and ¥600 ($5.70) for a massage chair. You have to wonder how many people actually work. Ladies take note: There's a section just for you.

A few places offer free Internet access, though waits can be long: **Marunouchi Café,** Shin Tokyo Building, 3–3–1 Marunouchi (© 03/3212-5025; station: Marunouchi, Tokyo), with six computers available Monday to Friday 8am to 9pm and Saturday and Sunday 11am to 8pm; and the **Apple Store,** Ginza, 3–5–12 Ginza (© 03/5159-8200; station: Ginza), with 18 Macs on the fourth floor offering free Internet access daily 10am to 9pm.

Although expensive, **Kinko's** has more than 30 locations throughout Tokyo, including one at Tokyo Station at the Yaesu north exit (© 03/3213-1811). Most Kinko's are open 24 hours and charge ¥210 ($2) per 10 minutes of computer time.

*Lost Property* If you've forgotten something on a subway, in a taxi, or on a park bench, don't assume it's gone forever—if you're willing to trace it, you'll probably get it back. If you can remember where you last saw it, the first thing to do is telephone the establishment or return to where you left it; there's a good chance it will still be sitting there. If you've lost something on the street, go to the nearest police box *(koban);* items found in the neighborhood will stay there for 3 days or longer.

If you've lost something in a taxi, have someone who speaks Japanese contact the **Tokyo Taxi Center,** 7–3–3 Minamisuma, Koto-ku (© 03/3648-0300). For JR trains, have someone who speaks Japanese call or go to the **Lost and Found Sections** at JR Tokyo Station (© 03/3231-1880) or at JR Ueno Station (© 03/3841-8069); or you can call the **JR East Infoline** (© 03/2016-1603). If you've lost something on a Tokyo Metropolitan subway or bus, immediately contact the nearest station where you think you lost it. After 3 days, contact the lost-and-found section of the **Tokyo Metropolitan Government,** 2–40–8 Hongo, Bunkyo-ku (© 03/3812-2011).

Eventually, every unclaimed item in Tokyo ends up at the Central Lost and Found Office of the **Metropolitan Police Board,** 1–9–11 Koraku, Bunkyo-ku (© 03/3814-4151; Mon–Fri 8:30am–5:15pm; station: Iidabashi).

*Luggage Storage & Lockers* Delivery service counters at Narita International Airport will send luggage to your hotel the next day (or from your hotel to the airport) for about ¥1,700 ($16) for bags up to 20 kilograms (44 lb.). Coin-operated lockers are located at all major JR stations, such as Tokyo, Shinjuku, and Ueno, as well as at most subway stations. Lockers cost ¥300 to ¥800 ($2.85–$7.60), depending on the size.

*Police* The national emergency telephone number is © 110. The Metropolitan Police Department also maintains a telephone counseling service for foreigners at © 03/3503-8484 Monday through Friday from 8:30am to 5pm.

*Post Offices* If your hotel cannot mail letters for you, ask the concierge where the nearest post office is. The **Central Post Office,** just southwest of Tokyo Station at 2–7–2 Marunouchi, Chiyoda-ku (© **03/3284-9527**), has longer business hours than most: Monday through Friday 9am to 9pm and Saturday, Sunday, and holidays 9am to 7pm. An after-hours counter remains open throughout the night for mail and packages, making this one of two 24-hour service facilities in town; the other is the Shibuya Central Post Office, 1–12–13 Shibuya (© **03/5469-9907**; station: Shibuya).

For English-language postal information, call © **03/3560-1139** Monday through Friday between 9:30am and 4:30pm or check the website www.post.japanpost.jp. Also see "Mail," under "Fast Facts: Japan," in chapter 2.

*Restrooms* If you need a restroom in Tokyo, your best bets are train and subway stations, big hotels, department stores, and fast-food chains like McDonald's. For an explanation of using Japanese toilets, see "Fast Facts: Japan" in chapter 2.

*Safety* Tokyo is one of the safest cities in the world. However, crime is on the increase, and there are precautions you should always take when traveling: Stay alert and be aware of your immediate surroundings. Be especially careful with cameras, purses, and wallets, particularly in crowded subways, department stores, or tourist attractions (such as the retail district around Tsukiji Fish Market), especially as pickpocketing has been on the rise. Some Japanese also caution women against walking through parks alone at night.

*Taxes* In addition to the national 5% consumption tax, which is already included in the price of goods and services, Tokyo levies a hotel tax on rooms costing ¥10,000 ($83) and up per person per night: ¥100 (95¢) is levied per person per night for rates between ¥10,000 ($95) and ¥14,999 ($142); rates of ¥15,000 and up are taxed at ¥200 ($1.90). See "Fast Facts: Japan" in chapter 2.

*Telephone* For information on how to make calls, see "Fast Facts: Japan" in chapter 2. For directory assistance in Tokyo, dial © **104.**

For information on renting a mobile phone in Japan, see "The 21st-Century Traveler" in chapter 2 for information.

## 3 Where to Stay

Tokyo has no old, grand hotels in the tradition of Hong Kong's Peninsula or Bangkok's Oriental; it has hardly any old hotels, period. But what the city's hotels may lack in quaintness or old grandeur is more than made up for by excellent service—for which Japanese are legendary—as well as cleanliness and efficiency. Be prepared, however, for small rooms. Space is at a premium in Tokyo, so with the exception of some of the upper-range hotels, rooms seem to come in only three sizes: minuscule, small, and barely adequate.

Unfortunately, Tokyo also doesn't have many first-class ryokan, or Japanese-style inns. I suggest, therefore, that you wait for your travels around the country to experience a first-rate ryokan. Otherwise, there are moderate and inexpensive Japanese-style inns in Tokyo. In fact, if you're traveling on a tight budget, a simple Japanese-style inn is often the cheapest way to go, though don't expect much in the way of service or

My, what an inefficient way to fish.

Ring toss, good. Horseshoes, bad.

Faster! Faster! Faster!

We take care of the fiddly bits, from providing over 43,000 customer reviews of hotels, to helping you find our best fares, to giving you 24/7 customer service. So you can focus on the only thing that matters. Goofing off.

travelocity®
You'll never roam alone.℠

# Akasaka

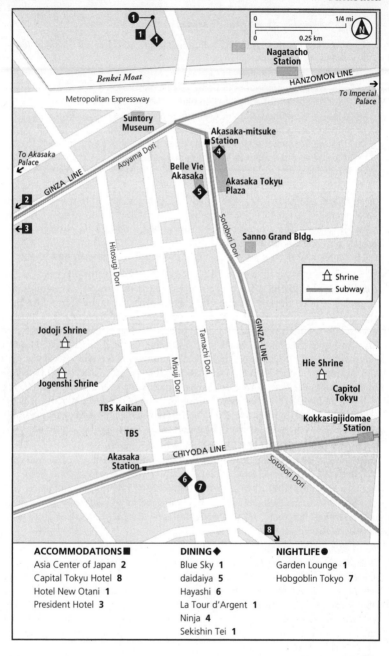

0       1/4 mi
0       0.25 km

Nagatacho Station

HANZOMON LINE

To Imperial Palace

Benkei Moat

Metropolitan Expressway

To Akasaka Palace

GINZA LINE

Suntory Museum

Aoyama Dori

Akasaka-mitsuke Station

Belle Vie Akasaka

Akasaka Tokyu Plaza

Sotobori Dori

Sanno Grand Bldg.

Hitosugi Dori

Jodoji Shrine

Jogenshi Shrine

Tamachi Dori

Misuji Dori

GINZA LINE

Hie Shrine

Capitol Tokyu

Kokkasigijidomae Station

⌂ Shrine
▬ Subway

TBS Kaikan

TBS

Akasaka Station

CHIYODA LINE

Sotobori Dori

Capitol Tokyu

**ACCOMMODATIONS** ■
Asia Center of Japan **2**
Capital Tokyu Hotel **8**
Hotel New Otani **1**
President Hotel **3**

**DINING** ◆
Blue Sky **1**
daidaiya **5**
Hayashi **6**
La Tour d'Argent **1**
Ninja **4**
Sekishin Tei **1**

**NIGHTLIFE** ●
Garden Lounge **1**
Hobgoblin Tokyo **7**

---

**⟨Tips⟩  Mapping Out Tokyo's Hotels**

Once you've chosen a hotel or inn that appeals to you, you can locate it using the following neighborhood maps:

- To locate accommodations in **Akasaka,** p. 119.
- To locate accommodations in **Ueno,** p. 125.
- To locate accommodations in **Shinjuku,** p. 128.
- To locate accommodations in **Asakusa,** p. 133.
- To locate accommodations in **Hibiya** and **Ginza,** p. 144.
- To locate accommodations in **Harajuku,** p. 157.
- To locate accommodations in **Roppongi,** p. 163.

---

amenities. In addition, most of the upper-bracket hotels offer at least a few Japanese-style rooms, with tatami mats, a Japanese bathtub (deeper and narrower than the Western version), and a futon. Although these rooms tend to be expensive, they're usually large enough for four people.

For more on available types of accommodations, see "Tips on Accommodations" in chapter 2.

**PRICE CATEGORIES**    The recommended hotels that follow are arranged first according to price, then by location. After all, since attractions are spread throughout the city, and Tokyo's public transportation service is fast and efficient (I've provided nearest subway or train stations for each listing)—and since this is one of the most expensive hotel cities in the world—the overriding factor in selecting accommodations will likely be cost. I've divided Tokyo's hotels into price categories based upon two people per night, including tax but excluding service charge: **Very Expensive** hotels charge ¥45,000 ($428) and above, **Expensive** hotels charge ¥30,000 to ¥44,000 ($285–$418), **Moderate** hotels offer rooms from ¥15,000 to ¥29,000 ($143–$275), and **Inexpensive** accommodations offer rooms for less than ¥15,000 ($143). Unless otherwise indicated, each unit comes with a private bathroom.

**TAXES & SERVICE CHARGES**    All hotels rates below include a 5% government **tax.** However, an additional local hotel tax will be added to bills that cost more than ¥10,000 ($95) per person per night: ¥100 (95¢) is levied per person per night for rates between ¥10,000 and ¥14,999 ($95–$142); rates of ¥15,000 ($143) and up are taxed at ¥200 ($1.90). Furthermore, upper-class hotels and most medium-range hotels will add a **service charge** of 10% to 15%. *Unless otherwise stated, the prices given in this chapter do not include the local tax or service.*

**RESERVATIONS**    Although Tokyo doesn't suffer from a lack of hotel rooms during peak holidays (when most Japanese head for the hills and beaches), rooms may be in short supply at other times because of conventions and other events. If possible, avoid coming to Tokyo in mid-February unless you book well in advance—that's when university entrance exams bring aspiring high-school students and their parents flocking to the capital for a shot at one of the most prestigious universities in the country. And in summer, when most foreign tourists visit Japan, the cheaper accommodations are likely to fill up first.

It's always best, therefore, to make your hotel reservations in advance, especially if you're arriving in Japan after a long transoceanic flight and don't want the hassle of

searching for a hotel room. See "Planning your Trip Online" in chapter 2 for tips on securing rooms on the Internet. If you arrive in Tokyo without reservations, stop by the **Tourist Information Center** (**TIC;** see "Visitor Information," earlier in this chapter), where its Welcome Inn Reservation Center will book an inexpensive room free of charge.

## VERY EXPENSIVE
### NEAR TOKYO STATION

**Four Seasons Hotel Tokyo at Marunouchi** 🌟🌟🌟   If it's your dream to stay in what may be Japan's most expensive hotel, this Four Seasons is for you, and with only 57 rooms, it offers the ultimate in service, privacy, and exclusivity. With a great location beside Tokyo Station (convenient to both the Shinkansen bullet train and Narita Airport) and within walking distance of the Ginza, it's buffered from the outside world with triple-glazed glass and a soothing, ultra-contemporary design that employs natural woods and color schemes of ecru and charcoal or off-white and black. Guests are escorted to rooms by guest-relations officers, and with good reason, as rooms are so high-tech it's almost impossible to figure out even such mundane tasks as double-locking the doors or engaging the bathtub stopper. At 44 sq. m (474 sq. ft.) and larger, the attractive rooms are among the largest in Tokyo, with such standouts as wall-mounted 42-inch plasma-screen TVs, leather-covered desks, bathrooms with separate tub and shower areas, and floor-to-ceiling windows. Unfortunately, the hotel's location on the lower levels of an office high-rise affords views only of Tokyo Station and its Shinkansen bullet trains or surrounding buildings, and at these prices, you have to wonder why there's no mini-TV in the bathroom. Still, this is a great place to stay— if you can get someone else to pay for it.

Pacific Century Place, 1–11–1 Marunouchi, Chiyoda-ku, Tokyo 100-6277. © 800/332-3442 in the U.S., or 03/5222-7222. Fax 03/5222-1255. www.fourseasons.com/marunouchi. 57 units. ¥57,750 – ¥68,250 ($549–$648) single; ¥63,000 –¥73,500 ($599–$698) double or twin; from ¥99,750 ($948) suite. Children under 18 stay free in parent's room. AE, DC, MC, V. Station: Tokyo (2 min.). **Amenities:** Restaurant (international); bar; lounge; 24-hr. exercise room (free); public bath with imported hot-springs mineral water and steam room (free); spa; concierge; 24-hr. small business center; 24-hr. room service; in-room massage; babysitting; same-day laundry/dry-cleaning service; nonsmoking rooms; complimentary shoeshine; free rental bikes. *In room:* A/C, cable TV w/on-demand pay movies and CD/DVD players, fax/printer/scanner/copier, high-speed dataport, minibar, hot-water pot w/tea and coffee, hair dryer, safe, bathroom scale, Washlet toilet.

### SHINJUKU

**Park Hyatt Tokyo** 🌟🌟🌟   Located in western Shinjuku on the 39th to 52nd floors of Kenzo Tange's granite-and-glass Shinjuku Park Tower, the Park Hyatt is among the most gorgeous and sophisticated hotels in Japan, a perfect reflection of high-tech, avant-garde Tokyo in the 21st century. If you can afford it, stay here. Check-in, on the 41st floor, is comfortably accomplished at one of three sit-down desks. Though it doesn't attract as much off-the-street foot traffic as Shinjuku's other hotels, the Park

---

*Tips*  **A Note on Prices**

The prices quoted in this book were figured at ¥105 = US$1. However, because of fluctuations in the exchange rate of the yen, the U.S. dollar equivalents given will probably vary during the lifetime of this edition. Be sure to check current exchange rates when planning your trip. In addition, the rates given below may increase, so be sure to ask the current rate when making your reservation.

Hyatt's debut in *Lost in Translation* assures a steady stream of fans to its lounges and restaurants. Book early, therefore, for the 52nd-floor New York Grill, one of Tokyo's best restaurants and offering a spectacular setting (p. 154). All rooms average at least 45 sq. m (484 sq. ft.; the largest in Tokyo) and have original artwork, stunning and expansive views (including Mount Fuji on clear days), bathrooms to die for with a deep tub (plus separate shower) and a 15-inch plasma-screen TV, walk-in closets, remote-control curtains, and even Japanese/English dictionaries. Despite the competition posed by Roppongi Hill's Grand Hyatt, this hotel isn't worried, as it considers itself in a higher class of its own.

3–7–1–2 Nishi-Shinjuku, Shinjuku-ku, Tokyo 163-1055. © 800/233-1234 in the U.S. and Canada, or 03/5322-1234. Fax 03/5322-1288. www.parkhyatttokyo.com. 178 units. ¥55,650–¥68,250 ($529–$648) single or double; from ¥126,000 ($1,197) suite. AE, DC, MC, V. Station: Shinjuku (a 13-min. walk or 5-min. free shuttle ride), Hatsudai on the Keio Line (7 min.), or Tochomae (8 min.). **Amenities:** 3 restaurants (French, contemporary Japanese, American); 2 bars; 1 lounge; health club w/fitness room and dramatic 20m (66-ft.) indoor swimming pool with great views (free for hotel guests); spa (fee: ¥4,000/$33); concierge; business center; salon; 24-hr. room service; in-room massage; babysitting; same-day laundry/dry-cleaning service; nonsmoking rooms; CD and book libraries; free shuttle service to Shinjuku Station 1–3 times an hour; complimentary shoeshine. *In room:* A/C, wide-screen plasma TV w/cable and pay movies, CD/DVD player (with free rentals), fax/printer, complimentary high-speed dataport, minibar, hot-water pot w/tea and coffee, hair dryer, safe, bathroom scale, Washlet toilet.

## EBISU

**Westin Tokyo** 🎔🎔 *(Value)*    A black marble floor, neoclassical columns and statuary, huge floral bouquets, and palm trees set this smart-looking hotel apart from other Tokyo hotels—in Hong Kong, it would fit right in. Opened in 1994 and set in the attractive Yebisu Garden Place (Tokyo's first planned community), it's still a hike from Ebisu Station, even with the aid of the elevated moving walkways. It's also far from Tokyo's business center. But the largely Japanese clientele (with North Americans accounting for 25% of hotel guests) favors it for its European ambience, relaxed atmosphere, Westin name, and Yebisu Garden Place with its shops and restaurants. The spacious, high-ceilinged rooms blend 19th-century Biedermeier styles with contemporary furnishings and boast Westin's trademark "Heavenly Beds" that are either king-size (in double rooms) or two double beds (in twins), oversize desks, separate lighted vanities, and large bathrooms with separate shower and tub areas. Guest Office rooms provide such additional features as laser printers, fax machines, and office supplies. Rooms on higher floors cost more, with the best views of Tokyo Tower, though on clear days those facing west are treated to views of Mount Fuji.

1–4–1 Mita, Meguro-ku, Tokyo 153-8580. © 800/WESTIN-1 in the U.S. and Canada, or 03/5423-7000. Fax 03/5423-7600. www.westin-tokyo.co.jp. 438 units. ¥53,200–¥56,200 ($505–$539) single; ¥58,400–¥62,400 ($555–$593) double or twin; from ¥120,400 ($1,144) suite. Guest Office or Executive Club ¥64,200–¥68,200 ($610–$648) single; ¥70,400–¥74,400 ($669–$707) double or twin. AE, DC, MC, V. Station: Ebisu (7 min. via Yebisu Sky Walk). **Amenities:** 6 restaurants; 3 bars and lounges; access to nearby health club w/heated indoor pool and gym (fee: ¥4,000/$38; ¥2,000/$19 for Starwood Preferred Guest members); concierge; business center; 24-hr. room service; in-room massage; babysitting; same-day laundry/dry-cleaning service; nonsmoking rooms; executive-level rooms. *In room:* A/C, cable TV w/on-demand pay movies, high-speed dataport, minibar, hot-water pot w/tea, hair dryer, iron, bathroom scale, Washlet toilet.

## ROPPONGI

**Grand Hyatt Tokyo** 🎔🎔🎔    Opened in 2003 and counting on the surrounding Roppongi Hills development with its 200-some shops and restaurants to act as a major draw, this ambitious hotel wows with a wide range of recreational and dining facilities of its own, as well as technically advanced rooms older hotels can only dream about. In

contrast to sister Park Hyatt's subdued, sophisticated atmosphere that attracts bigwigs hoping to escape the limelight, the Grand Hyatt strives for a livelier clientele who relish being in the center of things. Still, key cards inserted into elevators block public access to guest floors, and those seeking pampering can opt for the Grand Club floor. Rooms, at 42 sq. m (452 sq. ft.) among Tokyo's largest, feature Italian furnishings, large mahogany desks, the fastest high-speed Internet connection currently available (free of charge), blackout blinds, 30-inch flatscreen TVs, safes designed for laptops with plug-ins for recharging, and a 24-hour in-house technology concierge to correct guests' computer woes. One-quarter of each unit's space is taken up by a huge bathroom equipped with separate shower and tub areas and a 13-inch flatscreen TV.

6–10–3 Roppongi, Minato-ku, Tokyo 106-0032. © 800/233-1234 in the U.S. and Canada, or 03/4333-1234. Fax 03/4333-8123. www.tokyo.grand.hyatt.com. 389 units. ¥47,250–¥54,600 ($449–$519) single; ¥52,500–¥59,850 ($499–$569) double; from ¥63,000 ($599) Grand Club double; from ¥94,500 ($893) suite. AE, DC, MC, V. Station: Roppongi (exit 1, 3 min.) or Azabu Juban (exit A3, 5 min.). **Amenities:** 7 restaurants; 1 bar; 20m (66-ft.) indoor pool with Jacuzzi and sauna (fee: ¥4,000/$38); fitness room (free); spa; concierge; business center; shopping arcade; salon; barbershop; 24-hr. room service; in-room massage; babysitting; same-day laundry/dry-cleaning service; nonsmoking rooms; executive-level rooms; free shoeshine. *In room:* A/C, cable TV w/on-demand pay movies and CD/DVD player (free DVD rentals), high-speed dataport, minibar, hot-water pot w/tea and coffee, hair dryer, safe, bathroom scale, Washlet toilet.

## NEAR IKEBUKURO

**Four Seasons Hotel Tokyo at Chinzan-So** ★★★ *Finds*    Although inconveniently located in northwest Tokyo (about a 15-min. taxi ride from Ikebukuro), this Four Seasons, built in 1992, is a superb hotel set in the luscious 6.8-hectare (17-acre), 100-year-old Chinzan-So Garden, making it extremely inviting after a bustling day in Tokyo. It also has one of Tokyo's best health clubs and spas, including a gorgeous glass-enclosed indoor pool surrounded by greenery with a glass ceiling that opens in summer, indoor and outdoor Jacuzzis (the outdoor one overlooks a small Japanese garden), and a Japanese hot-springs bath (the water is shipped in from Izu Peninsula)—all free for hotel guests. The health club, with personal-size TVs at most workstations, even offers free continental breakfasts. In contrast to the starkly modern Four Seasons at Marunouchi, the luxurious interiors here make this one of the most beautiful European-style hotels in Japan. Since the hotel embraces the park, most rooms have peaceful garden views from their V-shaped bay windows. Even the smallest rooms, which occupy the lower floors, boast king-size beds and are twice the size of most Japanese hotel rooms. Bathrooms have mini-TVs and separate shower and tub areas. Don't miss a stroll through the garden.

2–10–8 Sekiguchi, Bunkyo-ku, Tokyo 112-8667. © 800/332-3442 in the U.S., 800/268-6282 in Canada, or 03/3943-2222. Fax 03/3943-2300. www.fourseasons.com/tokyo. 283 units. ¥45,150–¥52,500 ($429–$499) single; ¥50,400–¥57,750 ($479–$549) double or twin; from ¥71,400 ($678) suite. AE, DC, MC, V. Station: Edogawabashi (exit 1a, a 10-min. walk or a 2-min. ride). **Amenities:** 3 restaurants (Italian, Japanese, French); 1 bar; 1 lounge; indoor pool and health club (free); concierge; business center; 24-hr. room service; in-room massage; same-day laundry/dry-cleaning service; nonsmoking rooms; executive-level rooms; complimentary shoeshine. *In room:* A/C, satellite TV w/on-demand pay movies, CD/DVD player, high-speed dataport (free), minibar, hot-water pot w/tea, hair dryer, safe, bathroom scale, Washlet toilet.

## EXPENSIVE
### GINZA & HIBIYA

**Imperial Hotel** ★★★ *Kids*    Located across from Hibiya Park, within walking distance of the Ginza and Imperial Palace, this is one of Tokyo's best-known hotels, with foreigners (mostly business executives) making up about 40% of the guests. Although

## _Kids_  Family-Friendly Hotels

**Hotel New Otani** (p. 127)  This huge hotel has both indoor and outdoor swimming pools, but best for parents is the babysitting room for children ages 1 month to 5 years. For a small fortune, you can even leave the darlings overnight.

**Imperial Hotel** (p. 123)  Although oriented toward business travelers, this famous hotel makes it easier to bring the family along, with its day-care center for children ages 2 weeks to 6 years, its babysitting service, and an indoor pool.

**National Children's Castle Hotel** (p. 139)  This is the absolutely top place to stay with kids, since the same building contains Tokyo's best indoor/outdoor playground and activity rooms for all ages, offering everything from building blocks and computer games to a swimming pool.

**Shinagawa Prince Hotel** (p. 136)  Japan's largest hotel boasts a children's day-care center, an IMAX theater, an amusement arcade, indoor and outdoor pools, aquarium, bowling alley, sports center, and much more.

the Imperial's history goes back to 1890 and it was rebuilt in 1922 by Frank Lloyd Wright, the present hotel dates from 1970, with a 31-story tower added in 1983. Unfortunately, Wright's legacy lives on only in the hotel's Art Deco Old Imperial Bar. (Part of Wright's original structure survives at Meiji-Mura, an architectural museum outside Nagoya.) On the plus side, the Imperial is one of the few hotels with a children's day-care center. Rooms in the main building are quite large for Tokyo, while Tower rooms, slightly smaller but pricier, are higher up, have floor-to-ceiling bay windows, and offer fantastic views of either Imperial Palace grounds or, my preference, the Ginza and Tokyo Bay. All rooms come with the amenities you'd expect from a first-class hotel, as well as such appreciated extras as a hands-free phone, bedside controls for the curtains, and free high-speed Internet access, with a private e-mail address for each guest. **_Tip:_** Become a member of the Imperial Club (membership is free), and you can use the small pool and gym free of charge.

1–1–1 Uchisaiwaicho, Chiyoda-ku, Tokyo 100-8558. © **800/223-6800** in the U.S. and Canada, or 03/3504-1111. Fax 03/3581-9146. www.imperialhotel.co.jp. 1,059 units. ¥31,500 – ¥58,800 ($299–$558) single; ¥36,750 – ¥64,050 ($349–$608) double or twin; from ¥63,000 ($599) suite. Imperial Floor ¥45,150 – ¥63,000 ($429–$599) single; ¥50,400 – ¥68,250 ($479–$648) double or twin. AE, DC, MC, V. Station: Hibiya (1 min.). **Amenities:** 13 restaurants; 2 bars; 2 lounges; 20th-floor indoor pool (fee: ¥1,000/$9.50; free for Imperial Club members); fitness room (fee: ¥1,000/$9.50; free for Imperial Club members); sauna; day-care center for children ages 2 weeks–6 years (fee: ¥5,250/$50 for 2 hr.); concierge; limousine and car-rental services; business center; impressive shopping arcade; salon; barbershop; 24-hr. room service; in-room massage; babysitting; same-day laundry/dry-cleaning service; nonsmoking rooms; executive-level rooms; in-house doctor and dentist; tea-ceremony room; post office. _In room:_ A/C, cable TV w/pay movies, fax, high-speed dataport, mini-bar, hot-water pot w/tea and coffee, hair dryer, large safe, bathroom scale, Washlet toilet.

## UENO

**Hotel Sofitel** 🌟🌟🌟 _(Finds)_  Located across from Shinobazu Pond in the heart of Ueno, this French-owned hotel is easily recognizable by its unique architecture: five pyramid-shaped trapeziums, stacked on top of each other. Inside, it's an oasis of refined beauty, excellent service, and great views. And with only a handful of rooms

# Ueno

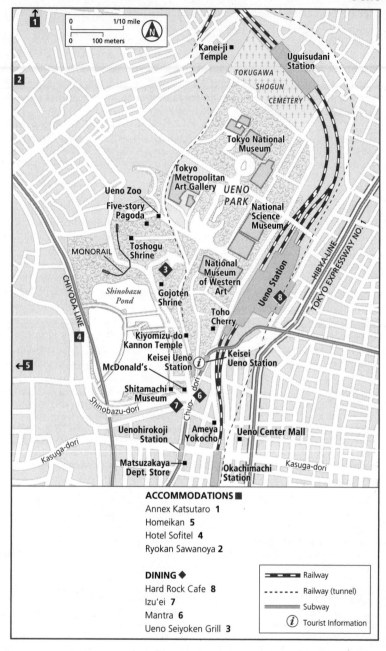

**ACCOMMODATIONS ■**

Annex Katsutaro **1**

Homeikan **5**

Hotel Sofitel **4**

Ryokan Sawanoya **2**

**DINING ◆**

Hard Rock Cafe **8**

Izu'ei **7**

Mantra **6**

Ueno Seiyoken Grill **3**

Railway

Railway (tunnel)

Subway

(i) Tourist Information

on each floor, it has the atmosphere of an intimate, luxury boutique hotel. Its restaurant, Provence, with a French chef, draws rave reviews. Chic rooms, with rates based on size, boast inlaid wood furniture, original artwork, and TVs that double as computers for Internet access (but no e-mail capabilities). Nothing beats the view over Shinobazu Pond with its bird refuge and the adjoining zoo (some rooms facing the opposite side have occasional views of Mount Fuji). I'm partial to the superior rooms on the 25th floor. Easy accessibility to Ueno Park and its museums make this unique hotel a natural for joggers and art lovers alike.

2–1–48 Ikenohata, Taito-ku, Tokyo 110-0008. Ⓒ 800/221-4542 in the U.S. and Canada, or 03/5685-7111. Fax 03/5685-6171. www.sofiteltokyo.com. 83 units. ¥30,000 ($285) single; ¥35,000 ($333) double; ¥41,000 ($390) twin; from ¥58,000 ($551) suite. Rates include local tax and service charge. AE, DC, MC, V. Station: Yushima (7 min.) or Ueno (13 min.). **Amenities:** Restaurant (French); bar; lounge; small exercise room (free); 24-hr. room service; in-room massage; same-day laundry/dry-cleaning service; nonsmoking rooms. *In room:* A/C, cable TV w/pay movies and Internet access, high-speed dataport, minibar, hot-water pot w/tea and coffee, hair dryer, safe, Washlet toilet.

## SHINJUKU

**Century Hyatt Tokyo** 🐾  Located on Shinjuku's west side next to Shinjuku Central Park (popular with joggers), this least expensive and oldest of the Hyatt's three Tokyo properties celebrated its 25th anniversary in 2005 with renovated restaurants and rooms. Remaining is the hotel's impressive seven-story atrium lobby with three of the most massive chandeliers you're likely to see anywhere. Many foreigners (mostly American) pass through the hotel's doors, ably assisted by the excellent staff with the Hyatt's usual high standards. However, since this hotel is popular with both business and leisure groups, those searching a quieter, more personalized experience will want to book elsewhere. Rates are based on size; even the cheapest units are adequate, but they do face another building and don't receive much sunshine. If you can afford it, spring for a more expensive room on a high floor with bay windows overlooking the park (in winter, you might also have a view of Mount Fuji).

2–7–2 Nishi-Shinjuku, Shinjuku-ku, Tokyo 160-0023. Ⓒ 800/233-1234 in the U.S. and Canada, or 03/3349-0111. Fax 03/3344-5575. www.tokyo.century.hyatt.com. 766 units. ¥30,030 ($288) single; ¥36,960–¥39,270 ($351–$373) double or twin. Regency Club from ¥41,580 ($395) single or double. Rates include service charge. AE, DC, MC, V. Station: Tochomae (1 min.), Nishi-Shinjuku (3 min.), or Shinjuku (a 10-min. walk, or a free 3-min. shuttle ride). **Amenities:** 6 restaurants; 1 bar; 1 lounge; health club with indoor pool (fee: ¥1,500/$14); concierge; tour desk; shopping arcade; salon; 24-hr. room service; in-room massage; same-day laundry/dry-cleaning service; nonsmoking rooms; executive-level rooms; free shuttle service to Shinjuku Station every 20 min. *In room:* A/C, cable TV w/pay movies, dataport (not all rooms), minibar, hot-water pot w/tea, hair dryer, safe, Washlet toilet.

**Hilton Tokyo** 🐾🐾  Located on Shinjuku's west side next to Century Hyatt, the 38-story Hilton Tokyo with its sensually curving facade opened in 1984 as the largest Hilton in the Asia/Pacific area. Today it keeps a lower profile than most of the other Shinjuku hotels, with a quiet, subdued lobby, and it remains popular with business and leisure travelers alike. Rooms are up-to-date and adequate in size. As with all Hiltons, the room decor reflects traditional native style, with shoji screens instead of curtains and simple yet elegant furnishings that include queen-size beds or larger in all rooms. Deluxe-floor rooms come with the extras of free high-speed Internet access, fax, and safe.

6–6–2 Nishi-Shinjuku, Shinjuku-ku, Tokyo 160-0023. Ⓒ 800/HILTONS in the U.S. and Canada, or 03/3344-5111. Fax 03/3342-6094. www.hilton.com. 806 units. ¥34,000–¥40,000 ($323–$380) single; ¥37,000–¥46,000 ($352–$437) twin or double. Executive floor from ¥45,500 ($432) twin or double; from ¥70,000 ($665) suite. Children stay free in parent's room. AE, DC, MC, V. Station: Nishi-Shinjuku (2 min.), Tochomae (3 min.), or Shinjuku (10-min. walk or free shuttle bus). **Amenities:** 5 restaurants; 1 bar; 1 lounge; 2 outdoor lighted tennis courts; health club w/indoor pool (fee: ¥3,000 ($29)); concierge; tour desk; shopping arcade; salon; 24-hr. room service; in-room massage; same-day

laundry/dry-cleaning service; nonsmoking rooms; executive-level rooms; Kinko's (open 24 hr.); free shuttle service to Shinjuku Station. *In room:* A/C, satellite TV w/on-demand pay movies, dataport, minibar, hot-water pot w/tea, hair dryer.

## AKASAKA & ROPPONGI

**Capitol Tokyu Hotel** ✰✰ *Finds*    This Tokyo old-timer is a popular choice for knowledgeable travelers seeking up-to-date accommodations with traditional touches. Built just before the 1964 Olympics, it's nestled against the wooded hillside leading to Hie Shrine, one of the city's most important Edo-Era shrines, yet is centrally located in Akasaka convenient to the city's many sights. A member of the Tokyu chain, it has the unique ability to make foreign guests feel as if they're in Asia and at home at the same time, making it a longtime local favorite. Fantastically large floral bouquets are the trademark of the dark, subdued lobby, which overlooks a small Japanese garden with a carp pond. The level of service is extraordinary. While double and twin rooms are comfortably large, the 50 single rooms are fairly small. All come with traditional shoji screens, as well as light-blocking sliding panels; the best ones overlook the greenery of Hie Shrine, while some pricier rooms also have high-speed Internet connections.

2–10–3 Nagata-cho, Chiyoda-ku, Tokyo 100-0014. ✆ **800/888-4747** in the U.S. and Canada, or 03/3581-4511. Fax 03/3581-5822. www.capitoltokyu.com. 455 units. ¥30,030–¥33,495 ($285–$318) single; ¥43,890–¥69,300 ($417–$658) double or twin; from ¥115,500 ($1,097) suite. Rates include service charge. AE, DC, MC, V. Station: Kokkai Gijido-mae (1 min.) or Tameikesanno (3 min.). **Amenities:** 5 restaurants; 1 cafe; 1 bar; 1 lounge; outdoor pool (free); small fitness room (free); concierge; travel agency; business center; shopping arcade; salon; barbershop; 24-hr. room service; in-room massage; babysitting; same-day laundry/dry-cleaning service; nonsmoking rooms; executive-level rooms; in-house dentist. *In room:* A/C, cable TV w/on-demand pay movies, dataport, minibar, hot-water pot w/tea, hair dryer, Washlet toilet.

**Hotel New Otani** ✰✰ *Kids*    If you like small, quiet hotels, this monolith is not for you. Like a city unto itself, the New Otani is so big that two information desks are needed to assist lost souls searching for a particular restaurant or shop in the meandering arcade; there are even two check-in desks. The hotel's most splendid feature is its garden, the best of any Tokyo hotel—a 400-year-old Japanese garden that once belonged to a feudal lord, with 4 hectares (10 acres) of ponds, waterfalls, bridges, bamboo groves, and manicured bushes. The outdoor pool, flanked by greenery, is also nice. A variety of rooms, in a main building and a newer tower, are available. Those in the main building are comfortable, with shojilike screens on the windows; more expensive rooms have such extras as bathroom scales, walk-in closets, and fax machines (otherwise, fax machines are available free of charge). Tower rooms range from chic ones done in jade, black, and chrome to "fusui healing" rooms with such extras as in-room humidifier, foot bath, and compact CD/MD player. The tower offers the best views—of the garden, the skyscrapers of Shinjuku, and, on clear days, Mount Fuji. Since rates are the same no matter which way you face, be sure to request a room overlooking the garden. Parents appreciate the 24-hour Baby Room and the fact that the pool is free for those who become (for free) Hotel Club members.

4–1 Kioi-cho, Chiyoda-ku, Tokyo 102-8578. ✆ **800/421-8795** in the U.S. and Canada, or 03/3265-1111. Fax 03/3221-2619. www.newotani.co.jp/en. 1,600 units. ¥36,005–¥54,485 ($342–$518) single; ¥41,980–¥62,770 ($399–$596) double or twin; from ¥86,825 ($825) suite. Rates include local tax and service charge. AE, DC, MC, V. Station: Akasakamitsuke or Nagatacho (3 min.). **Amenities:** 37 restaurants and cafes; 6 bars and lounges; outdoor pool (fee: ¥2,000/$19; free for Hotel Club members); small exercise room (free); health club w/indoor pool and lighted outdoor tennis courts (fee: ¥5,000/$48); day-care center for children 1 month–5 years old (fee: ¥6,000/$57 for 2 hr.); concierge; tour desk; business center; shopping arcade with 120 stores; salon; room service (6am–1am); in-room massage; same-day laundry/dry-cleaning service; medical and dental clinics; post office; tea-ceremony room; art museum (free for hotel guests); nonsmoking rooms. *In room:* A/C, cable TV w/pay movies, high-speed dataport, minibar, hot-water pot w/tea, hair dryer, safe, Washlet toilet.

# Shinjuku

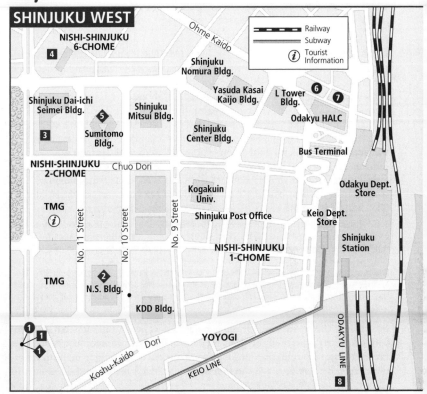

**SHINJUKU WEST**

NISHI-SHINJUKU 6-CHOME

4

Ohme Kaido

Shinjuku Nomura Bldg.

Yasuda Kasai Kaijo Bldg.

L Tower Bldg.

6  7

Odakyu HALC

Shinjuku Dai-ichi Seimei Bldg.

Shinjuku Mitsui Bldg.

5

3

Sumitomo Bldg.

Shinjuku Center Bldg.

Bus Terminal

NISHI-SHINJUKU 2-CHOME

Chuo Dori

Odakyu Dept. Store

TMG

Kogakuin Univ.

Keio Dept. Store

Shinjuku Post Office

Shinjuku Station

No. 11 Street

No. 10 Street

No. 9 Street

NISHI-SHINJUKU 1-CHOME

TMG

2

N.S. Bldg.

KDD Bldg.

YOYOGI

ODAKYU LINE

1  1

1

Koshu-Kaido Dori

KEIO LINE

8

Railway
Subway
Tourist Information

**Hotel Okura** ✿✿✿  Located across from the U.S. embassy and long considered one of Tokyo's most venerable hotels, the Okura is struggling to keep up with pricier—and newer—top-rated hotels in the city, recently adding a spa to increase its appeal. It remains a favorite home-away-from-home of visiting U.S. dignitaries, and the service is gracious and impeccable. Rich decor elegantly combines ikebana and shoji screens with an old-fashioned Western spaciousness. The atmosphere is low key, almost Zen-like, with none of the flashiness inherent in some younger hotels. All rooms are comfortable, with clean, crisp furnishings of maple and chrome. My favorite rooms are in the main building facing the garden; some on the fifth floor here have balconies overlooking the garden and pool. Other rooms have views of a rooftop garden or Tokyo Tower, while Grand Comfort rooms on the 9th and 10th floors offer free entrance to the spa. *Tip:* Although fees are charged for use of the health club and pools, hotel guests can use these facilities for free simply by becoming members of Okura Club International—there's no charge for membership, which starts immediately upon filling out an application at the guest relations desk.

2–10–4 Toranomon, Minato-ku, Tokyo 105-0001. © **800/223-6800** in the U.S., or 03/3582-0111. Fax 03/3582-3707. www.okura.com. 834 units. ¥30,450–¥44,100 ($289–$419) single; ¥39,375–¥61,950 ($374–$589) double; ¥42,000–¥61,950 ($399–$589) twin; from ¥82,950 ($788) suite. Grand Comfort rooms ¥52,500 ($499) single; ¥66,150 ($628) double. AE, DC, MC, V. Station: Toranomon or Kamiyacho (5 min.). **Amenities:** 10 restaurants; 2 bars; nicely landscaped

**SHINJUKU EAST**

| ACCOMMODATIONS ■ | | DINING ◆ | | NIGHTLIFE ● |
|---|---|---|---|---|
| Century Hyatt Tokyo **3** | | Ban-Thai **9** | | Advocates **17** |
| Hilton Tokyo **4** | | daidaya **21** | | Christon Café **14** |
| Hotel Century Southern Tower **8** | | Donto **5** | | Code **10** |
| Park Hyatt Tokyo **1** | | Hakkaku **2** | | Dubliners **19** |
| | | Hayashi **11** | | Kangaroo Court Decision **12** |
| | | Kakiden **20** | | Kento's **13** |
| | | New York Grill **1** | | Kinsmen **17** |
| | | Ten-ichi **15** | | Kinswomyn **17** |
| | | Tsunahachi **18** | | New York Bar **1** |
| | | | | Shinjuku Pit Inn **16** |
| | | | | Vagabond **7** |
| | | | | Volga **6** |

outdoor pool and health club (fee: ¥3,500/$29 to use everything; ¥2,000/$17 for indoor pool only); spa (fee: ¥12,600/$120); concierge; tour desk; comprehensive business center; shopping arcade; salon; barbershop; 24-hr. room service; in-room massage; same-day laundry/dry-cleaning service; nonsmoking rooms; free shuttle service to the nearest subways and Roppongi Hills (weekends only); tea-ceremony room; private museum showcasing Japanese art (free for hotel guests); pharmacy; in-house doctor and dentist; post office; packing and shipping service. *In room:* A/C, satellite TV w/on-demand pay movies that doubles as a computer w/Internet access, high-speed dataport, minibar, hot-water pot w/tea, hair dryer, bathroom scale, Washlet toilet.

## NEAR SHINAGAWA

**Miyako Hotel Tokyo** *展展 Value*    A Radisson affiliate, this hotel is one of my favorites in Tokyo, for its calm peacefulness as well as its small-luxury-hotel service. Because it's a bit off the beaten path, it has a quieter, more relaxed atmosphere than those found at more centrally located hotels, evident the moment you step into its lobby lounge with its gas-flame fireplace on one end and the greenery of a garden on the other. Attracting mostly Japanese guests, it offers average-size rooms, the best of which are renovated rooms on higher floors with beds so comfortable you'd sneak them into your luggage if you could, pinpoint reading lights, and huge floor-to-ceiling windows overlooking the hotel's own lush garden, a famed garden next door, or Tokyo Tower.

1–1–50 Shirokanedai, Minato-ku, Tokyo 108-8640. ✆ **800/333-3333** in the U.S. and Canada, or 03/3447-3111. Fax 03/ 3447-3133. www.radisson.com/tokyojp_miyako. 492 units. ¥28,350–¥44,100 ($269–$419) single; ¥31,500–¥47,250

($299–$449) double or twin; from ¥105,000 ($998) suite. AE, DC, MC, V. Station: Shirokanedai (4 min.), Shirokane-Takanawa (5 min.), or free shuttle from Meguro station. **Amenities:** 3 restaurants (Japanese, Chinese, fusion); 1 bar; 1 lounge; health club w/25m (82-ft.) indoor heated pool and sauna (fee: ¥735/$7); concierge; tour desk; shopping arcade; convenience store; salon; 24-hr. room service; in-room massage; same-day laundry/dry-cleaning service; nonsmoking rooms; free shuttle service to Meguro Station every 15 min. and Shinagawa Station (mornings only); dental/medical clinics. *In room:* A/C, cable TV w/pay movies, free high-speed dataport, minibar, hot-water pot w/tea, hair dryer, safe, Washlet toilet, trouser press.

## ODAIBA

**Hotel Nikko Tokyo** ✿✿    This is by far the most un-Tokyo-like hotel in the city. Opened in 1996 as the first hotel on Odaiba, an island of reclaimed land with a convention center, shopping malls, and sightseeing attractions, this grand, elegant lodging is surrounded by parks and gardens that give it a relaxed, resort-evoking atmosphere. Billing itself as an "urban resort," it's especially popular with young well-to-do Japanese in search of an exotic weekend getaway. A curved facade assures water-front views from most rooms, which have the added benefit of private balconies with two chairs. The most expensive rooms offer commanding views of Tokyo Bay, Rainbow Bridge, and the city skyline (impressive at night); the least expensive rooms, smaller in size, face another hotel or the Maritime Museum and Haneda Airport across the bay. This is a great choice if you want to get away from the bustle of Tokyo, but the location can be a disadvantage; it's served only by the monorail Yurikamome Line, the JR Saikyo Line to Shibuya, and the inconvenient Rinkai Fukutoshin Line, which can be quite crowded on weekends, as can bus and taxi travel via the Rainbow Bridge or harbor tunnel.

1–9–1 Daiba, Minato-ku, Tokyo 135-8625. ✆ **800/645-5687** in the U.S. and Canada, or 03/5500-5500. Fax 03/5500-2525. www.hnt.co.jp. 453 units. ¥32,340–¥46,200 ($307–$439) single; ¥38,115–¥51,975 ($362–$494) double or twin; from ¥92,400 ($878) suite. All rates include service charge. AE, DC, MC, V. Station: Daiba (1 min.) or Tokyo Teleport Station (10 min.). **Amenities:** 8 restaurants; 1 bar; 1 lounge; spa with indoor pool linked to outdoor heated tub, Jacuzzi, and sun terrace overlooking Rainbow Bridge (fee: ¥3,000/$29 the 1st day; thereafter ¥1,000/$9.50); concierge; business center; room service (6am–11:30am and 5pm–1am); in-room massage; babysitting; same-day laundry/dry-cleaning service; nonsmoking rooms. *In room:* A/C, cable TV w/pay movies, dataport, minibar, hot-water pot w/tea, hair dryer, safe, Washlet toilet.

## MODERATE
### GINZA & SHIODOME

**Hotel Monterey La Soeur** ✿✿ *Finds*    The Monterey chain targets female travelers with its feminine decor, and this hotel—designed by a woman—is no exception. A small, boutiquelike hotel with a slight European ambience (note the display of Art Deco perfume bottles in the tiny lobby), it rises above the ordinary business hotel with small but comfortable rooms that show a woman's touch without being fussy. Specially designated ladies' rooms contain amenities geared toward women. If rooms here are full, try the nearby sister **Hotel Monterery Ginza** (✆ **03/3544-7111**), with the same boutique-hotel concept and similar prices.

1–10–18 Ginza, Chuo-ku, Tokyo 104-0061. ✆ **03/3562-7111.** Fax 03/3544-1600. 141 units. ¥16,370–¥17,525 ($156–$166) single; ¥23,300 ($221) double; ¥30,230–¥35,050 ($287–$333) twin. Rates include local tax and service charge. AE, DC, MC, V. Station: Ginza Itchome (2 min.) or Ginza (4 min.). **Amenities:** Restaurant (French/Italian); same-day laundry/dry-cleaning service; nonsmoking rooms. *In room:* A/C, TV w/pay movies, minibar, hot-water pot w/tea, hair dryer, Washlet toilet.

**Mitsui Urban Hotel Ginza** ✿ *Value*    Because of its great location, convenient to the Ginza, Shimbashi, and Hibiya shopping and business centers, this attractive hotel caters mostly to business travelers but appeals to tourists as well. The lobby, on the

second floor, has a friendly staff. The bright and snazzy guest rooms are tiny but feature a few amenities usually found at more expensive hotels, including decent-size bathrooms with no-fog mirrors. Note, however, that the cheapest rooms have no closets and no space to unpack: a good example of what $238 buys in Tokyo. I suggest asking for a room away from the highway overpass beside the hotel.

8–6–15 Ginza, Chuo-ku, Tokyo 104-0061. © **03/3572-4131.** Fax 03/3572-4254. www.mitsuikanko.co.jp. 265 units. ¥14,500–¥20,500 ($138–$195) single; ¥25,000–¥28,800 ($238–$274) double; ¥25,000–¥34,800 ($238–$331) twin. AE, DC, MC, V. Station: Shimbashi (2 min.). **Amenities:** 3 restaurants (Western, Japanese, Chinese); 1 bar; 1 lounge; room service (Mon–Fri 10pm–1am); same-day laundry service. *In room:* A/C, cable TV w/pay movies, dataport, hot-water pot w/tea, hair dryer, trouser press, Washlet toilet.

## Park Hotel Tokyo ★★ *Finds*

Opened in 2003 and occupying 10 floors of a building it shares with international media organizations, this hotel boasts a 25th-floor lobby bathed in natural light afforded by a 10-story atrium topped with an opaque ceiling. Its front desk is one of the most dramatic I've seen, backed by nothing but great views of Tokyo Tower and the city. Small rooms also provide views, the best from those from the 30th floor and above facing Hama Rikyu garden and Tokyo Bay or those facing Tokyo Tower (and Mount Fuji on clear winter days). Each room, with whitewashed walls and wood furniture, has its own original artwork, and bathrooms have light dimmers so as not to awaken sleeping roommates. The hotel even has a trained "pillow fitter," who can take your measurements and provide one especially made to fit, at no extra cost. Its restaurants follow a natural-foods concept, using organic ingredients. In short, this hotel is a fine choice in the Shiodome district of downtown Tokyo, just a few minutes' walk from the Ginza.

Shiodome Media Tower, 1–7–1 Higashi Shimbashi, Minato-ku, Tokyo 105-7227. © **03/6252-1111.** Fax 03/6252-1001. www.parkhoteltokyo.com. 273 units. ¥22,145 ($210) single; ¥26,765–¥27,920 ($254–$265) double; ¥26,765–¥38,515 ($254–$366) twin. Rates include local tax and service charge. AE, DC, MC, V. Station: Shiodome (1 min.) or Shimbashi (8 min.). **Amenities:** 3 restaurants (Japanese, French, coffee shop); 1 bar; 1 lounge; aromatherapy massage room; business center (free Internet use); 24-hr. room service; in-room massage; same-day laundry service; nonsmoking rooms. *In room:* A/C, cable TV w/pay movies, free high-speed dataport, minibar, hot-water pot w/tea and coffee, hair dryer, Washlet toilet.

## Renaissance Tokyo Hotel Ginza Tobu ★

This small, classy, and personable hotel, located on Showa Dori behind the Ginza Matsuzakaya department store and within easy walking distance of shopping and the Kabuki theater, attracts a foreign clientele as high as 60%, due mainly to its association with Marriott. Primarily a business hotel (a whopping 90% of its guests are business travelers), it has limited facilities; you clearly pay for location here. Interestingly, the cheapest singles (which have single-size beds) are not offered to foreigners—they're considered too small—but if you insist, they'll let you have one (contact the hotel directly); though indeed small, I find them more nicely appointed than those offered by most business hotels. Be sure to pick up the hotel's sightseeing leaflets at the concierge's desk, with advice on what to see and how to get there.

6–14–10 Ginza, Chuo-ku, Tokyo 104-0061. © **888/236-2427** in the U.S. and Canada, or 03/3546-0111. Fax 03/3546-8990. www.marriott.com/tyorn. 206 units. ¥17,850–¥24,150 ($170–$229) single; ¥29,400 ($279) double or twin. Renaissance Floor ¥25,200–¥31,500 ($239–$299) single; ¥36,750 ($349) double or twin. AE, DC, MC, V. Station: Ginza (5 min.) or Higashi-Ginza (1 min.). **Amenities:** 2 restaurants (Japanese, coffee shop); 1 bar; 1 lounge; concierge; 24-hr. business center; salon; room service (6:30am–11:30pm); in-room massage; same-day laundry/dry-cleaning service; nonsmoking rooms; executive-level rooms. *In room:* A/C, cable TV w/on-demand pay videos, free high-speed dataport, minibar, hot-water pot w/tea, hair dryer.

## AROUND TOKYO STATION

**Hotel Yaesu Ryumeikan** ★ *Value*    This 40-year-old, nondescript hotel is your best bet for reasonably priced lodging just minutes away from Tokyo Station. From the north Yaesu exit, turn left onto Sotobori Dori; it will be on your right, just before Eitai Dori. Surprising for this location, it offers mostly Japanese-style tatami rooms, along with some Western-style rooms with beds. I prefer the Japanese-style rooms, especially the most expensive ones, which have a nice, traditional feel and come with sitting alcove and Japanese-style deep tub. Only Japanese breakfasts are available; if you can't stomach rice and fish in the morning, opt for a room without breakfast and subtract ¥800 ($7.60) per person from the rates below.

1–3–22 Yaesu, Chuo-ku 103-0028. ⓒ **03/3271-0971.** Fax 03/3271-0977. www.ryumeikan.co.jp. 30 units (23 with bathroom, 5 with toilet only, 2 without bathroom). ¥8,500 ($81) single without bathroom, ¥10,500–¥13,500 ($100–$128) single with bathroom; ¥9,500 ($90) single with toilet only; ¥15,000 ($143) double with toilet only, ¥17,600–¥19,000 ($167–$181) double with bathroom. Rates include Japanese breakfast, local tax, and service charge. AE, DC, MC, V. Station: Tokyo (3 min. from the north Yaesu exit) or Nihombashi (exit A3, 1 min.). On the corner of Eitai Dori and Sotobori Dori. **Amenities:** 2 restaurants (Italian, Japanese). *In room:* A/C, TV, high-speed dataport, fridge, hot-water pot w/tea, hair dryer.

## ASAKUSA

**Asakusa View Hotel**    This is the only upper-bracket, modern hotel in the Asakusa area, and it looks almost out of place rising 28 stories above this famous district's older buildings. It's a good place to stay if you want to be in Tokyo's old downtown but don't want to sacrifice any creature comforts. The medium-size guest rooms are pleasant, with sleek, contemporary furnishings and bay windows that let in plenty of sunshine (and smaller windows that can be opened, a rarity in Tokyo); rooms facing the front have views over the famous Sensoji Temple. Eight Japanese-style rooms are also available, sleeping up to five people; on the same floor are a small, rooftop Japanese garden and Japanese-style public baths featuring tubs made of 2,000-year-old cypress.

Kokusai Dori, 3–17–1 Nishi-Asakusa, Taito-ku, Tokyo 111-8765. ⓒ **03/3847-1111.** Fax 03/3842-2117. www.viewhotels.co.jp/Asakusa. 337 units. ¥13,650–¥18,000 ($130–$171) single; ¥24,150–¥31,000 ($229–$295) double; ¥27,300–¥31,000 ($260–$295) twin. Japanese-style rooms from ¥45,150 ($429) for 2. Executive floor from ¥33,600 ($319) double. AE, DC, MC, V. Station: Tawaramachi (8 min.). **Amenities:** 5 restaurants; 2 bars; 1 lounge; 20m (66-ft.) indoor pool w/retractable roof (fee: ¥3,000/$29, but request a 50% discount coupon at the front desk); shopping arcade; salon; Japanese-style public baths (fee: ¥1,050/$10); room service (7am–11pm); same-day laundry/dry-cleaning service; nonsmoking rooms; executive-level rooms. *In room:* A/C, cable TV w/pay movies, minibar, hot-water pot w/tea, hair dryer.

**Hotel Sunroute Asakusa** ★    Located on Kokusai Dori, this modern, pleasant hotel opened in 1998 as a business hotel but is a good choice for leisure travelers as well. Not only does it boast a good location near the sightseeing attractions of Asakusa, but it is classier than most business hotels, with Miró reprints in the lobby and modern artwork in each guest room. Though small, the (mostly single) rooms come with all the comforts, with slightly larger beds and bathrooms than those found at most business hotels. The hotel's one coffee shop, a chain called Jonathan's serving both Japanese and Western food, is open daily 24 hours.

1–8–5 Kaminarimon, Taito-ku, Tokyo 111-0034. ⓒ **03/3847-1511.** Fax 03/3847-1509. www.sunroute-asakusa.jp. 120 units. ¥8,925–¥11,025 ($85–$105) single; ¥15,225 ($145) double; ¥17,325–¥19,950 ($165–$186) twin. AE, DC, MC, V. Station: Tawaramachi (1 min.) or Asakusa (8 min.). **Amenities:** Restaurant; same-day laundry service; nonsmoking rooms. *In room:* A/C, TV, hot-water pot w/tea, hair dryer, Washlet toilet, trouser press.

# Asakusa

**Legend:**
Railway
Subway
Tourist Info ⓘ

ASAKUSA 3-CHOME

NISHI-ASAKUSA 3-CHOME

ASAKUSA 2-CHOME

Kototoi Dori

Hisago Dori

Kokusai Dori

HANAYASHIKI AMUSEMENT PARK

Asakusa Shrine

Sensoji Temple

Five-storied Pagoda

Horizon Gate

HANAKAWADO 2-CHOME

HANAKAWADO 1-CHOME

NISHI-ASAKUSA 2-CHOME

Dempoin Temple

Sushiya Dori

Umamichi Dori

TOBU ASAKUSA LINE

ASAKUSA 1-CHOME

Orange Dori

Chinyoko Dori

Nakamise Dori

Kannon Dori

Asakusa Station

Matsuya Dept. Store

Edo Dori

SUMIDA PARK

Drum Museum

Kaminarimon Dori

Ferry Pier

KAMINARIMON 1-CHOME

Asakusa Information Center ⓘ

Asakusa Station

AZUMA BRIDGE

Tarawamachi Station

Edo Dori

ASAKUSA LINE

Asahi Beer Tower

Asakusa Dori

GINZA LINE

Sumida River

METROPOLITAN EXPWY

Asakusa Station

KOMAGATA BRIDGE

0    1/10 mile
0    100 meters

N

133

## ACCOMMODATIONS ■
Asakusa View Hotel **1**
Hotel Sunroute Asakusa **7**
Ryokan Shigetsu **3**

## NIGHTLIFE ●
Sky Room **9**

## DINING ◆
Chinya **4**
Kamiya Bar **6**
Komagata Dojo **11**
La Ranarita Azumabashi **9**
Mugitoro **10**
Namiki Yabusoba **8**
Sansado **5**
Sometaro **2**

## SHINJUKU

**Hotel Century Southern Tower** ✿✿✿ *(Finds)*    Opened in 1998 as a welcome addition to the Shinjuku hotel scene, this sleek, modern hotel is located just south of the station and just a footbridge away from the huge Takashimaya Times Square shopping complex. Because it occupies the top floors of a sleek white building, it seems far removed from the hustle and bustle of Shinjuku below. Its 20th-floor lobby is simple and uncluttered and boasts almost surreal views of Tokyo stretching in the distance. Also on the 20th floor is Tribecks, a contemporary restaurant offering Asian- and European-influenced American food and great views of Shinjuku. Ask for a room on a high floor. Rooms facing east are considered best (and are therefore more expensive), especially at night when neon is in full regalia. Rooms facing west have views of Shinjuku's skyscrapers and, on clear days (mostly in winter), of Mount Fuji. A playful touch: the maps in each room outlining the important buildings visible from your room.

2–2–1 Yoyogi, Shibuya-ku, Tokyo 151-8583. ✆ **03/5354-0111.** Fax 03/5354-0100. www.southerntower.co.jp. 375 units. ¥18,480 – ¥20,790 ($176–$198) single; ¥25,410 – ¥32,340 ($241–$307) double; ¥25,410 – ¥27,720 ($241–$263) twin. Rates include service charge. AE, DC, MC, V. Station: Shinjuku (south exit, 3 min.). **Amenities:** 3 restaurants (Japanese, Chinese, contemporary American); 1 lounge; exercise room (free); convenience store; 24-hr. Kinko's; same-day laundry/dry-cleaning service; nonsmoking rooms. *In room:* A/C, cable TV w/pay movies, free high-speed dataport, fridge, hot-water pot w/tea, hair dryer, safe, Washlet toilet.

## AOYAMA

**President Hotel** ✿ *(Value)*    This small hotel is a good choice for the budget-conscious business traveler, not only because it's a respected address in Tokyo but also thanks to its reasonable prices and great location, between Akasaka, Shinjuku, Aoyama, and Roppongi. The unpretentious lobby has a comfortable European atmosphere—you don't have to be embarrassed about meeting business clients here—with a smart restaurant off to one side specializing in organic dishes. Units, which are mostly singles, are tiny but cheerful, though you'll take your life in your own hands trying to shave in the dark bathrooms. Ask for a unit on a high floor facing the front, and since not all rooms have dataports, be sure to reserve one in advance if it matters.

Aoyama Dori, 2–2–3 Minami Aoyama, Minato-ku, Tokyo 107-8545. ✆ **03/3497-0111.** Fax 03/3401-4816. www.president-hotel.co.jp. 210 units. ¥12,600 – ¥13,650 ($120–$130) single; ¥17,850 ($170) double; ¥17,850 – ¥22,050 ($170–$209) twin. AE, DC, MC, V. Station: Aoyama-Itchome (1 min.). **Amenities:** 3 restaurants (Japanese, organic/vegetarian, coffee shop); same-day laundry/dry-cleaning service, nonsmoking rooms. *In room:* A/C, cable TV, free high-speed dataport (not all rooms), minibar, hot-water pot w/tea, hair dryer, Washlet toilet.

## ROPPONGI

**Hotel Ibis**    The Ibis is about as close as you can get to the night action of Roppongi, just a minute's walk away from Roppongi Crossing. It caters to both businessmen and couples who come to Roppongi's discos and don't make (or don't want to make) the last subway home. The lobby, with public computers available for accessing the Internet (and costing ¥500/$4.75 for 25 min.), is on the fifth floor, with the guest rooms above. Tiny but comfortable, the rooms feature modern furniture and windows that you can open—though with a freeway nearby, I'm not sure you'd want to. The cheapest doubles come with semi-double-size beds, just slightly wider than a single. On the 13th floor is the reasonably priced Italian restaurant Sabatini, with views of the city.

7–14–4 Roppongi, Minato-ku, Tokyo 106-0032. ✆ **03/3403-4411.** Fax 03/3479-0609. www.ibis-hotel.com. 182 units. ¥13,382 – ¥15,461 ($127–$147) single; ¥16,285 – ¥26,765 ($155–$254) double; ¥22,145 – ¥26,765 ($210–$254) twin. Rates include service charge. AE, DC, MC, V. Station: Roppongi (1 min.). **Amenities:** 3 restaurants (Italian, Vietnamese, coffee shop); room service (Mon–Sat 11:30am–3am); same-day laundry/dry-cleaning service;

nonsmoking rooms. *In room:* A/C, cable TV w/pay movies, free high-speed dataport (not all rooms), minibar, hot-water pot w/tea, hair dryer.

## SHIBUYA

**Shibuya Excel Hotel Tokyu** 🕬🕬    Across from bustling Shibuya Station and connected by a footbridge and underground passage, this busy, modern hotel opened in 2000, the first new hotel to debut in Shibuya in many years. It's been so successful (I don't know why no one thought of locating hotels in Shibuya before), Tokyu promptly built another one farther from the station. With an excellent location above Mark City shopping mall (reception is on the fifth floor), the Excel tries hard to appeal to everyone: For business travelers, there are "Excel" twin rooms that feature high-speed dataports. For women, there are two floors reserved only for females and accessed by a special key, with in-room amenities—such as face cream, jewelry boxes, and plants—also geared toward women. There are also rooms for those with limited mobility, and almost half the rooms are for nonsmokers. Rooms, on the 7th to 24th floors, are comfortable. Ask for an upper-floor room facing Shinjuku; the night view is great. In-room refrigerators are empty so that you can stock them yourself from hotel vending machines, which, by the way, management claims are the largest in Japan.

1–12–2 Dogenzaka, Shibuya-ku 150-0043. ✆ **800/428-6598** in the U.S., or 03/5457-0109. Fax 03/5457-0309. www.tokyuhotels.co.jp. 408 units. ¥20,790–¥21,945 ($198–$208) single; ¥26,565–¥28,875 ($252–$274) double; ¥28,875–¥41,580 ($252–$395) twin. Rates include service charge. AE, DC, MC, V. Station: Shibuya (1 min. by footbridge). **Amenities:** 2 restaurants (Japanese, French) plus many more in Mark City mall; shopping mall beneath hotel; room service (7–9am and 9pm–midnight); same-day laundry/dry-cleaning service; nonsmoking rooms; public fax and copy machine. *In room:* A/C, satellite TV w/pay movies, dataport (not all rooms), fridge, hot-water pot w/tea, hair dryer, trouser press, Washlet toilet.

## SHINAGAWA

**Le Meridien Pacific Tokyo** 🕬    This aging hotel across the street from Shinagawa Station occupies grounds that once belonged to Japan's imperial family, a reminder of which remains in the peaceful, tranquil garden with pond and waterfall that serves as a dramatic backdrop for the lobby lounge. Approximately 50% of the hotel's guests are foreigners, mostly French, German, and American. Its location on the Yamanote Line makes it convenient for travel in the city, while trains to Kamakura and other points west and south, as well as the Shinkansen bullet train, make it convenient for travel farther afield. I also like its glass-enclosed coffee shop serving buffet meals and with views of the garden. Room rates are based mostly on room size, with those facing the front slightly larger and offering partial views of Tokyo Bay between buildings. Smaller rooms at the back are a bargain, as they face the garden and are quieter. In any case, rooms offer nothing out of the ordinary, and most bathrooms are surprisingly small, with almost no counter space to speak of. *Tip:* The outdoor pool's fee is for use of a locker; forgo that, and you can use the pool free of charge.

3–13–3 Takanawa, Minato-ku, Tokyo 108-8567. ✆ **800/543-4300** in the U.S., or 03/3445-6711. Fax 03/3445-5733. www.lemeridien.com. 954 units. ¥24,255–¥27,142 ($230–$258) single; ¥28,875–¥43,890 ($274–$417) double; ¥33,495–¥43,890 ($318–$417) twin; from ¥57,750 ($549) suite. Rates include service charge. AE, DC, MC, V. Station: Shinagawa (1 min.). **Amenities:** 7 restaurants; 2 bars; 2 lounges; outdoor pool (locker fee: ¥1,500/$14); access to fitness center at Le Meridien Grand Pacific in Odaiba (fee: ¥1,050/$10); concierge; business center; small shopping arcade; salon; room service (6am–midnight); in-room massage; babysitting; same-day laundry/dry-cleaning service; nonsmoking rooms; free shuttle bus to Le Meridien Grand Pacific Tokyo Hotel in Odaiba and Tokyo Disneyland. *In room:* A/C, cable TV w/pay movies, free high-speed dataport (not all rooms), minibar, hot-water pot w/tea, hair dryer, Washlet toilet.

**Shinagawa Prince Hotel** *(Kids)*    With four gleaming white buildings added at various stages (each with its own check-in), the Shinagawa Prince is the largest sleep factory in Japan. It's a virtual city within a city, with more than a dozen food and beverage outlets, a 10-screen cinema complex, an aquarium, a large sports center with nine indoor tennis courts, an 80-lane bowling center, an indoor golf practice center, a SEGA amusement/arcade-game center, indoor and outdoor pools, and a fitness center. It caters to Japanese businessmen on weekdays and to students and family vacationers on weekends and holidays. Rooms vary widely depending on which building you select: The Main Tower has only very small singles, at the cheapest rates; the Annex has singles, twins, and doubles in a medium price range; the 39-story New Tower, with its outdated pastel colors and mostly twins, is no longer very new; the upscale Executive Tower, with only doubles, has the smartest-looking rooms and the highest prices. Assuming you can find it, be sure to have a drink or meal at the 39th-floor Top of Shinagawa; its views of Tokyo Bay and the city are among the best in town. With its many diversions, this hotel is like a resort getaway but is too big and busy for my taste.

4–10–30 Takanawa, Minato-ku, Tokyo 108-8611. ✆ **800/542-8686** or in the U.S. and Canada, or 03/3440-1111. Fax 03/3441-7092. www.princehotelsjapan.com/shinagawaprincehotel. 3,680 units. ¥9,300–¥20,500 ($88–$195) single; ¥16,300–¥34,000 ($155–$323) twin; ¥17,000–¥36,000 ($162–$342) double; AE, DC, MC, V. Station: Shinagawa (2 min.). **Amenities:** 14 restaurants; 1 bar; 24-hr. Internet cafe; sports center (various fees charged, ¥1,050/$10 for indoor pool, ¥1,100/$10 for outdoor pool); tour desk; business center; shopping arcade; convenience store; salon; same-day laundry/dry-cleaning service; nonsmoking rooms; cinema complex; IMAX; amusement arcade; aquarium; children's day-care center. *In room:* A/C, TV, fridge, hot-water pot w/tea, hair dryer.

## OTHER NEIGHBORHOODS

**The Hilltop Hotel (Yama-no-Ue Hotel)** *(★★)* *(Finds)*    This is a delightfully old-fashioned, unpretentious (some might say dowdy) hotel with character. Opened in 1937 and boasting an Art Deco facade, it was once the favorite haunt of writers, including novelist Mishima Yukio. Avoid the cheaper, more boring rooms in the annex unless you spring for the higher-priced Art Septo rooms on the seventh floor with their flower boxes outside the windows, black leather furnishings, LCD TV with CD player, and fancier bathrooms. Otherwise, rooms in the main building have such endearing, homey touches as fringed lampshades, doilies, cherrywood furniture (and mahogany desks), velvet curtains, vanity tables, and old-fashioned heaters with intricate grillwork. Some twins even combine a tatami area and shoji with beds; the most expensive twin overlooks its own Japanese garden. Don't be surprised if the reception desk remembers you by name. Although the Hilltop is not as centrally located or up-to-date as other hotels, nearby Meiji University brings lots of young people to the area.

1–1 Surugadai, Kanda, Chiyoda-ku, Tokyo 101-0062. ✆ **03/3293-2311.** Fax 03/3233-4567. www.yamanoue-hotel. co.jp. 74 units. ¥17,850–¥21,000 ($170–$200) single; ¥23,100–¥29,400 ($219–$279) double; ¥23,100–¥33,600 ($219–$319) twin. AE, DC, MC, V. Station: Ochanomizu or Shin-Ochanomizu (8 min.) or Jimbocho (5 min.). **Amenities:** 7 restaurants; 3 bars; room service (7am–2am); same-day laundry/dry-cleaning service. *In room:* A/C, cable TV, high-speed dataport, minibar, hot-water pot w/tea, hair dryer, Washlet toilet.

## INEXPENSIVE
### NIHOMBASHI

**Hotel Kitcho** *(★)* *(Finds)*    This great-value hotel, open since the mid-1970s, is located in a charming, old-fashioned neighborhood called Ningyo-cho, near the Suitengu Shrine (popular with expectant mothers hoping for a safe delivery). During cherry-blossom season, try to get a room facing the front with its tree-lined median. Rooms,

## Narita Stopover

An early departure out of Narita Airport? A late-night arrival? It might make sense to spend the night near the airport. Topping the list is the **Hilton Narita**, 456 Kosuge, Narita, Chiba 286-0127 (© **800/HILTONS** in the U.S. and Canada, or 0476/33-1121; fax 0476/33-0369; www.hilton.com), a 10-minute free shuttle ride from the airport. With a glass-enclosed garden and waterfall centered in its lobby, it's the only airport hotel that imparts an Asian flair. Facilities include three restaurants (Japanese, Chinese, coffee shop), a top-floor bar with views of the airport, a health club with gym and outdoor pool, and 540 good-size rooms with all the amenities you'd expect. Rates range from ¥20,000 to ¥25,000 ($190–$236) for one person and ¥24,000 to ¥29,000 ($228–$276) for two.

The 500-room **Holiday Inn Tobu Narita**, 320–1 Tokko, Narita, Chiba 286-0106 (© **800/HOLIDAY** or 0476/32-1234; fax 0476/32-0617; www.holidayinntobunarita.com), a 5-minute free shuttle ride from the airport, offers singles starting at ¥11,550 ($110) on weekdays and ¥12,600 ($120) on weekends. Twins are ¥18,900 ($180) and ¥21,000 ($200) respectively. Prices include breakfast and service charge, and facilities include a coffee shop, a Chinese restaurant, and a health club with indoor pool and gym.

If you have 3 hours to spare, consider an excursion to **Narita** (10 min. by train from the airport; most airport hotels also offer shuttle buses), a quaint village with a winding, shop-lined street leading to Narita-san Temple, an impressive complex consisting of a main hall, several pagodas, and a nice park.

mostly single and twins, are tiny but tidy. There's even a Japanese-style room, costing ¥12,000 ($114) for one or two persons, and the hotel goes the extra mile by providing a small library, tea ceremonies in its Japanese restaurant Friday through Sunday afternoons, free use of bikes (reserve in advance), and even a choice of pillows.

2–32–8 Ningyo-cho, Nihombashi, Chuo-ku, Tokyo 103-0013. © **03/3666-6161.** Fax 03/3666-6162. www.kitcho. co.jp. 24 units. ¥7,000–¥9,000 ($67–$86) single; ¥9,000 ($86) double; ¥9,000–¥10,000 ($86–$95) twin. AE, DC, MC, V. Station: Hamacho (3 min.), Suitengu-mae or Ningyo-cho (5 min.). **Amenities:** 2 restaurants (Japanese, coffee shop); small library; in-room massage; coin-op washer and dryer; complimentary bikes. *In room:* A/C, TV, dataport, minibar, hot-water pot w/tea and coffee.

### ASAKUSA

**Ryokan Shigetsu** 🌶🌶 *(Finds)*    Whenever a foreigner living in Tokyo, soon to play host to first-time visitors to Japan, asks me to recommend a moderately priced ryokan in Tokyo, this is the one I most often suggest. It has a great location in Asakusa just off Nakamise Dori, a colorful, shop-lined pedestrian street leading to the famous Sensoji Temple—an area that gives you a feel for the older Japan. A member of the Japanese Inn Group, it represents the best of modern yet traditional Japanese design—simple yet elegant, with shoji, unadorned wood, and artwork throughout. Traditional Japanese music or the recorded chirping of birds play softly in the public spaces. Two public Japanese baths have views of the nearby five-storied pagoda. A Japanese restaurant serves excellent Japanese breakfasts, as well as mini-kaiseki dinners (discounts

given to hotel guests; reserve 1 week in advance; closed Sun–Mon) and lunches. There are 11 Western-style rooms, but I prefer the 12 slightly more expensive Japanese-style tatami rooms, which include Japanese-style mirrors and comfortable chairs for those who don't like relaxing on the floor. In short, this establishment costs no more than a regular business hotel but has much more class.

1–31–11 Asakusa, Taito-ku 111-0032. © **03/3843-2345.** Fax 03/3843-2348. www.shigetsu.com. 23 units. ¥7,665– ¥9,450 ($73–$90) single; ¥14,700–¥26,250 ($140–$249) twin. Japanese or Western breakfast ¥1,300 ($12) extra, Japanese dinner ¥4,200 ($40) extra. AE, MC, V. Station: Asakusa (4 min.). **Amenities:** Restaurant (Japanese); Mac laptop in lobby providing free Internet access; nonsmoking rooms. *In room:* A/C, TV, minibar, hot-water pot w/tea, hair dryer.

## UENO

**Annex Katsutaro** ★★ *(Finds)*   Opened in 2001, this thoroughly modern concrete ryokan is a standout for its simple yet chic designs, spotless Japanese-style rooms (all with bathroom), and location—right in the heart of Yanaka with its old-fashioned neighborhood and about a 20-minute walk northwest of Ueno Park. The Keisei Skyliner from Narita Airport stops at nearby Nippori Station. If you have your own laptop and LAN card, you can tap into the Internet free of charge from your room; or you can use a public computer for free. If the ryokan is full, don't let management talk you into taking a room in its much older main Ryokan Katsutaro; it's not nearly as nice as the annex.

3–8–4 Yanaka, Taito-ku, Tokyo 110-0001. © **03/3828-2500.** Fax 03/3821-5400. www.katsutaro.com. 17 units. ¥6,300 ($60) single; ¥10,500–¥12,600 ($100–$120) twin; ¥14,700–¥16,800 ($140–$160) triple. Continental breakfast ¥840 ($8) extra. AE, MC, V. Station: Sendagi (2 min.) or Nippori (7 min.). **Amenities:** Computer w/Internet access free for guest use; coin-op washers and dryers. *In room:* A/C, TV w/cable, fridge, hot-water pot w/tea and coffee, hair dryer.

**Homeikan** ★★★ *(Finds)*   Although a bit of a hike from Ueno Park (about 30 min.) and not as conveniently located as the other ryokan, this lovely place is my number-one choice if you want to experience an authentic, traditional ryokan in a traditional neighborhood. It consists of three separate buildings acquired over the last century by the present owner's grandfather. Homeikan, the main building (Honkan), was purchased almost 100 years ago; today it is listed as a "Tangible Cultural Property" and is used mainly by groups of students and seniors. Across the street is Daimachi Bekkan, built after World War II to serve as the family home. A beautiful, 31-room property, it boasts a private Japanese garden with a pond, public baths (including one open 24 hr.), and wood-inlaid and pebbled hallways leading to nicely detailed tatami rooms adorned with such features as gnarled wood trim and sitting alcoves, as well as simpler tatami rooms for budget travelers. This is where most foreigners stay, and if you opt for meals, they will be served in your room in true ryokan fashion. The third building, Morikawa Bekkan, about a 5-minute walk away, was built as an inn about 45 years ago and, with 35 rooms, is the largest. Owner Koike-san, who speaks excellent English, points out that travelers who need the latest in creature comforts (including private bathrooms) should go elsewhere; those seeking a traditional ryokan experience, however, will not be disappointed.

5–10–5 Hongo, Bunkyo-ku, Tokyo 113-0033. © **03/3811-1181** or 03/3811-1187. Fax 03/3811-1764. www. hostelworld.com. 91 units (none with bathroom). ¥6,500–¥7,000 ($62–$67) single; ¥11,000–¥12,000 ($105–$114) double; ¥13,500–¥15,000 ($128–$143) triple. ¥500 more per person in peak season; ¥500 less per person in off season. Rates do not include consumption tax. Western- or Japanese-style breakfast ¥1,000 ($9.50); Japanese dinner ¥2,000 ($19; not available 1st night of stay). AE, DC, MC, V. Station: Hongo Sanchome (8 min.) or Kasuga (5 min.). *In room:* A/C, TV, minibar, hot-water pot w/tea, safe.

**Ryokan Sawanoya** ★   Although this family-run ryokan is relatively modern looking and unexciting, it's delightfully located in a wonderful residential area of old Tokyo, northwest of Ueno Park and within walking distance of the park's many

attractions and Nezu Shrine. Upon your arrival, the owner, English-speaking Sawa-san, will give you a short tour of the establishment before taking you to your tatami room; throughout the ryokan are written explanations to help the novice. The owner also gives you a map outlining places of interest in the vicinity. Once a week or so, Sawa-san's son provides guests with a special treat—a traditional Japanese lion dance, free of charge. His daughter-in-law sometimes gives demonstrations of the tea cere-mony. In short, this is a great place to stay thanks to Sawa-san's enthusiastic devotion to his neighborhood, which he readily imparts to his guests. Highly recommended.

2–3–11 Yanaka, Taito-ku, Tokyo 110-0001. ⓒ 03/3822-2251. Fax 03/3822-2252. www.sawanoya.com. 12 units (2 with bathroom). ¥4,935–¥5,250 ($47–$50) single without bathroom; ¥9,240 ($88) double without bathroom, ¥9,879 ($94) double with bathroom; ¥12,600 ($120) triple without bathroom, ¥14,175 ($144) triple with bathroom. Breakfast of toast and fried eggs ¥315 ($3) extra, Japanese breakfast ¥945 ($9) extra. AE, MC, V. Closed Dec 29–Jan 3. Station: Nezu (exit 1, 7 min.). **Amenities:** Computer w/Internet access free for guest use; coin-op washers and dry-ers (free laundry detergent); ironing board, iron, and trouser press (on 3rd floor); free coffee/tea service; public fridge. In room: A/C, TV, dataport, hot-water pot w/tea, hair dryer.

## SHINJUKU

**Tokyo International Youth Hostel** (Value)   This spotless hostel, operated by the Tokyo Metropolitan Government and situated in a high-rise, is definitely the best place to stay in its price range—it offers fantastic Tokyo views. Even the public baths boast good views (especially at night). All beds are dormitory style, with two, four, or five bunk beds to a room. Rooms are very pleasant, with big windows, and each bed has its own curtain for privacy. If there are vacancies, you can stay longer than the normal 6-day maximum. In summer, it's a good idea to reserve about 2 months in advance. The hostel is closed from 10am to 3pm and locked at 10:30pm (lights out at 11pm).

1–1 Kagura-kashi, Shinjuku-ku, Tokyo 162-0823. ⓒ 03/3235-1107. Fax 03/3264-4000. www.tokyo-yh.jp. 158 beds. ¥3,500 ($33) adult; ¥2,000 ($19) child. Breakfast ¥400 ($3.80); dinner ¥900 ($8.55). No youth-hostel card required; no age limit. No credit cards. Closed Dec 29–Jan 3. Station: Iidabashi (2 min.). Reception is on the 18th floor of the Central Plaza Building. **Amenities:** Coin-op computer w/Internet access; shopping mall on 1st and 2nd floors of same building; coin-op washers and dryers; communal kitchen. In room: A/C, no phone.

## SHIBUYA & AOYAMA

**National Children's Castle Hotel (Kodomo-no-Shiro Hotel)** (Kids)   The National Children's Castle, located on Aoyama Dori about halfway between Aoyama and Shibuya (and a bit of a trek from either station), is a great place to stay if you're traveling with young children. Located on the sixth and seventh floors, the hotel is plain rather than playful, but the complex boasts Tokyo's best and most sophisticated indoor/outdoor playground for children. Guests range from businesspeople on week-days to families and young college students on weekends. The rooms—mainly twins—are simple and of adequate size, with large windows. The most expensive twins, which face Shinjuku, have the best views and are a great value. Note that the hotel's three singles do not have windows, but you can pay extra to stay in a twin. The three Japanese-style rooms, available for three or more people, are a good way for fam-ilies to experience the traditional Japanese lifestyle. Make reservations at least 2 months in advance, especially if you plan on being in Tokyo in the summer. Note that there's an 11pm curfew, check-in isn't until 3pm, and not much English is spoken.

5–53–1 Jingumae, Shibuya-ku, Tokyo 150-0001. ⓒ 03/3797-5677. Fax 03/3406-7805. www.kodomono-shiro. or.jp/hotel. 27 units. ¥6,720 ($64) single; ¥14,700–¥16,170 ($140–$154) twin; ¥7,140 ($68) per person Japanese-style room. AE, DC, MC, V. Station: Omotesando (8 min.) or Shibuya (10 min.). Front desk on the 7th floor. **Amenities:** Restaurant (Japanese/Western); National Children's Castle; indoor swimming pool. In room: A/C, TV, hot-water pot w/tea, Washlet toilet.

## ROPPONGI & AKASAKA

**Arca Torre** *(Value)*    This smart-looking, 10-story property looks expensive from the outside but is actually a business hotel. Opened in 2002, it has a great location on Roppongi Dori, between Roppongi Crossing and Roppongi Hills, making it popular with both business types and tourists on a budget. Its (mostly single) rooms are small but cheerful, with flat-panel TVs and complimentary bottled water in the otherwise empty fridge. Rooms facing the back are quiet but face another building. If you opt for a room facing the front, ask for a high floor above the freeway; otherwise, your view will be of cars and, at certain times of the day, traffic jams.

6–1–23 Roppongi, Minato-ku, Tokyo 106-0032. (C) 03/3404-5111. Fax 03/3404-5115. 77 units. ¥11,000–¥13,000 ($105–$124) single; ¥14,000–¥17,000 ($133–$162) double; ¥21,000 ($200) twin. Rates do not include consumption tax. AE, DC, MC, V. Station: Roppongi (1 min.). **Amenities:** Restaurant (coffee shop); same-day laundry/dry-cleaning service; nonsmoking rooms. *In room:* A/C, TV w/cable, fridge, hot-water pot w/tea, hair dryer, Washlet toilet.

**Asia Center of Japan** *(Value)*    Great rates make this a top choice if you're looking for inexpensive Western-style accommodations in the center of town (it's wise to reserve months in advance). Everyone—from businessmen to students to travelers to foreigners teaching English—stays here; I know one teacher who lived here for years. Resembling a college dormitory, the Asia Center is popular with area office workers for its inexpensive cafeteria with outdoor seating. Accommodations are basic, with few frills, and in the singles you can almost reach out and touch all four walls. The cheapest doubles are actually single rooms with small, semi-double-size beds (not quite full size but larger than single/twin size). Avoid rooms on the ground floor—windows can open and in Japan there are no screens. Tucked on a side street off Gaien-Higashi Dori not far from Aoyama Dori, the center is a 15-minute walk to the nightlife of Roppongi or Akasaka, one station away by subway.

8–10–32 Akasaka, Minato-ku, Tokyo 107-0052. (C) 03/3402-6111. Fax 03/3402-0738. www.asiacenter.or.jp. 173 units. ¥8,610–¥10,290 ($82–$98) single; ¥12,390–¥14,490 ($118–$138) double; ¥16,590–¥18,690 ($158–$178) twin. AE, MC, V. Station: Aoyama-Itchome (exit 4, 5 min.) or Nogizaka (exit 3, 5 min.). **Amenities:** Restaurant (international); coin-op computer w/Internet access; coin-op washers and dryers, nonsmoking rooms. *In room:* A/C, cable TV w/pay movies, high-speed dataport (not all rooms), fridge, hot-water pot w/tea, hair dryer, Washlet toilet.

## SHINAGAWA

**Toyoko Inn Shinagawa-Eki Takanawaguchi** *(Value)*    I like this hotel chain for its clean functional rooms, complimentary breakfast of coffee and pastries served in the lobby, free use of dataports, free wireless LAN access in the lobby (and for those who don't have their own laptop, free use of computers in the lobby), and complimentary movies (only occasionally English-language). Rooms are all very small singles and doubles.

4–23–2 Takanawa, Minato-ku, Tokyo 108-0074. (C) 03/3280-1045. Fax 03/3280-1046. www.toyoko-inn.com. 181 units. ¥7,140 ($68) single; ¥8,190–¥9,240 ($78–$88) double. Rates include continental breakfast. AE, DC, MC, V. Station: Shinagawa (3 min.). From JR Station's Takanawa (west) exit, turn left. **Amenities:** Computers w/Internet access free for hotel guests; laundry/dry-cleaning service; nonsmoking rooms. *In room:* A/C, TV w/free movies, free dataport, fridge, hot-water pot w/tea, hair dryer, trouser press.

## IKEBUKURO

**Kimi Ryokan** *(Finds)*    This has long been a Tokyo favorite for inexpensive Japanese-style lodging. Spotlessly clean and with such Japanese touches as sliding screens, a cypress public bath, flower arrangements in public spaces, and traditional Japanese music playing softly in the hallways, it caters almost exclusively to foreigners (mostly

20-somethings) and is so popular there's sometimes a waiting list. A bulletin board lists rental apartments and job opportunities (primarily teaching English); a lounge with cable TV is a favorite hangout and a good place to network with other travelers. Rooms are Japanese style, with singles and the cheapest doubles the size of 4½ tatami mats, and the larger doubles the size of six tatami mats (a single tatami measures 1×1.8m/3×6 ft.). Note that there's a 1am curfew.

2–36–8 Ikebukuro, Toshima-ku, Tokyo 171-0014. © 03/3971-3766. Fax 03/3987-1326. www.kimi-ryokan.jp. 38 units (none with bathroom). ¥4,500 ($43) single; ¥6,500–¥7,500 ($62–$71) double; ¥10,000–¥12,000 ($95–$114) triple. No credit cards. Station: Ikebukuro (west exit, 7 min.). The police station (take the west exit from Ikebukuro Station and turn right) has maps that will guide you to Kimi. *In room:* A/C.

## 4 Where to Dine

From stand-up noodle shops and pizzerias to exclusive kaiseki restaurants and sushi bars, there are at least 80,000 restaurants in Tokyo—which gives you some idea of how fond Japanese are of eating out. In a city where apartments are so small and cramped that entertaining at home is almost unheard of, restaurants serve as places for socializing, meeting friends, and wooing business associates—as well as great excuses for drinking a lot of beer, sake, and whiskey.

**HOW TO DINE IN TOKYO WITHOUT SPENDING A FORTUNE** I know people in Tokyo who claim they haven't cooked in years—and they're not millionaires. They simply take advantage of one of the best deals in Tokyo—the fixed-price lunch, usually available from 11am to 2pm. Called a *teishoku* in a Japanese restaurant, a fixed-price meal is likely to include soup, a main dish such as tempura or whatever the restaurant specializes in, pickled vegetables, rice, and tea. In restaurants serving Western food, the fixed-price lunch is variously referred to as a set lunch, *seto coursu* or simply *coursu*, and usually includes an appetizer, a main course with one or two side dishes, coffee or tea, and sometimes dessert. Even restaurants listed under **Very Expensive**—where you'd otherwise spend at least ¥13,000 ($124) or more for dinner (excluding drinks)—and **Expensive**—where you can expect to pay ¥9,000 to ¥13,000 ($86–$124) for dinner—usually offer set-lunch menus, allowing you to dine in style at very reasonable prices. To keep your costs down, therefore, try having your biggest meal at lunch, avoiding, if possible, the noon-to-1pm weekday crush when Tokyo's army of office workers flood area restaurants. Because Japanese tend to order fixed-price meals rather than a la carte, set dinners are also usually available (though they're not as cheap as set lunches). All-you-can-eat buffets (called *viking* in Japanese), offered by many hotel restaurants, are also bargain meals for hearty appetites.

So many of Tokyo's good restaurants fall into the **Moderate** category that it's tempting to simply eat your way through the city—and the range of cuisines is so great you could eat something different at each meal. A dinner in this category will average ¥4,000 to ¥8,000 ($38–$86). Lunch is likely to cost half as much.

Many of Tokyo's most colorful, noisy, and popular restaurants fall into the **Inexpensive** category, where meals usually go for less than ¥4,000 ($38); indeed, many offer meals for less than ¥2,000 ($19) and lunches for ¥1,000 ($9.50) and less. The city's huge working population heads to these places to catch a quick lunch or to socialize with friends after hours. In the past few years, a number of excellent yet inexpensive French bistros and Italian trattorie have burst onto the culinary scene. Ethnic restaurants, particularly those serving Indian, Chinese, and other Asian cuisines, are also plentiful and usually inexpensive. Hotel restaurants are also good bargains for

---

## ⟨Tips⟩ Mapping Out Tokyo's Restaurants

You can locate the restaurants reviewed below using the following neighborhood maps:

- To locate restaurants in **Akasaka,** p. 119.
- To locate restaurants in **Ueno,** p. 125.
- To locate restaurants in **Shinjuku,** p. 128.
- To locate restaurants in **Asakusa,** p. 133.
- To locate restaurants in **Hibiya** and **Ginza,** p. 144.
- To locate restaurants in **Harajuku & Aoyama,** p. 157.
- To locate restaurants in **Roppongi,** p. 163.

---

inexpensive set lunches. Finally, see "Tokyo After Dark" in chapter 5 for suggestions on inexpensive drinking places that serve food.

**OTHER DINING NOTES**   The restaurants listed below are organized first by neighborhood and then by price category. For information on Japanese food, refer to "Tips on Dining, Japanese Style" in chapter 2.

Note that the 5% consumption tax is now included in menu prices. However, many first-class restaurants, as well as hotel restaurants, will add a 10% to 15% service charge to the bill. Unless otherwise stated, the prices given below include the tax but not the service charge.

Note that restaurants that have no signs in English letters are preceded by a numbered icon, which is keyed to a list of **Japanese symbols** in appendix C.

Finally, keep in mind that the **last order** is taken at least 30 minutes before the restaurant's actual closing time, sometimes even an hour before closing at the more exclusive restaurants.

## HIBIYA & GINZA
### EXPENSIVE

**Kamon** 𝒶𝒶𝒶 TEPPANYAKI   Kamon, which means "Gate of Celebration," has an interior that could be a statement on Tokyo itself—traditionally Japanese yet ever so high-tech. Located on the 17th floor of the Imperial Hotel, the restaurant offers seating at one of several large counters (some with views over Hibiya) centered around grills where expert chefs prepare excellent teppanyaki before your eyes. Japanese sirloin steaks or filets, cooked to perfection, are available, as well as seafood ranging from fresh prawns and scallops to crabmeat and fish, and seasonal vegetables. The service is, of course, imperial.

On the 17th floor of the Imperial Hotel, 1-1-1 Uchisaiwai-cho. ⓒ **03/3504-1111.** www.imperialhotel.co.jp. Reservations recommended for dinner. Set dinners ¥9,450–¥18,900 ($90–$180); set lunches ¥3,675–¥7,350 ($35–$70). AE, DC, MC, V. Daily 11:30am–2:30pm and 5:30–9:30pm. Station: Hibiya (1 min.).

**Ten-ichi** 𝒶 TEMPURA   In this restaurant, located on Namiki Dori in the heart of Ginza's nightlife, you can sit at a counter and watch the chef prepare your meal. This is the main outlet of a 75-year-old restaurant chain that helped the tempura style of cooking gain worldwide recognition by serving important foreign customers. Today Ten-ichi still has one of the best reputations in town for serving the most delicately fried foods, along with its special sauce (or, if you prefer, you can dip the morsels in lemon juice with a pinch of salt).

There are a dozen Ten-ichi restaurants in Tokyo. Locations include the Ginza Sony Building at the intersection of Harumi Dori and Sotobori Dori (𝄞 **03/3571-3837;** station: Hibiya or Ginza); the Imperial Hotel's Tower basement (𝄞 **03/3503-1001;** station: Hibiya); Akasaka Tokyu Plaza (𝄞 **03/3581-2166;** station: Akasaka-mitsuke); and Isetan department store, 3–14–1 Shinjuku (𝄞 **03/5379-3039;** station: Shinjuku Sanchome).

6–6–5 Ginzai. 𝄞 **03/3571-1949.** Reservations recommended for lunch, required for dinner. Set dinners ¥10,500– ¥18,000 ($100–$171); set lunches ¥7,350–¥10,500 ($70–$100). AE, DC, MC, V. Daily 11:30am–9:30pm. Station: Ginza (3 min.). On Namiki Dori.

## MODERATE

① **Donto** 🌟🌟 *finds* VARIED JAPANESE   Located in Hibiya on Harumi Dori in the basement of an unlikely looking office building, this is a great place for lunch. Popular with the local working crowd (and therefore best avoided noon–1pm), it's pleasantly decorated in a rustic style with shoji screens, wooden floors, and an open kitchen. Take off your shoes at the entryway and put them into one of the wooden lockers. Choose what you want from the plastic display case, which shows various teishoku and set meals. Everything from noodles, sashimi, tempura, and obento to kaiseki is available. Unfortunately, the best deals are daily specials written in Japanese only; ask about them or look around at what others are eating.

There's another Donto on the 49th floor of the Sumitomo Building in Shinjuku (𝄞 **03/3344-6269;** station: Tochomae), open the same hours.

Yurakucho Denki Building basement, 1–7–1 Yurakucho, on Harumi Dori. 𝄞 **03/3201-3021.** Set dinners ¥3,500– ¥4,500 ($33–$43); set lunches ¥750–¥950 ($7.15–$9.05). AE, DC, MC, V. Mon–Sat 11am–2pm and 5–11pm. Closed holidays. Station: Hibiya (1 min.).

② **Ginza Daimasu** KAISEKI/OBENTO   This 90-year-old restaurant has a simple, modern decor with Japanese touches. Experienced, kimono-clad waitresses serve artfully arranged set meals from the English-language menu. The *Fukiyose-zen obento*— many delicate dishes served in three courses—includes beautiful tempura delicacies and a menu (in Japanese) explaining what you're eating. A plastic-food display in the front window will help you recognize the restaurant. Set lunches are served until 4pm.

6–9–6 Ginza. 𝄞 **03/3571-3584.** Reservations required for kaiseki. Kaiseki ¥5,250–¥12,600 ($50–$120); obento ¥2,415–¥3,675 ($23–$35); set lunches ¥2,100–¥2,500 ($20–$24). AE, DC, MC, V. Daily 11:30am–9:30pm (last order 8:30pm). Station: Ginza (2 min.). Across from Matsuzakaya department store on Chuo Dori.

**Kihachi** 🌟 FUSION-CROSSOVER   With a cool, crisp interior accented with Art Nouveau trimmings, this restaurant offers an interesting French menu that combines flavors of the West with Japanese and Asian ingredients, creations of its French-trained chef. Past choices on the English-language menu have included starters like seared foie gras and bamboo shoot with miso mustard sauce; mains have included braised beef with red-wine and miso sauce, and fried veal crusted spicy sesame and black peppers with hot vegetable salad. The hardest part of dining here? Limiting yourself to one meal—you just might have to come back.

2–2–6 Ginza. 𝄞 **03/3567-6281.** Main dishes ¥2,625–¥4,410 ($25–$42); set dinners ¥4,000–¥10,000 ($38–$95); set lunches ¥2,500–¥5,000 ($24–$48). AE, DC, MC, V. Daily 11:30am–3pm and 6–9:30pm (last order). Station: Yurakucho (5 min.). Near the Tourist Information Center and Printemps department store.

③ **Ohmatsuya** 🌟🌟 *finds* JAPANESE GRILL   Enter this second-floor restaurant of a nondescript building and you're instantly back in time: After you're greeted by

# Hibiya & Ginza

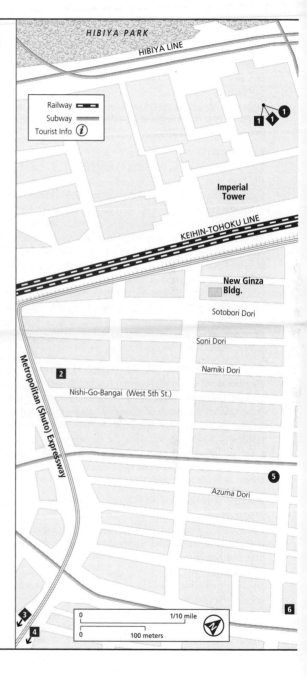

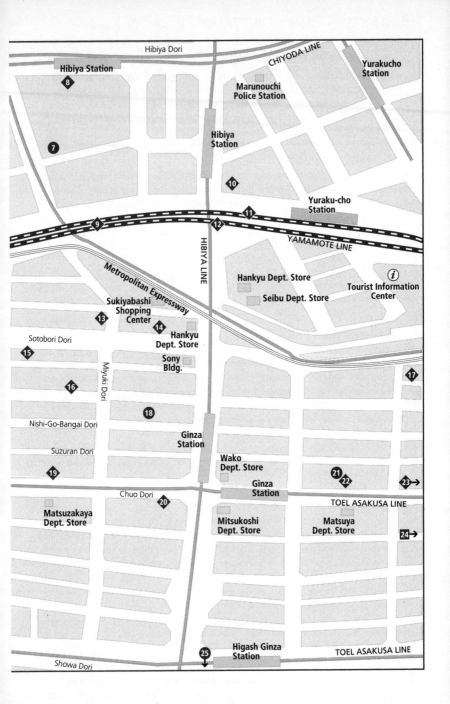

---

*Tips*  **A Note on Japanese Symbols**

Many establishments and attractions in Japan do not have signs in Roman (English-language) letters. Those that don't are indicated in this guide by an oval with a number that corresponds to a number in appendix C showing the Japanese symbols. Thus, to find the Japanese symbol for, say, **Rangetsu** (below), refer to no. 4 in appendix C.

---

waitresses clad in traditional country clothing, you'll find yourself enveloped in an old farmhouse atmosphere. (Part of the decor is from a 17th-c. samurai house in northern Japan.) Even the style of cooking is traditional, as customers grill their own food over a hibachi. Sake, served in a length of bamboo, is drunk from bamboo cups. Dinner menus (English-language) include such delicacies as grilled fish, skewered meat, and vegetables. This true find—and easy to find at that—is located on Sony Street, the small side street behind the Sony Building.

6–5–8 Ginza. ⓒ 03/3571-7053. Reservations required. Set dinners ¥5,040–¥9,450 ($48–$90), plus a ¥500 ($4.75) table charge. AE, DC, MC, V. Mon–Fri 5–10pm; Sat 4:30–9pm (last order). Closed holidays. Station: Ginza (3 min.). On the 2nd floor of the modern Ail D'Or Building behind the Sony Building on Sony St.

④ **Rangetsu** SUKIYAKI/SHABU-SHABU/KAISEKI/OBENTO  This well-known Ginza restaurant has been dishing out sukiyaki, shabu-shabu, obento, and steaks since 1947. It uses only Matsuzaka beef (bought whole and carved up by the chefs), which ranges from costlier fine-marbled beef to cheaper cuts with thick marbling. There are also crab dishes (including a crab sukiyaki), kaiseki, sirloin steaks, and eel dishes. Especially good deals are the obento box meals (available day and night and offering a variety of small dishes) and the set lunches served until 2:30pm. In the basement is a sake bar with more than 80 different kinds of sake from all over Japan, which you can also order with your meal.

3–5–8 Ginza. ⓒ 03/3567-1021. Reservations recommended. Beef sukiyaki or shabu-shabu set meals from ¥7,500 ($71) for dinner, ¥2,200 ($21) for lunch; obento meals and mini-kaiseki ¥2,200–¥5,500 ($21–$52); set lunches ¥1,200–¥3,800 ($11–$36). AE, DC, MC, V. Daily 11:30am–10pm. Station: Ginza (3 min.). On Chuo Dori across from the Matsuya department store.

**Sal Imperial Viking** ⚘ INTERNATIONAL  No, this has nothing to do with Scandinavian invaders; rather, *viking* is the Japanese word for "all-you-can-eat buffet." Although lots of Tokyo hotels now offer such spreads, this 17th-floor restaurant has been serving buffets for more than 40 years. It offers more than 40 mostly European and some international dishes, which vary according to seasonal food promotions spotlighting a country's cuisine, from Indonesian to Swiss. Views are of Ginza and Hibiya Park, and there's live jazz in the evenings. This restaurant has enjoyed great popularity for decades, making reservations a must.

Imperial Hotel, 17th floor, 1–1–1 Uchisaiwai-cho. ⓒ 03/3504-1111. www.imperialhotel.co.jp. Reservations recommended. Buffet dinner ¥7,875 ($75); buffet lunch ¥5,250 ($50). AE, DC, MC, V. Daily 11:30am–2:30pm and 5:30–9:30pm. Station: Hibiya (1 min.).

**Zipangu** VARIED JAPANESE  Just outside the Ginza and located high in the sky—on the 47th floor of the new Caretta Shiodome Building with shimmering views over Tokyo Bay—this contemporary Japanese restaurant offers set meals for lunch that

are difficult to describe—the constantly changing presentations border on nouvelle Japanese cuisine, with international influences. In the evenings, the stone-and-wood venue is more of a drinking bar, with an a la carte menu offering charcoal-grilled steak, yakitori, dim sum, and dishes that go well with wine. In any case, this is a great choice if you're visiting nearby Hama Rikyu Garden.

Caretta Shiodome, 1–8–1 Higashi-Shimbashi. ⓒ 03/6215-8111. Reservations required. Main dishes ¥1,260 – ¥2,625 ($12–$25); set lunches ¥3,000–¥8,400 ($29–$80). AE, DC, MC, V. Daily 11:30am–2:30pm and 5–10pm (last order). Station: Shiodome (2 min.) or Shimbashi (5 min.).

## INEXPENSIVE

In addition to the restaurants here, there's a branch of the tonkatsu restaurant **Maisen** in the Mitsui Building at 1–1–2 Yurakucho, near the Imperial Hotel (ⓒ **03/ 3503-1886**; see review in "Harajuku & Aoyama," later in this chapter). In addition, a number of restaurants on the eighth floor of **Matsuya Ginza department store** serve everything from French and Chinese food to sushi, tempura, noodles, and more.

For atmospheric dining, head to an arch underneath the elevated Yamanote railway tracks located about halfway between Harumi Dori and the Imperial Hotel Tower; it has a handful of **tiny yakitori stands,** each with a few tables and chairs. They cater to a rather boisterous working-class clientele, mainly men. The atmosphere, unsophisticated and dingy, harks back to prewar Japan, somewhat of an anomaly in the otherwise chic Ginza. Stalls are open from about 5pm to midnight Monday to Saturday.

**Andy's Shin Hinomoto** ⟨Value⟩ VARIED JAPANESE   Occupying its own arch underneath the Yamanote tracks, this Japanese-style pub is owned by Andy, a Brit, who buys all his seafood and vegetables fresh daily at Tsukiji market. The upstairs is the place to be, with its arched ceiling and mixed foreign and Japanese crowd. If you don't have reservations, you'll be shunted into the less ambient downstairs, where you'll feel like a refugee in a fallout shelter as you sit elbow-to-elbow with local office workers at long tables under fluorescent lighting. Sashimi, grilled fish, tempura, sautéed vegetables, deep-fried chicken, tofu, salad, and much more is offered on the English-language menu.

2–4–4 Yurakucho. ⓒ 03/3214-8021. Main dishes ¥500–¥1,600 ($4.75–$15). No credit cards. Daily 5pm–midnight. Station: Yurakucho or Ginza (1 min.). Underneath the Yamanote elevated tracks, across from the Yurakucho Denki Building.

---

## ⟨Kids⟩ Family-Friendly Restaurants

**Cafe Creperie Le Bretagne (p. 159)**   If sweet bean paste is not your child's idea of dessert, then perhaps the crepes at this casual establishment will do the trick, filled with fruit, chocolate, and other yummy concoctions.

**Hard Rock Cafe (p. 166)**   This internationally known establishment should pacify grumbling teenagers. They can munch on hamburgers, gaze at famous guitars and other rock-'n'-roll memorabilia and, most importantly, buy that Hard Rock Cafe T-shirt.

**Kua' Aina (p. 161)**   When your kids start asking for "real food," take them here for the best burgers in town.

⑤ **Fukusuke** SUSHI   In this basement full of cheap restaurants, called Ginza Palmy, walk all the way to the back (away from Harumi Dori) to this very inexpensive sushi bar, popular with area office workers. It has an exceptionally long counter, which makes it a good choice if you're looking for an empty seat during the noon-to-1pm rush. (A branch of the same restaurant lies catty-corner.) A counter outside displays set meals. The ¥893 ($8.50) set lunch includes soup, sushi, Japanese pickles, and tea.

Mosaic Building B2, 5–2–1 Ginza. ⓒ 03/3573-0471. Sushi a la carte ¥150–¥500 ($1.45–$4.75); set dinners ¥1,365–¥3,360 ($13–$32); set lunches ¥893–¥2,940 ($8.50–$28). AE, DC, MC, V. Daily 11am–10pm. Station: Ginza or Hibiya (4 min.). In the 2 basement on Sotobori Dori at Sukiyabashi Crossing.

**La Boheme** ITALIAN   The food is passable, but what sets La Boheme apart is that it's open every day until 5am, making it a good bet for a late-night meal. I also like its huge, open kitchen in the middle of the room, surrounded by a U-shaped counter that provides a ringside view of the action. The pasta ranges from spaghetti with eggplant and tomato sauce to spaghetti Bolognese, along with Japanese-style versions like steamed breast of chicken with Japanese baby leek, spinach, and sesame oil.

You'll find other La Boheme restaurants at many popular spots around Tokyo, including the Ginza at 1–2–3 Ginza (ⓒ **03/5524-3616**); in Harajuku at 6–8–18 Jingumae (ⓒ **03/3400-3406**) and 5–8–5 Jingumae (ⓒ **03/5467-5666**); in Aoyama at 6–2–2 Minami Aoyama (ⓒ **03/6418-4242**); in Shibuya at 1–6–8 Jinnan (ⓒ **03/3477-0481**); in Nishi Azabu at 2–25–18 Nishi Azabu (ⓒ **03/3407-1363**); in Meguro at 4–19–17 Shirokanedai (ⓒ **03/3442-4488**); and on the fourth floor of Mediage on Odaiba (ⓒ **03/3599-4801**). All are open daily from 11:30am to 5am.

6–4–1 Ginza ⓒ 03/3572-5005. www.global-dining.com Pizza and pasta ¥550–¥1,400 ($5.25–$13); set lunches ¥900–¥1,300 ($8.55–$12). AE, DC, MC, V. Daily 11:30am–5am. Station: Hibiya (5 min.) or Ginza (10 min.). Behind Mosaic, on a corner.

**Manpuku** ⟨Value⟩ YAKITORI   This yakitori restaurant is different from the others under the Yamanote tracks in that it offers tables along a covered passageway where you can watch office workers bustling by. With its old posters both inside and out, it has a slight post–World War II retro feel (it's sign boasts "Retro Dining") and offers an English-language menu with yakitori, tuna cutlet with wasabi, braised tofu with meat, and other pub grub, along with some more unusual choices like stir-fried garlic horse meat and "grilled aborigine" (which turns out to be eggplant—you have to wonder, did they mean aubergine?).

2–4–1 Yurakucho. ⓒ 03/3211-6001. Main dishes ¥504–¥1,239 ($4.80–$12). No credit cards. Open 24 hr., except Sat–Mon night when it's closed nightly 1am–11am. Station: Yurakucho or Hibiya (1 min.). On Harumi Dori, underneath the elevated Yamanote tracks between the Sony Building and Yurakucho Denki building.

⑥ **Shabusen** ⟨Value⟩ SHABU-SHABU   Located on the second floor of a fashion department store just a stone's throw from Ginza 4–chome Crossing (the Harumi Dori–Chuo Dori intersection), this is a fun restaurant where you can cook your own sukiyaki or shabu-shabu in a boiling pot as you sit at a round counter. It's also one of the few restaurants that caters to individual diners (shabu-shabu is usually shared by a group). Orders are shouted back and forth among the staff, service is rapid, and the place is lively. There's an English-language menu complete with cooking instructions, so it's user-friendly. The special shabu-shabu dinner for ¥4,147 ($39), with appetizer, tomato ("super dressing") salad, beef, vegetables, noodles or rice porridge, and dessert, is enough for most voracious appetites.

You'll find a branch of Shabusen in the basement of the same building (© **03/ 3572-3806**).

Core Building 2F, 5–8–20 Ginza. © **03/3571-1717**. Set dinners ¥2,310–¥5,880 ($22–$56); set lunches ¥976–¥3,150 ($9.25–$30). AE, DC, MC, V. Daily 11am–10pm. Station: Ginza (1 min.). On Chuo Dori next to the Nissan Building.

**Zest Cantina** TEX-MEX  You can probably find better Mexican restaurants at home, but this will do for a quick fix, especially once the margaritas kick in. It offers chicken and cheese burritos, shrimp enchiladas, tacos, and other Tex-Mex fare, as well as steaks, hamburgers, and very good salads in a rustic, cowboy-themed setting. This restaurant is actually one of four restaurants ensconced under a freeway in a nifty dining complex called **G-Zone**, all part of a chain belonging to the Global Dining group (www.global-dining.com). Southeast Asian fare is offered in **Monsoon** (© **03/ 5524-3631**); pizza and pasta in Italian-themed **La Boheme** (© **03/5524-3616;** see above); and Japanese food in **Gonpachi** (© **03/5524-3641;** see "Roppongi" later in this chapter for a review). English-language menus, inexpensive food, friendly and polished staff, and late opening hours make all Global Dining restaurants winners whether you're a Tokyo novice or a pro.

You'll find other Zest Cantinas, all open 11:30am to 5am, in Harajuku at 6–7–18 Jingumae (© **03/3409-6268**); in Shibuya at 1–6–8 Jinnan (© **03/5489-3332**); in Ebisu at 1–22–19 Ebisu (© **03/5475-6291**); and in Odaiba on the fourth floor of Mediage (© **03/3599-4803**).

1–2–3 Ginza. © **03/5524-3621**. www.global.dining.com. Main dishes ¥1,000–¥1,800 ($9.50–$17); set lunches ¥800–¥1,500 ($7.60–$14). AE, DC, MC, V. Daily 11:30am–5am. Station: Kyobashi (exit 3, 2 min.) or Ginza-Itchome (exit 7, 1 min.). On Chuo Dori, at the northern edge of Ginza.

## AROUND TOKYO STATION
### MODERATE
**Aux Amis Tokyo** ⚜ FRENCH  This small, tony restaurant specializing in creative French cuisine is one of several on the top two floors of the newly remodeled Marunouchi Building (called *Maru Biru* by locals), located on the Marunouchi (west) side of Tokyo Station. Sweeping views make it a dining hot spot (reserve one of the few coveted window seats), as do an extensive wine list and a changing French/Japanese menu that might include such entrees as roast lamb with herbs of Provence, pork filet in a red-wine sauce, or fish of the day. It's also a great spot for lunch, but note that the rather bare dining room fails to absorb the constant chatter of this popular venue. Other restaurants on the two floors serve shabu-shabu, sushi, tempura, and kaiseki, as well as Italian, Thai, French, and Chinese cuisines. There are many more inexpensive eateries in the basement.

Marunouchi Building, 35th floor, 2–4–1 Marunouchi. © **03/5220-4011**. Main dishes ¥3,675–¥4,515 ($35–$43); set dinners ¥6,300–¥12,600 ($60–$120); set lunches ¥2,940–¥8,400 ($23–$42). AE, DC, MC, V. Daily 11am–2:30pm and 5:30–11pm (last order). Station: Tokyo (Marunouchi exit, 2 min.).

### INEXPENSIVE
In addition to the choices here, there's a **Kua' Aina** outlet selling hamburgers in the Marunouchi Building across from Tokyo Station at 2–4–1 Marunouchi (© **03/5220-2400;** see "Harajuku & Aoyama," later in this chapter, for a review).

**Central Mikuni's** ⚜ VARIED JAPANESE/SUSHI/FUSION/INTERNATIONAL This is my top pick for a reasonably priced Japanese meal in Tokyo Station. Owned by popular local chef Mikuni, it resembles an early-20th-century diner and is divided

into themed sections flanking a central open kitchen. The conveyor-belt sushi counter, with dishes color-coded according to price, offers standards as well as original creations, including Mexican and Californian rolls. Diners help themselves to dishes that appeal to them. There are also so-called "compartment" set meals featuring French/Italian/Japanese fusion cuisine, served in retro-style booths, as well as inexpensive noodle and rice dishes served cafeteria-style. Weekday Continental lunches start at ¥1,050 ($10), while in the evening part of the restaurant transforms into a Japanese-style pub with drinks and snacks. There's also a wine bar. In short, this restaurant's offerings are so varied that you could dine here several days in a row, each time with a different dining experience.

Basement of Tokyo Station, 1–9–1 Marunouchi. ⓒ **03/5218-5123.** Sushi a la carte ¥150–¥500 ($1.45–$4.75) for lunch, ¥550–¥950 ($5.25–$9.05) for dinner; compartment lunches ¥2,100–¥3,800 ($20–$36); compartment dinners ¥2,500–¥5,800 ($24–$55). AE, DC, MC, V. Daily 11am–10pm. Station: Tokyo. Underneath Tokyo Station, with an entrance on the south end of the Marunouchi side.

## TSUKIJI

Since Tsukiji is home to the nation's largest wholesale fish market, it's not surprising that this area abounds in sushi and seafood restaurants. In addition to the recommendations here, don't neglect the many stalls in and around the market where you can eat everything from noodles to fresh sashimi.

### MODERATE

⑦ **Tentake** FUGU   People who really know their *fugu,* or blowfish, will tell you that the only proper time to eat it is October through March, when it's fresh. You can eat fugu year-round, however, and a good place to try this Japanese delicacy is Tentake, popular with the Tsukiji working crowd. An English-language menu lists dishes such as tempura fugu, along with complete fugu dinners with all the trimmings. Otherwise, if you want suggestions, try the *fugu-chiri* for ¥2,800 ($27), a do-it-yourself meal in which you cook raw blowfish, cabbage, dandelion leaves, and tofu in a pot of boiling water in front of you—this was more than I could eat, but you can make a complete meal of it by ordering the fugu-chiri course for ¥6,500 ($62), which adds tempura, yakitori, and other dishes. You can wash it all down with fugu sake. If someone in your party doesn't like fugu, I recommend the crab set menu for ¥4,090 ($39). And yes, that's fugu swimming in the fish tank.

Before you eat here, be sure you read about fugu in "Tips on Dining, Japanese Style," in chapter 2.

6–16–6 Tsukiji. ⓒ **03/3541-3881.** Fugu dishes ¥1,000–¥3,900 ($9.50–$37); fugu set courses ¥4,800–¥13,500 ($46–$128); set lunches ¥840–¥1,050 ($8–$10). AE, MC, V. Daily 11:30am–9:30pm (last order). Station: Tsukiji (7 min.). From the Harumi Dori/Shinohashi intersection, walk on Harumi Dori in the opposite direction of Ginza; the restaurant is on the left just before the bridge in a modern building.

### INEXPENSIVE

⑧ **Edogin** SUSHI   There are four Edogin sushi restaurants in Tsukiji, all located within walking distance of one another. Since they're close to the famous fish market, you can be sure that the fish will be fresh. There's nothing aesthetic about the main Edogin, first established about 80 years ago—the lights are bright, it's packed with the locals, and it's noisy and busy. It's particularly crowded during lunch and dinnertime because the food is dependably good and plentiful. The menu is in Japanese only, but an illustrated menu outside displays some of the set meals, with prices for most ¥3,000 ($29) or less. As an alternative, look at what the people around you are eating or, if it's

lunchtime, order the teishoku (served until 2pm). The nigiri-zushi teishoku for ¥1,050 ($10) offers a variety of sushi, along with soup and pickled vegetables; if you're really hungry, a more plentiful nigiri-zushi teishoku is available for ¥1,470 ($14).

4–5–1 Tsukiji. ✆ 03/3543-4401. Set meals ¥1,600–¥4,200 ($15–$40); lunch teishoku ¥1,050–¥1,470 ($10–$14). AE, DC, MC, V. Mon–Sat 11:30am–9:30pm; Sun and holidays 11:30am–9pm. Station: Tsukiji (3 min.). Located near the Harumi and Shinohashi Dori intersection behind McDonald's; anyone in the neighborhood can point you in the right direction.

⑨ **Sushi Dai** ✻ SUSHI    Located right in the Tsukiji Fish Market, this sushi bar boasts some of the freshest fish in town (and often a long line of people queuing to get in; waits can be up to an hour). The easiest thing to do is order the *seto*, a set sushi course that usually comes with tuna, eel, shrimp, and other morsels, plus six rolls of tuna and rice in seaweed *(onigiri)*. You won't get plates here—food is served directly on the raised counter in front of you.

Tsukiji Fish Market. ✆ 03/3547-6797. Sushi a la carte ¥220–¥1,000 ($2.10–$10); sushi seto ¥2,100–¥3,760 ($20–$36). No credit cards. Mon–Sat 5am–2pm. Closed Wed if the market is closed, and also on holidays. Station: Tsukijijo (2 min.) or Tsukiji (10 min.). Located in a row of barracks housing other restaurants and shops beside the covered market, in Building 6 in the 3 alley (just past the mailbox); it's the 3rd shop on the right.

## ASAKUSA
### MODERATE
⑩ **Komagata Dojo** ✻ *Finds* DOJO    This is a restaurant very much out of the Edo Period. Following a tradition spanning 200 years and now in its sixth generation of owners, this old-style dining hall specializes in *dojo,* a tiny sardinelike river fish that translates as "loach." It's served in a variety of styles, from grilled to stewed. Easiest is to order one of the set meals, which includes a popular *dojo nabe,* cooked on a charcoal burner at your table (dojo nabe ordered a la carte costs ¥1,500/$14). Otherwise, look around and order what someone else is eating. The dining area is a single large room of tatami mats, with ground-level boards serving as tables and waitresses in traditional dress moving quietly about.

1–7–12 Komagata, Taito-ku. ✆ 03/3842-4001. Reservations recommended for dinner. Dojo dishes ¥1,250–¥1,470 ($12–$14); set meals ¥2,200–¥6,800 ($21–$65). AE, DC, MC, V. Daily 11am–9pm. Station: Asakusa (3 min.). To reach the restaurant, walk south on Edo Dori (away from Kaminarimon Gate and Sensoji Temple); the restaurant—a large, old-fashioned wood house on a corner, with blue curtains at its door—is on the right side of the street, about a 5-min. walk from Kaminarimon Gate, past the UFJ Bank.

**La Ranarita Azumabashi** ✻ ITALIAN    The Asahi Beer Tower may not mean anything to you, but if I mention the building with the golden hops poised on top, you'll certainly know it when you see it (the building was designed by Philippe Starck). The Asahi Beer Tower is the high-rise beside the golden hops, looking like . . . a foaming beer mug? On the top floor (in the foam) is this Italian restaurant with soaring walls and great views of Asakusa. It's a perfect perch from which to watch barges on the river or the sun set over Asakusa as you dine on everything from pizza to pasta to grilled scampi. The set lunches, which begin at ¥1,000 ($9.50) on weekdays and ¥1,800 ($17) on weekends and holidays, include an antipasto, salad, main dish, and coffee. If you want a ringside seat, make a reservation at least 3 days in advance or avoid the weekends.

Asahi Beer Tower (on the opposite side of the Sumida River from Sensoji Temple), 22nd floor, 1–23–1 Azumabashi. ✆ 03/5608-5277. Reservations recommended on weekends. Pizza ¥1,550–¥2,200 ($15–$21); pasta ¥1,100– ¥1,900 ($11–$18); main dishes ¥1,900–¥3,900 ($18–$37). AE, DC, MC, V. Mon–Sat 11:30am–2pm (last order) and 5–9pm (last order); Sun and holidays 11:30am–3pm and 4–8pm (last order). Station: Asakusa (4 min.).

⑪ **Mugitoro** YAM/KAISEKI Founded about 60 years ago but now housed in a new building, this restaurant specializes in yam *(tororo-imo)* kaiseki and has a wide following among middle-aged Japanese women. Popular as a health food, the yams used here are imported from the mountains of Akita Prefecture and are featured in almost all the dishes. If you're on a budget or want a quick meal, come for the weekday lunch buffet offered until 1pm; it includes a main dish like fish or beef, yam in some form, vegetable, soup, and rice. Deposit ¥1,000 ($9.50) into the pot on the table and help yourself.

2–2–4 Kaminarimon. Ⓒ 03/3842-1066. Reservations recommended. Set dinners ¥4,000–¥10,500 ($38–$100); set lunches weekends/holidays ¥2,500–¥3,500 ($24–$33). AE, DC, MC, V. Mon–Fri 11:30am–9pm (last order); Sat–Sun and holidays 11am–9pm. Station: Asakusa (2 min.). From Sensoji Temple, walk south (with your back to Kaminarimon Gate) until you reach the big intersection with the stoplight. Komagata-bashi Bridge will be to your left; Mugitoro is right beside the bridge on Edo Dori, next to a tiny temple and playground. Look for the big white lantern hanging outside.

## INEXPENSIVE

⑫ **Chinya** ⓡ (Value) SHABU-SHABU/SUKIYAKI Established in 1880, Chinya is an old sukiyaki restaurant with a new home in a seven-story building to the left of Kaminarimon Gate. The entrance to this place is open-fronted; all you'll see is a man waiting to take your shoes and a hostess in a kimono ready to lead you to one of the tatami-floored dining areas above. Chinya offers very good shabu-shabu or sukiyaki set lunches for ¥2,415 ($23), available until 4pm and including soup and side dishes. Otherwise, dinner set meals of shabu-shabu or sukiyaki, including rice and soup, begin at ¥2,625 ($25). A display case out front shows a few options, but the very good English-language menu includes instructions, making this a good bet for the sukiyaki/shabu-shabu novice.

1–3–4 Asakusa. Ⓒ 03/3841-0010. Set meals ¥2,625–¥12,600 ($25–$120). AE, DC, MC, V. Mon–Sat 11:45am–9:15pm; Sun and holidays 11:30am–9pm. Station: Asakusa (1 min.). On Kaminarimon Dori; located to the left of the Kaminarimon Gate if you stand facing Asakusa Kannon Temple (look for the SUKIYAKI sign).

**Kamiya Bar** VARIED JAPANESE/WESTERN This inexpensive restaurant, established in 1880 as the first Western bar in Japan, serves both Japanese and Western fare on its three floors. The first floor is the bar, popular with older, tobacco-smoking Japanese men. The second floor offers Western food of a sort (that is, the Japanese version of Western food), including fried chicken, smoked salmon, spaghetti, fried shrimp, and hamburger steak; the third floor serves Japanese food ranging from udon noodles and yakitori to tempura and sashimi. I personally prefer the third floor for both its food and its atmosphere. Although the menus are in Japanese only, extensive plastic-food display cases show set meals of Japanese food costing ¥1,500 to ¥3,500 ($14–$33). This is a very casual restaurant, very much a place for older locals, and it can be quite noisy and crowded.

1–1–1 Asakusa. Ⓒ 03/3841-5400. Main dishes ¥610–¥1,500 ($5.80–$14). No credit cards. Wed–Mon 11:30am–9:30pm (last order). Station: Asakusa (1 min.). Located on Kaminarimon Dori in a plain, brown-tiled building between Kaminarimon Gate and the Sumida River.

⑬ **Namiki Yabusoba** ⓡ NOODLES Asakusa's best-known noodle shop, founded in 1913, offers plain buckwheat noodles in cold or hot broth as well as more substantial tempura with noodles, all listed on an English-language menu. Seating is at tables or on tatami mats, and it's a small place, so you won't be able to linger if people are waiting.

2–11–9 Kaminarimon. ✆ **03/3841-1340.** Dishes ¥650–¥1,600 ($6.20–$15). No credit cards. Fri–Wed 11:30am–7:30pm. Station: Asakusa (2 min.). From Kaminarimon Gate, walk south (away from Sensoji Temple) 1 min.; Namiki is on the right side of the street, a brown building with bamboo trees, a small maple, and a stone lantern by the front door.

⑭ **Sansado** TEMPURA   Located right beside Kaminarimon Gate, next to the Kurodaya paper shop, this simple tempura restaurant specializes in Edo-style tempura, fried in a light oil. On the first floor, seating is either at tables or on tatami, while the upstairs is more traditional with tatami seating, with one room even overlooking the temple gate. It's run by an army of very able grandmotherly type women, and because the menu is in Japanese only, they're more than happy to go outside with you to help you make a selection from the plastic display case.

1–2–2 Asakusa. ✆ **03/3841-3400.** Set meals ¥1,260–¥2,940 ($12–$28). AE, DC, MC, V. Daily 11:30am–9:30pm (last order). Station: Asakusa (1 min.). Next to Kaminarimon Gate, with entrances beside Kurodaya paper shop and on Kaminarimon Dori.

⑮ **Sometaro** � *Finds* OKONOMIYAKI/YAKISOBA   This very atmospheric neighborhood restaurant specializes in *okonomiyaki,* a working-class meal that is basically a Japanese pancake filled with beef, pork, and vegetables, and prepared by the diners themselves as they sit on tatami at low tables inset with griddles. Realizing that some foreigners may be intimidated by having to cook an unfamiliar meal, this restaurant makes the process easier with an English-language menu complete with instructions. The busy but friendly staff can also help you get started. In addition to okonomiyaki, fried noodles *(yakisoba)* with meat or vegetables and other do-it-yourself dishes are available. This is a fun, convivial way to enjoy a meal. Before entering the restaurant, be sure to deposit your shoes in the proffered plastic sacks by the door.

2–2–2 Nishi-Asakusa. ✆ **03/3844-9502.** Main dishes ¥500–¥734 ($4.75–$6.95); set meals ¥1,575 ($15). No credit cards. Daily noon–10pm (last order). Station: Tawaramachi (2 min.) or Asakusa (5 min.). Just off Kokusai Dori, on the side street that runs between the Drum Museum and the police station, on the 2nd block on the right.

# UENO
## EXPENSIVE
**Ueno Seiyoken Grill** 🌟 CLASSIC FRENCH   Seiyoken opened in 1876 as one of Japan's first restaurants serving Western food. Now a nondescript building dating from the 1950s, it nonetheless remains the best place to eat in Ueno Park, serving pricey but quite good classic French cuisine, with a relaxing view of greenery outside its large windows and classical music playing softly in the background. The English-language menu includes seafood such as sole stuffed with shrimp in white-wine sauce, and meat dishes ranging from filet mignon in red-wine sauce to roast duck in green-pepper sauce. There's a varied selection of French wines as well as wines from Germany, California, and Australia. The Grill is located to the right as you enter the building and is not to be confused with the much cheaper utilitarian restaurant to the left.

In Ueno Park between Kiyomizu Temple and Toshogu Shrine. ✆ **03/3821-2181.** Main dishes ¥3,150–¥7,350 ($30–$70); set dinners ¥7,000–¥12,600 ($67–$120); set lunches ¥3,675–¥9,450 ($35–$90). AE, DC, MC, V. Daily 11am–8pm (last order). Station: JR Ueno (6 min.).

## MODERATE
⑯ **Izu'ei** EEL   Put aside all your prejudices about eels and head for this modern yet traditionally decorated multistoried restaurant with a 260-year history dating from the Edo Period and views of Shinobazu Pond. Because eels are grilled over charcoal, Japanese place a lot of stock in the quality of the charcoal used, and this place boasts

its own furnace in the mountains of Wakayama Prefecture, which is said to produce the best charcoal in Japan. Rice topped with strips of eel *(Unagi donburi)*, tempura, and sushi are available, as well as set meals. There's no English-language menu, but there is a display case outside, and the menu has some pictures.

2–12–22 Ueno. ⓒ **03/3831-0954.** Reservations recommended. Main dishes ¥1,585–¥3,045 ($15–$29); set meals ¥2,100–¥10,500 ($20–$100). AE, DC, MC, V. Daily 11am–9:30pm (last order). Station: JR Ueno (3 min.). On Shinobazu Dori, across the street from Shinobazu Pond and the Shitamachi Museum, next to KFC Home Kitchen.

## INEXPENSIVE

In addition to the restaurant below, try **Hard Rock Cafe Ueno,** located in JR Ueno Station (ⓒ **03/5826-5821**); see p. 166 for a review.

**Mantra** INDIAN Decorated in pink with etched mirrors and lots of brass, this tiny, spotless restaurant offers curries and tandoori at inexpensive prices. A good way for lone diners to try a variety of dishes is the all-you-can-eat lunch buffet served from 11am to 3pm; or try one of the meat or vegetarian set meals *(thali)*.

Nagafuji Building Annex, 3rd floor, 4–9–6 Ueno. ⓒ **03/3835-0818.** Main dishes ¥980–¥1,200 ($9.30–$11); set meals ¥1,600–¥3,600 ($15–$34); lunch buffet ¥998 ($9.50) weekdays, ¥1,300 ($12) weekends and holidays. AE, DC, MC, V. Daily 11am–9:30pm (last order). Station: JR Ueno (2 min.). From the south end of Ueno Park, look for the modern Nagafuji Building on Chuo Dori; the annex is in the back, facing the north end of Ameyokocho shopping street.

# SHINJUKU

In addition to the suggestions below, be sure to check out the restaurant floors of several buildings in Shinjuku, where you can find restaurants in all price categories serving a variety of Japanese and international cuisine, some with very good views. These include the 29th and 30th floors of the **N. S. Building** where, in addition to Hakkaku (described below), there are restaurants serving tempura, tonkatsu, teppanyaki, sushi, and Italian, German, and French food; the top four floors of the **Sumitomo Building** where, in addition to Donto (see review under "Hibiya & Ginza," earlier in this chapter), you'll find more than 20 outlets offering everything from tempura to Chinese cuisine; and the 12th, 13th, and 14th floors of **Takashimaya Times Square** where there are restaurants serving sushi, tonkatsu, noodles, and more.

## VERY EXPENSIVE

**New York Grill** ✿✿✿ AMERICAN On the 52nd floor of Tokyo's most exclusive hotel, the New York Grill has remained *the* place to dine ever since its 1994 opening; some swear it's the most sophisticated restaurant in all of Japan. Surrounded on four sides by glass, it features stunning views (especially at night), artwork by Valerio Adami, live jazz in the evenings, and a 1,600-bottle wine cellar (with an emphasis on California wines). The restaurant backs up its dramatic setting with generous portions of steaks, seafood, and other fare ranging from delectable roast duck to rack of "certified organically raised" lamb, all prepared in an open kitchen. Both the set lunch and the weekend and holiday brunches are among the city's best and most sumptuous (reservations required)—and are great options for those who don't want to pawn their belongings to eat dinner here. I wouldn't miss it.

Park Hyatt Hotel, 3–7–1–2 Nishi-Shinjuku. ⓒ **03/5322-1234.** www.parkhyattthokyo.com. Reservations required. Main dishes ¥4,500–¥8,500 ($43–$81); set lunch ¥4,800 ($46); set dinners ¥11,000–¥21,000 ($105–$196); Sat–Sun and holiday brunch ¥6,200 ($59). AE, DC, MC, V. Daily 11:30am–2:30pm and 5:30–10:30pm. Station: Shinjuku (west exit, a 13-min. walk or a 5-min. free shuttle ride), Hatsudai on the Keio Line (7 min.), or Tochomae on the Oedo Line (8 min.).

## EXPENSIVE

In addition to the listing here, there's a branch of the famous tempura restaurant **Ten-ichi** on the seventh floor of Isetan department store, 3–14–1 Shinjuku (© **03/ 5379-3039;** see the "Hibiya & Ginza" section, earlier in this chapter, for a review).

⑰ **Kakiden** 🌣🌣 KAISEKI   Although it's located on the eighth floor of a rather uninspiring building, Kakiden has a relaxing teahouse atmosphere with low chairs, shoji screens, bamboo trees, and soothing traditional Japanese music playing softly in the background. Sibling restaurant to one in Kyoto founded more than 260 years ago as a catering service for the elite, this kaiseki restaurant serves set meals that change with the seasons according to what's fresh and available. An English-language menu lists the set meals, but it's probably best to simply pick a meal to fit your budget. The set lunch is available until 3pm. Set dinners include box kaiseki starting at ¥5,100 ($48), mini-kaiseki for ¥8,400 ($80), and kaiseki courses ranging from ¥8,400 to ¥15,750 ($80–$149). Some of the more common dishes here include fish, seasonal vegetables, eggs, sashimi, shrimp, and mushrooms, but don't worry if you can't identify everything—I've found that even Japanese don't always know what they're eating.

3–37–11 Shinjuku, 8th floor. © **03/3352-5121.** Reservations recommended for lunch. Set dinners ¥5,100–¥15,750 ($48–$149); set lunches ¥4,200–¥6,300 ($40–$60). AE, DC, MC, V. Daily 11am–9pm (last order). Station: Shinjuku (east exit, 1 min.). On the east side of Shinjuku Station next to My City shopping complex.

## MODERATE

In addition to the suggestions here, an excellent choice for nouvelle Japanese cuisine is **daidaiya,** located next to the east exit of Shinjuku station on the third floor of the Nowa Building, 3–37–12 Shinjuku (© **03/5362-7173**), open daily 5pm to midnight (see review under "Akasaka," later in this chapter).

⑱ **Ban-Thai** THAI   One of Tokyo's longest-running Thai restaurants and credited with introducing authentic Thai food to Japanese, Ban-Thai still prepares excellent Thai fare, with 90 mouthwatering items listed on the menu. My favorites are the cold and spicy meat salad, the chicken soup with coconut and lemon grass, and the *pad Thai.* Note that set dinners are available only for parties of two or more; also, portions are not large, so if you order several portions and add beer, your tab can really climb. Finally, the service is indifferent. Yet this place is packed every time I come here.

1–23–14 Kabuki-cho, 3rd floor. © **03/3207-0068.** Reservations recommended. Main dishes ¥1,200–¥1,800 ($11–$17); set dinners ¥2,500–¥6,000 ($24–$57); set lunches ¥630–¥945 ($6–$9) weekdays, ¥1,600–¥2,200 ($15–$21) weekends and holidays. AE, MC, V. Mon–Fri 11:30am–3pm and 5–11pm (last order); Sat–Sun and holidays 11:30am–11pm. Station: Shinjuku (east exit, 7 min.). In East Shinjuku in the seediest part of Kabuki-cho (don't worry, the interior is nicer than the exterior) on a neon-lit pedestrian street connecting the Koma Building with Yasukuni Dori (look for the red neon archway and Pronto coffee shop), about halfway down, next to a game arcade.

⑲ **Hayashi** 🌣🌣 *(Finds* JAPANESE GRILL   This restaurant specializes in Japanese set meals cooked over your own hibachi grill. It's small and cozy, with only five grills and women in kimono overseeing the cooking operations, taking over if customers seem the least bit hesitant. The rustic interior was imported intact from the mountain region of Takayama. Four set meals are offered (vegetarian meals are available on request). My ¥5,250 ($50) meal came with sashimi, yakitori, tofu steak, scallops

cooked in their shells, shrimp, and vegetables, all grilled one after the other. Watch your alcohol intake—drinks can really add to your bill.

Jojoen Daini Shinjuku Building, 2–22–5 Kabuki-cho. ⓒ 03/3209-5672. Reservations recommended. Set dinners ¥4,200–¥7,350 ($40–$70). AE, MC, V. Mon–Sat 5–11:30pm. Closed holidays. Station: Shinjuku (east exit, 10 min.). On the northern edge of Kabuki-cho; you'll know you're getting close when you see Godzilla hanging from a building; the restaurant is just a bit farther to the north, on a corner.

⑳ **Tsunahachi** TEMPURA   Inside a small, old-fashioned brown building in the heart of fashionable East Shinjuku is the main branch of a restaurant that has been serving tempura since 1923. Now there are more than 40 outlets in Japan, including one on the 13th floor of Takashimaya Times Square (ⓒ 03/5361-1860), but this is the largest outlet, and though it has an English-language menu, the easiest option is to order the teishoku, the least expensive of which includes six pieces of tempura, including deep-fried shrimp, cuttlefish, white fish, green pepper, conger eel, and Japanese pickles.

3–31–8 Shinjuku. ⓒ 03/3352-1012. Reservations recommended. Tempura a la carte ¥470–¥1,200 ($4.45–$11); teishoku ¥1,365–¥5,775 ($13–$55). AE, DC, V. Daily 11am–10pm. Station: Shinjuku Sanchome (2 min.) or Shinjuku (east exit, 5 min.). Off Shinjuku Dori on the side street that runs along the east side of Mitsukoshi department store.

## INEXPENSIVE

㉑ **Hakkaku** ⚜ (Finds) VARIED JAPANESE/ROBATAYAKI   This lively, crowded establishment has a lot going for it: a corner location in a skyscraper with expansive views over Yoyogi Park, inexpensive dishes and meals, and Kirin beer on tap. Although its decor and food resemble those of a bar, it's open for lunch, when only set meals are available; choose grilled fish, breaded pork cutlet *(hirekatsu),* or from the display case. Dinner offers a wider range of possibilities, including sashimi, grilled fish, a very tasty beef and potato stew called *nikujaga,* and salads. Yakitori, beginning at ¥300 ($2.50) per skewer, includes asparagus wrapped in bacon and *tsukune* (chicken meatballs), two of my favorites. Since the menu is in Japanese only, perhaps you'll want to sit at the *robatayaki* counter, where you can point at various dishes, watch them be prepared on the open grill, and then receive them from a wooden paddle passed in your direction.

N. S. Building, 29th floor, 2–4–1 Nishi-Shinjuku. ⓒ 03/3345-1848. Main dishes ¥500–¥850 ($4.75–$8.10); set lunches ¥780–¥850 ($7.40–$8.10). AE, DC, MC, V. Daily 11am–2:30pm and 5–9:30pm. Station: Tochomae (3 min.) or Shinjuku (west exit, 8 min.).

## HARAJUKU & AOYAMA
### EXPENSIVE

**Casita** ⚜⚜⚜ (Finds) PACIFIC RIM/FUSION-CROSSOVER   One of the reasons I'm a great fan of Casita's is that I feel truly pampered here. Who wouldn't, with a staff that proffers flashlights to the aged among us who have difficulty reading menus in dim lighting, stands ready to carry out every whim and, on chilly nights, tucks us in under electric blankets so we can enjoy after-dinner drinks on the deck before we head over to the massage chairs? Casita aims to please, carving its own niche in Tokyo's fiercely competitive market by creating a tropical, resortlike atmosphere bolstered by great service and a year-round outdoor deck that's heated in winter and covered when it rains. Of course, none of that matters if the food falls short, but Casita turns out dishes that border on awesome, whether it's the Caesar salad with serious shavings of Parmesan, the caramelized foie gras with sweet-and-spicy chutney, the

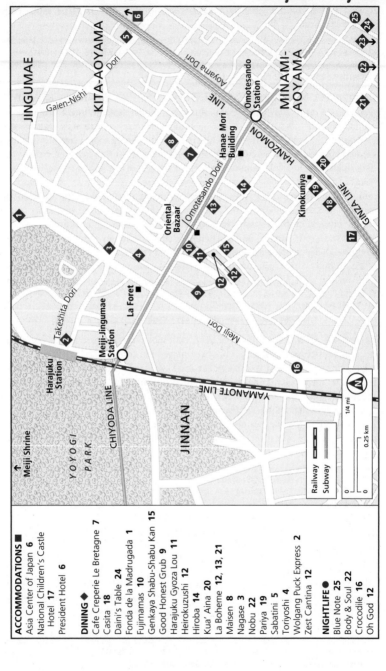

# Harajuku & Aoyama

ACCOMMODATIONS ■
Asia Center of Japan 6
National Children's Castle
  Hotel 17
President Hotel 6

DINING ◆
Cafe Creperie Le Bretagne 7
Casita 18
Daini's Table 24
Fonda de la Madrugada 1
Fujimamas 10
Genkaya Shabu-Shabu Kan 15
Good Honest Grub 9
Harajuku Gyoza Lou 11
Heirokuzushi 12
Hiroba 14
Kua' Aina 20
La Boheme 12, 13, 21
Maisen 8
Nagase 3
Nobu 22
Pariya 19
Sabatini 5
Toriyoshi 4
Wolgang Puck Express 2
Zest Cantina 12

NIGHTLIFE ●
Blue Note 25
Body & Soul 22
Crocodile 16
Oh God 12

157

roasted lobster, or the Japanese beef flavored with a Thai barbecue sauce. Who wouldn't be a fan?

La Porte Aoyama, 5th floor, 5–51–8 Jingumae. ✆ 03/5485-7353. www.casita.jp. Reservations required. Main dishes ¥2,600–¥4,500 ($25–$43); set dinners ¥8,000–¥10,000 ($76–$95). AE, DC, MC, V. Daily 5–11:30pm (last order). Station: Omotesando (3 min.). Head toward Shibuya on Omotesando Dori; it will be on your right, in an unlikely looking building past the stoplight.

**Nobu** 🎔🎔🎔 NOUVELLE JAPANESE/PACIFIC RIM FUSION-CROSSOVER
Sister restaurant to New York's Nobu, this classy, modern establishment is the place to see and be seen—and you can count on being seen since the staff yells *"Irashaimase!"* ("Welcome!") the minute anyone is ushered into the dining room. Jazz plays softly in the background, flowers sit atop each table, and the efficient staff keeps everything running smoothly. The food, beautifully presented and served one dish at a time, is a unique blend of Pacific Rim ingredients (not quite Japanese) with decidedly American/Latin influences. Sushi and sashimi are served, as well as sushi rolls like California rolls (with avocado) and soft-shell-crab rolls. Other dishes include toro sashimi with jalapeño and vinegar mustard miso sauce, and black cod with miso. If ordering is too much of a chore, you can leave your meal to the discretion of Chef Matsuhisa by ordering the *omakase,* a complete chef's-choice dinner starting at ¥10,500 ($100). Prices are less expensive at lunch. In fine weather, you can dine on an outdoor patio with a retractable roof.

6–10–17 Minami Aoyama. ✆ 03/5467-0022. Reservations recommended. Sushi and sashimi (per piece) ¥500–¥1,000 ($4.75–$9.50); set dinners ¥5,300–¥21,000 ($50–$200); set lunches ¥2,800–¥10,000 ($27–$95). AE, DC, MC, V. Mon–Fri 11:30am–2pm; daily 6–10:30pm (last order). Closed for lunch holidays. Station: Shibuya or Omotesando (15 min.). On Roppongi Dori near Komazawa Dori and Kotto Dori.

**Sabatini** 🎔 ITALIAN   This restaurant, with its Italian furniture and tableware and strolling musicians, seems as if it has been moved intact from the Old World. In fact, the only thing to remind you that you're in Tokyo is your Japanese waiter. The Italian family that owns Sabatini has had a restaurant in Rome for more than 40 years (this restaurant has no relation to the Sabatini restaurants in the Ginza and Roppongi), and family members take turns overseeing the Tokyo restaurants, so one of them is always here. The menu includes seafood, veal, steak, lamb, and a variety of vegetables; many of the ingredients, like olive oil, ham, salami, tomato sauce, and Parmesan, are flown in fresh from Italy. Naturally, there's a wide selection of Italian wines.

Suncrest Building, 2–13–5 Kita-Aoyama. ✆ 03/3402-3812. Reservations recommended for dinner. Pasta ¥1,890–¥3,360 ($18–$32); main dishes ¥3,885–¥7,900 ($37–$75); set dinner ¥15,750 ($150); set lunch ¥3,990–¥4,200 ($38–$40). AE, DC, MC, V. Daily 11:30am–2:30pm and 5:30–11pm. Station: Gaienmae (2 min.). On Aoyama Dori near Gaien-Nishi Dori.

## MODERATE
**Daini's Table** 🎔🎔 NOUVELLE CHINESE   This elegant Chinese restaurant, located next to the Blue Note jazz club off Kotto Dori, serves intriguing dishes that are nicely presented one dish at a time rather than all at once as in most Chinese restaurants. It offers both traditional dishes (roast Peking duck, boiled prawns with red chile sauce, and hot-and-sour Peking-style soup) and more unusual combinations that change with the seasons. Everything I've had here has been delicious, though note that set dinners require a two-person minimum. Lone diners, therefore, should come for lunch.

6–3–14 Minami Aoyama. ✆ 03/3407-0363. Reservations recommended. Main dishes ¥2,000–¥3,800 ($19–$36); set dinners ¥5,250–¥15,750 ($50–$150); set lunches ¥1,100–¥2,800 ($10–$27). AE, DC, MC, V. Mon–Fri 11:30am–2pm; daily 5:30–11pm (last order). Station: Omotesando (6 min.).

**Fujimamas** ⚘ PACIFIC RIM/FUSION   This airy restaurant employs lots of wood to impart a beach-shack atmosphere, but naturally at Tokyo prices. The culinary cross-road of cuisines presented on the changing English-language menu may include salads like a Thai-style Caesar salad with crispy calamari croutons, or smoked chicken salad with sweet potatoes and spicy mint chutney. Main dishes may include such tempting choices as seared lamb with tomatoes and mint or grilled swordfish with orange, red onion, and dill salad with ponzu dressing. Lunch offers lighter fare, including sandwiches, stir-fries, and curries.

6–3–2 Jingumae. ✆ 03/5485-2262. Reservations recommended. Main dishes ¥1,365–¥1,890 ($13–$18); set lunch ¥1,050 ($10). AE, DC, MC, V. Mon–Fri noon–3pm and 6–10pm; Sat–Sun and holidays 11am–4pm and 6–10pm. Station: Meiji-Jingumae (2 min.) or Harajuku (5 min.). From the Meiji Dori/Omotesando intersection, walk on Omotesando toward Aoyama and take the first right.

### INEXPENSIVE

In addition to the choices below, consider Tex-Mex restaurant **Zest Cantina,** 6–7–18 Jingumae (✆ **03/3409-6268**), open daily from 11:30am to 5pm. Here, too, is **La Boheme,** with three locations at 6–8–18 Jingumae (✆ **03/3400-3406**), 6–2–2 Minami Aoyama (✆ **03/6418-4242**), and on Omotesando Dori at 5–8–5 Jingumae (✆ **03/5467-5666**); all serve pizza and pasta and are open daily from 11:30am to 5pm. See "Hibiya & Ginza," earlier in this chapter, for a review of both.

**Cafe Creperie Le Bretagne** *Kids* FRENCH/CREPES   With an inviting open-fronted shop, posters of Brittany, natural wood and brick, and a French staff, this is *the* place for authentic buckwheat galettes and crepes filled with yummy fruit or chocolate (or with such irresistible combinations as banana, chocolate, and rum). Kids will love this place, too.

4–9–8 Jingumae. ✆ 03/3478-7855. Crepes ¥700–¥1,200 ($6.65–$11); set lunches ¥1,280–¥2,680 ($12–$25). No credit cards. Mon–Thurs 11:30am–11pm; Fri–Sat 11:30am–midnight; Sun 11:30am–10pm (last order). Station: Omotesando (3 min.). Off Omotesando Dori; take the side street opposite the Hanae Mori Building (the one between McDonald's and Ito Hospital, with a HARAJUKU sign above it), walk to the end of the block.

**Fonda de la Madrugada** MEXICAN   Serving what is probably Tokyo's most authentic Mexican food, this dark basement restaurant has a cavernous main dining room, several small and cozy offshoots, and a strolling mariachi band, making it seem like you're dining in a Mexican villa. Shrimp marinated in tequila, chicken mole, and soft-tortilla tacos served with chicken, fish, beef, or pork are just some of the items on the trilingual (Japanese/Spanish/English) menu, along with the requisite Mexican beers; tequila shots and shooters; margaritas; rum and vodka cocktails; and wine from Mexico, Chile, and Argentina.

2–33–12 Jingumae. ✆ 03/5410-6288. Main dishes ¥1,050–¥2,900 ($10–$28). AE, DC, MC, V. Sun–Thurs 5pm–2am; Fri–Sat 5pm–5am. Station: Meiji-Jingumae (10 min.). From the Meiji Dori/Omotesando intersection, walk north on Meiji Dori (toward Shinjuku); it will be on your right after the pedestrian overpass.

㉒ **Genkaya Shabu-Shabu Kan** *Value* SHABU-SHABU/SUKIYAKI   This casual restaurant with a rustic interior is one of the cheapest I've ever seen for shabu-shabu and sukiyaki. For ¥1,680 ($16) you can have all the shabu-shabu or sukiyaki you can eat in 90 minutes; for ¥1,260 ($12) you can add all you can drink. For real gluttons, for ¥3,150 ($30) you can eat and drink all you can consume, including side dishes like rice, *kimchi* (traditional pickled cabbage), and other pickled vegetables, for 100 minutes. For ¥3,675 ($35), it's all you can consume for 120

minutes. Thank goodness there's a time limit; otherwise, you might have to be air-lifted out.

6–7–8 Jingumae. C 03/3406-6500. All-you-can-eat shabu-shabu or sukiyaki from ¥1,680 ($16). No credit cards. Mon–Fri 5pm–midnight; Sat–Sun 5pm–2am. Station: Meiji-Jingumae (3 min.) or Harajuku (5 min.). From the Meiji/Omotesando Dori intersection, walk on Omotesando Dori toward Aoyama and take the 3rd right (just before Kiddy Land); it's at the end of this street, to the left.

**Good Honest Grub** AMERICAN/VEGETARIAN   The owner is Canadian and the food is a compilation of all the homegrown favorites expatriates—including the health conscious—are likely to crave: eggs Benedict, pancakes, and a tofu-vegetable combination for brunch; sandwiches (including many vegetarian choices) for lunch; and, for dinner, everything from pizza, pasta, and yummy salads to chicken breast stuffed with ham and mushroom dipped in egg and cheese batter and served with a demi-glaze sauce, or eggplant and tofu topped with tomatoes and garlic. Decorated in bright, happy colors, it would be right at home at any North American college campus. Heck, Honest Grub even supplies the canteen of the U.S. embassy. There's a branch in Ebisu at 1–11–11 Ebisu-Minami (C **03/3710-0400**).

6–6–2 Jingumae. C 03/3406-6606. www.goodhonestgrub.com. Lunch dishes ¥1,450–¥1,600 ($14–$15); dinner entrees ¥1,800–¥2,000 ($17–$19). DC, MC, V. Mon–Fri 11am–11pm; Sat–Sun and holidays 9am–11pm. Station: Meiji-Jingumae (2 min.) or Harajuku (5 min.). From the Meiji Dori/Omotesando intersection, walk on Omotesando toward Aoyama and take the 1st right.

㉓ **Harajuku Gyoza Lou** ✦ GYOZA   If you like pork dumplings *(gyoza)*, you owe yourself a meal here. Unlike most greasy spoons that specialize in fast-food Chinese (and tend to be on the dingy side), this restaurant in the heart of Harajuku is hip yet unpretentious and draws a young crowd with its straightforward menu posted on the wall. Only four types of gyoza are offered: boiled *(sui-gyoza)* or fried *(yaki-gyoza)*, and with or without garlic *(ninniku)*. A few side dishes, such as cucumber, boiled cabbage with vinegar, sprouts with a spicy meat sauce, and rice, are available, as are beer and sake. A U-shaped counter encloses the open kitchen, giving diners something to watch as they chow down on the very good gyoza.

6–2–4 Jingumae. C 03/3406-4743. Gyoza ¥290 ($2.75) for a plate of 6. No credit cards. Mon–Sat 11:30am–4:30am; Sun and holidays 11:30am–11:30pm. Station: Meiji-Jingumae (3 min.) or Harajuku (5 min.). From the Meiji/Omotesando Dori intersection, walk on Omotesando Dori toward Aoyama and take the 3rd right (just before Kiddy Land); it's at the end of this street, on the right.

㉔ **Heirokuzushi** SUSHI   Bright (a bit too bright), clean, and modern, this is one of those fast-food sushi bars where plates of food are conducted along a conveyor belt on the counter. Customers help themselves to whatever strikes their fancy. To figure your bill, the cashier counts the number of plates you took from the conveyor belt: pink plates cost ¥126 ($1.20), green ones ¥168 ($1.35), blue ones ¥252 ($2.40), black ones ¥367 ($3.50), and gold ones ¥525 ($5). There's a plastic display case of takeout sushi; you might want to eat in nearby Yoyogi Park.

5–8–5 Jingumae. C 03/3498-3968. Sushi ¥126–¥525 ($1.20–$5) each. No credit cards. Daily 11am–9pm. Station: Meiji-Jingumae (2 min.) or Omotesando (5 min.). On Omotesando Dori close to the Oriental Bazaar.

**Hiroba** JAPANESE HEALTH FOOD/VEGETARIAN   Located in the basement of the Crayon House, which specializes in Japanese children's books, this natural-food restaurant offers a buffet lunch of organic veggies, fish, brown rice, and other health foods. For dinner only, set meals are available along with a few simple dishes like vegetable tempura or seaweed salad. The dining hall is very simple (its atmosphere

reminds me of a potluck supper in a church basement), and because of the upstairs bookstore, there are likely to be families here. Sharing the same phone, open hours, and cash register is **Home,** which offers waitress service and the same wholesome meals using organic ingredients, including vegetarian choices. Set lunches here are ¥2,000 ($19) and up, set dinners ¥3,000 ($29).

Crayon House, 3–8–15 Kita Aoyama. ℂ **03/3406-6409.** Lunch buffet ¥1,260 ($12); set dinners ¥1,200–¥1,500 ($11–$14). No credit cards. Daily 11am–2pm and 5–10pm. Station: Omotesando (2 min.). Off Omotesando Dori on the side street to the right of the Hanae Mori Building.

**Kua' Aina** *Value* *Kids* AMERICAN/HAMBURGERS/SANDWICHES How far will you go for a great burger? Quite simply, the best burgers in town make this Hawaiian import a smashing success. In fact, if you come at mealtime you'll probably have to wait for a table in one of the tiny upstairs dining rooms. Burgers come as third- and (whopping) half-pounders. There are also sandwiches ranging from BLTs with avocado to roast beef to tuna. A good carnivore fix.

Branches can be found at 1–10–4 Shibuya (ℂ **03/3409-3200**), in the Marunouchi Building across from Tokyo Station at 2–4–1 Marunouchi (ℂ **03/5220-2400**), and in Aqua City in Odaiba (ℂ **03/3599-2800**).

5–10–21 Minami Aoyama. ℂ **03/3407-8001.** Burgers and sandwiches ¥610–¥1,300 ($5.80–$12). No credit cards. Mon–Sat 11am–11pm; Sun 11am–10pm. Station: Omotesando (2 min.). On Aoyama Dori at its busy intersection with Kotto Dori, catty-corner from Kinokuniya grocery store (undergoing reconstruction).

㉕ **Maisen** *Value* *Finds* TONKATSU Extremely popular with the locals, this restaurant has been dishing out *tonkatsu* (deep-fried breaded pork cutlet) for more than 20 years and is especially known for its black pork, originally from China and prized for its sweet, intense flavor. But what makes this restaurant a real standout is that it occupies a former pre–World War II public bathhouse; its main dining hall used to the changing room and sports a tall ceiling and original architectural details. There's an English-language menu, but lunch specials (available until 6pm) are listed in Japanese only, though there are photographs. It's easiest to order a set meal.

There's a branch in the Mitsui Building, 1–1–2 Yurakucho (ℂ **03/3503-1886**), near the Imperial Hotel.

4–8–5 Jingumae. ℂ **03/3470-0071.** Set meals ¥1,207–¥1,732 ($11–$16); set lunches ¥735–¥1,260 ($7–$12). AE, DC, MC, V. Daily 11am–10pm (last order). Station: Omotesando (4 min.). Take the A2 exit and turn right on the side street between Ito Hospital and McDonald's (the one with a HARAJUKU above it); take the 1st left and then an immediate right. It will be in the next block on the left.

**Nagase** *Value Value* *Finds* FRENCH This is another one of those casual neighborhood bistros offering great food at very reasonable prices that made its debut following the economic recession. Like most of the others, a cut in prices means a crowding of tables to accommodate as many diners as possible, but except for the most special of occasions, I'll gladly settle for cheaper prices over spaciousness. Set dinner menus give a choice of a half-dozen main dishes, which might include the fish of the day, beef Burgundy, *confit de canard,* or *noisettes de lamb au thym,* along with a salad or side dish, bread, and coffee. My ¥1,050 ($10) lunch was one of the best Western meals I've had in Japan at that price—a salad with boiled egg, chicken, mushrooms, and tomato, followed by whitefish on mashed potatoes with an eggplant-tomato sauce subtly flavored with curry.

3–21–12 Jingumae. ℂ **03/3423-1925.** Reservations required on weekends. Set dinners ¥2,500 and ¥3,500 ($24–$33); set lunches ¥1,050–¥2,400 ($10–$23). No credit cards. Tues–Fri 11:30am–2pm and 5:30–9:30pm; Sat–Sun and holidays 11:30am–8:30pm (last order). Station: Meiji-Jingumae (3 min.) or Harajuku (8 min.). On the opposite side of Meiji Dori from Takeshita St., on a side street nicknamed Harajuku Dori; it's on the left side of the street, up on the 2nd floor.

**Pariya** ✦ VARIED JAPANESE/INTERNATIONAL   What a clever concept: Design a chic, airy restaurant sure to draw in the fashionable Aoyama crowd, and then keep 'em coming with set lunches that change weekly. Diners compose their own meals from choices of a main course, one side dish, a salad, unpolished brown rice *(genmai)* or polished white rice *(hakumai),* soup, and coffee and tea. Ethnic-influenced offerings have included grilled chicken, salmon, and sukiyaki beef, while side dishes have ranged from sweet potatoes to pasta. At dinner, the establishment is a combination bar/restaurant, with an English-language menu listing salads (a standout is the Asian Caesar salad with fried sea eel and poached egg, as well as the compose-your-own salads), noodle and rice dishes (recommended are the gyoza with leek or the pumpkin gnocchi with porcini cream sauce), pizza, and other fare that changes with the season.

3–12–14 Kita Aoyama. ✆ 03/3486-1316. Set lunches ¥1,150 ($11) with genmai, ¥1,050 ($10) with hakumai; dinner main courses ¥1,050–¥2,100 ($10–$20). AE, MC, V. Daily 11:30am–3pm and 6–10pm (last order). Station: Omotesando (4 min.). On a side street off Aoyama Dori, past Kinokuniya grocery store (presently undergoing renovation).

㉖ **Toriyoshi** VARIED JAPANESE/INTERNATIONAL   Open and airy and decorated like a traditional warehouse *(kura)* with its gleaming woods, shoji screens, and tatami seating (with leg wells for those errant legs), this chain has an English-language menu listing a variety of Japanese and Asian pub fare, including salads, yakitori, tofu (I love the black sesame tofu, called *kuroi gomadofu*), chicken dishes, spicy Korean cabbage *(kimchi)*, and more. A good place for a convivial evening.

4–28–21 Jingumae. ✆ 03/3470-3901. Main dishes ¥620–¥1,500 ($5.90–$14). AE, DC, MC, V. Mon–Fri 5–11pm; Sat–Sun 4–11pm (last order). Station: Meiji-Jingumae (3 min.). From the Meiji Dori/Omotesando intersection, walk on Omotesando toward Aoyama and take the 1st left (there's a Wendy's here); Toriyoshi is down this street, on the right side beside a willow tree. Look for its lit signboard with photos.

**Wolfgang Puck Express** AMERICAN   This is the most casual and least expensive of Puck's invasion of eateries in Japan. It concentrates on burgers, pizza, pasta, salads, and other fast foods. What I like about this location is that it's right at the top of Takeshita Dori (Harajuku's most popular shopping street) across from the station, and it's more stylish than other fast-food competitors that shall remain nameless. Fast service, pop music, and beer—what more could you ask for?

1–17–1 Jingumae. ✆ 03/5786-4690. Main dishes ¥780–¥1,480 ($7.40–$14); set lunch ¥1,280 ($12). AE, DC, MC, V. Daily 11am–11pm. Station: Harajuku (1 min.). Across the street from Harajuku Station's north exit, at the top of Takeshita Dori.

## ROPPONGI

Because Roppongi is such a popular nighttime hangout for young Tokyoites and foreigners, it boasts a large number of both Japanese and Western restaurants. To find the location of any of the Roppongi addresses below, stop by the tiny police station on Roppongi Crossing (Roppongi's main intersection of Roppongi Dori and Gaien-Higashi Dori), where you'll find a map of the area. If you still don't know where to go, ask one of the policemen.

About a 10-minute walk west of Roppongi (via Roppongi Dori in the direction of Shibuya) is another popular nighttime area—**Nishi Azabu.** Once primarily a residential neighborhood, Nishi Azabu has slowly changed over the years as it began absorbing the overflow of Roppongi. It has restaurants and bars yet remains mellower and much less crowded than Roppongi.

# Roppongi

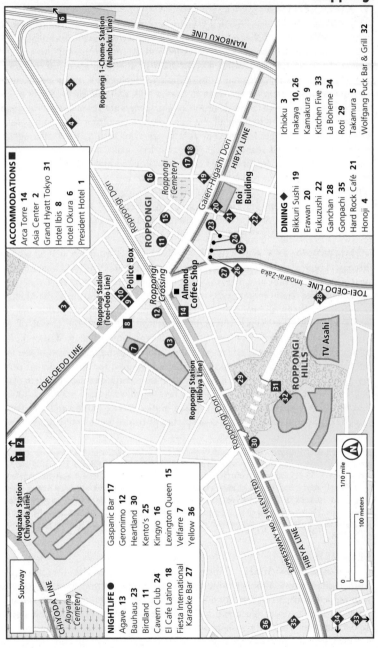

**ACCOMMODATIONS ■**
Arca Torre **14**
Asia Center **2**
Grand Hyatt Tokyo **31**
Hotel Ibis **8**
Hotel Okura **6**
President Hotel **1**

**NIGHTLIFE ●**
Agave **13**
Bauhaus **23**
Birdland **11**
Cavern Club **24**
El Cafe Latino **18**
Fiesta International
  Karaoke Bar **27**
Gaspanic Bar **17**
Geronimo **12**
Heartland **30**
Kento's **25**
Kingyo **16**
Lexington Queen **15**
Velfarre **7**
Yellow **36**

**DINING ◆**
Bikkuri Sushi **19**
Erawan **20**
Fukuzushi **22**
Ganchan **28**
Gonpachi **35**
Hard Rock Café **21**
Honoji **4**
Ichioku **3**
Inakaya **10, 26**
Kamakura **9**
Kitchen Five **33**
La Boheme **34**
Roti **29**
Takamura **5**
Wolfgang Puck Bar & Grill **32**

Subway

163

## VERY EXPENSIVE

㉗ **Inakaya** 🖉🖉 ROBATAYAKI    Whenever I'm playing hostess to first-time foreign visitors in Tokyo, I always take them to this festive restaurant, and they've never been disappointed. Although tourist-oriented and overpriced, it's still great fun; the drama of the place alone is worth it. Customers sit at a long, U-shaped counter, on the other side of which are mountains of fresh vegetables, beef, and seafood. And in the middle of all that food, seated in front of a grill, are male chefs—ready to cook whatever you point to in the style of robatayaki. Orders are yelled out by your waiter and are repeated in unison by all the other waiters, resulting in ongoing, excited yelling. Sounds strange, I know, but actually it's a lot of fun. Food offerings may include yellowtail, red snapper, sole, king crab legs, giant shrimp, steak, meatballs, gingko nuts, potatoes, eggplant, and asparagus, all piled high in wicker baskets and ready for the grill. There's another nearby branch at 5–3–4 Roppongi (② **03/3408-5040**), open daily 5pm to 5am.

4–10–11 Roppongi. ② **03/5775-1012**. Meals average ¥12,000 ($114). AE, DC, MC, V. Daily 5–11pm. Station: Roppongi (2 min.). Off Gaien-Higashi Dor on a side street opposite Ibis Hotel; from Roppongi Crossing, walk on Gaien-Higashi Dori in the direction of Aoyama and take the 2nd right.

㉘ **Takamura** 🖉🖉🖉 *(Finds* KAISEKI    Takamura is a must for anyone who can afford it. Located at the edge of Roppongi, this wonderful 60-year-old house, perched on a hill and hidden by greenery, is a peaceful oasis that time forgot. You'll dine in one of eight private tatami rooms, each one different. Charcoal hearths in the rooms are built into the floors, and windows look out onto miniature gardens. Takamura has a very Japanese feeling, which intensifies proportionately with the arrival of your meal—seasonal kaiseki food arranged so artfully you almost hate to destroy it. Your pleasure increases, however, as you savor the various textures and flavors of the food. Specialties may include quail, sparrow, or duck, grilled on the hearth in your private tatami room. Seating is on the floor, as it is in most traditional Japanese restaurants, but with leg wells. The price of dinner here usually averages about ¥27,000 to ¥33,000 ($257–$314) by the time you add drinks, service charge, and table charge (¥2,000/$19 per person). Dinner is for parties of two or more, while lunch is available only for parties of four or larger.

3–4–27 Roppongi. ② **03/3585-6600**. Reservations required (1 day in advance for lunch, a week in advance for dinner, at which time you must order your meal). Set dinners ¥17,850, ¥21,000, and ¥26,250 ($170, $200, and $249); set lunches ¥15,750, ¥17,850, and ¥21,000 ($150, $170, and $200). AE, DC, MC, V. Tues–Sat noon–3pm and Mon–Sat 5–10:30pm. Closed for lunch the day following a holiday, 1 week in Jan, and 1 week in mid-Aug. Station: Roppongi (4 min.). The restaurant has 2 entrances, each marked by a wooden gate with a little roof. The sign on the restaurant is in Japanese only, but look for the credit card signs. From Roppongi Crossing, take Roppongi Dori in the direction of Kasumigaseki; at the bottom of the hill, turn right on the side street between HMV and Somerset Roppongi residential building.

## EXPENSIVE

㉙ **Fukuzushi** 🖉🖉 SUSHI    This is one of Tokyo's classiest sushi bars, attracting a cosmopolitan crowd. Although it has a traditional entrance through a small courtyard with lighted lanterns and the sound of trickling water, the interior is slick and modern with bold colors of black and red. Some people swear it has the best sushi in Tokyo, although with 7,000 sushi bars in the city, I'd be hard-pressed to say which one is tops. Certainly, you can't go wrong here. Three different set lunches are available, which feature sushi, assorted sashimi with rice *(chirashi-zushi),* or eel as the main course. Dinners are more extensive, with the ¥8,400 ($80) set course consisting of

salad, sashimi, steamed egg custard, grilled fish, sushi, miso soup, dessert, and coffee (set dinners require orders by a minimum of two people).

5–7–8 Roppongi. ✆ **03/3402-4116.** www.roppongifukuzushi.com. Reservations recommended, especially for dinner. Set dinners ¥6,300–¥8,400 ($60–$80); set lunches ¥2,625–¥4,725 ($25–$45). AE, DC, MC, V. Mon–Sat 11:30am–2pm and 5:30–11pm; holidays 5:30–10pm. Station: Roppongi (4 min.). From Roppongi Crossing, walk toward Tokyo Tower on Gaien-Higashi Dori, turning right after McDonald's and left in front of Hard Rock Cafe.

## MODERATE

**Erawan** 🎜🎜 THAI   Perched 13 floors above the Roppongi madness and offering cool, aloof views on three sides (ask for the Tokyo Tower side), this restaurant is massive but does a good job of sectioning the floor space into intimate dining areas and re-creating its native homeland with dark gleaming woods, woodcarvings, plants, bamboo screens, and a smiling Thai staff. The food lives up to its reputation, with plenty of seafood and curry selections, including deep-fried prawns with chile sauce, steamed whitefish with Thai sauce, and red curry with beef and eggplant.

Roi Building, 13th floor, 5–5–1 Roppongi. ✆ **03/3404-5741.** Main dishes ¥1,200–¥2,000 ($11–$19); set dinners ¥3,500–¥3,800 ($33–$36). AE, DC, MC, V. Mon–Fri 5:30–11:30pm; Sat–Sun and holidays 5–11:30pm. Station: Roppongi (3 min.). From Roppongi Crossing, Erawan is on the right side of Gaien-Higashi Dori (the road leading to Tokyo Tower), just past McDonald's.

**Wolfgang Puck Bar & Grill** 🎜🎜 AMERICAN/FUSION-CROSSOVER   This restaurant, launched in 2003 in Roppongi Hills, is the flagship operation of Wolfgang Puck's successful foray into the Japan culinary market. Austrian-born Puck, who jump-started nouveau American cooking with his innovative California cuisine, has ambitious plans to open a mind-boggling 100 more outlets in Japan over the next 10 years (including lower-priced cafes focusing on pizzas, sandwiches, and salads). Stylishly chic and laid-back, with a slight retro feel and an inviting outdoor patio, the Bar & Grill attracts both business types and families alike with its East-meets-West fusion cuisine, including original recipes designed for Japan. Dinner features dishes like grilled soy and maple-syrup marinated lamb chop with stir-fried eggplant and mint cilantro vinaigrette, while lunch is more casual, with everything from grilled hamburgers to pizza.

Roppongi Hills, Hollywood Plaza 2nd floor, 6–4–1 Roppongi. ✆ **03/5786-9630.** Reservations recommended. Main dishes ¥2,600–¥3,800 ($25–$36); set lunches ¥2,000–¥3,800 ($19–$36). AE, DC, MC, V. Daily 11am–3:30pm and 6–10pm (last order). Station: Roppongi (Roppongi Hills exit, 1 min.).

## INEXPENSIVE

In addition to the recommendations below, **La Boheme,** 2–25–18 Nishi Azabu (✆ **03/3407-1363**), serves pizza and pasta (see "Hibiya & Ginza," earlier in this chapter, for a review).

㉚ **Bikkuri Sushi** 🎜🎜 SUSHI   This is one of the cheapest places to eat in this popular nightlife district. Plates of sushi move along a conveyor belt past customers seated at the counter, who help themselves to whichever plates strike their fancy; this makes dining a cinch since it's not necessary to know the name of anything. The white plates of sushi are all priced at ¥136 ($1.30), while the colored dishes run ¥262 ($2.50) and ¥682 ($6.50). Your bill is tallied according to the number of plates you've taken.

3–14–9 Roppongi. ✆ **03/3403-1489.** Dishes ¥136–¥682 ($1.30–$6.50). No credit cards. Daily 11am–5am. Station: Roppongi (3 min.). On the left-hand side of Gaien-Higashi Dori (the road leading to Tokyo Tower), across the street from the Roi Building.

㉛ **Ganchan** ⚑ YAKITORI    This is one of my favorite yakitori-ya. Small and intimate, it's owned by a friendly and entertaining man who can't speak English worth a darn but keeps trying with the help of a worn-out Japanese-English dictionary he keeps behind the counter. His staff is young and fun-loving. There's an eclectic cassette collection—I never know whether to expect Japanese pop tunes or American oldies. Seating is along just one counter with room for only a dozen or so people. Though there's an English-language menu, it's easiest to order the yakitori *seto*, a set course that comes with salad and soup and eight skewers of such items as chicken, beef, meatballs, green peppers, and asparagus rolled with bacon. Be aware that there's a table charge of ¥600 ($5.70) per person, which includes an appetizer.

6–8–23 Roppongi. ✆ 03/3478-0092. Yakitori skewers ¥263–¥525 ($2.50–$5); yakitori set course ¥2,625 ($25). AE, MC, V. Mon–Sat 5:30pm–1:30am; Sun and holidays 5:30pm–midnight. Station: Roppongi (7 min.). From Roppongi Crossing, take the small street going downhill to the left of the Almond Coffee Shop; Ganchan is at the bottom of the hill on the right.

**Gonpachi** ⚑⚑ *Value* VARIED JAPANESE    Housed in a re-created *kura* (traditional Japanese warehouse) with a high ceiling and an open kitchen in the middle, this is one of Tokyo's most imaginative inexpensive Japanese restaurants. It offers a wide variety of dishes, including yakitori (like skewered albacore with Gorgonzola tartar sauce), fish (like miso-glazed black cod), sushi (on the third floor), noodles, and more. From the outside, you'd expect this place to be much more exclusive than it is—and you probably will be excluded if you fail to make reservations for dinner.

There are branches of Gonpachi at the G-Zone, 1–2–3 Ginza (✆ **03/5524-3641**), and at Mediage on Odaiba (✆ **03/3599-4807**), all open from 11:30am to 5am. However, they don't match the Nishi Azabu location's atmosphere.

1–13–11 Nishi Azabu. ✆ 03/5771-0170. www.global-dining.com. Yakitori ¥250–¥580 ($2.40–$5.50); main dishes ¥980–¥2,300 ($9.30–$22); set lunches ¥650–¥1,200 ($6.20–$11). AE, DC, MC, V. Daily 11:30am–5am. Station: Roppongi (10 min.). From Roppongi Crossing, walk toward Shibuya on Roppongi Dori. It will be on your right, at Gaien-Nishi Dori.

**Hard Rock Cafe** *Kids* AMERICAN    Founded by two American expatriates in London in 1971, Hard Rock Cafe now has half a dozen locations in Japan; this was the first. If you have disgruntled teenagers in tow, bring them to this world-famous hamburger joint dedicated to rock 'n' roll to ogle the memorabilia on the walls, chow down on burgers, and look over the T-shirts for sale. In addition to hamburgers, the menu includes salads, sandwiches, steak, barbecued ribs, barbecued chicken, fish of the day, and fajitas. The music, by the way, is loud.

A branch is located in JR Ueno Station at 7–1–1 Ueno (✆ **03/5826-5821**), open daily 7am to 11pm.

5–4–20 Roppongi. ✆ 03/3408-7018. Main dishes ¥1,478–¥3,465 ($14–$33). AE, DC, MC, V. Mon–Thurs 11:30am–2am; Fri–Sat 11:30am–4am; Sun and holidays 11:30am–11:30pm. Station: Roppongi (3 min.). From Roppongi Crossing, walk on Gaien-Higashi Dori toward Tokyo Tower and take a right at McDonald's.

㉜ **Honoji** ⚑ *Finds* VARIED JAPANESE    A plain wooden facade and a stark interior of concrete walls with wire-mesh screens set the mood for what this restaurant offers: good, home-style Japanese cooking. Although it looks small at first glance (an open kitchen takes up half the space), back-room nooks and crannies give diners a sense of privacy as they enjoy grilled fish, sashimi, yakitori, grilled eggplant with miso, deep-fried tofu, stir-fried dishes like cabbage with oyster sauce, and seasoned pork

with potatoes. Honoji serves the kinds of food offered by neighborhood drinking establishments *(nomiya)* all over Japan, which isn't exactly the kind of fare you'd expect to find in trendy Roppongi (you might want to steer clear of the grilled cow diaphragm with salt listed on the English-language menu). Still, the crowds that wait at the door, especially on weekend nights, attest to its success. Note that there's a dinner table charge of ¥450 ($4.30), though I was told it will be waived if foreigners don't like the snack that comes with it. The lunch teishoku, available for ¥945 ($9) and the only item offered for lunch, draws Japanese from all walks of life.

3–4–33 Roppongi. ✆ 03/3588-1065. Main dishes ¥480 – ¥1,000 ($4.55–$9.50). AE, DC, MC, V. Mon–Fri 11:30am–1:30pm (last order); Mon–Sat 5:30–11pm (last order 10:15pm). Closed holidays. Station: Roppongi (3 min.). On the right side of Roppongi Dori as you walk from Roppongi Crossing in the direction of Akasaka, at the bottom of the hill just past 7-Eleven.

㉝ **Ichioku** ✦ JAPANESE ORIGINALS   This is one of my favorite restaurants in Roppongi for casual dining. It's a tiny, cozy place with only eight tables, and you fill out your order yourself using the English-language menu—complete with pictures—which is glued underneath the clear glass tabletop. The food, featuring organically grown vegetables, can best be called Japanese nouvelle cooking, with original creations offered at very reasonable prices. About 25 dishes are offered, including tuna and ginger sauté, mushroom sauté, shrimp spring rolls, Thai curry, asparagus salad, fried potatoes, sautéed eggplant, and a dish of grated radish and tiny fish. I recommend the tofu steak (fried tofu and flakes of dried fish) as well as the cheese gyoza (a fried pork dumpling with cheese melted on it).

4–4–5 Roppongi. ✆ 03/3405-9891. Main dishes ¥350–¥2,450 ($3.35–$23). AE, DC, MC, V. Mon–Fri 11:30am–2pm and 5pm–12:30am (last order); Sat 5pm–1am; holidays 5–11pm. Station: Roppongi (4 min.). On a side street in the neighborhood behind the police station.

**Kamakura** YAKITORI   Much more refined than most yakitori-ya, this basement establishment is decorated with paper lanterns and sprigs of fake but cheerful spring blossoms, with traditional koto music playing softly in the background. The English-language menu lists yakitori set courses, and a la carte sticks are skewered with shrimp, meatballs, gingko, squid, eggplant, or mushrooms.

4–10–11 Roppongi. ✆ 03/3405-4377. Yakitori skewers ¥240 – ¥280 ($2.30–$2.65); set dinners ¥2,300 – ¥4,300 ($22–$41). AE, DC, MC, V. Mon–Sat 5–11:30pm. Station: Roppongi (2 min.). Off Gaien-Higashi Dori on a side street opposite Ibis Hotel; from Roppongi Crossing, walk on Gaien-Higashi Dori in the direction of Aoyama and take the 2nd right.

**Kitchen Five** ✦ *Finds* MEDITERRANEAN/ETHNIC   If it's true that love is the best spice for cooking, then perhaps that's why Yuko Kobayashi's 15-year-old, 16-seat restaurant is so popular. She goes to market every morning to fetch ingredients for a dozen main dishes, which may include stuffed eggplant, moussaka, and other casseroles and curries. Every summer Kobayashi goes off to search for recipes in Sicily, South America, northern Africa, and other countries that feature garlic, tomatoes, and olive oil in their cuisine. The love for what she does shines in her eyes as she cooks, serves, and walks you through the menu of daily dishes displayed. Highly recommended. *A word of warning:* The food is so delicious, it's tempting to overorder.

4–2–15 Nishi Azabu. ✆ 03/3409-8835. Dishes ¥1,300–¥1,900 ($12–$18). No credit cards. Tues–Sat 6–9:45pm (last order). Closed holidays, Golden Week, and late July to early Sept. Station: Hiroo (7 min.) or Roppongi (15 min.). Opposite Gaien-Nishi Dori from the gas station, down a side street.

**Roti** AMERICAN    A casual brasserie with both indoor (nonsmoking) and outdoor seating, Roti counts many ex-pats among its loyal customers, due in part to its quiet, tucked-away location just a minute's walk from Roppongi Hills and also to its bilingual staff and modern American fare, including free-range rotisserie chicken, grilled steaks and burgers, lobster risotto, serious Caesar salads, and delectable New York cheesecake. More than 90 bottles of New World, Australian, and New Zealand wines, as well as American ales and Belgian microbrews, are on offer, as well as a Sunday breakfast menu (served until 3pm) that includes eggs Benedict, blueberry pancakes, and omelets, along with a bottomless cup of coffee.

6–6–9 Roppongi. ✆ 03/5785-3671. www.rotico.com. Main dishes ¥1,600–¥3,800 ($15–$36); set lunches ¥1,400–¥1,650 ($13–$16). No credit cards. Mon–Fri 11:30am–2:30pm; Sat 11:30am–5pm; Sun 11am–5pm; daily 6–11pm. Station: Roppongi (5 min.). From Roppongi Crossing, take the side street beside Almond coffee shop and take the first right. It's near the end of this street, on the left before Roppongi Hills.

## AKASAKA
### VERY EXPENSIVE

**La Tour d'Argent** 🎭🎭 CLASSIC FRENCH    Here's the place to dine if you're celebrating a very special occasion, are on a hefty expense account, or fancy yourself a jet-setter. Opened in 1984, La Tour d'Argent is the authentic sister to the one in Paris, which opened back in 1582 and was visited twice by Japan's former emperor, Hirohito. Entrance to the Tokyo restaurant is through an impressive hallway with a plush interior and displays of tableware used in the Paris establishment throughout the centuries. The dining hall looks like an elegant Parisian drawing room. The service is superb, and the food is excellent. The specialty here is roast duckling—it meets its untimely end at the age of 3 weeks and is flown to Japan from Brittany. Other dishes on the menu, which changes seasonally, may include lobster or Kobe beef sirloin.

Hotel New Otani, 4–1 Kioi-cho. ✆ 03/3239-3111. www.newotani.co.jp/en. Reservations required. Main dishes ¥5,600–¥13,000 ($53–$124). AE, DC, MC, V. Tues–Sun 5:30–10:30pm (last reservation accepted for 8:30pm). Station: Akasaka-mitsuke or Nagatacho (3 min.).

**Sekishin Tei** 🎭🎭 TEPPANYAKI    Nestled in the New Otani's 400-year-old garden (which is the reason this is the hotel's most popular restaurant), this glass-enclosed teppanyaki pavilion has an English-language menu for Kobe beef, fish, lobster, and vegetables, cooked on a grill right in front of you. If you order a salad, try the soy sauce dressing; it's delicious. You'll eat surrounded by peaceful views, making this place a good lunchtime choice.

Hotel New Otani, 4–1 Kioi-cho, Chiyoda-ku. ✆ 03/3238-0024. www.newotani.co.jp/en. Reservations required. Set dinners ¥13,600–¥18,000 ($129–$171); set lunches ¥3,675–¥6,300 ($35–$60). AE, DC, MC, V. Mon–Fri 11:30am–2pm and 6–9pm; Sat–Sun and holidays 11:30am–3pm and 6–9pm. Station: Nagatacho or Akasaka-mitsuke (3 min.).

### EXPENSIVE

In addition to the recommendations here, there's a branch of **Ten-ichi,** specializing in tempura, in Akasaka Tokyu Plaza, 2–14–3 Nagata-cho (✆ **03/3581-2166**), open daily 11am to 9:30pm (see "Hibiya & Ginza," earlier in this chapter, for a review).

㉞ **Hayashi** 🎭🎭🎭 *Finds* JAPANESE GRILL/RICE CASSEROLES    One of the most delightful old-time restaurants I've been to in Tokyo, this cozy, rustic-looking place serves home-style country cooking and specializes in grilled food that you prepare over your own square hibachi. Altogether, there are eight grills in this small restaurant, some of them surrounded by tatami mats and some by wooden stools or

chairs. As the evening wears on, the one-room main dining areas can get quite smoky, but that just adds to the ambience. Other nice touches are the big gourds and memorabilia hanging about and the waiters in traditional baggy pants. Hayashi serves three set menus, which change with the seasons. The ¥6,300 ($60) meal—which will probably end up being closer to ¥8,000 ($76) by the time you add drinks and service charge—may include such items as sashimi and vegetables, chicken, scallops, and gingko nuts, which you grill yourself. At lunch, only *oyakodonburi* is served: literally, "parent and child," a simple rice dish topped with egg and chicken.

Sanno Kaikan Building, 4th floor, 2–14–1 Akasaka. ✆ 03/3582-4078. Reservations required for dinner. Set dinners ¥6,300, ¥8,400, and ¥10,500 ($60, $80, and $100); set lunches ¥900 ($8.55). AE, DC, MC, V. Mon–Fri 11:30am–2pm and 5:30–11pm; Sat 5:30–11pm. Closed holidays. Station: Akasaka (exit 2, 1 min.). Just south of Misuji Dori on the 3rd and 4th floors of a nondescript, improbable-looking building.

**Ninja** ✿ VARIED JAPANESE   At this themed restaurant, diners enter the secret world of the ninja as soon as they step inside the darkened entrance, where costumed waiters appear out of nowhere to lead the hungry through a series of twisting passageways to private dining nooks. A scroll unrolls to reveal an English-language menu listing various set dinner menus that may include shabu-shabu, as well as a la carte items like sweet-and-sour pork with asparagus, sole baked with herbs in saffron sauce, and grilled tenderloin beef and foie gras wrapped in *yuba* (soymilk skin). A fun place for a meal, but book early to reserve a seat.

Akasaka Tokyu Plaza, 1st floor, 2–14–3 Nagata-cho. ✆ 03/5157-3936. Reservations required. Main dishes ¥1,800–¥3,500 ($17–$33); set dinners ¥7,000–¥20,000 ($67–$190). AE, DC, MC, V. Mon–Sat 5pm–2am; Sun and holidays 6–11pm. Station: Akasaka-mitsuke (1 min.). In the candy-cane-striped building, below the Akasaka Excel Tokyu Hotel.

## MODERATE

**Blue Sky** CHINESE   Located on the 17th floor of the New Otani's main building with great views of the city, this revolving restaurant provides panoramic views and all-you-can eat buffets, primarily Chinese. The food, tasty and varied, consists of approximately 40 different items for lunch and 50 for dinner, and includes spicy Szechuan cuisine, dim sum, Japanese food, and freshly baked pizza. My only complaint is that the restaurant revolves at such breakneck speed—making a complete turn every 45 minutes—that it almost matches fast-paced Tokyo. If the thought makes you dizzy, another buffet-style restaurant called **Top of the Tower,** on the 40th floor of the New Otani's tower, also has spectacular views of the city and offers Continental buffet lunches for ¥5,040 ($48) and dinners for ¥7,875 ($75).

Hotel New Otani, 4–1 Kioi-cho, Chiyoda-ku. ✆ 03/3238-0028. www.newotani.co.jp/en. Dinner buffet ¥6,615 ($63); lunch buffet ¥3,675 ($35). AE, DC, MC, V. Daily 11:30am–2pm and 5–9pm. Station: Akasaka-mitsuke or Nagatacho (3 min.).

**daidaiya** ✿ *Finds* VARIED JAPANESE/NOUVELLE JAPANESE   Upon exiting the elevator, you'll be forgiven for confusedly thinking you've landed in a nightclub rather than a restaurant—daidaiya's dark, theatrical entrance is the first clue that this is not your ordinary Japanese restaurant. The dining room, a juxtaposition of modern and traditional with a slate stone floor, shoji screens, warm woods, and black furniture, is rather like the cuisine—a curious mix of traditional Japanese food and original nouvelle creations, all mouthwateringly good. Pop music or jazz plays in the background, and for dinner, gauzy sheets of fabric are hung from the ceiling to create tiny, tête-à-tête dining cubicles for couples. Tatami seating is also available, with views

over Akasaka. An English-language menu lists such intriguing entrees as sashimi and vegetables rolled in kimchi; skewered chicken rolled in lettuce; foie gras steak; and prime beef on magnolia *(hoba)* leaf grilled over charcoal with a citrus-flavored soy sauce. Lunch sets, including obento, are equally satisfying. I love this place.

There's a branch located on the third floor of the Nowa building, 3–37–12 Shinjuku (𝓒 **03/5362-7173**).

Bellevie Akasaka Building, 9th floor, 3–1–6 Akasaka. 𝓒 **03/3588-5087**. Reservations recommended for dinner. Main dishes ¥1,100–¥2,300 ($10–$22); set dinners ¥5,000–¥8,000 ($48–$76); set lunches ¥1,000–¥3,500 ($9.50–$33). AE, DC, MC, V. Mon–Fri 11:30am–2pm and 5pm–midnight (last order); Sat–Sun 11:30am–3pm and 5–11pm. Station: Akasaka-mitsuke (1 min., underneath the Bellevie Akasaka Building).

# Exploring Tokyo

Tokyo hasn't fared very well over the centuries. Fires and earthquakes have taken their toll, old buildings have been torn down in the zeal of modernization, and World War II left most of the city in ruins. The Tokyo of today has very little remaining of historical significance. Save your historical sightseeing for places like Kyoto, Nikko, and Kamakura, and consider Tokyo your introduction to the newest of the new in Japan, the showcase of the nation's accomplishments in the arts, technology, fashion, pop art, and design. It's also the best place in the world to take in Japan's performing arts, such as Kabuki, and such diverse activities as the tea ceremony, flower arranging, and sumo. Tokyo also has more museums than any other city in Japan, as well as a wide range of other attractions, including parks and temples. In Tokyo you can explore mammoth department stores, experiment with restaurants, walk around the various neighborhoods, revel in kitsch, and take advantage of glittering nightlife. There's so much to do in Tokyo that I can't imagine ever being bored there—even for a minute.

**SEEING THE CITY BY GUIDED TOUR** With the help of this book and a good map, you should be able to visit Tokyo's major attractions easily on your own. Should you be pressed for time, however, consider taking one of several group tours of Tokyo and its environs offered by the **Japan Travel Bureau (JTB;** ✆ **03/5796-5454;** www.jtb.co.jp/sunrisetour) or **Japan Gray Line** (✆ **03/3433-5745;**

www.jgl.co.jp/inbound/index.htm). Day tours may include Tokyo Tower, the Imperial Palace district, Asakusa Sensoji Temple, Meiji Jingu Shrine, a harbor or river cruise, and the Ginza. A number of organized evening tours take in such activities as Kabuki or entertainment by geisha. Be warned, however, that tours are very tourist-oriented and are more expensive than touring Tokyo on your own. Prices range from about ¥5,000 ($48) for a half-day tour to about ¥9,800 ($93) for a night tour with dinner and Kabuki. You can easily book tours through most tourist hotels and travel agencies.

Although they cover less ground, 10 tours offered by the Tokyo Metropolitan Government concentrate on specific areas or themes, such as Japanese gardens or Harajuku. Lasting 2 to 3 hours, they are conducted mostly on foot and vary in price from free to ¥2,860 ($27), plus admission costs of the volunteer guides. Tours depart from the Tokyo Tourist Information Center in Shinjuku or the TCVB office in Yurakucho at 1pm Monday to Friday, and pre-registration is required. For more information, check the website www.tourism.metro.Tokyo.jp/English/guideservice/index.html or contact the tourist offices (see chapter 4 for locations and open hours).

Volunteer guides are also on hand at the Ueno Green Salon in Ueno Park every Wednesday, Friday, and Sunday for 90-minute walking tours departing at 10:30am and 1:30pm. No registration is required. For more information, call ✆ **03/5246-1151.**

Otherwise, one tour I especially like is a **boat trip on the Sumida River** between Hama Rikyu Garden and Asakusa. Commentary on the 40-minute trip is in both Japanese and English (be sure to pick up the English-language leaflet, too). You'll get descriptions of the 12 bridges you pass along the way and views of Tokyo you'd otherwise miss. Boats depart Hama Rikyu Garden hourly or more frequently between 10:20am and 4:20pm, with the fare to Asakusa costing ¥620 ($5.90) one-way. Other cruises are available from Hinode Pier (closest station: Hinode, about a 1-min. walk) to Asakusa (fare: ¥660/$6.25), Tokyo Sea Life Park in Kasai (fare: ¥800/$7.60), and Odaiba (fare: ¥500/$4.75). For more information, contact the **Tourist Information Center** (© **03/3201-3331**) or the **Tokyo Cruise Ship Co.** (© **03/5733-4812;** www.suijobus.co.jp).

For personalized, one-on-one tours of Tokyo, contact **Jun's Tokyo Discovery Tours,** managed by Tokyoite Junko Matsuda, which offers tailored sightseeing trips to Tsukiji, Asakusa, Yanaka, Harajuku, Aoyama, Shibuya, and Shinjuku, as well as shopping trips and special trips designed to fit your interests. Tours, which are especially useful if you wish to communicate with shopkeepers and the locals, want to learn more about what you're seeing, or are timid about finding your way on public transportation (if you wish, you'll be met at your hotel), cost ¥20,000 ($190) for 1 day (8 hr.) and are available for up to four adults or a family. Reserve tours at least 3 days in advance (1 week preferred) by fax (03/3749-0445) or e-mail (me2@gb3.so-net.ne.jp), stating the desired tour date and what you'd like to see; messages can also be left at © **03/3749-0445.**

## 1 The Top Attractions

There are two things to remember when planning your sightseeing itinerary: The city is huge, and it takes time to get from one end to the other. Plan your days so you cover Tokyo neighborhood by neighborhood, coordinating sightseeing with dinner and evening plans. The suggestions below will guide you to the most important attractions, but note that some attractions are closed 1 day of the week.

**Edo-Tokyo Museum (Edo-Tokyo Hakubutsukan)** ✸✸✸ (Kids)   The building housing this impressive museum is said to resemble a rice granary when viewed from afar, but to me it looks like a modern *torii,* the entrance gate to a shrine. This is the metropolitan government's ambitious attempt to present the history, art, disasters, science, culture, and architecture of Tokyo from its humble beginnings in 1590—when the first shogun, Tokugawa Ieyasu, made Edo (old Tokyo) the seat of his domain—to 1964, when Tokyo hosted the Olympics. All in all, the museum's great visual displays create a vivid portrayal of Tokyo through the centuries. I wouldn't miss it. Plan on spending 2 hours here.

After purchasing your tickets and taking the escalator to the sixth floor, you'll enter the museum by walking over a replica of Nihombashi Bridge, the starting point for all roads leading out of old Edo. Exhibits covering the Edo Period portray the lives of the shogun, merchants, craftsmen, and townspeople. The explanations are mostly in Japanese only, but there's plenty to look at, including a replica of an old Kabuki theater, a model of a *daimyo's* (feudal ruler's) mansion, portable floats used during festivals, maps and photographs of old Edo, and—perhaps most interesting—a row house tenement where Edo commoners lived in cramped quarters measuring only 10 sq. m (108 sq. ft.). Other displays cover the Meiji Restoration, the Great Kanto Earthquake

of 1923, and the bombing raids of World War II (Japan's own role as aggressor is disappointingly glossed over).

If you wish, take advantage of a free museum tour offered by volunteers daily 10am to 3pm (last tour). Most tours last 1 to 2 hours, depending on the level of visitor interest, and are insightful for their explanations of the Japanese-only displays. However, tours are necessarily rushed and focus on particular displays; you may wish to tour the museum afterward on your own.

1–4–1 Yokoami, Sumida-ku. (© 03/3626-9974. www.edo-tokyo-museum.or.jp. Admission ¥600 ($5.70) adults, ¥480 ($4.55) students, ¥300 ($2.50) seniors and children junior high–high school, free for children. Tues–Wed and Sat–Sun 9:30am–5:30pm; Thurs–Fri 9:30am–8pm. Station: Ryogoku on the JR Sobu and Oedo lines (2 min.).

**The Imperial Palace (Kyokyo)** ✿    The Imperial Palace, home of the imperial family, is the heart and soul of Tokyo. Built on the very spot where Edo Castle used to stand during the days of the Tokugawa shogunate, it became the imperial home upon its completion in 1888 and is now the residence of Emperor Akihito, 125th emperor of Japan. Destroyed during air raids in 1945, the palace was rebuilt in 1968 using the principles of traditional Japanese architecture. But don't expect to get a good look at it; most of the palace grounds' 114 hectares (284 acres) are off-limits to the public, with the exception of 2 days a year when the royal family makes an appearance before the throngs: January 2 and December 23 (the emperor's birthday). Or you can visit imperial grounds on free **guided tours** Monday through Friday at 10am and 1:30pm, but you must register at least 1 day in advance (reservations are accepted up to 1 month in advance) by calling (© **03/3213-111,** ext. 485 or 486, and then stopping by the Imperial Household (located at the Sakashita-mon Gate, on the east side of palace grounds) to provide your passport number, nationality, name, age, occupation, and address in Tokyo. Tours, conducted in Japanese but with English-language audio guides available, last about 75 minutes and lead past official buildings, the inner moat and historic fortifications, and Nijubashi Bridge. I recommend this tour only if you have time to spare and have already seen Tokyo's other top attractions.

Otherwise, you'll have to console yourself with a camera shot of the palace from the southeast side of **Nijubashi Bridge,** where the moat and the palace turrets show above the trees. Most Japanese tourists make brief stops here to pay their respects. The wide moat, lined with cherry trees, is especially beautiful in the spring. You might even want to spend an hour strolling the 4.8km (3 miles) around the palace and moat. But the most important thing to do in the vicinity of the palace is to visit its **Higashi Gyoen (East Garden),** where you'll find what's left of the central keep of old Edo Castle, the stone foundation; see "Parks & Gardens," later in this chapter.

Hibiya Dori Ave. Station: Nijubashi-mae (1 min.) or Hibiya (5 min.).

**Meiji Jingu Shrine** ✿✿    This is Tokyo's most venerable Shinto shrine, opened in 1920 in honor of Emperor and Empress Meiji, who were instrumental in opening Japan to the outside world more than 120 years ago. Japan's two largest *torii* (the traditional entry gate of a shrine), built of cypress more than 1,700 years old, give dramatic entrance to the grounds, once the estate of a *daimyo* (feudal lord). The shaded pathway is lined with trees, shrubs, and dense woods. In late May/June, the **Iris Garden** is in spectacular bloom (separate admission fee charged). About a 10-minute walk from the first torii, the shrine is a fine example of dignified and refined Shinto architecture. It's made of plain Japanese cypress and topped with green-copper roofs.

# Tokyo Attractions

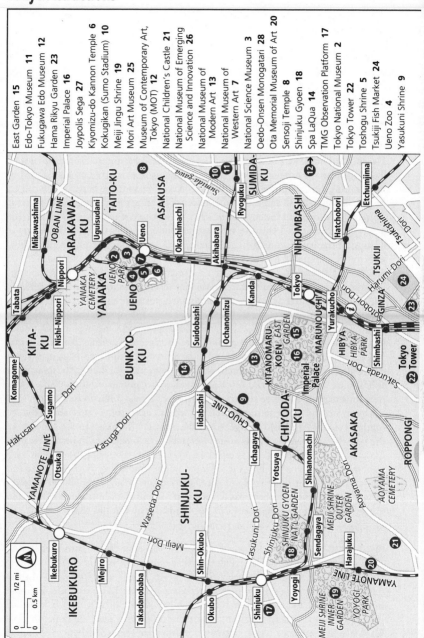

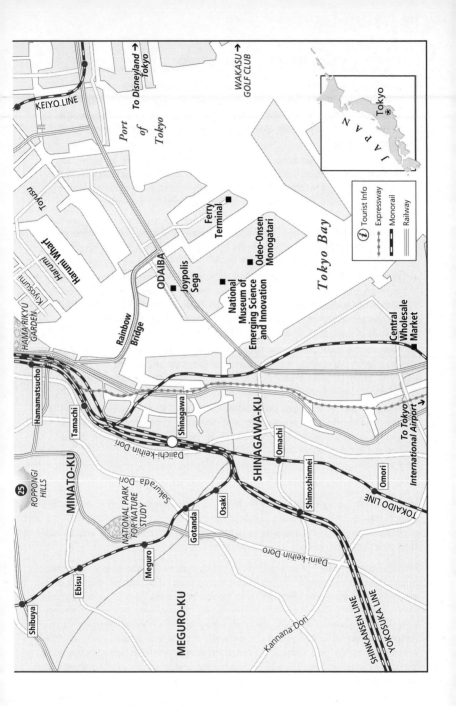

175

## Frommer's Favorite Tokyo Experiences

**Strolling through Asakusa**   Asakusa conveys the atmosphere of old Tokyo better than any other place in the city. Sensoji Temple is the city's oldest and most popular temple, and Nakamise Dori, the pedestrian lane leading to the temple, is lined with open-fronted stalls selling souvenirs and traditional Japanese goods.

**Taking in the Early Morning Action at Tsukiji Fish Market**   Get up early your first morning in Japan (you'll probably be wide awake with jet lag anyway) and head straight for the country's largest fish market, where you can watch the tuna auctions, browse through stalls of seafood, and sample the freshest sushi you'll ever have.

**Spending an Evening in a Yakitori-ya**   There's no better place to observe Tokyo's army of office workers at play than at a yakitori-ya, a drinking place that serves skewered foods and bar snacks. They're fun and noisy.

**Watching a Kabuki Play at the Kabukiza Theater**   Kabuki has served as the most popular form of entertainment for the masses since the Edo Period. Watch the audience members as they yell their approval; watch the stage for gorgeous costumes, stunning stage settings, and easy-to-understand dramas of love, duty, and revenge.

**Viewing the Treasures at the Tokyo National Museum**   There's a feast for the eyes at the world's largest museum of Japanese art, packed with everything from samurai armor and lacquerware to kimono and woodblock prints. If you visit only one museum in Tokyo, this should be it.

**Hanging Out in Harajuku on Sunday**   Start with brunch and then stroll Omotesando Dori for people-watching. Shop the area's boutiques, visit a couple of museums and the Meiji Shrine, or just sit back and take in all the action from a sidewalk cafe.

Meiji Jingu Shrine is the place to be on New Year's Eve, when more than two million people crowd onto the grounds to usher in the New Year.

Meiji Shrine Inner Garden, 1–1 Kamizono-cho, Yoyogi, Shibuya-ku. ✆ 03/3379-5511. Free admission. Daily sunrise–sunset (until 4:30pm in winter). Station: Harajuku (2 min.).

**Sensoji Temple** *ᏗᏗᏗ*   Also popularly known as Asakusa Kannon, this is Tokyo's oldest and most popular temple, with a history dating from 628. That was when, according to popular lore, two brothers fishing in the nearby Sumida River netted the catch of their lives—a tiny golden statue of Kannon, the Buddhist goddess of mercy and happiness who is empowered with the ability to release humans from all suffering. Sensoji Temple was erected in her honor, and although the statue is housed here, it's never shown to the public. Still, through the centuries, worshippers have flocked here seeking favors of Kannon; and when Sensoji Temple burned down during a 1945 bombing raid, the present structure was rebuilt with donations from the Japanese people.

Colorful **Nakamise Dori,** a pedestrian lane leading to the shrine, is lined with traditional shops and souvenir stands, while nearby **Demboin Garden** remains an

**Seeing Sumo** Nothing beats watching huge sumo wrestlers (most weigh well over 135kg/300 lb.) throw each other around. Matches are held in Tokyo in January, May, and September; catch one on TV if you can't make it in person.

**Shopping the Department Stores** Tokyo's department stores are huge, spotless, and filled with merchandise, some of which you never knew existed; many also have first-rate art galleries. Shibuya and Ginza boast the greatest concentration of department stores. Tobu, in Ikebukuro, is the city's largest—a virtual city in itself. Be there when the doors open in the morning and you can witness a sight you'll never see back home: employees lined up in a row, bowing to incoming customers.

**Soaking in Hot-Spring Baths at Oedo-Onsen Monogatari** This Edo-themed public bath features hot-spring waters pumped up from the deep outdoor tubs, massage, souvenirs, and restaurants, making this a standout for soaking away urban stress.

**Feasting on a Kaiseki Meal** A kaiseki meal, consisting of dish after dish of artfully displayed delectables, goes for big bucks—but it may well be the most beautiful and memorable meal you'll ever have. Splurge at least once on the most expensive kaiseki meal you can afford, and you'll feel like royalty.

**Taking a Spin through Kabuki-cho** Shinjuku's Kabuki-cho has the craziest nightlife in all of Tokyo, with countless strip joints, porn shops, restaurants, bars, and the greatest concentration of neon you're likely to see anywhere. It's a fascinating place for an evening stroll.

**Clubbing in Roppongi** You can dance and party the night away in the madness that's Roppongi; most revelers party 'til dawn.

insider's favorite as a peaceful oasis away from the bustling crowds. Asakusa is one of my favorite neighborhoods, and you can easily spend half a day here; see the walking tours below for more on this fascinating part of old Tokyo.

2–3–1 Asakusa, Taito-ku. © 03/3842-0181. Free admission. Daily 6am–5pm. Station: Asakusa (2 min.).

## Tokyo National Museum (Tokyo Kokuritsu Hakubutsukan) ✷✷✷ The
National Museum not only is the largest and oldest museum in Japan, it also boasts the largest collection of Japanese art in the world. This is where you go to see antiques from Japan's past—old kimono, samurai armor, priceless swords, lacquerware, metalwork, pottery, scrolls, screens, *ukiyo-e* (woodblock prints), calligraphy, ceramics, archaeological finds, and more. Items are shown on a rotating basis with about 4,000 on display at any one time—so no matter how many times you visit the museum, you'll always see something new. Schedule at least 2 hours to do the museum justice.

The museum is composed of five buildings. The **Main Gallery (Honkan),** straight ahead as you enter the main gate, is the most important one, devoted to Japanese art.

Here you'll view Japanese ceramics; Buddhist sculptures dating from about A.D. 538 to 1192; samurai armor, helmets, and decorative sword mountings; swords, which throughout Japanese history were considered to embody spirits all their own; textiles and kimono; lacquerware; ceramics; and paintings, calligraphy, ukiyo-e, and scrolls. Be sure to check out the museum shop in the basement; it sells reproductions from the museum's collections as well as traditional crafts by contemporary artists.

The **Gallery of Eastern Antiquities (Toyokan)** houses art and archaeological artifacts from everywhere in Asia outside Japan. There are Buddhas from China and Gandhara, stone reliefs from Cambodia, embroidered wall hangings and cloth from India, Iranian and Turkish carpets, Thai and Vietnamese ceramics, and more. Chinese art—including jade, paintings, calligraphy, and ceramics—makes up the largest part of the collection, illustrating China's tremendous influence on Japanese art, architecture, and religion. You'll also find Egyptian relics, including a mummy dating from around 751 to 656 B.C. and wooden objects from the 20th century B.C.

The **Heiseikan Gallery** is where you'll find archaeological relics of ancient Japan, including pottery and Haniwa clay burial figurines of the Jomon Period (10,000 B.C.–1,000 B.C.) and ornamental, keyhole-shaped tombs from the Yayoi Period (400 B.C.–A.D. 200). The **Gallery of Horyuji Treasures (Horyuji Homotsukan)** displays priceless Buddhist treasures from the Horyuji Temple in Nara, founded by Prince Shotoku in 607. Although the building's stark modernity (designed by Taniguchi Yoshio, who also designed the expansion of the New York Museum of Modern Art) seems odd for an exhibition of antiquities, the gallery's low lighting and simple architecture lend dramatic effect to the museum's priceless collection of bronze Buddhist statues, ceremonial Gigaku masks used in ritual dances, lacquerware, and paintings. The **Hyokeikan,** built in 1909 to commemorate the marriage of Emperor Taisho, holds special exhibitions.

Ueno Park, Taito-ku. © 03/3822-1111. www.tnm.jp. Admission ¥420 ($4) adults, ¥130 ($1.25) students, free for seniors (except during special exhibitions), free for children. Oct–Mar Tues–Sun 9:30am–5pm (enter by 4:30pm); Apr–Sept Tues–Fri and Sat–Sun 9:30am–6pm (Fri open to 8pm during special exhibitions). Closed Dec 26–Jan 3. Station: Ueno (10 min.).

**Tsukiji Fish Market** 🐟🐟🐟    This huge wholesale fish market—the largest in Japan and one of the largest in the world—is a must for anyone who has never seen such a market in action. And the action here starts early: At about 3am, boats begin arriving from the seas around Japan, from Africa, and even from America, with enough fish to satisfy the demands of a nation where seafood reigns supreme. To give you some idea of its enormity, this market handles almost all the seafood—about 450 kinds of seafood—consumed in Tokyo. The king is tuna, huge and frozen, unloaded from the docks, laid out on the ground, and numbered. Wholesalers walk up and down the rows, jotting down the numbers of the best-looking tuna, and by 5:30am, the tuna auctions are well under way (however, too many tourists prompted authorities to close tuna auctions to visitors in 2005). The entire auction of sea products takes place about 4:40 to 6:30am, with auctions of vegetables at a corner of the market starting at 6:30am (refrain from photographing auctions). The wholesalers then transfer what they've bought to their own stalls in the market, subsequently selling fish and produce to their regular customers, usually retail stores and restaurants.

The market is held in a cavernous, hangarlike building, which means you can visit it even on a dismal rainy morning. There's a lot going on—men in black rubber boots rushing wheelbarrows and carts through the aisles, hawkers shouting, knives chopping

and slicing. Wander the aisles and you'll see things you never dreamed were edible. This is a good place to bring your camera: The people working here burst with pride if you single them out for a photograph. The floors are wet, so leave your fancy shoes at the hotel.

Tsukiji is also a good place to come if you want sushi for breakfast. Alongside the covered market are rows of barracklike buildings divided into sushi restaurants and shops related to the fish trade. In addition, as you walk the distance between the Tsukiji subway station and the fish market, you'll find yourself in a delightful district of tiny retail shops and stalls where you can buy the freshest seafood in town, plus dried fish and fish products, seaweed, vegetables, knives, and other cooking utensils. *Warning:* While walking through the retail district on our way from Tsukiji Market, my Japanese friend and I were warned several times by local shopkeepers to keep watch over our purses, advice we didn't take lightly. Apparently, pickpockets have been at work here on unsuspecting tourists.

5–2–1 Tsukiji, Chuo-ku. (𝒞 03/3542-1111. Free admission. Mon–Sat 5–11am (best time 5:30–9am). Closed some Wed, holidays, Dec, New Year's, and Aug 15–16. Station: Tsukijishijo (exit A2, 2 min.) or Tsukiji (Honganji Temple exit, 10 min.).

## 2 Five Unforgettable Ways to Immerse Yourself in Japanese Culture

Just walking down the street could be considered a cultural experience in Japan, but there are more concrete ways to learn more about this country's cultural life: The best is by participating in some of its time-honored rituals and traditions. For some background information on Japanese flower arranging, the tea ceremony, and other activities recommended below, see "Cultural Snapshots: Japanese Arts in a Nutshell," in appendix A.

**IKEBANA**   Instruction in *ikebana,* or Japanese flower arranging, is available at several schools in Tokyo, a few of which offer classes in English on a regular basis. (Note that you should call beforehand to enroll.) **Sogetsu Ikebana School,** 7–2–21 Akasaka (𝒞 03/3408-1151; www.sogetsu.or.jp; station: Aoyama-Itchome, a 5-min. walk from exit 4), offers instruction in English on Monday from 10am to noon (closed in Aug). The cost of one lesson for first-time participants is ¥3,800 ($36). The **Ohara Ikebana School,** 5–7–17 Minami Aoyama (𝒞 03/5774-5097; www.ohararyu.or.jp; station: Omotesando, 3-min. walk from exit B1), offers 2-hour English-language instruction at 10am on Wednesday and 10am and 1:30pm on Thursday, charging ¥2,000 ($19) for instruction, plus extra cost for flowers (no classes July 20–Sept 8).

If you wish to see ikebana, ask at the **Tourist Information Office** whether there are any special exhibitions. Department stores sometimes have special ikebana exhibitions in their galleries. Another place to look is **Yasukuni Shrine,** located on Yasukuni Dori northwest of the Imperial Palace (closest station: Ichigaya or Kudanshita). Dedicated to Japanese war dead, the shrine is also famous for ongoing ikebana exhibitions on its grounds.

**TEA CEREMONY**   Several first-class hotels hold tea-ceremony demonstrations in special tea-ceremony rooms. Reservations are usually required, and since the ceremonies are often booked by groups, you'll want to call in advance to see whether you can participate. **Seisei-an,** on the seventh floor of the Hotel New Otani, 4–1 Kioi-cho, Chiyoda-ku (𝒞 03/3265-1111, ext. 2443; station: Nagatacho or Akasaka-mitsuke, a

3-min. walk from both), holds 20-minute demonstrations Thursday through Saturday from 11am to 4pm. The cost is ¥1,050 ($10), including tea and sweets. **Chosho-an,** on the seventh floor of the Hotel Okura, 2–10–4 Toranomon, Minato-ku (© 03/ 3582-0111; station: Toranomon or Kamiyacho, a 10-min. walk from both), gives 30-minute demonstrations anytime between 11am and noon and between 1 and 4pm Monday through Saturday except holidays. Appointments are required; the cost is ¥1,050 ($10) for tea and sweets. At **Toko-an,** on the fourth floor of the Imperial Hotel, 1–1–1 Uchisaiwaicho, Chiyoda-ku (© 03/3504-1111; station: Hibiya, 1 min.), demonstrations are given from 10am to noon and 1 to 4pm Monday through Saturday except holidays. Reservations are required. The fee is ¥1,500 ($14) for tea and sweets.

**ACUPUNCTURE & SHIATSU**   Although most Westerners have heard of acupuncture, they may not be familiar with *shiatsu* (Japanese pressure-point massage). Most first-class hotels in Japan offer shiatsu in the privacy of your room. There are acupuncture clinics everywhere in Tokyo, and the staff of your hotel may be able to tell you of one nearby. As it's not likely the clinic's staff will speak English, it might be a good idea to have the guest relations officer at your hotel not only make the reservation but specify the treatment you want. Otherwise, English is spoken at **Yamate Acupuncture Clinic,** second floor of the ULS Nakameguro Building, 1–3–3 Higashiyama, Meguro-ku (© 03/3792-8989; station: Nakameguro, 6 min.), open Monday to Friday 9am to 8pm and Saturday 9am to 2pm and charging ¥3,000 ($29) for a specific treatment or ¥5,000 ($48) for the whole body, plus a ¥1,000 ($9.50) initial fee. English is also spoken at **Tani Clinic,** third floor of the Taishoseimei Hibiya Building, 1–9–1 Yurakucho, Chiyoda-ku (© 03/3201-5675; station: Hibiya, 1 min.), open Monday, Tuesday, Wednesday, Friday, and Saturday 9am to noon and 2 to 5pm and charging ¥10,500 ($100) for the first visit, ¥6,300 ($60) for each subsequent visit.

**PUBLIC BATHS**   Tokyo has more than 1,000 *sento* (public baths)—which may sound like a lot but is nothing compared to the 2,687 the city used to have in the 1970s. Easily recognizable by a tall chimney and shoe lockers just inside the door, a sento sells just about anything you might need at the bathhouse—soap, shampoo, towels, even underwear.

For a unique bathing experience, nothing beats a 3- or 4-hour respite at the **Oedo-Onsen Monogatari,** 2–57 Aomi on Odaiba (© 03/5500-1126; station: Telecom Center Station, 2 min.), which tapped mineral-rich hot-spring waters 1,380m (4,600 ft.) below ground to supply this re-created Edo-Era bathhouse village. After changing into *yukata* (cotton kimono) and depositing your belongings in a locker (your key is bar-coded so there's no need to carry any money), you'll stroll past souvenir shops and restaurants on your way to massage rooms, sand baths (extra fee charged), and *onsen* (hot-spring baths) complete with outdoor baths, Jacuzzi, steam baths, and saunas. Since as many as 6,500 bathers pour into this facility on weekends, try to come on a weekday, and since signs in the English-language are virtually nonexistent, observe gender before entering bathing areas (a hint: women's baths usually have pink or red curtains, men's blue). Open daily 11am to 9am the next day. Admission is ¥2,827 ($27) for adults and ¥1,570 ($15) for children, with reduced prices after 6pm.

Not quite as colorful is the upscale **Spa LaQua,** 1–1–1 Kasuga (© 03/3817-4173; www.laqua.jp; station: Kasuga, 2 min.), located in the heart of Tokyo at Korakuen's Tokyo Dome City complex. It, too, has hot-spring indoor/outdoor baths, saunas, and massage options, but an adjoining amusement park with roller coasters (and screaming

passengers) makes this a less relaxing alternative. It's open daily 11am to 9am the next day, with admission priced at ¥2,565 ($24) for adults and ¥1,785 ($17) for children. Note that no children under 6 are allowed and no minors under 18 are allowed after 6pm.

**ZAZEN**   A few temples in the Tokyo vicinity occasionally offer sitting meditation with instruction in English. Approximately 30 minutes east of Akihabara on the Sobu Line is **Ida Ryogoku-do Zazen Dojo** of the Sotoshu Sect, 5–11–20 Minami Yawata, Ichikawa City (© **0473/79-1596;** station: Moto-Yawata, 5 min.). Zazen is held daily at 5:30 and 10am and 3 and 8:30pm, generally for 45 minutes (call to confirm times). A Dogen-Sangha meeting is held the fourth Saturday of the month from 1 to 2:30pm, consisting of 30 minutes for zazen followed by a 1-hour lecture. Participation is free, and if you call from Moto-Yawata Station, someone will come for you. You can also stay here for longer periods to practice Zen; call Mr. Nishijima at © **03/3435-0701** for more information.

In addition, the **Young Men Buddhist Association of Tokyo University,** of the Sotoshu Sect, second floor of the Nippon Shimpan Building, 3–33–5 Hongo (© **03/ 3235-0701;** station: Hongo-Sanchome, 3 min.) holds a Dogen-Sangha meeting the first, third, and fifth Saturday of each month from 1 to 2:30pm, which includes 30 minutes of zazen and a 1-hour lecture in English. There's a ¥400 ($3.80) fee. This one, too, allows long-term stays.

## 3 Parks & Gardens

Although Japan's most famous gardens are not in Tokyo, the first three places listed below use traditional principles of landscaping and give visitors an idea of the scope and style of Japanese gardens. (Nearby skyscrapers, however, detract from their charm; there ought to be a law.) The fourth listing, Ueno Park, is Tokyo's largest city park and contains a number of museums and attractions, making it one of the city's most visited places.

**Hama Rikyu Garden** 🕮🕮   Considered by some to be the best garden in Tokyo (but marred, in my opinion, by nearby buildings that detract from its charm), this peaceful oasis has origins stretching back 300 years, when it served as a retreat for a former feudal lord and as duck-hunting grounds for the Tokugawa shogun. In 1871, possession of the garden passed to the imperial family, who used it to entertain such visiting dignitaries as Gen. Ulysses S. Grant. Come here to see how the upper classes enjoyed themselves during the Edo Period. Located on Tokyo Bay and surrounded by water on three sides, the garden contains an inner tidal pool, spanned by three bridges draped with wisteria. There are also other ponds; a refuge for ducks, herons, and migratory birds; a promenade along the bay lined with pine trees and offering views of Rainbow Bridge; a 300-year-old pine; moon-viewing pavilions; and teahouses. Plan on at least an hour's stroll to see everything. From a boarding pier on the garden's grounds, ferries depart for Asakusa every hour (or more often) between 10:20am and 4:20pm; the fare is ¥620 ($5.90) one-way.

1–1 Hamarikyuteien, Chuo-ku. © **03/3541-0200.** Admission ¥300 ($2.85). Daily 9am–5pm. Station: Shiodome (exit 5, 5 min.) or Shimbashi (12 min.).

**East Garden (Higashi Gyoen)** 🕮🕮   The 21 hectares (53 acres) of the formal Higashi Gyoen—once the main grounds of Edo Castle and located next to the Imperial Palace— are a wonderful respite in the middle of the city. Yet surprisingly, this garden is hardly

ever crowded. **Ninomaru** ✦✦✦, my favorite part, is laid out in Japanese style with a pond, steppingstones, and winding paths; it's particularly beautiful when the wisteria, azaleas, irises, and other flowers are in bloom. Near Ninomaru is the **Sannomaru Shozokan,** with free changing exhibitions of art treasures belonging to the imperial family.

On the highest spot of Higashi Gyoen is the **Honmaru** (inner citadel), where Tokugawa's main castle once stood. Built in the first half of the 1600s, the castle was massive, surrounded by a series of whirling moats and guarded by 23 watchtowers and 99 gates around its 16km (10-mile) perimeter. At its center was Japan's tallest building at the time, the five-story castle keep, soaring 50m (168 ft.) above its foundations and offering an expansive view over Edo. This is where Tokugawa Ieyasu would have taken refuge, had his empire ever been seriously threatened. Although most of the castle was a glimmering white, the keep was black with a gold roof, which must have been quite a sight in old Edo as it towered above the rest of the city. All that remains today of the shogun's castle are a few towers, gates, stone walls, moats, and the stone foundations of the keep.

1–1 Chiyoda, Chiyoda-ku. 📞 03/3213-1111. Free admission. Mar–Oct Tues–Thurs and Sat–Sun 9am–4:30pm (enter by 4pm); Nov–Feb Tues–Thurs and Sat–Sun 9am–4pm (enter by 3:30pm). Closed Dec 23 and Dec 28–Jan 3; open other national holidays. Station: Otemachi, Takebashi, or Nijubashi-mae.

**Shinjuku Gyoen** ✦✦ *(Kids)*   Formerly the private estate of a feudal lord and then of the imperial family, this is considered one of the most important parks of the Meiji Era. It's wonderful for strolling because of the variety of its planted gardens; styles range from French and English to Japanese traditional. This place amazes me every time I come here. The park's 58 hectares (144 acres) make it one of the city's largest, and each bend in the pathway brings something completely different: Ponds and sculpted bushes give way to a promenade lined with sycamores that opens onto a rose garden. Cherry blossoms, azaleas, chrysanthemums, and other flowers provide splashes of color from spring through autumn. There are also wide grassy expanses, popular for picnics and playing, and a greenhouse filled with tropical plants. You could easily spend a half-day of leisure here, but for a quick fix of rejuvenation, 1½ hours will do.

11 Naitocho, Shinjuku-ku. 📞 03/3350-0151. Admission ¥200 ($1.90). Tues–Sun 9am–4:30pm (enter by 4pm). Station: Shinjuku Gyoen-mae (2 min.).

**Ueno Park**   Ueno Park—on the northeast edge of the Yamanote Line—is one of the largest parks in Tokyo and one of the most popular places in the city for Japanese families on a day's outing. It's a cultural mecca with a number of attractions, including the prestigious Tokyo National Museum; the National Museum of Western Art; the delightful Shitamachi Museum with its displays of old Tokyo; Ueno Zoo; and Shinobazu Pond, a bird sanctuary. For a map of the Ueno area, see p. 125.

A landmark in the park is the small **Toshogu Shrine.** Erected in 1651, it's dedicated to Tokugawa Ieyasu, founder of the Tokugawa shogunate. Stop here to pay respects to the man who made Edo (present-day Tokyo) the seat of his government and thus elevated the small village to the most important city in the country. The pathway to the shrine is lined with massive stone lanterns, as well as 50 copper lanterns donated by *daimyo* (feudal lords) from all over Japan. Entrance to the shrine itself is to the left of the main building, where you can see examples of exquisite art, including murals by a famous Edo artist, Kano Tan-yu, and samurai armor worn by Ieyasu. The shrine is open daily from 9am to 6pm (to 4:30pm in winter); admission is ¥200 ($1.90). On a more somber note, there's also a display on the shrine grounds appealing for world

peace, with photographs of Hiroshima following its destruction by the atomic bomb and of victims dead and alive.

Also in the park is **Kiyomizu Kannon-do Temple,** completed in 1631 as a copy of the famous Kiyomizu Temple in Kyoto (but on a much less grand scale). It enshrines Kosodate Kannon, protector of childbearing and child-raising. Women hoping to become pregnant come here to ask for the goddess's blessing; those whose wishes have been fulfilled return to pray for their children's good health and protection. Many leave behind dolls as symbols of their children—if you take your shoes off and walk to the door to the right of the inner shrine, you'll see some of those dolls. Once a year, a requiem service is held for all the dolls at the temple, after which they are cremated.

The busiest time of the year at Ueno Park is April, during the **cherry-blossom season,** when people come en masse to celebrate the birth of the new season. It's not the spiritual communion with nature that you might think, however. On weekends and in the evenings during cherry-blossom time (which only lasts for a few days), havoc prevails as office workers break out of their winter shells. Whole companies converge on the park to sit under the cherry trees on plastic or cardboard, and everyone drinks sake and beer and gets drunk and rowdy and—worst of all—sings karaoke. At any rate, visiting Ueno Park during cherry-blossom season is an experience no one should miss. More than likely, you'll be invited to join one of the large groups—and by all means, do so.

Taito-ku. Free admission to the park; separate admissions to each of its attractions. Daily 24 hr. Station: Ueno (1 min.).

## 4 More Museums

In addition to the museums listed below, Tokyo has a wealth of small museums specializing in everything from woodblock prints to architecture; for a more complete list of Tokyo museums, see *Frommer's Tokyo*. For details on the **Tokyo National Museum** and the **Edo-Tokyo Museum,** see "The Top Attractions," earlier in this chapter.

**Fukagawa Edo Museum (Fukagawa Edo Shiryokan)** ⚑ *Kids*   This is the Tokyo of your dreams, the way it appears in all those samurai flicks on Japanese TV: a reproduction of a 19th-century neighborhood in Fukagawa, a prosperous community on the east bank of the Sumida River during the Edo Period. This delightful museum is located off Kiyosumi Dori on a pleasant tree-lined, shop-filled street called Fukagawa Shiryokan Dori. The museum's hangarlike interior contains 11 full-scale replicas of traditional houses, vegetable and rice shops, a fish store, two inns, a fire watchtower, and tenement homes, all arranged to resemble an actual neighborhood. There are lots of small touches and flourishes to make the community seem real and believable—a cat sleeping on a roof, a snail crawling up a fence, a dog relieving itself on a pole, sounds of birds, and a vendor shouting his wares. The village even changes with the seasons (with trees sprouting cherry blossoms in spring and threatened by thunderstorms in summer) and, every 45 minutes or so, undergoes a day's cycle from morning (roosters crow, lights brighten) to night (the sun sets, the retractable roof closes to make everything dark). Of Tokyo's museums, this one is probably the best for children; plan on spending about an hour here. Don't confuse this museum with the much larger Edo-Tokyo Museum, which traces the history of Tokyo.

1–3–28 Shirakawa, Koto-ku. ⓒ **03/3630-8625.** Admission ¥300 ($2.85) adults, ¥50 (50¢) children 6–14. Daily 9:30am–5pm. Closed 2nd and 4th Mon of each month. Station: Kiyosumi-Shirakawa (3 min.).

*Tips* **Museum Holidays**

Most museums in Tokyo are closed on Mondays and for New Year's, generally the last few days in December and the first 3 days of January. If Monday happens to be a national holiday, most museums will remain open but will close Tuesday instead. Some of the privately owned museums, however, may also be closed on national holidays, as well as for exhibition changes. Call beforehand to avoid disappointment. Remember, too, that you must enter museums at least 30 minutes before closing time. For a listing of current special exhibitions, including those being held at major department stores, consult *Metropolis,* published weekly.

**Museum of Contemporary Art, Tokyo (MOT; Tokyo-to Gendai Bijutsukan)** ⚘
The MOT is inconveniently located but is well worth the trek if you're a fan of the avant-garde (you'll pass the Fukagawa Edo Museum, described above, on the way, so you may wish to visit both). This modern structure of glass and steel, with a long corridor entrance that reminds me of railroad trestles, houses both permanent and temporary exhibits of Japanese and international postwar art in large rooms that lend themselves to large installations. Although temporary exhibits, which occupy most of the museum space, have ranged from Southeast Asian art to a retrospective of Jasper Johns, the smaller permanent collection presents a chronological study of 50 years of contemporary art, beginning with Japanese postwar avant-garde and continuing with anti-artistic trends and pop art in the 1960s, minimalism, and art after the 1980s, with about 100 works displayed on a rotating basis. Included may be works by Andy Warhol, Gerhard Richter, Roy Lichtenstein, David Hockney, Frank Stella, Sandro Chia, and Julian Schnabel. Depending on the number of exhibits you visit, you'll spend anywhere from 1 to 2 hours here. Bonus: A computer room lets you surf the Internet for free.

4–1–1 Miyoshi, Koto-ku. ⓒ 03/5245-4111. www.mot-art-museum.jp. Admission to permanent collection ¥500 ($4.75) adults, ¥400 ($3.80) students, ¥250 ($2.10) high-school students and seniors, free for children; special exhibits ¥1,000 ($9.50) or more. Tues–Sun 10am–6pm. Station: Kiyosumi-Shirakawa (exit A3, 13 min.). On Fukagawa Shiroyokan-dori St., just off Mitsume Dori.

**Miraikan–National Museum of Emerging Science and Innovation (Nippon Kagaku Miraikan)** ⚘⚘ *(Kids)*   Opened in 2001 on Odaiba, this fascinating, educational museum provides hands-on exploration of the latest developments in cutting-edge science and technology, including interactions with robots, virtual-reality rides, a planetarium, and displays that suggest future applications such as non-invasive medical procedures and an environmentally friendly home. Everything from nanotechnology to genomes are explained in detail; touch-screens in English and a volunteer staff eager to assist in demonstrations and answer questions catapult this to one of the most user-friendly technology museums I've seen. A great place to get your brain cells up and running whether you're 4 years old or 80, this museum deserves at least 3 hours.

2–41 Aomi, Koto-ku. ⓒ 03/3570-9151. www.miraikan.jst.go.jp. Admission ¥500 ($4.75) adults, ¥200 ($1.90) children. Wed–Mon 10am–5pm. Station: Telecom Center or Fune-no-Kagakukan (5 min.). On Odaiba.

**Mori Art Museum (Mori Bijutsukan)** ⚘   This is Tokyo's highest museum, on the 53rd floor of the Roppongi Hills Mori Tower. Opened in 2003, it features state-of-the

art galleries with 6m-tall (20-ft.) ceilings, controlled natural lighting, and great views of Tokyo. Innovative exhibitions of emerging and established artists from around the world are shown four times a year, with past shows centering on contemporary Asian, African, and Japanese art. Although the installations are alone worth a visit, an extra incentive is the attached Tokyo City View observatory, usually included in the museum admission and providing eye-popping views over Tokyo. Plan on at least 90 minutes up here.

Roppongi Hills Mori Tower, 6–10–1 Roppongi, Minato-ku. ⟨© 03/5777 8600. www.mori.art.museum. Admission varies according to the exhibit but averages ¥1,500 ($14) adults, ¥1,000 ($9.50) students, and ¥500 ($4.75) children. Mon and Wed–Sun 10am–10pm; Tues 10am–5pm. Station: Roppongi (Roppongi Hills Exit, 1 min.).

## National Museum of Modern Art (Tokyo Kokuritsu Kindai Bijutsukan) 𝕲𝕲

This museum houses the largest collection of modern Japanese art under one roof, including both Japanese- and Western-style paintings, prints, watercolors, drawings, and sculpture, all dating from the Meiji Period to World War II. Names to look for include Munakata Shiko, Kuroda Seiki, and Yokoyama Taikan. To provide a wider context, a few Western artists are also represented, among them Klee and Kandinsky. Expect to spend about 1½ hours here.

3 Kitanomaru Koen Park, Chiyoda-ku. ⟨© 03/3214-2561. www.momat.go.jp. Admission ¥420 ($4) adults, ¥130 ($1.25) students, free for children; special exhibits cost more. Tues–Thurs and Sat–Sun 10am–5pm; Fri 10am–8pm. Station: Takebashi (5 min.).

## National Museum of Western Art (Kokuritsu Seiyo Bijutsukan) 𝕲

Japan's only national museum dedicated to Western art is housed in a main building designed by Le Corbusier and in two more recent additions. It presents a chronological study of sculpture and art from the end of the Middle Ages through the 20th century, beginning with works by old masters, including Lucas Cranach the Elder, Rubens, El Greco, Murillo, and Tiepolo. French painters and Impressionists of the 19th and 20th centuries are well represented, including Delacroix, Monet (with a whole room devoted to his work), Manet, Renoir, Pissarro, Sisley, Courbet, Cézanne, and Gauguin. The museum's 20th-century collection includes works by Picasso, Max Ernst, Miró, Dubuffet, and Pollock. The museum is also famous for its 50-odd sculptures by Rodin, one of the largest collections in the world, encompassing most of his major works including *The Kiss, The Thinker, Balzac,* and *The Gates of Hell.* Plan on spending at least an hour here.

Ueno Park, Taito-ku. ⟨© 03/3828-5131. www.nmwa.go.jp. Admission ¥420 ($4) adults, ¥130 ($1.25) students, ¥70 (65¢) high-school students, free for children and seniors; special exhibits require separate admission fee. Free admission to permanent collection 2nd and 4th Sat of the month. Tues–Thurs and Sat–Sun 9:30am–5pm; Fri 9:30am–8pm. Station: Ueno (4 min.).

## National Science Museum (Kokuritsu Kahaku Hakubutsukan) 𝕲 𝕂𝕚𝕕𝕤

Japan's largest science museum has been undergoing renovation that should bring it up to par with some of the world's top national science museums (the main building, with a focus on Japan, is scheduled to reopen in autumn 2006). Everything from the evolution of life to Japanese inventions and technology are covered in expansive, imaginative displays, with plenty of plenty of exhibits geared toward children. A highlight is an entire arena of 100-some stuffed animals from around the world, including a polar bear, camel, gorilla, tiger, bear, and other creatures (some are animals that died at Ueno Zoo). Other highlights include a dinosaur display, a hands-on discovery room for children exploring sound, light, magnetism, and other scientific phenomena,

re-created wood and marine habitats, and an extensive exhibition that allows visitors to stroll through some 4 billion years of evolutionary history. You'll want to spend about 2 hours here, more if you have children in tow.

Ueno Park, Taito-ku. ✆ 03/3822-0111. www.kahaku.go.jp. Admission ¥500 ($4.75) adults, free for children. Tues–Sun 9am–4:30pm. Station: Ueno (5 min.).

### Open-Air Folk House Museum (Nihon Minka-en) 🅱🅱 Finds   Whereas the Edo-Tokyo Tatemono-en (a branch of the Edo-Tokyo Museum stationed in Tokyo Metropolitan Koganei Park) is an open-air museum of traditional and modern Tokyo homes and buildings mostly dating from the late 1800s to the 1950s, this architectural museum concentrates on rural Japan from centuries past. Located in the neighboring city of Kawasaki, 30 minutes by express train from Shinjuku, it features 23 traditional houses and other historical buildings, in a lovely setting along wooded hillsides. Most buildings are heavy-beamed thatched houses (the oldest are 300 years old), but there are also warehouses, a samurai's residential gate, a water wheel, and a Kabuki stage from a small fishing village, all originally from other parts of Honshu and reconstructed here. An English-language pamphlet and numerous signs explain each of the buildings, all open to the public so you can wander in and inspect the various rooms, gaining insight into rural Japanese life in centuries past. Plan on spending a half-day here, including transportation back and forth.

7–1–1 Masugata, Tama-ku, Kawasaki. ✆ 044/922-2181. Admission ¥500 ($4.75) adults, ¥300 ($2.85) students, free for children. Tues–Sun 9:30am–4pm. From Shinjuku Station, take the express Odakyu Line 30 min. to Mukogaoka Yuen Station, from which it's a 15-min. walk.

### Ota Memorial Museum of Art (Ota Kinen Bijutsukan) 🅱 Finds   This great museum features the private *ukiyo-e* (woodblock print) collection of the late Ota Seizo, who early in life recognized the importance of ukiyo-e as an art form and dedicated himself to its preservation. Although the collection contains 12,000 prints, only 80 to 100 are displayed at any given time, in thematic exhibitions that change monthly and include English-language descriptions. The museum itself is small but delightful, with such traditional touches as bamboo screens and stone pathways. You can tour the museum in about 30 minutes.

1–10–10 Jingumae, Shibuya-ku. ✆ 03/3403-0880. www.ukiyoe-ota-muse.jp. Admission ¥700 – ¥1,000 ($6.65–$9.50) adults, ¥500–¥700 ($4.75–$6.65) high-school and college students, ¥200–¥400 ($1.90–$3.80) junior high students, free–¥200 ($1.90) children; price depends on the exhibit. Tues–Sun 10:30am–5:30pm (enter by 5pm). Closed from the 27th to end of each month. Station: Harajuku (2 min.) or Meiji-Jingumae (1 min.). Near the Omotesando Dori and Meiji Dori intersection, behind La Forêt.

### Yushukan 🅱   Located on the grounds of Yasukuni Shrine, built in 1869 to commemorate some 2.5 million Japanese war dead, this war memorial museum chronicles the rise and fall of the samurai, Sino-Japanese War, Russo-Japanese War, and World Wars I and II, though English-language explanations are rather vague and Japan's military aggression in Asia is glossed over. Still, a fascinating 90 minutes can be spent here gazing at samurai armor, uniforms, tanks, guns, and artillery, as well as such thought-provoking displays as a human torpedo (a tiny submarine guided by one occupant and loaded with explosives) and a suicide attack plane. But the most chilling displays are the seemingly endless photographs of war dead, some of them young teenagers. In stark contrast to the somberness of the museum, temporary exhibits of beautiful

ikebana (Japanese flower arrangements) and bonsai are often held on shrine grounds in rows of glass cases. The shrine is also famous for its cherry blossoms. Yasukuni Shrine is most well known, however, for the controversy that erupts every August 15 when World War II memorials are held and top government officials stop by, causing outrage among Japan's Asian neighbors.

Yasukuni Shrine, 3–1–1 Kudan-kita, Chiyoda-ku. ✆ 03/3261-8326. www.yasukuni.or.jp. Admission ¥800 ($7.60) adults, ¥500 ($4.75) high-school and college students, ¥300 ($2.85) children. Daily 9am–5:30pm (to 5pm Nov–Feb). Station: Kudanshita (3 min.); Ichigayaumae or Iidabashi (7 min.). On Yasukuni Dori.

## 5 Spectacular City Views

**Tokyo Metropolitan Government Office (TMG)** ✿✿✿ *Kids*    Tokyo's city hall—designed by one of Japan's best-known architects, Kenzo Tange—is an impressive addition to the skyscrapers of west Shinjuku. Three buildings comprise the complex—TMG No. 1, TMG No. 2, and the Metropolitan Assembly Building—and together they contain everything from Tokyo's Disaster Prevention Center to the governor's office. Most important for visitors is TMG No. 1, the tall building to the north that offers one of the best views of Tokyo. This 48-story, 240m (800-ft.) structure, the tallest building in Shinjuku, boasts two observatories located on the 45th floors of both its North and South towers, with access from the first floor. Both observatories offer the same spectacular views—on clear winter days you can even see Mount Fuji—as well as a small souvenir shop and coffee shop. In expensive Tokyo, this is one of the city's best bargains, and kids love it. On the first floor is a Tokyo Tourist Information Center, open daily 10am to 6:30pm.

2–8–1 Nishi-Shinjuku. ✆ 03/5321-1111. Free admission. Daily 9:30am–10:30pm. Closed Dec 29–Jan 3. Station: Tochomae (1 min.), Shinjuku (10 min.), or Nishi-Shinjuku (4 min.).

**Tokyo Tower** ✿ *Kids*    Japan's most famous observation tower was built in 1958 and was modeled after the Eiffel Tower in Paris. Lit up at night, this 330m (1,099-ft.) tower, a relay station for TV and radio stations, is a familiar and beloved landmark in the city's landscape; but with the construction of skyscrapers over the past few decades (including the TMG, above, with its free observatory), it has lost some of its appeal as an observation platform and seems more like a relic from the 1950s. With its tacky souvenir shops and assorted small-time attractions, this place is as about as kitsch as kitsch can be.

The tower has two observatories: the main one at 149m (495 ft.) and the top observatory at 248m (825 ft.). The best time of year for viewing is said to be during Golden Week at the beginning of May. With many Tokyoites gone from the city and most factories and businesses closed down, the air at this time is thought to be the cleanest and clearest. There are several offbeat tourist attractions in the tower's base building, including a wax museum (where you can see the Beatles, a wax rendition of Leonardo's *Last Supper*, Hollywood stars, and a medieval torture chamber), a small aquarium, a museum of holography, and a trick art gallery, all with separate admission fees and appealing mainly to children.

4–2 Shiba Koen, Minato-ku. ✆ 03/3433-5111. www.tokyotower.co.jp. Admission to main observatory ¥820 ($7.80) adults, ¥460 ($4.35) children; top observatory ¥1,420 ($13) adults, ¥860 ($8.15) children. Daily 9am–10pm. Station: Onarimon or Kamiyacho (6 min.).

## 6 City Strolls

**WALKING TOUR 1**   SEARCHING FOR OLD EDO: A WALKING TOUR OF ASAKUSA

**Start:** Hama Rikyu Garden (Shiodome Station) or Asakusa Station (exit 1 or 3).

**Finish:** Kappabashi Dori (station: Tawaramachi).

**Time:** Allow approximately 5 hours, including the boat ride.

**Best Times:** Tuesday through Friday, when the crowds aren't as big.

**Worst Times:** Sunday, when Demboin Garden and the shops on Kappabashi Dori are closed.

If anything remains of old Tokyo, Asakusa is it. This is where you'll find narrow streets lined with small residential homes, women in kimono, Tokyo's oldest and most popular temple, and quaint shops selling boxwood combs, fans, kitchen knives, sweet pastries, and other products of yore. With its temple market, rickshaw drivers vying for the tourist trade, old-fashioned amusement park, traditional shops, and restaurants, Asakusa preserves the charm of old downtown Edo better than anyplace else in Tokyo. For many older Japanese, a visit to Asakusa is like stepping back to the days of their childhood; for tourists, it provides a glimpse of the way things were.

Pleasure-seekers have been flocking to Asakusa for centuries. Originating as a temple town back in the 7th century, it grew in popularity during the Tokugawa regime as merchants grew wealthy and whole new forms of popular entertainment arose to cater to them. Theaters for Kabuki and Bunraku flourished in Asakusa, as did restaurants and shops. By 1840, Asakusa had become Edo's main entertainment district. In stark contrast to the solemnity surrounding places of worship in the West, Asakusa's temple market had a carnival atmosphere reminiscent of medieval Europe, complete with street performers and exotic animals. It retains some of that festive atmosphere even today.

---

The most dramatic way to arrive in Asakusa is by boat from Hama Rikyu Garden (see stop no. 1 below), just as people used to arrive in the olden days. If you want to forgo the boat ride, take the subway to Asakusa Station and start your tour from there. Otherwise, head to:

**① Hama Rikyu Garden**

The garden is at the south end of Tokyo (station: Shiodome, exit 5, then a 5-min. walk). Considered by some to be Tokyo's finest garden, it was laid out during the Edo Period in a style popular at the time, in which surrounding scenery was incorporated into its composition. (See p. 181 for more details.)

Boats depart the garden to make their way along the Sumida River hourly or more frequently between 10:20am and 4:20pm, with the fare to Asakusa costing ¥620 ($5.90). Although much of what you see along the working river today is only concrete embankments, I recommend the trip because it affords a different perspective of Tokyo—barges making their way down the river, high-rise apartment buildings with laundry fluttering from balconies, warehouses, and superhighways. The boat passes under approximately a dozen bridges during the 40-minute trip, each one completely different. During cherry-blossom season, thousands of cherry trees lining the bank make the trip particularly memorable.

# Walking Tour 1—Asakusa

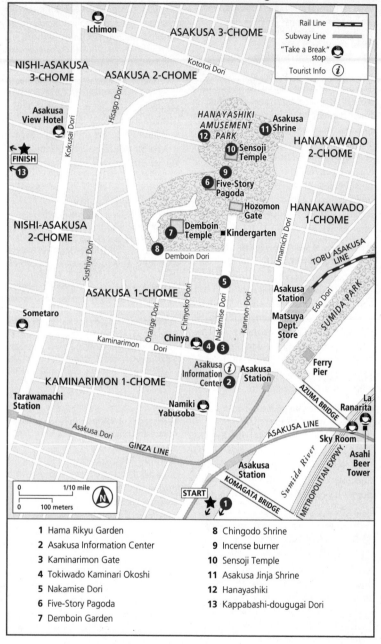

Rail Line
Subway Line
"Take a Break" stop
Tourist Info (i)

Ichimon

ASAKUSA 3-CHOME

NISHI-ASAKUSA 3-CHOME

ASAKUSA 2-CHOME

Kototoi Dori

Hisago Dori

Asakusa View Hotel

Kokusai Dori

FINISH

13

HANAYASHIKI AMUSEMENT PARK

12

Asakusa Shrine

11

HANAKAWADO 2-CHOME

10 Sensoji Temple

9

6 Five-Story Pagoda

Hozomon Gate

HANAKAWADO 1-CHOME

NISHI-ASAKUSA 2-CHOME

Sushiya Dori

7 Demboin Temple

Kindergarten

Umamichi Dori

TOBU ASAKUSA LINE

8

Demboin Dori

SUMIDA PARK

Edo Dori

Orange Dori

Chinyoko Dori

Nakamise Dori

Kannon Dori

ASAKUSA 1-CHOME

5

Asakusa Station

Sometaro

Matsuya Dept. Store

Kaminarimon Dori

Chinya

4 3

Ferry Pier

La Ranarita

KAMINARIMON 1-CHOME

Asakusa Information Center 2

Asakusa Station

AZUMA BRIDGE

Tarawamachi Station

Namiki Yabusoba

ASAKUSA LINE

Sky Room

Asahi Beer Tower

Asakusa Dori

GINZA LINE

Asakusa Station

Sumida River

METROPOLITAN EXPWY.

0     1/10 mile

0     100 meters

N

START

1

KOMAGATA BRIDGE

1  Hama Rikyu Garden
2  Asakusa Information Center
3  Kaminarimon Gate
4  Tokiwado Kaminari Okoshi
5  Nakamise Dori
6  Five-Story Pagoda
7  Demboin Garden

8  Chingodo Shrine
9  Incense burner
10 Sensoji Temple
11 Asakusa Jinja Shrine
12 Hanayashiki
13 Kappabashi-dougugai Dori

Upon your arrival in Asakusa, walk away from the boat pier a couple of blocks inland, where you'll soon see the colorful Kaminarimon Gate. Across the street is the:

## ② Asakusa Information Center

Located at 2–18–9 Kaminarimon (© **03/3842-5566**), the center is open daily from 9:30am to 8pm and is staffed by English-speaking volunteers from 10am to 5pm. Stop here to pick up a map of the area and to ask directions to restaurants and sights. In addition, note the huge Seiko clock on the center's facade—a musical clock that performs (mechanical dolls reenact scenes from several of Asakusa's most famous festivals) every hour on the hour from 10am to 7pm.

Then it's time to head across the street to the:

## ③ Kaminarimon Gate

The gate is unmistakable with its bright red colors and 100-kilogram (220-lb.) lantern hanging in the middle. The statues inside the gate are the god of wind to the right and the god of thunder to the left, ready to protect the deity enshrined in the temple. The god of thunder is particularly fearsome—he supposedly has an insatiable appetite for navels.

To the left of the gate, on the corner, is:

## ④ Tokiwado Kaminari Okoshi

This open-fronted confectionery has been selling rice-based sweets *(okoshi)* for 250 years and is popular with visiting Japanese buying gifts for the folks back home. It's open daily from 9am to 9pm.

Once past Kaminarimon Gate, you'll find yourself immediately on a pedestrian lane called:

## ⑤ Nakamise Dori

The lane leads straight to the Sensoji Temple. *Nakamise* means "inside shops," and historical records show that vendors have sold wares here since the late 17th century. Today Nakamise Dori is lined on both sides with tiny stall after tiny stall, many owned by the same family for generations. If you're expecting austere religious artifacts, however, you're in for a surprise: sweets, shoes, barking toy dogs, Japanese crackers (called *sembei*), bags, umbrellas, Japanese dolls, T-shirts, fans, masks, and traditional Japanese accessories are all sold. How about a brightly colored straight hairpin—and a black hairpiece to go with it? Or a temporary tattoo in the shape of a dragon? This is a great place to shop for souvenirs, gifts, and items you have no earthly need for— a little bit of unabashed consumerism on the way to spiritual purification.

**TAKE A BREAK**
If you're hungry for lunch, there are a number of possibilities in the neighborhood. **Chinya**, 1–3–4 Asakusa, just west of Kaminarimon Gate on Kaminarimon Dori, has been serving sukiyaki and shabu-shabu since 1880. To the south of Kaminarimon Gate is **Namiki Yabusoba**, 2–11–9 Kaminarimon, Asakusa's best-known noodle shop. For Western food, head to the other side of the Sumida River, where on the 22nd floor of the Asahi Beer Tower is **La Ranarita Azumabashi**, 1–23–1 Azumabashi, a moderately priced Italian restaurant with great views of Asakusa. (See p. 152 and 151 for complete reviews.)

Near the end of Nakamise Dori, as you head toward the temple, you'll pass a kindergarten on your left, followed by a five-story red-and-gold:

## ⑥ Pagoda

This is a 1970 remake of one constructed during the time of the third shogun, Iemitsu, in the 17th century.

A low-lying building connected to the pagoda is the gateway to the gem of this tour: a **hidden garden,** one of Asakusa's treasures, just a stone's throw from Nakamise Dori but barely visible on the other side of the kindergarten. Most visitors to Asakusa pass it by, unaware of its existence, primarily because it isn't open to the general public. However, anyone can visit it simply by asking for permission, which you can obtain by entering the building connected to the pagoda at

the left. Go inside, turn right, and walk to the third door to the left; you'll be asked to sign your name and given a map showing the entrance to the garden, open Monday through Saturday from 9am to 3pm. However, because the garden is on private grounds belonging to the Demboin Monastery, it's often closed for functions (call ✆ **03/3842-0181** to see whether it's open, or trust to luck).

Once you've obtained permission, retrace your steps down Nakamise past the kindergarten, take the first right onto Demboin Dori (you'll pas some interesting stalls selling antiques here), and then enter the second gate on your right. This is the entrance to:

### ➐ Demboin Garden

The gate to Demboin Garden (also spelled Dempoin Garden) may be locked. If so, ring the doorbell to be let in. You'll find yourself in a peaceful oasis in the midst of bustling Asakusa, in a countryside setting that centers on a pond filled with carp and turtles. Enshu Kobori, a tea-ceremony master and famous landscape gardener who also designed a garden for the shogun's castle, designed the garden in the 17th century. Because most people are unaware that the garden exists, you may find yourself the sole visitor. The best view is from the far side of the pond, where you can see the temple building and pagoda above the trees.

If the garden is closed, you can still see a glimpse of it by continuing past the garden gate on Demboin Dori until you come to a small red gate on your right. This is:

### ➑ Chingodo Shrine

Dedicated to Chingodo, the so-called raccoon dog and guardian against fires and burglars, it affords a view of part of Demboin Garden through a fence.

Return to Nakamise Dori and resume your walk north to the second gate, which opens onto a square filled with pigeons and a large:

### ➒ Incense Burner

This is where worshippers "wash" themselves to ward off or help cure illness. If,

for example, you have a sore throat, be sure to rub some of the smoke over your throat for good measure.

The building dominating the square is:

### ➓ Sensoji Temple

Sensoji is Tokyo's oldest temple. Founded in the 7th century and therefore already well established long before Tokugawa settled in Edo, Sensoji Temple is dedicated to Kannon, the Buddhist goddess of mercy, and is therefore popularly called the Asakusa Kannon Temple. According to legend, the temple was founded after two fishermen pulled a golden statue of Kannon from the sea. The sacred statue is still housed in the temple, carefully preserved inside three boxes; even though it's never on display, an estimated 20 million people flock to the temple annually to pay their respects.

Within the temple is a counter where you can buy your fortune by putting a 100-yen coin into a wooden box and shaking it until a long bamboo stick emerges from a small hole. The stick will have a Japanese number on it, which corresponds to one of the numbers on a set of drawers. Take the fortune, written in both the English language and Japanese, from the drawer that has your number. But don't expect the translation to clear things up; my fortune contained such cryptic messages as "Getting a beautiful lady at your home, you want to try all people know about this" and "Stop to start a trip." If you find that your fortune raises more questions than it answers or you simply don't like what it has to say, you can conveniently negate it by tying it to one of the wires provided for this purpose just outside the main hall.

If you walk around the temple to the right, on the northeast corner of the grounds is the small orange:

### ⓫ Asakusa Jinja Shrine

This shrine was built in 1649 by Iemitsu Tokugawa, the third Tokugawa shogun,

to commemorate the two fishermen who found the statue of Kannon and their village chief. Its architectural style, called *Gongen-zukuri,* is the same as the style of Toshogu Shrine in Nikko. West of Sensoji Temple is a gardenlike area of lesser shrines and memorials, flowering bushes, and a stream filled with carp.

**Farther west still is:**

### ⑫ Hanayashiki

This is a small and corny amusement park that first opened in 1853 and still draws in the little ones. (See p. 196 for more details.)

Most of the area west of Sensoji Temple (the area to the left if you stand facing the front of the temple) is a small but interesting part of Asakusa popular among Tokyo's older working class. This is where several of Asakusa's old-fashioned pleasure houses remain, including bars, restaurants, strip shows, traditional Japanese vaudeville, and so-called "love hotels," which rent rooms by the hour.

**If you keep walking west, past the Asakusa View Hotel, within 10 minutes you'll reach:**

### ⑬ Kappabashi-dougugai Dori

This district, generally referred to as Kappabashi Dori, is Tokyo's wholesale district for restaurant items. Shop after shop sells pottery, chairs, tableware, cookware, lacquerware, rice cookers, *noren* (short curtains hung outside shops and restaurants to signify they are open), and everything else needed to run a restaurant. And yes, you can even buy those models of plastic food you've been drooling over in restaurant displays. Ice cream, pizza, sushi, mugs foaming with beer—they're all here, looking like the real thing. (Stores close about 5pm.)

> **WINDING DOWN**
> The **Asakusa View Hotel,** on Kokusai Dori Avenue between Sensoji Temple and Kappabashi Dori, has several restaurants and bars. In the basement is the clubby **Ice House,** the hotel's main bar.

---

| WALKING TOUR 2 | IN THE HEART OF TRENDY TOKYO: A STROLL THROUGH HARAJUKU & AOYAMA |
|---|---|

| | |
|---|---|
| **Start:** | Meiji Jingu Shrine (station: Harajuku). |
| **Finish:** | Aoyama (station: Omotesando). |
| **Time:** | Allow approximately 4 hours. |
| **Best Times:** | The first and fourth Sundays of every month, when there's an antiques/flea market at Togo Shrine. |
| **Worst Times:** | Monday, from the 27th to the end of every month (when the Ota Memorial Museum of Art is closed), and Thursday (when the Oriental Bazaar is closed). |

**Harajuku** is one of my favorite neighborhoods in Tokyo, though I'm too old to really fit in. In fact, anyone over 25 is apt to feel ancient here, since this is Tokyo's most popular hangout for Japanese high-school and college students. The young come here to see and be seen; you're sure to spot Japanese punks, girls decked out in the fashions of the moment, and young couples out on dates. I like Harajuku for its vibrancy, its sidewalk cafes, its street hawkers, and its trendy clothing boutiques. It's also the home of Tokyo's most important Shinto shrine, as well as a delightful woodblock-print museum and an excellent souvenir shop of traditional Japanese items.

# Walking Tour 2—Harajuku & Aoyama

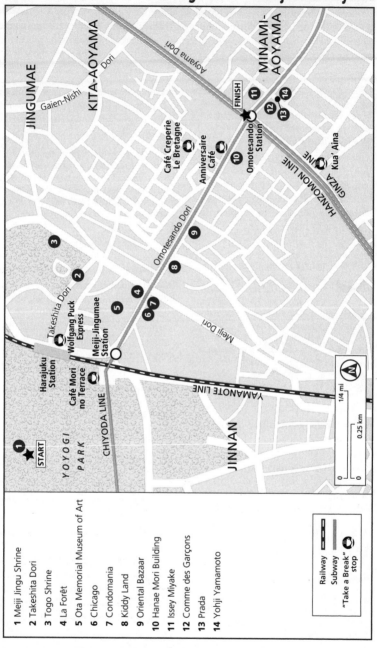

1 Meiji Jingu Shrine
2 Takeshita Dori
3 Togo Shrine
4 La Forêt
5 Ota Memorial Museum of Art
6 Chicago
7 Condomania
8 Kiddy Land
9 Oriental Bazaar
10 Hanae Mori Building
11 Issey Miyake
12 Comme des Garçons
13 Prada
14 Yohji Yamamoto

Railway
Subway
"Take a Break"
   stop

Nearby is **Aoyama,** a yuppified version of Harajuku, where the upwardly mobile dine and shop for designer clothing. Connecting Harajuku and Aoyama is **Omotesando Dori,** a wide, tree-lined, European-style shopping boulevard that forms the heart of this area; its many sidewalk cafes make it a popular promenade for people-watching.

From Harajuku Station, take the south exit (the one closer to Shibuya) and turn right over the bridge, where you will immediately see the huge cypress torii marking the entrance to:

### ➊ Meiji Jingu Shrine

This is the most venerable shrine in Tokyo (p. 173), dedicated to Emperor and Empress Meiji. On the 10-minute walk along the tree-shaded path to the shrine, stop off at the Iris Garden, spectacular for its irises in June.

**TAKE A BREAK**
If the hike to Meiji Shrine has made you thirsty, stop off at the rustic **Café Mori no Terrace** outdoor pavilion just inside the entryway to the shrine grounds. Open daily 9am to sunset, it offers coffee, beer, pastries, and ice cream. For something more substantial, wait until you get to Takeshita Dori (described below), where you'll find a **Wolfgang Puck Express**, 1-17-1 Jingumae, good for burgers and pizza (p. 162).

After visiting the shrine, retrace your steps to Harajuku Station. If it's Sunday, you'll see groups of teenagers—many bizarrely dressed—gathered on the bridge over the train tracks. They're all that's left of the masses of teens that used to congregate on nearby Yoyogi Dori back when it was closed to vehicular traffic on Sundays. Sadly, authorities decided to open Yoyogi and Omotesando Dori streets to traffic, thereby putting an end to Tokyo's most happening Sunday scene.

At Harajuku Station, continue walking north beside the station to its north exit. Across the street from Harajuku Station's north exit is:

### ➋ Takeshita Dori

This pedestrian-only street is lined nonstop with stores that cater to teenagers. It's packed—especially on Sunday afternoons—with young people hunting for bargains on inexpensive clothing, shoes, music, sunglasses, jewelry, watches, cosmetics, and more.

After inching your way through the flow of humanity along this narrow lane, you'll eventually find yourself on a busy thoroughfare, Meiji Dori. If it's the first or fourth Sunday of the month, turn left (north) onto Meiji Dori. In a couple of minutes, on your left you'll see:

### ➌ Togo Shrine

Togo Shrine is dedicated to Admiral Togo, who was in charge of the fleet that defeated the Russian navy in 1905 in the Russo-Japanese War. Nowadays, the shrine is most popular for its flea market held the first and fourth Sundays, morning til 2pm, when everything from old chests, dolls, porcelain, and kimono are for sale, all spread out on a tree-shaded sidewalk that meanders around the shrine.

Head back south on Meiji Dori. To your right, just before the big intersection, is:

### ➍ La Forêt

La Forêt is filled with trendy shoe and clothing boutiques. The less expensive boutiques tend to be on the lower floors; the more exclusive are higher up. (See "Shopping," later in this chapter, for details on many of the shops and department stores listed in this walking tour.)

Behind La Forêt is one of my favorite museums, the:

### ➎ Ota Memorial Museum of Art

This museum at 1–10–10 Jingumae features the private Ukiyo-e (woodblock prints) collection of the late Ota Seizo. (See p. 186 for more details.)

Across Omotesando Dori is:

### ➏ Chicago

This store specializes in used American clothing but also stocks hundreds of used

and new kimono and yukata in a corner of its basement.

Near La Forêt is Harajuku's major intersection, Meiji Dori and Omotesando Dori. Here, on the intersection near Chicago, is one of Harajuku's more unusual shops:

### ❼ Condomania

This store at 6–30–1 Jingumae sells condoms in a wide range of sizes, colors, and styles, from glow-in-the-dark to scented. It's open daily 11am to 11pm.

Heading east on Omotesando Dori (away from Harajuku Station), you'll soon see, to your right:

### ❽ Kiddy Land

Located at 6–1–9 Jingumae, this store sells gag gifts and a great deal more than just toys, including enough to amuse less-discerning adults. You could spend an hour browsing here, but the store is so crowded with teenagers that you may end up rushing for the door.

Continue east on Omotesando Dori (where sidewalk vendors selling jewelry and ethnic accessories set up shop on weekends); to your right will soon be Harajuku's most famous store:

### ❾ Oriental Bazaar

At 5–9–13 Jingumae, you'll find the Oriental Bazaar, Tokyo's best one-stop shopping for Japanese souvenirs. Four floors offer antique chinaware, old kimono, Japanese paper products, fans, jewelry, woodblock prints, dolls, screens, china, and much more, all at reasonable prices. I always stock up on gifts here for the folks back home.

Continue walking east on Omotesando Dori, past the construction area on your left (soon to be a residential and commercial complex designed by Tadao Ando). Near the end of Omotesando Dori, to your right, is the:

### ❿ Hanae Mori Building

This building was designed by Japanese architect Kenzo Tange (who also designed the Akasaka Prince Hotel and the TMG city hall in Shinjuku). It houses the entire collection of the designer Hanae Mori, from casual wear to evening wear. In the basement is the Antique Market where

individual stalls sell china, jewelry, clothing, watches, swords, and items from the 1930s.

**TAKE A BREAK**
Harajuku and Aoyama have more sidewalk cafes than any other part of Tokyo. Most conspicuous is the fancy **Anniversaire Café**, 3–5–30 Kita-Aoyama, across from the Hanae Mori Building (see no. 10, above). If you backtrack a bit and take the small side street that runs beside McDonald's (underneath the "Harajuku" arch) and then turn left, you'll come to **Café Creperie Le Bretagne**, 4–9–8 Jingumae, selling buckwheat *galettes* and crepes filled with fruit and chocolate combinations.

At the end of Omotesando Dori, where it connects with Aoyama Dori, is Omotesando Station. You can board the subway here or, for more shopping, cross Aoyama Dori and continue heading east, where you'll pass a number of designer shops. First, on the left at 3–18–11 Minami-aoyama, is:

### ⓫ Issey Miyake

The clothes here are known for their richness in texture and fabrics.

To the right, at 5–2–1 Minami-Aoyama, is:

### ⓬ Comme des Garçons

Rei Kawakubo's designs for both men and women are showcased here.

Farther down the street, on the right at 5–3–6 Minami-Aoyama, is:

### ⓭ Yohji Yamamoto

As with all Yamamoto shops, this store has an interesting avant-garde interior.

**WINDING DOWN**
The cafes listed above are just a few minutes' walk away, but if you're dying for a burger, look no farther than **Kua' Aina**, 5–10–21 Minami Aoyama, on the corner of the Aoyama Dori and Kotto Dori intersection. It boasts the most satisfying burgers in town, along with sandwiches and soft drinks.

## 7 Especially for Kids

In addition to its observatories, **Tokyo Tower** (p. 187) contains a few other attractions that might be worth a visit if you have children in tow, including a small **aquarium** and a **wax museum.** Other attractions listed earlier that are good for children include the **Edo-Tokyo Museum, Fukagawa Edo Museum, National Museum of Emerging Science and Innovation, National Science Museum**, and the **observatory** of the Tokyo Metropolitan Government Office.

**Hanayashiki**    Opened in 1853, this small and rather corny amusement park is Japan's oldest. It offers a small roller coaster, a kiddie Ferris wheel, a carousel, a haunted house, a 3-D theater, and other diversions that appeal to children. Note, however, that after paying admission, you must still buy tickets for each ride; tickets are ¥100 (95¢) each, and most rides require two or three.

2–28–1 Asakusa (northwest of Sensoji Temple), Taito-ku. ℂ 043/3842-8780. Admission ¥900 ($8.55) adults, ¥400 ($3.80) children 5–12 and seniors, free for children 4 and under. Wed–Mon 10am–6pm (to 5pm in winter). Station: Asakusa (5 min.).

**Joypolis Sega**    Bored teenagers in tow, grumbling at yet another temple or shrine? Bring them to life at Tokyo's most sophisticated virtual amusement arcade, outfitted with the latest in video games and high-tech virtual-reality attractions, courtesy of Sega. Video games include bobsledding and car races, in which participants maneuver curves utilizing virtual-reality equipment, as well as numerous aeronautical battle games. There's also a 3-D sightseeing tour with seats that move with the action on the screen, several virtual reality rides (sky diving, anyone?), and much, much more. Most harmless are the Print Club machines, which will print your face on stickers with the background (Mount Fuji, perhaps?) of your choice. If you think your kids will want to try everything, buy them a passport for ¥3,300 ($31).

There's a smaller Sega on Dogenzaka slope in Shibuya at 2–6–16 Dogenzaka (ℂ **03/5458-2201;** station: Shibuya, 2 min.), open daily 10am to midnight and offering arcade and virtual-reality games, but note that children under 16 aren't allowed after 6pm.

Tokyo Decks, 3rd floor, Odaiba. ℂ 03/5500-1801. Admission ¥500 ($4.75) adults, ¥300 ($2.85) children; individual attractions an additional ¥200–¥700 ($1.90–$6.65) each. Daily 10am–11pm. Station: Odaiba Kaihin Koen (2 min.). On Odaiba.

**National Children's Castle (Kodomo-no-Shiro)** ⚝    Here's a great place to bring the kids. Conceived by the Ministry of Health and Welfare to commemorate the International Year of the Child in 1979, the Children's Castle holds various activity rooms for children of all ages (though most are geared to elementary-aged kids and younger). The third floor, designed for spontaneous and unstructured play, features a large climbing gym, a computer playroom, building blocks, a playhouse, dolls, books, and a teen corner with table tennis and other age-appropriate games; there's also an art room staffed with instructors to help children with projects suitable for their ages. On the fourth floor is a music room with instruments the kids are invited to play, as well as a video room with private cubicles where visitors can make selections from a library of Japanese- and English-language videos. On the roof is an outdoor playground complete with tricycles and a small wading pool for toddlers (¥200/$1.90 extra), while in the basement is the family swimming pool (¥300/$2.85 for adults,

¥200/$1.90 for children). Various programs are offered throughout the week, including puppet shows, fairy tales, and origami presentations.

5–53–1 Jingumae, Shibuya-ku. © 03/3797-5666. www.kodomono-shiro.or.jp. Admission ¥500 ($4.75) adults, ¥400 ($3.80) children 3–17, free for children under 3. Tues–Fri 12:30–5:30pm; Sat–Sun and holidays (including school holidays) 10am–5:30pm. Station: Omotesando (exit B2, 8 min.) or Shibuya (10 min.). On Aoyama Dori between Omotesando and Shibuya stations.

**Tokyo Disneyland and Tokyo DisneySea** 𝕲𝕲𝕲   If you (or your kids) have your heart set on visiting all the world's Disney parks, head to **Tokyo Disneyland.** Virtually a carbon copy of the back-home version, this one also boasts the Jungle Cruise, Pirates of the Caribbean, Haunted Mansion, and Space Mountain. Other hot attractions include Toontown, a wacky theme park where Mickey, Minnie, Donald, and other Disney characters work and play; MicroAdventure, which features 3-D glasses and special effects; and Star Tours, a thrill adventure created by Disney and George Lucas.

Opened in 2001 adjacent to Disneyland, **DisneySea,** a theme park based on ocean legends and myths, offers seven distinct "ports of call," including the futuristic Port Discovery marina with its StormRider that flies straight into the eye of a storm; the Lost River Delta with its Indiana Jones Adventure; Mermaid Lagoon based on the film *The Little Mermaid;* and the Arabian Coast, with its Sindbad's Seven Voyages boat ride.

1–1 Maihama, Urayasu-shi, Chiba. © 045/683-3777. www.tokyodisneyresort.co.jp. Tickets can be purchased in advance daily 10am–7pm at the Tokyo Disneyland Reservation Center, Hibiya Mitsui Building, 1–1–2 Yurakucho (© 03/3595-1777; station: Hibiya). 1-day passport to either Disneyland or DisneySea, including entrance to and use of all attractions ¥5,500 ($52) adults, ¥4,800 ($46) seniors and children 12–17, ¥3,700 ($35) children 4–11, free for children under 4. Daily 8 or 9am–10pm, with slightly shorter hours in winter. Station: Maihama Station on the JR Keiyo Line from Tokyo Station (1 min.).

**Ueno Zoo**   Founded back in 1882, Japan's oldest zoo is small by today's standards but remains one of the most well-known zoos in Japan, due in part to its giant panda, donated by the Chinese government to mark the reestablishment of diplomatic relations between the two countries following World War II. A vivarium, opened in 1999, houses amphibians, fish, and reptiles, including Komodo dragons, green tree pythons, and dwarf crocodiles. I can't help but feel sorry for some of the animals in their small spaces, but children will enjoy the Japanese macaques, polar bears, California sea lions, penguins, gorillas, giraffes, zebras, elephants, deer, and tigers. Expect to spend a minimum of 2 hours here.

Ueno Park, Taito-ku. © 03/3828-5171. www.tokyo-zoo.net/english. Admission ¥600 ($5.70) adults, ¥300 ($2.85) seniors, ¥200 ($1.90) children 13–15, free for children under 12. Tues–Sun 9:30am–5pm (enter by 4pm). Closed some holidays. Station: Ueno (4 min.).

## 8 Spectator Sports

For information on current sporting events taking place in Tokyo, ranging from kick-boxing and pro wrestling to soccer, table tennis, martial arts, and golf classics, contact the Tourist Information Center or pick up a copy of the free weekly *Metropolis* magazine. Tickets for many events, including baseball and sumo, can be purchased at **Ticket Pia** (© **0570/02-9999**), as well as convenience stores like Lawson, Family Mart, and 7-Eleven.

**SUMO**   Sumo matches are held in Tokyo at the **Kokugikan,** 1–3–28 Yokoami, Sumida-ku (© **03/3623-5111;** station: Ryogoku, then a 1-min. walk). Matches are held in January, May, and September for 15 consecutive days, beginning at around

## For It's Ichi, Ni, San Strikes You're Out . . .

Japanese are so crazy about baseball, you'd think they invented the game. Actually, it was introduced to Japan by the United States way back in 1873. Today, it's as popular among Japanese as it is among Americans. Even the annual high-school playoffs keep everyone glued to the TV set.

As with other imports, Japanese have added their own modifications: Some of the playing fields are smaller (though newer ones tend to have American dimensions) and, borrowing from American football, each team has its own cheerleaders. There are several American players who have proved very popular with local fans; but according to the rules, no more than four foreigners may play on any one team. On the other hand, recent years have also seen an exodus of top Japanese players defecting to American teams, including the hugely popular and successful Suzuki Ichiro, leadoff hitter and right fielder for the Seattle Mariners; and Matsui Hideki, a power-hitting outfielder with the New York Yankees. In fact, Japanese fans have been so mesmerized by the Mariners and Yankees (whose games are broadcast on Japanese TV) that television ratings for Japanese games have fallen.

Although playing one's hardest is at a premium in the United States, in Japan, any attempt at excelling individually is frowned upon. As in other aspects of life, it is the group, the team, that counts. To what extent that's so may be illustrated by the case of an American player: When he missed opening day at training camp due to a life-or-death operation on his son at a hospital, his contract was immediately canceled. And rather than let a foreign player excel by breaking the hitting record set by a Japanese, American Randy Bass was thrown only balls and walked.

There are two professional leagues, the Central and the Pacific, which play from April to October and meet in the final Japan Series playoffs. In Tokyo, the home teams are the **Yomiuri Giants,** which play at the Tokyo Dome (© 03/5800-9999; station: Korakuen), and the **Yakult Swallows,** which play at Jingu Stadium (© 03/3404-8999; station: Gaienmae). Other teams playing in the vicinity of Tokyo are the **Chiba Lotte Marines,** who play at Chiba Marine Stadium in Chiba (© 043/296-8900), and the **Yokohama Bay Stars,** who play in downtown Yokohama Stadium (© 045/661-1251). Advance tickets go on sale Friday, 2 weeks prior to the game, and can be purchased at **Ticket Pia** (© 0570/02-9999), except for the Giants, where tickets can be purchased only at Tokyo Dome. Prices for the Tokyo Dome and Jingu Stadium range from ¥1,800 ($17) for an unreserved seat in the outfield to ¥6,000 ($57) for seats behind home plate. The Giants are so popular, however, that tickets are hard to come by.

9:30am and lasting until 6pm; the top wrestlers compete after 3:30pm. The best seats are ringside box seats, but they're bought out by companies and by friends and families of sumo wrestlers. Usually available are balcony seats, which can be purchased at **Ticket Pia** (© 0570/02-9999). You can also purchase tickets directly at the Kokugikan ticket office beginning at 9am every morning of the tournament. Prices

range from about ¥2,100 ($18) for an unreserved seat (sold only on the day of the event at the stadium, with about 400 seats available) to ¥8,200 ($78) for a good reserved seat.

If you can't make it to a match, watching on TV is almost as good. Tournaments in Tokyo, as well as those that take place annually in Osaka, Nagoya, and Fukuoka, are broadcast on the NHK channel from 4 to 6pm daily during matches. For more information on sumo, see appendix A.

## 9 Shopping

It won't take you long to become convinced that shopping is the number-one pastime in Tokyo. Women, men, couples, and even whole families go on buying expeditions in their free time, making Sunday the most crowded shopping day of the week.

### THE SHOPPING SCENE

**BEST BUYS**   Tokyo is the country's showcase for everything from the latest in camera, computer, or stereo equipment to original woodblock prints. Traditional Japanese crafts and souvenirs that make good buys include toys (both traditional and the latest in technical wizardry), kites, Japanese dolls, carp banners, swords, lacquerware, bamboo baskets, ikebana accessories, ceramics, chopsticks, fans, masks, knives, scissors, sake, and silk and cotton kimono. And you don't have to spend a fortune: You can pick up handmade Japanese paper *(washi)* products, such as umbrellas, lanterns, boxes, stationery, and other souvenirs for a fraction of what they would cost in import shops at home. In Harajuku, it's possible to buy a fully lined dress in the latest fashion for $80, and I can't even count the number of pairs of fun, casual shoes I've bought in Tokyo for a song. Used cameras can be a good buy, reproductions of famous woodblock prints make great inexpensive gifts, and many items—from pearls to electronic video and audio equipment—can be bought tax free (see "Taxes," below).

Japan is famous for its electronics, but if you're buying new, you can probably find these products just as cheaply, or even more cheaply, in the United States. If you think you want to shop for electronic products while you're in Tokyo, it pays to do some comparison shopping before you leave home so you can spot a deal when you see one. On the other hand, one of the joys of shopping for electronics in Japan is discovering new, advanced models; you might decide you want that new Sony MP3 player simply because it's the coolest thing you've ever seen, no matter what the price.

**GREAT SHOPPING AREAS**   Another enjoyable aspect of shopping in Tokyo is that specific areas are often devoted to certain goods, sold wholesale but also available to the individual shopper. **Kappabashi Dori** (station: Tawaramachi), for example, is where you'll find shops specializing in kitchenware, while **Kanda** (station: Jimbocho) is known for its bookstores. **Akihabara** (station: Akihabara) is packed with stores selling the latest in electronics. **Ginza** (station: Ginza) is the chic address for clothing boutiques as well as art galleries. **Aoyama** (station: Omotesando) boasts the city's largest concentration of designer clothing stores, while nearby **Harajuku** (stations: Harajuku, Meiji-Jingumae, or Omotesando) and **Shibuya** (station: Shibuya) are the places to go for youthful, fun, and inexpensive fashions.

**SALES**   Department stores have sales throughout the year, during which you can pick up bargains on everything from electronic goods and men's suits to golf clubs, toys, kitchenware, food, and lingerie; there are even sales for used wedding kimono. The most popular sales are for **designer clothing,** usually held twice a year in July and

December or January. Here you can pick up fantastic clothing at cut-rate prices—but be prepared for the crowds. Sales are generally held on one of the top floors of the department store in what's usually labeled the "Exhibition Hall" or "Promotion Hall" in the store's English-language brochure. Stop by the department store's information desk, usually located near the main entrance, for the English-language brochure as well as flyers listing their sale promotions.

**TAXES** A 5% consumption tax is included in the price of marked goods, but all major department stores in Tokyo will refund the tax to foreign visitors if total purchases amount to more than ¥10,001 ($95) on that day. Exemptions include food, beverages, tobacco, pharmaceuticals, cosmetics, film, and batteries. When you've completed your shopping, take the purchased goods and receipts to the tax refund counter in the store. There are forms to fill out (you will need your passport). Upon completion, a record of your purchase is placed on the visa page of your passport and you are given the tax refund on the spot. When you leave Japan, make sure you have your purchases with you (pack them in your carry-on); you may be asked by Customs to show them, though I've never been asked.

**SHIPPING IT HOME** Many first-class hotels in Tokyo provide a packing and shipping service. In addition, most large department stores, as well as tourist shops such as the Oriental Bazaar and antiques shops, will ship your purchases overseas.

If you wish to ship packages yourself, the easiest method is to go to a post office and purchase an easy-to-assemble cardboard box, available in various sizes (along with the necessary tape). Keep in mind that packages mailed abroad cannot weigh more than 20 kilograms (about 44 lb.) and that only the larger international post offices accept packages to be mailed overseas. Remember, too, that mailing packages from Japan is expensive. Ask your hotel concierge for the closest international post office.

## SHOPPING FROM A TO Z
### ANTIQUES & CURIOS

In recent years, it has become a buyer-beware market in Japan, with fake antiques produced in China infiltrating the Japanese market. You shouldn't have any problems with the reputable dealers listed here, but if you're buying an expensive piece, be sure to ask whether there are any papers of authenticity.

In addition to the listings here, other places to look for antiques include the **Oriental Bazaar** (p. 202); and Tokyo's outdoor **flea markets** (see later in this section).

**Antique Mall Ginza** Japanese, European, and some American antiques, collectibles, and odds and ends crowd several floors of Tokyo's largest antiques mall, where you could spend hours browsing among furniture, jewelry, watches, porcelain, pottery, dolls, scrolls, glassware, kimono, and much more. Open Thursday to Tuesday 11am to 7pm. 1–13–1 Ginza, Chuo-ku. ✆ 03/3590-3401. Station: Higashi-Ginza or Ginza-Itchome (4 min.). Near Hotel Seiyo Ginza.

**Fuji-Torii** Open since 1948, this small, one-room shop in Harajuku specializes in traditional Japanese works of art and antiques, including screens, scrolls, woodblock prints, and ceramics. Open Wednesday to Monday from 11am to 6pm; closed third Monday of the month. 6–1–10 Jingumae, Shibuya-ku. ✆ 03/3400-2777. Station: Meiji-jingumae (2 min.). On Omotesando Dori, next to Kiddy Land.

**Kurofune** *Finds* Located in a large house in Roppongi, Kurofune is owned by an American, John Adair, who for more than 25 years has specialized in Japanese antique

furniture in its original condition. The largest collection here is of mid- to top-quality pieces, but browsing is a delight even if you can't afford to buy; stock includes hibachi, fabrics, prints, maps, lanterns, screens, folk art, and the country's largest collection of Japanese baskets. Fax Adair (03/3479-0719) for a map of how to get here. Open Monday to Saturday from 10am to 6pm. 47–7–4 Roppongi. ✆ **03/3479-1552.** www. kurofuneantiques.com. Station: Roppongi (5 min.). From Roppongi Crossing, walk away from Tokyo Tower on Gaien-Higashi Dori, take the *diagonal* street to the left (across from the huge urban renewal project underway), and then take a right at 7-Eleven.

## ARCADES & SHOPPING MALLS

**UNDERGROUND ARCADES**    Underground shopping arcades are found around several of Tokyo's train and subway stations; the biggest are at **Tokyo Station** (the Yaesu side) and **Shinjuku Station** (the east side). They often have great sales and bargains on clothing, accessories, and electronics. My only complaint is that once you're in them, it sometimes seems like you'll never find your way out again.

**SHOPPING MALLS    Sunshine City** (station: Higashi Ikebukuro or Ikebukuro) is one of Tokyo's oldest shopping malls, with more than 300 shops and restaurants spread through several adjoining buildings. Its popularity, however, is now challenged by newer and grander shopping malls in recently developed Odaiba (station: Odaiba Kaihin Koen). Palette Town is an amusement/shopping center that contains the Italian-themed **Venus Fort,** an indoor mall that evokes scenes from Italy with its store-fronted lanes, painted sky, fountains, plazas, and Italian name-brand boutiques. Nearby **Tokyo Decks** specializes in international household goods, including imports from the United States, Europe, China, and Hong Kong; I especially like its Daiba 1-chome Syoutengai section on the fourth floor, a remake of mid-1900s Japan, with goods, food, songs, and TV shows of the period; and the sixth-floor Daiba Little Hong Kong department with its Chinese accessories, souvenirs, and restaurants.

## BOOKS

**Yasukuni Dori** in Jimbocho-Kanda (station: Jimbocho) is lined with bookstores selling both new and used books, with several dealing in English-language books. Keep in mind, however, that English-language books are usually more expensive in Japan than back home. Still, no bibliophile should pass this street up. Stores are closed on Sunday; most are closed holidays as well. **Kitazawa** (✆ **03/3263-0011**), the most spacious of the three listed here, boasts an overwhelming selection of books, including the most recently published novels, American and English-language classic literature, topical books ranging from history to politics, books on Japan, and antiquarian books. **Tokyo Random Walk** (✆ **03/3291-7071**), the Tokyo branch of the Tuttle publishing firm in Vermont, carries a wide selection of books on Japan and the Far East written in English, including English-language translations of Japanese novels. Established in 1882, **Ohya Shobo** (✆ **03/3291-0062**) doesn't have any English-language books, but it does claim to have the world's largest stock of 18th- and 19th-century Japanese illustrated books, woodblock prints, and maps, including maps from the Edo Period. (Credit cards are not accepted.)

**Kinokuniya**    This is one of Tokyo's best-known bookstores, with one of the city's largest selections of English-language books and magazines—including books on Japan, dictionaries and textbooks for students of Japanese, and novels—on its sixth floor. Open daily 10am to 8pm; closed some Wednesdays. Takashimaya Annex, Takashimaya Times Sq. complex. ✆ **03/5361-3301.** Station: Shinjuku (south exit, 2 min.).

**Maruzen** This is Japan's oldest bookstore, founded in 1869 but recently ensconced in the very new Oazo building across from Tokyo Station's Marunouchi exit. Its English-language section, on the fourth floor, is huge and well laid out, with everything from dictionaries to travel guides to special-interest books on Japan. It also carries books on science, politics, and history, as well as magazines and paperbacks. If you're searching for a specific title, you'll probably want to come here first. Open daily 9am to 9pm. 1–6–4 Marunouchi. ✆ **03/5288-8881**. Station: Tokyo (1 min.). Take the Marunouchi exit from Tokyo Station and turn right (north); it's across the street.

**Tower Records and Books** My friends in Tokyo don't shop anywhere else for their books and magazines, as prices are usually lower here than elsewhere. The seventh floor is devoted to imported publications, with a good selection of English-language books, more than 3,000 different kinds of magazines, and the Sunday editions of major newspapers. Open daily 10am to 11pm; closed some Mondays. 1–22–14 Jinnan. ✆ **03/3496-3661**. Station: Shibuya (Hachiko exit, 5 min.).

## CRAFTS & TRADITIONAL JAPANESE PRODUCTS

If you want to shop for traditional Japanese folk crafts in the right atmosphere, nothing beats **Nakamise Dori** (station: Asakusa; 1 min.), a pedestrian lane leading to Sensoji Temple in Asakusa. It's lined with stall after stall selling souvenirs galore, from wooden *geta* shoes and hairpins worn by geisha to T-shirts, fans, umbrellas, toy swords, and dolls. Most are open from 10am to 6pm; some may close 1 day a week.

Another good place to search for traditional crafts are **department stores,** which usually have sections devoted to ceramics, pottery, bambooware, flower-arranging accessories, and fabrics.

**Japan Sword** This is the best-known sword shop in Tokyo, with an outstanding collection of fine swords, daggers, sword guards and fittings, and other sword accessories, as well as some antique samurai armor. Coming here is like visiting a museum. The place also sells copies and souvenir items of traditional swords at prices much lower than the very expensive historic swords. You can also have swords cleaned and polished here. Open Monday through Friday 9:30am to 6pm; Saturday 9:30am to 5pm. Closed holidays. 3–8–1 Toranomon, Minato-ku. ✆ **03/3434-4321**. Station: Toranomon (exit 2, 5 min.).

**Japan Traditional Craft Center (Zenkoku Dentoteki Kogeihin Senta)** *Finds* This store is worth a trip even if you can't afford to buy anything. Established to publicize and distribute information on Japanese crafts and to promote the country's artisans, the center is a great introduction to both traditional and contemporary Japanese design. It sells various top-quality crafts from all over Japan on a rotating basis, so there are always new items on hand. Crafts for sale usually include lacquerware, ceramics, fabrics, paper products, bamboo items, writing brushes and ink stones, metalwork, furniture, and sometimes even stone lanterns or Buddhist family altars. Prices are high, but rightfully so. Unfortunately, its location in out-of-the-way Ikebukuro makes a trip here feasible only if you have time; otherwise, you're probably better off shopping in the crafts section of a department store. Daily 11am to 7pm. 1st floor of Metropolitan Plaza Building, 1–11–1 Nishi-Ikebukuro. ✆ **03/5954-6066**. Station: Ikebukuro (1 min.).

**Oriental Bazaar** If you have time for only one souvenir shop in Tokyo, this should be it. This is the city's best-known and largest souvenir/crafts store, selling products at reasonable prices and offering four floors of souvenir and gift items, including cotton yukata, kimono (new and used), woodblock prints, paper products, wind chimes,

stationery, fans, chopsticks, lamps and vases, Imari chinaware, sake sets, Japanese dolls, pearls, and even books on Japan and a large selection of antique furniture. This store will also ship things home for you. Open Friday through Wednesday 10am to 7pm. 5–9–13 Jingumae, Shibuya-ku. ✆ **03/3400-3933**. Station: Meiji-Jingumae (3 min.), Harajuku (4 min.), or Omotesando (5 min.). On Omotesando Dori in Harajuku; look for an Asian-looking facade of orange and green.

**Sakai Kokodo Gallery**    This gallery claims to be the oldest woodblock print shop in Japan. The first shop was opened in 1870 in the Kanda area of Tokyo by the present owner's great-grandfather, and altogether four generations of the Sakai family have tended the store. Open daily 11am to 6pm, it's a great place for original prints, as well as for reproductions of such great masters as Hiroshige. (If you're really a woodblock-print fan, you'll want to visit the Sakai family's excellent museum, Japan Ukiyo-e Museum, in the small town of Matsumoto in the Japan Alps; see p. 259.) 1–2–14 Yuraku-cho, Chiyoda-ku (across from the Imperial Hotel's Tower). ✆ **03/3591-4678**. Station: Hibiya (1 min.).

## DEPARTMENT STORES

Japanese department stores are institutions in themselves. Usually enormous, well-designed, and chock-full of merchandise, they have about everything you can imagine, including museums and art galleries, pet stores, rooftop playgrounds or greenhouses, travel agencies, restaurants, grocery markets, and flower shops. You could easily spend a whole day in a department store—eating, attending cultural exhibitions, planning your next vacation, having your neck massaged, and, well, shopping.

One of the most wonderful aspects of the Japanese department store is the **courteous service.** If you arrive at a store as its doors open at 10 or 10:30am, you'll witness a daily rite: Lined up at the entrance are staff who bow in welcome. Some Japanese shoppers arrive just before opening time so as not to miss this favorite ritual. Sales clerks are everywhere, ready to help you. In some stores, you don't even have to go to the cash register once you've made your choice; just hand over the product, along with your money, to the sales clerk, who will return with your change, your purchase neatly wrapped, and an *"Arigatoo* (the double oo is used to mean that you hold the "o" sound, not that it's a u sound) *gozaimashita"* (Thank you very much). A day spent in a Japanese department store could spoil you for the rest of your life.

The basement of the store is usually devoted to **foodstuffs:** fresh fish, produce, and prepared snacks and dinners. There are often free samples of food; if you're feeling slightly hungry, walking through the food department can do nicely for a snack. Many department stores include **boutiques** by such famous Japanese and international fashion designers as Issey Miyake, Rei Kawakubo (creator of Comme des Garçons), Hanae Mori, Takeo Kikuchi, Vivienne Westwood, and Paul Smith, as well as a department devoted to the kimono. Near the **kimono department** may also be the section devoted to **traditional crafts;** department stores are convenient places to shop for these. To find out what's where, stop by the store's information booth located on the ground floor near the front entrance and ask for the floor-by-floor English-language pamphlet. Be sure, too, to ask about **sales** on the promotional floor—you never know what bargains you may chance upon.

**Hours** are generally from 10 or 10:30am to 7:30, or 8pm. Department stores used to close 1 day a week, but now they rarely close or close irregularly, but always on the same day of the week (say, on Tues) but in no apparent pattern. One month they may be closed the second and third Tuesday of the month, but the next month only the

first or not at all. In any case, you can always find several department stores that are open, even on Sundays and holidays (major shopping days in Japan). All major credit and charge cards are accepted.

**Isetan**   Isetan is a favorite among foreigners living in Tokyo. It has a good line of conservative clothing appropriate for working situations, as well as contemporary and fashionable styles, including designer clothes (Issey Miyake, Yohji Yamamoto, Tsumori Chisato, Comme des Garçons, Marc Jacobs, and Sonia Rykiel) and large dress sizes (on the second floor). It also has a great kimono section along with all the traditional accessories (obi, shoes, purses). In the annex, which carries mostly men's clothing, is a New Creator's Space on the ground floor, unique among Japanese department stores (which are generally reluctant to carry anything but the tried and true), that showcases clothing by up-and-coming Japanese designers of men's clothing. Open daily 10am to 8pm; closed some Wednesdays. 3–14–1 Shinjuku, Shinjuku-ku. © 03/3352-1111. Station: Shinjuku Sanchome (1 min.) or Shinjuku (east exit, 6 min.). On Shinjuku Dori, east of Shinjuku Station.

**Matsuya**   This is one of my favorite department stores in Tokyo; if I were buying a wedding gift, Matsuya is one of the first places I'd look. It has a good selection of Japanese folk crafts items, kitchenware, kimono, and beautifully designed contemporary household goods, in addition to the usual designer clothes and accessories. I always make a point of stopping by the seventh floor's Design Collection, which displays items from around the world selected by the Japan Design Committee as examples of fine design, from the Alessi teapot to Braun razors. Open Monday and Tuesday 10am to 7:30pm; Wednesday, Thursday, Saturday, and Sunday 10am to 8pm; Friday 10am to 9pm. 3–6–1 Ginza, Chuo-ku. © 03/3567-1211. Station: Ginza (2 min.). On Chuo Dori Ave., just a long block north of Ginza 4–chome Crossing.

**Mitsukoshi**   This Nihombashi department store is one of Japan's oldest and grandest, founded in 1673 by the Mitsui family as a kimono store. In 1683, it became the first store in the world to deal only in cash sales; it was also one of the first stores in Japan to display goods on shelves rather than have merchants fetch bolts of cloth for each customer, as was the custom of the time. It was one of the first shops to employ female clerks. Today, housed in a building dating from 1914, it remains one of Tokyo's loveliest department stores, with a beautiful and stately Renaissance-style facade and an entrance guarded by two bronze lions, replicas of the lions in Trafalgar Square. The store carries many name-brand boutiques, including Givenchy, Dunhill, Chanel, Hanae Mori, Oscar de la Renta, Christian Dior, and Tiffany. Its kimono, by the way, are still hot items. Open daily 10am to 7:30pm; closed some Mondays.

Another branch, located right on Ginza 4–chome Crossing (© 03/3562-1111; Mon–Sat 10am–8pm; Sun 10am–7:30pm), is popular with young shoppers. 1–4–1 Nihombashi Muromachi, Chuo-ku. © 03/3241-3311. Station: Mitsukoshimae (1 min.).

**Seibu**   Once the nation's largest department store—and still one of the biggest—Seibu has 47 entrances, thousands of sales clerks, dozens of restaurants, 12 floors, 31 elevators, and an average of 170,000 shoppers a day. Two basement floors are devoted to foodstuffs—you can buy everything from taco shells to octopus to seaweed there. Dishes are set out so you can nibble the food as you move along, and hawkers yelling out their wares give the place a marketlike atmosphere. Fast-food counters sell salads, grilled eel, chicken, sushi, and other ready-to-eat dishes. The rest of the floors offer clothing, furniture, art galleries, kitchenware, and a million other things. Loft, Seibu's department for

household goods and interior design, and Wave, Seibu's CD department, occupy the top four floors of the main building. Many of the best Japanese and Western designers have boutiques here; Size World (on the third floor) and Queen's Coordination (on the fourth floor), specialize in large and petite women's sizes respectively.

There's another Seibu in **Ginza** near the elevated tracks of the JR Yamanote Line (© 03/3286-0111; daily 11am–8pm; closed some Tues; station: Yurakucho [between the Hibiya and Ginza subway stations], 1 min.). It specializes in men's and women's clothing and accessories, from casual to formal wear. Next to it is Hankyu, another large department store. Also look for Seibu in **Shibuya** at 21–1 Udagawacho (© 03/3462-0111; open Sun–Wed 10am–8pm, Thurs–Sat 10am–9pm, closed some Wed; station: Shibuya, Hachiko exit, 2 min.), which is similar to the main store in Ikebukuro. This Seibu consists of two buildings connected by pedestrian skywalks, and it offers lots of designer boutiques; a branch of Loft (behind Seibu B), Seibu's interior design and household goods shop; and Parco and Movida fashion department stores.

Open Monday through Saturday 10am to 9pm; Sunday and holidays 10am to 8pm. Closed some Tuesdays. 1–28–1 Minami Ikebukuro, Toshima-ku. © 03/3981-0111. Station: Ikebukuro (underneath the store).

**Takashimaya**   This department store provides stiff competition for Mitsukoshi, with a history just as long. It was founded as a kimono shop in Kyoto during the Edo Period and opened in Tokyo in 1933. Today it's one of the city's most attractive department stores, with white-gloved elevator operators whisking customers to eight floors of shopping and dining. Naturally, it features boutiques by such famous designers as Chanel, Louis Vuitton, Gucci, Issey Miyake, and more. Its sale of used kimono (look for advertisements in the *Japan Times*) draws huge crowds. Daily 10am to 8pm. 2–4–1 Nihombashi (on Chuo Dori Ave.), Chuo-ku. © 03/3211-4111. Station: Nihombashi (1 min.).

**Takashimaya Times Square**   Since its opening in 1996, Takashimaya Times Square has been the number-one draw in Shinjuku and is packed on weekends. Much larger than Takashimaya's Nihombashi flagship, this huge complex is anchored by the Takashimaya department store, which boasts 10 floors of clothing and restaurants (petite and "queen-size" clothing are on the sixth floor). There's also Tokyu Hands with everything imaginable for the home hobbyist, and Kinokuniya bookstore with English-language books on the sixth floor. Open daily 10am to 8pm; closed some Wednesdays. 5–24–2 Sendagaya, Shinjuku-ku. © 03/5361-1122. Station: Shinjuku (1 min.). Across the street from Shinjuku Station's south exit.

**Wako**   This is one of Ginza's smallest department stores but also one of its classiest, housed in one of the few area buildings that survived World War II. It was erected in 1932 and is famous for its distinctive clock tower, graceful curved facade, and innovative window displays. The owners are the Hattori family, founders of the Seiko watch company. The store's ground floor carries a wide selection of Seiko watches and handbags, while the upper floors carry imported and domestic fashions and luxury items with prices to match. It caters to older, well-to-do customers; you won't find hordes of young Japanese girls shopping here. Open Monday to Saturday 10:30am to 6pm; closed holidays. 4–5–11 Ginza (at Ginza 4–chome Crossing), Chuo-ku. © 03/3562-2111. Station: Ginza (1 min.).

## ELECTRONICS

The largest concentration of electronics and electrical-appliance shops in Japan is in an area of Tokyo called **Akihabara Electric Town (Denkigai),** centered around Chuo

Dori. Although you can find good deals on video and audio equipment elsewhere (especially just west of Shinjuku Station, where Yodobashi—see "Cameras" below—dominates with several stores devoted to electronics), Akihabara is a must-see simply for its sheer volume. With more than 600 multilevel stores, shops, and stalls, Akihabara accounts for one-tenth of the nation's electronics and electrical-appliance sales. An estimated 50,000 shoppers come here on a weekday, 100,000 per day on a weekend. Even if you don't buy anything, it's great fun walking around. If you do intend to buy, make sure you know what the item would cost back home. Or, you may be able to pick up something that's unavailable back home. Most of the stores and stalls are open-fronted, and many are painted neon green and pink. Inside, lights flash, fans blow, washing machines shimmy and shake, and stereos blast. Salespeople yell out their wares, trying to get customers to look at their rice cookers, refrigerators, computers, cellular phones, video equipment, digital cameras, CD and DVD players, TVs, calculators, and watches. This is the best place to see the latest models of everything electronic; it's an educational experience in itself. In recent years, some shops have branched out to include anime products and *manga* (Japanese comic books).

If you are buying, be sure to bargain and don't buy at the first place you go to. One woman I know who was looking for a portable music device bought it at the third shop she went to for ¥4,000 ($38) less than what was quoted to her at the first shop. Make sure, too, that whatever you purchase is made for export—that is, with instructions in English, an international warranty, and the proper electrical connectors. All the larger stores have duty-free floors where products are made for export. Two of the largest are **Yamagiwa,** 3–13–10 Soto-Kanda (© **03/3253-2111**); and **Laox,** 15–3 Soto-Kanda (© **03/3255-5301**). Also worth a browse is **AKKY International,** 1–12–5 Soto-Kanda (© **03/5207-5027**), with its knowledgeable salespeople and inexpensive Japanese souvenirs in the basement. If you're serious about buying, check these stores first.

The easiest way to get to Akihabara is via the Yamanote Line or Sobu Line to the JR Akihabara Station. You can also take the Hibiya subway line to Akihabara Station, but it's farther to walk. In any case, take the Akihabara Electric Town exit. Most shops are open daily from about 10:30am to 8pm.

### Cameras

You can purchase cameras at many duty-free shops, including those in Akihabara, but if you're really serious about photographic equipment, make a trip to a shop dealing specifically in cameras. If a new camera is too formidable an expense, consider buying a used camera. New models come out so frequently in Japan that older models can be grabbed up for next to nothing.

**Bic Camera**   This huge, eight-floor store near the Ginza offers not only single-lens reflex, large and medium format, and digital cameras, but also computers, DVD and MP3 players, video cameras, watches, toys, and much more. Note, however, that it caters primarily to Japanese; English-speaking sales clerks are scarce and export models are limited. Ask for the English-language brochure, and if you're buying sensitive equipment, make sure it will work outside Japan and comes with English-language instructions. Open daily 10am to 9pm. There's a branch in Shibuya at 1–24–12 Shibuya (© **03/5466-1111;** open daily 10am–8pm; station: Shibuya, 2 min.). 1–11–1 Yurakucho, Chiyoda-ku. © 03/5221-1112. Station: Yurakucho (1 min.).

㉟ **Lemon**   Its name doesn't inspire confidence, but this company specializes in used and new cameras from around the world. On the first floor are both new and used

Japanese cameras, including digital cameras, while the second floor sells only Japanese-made cameras. An annex, at 4–2–2 Ginza, sells foreign large-format new and used models on the eighth floor, including Leica, Hasselblad, and others. A camera buff's paradise. Open Monday to Saturday 11am to 8pm, Sunday 11am to 5pm. 4–3–14 Ginza, Chuo-ku. (𝄡 03/3567-4581. Station: Ginza (1 min.). Look for the yellow sign and picture of a lemon.

**Yodobashi Camera**    Shinjuku is the photographic equipment center for Tokyo, and this store, 1 block west of the station, is the biggest in the area. In fact, it ranks as one of the largest discount camera shops in the world, with around 30,000 items in stock, and it reputedly sells approximately 500 to 600 cameras daily. Although prices are marked, you can bargain here. This is the place to stock up on film; you can also have film developed here. In addition to cameras, it sells watches, calculators, computers, and other electronic equipment, though if you're interested specifically in watches, clocks, audio/video equipment, games, and other wares, nearby branches specialize in all of these (ask at the main shop for a map of the area). Open daily 9:30am to 9pm. 1–11–1 Nishi-Shinjuku, Shinjuku-ku. (𝄡 03/3346-1010. Station: Shinjuku (west exit, 3 min.).

## FASHIONS

The **department stores** and **shopping malls** listed earlier are all good places to check out the latest trends. For inexpensive, basic clothing (think Japanese version of Gap), look for one of the 40 **Uniqlo** shops in Tokyo selling T-shirts, jeans, socks, shirts, and other clothing for the whole family. Convenient locations include 5–7–10 Ginza, on the fifth floor of the New Melsa building on Chuo Dori (𝄡 03/5537-6795; station: Ginza); 6–10–8 Jingumae (𝄡 03/5468-7313; station: Meiji-Jingumae, on Meiji Dori in the direction of Shibuya); and 16–17 Udagawacho (𝄡 03/5728-8431; station: Shibuya).

Otherwise, Harajuku and Shibuya are the places to go for hundreds of small shops selling inexpensive designer knockoffs, as well as fashion department stores—multistoried buildings filled with concessions of various designers and labels. The stores below are two of the best known and largest.

**La Forêt**    This is not only the largest store in Harajuku but also one of the most fashionable, appealing mostly to teenage and 20-something shoppers. Young and upcoming Japanese designers are here as well as established names, in boutiques spread on several floors. There's so much to see, you can easily kill a few hours here. Open daily 11am to 8pm. 1–11–6 Jingumae, Shibuya-ku. (𝄡 03/3475-0411. Station: Meiji-Jingumae (1 min.) or Harajuku (3 min.). Just off Harajuku's main intersection of Omotesando Dori and Meiji Dori.

**Parco**    A division of Seibu, Parco is actually three buildings clustered together and called Parco Part 1, Part 2, and Part 3. Parco Part 1 is the place to go for designer boutiques for men and women, with clothes by Japanese designers like Yohji Yamamoto and Tsumori Chisato and foreign designers like Anna Sui and Vivienne Westwood. Part 2 has furniture and household goods, while Part 3 is devoted to casual, young fashions. Parco has two sales a year that you shouldn't miss if you're here—one in January and one in July. Open daily 10am to 9pm. 15–1 Udagawacho, Shibuya-ku. (𝄡 03/3464-5111. Station: Shibuya (Hachiko exit, 4 min.).

### Designer Boutiques

The block between Omotesando Crossing and the Nezu Museum (currently undergoing renovation) in **Aoyama** (station: Omotesando, 2 min.) has become the Rodeo Drive of Japan, the showcase of top designers. Even if you can't buy here (steep prices

for most pocketbooks), a stroll is de rigueur for clothes hounds and those interested in design. Most shops are open daily from 11am to 8pm. **Comme des Garçons,** on the right side as you walk from Aoyama Dori (© 03/3406-3951), is Rei Kawakubo's showcase for her daring—and constantly evolving—men's and women's designs. The goddess of Japanese fashion and one of the few females in the business, Kawakubo has remained on the cutting edge of design for more than 2 decades. Across the street is **Issey Miyake** (© 03/3423-1408), with two floors of cool, spacious displays of Miyake's interestingly structured designs for men and women. (His very popular Pleats Please line is around the corner on Aoyama Dori, 3–13–21 Minami Aoyama; © 03/5772-7750.) Of the many non-Japanese designers to have invaded this trendy neighborhood in recent years, none stands out as much as **Prada** (© 03/6418-0400), a bubble of convex/concave windows on the right side of the street. One of Japan's newer designers, **Tsumori Chisato,** has a shop on the left side of the street (© 03/3423-5170). Also worth seeking out along this stretch is **Yohji Yamamoto** on the right (© 03/3409-6006), where Yamamoto's unique, classically wearable clothes are sparingly hung, flaunting the avant-garde interior space.

On the other side of Aoyama Dori, on Omotesando Dori, is **Hanae Mori** (© 03/3400-3301), the grande dame of Japanese design, with everything from separates and men's golf wear to haute couture and wedding gowns on display on three floors of a building designed by Japanese architect Kenzo Tange.

## FLEA MARKETS

Flea markets are good opportunities to shop for antiques as well as delightful junk. You can pick up secondhand kimono at very reasonable prices, as well as kitchenware, vases, cast-iron teapots, small chests, dolls, household items, and odds and ends. (Don't expect to find any good buys in furniture.) The markets usually begin as early as dawn or 6am and last until 3 or 4pm or so, but go early if you want to pick up bargains. Bargaining is expected. Note that because most are outdoors, they tend to be canceled if it rains. Tokyo also has huge antiques fairs several times a year, including the Heiwajima Antique Fair, held for several days in May, June, July, September, and December near Ryutsu Center Station on the Tokyo Monorail Line; and an antiques fair held at Ueno Shinobazu Pond for several weeks in April, July, August, and October. Contact the Tourist Information Center for an update.

**Togo Shrine,** on Meiji Dori in Harajuku (near Meiji-Jingumae and Harajuku stations), has an antiques market on the first, fourth and, when there is one, fifth Sunday of every month from 4am to 2pm. Great for used kimono as well as small furniture and curios, it's one of my favorites. **Nogi Shrine,** a 1-minute walk from Nogizaka Station, has an antiques flea market from dawn to about 2pm the second Sunday of each month except November.

**Hanazono Shrine,** near the Yasukuni Dori/Meiji Dori intersection east of Shinjuku Station (a 5-min. walk from Shinjuku Sanchome Station), has a flea market every Sunday from dawn to about 2pm (except in May and Nov due to festivals). But it's **Oedo Antique Fair,** held in the courtyard of the Tokyo International Forum beside Yurakucho Station, that claims to be Tokyo's largest fair of international antiques. Held the first and third Sunday of the month from 8am to 5pm, it features Western antiques (at highly inflated prices), as well as Japanese furniture, ceramics, furniture, kimono, woodblock prints, and more.

Finally, the closest thing Tokyo has to a permanent flea market is **Ameya Yokocho** (also referred to as Ameyokocho or Ameyacho), a narrow street near Ueno Park that

runs along and underneath the elevated tracks of the JR Yamanote Line between Ueno and Okachimachi stations. There are about 400 stalls here selling discounted items ranging from fish, seaweed, and vegetables to handbags, tennis shoes, cosmetics, watches, and casual clothes. The scene retains something of the *shitamachi* spirit of old Tokyo. Although housewives have been coming here for years, young Japanese recently discovered the market as a good bargain spot for fashions, accessories, and cosmetics. Some shops close on Wednesdays, but hours are usually daily from 10am to 7pm; early evening is the most crowded time. Don't even think of coming here on a holiday—it's a standstill pedestrian traffic jam.

## KIMONO

**Chicago,** on Omotesando Dori in Harajuku (☏ 03/3409-5017; station: Meiji-Jingumae, 1 min., or Harajuku, 2 min.), is the place to go for used kimono. It stocks hundreds of affordable used kimono, cotton yukata, and obi (sashes) toward the back left corner of the basement shop, past the 1950s clothes, in its Kimono Corner. It's open daily from 11am to 8pm. The nearby **Oriental Bazaar** (p. 202) also has a decent selection of new and used kimono at affordable prices, including elaborate wedding kimono.

In addition, department stores sell new kimono, notably **Takashimaya** and **Mitsukoshi** in Nihombashi and **Isetan** in Shinjuku. They also hold sales for rental wedding kimono. Flea markets are also good for used kimono and yukata, particularly the antiques market at **Togo Shrine.**

Established in 1913, **Hayashi Kimono** (☏ 03/3501-4012), with two locations in the International Arcade (near the Imperial Hotel under the elevated JR Yamamote train tracks; station: Hibiya), sells all manner of kimono, including antique kimono, cotton yukata, and *tanzen* (the heavy winter overcoat that goes over the yukata). If you're buying a gift for someone back home, this is a good place to start. Open daily from 10am to 7pm (to 6pm on Sun).

## KITCHENWARE & TABLEWARE

In addition to the department stores listed above, the best place to shop for items related to cooking and serving is **Kappabashi-dougugai Dori** (station: Tawaramachi), popularly known as Kappabashi; this is Japan's largest wholesale area for cookware. There are approximately 150 specialty stores here selling cookware, including sukiyaki pots, woks, lunch boxes, pots and pans, aprons, knives, china, lacquerware, rice cookers, and disposable wooden chopsticks in bulk. Although stores are wholesalers selling mainly to restaurants, you're welcome to browse and purchase as well. Stores are closed on Sunday but are otherwise open from about 10am to 5pm.

## PEARLS

**Mikimoto,** on Chuo Dori not far from Ginza 4-chome Crossing, past Wako department store (☏ 03/3535-54611; station: Ginza, 1 min.), is Japan's most famous pearl shop. It was founded by Mikimoto Koichi, the first to produce a really good cultured pearl, in 1905. Open daily 11am to 7:30pm; closed occasionally on Wednesday. Otherwise, there's a Mikimoto branch (☏ 03/3591-5001) in the **Imperial Hotel Arcade,** under the Imperial Hotel (station: Hibiya), where you'll also find **Asahi Shoten** (☏ 03/3503-2528), with a good selection in the modest-to-moderate price range; and **K. Uyeda Pearl Shop** (☏ 03/3503-2587), with a wide selection of pearls in many different price ranges.

## 10 Tokyo After Dark

By day, Tokyo is arguably one of the least attractive cities in the world. Come dusk, however, Tokyo comes into its own. The drabness fades, the city blossoms into a profusion of giant neon lights and paper lanterns, and its streets fill with millions of overworked Japanese out to have a good time. If you ask me, Tokyo at night is one of the craziest cities in the world, a city that never gives up and never seems to sleep. Entertainment districts are as crowded at 3am as they are at 10pm, with many establishments open until the first subways start running after 5am. Whether it's jazz, reggae, gay bars, sex shows, dance clubs, mania, or madness that you're searching for, Tokyo has it all.

**GETTING TO KNOW THE SCENE**    Tokyo has several nightlife districts spread throughout the city, each with its own atmosphere, price range, and clientele. Most famous are probably **Kabuki-cho** in Shinjuku, and **Roppongi.** Before visiting any of the locales suggested below, be sure to just walk around one of these neighborhoods and absorb the atmosphere. The streets will be crowded, the neon lights will be overwhelming, and you never know what you might discover on your own.

Although there are many bars, discos, and clubs packed with young Japanese of both sexes, nightlife in Japan for the older generations is still pretty much a man's domain, just as it has been for centuries. At the high end of this domain are the **geisha bars,** concentrated primarily in Kyoto. All Japanese cities, however, have so-called **hostess bars;** in Tokyo these are concentrated in Ginza, Roppongi, Shinjuku, and Akasaka. A woman will sit at your table, talk to you, pour your drinks, listen to your problems, and boost your ego. You buy her drinks as well, which is one reason the tab can be so high. Hostess bars in various forms have been a part of Japanese society for centuries. Most of you will probably find the cost of visiting a hostess bar not worth the price since hostesses usually speak Japanese only, but such places provide Japanese males with sympathetic ears and the chance to escape the world of both work and family. Men usually have their favorite hostess bar, often a small place with just enough room for regular customers. In the more exclusive hostess bars, only those customers with an introduction are allowed entrance.

The most popular nightlife spots are **drinking establishments,** where the vast majority of Japan's office workers, college students, and expatriates go for an evening out. These places include Western-style bars as well as Japanese-style watering holes, called *nomi-ya. Yakitori-ya,* restaurant-bars that serve yakitori and other snacks, are included in this group. Dancing and live-music venues are also hugely popular with young Tokyoites. At the low end of the spectrum are Tokyo's topless bars, sex shows, massage parlors, and porn shops, with the largest concentration of such places in Shinjuku's **Kabuki-cho District.**

In addition to the establishments listed below, be sure to check the restaurants listed in the inexpensive category under "Where to Dine" in chapter 4 for a relatively cheap night out on the town. Many places serve as both eateries and watering holes, especially yakitori-ya.

**EXTRA CHARGES & TAXES**    One more thing you should be aware of is the "table charge" that some bars and many cocktail lounges charge their customers. Included in the table charge is usually a small appetizer—maybe nuts, chips, or a vegetable. For this reason, some places call it an *otsumami,* or a snack charge. At any rate, the charge is usually between ¥300 and ¥500 ($2.85–$4.75) per person. Some establishments levy a table charge only after a certain time in the evening; others may add

it only if you don't order food from the menu. If you're not sure and it matters to you, be sure to ask before ordering anything. Remember, too, that there's a 5% consumption tax, though most menus already include it in their price. Some higher-end establishments, especially nightclubs, hostess bars, and some dance clubs, will also add a 10% to 20% service charge.

**FINDING OUT WHAT'S ON**   To find out what's happening in the entertainment scene—contemporary and traditional music and theater, films, and special events—keep an eye out for the free weekly *Metropolis* (www.metropolis.japantoday.com), which carries a nightlife section covering concerts and events and is available at bars, restaurants, and other venues around town. The *Japan Times* and *Daily Yomiuri* also carry entertainment sections.

**GETTING TICKETS FOR EVENTS**   If you're staying in one of the higher-class hotels, the concierge or guest-relations manager can usually get tickets for you. Otherwise, you can always head to the theater or hall itself. It's easier, however, to go through a ticket service such as **Ticket PIA** (© **0570/02-999**), which has outlets at the Sony Building in the Ginza (5–3–1 Ginza), the Isetan department store annex in Shinjuku, and many other locations in Tokyo. Another good service is provided by **CN Playguide** (© **03/5802-9999**).

## THE PERFORMING ARTS

For descriptions of Japanese traditional performance arts such as Kabuki and Noh, see "Cultural Snapshots: Japanese Arts in a Nutshell," in appendix A. In addition to the performance art listings below, Tokyo also has occasional shows of more avant-garde or lesser-known performance art productions, including highly stylized Butoh dance performances from companies like Sankai Juku and percussion demonstrations by Kodo drummers and other Japanese drum groups. See one of the publications listed above for complete listings.

**KABUKI**   Tokyo's most prestigious Kabuki theater is **Kabukiza** ���, 4–12–15 Ginza (© **03/5565-6000** for advance reservations; www.shochiku.co.jp/play/kabukiza/theater/index.html). Conveniently located within easy walking distance of the Ginza 4–chome Crossing (directly above the Higashi-Ginza Station), this impressive theater with a Momoyama-style facade (influenced by 16th-c. castle architecture) is a remake of the 1924 original building. It seats almost 2,000 and features the usual Kabuki stage fittings, including a platform that can be raised above and lowered below the stage for dramatic appearances and disappearances of actors, a revolving stage, and a runway stage extending into the audience.

The Kabukiza stages about eight or nine Kabuki productions a year. Each production begins its run between the first and third of each month and runs about 25 days (there are no shows in Aug). Usually, two different programs are shown; matinees run from about 11 or 11:30am to 4pm, and evening performances run from about 4:30 or 5pm to about 9pm. It's considered perfectly okay to come for only part of a performance.

Of course, you won't be able to understand what's being said, but that doesn't matter; the productions themselves are great entertainment. For an outline of the plot, you can purchase an **English-language program,** which costs ¥1,000 ($9.50); you also can rent **English-language earphones** for ¥650 ($6.20), plus a ¥1,000 ($9.50) refundable deposit—these provide a running commentary on the story, music, actors, stage properties, and other aspects of Kabuki. Buying a program or renting earphones will add immensely to your enjoyment of the play.

Tickets generally range from ¥3,500 to ¥22,000 ($33–$209), depending on the program and seat location. Advance tickets can be purchased at the **Advance Ticket Office** to the right side of Kabukiza's main entrance from 10am to 6pm. You may also make advance reservations by phone (same-day bookings are not accepted). Otherwise, tickets for each day's performance are placed on sale 1 hour before the start of each performance.

If you don't have time for an entire performance or you wish to view Kabuki only for a short while, it's possible to watch only one act *(makumi)*. One-acts generally last about 1 or 1½ hours, with tickets per act costing ¥800 to ¥1,300 ($7.60–$12) depending on the time of day and length of the show. English-language earphones here cost ¥400 ($3.80) for one act, and you can also buy an English-language program. Note that seats are a bit far from the stage, on the very top two rows of the theater (on the fourth floor; there is no elevator). On the other hand, I have seen several acts this way, sometimes simply dropping by when I'm in the area; it's a marvelous midday break from the rigors of shopping. These tickets, sold at the smaller entrance to the left of the main entrance, are available on a first-come, first-served basis and go on sale 20 minutes before each act. If you liked the act so much that you wish to remain for the next one, it's possible to do so if the act is not sold out; tickets in these cases are usually available on the fourth floor.

If there are no shows at Kabukiza, you may be able to see Kabuki at the **National Theater of Japan (Kokuritsu Gekijo),** 4–1 Hayabusacho, Chiyoda-ku (**©️ 03/3230-3000;** www.ntj.go.jp; station: Hanzomon, 6 min.). Kabuki is scheduled here throughout the year except during February, May, August, and September, when Bunraku (see below) is being staged instead. Matinees usually begin at 11am or noon, and afternoon performances at 2:30 or 5pm. Most tickets range from about ¥1,500 to ¥3,800 ($14–$36), with earphones available for ¥700 ($6.65) plus a ¥1,000 ($9.50) deposit.

**NOH**    Noh is performed at a number of locations in Tokyo, but most famous is the **National Noh Theater (Kokuritsu Nohgakudo),** 4–18–1 Sendagaya, Shibuya-ku (**©️ 03/3423-1331;** station: Sendagaya, 5 min.). Opened in 1983, it is dedicated to presenting classical Noh and kyogen, with about three to five performances monthly. Tickets range from about ¥2,300 to ¥4,300 ($22–$41) but are often sold out in advance. However, about 30 tickets are held back to be sold on the day of the performance. In addition, privately sponsored Noh performances are also held here, for which the admission varies. Check the *Japan Times* or *Daily Yomiuri* for performance dates and times.

**BUNRAKU**    Four Bunraku performances a year—in February, May, August, and September—are staged at The National Theater of Japan (Kokuritsu Gekijo), 4–1 Hayabusacho, Chiyoda-ku (**©️ 03/3265-7411;** station: Hanzomon, 6 min.). There are usually two to three performances daily, beginning at 11am, with tickets averaging ¥1,500 to ¥6,500 ($14–$62). Earphones with English-language explanations are available for ¥650 ($6.20).

**TAKARAZUKA KAGEKIDAN**    This world-famous, all-female troupe stages elaborate musical revues with dancing, singing, and gorgeous costumes, with performances ranging from Japanese versions of Broadway hits to original Japanese works based on local legends. The first Takarazuka troupe, formed in 1912 at a resort near Osaka, gained instant notoriety because all its performers were women, in contrast to

the all-male Kabuki. When I went to see this troupe perform, I was surprised to find that the audience also consisted almost exclusively of women; indeed, the troupe has an almost cultlike following.

Performances, with story synopses available in English, are held generally in March, April, July, August, November, December, and sometimes in June at **Tokyo Takarazuka Gekijo,** 1–1–3 Yurakucho (© **03/5251-2001;** station: Hibiya, 1 min.). Tickets, available at the box office or through Ticket Pia (© **0570/02-9999**), generally range from about ¥3,500 to ¥10,000 ($33–$95).

**KINGYO** ℜ    This sophisticated nightclub stages one of the most high-energy, visually charged acts I've ever seen—nonstop action of ascending and receding stages and stairs, fast-paced choreography, elaborate costumes, and loud music. There are a few female dancers, but most of the dancers are males assuming female parts, just like in Kabuki. In fact, many of the performances center on traditional Japanese themes with traditional dress and kimono, but the shows take place in a very technically sophisticated setting. There are also satires: One past performance included a piece on Microsoft vs. Apple; another featured aliens from outer space—great fun. It's located in the heart of the Roppongi nightlife district at 3–14–17 Roppongi (© **03/ 3478-3000;** station: Roppongi, 4 min.), near the Roppongi cemetery (from Roppongi Crossing, walk toward Tokyo Tower on Gaien-Higashi Dori and turn left at Freshness Burger). Cover is ¥4,000 ($38) for daily shows at 7:20 and 9:50pm, with additional shows Friday and Saturday at 1:20am. Reservations are advised, as this is a very popular show.

## THE CLUB & MUSIC SCENE
### THE MAJOR ENTERTAINMENT DISTRICTS
**GINZA**    A chic and expensive shopping area by day, Ginza transforms itself into a dazzling entertainment district of restaurants, bars, and first-grade hostess bars at night. It's the most sophisticated of Tokyo's nightlife districts and is also one of the most expensive. Almost all Japanese businessmen you see out carousing in Ginza are paying by expense account; the prices are ridiculously high.

Because I'm not wealthy, I prefer Shinjuku and Roppongi. However, because Ginza does have some fabulous restaurants and several hotels, I've included some reasonably priced recommendations for a drink in the area if you happen to find yourself here after dinner. The cheapest way to absorb the atmosphere in Ginza is simply to wander about, particularly around **Namiki Dori** and its side streets.

**SHINJUKU**    Northeast of Shinjuku Station is an area called **Kabuki-cho,** which undoubtedly has the craziest nightlife in all of Tokyo, with block after block of strip joints, massage parlors, pornography shops, peep shows, bars, restaurants, and, as the night wears on, lots of drunk revelers. A world of its own, it's sleazy, chaotic, crowded, vibrant, and fairly safe. Despite its name, Shinjuku's primary night hot spot has nothing to do with Kabuki. At one time, there was a plan to bring some culture to the area by introducing a Kabuki theater; the plan never materialized but the name stuck. Although Kabuki-cho used to be the domain of businessmen out on the town, in recent years young Japanese, including college-age men and women, have claimed parts of it as their own and now outnumber businessmen; the result is that there are a growing number of inexpensive drinking establishments well worth a visit.

To the east of Kabuki-cho, just west of Hanazono Shrine, is a smaller district called **Goruden Gai,** which is "Golden Guy" mispronounced. It's a warren of tiny alleyways

leading past even tinier bars, each consisting of just a counter and a few chairs. Many of these closet-size bars are closed to outsiders, catering to regular customers, though others welcome strangers as well. Although many thought Goruden Gai would succumb to land-hungry developers in the 1980s, the economic recession has brought a stay of execution. In fact, in recent years Goruden Gai has experienced a revival, with more than 100 tiny drinking dens lining the tiny streets. Still, it occupies such expensive land that I still fear for the life of this tiny enclave, one of Tokyo's most fascinating.

Even farther east is **Shinjuku 2-chome** (pronounced "knee-chomay"), officially recognized as the gay-bar district of Shinjuku. Its lively street scene of mostly gays and some straights of all ages (but mostly young) make this one of the most vibrant nightlife districts. It's here that I was once taken to a host bar featuring young men in crotchless pants. The clientele included both gay men and groups of young, giggling office girls. That place has since closed down, but Shinjuku is riddled with other spots bordering on the absurd.

The best thing to do in Shinjuku is to simply walk about. In the glow of neon light, you'll pass everything from smoke-filled restaurants to hawkers trying to get you to step inside so they can part you from your money. If you're looking for strip joints, topless or bottomless coffee shops, peep shows, or porn, I leave you to your own devices, but you certainly won't have any problems finding them. In Kabuki-cho alone, there are an estimated 200 sex businesses in operation, including bathhouses where women are available for sex at a high price. Although prostitution is illegal in Japan, everyone seems to ignore what goes on behind closed doors. Just be sure you know what you are getting into; your bill at the end may add up to much more than you figured.

**ROPPONGI**   To Tokyo's younger crowd, Roppongi is the city's most fashionable place to hang out. It's also a favorite with the foreign community, including models, business types, and English-language teachers. Roppongi has more than its fair share of live-music houses, restaurants, discos, expatriate bars, and pubs. Some Tokyoites complain that Roppongi is too crowded, too crass, and too commercialized (and has too many foreigners), but for the casual visitor I think Roppongi offers an excellent opportunity to see what's new and hot in the capital city, and it's easy to navigate because nightlife activity is so concentrated.

The center of Roppongi is **Roppongi Crossing** (the intersection of Roppongi Dori and Gaien-Higashi Dori), at the corner of which sits the garishly pink Almond Coffee Shop. The shop itself has mediocre coffee and desserts at terribly inflated prices, but the sidewalk in front of the store is the number-one meeting spot in Roppongi.

If you need directions, there's a conveniently located *koban* (police box) catty-corner from the Almond Coffee Shop and next to the Bank of Tokyo-Mitsubishi. It has a big map of the Roppongi area showing the address system, and someone is always there.

If the buzz of Roppongi is too much, a quieter, saner alternative is neighboring **Nishi-Azabu,** which has restaurants and bars catering to both Japanese and foreigners. The center of Nishi-Azabu is the next big crossroads, Nishi-Azabu Crossing (the intersection of Roppongi Dori and Gaien-Nishi Dori). Nishi Azabu is about a 10-minute walk from Roppongi Station, past Roppongi Hills in the direction of Shibuya. **Roppongi Hills** is a massive urban development with many restaurants and some bars of its own.

> **Tips  Mapping Out Tokyo's Nightlife**
>
> Once you've chosen a nightlife spot that appeals to you, you can locate it using
> the following neighborhood maps:
>
> • To locate bars and clubs in **Akasaka**, p. 119.
> • To locate bars and clubs in **Shinjuku**, p. 128.
> • To locate bars and clubs in **Asakusa**, p. 133.
> • To locate bars and clubs in **Hibiya and Ginza**, p. 144.
> • To locate bars and clubs in **Harajuku & Aoyama**, p. 157.
> • To locate bars and clubs in **Roppongi**, p. 163.

## LIVE MUSIC

The live-music scene exploded in the 1990s and is now located throughout the metropolis. In addition to the dedicated venues below, several bars offer live music most nights of the week, including What the Dickens (see "The Bar Scene," below).

**Bauhaus**   Since 1981, this small club has the same great house band that plays mostly 1970s and 1980s British and American hard rock (Deep Purple, ZZ Top, Aerosmith, Queen, the Rolling Stones, Led Zeppelin), with five sets beginning at 8pm. The band puts on quite a show—a bit raunchy at times but very polished. Hours are Monday to Saturday 7pm to 1am. Closed holidays. Reine Roppongi, 2nd floor, 5–3–4 Roppongi. ⓒ 03/3403-0092. Cover ¥2,835 ($27). Station: Roppongi (3 min.). From Roppongi Crossing, walk toward Tokyo Tower on Gaien-Higashi Dori and turn right at McDonald's.

**Birdland**   Down to earth and featuring good jazz (with an emphasis on 1940s swing) performed by Japanese musicians, as well as other types of music such as Hawaiian folk, Birdland has been a welcome refuge from Roppongi's madding crowd for more than a quarter of a century. It's small and cozy with candles and soft lighting and attracts an older, knowledgeable, and appreciative crowd. Incidentally, the official cover price is ¥3,500 ($33), but management told me if you show your *Frommer's* guide, you can get in for ¥1,500 ($13). Hours are Monday to Saturday 6pm to midnight (music begins at 7pm). Square Building (in the basement), 3–10–3 Roppongi. ⓒ 03/3478-3456. www.birdland-tokyo.jp. Cover ¥3,500 ($33) plus ¥900 ($8.55) drink minimum and 10% service charge. Station: Roppongi (2 min.). From Roppongi Crossing, walk toward Tokyo Tower on Gaien-Higashi Dori and take the 1st left.

**Blue Note**   Tokyo's most expensive, elegant jazz venue is cousin to the famous Blue Note in New York. The musicians are top-notch; Oscar Peterson, Sarah Vaughan, Tony Bennett, David Sanborn, and the Milt Jackson Quartet have all performed here. However, the 300-seat establishment follows the frustrating practice of selling tickets good for only one set. There are usually two sets nightly, generally at 6:30 and 9pm. 6–3–16 Minami Aoyama. ⓒ 03/5485-0088. www.bluenote.co.jp. Cover ¥8,400 ($80) for most performances, more for top names. Station: Omotesando (8 min.). Off Kotto Dori.

**Body & Soul**   Since 1974, this low-ceilinged, tiny but cozy basement club with only a few tables and a long bar gives everyone a good view of its mostly jazz performances by Japanese and foreign musicians. Hours are Monday to Saturday 7pm to midnight, with performances at 8:30 and 10:20pm. 6–13–9 Minami Aoyama. ⓒ 03/5466-3348. www.bodyandsoul.co.jp. Cover ¥3,500–¥5,000 ($33–$48) for most performances. Station: Omotesando (7 min.). Off Roppongi Dori, a stone's throw from Nobu.

**Cavern Club**   If you know your Beatles history, you'll know Cavern is the name of the Liverpool club where the Fab Four got their start. The Tokyo club features Beatles memorabilia and house bands performing Beatles music exclusively and very convincingly at that. Close your eyes—and you'll swear you're listening to the real thing. Extremely popular with both Japanese and foreigners, it's packed on weekends—expect long lines, or call to reserve a table. Hours are Monday to Saturday 6pm to 2:30am; Sunday and holidays 6pm to midnight. 5–3–2 Roppongi. ✆ 03/3405-5207. Cover ¥1,575 ($15), plus a 1-drink minimum and 10% service charge. Station: Roppongi (4 min.). Take the side street going downhill on the left side of Almond Coffee Shop and then take the 1st left; the club will be on the right.

**Crocodile**   Popular with a young Japanese crowd, the eclectic Crocodile describes itself as a casual rock-'n'-roll club, with live bands ranging from rock and blues to jazz-fusion, reggae, soul, experimental, and even country and salsa; it's a good place to check out new Japanese bands (a live-action video of the performing band at the front door helps you decide if it's a band you want to see). It has an interesting interior and a good, laid-back atmosphere; depending on the music, the clientele ranges from Japanese with bleached-blond hair and body piercings to a grunge and even middle-aged crowd. Hours are daily 6pm to 2am; music starts at 8pm. 6–18–8 Jingumae. ✆ 03/3499-5205. Cover ¥2,000–¥3,000 ($19–$29), occasionally more for big acts. Station: Meiji-Jingumae or Shibuya (10 min.). On Meiji Dori halfway between Harajuku and Shibuya.

**JZ Brat**   This hotel club promotes both domestic and international jazz performers, including many vocalists, in a breezy setting reminiscent of the '60s. It's open Monday to Thursday 6pm to midnight, Friday 6pm to 4am, and Saturday 8pm to 4am, but is sometimes closed for private events (phone first). Live music starts at 7:30pm. Cerulean Tower Tokyu Hotel, 26–1 Sakurgaoka-cho. ✆ 03/5728-0168. Cover ¥4,200–¥5,250 ($40–$50) for most bands. Station: Shibuya (5 min.).

**New York Bar**   This is one of Tokyo's most sophisticated venues, boasting Manhattan-style jazz and breathtaking views of glittering west Shinjuku. Unfortunately, it's also one of the city's smallest. Consider coming for dinner in the adjacent **New York Grill** (p. 154); it costs a small fortune, but you'll save the cost of the cover. Hours are daily from 5pm (from 7pm Sunday), with live music 8pm to midnight. Park Hyatt Hotel, 52nd floor, 3–7–1–2 Nishi-Shinjuku. ✆ 03/5322-1234. Cover ¥2,000 ($19). Station: Shinjuku (13 min.), Hatsudai on the Keio Line (7 min.), or Tochomae (8 min.).

**Ruby Room**   I've seen living rooms larger than this second-floor venue, home to local acts, open mic on Tuesdays, house and techno DJs, and other events. The crowd depends on the music, but since there's no room to move, people just dance where they are, and the band is close, close, close—any closer and you'd be in the drummer's lap. Hours are Monday to Saturday from 7pm to 5am. 2–25–17 Dogenzaka, Shibuya-ku. ✆ 03/3780-3022. www.rubyroomtokyo.com. Cover ¥1,500 ($14) Fri–Sat only, including 1 drink. Station: Shibuya (2 min.). Take the Hachiko exit to Dogenzaka and turn right at Vodafone.

**Shinjuku Pit Inn**   This is one of Tokyo's most famous and longest-running jazz, fusion, and blues clubs, featuring both Japanese and foreign musicians. There are two programs daily—from 2:30 to 5pm and from 7:30pm—making it a great place to stop for a bit of music in the middle of the day. 2–12–4 Shinjuku, southeast of the Yasukuni Dori/Meiji Dori intersection. ✆ 03/3354-2024. www.pit-inn.com. Cover from ¥1,300 ($12), including 1 drink, for the 2:30pm show (¥2,500/$24 weekends and holidays), ¥3,000–¥4,000 ($29–$38) for the evening shows, including 1 drink. Station: Shinjuku Sanchome (4 min.).

## DANCE CLUBS & DISCOS

Discos lost popularity after their 1980s heyday, but with the rise of almost cult-figure DJs, dance clubs have witnessed a resurgence in recent years, with Roppongi still boasting more dance clubs than anywhere else in the city. Sometimes the set cover charge includes drinks and occasionally even food, which makes for an inexpensive way to spend an evening. Keep in mind, however, that prices are usually higher on weekends and are sometimes higher for men than for women. Although discos are required by law to close at midnight, many of them ignore the rule and stay open until dawn. Finally, you must be at least 20 years old (the legal drinking age in Japan) to enter most clubs.

**Code**   Known for its frequent trance and techno events, Kabuki-cho's largest club brings in both Japanese and foreign DJs to keep things hopping on its massive dance floor. Open daily 6pm to 1am, though Fridays through Mondays it often reopens at 5am for all-night revelers who just can't call it quits. Shinjuku Toho-Kaikan, 4th floor, 1–19–2 Kabuki-cho. ✆ 03/3209-0702. Cover ¥2,500 ($24) for males and ¥2,000 ($19) for females, including 1 drink; 5am admission ¥2,000–¥3,000 ($19–$29), including 1 drink. Station: Shinjuku (east exit, 10 min.). Beside Koma Stadium, a Shinjuku landmark.

**El Café Latino**   All the smooth Latin moves make their way to the tiny dance floor of this happening club. It's fun to watch, even if you don't know how to perform the salsa, rhumba, or other Latin dances. Open daily 6pm to 5am. 3–15–24 Roppongi. ✆ 03/3402-8989. Cover Fri–Sat only, ¥1,500 ($14). Station: Roppongi (4 min.). From Roppongi Crossing, walk toward Tokyo Tower on Gaien-Higashi Dori, turning left at Hamburger Inn and right at Gaspanic.

**Kento's**   Kento's was one of the first places to open when the wave of 1950s nostalgia hit Japan in the 1980s; it has even been credited with creating the craze. This is the place to come to if you feel like dancing the night away to tunes of the 1950s and 1960s played by live bands. Although there's hardly room to dance, that doesn't stop the largely over-30 Japanese audience from twisting in the aisles to the tunes of Elvis, Little Richard, The Temptations, Chuck Berry, and others. Hours are Monday to Saturday from 6pm to 2:30am; Sunday and holidays from 6pm to midnight. Daini Reine Building, 5–3–1 Roppongi. ✆ 03/3401-5755. (Also at 6–7–12 Ginza, ✆ 03/3572-9161; and in east Shinjuku at 3–18–4 Shinjuku, ✆ 03/3355-6477.) Cover ¥1,000 ($8.35) for females, ¥1,575 ($15) for males, plus 10% service charge and 1 drink minimum. Station: Roppongi (4 min.). Take the side street going downhill on the left side of Almond Coffee Shop and then take the 1st left; the club will be on the right.

**Lexington Queen**   Opened in 1980, Lexington Queen has been the reigning queen of disco in Tokyo for more than 2 decades. In fact, it's so much smaller than the newer, glitzier discos, it seems almost quaint. The music played here covers many genres, from pop and rock to R&B, with requests taken every night except Friday and Saturday. The club's list of past guests reads like a who's who of foreign movie and rock stars to have visited Tokyo, from Rod Stewart to Stephen Dorff to Dustin Hoffman to Marilyn Manson; one night when I was there, Duran Duran walked in. This is the best place to be on Halloween and New Year's, if you can stand the crowds. Women pay only ¥100 (95¢) admission Thursday, including all they can drink. Sunday to Wednesday 10pm to 5am; Thursday and Friday 9pm to 5am. Daisan Goto Building, 3–13–14 Roppongi. ✆ 03/3401-1661. Cover ¥3,000 ($29) for women, ¥4,000 ($38) for men, including free drinks. Station: Roppongi (3 min.). From Roppongi Crossing, walk toward Tokyo Tower on Gaien-Higashi Dori and take the 2nd left.

**Velfarre** If you're looking for the disco scene, search no further. This huge, plush venue—run by a record group famous for its Eurobeat recordings—claims to be Japan's largest disco and has all the latest technical gadgetry to match. Tokyo's disco of the moment, it attracts young Japanese dressed to kill (there's even a dress code: smart casual). The staff is stylishly dressed, too. The dance floor is absolutely gigantic; stage dancers help set the pace. Leading DJs from Tokyo and abroad play everything from pop and retro to techno, hard house, and—what else?—Eurobeat. *Note:* Unlike other discos, this one closes promptly at 1am, though it does reopen Saturday at 5am to round up all those who never went home Friday night. Otherwise, hours are Thursday to Saturday 7pm to 1am. 7–14–22 Roppongi. © 03/3402-8000. Cover Thurs ¥2,000 ($19) for women and ¥3,000 ($29) for men, including 1 drink; Fri–Sat usually ¥3,500 ($33), including 2 drinks. Station: Roppongi (3 min.). From Roppongi Crossing, take the 1st left after Ibis Hotel.

**Yellow** Closed on and off by the boys in blue during its infant rebellious years, this is the closest thing Tokyo has to a true underground disco, staging the city's most progressive events from Butoh performances (a modern minimalist form of dance) to gay nights. Guest DJs from abroad make appearances, playing a variety of music from jazz and reggae to hip-hop, soul, and techno. Only those in the know are supposed to come here, so there's no sign—just a blank, yellow neon square. Hours are daily 10pm to 2 or 4am, but it's often closed for private functions on weekdays, so call ahead. 1–10–11 Nishi-Azabu. © 03/3479-0690. Cover ¥2,500–¥4,000 ($24–$38) including 1 drink, depending on the DJ and the event. Station: Roppongi (10 min.). From Roppongi Crossing, head toward Shibuya on Roppongi Dori. Turn right at the next-to-last street before Gaien-Nishi Dori; it's in the 2nd block on the right.

## THE BAR SCENE

**GINZA** If you're looking for a quiet place for a drink, you can't do better than ㊱ **Lupin** ✒, 5–5–11 Ginza (© 03/3571-0750; station: Ginza, 2 min.), located in a tiny alley between Namiki and Ginza West 5th Street. This tiny basement bar first opened back in 1928 and has changed little over the decades. Even the staff looks like they've been here since it opened. Because no music is played, it's is a good place to come if you want to talk. Note that there's a ¥700 ($6.65) snack/table charge. The bar is closed Sunday and Monday. Another good bar is the **Old Imperial** in the Imperial Hotel (© 03/3504-1111; station: Hibiya, 1 min.); the bar is the hotel's tribute to its original architect, Frank Lloyd Wright, and is the only place in the hotel with some Wright originals, including an Art Deco terra-cotta wall and a mural. With its low lighting and comfortable chairs and tables that are copies of Wright originals, it has a clubby, masculine atmosphere. Try a Mount Fuji, the bar's own cocktail original.

Sapporo beer is the draw at **Sapporo Lion,** a large beer hall with a mock Gothic ceiling and kitschy decor, on Chuo Dori not far from Matsuzakaya department store (© 03/3571-2590; station: Ginza, 3 min.). A large display of plastic foods and an English-language menu help you choose from snacks ranging from yakitori to sausage and spaghetti. If you want to rub elbows with Ginza's office workers, head to the yakitori-ya ㊲ **Atariya,** 3–5–17 Ginza (© 03/3564-0045; station: Ginza, 3 min.), located on the small side street behind Wako department store, in the second block on the right. It offers yakitori skewers in a convivial setting (avoid the yakitori set course, as it contains almost all parts of the chicken).

**ASAKUSA** **Sky Room,** on the 22nd floor of the Asahi Beer Tower, across the Sumida River from Sensoji Temple and next to the building that looks like a mug of beer (© 03/5608-5277; station: Asakusa, 4 min.), is a great place for an inexpensive drink

after an active day in historic Asakusa. A simple cafeteria-type place, it offers great views as well as different kinds of Asahi beer, wine, coffee, and other drinks, all priced at only ¥550 ($5.25). It can be crowded on weekends, and note that the last order is taken at 8:30pm.

**SHINJUKU**   Tiny **Kangaroo Court Decision,** 1–1–6 Kabuki-cho (© **03/3204-6086;** station: Shinjuku Sanchome, 8 min.), with room for only five or so patrons, is typical of a multitude of miniature establishments that line the alleyways of Goruden Gai (see "The Major Entertainment Districts," earlier in this section). Also near Hanazono Shrine, on the eighth floor of the Oriental Wave building on Yasukuni Dori, is one of weirdest theme bars I've seen in Tokyo, **Christon Café,** 5–17–13 Shinjuku (© **03/5287-2426;** station: Shinjuku Sanchome, 5 min.). Decorated like a church with its stained-glass windows, vaulted ceiling, organ music, crosses, and a statue of Jesus, it's packed to the rafters despite the ¥300 ($2.85) cover charge. What to order? A bloody mary, of course. More down-to-earth is the Irish bar **Dubliners,** behind Mitsukoshi on the second floor above Lion, 3–28–9 Shinjuku (© **03/3352-6606;** station: Shinjuku, 3 min.), which attracts a mixed Japanese/ex-pat crowd.

Although most of Shinjuku's night action is east of the station, **Vagabond,** 1–4–20 Nishi-Shinjuku on the second floor in the second alley behind—north of—Odakyu Halc (© **03/3348-9109;** station: Shinjuku, west exit, 2 min.), is on the west side. It features a jazz pianist nightly and is popular with foreigners (especially Brits, who come for the Guinness). The place has been in operation for more than 25 years and is now managed by the original owner's son, Matsuoka Takahiko. Closed on Sunday. Just down the street is ㊳ **Volga,** 1–4–18 Nishi Shinjuku (© **03/3342-4996;** station: Shinjuku, west exit, 2 min.), a yakitori-ya in an ivy-covered, two-story brick building on the corner. Its unrefined atmosphere has changed little since its opening in the 1950s; the place is popular with middle-aged and older Japanese. Closed on Sunday.

**HARAJUKU**   Mellow, dimly lit **Oh God,** 6–7–18 Jingumae (© **03/3406-3206;** station: Meiji-Jingumae, 4 min.), features a mural of a city at sunset and shows free foreign films every night at 9pm, midnight, and 3am (also at 6pm Fri–Sun and holidays). I've seen everything from James Bond to Fassbinder to grade-B movies here; most of the "recent" releases are several years old. There are also two pool tables. This place is a godsend for travelers on a budget and is a good place to hang out.

**EBISU**   Ebisu's most popular bar (especially with ex-pats) is **What the Dickens,** 1–13–3 Ebisu Nishi (© **03/3780-2088;** station: Ebisu, west exit, 2 min.), which features free live bands nightly, English and Irish beer, and British pub grub. Take the side street that runs between Wendy's and KFC; the bar is at the end of the second block on the left on the fourth floor. It's closed on Monday. Personally, my favorite bar is the inimitable **Enjoy House,** 2–9–9 Ebisu Nishi (© **03/5489-1591;** station: Ebisu, west exit, 3 min.), with its 1960s-reminiscent decor, efficient yet relaxed and funky staff, friendly atmosphere, and tiny dance floor. Everyone here seems high and happy; the place is aptly named. Closed on Monday.

**ROPPONGI**   **Gaspanic Bar,** 3–15–24 Roppongi (© **03/3405-0633;** station: Roppongi, 3 min.), epitomizes Roppongi frenzy, attracting foreign and Japanese 20-somethings. The music is loud, and after midnight, this place can get so crowded that women have been known to dance on the countertops. Thursdays are especially crowded since all drinks go for only ¥400 ($3.80). **Gaspanic Cafe,** downstairs, sells pizza by the slice, while in the basement is **Club 99,** open only on Thursday, Friday,

and Saturday for dancing. Large bouncers at the door serve as clues that this place can get rough. From Roppongi Crossing, walk toward Tokyo Tower on Gaien-Higashi Dori, turning left at Hamburger Inn.

I'm more partial to **Geronimo,** 7–14–10 Roppongi (© **03/3478-7449;** Roppongi, 1 min.), on Roppongi Dori opposite Almond Coffee Shop. A tiny place with a bar in the middle and ex-pats practically two-deep everywhere else, it's the kind of place where people dance, drink way too much, and party 'til they can't party anymore. When the gong rings, it means someone is buying shots for everyone at the bar. I also like the more upscale **Heartland,** 6–10–1 Roppongi (© **03/5772-7600;** Roppongi, 3 min.), on Roppongi Dori just past Roppongi Hills. Attracting everyone from bankers to artistic types, it offers cocktails and its own Heartland microbrew and is packed with ex-pats on the prowl.

But the most sane, sophisticated place for a drink is surely **Agave,** 7–15–10 Roppongi (© **03/3497-0229;** station: Roppongi, 3 min.), a cellar bar boasting Japan's largest selection of tequila (more than 350 kinds), as well as cigars from the Dominican Republic, Nicaragua, Honduras, Mexico, and Jamaica. Closed on Sunday. And if *Lost in Translation* makes you yearn for a chance in the spotlight, head to **Fiesta International Karaoke Bar,** 6–7–14 Roppongi (© **03/5410-3008;** Roppongi, 3 min.), on the right side of the small road leading downhill from Almond Coffee Shop's left side. For ¥3,000 ($29) you get three drinks and all the songs you care to sing from the 10,000 English-language song menu. Closed on Sunday.

**AKASAKA**    If your idea of a wild night is relaxing over a drink in a sophisticated lounge, head to the **Garden Lounge** at the Hotel New Otani (© **03/3265-1111;** station: Nagatacho or Akasaka-mitsuke, 3 min.) before sunset. The bonus here is a view of a 400-year-old Japanese landscape garden, complete with a waterfall, a pond, bridges, and manicured bushes. For a more casual setting, try **Hobgoblin Tokyo Brewery Pub and Restaurant,** 2–13–19 Akasaka (© **03/3585-3681;** station: Akasaka, exit 2, 2 min.), a British chain offering more draft beers than any other bar in town, major sporting events from its satellite TVs, darts, and hearty pub meals.

## GAY & LESBIAN BARS

**Shinjuku 2-chome** (station: Shinjuku Sanchome), southeast of the Yasukuni-Gyoen Dori intersection, is Tokyo's gay and lesbian quarter, with a lively street scene and numerous establishments catering to a variety of age groups and preferences. The following are good starting points, but you'll find a lot more in the immediate area by exploring on your own. Attracting both gays and straights, **Advocates,** 2–18–1 Shinjuku (© **03/3358-3988**), is a crowded, small bar open to the street with a few sidewalk tables, making this a good vantage point from which to watch the street action. It's also a good place to network and find out about neighboring bars. **Kinsmen,** on the second floor at 2–18–5 Shinjuku (© **03/3354-4949**), welcomes customers of all persuasions. It's a pleasant oasis, small and civilized, with a huge flower arrangement dominating the center of the room. It's closed on Monday. The casual, laid-back, women-only **Kinswomyn,** 2–15–10 Shinjuku (© **03/3354-8720**), attracts a regular clientele of mainly Japanese lesbians and has a friendly, welcoming atmosphere. It's closed on Tuesday.

# 6

# Side Trips from Tokyo

If your stay in Tokyo is long enough, you should consider taking an excursion or two. **Kamakura** and **Nikko** rank as two of the most important historical sites in Japan, while the **Fuji-Hakone-Izu National Park** serves as a huge recreational playground for the residents of Tokyo. **Yokohama,** with its thriving port, waterfront development, and several museums and attractions, is an interesting day trip from Tokyo. For overnight stays,

I recommend **Hakone** or **Izu Peninsula,** since these resorts boast Japanese-style inns *(ryokan)* where you'll be able to experience the atmosphere of old Japan.

Before departing Tokyo, stop by the **Tourist Information Center (TIC)** for pamphlets on Kamakura, Nikko, Hakone, and the Mount Fuji area, some of which give train schedules and other useful information; see "Visitor Information" in chapter 4 for the TIC location.

## 1 Kamakura, Ancient Capital ✦✦✦

51km (32 miles) S of Tokyo

If you take only one day trip outside Tokyo, it should be to Kamakura, especially if you're unable to include the ancient capitals of Kyoto and Nara in your travels. (If you're going to Kyoto and Nara, I would probably choose Nikko, below.) Kamakura is a delightful hamlet with no fewer than 65 Buddhist temples and 19 Shinto shrines spread throughout the village and surrounding wooded hills. Most of these were built centuries ago, when a warrior named Yoritomo Minamoto seized political power and established his shogunate government in Kamakura in 1192. Wanting to set up his seat of government as far away as possible from what he considered to be the corrupt imperial court in Kyoto, Yoritomo selected Kamakura because it was easy to defend. The village is enclosed on three sides by wooded hills and on the fourth by the sea—a setting that lends a dramatic background to its many temples and shrines.

Although Kamakura remained the military and political center of the nation for a century and a half, the Minamoto clan was in power for only a short time. After Yoritomo's death, both of his sons were assassinated, one after the other, after taking up military rule. Power then passed to the family of Yoritomo's widow, the Hojo family, who ruled until 1333, when the emperor in Kyoto sent troops to crush the shogunate government. Unable to stop the invaders, 800 soldiers retired to the Hojo family temple at Toshoji, where they all disemboweled themselves in ritualistic suicide known as *seppuku.*

Today a thriving seaside resort with a population of 175,000, Kamakura—with its old wooden homes, temples, shrines, and wooded hills—makes a pleasant 1-day trip from Tokyo. (There's also a beach in Kamakura called Yuigahama Beach, but I find it unappealing; it's often litter-strewn and unbelievably crowded in summer. Skip it.)

## ESSENTIALS

**GETTING THERE**   Take the **JR Yokosuka Line** bound for Zushi, Kurihama, or Yokosuka; it departs every 10 to 15 minutes from the Yokohama, Shinagawa, Shimbashi, and Tokyo JR stations. The trip takes almost 1 hour from Tokyo Station and costs ¥890 ($8.50) one-way to Kamakura Station.

**VISITOR INFORMATION**   In Kamakura, there's a **tourist information window** (*©* **0467/22-3350;** www.city.kamakura.kanagawa.jp/English.htm; daily 9am–5:30pm, to 5pm in winter) immediately to the right outside Kamakura Station's east exit in the direction of Tsurugaoka Hachimangu Shrine. It sells a color brochure with a map of Kamakura for ¥200 ($1.90); there's also a free map (in both English and Japanese), but it's not always in stock. Ask here for directions on how to get to the village's most important sights and restaurants.

**ORIENTATION & GETTING AROUND**   Kamakura's major sights are clustered in two areas: **Kamakura Station,** the town's downtown with the tourist office, souvenir shops spread along Komachi Dori and Wakamiya Oji, restaurants, and Tsurugaoka Hachimangu Shrine; and **Hase,** with the Great Buddha and Hase Kannon Temple. You can travel between Kamakura Station and Hase Station via the **Enoden Line,** a wonderful small train, or you can walk the distance in about 20 minutes. Destinations in Kamakura are also easily reached by buses that depart from Kamakura Station.

## SEEING THE SIGHTS

Keep in mind that most temples and shrines open at about 8 or 9am and close between 4 and 5pm.

**AROUND KAMAKURA STATION**   About a 10-minute walk from Kamakura Station, **Tsurugaoka Hachimangu Shrine** ⟨⟨⟨ (*©* **0467/22-0315**) is the spiritual heart of Kamakura and one of its most popular attractions. It was built by Yoritomo and dedicated to Hachiman, the Shinto god of war who served as the clan deity of the Minamoto family. The pathway to the shrine is along Wakamiya Oji, a cherry tree–lined pedestrian lane that was also constructed by Yoritomo in the 1190s so that his oldest son's first visit to the family shrine could be accomplished in style with an elaborate procession. The lane stretches from the shrine all the way to Yuigahama Beach, with three massive *torii* gates set at intervals along the route to signal the approach to the shrine. On both sides of the pathway are souvenir and antiques shops selling lacquerware, pottery, and folk art (I suggest you return to Kamakura Station via Komachi Dori, a fun pedestrian shopping lane that parallels Wakamiya Oji to the west).

At the top of the stairs, which afford a panoramic view toward the sea, is the vermilion-colored shrine with its small shrine museum, not worth the ¥100 (95¢) admission. However, you can get your fortune in English for ¥100 by shaking out a bamboo stick with a number on it and giving it to the attendant. You can also buy a charm to assure good luck in health, driving a car, business, or other ventures. Shrine grounds are free to the public and are always open.

Although it's a bit out-of-the-way, it might pay to visit **Zeniarai-Benten Shrine** (*©* **0467/25-1081**), about a 20-minute walk west of Kamakura Station. This shrine is dedicated to the goddess of good fortune. On the Asian zodiac's Day of the Snake, worshippers believe that if you take your money and wash it in spring water in a small cave on the shrine grounds, it will double or triple itself later on. This being modern Japan, don't be surprised if you see a bit of ingenuity; my Japanese landlady told me that when she visited the shrine she didn't have much cash on her, so she washed

# Side Trips from Tokyo

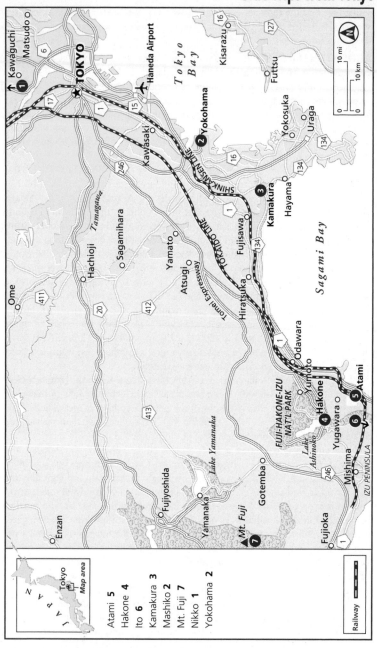

Atami **5**
Hakone **4**
Ito **6**
Kamakura **3**
Mashiko **2**
Mt. Fuji **7**
Nikko **1**
Yokohama **2**

Railway

something that she thought would be equally as good—her credit card. Because the shrine is dedicated to the goddess of fortune, it's fitting that admission is free. Open daily 8am to 5pm.

**AROUND HASE STATION**   To get to these attractions, you can go by bus, which departs from in front of Kamakura Station (take any bus from platform 1 or 6 to the Daibutsuen-mae stop). Or, for a more romantic adventure, you can go by the **JR Enoden Line,** a tiny train that putt-putts its way seemingly through backyards on its way from Kamakura Station to Hase and beyond. Since it's mostly only one track, trains have to take turns going in either direction. I suggest that you take the bus from Kamakura Station directly to the Great Buddha, walk to Hase Shrine, and then take the Enoden train back to Kamakura Station.

Probably Kamakura's most famous attraction is the **Great Buddha** ✿✿✿ (© 0467/ 22-0703), called the Daibutsu in Japanese and located at **Kotokuin Temple.** Eleven meters (37 ft.) high and weighing 93 tons, it's the second-largest bronze image in Japan. The largest Buddha is in Nara, but in my opinion, the Kamakura Daibutsu is much more impressive. For one thing, the Kamakura Buddha sits outside against a dramatic backdrop of wooded hills. Cast in 1252, the Kamakura Buddha was indeed once housed in a temple like the Nara Buddha, but a huge tidal wave destroyed the wooden structure—and the statue has sat under sun, snow, and stars ever since. I also prefer the face of the Kamakura Buddha; I find it more inspiring and divine, as though with its half-closed eyes and calm, serene face it's above the worries of the world. It seems to represent the plane above human suffering, the point at which birth and death, joy and sadness merge and become one. Open daily from 7am to 6pm (to 5:30pm in winter). Admission is ¥200 ($1.90) for adults and ¥150 ($1.45) for children, and your entry ticket is a bookmark, a nice souvenir. If you want, you can pay an extra ¥20 (20¢) to go inside the statue—it's hollow.

About a 10-minute walk from the Daibutsu is **Hase Kannon Temple** ✿✿✿ or Hasedera (© 0467/22-6300), located on a hill with a sweeping view of the sea. This is the home of an 11-headed gilt statue of Kannon, the goddess of mercy, housed in the Kannon Hall *(Kannon-do).* More than 9m high (30 ft.) and the tallest wooden image in Japan, it was made from a single piece of camphor wood in the 8th century. The legend surrounding this Kannon is quite remarkable. Supposedly, two wooden images were made from the wood of a huge camphor tree. One of the images was kept in Hase, not far from Nara, while the second was given a short ceremony and then duly tossed into the sea to find a home of its own. The image drifted 483km (300 miles) eastward and washed up on shore but was thrown back in again because all who touched it became ill or incurred bad luck. Finally, the image reached Kamakura, where it gave the people no trouble. This was interpreted as a sign that the image was content with its surroundings, and Hase Kannon Temple was erected at its present site. Note how each face has a different expression, representing the Kannon's compassion for various kinds of human suffering. In the Kannon-do, you'll also find a museum with religious treasures from the Kamakura, Heian, Muromachi, and Edo periods.

Another statue housed here is of **Amida,** a Buddha who promised rebirth in the Pure Land to the West to all who chanted his name. It was created by order of Yoritomo Minamoto upon his 42nd birthday, which is considered an unlucky year for men. You'll find it housed in the Amida Hall *(Amida-do)* beside the Kannon-do to the right. Also of interest is the **Kyozo,** with rotating bookracks containing sutras (if you give the bookracks a spin, it's considered just as auspicious as reading the sutras).

# Kamakura

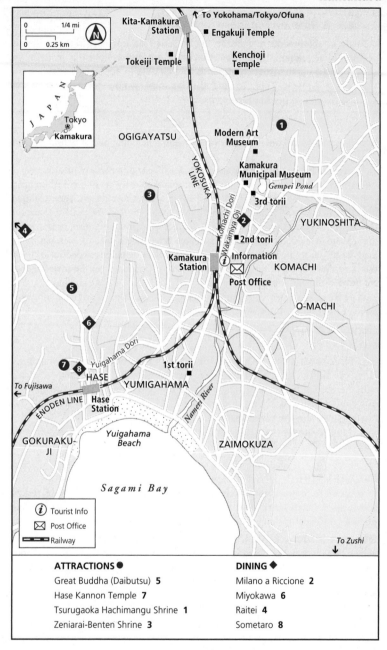

Kita-Kamakura Station

↑ To Yokohama/Tokyo/Ofuna

Engakuji Temple

Tokeiji Temple

Kenchoji Temple

**JAPAN**

Tokyo

**Kamakura**

OGIGAYATSU

Modern Art Museum

**❶**

Kamakura Municipal Museum

*Gempei Pond*

3rd torii

**❸**

**❷**

YUKINOSHITA

**❹**

2nd torii

YOKOSUKA LINE

Komachi Dori

Wakamiya Oji

Kamakura Station

Information

KOMACHI

Post Office

O-MACHI

**❺**

**❻**

Yuigahama Dori

**❼** **❽**

HASE

To Fujisawa

YUMIGAHAMA

1st torii

Nameri River

ENODEN LINE

Hase Station

Yuigahama Beach

GOKURAKU-JI

ZAIMOKUZA

*Sagami Bay*

*ⓘ* Tourist Info

⊠ Post Office

▭▭ Railway

To Zushi ↓

| ATTRACTIONS ● | DINING ◆ |
|---|---|
| Great Buddha (Daibutsu) **5** | Milano a Riccione **2** |
| Hase Kannon Temple **7** | Miyokawa **6** |
| Tsurugaoka Hachimangu Shrine **1** | Raitei **4** |
| Zeniarai-Benten Shrine **3** | Sometaro **8** |

0    1/4 mi
0    0.25 km
N

*Tips*  **A Note on Japanese Symbols**

Many establishments and attractions in Japan do not have signs in Roman (English-language) letters. Those that don't are indicated in this guide by an oval with a number that corresponds to a number in appendix C showing the Japanese symbols. Thus, to find the Japanese symbol for, say, **Miyokawa** (below), refer to no. 39 in appendix C.

**Benten-kutsu Cave** contains many stone images, including one of Benzaiten (seated, with a lute).

As you climb the steps to the Kannon-do, you'll encounter statues of a different sort. All around you will be likenesses of **Jizo,** the guardian deity of children. Although parents originally came to Hase Temple to set up statues to represent their children in hopes the deity would protect and watch over them, through the years the purpose of the Jizo statues has changed. Now they represent miscarried, stillborn, or aborted children. More than 50,000 Jizo statues have been offered here since the war, but the hundreds or so you see now will remain only a year before being burned or buried to make way for others. Some of the statues, which can be purchased on the temple grounds, are fitted with hand-knitted caps and sweaters. The effect is quite chilling.

Hase Temple is open daily 8am to 5:30pm (to 4:30pm in winter); admission is ¥300 ($2.85) for adults, ¥100 (95¢) for children.

## WHERE TO DINE
### MODERATE

㊴ **Miyokawa** MINI-KAISEKI/OBENTO    This modern, casual restaurant specializes in kaiseki, including beautifully prepared mini-kaiseki set meals that change with the seasons. It also offers great obento lunch boxes (my favorite is the one served in a container shaped like a gourd, costing ¥2,415/$23), as well as set meals. Color photographs show the various options.

1–16–17 Hase. ℂ 0467/25-5556. Reservations recommended. Mini-kaiseki ¥5,775–¥10,500 ($55–$100); obento and set meals ¥1,995–¥3,990 ($19–$38). AE, MC, V. Daily 11am–9pm. Station: Hase (5 min.). On the main road (east side) leading from Hase Station to the Great Buddha (about a 5-min. walk from each).

### INEXPENSIVE

In addition to the suggestions below, a simple restaurant at **Hase Temple,** described above, serves noodles, beer, and soft drinks, with both indoor and outdoor seating. It offers a great view, making it a good place for a snack on a fine day.

**Milano a Riccione** ITALIAN    This is the Japanese branch of a restaurant from Milan known for its handmade pasta, seafood, and good selection of wines. Although located in a basement, it opens onto a subterranean courtyard, making it brighter and more cheerful than you would expect. There's an English-language seasonal menu, but the best bargain is the daily set lunch for ¥1,365 ($13), which gives a choice of pasta or pizza, an appetizer, and coffee, espresso, or tea. It's also the quickest meal you can order; otherwise, if you're in a hurry, you should dine elsewhere, as care and time are devoted to the preparation of such meals as grilled scallops with leeks and sautéed chicken with basil and tomato sauce.

2–12–30 Komachi. ℂ 0467/24-5491. Reservations required for lunch. Pizza and pasta ¥1,050–¥1,680 ($10–$16); main dishes ¥1,785–¥2,205 ($17–$21); set dinners ¥3,990–¥4,725 ($38–$45); set lunches ¥1,365–¥2,625

($13–$25). AE, DC, MC, V. Thurs–Tues 11:30am–3pm and 5:30–9:30pm (last order). Station: Kamakura (6 min.). On the left side of Wakamiya Oji when walking from Kamakura Station to Tsurugaoka Hachimangu Shrine.

40 **Raitei** ✦✦✦ (Finds) NOODLES/OBENTO    Though it's a bit inconveniently located, this is the absolute winner for a meal in Kamakura. Visiting Raitei is as much fun as visiting the city's temples and shrines. The restaurant is situated in the hills on the edge of Kamakura, surrounded by verdant countryside, and the wonder is that it serves inexpensive Japanese noodles *(soba)* as well as priestly kaiseki feasts, which you must reserve in advance. If you're here for soba or one of the obento lunch boxes, go down the stone steps on the right to the back entry, where you'll be given an English-language menu with such offerings as noodles with chicken, mountain vegetables, tempura, and more. The pottery used here comes from the restaurant's own specially made kiln, and you'll dine while sitting on roughly hewn wood stools or on tatami. If you opt for kaiseki, you'll dine upstairs in a refined traditional setting with great views. The house, once owned by a wealthy landowner, was moved to this site in 1929.

> **(Moments  A Special Stroll**
>
> When you've finished your meal at Raitei, be sure to walk the loop through the garden past a bamboo grove, stone images, and a miniature shrine. The stroll takes about 20 minutes, unless you stop for a beer at the refreshment house, which has outdoor seating and a view of the countryside.

Takasago. © 0467/32-5656. Reservations required for kaiseki. Noodles ¥700–¥1,200 ($6.65–$11); obento lunch boxes ¥3,500–¥4,500 ($33–$43); soba set meals ¥2,500 ($24); kaiseki feasts from ¥6,300 ($60). At the front gate, you must pay an entry fee of ¥500 ($4.75), which counts toward the price of your meal. AE, DC. Daily 11am–sundown (about 7pm in summer). Bus: 4 or 6 from platform 6 at Kamakura Station to Takasago stop (or a 15-min. taxi ride).

41 **Sometaro** (Value) OKONOMIYAKI    Located near the approach to Hase Temple, this small, second-floor restaurant offers *okonomiyaki* (a kind of Japanese pancake) filled with cabbage, bean sprouts, and a choice of main ingredient like beef, pork, or shrimp, as well as fried noodles *(yakisoba)* and teppanyaki, all from an English-language menu.

3–12–11 Hase. © 0467/22-8694. Reservations recommended for lunch. Main dishes ¥900–¥1,200 ($8.55–$11). No credit cards. Thurs–Tues 11:30am–10pm. Station: Hase (2 min.). On the slope leading to the entrance of Hase Temple, at the beginning on the left side.

## 2 Shogun Country: Nikko ✦✦✦

150km (93 miles) N of Tokyo

Since the publication of James Clavell's novel *Shogun,* many people have become familiar with Tokugawa Ieyasu, the powerful real-life shogun of the 1600s on whom Clavell's fictional shogun was based. Quashing all rebellions and unifying Japan under his leadership, Tokugawa established such a military stronghold that his heirs continued to rule Japan for the next 250 years without serious challenge.

If you'd like to join the millions of Japanese who through the centuries have paid homage to this great man, travel 150km (93 miles) north of Tokyo to Nikko, where **Toshogu Shrine** ✦✦✦ was constructed in his honor in the 17th century and where Tokugawa's remains were entombed in a mausoleum. Nikko means "sunlight"—an apt description of the way the sun's rays play upon this sumptuous shrine of wood and

gold leaf. In fact, nothing else in Japan matches Toshogu Shrine for its opulence. Nearby is another mausoleum containing Tokugawa's grandson, as well as a temple, a shrine, and a garden. Surrounding the sacred grounds, known collectively as Nikko Sannai and designated a World Heritage Site by UNESCO in 1999, are thousands of majestic cedar trees in the 80,000-hectare (200,000-acre) **Nikko National Park** ⚏⚏. Another worthwhile sight is the **Nikko Tamozawa Imperial Villa,** built in 1899.

I've included a few recommendations for an overnight stay. Otherwise, you can see Nikko in a full day. Plan on 4 to 5 hours to Nikko and back, 2½ hours to see Toshogu Shrine and vicinity, and 1 hour to see the imperial villa.

## ESSENTIALS

**GETTING THERE** The easiest, fastest, and most luxurious way to get to Nikko is on the privately owned Tobu Line's Limited Express, called the **Spacia,** which departs every hour or more frequently from Asakusa Station and costs ¥2,620 ($25) one-way for the 2-hour trip on weekdays and ¥2,720 ($26) on weekends and holidays (most trains require a transfer at Shimo-Imaichi Station). All seats are reserved, which means you are guaranteed a seat; if you're traveling on a holiday or a summer weekend, you may wish to purchase and reserve your ticket in advance. Another plus is that there's usually an English-speaking hostess on board who passes out pamphlets on the area and can answer sightseeing questions about Nikko.

Otherwise, you can reach Nikko on Tobu's slower **rapid train** from Asakusa, which costs ¥1,320 ($13) one-way and takes 2 hours and 10 minutes, with trains departing every hour or more frequently. There are no reserved seats, which means you might have to stand if trains are crowded.

You can also travel to Nikko via JR train. If you're visiting **Mashiko,** you can save yourself the hassle of buying train tickets from different rail companies by taking the JR Tohoku Honsen line from Shinjuku to JR Utsunomiya Station for the bus to Mashiko, and then continuing onward from JR Utsunomiya Station to Nikko (the Tobu line does not travel between Utsunomiya and Nikko). Slightly faster but more expensive is the Shinkansen bullet train from Tokyo to Utsunomiya (there are departures every 15–30 min. and the trip takes about 47 min.), where you change for the train to Nikko (45 min.).

**VISITOR INFORMATION** Before leaving Tokyo, pick up the leaflet "Nikko" from the Tourist Information Center (TIC). It gives the train schedule for both the Tobu Line, which departs from Asakusa Station, and the JR trains that depart from Ueno Station. The TIC also has color brochures with maps of the Nikko area.

Nikko's Tobu and JR stations are located almost side by side in the village's downtown area. The **Nikko Tobu Station tourist information counter** (© 0288/ 53-4511; www.nikko-jp.org), located inside Tobu Station to the right after you pass through the wicket gate, is staffed by a friendly woman who speaks enough English to give you a map, answer basic questions, and point you in the right direction. You can also make hotel and ryokan reservations here for free. Open daily 8:30am to noon and 1 to 5pm.

Another tourist office, the **Nikko Information Center** (© 0288/54-2496), is located on the left side of the main road leading from the train station to Toshogu Shrine (next to Eneos gas station). It has English-speaking staff and lots of information in English about Nikko, including information on public hot springs. Open daily from 9am to 5pm.

# Nikko

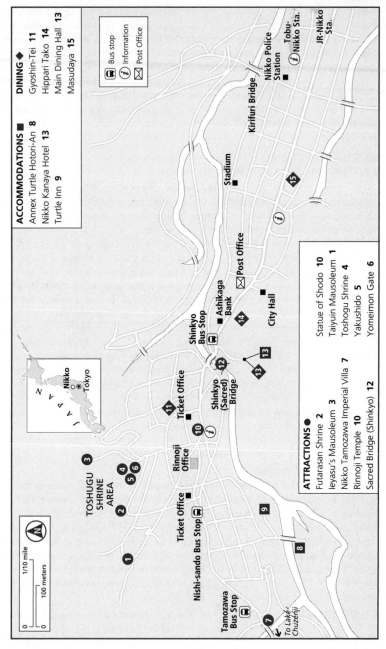

**ACCOMMODATIONS ■**

Annex Turtle Hotori-An **8**
Nikko Kanaya Hotel **13**
Turtle Inn **9**

**DINING ◆**

Gyoshin-Tei **11**
Hippari Tako **14**
Main Dining Hall **13**
Masudaya **15**

**ATTRACTIONS ●**

Futarasan Shrine **2**
Ieyasu's Mausoleum **3**
Nikko Tamozawa Imperial Villa **7**
Rinnoji Temple **10**
Sacred Bridge (Shinkyo) **12**

Statue of Shodo **10**
Taiyuin Mausoleum **1**
Toshogu Shrine **4**
Yakushido **5**
Yomeimon Gate **6**

■ Bus stop
ⓘ Information
⊠ Post Office

TOSHUGU
SHRINE
AREA

Rinnoji
Office

Ticket Office

Nishi-sando Bus Stop

Tamozawa
Bus Stop

To Lake
Chuzenji

Shinkyo
(Sacred)
Bridge

Shinkyo
Bus Stop

Ashikaga
Bank

Post Office

City Hall

Stadium

Kirifuri Bridge

Nikko Police
Station

Tobu-
Nikko Sta.

JR-Nikko
Sta.

JAPAN

Nikko
Tokyo

1/10 mile
100 meters

**GETTING AROUND**    Toshogu Shrine and its mausoleum are on the edge of town, but you can walk from either the JR or Tobu train stations to the shrine in about half an hour. Head straight out the main exit, pass the bus stands, and then turn right. Signs in English point the way throughout town. Keep walking on this main road (you'll pass the Nikko Information Center about halfway down on the left side, as well as souvenir shops) until you come to a T intersection with a vermilion-colored bridge spanning a river (about a 15-min. walk from the train stations). The stone steps opposite lead up the hill into the woods and to Toshogu Shrine. You can also travel from Tobu Station by bus, getting off at either the Shinkyo (a 7-min. ride) or Nishi Sando (a 10-min. ride) bus stop.

## SEEING THE SIGHTS

**ON THE WAY TO THE SHRINE**    The first indication that you're nearing the shrine is the vermilion-painted **Sacred Bridge (Shinkyo)** arching over the rushing Daiyagawa River. It was built in 1636, and for more than 3 centuries only shogun and their emissaries were allowed to cross it. Today, you can cross it by paying ¥500 ($4.75), or take the modern vehicular bridge for free.

Across the road from the Sacred Bridge are some steps leading uphill into a forest of cedar where, after a 5-minute walk, you'll see a statue of **Shodo,** a priest who founded Nikko 1,200 years ago at a time when mountains were revered as gods. In the centuries that followed, Nikko became one of Japan's greatest mountain Buddhist retreats, with 500 sub-temples spread through the area. Behind Shodo is the first major temple, Rinnoji Temple, where you can buy a **combination ticket** for ¥1,000 ($9.50) that allows entry to Rinnoji Temple, Toshogu Shrine, neighboring Futarasan Shrine, and the other Tokugawa mausoleum, Taiyuin. Once at Toshogu Shrine, you'll have to pay an extra ¥520 ($4.95) to see Ieyasu's tomb. Combination tickets sold at the entry to Toshogu Shrine already include Ieyasu's tomb. It doesn't really matter where you buy your combination ticket since you can always pay the extra fee to see sights not covered. *A note for bus riders:* If you take the bus to the Nishi Sando bus stop, the first place you'll come to is the Taiyuin Mausoleum, where you can also purchase a combination ticket.

Toshogu Shrine and the other sights in Nikko Sannai are open daily April to October from 8am to 5pm (to 4pm the rest of the year); you must enter at least 30 minutes before closing time.

**RINNOJI TEMPLE**    Rinnoji Temple was founded by the priest Shodo in the 8th century, long before the Toshogu clan came onto the scene. Here you can visit the **Sanbutsudo Hall,** a large building that enshrines three 8.4m-high (28-ft.), gold-plated wooden images of Buddha, considered the "gods of Nikko"; today people pray here for world peace. Perhaps the best thing to see at Rinnoji Temple, however, is its **Shoyo-en Garden** (opposite Sanbutsudo Hall), which requires a separate ¥300 ($2.85) admission. Completed in 1815 and typical of Japanese landscaped gardens of the Edo Period, this small strolling garden provides a different vista with each turn of the path, making it seem much larger than it actually is.

**TOSHOGU SHRINE**  🕹🕹🕹    The most important and famous structure in Nikko is Toshogu Shrine, built by Tokugawa's grandson (and third Tokugawa shogun), Tokugawa Iemitsu, as an act of devotion. It seems that no expense was too great in creating the monument: Some 15,000 artists and craftspeople were brought to Nikko

from all over Japan, and after 2 years' work, they erected a group of buildings more elaborate and gorgeous than any other Japanese temple or shrine. Rich in colors and carvings, Toshogu Shrine is gilded with 2.4 million sheets of gold leaf (they could cover an area of almost 2.4 hectares/6 acres). The mausoleum was completed in 1636, almost 20 years after Ieyasu's death, and was most certainly meant to impress anyone who saw it as a demonstration of the Tokugawa shogunate's wealth and power.

Toshogu Shrine is set in a grove of magnificent ancient **Japanese cedars** planted over a 20-year period during the 1600s by a feudal lord named Matsudaira Masatsuna. Some 13,000 of the original trees are still standing, adding a sense of dignity to the mausoleum and the shrine.

You enter Toshogu Shrine via a flight of stairs that passes under a huge stone torii gateway, one of the largest in Japan. On your left is a five-story, 35m-high (115-ft.) **pagoda.** Although normally pagodas are found only at temples, this pagoda is just one example of how both Buddhism and Shintoism are combined at Toshogu Shrine. After climbing a second flight of stairs, turn left and you'll see the **Sacred Stable,** which houses a sacred white horse. Horses have long been dedicated to Shinto gods and are kept at shrines. Shrines also kept monkeys as well, since they were thought to protect horses from disease; look for the three monkeys carved above the stable door, fixed in the poses of "see no evil, hear no evil, speak no evil"—they're considered guardians of the sacred horse. Across from the stable is **Kami-Jinko,** famous for its carving by Kano Tanyu, who painted the images of the two elephants after reading about them but without seeing what they actually looked like.

Up the next flight of stairs, to the left, is **Yakushido,** famous for its dragon paint-ing on the ceiling. If you clap your hands under the painting, the echo supposedly resembles a dragon's roar. You also can visit the shrine's main sanctuary, the **Hai-den,** comprising three halls: One was reserved for the imperial family, one for the shogun, and one (the central hall) for conducting ceremonies. You can buy good-luck charms here that will guard against such misfortunes as traffic accidents, or that will ensure good health, success in business, easy childbirth, or other achievements in daily life.

But the central showpiece of Nikko is **Yomeimon Gate,** popularly known as the Twilight Gate, implying that it could take you all day (until twilight) to see everything carved onto it. Painted in red, blue, and green and decorated with gilding and lacquer-work, this gate has about 400 carvings of flowers, dragons, birds, and other animals. It's almost too much to take in at once and is very un-Japanese in its opulence, hav-ing more in common with Chinese architecture than the usual austerity of most Japanese shrines.

To the right of the main hall is the entrance to **Tokugawa Ieyasu's mausoleum.** If it's not already included in your combination ticket, admission is ¥520 ($4.95). After the ticket counter, look for the carving of a sleeping cat above the door, dating from the Edo Period and famous today as a symbol of Nikko (you'll find many reproductions in area souvenir shops). Beyond that are 200 stone steps leading past cedars to Tokugawa's tomb. After the riotous colors of the shrine, the tomb seems surprisingly simple.

**FUTARASAN SHRINE**    Directly to the west of Toshogu Shrine is Futarasan Shrine, the oldest building in the district (from 1617), which has a pleasant garden and is ded-icated to the gods of mountains surrounding Nikko. You'll find miniature shrines dedicated to the god of fortune, god of knowledge, god of health, and god of good marriages. On the shrine's grounds is the so-called **ghost lantern,** enclosed in a small

wooden structure. According to legend, it used to come alive at night and sweep around Nikko in the form of a ghost. It apparently scared one of the guards so much that he struck it with his sword 70 times; the marks are still visible on the lamp's rim. Entrance to the miniature shrines and ghost lantern is ¥200 ($1.90) extra.

**TAIYUIN MAUSOLEUM** ⋆    Past Futarasan Shrine is **Taiyuin Mausoleum,** the final resting place of Iemitsu, the third Tokugawa shogun (look for his statue). Completed in 1653, it's not nearly as large nor as crowded as Toshogu Shrine, but is ornate and serenely elegant nevertheless, making it a pleasant last stop on your tour of Nikko Sannai.

**NIKKO TAMOZAWA IMPERIAL VILLA (Tamozawa Goyoutei Kinen Koen)** ⋆⋆⋆    If you haven't seen the imperial villas of Kyoto (which require advance planning), the Nikko Tamozawa Imperial Villa, 8–27 Honcho (© **0288/53-6767**), is a great alternative. Though not as old (it was built in 1899 for Prince Yoshihito, who later became the Taisho emperor) and recently painstakingly restored so that it looks brand new, it has the distinction of being the largest wooden imperial villa of its era, with 106 rooms (37 of which are open to the public). The central core of the villa is actually much older, constructed in 1632 by a feudal lord and brought to Nikko from Edo (present-day Tokyo). A self-guided tour of the villa provides insight into traditional Japanese architectural methods—from its 11 layers of paper-plastered walls to its nail-less wood framing—as well as the lifestyle of Japan's aristocracy. Be sure to wander the small, outdoor garden. Admission is ¥500 ($4.75) for adults, half price for children. Open Wednesday to Monday 9am to 4:30pm. It's about a 20-minute walk from Toshogu Shrine; or take the bus to Tamozawa stop.

## WHERE TO STAY

If it's peak season (May, Aug, and Oct) or a weekend, it's best to reserve a room in advance, which you can do by calling a lodging either directly or through a travel agency in Tokyo. Otherwise, if it's not peak season, you can make a reservation upon arrival at Nikko Tobu Station, either at the **tourist information counter,** where the service is free, or at the **accommodations-reservation window** (© **0288/54-0864;** open daily 9am–5pm), which charges a ¥200 to ¥500 ($1.90–$4.75) fee but is familiar with the accommodations in the area and will make all arrangements for you.

### MODERATE

**Nikko Kanaya Hotel** ⋆⋆ *(Finds*    This distinguished-looking, old-fashioned place on a hill above the Sacred Bridge is the most famous hotel in Nikko, combining the rustic heartiness of a European country lodge with elements of old Japan. It was founded in 1873 by the Kanaya family, who wished to offer accommodations to foreigners, mainly missionaries and businessmen looking to escape the heat and humidity of Tokyo. The present complex, built in spurts over the past 100 years, has a rambling, delightfully old-fashioned atmosphere that fuses Western architecture with Japanese craftsmanship. Through the decades it has played host to a number of VIPs, from Charles Lindbergh to Indira Gandhi to Shirley MacLaine; Frank Lloyd Wright left a sketch for the bar fireplace, which was later built to his design. Even if you don't stay here, you might want to drop by for lunch (see review below). Pathways lead to the Daiyagawa River and several short hiking trails.

All rooms are Western-style twins, with the differences in price based on room size, view (river view is best), and facilities. They're simple but cozy and have character; some have antiques and claw-foot tubs. If you want to stay in the best room in the

house, a corner room in the 70-year-old wing where the emperor once stayed, you'll pay the highest price below.

1300 Kami-Hatsuishi, Nikko City, Tochigi 321-1401. (C) **0288/54-0001.** Fax 0288/53-2487. www.kanayahotel.co.jp. 70 units (68 with tub/shower and toilet, 2 with toilet only). ¥8,400 ($80) single with toilet only, ¥10,500 ($100) single with shower and toilet, ¥11,550–¥36,750 ($110–$349) single with bathroom; ¥10,500 ($100) twin with toilet only, ¥12,600 ($120) twin with shower and toilet, ¥13,650–¥42,000 ($130–$399) twin with bathroom. ¥2,000–¥3,000 ($19–$29) extra on Sat and national holidays; ¥3,000–¥5,000 ($29–$48) extra in peak season. AE, DC, MC, V. Bus: From Nikko Tobu Station to the Shinkyo stop, a 5-min. ride. Bus: From Nikko Tobu Station to the Shinkyo stop, 5 min. On foot: 15 min. from Tobu Station. **Amenities:** 3 restaurants (shabu-shabu, Western, and coffee shop); 1 bar; small outdoor heated pool (open only in summer and free for hotel guests); outdoor skating rink (in winter); souvenir shops; in-room massage. *In room:* A/C, TV, minibar.

## INEXPENSIVE

**Annex Turtle Hotori-An** 🐢🐢 (Kids)    Owned by the superfriendly family that runs Turtle Inn (see below), this is one of my favorite places to stay in Nikko. One dip in the hot-springs bath overlooking the Daiyagawa River (which you can lock for privacy) will tell you why; at night, you're lulled to sleep by the sound of the rushing waters. A simple but spotless modern structure (all nonsmoking), it's located in a nice rural setting on a quiet street with a few other houses; an adjoining park and playground provide plenty of space for kids to play. All its rooms except one are Japanese style. A plentiful Western-style breakfast costs ¥1,050 ($10) in the pleasant living area/dining room. For dinner, you can go to the nearby Turtle Inn (not available Sun, Tues, and Thurs; reservations should be made the day before), or buy a pizza from the freezer and microwave it yourself. There's also a communal refrigerator where you can store food.

8–28 Takumi-cho, Nikko City, Tochigi 321-1433. (C) **0288/53-3663.** Fax 0288/53-3883. www.turtle-nikko.com. 11 units (all with bathroom). ¥6,500 ($62) single; ¥12,400 ($119) double. Special rates for children. AE, MC, V. Bus: From Nikko Station to the Sogo Kaikan-mae stop, a 7-min. ride; then a 9-min. walk. **Amenities:** Computer w/free Internet access at Turtle Inn; hot-spring baths; coin-op washer and dryer. *In room:* A/C, TV.

**Turtle Inn** 🐢    This excellent, nonsmoking pension, a Japanese Inn Group member, is located within walking distance of Toshogu Shrine in a newer two-story house on a quiet side street beside the Daiyagawa River. It's run by the very friendly Fukuda family. Mr. Fukuda speaks English and is very helpful in planning a sightseeing itinerary for the area. Rooms are bright and cheerful in both Japanese and Western styles; the five tatami rooms are without bathroom. Excellent Japanese dinners are available for ¥2,100 ($20), as are Western breakfasts for ¥1,050 ($10). Be sure to order the day before and note that it's not available on Sunday, Tuesday, and Thursday.

2–16 Takumi-cho, Nikko City, Tochigi 321-1433. (C) **0288/53-3168.** Fax 0288/53-3883. www.turtle-nikko.com. 10 units (3 with bathroom). ¥4,800 ($46) single without bathroom, ¥5,600 ($53) single with bathroom; ¥9,000 ($86) double without bathroom, ¥10,600 ($101) double with bathroom. Special rates for children. AE, MC, V. Bus: From Nikko Station to the Sogo Kaikan-mae stop, a 7-min. ride; then a 5-min. walk. **Amenities:** Computer w/free Internet access; coin-op washer and dryer. *In room:* A/C, TV, no phone.

## WHERE TO DINE
### EXPENSIVE
**Main Dining Hall at Nikko Kanaya Hotel** 🐢🐢 (Finds) CONTINENTAL    Even if you don't spend the night here, you might want to come for a meal in the hotel's quaint dining hall with its wood-carved pillars. It's one of the best places in town for lunch. Since it's beside the Sacred Bridge, only a 10-minute walk from Toshogu Shrine, you can easily combine it with your sightseeing tour of Nikko. I suggest

Nikko's specialty, locally caught rainbow trout available in three different styles of cooking. I had mine cooked Kanaya style, covered with soy sauce, sugar, and sake, grilled and served whole. The best bargain is the set lunch for ¥2,940 ($28) available until 3pm, which comes with soup, salad, a main dish such as trout, bread or rice, and dessert. Steak, lobster, salmon, chicken, and other Western fare are also listed on the English-language menu.

Nikko Kanaya Hotel, 1300 Kami-Hatsuishi. ✆ 0288/54-0001. Reservations recommended during peak season. Main dishes ¥2,600–¥8,400 ($25–$80); set lunches ¥2,940–¥10,500 ($28–$100); set dinners ¥7,350 ($70). AE, DC, MC, V. Daily noon–3pm and 6–8pm. A 15-min. walk from Nikko Tobu Station.

## MODERATE

**Gyoshin-Tei** 🦋🦋 VEGETARIAN/KAISEKI    This lovely Japanese restaurant, with a simple tatami room and a view of pines, moss, and bonsai, serves two kinds of set meals—kaiseki and Buddhist vegetarian cuisine—both of which change monthly and include the local specialty, *yuba*. (See Masudaya, below.) It's one of several restaurants in a parklike setting all under the same management and with the same open hours. Meiji-no-Yakata (closed Wed), occupying a stone house built 110 years ago as the private retreat of an American businessman, serves Western food such as grilled rainbow trout, veal cutlet, and steak, with set meals ranging from ¥3,990 to ¥8,400 ($38–$80). Fujimoto (closed Thurs), in a small stone cottage, serves French food created with Japanese ingredients and eaten with chopsticks. The drawback: This place is harder to find than this book's other recommendations, but it's only a 4-minute walk northeast of Rinnoji Temple.

2339-1 Sannai. ✆ 0288/53-3751. Reservations recommended. Vegetarian/kaiseki meals ¥3,675 ($35) and ¥5,250 ($50). AE, DC, MC, V. Thurs–Tues 11am–7pm (from 11:30am in winter). A 25-min. walk from Nikko Tobu Station; or bus from Nikko Station to Seikoen (then a 1-min. walk).

**Masudaya** 🦋 YUBA    Only two fixed-price meals are served at this Japanese-style, 80-year-old restaurant, both featuring *yuba*. A high-protein food made from soybeans, yuba is a local specialty produced only in Kyoto and Nikko. Until 100 years ago, it could be eaten only by priests and members of the imperial family. Now you can enjoy it, too, along with such sides as rice, sashimi, soup, fried fish, and vegetables. Dining is either in a common dining hall (make reservations 2 days in advance) or, for the more expensive meals, in private tatami rooms upstairs, for which you should make a reservation 1 week in advance.

439 Ichiyamachi. ✆ 0288/54-2151. Reservations required. Yuba kaiseki meals ¥3,990 ($38) and ¥5,450 ($52). No credit cards. Fri–Wed 10:30am–4pm (open Thurs if a holiday). A 5-min. walk from Nikko Tobu Station. On the left side of the main street leading from Tobu Station to Toshogu Shrine, just before the fire station.

## INEXPENSIVE

㊷ **Hippari Tako** NOODLES    This tiny, three-table establishment is under the caring supervision of motherly Miki-san, who serves a limited selection of noodle dishes, including ramen and stir-fried noodles with vegetables as well as rice balls (*onigiri*) and yakitori. There's an English-language menu, and the walls, covered with business cards and messages left by appreciative guests from around the world, are testimony to both the tasty meals and Miki-san's warm hospitality.

1011 Kami-Hatsuishi. ✆ 0288/53-2933. Main dishes ¥550–¥840 ($5.25–$8). No credit cards. Daily 11:30am–7pm (last order). A 15-min. walk from Nikko Tobu Station. On the left side of the main street leading from Toshogu Shrine, 1 min. before the Nikko Kanaya Hotel and the Sacred Bridge.

## 3 Yokohama: City of the 21st Century

29km (18 miles) S of Tokyo

Few attractions in Yokohama warrant a visit if you're just in Japan for a short time. If you find yourself in Tokyo for an extended period, however, Yokohama is a pleasant destination for an easy day trip. Be sure to make time for wonderful Sankeien Garden; although a mere 90-some years old, it ranks on my long list as one of the top gardens in Japan.

A rather new city in Japan's history books, Yokohama was nothing more than a tiny fishing village when Commodore Perry arrived in the mid-1800s and demanded that Japan open its doors to the world. The village was selected by the shogun as one of several ports to be opened for international trade, transforming it from a backwater to Japan's most important gateway. Yokohama subsequently grew by leaps and bounds, and was a pioneer when it came to Western goods and services, boasting Japan's first bakery (1860), photo studio (1862), telephone (1869), beer brewery (1869), cinema (1870), daily newspaper (1870), public restroom (1871), and ice cream (1879).

Now Japan's second-largest city with a population of almost 3.5 million, Yokohama remains the nation's largest international port and supports a large international community, with many foreigners residing in the section called the Bluff. Yokohama has an especially large Chinese population and Japan's largest Chinatown, whose restaurants serve as a mecca for hungry Tokyoites. Befitting a city known for its firsts, Yokohama began constructing Japan's first and largest urban development project more than a decade ago—**Minato-Mirai,** with a conference center, museums, hotels, and restaurants. Hard to imagine that a mere 140-some years ago, Yokohama was a village of 100 houses.

## ESSENTIALS

**GETTING THERE**    Because many Yokohama residents work in Tokyo, it's as easy to get to Yokohama as it is to get around Tokyo. Although Yokohama Station is the city's main train station, I suggest taking a train from Tokyo that will take you farther to Sakuragicho, Minato Mirai, or Motomachi Chukagai station, since most attractions are clustered here (however, if you're headed first to Sankeien Garden, you'll want to disembark at Yokohama Station and transfer to bus no. 8). Best is the **Minato Mirai Line** (of the Tokyu-Toyoko private company), which departs from Shibuya and reaches Minato Mirai in about 30 minutes, with a one-way fare costing ¥460 ($4.35) or an all-day Minato Mirai Line pass, including transportation from Shibuya and back, costing ¥840 ($9). Alternatively, the **JR Keihin-Tohoku Line** travels through Ueno, Tokyo, Yurakucho, Shimbashi, and Shinagawa stations before continuing on to Sakuragicho, with the journey from Tokyo Station taking approximately 40 minutes and costing ¥450 ($4.30) one-way.

**VISITOR INFORMATION**    There are several tourist information centers in Yokohama, but probably the most convenient and easiest to find is the **Sakuragicho Station Tourist Information Center** (© 045/211-0111; open daily 9am–7pm), located in a kiosk outside Sakuragicho Station in the direction of Minato-Mirai and its Landmark Tower. The main office, the **Yokohama Convention & Visitors Bureau,** is located in the Sangyo Boeki Center (nicknamed Sambo Center), 2 Yamashita-cho, Naka-ku (© **045/641-4759;** www.welcome.city.yokohama.jp; open Mon–Fri 9am–5pm), close to the Silk Center and Yamashita Park. Both have excellent city maps and brochures.

Next door to the Convention and Visitors Bureau, in the Silk Center, is the **Kanagawa Prefectural Tourist Office** (© 045/681-0007; open Tues–Sun 10am–6pm), where you can also get information on Hakone and Kamakura, both in Kanagawa Prefecture.

**GETTING AROUND**    If you start your day in Yokohama at either Sakuragicho or Minato Mirai station, you can visit the museums and attractions there and then walk onward to Yamashita Park via a waterfront promenade (about a 30-min. walk, stopping, perhaps, at the Red Brick Warehouse on the way). If you prefer not to walk, there's a red Tourist Spot Round-trip Bus which makes the rounds of central Yokohama, including Sakuragicho Station, Minato Mirai, Yamashita Park, and Chinatown throughout the year, with departures every 20 to 30 minutes and costing ¥300 ($2.85) for an all-day pass (pick up a map and timetable at the Sakuragicho Station tourist office). To reach Sankeien Garden, take bus no. 8, which departs from Yokohama Station and also passes Minato-Mirai, Chinatown, and Yamashita Park on its way to the garden. If you end the day with a meal at Chinatown, you can catch the Minato Mirai Line back to Shibuya at nearby Motomachi station.

## SEEING THE SIGHTS

**MINATO-MIRAI**    There's no mistaking **Minato-Mirai** when you see it—it looks like a vision of the future with its dramatic monolithic buildings. It boasts a huge state-of-the-art convention facility, three first-class hotels, Japan's tallest building, office buildings, two great museums, and an amusement park. It's all a bit too sterile for my taste, but its two museums make a visit here worthwhile.

If you arrive at Sakuragicho Station, take the moving walkway that connects Sakuragicho Station to the Landmark Tower in Minato-Mirai in 5 minutes. Otherwise, the Minato Mirai Line will deposit you directly in the middle of the massive urban development.

There are several shopping malls in Minato-Mirai, including Queen's Square, Yokohama World Porter's, Landmark Plaza, Jack Mall, and the restored Red Brick Warehouse, but the area's most conspicuous building is the **Landmark Tower,** Japan's tallest building. The fastest elevator in the world will whisk you up 270m (900 ft.) in about 40 seconds to the 69th floor, where there's an observation room called **Sky Garden** (© 045/222-5030), open daily from 10am to 9pm (to 10pm Sat). From here you can see the harbor with its container port and Yokohama Bay Bridge, as well as almost the entire city and even, on clear days in winter, Mount Fuji. However, its admission fees—¥1,000 ($9.50) for adults, ¥800 ($7.60) for seniors and high-school students, ¥500 ($4.75) for elementary and junior-high students, and ¥200 ($1.90) for children—make it too expensive in my book. Better is the Landmark Tower's 70th-floor **Sirius Sky Lounge;** although there's a cover charge, its atmosphere is more relaxing. (See below.)

It would be hard to miss **Yokohama Cosmo World** (© 045/641-6591), an amusement park spread along both sides of a canal: It boasts one of the largest Ferris wheels in the world. Other diversions include a roller coaster that looks like it dives right into a pond (but vanishes instead into a tunnel), a haunted house, a simulation theater with seats that move with the action, kiddie rides, a games arcade, and much more. Admission is free but rides cost ¥300 to ¥700 ($2.85–$6.65) each. The park is open 11am to 8pm in winter and 11am to 10pm in summer; closed most Thursdays (except summer), plus weekdays in February.

# Yokohama

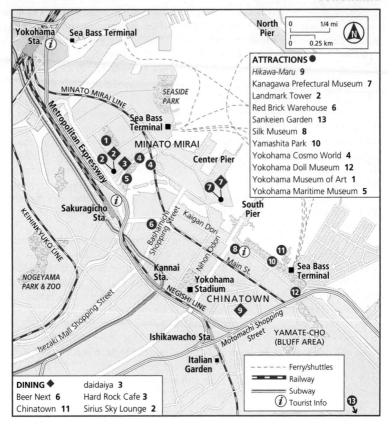

The most important thing to see in Minato-Mirai is the **Yokohama Museum of Art** 𝒢, 3-4-1 Minato-Mirai (𝒞 **045/221-0300;** www.yma.city.yokohama.jp), which emphasizes works by Western and Japanese artists since the 1850s. The museum's ambitious goal is to collect and display works reflecting the mutual influence between the modern art of Europe and that of Japan since the opening of Yokohama's port in 1859. The light and airy building, designed by Kenzo Tange and Urtec Inc., features exhibits from its permanent collection—which includes works by Cézanne, Picasso, Matisse, Leger, Max Ernst, Dalí, and Japanese artists—that change three times a year (you can tour its four rooms in about 30 min.), as well as special exhibits on loan from other museums. Open Friday through Wednesday from 10am to 6pm (closed the day following a national holiday). Admission for the permanent collection is ¥500 ($4.75) for adults, ¥300 ($2.85) for high-school and college students, and ¥100 (95¢) for children. Special exhibitions cost more. You'll spend at least an hour here.

Maritime buffs should check out the **Yokohama Maritime Museum,** 2-1-1 Minato-Mirai (𝒞 **045/221-0280**), which concentrates on Yokohama's history as a port, beginning with the arrival of Perry's "Black Ships." Other displays chart the evolution of ships from Japan and around the world from the 19th century to the

present, with lots of models of everything from passenger ships to oil tankers. Kids like the three telescopes connected to cameras placed around Yokohama and the captain's bridge with a steering wheel; sailing fans enjoy touring the 96m (320-ft.), four-mast *Nippon-Maru* moored nearby, built in 1930 as a sail-training ship for students of the merchant marines. Admission is ¥600 ($5.70) for adults and ¥300 ($2.85) for children. Open 10am to 5pm (to 6:30pm in July–Aug, to 4:30pm Nov–Feb). The museum is closed the fourth Monday of every month; the *Maru* is closed every Monday. It takes more than an hour to see everything.

**IN & AROUND YAMASHITA PARK**    You can walk to Yamashita Park from Minato-Mirai in less than 30 minutes along a waterfront promenade. Along the way you'll pass the **Red Brick Warehouse (Aka Renga),** located in the Shinko-cho District of Minato-Mirai (© **045/227-2002**). This restored waterfront warehouse is home to dozens of shops selling crafts, furniture, housewares, clothing, and jewelry, as well as restaurants, with most shops open daily 11am to 8pm. Otherwise, Yamashita Park is closest to Nihon Odori and Motomachi stations on the Minato Mirai Line, about a 5-minute walk from either.

Laid out after the huge 1923 earthquake that destroyed much of Tokyo and Yoko-hama, Yamashita Park is Japan's first seaside park, a pleasant place for a stroll along the waterfront where you have a view of the city's mighty harbor and Bay Bridge. Moored alongside the park is the *Hikawa-Maru* (© **045/641-4361**), a 1930 ocean liner that transported 25,000 passengers between Yokohama and North America before being called to military service during World War II. One of the few Japanese ships to survive the war, it now serves as a museum, with its engine room, bridge, sleeping quarters (including the captain's room and a stateroom once occupied by Charlie Chaplin), deck, and more, on display. It's open daily 9:30am to 9:30pm in summer and 9:30am to 6:30pm in winter. Admission is ¥800 ($7.60) for adults, ¥400 ($3.80) for children 6 to 15 years old, and ¥300 ($2.85) for children 3 to 5. It takes about 30 minutes to walk through the ship.

Across the gingko-lined street from Yamashita Park are two worthwhile special-interest museums. At the west end (closest to Minato-Mirai) is the Silk Center, where you'll find both the prefectural tourist office and the excellent **Silk Museum** ⋆⋆, 1 Yamashita-cho, Naka-ku (© **045/641-0841**). For many years after Japan opened its doors, silk was its major export, and most of it was shipped to the rest of the world from Yokohama, the nation's largest raw-silk market. In tribute to the role silk has played in Yokohama's history, this museum has displays showing the metamorphosis of the silkworm and the process by which silk is obtained from cocoons, all well documented in English; from April to October you can even observe live cocoons and silkworms at work (compared to the beauty they produce, silkworms are amazingly ugly). The museum also displays various kinds of silk fabrics, as well as gorgeous kimono and reproduction Japanese costumes from the Nara, Heian, and Edo periods. Don't miss this museum, which takes about 30 minutes to see; surprisingly, it's never crowded. Open Tuesday through Sunday from 9am to 4:30pm; admission is ¥500 ($4.15) for adults, ¥300 ($2.50) for seniors, ¥200 ($1.65) for students, and ¥100 (85¢) for children 6 to 11.

At the opposite end of Yamashita Park is the **Yokohama Doll Museum,** 18 Yamashita-cho (© **045/671-9361**), which houses approximately 9,000 dolls from 139 countries around the world. Its main floor displays antique dolls, including those produced by such famous doll makers as Lenci and Jumeau, as well as dolls from

around the world dressed in native costume. The upstairs floor is devoted to Japanese dolls, including folk dolls traditionally sold at shrines and temples, classical Edo-Period dolls, *hina* (elaborate dolls representing the empress and emperor, used for the March Hina Festival), and *kokeshi* (simple wooden dolls). Open 10am to 6:30pm; closed third Monday of every month. Admission is ¥300 ($2.85) for adults and ¥150 ($1.45) for children. Plan on spending about 30 to 45 minutes here.

Not far from Yamashita Park is **Chukagai,** Japan's largest Chinatown with hundreds of souvenir shops and restaurants; see "Where to Dine," below.

**SANKEIEN GARDEN** ✿✿✿   In my opinion, **Sankeien Garden** (𝄞 045/621-0634; www.sankeien.or.jp) is the best reason to visit Yokohama. Although not old itself, this lovely park contains more than a dozen historical buildings that were brought here from other parts of Japan, including Kyoto and Nara, all situated around streams and ponds and surrounded by Japanese-style landscape gardens. The park, which is divided into an Inner Garden and Outer Garden, was laid out in 1906 by Tomitaro Hara, a local millionaire who made his fortune exporting silk. As you wander along the gently winding pathways, you'll see a villa built in 1649 by the Tokugawa shogunate clan, tea arbors, a 500-year-old three-story pagoda, and a farmhouse built in 1750 without the use of nails. The gardens are well known for their blossoms of plums, cherries, wisteria, azaleas, irises, and water lilies, but no matter what the season, the views here are beautiful.

Plan on at least 2 hours to see both gardens. Sankeien is open daily from 9am to 5pm (you must enter the Inner Garden by 4pm, the Outer Garden by 4:30pm). Admission is ¥500 ($4.75) for adults, ¥200 ($1.90) for children. The easiest way to reach Sankeien Garden is by bus no. 8, which departs from platform no. 2 at Yokohama Station's east exit (near Sogo department store) and winds its way past Sakuragicho Station, past Chinatown, and through Kannai before it reaches the Honmoku-Sankeien-mae bus stop 30 minutes later (the bus stop is announced in English).

## WHERE TO DINE

**MINATO-MIRAI**   For sophisticated surroundings or just a romantic evening cocktail (no children allowed after 5pm), take the elevator up to the 70th floor of Landmark Tower, where you'll find the Yokohama Royal Park Hotel Nikko's **Sirius Sky Lounge** ✿ (𝄞 045/221-1111) with stunning seaside views. It serves a buffet lunch for ¥3,500 ($33) daily from 11:30am to 2:30pm, which often centers on a changing, ethnic cuisine but also offers items like salmon, lamb, pizza, and more. After lunch, it's teatime until 5pm. From 5pm to 1am daily, Sirius is a cocktail lounge and levies a cover charge: ¥1,050 ($10) per person from 5 to 7pm and again from 11pm to 1am; ¥2,100 ($20) for live music from 7 to 11pm. It offers a small, a la carte dinner menu, as well as set dinners for ¥6,300 ($60) and ¥9,450 ($90).

The 1911 renovated Red Brick Warehouse (see above) also has fast-food outlets, but for something more substantial, head to the third floor for **Beer Next** (𝄞 045/226-1961), which admirably strives to create an international cuisine that goes down well with beer. Pizza, pasta, rotisserie roast chicken, pork knuckle *(Schweinshaxe),* and seared tuna with garlic oil and soy sauce are just some of the dishes offered, with prices ranging from ¥1,155 to ¥2,310 ($11–$22). Beer Next is open daily 11am to 10pm (last order)

Another good place for a drink or a hamburger is the local branch of the **Hard Rock Cafe,** located on the first floor of Queen's Square Yokohama Tower A

(© **045/682-5626**; open daily 11am–11:30pm). Nearby, on the fourth and fifth floors of the Queen's Square Yokohama, is a branch of **daidaiya** (© **045/228-5035**). See chapter 4, the "Roppongi" and "Akasaka" sections respectively, for reviews of these restaurants.

**CHUKAGAI (CHINATOWN)**　Located in Yamashita-cho, a couple of blocks inland from Yamashita Park and next to Motomachi Station of the Minato Mirai Line, Chinatown has more than 500 restaurants and shops lining one main street and dozens of offshoots. Tokyoites have long been coming to Yokohama just to dine here; many of the restaurants have been owned by the same families for generations. Most serve Cantonese food and have plastic-food displays, English-language menus, or pictures of their dishes, so your best bet is to wander around and let your budget be your guide. Most dishes run ¥850 to ¥3,000 ($8.10–$29), and set lunches go for ¥900 to ¥1,200 ($8.55–$11). Larger restaurants accept credit cards; those that do display them on the front door. Most Chinatown restaurants are open from 11 or 11:30am to 9:30pm or later; some close Tuesday or Wednesday, but there are always restaurants open.

While here, you might want to take a spin through the **China Museum (Yokohama Daisekai)**, 97 Yamashita-cho (© **045/681-5588**), an eight-story building with an interior that replicates Shanghai of the 1920s and 1930s (Shanghai and Yokohama are sister cities), with re-created street scenes, artisans producing traditional crafts, a stage with musical and theatrical performances, and a food court with stalls offering dishes from various parts of China, most priced less than ¥800 ($7.60). It's open daily 10am to 10pm; admission is ¥500 ($4.75) for adults and ¥400 ($3.80) for children.

## 4 Climbing Japan's Most Famous Mountain: Mount Fuji ★★

100km (62 miles) SW of Tokyo

**Mount Fuji,** affectionately called "Fuji-san" by Japanese, has been revered since ancient times. Throughout the centuries, Japanese poets have written about it, painters have painted it, pilgrims have flocked to it, and more than a few people have died on it. Without a doubt, this mountain has been photographed more than anything else in Japan.

Mount Fuji is stunningly impressive. At 3,716m (12,388 ft.), it's the tallest mountain in Japan, towering far above anything else around it, a cone of almost perfectly symmetrical proportions. Mount Fuji is majestic, grand, and awe-inspiring. To Japanese, it symbolizes the very spirit of their country. Though it's visible on clear days (mostly in winter) from as far as 161km (100 miles) away, Fuji-san is, unfortunately, almost always cloaked in clouds. If you catch a glimpse of this elusive mountain (which you can sometimes do from the bullet train between Tokyo and Nagoya), consider yourself extremely lucky. One of the best spots for views of Mount Fuji is **Hakone** (see below).

### ESSENTIALS

There are six ascending trails to the summit of Mount Fuji (and six descending trails), each divided into 10 stages of unequal length, with most climbs starting at the Go-go-me, or the Fifth Stage. From Tokyo, **Kawaguchiko Trail** is the most popular and most easily accessible, as well as the least steep. Although the "official" climbing season is from mid-July to the end of August, you can climb Mount Fuji April through October, weather permitting.

**GETTING THERE** The easiest way to reach Kawaguchiko Trail's Fifth Stage is by **bus** from Shinjuku Station, and most trips require a change of buses at Kawaguchiko Station. There are some 13 buses a day in operation between Shinjuku and Kawaguchiko Station from mid-July to the end of August, with less frequent service April through mid-July and September through October. The bus ride from Shinjuku Station, with departures a 2-minute walk from the west side of the station in front of the Yasuda Seimi no. 2 Building at bus platform no. 50, takes about 1 hour and 45 minutes and costs ¥1,700 ($16) one-way to Kawaguchiko Station. Note that you must make a reservation for this bus through **Keio Kosoku Bus Yoyaku Center** (© **03/5376-2222**) or a travel agency such as JTB. Less frequent buses also depart from Tokyo Station's Yaesu south exit for the same price.

From Kawaguchiko Station there are buses onward to the Fifth Stage, with the trip taking approximately 45 minutes and costing another ¥1,700 ($16). During the official climbing season, a handful of buses travel directly from Shinjuku Station to Kawaguchiko Trail's Fifth Stage, costing ¥2,600 ($25) one-way and taking almost 2½ hours. Note that bus service is suspended in winter, when Mount Fuji is blanketed in snow and is considered too dangerous for novice climbers. Otherwise, buses generally run April through October to the Fifth Stage unless there is inclement weather (including snow), though they run far less frequently than during the official season.

If you want to use your Japan Rail Pass, you can leave from Tokyo's Shinjuku Station via the **JR Chuo Line** to Otsuki, where you change to the **Fuji Kyuko Line** for Kawaguchiko Station (note, however, that you must pay an extra ¥1,100/$10 for the last leg of the journey). The entire trip takes more than 2 hours. From Kawaguchiko Station, you can then take the 45-minute bus ride onward to the Fifth Stage.

**VISITOR INFORMATION** More information and train and bus schedules can be obtained from the **Tokyo Tourist Information Center,** including a leaflet called "Mount Fuji and Fuji Five Lakes." See "Visitor Information" in chapter 4.

## CLIMBING MOUNT FUJI

Mount Fuji is part of a larger national park called **Fuji-Hakone-Izu National Park.** Of the handful of trails leading to the top, most popular for Tokyoites is the **Kawaguchiko Trail,** which is divided into 10 different stages; the Fifth Stage, located about 2,475m (8,250 ft.) up and served by bus, is the usual starting point. From here it takes about 6 hours to reach the summit and 3 hours for the descent.

**PREPARING FOR YOUR CLIMB** You don't need climbing experience to ascend Mount Fuji (you'll see everyone from grandmothers to children making the pilgrimage), but you do need stamina and a good pair of walking shoes. The climb is possible in tennis shoes, but if the rocks are wet, they can get awfully slippery. You should also bring a light plastic raincoat (which you can buy at souvenir shops at the Fifth Stage) since it often rains on the mountain, a sun hat, a bottle of water, a sweater for the evening, and a flashlight if you plan on hiking at night. It gets very chilly on Mount Fuji at night. Even in August, the average temperature on the summit is 42.5°F (5.8°C).

Because of snow and inclement weather from fall through late spring, the best time to make an ascent is during the "official" climbing season from mid-July to August 31. This is also when buses run most frequently. However, it's the most crowded time of the year. Consider the fact that there are more than 120 million Japanese, most of whom wouldn't dream of climbing the mountain outside the "official" 1½ months it's open, and you begin to get the picture. About 600,000 people climb Fuji-san every

---

*Fun Fact* **Mount Fuji or Bust**

The first documented case of someone scaling Mount Fuji is from the early 8th century. During the Edo Period, pilgrimages to the top were considered a purifying ritual, with strict rules governing dress and route. Women, thought to defile sacred places, were prohibited from climbing mountains until 1871.

---

year, mostly in July and August and mostly on weekends—so if you plan on climbing Mount Fuji on a Saturday or a Sunday in summer, go to the end of the line, please.

Don't be disappointed when your bus deposits you at **Kawaguchiko Fifth Stage,** where you'll be bombarded with souvenir shops, restaurants, and busloads of tourists; most of these tourists aren't climbing to the top. As soon as you get past them and the blaring loudspeakers, you'll find yourself on a steep rocky path, surrounded only by scrub brush and the hikers on the path below and above you. After a couple of hours, you'll probably find yourself above the roily clouds, which stretch in all directions. It will be as if you are on an island, barren and rocky, in the middle of an ocean.

**STRATEGIES FOR CLIMBING TO THE TOP**    The usual procedure for climbing Mount Fuji is to take a morning bus, start climbing in early afternoon, spend the night near the summit, get up early in the morning to climb the rest of the way to the top, and then watch the sun rise (about 4:30am) from atop Mount Fuji. (You can, of course, also wake up in time to see the sun rise and then continue climbing.) At the top is a 1-hour hiking trail that circles the crater. Hikers then begin the descent, reaching the Fifth Stage about noon.

There are about 20 **mountain huts** along the Kawaguchiko Trail above the Fifth Stage, but they're very primitive, providing only a futon and toilet facilities, and some with a capacity to house 500 hikers. The cost is ¥5,250 ($50) per person without meals, ¥7,350 ($70) with meals. When I stayed in one of these huts, dinner consisted of dried fish, rice, bean-paste soup, and pickled vegetables; breakfast was exactly the same. Still, unless you want to carry your own food, I'd opt for the meals. Note that huts are open only in July and August; book as early as you can to assure a place. I recommend the **Toyokan Hut** at the Seventh Stage (© 0555/22-1040) or the **Taishikan Hut** at the Eighth Stage (© 0555/22-1947). Call the **Japanese Inn Union of Mount Fuji** at © 0555/22-1944 for more information.

In the past few decades, there's been a trend in which climbers arrive at the Fifth Stage late in the evening and then climb to the top during the night with the aid of flashlights. After watching the sunrise, they then make their descent. That way, they don't have to spend the night in one of the huts.

Climbing Mount Fuji is definitely a unique experience, but there's a saying in Japan: "Everyone should climb Mount Fuji once; only a fool would climb it twice."

## 5 Hakone: By Mountain Streetcar, Cable Car, Ropeway & Boat *(★(★(★*

97km (60 miles) SW of Tokyo

Part of the **Fuji-Hakone-Izu National Park** *(★(★*, Hakone is one of the closest and most popular destinations for residents of Tokyo. Beautiful Hakone has about everything a vacationer could wish for—hot-spring resorts, mountains, lakes, breathtaking views of

# Hakone

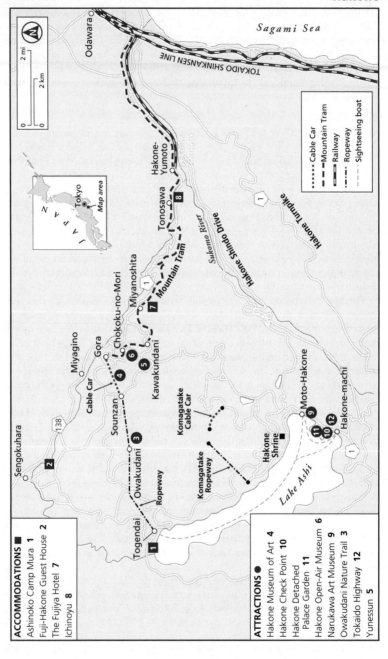

**ACCOMMODATIONS ■**
Ashinoko Camp Mura **1**
Fuji-Hakone Guest House **2**
The Fujiya Hotel **7**
Ichinoyu **8**

**ATTRACTIONS ●**
Hakone Museum of Art **4**
Hakone Check Point **10**
Hakone Detached
   Palace Garden **11**
Hakone Open-Air Museum **6**
Narukawa Art Museum **9**
Owakudani Nature Trail **3**
Tokaido Highway **12**
Yunessun **5**

Mount Fuji, and interesting historical sites. You can tour Hakone as a day trip if you leave early in the morning and limit your sightseeing to a few key attractions, but adding an overnight stay—complete with a soak in a hot-spring tub—is much more pleasant. If you plan to return to Tokyo, I suggest that you leave your luggage in storage at your Tokyo hotel or Shinjuku Station and travel to Hakone with only an overnight bag. If you're traveling onward, say, to Kyoto, leave your bags at a check-in counter at Hakone Yumoto Station.

## ESSENTIALS

**GETTING THERE & GETTING AROUND**    Getting to and around Hakone is half the fun! An easy loop tour you can follow through Hakone includes various forms of unique transportation: Starting out by train from Tokyo, you switch to a small two-car streetcar that zigzags up the mountain, change to a cable car and then to a smaller ropeway, and end your trip with a boat ride across Lake Ashi, stopping to see major attractions along the way. From Lake Ashi (that is, from the villages of Togendai, Hakone-machi, or Moto-Hakone), you can then board a bus bound for Odawara Station (an hour's ride), where you board the train back to Tokyo. These same buses also pass by all the recommendations listed below, which is useful if you wish to complete most of your sightseeing the first day before going to your hotel for the evening. There is also a bus that travels directly between Togendai and Shinjuku in about 2 hours (fare: ¥1,960/$19).

**Odakyu** operates the most convenient network of trains, buses, streetcars, cable cars, and boats to and around Hakone. The most economical and by far easiest way to see Hakone is with Odakyu's **Hakone Free Pass,** which, despite its name, isn't free but does give you a round-trip ticket on the express train from Shinjuku Station to Hakone Yumoto and includes all modes of transportation in Hakone listed above and covered below. The pass lets you avoid the hassle of buying individual tickets and also gives nominal discounts on most Hakone attractions. Several variations of the pass are available; the most common, valid for 3 days, costs ¥5,500 ($52) for adults (half fare for children). You'll save money, however, by traveling on a weekday. The **Hakone Weekday Pass,** which is good only Monday through Thursday, is valid for 2 days and costs ¥4,700 ($45) for adults, half price for children. Not only are weekdays less crowded, but some hotels offer cheaper weekday rates, which means you'll save all around. Note, however, that the Weekday Pass is not available during peak times, including Golden Week and summer school vacation (mid-July through Aug).

The trip from Shinjuku to Hakone Yumoto, where you can then board the mountain streetcar, takes 2 hours, with departures approximately every 30 minutes. If time is of the essence or if you want to be assured a seat during peak season, you can reserve a seat on the faster and more luxurious **Odakyu Romance Car,** which travels from Shinjuku all the way to Hakone Yumoto in 1½ hours and costs an extra ¥870 ($8.25) one-way.

If you have a **Japan Rail Pass,** you should take the Shinkansen bullet train first to Odawara (not all bullet trains stop here, so make sure yours does). From there, you can buy a Hakone Free Pass that includes travel onward through Hakone on Odakyu private railways, cable cars, buses, and boats for ¥4,130 ($39), valid for 3 days. The Weekday Pass costs ¥3,410 ($26).

All passes described above can be purchased at any station of the Odakyu Railway, including Shinjuku and Odawara. In Tokyo, the best place to purchase Hakone Free Pass tickets is at the **Odakyu Sightseeing Service Center** (located on the ground floor

near the west exit of Odakyu Shinjuku Station; © **03/5321-7887**; www.odakyu-group.
co.jp/english; open daily 8am–6pm), where you can obtain sightseeing information in
English in addition to purchasing tickets.

**VISITOR INFORMATION**   Before leaving Tokyo, pick up the "Hakone and
Kamakura" leaflet available from the Tourist Information Center; it lists the schedules
for the extensive transportation network throughout the Hakone area. There's also a
color brochure called "Hakone National Park," which includes sightseeing information and contains a map of the Hakone area. See "Visitor Information" in chapter 4
for TIC locations.

In Hakone Yumoto, the **Yumoto Tourist Office** (© **0460/5-8911;** open daily
9:30am–5:30pm) is a 2-minute walk from the Hakone Yumoto Station. Take a right
out of the station onto the town's main street; the office is on the left. If you want to
leave luggage, you can do so at a counter inside the Hakone Yumoto train station,
open daily 6am to 10pm.

## EXPLORING HAKONE

**STRATEGIES FOR SEEING HAKONE**   If you plan on spending only a day in
Hakone, you should leave Tokyo very early in the morning and plan on visiting only
a few key attractions—I recommend the **Hakone Open-Air Museum, Owakudani
Nature Trail,** and, if time permits, **Hakone Check Point** and/or **Narukawa Art
Museum.** Keep in mind that most forms of transportation (like the ropeway), as well
as museums, close at 5pm.

If you're spending the night—and I strongly urge that you do—you can arrange
your itinerary in a more leisurely fashion and devote more time to Hakone's attractions. You may wish to travel only as far as your hotel the first day, stopping at sights
along the way and in the vicinity. The next day you could continue with the rest of
the circuit through Hakone. Or, you can opt to complete most of your sightseeing the
first day, and then backtrack to your accommodations or reach it by bus from
Togendai, Hakone-machi, or Moto-Hakone.

**SCENIC RAILWAY TO GORA**   Regardless of whether you travel via the Odakyu
Romance Car or the ordinary Odakyu express, you'll end up at Hakone Yumoto Station. Here you'll transfer to the **Hakone Tozan Railway,** a delightful, mountain-
climbing, two-car electric streetcar that winds its way through forests and over streams
and ravines as it travels upward to Gora, making several switchbacks along the way.
The entire trip from Hakone Yumoto Station to Gora takes only 45 minutes, but it's
a beautiful ride on a narrow track through the mountains. This is my favorite part of
the whole journey. The trains, which run every 10 to 15 minutes, make about a half-
dozen stops before reaching Gora, including **Tonosawa** and **Miyanoshita,** two hot-
spring spa resorts with a number of old ryokan and hotels. Some of these ryokan date
back several centuries to the days when they were on the main thoroughfare to Edo,
called the old Tokaido Highway. Miyanoshita is also the best place for lunch. See
"Where to Dine," and "Where to Stay," below.

For some relaxing hot-springs bathing en route, stop at the thoroughly modern,
sophisticated public bath called **Yunessun** ✿✿ (© **0460/2-4126;** www.yunessun.com).
To reach it, disembark the Hakone Tozan Railway at Kowakudani, then take a 15-
minute taxi or bus ride (bus stop: Kowaki-en). This self-described "Mediterranean Style
Spa Resort" offers a variety of both indoor and outdoor family baths, which means you
wear your bathing suit. In addition to indoor Turkish, Roman, and salt baths, there's also

a small children's play area with slides and a large outdoor area with a variety of small baths, including those mixed with coffee, sake, wine, rose petals, or healthy minerals. For those who desire more traditional bathing, there's the Mori No Yu, with both indoor and outdoor baths separated for men and women (you don't wear your suit here). Most people who come stay 2 to 3 hours. Admission is ¥3,500 ($33) to Yunessun, ¥1,800 ($17) to Mori No Yu, or ¥4,000 ($38) to both; children pay half fare. Upon admission, you'll be given a towel, robe, and wristband to pay for drinks and extras (rental suits are available), so you can leave all valuables in your assigned locker. Yunessun is open daily 9am to 7pm in summer, 9am to 6pm in winter (Mori No Yu is open 9am–8pm year-round).

The most important stop on the Hakone Tozan Railway is the next-to-the-last stop, Chokoku-no-Mori, where you'll find the famous **Hakone Open-Air Museum (Chokoku-no-Mori Bijutsukan)** ★★★ (© **0460/2-1161;** www.hakone-oam.or.jp), a minute's walk from the station. With the possible exception of views of Mount Fuji, this museum is, in my opinion, Hakone's number-one attraction. Using nature itself as a dramatic backdrop, it showcases sculpture primarily of the 20th century in a spectacular setting of glens, formal gardens, ponds, and meadows. There are 400 sculptures on display, both outdoors and in several buildings, with works by Carl Milles, Manzu Giacomo, Jean Dubuffet, Willem de Kooning, Barbara Hepworth, Joan Miró, and more than 25 pieces by Henry Moore, shown on a rotating basis. The Picasso Pavilion contains works by Picasso from pastels to ceramics (it's one of the world's largest collections), while the Picture Gallery displays paintings by Miró, Renoir, Kandinsky, Vlaminck, Utrillo, and others. Several installations geared toward children allow them to climb and play. I could spend all day here; barring that, count on staying at least 2 hours. Be sure to stop off at the "foot onsen," where you can immerse your tired feet in soothing, hot water. The museum is open daily 9am to 5pm (to 4pm Dec–Feb); admission is ¥1,600 ($15) adults, ¥1,100 ($10) university and high-school students and seniors, and ¥800 ($7.60) children. Your Hakone Free Pass gives you a ¥200 ($1.90) discount.

**BY CABLE CAR TO SOUNZAN**   Cable cars leave Gora every 20 minutes or so and arrive 9 minutes later at the end station of Sounzan, making several stops along the way as they travel steeply uphill. One of the stops is Koen-Kami, from which it's only a minute's walk to the **Hakone Museum of Art** (© **0460/2-2623**). This five-room museum displays Japanese pottery and ceramics from the Jomon Period (around 4000–2000 B.C.) to the Edo Period, including terra-cotta *haniwa* burial figures, huge 16th-century Bizen jars, and Imari ware. What makes this place particularly rewarding are the bamboo grove and small but lovely moss garden, shaded by Japanese maples, with a teahouse where you can sample Japanese tea for ¥630 ($6). It is most beautiful in autumn. Open Friday through Wednesday from 9:30am to 4:30pm (to 4pm in winter); admission is ¥900 ($8.55) for adults, ¥400 ($3.80) for university and high-school students and seniors, and free for children. The Hakone Free Pass gives you a ¥200 ($1.90) discount. Plan on spending about a half-hour here, more if you opt for tea.

**BY ROPEWAY TO TOGENDAI**   From Sounzan, you board a ropeway with gondolas for a long, 30-minute haul over a mountain to Togendai on the other side, which lies beside Lake Ashi, known as Lake Ashinoko in Japanese. Note that the ropeway stops running at around 5:15pm in summer and 4pm in winter.

Before reaching Togendai, however, get off at the first stop, Owakudani, the ropeway's highest point, to hike the 30-minute **Owakudani Nature Trail** ★. Owakudani means "Great Boiling Valley," and you'll soon understand how it got its name when

you see (and smell) the sulfurous steam escaping from fissures in the rock, testimony to the volcanic activity still present here. Most Japanese commemorate their trip by buying boiled eggs cooked here in the boiling waters, available at the small hut midway along the trail.

**ACROSS LAKE ASHI BY BOAT**    From Togendai you can take a pleasure boat across Lake Ashi, also referred to as "Lake Hakone" in some English-language brochures. Believe it or not, a couple of the boats plying the waters are replicas of a man-of-war pirate ship. It takes about half an hour to cross the lake to Hakone-machi (also called simply Hakone; *machi* means city) and Moto-Hakone, two resort towns right next to each other on the southern edge of the lake. This end of the lake affords the best view of Mount Fuji, one often depicted in tourist publications. Boats are in operation year-round (though they run less frequently in winter and not at all in stormy weather); the last boat departs around 5pm from the end of March to the end of November. Buses connect Togendai with Moto-Hakone, Odawara, and Shinjuku.

If you're heading back to Tokyo, buses depart for Odawara near the boat piers in both Hakone-machi and Moto-Hakone. Otherwise, for more sightseeing, get off the boat in Hakone-machi, turn left, and walk about 5 minutes on the town's main road, following the signs and turning left to the **Hakone Check Point (Hakone Seki-sho)** ✆ (© **0460/3-6635**), on a road lined with souvenir shops. This is a reconstructed guardhouse originally built in 1619 to serve as a checkpoint along the famous Tokaido Highway, which connected Edo (present-day Tokyo) with Kyoto. In feudal days, local lords, called *daimyo,* were required to spend alternate years in Edo; their wives were kept on in Edo as virtual hostages to discourage the lords from planning rebellions while in their homelands. This was one of several points along the highway to guard against the transport of guns, spies, and female travelers trying to flee Edo. Passes were necessary for travel, and although it was possible to sneak around it, male violators who were caught were promptly executed, while women suffered the indignity of having their heads shaven and then being given away to anyone who wanted them. Inside the reconstructed guardhouse, you'll see life-size models reenacting scenes inside a checkpoint. Your ticket also allows admission to a small museum with displays relating to the Edo Period, including items used for travel, samurai armor, and gruesome articles of torture. Open daily from 9am to 5pm (until 4:30pm in winter); admission is ¥300 ($2.85) for adults and ¥150 ($1.45) for children. It shouldn't take more than 20 minutes to see everything.

Just beyond the Hakone Check Point, at the big parking lot with the traditional gate, is the **Hakone Detached Palace Garden (Onshi-Hakone-Koen),** which lies on a small promontory on Lake Ashi and has spectacular views of the lake and, sometimes, Mount Fuji. Originally part of an imperial summer villa built in 1886, the garden is open free to the public 24 hours daily. It's a great place for wandering. On its grounds is the **Lakeside Observation Building** (open daily 9am–4:30pm), with displays relating to the Hakone Palace, which was destroyed by earthquakes.

If you take the northernmost exit from the garden, crossing a bridge, you'll see the neighboring resort town, **Moto-Hakone.** Across the highway and lined with ancient and mighty cedars is part of the old **Tokaido Highway** itself. During the Edo Period, more than 400 cedars were planted along this important road, which today stretches 2.5km (1½ miles) along the curve of Lake Ashi and makes for a pleasant stroll (unfortunately, though, a modern road has been built right beside the original one). Moto-Hakone is a 5-minute walk from the Detached Palace Garden.

In Moto-Hakone, the **Narukawa Art Museum** 𝒢𝒢 (𝒞 **0460/3-6828**) is very worthwhile and located just after you enter town, up the hill to the right when you reach the orange torii gate. It specializes in modern works of the *Nihonga* style of painting, developed during the Heian period (794–1185) and sparser than Western paintings (which tend to fill in backgrounds and every inch of canvas). Large paintings and screens by contemporary Nihonga artists are on display, including works by Yamamoto Kyujin, Maki Susumu, Kayama Matazo, Hirayama Ikuo, and Hori Fumiko. Changing exhibitions feature younger up-and-coming artists, as well as glassware. I wouldn't miss it; views of Lake Ashi and Mount Fuji are a bonus. Open daily 9am to 5pm; admission is ¥1,200 ($11) for adults and ¥600 ($5.70) for children.

**WHEN YOU'RE DONE SIGHTSEEING FOR THE DAY**    Buses depart for Hakone Yumoto and Odawara from both Hakone-machi and Moto-Hakone two to four times an hour. Be sure to check the time of the last departure; generally it's around 8pm, but this can change with the season and the day of the week. (The bus also passes two of the accommodations recommended below, The Fujiya Hotel and Ichinoyu, as well as Yunessun hot-springs baths; another bus will take you to Fuji-Hakone Guest House.) Otherwise, the trip from Moto-Hakone takes approximately 30 minutes to Hakone Yumoto and 50 minutes to Odawara, where you can catch the Odakyu train back to Shinjuku.

## WHERE TO STAY

**Ashinoko Camp Mura** *(Kids)*    Since you're in a national park, you might be inclined to enjoy nature by roughing it in a cabin beside Lake Ashi, just a 10-minute walk from the ropeway to Sounzan and the boat to Hakone-machi. Operated by Kanagawa Prefecture and also with tent camping, it offers row and detached (more expensive and closer to the lake) cabins that sleep up to six persons, each with two bedrooms, a bathroom, a living room with cooking facilities and tableware, and a deck with picnic table. However, there is no supermarket in nearby Togendai, so you'll want to either bring your own food or dine at the camp's restaurant with both Japanese and Western selections (reservations required for lunch and dinner). There's a hiking trail around the lake. A great place for kids. Open year-round.

164 Hakone-machi, Moto-Hakone, Ashigarashimo-gun, Kanagawa 250-0522. 𝒞 **0460/4-8279.** Fax 0460/4-6489. 36 units. Peak season ¥26,250 ($249) row cabin; ¥31,500 ($299) detached cabin. Off season ¥15,750 ($149) row cabin; ¥21,000 ($200) detached cabin. No credit cards. Bus: Togendai, from Odawara (1 hr.) or Shinjuku (2 hr.), then a 10-min. walk. **Amenities:** Restaurant; rental bikes; barbecue grills. *In room:* Kitchenette, fridge.

**Fuji-Hakone Guest House**    It's a bit isolated, but this Japanese Inn Group member offers inexpensive, spotlessly clean lodging in tatami rooms, all nonsmoking. A 20-year-old house, situated in tranquil surroundings set back from a tree-shaded road, is run by a man who speaks very good English and is happy to provide sightseeing information, including a map of the area with local restaurants. Some of the rooms face the Hakone mountain range. Pluses are the communal lounge area with TV and even a piano and a guitar; and the outdoor hot-spring bath (for which there's an extra ¥500/$4.15 charge).

912 Sengokuhara, Hakone, Kanagawa 250-0631. 𝒞 **0460/4-6577.** Fax 0460/4-6578. www.fujihakone.com. 14 units (none with bathroom). ¥5,250–¥6,300 ($50–$60) single; ¥10,500–¥12,600 ($100–$120) double; ¥15,750–¥16,800 ($150–$160) triple. Plus ¥150 ($1.45) local tax per person. Peak season and weekends ¥1,000–¥2,000 ($9.50–$19) extra. Minimum 2-night stay preferred. Western breakfast ¥840 ($8) extra. AE, MC, V. Bus: Hakone Tozan (included in the Hakone Free Pass) from Togendai (15 min.) or from Odawara Station (50 min.) to the Senkyoro-mae stop (announced in English), then a 1-min. walk. **Amenities:** Hot-spring bath; coin-op laundry and dryer; communal fridge and microwave. *In room:* A/C, TV.

**The Fujiya Hotel** *ααα* *finds*   The Fujiya, which was established in 1878, is quite simply the grandest, most majestic old hotel in Hakone; indeed, it might be the loveliest historic hotel in Japan. I love this hotel for its comfortably old-fashioned atmosphere, including such Asian touches as a Japanese-style roof, lots of windows, and long wooden corridors with photographs of famous guests, from Einstein to Eisenhower. Staying here transports me to a gentler, and more genteel, past. There are five separate buildings, all different and added on at various times in the hotel's long history, but management has been meticulous in retaining its historical traditions. A landscaped garden out back, with a waterfall, a pond, a greenhouse, and stunning views over the valley, is great for strolls and meditation. An outdoor pool, fed by river water, occupies a corner of the garden, and there's also an indoor thermal pool and hot-spring public baths. Even the private bathroom in each room has piped in hot-spring water.

Rooms are old-fashioned and spacious with high ceilings and antique furnishings; some even have claw-foot tubs. The most expensive rooms are the largest, but my favorites are those in the Flower Palace, which has an architectural style that reminds me of a Japanese temple and seems unchanged since its 1936 construction. Even if you don't stay here, do come for a meal or tea. Highly recommended.

*Note:* A limited number of the least expensive rooms are available for foreigners at a special discounted rate, based on the hotel's age. Note, however, that the special rate is not available on Saturday and during Golden Week, the month of August, or New Year's. And if these discounted rooms are sold out, you'll pay regular fare.

359 Miyanoshita, Hakone-machi, Ashigarashimo-gun 250-0404. © **0460/2-2211.** Fax 0460/2-2210. www.fujiya hotel.co.jp. 149 units. Special foreigners' rate $127 single or double in 2006, $128 in 2007. Regular rates ¥21,090–¥43,035 ($200–$409) single or double; ¥5,775 ($55) extra on Sat or night before holiday; ¥11,550 ($110) extra mid-Aug and New Year's. AE, DC, MC, V. Station: Miyanoshita, Hakone Tozan Railway (5 min.). Bus: From Odawara or Moto-Hakone to Miyanoshita Onsen stop (1 min.). **Amenities:** 3 restaurants (Continental, grill, traditional Japanese); 1 bar; indoor and outdoor pools (free for hotel guests); hot-spring baths; Jacuzzi; sauna; souvenir shops; game room; golf course; room service (9am–10pm); in-room massage; same-day laundry service; landscaped garden. *In room:* A/C, TV, minibar, hair dryer.

㊸ **Ichinoyu** *αα*   Located near Tonosawa Station (on the Hakone Tozan Line) next to a roaring river, this delightful, rambling, wooden building stands on a tree-shaded winding road that follows the track of the old Tokaido Highway. First opened more than 375 years ago, Ichinoyu is now in its 15th generation of owners. It claims to be the oldest ryokan in the area and was once honored by the visit of a shogun during the Edo Period. Old artwork, wall hangings, and paintings decorate the place.

The ryokan has only tatami rooms. The oldest date from the Meiji Period, more than 100 years ago. My favorites are the Take, Kotobuki, and Matsue rooms, old-fashioned and consisting mainly of seasoned and weathered wood; they face the river and even have their own private outdoor baths, also with views of the river (rooms with private *rotenburo,* or outdoor hot-spring bath, cost ¥3,000/$29 extra). Both the communal tubs and the tubs in the rooms are supplied with hot water from a natural spring. The price you pay depends on your room, the meals you select, and the time of year.

90 Tonosawa, Hakone-machi, Ashigarashimo-gun 250-0315. © **0460/5-5331.** Fax 0460/5-5335. 24 units (12 with bathroom). ¥7,800–¥10,800 ($74–$103) per person including 2 meals. ¥2,000 ($19) extra per person in Aug and on weekends and holidays. AE, DC, MC, V. Station: Tonosawa, Hakone Tozan Railway (6 min.). Bus: From Odawara or Moto-Hakone to Tonosawa bus stop (2 min.). **Amenities:** Indoor and outdoor hot-spring baths. *In room:* A/C, TV, fridge, safe.

## WHERE TO DINE

For casual dining, the Hakone Open-Air Museum has a pleasant restaurant, **Bella Foresta**, overlooking the park's fantastic scenery and offering a buffet lunch daily from 11am to 3pm for ¥1,680 ($16). Also sporting a view is the even less formal restaurant on the third floor of the Owakudani Ropeway Station, serving spaghetti, tempura, and other inexpensive fare.

**Main Dining Room** *ⓒⓒ* CONTINENTAL   Hakone's grandest, oldest hotel, conveniently located near a stop on the two-car Hakone Tozan Railway, is a memorable place for a good Western meal. The main dining hall, dating from 1930, is very bright and cheerful, with a high and intricately detailed ceiling, large windows with Japanese screens, a wooden floor, and white tablecloths. The views of the Hakone hills are impressive, and the service by the bow-tied waitstaff is attentive. For lunch you can have such dishes as spaghetti, sandwiches, fried chicken, rainbow trout, and sirloin steak. The excellent dinners feature elaborate set courses or a la carte dishes ranging from scallops and sole to grilled lamb, chicken, rainbow trout, and steaks. Afterward, be sure to tour the landscaped garden.

In The Fujiya Hotel, 359 Miyanoshita. ⓒ **0460/2-2211.** Reservations required for dinner. Main dishes ¥2,541–¥7,854 ($24–$75); set dinners ¥13,860–¥23,100 ($132–$219); lunch main dishes ¥1,732–¥6,699 ($16–$64). AE, DC, MC, V. Daily noon–2pm and 6–8:30pm. Station: Miyanoshita on the Hakone Tozan Railway (5 min.).

## 6 Izu Peninsula: Tokyo's Playground

Atami: 107km (66 miles) SW of Tokyo; Ito: 120km (75 miles) SW of Tokyo

Whenever Tokyoites want to spend a night or two at a hot-spring spa on the seashore, they head for Izu Peninsula. Jutting into the Pacific Ocean southwest of Tokyo, Izu boasts some fine beaches, verdant and lush countryside, and a dramatic coastline marked in spots by high cliffs and tumbling surf. Even though the scenery is at times breathtaking, there's little of historical interest to lure a short-term visitor to Japan; make sure you've seen both Kamakura and Nikko before you consider coming here. Keep in mind also that Izu's resorts are terribly crowded during the summer vacation period from mid-July to the end of August.

The best way to enjoy Izu Peninsula, which is in Shizuoka Prefecture, is to drive, making this one of the few times when it may be worthwhile to rent your own car. A road hugs the coast all the way around the peninsula; you can drive it easily in a day (but beware: it's awfully narrow in parts). Rather than rent a car in Tokyo, I suggest you wait until you reach Atami or Ito, both of which have many car-rental agencies near their train stations. Ito, especially, warrants a car because attractions are rather far-flung and poorly served by public transportation.

If you're traveling during the peak summer season (July–Aug), you should make accommodations reservations at least several months in advance. Otherwise, there are hotel, ryokan, and *minshuku r*eservation offices in all of Izu's resort towns that will arrange accommodations for you. Be aware, however, that if a place has a room still open at the last minute in August, there's probably a reason for it—poor location, poor service, or unimaginative decor.

Before you leave Tokyo, be sure to pick up the leaflet "The Izu Peninsula" at the Tourist Information Center.

# ATAMI

Atami means "hot sea." According to legend, once upon a time local fishermen, concerned about a geyser spewing forth into the sea and killing lots of fish and marine life, asked a Buddhist monk to intervene on their behalf and to pray for a solution to the problem. The prayers paid off when the geyser moved itself to the beach; not only was the marine life spared, but Atami was blessed with hot-spring water the townspeople could henceforth bathe in.

Today, Atami—with a population of 44,000—is a conglomeration of hotels, ryokan, restaurants, pachinko parlors, souvenir shops, and a sizable red-light district, spread along narrow, winding streets that hug steep mountain slopes around Atami Bay. The city itself isn't very interesting—in fact, its economy is severely depressed, and since it has none of the fancy shops and nightlife to attract a younger generation, mostly older Japanese vacation here, giving the town an old-fashioned, unpretentious atmosphere. In any case, this is the most easily accessible hot-spring resort from Tokyo, and it has a wide beach flanked by a half-mile boardwalk and a wonderful art museum that even Tokyoites make a day trip to see.

## ESSENTIALS

**GETTING THERE**    From Tokyo Station, it's 55 minutes by **Shinkansen bullet train;** since not all bullet trains stop in Atami, be sure to check beforehand. If you don't have a Japan Rail Pass, the fare is ¥3,570 ($34) for an unreserved seat. You can also take the slower, 2-hour **JR Tokaido Local Line** for ¥1,890 ($18).

**VISITOR INFORMATION**    The **JR Travel Service Center** (adjacent to a coffee shop) is to the left as you exit the train station (© 0557/81-6002; Fri–Tues 10am–1:30pm and 2:50–5:30pm). No English is spoken, but English-language literature and a map are available.

**GETTING AROUND**    Buses serve major sightseeing attractions in Atami. If you're spending the day here, you might wish to purchase a 1-day ticket for the **YuYu Bus,** which has two routes, both making circuitous trips through town and departing Atami Station every 30 minutes. You can leave and reboard as often as you wish, or you can stay on for a tour of the city. The cost is ¥800 ($7.60) for adults and ¥400 ($3.80) for children. There's also a **Toyota Rental Car** office in front of Atami Station (© 0557/81-0100), open daily 8am to 8pm.

## SEEING THE SIGHTS

Atami's must-see is the **MOA Art Museum** ✦, 26–2 Momoyama-cho (© 0557/ 84-2511), housed in a modern building atop a hill with sweeping views of Atami and the bay. It's a 5-minute bus ride from Atami Station on the YuYu Bus; or take a bus from platform 4 to the last stop (one-way fare is ¥160/$1.50). The museum's entrance is dramatic—a long escalator ride through a tunnel followed by a 7-minute laser show (given every hour). The museum itself, however, concentrates on traditional Asian art, including woodblock prints by Hokusai, Hiroshige, and their contemporaries; Chinese ceramics; Japanese bronze religious art; and lacquerware. Although some 200 items from the 3,500-piece private collection are changed monthly, look for two National Treasures almost always on display: a tea-storage jar with a wisteria design by Edo artist Ninsei, and a gold-leaf screen of red and white plum blossoms by Ogata Korin. It takes about an hour to tour the museum, open Friday through Wednesday

from 9:30am to 5pm; admission is ¥1,600 ($15) for adults, ¥1,200 ($11) for seniors, ¥800 ($7.60) for university and high-school students, and free for children.

Another worthwhile attraction is ㊹ **Kiunkaku,** 4–2 Showa-cho (𝒞 **0557/86-3101;** YuYu Bus: Kiunkaku stop), built in 1918 as the private villa of a shipping magnate, converted to a ryokan in 1947, and now open to the public. It's an eclectic mix of Japanese and Western architectural styles, with stained-glass windows, fireplaces, parquet floors, gaily painted European furniture, and tatami rooms, wrapped around a lovely inner garden. It was once a favorite haunt of famous Japanese writers (including Mishima Yukio); who wouldn't feel inspired here? Allow 30 minutes to tour the facilities, open Thursday to Tuesday from 9am to 5pm. Admission is ¥310 ($2.95) for adults, ¥210 ($2) for university and high-school students, and ¥100 (95¢) for children.

Finally, if you're here on a weekend, try to catch the 11am dancing performance of the **Atami Geisha,** in front of City Hall at Geigi Kenban, 17–13 Chuo-cho (𝒞 **0557/81-3575;** YuYu Bus: Shiyakusho-mae). Admission, including tea and refreshments, is ¥1,300 ($12).

## WHERE TO STAY

㊺ **Taikanso** ✿✿    Located on a pine-shaded mountain slope above the city, this beautiful ryokan was built in 1938 as the private villa of a steelworks owner and was named after his friend Yokoyama Taikan, a famous Japanese painter. Ten years later it was converted to a Japanese inn; since then, it's been expanded into several buildings connected by covered pathways and meandering streams, adhering to a Kyoto style of architecture popular in the 16th century. Various styles of rooms are available (most with Washlet toilets and massage chairs), with the most expensive offering the best views, the most space, and the best meals (Western-style breakfasts available on request). The ultimate in luxury is the oldest unit, a three-room suite with a sitting alcove and cypress tub. Queen Beatrix of the Netherlands stayed here with her husband and three sons. Although all the rooms boast hot-spring water for the tubs, there are three public baths with open-air bathing. Be sure to wander the corridors and grounds.

7–1 Hayashigaoka-cho, Atami City, Shizuoka 413-0031. 𝒞 0557/81-8137. Fax 0557/83-5308. www.heartonhotel. com/taikanso. 44 units. ¥29,000–¥70,000 ($276–$665) per person. Rates include 2 meals and a service charge. ¥3,000–¥5,000 ($29–$48) extra per person weekends, holidays, and peak season. AE, DC, V. Take a taxi from Atami Station, a 4-min. ride. **Amenities:** Sushi bar; coffee shop; nightclub w/live band; outdoor swimming pool (free for hotel guests); indoor/outdoor hot-spring baths; sauna; in-room massage. *In room:* A/C, TV, minibar, hot-water pot w/tea, hair dryer, safe.

## WHERE TO DINE

㊻ **Home Run Sushi** *Value* SUSHI    For excellent sushi, head to this simple, one-room restaurant near the waterfront with both counter and table seating. There's no English-language menu, but pictures show various kinds of sushi a la carte. I have no idea why this place is called Home Run—one of Japan's many mysteries.

5–1 Nagisacho. 𝒞 0557/82-7300. Sushi a la carte ¥200–¥630 ($1.90–$6). No credit cards. Daily 11:30am–11pm. A 13-min. walk from Atami Station, at the end of Ginza Dori street on a corner to the left.

# ITO

Just 18km (11 miles) south of Atami, Ito is a hot-spring spa, hemmed in on one side by steeply wooded mountains and on the other by the sea. Its 75,000 inhabitants are unusually spread along the coast in a string of hamlets, separated by beautiful scenery but connected by winding roads, private railway, and buses. Its lush, tropical atmosphere with palm trees and flowering bushes comes as a surprise this close to Tokyo,

but what makes this town truly unique is that it supports an astonishing number of private museums, most of them Western and some quite odd. I don't think I could come up with a more bizarre collection of museums even if I tried.

## ESSENTIALS

**GETTING THERE**    From Tokyo Station it's approximately 1 hour and 45 minutes to Ito Station aboard the **JR Odoriko** (¥3,820/$36); or 1 hour and 20 minutes aboard the **Super View Odoriko JR** (¥4,390/$42), with five daily runs. Otherwise, a slower local line takes approximately 2½ hours and costs ¥2,210 ($21) one-way. From Atami, the trip costs ¥320 ($3.05) and takes almost a half-hour aboard the **JR Ito Local Line.**

**VISITOR INFORMATION**    The **Ito Tourist Information Office** (© 0557/37-6105) has two locations: across the street from the train station's exit (open daily 9am–5pm) and in Marine Town on the waterfront (open daily 10am–5:30pm).

**GETTING AROUND**    The Ito Local Line travels south from Ito Station to **Jogasaki,** the site of Izu's famous Jogasaki Coast. However, since most museums are located inland from Jogasaki, it's best to rent a car (avoid weekends and peak season). There are many agencies around Ito Station, including **Toyota Rental Car** (© 0557/37-0100), **JR Eki Rent-A-Car** (© 0557/37-2866), and **Avis** (© 0557/36-1150). Otherwise, a **bus** departing Ito Station for Shaboten Koen makes stops at both the Ikeda Museum of 20th Century Art and the Izu Glass & Craft Museum. A **Free Pass** for ¥1,300 ($12) allows unlimited 1-day travel by bus.

## SEEING THE SIGHTS

Of Ito's two dozen museums, the most well known, and one of the oldest, is the **Ikeda Museum of 20th Century Art** ✻✻, 614 Totari (© 0557/45-2211; bus stop: Ikeda Nijuseki Bijutsukan). Though small, it boasts an impressive collection by both Western and Japanese artists, including Warhol, Salvador Dalí, Picasso, Renoir, Roy Lichtenstein, Edvard Munch, Emil Nolde, Willem de Kooning, Miró, Kokoshka, Matisse, and Chagall as well as Kimura Issho, Tatsuoki Nambata, and Junzo Watanabe. Plan on spending about 40 minutes here. Open Thursday to Tuesday 10am to 5pm; admission is ¥900 ($8.55) for adults, ¥700 ($6.65) for high-school students, and ¥500 ($4.75) for elementary and junior-high students.

Another personal favorite is the **Izu Glass & Craft Museum** ✻, 11–300 Omurokogen (© 0557/51-7222; bus stop: Risokyo), with its exquisite collection of Art Nouveau and Art Deco glass art, including figurines, perfume bottles, jewelry, vases, and lamps by such artists as Galle, Lalique, Erté, and Daum. Although at first thought it seems strange to find such a collection here, the use of dragonflies, water lilies, orchids, and other motifs show decided Japanese influence. You'll want to spend at least an hour here. Open 9am to 5pm daily; admission is ¥850 ($8.10) for adults and ¥450 ($4.30) for children.

Other art and decorative-art museums include the **Izu Lake Ippeki Museum** with works by Jean-Pierre Cassigneaul (© 0557/45-5500), the **Izu Kogen Ceramic Glass Art Museum** (© 0557/54-9600) with Chinese works, the **Izu Lake Ippeki Museum of Perfume** (© 0557/45-7700) with early-20th-century American and European perfume bottles, the **Brian Wild Smith Museum** (© 0557/51-7330) with original pictures and books including *Mother Goose,* the **Bohemian Glass Museum** (© 0557/53-4630), and the **Antique Jewelry Museum** (© 0557/54-5566) with Victorian brooches, rings, and more. There are also special-interest museums with collections

dedicated to Santa, the teddy bear, dolls, music boxes and automatic musical instruments, stained glass, antique clocks, ammonites, cats, and even penguins. A wax museum boasts likenesses of Elvis, the Beatles, Charlie Chaplin, Michael Jackson, presidents Lincoln and Clinton, and other celebrities. Contact the **Ito Tourist Office** for more information.

To see the **Jogasaki Coast** with its dramatic, rugged, cliff-lined coast and hiking paths, take the train to Jogasaki Station; from there it's a 20-minute walk. For bathing, there's the **Ito Orange Beach** not far from Ito Station.

## HOT-SPRING BATHING

Although many accommodations boast hot-spring baths, Japanese think nothing of visiting additional hot-spring facilities during the day. Unique is ㊼ **Tokaikan,** 12–10 Higashimatsubara-cho (© **0557/36-2004**), located next to Ryokan Inaba (see below). A beautiful Japanese inn built in 1928 and boasting superior wood craftsmanship, it was in danger of becoming a parking lot before it was rescued by the city and opened to the public. You can wander its halls for free, but taking the waters in the tiny public baths costs ¥500 ($4.75). It's open daily 11am to 8pm; closed the third Tuesday of every month.

**Seaside Spa,** located in a small, waterfront shopping/dining complex called Marine Town, 571–19 Yukawa (© **0557/38-1811**), offers indoor and outdoor baths with views of the sea, whirlpools, and saunas daily from 10am to 10pm; admission is ¥1,500 ($14). It's about a 25-minute walk from Ito Station; turn left out of the station and left again at the coast.

## WHERE TO STAY

㊽ **Ito-en Hotel** *Value*    Located on the Matsukawa River, this modern, simple hotel opened in 2002 and offers mostly Japanese-style rooms that can sleep two to six people, all with small balconies and—I like this—*manga* comic books. There are also huge Western-style twin rooms and combination bed/tatami rooms that are great for families. Other pluses include its hot-spring indoor/outdoor baths and breakfast served until a late 11am. The downside: Only parties of two or more are accepted.

1–12 Matsukawa-cho, Ito City, Shizuoka 414-0001. © 0557/35-1234. Fax 0557/35-2003. 66 units. ¥7,800 ($74) per person. Rates include 2 buffet meals and service charge. AE, MC, V. Station: Ito (8 min.). Go straight out of the station to the 3rd stoplight, and turn right on the last street before the river; it's on the left. **Amenities:** Indoor/outdoor hot-spring baths; sauna; lobby computer with free Internet access. *In room:* A/C, TV, fridge, safe, Washlet toilet.

**Kawana Hotel** *ᴋᴋ*    This grand old hotel is a good choice for relaxation, golf, and swimming. With its whitewashed walls, red roof tiles, and manicured lawns sloping gently toward the sea, the place seems little changed since it opened in 1936. Even the lobby lounge, built in the theme of an English country estate, remains faithful to the era with its soaring ceiling, large fireplace, coat of arms, heavy wood detailing, and antique furniture. The hotel's seclusion drew Joe Dimaggio and Marilyn Monroe on their honeymoon. Today, its two 18-hole golf courses make it famous among golfers—the hotel is often fully booked a half year in advance. Nevertheless, the hotel shows its age in places, with unimaginative, mediocre rooms that could use some updating. Best are those facing the sea, with small balconies, automatic curtain controls, and large bathrooms, most with two sinks. The least expensive rooms are smaller in size and face inland toward the mountains; double rooms are cramped for two large people. Don't forget to climb to the top of the hotel's observation tower for a view of the grounds

and their 10,000 cherry trees. Since the hotel is rather isolated, you'll probably want to dine at one of its restaurants: the old-fashioned main dining room serving Continental cuisine; a 370-year-old, thatched-roof farmhouse specializing in Japanese food; and the casual, oval-shaped Sun Parlor with windows on three sides that offer views of the sea and, on clear days, Mount Fuji rising above the mountains.

1459 Kawana, Ito City, Shizuoka 414-0044. ⓒ 0557/45-1111. Fax 0557/45-3834. www.princehotels.co.jp/kawana-e. 140 units. ¥29,400–¥30,450 ($279–$289) single; ¥37,000–¥41,600 ($312–$352) double; ¥32,400–¥57,800 ($308–$549) twin. Rates include service charge. AE, DC, MC, V. A 15-min. taxi ride from Ito Station. **Amenities:** 3 restaurants (Continental, Japanese, casual); 3 outdoor swimming pools, including a children's pool (fee: ¥1,680/$16); 2 18-hole golf courses (greens fees: ¥13,000–¥16,000/$124–$152 weekdays, ¥20,000–¥23,000/$190–$219 weekends and holidays); unlit outdoor tennis courts; in-room massage; room service (8–10am and 3–10:30pm); laundry service; nonsmoking rooms. *In room:* TV, minibar, hair dryer.

㊾ **Ryokan Inaba** 🐟🐟 *Finds*    This 85-year-old traditional ryokan, a registered National Treasure under the kind guidance of English-speaking Mrs. Inaba, has a lovely spot on the Matsukawa River not far from Ito Orange Beach. Each room is different (even a different kind of wood is employed in each room), with such traditional touches as sitting balconies over the river or woodcarvings adorning windows, transoms, or shoji screens. All rooms boast river views (making this the best place for viewing the annual tub race held here the first Sun in July or the riverside Noh theater in May). Across the river is a tiny, chest-deep, hot spring–fed pool, open only to inn guests (May–Nov). Meals are served either in your room or in a communal dining room facing the river, according to your preference (vegetarian meals available). Photo op: The best view of the ryokan is from across the river.

12–13 Higashimatsubara-cho, Ito City, Shizuoka 414-0022. ⓒ **0557/37-3178.** Fax 0557/37-3180. inaba-r@mtd. biglobe.ne.jp. 16 units (2 with bathroom, 8 with toilet only). Peak season, Sat, and holidays ¥15,000–¥25,000 ($142–$238) per person; off season and Sun–Fri ¥13,000–¥20,000 ($126–$190) per person. Rates include 2 meals and service charge. MC, V. Station: Ito (10 min.). Go straight out of the station to the 3rd stoplight (just before the bridge) and turn left; keep to the right on the small lane that parallels the river; it will be on the right. **Amenities:** 24-hr. hot-spring public baths; in-room massage. *In room:* A/C, TV, minibar, hot-water pot w/tea, hair dryer.

## WHERE TO DINE

㊿ **Fujiichi** FISH    This family-owned establishment near the public fish market and marina operates a fish shop on the ground floor and a simple restaurant on the second floor with views of the small Ito harbor. Popular with the locals, it also attracts tourists who have heard about its reputation for fresh fish. The *teishoku* gives a choice of main dish (like grilled fish, tempura, or sashimi) along with rice and soup, while set courses include more side dishes.

7–6 Shizumicho. ⓒ **0557/37-4705.** Teishoku ¥1,000–¥2,000 ($9.50–$19); set courses ¥3,000–¥5,000 ($29–$48); *donburi* rice casseroles ¥1,200–¥2,000 ($11–$19). AE, MC, V. Mon–Fri 10am–3pm; Sat–Sun 10am–7pm (last order). Station: Ito (20 min.). Turn left out of the station, walk to the coast, and turn right. After you cross the bridge, it will be on the right across from Denny's.

# 7

# The Japan Alps

The several volcanic mountain ranges that lie in central Honshu together comprise **Japan Alps National Park** 🎿🎿🎿 (called Chubu Sangaku National Park in Japanese). With the exception of Japan's tallest mountain, Mount Fuji (see section 4 of chapter 6, beginning on p. 240), all of Japan's loftiest mountains are in these ranges, making the Japan Alps a popular destination for hikers in summer and skiers in winter (Nagano, near Matsumoto, hosted the XVIII Winter Olympics in 1998). In addition, since some of the villages nestled in these mountains retain much of their traditional architecture, the Japan Alps provide a unique look at mountain life both past and present.

**A GOOD STRATEGY FOR SEEING THE JAPAN ALPS**  Because towns and villages in this region are spread out— with lots of mountains in between—traveling isn't as fast in this part of the country as on Honshu's broad plains. Your best strategy for visiting all the destinations covered in this chapter is to start from Nagoya Station by taking the JR Shinano train in the morning to Nakatsugawa, where you can then board a bus for Magome and spend the day hiking to Tsumago. From Tsumago, it's only a short bus ride to Nagiso, where you can then reboard the Shinano train bound for Matsumoto. From Matsumoto, you'll travel by bus onward to Takayama and then on to Ogimachi (in Shirakawago).

## 1 Matsumoto, Gateway to the Japan Alps 🎿

235km (146 miles) NW of Tokyo

Located in the middle of a wide basin about 198m (660 ft.) above sea level and surrounded on all sides by mountain ranges, **Matsumoto** 🎿 boasts a fine feudal castle with the oldest existing keep *(donjon)* in Japan, as well as an outstanding woodblock-print museum. Although the city itself (pop. 202,000) is modern with little remaining from its castle days, it does boast approximately 100 storehouses *(kura)* scattered throughout town, built a century ago after a devastating fire destroyed most homes and businesses. Some of the kura, made of earth and straw and then painted many times to protect valuables against future flames, have been renovated into shops, restaurants, and other establishments.

In any event, I find Matsumoto pleasant, the air fresh, and its people among the nicest I've encountered in Japan. Encircled by towering peaks, sparkling mountain lakes, and colorful wildflowers, Matsumoto also serves as the gateway to the hiking trails of Japan Alps National Park; most travelers heading to the more remote regions of the Japan Alps pass through here on their way.

# The Japan Alps

Sea of Japan

Takojima
Suzu
Wajima
Noto
Anamizu
Toyama-wan
Nanao
Himi
Hakiu
Takaoka
Toyama
Tsubata
Kanazawa
Matto
Komatsu
Ogimachi
Furukawa
Kaga
Shirakawago
HAKUSAN
NATIONAL
PARK
Yamanaka
Katsuyama
Hokuno
Fukui
Ono
Imago
Tsuruga
Seki
Mihama
Ibigawa
Gifu
Imazu
Biwa-ko
Nagoya
Tsushima
Chiryu
Ohara
Moriyama
Komono
Nishio

Tokamachi

JAPAN
Tokyo
Map area

0    25 mi
0    25 km

KOGEN
NATIONAL
PARK

Nakano
Nagano
Suzaka
Koshoku
Ueda
CHUBU
SANGAKU
NATIONAL
PARK
Matsumoto
Kamikochi
Kamioka
Okaya
Ina
Takayama
Kisofukushima
Gero
Tsumago
Tsukechi
Magome
Nakatsugawa
Namiai
Yaotsu
Akechi
Seto
Shitara
Toyota
Tokai
Toyokawa
Kuwana
Ise-wan
Mikawa-wan
Enshu-nada

Chikuma-gawa
Hime-kawa
Kurobe-gawa
Sai-gawa
Sho-gawa
Kuzuryu-gawa
Nagara-gawa
Kiso-gawa
Tenryu-gawa
Yahagi-gawa

## ESSENTIALS

**GETTING THERE   By Train**   The **JR Chuo Honsen Line** runs directly to Matsumoto from Tokyo's Shinjuku Station. Its *Limited Express Azusa,* departing every hour or less, reaches Matsumoto in about 2½ to 3½ hours and costs ¥6,200 ($59) one-way for an unreserved seat. There's also a direct JR train from Nagoya, the *Limited Express Shinano,* which takes about 2 hours and costs ¥5,360 ($51).

**By Bus**   From Tokyo's Shinjuku Station, buses depart for Matsumoto approximately every hour, taking about 3¼ hours and costing ¥3,400 ($32). From Nagoya, the ride is 2½ hours and ¥3,460 ($33); from Osaka, the ride is 5½ hours and ¥5,710 ($54); from Takayama, the ride is 2¼ hours and ¥3,100 ($29).

**VISITOR INFORMATION**   Before you depart from Tokyo, pick up a sheet called "Nagano" at the **Tourist Information Center** (p. 101). It provides information on buses and trains to Matsumoto, as well as information on sights in and around Matsumoto. It also recommends 2- to 4-hour hiking trips from **Kamikochi** ✿, the Japan Alps' most popular destination for serious hikers; the small village is a little more than 2 hours from Matsumoto via train and then bus.

In Matsumoto, you'll find the **Matsumoto Tourist Information** window (© **0263/ 32-2814;** www.city.matsumoto.nagano.jp; open daily 9:30am–6pm Apr–Oct, to 5:30pm Nov–Mar) by taking the main (east) exit out of Matsumoto Station and turning right. It has a good English-language map of the city, and its excellent English-speaking staff will also help with accommodations and can provide information on nearby skiing destinations.

**GETTING AROUND**   You can **walk** to Matsumoto Castle, about 1.5km (1 mile) northeast of the station, in about 20 minutes. Alternatively, the Town Sneaker Bus departs from in front of Matsumoto Station every 30 minutes and makes a circular trip to all city sights; it costs ¥100 (95¢) each time you get off. To visit the Japan Ukiyo-e Museum, however, you'll have to go by **train** or **taxi.** Alternatively, free bicycles are available daily 8:30am to 5pm at various locations throughout town, including the Matsumoto City Museum next to Matsumoto Castle and the Kaichi Gakko Primary School. They're convenient for visiting sights not accessible by Sneaker Bus; ask the Matsumoto Tourist Information staff for details. Otherwise, you can rent a **bike** from JR Eki Rent-A-Car (© **0263/32-4690**) beside the station for ¥1,500 ($14) per day from 8am to 6pm.

## SEEING THE SIGHTS

In addition to the sights below, good places for strolling and shopping include the **Nakamachi** district in the heart of the city with its kura, restaurants, and shops selling Matsumoto furniture, crafts, and antiques; and **Nawate Dori,** a narrow pedestrian lane flanking the Metoba River where vendors sell fruit, vegetables, flowers, and crafts.

Unless otherwise noted, all directions below are from Matsumoto Station.

### MATSUMOTO CASTLE & ENVIRONS

**Matsumoto Castle** ✿✿   Originally built in 1504 when Japan was in the throes of continuing and bloody civil wars, Matsumoto Castle is a fine specimen of a feudal castle with a 400-year-old donjon that's the oldest existing keep in the country. Surrounded by a moat with ducks and white swans and lined with willow and cherry trees, the outside walls of the donjon are black, earning the place the nickname of Karasu-jo, or Crow

Castle. It's rather small as castles go, but English-speaking Goodwill Guides stand ready daily to provide free, 1-hour tours outlining the castle's history and architectural features. Take your shoes off at the entrance and walk in stocking feet over worn wooden floors and up steep and narrow steps until you finally reach the sixth floor, from which you have a nice view of the city. This would have served as the feudal lord's *(daimyo's)* headquarters in case of enemy attack, while the fifth floor, with views in all directions, was where the generals would have conferred during war. Although the Ishikawa clan rebuilt the castle in 1593 in anticipation of gun warfare (guns were introduced to Japan in 1543) with many arrow and gun slots and walls thick enough to withstand bullets, the castle was never attacked because the civil wars ended with the coming of the Edo Period (1603–1867). Nevertheless, guns were manufactured in Japan throughout the Edo Period, and on display inside the castle are approximately 370 matchlocks, armor, and other arms manufactured in Japan from 1543 to the late Edo Era, providing interesting insight into how the import was adapted for domestic use. With war no longer a threat, a moon-viewing room was added to the castle in 1635.

Included in your castle ticket is admission to the **Matsumoto City Museum** ⚔ next to the castle. This rather eclectic museum has displays relating to archaeology, history, and folklore of the surrounding region, including samurai armor, an ornate palanquin, farming equipment, and items relating to Matsumoto's many festivals. Among these are the summer Tanabata Festival and a fertility festival held in September featuring, well, phalluses. You can tour both castle and museum in about 75 minutes.

4–1 Marunouchi. ⓒ 0263/32-2902. Admission ¥600 ($5.70) adults, ¥300 ($2.85) children. Daily 8:30am–5pm. Town Sneaker Bus: Matsumotojo Kuromon. To walk, take Ekimae Dori, the main road leading away from the station, and turn left onto Honmachi Dori.

**Kaichi Gakko Primary School**   Japan's public school system was founded in 1872 (before that, Buddhist temples were the only source of education). In 1876, this handsome white mortar building of black tile topped by an octagonal turret opened its doors, making it one of the oldest Western-style schools still in existence and a fine example of Meiji Era architecture. Serving as an elementary school for 90 years, it remains much as it was, with displays of books, games, desks, abacuses, and other educational items. Most fascinating are the photographs of former pupils (showing how many young girls came to school with young siblings strapped to their backs, since parents were hard at work) and the children's books dating from World War II, with offending passages blackened out by demand of Allied occupational forces after the war. You can see everything here in about 30 minutes.

2–4–12 Kaichi. ⓒ 0263/32-5725. Admission ¥310 ($2.95) adults, ¥150 ($1.45) children. Daily 8:30am–5pm. Closed Mon Dec–Feb. Town Sneaker Bus: Takajomachi. Behind the castle, about a 7-min. walk north.

## MORE TO SEE & DO
**Japan Ukiyo-e Museum** ⚔⚔⚔ *Finds*   Don't miss this ultramodern building housing the private collection of the Sakai family, quite simply one of the best museums of woodblock prints in Japan. With more than 100,000 prints, it's believed to be the largest collection of its kind in the world and includes representative masterpieces of all known Ukiyo-e artists. The exhibition changes every 3 months, with approximately 100 prints on display at any one time. A 10-minute slide show with English-language explanations introduces the current exhibition, and an English-language pamphlet describes the history of the collection and how woodblock prints are made.

You'll want to spend at least 45 minutes here, longer if you browse the museum shop of reproduction and original prints.

2206–1 Koshiba, Shimadachi. (© 0263/47-4440. www.ukiyo-e.co.jp. Admission ¥1,050 ($10) adults, ¥530 ($5.05) children. Tues–Sun 10am–5pm. From platform 7, take the local Kamikochi Line 10 min. to Oniwa Station (¥170/$1.60; JR Rail Pass not accepted) and then walk 15 min. (turn left out of the station, then left at the T-intersection with the post office; after passing under the bridge, take the 3rd right at the small cemetery and continue straight on, past the underpass); or take a ¥1,500 ($14) taxi ride; or, better yet, come by bike (about 20 min. from Matsumoto Station).

� **Matsumoto Folkcraft Museum (Matsumoto Mingei-kan)** *ᖶ*    Here's one more museum worth visiting if you have an extra hour (including the bus ride). Housed in a kura built to store fish, it contains folk art made primarily of wood, glass, bamboo, and porcelain from Japan and other countries, with exhibits changed three times a year. On display may be items as diverse as combs from around the world to Japanese store signs designed during the Edo Period for people who couldn't read. Particularly beautiful are the wooden chests.

1313–1 Satoyamabe. (© 0263/33-1569. Admission ¥300 ($2.85) adults, free for children 15 and younger. Tues–Sun 9am–5pm. About 15 min. by bus (¥290/$2.75; take the platform 1 bus and get off at the Shimoganai Mingeikan Guchi) or taxi.

**Matsumoto City Museum of Art (Matsumoto-shi Bijutsukan)**    Opened in 2002, this inviting museum showcases the talents of artists who have connections to Matsumoto, including Kamijyo Shinzan, who elevated calligraphy to an art, landscape artist Tamura Kazuo, and Kusama Yayoi, a female artist known for her exuberant colors and polka-dot modern art. Expect to spend about 30 minutes here.

4–2–22 Chuo. (© 0263/39-7400. Admission ¥800 ($7.60) adults, ¥500 ($4.75) university and high-school students, free for children and seniors. Tues–Sun 9am–5pm. Town Sneaker Bus: Matsumoto-shi Bijutsukan or a 15-min. walk east of Matsumoto Station on Ekimae Dori.

㊾ **Suzuki Shinichi Memorial Hall (Suzuki Shinichi Kinenkan)** *ᖶ*    If you studied violin when you were young, maybe you were one of the countless children around the world who learned by the Suzuki Method, named after its creator, Dr. Suzuki Shinichi, who died in 1998 at the age of 99. From 1946 to 1994, Suzuki lived in this simple home. You can see his study, where he spent 6 hours every morning reviewing tapes sent by pupils from around the world. You can also view short films in which Dr. Suzuki discusses his revolutionary teaching theory based on the belief that any child can be taught to play an instrument. Especially interesting is the 1955 film showing 1,000 Japanese children performing—in unison—Bach's Concerto for Two Violins, which is credited with spreading the theory to the United States when Mochizuki Kenji, a graduate student at Oberlin College in Ohio, showed it to one of his professors. Mr. Mochizuki now serves as the memorial hall's director. Matsumoto is also home of the **Suzuki Shinichi Talent Education Institute,** 3–10–15 Fukashi

(© **0263/32-1611**), where you can watch group lessons (advance reservations required) or see periodic concerts given by graduating musicians of the institute.

2–11–87 Asahi. © **0263/34-6645**. Free admission. Tues–Sun 9am–5pm. About 10 min. by bus from platform 6 (bound for Osama Onsen) to Motoharacho, then a 5-min. walk.

## WHERE TO STAY

Because Matsumoto is popular primarily with hikers used to roughing it along nature trails, accommodations are geared mainly toward convenience. Directions are from Matsumoto Station.

### EXPENSIVE

**Buena Vista** ℱ    Matsumoto's biggest and fanciest hotel is a white gleaming struc-
ture popular for its conference and wedding facilities and with those attending the Saito Kinen Festival. Otherwise, it's a rather ordinary hotel, though it does boast more facilities than Matsumoto's other hotels. The singles are very small, though windows can be opened. Rooms on higher floors have views of mountains in the distance. The rates below reflect the seasons, with the highest prices charged in summer peak season (July 20–Sept 15).

1–2–1 Honjo, Matsumoto, Nagano 390-0184. © **0263/37-0111**. Fax 0263/37-0666. www.buena-vista.co.jp. 200 units. ¥8,400–¥11,550 ($80–$110) single; ¥18,900–¥23,100 ($180–$219) double; ¥17,850–¥29,400 ($170–$279) twin. AE, DC, MC, V. A 7-min. walk from the station. Turn right out of Matsumoto Station onto Shirakaba Dori; the hotel will be on a side street to the left. **Amenities:** 4 restaurants (Japanese, Chinese, French, coffee shop); 1 lounge; 2 computers w/free Internet service in the lobby; gift shop; salon; room service (7:30–10am and 5:30–10pm); in-room massage; same-day laundry/dry cleaning; nonsmoking rooms. *In room:* A/C, cable TV, high-speed dataport, minibar, hot-water pot w/tea, hair dryer, Washlet toilet.

�53 **Kurano Yado Ichiyama** ℱℱ *Finds*    The Meiji-Era *kura* that used to stand here was torn down, and in its place is this six-story kura replica, which nonetheless imparts a homey atmosphere with its whitewashed walls, dark wooden beams, Asian folkcrafts, and architectural features common to the region. The five Japanese-style rooms have pleasing architectural features such as wood and bamboo ceilings, salvaged from the original building, while the eight Western-style rooms are spacious and uncluttered. All come with heavy shades to block light and windows that can be opened. Full Western breakfasts are served in the pleasant ground-floor dining room, though you can opt out of breakfast and deduct ¥1,000 ($9.50) from the rates below. In short, Ichiyama has more charm than most accommodations and is quiet despite its central location.

2–1–12 Chuo, Matsumoto, Nagano 390-0811. © **0263/32-0122**. Fax 0263/32-3968. 13 units. ¥10,500–¥12,600 ($100–$120) single; ¥16,800–¥23,100 ($160–$219) double. Winter discounts available. Rates include breakfast and service charge. AE, DC, MC, V. A 5-min. walk from the station. Turn left out of the station and then turn right onto Koen Dori (there's a McDonald's on the corner); it will be on the right, just past Parco department store and the park plaza. **Amenities:** Laundry/dry-cleaning service. *In room:* A/C, TV, fridge, hot-water pot w/tea, hair dryer.

### MODERATE

�54 **Marumo** ℱℱ *Finds*    This is my top pick for accommodations that epitomize the old-fashioned atmosphere of Matsumoto during the Meiji Era. Located in the traditional district of Nakamachi and occupying a kura and traditional Japanese inn con-
structed after the great 1888 fire that destroyed much of Matsumoto, it boasts a diminutive but eye-catching entryway of polished woods and antiques, very narrow stairs and corridors leading to Japanese-style rooms, and a wonderful coffee shop which has changed little over the decades. Rooms are simple and without the usual

creature comforts, but the location is great and the atmosphere is truly one of a kind. If you're searching for "traditional Japan," this is where you'll want to stay.

3-3-10 Chuo, Matsumoto, Nagano 390-0811. (© 0263/32-0115. 8 units, none with bathroom. ¥5,250 ($44) per person without breakfast; ¥6,300 ($53) per person with Japanese breakfast. Rates include service charge. No credit cards. Town Sneaker Bus: Nakamachi (12 min.). Walk down Koen Dori (left of the station; there's a McDonald's on the corner) to Honmachi, turn left, and then turn right at Nakamachi. *In room:* A/C, TV, hot-water pot w/tea.

**Matsumoto Tokyu Inn**   Visible from the station, this practical and clean business hotel's main selling point is its convenient location, which probably accounts for rates that are a bit higher than you would expect in Matsumoto (the highest rates below are charged in summer). The majority of rooms are singles and twins, all with semi-double-size beds with feather quilts. There are also six doubles and five deluxe twins, the latter with sofa, chairs, and a separate vanity area with its own sink. Of special note are rooms designated for women (request one when making a reservation) that add humidifiers, irons, nightshirts, and female-oriented toiletries. Some rooms also have high-speed Internet access. On clear days, rooms facing west have views of the Japan Alps.

1-3-21 Fukashi, Matsumoto, Nagano 390-0185. (© 0263/36-0109. Fax 0263/36-0883. www.tokyuhotels.co.jp/en. 160 units. ¥8,190–¥10,185 ($78–$97) single; ¥13,650–¥25,200 ($117–$239) twin; ¥15,750–¥19,110 ($150–$182) double. AE, DC, MC, V. Turn right out of the station, then take a 3-min. walk. **Amenities:** Restaurant (Western/Japanese); bar; salon; same-day laundry/dry-cleaning service; nonsmoking rooms. *In room:* A/C, TV, minibar, hot-water pot w/tea, hair dryer, Washlet toilet, trouser press.

### INEXPENSIVE

**Enjyoh Bekkan**   Although it's a bit far from the center of Matsumoto in a community called Utusukushigara-Onsen (Utusukushigara Spa), this 32-year-old ryokan is worth recommending for its free access to the nearby hot-spring public baths, only a 3-minute walk away with both indoor and outdoor baths. Facing a field of paddies, it also has good views of the Japan Alps from some of its rooms. Eight of the clean and spacious tatami rooms have toilets and sinks, while the rest have bathrooms. Dinner is served in your room, while both Japanese and Western breakfasts are served communally in the dining hall. The ryokan also has its own hot-spring baths, open 24 hours and with views of a garden.

110 Utusukushigahara-Onsen, Satoyamabe, Matsumoto, Nagano 390-0221. (© 0263/33-7233. Fax 0263/36-2084. www.mcci.or.jp/www/enjyoh. 19 units (11 with bathroom, 8 with toilet). ¥5,565 ($53) single with toilet only, ¥6,915 ($66) single with bathroom; ¥10,290 ($98) twin with toilet only, ¥11,970 ($114) twin with bathroom; ¥13,860 ($132) triple with toilet only, ¥16,170 ($154) triple with bathroom. Spa tax ¥150 ($1.45) extra. Breakfast ¥840 ($8) extra; Japanese-style dinner ¥4,725 ($45) extra. AE, MC, V. Bus: 20 min. to Utusukushigahara-Onsen bus terminal (the last stop), then a 5-min. walk straight ahead. **Amenities:** Hot-spring baths; in-room massage; laundry service. *In room:* A/C, TV w/pay computer games, fridge, hot-water pot w/tea.

## WHERE TO DINE

Matsumoto is famous for its buckwheat noodles, which are fairly thick with a hearty flavor and can be served hot or cold, with several kinds of dips and sauces. It is also known for its *basashi*—raw horse meat.

⑤⑤ **Kura** ✦✦✦ *(Finds)* TEMPURA   This convivial restaurant occupies the ground floor of one of the largest *kura* in Matsumoto, built in the late Meiji Period and rare for its three stories (most kura are two-storied). Enter the dining room through the thick vault-like door and sit at the dark wood counter (an excellent way to meet the locals) or at one of the tables. The restaurant is known for its delicious tempura, though it also offers sushi, grilled fish, basashi, and the local cold noodles *(zaru soba)*

on its English-language menu. Your best bet is to order one of the set meals; kaiseki is available only with prior reservations.

1–10–22 Chuo. ⓒ **0263/33-6444.** Kaiseki ¥3,675 – ¥6,300 ($35–$60); tempura and sashimi set dinners ¥1,260 – ¥2,100 ($12–$20); set lunches ¥735 – ¥2,100 ($7–$29). AE, DC, V. Thurs–Tues 11:30am–2pm and 5:30–10pm. A 5-min. walk from the station. Walk down Koen Dori (left of the station; there's a McDonald's on the corner) and take the 1st left past the Parco department store.

㊚ **Nomugi** ⚔ NOODLES   There are only three tables in this well-known eatery popular with the locals, which means you may have to wait for a seat and can't dawdle over a meal. Its handmade buckwheat noodles are served until they run out, which is why the restaurant has a flexible closing time. You'll be given a sauce to pour into a cup; add green onion, wasabi, and daikon radish, then dip your soba into the mix. At the end of your meal, make a soup from the soba water stock (served in a teapot) and the soba sauce. In winter, the soba is served with boiled toppings.

2–9–11 Chuo. ⓒ **0263/36-3753.** Soba ¥1,100 ($10); half portion ¥700 ($6.65). No credit cards. Thurs–Mon 11:30am–around 2pm. Town Sneaker Bus stop: Nakamachi. A 12-min. walk from the station. Walk down Koen Dori (left of the station; there's a McDonald's on the corner), turn left at Honmachi, turn right at Nakamachi, and then take the 1st right; it will be on the left.

㊹ **Sano-Haru** (Finds) LOCAL SPECIALTIES   Dining in this cozy, one-room establishment, opened more than 60 years ago by the present proprietor's mother, is like being an invited guest in the Nishimura home, with Mr. Nishimura behind the counter and his wife serving the meals. Tempura, sashimi, grilled fish *(yakizakana),* basashi, tofu, and seasonal dishes are available, ranging from bamboo shoots in spring (which are grilled in their husks and served with miso paste) to mushrooms in autumn, both gathered from the nearby mountain forests by Mr. Nishimura himself. He also grates his own wasabi. The best thing to do is to tell him what kinds of food you like and how much you want to spend, then leave the rest to him.

4–12–8 Ote. ⓒ **0263/36-4943.** Meals start at ¥3,000 ($29) and go up. No credit cards. Mon–Sat 5–11pm. Town Sneaker Bus: Agetsuchi to the Nakamachi stop. A 20-min. walk from the station. Walk down Koen Dori (left of the station; there's a McDonald's on the corner), turn left at Honmachi, and turn right when you reach the castle; it's down this street, on the right.

㊺ **Shikimi** ⚔ EEL/SUSHI   For inexpensive Japanese fare close to Matsumoto Station, try this place specializing in eel and sushi. An atmosphere of old Japan is evoked by its traditional tiled roof, cast-iron lanterns, and interior with wooden sliding doors, small tatami rooms, wooden counter, and paper lanterns. I recommend the *unagi donburi* (strips of eel on rice), which comes with soup and pickled vegetables. If sushi is more to your liking, try one of Shikimi's platters of assorted sushi, called *moriawase.*

1–5–5 Chuo. ⓒ **0263/35-3279** or 0263/36-7716. Unagi donburi ¥1,680 – ¥1,995 ($16–$19); platters of assorted sushi (moriawase) ¥1,680 – ¥3,150 ($16–$30). No credit cards. Mon–Wed and Fri 11:45am–3pm and 4:30–9:30pm; Sat–Sun 11:45am–9pm. A 3-min. walk from the station. Walk straight east out of the station on Ekimae Dori 1 block, turn left, and walk 3 blocks; it will be on the left.

**Taiman** ⚔⚔⚔ FRENCH   If you feel like treating yourself, this ivy-covered, rustic yet elegant restaurant with a view of a garden is an excellent choice. In business for half a century and located just south of Matsumoto Castle, it offers wonderful French cuisine from a changing menu that might include grilled duck, whitefish in a shrimp cream sauce, scallops, lamb cutlet with pistachio, or grilled steak in a red-wine sauce. My yummy ¥5,250 ($50) lunch—which included bread or rice plus salad, dessert, and coffee—started with an hors-d'oeuvre plate of marinated squid, lox, cream cheese,

capers, and grated onion; the next course was crab gratin cooked in a cheese-and-tomato base resembling lasagna; and the main dish was sautéed pork wrapped in bacon and topped with cheese.

4-2-4 Ote. ⓒ 0263/32-0882. Reservations recommended. Main dishes ¥3,885–¥8,400 ($37–$80); set lunches ¥5,250–¥9,450 ($50–$90). AE, DC, MC, V. Thurs–Tues 11:30am–2pm and 5–9pm (last order 8pm). A 12-min. walk from the station. Walk straight ahead (east) on Ekimae Dori and turn left on Honmachi Dori with its post office; after the bridge, turn right at the 2nd stoplight where the NTT Building is.

## 2 Along the Nakasendo Highway: Tsumago & Magome

About 98km (61 miles) E of Nagoya; 88km (55 miles) SW of Matsumoto

If you're traveling between Nagoya and Matsumoto, you'll most likely pass through Kiso Valley in mountainous Nagano Prefecture. Formed by the Kiso River, the valley has always served as a natural passageway through the Japan Alps and was, in fact, one of two official roads linking Kyoto with Edo (Tokyo) back in the days of the Tokugawa shogunate (the other route was the Tokaido Hwy., which passes through Hakone). Known as the **Nakasendo Highway** 𝒜𝒜, it was the route of traveling *daimyo* and their entourages of samurai retainers journeying between Japan's two most important towns. To serve their needs, 11 post towns sprang up along the Nakasendo Highway. Back then, it took 3 days to travel through the valley.

Of the old post towns, ㉟ **Tsumago** 𝒜𝒜 and ㉠ **Magome** 𝒜 are two that still survive, with many of the old buildings left intact. An 8km (5-mile) pathway skirting the Kiso River links the two villages, providing hikers with the experience of what it must have been like to travel the 400-year-old Nakasendo Highway back in the days of the shogun. You can easily visit the two picturesque villages and take the hike in a 1-day excursion from Nagoya or Matsumoto, but I've included an overnight recommendation in case you want to linger.

### ESSENTIALS

**GETTING THERE**   Since neither Magome nor Tsumago is directly on a train line, you'll have to make the final journey by bus.

To reach **Magome,** take the **JR Shinano train** (which connects Nagoya and Matsumoto and departs hourly) to Nakatsugawa Station. Trains from Nagoya take about 50 minutes and cost ¥2,430 ($23) for an unreserved seat; from Matsumoto it takes about 75 minutes and costs ¥3,670 ($35). The 30-minute bus ride onward to Magome costs ¥540 ($4.15), with buses departing once or twice an hour.

To reach Tsumago, take the **JR Shinano train** to Nagiso Station and then take a 10-minute bus ride (¥270/$2.55). A taxi ride between Tsumago and Nagiso costs about ¥1,200 ($11).

Not all trains stop in Nagiso or Nakatsugawa, so make certain your train does (trains stop in Nagiso less frequently, only five times a day). Note also that buses are infrequent; be sure to inquire about bus schedules beforehand (the Matsumoto Station tourist office has information on bus schedules; see "Visitor Information," on p. 258).

**VISITOR INFORMATION**   The best way to obtain information about Kiso Valley is to stop by the **Tourist Information Center** in Tokyo or Narita or Kansai international airports to pick up a leaflet called "Kiso Valley," which provides a rough sketch of the 8km (5-mile) hiking path between Magome and Tsumago and gives some basic information about the villages; you can also stop by the tourist office in Matsumoto.

Otherwise, there's a tourist office in Tsumago (© **0264/57-3123;** open daily 8:30am–5pm) and one in Magome (© **0264/59-2336;** open daily 9am–5pm except in summer when it opens at 8:30am). No English is spoken.

**TRAVELING BETWEEN TSUMAGO & MAGOME**    If you can't walk the entire distance between Tsumago and Magome, a **bus** travels between the two villages, so you could walk around Tsumago and then take a bus to Magome for ¥650 ($6.20).

Especially useful for hikers is a **luggage-transfer service** available between Magome and Tsumago on weekends and national holidays from mid-March to mid-November (offered daily during peak season, July 20–Aug 31). Luggage is accepted at either town's tourist office no later than 11:30am, at a charge of ¥500 ($4.75) per bag, and must be picked up after your hike by 5pm.

## WALKING THE NAKASENDO HIGHWAY BETWEEN TSUMAGO & MAGOME

Allow about 3 hours for the 8km (5-mile) hike between Tsumago and Magome. It doesn't matter which town you start from, though starting from Tsumago is easier if you have heavy luggage being sent via transfer service, since starting in Magome requires an 8-minute walk from the bus stop up a steep slope to the tourist office. In any case, the trail is mainly a footpath tracing the contours of the Kiso Valley and crisscrossing the stream over a series of bridges. At times the trail follows a paved road and leads through interesting farming villages. There are public toilets along the way. Since the trail does go up some steep inclines, be sure to wear your walking shoes. And have fun—this is a great walk!

**TSUMAGO** 🐾🐾    Tsumago, the second post town from the south, is the more beautiful and authentic of the two towns. Threatened with gradual decline and desertion after the train line was constructed in 1911, bypassing Tsumago, the town experienced decades of neglect—and that's probably what ultimately saved it. Having suffered almost no modernization in the rebuilding zeal of the 20th century, Tsumago was a perfect target for renovation and restoration in the early 1970s, and in a rare show of insight, electrical wires, TV antennas, and telephone poles were hidden from sight along the main road. Thus, Tsumago looks much as it did back in the days of Edo. There are, of course, the ubiquitous souvenir shops, but many sell locally made crafts made of wood and bamboo.

On the main street of Tsumago, be sure to stop at the **Tsumagojuku Honjin** (© **0264/57-3322**), an officially appointed inn that once served as a way station for the 30 or so daimyo who used the Nakasendo Highway to travel to and from Edo. Like all *honjin* (an inn designated as the resting place for daimyo), it's divided into two parts: a large, grand area for the feudal lord and his attendants, and a few smaller, simpler rooms for the Shimazaki family, who managed the inn.

Apparently, the Shimazaki family had plans drawn up to rebuild their inn back in 1830. Renovation, however, didn't take place until 160 years later when an heir discovered the plans and gave them to the township, which rebuilt the inn according to the original plans using techniques dating from the period. You'd swear it's the original.

Across the lane is the **Waki-honjin Okuya,** the town's secondary inn, used by court nobles or by daimyo when the Honjin was already occupied. The present house, a lovely traditional structure with a garden, dates from 1877 and was rebuilt with *hinoki* cypress trees, a fact that has a special significance for this region. For centuries, all the

way through the Edo Period, wood in the Kiso Valley was as good as gold and was used instead of rice to pay taxes. Commoners, therefore, were prohibited from cutting down trees, and those who did so literally lost their heads. When the Meiji Period dawned and the ban was finally lifted, wealthy landowners were quick to rebuild in a more stately manner. Emperor Meiji himself visited the inn in 1880, and though a special tub and toilet were built just for the occasion, he stayed only 30 minutes. Next door is the **Rekishi Shiryokan,** which serves as a local history museum with displays of lacquerware, a model of how the Waki-honjin looked during the Edo Period, diagrams showing how trees were felled and transported from the steep mountainsides, and photographs of buildings in Tsumago before and after they were renovated. A ¥700 ($6.65) ticket allows admission to all three museums; all are open daily 9am to 5pm.

---

**Fun Fact  Daimyo Paranoia**

Daimyo (feudal lords) almost never ate meals prepared by local innkeepers. Rather, feudal lords traveled with their own cooks, who shopped for provisions in the village and then prepared meals in the inn's kitchen. Even then the food was first tested by a taster before the daimyo himself ate, to make sure it wasn't poisoned.

---

**MAGOME**    The southernmost post town, Magome has old inns and souvenir shops that line both sides of a steeply sloping, cobblestone road. It takes about 20 minutes to stroll through the town.

## WHERE TO STAY & DINE

Both Tsumago and Magome have simple minshuku and ryokan. I'm partial to ⑥ **Ryokan Fujioto,** Tsumago, Nagiso-machi 399-5302 (© **0264/57-3009;** fax 0264/57-2239), set back from the main road of Tsumago and buffered from foot traffic by a nice Japanese garden. The 100-year-old inn offers nine tatami rooms (none with bathroom) for ¥10,500 to ¥12,600 ($100–$120) per person, including two meals. No credit cards are accepted. What makes this a particularly good place to stay is the English-speaking owner, whose daughter volunteers as a free guide around town (you can request her services when making a reservation).

Even if you don't spend the night, you can sample the inn's meal of local specialties during lunch, served from 11am to 2:30pm daily. An English-language menu with pictures offers broiled trout, carp sashimi, raw horse meat, and other fare, as well as set meals for ¥950 to ¥1,400 ($9.05–$13).

## 3 Takayama, Little Kyoto of the Mountains ★★★

533km (331 miles) NW of Tokyo; 165km (103 miles) NE of Nagoya

Located in the Hida Mountains (part of the Japan Alps National Park), **Takayama** is surrounded by 3,000m (10,000-ft.) peaks, making the train ride here breathtaking. The town, situated along a river on a wide plateau with a population of 67,600, was founded back in the 16th century by Lord Kanamori, who selected the site because of the impregnable position afforded by the surrounding mountains. Modeled after Kyoto but also with strong ties to Edo (Tokyo), Takayama borrowed from both cultural centers in developing its own architecture, food, and crafts, all well preserved today thanks to centuries of isolation. With a rich supply of timber provided by surrounding forests,

its carpenters were legendary, creating not only beautifully crafted traditional merchants' homes in Takayama but also the Imperial Palace and temples in Kyoto.

Today, Takayama boasts a delightful and elegant historic district, called **San-machi Suji**, with homes of classical design typical of 18th-century Hida. The streets are narrow and clean and are flanked on both sides by tiny canals of running water, which in centuries past were useful for fire prevention, washing clothes, and dumping winter snow, but which now give the town its distinct character. Rising from the canals are one- and two-story homes and shops of gleaming dark wood with overhanging roofs; latticed windows and slats of wood play games of light and shadow in the white of the sunshine. In the doorways of many shops, blue curtains flutter in the breeze.

With its quaint old character, great shopping (including a lively city market), and museums, Takayama is a town that invites exploration. As you walk down the streets, you'll also notice huge cedar balls hanging from the eaves in front of several shops, indicating one of Takayama's sake breweries. Altogether there are six of them in Takayama, most small affairs. Go inside, sample the sake, and watch the men stirring rice in large vats. There are also a surprising number of museums, most housed in traditional homes and filled with historical relics and antiques.

## ESSENTIALS

**GETTING THERE   By Train**   The easiest way to reach Takayama is by direct train from Nagoya, with about 10 departures daily for the 2¼-hour trip that costs ¥5,360 ($51) for an unreserved seat. There's also one direct train a day from Osaka via Kyoto, which takes about 5 hours and costs ¥7,560 ($72).

**By Bus**   Buses depart Tokyo's Shinjuku Station four to six times daily spring through autumn, arriving in Takayama 5½ hours later and costing ¥6,500 ($62). There are fewer departures in winter, when snowfall sometimes makes roads unpassable. From Matsumoto, the **Highland Express Bus** (© 0263/35-7400 in Matsumoto, or 0577/32-1160 in Takayama) passes through mountain scenery on the 2¼-hour trip and costs ¥3,100 ($29).

**VISITOR INFORMATION**   Before you depart from Tokyo or Narita or Kansai airports, stop by the **Tourist Information Center** for the excellent "Takayama and Shirakawago" leaflet, which contains maps and travel and sightseeing information. In Takayama, the local **tourist office** (© **0577/32-5328;** open daily 8:30am–6:30pm, to 5pm Nov–Mar) is housed in a wooden booth just outside the main (east) exit of Takayama Station. You can pick up an English-language brochure with a map of the town showing the location of all museums and attractions. You can also use the tourist office's laptop for free Internet access, but you have to stand.

More information is available at **www.hidatakayama.or.jp**.

**GETTING AROUND**   Takayama is one of Japan's easiest towns to navigate. Most of Takayama's attractions lie to the east of the train station in **San-machi Suji** and are easily reached from the station in about 10 to 15 minutes **on foot.** Throughout the town are English-language signs pointing directions to the many attractions; they're even embedded in sidewalks and streets.

An alternative to walking is to rent a **bicycle** from one of the many shops ringing the station; the cost averages ¥300 ($2.85) for the first hour and ¥200 ($1.90) per additional hour.

To reach Hida Folk Village and Hida Takayama Museum of Art (see below for both), you'll have to go by **bus,** which departs from platform 6 at the bus station to

the left of the main exit of the train station. Better yet, take the free London Bus operated by the Museum of Art, with three departures daily from Takayama Station in peak season (ask the Tourist Information Center for a schedule). If you don't plan on visiting the museum, at least wander into the museum shop or have a cup of coffee on the outdoor terrace; from here it's about a 10-minute walk to the folk village.

## SEEING THE SIGHTS

Takayama's main attraction is its old merchants' houses, which are clustered together in San-machi Suji on three narrow streets called **Ichino-machi, Nino-machi,** and **Sanno-machi.** Be sure to allow time to wander around. In addition to the district's many museums, there are also shops selling Takayama's specialties, including sake, yew woodcarvings, and a unique lacquerware called *shunkei-nuri.*

Be sure, too, to visit the **Miyagawa Morning Market,** which stretches on the east bank of the Miyagawa River between Kajibashi and Yayoibashi bridges. Held every morning from 7am (6am in summer) to noon, it's very picturesque, with cloth-covered stalls selling fresh vegetables, flowers, pickled vegetables, locally made crafts, and toys.

And if you have more free time still, consider the **Higashiyama Hiking Course,** which takes you to a string of 13 temples and five shrines, nestled on a wooded hill on the east edge of town in an area called Higashiyama Teramachi. The path here stretches 3.5km (2¼ miles) end to end, but English-language signs are few and far between and the map provided by the tourist office is hopeless; you could consider getting lost part of the fun. The Higashiyama Hiking Course then continues through Shiroyama Park, site of the Kanamori clan castle until it was torn down in 1695 by order of the Tokugawa shogunate. Parts of its stone foundations still remain.

## THE TOP ATTRACTIONS

Note that the attractions listed below are closed during the New Year's holiday.

**Hida Minzoku Mura Folk Village (Hida no Sato)** ★★★ This is an open-air museum of more than 30 old thatched and shingled farmhouses, sheds, and buildings, many of which were brought here from other parts of the region to illustrate how farmers and artisans used to live in the Hida Mountain range. The whole village is picturesque, with swans swimming in the central pond, green moss growing on the thatched roofs, and flowers blooming in season. Some of the houses have *gassho-zukuri-*style roofs, built steeply to withstand the region's heavy snowfalls; the tops of the roofs are said to resemble hands joined in prayer. All the structures, which range from 100 to 500 years old, are open to the public and are filled with furniture, old spindles and looms, utensils for cooking and dining, instruments used in the silk industry, farm tools, sleds, and straw boots and snow capes for winter.

Workshops have been set up in one corner of the village grounds to demonstrate Takayama's well-known woodcarving, tie-dying, weaving, and lacquerwork industries; some of the artisans even live here. You'll probably want to spend about 1½ hours here, but if you're heading to Shirakawago, skip it; there's a similar, more accessible open-air museum there.

ⓒ 0577/34-4711. Admission ¥700 ($6.65) adults, ¥200 ($1.90) children under 15. Daily 8:30am–5pm. Either take the bus from platform 6 next to Takayama Station (a 10-min. ride) or the free London Bus to the Hida Takayama Museum of Art (then a 10-min. walk); or walk 30 min. southwest from the train station.

**Merchants' Houses** ★★★ In contrast to other castle towns during the Edo Period, Takayama was under the direct control of the Tokugawa government rather than a

feudal lord, which meant its homes were built and owned by merchants and common-ers rather than the samurai class that dominated other Japanese cities. Located side by side in San-machi Suji and both toured easily in less than 30 minutes, **Yoshijima-ke** or Yoshijima House (© 0577/32-0038) and **Kusakabe Mingeikan** (© 0577/32-0072) are merchants' mansions that once belonged to two of the richest families in Takayama. Of the two, the Yoshijima House is my favorite: With its exposed attic, heavy crossbeams, sunken open-hearth fireplace, and sliding doors, it's a masterpiece of geometric design. It was built in 1907 as both the home and factory of the Yoshi-jima family, well-to-do brewers of sake. Notice how the beams and details of the home gleam, a state attained through decades of polishing as each generation of women did their share in bringing the wood to a luster. Yoshijima-ke is also famous for its lattices, typical of Takayama yet showing an elegance influenced by Kyoto. But one of the main reasons I like this house is that its walls serve as an art gallery for the lithographs of female artist Shinoda Toko, one of my favorite Japanese artists (and a distant rela-tive of present owner Yoshijima Tadao, who also uses the house for his other passion, jazz, heard softly in the back gallery).

The Kusakabe Mingeikan, built in 1879 for a merchant dealing in silk, lamp oil, and finance, is more refined and imposing. Its architectural style is considered unique to Hida but has many characteristics common during the Edo Period, including a two-story warehouse with open beams and an earthen floor. On display are personal items such as lacquerware and chests from Japan and imports from other countries, handed down through the generations and arranged just as they would have been in the 18th and 19th centuries.

North end of Nino-machi St., Oshinmachi. Separate admission to each house: ¥500 ($4.75) for adults, ¥300 ($2.85) for children. Summer: Both open daily 9am–5pm. Winter (Dec–Feb): Yoshijima-ke Wed–Mon 9am–4:30pm; Kusakabe Mingeikan daily 9am–4:30pm.

## MORE MUSEUMS

**Fujii Folk Craft Museum (Fujii Bijutsu Mingei-Kan)** ⚔  This gallery in the heart of San-Machi Suji occupies a traditional merchant's storehouse; its entrance is a copy of an outer gate that once led to Takayama Castle. The eclectic collection from the Edo Period includes beautiful chests *(tansu)* inlaid with mother-of-pearl, sake and wine glasses, lacquerware, Imari and Kutani porcelain, tortoise-shell combs, ceremonial dolls, kimono, teakettles, paper lanterns, rice barrels, smoking utensils, matchlocks, swords, farming tools, spinning wheels, and more. Many items are identified in Eng-lish, making this a very worthwhile museum; you can see it all in about 15 minutes.

Sanno-machi St., 69 Kamisanno-machi. © 0577/35-3778. Admission ¥700 ($6.65) adults, ¥350 ($3.35) children. Daily 9am–5pm. A 12-min. walk from the train station.

㉒ **Hida Takayama Museum of Art (Hida Takayama Bijutsukan)**  Serious glass lovers will not want to miss this museum with its collection of mostly European antique and contemporary glassware from the 16th to the 20th centuries, including works by Tiffany, Lalique, and Gallé. Several rooms are furnished in decorative and applied arts by masters like Louis Majorelle, Mackintosh, and Vienna's Secessionist artists. Don't miss the museum shop, with its Japanese and imported glassware and crafts; I also like the Mackintosh-inspired tearoom with outdoor terrace seating. Plan on spending about 45 minutes here.

1–124–1 Kamiokamoto-cho. © 0577/35-3535. www.htm-museum.co.jp. Admission ¥1,300 ($12) adults, ¥1,000 ($9.50) university and high-school students, ¥800 (7.605) junior-high age and younger. Apr–Nov daily 9am–5pm;

Dec–Mar daily 9am–5pm (irregular holidays; call first). Take the bus from platform 6 to Hida Takayama Bijutsukan, or take the free London Bus.

**Hirata Folk Art Museum (Hirata Kinen-kan)** ★★    Here you'll find what is probably Takayama's most varied and extensive collection of folk art. It vividly conveys what life was like during the Edo Period by displaying household utensils, crafts, and fine arts found in a typical middle-class home; the house itself, built in 1897 in the traditional style with a sunken hearth and both living and working quarters, belonged to a candlemaker. Items are identified in English. On display are folk toys, coin boxes, mirrors, toiletry sets, *geta*, spectacles, hair adornments, *shunkei* lacquerware, and paper and kerosene lamps; my favorite is the room outfitted with items used for travel, including guide maps, portable abacuses, compasses, a traveling pillow, a folding lantern, and even a folding hat. You'll probably spend 20 minutes here.

Ichino-machi St., 39 Kaminino-machi. ✆ 0577/33-1354. Admission ¥300 ($2.85) adults, ¥150 ($1.45) children. Daily 9am–5pm.

**Historical Government House (Takayama Jinya)** ★★★    I highly recommend a visit here to anyone interested in Japanese history. The building served as the Tokugawa government's administrative building for 177 years (1692–1868). Of some 60 local government offices that were once spread throughout Japan, this is the only one still in existence. Resembling a miniature palace with its outer wall and an imposing entrance gate, the sprawling complex consists of both original buildings and reconstructions. In addition to administrative offices, chambers, and courts, the complex contained living quarters, a huge kitchen, an interrogation room with torture devices, and a 400-year-old rice granary, the oldest and biggest in Japan, where rice collected from farmers as a form of taxation was stored.

What makes a visit here especially educational are the free guided tours available in English, which last about 30 to 40 minutes and provide fascinating insight into administrative life during the Edo Period.

1–5 Hachi-ken-machi. ✆ 0577/32-0643. Admission ¥420 ($4) for adults, free for high-school age and younger. Mar–Oct daily 8:45am–5pm; Nov–Feb daily 8:45am–4:30pm. A 10-min. walk from the train station.

**Inro Museum (Inro Bijitsukan)** ★★★ *Finds*    If you're an enthusiast of the tiny, intriguing *inro,* a small portable medicine case, you must not miss this museum. If you're not yet a fan, you probably will be after visiting here. The museum displays Japan's largest collection of 18th-century inro and *netsuke,* toggles or counterweights used for hanging inro (as well as purses and tobacco pouches) from kimono sashes. All inro are displayed with their original and thematically matching netsuke intact, and some of the designs display a great sense of humor. More than 300 rare inro and netsuke are on display, and they're all wonderful works of art, with an astounding attention to detail. You'll probably want to stay at least 30 minutes, though I could spend hours here.

1–98 Oshinmachi. ✆ 0577/32-8500. Admission ¥500 ($4.75) for adults, ¥300 ($2.85) for high-school, junior-high, and elementary students. Wed–Mon 9am–5pm. Closed Dec–Mar. In a beautiful *kura* just off Omotesando Dori, not far from Yoshijima-ke.

**Lacquerware Museum (Hida Takayama Shunkei Kaikan)**    This museum, which can be toured in 15 minutes, displays Takayama lacquerware, known for the transparency of its finish, which enhances the grain of the wood. Takamaya lacquerware is admired all over Japan for its honey-colored sheen, which becomes lighter and more beautiful over time. The museum displays some 1,000 items dating from the

17th century to the present, including beautifully crafted trays, furniture, vases, rice containers, and lunch boxes; one exhibit explains the multistage production technique and tools of the craft. There's also a shop—and after seeing the time-consuming process to produce shunkei ware, you'll know why prices are high.

1–88 Kanda-cho. ✆ 0577/32-3373. Admission ¥300 ($2.85) adults, ¥200 ($1.90) high-school and junior-high students, free for children. Summer daily 8am–5:30pm; winter daily 9am–5pm. A 15-min. walk from the train station.

63 **Lion Dance Ceremony Exhibition Hall (Shishi-Kaikan)**    More than 200 lion masks from all over Japan, used to perform the lion dance in Japanese festivals, are on display here, as well as Edo-Period screens, ceramics, scrolls, coins, samurai armor, and swords. Best, however, are the 15-minute performances given every half-hour by marionettes, which decorate many of Takayama's floats in its two festivals; they're capable of wonderful acrobatics.

53–1 Sakura-machi. ✆ 0577/32-0881. Admission ¥600 ($5.70) adults, ¥400 ($3.80) junior-high age and younger. Summer daily 8:30am–5:30pm; winter daily 9am–5pm. A 1-min. walk from Takayama Festival Float Exhibition Hall (see below).

**Takayama Festival Float Exhibition Hall (Takayama Yatai Kaikan)** 𝒜    This exhibition hall displays four of the huge, elaborate floats used for Takayama's famous Takayama Matsuri (Autumn Festival). Dating mostly from the 17th century and colorfully decorated with carvings, hanging lanterns, and sometimes marionettes, floats are as high as 6.9m (23 ft.) and are mounted on wheels. Free 20-minute guided tours in English are available, making the festival hall an interesting stop if you're unable to see the festival itself.

The admission price also allows entrance to **Sakurayama Nikko Kan** next door, which houses a replica of the Toshogu Shrine in Nikko (p. 230), built almost 100 years ago at one-tenth the scale. I was initially skeptical, but the 28 buildings—complete with computerized sunsets and sunrises—are works of art.

178 Sakura-machi. ✆ 0577/32-5100. Admission ¥820 ($7.80) adults, ¥510 ($4.85) high-school students, ¥410 ($3.90) junior-high age and younger. Summer daily 8:30am–5pm; winter daily 9am–4:30pm. In the precincts of Sakurayama Hachimangu Shrine, about a 10-min. walk north of San-machi Suji or a 25-min. walk from the train station.

## WHERE TO STAY

There are more minshuku and ryokan in Takayama than hotels, making it the perfect place to stay in a traditional inn. In fact, staying in a tatami room and sleeping on a futon is the best way to immerse yourself in the life of this small community, and the best news is that there are places to fit all budgets.

You should be aware that in peak season—Golden Week (Apr 29–May 5), August, festival times in April and October, and New Year's—prices will be higher, generally between 10% and 20%.

All directions are from Takayama Station.

### EXPENSIVE

64 **Nagase** 𝒜𝒜𝒜 𝐹𝑖𝑛𝑑𝑠    The Nagase family has been running this traditional inn for 250 years, spanning 10 generations. A renovated merchant's home not far from the Historical Government House that highlights the region's strong architectural identity, it's filled with antiques. Each of the tatami guest rooms is unique, made special by carved wooden transoms, bamboo detailing, shunkei lacquer furniture, flower arrangements, and hanging scrolls in alcoves. Best of all, each room has views of one of six perfectly crafted miniature gardens, complete with small waterfalls and streams

fed by natural springs that provide their own serenade throughout the ryokan. Kyoto-style cuisine and local specialties, served on beautiful lacquerware and ceramics, are brought to your room. If you are looking for an authentic Japanese experience (not to mention Takayama's most venerable inn), look no further.

10 Kami-Nino-machi, Takayama, Gifu 506-0845. © **0577/32-0068.** Fax 0577/32-1068. 10 units (8 with bathroom, 2 with toilet only). ¥15,750–¥17,850 ($55–$170) per person with toilet only; ¥18,900–¥31,500 ($180–$299) per person with bathroom. Rates include breakfast, dinner, and service. MC, V. Just south of San-machi Suji, on Nino-machi St., a 10-min. walk from the train station. **Amenities:** Jacuzzi; in-room massage. *In room:* A/C, TV, mini-bar, hot-water pot w/tea, safe.

## MODERATE

⑥⑤ **Antique Inn Sumiyoshi** ✦✦✦ *(Finds* This calls itself a ryokan, but its price and homey atmosphere make it seem more like a minshuku. Built almost 100 years ago by a well-known local carpenter to house a silkworm industry, it opened in 1950 as a ryokan and probably hasn't changed a bit since then. An open-hearth fireplace, samurai armor, and antiques fill the reception area, where you are invited to have tea or coffee, and on the second floor there's an outdoor deck facing the river. Rooms are comfortable and old-fashioned, and many have painted screens and antiques; request one facing the river, across which you have a view of the morning market. The older women running the place don't speak English, but they're very sweet.

Honmachi 4–21, Takayama, Gifu 506-0011. © **0577/32-0228.** Fax 0577/33-8916. 10 units (1 with bathroom). ¥8,400–¥13,650 ($80–$130) per person. Rates include breakfast, dinner, and service. No credit cards. Across from historic San-machi Suji on the Miyagawa River, a 10-min. walk northeast of the station. **Amenities:** In-room massage; laundry/dry-cleaning service. *In room:* A/C, TV, minibar, hot-water pot w/tea.

**Best Western Hotel Takayama** ✦ Purists might decry the size of this 1998 chain hotel in such a historic town, but it does have a convenient location just a minute's walk from the train station and could be a lifesaver for those who do not like sleeping on the floor. Besides, at seven stories, it's not even the tallest building around, and its facade, with a replica Meiji-Era design, could be worse. Otherwise, its mostly twin rooms are fairly small and ordinary, though cheerful and bright; ask for a room on a higher floor facing east, where you have a view of mountains in the distance. The rates below reflect the season.

Hanasatocho 6–6, Takayama, Gifu 506-0026. © **0577/37-2000.** Fax 0577/37-2005. www.bestwestern.com. 78 units. ¥10,500–¥14,000 ($100–$133) single; ¥15,750–¥18,900 ($150–$180) double; ¥17,850–¥21,000 ($170–$200) twin. Rates include breakfast. AE, MC, V. Walk straight out of the station for 1 block and turn left (1 min.). **Amenities:** 3 restaurants (steak, seafood, Western); 1 lounge; in-room massage; same-day laundry/dry-cleaning service; nonsmoking rooms. *In room:* A/C, cable TV w/pay movies, fridge, hot-water pot w/tea, hair dryer, Washlet toilet.

**Four Seasons** *(Value* Although this modern-looking building with an arched roof looks out of place in Takayama, the hotel is a good choice in terms of price. Catering to business travelers during the week and tourists on weekends, it has an accommodating staff, free coffee and tea in the lobby, and a slightly feminine touch in its public spaces and rooms, which come with all the basics. Avoid the cheaper rooms on the second and third floors, as these have glazed windows. Rooms on the fourth through sixth floors have views over the city (request a corner room), with those on the sixth floor decorated with wooden furniture and wooden floors (important for the allergy conscious). A large Japanese bath with Jacuzzi and sauna overlooking a small garden is a plus. (By the way, as you may have guessed by its rates, this place is not part of the famous Four Seasons hotel chain.)

Kanda-machi 1–1, Takayama, Gifu 506-0006. © **0577/36-0088.** Fax 0577/36-0080. fseasons@aioros.ocn.ne.jp. 46 units. ¥6,900–¥7,500 ($66–$71) single; ¥13,500–¥14,500 ($128–$138) twin. Rates approximately 20% higher

per person during festival times. Rates include service charge. AE, MC, V. A 10-min. walk northeast of the train station. **Amenities:** Restaurant (local Japanese food); hot-spring indoor bath; Jacuzzi; sauna; rental bikes; in-room massage; coin-op washers and dryers; same-day laundry/dry-cleaning service. *In room:* A/C, TV, minibar, hot-water pot w/tea, hair dryer, Washlet toilet.

**Yamakyu** *&* This spotless minshuku has a deserved reputation for serving the best meals in town in its price range, though everything operates so slickly that service seems rather impersonal. Although it's a bit far from the station—about a 20-minute walk or a 5-minute taxi ride—it's located in a quiet residential area near Takayama's many temples and shrines and is only a 10-minute walk or short bike ride to the historic district. Its hallways boast a good collection of folk art, antique clocks, glassware, and lamps, and eaves above all guest-room doors give it a slight "village" atmosphere. In the mornings, free coffee is available from the small lobby lounge, where you have a view of a small courtyard garden. As with most minshuku, the Japanese-style rooms—nicely done with natural woods and artwork—are without private bathrooms (though some do have toilets), but the public baths are large and pleasant and feature turning water wheels.

Tenshoji-machi 58, Takayama, Gifu 506-0832. ⓒ **0577/32-3756.** Fax 0577/35-2350. 28 units (15 with toilet only, 13 without bathroom). ¥7,980 ($76) per person; ¥945 ($9) extra for special meals featuring festival favorites at twice-yearly festival times (mid-Apr, Oct). Rates include breakfast, dinner, and service. No credit cards. Walk straight up San-machi Suji (20 min.). **Amenities:** Rental bikes (¥500/$4.75 per day); in-room massage. *In room:* A/C, TV, hot-water pot w/tea, safe.

## INEXPENSIVE

**Minshuku Sosuke**   The entryway of this warm and friendly minshuku is filled with country knickknacks. There's an open hearth *(irori)* in the communal room to the left as you enter—if it's chilly, you'll be invited to sit down and warm yourself. Although the building housing the minshuku is 170 years old, the inside has been remodeled, and all the rooms, though simple, are clean and are nonsmoking. Note, however, that some have skylights, and that morning arrives awfully early in summer. Also, though it's not far from the station, it's in the opposite direction from the town center, making it less convenient for sightseeing.

Okamoto-machi 1–64, Takayama, Gifu 506-0054. ⓒ **0577/32-0818.** Fax 0577/33-5570. www.irori-sosuke.com. 13 units (none with bathroom). ¥7,875–¥9,450 ($75–$90) per person with 2 meals; ¥5,040 ($48) per person without meals. No credit cards. An 8-min. walk west of the station. Turn right out of the station and then take the 1st right (at the T intersection); it's over the bridge on the right side of the street, across from the Green Hotel. *In room:* A/C, TV, hot-water pot w/tea, no phone.

**Rickshaw Inn** *&& Kids*   In a modern house, centrally located between the train station and San-machi Suji, the Rickshaw Inn is welcoming and homey, due in no small part to the friendly owner, Setoyama Eiko, a Takayama native who lived in the United States and speaks flawless English. A communal living room—with sofas, TV, newspapers, a table, and an adjoining kitchen complete with refrigerator, hot plate, microwave, and toaster—is a good place to relax with fellow guests. Simple Japanese- and Western-style rooms with sinks are available, with Asian artwork on the walls and batik shades to block out light. Good for families is the one Japanese-style suite, complete with kitchenette and bathroom, that sleeps up to five people. No dinner is served, but Eiko-san is happy to recommend nearby restaurants (ask for her map) and is also knowledgeable about museums, crafts, and Takayama's history. A crafts shop with goods from all over Japan, Asia, and Africa occupies the ground floor.

Suehiro-cho 54. Takayama, Gifu 506-0016. ⓒ **0577/32-2890.** Fax 0577/32-2469. www.rickshawinn.com. 10 units (7 with bathroom). ¥4,900 ($47) single without bathroom, ¥6,500 ($62) single with bathroom; ¥9,800 ($93) twin

without bathroom, ¥11,600–¥12,600 ($110–$120) twin with bathroom. Western breakfast ¥550 ($5.25) extra. AE, DC, MC, V. A 6-min. walk east of the station, just off Kokubunji St. **Amenities:** Coin-op washer and dryer; nonsmoking rooms; communal kitchen. *In room:* A/C, TV, hot-water pot w/tea, no phone.

# WHERE TO DINE

Takayama has some local specialties you should try while you're here (they may well be served at your ryokan or minshuku). The best known is *hoba miso,* which is soybean paste mixed with dried scallions, ginger, and mushrooms and cooked on a dry magnolia leaf at your table above a small clay burner. *Sansai* are mountain vegetables, including edible ferns and other wild plants; and *ayu* is river fish, grilled with soy sauce or salt. Other favorite dishes include Takayama's own style of buckwheat noodles *(soba), mitarashi-dango* (grilled rice balls with soy sauce), and Hida beef.

All directions given are from Takayama Station.

## VERY EXPENSIVE

⑥⑥ **Kakusho** ★★★ *(Finds)* VEGETARIAN    For a big splurge, dine at Kakusho, established 180 years ago and offering local vegetarian fare called *shojin-ryori,* typically served at Buddhist temples. Situated on the slope of a hill in the eastern part of the city, a 5-minute walk from San-machi Suji, this delightful restaurant serves meals either in small, private tatami rooms dating from the Edo Period or in a larger room from the Meiji Period that can be opened to the elements on three sides, all of which overlook a dreamy, mossy garden enclosed by a clay wall. You must make a reservation to dine here. The least expensive meals consist of various mountain vegetables, mushrooms, nuts, tofu and other dishes; more dishes are added for the more expensive set meals.

2-98 Babacho. ☎ 0577/32-0174. Reservations required. Kaiseki shojin-ryori ¥10,000–¥20,000 ($95–$190); set lunches ¥5,500 ($52). No credit cards. Daily 11:30am or 1:30pm (2 lunch seatings) and 5:30–about 7pm (flexible closing time). Closed some Wed, some Thurs. Just north off of San-machi and 1 block east of Kami-ichino-machi (15 min.).

## MODERATE

⑥⑦ **Suzuya** ★★ LOCAL SPECIALTIES    Darkly lit with traditional Takayama country decor, this restaurant specializing in Takayama cuisine is so popular that if you come for lunch between noon and 1pm, you'll probably have to wait for a table. There's an English-language menu complete with photographs and explanations of each dish, including such local specialties as mountain vegetables, hoba miso, Hida beef, and *tobanyaki,* which is a stew of leeks, Japanese green peppers, mushrooms, and various chicken parts (including liver, gizzard, skin, and meat) that you cook at your table. Also cooked at the table is *sansai-misonabe,* a stew of Chinese cabbage, chicken, and various mountain vegetables flavored with miso.

Hanakawa-cho 24. ☎ 0577/32-2484. Reservations recommended in summer and during festivals. Set meals ¥1,500–¥4,000 ($14–$38). AE, DC, MC, V. Wed–Mon 11am–3pm and 5–8pm. Just off Kokubunji St., halfway between the station and the Miyagawa River (6 min.); look for the curtains with bells hanging above the front door and the cedar ball hanging from the eaves.

## INEXPENSIVE

**Agura** ★★ *(Finds)* LOCAL SPECIALTIES/PIZZA    A converted rice *kura,* with a high-beamed ceiling, wooden floors, slabs of wood for tables, and locally crafted bent-wood chairs, makes for a lovely, airy setting, heightened by eclectic cuisine, hip waiters, and jazz. The English-language menu has lots of great salads (I especially like the "Agura Original Salad" with lettuce, spinach, boiled egg, tomato, ham, tuna, and sprouts), pizzas fired in a wood-burning stove, and food that goes down well with beer, including roasted tuna with a honey sauce, Vietnamese spring rolls, and steaks served with garlic soy sauce.

4–7 Shinmeicho ✆ **0577/37-2666.** Main dishes ¥880–¥1,500 ($8.35–$14). AE, MC, V. Tues–Sun 6pm–midnight. On the road that runs to the south of Takayama City Memorial Hall, on the right side (look for the green sign with the yellow seated Buddha; 12 min.).

⑥⑧ **Myogaya** VEGETARIAN    Just a minute's walk east of the train station, this tiny shop packed with books and some health foods offers a limited selection of organic set meals (only available until 3pm) from an English-language menu, including chicken or veggie curry and stir-fried rice, which come with salad, miso soup, and vegetables. Drinks range from organic coffee to plum juice and wine made from organic grapes. The friendly proprietress makes this a pleasant place to come even for just a drink or a snack, served from 3 to 5pm.

Hanasato-cho 5–15. ✆ **0557/32-0426.** Set meals ¥950 – ¥1,000 ($8.10–$9.50). No credit cards. Wed–Mon 11:30am–5pm.

## 4 Rural Shirakawago & Ogimachi

555km (347 miles) NW of Tokyo

With its thatched-roof farmhouses, paddies trimmed with flower beds, roaring river, and pine-covered mountains rising on all sides, **Shirakawago** is one of the most picturesque regions in Japan. Unfortunately, it also has more than its fair share of tour buses (especially in May, Aug, and Oct), but because of its rather remote location and because it's accessible only by car or bus, Shirakawago still remains off the beaten path for most foreign tourists. A visit to this rural region could well be the highlight of your trip.

Although Shirakawago stretches about 39km (24 miles) beside the Shokawa River and covers 229 sq. km (142 sq. miles), mountains and forest account for 95% of the region, and Shirakawago's 2,000 residents and cultivated land are squeezed into a valley averaging less than 3.2km (2 miles) in width. Thus, land in Shirakawago for growing rice and other crops has always been scarce and valuable. As a result, farmhouses were built large enough to hold extended families, with as many as several dozen family members living under one roof. Because there wasn't enough land available for young couples to marry and build houses of their own, only the eldest son was allowed to marry; the other children were required to spend their lives living with their parents and helping with the farming. But even though younger children weren't allowed to marry, a man was allowed to choose a young woman, visit her in her parents' home, and father her children. The children then remained with the mother's family, becoming valuable members of the labor force.

Before the roads came to Shirakawago, winter always meant complete isolation as snow 2m (6 ft.) deep blanketed the entire region. Open-hearth fireplaces *(irori)* in the middle of a communal room were used both for cooking and for warmth, and because there were no chimneys, smoke simply rose into the levels above. The family lived, therefore, on the ground floor, while upper floors were used for silk cultivation and storage of utensils. Because of the heavy snowfall, thatched roofs were constructed at steep angles, known as *gassho-zukuri* in reference to the fact that the tops of the roofs look like hands joined in prayer. The steep angle also allowed rain to run off quickly, and the thatch (Japanese pampas grass) dried quickly in the sun, preventing decay.

Today, there are about 115 thatched farmhouses, barns, and sheds in Shirakawago, most of them built about 200 to 300 years ago. The thatched roofs are about .6m (2 ft.) thick and last some 40 years. The old roofs are replaced in Shirakawago every April,

when one to four roofs are changed on successive weekends. The whole process involves about 200 people, who can replace one roof in a couple of days.

Shirakawago's inhabitants live in several small villages. Of these, **Ogimachi** 🌟🌟🌟, declared a UNESCO World Cultural and Natural Heritage site in 1995, boasts the greatest concentration of thatched-roof buildings. With just 600 residents, it's a delightful hamlet of narrow lanes winding past thatched-roof farmhouses, which stand like island sentinels surrounded by paddies. Many of the farmhouses have been turned into minshuku, souvenir shops, restaurants, and museums, including an **open-air museum** that depicts life in the region before roads opened it to the rest of the world.

## ESSENTIALS

**GETTING THERE**    The most common way to reach Ojimachi is by **bus** from Takayama, which takes about 1¾ hours and costs ¥2,400 ($23). There are usually six departures from Takayama daily April through November, less frequently in winter (heavy winter snowfall sometimes renders the road impassable). Reservations are required (𝄞 **0577/32-1688**). From Kanazawa, a bus operates twice daily mid-March through November; the fare is ¥1,800 ($17) for the 1¼-hour trip. In any case, buses arrive at a parking lot next to the Gassho zukuri Minkaen open-air museum (below); minshuku are located on the other side of the river, reached via footbridge.

**VISITOR INFORMATION**    There are two **tourist offices** (𝄞 **05769/6-1751** or 05769/6-1013; both open daily 9am–5pm). If you're arriving by bus, most convenient is the one located at the edge of the parking lot; the other one is across the river on the main road in the center of town. Both will reserve a room in a minshuku if you haven't already done so, and you can pick up an English-language map.

**GETTING AROUND**    Your own two feet can do it best. You can **walk** from one end of the village to the other in about 15 minutes; English-language signs direct you to the various attractions.

## SEEING THE SIGHTS IN & AROUND OGIMACHI

In addition to an open-air museum, several old farmhouses in Ogimachi are open to the public. *Note:* Since Ogimachi is so small, no addresses are given in this section. This is a very small village, basically just one main street and some side streets.

⑥⑨ **Doburoku Matsuri no Yakata (Festival Hall)**    This Festival Hall was erected in honor of the Doburoku Matsuri Festival held in Shirakawago every year from October 14 to October 19. Centering on a locally produced, potent sake, the festival is held just outside the museum's grounds at Hachimanjinja Shrine. If you've never seen a Japanese festival, you might want to come here to see some of the costumes worn during the festival, sample the festive sake, and watch a 20-minute video of the yearly festivities.

𝄞 05769/6-1655. Admission ¥300 ($2.85) adults, ¥100 (95¢) junior-high and elementary students. Daily 9am–4pm. Closed Oct 13–16 and Dec–Mar.

⑦⓪ **Gasshozukuri Seikatsu Shiryokan** 🌟🌟 *Finds*    This thatched-roof farmhouse is the best museum in town for seeing local farm and household implements and folkcrafts, including cooking utensils, lacquerware, pottery, obento lunch boxes, coins, clothing, and other personal items. Note the bamboo pipe for bringing running water into the house, the Buddhist family altar, the samurai outfits, and photographs of the imperial family. The upstairs is crammed with all kinds of farming tools and items used in everyday life, from mountain backpacks and handmade skis to the

*Moments* **A View of Ogimachi**

For an overview (and the best vantage point for photographs) of the entire village, walk along the gently sloping road that leads from the north side of Ogimachi to the **Shirayama Viewing Point** ☞☞. There's a souvenir shop/restaurant here, but the best thing to do is to turn left at the crest of the hill and walk to the hill's westernmost point (toward the river), where there are some secluded benches. From here, you'll have a marvelous view of the whole valley. If you're thirsty or hungry, go to the restaurant to buy a drink or a snack and then take it with you to the lookout.

wooden hammers used for pounding rice and the implements used for silk cultivation. The fascinating collection makes it easy to spend 20 minutes here.

© **05769/6-1818.** Admission ¥300 ($2.85) adults, ¥150 ($1.45) children. Apr–Nov daily 9am–5pm. Closed Dec–Mar. Located on the southern edge of town past the Jyuemon minshuku (see "Where to Stay," below).

**Shirakawago Gassho Zukuri Minkaen** ☞☞☞  To see how rural people lived in centuries past, visit Shirakawago's top attraction, this open-air museum with 25 *gasshozukuri* houses and sheds that were relocated and restored here. Filled with the tools of everyday life, the buildings are picturesquely situated around ponds, paddies, flower beds, and streams, a photographer's dream. The museum also serves as an artists' colony, where artisans engage in such traditional handicrafts as woodworking, pottery, and weaving; their products are for sale on-site. You can easily spend an hour here.

© **05769/6-1231.** Admission ¥500 ($4.75) adults, ¥300 ($2.85) children 7–15. Apr–July and Sept–Nov daily 8:40am–5pm; Aug daily 8am–5:30pm; Dec–Mar Fri–Wed 9am–4pm. If Thurs is a national holiday, the museum remains open but closes Wed instead. Across the Shokawa River from Ogimachi, over a pedestrian suspension bridge.

㋛ **Wada Ke** ☞  This thatched-roof home is Ogimachi's finest, not surprising since it belonged to the wealthy Wada family who served as the region's top officials. Still occupied by the Wada family, the 300-year-old house boasts carved transoms, painted sliding doors, lacquerware passed down through generations, a family altar, and tatami rooms overlooking a private garden. Upstairs you can see how the heavy roof beams are held together using only rope (no nails were used), as well as containers once used in silkworm cultivation. It takes only 10 minutes to see everything.

© **05769/6-1058.** Admission ¥300 ($2.85) adults, ¥150 ($1.45) children. Daily 9am–5pm. Occasionally closed. Just north of the main street.

## WHERE TO STAY

Because huge extended families living under one roof are a thing of the past, many residents of Ogimachi have turned their gassho-zukuri homes into **minshuku.** Staying in one gives you the unique chance to lodge in a thatched farmhouse with a family that might consist of grandparents, parents, and children. English is often limited to the basics of "bath," "breakfast," and "dinner," but smiles go a long way. Most likely, the family will drag out their family album with its pictures of winter snowfall and the momentous occasion when their thatched roof was repaired. What I like best about staying overnight in Ogimachi is that most Japanese tourists (about 4,000 on average daily), are day-trippers, which means you have the village pretty much to yourself by late afternoon. Be sure to take an evening or early morning stroll.

Most minshuku are fairly small, with about four to nine tatami rooms open to guests. Rooms are basic without bathroom or toilet (the communal toilets are sometimes nonflush style), and you may be expected to roll out your own futon. Privacy may be limited, as only a flimsy sliding partition may separate you from the guest next door. All recommended minshuku below are in thatch-roofed homes; rates include breakfast and dinner (add ¥400/$3.80 in winter for heating charges), and none accept credit cards or have private bathrooms. The tourist office can make a reservation for you at these or any of the others around town.

72 **Jyuemon** 🌟🌟   Jyuemon is a favorite among foreigners traveling in Japan. This attractive minshuku, in a 270-year-old farmhouse, features a stone-ringed pond with flowering shrubs and a couple of benches where you can relax and enjoy the view. In addition, there's an irori in the dining room, and the bathroom facilities feature flush toilets. The outgoing 70-something Mrs. Sakai who runs this place is quite a character; don't be surprised if she serenades you during dinner with a *shamisen* and folk songs.

Shirakawa Mura, Ogimachi, Ono-gun, Gifu 501-5627. ✆ **05769/6-1053**. 6 units. ¥8,400 ($80) per person. A 10-min. walk from the bus stop, on the south edge of Ogimachi past Doburoku Festival Hall.

73 **Koemon** 🌟🌟🌟   This is my top choice for accommodations, mainly because of fifth-generation innkeeper Otani Shoji and his wife Mutsuko. Otani-san speaks English and is enthusiastic about imparting information about his 200-year-old farmhouse, which became a minshuku 30 years ago and was recently modernized with a heated floor, automatic sensor lights, communal Washlet toilets, and even dim switches to enhance the mood around his irori fireplace. Best of all, he has transformed his attic into a theater where he's happy to show his guests 100 slides of Shirakawago through the seasons. Rooms are spotless, with the best one facing a pond.

Shirakawa Mura, Ogimachi, Ono-gun, Gifu 501-5627. ✆ **05769/6-1446**. Fax 05769/6-1748. 4 units (none with bathroom). ¥8,400 ($80) per person. A 2-min. walk from the bus stop, beside the footbridge over the Shokawa River. *In room:* Hot-water pot w/tea.

74 **Nodaniya** 🌟🌟   Life in this minshuku centers around the irori, where you dine on what coauthor Janie considers some of the best food she's ever had in a minshuku. The family is very friendly. The minshuku is equipped with flush toilets and a communal cedar bath.

Shirakawa Mura, Ogimachi, Ono-gun, Gifu 501-5627. ✆ **05769/6-1011**. Fax 05769/6-1218. 5 units. ¥8,200 ($78) per person. A 7-min. walk from the bus stop, across from Hachimanjinja Shrine.

## WHERE TO DINE

Since all minshuku and ryokan serve breakfast and dinner, you'll only need to find a place for lunch.

75 **Irori** LOCAL SPECIALTIES   A huge block of gnarled wood sits outside Irori's front door. Inside, this gassho-zukuri house is appropriately rustic and has an irori. The menu, in Japanese only, includes fresh river fish *(ayu)*, wild mountain vegetables *(sansai)*, hoba miso (soybean paste cooked on a magnolia leaf over a small clay pot), and sansai soba. I opted for the *yakidofu teishoku* set meal, which consisted of fried tofu covered with fish flakes, vegetables, rice, and soup. The food here is not sensational, but it is good for lunch and includes local specialties. In any case, there are hardly any restaurant choices in the village.

✆ **05769/6-1737**. Set meals ¥1,200–¥2,000 ($11–$19). No credit cards. Wed–Mon 9am–3 or 5pm, depending on whether there are customers. A 5-min. walk from the bus stop, on Ogimachi's main road in the direction of the Shirayama Viewing Point.

# Kyoto & Nara

If you go to only one place in all of Japan, **Kyoto** ✿✿✿ should be it. Not only is it the most historically significant town in the nation, this former capital was also the only major Japanese city spared from the bombs of World War II. As such, it's rife with temples, shrines, imperial palaces, and traditional wooden homes. In nearby **Nara** ✿✿, another former capital—one even more ancient than Kyoto—is Japan's largest bronze Buddha and more historic temples.

Even though its well-preserved architecture and relics are what put Kyoto on the sightseeing map, I've always felt that its scenes from daily life are what make the city exceptional. Kyoto is home to 20% of Japan's national treasures. It is also home to the nation's greatest concentration of craft artisans, making Kyoto famous for its shops dealing in textiles, dyed fabrics, pottery, bambooware, cutlery, metalwork, fans, umbrellas, and other goods.

As your Shinkansen bullet train glides toward Kyoto Station, however, your first reaction is likely to be great disappointment. There's Kyoto Tower looming in the foreground like some misplaced spaceship. Kyoto Station itself is strikingly modern and unabashedly high tech, looking as though it was airlifted straight from Tokyo. Modern buildings and hotels surround the station on all sides, making Kyoto look like any other Japanese town.

In other words, as Japan's seventh-largest city with a population of about 1.5 million people, Kyoto hasn't escaped the afflictions of the modern age. Yet it has always led a rather fragile existence, as

a look at any of its temples and shrines will tell you. Made of wood, they've been destroyed through the years by man, fire, and earthquake and have been rebuilt countless times. Come and explore—you'll soon understand why I consider Kyoto to be Japan's most romantic city despite modernization. No one who comes to this country should miss the wealth of experiences this ancient capital has to offer.

**A LOOK AT THE PAST** Kyoto served as Japan's capital for more than 1,000 years from 794 to the Meiji Restoration in 1868. Originally known as Heian-kyo, it was laid out in a grid pattern borrowed from the Chinese with streets running north, south, east, and west. Its first few hundred years—from about A.D. 800 to the 12th century—were perhaps its grandest, a time when culture blossomed and court nobility led luxurious and splendid lives dotted with poetry-composing parties and moon-gazing events. Buddhism flourished and temples were built. A number of learning institutions were set up for the sons and daughters of aristocratic families, and scholars were versed in both Japanese and Chinese.

Toward the end of the Heian Period, military clans began clashing for power as the samurai class grew more powerful, resulting in a series of civil wars that eventually pushed Japan into the Feudal Era of military government that lasted nearly 680 years—until 1868. The first shogun to rise to power was Minamoto Yoritomo, who set up his shogunate government in

Kamakura. With the downfall of the Kamakura government in 1336, however, Kyoto once again became the seat of power, home to both the imperial family and the shogun. The beginning of this era, known as the Muromachi and Azuchi-Momoyama periods, was marked by extravagant prosperity and luxury, expressed in such splendid shogun villas as Kyoto's Gold Pavilion and Silver Pavilion. Lacquerware, landscape paintings, and the art of metal engraving came into their own. Zen Buddhism was the rage, giving rise to such temples as Saihoji Temple and the Ryoanji rock garden. And despite the civil wars that rocked the nation in the 15th and 16th centuries and destroyed much of Kyoto, culture flourished. During these turbulent times, Noh drama, the tea ceremony, flower arranging, and landscape gardening gradually took form.

Emerging as victor in the civil wars, Tokugawa Ieyasu established himself as shogun and set up his military rule in Edo (presently Tokyo) far to the east. For the next 250 years, Kyoto remained the capital in name only, and in 1868 (which marked the downfall of the shogunate and the restoration of the emperor to power), the capital was officially moved from Kyoto to Tokyo.

## 1 Orientation

### GETTING THERE

**FROM KANSAI AIRPORT**   If you arrive in Japan at Kansai International Airport (KIX) outside Osaka, the **JR Haruka Super Express train** has direct service every 30 minutes to Kyoto Station; the trip takes approximately 75 minutes. It costs ¥3,490 ($33) for a reserved seat (recommended during busy departure times or peak season) and ¥2,980 ($28) for a nonreserved seat, or you can ride free with your JR Rail Pass. A cheaper (¥1,830/$17), though less convenient, alternative is the **JR Kanku Kaisoku,** which departs every 30 minutes or so from Kansai Airport and arrives in Kyoto 100 to 120 minutes later with a change at Osaka Station.

If you have a lot of luggage, I recommend taking the **Airport Limousine Bus** (© 075/682-4400) from Kansai Airport; buses depart every hour or less for the 105-minute trip to Kyoto Station. Fare is ¥2,300 ($22) one-way.

**BY TRAIN FROM ELSEWHERE IN JAPAN**   Kyoto is one of the major stops on the Shinkansen bullet train; trip time from **Tokyo** is 2½ hours, with the fare for a nonreserved seat ¥12,710 ($121) one-way if you don't have a rail pass. Kyoto is only 20 minutes from Shin-Osaka Station in **Osaka,** but you may find it more convenient to take one of the local commuter lines that connect Kyoto directly with Osaka Station. From **Kobe,** you can reach Kyoto from Sannomiya and Motomachi stations. The strikingly modern **Kyoto Station,** which is like a city in itself with tourist offices, restaurants, a hotel, a department store, a shopping arcade, a theater, and stage events, is connected to the rest of the city by subway and bus.

**BY BUS FROM TOKYO**   Night buses depart from Tokyo every evening for Kyoto, arriving the next morning. Buses depart from Tokyo Station at both 10 and 10:50pm, arriving in Kyoto at 5:51am and 6:41am respectively, and from Shinjuku Station at 11:10 and 11:50pm, arriving in Kyoto at 6:51 and 7:31am. The fare for these buses is ¥8,180 ($78) one-way or ¥14,480 ($138) round-trip. Cheaper still are the Seishun Dream buses that depart Tokyo Station at 8:50pm and Shinjuku Station at 9:10pm, arriving in Kyoto at 5am and 5:11am respectively and costing ¥5,000 ($48) one-way. In addition, day buses depart Tokyo Station several times daily, with fares starting at

## Frommer's Favorite Kyoto Experiences

**Spending a Night in a Ryokan**   Kyoto is one of the best places in Japan to experience the traditional inn, where you'll sleep on a futon in a tatami room and be treated to a beautifully presented multicourse kaiseki feast, perhaps with a view of your own private garden. Though expensive, it's the utmost in simple elegance.

**Dining on a Tofu Vegetarian Meal in a Garden Setting**   *Shojin ryori,* vegetarian meals served at Buddhist temples, are one of Kyoto's specialties. There are a number of rustic restaurants with outdoor garden seating throughout Kyoto.

**Visiting a Japanese Garden**   Kyoto has a wide range of traditional gardens, from austerely beautiful Zen rock gardens used by Buddhist priests for meditation to the miniature bonsai-like landscape gardens of the ruling classes.

**Strolling through Eastern Kyoto**   Temples, shrines, gardens, craft shops, traditional neighborhoods—these are highlights of a day spent walking through this historic part of Kyoto. You won't find a slice of old Japan like this in other Japanese cities.

**Shopping for Traditional Crafts**   Traditional arts and crafts thrive in Kyoto, where skills are passed down from generation to generation. You'll find small specialty shops selling everything from fans to wooden combs.

**Seeing How the Upper Class Lived**   Kyoto has more imperial palaces and villas than any other Japanese city. Walk through the shogun's digs at Nijo Castle and if you have time, visit the Kyoto Imperial Palace, Katsura Imperial Villa, or Shugakuin Imperial Villa with their splendid gardens.

**Exploring Gion**   Kyoto's traditional pleasure quarter is fascinating for its austere architecture, hushed atmosphere, and the sight of heavily made-up geisha in traditional kimono hurrying to their evening appointments. Though touristy, Gion Corner is your best bet for observing performances of traditional dance, puppetry, and other cultural presentations.

**Watching Cormorant Fishing along the Oi River in Arashiyama**   There's no more romantic way to spend a summer's evening than drifting down the river in a wooden boat decorated with paper lanterns, watching the fishermen and their cormorants at work. It's simply magical.

**Taking an Evening Stroll through Pontocho**   A small, narrow pedestrian lane, Pontocho is lined with a dazzling collection of brightly lit hostess bars, restaurants, and drinking establishments. If it's a warm night, end the evening by sitting for a while along the banks of the nearby Kamo River, a popular spot for Kyoto's young couples.

¥5,700 ($54). Tickets can be purchased at any major JR station or a travel agency. Contact the **Tourist Information Center (TIC)** in Tokyo for more information (see "Visitor Information" in chapter 4).

## VISITOR INFORMATION

Although there's a **Kyoto City Tourist Information Office** (© 075/343-6656; open daily 8:30am–7pm) on the second floor of Kyoto Station, it's for Japanese only. Foreign visitors are requested to visit the roomier but less convenient **Kyoto Tourist Information** on the ninth floor of Isetan department store in Kyoto Station (© 075/ 344-3300), which can prove quite a challenge if you're toting luggage and battling shoppers for space in the crowded elevators. Surprisingly, there are no brochure racks here to peruse, so you have to wait your turn to ask English-speaking staff for city and bus maps and sightseeing pamphlets. It's open daily 10am to 6pm, closed the second and fourth Tuesday of every month. You can also make reservations here for inexpensive lodging throughout Japan free of charge.

**ON THE WEB**   Check out the city's website at raku.city.kyoto.jp/sight_e.phtml and Kyoto Prefecture's website at www.pref.Kyoto.jp/visitkyoto/en.

**TOURIST PUBLICATIONS**   In addition to the brochures and leaflets distributed by the Kyoto Tourist Information office, a monthly tabloid distributed free at hotels, restaurants, and the tourist office is the *Kyoto Visitor's Guide* (www.kyotoguide. com), with maps, a calendar of events, and information on sightseeing and shopping. *Kansai Scene* (www.kansaiscene.com) is a monthly giveaway with information on nightlife, festivals, and other events in Kyoto, Osaka, and Kobe. In addition, a monthly English-language magazine, *Kansai Time Out,* carries information and articles on Kyoto, Osaka, and Nara. It's available in Kyoto for ¥300 ($2.85) at Junkudo Kyoto BAL bookstore, located in the BAL department store, on the east side of Kawaramachi Dori north of Shijo Dori (© 075/253-6460; open daily 11am–8pm).

## CITY LAYOUT

Most of Kyoto's attractions and hotels are north of Kyoto Station (take the Central exit), spreading like a fan toward the northeast and northwest. The **northern and eastern edges** of the city contain the most famous temples. The heart of the city is in **central Kyoto (Nakagyo-ku ward),** which boasts the largest concentration of restaurants, shops, and bars and which radiates outward from the intersection of Kawaramachi Dori and Shijo Dori. It includes a narrow street called Pontocho, a nightlife mecca that runs along the western bank of the Kamo River. Across the Kamo River to the east is the ancient geisha district of Gion.

**FINDING AN ADDRESS**   Kyoto's streets are laid out in a grid pattern with named streets (a rarity in Japan) and an address system that's actually quite easy to understand once you get to know the directional terms. Streets north of Kyoto Station that run east-west are numbered; for example, the *shi* of Shijo Dori means "Fourth Avenue." *Agaru* means "to the north," *sagaru* means "to the south," *nishi-iru* means "to the west," and *higashi-iru* means "to the east." Thus, an address that reads Shijo-agaru means "north of Fourth Avenue."

Many addresses also indicate which cross streets a building is near. Take the Hotel Gimmond, for example: Its address is Takakura Oike Dori, which tells you that the hotel is near the intersection of Takakura Dori and Oike Dori. Complete addresses include the ward, or *ku,* such as Higashiyama-ku.

# KYOTO'S NEIGHBORHOODS IN BRIEF

The following are Kyoto's main tourist areas; to locate them, see the "Kyoto" map on p. 288.

**Around Kyoto Station** The southern ward of **Shimogyo-ku,** which stretches from Kyoto Station north to Shijo Dori Avenue, caters to tourists with its cluster of hotels and to commuters with its shops and restaurants. Kyoto Station, which caused quite a controversy when built because of its size, height, and futuristic appearance, is now this area's top attraction with Isetan department store, a shopping arcade, restaurants, a cinema, a theater, and dramatic public spaces, including a rooftop plaza.

**Central Kyoto Nakagyo-ku,** the central part of Kyoto west of the Kamo River and north of Shimogyo-ku, embraces Kyoto's main shopping and nightlife districts, with most of the action on **Kawaramachi** and **Shijo Dori** avenues and **Teramachi** and **Shin-kyogoku** covered shopping arcades. Most of Kyoto's legendary craft stores are located here, along with numerous restaurants and bars. Home also to **Nijo Castle,** Nakagyo-ku has a number of exclusive ryokan tucked away in delightful neighborhoods typical of old Kyoto. But downtown is changing fast, as Kyoto's younger generation lays claim to new shopping and entertainment complexes, such as **Shin-Puh-Kan,** a renovated telephone company building on Karasuma Dori filled with shops and restaurants and an open stage for concerts. Nakagyo-ku is one of the most desirable places to stay in terms of convenience and atmosphere.

**Pontocho,** a narrow lane that parallels the Kamo River's western bank just a stone's throw from the Kawaramachi-Shijo Dori intersection, is Kyoto's most famous street for nightlife. It's lined with bars and restaurants that boast outdoor verandas extending over the Kamo River in summer.

**Eastern Kyoto** East of the Kamo River, the wards of **Higashiyama-ku** and **Sakyo-ku** boast a number of the city's most famous temples and shrines, as well as restaurants specializing in Kyoto cuisine and Buddhist vegetarian dishes, and shops selling local pottery and other crafts. Eastern Kyoto is a great area for walking and shopping, particularly Higashiyama-ku, and boasts several ryokan as well. **Gion,** Kyoto's most famous geisha entertainment district, is part of Higashiyama-ku. Customers are entertained in traditional wooden geisha houses that are not open to the public (you can only gain entry through introductions provided by someone who is already a customer)—but the area makes for a fascinating stroll.

**Northern Kyoto** Embracing the **Kita-ku, Kamigyo-ku,** and **Ukyo-ku** wards, northern Kyoto is primarily residential but contains a number of Kyoto's top sights, including the Kyoto Imperial Palace, Kinkakuji (Temple of the Golden Pavilion), and Ryoanji Temple, site of Kyoto's most famous Zen rock garden.

## 2 Getting Around

Kyoto is Japan's most visitor-friendly city, with lots of English-language signs and an easy-to-navigate transportation system.

**BY PUBLIC TRANSPORTATION**    Kyoto's subway and bus networks are efficient and quite easy to use, but one of the best ways to explore is by foot.

**By Subway**   Kyoto is growing by leaps and bounds—there are now two subway lines. The older **Karasuma Line** runs north and south, from Takeda in the south to Kokusai Kaikan in the north, with stops at Kyoto Station and Imadegawa Station (convenient for visiting the Imperial Palace). The newer **Tozai Line** runs in a curve from east to west and is convenient for visiting Nijo Castle and Higashiyama-ku. Stops are announced in English. The subway lines intersect in central Kyoto at Karasuma Oike Station. Fares start at ¥200 ($1.90), and service runs from 5:30am to about 11:30pm. Although buses are generally more convenient (they usually get you closer to where you want to go), I sometimes opt for the subway even if I have to walk a bit, simply to avoid hassling with buses and their unknown stops.

**By Bus**   The easiest way to get around Kyoto and to most of its attractions is by bus. Buses depart from Kyoto Station's Central (north/Karasuma) exit, with platforms clearly marked in English listing the bus destinations. The Kyoto Tourist Information office gives out an excellent map showing major bus routes (see "Visitor Information," above). Some of the buses loop around the city, while others go back and forth between two destinations. Most convenient for sightseeing is Raku bus no. 100 (some of which look like old-fashioned trolleys), which makes a run every 10 minutes from Kyoto Station to major attractions in east Kyoto, including the Kyoto National Museum, Gojo-zaka (the approach to Kiyomizu Temple), Gion, Heian Shrine, Nanzenji, and Ginkakuji. Raku bus no. 101 departs Kyoto Station for Nijo Castle and Kinkakuji.

The fare for traveling in central Kyoto is ¥220 ($2.10) for a single ride or ¥500 ($4.75) for a 1-day pass (good for all local buses). Board the bus at the rear entrance and pay when you get off. If the bus is traveling a **long distance** out to the suburbs, there will be a ticket machine right beside the back door—take the ticket and hold onto it. It has a number on it and will tell the bus driver when you got on and how much you owe. You can see for yourself how much you owe by looking for your number on a lighted panel at the front of the bus; the longer you stay on the bus, the higher the fare.

**TRANSIT PASSES**   If you think you'll be doing a lot of sightseeing in 1 or 2 days, it may pay to buy a pass. A **day pass** only for buses costs ¥500 ($4.75). Passes for both buses and subways cost ¥1,200 ($11) for 1 day or ¥2,000 ($19) for 2 days. You can purchase passes at subway stations, the city bus center at Kyoto Station, and major hotels. In addition, **prepaid cards** are available in different values and can be used for the subway and most city buses. Because there is no time limit, they're convenient if you're staying in Kyoto for several days.

**BY TAXI**   Taxis in Kyoto come in two different sizes with only slightly different fares. Small ones are ¥580 ($5.50) for the first 2km (1¼ miles), and large ones are ¥640 ($6.10). Taxis can be waved down or, in the city center, boarded at marked taxi stands or at hotels. **MK Taxi** (⌀ 075/721-4141) has the cheapest fares and also offers individualized English-language guided tours.

**BY BICYCLE**   A popular way to get around Kyoto is by bike, made easy because there are few hills and because most streets are named. You do, however, have to be on guard for vehicular traffic. **Kyoto Cycling Tour Project,** a 3-minute walk from the Central (north) Exit of Kyoto Station (turn left upon exiting the station and walk past the post office and APA Hotel; ⌀ 075/354-3636; www.kctp.net), open daily 9am to 7pm, rents bikes beginning at ¥1,000 ($9.50) a day.

## FAST FACTS: Kyoto

*Area Code* If you're calling a Kyoto number from outside Kyoto but within Japan, the area code for Kyoto is **075**. For calls within Kyoto, don't dial the area code. For details on calling Kyoto from outside Japan, see "Telephones," in "Fast Facts: Japan," in chapter 2.

*Climate* Kyoto is generally hotter and more humid than Tokyo in summer and colder than Tokyo in winter. For more information, see "When to Go" in chapter 2.

*Currency Exchange* In addition to banks, good places to exchange money after banks close are large department stores like Isetan, Takashimaya, and Daimaru, and the Kyoto Handicraft Center (p. 333). You can also exchange money at the World Currency Shop on the eighth floor of Kyoto Station (ⓒ **075/365-7750**), open Monday to Friday 11am to 5pm. When changing money, be sure to bring your passport. The most convenient ATMs accepting foreign credit cards are at Kyoto Central Post Office next to Kyoto Station and at the Nakagyo-ku Post Office (see "Post Offices," below) in central Kyoto.

*Dentists & Doctors* **Sakabe International Clinic,** Gokomachi, Nijo-sagaru, Nakagyo-ku (ⓒ **075/231-1624**), has an English-speaking staff. Otherwise, ask Kyoto Tourist Information or the concierge of your hotel for a list of English-speaking doctors.

*Electricity* In both Kyoto and Nara it's 100 volts, 60 cycles, almost the same as in the United States (110 volts, 60 cycles); your two-pronged appliances should work, but they'll run a little slowly (there are no three-pronged plugs in Japan).

*Hospitals* Most hospitals are not equipped to handle emergencies 24 hours a day, but a system has been set up in which hospitals handle emergencies on a rotating basis. English is spoken at **Japan Baptist Hospital (Nihon Baputesuto Byoin),** north of Kikage, east of Shirakawa, Sakyo-ku (ⓒ 075/781-5191). Also in Kyoto are **Kyoto University Hospital (Kyoto Daigaku Byoin),** Shogoin Kawahara-cho, Sakyo-ku (ⓒ 075/751-3111), and **Kyoto Municipal Hospital (Kyoto Shiritsu Byoin),** Gojo Dori Onmae, Nakagyo-ku (ⓒ 075/311-5311). There's also a **holiday emergency clinic** on Shichihonmatsu Street, north of Marutamachi (ⓒ 075/811-5072).

*Internet Access* **Media Café Popeye,** in central Kyoto next to the Kyoto Royal Hotel & Spa at Sanjo Kawaramachi (ⓒ **075/253-5300**), is open 24 hours and offers 1 hour of Internet surfing for ¥420 ($4), plus ¥95 (90¢) for each additional 15 minutes. Across from Kyoto Station's south (Hachijo) exit is **Topscafe,** on the corner of Karasuma and Hachijo Dori (ⓒ **075/681-9270**), open 24 hours. You have to become a member here for ¥200 ($1.90; ID required), after which you pay ¥120 ($1.15) for every 15 minutes.

*Lost Property* If you leave something on the **Shinkansen bullet train,** call ⓒ **075/691-1000** to see whether it has been found. Items lost at **Kyoto Station** are turned in to the lost-and-found office (ⓒ **075/371-0134**). If you lost something along a street or outside, contact the **Shichijo Police Station** (ⓒ **075/342-0110**). **Taxi Kyodo Center** (ⓒ **075/672-1110**) handles lost and found for all taxi companies.

*Luggage Storage & Lockers* Kyoto Station has lockers for storing luggage beginning at ¥300 ($2.50) for 24 hours, including lockers large enough for big suitcases on its south (Shinkansen) side.

*Police* The national emergency telephone number is ✆ 110.

*Post Offices* The **Kyoto Central Post Office,** located just west of Kyoto Station's Central (north) Exit (✆ **075/365-2471**), is open Monday to Friday 9am to 7pm, Saturday 9am to 5pm, Sunday and holidays 9am to 12:30pm. You can mail packages bound for international destinations here. To the south of the Central Post Office's main entrance is a counter offering 24-hour service (but not for packages or currency exchange); stamps for letters are sold from vending machines. There are also ATMs here, where you can obtain currency Monday to Saturday from 5am to 11:55pm and Sundays and holidays 5am to 8pm. The **Nakagyo-ku Post Office,** at Sanjo and Higashinotoin streets in central Kyoto, is open Monday to Friday 9am to 7pm and Saturday 9am to 3pm; its ATMs are open Monday to Friday 8am to 9pm and weekends 9am to 5pm.

## 3 Where to Stay in Kyoto

If you've never stayed in a **ryokan,** Kyoto is probably the best place to do so. With the exception of hot-spring resorts, Kyoto has more choices of ryokan in all price categories than any other city in Japan. Small, usually made of wood, and often situated in delightfully quaint neighborhoods, these ryokan can enrich your stay in Kyoto by putting you in direct touch with the city's traditional past. Remember that in upper- and medium-priced ryokan, the room charge is per person, and though the prices may seem prohibitive at first glance, they do include two meals, tax, and usually a service charge. These meals are feasts, not unlike kaiseki meals you'd receive at a top restaurant where they could easily cost ¥10,000 ($95). Ryokan in the budget category, on the other hand, usually don't serve meals unless stated otherwise, and they often charge per room rather than per person.

Be sure to make reservations in advance, particularly in spring when flowers bloom, in autumn for the changing of the leaves, during summer vacation from mid-July through August, and during major festivals (see "Calendar of Events" in chapter 2). Some accommodations raise their rates during these times. In any case, accommodations are expensive in Kyoto, almost on par with Tokyo.

Because Kyoto is relatively small and has such good bus and subway systems, no matter where you stay, you won't be too far away from the heart of the city. Most hotels and ryokan are concentrated around Kyoto Station (Shimogyo-ku Ward), in central Kyoto not far from the Kawaramachi-Shijo Dori intersection (Nakagyo-ku Ward), and east of the Kamo River (in the Higashiyama-ku and Sakyo-ku wards).

**TAXES & SERVICE CHARGES**   The 5% tax levied by hotels is included in room rates. Medium- and upper-range hotels, however, add a 10% to 15% service charge to the prices below unless noted otherwise.

## AROUND KYOTO STATION
### EXPENSIVE

**Hotel Granvia Kyoto** ⚜⚜   Opened in 1997 and owned by the Japan Railways group (holders of a Japan Rail Pass get discounts), this hotel boasts Kyoto's most convenient

location for travelers arriving by train: It's right atop the futuristic-looking Kyoto Station. Only a minute's walk from city buses and trains, it's a great base for exploring Kyoto, Nara, and beyond. Thankfully, the dimly lit hotel lobby is on the second floor, removed from the foot traffic of the station, and excellent insulation contributes to the tranquillity. A very good guest-relations desk helps with everything from sightseeing to restaurant reservations (a huge plus given the inconvenience of the local tourist office), and although there's no business center, behind the guest-relations desk are a workstation and computer with Internet access for hotel guests (¥100/95¢ per 10 min). If you can, avoid the least expensive rooms—they have rather unexciting views of the station's glass roof. Otherwise, modern rooms on higher floors facing north have great Kyoto views. Hotel packages are available that include cooking classes, a visit to the inner sanctums of a Shinto shrine, or the opportunity to spend the evening with a geisha.

JR Kyoto Station Building, Central Exit, Karasuma Dori Shiokoji-sagaru, Shimogyo-ku, Kyoto 600-8216. ✆ **075/344-8888.** Fax 075/334-4400. www.granvia-kyoto.co.jp. 539 units. ¥23,100–¥34,650 ($220–$330) double; ¥25,410–¥34,650 ($242–$330) twin. Executive units from ¥35,805 ($341) double, ¥40,425 ($385) twin. Prices include service charge. 10% discount for holders of Japan Rail Pass. AE, DC, MC, V. **Amenities:** 11 restaurants; 1 bar; 2 lounges; health club w/indoor swimming pool, fitness gym, and sauna (fee: ¥1,050/$10); concierge; shopping arcade (in same building); salon; room service (6am–midnight); in-room massage; same-day laundry/dry-cleaning service; nonsmoking rooms; executive-level rooms. *In room:* A/C, cable TV w/pay movies, free high-speed dataport, minibar, hot-water pot w/tea, hair dryer, Washlet toilet.

**New Miyako Hotel**   With the Miyako name behind it (it's a sister hotel to the famous Westin Miyako in eastern Kyoto), this is a popular choice near Kyoto Station due in part to its convenient location near the terminus of both the Shinkansen and Kintetsu trains (the city bus terminus, however, is a 5-min. walk away on the other side of Kyoto Station). Opened in 1975 but updated and adding a new wing in 2005 that gave it the dubious honor of being Kyoto's largest hotel, it has a utilitarian, almost spartan lobby and rooms that vary in price according to floor and size, though the view is nothing special (children may like rooms facing the front, where they can see the Shinkansen trains arrive). The cheapest twins are so small that couples may fight over who gets the lone luggage rack, while those in the pricier new wing seem like a different hotel altogether, with tall ceilings, mock balconies, and upbeat colors (some rooms face the hotel's courtyard glass-prism chapel, lit at night). A plus to staying here is the free shuttle to The Westin Miyako, which is near the many temples of eastern Kyoto. I also like the rooftop summer beer garden with its all-you-can-eat buffet.

Hachijo-guchi, Kyoto Station, Kyoto 601-8412. ✆ **800/336-1136** in the U.S., or 075/661-7111. Fax 075/661-7135. www.miyakohotels.ne.jp/newmiyako. 986 units. ¥10,395–¥12,705 ($99–$121) single; ¥20,790–¥32,340 ($198–$308) double; ¥21,945–¥36,960 ($209–$352) twin. Rates include service charge. AE, DC, MC, V. Across the street and to the right from Kyoto Station's south side (Hachijo exit). **Amenities:** 6 restaurants; 1 bar; 1 lounge; beer garden; work station w/free computer access; souvenir and gift shops; salon; room service (5am–11pm); in-room massage; same-day laundry/dry-cleaning service; nonsmoking rooms. *In room:* A/C, cable TV w/on-demand pay movies, minibar, hot-water pot w/tea, hair dryer, trouser press, Washlet toilet.

# Kyoto

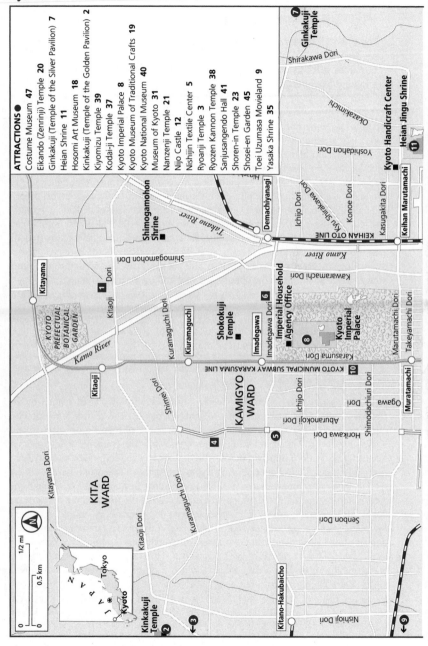

## ATTRACTIONS ●

Costume Museum **47**
Eikando (Zenrinji) Temple **20**
Ginkakuji (Temple of the Silver Pavilion) **7**
Heian Shrine **11**
Hosomi Art Museum **18**
Kinkakuji (Temple of the Golden Pavilion) **2**
Kiyomizu Temple **39**
Kodai-ji Temple **37**
Kyoto Imperial Palace **8**
Kyoto Museum of Traditional Crafts **19**
Kyoto National Museum **40**
Museum of Kyoto **31**
Nanzenji Temple **21**
Nijo Castle **12**
Nishijin Textile Center **5**
Ryoanji Temple **3**
Ryozen Kannon Temple **38**
Sanjusangendo Hall **41**
Shoren-in Temple **23**
Shosei-en Garden **45**
Toei Uzumasa Movieland **9**
Yasaka Shrine **35**

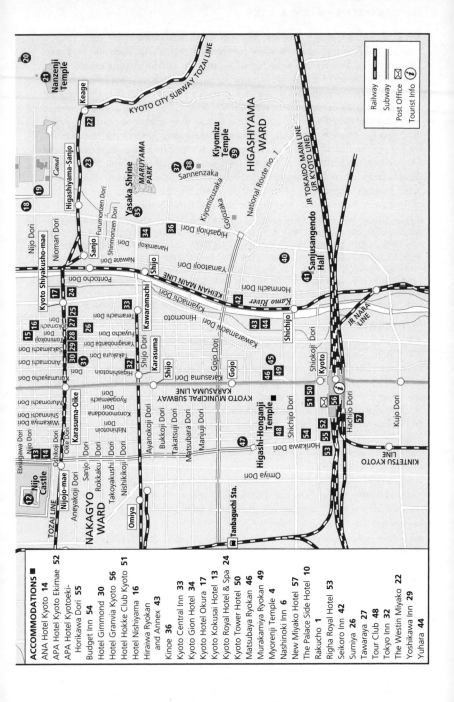

**ACCOMMODATIONS ■**

ANA Hotel Kyoto **14**
APA Hotel Kyoto Ekimae **52**
APA Hotel Kyotoeki-Horikawa Dori **54**
Budget Inn **55**
Hotel Gimmond **30**
Hotel Granvia Kyoto **56**
Hotel Hokke Club Kyoto **51**
Hotel Nishiyama **16**
Hiraiwa Ryokan
  and Annex **43**
Kinoe **36**
Kyoto Central Inn **33**
Kyoto Gion Hotel **34**
Kyoto Hotel Okura **17**
Kyoto Kokusai Hotel **13**
Kyoto Royal Hotel & Spa **24**
Kyoto Tower Hotel **50**
Matsubaya Ryokan **46**
Murakamiya Ryokan **49**
Myorenji Temple **4**
Nashinoki Inn **6**
New Miyako Hotel **57**
The Palace Side Hotel **10**
Rakucho **1**
Righa Royal Hotel **53**
Seikoro Inn **42**
Sumiya **26**
Tawaraya **27**
Tour Club **48**
Tokyo Inn **32**
The Westin Miyako **22**
Yoshikawa Inn **29**
Yuhara **44**

289

**Rihga Royal Hotel** ✆    This has been one of Kyoto's grand hotels since 1969, a familiar landmark topped by the city's only revolving restaurant, open also for breakfast (see p. 301 for a review of the Top of Kyoto). The building's aging exterior offers a modern rendition of traditional Japanese architecture with its railed ledges, but the lobby is rather confining and uninteresting, with a row of chairs near the checkout desk testimony to the sometimes long queues. Still, rooms are comfortable enough, with adequately sized standard rooms that feature shoji screens and window panels that close for darkness. The most expensive rooms—recently renovated and occupying the top two floors—have smart-looking Italian-style furnishings, better views, and spacious modern bathrooms. To aid the foreigners who make up about 30% of hotel guests, there's an English-language guest-relations coordinator on staff. Another plus is the frequent shuttle bus to Kyoto Station, though it delivers you to the south side of the station (buses depart from the north side of Kyoto Station).

Horikawa-Shiokoji, Shimogyo-ku, Kyoto 600-8237. ✆ **075/341-1121.** Fax 075/341-3073. www.rihga.com/ Kyoto/index.html. 494 units. ¥15,015–¥24,255 ($143–$231) single; ¥25,945–¥38,115 ($247–$363) double; ¥21,945¥38,115 ($209–$363) twin; Japanese-style units ¥40,425 ($385) single or double. Rates include service charge. AE, DC, MC, V. Free shuttle bus 8 times an hour 7:30am–9pm from Kyoto Station's Hachijo exit (turn left and walk to the end of the parking lot, past McDonald's), or a 7-min. walk from Kyoto Station. **Amenities:** 7 restaurants; 2 bars; 1 lounge; indoor pool (fee: ¥1,050/$10); sauna (men only; fee: ¥2,625/$25); concierge; complimentary shuttle to station; salon; room service (6am–midnight); in-room massage; same-day laundry/dry-cleaning service; nonsmoking rooms. *In room:* A/C, cable TV w/pay movies, dataport, minibar, hot-water pot w/tea, hair dryer, trouser press.

## MODERATE

**APA Hotel Kyoto Ekimae**    Opened in 1999, this smart-looking business hotel is a good choice for its location. Rooms, however, are very small (the cheapest singles are minuscule) but pleasantly decorated and, though close to the train tracks, are relatively quiet. In short, stay here or one of its sister hotels below only if this book's top choices are full or if you don't plan on spending any quality time with your room.

Other choices include the nearby APA Hotel Kyotoeki-Horikawa Dori (✆ **075/342-6111**), opened in 2005 just a 2-minute walk farther west at Nishi Aburakojicho, Shiokoji, across the street from the Rihga Royal Hotel. It offers similarly miniature rooms at cheaper prices, beginning at ¥9,000 ($86) for a single, ¥13,000 ($124) for a double, and ¥16,000 ($153) for a twin. The cheapest rooms face an inner courtyard (read: no sunshine), and you'll be climbing over your partner to get out of bed in the cheapest double rooms. Note that ¥500 ($4.75) per person is added to all APA hotels on Saturday and nights before public holidays; ¥1,000 ($9.50) per person is added in peak season.

806 Minami Fudodocho, Shiokoji-sagaru, Aburakoji Dori, Shimogyo-ku, Kyoto 600-8234. ✆ **075/365-4111.** Fax 075/ 365-8720. www.apahotel.com 192 units. ¥10,000–¥10,500 ($95–$100) single; ¥19,000–¥21,000 ($180–$200) twin. AE, MC, V. A 3-min. walk from Kyoto Station's north Central exit; turn left out of the station and walk between the post office and train station. **Amenities:** Restaurant (Western); in-room massage; same-day laundry/dry-cleaning service; nonsmoking rooms. *In room:* A/C, TV, fridge, hot-water pot w/tea, hair dryer, Washlet toilet.

**Kyoto Tower Hotel**    There's no problem finding this hotel, located under Kyoto Tower and in business for more than 40 years. It doesn't have a lot to offer, other than convenient access and reasonable prices. Check-in is on the ground floor, and though there's a functional lobby on the eighth floor, it's doubtful you'll want to spend a lot of time here. Guest rooms are long and narrow, with shoji screens, but only the higher-priced rooms afford a view of the station (the rest face other buildings).

Even cheaper prices are available at the nearby Kyoto Tower Hotel Annex, Shinmachi Dori, Shichijo-sagaru (✆ **075/343-3111**), where twins start at ¥12,500 ($119), and at

the Kyoto Dai-Ni Tower Hotel, Higashinotoin Dori, Shichijo-sagaru (© **075/361-3261**), with twins starting at ¥13,000 ($124). Both are within a 4-minute walk from the station.

806 Minami Fudodocho, Shiokoji-sagaru, Aburakoji Dori, Shimogyo-ku, Kyoto 600-8234. © **075/365-4111**. Fax 075/365-8720. www.apahotel.com 192 units. ¥10,000–¥10,500 ($95–$100) single; ¥19,000–¥21,000 ($181–$200) twin. AE, MC, V. A 3-min. walk from Kyoto Station's north Central exit; turn left out of the station and walk between the post office and train station. **Amenities:** Restaurant (Western); in-room massage; same-day laundry/dry-cleaning service; nonsmoking rooms. *In room:* A/C, TV, fridge, hot-water pot w/tea, hair dryer, Washlet toilet.

## INEXPENSIVE

**Budget Inn** *★★ Finds*    Keiji and his wife, Hiromi, opened this hostelry in 2003 in a former apartment building with six tatami rooms (three of which are gilded in gold and have refrigerators) complete with private bathrooms and balconies, plus two dormitory rooms with beds that sleep up to five persons. But it's the level of caring that impresses me the most, with little maps of the neighborhood given to guests that show the location of restaurants, supermarkets, and more; tips dispensed on what's going on and how to spend rainy days; free coffee and tea in the communal kitchen; and the chance to try on a kimono. With its convenient location, English-speaking staff, clean rooms, free wireless WAN, and other amenities, this place beats most other budget accommodations hands down.

Keiji offers an additional 13 rooms (including Western-style twins) and three dormitory rooms at his nearby **Tour Club,** 362 Momiji-cho, Kitakoji-agaru, Higashi-Nakasuji Dori (© **075/353-6968;** www.kyotojp.com), a 9-minute walk from the station. With similar facilities and amenities, it offers twin/double rooms for ¥7,770 ($74), triples for ¥9,345 ($89), and dormitory beds for ¥2,415 ($23).

295 Aburanokoji-cho, Aburanokoji, Shichijo-sagaru, Shimogyo-ku, Kyoto 600-8231. ©/fax **075/344-1510**. 8 units. ¥8,990 ($86) double; ¥9,990–¥10,990 ($95–$105) triple; ¥11,990–¥12,990 ($114–$123) quad; ¥2,500 ($24) dormitory bed. ¥150 ($14) extra for 1-night stays; discounts available for longer stays. No credit cards. A 6-min. walk from Kyoto Station's Central (north) exit; turn left on Shiokoji Dori and right at the Esso gas station. **Amenities:** Lobby computer with Internet access (¥100/¢95 per 15 min.); coin-op washer and dryer; communal kitchen; rental bikes (¥630/$6 per day). *In room:* A/C, TV, hot-water pot, no phone.

**Hiraiwa Ryokan and Annex**    This inexpensive ryokan, halfway between Kyoto Station and downtown, is one of the best-known and oldest members of the Japanese Inn Group. Although they speak limited English, the Hiraiwa family has been welcoming foreigners from all over the world since opening their doors in 1973. The tatami guest rooms, spread through the 80-year-old traditional main building and a newer annex, are spotless. Note that a Japanese breakfast, which includes *kamameshi* (rice casserole), miso soup, and tofu, must be ordered a day in advance, but you can have coffee and toast until 9am. Shower and bathing facilities are limited (you might opt for the neighborhood public bath and sauna just around the corner) and toilet stalls are unisex, affording little privacy for the shy. And since there's no lounge, there's no chance to meet other guests unless you pass them shuffling down the hall to the bathroom. If you're traveling with a group of friends and would like to hang out in a communal room, stay elsewhere.

314 Hayao-cho, Kaminoguchi-agaru, Ninomiyacho Dori, Shimogyo-ku, Kyoto 600-8114. © **075/351-6748**. Fax 075/351-6969. www2.odn.ne.jp/hiraiwa. 21 units (none with bathroom). ¥4,200–¥5,250 ($40–$50) single; ¥8,400–¥9,450 ($80–$90) double. Western breakfast (toast and coffee) ¥320 ($3) extra; Japanese breakfast ¥1,050 ($10) extra. AE, MC, V. Bus: 17 or 205 (don't take the express 205) to Kawaramachi-Shomen (3rd stop) and then a 4-min. walk from the bus stop (look for the side street beside Tony Lama), or a 15-min. walk from Kyoto Station. **Amenities:** Computer in annex lobby w/free 30-min. Internet access; coin-op washers and dryers; communal fridge. *In room:* A/C, TV, hot-water pot w/tea.

**Hotel Hokke Club Kyoto** *Value*    Popular with tourists thanks to its great location just opposite Kyoto Station and its reasonable rates, this chain hotel opened 80 years ago but underwent a much-needed renovation in 2000 and now offers clean and pleasantly decorated Western-style rooms, all with feather quilts and smallish bathrooms. Note that all the singles have tiny glazed windows (which could drive the claustrophobic over the brink) but do have semi-double-size beds. The most expensive twins, large for this price category, face Kyoto Station.

Kyoto Eki-mae, Shomen Chuoguchi, Karasuma, Shimogyo-ku, Kyoto 600-8216. © **075/361-1251.** Fax 075/361-1255. 188 units. ¥7,700 ($73) single; ¥11,550 ($110) double; ¥13,650–¥18,900 ($130–$180) twin. AE, DC, MC, V. Across from Kyoto Station's Central (north) exit. **Amenities:** 2 restaurants (Japanese, coffee shop); business center with free Internet access; in-room massage; coin-op washers and dryers; same-day laundry/dry-cleaning service; nonsmoking rooms. *In room:* A/C, TV, fridge, hot-water pot w/tea, hair dryer, Washlet toilet.

**Matsubaya Ryokan** *Finds*    A member of the Japanese Inn Group, this highly-recommended traditional ryokan just east of Higashi Honganji Temple is a great choice in this category. First opened in 1885, it's owned and managed by the friendly and irrepressibly energetic octogenarian Mrs. Hayashi, representing the fifth generation of innkeepers. She'll talk on and on to you in Japanese even if you don't understand, making you wish you did. Her best, slightly higher-priced rooms have wooden balconies facing a miniature inner courtyard or a tiny enclosed garden. All are tatami rooms with sitting alcoves. Telephone cards sold at the inn can be used from your room for international calls. Note that curfew here is 11pm, and when faxing to the ryokan, please be respectful of the time difference—Mrs. Hayashi isn't getting any younger, and she's been so kind to so many travelers.

Higashinotoin Nishi, Kamijuzuyamachi Dori, Shimogyo-ku, Kyoto 600-8150. © **075/351-3727** or 075/351-4268. Fax 075/351-3505. www.matsubayainn.com. 11 units (none with bathroom). ¥5,200 ($49) single; ¥10,400 ($99) double; ¥14,600 ($139) triple. Reservations require a 1-night deposit, payable by cashier's check, international money order, or credit card. AE, MC, V. A 10-min. walk north of Kyoto Station's Central exit; walk north on Karasuma Dori and take the 3rd right after passing Shichijo Dori. **Amenities:** Lobby computer w/free Internet access; coin-op washer and dryer; communal fridge. *In room:* A/C, cable TV, hot-water pot w/tea.

**Murakamiya Ryokan** *Finds*    Near the Matsubaya (above), this pleasant and spotlessly clean member of the Japanese Inn Group offers nicely decorated rooms—some with old-style ceilings and woodwork—in a 80-year-old traditional wooden building with an inner courtyard garden. The owner, who inherited the inn from her grandfather, is friendly and accommodating and does her best to communicate, even though her English is limited. There's an international phone that accepts credit cards. A Japanese breakfast is available if you order it the night before. The ryokan locks its doors at 11pm.

270 Sasaya-cho, Shichijo-agaru, Higashinotoin Dori, Shimogyo-ku, Kyoto 600-8156. © **075/371-1260.** Fax 075/371-7161. www2.odn.ne.jp/ryokanmurakamiya. 8 units (none with bathroom). ¥4,700–¥5,000 ($45–$48) single; ¥8,400 ($80) double; ¥12,600 ($120) triple. AE, MC, V. A 9-min. walk north of Kyoto Station's Central exit; walk north on Karasuma Dori, take the 1st right after passing Shichijo Dori, and then the 1st left. **Amenities:** Coin-op washer and dryer (w/free detergent). *In room:* A/C, TV, hot-water pot w/tea, no phone.

**Yuhara** *Finds*    This small ryokan has been welcoming guests from all over the world for more than 50 years and seems to be a favorite of visiting journalists, as evidenced by the many framed newspaper articles written about the ryokan that line the corridor walls. It has one of the most picturesque, pleasant settings in all of Kyoto—beside the tree-lined narrow Takasegawa canal in a quiet residential area that's a 13-minute walk from Kyoto Station—and is run by an enthusiastic woman who speaks some English. There are nice touches everywhere, from shoji screens and artwork in the

rooms to plants and bamboo decorations in the hallways. One of the rooms is Western style, and three come with a sink. The largest room looks out onto a miniature courtyard. Guests are requested to vacate their rooms from 10am to 3pm, and there's an 11pm curfew.

188 Kagiyacho, Shomen-agaru, Kiyamachi Dori, Shimogyo-ku, Kyoto 600-8126. ⓒ 075/371-9583. Fax 075/371-9583. 8 units (none with bathroom). ¥4,200 ($40) per person. AE, MC, V. Bus: 17 or 205 (don't take the express bus) to Kawaramachi-Shomen (the 3rd stop), and then a 2-min. walk (take the side street beside Tony Lama and turn right after crossing the canal), or a 13-min. walk from the station. *In room:* A/C, coin-op TV, hot-water pot w/tea, no phone.

# CENTRAL KYOTO
## VERY EXPENSIVE

**Hiiragiya Ryokan** 🏵🏵🏵   This exquisite ryokan is as fine an example of a traditional inn as you'll find in Japan. Situated in the heart of old Kyoto, it offers the ultimate in Japanese-style living, with a very accommodating staff that's helpful in initiating foreigners unfamiliar with Japan to the joys of a ryokan. Noteworthy former guests include princes of the Japanese royal family, Charlie Chaplin, and Pierre Cardin. If you're going to splurge just once in Japan, this is one of my top choices.

Built in 1818 and an inn since 1861—Ms. Nishimura is the sixth-generation innkeeper—Hiiragiya is a haven of simple design that makes artful use of wood, bamboo, screens, and stones in its spacious, traditionally arranged rooms. Even the remote controls for the lights and curtains are cleverly concealed in specially made lacquered boxes shaped like gourds (invented by the present owner's great-grandfather). Rooms, each one unique, are also outfitted with art and antiques such as gold-painted folding screens or lacquered bathrooms, and most offer garden views and cypress baths. Even the least expensive room—a former tearoom only 4½ tatami mats big, with a sink but no bathroom and a view of the garden—is good enough for me. A recent addition added seven new but elegant rooms. Dinners are exquisite multicourse kaiseki feasts; Western-style breakfasts are available upon request.

Oike-kado, Fuyacho, Nakagyo-ku, Kyoto 604-8094. ⓒ **075/221-1136.** Fax 075/221-1139. www.hiiragiya.co.jp. 28 units (24 with bathroom; 2 with toilet only). ¥26,250–¥60,000 ($250–$571) per person. Rates include 2 meals and service charge. AE, DC, MC, V. Located on the corner of Fuyacho and Oike sts. Subway: Kyoto Shiyakusho-mae (4 min.) or Karasuma-Oike (7 min.). Bus: 17 or 205 to Kyoto Shiyakusho-mae (5 min.). Taxi: 10 min. **Amenities:** In-room massage. *In room:* A/C, TV, minibar, hot-water pot w/tea, hair dryer.

**Sumiya** 🏵🏵🏵   Like the other traditional Japanese inns listed here, the 100-year-old Sumiya has a great location in a typical Kyoto neighborhood just a few minutes' walk from bustling downtown. Offering excellent service amid simple yet elegant surroundings, including wooden corridors that wrap around courtyard gardens and several tearooms (a tea ceremony is performed after dinner on the 7th and 17th of each month), it has a variety of rooms, most with wooden tubs and some with wonderful views of tiny private gardens with outdoor benches and platforms for sitting. The oldest rooms employ a striking variety of different woods in their design (be sure, too, to notice the Edo-Era designs on the sliding doors), while rooms in a 45-year-old addition may have sliding screen doors that open onto a private garden. Meals feature Kyoto kaiseki cuisine; Western breakfasts are also available.

Sanjo-sagaru, Fuyacho, Nakagyo-ku, Kyoto 604-8075. ⓒ **075/221-2188.** Fax 075/221-2267. sumiyaryokan@par.odn. ne.jp. 23 units (17 with bathroom). ¥27,500–¥63,000 ($262–$600) per person, including 2 meals. AE, DC, MC, V. On Fuyacho Dori just south of Sanjo St. Subway: Kyoto Shiyakusho-mae (6 min.) or Karasuma-Oike (9 min.). Bus: 5, 17, or 205 to Kawaramachi Sanjo (5 min.). Taxi: 10 min. **Amenities:** In-room massage. *In room:* A/C, TV, minibar, hot-water pot w/tea, hair dryer, safe.

**Tawaraya** 🍁🍁🍁    Across the street from the Hiiragiya (see above) is another distinguished, venerable old inn, which has been owned and operated by the same family since it opened in the first decade of the 1700s (the present owner, Mrs. Toshi Okazaki Sato, is the 11th generation of innkeepers). Unfortunately, fire consumed the original building, so the oldest part of the ryokan now dates back a mere 175 years. This inn has had an impressive list of former guests, from former Canadian Prime Minister Pierre Trudeau to Leonard Bernstein and Alfred Hitchcock. Saul Bellow wrote in the ryokan's guest book, "I found here what I had hoped to find in Japan—the human scale, tranquility, and beauty."

With refined taste reigning supreme, each room is different and exquisitely appointed. Some, for example, have glass sliding doors opening onto a mossy garden of bamboo, stone lanterns, and manicured bushes, with cushions on a wooden veranda where you can sit and soak in the peacefulness.

Oike-Sagaru, Fuyacho, Nakagyo-ku, Kyoto 604-8094. ✆ **075/211-5566.** Fax 075/211-2204. 18 units. ¥48,300–¥84,000 ($460–$800) per person, including 2 meals. AE, DC, MC, V. Subway: Kyoto Shiyakusho-mae (4 min.) or Karasuma-Oike (7 min.). Bus: 17 or 205 to Shiyakusho-mae (5 min.) Taxi: 10 min. **Amenities:** In-room massage. *In room:* A/C, TV, minibar, hot-water pot w/tea, hair dryer.

**Yoshikawa Inn** 🍁    Known for its tempura (see "Where to Dine in Kyoto," later in this chapter), this inn also offers tatami rooms, the best of which offer views of the largest garden I've seen in a downtown Kyoto ryokan. Built more than 100 years ago and opening as an inn a half-century ago, it offers the extra benefit of leg wells under the tables of its tatami rooms, making dining easier for foreigners not used to sitting on the floor. Otherwise, it offers the usual elegance you'd expect from an inn of this caliber.

Tominokoji Dori Oike-sagaru, Nakagyo-ku, Kyoto 604-8093. ✆ **075/211-5544.** Fax 075/211-6805. www.kyoto-yoshikawa.co.jp. 8 units. ¥33,000–¥66,000 ($314–$629) per person, including 2 meals. AE, DC, MC, V. Subway: Subway: Karasuma Oike Station (6 min.; on Tominokoji St. just south of Oike Dori). Taxi: 10 min. **Amenities:** In-room massage. *In room:* A/C, TV, hot-water pot w/tea, hair dryer.

### EXPENSIVE

**ANA Hotel Kyoto (Zenniku Hotel Kyoto)** 🍁🍁    Just across the street from Nijo Castle and offering rooms with castle views, this hotel has one of the most eye-catching lobby lounges in town, complete with a glass wall overlooking an impressive waterfall and tiny landscape garden, all to the accompaniment of koto music (a Japanese stringed instrument). Kimono-clad hostesses greeting guests as they enter the lobby is a welcoming touch. Rooms are attractive if a bit cramped, with well-crafted, Asian-accented furniture, roomy bathrooms, and unusual extras like shoe dryers and de-humidifiers (both handy during the rainy season), and ion-free hair dryers and hair brushes. None of the singles face the castle; double rooms that do—with floor-to-ceiling windows—start at ¥27,720 ($264) during the regular season. Another plus: a complimentary shuttle bus four times an hour to and from Kyoto Station from 8am to 7:45pm.

Nijojo-mae, Horikawa Dori, Nakagyo-ku, Kyoto 604-0055. ✆ **800/ANA-HOTELS** in the U.S. and Canada, or 075/231-1155. Fax 075/231-5333. www.anahotels.com/eng/hotels/uky. 301 units. ¥15,015 ($143) single; ¥21,945–¥27,720 ($209–$264) double; ¥21,945–¥32,340 ($209–$308) twin. ¥1,155–¥2,310 ($11–$22) extra per person Apr–May, Oct–Nov, Sat, and nights before holidays. Rates include service charge. AE, DC, MC, V. Subway: Nijojo-mae (1 min.). Free shuttle bus from Kyoto Station; or bus: 9, 50, or 101 to Nijojo-mae. **Amenities:** 4 restaurants (Japanese, French, Chinese, coffee shop); 1 bar; 1 lounge; indoor pool and sauna (fee: ¥1,500/$14); computer w/free Internet access in the lobby; shopping arcade; salon; room service (7am–midnight); in-room massage; same-day laundry/dry-cleaning service; nonsmoking rooms. *In room:* A/C, cable TV w/pay movies, minibar, hot-water pot w/tea, ion-free hair dryer, bathroom scale, Washlet toilet, shoe dryer, dehumidifier.

**Kyoto Hotel Okura** ✿✿✿    First built in 1888, one of Kyoto's oldest hotels underwent a complete metamorphosis and reopened in 1994 as the city's tallest building, with 17 floors. Its height caused a stir of protest by those who advocate stricter height restrictions; though I usually side with historical preservationists, I must admit that no finer building could have violated the skyline. Its modern facade hints at traditional Japanese latticework, while the spacious lobby, designed after the hotel's original 1920s ballroom, exudes a gracefully elegant old-world ambience. Restaurants on the top floor offer stunning views.

Luxurious accommodations, a convenient location in the heart of Kyoto, and an English-speaking staff that makes a special effort to be hospitable (their motto is "Service with a Smile") come together to make this an excellent choice. Rooms, built around a central atrium, are the utmost in comfort and grandeur, with deep carpeting, rich textiles, vanities, and large bathrooms that, with the exception of single rooms, have separate shower stalls and tubs. The best views are of the Kamo River, especially from the most expensive rooms on upper floors that also take in the hills of Higashiyama-ku beyond the city. The only drawback is that the indoor pool and related facilities are open to guests only from 7 to 10am (people under 20 not allowed), after which they become a private club (if they're not crowded you may get in, but it costs more).

Kawaramachi-Oike, Nakagyo-ku, Kyoto 604-8558. ✆ **075/211-5111**, or 075/223-2333 for reservations. Fax 075/221-7770. www.kyotohotel.co.jp. 322 units. ¥18,480–¥20,790 ($176–$198) single; ¥35,805–¥51,975 ($341–$495) double; ¥28,875–¥51,975 ($275–$495) twin; from ¥43,890 ($418) executive twin or double. Rates include service charge. AE, DC, MC, V. Subway: Kyoto Shiyakusho-mae (1 min., below the hotel). Bus: 17 or 205 to Shiyakusho-mae (2 min.). **Amenities:** 8 restaurants; 2 bars; 1 lounge; indoor pool with Jacuzzi and sauna (fee: ¥2,100/$20); children's day-care center open daily 10am–5pm (¥5,250/$50 for 2 hr.); concierge; shopping arcade; salon; room service (6:30am–midnight); in-room massage; babysitting room; same-day laundry/dry-cleaning service; nonsmoking rooms; executive-level rooms. *In room:* A/C, satellite TV w/pay movies, dataport, minibar, hot-water pot w/tea, hair dryer, safe, Washlet toilet.

**Kyoto Royal Hotel & Spa** ✿    The main reason to stay here? Location, location, location. In the heart of Kyoto on Kawaramachi Dori, this typical tourist hotel has a friendly staff, was stylishly renovated in 2001 to achieve a top-class atmosphere, and added a spa in 2005—yet it still can't compete with the facilities and grandeur of Kyoto's other top hotels. However, it's a convenient base for sightseeing and has an information desk to answer guest questions. Chic blonde-and-black furnished rooms feature focused bedside reading lamps but are otherwise fairly basic. Note that most single rooms and some doubles face an inner courtyard, which cuts down on noise but also on sunshine, while rooms that face the Kamo River have better views but are minuscule. Again, the best reason to stay here is location, though the spa might help you get over jet lag.

Sanjo-agaru Kawaramachi, Nakagyo-ku, Kyoto 604-8005. ✆ **075/223-1234.** Fax 075/223-1702. www.ishinhotels.com/Kyoto-royal/en. 335 units. ¥20,000 ($190) single; ¥30,000 ($286) double; ¥32,000 ($305) twin; from ¥35,000 ($333) executive twin. Rates include service charge. AE, DC, MC, V. Subway: Kyoto Shiyakusho-mae (2 min.). Bus: 5, 17, or 205 to Kawaramachi Sanjo (2 min.). **Amenities:** 2 restaurants (Chinese, coffee shop); 1 bar; 1 lounge; concierge; salon; room service (7am–10:30pm); in-room massage; same-day laundry/dry-cleaning service; nonsmoking rooms. *In room:* A/C, cable TV w/pay movies, dataport, minibar, hot-water pot w/tea, hair dryer, Washlet toilet.

## MODERATE

**Hotel Alpha Kyoto**    This small and unassuming but pleasant brick business hotel has a great, hidden location near the Kawaramachi-Shijo Dori intersection, and I have always found the staff accommodating. Most rooms, including singles, are outfitted

with double-size beds, but since the cheapest singles face an inner courtyard and are fairly dark, it may be worthwhile to dish out the extra yen for a brighter room. My favorite rooms are those that overlook a quiet temple and Buddhist cemetery—a fitting view in a town that boasts so many religious structures. The handmade origami crane in each room is a nice touch. In short, this is a good choice if you like to be in the thick of things and are willing to sacrifice space and facilities to be there.

Kawaramachi, Sango-agaru, Nakagyo-ku, Kyoto 604-8006. (C) 075/241-2000. Fax 075/211-0533. hotel-alpha@joytel.co.jp. 119 units. ¥7,500–¥8,900 ($75–$85) single; ¥12,400–¥16,100 ($118–$153) double; ¥13,100–¥18,100 ($125–$172) twin. AE, DC, MC, V. Subway: Kyoto Shiyakusho-mae (2 min.). Bus: 5, 17, or 205 to Kawaramachi Sanjo (1 min.). Just off Kawaramachi Dori not far from Sanjo Dori; entrance is on a side street called Aneyakoji Dori. **Amenities:** Restaurant (Japanese); computer w/free Internet access in lobby; in-room massage; same-day laundry service; nonsmoking rooms (single and twin only). *In room:* A/C, TV, fridge, hot-water pot w/tea, hair dryer.

**Hotel Gimmond** This small hotel on Oike Dori was built some 30 years ago, but it achieves an even older ambience in its lobby with the clever use of antique-looking lighting and decor. Though the hotel calls itself a tourist hotel and offers mainly twins, its accommodations and lack of services and facilities place it in the category of business hotel. Simple rooms show their age and are soundproof, but I still think those that face away from Oike Dori are quieter; ask for one on a higher floor. The cheapest rooms are quite small.

Takakura, Oike Dori, Nakagyo-ku, Kyoto 604-8105. (C) **075/221-4111.** Fax 075/221-8250. www.gimmond.co.jp. 140 units. ¥9,586–¥10,741 ($91–$102) single; ¥16,170 ($154) double; ¥16,747–¥23,100 ($159–$220) twin. AE, DC, MC, V. Subway: Karasuma-Oike (2 min.). **Amenities:** 2 restaurants (Japanese, Italian); 1 bar; in-room massage; same-day laundry/dry-cleaning service; nonsmoking rooms. *In room:* A/C, TV, fridge, hot-water pot w/tea, hair dryer.

**Kyoto Kokusai Hotel** *&* I like this hotel across from Niji Castle because it offers a few surprises you wouldn't expect in medium-range accommodations. Billing itself as a Western-style hotel with a Japanese atmosphere, it has a very nice lobby overlooking a pleasant, lush garden, which you can gaze upon from either the lobby tea lounge or the buffet-style restaurant, Azalea (p. 307). Every Friday and Saturday evening at 7:30pm, the garden also serves as a stage for a free 15-minute dance presentation given by *maiko* (geisha apprentices). Room rates are based on decor and amenities, with higher-priced rooms offering such luxuries as Internet connections and bathroom scales along with views of Nijo Castle (note, however, that about 50 twins and two doubles face the castle, but none of the singles do). All rooms are comfortable and are outfitted with shoji screens. Despite the hotel's name, which translates as the International Hotel, more than 90% of its guests are Japanese.

Nijojo-mae, Horikawa Dori, Nakagyo-ku, Kyoto 604-8502. (C) **075/222-1111.** Fax 075/231-9381. www.kyoto-kokusai.com. 274 units. ¥8,085–¥17,325 ($77–$165) single; ¥18,480–¥31,185 ($176–$297) double; ¥16,170–¥38,115 ($154–$363) twin. AE, DC, MC, V. Subway: Nijojo-mae (2 min.). Bus: 9, 50, or 101 to Nijojo-mae (2 min.). Across from Nijo Castle. **Amenities:** 4 restaurants; concierge; shopping arcade; salon; room service (11:30am–9:45pm); in-room massage; same-day laundry/dry-cleaning service; nonsmoking rooms. *In room:* A/C, TV, minibar, hot-water pot w/tea, hair dryer, Washlet toilet.

**Hotel Nishiyama** Located just a few minutes' walk north of downtown Kyoto, this 35-year-old property has a traditional atmosphere, from the old lantern above its front door to the small courtyard garden just beyond the lobby. Although the building itself is fairly plain and nondescript, it has more soul than a chain hotel and, despite its name, offers mostly Japanese-style tatami rooms and four small Western-style twins. A public bath boasts views of a garden waterfall. Low rates make this a popular choice for school groups, but if you don't mind the youthful clientele this makes for a good

choice for moderately priced Japanese-style accommodation in the heart of the city. Manager Mr. Nishiyama speaks good English.

Gokomachi, Nijo-sagaru, Nakagyo-ku, Kyoto 604-0933. ☎ **075/222-1166.** Fax 075/231-3558. nishiyama@ryokan. or.jp. 32 units (28 with bathroom, 4 with toilet only). ¥6,300 ($60) single with toilet only; ¥7,350 ($70) single with bathroom; ¥10,500 ($100) Western twin; ¥14,700 ($140) Japanese double. Japanese room with 2 meals from ¥13,650 ($130) per person. Rates ¥1,000–¥3,000 ($9.50–$28) higher in peak season. AE, DC, MC, V. Subway: Shiyakusho-mae (3 min.). Bus: 17 or 205 to Shiyakusho-mae (3 min.). 2 blocks northwest of City Hall. **Amenities:** Restaurant (Japanese); computer w/free Internet access in lobby; in-room massage; free washer/dryer. *In room:* A/C, TV.

## INEXPENSIVE

**Hirota Guest House** ★★ *Finds*    Although it looks rather ordinary from the outside, this guesthouse is actually a reconstructed, 130-year-old former sake brewery, located on a quiet residential street in the heart of the city. It's the home of Hirota Harumi, a retired interpreter/tour guide who speaks perfect English and is happy to impart valuable sightseeing information about the town she knows so well. All the rooms she rents out are tatami style; the cheapest are equipped only with fans (no air-conditioning) and face the front street, which can be noisy, while the most expensive add the comfort of air-conditioning and face the garden. Best of all is the detached, two-story cottage, which is actually a converted *kura* (warehouse) standing in a corner of the garden, with sliding screens that open to the outdoors, bathroom, kitchenette, table with leg wells, and enough room to sleep a family of seven. Japanese breakfasts are served in a pleasant room with a view of the garden.

665 Seimei-cho, Nijo Dori, Tominokoji-nishi, Nakagyo-ku, Kyoto 604-0951. ☎ **075/221-2474.** Fax 075/221-2627. h-hirota@msi.biglobe.ne.jp. 5 units (none with bathroom), 1 cottage. ¥6,300–¥8,925 ($60–$85) single; ¥11,550–¥14,700 ($110–$140) double. Cottage: ¥9,450 ($90) per person for 2, ¥8,400 ($80) per person for 3–4, ¥7,350 ($70) per person for 5–7. Japanese breakfast ¥1,050 ($10) extra. No credit cards. Subway: Oike Station (exit 1, 12 min.). Walk north on Tominokoji-nishi Dori and turn left on Nijo. **Amenities:** Rental bikes (¥500/$4.75 per day); in-room massage; babysitting; dry-cleaning/laundry service; nonsmoking rooms. *In room:* A/C, TV, fridge, hot-water pot w/tea and coffee.

**Kyoto Central Inn**    As the name implies, this inn is centrally located in the heart of the city, near the intersection of Shijo Dori and Kawaramachi Dori. It resembles a business hotel, but thanks to its great location, about 50% of its guests are tourists, with twins making up the vast majority of its rooms. However, rooms are worn and dated, with the only difference between those in the newer and older wing being that the newer-wing rooms are slightly larger and therefore more expensive. Since those facing the front or side of the building are plagued by traffic noise, ask for a room on a high floor facing the back, where you might have a view over surrounding buildings. Clearly, the best thing this aged hotel has going for it are its prices and its location. You even have to fetch your own tea from the lobby.

Shijo Kawaramachi, Nishi-iru, Shimogyo-ku, Kyoto 600-8002. ☎ **075/211-1666.** Fax 075/241-2765. 150 units. ¥7,350–¥9,450 ($70–$90) single; ¥11,550–¥13,650 ($110–$130) double or twin. AE, DC, MC, V. Bus: 4, 5, 17, or 205 to Shijo Kawaramachi (1 min.). **Amenities:** In-room massage; nonsmoking rooms. *In room:* A/C, TV, fridge.

**The Palace Side Hotel** ★ *Finds*    Budget-conscious travelers in the know have been flocking to this modest hotel with its contemporary lobby and cafe for more than 3 decades. Although its location just west of the Imperial Palace is not as convenient as my other inexpensive recommendations in central Kyoto, it's near a subway line and offers more facilities than most (joggers like running on palace grounds). With the exception of original artwork that graces half the rooms by artists who actually stayed in them, rooms (all nonsmoking) resemble those in a dormitory, small with just the

basics of a desk too tiny for any serious work, windows that open, and old tiled bathrooms. More expensive twins add a sofa bed, while the most expensive twins have both sofas and kitchenettes (these are also sold as triples but are cramped). Long-term rates attract many who come to Kyoto to study or work.

Karasuma Shimodachiuri-agaru, Kamigyo-ku, Kyoto 602-8011. ✆ 075/415-8887. Fax 075/415-8889. www. palacesidehotel.co.jp. 120 units. ¥5,040–¥6,090 ($48–$58) single; ¥6,825–¥8,400 ($65–$80) double; ¥7,350–¥10,500 ($70–$83) twin. Long-term rates available. AE, DC, MC, V. Subway: Marutamachi (3 min.). **Amenities:** Restaurant (Western); bar (Sat. only, staffed by volunteers); Thai massage room; 2 computers w/free Internet access in the lobby; rental bikes (free the first hour, then ¥300/$2.85) for up to 6 hr.); coin-operated washers and dryers; nonsmoking rooms; communal kitchen. *In room:* A/C, TV, fridge, hot-water pot w/tea.

**Toyoko Inn** *Value* This popular budget chain has easy subway access from Kyoto Station, is located in the heart of downtown, and offers Toyoko Inn's usual free computers in the lobby, free domestic phone calls from lobby telephones, two free movie channels, and tiny rooms with all the necessities.

28, Naginataboko-cho, Shijo Dori, Karasuma-higashi-iru, Shimogyo-ku, Kyoto 600-8008. ✆ 075/212-1045. Fax 075/212-1049. www.toyoko-inn.com. 223 units. ¥6,720 ($64) single; ¥8,820 ($84) double or twin. Rates include Japanese breakfast. AE, DC, MC, V. Subway: Shijo-Karasima (1 min.). On Shijo Dori, west of Daimaru department store. **Amenities:** Computers w/free Internet access in the lobby; nonsmoking rooms. *In room:* A/C, TV, fridge, hot-water pot w/tea, hair dryer, trouser press.

## EASTERN KYOTO
### VERY EXPENSIVE

⑦⑥ **Kinoe** *Finds* This ryokan is different from my other high-end Japanese inn recommendations in that it's been in operation only half a century and occupies a modern, 12-year-old building. However, there may be room at this inn when more famous establishments are full, and it has an interesting location on the edge of the Gion geisha district. Under the able management of Ms. Chizuyo Miyata, it offers simple but elegant tatami rooms with all the traditional flourishes like shoji screens, sliding paper doors, calligraphy in the tokonoma alcove, and a seating area beside the window. Meals, including Western breakfasts on request, are served in your room. Rates below, based on two persons occupying a room, reflect the seasons, with higher rates charged on weekends and the highest rates in spring and autumn.

Yasui, Higashioji, Higashiyama-ku, Kyoto 605-0812. ✆ 075/561-1230. Fax 075/561-8719. info@kinoe.co.jp. 13 units. ¥25,250–¥34,650 ($240–$330) per person, including 2 meals and service charge. AE, DC, MC, V. On Higashioji Dori, south of Yasaka Shrine. Bus: 207 to Higashiyama Yasui (1 min.). Taxi: 10 min. **Amenities:** In-room massage. *In room:* A/C, TV, hot-water pot w/tea, hair dryer, Washlet toilet.

**Seikoro Inn** *Finds* This ryokan just east of the Kamo River was established in 1831, with the present building dating from a century ago. After passing through a

---

**Tips** **A Note on Japanese Symbols**

Many hotels, restaurants, attractions, and other establishments in Japan do not have signs giving their names in Roman (English-language) letters. Appendix C in this book lists the Japanese symbols for all such places described in this guide. Each set of characters representing an establishment name has a number in the appendix that corresponds to the number that appears inside the oval before the establishment's name in the text. Thus, to find the Japanese symbol for, say, the **Kinoe** (above), refer to no. 76 in appendix C.

traditional front gate and small courtyard, you'll find yourself in one of the most charming entryways I've seen in Japan, which adjoins a cozy parlor replete with an eclectic mix of Japanese and Western antiques, including an old grandfather clock. The rooms, also decorated in antiques, are very homey and comfortable; some open onto a garden with sliding doors and shoji screens. Rooms in an annex built just before the 1964 Olympics are high enough that you can see over the surrounding rooftops, but most of these don't have garden views so I prefer the ones in the oldest buildings. The nice public bath boasts a tub made of 400-year-old black pine, making it one of the inn's most treasured possessions. The owner, who speaks English well, doesn't mind if you take your meals elsewhere, especially if you're going to be here for a while. The staff is warm and welcoming.

Gojo-sagaru, Tonyamachi, Higashiyama-ku, Kyoto 605-0907. © 075/561-0771. Fax 075/541-5481. www.seikoro.com. 22 units. ¥28,875 ($275) double room without meals; ¥28,875–¥57,750 ($275–$540) per person including 2 meals. Rates include service charge. AE, DC, MC, V. Bus: 17 or 205 to Kawaramachi Gojo and then a 5-min. walk; cross the bridge over the Kamo River and after Kawabata Dori take the 1st right. Keihan Electric Railway: Gojo Station (2 min.). **Amenities:** Computer w/free Internet access in parlor. *In room:* A/C, TV, hot-water pot w/tea, hair dryer, Washlet toilet.

## EXPENSIVE

**The Westin Miyako** ⭐⭐⭐ (Kids)    This is the place to stay if you're looking for a hotel with history. One of the best-known hotels in Japan, the Miyako first opened back in 1890 and boasts a guest list that reads like a who's who of visitors to Japan: Douglas Fairbanks, Queen Elizabeth II, Prince Charles and Princess Diana, Anwar el-Sadat, and Ted Kennedy. Even today, half of the guests staying here are foreigners.

You'd be hard-pressed to find evidence of that history today. Rather, the newly renovated Westin Miyako is like a butterfly finally emerging from a series of past renovating blunders which obliterated all vestiges of its historic past. It is now the most smartly appointed hotel in Kyoto, on par with the best of Tokyo's hotels. In addition, the setting is as good as it gets: The hotel sprawls over more than 6.4 hectares (16 acres) of hilltop at the northeastern end of the city, close to some of Kyoto's most famous temples (and a subway station) and commanding a good view of the surrounding hills. Other pluses include a Japanese garden and a registration satellite at Kyoto Station (at the Hachijo/Shinkansen exit) where you can check in and deposit your bags (for a ¥200/$1.90 fee per bag, they'll be forwarded to the hotel), leaving you free to explore Kyoto or to take the complimentary bus to the hotel unencumbered by baggage. Families appreciate the free use of indoor and outdoor pools and a small playroom equipped with billiards, video games, and an activity corner just for toddlers.

Western-style rooms, which come with Westin's trademark Heavenly beds and one-touch express service for everything from room service to messages, come in a variety of styles and price ranges, with the least expensive rooms occupying the oldest wing and the most expensive featuring updated, modern furnishings. Best of all are rooms on the fifth floor with large terraces overlooking the valley. And for those who wish to experience the pleasures of a traditional tatami room but with all the nearby conveniences of a first-rate hotel, the Japanese-style Kasui-en annex is a good bet for ryokan first-timers. Built in 1959, the annex offers 20 modern, elegant rooms with views of a Japanese garden and cypress baths.

Keago, Sanjo, Higashiyama-ku, Kyoto 605-0052. © 800/WESTIN-1 in the U.S. and Canada, or 075/771-7111. Fax 075/751-2490. www.westinmiyako-kyoto.com. 502 units. ¥28,900–¥52,000 ($275–$495) single or double; from ¥57,800 ($550) Executive Club floor; ¥46,200 ($440) double in Kasui-en. AE, DC, MC, V. Free shuttle every 30 min. from Kyoto Station's Hachijo exit (9am–6:30pm). Subway: Keage (2 min.). **Amenities:** 6 restaurants; 1 bar; 2 lounges; 20m (66-ft.) indoor pool; shallow outdoor pool; grass tennis court (¥5,250/$50 per hour); Jacuzzi, sauna, and gym

(free for hotel guests); sun decks (available also for viewing the full moon); observation deck; wild-bird sanctuary and bird-watching trail; jogging trail; tea ceremony room open daily 10am–7pm (fee: ¥1,050/$10); game room; concierge; salon; 24-hr. room service; in-room massage; babysitting, same-day dry-cleaning/laundry; nonsmoking rooms; executive-level rooms. *In room:* A/C, cable TV w/pay movies on demand, dataport, minibar, hot-water pot w/tea, hair dryer, Washlet toilet, complimentary bottled water.

## MODERATE

**Kyoto Gion Hotel**  This older, simple hotel has no frills but a great location in the heart of Gion, within easy walking distance of the city center, shops, nightlife, and the many sights in Higashiyama-ku. Rooms were renovated in 2001, but the single rooms are still among the smallest I've seen (I'm not sure there's even room to unpack). There's no view to speak of, but I prefer the rooms facing west, which have floor-to-ceiling windows overlooking the quaint tiled roofs of Gion (corner rooms are best). A plus is the rooftop beer garden, open in summer.

555 Minamigawa, Gion, Higashiyama-ku, Kyoto 605-0074. © **075/551-2111.** Fax 075/551-2200. www.apahotel.com. 154 units. ¥9,500–¥10,000 ($90–$95) single; ¥16,500–¥23,000 ($157–$219) twin. ¥500 ($4.15) per person more on Sat and nights before holidays; ¥1,000–¥2,000 ($8.35–$17) more per person during spring, autumn, and major holidays. AE, DC, MC, V. Bus: 100 or 206 to Gion (2 min.). On Shijo Dori, west of Yasaka Shrine. **Amenities:** Restaurant (Japanese); bar; Starbucks; beer garden; in-room massage; same-day laundry service; nonsmoking rooms. *In room:* A/C, TV, dataport, fridge, hot-water pot w/tea, hair dryer, Washlet toilet.

# NORTHERN KYOTO
## INEXPENSIVE

⑦ **Myorenji Temple** 🕸🕸 *Finds*  If you don't mind the austerity of life in a temple (early to bed, early to rise), you'll like the tranquillity of this place. Located northwest of the Horikawa-Ternanouchi intersection in a pleasant, quiet neighborhood, Myorenji Temple was founded more than 700 years ago and is now run by a jolly woman named Chizuko-san, who speaks a little English. Since she manages this place virtually single-handedly, she prefers guests who stay 2 or 3 days and requests that they make reservations at least a week in advance (a month in advance would be even better). The temple buildings, about 200 years old and containing several important cultural properties (including paintings from the Momoyama Period that you can see upon request), are beautifully laid out. Cherry blossoms bloom from October to April, and there's even a rock garden, laid out by the same priest who directed the construction of the gardens of Katsura Imperial Villa. Sleeping is in bare, simple tatami rooms, and since there are no bathing facilities on the temple grounds, you're given a ticket to use the neighborhood bath. Services are held every morning at 6:30am.

Teranouchi Omiya Higashi-iru, Horikawa, Kamigyo-ku, Kyoto 602-8418. **075/451-3527.** Fax 075/451-3597. 6 units (none with bathroom). ¥3,800 ($36) per person. Rates include tax and a ticket for the neighborhood public bath. No credit cards. Bus: 9 to Horikawa Teranouchi stop (5 min.). *In room:* A/C, hot-water pot w/tea (coffee on request), no phone.

**Nashinoki Inn** 🕸 *Kids*  In a quiet, peaceful neighborhood north of the Kyoto Imperial Palace, this ryokan has been run by a warm, friendly older couple that speaks some English since 1970. Staying here is like living with a Japanese family, since the home looks very lived-in and is filled with the personal belongings of a lifetime. Some of the tatami rooms, which feature touches such as vases, Japanese dolls, and pictures, are quite large and adequate for families. Breakfast is served in your room.

Agaru Imadegawa Nashinoki St., Kamigyo-ku, Kyoto 602-0838. © **075/241-1543.** Fax 075/211-0854. www. nande.com/nashinoki/english.htm. 7 units (none with bathroom). ¥5,250 ($50) single; ¥9,450 ($90) double. Japanese or Western breakfast ¥735–¥945 ($7–$9) extra. No credit cards. Subway: Imadegawa Station (7 min. from exit 3); walk past Doshisha University and turn left at Yaomon coffee shop. *In room:* A/C, TV, hot-water pot w/tea.

**Rakucho** *(Finds)* This member of the Japanese Inn Group isn't as conveniently situated as most of the other inns listed above, but that shouldn't stop anyone from staying in this well-kept 70-year-old ryokan, managed by English-speaking Kimiko Urade and her son. All but one of the spotless tatami rooms, decorated with such traditional touches as scrolls, have views of a small peaceful garden. Entrance to the ryokan is through a well-tended tiny courtyard filled with plants. There's a computer in the lobby with free Internet access and an international phone, as well as two communal refrigerators, a toaster, a microwave, and free instant coffee.

67 Higashihangi-cho, Shimogamo, Sakyo-ku, Kyoto 606-0824. ⓒ 075/721-2174. Fax 075/791-7202. www.rakucho-ryokan.com. 8 units (none with bathroom). ¥5,300 ($50) single; ¥8,400–¥9,240 ($80–$88) double; ¥12,600 ($120) triple. MC, V. Subway: Kitaoji Station (10 min.); walk east on Kitaoji Dori and turn left at the 5th traffic light. Bus: 205 to Furitsudaigaku-mae (2 min. to the north). **Amenities:** Coin-op washers and dryers; lobby computer w/free Internet access; communal kitchenette. *In room:* A/C, hot-water pot w/tea.

## 4 Where to Dine in Kyoto

Kyoto cuisine, known as *Kyo-ryori,* is linked to Kyoto's long history and to seasonal foods produced in the surrounding region. Among the various types of Kyo-ryori available, most famous are probably the vegetarian dishes, which were created to serve the needs of Zen Buddhist priests and pilgrims making the rounds of Kyoto's many temples. Called *shojin ryori,* these vegetarian set meals may include tofu simmered in a pot at your table *(yudofu),* filmy sheets of soy milk curd *(yuba),* and an array of local vegetables. Kyoto is also renowned for its own style of kaiseki *(Kyo-kaiseki),* originally conceived as a meal to be taken before the tea ceremony but eventually becoming an elaborate feast enjoyed by the capital's nobility with its blend of ceremonial court cuisine, Zen vegetarian food, and simple tea-ceremony dishes. Today, Kyoto abounds in restaurants serving both vegetarian tofu dishes and kaiseki meals fit for an emperor (Kyoto's better ryokan also serve kaiseki as the evening meal). Simpler restaurants specialize in *Obanzai,* home-style Kyoto cooking using traditional seasonal ingredients. Otherwise, any restaurant advertising that it serves Kyo-ryori generally offers a variety of Kyoto specialties. For more on kaiseki and other Japanese-style meals, see "Tips on Dining, Japanese Style," beginning on p. 68.

*Remember:* Last orders are taken 30 to 60 minutes before the restaurant's actual closing time, even earlier for some kaiseki restaurants (which often require a reservation). Bus information to each restaurant is from Kyoto Station.

### AROUND KYOTO STATION

In addition to the restaurants listed here, a good place for inexpensive dining is **Kyoto Station,** which houses approximately 70 restaurants in underground arcades, at major exits, at Isetan department store (there are more than 20 outlets here alone, mostly on the 11th floor), and at Hotel Granvia.

### EXPENSIVE

**Top of Kyoto** *(*  CONTINENTAL Kyoto's only revolving restaurant, located on the 14th floor of the Rihga Royal Hotel, is a good choice for a romantic dinner. Unlike most other revolving restaurants in Japan, which usually move so fast that you fear being flung against the windows by centrifugal force, this one, I'm happy to report, takes a leisurely 90 minutes to revolve, affording excellent views over the tops of Kyoto's temples to the mountains surrounding the city. With a smart Italian marble decor, it offers a seasonal menu that may include roasted lobster with vegetables

# Where to Dine in Kyoto

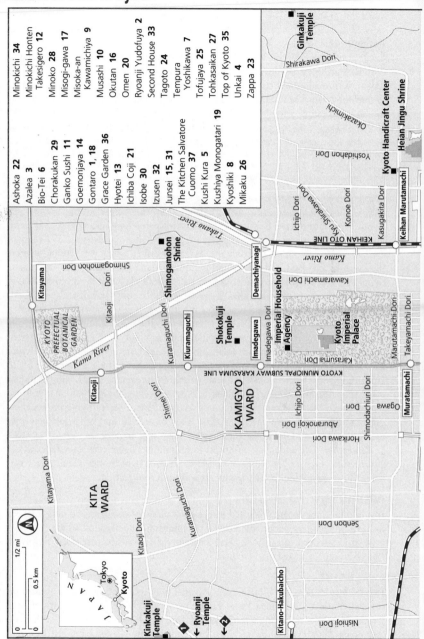

Ashoka **22**
Azalea **3**
Bio-Tei **6**
Chorakukan **29**
Ganko Sushi **11**
Goemonjaya **14**
Gontaro **1, 18**
Grace Garden **36**
Hyotei **13**
Ichiba Coji **21**
Isobe **30**
Izusen **32**
Junsei **15, 31**
The Kitchen Salvatore
   Cuomo **37**
Kushi Kura **5**
Kushiya Monogatari **19**
Kyoshiki **8**
Mikaku **26**

Minokichi **34**
Minokichi Honten
   Takesigero **12**
Minoko **28**
Misogi-gawa **17**
Misoka-an
   Kawamichiya **9**
Musashi **10**
Okutan **16**
Omen **20**
Ryoanji Yudofuya **2**
Second House **33**
Tagoto **24**
Tempura
   Yoshikawa **7**
Tofujaya **25**
Tohkasaikan **27**
Top of Kyoto **35**
Unkai **4**
Zappa **23**

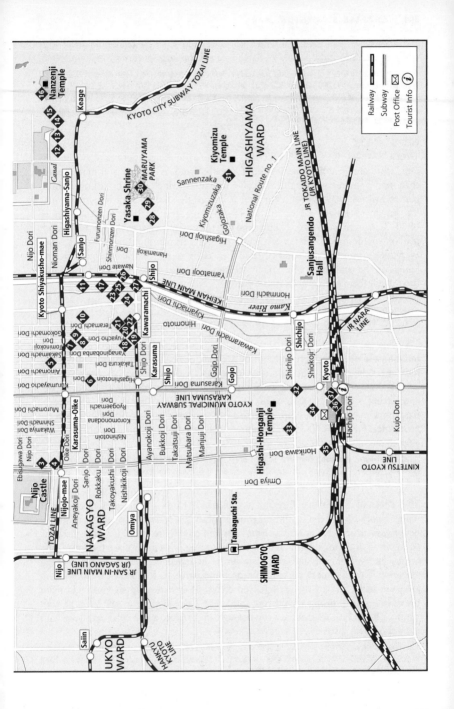

**Legend**
- Railway
- Subway
- Post Office
- Tourist Info (i)

**KYOTO CITY SUBWAY TOZAI LINE**

Nanzenji Temple
16
Keage
15
14
13
12

Canal

Higashiyama-Sanjo

MARUYAMA PARK

Kiyomizu Temple
31

HIGASHIYAMA WARD

Sannenzaka

Yasaka Shrine
30
29
28

Furumonzen Dori
Shinmonzen Dori
Nawate Dori

Nijo Dori
Nioman Dori
Higashioji Dori

Kiyomizuzaka
Gojozaka

National Route no. 1

Kyoto Shiyakusho-mae
Sanjo
17    17

23 25 26
24 27

18 20 22
19 21

Shijo
Kawaramachi

Shijo Dori
Karasuma
Shijo

Karasuma Dori

Gojo

Teramachi Dori
Gokomachi Dori
Fuyacho Dori
Yanaginobaba Dori
Sakaimachi Dori
Tominokoji Dori

10
9  8

6

Higashinotoin Dori
Takakura Dori

Ainomachi Dori
Kurumayacho Dori

SANJO Dori
Higashioji Dori
Yamatooji Dori
Hanamikoji Dori
Nawate Dori

KEIHAN MAIN LINE

Kiyamachi Dori
Kawaramachi Dori
Kamo River

Kawaramachi Dori
Hinomoto
Hinomoto

Higashi-Honganji Temple

KYOTO MUNICIPAL SUBWAY KARASUMA LINE

Ayanokoji Dori
Bukkoji Dori
Takatsuji Dori
Matsubara Dori
Manjuji Dori

Shichijo Dori
Shiokoji Dori
Horikawa Dori

Shichijo
Shichijo

Gojo Dori

Sanjusangendo Hall

JR TOKAIDO MAIN LINE (JR KYOTO LINE)

JR NARA LINE

Kyoto
(i)
Hachijo Dori
Kujo Dori

32
34
35
33

Omiya Dori
Nishitoin Dori
Muromachi Dori
Koromonodana Dori
Ryogaemachi Dori
Karasuma-Oike

Karasuma-Oike
Oike Dori
Sanjo Dori
Rokkaku Dori
Takoyakushi Dori
Nishikikoji Dori
Aneyakoji Dori

Nijojo-mae
3
4

Nijo Castle

Ebisugawa Dori
Nijo Dori

Wakamiya Dori
Shinmachi Dori
Muromachi Dori

TOZAI LINE

NAKAGYO WARD

Nijo
JR SAN-IN MAIN LINE (JR SAGANO LINE)

Omiya

Tanbaguchi Sta.

SHIMOGYO WARD

Saiin

UKYO WARD

HANKYU KYOTO LINE

KINTETSU KYOTO LINE

303

and herb sauce, pan-fried veal with basil sauce, and Japanese tenderloin steak with truffle sauce, with most entrees available in small and large portions.

Rihga Royal Hotel, Horikawa-Shiokoji. © 075/341-2311. Reservations recommended. Main dishes ¥2,000–¥8,000 ($19–$76); set lunches ¥3,000–¥5,500 ($29–$52); set dinners ¥6,930–¥15,015 ($66–$143). AE, DC, MC, V. Daily 11:30am–2:30pm and 5–9:30pm (last order). Free shuttle bus 8 times an hour until 9pm from Kyoto Station's Hachijo (south) exit (turn left out of the station and walk to the end of the parking lot, past McDonald's), or a 7-min. walk west of Kyoto Station to the Horikawa-Shiokoji intersection.

## MODERATE

**Grace Garden** ✿ CONTINENTAL   This smart-looking, bright, and airy restaurant, with large windows overlooking southern Kyoto, is trendier and more upbeat than most hotel restaurants that specialize in buffets (which tend toward the utilitarian) and is also smaller, with fewer than 100 seats. Because of that, there are seatings for lunch (11:30am–12:30pm, 12:45–2:15pm, and 2:30–4pm) and dinner (5:30–7pm and 7:30–9pm). Though you don't have to arrive at the beginning of each seating, you do have to leave when your time is up. Its plentiful spreads offer a bit of everything, from fish to pasta. After dinner, retire to the Southern Court cocktail lounge on the same floor, which offers the same view over Kyoto and live piano music (best of all, there's no cover or music charge).

15th floor, Hotel Granvia Kyoto, Kyoto Station. © 075/342-5522. Reservations strongly recommended. Buffet dinner ¥4,000 ($38) weekdays, ¥4,300 ($41) weekends; buffet lunch ¥2,700 ($26) weekdays, ¥3,000 ($29) weekends. AE, DC, MC, V. Daily 11:30am–4pm and 5:30–9pm. Above Kyoto Station.

⑦⑧ **Izusen** ✿ KYO-RYORI/VEGETARIAN   Although located in a nondescript building and decorated very simply, this is a good choice for inexpensive Japanese set meals near the station. The food, which features local and vegetarian dishes, is delicious and beautifully presented. There's an English-language menu with photographs, and seating is either at tables or on tatami mats. You can choose from a variety of fixed-price meals offering soup, appetizer, rice, a main dish, and side dishes. A vegetarian meal for ¥2,400 ($23), for example, is the kind of light meal usually served at a tea ceremony.

Surugaiya Building, 2nd floor, Karasuma Shichijo Dori-sagaru. © 075/343-4211. Set meals ¥2,400–¥5,000 ($23–$48). No credit cards. Daily 11am–8pm. On the west side of Karasuma Dori above a McDonald's, a 1-min. walk from Kyoto Station's Central (north) exit.

**The Kitchen Salvatore Cuomo** ✿✿ *Finds* ITALIAN   Whereas Grace Garden (above) looks toward the south, this contemporary eatery with an open kitchen has a better view toward the north, over rooftops and temples to the hills in the distance. At night, with dimmed lights and an elegant setting, it's a good place for a romantic meal. The well-trained staff greets customers in Italian and keeps things running smoothly. Three set meals are available for dinner, with the least expensive offering an antipasto plate, pizza, pasta, dessert, and coffee. More expensive set meals add main dishes like grilled shrimp with thyme and lemon-flavored sauce or sautéed tuna with risotto. The set lunches include a trip through an antipasto and a salad bar, along with choices of main dishes.

10th floor, Isetan department store, Kyoto Station. © 075/365-7765. Reservations recommended. Set dinners ¥3,800–¥7,800 ($36–$74); set lunches ¥1,800–¥4,500 ($17–$43). AE, DC, MC, V. Daily 11am–3pm and 5–10pm (last order). Above Kyoto Station.

**Minokichi** ✿✿ *Value* KYO-KAISEKI/KYO-RYORI   A branch of the famous Minokichi restaurant first established in Kyoto 287 years ago, this place is designed to

resemble a lane in a typical traditional Japanese village; waitresses are dressed in kimono and Japanese music plays in the background to help set the mood. The menu includes Kyo-kaiseki cuisine and typical Kyoto dishes, as well as such Japanese favorites as obento lunch boxes and shab-shabu. Set lunches, served daily until 2pm, are especially good bargains, featuring everything from eel to mini-kaiseki. The English-language menu is limited, so be sure to ask for the Japanese menu as well; it has pictures of the various offerings.

Basement, Hotel New Hankyu Kyoto, Shiokoji Dori. ✆ 075/343-5300. Reservations recommended. Set meals ¥2,310–¥10,000 ($22–$953); set lunches ¥2,079–¥3,500 ($20–$33). AE, DC, MC, V. Daily 11:30am–9pm (last order). Across the street from Kyoto Station's Central (north) exit.

## INEXPENSIVE

⑦⑨ **Ichiba Coji** VARIED JAPANESE/INTERNATIONAL    This inexpensive beer hall offers a variety of snacks and dishes that go well with its long list of locally brewed beer and sake, as well as shochu, wine, and cocktails, listed on an English-language menu. Sashimi, skewered shrimp and scallops, baked white fish wrapped in bacon in an olive oil sauce, fried chicken, spareribs served with miso sauce, gyoza, Vietnamese spring rolls, salads, and more are offered, along with views north over the city from its 9th-floor perch.

There's another Ichiba Coji in the heart of central Kyoto in the Teramachi covered shopping arcade, basement of the Withyou Building (✆ **075/252-2008**), with a hip, modern decor and set lunches priced from ¥950 to ¥1,350 ($9.05–$13). It's open Monday to Friday 11:30am to 3pm and 5 to 10:15pm; Saturday and Sunday 11:30am to 10:15pm (last order).

9th floor, Isetan department store, Kyoto Station. ✆ 075/365-3388. Dishes ¥578–¥1,680 ($5.50–$16). AE, DC, MC, V. Daily 11am–11pm. Above Kyoto Station.

**Second House** PASTA    Occupying a former bank with tall ceilings, a large non-smoking section, and a young staff, this casual restaurant is part of a local chain offering a variety of pasta dishes, like spaghetti with eggplant, tomato, and bacon or spaghetti with mushrooms and baby clams, as well as quiche, lunch specials, and homemade cakes and pastries, listed on an English-language menu.

Higashi-Nakasuji Dori, Shijo-agaru. ✆ 075/342-2555. Dishes ¥810–¥1,900 ($7.70–$18). AE, DC, MC, V. Daily 10am–10pm (last order). A 7-min. walk north of Kyoto Station; from Kyoto Station's Central (north) exit, walk north on Karasuma Dori and turn left on Shijo Dori (it will be on your right).

# CENTRAL KYOTO

The heart of Kyoto's shopping, dining, and nightlife district is in Nakagyo-ku, especially on Kawaramachi and Shijo Dori and along the many side streets. In summer, restaurants on the west bank of the Kamo River erect large wooden outdoor platforms that extend over the water and offer open-air dining.

## EXPENSIVE

⑧⓪ **Misogi-gawa** ✦✦✦ *Finds* FRENCH KAISEKI    Dining here could well be the culinary highlight of your trip. For more than 25 years—long before fusion cuisine burst onto the scene—this lovely and exclusive restaurant has been serving nouvelle French cuisine that utilizes the best of Japanese style and ingredients in what could be called French kaiseki. It's located on narrow Pontocho, which parallels the Kamo River and is one of Kyoto's most famous nightlife districts, in a century-old renovated wooden building that once belonged to a geisha. Dishes are the creations of

owner/master-chef Teruo Inoue, who trained with a three-star Michelin chef and successfully blends the two cuisines into dishes that are arranged like a work of art and served on Japanese tableware. Although four set meals are offered, diners are often asked for their preferences and dislikes, with favorite foods incorporated into at least one dish. The dining experience is enhanced by an English-speaking staff, who explain the ingredients of each dish as it's presented, and by an extensive wine list, culled from Inoue's annual visits to France. Seating options include an L-shaped counter with tatami seating and leg wells; an informal counter for customers who prefer to order a la carte dishes (written in French and changing regularly) while watching chefs at work; private tatami rooms; and my favorite, an outdoor summer veranda overlooking the river. Note that the L-shaped counter and veranda add a 10% service charge and private rooms add a 15% service charge, but no service charge is added for the a la carte counter. This is a great place for a splurge.

Sanjo-sagaru, Pontocho. C **075/221-2270.** http:/homepage2nifty.com/misoguigawa. Reservations required. Set dinners ¥12,600–¥31,500 ($120–$300); set lunches ¥4,725–¥10,500 ($45–$100). AE, DC, MC, V. Tues–Sun 11:30–2pm and 5:30–8:30pm (last order). Bus: 5, 17, or 205 to Kawaramachi Sanjo (5 min.); on Pontocho, north of the playground.

**Tempura Yoshikawa** 🌸🌸 TEMPURA  If you're hungering for tempura, this restaurant has a sign in English and is easy to find. Located in an old-fashioned part of Kyoto that boasts a number of expensive ryokan, it's a tiny, intimate place with a traditional atmosphere. The tempura counter, where you can watch the chefs prepare delicate deep-fried morsels, seats only 12 and offers tempura lunches beginning at ¥2,100 ($20) and dinners beginning at ¥6,300 ($60). Meals in tatami rooms, with views of an expansive garden (lit at night), are more expensive, with tempura lunches beginning at ¥6,300 ($60), tempura dinners beginning at ¥12,600 ($120), and Kyo-kaiseki meals costing ¥21,000 ($200).

Tominokoji Dori, Oike-sagaru. C **075/221-5544.** Reservations required. Set dinners ¥6,300–¥21,000 ($60–$200); set lunches ¥2,100–¥6,300 ($20–$60). AE, DC, MC, V. Daily 11am–1:30pm and 5–8:30pm (last order). Counter seating closed Sun. Subway: Karasuma Oike Station (6 min.). On Tominokoji St. just south of Oike Dori.

**Unkai** 🌸 KAISEKI/SHABU-SHABU/VEGETARIAN  A convenient place for a meal if you're visiting Nijo Castle (across the street), Unkai has a modern and refined decor, floor-to-ceiling windows overlooking greenery, and kimono-clad waitresses. The English-language menu has photos illustrating shabu-shabu, kaiseki, tempura, and *shojin ryori* (a vegetarian set meal typical of Kyoto). The ¥5,250 ($50) Miyako Course is the one most often recommended for foreigners and includes an appetizer, sashimi, custard, grilled fish, tempura, miso soup, and rice.

ANA Hotel Kyoto, Nijojo-mae, Horikawa Dori. C **075/231-1155.** Set dinners ¥5,040–¥8,400 ($48–$80); set lunches ¥2,100–¥8,400 ($20–$80). AE, DC, MC, V. Daily 11:30am–2:30pm and 5–10pm. Subway: Nijojo-mae (1 min.). Bus: 9, 50, or 101 to Nijojo-mae. On Horikawa Dori across from Nijo Castle's main entrance.

## MODERATE

**Ashoka** 🌸 INDIAN  One of Kyoto's most popular and longest-running Indian restaurants, in business about 30 years, serves vegetarian and meat curries prepared by Indian chefs, including mutton, chicken, fish, vegetable, and shrimp selections, as well as tandoori. On weekdays it offers an even cheaper set lunch than given below, only ¥950 ($9.05).

Kikusui Building, 3rd floor, Teramachi Dori. C **075/241-1318.** Main dishes ¥1,200–¥2,400 ($11–$23); set dinners ¥3,500–¥6,000 ($33–$57); set lunches ¥1,250–¥2,100 ($12–$20). AE, DC, MC, V. Mon–Sat 11:30am–2:30pm and

5–9pm (last order); Sun and holidays 11:30am–2:30pm and 5–8:30pm. Bus: 4, 5, 17, or 205 to Shijo Kawaramachi (1 min.). On the north side of Shijo Dori, to the right at the entrance of the Teramachi covered shopping arcade.

**Azalea** CONTINENTAL   Azalea is a pleasant place for a casual Western meal if you're visiting nearby Nijo Castle. Offering an English-language menu and a view of its small, Japanese landscaped garden, it has inexpensive set lunches that may include a pasta or risotto dish as the main course, along with a la carte selections like club sandwiches and beef curry rice. Dinner entrees include grilled scallops, steaks, and heavier fare starting at ¥1,510 ($14). Obviously, at these prices you can't expect perfection, but the setting is nice and it's easy to find.

Kyoto Kokusai Hotel, Nijojo-mae, Horikawa Dori. ✆ 075/222-1111. Set dinners ¥2,900–¥5,085 ($28–$48); set lunches ¥1,500–¥3,500 ($14–$33). AE, DC, MC, V. Daily 11:30am–2:30pm and 5–9pm. Subway: Nijojo-mae (2 min.). Bus: 9, 50, or 101 to Nijojo-mae. On Horikawa Dori across from Nijo Castle's main entrance.

⑧⑴ **Kushi Kura** YAKITORI   Housed in a 100-year-old warehouse with heavy-beamed, dark-polished wood and whitewashed walls, this refined yakitori-ya serves specially raised chicken grilled over top-grade charcoal, with an English-language menu offering various set meals and a la carte selections. You can watch the action while you're comfortably seated at the counter with its leg wells. A large selection of sake (including the local Fushimi brew) adds to the great atmosphere here.

Takakura Dori, Oike-agaru ✆ 075/213-2211. Yakitori set meals ¥2,800–¥3,500 ($27–$33); yakitori skewers ¥160–¥680 ($1.50–$6.50). AE, DC, MC, V. Daily 5–11pm. Subway: Karasuma-Oike (2 min.). Just north of Oike Dori on Takakura Dori.

**Kyoshiki** ✿ KAISEKI/KYO-RYORI   This reasonably priced kaiseki restaurant, with a small garden in the back, was converted from a Meiji-Era private home more than 30 years ago. I recommend the Hisago obento for ¥3,465 ($33) offered on the English-language menu. It consists of a variety of seasonal foods served in individual dishes that stack neatly on top of one another to form a gourd; you take the bowls apart to eat. The atmosphere here is relaxed and comfortable, with both tatami and table seating.

Fuyacho Dori, Sanjo-agaru (just north of Sanjo Dori). ✆ 075/221-4840. Set meals ¥3,465–¥10,500 ($33–$100); set lunches ¥3,300–¥3,465 ($31–$33). AE, DC, MC, V. Tues–Sun 11:40am–2pm and 5–8pm (last order). Bus: 5 to Shijo-Fuyacho (1 min.). On Fuyacho Dori, just north of Sanjo Dori.

⑧⑵ **Tagoto** ✿ KYO-RYORI/KAISEKI/OBENTO   Nestled in an inner courtyard off busy Shijo Dori and offering a peaceful retreat in the heart of downtown Kyoto, this restaurant has been serving a variety of Japanese dishes at moderate prices since 1868. The English-language menu (with photos) includes Kyo-ryori set meals, tempura, sashimi, obento lunch boxes, seasonal kaiseki courses, and *yuba* (a low-calorie curd made from soy milk). Seating is either at tables or on tatami.

Shijo-Kawaramachi, Nishi-iru, Kitagawa. ✆ 075/221-1811. Set meals ¥3,150–¥7,350 ($30–$70). AE, DC, MC, V. Daily 11:30am–3pm and 4–8:30pm (last order). Bus: 4, 5, 17, or 205 to Shijo Kawaramachi (1 min.). The entrance is on Shijo Dori just west of Kawaramachi, east of Kyoto Central Inn (look for a tiny door with a white sign; step through it and follow the passageway to the back courtyard).

⑧⑶ **Tofujaya** *finds* TOFU   After inheriting a tofu shop, owner Hamano-san opened this small, casual restaurant to promote tofu's nutritious qualities. Look for a tiny tofu shop on narrow Pontocho; the entrance to the second-floor restaurant is around the corner to the right. The restaurant, with room for only a dozen or so diners, has an open kitchen and an English-language menu listing *dengaku* (broiled tofu with a miso coating), fried tofu, sesame tofu, and other dishes priced under ¥1,000

($9.50). It's easiest, however, to order one of the tofu kaiseki courses, which come with a variety of tofu and side dishes. You'll probably feel healthy after eating here.

Shijo-agaru, Pontocho. ⟨ 075/212-7706. Reservations required. Set courses ¥3,150–¥4,700 ($30–$45). No credit cards. Wed–Mon 5–9pm (until 9:30pm Sat–Sun and holidays). Bus: 4, 5, 17, or 205 to Shijo Kawaramachi (4 min.). On Pontocho's western side about halfway between Shijo and Sanjo sts. (north of the playground; look for the tofu shop).

## INEXPENSIVE

In addition to the choices here, there's a branch of **Ichiba Coji** in the Teramachi covered shopping arcade, with a modern, hip decor and offering pub food that goes good with beer, sake, and spirits. See "Around Kyoto Station," above, for a review.

⟨84⟩ **Bio-Tei** VEGETARIAN/HEALTH FOOD   If you're yearning for a meal in a health-food restaurant, head to this very informal second-floor restaurant down the street from the Museum of Kyoto and catty-corner from the post office. Using organic, preservative-free ingredients, it serves only one thing at lunch: a great teishoku. Last time I was there it came with *genmae* (brown rice), salad, miso soup, pickles, and a curry-based tofu stew with potatoes and carrots. For dinner, a set meal and vegetarian a la carte dishes are offered from a Japanese-language menu. Seating is at sturdy wooden tables hewn from Japanese cypress, and meals are served on tableware from local kilns. As befits a health-food restaurant, smoking is not allowed.

Sanjo Dori Higashinotoin. ⟨ 075/255-0086. Lunch teishoku ¥840 ($8); set dinner ¥1,260 ($12); dinner main courses ¥700–¥800 ($6.65–$7.60). No credit cards. Tues–Fri 11:30am–2pm; Tues–Wed and Fri–Sat 5–8:30pm (last order). Closed holidays. Subway: Karasuma-Oike (exit 5, 3 min.). On the southwest corner of Sanjo-Higashinotouin intersection on the 2nd floor.

⟨85⟩ **Ganko Sushi** SUSHI   This popular, lively sushi restaurant offers the usual raw fish selections, as well as such items as grilled yakitori, shabu-shabu, tempura, tofu (ranging from fried to grilled), and shrimp or crab dishes on an English-language menu. Behind the sushi counter is a fish tank with some rather large specimens swimming around happily until their numbers come up. On the second floor is a *robatayaki* restaurant popular with office workers after work; an English-language menu here lists grilled vegetables and meats, all priced at ¥380 ($3.60). In the basement is a Japanese-style pub, with all menu items—like dim sum, ramen noodles, sushi—priced at ¥399 ($3.80).

Kawaramachi-Sanjo, Higashi-iru. ⟨ 075/255-1128. Sushi a la carte ¥50–¥780 (50¢–$7.40); set meals ¥1,150–¥2,580 ($11–$26). MC, V. 1st floor daily 11:30am–10pm; 2nd floor and basement daily 4:30–11pm. Subway: Kyoto Shiyakusho-mae (4 min.). Bus: 4, 17, or 205 to Kawaramachi Sanjo (2 min.). On Sanjo Dori just west of the Kamo River (look for its logo of a face with glasses and a bandanna).

⟨86⟩ **Gontaro** NOODLES   This noodle shop has been serving its own handmade noodles for a mere 100-some years. A small place with a modern yet traditional interior and an English-language menu, it offers various noodle dishes of either *soba* (buckwheat) or *udon* (a thicker, wheat noodle) with such toppings as tempura, as well as *donburi* (a rice casserole with tempura, yakitori, or other topping) and *nabe* (udon boiled in broth with seafood, chicken, and vegetables). Those with insatiable appetites should have it all with the Okimori set meal for ¥5,500 ($52), which comes with nabe, tempura, barbecue chicken, and noodles.

Fuyacho Dori, Shijo-agaru. ⟨ 075/221-5810. Noodles ¥700–¥1,250 ($6.65–$12); donburi ¥1,200–¥1,350 ($11–$13); nabe ¥3,800 ($36). AE. Thurs–Tues 11am–10pm. Bus: 5 to Shijo-Fuyacho (1 min.). On the west side of Fuyacho Dori just north of Shijo Dori; look for a tiny recessed courtyard, white curtains, and a lone pine tree.

**Kushiya Monogatari** (Value) KUSHIYAKI    This is the first all-you-can-eat, do-it-yourself kushiyaki restaurant I've seen. After choosing skewers of chicken, beef, salmon, scallops, fish, mushrooms, onions, potatoes, and other meats and vegetables from refrigerated cases, you cook them yourself by dipping them in a paste, covering them with bread crumbs and then deep frying them at your table (there are English-language instructions to help you along). There's also rice, noodles, and a dessert and salad bar. Gluttony is restricted to 90 minutes, and you can add all-you-can drink alcohol and soft drinks for an additional ¥1,050 ($10).

5th Floor, Sakizo Plaza Building, Shijo-agaru, Nishi-Fuyacho. ✆ 0120/194-948 (toll-free). All-you-can eat kushiyaki ¥2,625 ($25). No credit cards. Daily 4–11pm. Bus: 5 to Shijo-Fuyacho (2 min.). On the north side of Shijo Dori west of Fuyacho Dori; look for the English-language billboard.

**Misoka-An Kawamichiya** ✿✿ NOODLES    Charming and delightful with a central courtyard and cubbyhole rooms, this tiny, 300-year-old noodle shop makes a great place for an inexpensive meal in the heart of traditional Kyoto. It offers hot or cold buckwheat noodles as well as noodles with such adornments as tempura and chicken and onions. Its specialty is a one-pot noodle dish prepared at your table called *hokoro,* which includes chicken, yuba, mushrooms, and vegetables for two. There's an English-language menu.

Fuyacho Dori, Sanjo-agaru. ✆ 075/221-2525. Noodles ¥580–¥1,450 ($5.50–$14); hokoro ¥8,000 ($76) for 2 people. AE, DC, MC, V. Fri–Wed 11am–7:30pm (last order). Bus: 5 to Shijo-Fuyacho (2 min.). On the west side of Fuyacho Dori just north of Sanjo Dori.

(87) **Musashi** (Value) SUSHI    For a cheap meal of raw fish, this conveniently located restaurant can't be beat. Morsels of sushi ranging from tuna to octopus are served via a conveyor belt that moves plates along the counter; reach out and take whatever strikes your fancy. Sushi is priced at ¥126 ($1.20) a plate. Takeout sushi is also available from the sidewalk front counter.

On the northwest corner of the Kawaramachi-Sanjo intersection. ✆ 075/222-0634. ¥126 ($1.20) per plate. No credit cards. Daily 11am–9:40pm (last order). Bus: 5, 17, or 205 to Kawaramachi Sanjo (1 min.).

(88) **Omen** UDON    A casual atmosphere and healthy food at reasonable prices make this tiny place popular. Vegetable udon *(omen)* is the specialty, and the house's traditional style is to serve the wheat noodles in a flat wooden bowl, the sauce in a pottery bowl, the vegetables delicately arranged (sushi style) on a handmade platter with a bowl of sesame seeds alongside. You dip and mix yourself, unlike at other udon shops where it all arrives like a stew swimming in one bowl. Tempura, lightly fried tofu, and *kamonasu dengaku* (fried eggplant topped with a rich miso sauce) are among the other dishes offered. Other branches are located just south of Ginkakuji (✆ 075/771-8994), open every day except Thursday from 11am to 10pm, and on Pontocho (✆ 075/253-0377), open daily 11:30am to 10pm. There's also one in New York.

Gokomachi Dori, Shijo-agaru. ✆ 075/255-2125. Main dishes ¥630–¥1,050 ($6–$10); set meal ¥1,600 ($15). No credit cards. Fri and Mon–Wed 11:30am–3pm and 4:30–9:30pm; Sat–Sun and holidays 11:30am–9:30pm. Subway: Shijo (5 min.). Bus: 4, 5, 17, or 205 to Shijo Kawaramachi (3 min.). On the east (right) side of Gokomachi Dori, just north of Shijo.

**Tohkasaikan** BEIJING CHINESE    This Beijing-style Chinese restaurant, which is popular with families, started life as a Western restaurant. The old building features an ancient, manually operated elevator, lots of wood paneling, high ceilings, old-fashioned decor, and a friendly staff. From June to mid-September, you can sit outside on a

wooden veranda over the Kamo River, one of the cheapest places along the river to do so. If it's winter or raining, consider sitting in the fifth-floor dining room, which has nice views of the city. The best views, however, are from the rooftop garden (open in summer), where you can order mugs of beer and dine on dishes from the extensive English-language menu, including sweet-and-sour pork, cooked shrimp with arrow-root, and chicken and green pepper. The service tends to be slow and I've had better Chinese food, but the atmosphere is great and is reminiscent of another era.

Nishizume, Shijo Ohashi. (C) 075/221-1147. Main dishes ¥1,260 – ¥2,630 ($12–$25). AE, DC, MC, V. Daily 11:30am–9pm (last order). Bus: 4, 5, 17, or 205 to Shijo Kawaramachi (2 min.). On Shijo Dori just west of the bridge spanning the Kamo River in a large yellow stone building.

**Zappa** INDONESIAN/ASIAN Named after Frank himself, this hole-in-the-wall eatery opened more than 25 years ago as a rock bar but metamorphosed into an Indonesian restaurant 10 years ago, inspired by the owner's frequent trips to Bali. Crammed full with knickknacks and photographs, it offers an eclectic mix of dishes from an English-language menu, like chicken with peanut sauce, sweet-and-spicy Thai chicken, yummy Mexican gyoza (filled with taco meat), Thai fried noodles, *nasi goreng* (fried rice), and *nasi campur* (rice, chicken, egg, and cabbage). You'll probably want to order at least two dishes per person.

Higashi-iru Takoyakushi, Kawaramachi. (C) 075/225-4437. Main dishes ¥450–¥950 ($4.30–$9.05). No credit cards. Mon–Sat 6–10:30pm (last order). Bus: 4, 5, 17, or 205 to Shijo Kawaramachi (2 min.). From Kawaramachi, walk east on Takoyakushi until you reach a small shrine and then turn right.

## EASTERN KYOTO

In addition to the restaurants discussed below, there are a lot of informal and inexpensive places near **Kiyomizu Temple** (p. 318). If the weather is nice, you may wish to stop for noodles and a beer on the Kiyomizu Temple grounds, where you'll find several open-air tatami pavilions.

### EXPENSIVE

89 **Hyotei** ★★★ *finds* KAISEKI/OBENTO This 300-year-old restaurant first opened its doors as a teahouse to serve pilgrims and visitors on their way to Nanzenji Temple. Today it consists of two parts: one offering expensive Kyo-kaiseki, which origi-nated with the tea ceremony but is now associated with Kyoto cooking, and an annex offering seasonal obento lunch boxes. The kaiseki meals are served in separate tiny houses situated around a beautiful garden with a pond, maple trees, and bushes; the old-est house, which resembles a small teahouse, is more than 3 centuries old. You'll dine seated on a tatami floor in a private room, the food brought to you by kimono-clad women. The annex *(bekkan),* to the left of the kaiseki restaurant and with its own entrance, serves delicious lunch boxes (Shokado Bento), which change with the season and are served in a communal tatami room with views of a garden. It also serves a sea-sonal breakfast: For the cold winter months (Dec–Mar), the ¥12,075 ($115) Uzuragayu set breakfast, served until 11am, warms the body and soul with a quail rice gruel, grilled skewers, sashimi, soup, and other dishes, while the ¥5,500 ($52) Asagayu, served until 10am in summer (July–Aug), features lighter fare, including a rice porridge.

35 Kusakawa-cho, Nanzenji. (C) 075/771-4116. Reservations required for kaiseki, recommended for obento. Kaiseki lunches from ¥22,580 ($215); dinners from ¥25,000 ($238); obento lunch boxes ¥4,625 ($44). AE, DC, MC, V. Kaiseki daily 11am–7:30pm; closed the 2nd and 4th Tues of each month. Shokado Bento Apr–Nov Fri–Wed 8am–4pm, Dec–Mar Fri–Wed 9am–5pm. Subway: Keage (5 min.). Bus: 5, 57, or 100 to Dobutsuen-mae (3 min.). West of Shirakawa Dori and south of Murin-an; look for a plain facade hidden behind a bamboo fence with a sign shaped like a gourd.

90 **Mikaku** *JAPANESE STEAKHOUSE*  Established almost a century ago by the present owner's grandfather, this restaurant, in the heart of Gion, is housed in a 100-year-old renovated building that was once a private home. It offers sukiyaki, shabu-shabu, oil-yaki (sliced beef cooked on an iron griddle and flavored with soy sauce, lemon, and Japanese radish), and teppanyaki, all made with high-grade Kobe beef.

Nawate Dori, Shijo-agaru, Gion. ✆ 075/525-1129. Reservations recommended. Set meals ¥10,000–¥23,500 ($95–$224); set lunch ¥2,625–¥3,150 ($25–$30). AE, DC, MC, V (no credit cards accepted for lunch). Prices include service charge. Mon–Sat 11:30am–1:30pm and 5–9pm (last order). Bus: 100 or 206 to Gion (5 min.) or 4, 5, 17, or 205 to Shijo Kawaramachi (5 min.). From Shijo Dori, go 1 block north on Nawate Dori and take the 1st left.

**Minokichi Honten Takesigero** *KYO-KAISEKI*  One of Japan's best-known restaurants for Kyoto cuisine, Minokichi was founded in 1719 as one of eight restaurants licensed to serve freshwater fish and is now in its 10th generation of restaurateurs. With several branches in Japan, including a handful in Kyoto, Osaka, and Tokyo, this flagship restaurant is an elegantly simple modern building, with tatami rooms reminiscent of those used in tea ceremonies, all with peaceful views of a graceful moss and bamboo garden. The specialty is Kyoto-style kaiseki *(Kyo-kaiseki);* emphasis is on the appearance of the food, and great care is given to the selection and preparation of seasonal ingredients. Although the dishes themselves change, a kaiseki meal here always consists of 10 items: appetizer, raw fish, light soup, food cooked in delicate broth, steamed food, broiled food, deep-fried food, vinegared food, fruit, and green tea with a sweet.

Sanjo-agaru, Dobutsuen-mae Dori. ✆ 075/771-4185. Reservations required for dinner, recommended for lunch. Kyo-kaiseki dinner ¥15,750–¥31,500 ($150–$300); kaiseki lunch ¥7,350–¥15,750 ($70–$150). AE, DC, MC, V. Daily 11:30am–2pm and 5–7:30pm (last order). Subway: Keage (10 min.). North of Sanjo Dori on the road to the Zoological Gardens.

91 **Minoko** *KAISEKI/OBENTO*  This former villa is an enclave of traditional Japan with a simple, austere exterior and an interior of winding wooden corridors, tatami rooms, and a garden. Opened about 90 years ago by the present owner's father, Minoko does its best to retain the spirit of the tea ceremony, specializing in an elaborate kind of kaiseki dinner called *cha-kaiseki,* usually served at tea-ceremony gatherings and utilizing seasonal ingredients that are beautifully arranged to please both the palate and the eye. If you come for dinner, when only kaiseki is served, you'll eat in a private tatami room. Lunch, which is served communally in a large tatami room with a view of a beautiful garden, is more economical and less formal but still draws on the tea ceremony for inspiration. The obento lunch box, for example, called *chabako-bento,* is named after the lacquered box it's served in, which is traditionally used to carry tea utensils to outdoor tea ceremonies. A *hiru-kaiseki,* or mini-kaiseki set meal, is also available at lunch.

480 Kiyoi-cho, Shimogawara-dori, Gion. ✆ 075/561-0328. Reservations recommended for lunch, required for dinner. Kaiseki ¥15,697 ($149); mini-kaiseki lunch ¥9,999 ($95); obento lunch box ¥3,500–¥5,198 ($33–$50). Prices include service charge. AE, DC, MC, V. Daily 11:30am–2:30pm and 5–10pm (last order 8pm). Closed irregularly 3 days a month. Bus: 100 or 206 to Gion (3 min.). A short walk south of Yasaka Shrine.

## MODERATE

92 **Isobe** KAISEKI/VARIED JAPANESE  A convenient place to stop for lunch if you're walking from Kiyomizu Temple to Gion, this modern, pleasant restaurant offers

a nice view of Maruyama Park from its dining room and has an English-language menu with photos listing a variety of set meals featuring sashimi, tempura, and kaiseki.

Maruyama Park, Ikenohata. (C) 075/561-2216. Set meals ¥3,150–¥8,400 ($30–$80). MC, V. Daily 11am–10pm. Bus: 100 or 206 to Gion (10 min.). On the southeastern edge of the park (if you're walking from Kiyomizu, take a right at the park entrance; if you're coming from Gion, walk past Yasaka Shrine and keep to the right); look for the outdoor red umbrella (up only in dry weather but also depicted on the sign).

**Junsei** *(finds)* TOFU/KAISEKI/OBENTO    Specializing in tofu dishes, Junsei opened in 1961, but the grounds and garden were originally part of a medical school established in the 1830s during the shogun era. Although tourist oriented and popular with tour groups, the food is good and an English-language menu makes ordering easy. There are several buildings spread throughout the grounds, and what you want determines where you go; as soon as you arrive, you'll be given a menu and asked what you'll be eating. I chose the house specialty, a *yudofu* (tofu) set meal, and was directed to an older building with a view of the garden and filled with antiques and tatami mats. My meal came with vegetable tempura and various tofu dishes, including fried tofu on a stick and yudofu (tofu boiled in a pot at my table). Other set meals include kaiseki (by reservation only), yuba, shabu-shabu, or sukiyaki.

There's a branch, Kiyomizudera Junsei ((C) **075/541-7111**), located just off Kiyomizu-zaka, the main slope leading to Kiyomizu Temple. Housed in a grand, 1914 former villa with high ceilings, wainscoting, and stained-glass windows, it offers just three set tofu meals priced ¥1,600 to ¥2,900 ($15–$28) and is open daily 10:30am to 5pm.

60 Kusakawa-cho, Nanzenji. (C) 075/761-2311. Reservations required for kaiseki. Yudofu set meal ¥3,000 ($29); yuba kaiseki meal ¥5,000–¥8,000 ($48–$76); shabu-shabu or sukiyaki ¥8,000 ($76); kaiseki set meal ¥10,000–¥20,000 ($95–$190). AE, DC, MC, V. Daily 11am–8pm (last order). Subway: Keage (5 min.). Bus: 5 to Nanzenji-Eikando-michi (7 min.). East of Shirakawa Dori on the road to Nanzenji Temple.

**93 Okutan** *(finds)* TOFU/VEGETARIAN    This is one of the oldest, most authentic, and most delightful tofu restaurants in Kyoto. Founded about 350 years ago as a vegetarian restaurant serving Buddhist monks, this thatched-roof wooden place in a peaceful setting with pond and garden serves just two things: a tofu set meal (*yudofu*) and a more traditional tofu meal originally from China. Okutan is very simple and rustic with seating either in tatami rooms or outdoors on cushioned platforms, making it especially delightful in fine weather. Women dressed in traditional rural clothing bring your food. The yudofu set meal, which changes slightly with the seasons, includes a pot of tofu boiled at your table, fried tofu on a stick, vegetable tempura, yam soup, and pickled vegetables. It's all highly recommended.

86–30 Fukuchi-cho, Nanzenji. (C) 075/771-8709. Reservations recommended (but not accepted in peak season). Yudofu set meal ¥3,150 ($30); traditional tofu meal ¥4,200 ($40). No credit cards. Fri–Wed 11am–5:30pm (last order). Bus: 5 or 100 to Nanzenji-Eikando-michi (6 min.). Just north of Nanzenji Temple's main gate (the San Mon Gate).

## INEXPENSIVE

**94 Chorakukan** WESTERN    Located on the edge of Maruyama Park and a good place to stop if you're walking from Kiyomizu Temple to Gion, this restaurant, housed in a building dating from the Meiji Period with elaborate woodwork and marble, is one of the few Western restaurants in eastern Kyoto. Although the inexpensive downstairs restaurant is nothing fancy, it's restful: Classical music plays in the background, and there's a view of some maple trees. Generic items on the menu include beef stew, fried prawns, beef curry, and steak, with a set lunch available until 3pm. After your

meal, you may wish to retire to the building's coffee shop, a beautiful room reminiscent of European coffee shops, open daily 8:30am to 9:30pm.

In the southwest corner of Maruyama Park. ℂ 075/561-0001. Main dishes ¥1,000–¥1,800 ($9.50–$17); set dinners ¥4,000–¥8,000 ($38–$76); set lunches ¥2,000–¥3,500 ($19–$33). No credit cards. Daily 11am–7:30pm (last order). Bus: 100 or 206 to Gion (7 min.); after passing Yasaka Shrine, look to the right for a large stone-and-brick, Western-style building with a huge stone lantern in its driveway.

⑨⑤ **Goemonjaya** TOFU/TEMPURA/NOODLES    Convenient if you're visiting Nanzenji, this typical Japanese restaurant specializes in tofu dishes and tempura. With tatami seating, a miniature garden, a waterfall, and a carp-filled pond, it offers a *yudofu* (tofu) set meal, a shrimp or vegetarian tempura teishoku and, in summer only, inexpensive noodle dishes ranging in price from ¥650 ($6.20) for *somen* (thin vermicelli served cold) to ¥800 ($7.60) for *zarusoba* (cold buckwheat noodles). You might also wish to try its desserts, including *mitarashi dango* (soy-flavored rice dumplings on a stick) and *zensai-mochi* (rice cake with black beans).

67 Kukasawa-cho, Nanzenji. ℂ 075/751-9638. Set meal ¥2,200–¥2,900 ($21–$28). No credit cards. Daily 11am–7pm (last order). Closed some Tues. Bus: 5 to Nanzenji-Eikando-michi (2 min.). Across the street from Yachiyo Inn on the road leading to Nanzenji Temple, look for a red lantern beside the road and a display case of plastic food; the restaurant is back off the main road past a smiling Buddha and a red paper umbrella (open only in dry weather).

## NORTHERN KYOTO

In addition to the selection here, there's a branch of the **Gontaro** noodle shop in this area, at Hinomiyashiki-cho 26 (ℂ 075/463-1039), with the same English-language menu as its main shop (p. 308). It's located about halfway down the street that runs between Ryoanji and Ginkakuji, on the west side; look for the red paper lantern. It's open Thursday to Tuesday from 11am to 10pm.

### INEXPENSIVE

**Ryoanji Yudofuya** 🐟🐟 *finds* TOFU/VEGETARIAN    If you're visiting Ryoanji Temple in northeastern Kyoto, there's no lovelier setting for a meal than this traditional restaurant, which calls itself the Ryoanji Seven Herb Tofu Restaurant in honor of the only thing it serves, *yudofu*, which is boiled tofu and vegetables topped with seven herbs. You can order it by itself, or as a set meal with side dishes. Entrance to the restaurant, situated beside the Kyoyoike Pond, is along a small path that takes you past a stream, a small pond, a grove of maple and pine, and moss-covered grounds, which are also what you look out on as you dine, seated on tatami. You'll know you're getting close to the restaurant when you hear the *thonk* of a bamboo trough fed by a stream, which fills and hits against stone as it empties. Note that if you wish to come here only for a beer after visiting the temple, you'll pay an extra ¥300 ($2.85) table charge in addition to ¥500 ($4.75) for the beer.

Ryoanji Temple. ℂ 075/462-4742. Yudofu ¥1,500 ($14); yudofu vegetarian set meal ¥3,300 ($31). No credit cards. Daily 10am–5pm. Bus: 59 to Ryoanji-mae (2 min.) or 12, 50, or 51 to Ritsumeikan Daigaku-mae (4 min.).

## 5 Exploring the City

Because Kyoto has so many worthwhile sights, you must plan your itinerary carefully. Even the most avid sightseer can become jaded after days of visiting yet another temple or shrine, no matter how beautiful or peaceful, so be sure to temper your visits to cultural and historical sights with time spent simply walking around. Kyoto is a city best seen on foot; take time to explore small alleyways and curio shops, pausing from

time to time to soak in the beauty and atmosphere. If you spend your days in Kyoto racing around in a taxi or a bus from one temple to another, the essence of this ancient capital and its charm may literally pass you by.

Before setting out, be sure to stop by **Kyoto City Tourist Information** on the ninth floor of Kyoto Station's Isetan department store (© **075/344-3300**) to get a detailed map of the city, a bus map, and the *Kyoto's Visitor's Guide* (which also contains maps).

Keep in mind, too, that you must enter Kyoto's museums, shrines, and temples at least a half-hour before closing time. Listings in this section give numbers not only for buses departing from Kyoto Station but from elsewhere as well.

For a map of Kyoto's attractions, see the map on p. 288, "Kyoto."

## AROUND KYOTO STATION

As strange as it sounds, the biggest tourist draw around Kyoto Station is **Kyoto Station** itself. Japan's second-largest station building (after Nagoya) is a futuristic-looking building with soaring glass atriums, space-age music, escalators rising to a rooftop observatory, and open stages for free concerts and other events. In a bold move to attract young Japanese (who nowadays prefer to take their vacations in more exotic or trendier climes), it also has a shopping center selling everything from clothing to Kyoto souvenirs, the fashionable Isetan department store, and restaurants galore. I see more tourists photographing Kyoto Station than any other modern building in town.

Just a 10- and 5-minute walk (respectively) north of Kyoto Station are two massive temple compounds, **Nishi-Honganji** and **Higashi-Honganji.** They were once joined as one huge religious center called Honganji, but they split after a disagreement several centuries ago. Higashi-Honganji is Kyoto's largest wooden structure, while Nishi-Honganji is an outstanding example of Buddhist architecture. Another good thing to do is visit Higashi-Honganji's garden, **Shosei-en** (© **075/371-2961**), a 2-minute walk to the east. Once the private villa of Higashi-Honganji's abbot and designed in part by famous landscape architect Kobori Enshu in the 17th century, it features a pond and several buildings in a parklike setting. Although there are far more beautiful and grander gardens in Kyoto, it provides a nice respite if you're in the area and, even better, it's free (though donations are strongly encouraged). It's open daily 9am to 4pm.

For a personalized English-language tour that takes in Higashi-Honganji, Shosei-en Garden, and several shrines before ending near Kiyomizu Temple, join **Johnnie Hillwalker's Kyoto Walking** tour, held every Monday, Wednesday, and Friday from 10am to 3pm March through November (no walks on national holidays). Led by Hajime Hirooka, with 44 years guide experience, the tour costs ¥2,000 ($19) for adults ¥1,000 ($9.50) for children. No reservations are required; pick up his brochure at the tourist office.

**Costume Museum**    This one-room museum is filled with an elaborate, quarter-size replica of the Spring Palace as immortalized by Murasaki Shikibu in *The Tale of Genji,* complete with scenes of ceremonies, rituals, and everyday court life depicted by dolls wearing gorgeous kimono and by miniature furniture and other objects of the Heian Period. The exhibit, including costumes, changes twice a year. In an adjoining room, life-size kimono and costumes can be donned for free, so be sure to bring your camera. You can see everything in about 15 minutes.

Izutsu Building, 5th floor, Shinhanayacho Dori, Horikawa Higashiiru (on the corner of Horikawa and Shinhanayacho sts. just northeast of Nishi-Honganji Temple). © 075/342-5345. Admission ¥400 ($3.80) adults, ¥300 ($2.85) students, ¥200 ($1.65) children 7–12. Mon–Sat 9am–5pm. Bus: 9 or 28 to Nishi-Honganji-mae (2 min.), or a 15-min. walk north from Kyoto Station.

# CENTRAL KYOTO

Much of Central Kyoto has been taken over by the 21st century, but there are a few interesting sites worth investigating.

If you've never been to a market in Japan, you'll probably want to take a stroll down **Nishiki-Koji Dori,** a fish-and-produce market right in the heart of town. A covered pedestrian lane stretching west from Teramachi Dori (and just north of Shijo Dori), Nishiki-Koji has been Kyoto's principal food market for more than 4 centuries. This is where the city's finest restaurants and inns buy their food; you'll find approximately 135 open-fronted shops and stalls selling seasonal vegetables, fish, beans, seaweed, and pickled vegetables, as well as crafts and cooking supplies. Shops are open from the early-morning hours until about 6pm; many close on either Wednesday or Sunday.

**Kyoto Imperial Palace (Kyoto Gosho)** 🕊🕊   This is where the imperial family lived from 1331 until 1868 when they moved to Tokyo. The palace was destroyed several times by fire but was always rebuilt in its original style; the present buildings date from 1855. Modestly furnished with delicate decorations, the palace shows the restful designs of the peaceful Heian Period. The emperor's private garden is graceful. You can visit the palace only on a free, 1-hour guided tour, but fair warning: Tours are conducted quickly, leaving little time for dawdling or taking pictures. In addition, tours view buildings only from the outside, though they do impart interesting information on court life and palace architecture.

Kyotogyoen-nai, Karasuma-Imadegawa. ℂ 075/211-1215. Free admission. Tours in English Mon–Fri at 10am and 2pm, also 3rd Sat of every month and every Sat Apr–May and Oct–Nov. Closed national holidays. Permission must be obtained from the Imperial Household Agency Office (ℂ 075/211-1215), either online at http://sankan. kunaicho.go.jp/order/index_EN.html at least 4 days in advance; or in person at palace grounds near the northeast corner, Mon–Fri 8:45am–noon and 1–4pm. Foreign visitors can apply in person in advance or on the day of the tour (before 9:40am for the 10am tour, before 1:40pm for the 2pm tour; 1-day advance application required for Sat tours), but tours can fill up (especially in spring and fall). You must be 18 or older (or accompanied by an adult) and you must present your passport; parties of no more than 8 may apply. Subway: Karasuma Line to Imadegawa (exit 3); then turn left and walk south on Karasuma Dori (5 min.).

**Museum of Kyoto (Kyoto Bunka Hakubutsukan)** 🕊   Through video displays, slides, and even holograms, this museum presents Kyoto's 1,200-year history from prehistoric relics to contemporary arts and crafts. I particularly like the various architectural models depicting a local market, merchants' homes, and a wholesale store, but best of all is the vermilion-colored Heian Shrine model with its holographic display of construction workers. The third floor features changing exhibitions of Kyoto arts and crafts as well as a Japanese-style room and garden. The annex, which occupies a 1906 bank with its original main hall (complete with teller cages), houses special exhibits and events.

Unfortunately, explanations are in Japanese only, but the museum does offer free English-language guides every day from 10am to 5pm; personal tours last between 30 and 60 minutes depending on your interest (since guides are volunteers, it's a good idea to make a reservation for one). A special feature of the museum is its film library, which houses hundreds of Japanese classics from silent movies to films made up to 20 years ago (the Japanese movie industry was based in Kyoto for decades). Movies are shown twice a day Thursday through Sunday (at 1:30 and 5pm at last check, but you'd be wise to confirm the time). Be sure, also, to browse the Roji Temple Mercantile Street, a re-created merchant's quarters with shops selling crafts and souvenirs and restaurants serving typical Kyoto dishes.

At Sanjo and Takakura sts. ℂ 075/222-0888. Admission ¥500 ($4.75) adults, ¥400 ($3.80) students, ¥300 ($2.85) children; movie admission included. Tues–Sun 10am–7:30pm. Subway: Karasuma-Oike (exit 5, 3 min.).

*Moments* **Cultural Immersion**

If you're interested in learning firsthand about the tea ceremony, flower arranging, origami, Japanese calligraphy, Japanese cooking, and other cultural pursuits, you can do so with the help of the members of the **Women's Association of Kyoto (WAK Japan).** Contact WAK (© **075/212-9993;** www.wakjapan. com) for information on private instruction, classes, and fees. Courses run 1½ to 2 hours and cost ¥3,150 to ¥15,000 ($30–$143) per person depending on the class and the number of people in your group. Reservations should be made 2 days in advance, if possible.

**Nijo Castle (Nijojo)** 🕮🕮🕮    The Tokugawa shogun's Kyoto home stands in stark contrast to most of Japan's other remaining castles, which were constructed purely for defense. Built by the first Tokugawa shogun, Ieyasu, in 1603, Nijo Castle is considered the quintessence of Momoyama architecture, built almost entirely of Japanese cypress and boasting delicate transom woodcarvings and paintings by the Kano School on sliding doors. Unfortunately, no photos are allowed.

I prefer Nijo Castle to the Imperial Palace because you can explore its interior on your own. The main building, **Ninomaru Palace,** has 33 rooms, some 800 tatami mats, and an understated elegance, especially compared with castles being built in Europe at the same time. All the sliding doors on the outside walls of the castle can be removed in summer, permitting breezes to sweep through the building. Typical for Japan at the time, rooms were unfurnished, and the mattresses were stored in closets.

One of the castle's most intriguing features is its so-called **nightingale floors.** To protect the shogun from real or imagined enemies, the castle was protected by a moat and stone walls. How deep the shogun's paranoia ran, however, is apparent by the installation of these special floorboards, which creaked when trod upon in the castle corridors. The nightingale floors were supplemented by hidden alcoves for bodyguards. Furthermore, only female attendants were allowed in the shogun's private living quarters.

Outside the castle is an extensive **garden,** designed by the renowned gardener Kobori Enshu, that's famous in its own right. The original grounds of the castle, however, were without trees—supposedly because the falling of leaves in autumn reminded the shogun and his tough samurai of life's transitory nature, making them terribly sad.

Ironically, it was from Nijo Castle that Emperor Meiji issued his 1868 decree abolishing the shogunate form of government. Plan on spending an hour here, especially if you decide to rent an audio guide for ¥500 ($4.75) extra, recommended since it describes the significance of what you're seeing.

On the corner of Horikawa Dori and Nijo Dori. © **075/841-0096.** Admission ¥600 ($5.70) adults, ¥350 ($3.35) high-school students, ¥200 ($1.90) children. Daily 8:45am–5pm (you must enter by 4pm). Closed Tues Dec–Jan and July–Aug. Subway: Nijojo-mae Station (1 min.). Bus: 9, 12, 50, or 101 to Nijojo-mae (1 min.).

**Nishijin Textile Center (Nishijin-Ori Kaikan)** 🕮    About a 10-minute walk west of the Imperial Palace is this museum dedicated to the weavers who for centuries produced elegant textiles for the imperial family and nobility. The history of Nishijin silk weaving began with the history of Kyoto itself back in 794; by the Edo Period, there

were an estimated 5,000 weaving factories in the Nishijin District. Today, the district remains home to one of Japan's largest handmade weaving industries. The museum regularly holds weaving demonstrations at its ground-floor hand looms, which use the Jacquard system of perforated cards for weaving. One of the most interesting things to do here is attend the free **Kimono Fashion Show,** held six or seven times daily, showcasing kimono that change with the seasons. Other activities—for which you need reservations—include dressing as a geisha apprentice *(maiko)* or professional entertainer *(geiko)* for ¥9,240 ($88), or trying your own hand at producing a textile on a small loom, which you can then take home with you (fee: ¥1,800/$17). There's also, naturally, a shop selling textile products and souvenirs.

On Horikawa Dori just south of Imadegawa Dori. ✆ 075/451-9231. www.nishijin.or.jp. Free admission. Daily 9am–5pm. Subway: Imadegawa (8 min.). Bus: 9, 12, 51, 59, or 101 to Horikawa Imadegawa (2 min.).

## EASTERN KYOTO

The eastern part of Kyoto, embracing the area of Higashiyama-ku with its Kiyomizu Temple and stretching up all the way to the Temple of the Silver Pavilion (Ginkakuji Temple), is probably the richest in terms of culture and charm. Although temples and gardens are the primary attractions, Higashiyama-ku also boasts several fine museums, forested hills and running streams, great shopping opportunities, and some of Kyoto's oldest and finest restaurants. I've included two **recommended strolls** through eastern Kyoto later in this chapter that will lead you to the region's best attractions as well as to some lesser-known sights that are worth a visit if you have the time.

### Ginkakuji (The Temple of the Silver Pavilion) 🕊🕊    Ginkakuji, considered one of the more beautiful structures in Kyoto, was built in 1482 as a retirement villa for Shogun Ashikaga Yoshimasa, who intended to coat the structure with silver in imitation of the Golden Pavilion built by his grandfather. He died before this could be accomplished, however, so the Silver Pavilion is not silver at all but remains a simple, two-story wood structure enshrining the goddess of mercy and Jizo, the guardian god of children. Note the sand mound in the garden, shaped to resemble Mount Fuji, and the sand raked in the shape of waves, created to enhance the views during a full moon.

Ginkakuji-cho. ✆ 075/771-5725. Admission ¥500 ($4.75) adults, ¥300 ($2.85) junior-high and elementary students. Mar–Nov daily 8:30am–5pm; Dec–Feb daily 9am–4:30pm. Bus: 5, 17, 102, 203, or 204 to Ginkakuji-michi (10 min.); or 32 or 100 to Ginkakuji-mae (5 min.).

### Heian Shrine 🕊🕊    Although it dates only from 1895, Kyoto's most famous shrine was built in commemoration of the 1,100th anniversary of the founding of Kyoto and is a replica of the main administration building of the Heian capital. It also deifies two of Japan's emperors: Emperor Kanmu, 50th emperor of Japan, who founded Heian-kyo in 794; and Emperor Komei, the 121st ruler of Japan, who ruled from 1831 to 1866. Although the orange, green, and white structure is interesting for its Heian-Era architectural style, the most important thing to see here is **Shinen Garden** 🕊🕊🕊, the entrance to which is on your left as you face the main hall. Typical of gardens constructed during the Meiji Era, it's famous for its weeping cherry trees in spring, its irises and water lilies in summer, and its changing maple leaves in the fall. Don't miss it.

Nishi Tennocho, Okazaki. ✆ 075/761-0221. Free admission to grounds; Shinen Garden ¥600 ($5.70) adults, ¥300 ($2.85) children. Daily 8:30am–6pm (to 5pm Nov–Feb). Subway: Higashiyama (10 min). Bus: 5, 32, 46, 57 or 100 to Kyoto Kaikan Bijutsukan-mae (2 min.).

**Hosomi Art Museum** ✿ This highly acclaimed private museum houses changing exhibits of Buddhist and Shinto art, primarily from temples and shrines in Kyoto and Nara, including Heian bronze mirrors, Buddhist paintings, lacquerware, tea-ceremony objects, scrolls, folding screens, and pottery. In contrast to the objects it contains, the building itself is starkly modern, complete with automatic doors that open and clang shut with the finality of a prison. The 30 minutes it takes to walk through are worthwhile; be sure to browse through the gift shop of finely crafted goods.

6–3 Okazaki, Saishoji-cho. ✆ **075/752-5555.** Admission ¥700 ($6.65) adults, ¥500 ($4.75) university students and children. Tues–Sun 10am–6pm. Subway: Higashiyama (exit 2, 5 min.). Bus: 31, 201, 202, or 206 to Higashiyama-Nijo (2 min.). Catty-corner from the Kyoto Museum of Traditional Crafts (Fureaikan).

**Kiyomizu Temple (Kiyomizudera)** ✿✿✿ This is Higashiyama-ku's most famous temple, known throughout Japan for the grand views afforded from its main hall. Founded in 798 and rebuilt in 1633 by the third Tokugawa shogun, Iemitsu, the temple occupies an exalted spot on Mount Otowa, with its main hall constructed over a cliff and featuring a large wooden veranda supported by 139 pillars, each 15m (49 ft.) high. The main hall is dedicated to the goddess of mercy and compassion, but most visitors come for the magnificence of its height and view, which are so well known to Japanese that the idiom "jumping from the veranda of Kiyomizu Temple" means that they're about to undertake some particularly bold or daring adventure. Kiyomizu's grounds are particularly spectacular (and crowded) in spring during cherry-blossom season and in fall during the turning of the maple leaves.

Also worth checking out are the three-story pagoda and Otowa Falls (known for the purity of its water; *kiyomizu* translates as "pure water"), but be sure not to spite the gods by neglecting to visit **Jishu Shrine** ✿✿ (✆ **075/541-2097**), a vermilion-colored Shinto shrine behind Kiyomizu's main hall that has long been considered the dwelling place of the god of love and matchmaking. Ask for the English-language pamphlet and be sure to take the ultimate test: On the shrine's grounds are two "love–fortune telling" stones placed 9m (30 ft.) apart; if you're able to walk from one to the other with your eyes closed, your desires for love will be granted.

✆ **075/551-1234.** Admission ¥300 ($2.85) adults, ¥200 ($1.90) children 7–15. Daily 6am–6pm (Jishu Shrine closes at 5pm). Bus: 100, 202, 206, or 207 to Gojo-zaka (10 min.).

**Kodai-ji Temple** Located between Kiyomizu Temple and Yasaka Shrine, this temple was founded by Toyotomi Hideyoshi's widow, popularly referred to as Nene, to commemorate her husband and to pacify his spirit. Shogun Tokugawa Ieyasu, who served under Toyotomi before becoming shogun, financed its construction. It contains lovely gardens laid out by Kobori Enshu, as well as teahouses designed by Sen no Rikyu, a famous 16th-century tea master. A memorial hall enshrines wooden images of Hideyoshi (to the left) and Nene. Nene, by the way, became a Buddhist nun after her husband's death, as was the custom of noblewomen at the time.

Yasakatorii-mae-saguru, Shimo-Kawaramachi. ✆ **075/561-9966.** Admission ¥600 ($5.70) adults, ¥250 ($2.40) children. Daily 9am–5pm. Bus: 100 or 206 to Higashiyama Yasui (5 min.).

**Kyoto Museum of Traditional Crafts (Fureaikan)** ✿✿ *Finds* Near Heian Shrine is this excellent museum dedicated to the many crafts that flourished during Kyoto's long reign as the imperial capital. Various displays and videos demonstrate the step-by-step production of crafts ranging from stone lanterns and fishing rods to textiles, paper fans, umbrellas, boxwood combs, lacquerware, Buddhist altars, and Noh masks.

The displays are fascinating, the crafts beautiful, and explanations in English, making even a 30-minute stop here well worth the effort. Crafts are sold in the museum shop.

In the basement of the Miyako Messe (International Exhibition Hall), 9–1 Seishoji-cho, Okazaki. ☎ 075/762-2670. Free admission. Daily 9am–5pm. Subway: Higashiyama (5 min.). Bus: 5, 32, 46, 57, or 100 to Kyoto Kaikan Bijutsukan-mae (2 min.).

**Kyoto National Museum (Kokuritsu Hakubutsukan)** 🍁🍁 This museum, housed in a French baroque–style building constructed in 1897, features changing exhibits highlighting magnificent art objects and treasures, many of which once belonged to Kyoto's many temples and the imperial court. Japanese and Chinese ceramics, sculpture, Japanese paintings, clothing and kimono, lacquerware, and metalworks are always on display, making this the best museum in town for viewing the ancient capital's priceless treasures. Plan on staying about an hour, but if you've seen the more extensive Tokyo National Museum, you may want to skip this one.

527 Chaya-machi (across the street from Sanjusangendo Hall). ☎ 075/541-1151. www.kyohaku.go.jp. Admission to permanent exhibit ¥420 ($4) adults, ¥130 ($1.25) university and high-school students, free for children. Free admission to permanent exhibit 2nd and 4th Sat of the month. Special exhibits cost more. Tues–Sun 9:30am–5pm (to 6pm during special exhibitions). Bus: 100, 206, or 208 to Hakubutsukan Sanjusangendo-mae (1 min.).

**Sanjusangendo Hall** 🍁🍁🍁 Originally founded as Rengeoin Temple in 1164 and rebuilt in 1266, Sanjusangendo Hall has one of the most visually stunning sights I've seen in a Japanese temple: 1,001 wooden statues of the thousand-handed Kannon. Row upon row, these life-size figures, carved from Japanese cypress in the 12th and 13th centuries, make an impressive sight; in the middle is a large seated Kannon carved in 1254 by Tankei, a famous sculptor from the Kamakura Period. Don't expect to actually see a thousand arms on each statue; there are only 40, the idea being that each hand has the power to save 25 worlds. To accommodate the thousand-handed Kannons as well as 30 other statues representing the Kannon's disciples, the hall stretches almost 120m (400 ft.), making it the longest wooden building in Japan (no photography or videos are allowed in the building). Its length was too hard to ignore—in the corridor behind the statues, archery competitions were held; standing here, you can easily imagine how hard it must have been to hit a piece of sacred cloth attached to the wall at the opposite end.

Shichijo Dori. ☎ 075/525-0033. Admission ¥600 ($5.70) adults, ¥400 ($3.80) junior-high and high-school students, ¥300 ($2.85) children. Apr to mid-Nov daily 8am–5pm; mid-Nov to Mar daily 9am–4pm. Bus: 100, 206, or 208 to Hakubutsukan Sanjusangendo-mae (1 min.).

## NORTHERN KYOTO

Two of Kyoto's most famous sights are in the northwestern corner of the city.

**Kinkakuji (Temple of the Golden Pavilion)** 🍁🍁🍁 One of Kyoto's best-known attractions—and the inspiration for the Temple of the Silver Pavilion (above)—Kinkakuji was constructed in the 1390s as a retirement villa for Shogun Ashikaga Yoshimitsu and features a three-story pavilion covered in gold leaf with a roof topped by a bronze phoenix. Apparently, the retired shogun lived in shameless luxury while the rest of the nation suffered from famine, earthquakes, and plague. If you come here on a clear day, the Golden Pavilion shimmers against a blue sky, its reflection captured in the waters of a calm pond. However, this pavilion is not the original; in 1950, a disturbed student monk burned Kinkakuji to the ground (the story is told by author

Mishima Yukio in his famous novel, *The Temple of the Golden Pavilion*). The temple was rebuilt in 1955 and in 1987 was recovered in gold leaf, five times thicker than the original coating: You almost need sunglasses. Be sure to explore the surrounding **park** with its moss-covered grounds and teahouses.

Kinkakuji-cho. © 075/461-0013. Admission ¥400 ($3.80) adults, ¥300 ($2.85) children. Daily 9am–5pm. Bus: 12, 59, 101, 102, 204, or 205 to Kinkakuji-michi (3 min.).

**Ryoanji Temple** 𝕽𝕽𝕽    About a 20-minute walk southwest of the Golden Pavilion is Ryoanji—home to what is probably the most famous **Zen rock garden** 𝕽𝕽𝕽 in all of Japan—laid out at the end of the 15th century during the Muromachi Period. Fifteen rocks set in waves of raked white pebbles are surrounded on three sides by a clay wall and on the fourth by a wooden veranda. Sit down here and contemplate what the artist was trying to communicate. The interpretation of the rocks is up to the individual. (Mountains above the clouds? Islands in the ocean?) My only objection to this peaceful place is that, unfortunately, it's not always peaceful—a loudspeaker on occasion extols the virtue of the garden, destroying any chance for peaceful meditation. If you get here early enough, you may be able to escape both the crowds and the noise.

After visiting the rock garden, be sure to take a walk around the temple grounds. There's a 1,000-year-old **pond,** on the rim of which sits a beautiful little restaurant, **Ryoanji Yudofuya** 𝕽𝕽, with tatami rooms and screens, where you can eat yudofu (p. 301) and enjoy the view. There's also a nice landscape garden, with moss so inviting you wish you could lie down and take a nap.

Goryoshita-cho. © 075/463-2216. Admission ¥500 ($4.75) adults, ¥300 ($2.85) children. Mar–Nov daily 8am–5pm; Dec–Feb daily 8:30am–4:30pm. Bus: 59 to Ryoanji-mae (2 min.); or 12 or 50 to Ritsumeikan Daigaku-mae (4 min.).

**Toei Uzumasa Eiga Mura (Toei Uzumasa Movieland)** 𝕽 (Kids)    If your kids are ready to mutiny because of yet another temple, get on their good side by coming to this studio park, one of Japan's three major film companies and where most of the samurai flicks are made. Don't expect the high-tech, polished glitz of American theme parks—rather, this is a working studio with indoor and outdoor movie sets recreating the mood, setting, and atmosphere of feudal and turn-of-the-20th-century Japan, complete with "villages" lined with samurai houses and old-time shops. Stagehands carry around props, hammers and saws, and rework sets. You may even see a famous star walking around dressed in samurai garb, or come upon a scene being filmed. There are, of course, other attractions, including a museum tracing the history of the film industry, a 20-minute Ninja show four times a day Monday through Friday, a special-effects show, a haunted house, a games arcade, and indoor rides and play areas for children. You can also have a photo taken of yourself decked out in a kimono or samurai gear. *Note:* Back lots are open only on weekends when there is no filming, but kids will prefer a weekday when there are Ninja shows and filming. Come here only if you have a lot of time (you'll probably spend a minimum of 2 hr. here), are a cinema buff, or have youngsters in tow.

10 Higashi-Hachigaokacho, Uzumasa, Ukyo-ku. © 075/864-7718. Admission ¥2,200 ($21) adults, ¥1,300 ($12) junior-high and high-school students, ¥1,100 ($10) children. Daily 9am–5pm (9:30am–4pm Dec–Feb). Closed Dec 26–Jan 1. Train: JR line to Uzumasa or Hanazono Station (8 min.) or Keifuku Line to Uzumasa (5 min.). Bus: 75 to Uzumasa Eigamuramichi (4 min.).

**Start:** Sanjusangendo Hall on Shichijo Dori a couple of blocks east of the Kamo River; to get there, walk 20 minutes from Kyoto Station or take bus no. 100, 206, or 208 to Hakubutsukan Sanjusangendo-mae.

**Finish:** Kyoto Craft Center, Shijo Dori, Gion.

**Time:** Allow approximately 5 hours, including stops for shopping and museums.

**Best Times:** Weekdays, when temples and shops aren't as crowded.

**Worst Times:** Monday, when the Kyoto National Museum is closed; Wednesday, when the Kyoto Craft Center is closed.

A stroll through Higashiyama-ku will take you to Kiyomizu Temple, one of Kyoto's most famous sights, and other worthwhile attractions like Sanjusangendo Hall and the Kyoto National Museum. It will also take you through some of Kyoto's most charming neighborhoods, with plenty of shopping opportunities en route.

Although the walking-tour leaflet ("Kyoto Walks") distributed by the Tourist Information Center in Tokyo claims that you can walk from Kiyomizu Temple to Heian Shrine in 50 minutes, I don't see how it's possible unless you run the whole way. I've walked this route almost a dozen times, and it's always taken me the better part of a day—perhaps I'm slow, but it's a pace that I've found does justice to this wonderful area of Kyoto.

*Note:* The second walk, "The Philosopher's Stroll" (below), includes several attractions that could be combined with this walk if you don't have time for two walks. If you continue walking north from Maruyama Park instead of heading west for Gion, for example, you could take in Heian Shrine and the Kyoto Handicraft Center (covered at the end of the second walk). In any case, since eastern Kyoto has some of the city's most traditional and beautiful restaurants, be sure to read through the dining section to decide beforehand where you want to eat lunch or dinner.

Start your stroll at:

### ① Sanjusangendo Hall

This hall dates from 1266 and is only about 15m (50 ft.) wide, but stretches almost 120m (400 ft.), making it the longest wooden building in Japan. However, it's not the building itself that impresses but what it contains—1,001 life-size images of the thousand-handed Kannon. Seeing so many of them—row upon row of gold figures, glowing in the dark hall—is stunning (unfortunately, no photographs or videos allowed). In the middle is a 3.3m-tall (11-ft.) seated figure of Kannon carved in 1254. At the back of the hall is a 117m (384-ft.) archery range where a competition is held every

January 15. (See "Exploring the City," earlier in this chapter, for more information on this and other major sights described in this stroll.)

Across the street is the:

### ② Kyoto National Museum (Kokuritsu Hakubutsukan)

In 1889, the Meiji government, fearful that Japan's cultural objects were going the way of the samurai with the increasing import of Western ways and products, established three national museums—one in Tokyo, one in Nara, and this one in Kyoto, which serves as a repository for art objects and treasures that once belonged to Kyoto's temples

and royal court. Individual items, most of which come from the museum's own collection, are rotated continuously, which means that no matter how many times you come here you'll always see something new. Always on display are ceramics, paintings, calligraphy, lacquerware, textiles, and sculptures. For ancient art, there's no better place in town than this.

East of the Kyoto National Museum (toward the wooded hills) are Higashioji Dori and a stoplight; take a left and walk about 5 minutes until you come to the second stoplight, at a small intersection with a Sunkus convenience store. Turn left here, take the first right down a narrow street, and to your right you'll soon see:

### ❸ Kawai Kanjiro Memorial House

Kawai Kanjiro Memorial House, Gojozaka (© **075/561-3585**), is the former home and studio of one of Japan's most well-known potters, Kawai Kanjiro (1890–1966). Inspired at a young age by Bernard Leach and one of the cofounders of the Japan Folk Crafts Museum in Tokyo, this versatile man handmade much of the furniture in this lovely home, which is a traditional Japanese house with an indoor open-pit fireplace and gleaming woodwork. Pottery, personal effects, and his outdoor clay kiln, built on a slope in the traditional Japanese method, are all on display, but this museum is worth seeing for the house alone, especially if you haven't had much opportunity to see the interiors of traditional Japanese homes. Admission is ¥900 ($8.55) for adults, ¥500 ($4.75) for students, and ¥300 ($2.85) for children. Open Tuesday to Sunday from 10am to 5pm.

Take a right out of the museum, walk to the busy road with the overpass, and turn right. When you get to the big intersection, look catty-corner across the intersection to the left and you'll see a slope leading uphill between two big stone lanterns This marks the entrance to the:

### ❹ Otani Mausoleum

It serves as a major mausoleum for members of Shin Buddhism (a Japanese religious sect). In addition to a memorial hall dedicated to victims of World War II, it holds many memorial services for deceased Shin Buddhists from throughout Japan. After passing through a wooden gate, you should turn left and then right for:

### ❺ Toribeyama

Since ancient times it has served as a cremation site and burial ground, with more than 15,000 tombs spread along the slopes.

Follow the pathway uphill through the cemetery for about 10 minutes to the top, where you should then turn left and follow the painted white arrow in the street to the vermillion-colored tower gate, which marks the entrance to:

### ❻ Kiyomizu Temple

This temple is the star attraction of this stroll. First founded in 798 and rebuilt in 1633 by the third Tokugawa shogun, Iemitsu, the temple occupies an exalted spot. The main hall is built over a cliff and features a large wooden veranda supported by 139 pillars, each 15m (49 ft.) high. Take in the view of Kyoto from its deck, but to fully appreciate the grandeur of the main hall with its pillars and dark wood, be sure to walk to the three-story pagoda, which offers the best view of the main hall, built without the use of a single nail. From the pagoda, descend the stone steps to Otowa Falls, where you'll see Japanese lined up to drink from the refreshing spring water. Kiyomizu's name, in fact, translates as "pure water." From here you'll also have the best view of the temple's impressive pillars.

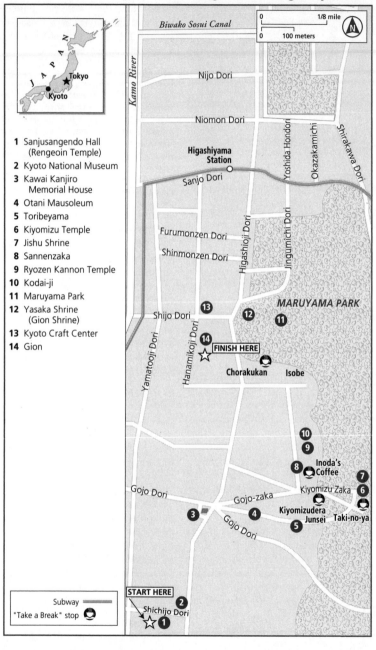

Biwako Sosui Canal

Kamo River

Nijo Dori

Niomon Dori

Higashiyama Station

Yoshida Hondori

Okazakamichi

Shirakawa Dori

Sanjo Dori

**1** Sanjusangendo Hall
   (Rengeoin Temple)
**2** Kyoto National Museum
**3** Kawai Kanjiro
   Memorial House
**4** Otani Mausoleum
**5** Toribeyama
**6** Kiyomizu Temple
**7** Jishu Shrine
**8** Sannenzaka
**9** Ryozen Kannon Temple
**10** Kodai-ji
**11** Maruyama Park
**12** Yasaka Shrine
   (Gion Shrine)
**13** Kyoto Craft Center
**14** Gion

Furumonzen Dori

Shinmonzen Dori

Higashioji Dori

Jingumichi Dori

MARUYAMA PARK

Shijo Dori

Yamatooji Dori

Hanamikoji Dori

FINISH HERE

Chorakukan    Isobe

Inoda's Coffee

Kiyomizu Zaka

Gojo Dori

Gojo-zaka

Kiyomizudera Junsei    Taki-no-ya

Gojo Dori

0        1/8 mile
0    100 meters

Subway
"Take a Break" stop

START HERE
Shichijo Dori

**TAKE A BREAK**
On the grounds of Kiyomizu Temple, just beside Otowa Falls, is **Taki-no-ya** (© 075/561-5117), an open-air pavilion where you can sit on tatami and enjoy noodles and a beer or flavored shaved ice from the English-language menu. This is a great place to stop (and now you know why this walk takes me all day). If you're lucky to be here in autumn, the fiery reds of the maple trees will set the countryside around you aflame. Open Friday through Wednesday from 10am to 5pm. Or, for something more substantial, wait until after your temple visit to dine on tofu at **Kiyomizudera Junsei**, located off Kiyomizu-zaka (see p. 312 for a complete review). On Sannenzaka (see below), keep your eyes peeled for **Inoda's Coffee** (© 075/532-5700), where you'll have views of a Japanese-style garden along with pastries, sandwiches, and coffee. It's open daily 9am to 5pm.

Before departing Kiyomizu Temple, be sure to make a stop at the vermilion-colored Shinto shrine located behind the temple's main hall:

### ⑦ Jishu Shrine

The shrine is regarded as a dwelling place of the deity in charge of love and match-making. Ask for the English-language leaflet that gives its history. Throughout the grounds are English-language signs and descriptions telling about its various parts; for once, you're not left in the dark about the purpose of the various statues and memorials and what Japanese are doing as they make their rounds. It's very enriching. You can buy good-luck charms for everything from a happy marriage to easy delivery of a child to success in passing an examination. On the shrine's grounds are two stones placed about 9m (30 ft.) apart—if you're able to walk from one stone to the other with your eyes closed, you're supposedly guaranteed success in your love life. It sure doesn't hurt to try. There's also a place where you can write down your troubles on a piece of paper and then submerge it in a bucket of water, which supposedly will cause both the paper and your troubles to dissolve. If you failed the rock test, you might make a point of stopping here.

From Kiyomizu Temple, retrace your steps to the vermillion-colored tower gate you passed earlier. From here, on a downhill slope called Kiyomizu-zaka, you'll pass shop after shop selling sweets, pottery, fans, ties, hats, souvenirs, and curios. It's okay to go crazy shopping here, but remember that you're going to have to carry whatever you buy. After passing a couple of small shrines nestled in among the shops, you'll come to a split in the road and a small shrine on the right shaded by trees in front. Just beside this shrine are stone steps leading downhill (north) to a stone-cobbled street called:

### ⑧ Sannenzaka

The slope leads past lovely antiques stores, upscale craft shops, and restaurants and winds through neighborhoods of wooden buildings reminiscent of old Kyoto. Keep your eyes peeled for downhill stairs to the right leading to Maruyama Park; after you take these, the street will wind a bit as it goes downhill and eventually end at a T intersection. Take the stairs opposite the road to:

### ⑨ Ryozen Kannon Temple

This temple (© 075/561-2205) has a 24m-high (80-ft.) white statue dedicated to unknown soldiers who died in World War II. Memorial services are conducted four times daily at a shrine that contains memorial tablets of the two million Japanese who perished during the war. There's also a Memorial Hall commemorating the more than 48,000 foreign soldiers who died on Japanese territory. Open daily from 8:30am to 4:20pm; since admission is ¥200 ($1.90), you may just want to take a peek at the statue. Just past Ryozen Kannon Temple, across the parking lot, is:

### ⑩ Kodaiji Temple

This temple was founded by the widow Nene in commemoration of her husband,

Toyotomi Hideyoshi, who succeeded in unifying Japan at the end of the 16th century. In addition to teahouses and a memorial hall containing wooden images of the couple, there's a beautiful garden designed by master gardener Kobori Enshu.

*Exit Kodai-ji Temple via the main steps leading downhill and turn right, continuing north.*

---

☕ **TAKE A BREAK**
Past Kodai-ji Temple and just before the street ends at a pagoda with a crane on top, keep your eyes peeled for a teahouse on your right with a garden, which you can glimpse from the street through a gate. The  **Kodaiji Rakusho Tea Room**, 516 Washiochiyo (𝄡 **075/561-6892**), is a lovely place and one of my favorite tearooms in Kyoto. It has a 100-year-old miniature garden with a pond that's home to some of the largest and most colorful carp I've ever seen, some of which are 20 years old and winners of the many medals displayed in the back room. In summer, stop for *somen* (finely spun cold noodles), tea, or traditional desserts, and refresh yourself with views of the small but beautiful garden from one of the tables or from the back tatami room. If you're a gardener, you'll probably want to give up the hobby after you've seen what's possible—but rarely achieved. Open from 9:30am to 5:30pm (until 6pm in summer); closed 1 day a week but, unfortunately, not a fixed day. For coffee or Western food, there's **Chorakukan**, located in a brick-and-stone Meiji-Era building at the southwest corner of Maruyama Park (described below; to the left as you enter the park). See p. 312 for a complete review.

---

*Continuing on your stroll north, turn right at the pagoda with the crane and then take an immediate left, which marks the beginning of:*

### ⓫ Maruyama Park

An unkempt field of shrubs and weeds until designated a public park in 1886, this is one of Kyoto's most popular outdoor respites, filled with ponds, pigeons, and gardens. In spring, it's one of the most popular spots for viewing cherry blossoms; to the left after you enter the park is one of the oldest, most famous cherry trees in Kyoto. Also farther west is:

### ⓬ Yasaka Shrine

Yasaka Shrine is also known as Gion Shrine because of its proximity to the Gion District. Its present buildings date from 1654; the stone *torii* (gates) on the south side are considered among the largest in Japan. But the reason most people come here is one of practicality—the shrine is dedicated to the gods of health and prosperity, two universal concerns. This shrine, which is free to the public and open 24 hours, is packed during the Gion Festival and on New Year's Eve.

*Exit Yasaka Shrine to the west; this brings you to a busy street called Higashioji. Cross it and continue walking west, on the right side of busy Shijo Dori, where you'll soon come to the:*

### ⓭ Kyoto Craft Center

The center carries beautifully crafted traditional items by local and famous artisans, including glassware, pottery, jewelry, baskets, and more (see p. 333 for more information).

*Across Shijo Dori is:*

### ⓮ Gion

Gion is one of Japan's most famous nightlife districts. It's centered primarily on Hanamikoji Dori, which translates as "Narrow Street for Flower Viewing." This is Kyoto's long-standing geisha district, an enclave of discreet, traditional, and almost solemn-looking wooden homes that reveal nothing of the gaiety that goes on inside—drinking, conversation, and business dealings with dancing, singing, and music provided by geisha and their apprentices, called *maiko*. If it's early evening, you might glimpse one of these women as she small-steps her way

in *geta*, a type of traditional wooden shoe, to an evening appointment, elaborately made up and wearing a beautiful kimono. You might also wish to visit **Gion Corner** on Hanamikoji Dori, which offers performances of dance, puppetry, and other traditional arts nightly; see "Kyoto After Dark," later in this chapter, for details.

**WINDING DOWN**
If all this sightseeing and shopping have made you thirsty, there are many restaurants and bars to the west across the Kamo River, on Pontocho, and near Shijo and Kawaramachi streets. See "Where to Dine in Kyoto" and "Kyoto After Dark" in this chapter for many suggestions in this area.

---

## WALKING TOUR 2    THE PHILOSOPHER'S STROLL

| | |
|---|---|
| **Start:** | Ginkakuji, the Temple of the Silver Pavilion; from Kyoto Station, take bus no. 100 to Ginkakuji-mae stop or bus no. 5 or 17 to Ginkakuji-michi stop. |
| **Finish:** | Kyoto Handicraft Center, Marutamachi Dori. |
| **Time:** | Allow about 5 hours, including stops along the way. |
| **Best Times:** | Early on weekdays, when crowds aren't as thick. |
| **Worst Times:** | There is no worst time for this walk. |

This stroll takes in the Temple of the Silver Pavilion as well as a couple of other temples, a museum dedicated to Kyoto's traditional crafts, Kyoto's most well-known shrine and its garden, and the best place in town for one-stop souvenir shopping. Linking the Silver Pavilion with the other sights is a canal lined by trees—a path known as the **Philosopher's Pathway.**

---

From the Ginkakuji-mae or Ginkakuji-michi bus stop, head east (toward the wooded hills) along the canal, and continue east when the canal veers to the (right) south, up the gentle slope to:

### ❶ Ginkakuji, the Temple of the Silver Pavilion

This temple is the architectural jewel of this stroll. Contrary to its name, however, it isn't silver at all. It was built in 1482 as a retirement villa for Shogun Ashikaga Yoshimasa, who intended to coat the structure with silver in imitation of the Golden Pavilion built by his grandfather. He died before this could be accomplished, however, which is just as well—the wood of the Silver Pavilion is spectacular just as it is. The whole complex is designed for enjoyment of the tea ceremony, moon viewing, and other aesthetic pursuits, with a beautiful garden of rippled sand, rocks, and moss. One of the small sand hills is in the image of Mount

Fuji. It's easy to imagine the splendor, formality, and grandeur of the life of Japan's upper class as you wander the grounds here. Be sure to take the hillside pathway with its lookout point, dozens of different kinds of moss, and streams; you might be able to escape the crowds that sometimes overwhelm this attraction.

Head back to that narrow canal you saw on the way to the temple, heading south lined with cherry, willow, and maple trees and flanked by a small pathway. It's known as the:

### ❷ Philosopher's Pathway

The name Philosopher's Pathway refers to the fact that, throughout the ages, philosophers and priests have strolled this tranquil canal thinking deep thoughts. It's a particularly beautiful sight in spring during the cherry-blossom season. The pathway runs almost a mile, allowing you to think your own deep thoughts.

# Walking Tour 2—The Philosopher's Stroll

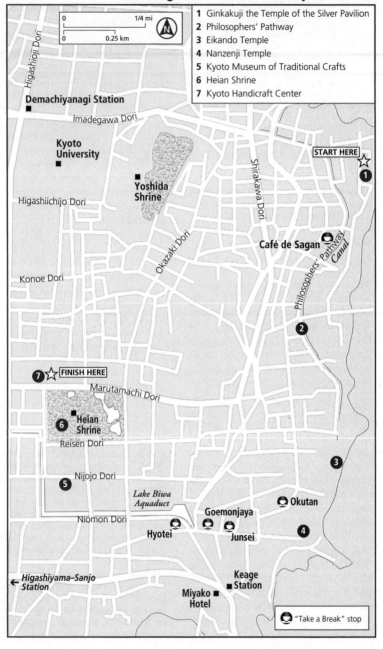

1 Ginkakuji the Temple of the Silver Pavilion
2 Philosophers' Pathway
3 Eikando Temple
4 Nanzenji Temple
5 Kyoto Museum of Traditional Crafts
6 Heian Shrine
7 Kyoto Handicraft Center

0 · · · 1/4 mi
0 · · · 0.25 km

Higashioji Dori

Demachiyanagi Station

Imadegawa Dori

Kyoto University

Yoshida Shrine

Higashiichijo Dori

Okazaki Dori

Shirakawa Dori

START HERE
1

Café de Sagan

Philosophers' Pathway
Canal

Konoe Dori

2

7 FINISH HERE

Marutamachi Dori

Heian Shrine
6

Reisen Dori

Nijojo Dori
5

3

Lake Biwa Aquaduct

Goemonjaya

Okutan

Niomon Dori

Hyotei

Junsei

4

← Higashiyama–Sanjo Station

Keage Station

Miyako Hotel

"Take a Break" stop

**TAKE A BREAK**
Approximately 5 minutes down the Philosopher's Pathway, to the right, is **Café de Sagan** (☎ 075/751-7968), a coffee shop with an English-language menu listing sandwiches, desserts, beer, and juices. It's open Friday to Wednesday from 7am to 5pm, with views of the shaded path through its windows.

At the end of the Philosopher's Pathway (a 30-min. walk), near Nyakuoji Shrine, turn right and walk for a few minutes through a residential area until you reach a street with some traffic on it (and a wooden sign pointing toward Eikando and Nanzenji). Here you should turn left. After a couple of minutes, on the left, you'll come to:

**❸ ⑨⑦ Eikando Temple**

Founded in 856, this temple (also known as **Zenrinji Temple;** ☎ 075/761-0007) derives its popular name from the seventh head priest Eikan (1032–1111), who was loved by the people for attending to the impoverished sick and for planting plum trees as sources of medicine. The temple is famous for a small statue of the Amida Buddha with his head turned, looking back over his shoulder. According to popular lore, it was carved after Eikan, who while walking and reciting chants he believed would propel him toward rebirth, was so astonished to see that the Amida Buddha had descended from the altar and was walking ahead of him that he stopped short in his tracks, whereupon the Buddha looked back over his shoulder and admonished, "Eikan, you are dawdling." How typically Zen. The Buddha facing backward is in the Amidado Hall. Otherwise, there isn't much to see unless it's autumn and the many maples here are at their most glorious. The temple's pagoda, up on a hillside, offers a view over the city. Open daily from 9am to 4pm; admission is ¥600 ($5.70), except in autumn when it's ¥1,000 ($9.50).

A few minutes' walk farther south brings you to:

**❹ Nanzenji Temple**

Nanzenji Temple (☎ 075/771-0365) is a Rinzai Zen temple set amid a grove of spruce. One of Kyoto's best-known Zen temples, it was founded in 1293, though its present buildings date from the latter part of the 16th century during the Momoyama Period. Attached to the main hall (Hojo) is a Zen rock garden attributed to Kobori Enshu; it's sometimes called "Young Tigers Crossing the Water" because of the shape of one of the rocks, but the association is a bit of a stretch for me. In the building behind the main hall is a sliding door with a famous painting by Kano Tanyu of a tiger drinking water in a bamboo grove. Spread throughout the temple precincts are a dozen other lesser temples and buildings worth exploring if you have the time, including Nanzen-in, which was built about the same time as Nanzenji Temple and served as the emperor's vacation house whenever he visited the temple grounds. The temple is open daily from 8:40am to 5pm (to 4:30pm in winter); admission to the main hall is ¥500 ($4.75) and to Nanzen-in ¥300 ($2.85).

**TAKE A BREAK**
Several traditional restaurants near Nanzenji reflect the settings of the temples themselves. **Okutan,** just north of Nanzenji and with a view of a peaceful pond, has been serving vegetarian tofu meals for 350 years. On the road leading west from Nanzenji are **Junsei,** serving tofu, obento lunch boxes, and kaiseki in a beautiful garden setting; **Goemonjaya,** which serves moderately priced set meals and noodles; and **Hyotei,** which opened more than 300 years ago to serve pilgrims to Nanzenji, offering obento lunches as well as expensive kaiseki. See "Where to Dine in Kyoto," earlier in this chapter, for details.

Head straight out (west) from Nanzenji until you see a body of water on your right, the Lake Biwa Aqueduct. Continue west on Niomon Dori (the water will be on your right) to the vermilion-colored bridge to your right, where you'll also see a vermilion-colored torii gate. Turn right here and continue straight ahead to Nijo Dori, where you turn left for one of my favorite museums, the:

### ❺ Kyoto Museum of Traditional Crafts (Fureaikan)

This museum displays all the Kyoto crafts you can think of, from combs, umbrellas, and fans to textiles, sweets, bambooware, and masks. English-language explanations and videos describe how the crafts are made (mostly by hand). The best news: The museum is free. For more details, see p. 318.

Farther north, it would be hard to miss:

### ❻ Heian Shrine

If orange and green are your favorite colors, you're going to love Heian Shrine, one of Kyoto's most famous. Although it was built as late as 1895 in commemoration of the 1,100th anniversary of the founding of Kyoto, Heian Shrine is a replica of the city's first administrative quarters, built in Kyoto in 794, giving you some idea of the architecture back then. The most important thing to see here is the **garden,** the entrance to which is on your left as you face the main hall. Typical of gardens constructed during the Meiji Era, it's famous for its weeping cherry trees in spring, its irises and water lilies in summer, and its changing maple leaves in the fall. I love sitting on the bench on the wooden bridge topped by a phoenix; you'll probably want to dawdle here, too.

Take a right out of the shrine's main exit onto Reisen Dori and then take the next right, which after 5 minutes will bring you to the:

### ❼ Kyoto Handicraft Center

This center is located behind the shrine on its north side. It's the best place in Kyoto for one-stop shopping for souvenirs of Japan, including pearls, kimono and the less-formal yukata, fans, paper products, toys, and more; see p. 333 for complete information. You may want to take advantage of the free hourly shuttle service the center provides to major hotels in Kyoto; the last bus departs at 6:05pm.

## 6 Imperial Villas & Temples within Easy Reach of Kyoto

If this is your first visit to Kyoto and you're here for only a couple days, you should concentrate on seeing sights in Kyoto itself. If, however, this is your second trip to Kyoto, you're here for an extended period of time, or you have a passion for traditional Japanese architecture or gardens, there are a number of worthwhile attractions in the region surrounding Kyoto. Foremost on my list is **Katsura Imperial Villa.**

*Note:* The Katsura Imperial Villa, **Shugakuin Imperial Villa,** and **Saihoji** (popularly called the Moss Temple) all require advance permission to visit. To see the Katsura Imperial Villa or Shugakuin Imperial Villa, which are free, you must apply for permission either online at http://sankan.kunaicho.go.jp/order/index_EN.html at least 4 days before your intended visit; or go in person to the **Imperial Household Agency Office** (© **075/221-1215;** no English is spoken and no reservations are accepted by phone, but you can call to see whether space is available), located on the northwest grounds of the **Kyoto Imperial Palace** near Inui Gomon Gate, a 5-minute walk from Imadegawa subway station. It's open Monday through Friday from 8:45am to noon and 1 to 4pm.

**Tours,** which take place weekdays and the third Saturday of every month year-round, as well as on Saturdays in April, May, October, and November (no tours on national holidays), are given at Katsura Imperial Villa at 10am and 2pm and at

Shugakuin Imperial Villa at 9am, 10am, 11am, 1:30pm, and 3pm. In the off season, you may be able to make a reservation for a tour on the same day, though keep in mind that it takes an hour to reach Katsura Imperial Villa and 30 minutes to reach Shugakuin by taxi from the Imperial Household Agency Office. It's always better, therefore, to make a reservation a day or two in advance; in spring and fall, try to make a reservation a week in advance. The time of your tour will be designated when you apply. Parties are limited to four persons, everyone must present their passports, and **participants must be at least 18 years old.** Tours are conducted in Japanese only, but an English-language video is shown.

For tours of Saihoji, see below.

**KATSURA IMPERIAL VILLA** ★★★    About a 15-minute walk from Katsura Station on the Hankyu railway line, or a 30-minute bus ride from Kyoto Station (take bus no. 33 to the Katsura Rikyu-mae stop) and then a 5-minute walk, this villa is considered the jewel of traditional Japanese architecture and landscape gardening. It was built between 1620 and 1624 by Prince Toshihito, brother of the emperor, with construction continued by Toshihito's son. The garden, markedly influenced by Kobori Enshu, Japan's most famous garden designer, is a "stroll garden" in which each turn of the path brings an entirely new view.

The first thing you notice upon entering Katsura is its simplicity—the buildings were all made of natural materials, and careful attention was paid to the slopes of the roofs and to the grain, texture, and color of the various woods used. A pavilion for moon viewing, a hall for imperial visits, a teahouse, and other buildings are situated around a pond; as you walk along the pathway, you're treated to views that literally change with each step you take. Islets; stone lanterns; various scenes representing seashores, mountains, and hamlets; manicured trees; and bridges of stone, earth, or wood that arch gracefully over the water—everything is perfectly balanced. No matter where you stand, the view is complete and in harmony. Every detail was carefully planned down to the stones used in the path, the way the trees twist, and how scenes are reflected in the water. Little wonder the Katsura Imperial Villa has influenced architecture not only in Japan but around the world. Sadly, tours are much too hurried (they last only 1 hr.), and no photography is allowed.

**SHUGAKUIN IMPERIAL VILLA** ★★    Northeast of Kyoto, about a 40-minute bus ride from Kyoto Station (take bus no. 5 from Kyoto Station to the Shugakuin Rikyu-michi bus stop) and then a 15-minute walk, this villa was built in the mid-1600s as a retirement retreat for Emperor Go-Mizunoo, who came to the throne at age 15 and suddenly abdicated 18 years later to become a monk, passing the throne to his daughter in 1629. Amazingly, though the villa was only 2 hours from the Imperial Palace, the emperor came here only on day trips; he never once spent the night. The 53-hectare (133-acre) grounds, among Kyoto's largest, are situated at the foot of Mount Hiei and are famous for the principle known as "borrowed landscape" in which the surrounding landscape is incorporated in the overall garden design. Grounds are divided into three levels (only two of which have compelling features): The **upper garden,** with its lake, islands, and waterfalls, is the most extensive of the three and offers grand views of the surrounding countryside from its hillside pavilion. The **middle garden,** built as a residence for the emperor's daughter, contains a villa with the famous "Shelves of Mist"; in keeping with the Japanese penchant for ranking the best three of everything, this is considered one of the three most beautiful shelves in Japan. The gardens are more spacious and natural than most Japanese-style

gardens, which are often small and contrived. Tours, which take 1 hour and 15 minutes and cover almost 3.2km (2 miles), allow ample time for photography.

**SAIHOJI**  Popularly known as **Kokedera (Moss Temple),** Saihoji was converted into a Zen temple in 1339 and is famous for its velvety-green moss garden spread underneath the trees. Altogether, there are more than 100 different varieties of moss throughout the grounds, with popular names like "velvet moss," "water moss," and "snake-stomach moss." They give off an iridescent and mysterious glow that's best just after a rain; indeed, Kyoto's rainy season and high summer humidity create the perfect breeding ground for moss. Before being allowed to visit the grounds, tour participants must first listen to a lecture (in Japanese).

*Note:* Because the monks are afraid that huge numbers of visitors will trample the moss to death, permission is needed to visit Saihoji, and you can obtain it only by writing to the temple at least 10 days in advance (applications up to 2 months in advance are accepted). Write to Saihoji Temple, 56 Matsuo Kamigatani-cho, Nishikyo-ku, Kyoto 615-8286 (© **075/391-3631**), and give your name, your address in Japan, your age, your occupation, and the date you'd like to visit (plus second and third choices). Include a self-addressed return envelope and International Reply Coupons for return postage. (If you're in Japan, you should send a double postcard or *ofuku hagaki*.) The cost of the visit, which includes a sutra-writing demonstration, is a "donation" of at least ¥3,000 ($29; no change given), payable when you pick up your ticket. To reach Saihoji, take the Karasuma subway line to Shijo Station, transferring there to bus no. 29 to the Kokedera-michi stop.

**BYODOIN TEMPLE**  Located in the town of Uji, about 18km (11 miles) southeast of Kyoto and a 15-minute ride by express JR train from Kyoto Station, Byodoin Temple (© **0774/21-2861**) is a good example of temple architecture of the Heian Period. Originally a villa, it was converted into a temple in 1053. Most famous is the main hall, known as **Phoenix Hall,** the only original building remaining. It has three wings, creating an image of the mythical bird of China, the phoenix; on the gable ends are two bronze phoenixes. On the temple grounds is a National Treasure: one of the most famous bells in Japan (there are no inscriptions on the bell, but it has reliefs of maidens and lions and is thought to contain Korean influences) as well as a monument to Minamoto Yorimasa, who took his own life here after being defeated by the rival Taira clan. Byodoin is best known to Japanese, however, for gracing the back of ¥10 coins. Byodoin is about a 10-minute walk from the Uji JR Station (there's a map of the town in front of the station). Admission to the grounds is ¥600 ($5.70), ¥500 ($4.75) more for Phoenix Hall. Open daily 9am to 5pm (to 4pm in winter).

**FUSHIMI-INARI SHRINE**  Just a minute's walk from the JR Inari Station (which is just two stops by local commuter train from Kyoto Station), Fushimi-Inari Shrine (© **075/641-7331**) has long been popular with merchants, who come here to pray for success and prosperity. One of Japan's most celebrated Shinto shrines, it was founded in 711 and is dedicated to the goddess of rice (rice was collected as taxes during the shogun era). The 4km (2½-mile) pathway behind the shrine is lined with more than 10,000 red torii gates, presented by worshippers throughout the ages; there are also stone foxes, which are considered messengers of the gods. It's a glorious—almost surreal—walk as you wind through the woods and the tunnel of vermilion-colored torii gates and then gradually climb a hill, where you'll have a good view of Kyoto. At several places along the path are small shops where you can sit down for a bowl of

noodles or other refreshments. Admission is free, and the expansive grounds never close. The most popular times to visit are the first day of each month and New Year's.

*Note:* Both Byodoin Temple and Fushimi-Inari Shrine are on the same JR line that continues to Nara. If you plan on spending the night in Nara, you could easily take in these two attractions on the way. Note, however, that the express train to Nara does not stop at JR Inari Station; for that you'll have to take a local train.

## 7 Shopping Kyoto

As the nation's capital for more than 1,000 years, Kyoto spawned a number of crafts and exquisite art forms that catered to the elaborate tastes of the imperial court and the upper classes. Kyoto today is still renowned for its **crafts,** including Nishijin textiles, Yuzen-dyed fabrics, Kyo pottery (pottery fired in Kyoto), fans, dolls, cutlery, gold-leaf work, umbrellas, paper lanterns, combs, Noh masks, cloisonné, and lacquerware.

**GREAT SHOPPING AREAS**    The majority of Kyoto's tiny specialty shops are situated in central Kyoto along Shijo Dori and in the area of Kawaramachi Dori. The square formed by **Kawaramachi Dori, Shijo Dori, Sanjo Dori,** and **Teramachi Dori** includes two covered shopping arcades and specialized shops selling lacquerware, combs and hairpins, knives and swords, tea and tea-ceremony implements, and more—including, of course, clothing and accessories.

If you're looking for antiques, woodblock prints, and art galleries, head toward **Shinmonzen Dori** and **Furumonzen Dori** in Gion, which parallel Shijo Dori to the north on the eastern side of the Kamo River. You'll find pottery and souvenir shops in abundance on the roads leading to Kiyomizu Temple in **Higashiyama-ku.**

For clothing, accessories, and modern goods, Kyoto's many **department stores** are good bets. They're conveniently located near Kyoto Station or in central Kyoto near the Shijo-Kawaramachi intersection. In addition, there's a big underground shopping mall beneath Kyoto Station selling everything from clothing and shoes to stationery and local souvenirs.

## CRAFTS & SPECIALTY SHOPS

**⑼ Aritsugu**    The fact that this family-owned business is located at the Nishiki-Koji market is appropriate since it sells hand-wrought knives and other handmade cooking implements, including sushi knives, bamboo steamers, pots, pans, and cookware used in the preparation of traditional Kyoto cuisine. In business for 400 years, the shop counts the city's top chefs among its customers. It also sells ikebana scissors. Open daily 9am to 5:30pm. Nishiki-Koji Dori, Gokomachi Nishi-iru, Nakagyo-ku. ℂ **075/221-1091.** Bus: 4, 5, 17, or 205 to Shijo Kawaramachi (5 min). 1 block north of Shijo Dori on the north side of Nishiki-Koji Dori, west of Gokomachi.

**Kasagen**    Kasagen has been making traditional umbrellas *(bangasa)* since 1861. They're more expensive than elsewhere but are of high quality and are made to last a lifetime. Open Thursday to Tuesday 10am to 8pm. 284 Gion-machi, Kitagawa. ℂ **075/561-2832.** Bus: 100, 206, or 208 to Gion. On the north side of Shijo Dori, just west of Yasaka Shrine.

**Kikuya**    Kikuya has a good selection of used kimono, *haori* (short kimono-like jackets, traditionally worn by men), geta, and kimono accessories for both adults and children. Although they're not antiques as Kikuya advertises but secondhand, the goods here are beautiful and timeless. Everything is in good condition (Japanese wear kimono only for special occasions), but be sure to look thoroughly for any defects. No

credit cards are accepted. Open Monday to Saturday 9am to 7pm. On Manjuji Dori, east of Sakaimachi. ⟨𝄞⟩ 075/351-0033. Take the Keihan Electric Line to Gojo (5 min.).

⑨⑨ **Kyoto Aburatorishi Senmontenzo**   I realize this is a bit odd, but this shop is dedicated to one of my favorite Japanese cosmetic products: face paper. Kyoto is famous for its face paper, long used by geisha and maiko, and this shop sells a bewildering choice of varieties, for everything from dry to troubled skin. I like it for blotting oily skin on hot, humid days. Daily 11am to 9pm. Kawaramachi, Shijo-aguru. ⟨𝄞⟩ 075/213-3322. Bus: Bus: 4, 5, 17, or 205 to Shijo Kawaramachi. On the east side of Kawaramachi Dori, north of Shijo Dori; look for its sign with an elephant.

**Kyoto Ceramics Center (Kyoto Tojiki Kaikan)**   This modern shop with a glass facade is operated by an association of Kyoto potters who display their wares of Kyo pottery (pottery fired locally). Approximately 10,000 items are on display, from sake cups and vases to bowls, plates, and chopstick rests. Daily 10am to 6pm. Higashioji Dori, Gojo-aguru. ⟨𝄞⟩ 075/541-1103. Bus: 100 or 206 to Gojozaka (one of the approaches to Kiyomizu Temple). On Higashioji Dori, north of Gojo Dori.

**Kyoto Craft Center**   Whereas the Kyoto Handicraft Center (below) is good for souvenirs and inexpensive gifts for the folks back home, this crafts center is the kind of place to which you head to buy a wedding gift or something really special for yourself. Featuring beautifully designed contemporary crafts by local and famous artisans, the Kyoto Craft Center devotes its two floors to a wide range of products, including jewelry, scarves, pottery, glass, fans, damascene, baskets, and much more. Since the products are continually changing, there's always something new. Open Thursday to Tuesday 11am to 7pm. 275 Gion, Kitagawa, Higashiyama-ku. ⟨𝄞⟩ 075/561-9660. Bus: 12, 31, 46, 80, 100, 201, 202, 203, 206, or 207 to Gion (3 min.). On Shijo Dori east of the Kamo River in the heart of Gion.

**Kyoto Handicraft Center**   For one-stop souvenir shopping, your best bet is Kyoto's largest craft, gift, and souvenir center. Five floors of merchandise contain almost everything Japanese imaginable: pearls, lacquerware, dolls, children's toys, kimono (including antique kimono), woodblock prints, pottery, cameras, paper products, swords, lanterns, silk and textile goods, painted scrolls, and music boxes—and that's just for starters. You can even buy the socks to be worn with geta wooden shoes and the obi sashes to be worn with the kimono.

You can easily spend an hour or two here just wandering around; artisans also demonstrate their various crafts, including woodblock printing and the production of damascene. You can even try your own hand at making woodblock prints, cloisonné, and dolls, with instruction provided. For this you should plan at least 1 hour; bookings are made at the information counter on the ground floor from 1 to 4pm daily. Lessons cost ¥1,500 ($13) and are a great way for older children to get creative while you shop. And if you spend more yen than you have, you can exchange money here at a favorable rate. Open daily from 10am to 6pm. Sakyo-ku. ⟨𝄞⟩ 075/761-8001. Bus: 93, 201, 202, 203, 204, or 206 to Kumano-jinja-mae (3 min.). Free hourly bus service (on the hour except noon) from the center to major hotels throughout Kyoto. Just north of Heian Shrine on Marutamachi Dori.

⑩⓪ **Miyawaki Baisen-an**   This elegant, open-fronted shop has specialized in handmade fans since 1823, particularly fans characteristic of Kyoto. A little English is spoken. Prices range from ¥2,000 ($19) for a small tea-ceremony fan to ¥50,000 ($476) for the best that money can buy. Open daily 9am to 7pm (to 6pm in winter). 102 Tominokoji-nishi, Rokkaku-dori, Nakagyo-ku. ⟨𝄞⟩ 075/221-0181. Subway: Karasuma Oike (6 min.). On Rokkaku-dori just west of Tominokoji, across from a playground.

## DEPARTMENT STORES

Department stores are good places to shop for Japanese items and souvenirs, including pottery, lacquerware, and kimono as well as clothing and everyday items.

**JR Kyoto Isetan,** located in Kyoto Station (© 075/352-1111; open daily 10am–8pm), is Kyoto's most fashionable department store for young people, specializing in women's imported and domestic clothing.

In central Kyoto, **Daimaru,** on Shijo Dori west of Takakura (© 075/211-8111; open daily 10am–8pm), is Kyoto's largest department store, with everything from clothing to food to electronic goods spread on nine floors. Nearby are **Hankyu,** on the southeast corner of Shijo-Kawaramachi intersection (© 075/223-2288; open daily at 11am, closing 8pm Mon–Wed and 9pm Thurs–Sun), with seven floors of fashion, housewares, and food; and **Takashimaya,** across the street at the southwest corner of the Shijo-Kawaramachi intersection (© 075/221-8811; open daily 10am–8pm), one of Japan's oldest and most respected department stores with a good selection of traditional crafts.

## MARKETS

On the 21st of each month, a flea market is held at **Toji Temple** (© 075/691-3325), about a 15-minute walk southwest of Kyoto Station. Japan's largest flea market, it's also one of the oldest; its history stretches back more than 700 years, when pilgrims began flocking to Toji Temple to pay their respects to Kobo Daishi, who founded the Shingon sect of Buddhism. Today, Toji Temple is still a center for the Shingon sect, and its market (popularly known as Kobo-san) is a colorful affair with booths selling Japanese antiques, old kimono, ethnic goods, odds and ends, and many other items. Worshippers come to pray before a statue of Kobo Daishi and to have their wishes written on wooden slats by temple calligraphers. Even if you don't buy anything, the festive atmosphere of the market and booths makes a trip here a memorable experience. The largest Kobo-san markets take place in December and January. All markets at Toji are held from about 6am to 4pm. A smaller market, devoted entirely to Japanese antiques, is held at Toji Temple on the first Sunday of each month.

Commemorating the scholar and poet Sugawara Michizane, the **Tenjin-san market** held at **Kitano Tenmangu Shrine** (© 075/461-0005) the 25th of every month is a large market offering a little bit of everything—antiques, used clothing, ceramics, food—in a beautiful setting. It's open from about 8am to dusk, but go as early as you can. Kitano Shrine is on Imadegawa Dori between Nishi-oji and Senbon; take bus no. 101 to the Kitano Tenmangu-mae stop.

Unlike the other temple markets, the **Chion-ji market** (© 075/691-3325), held the 15th of each month from 9am to 4pm, is devoted to handmade goods and crafts, including pottery and clothing. To reach it, take bus no. 206 to Hyakumanben at the Higashioji and Imadegawa intersection; **Chion-ji Temple** is just to the northeast.

On the first Sunday of every month (though sometimes the date changes), a flea market is held in front of **City Hall** from 10am to 4pm, with local citizens selling unwanted stuff, mostly clothing. Although you may not buy anything to take home with you, a stroll through the **Nishiki-Koji Dori market** is worthwhile just for the atmosphere. Kyoto's 400-year-old city produce market, this covered shopping arcade 1 block north of Shijo Dori in the heart of old Kyoto is lined with vendors selling fish, flowers, eggs, pickled vegetables, fruit, and takeout foods, as well as crafts. It's open from 10am to about 6pm; some shops close on either Wednesday or Sunday.

## 8 Kyoto After Dark

Nothing beats a fine summer evening spent strolling the streets of Kyoto. From the geisha district of Gion to the bars and restaurants lining Pontocho, Kyoto is utterly charming and romantic at night. Begin with a walk along the banks of the Kamo River—it's a favorite place for young couples in love. In summer, restaurants stretching north and south of Shijo Dori along the river erect outdoor wooden platforms on stilts over the water.

**FINDING OUT WHAT'S ON**    There are many annual events and dances, including the very popular geisha area dances held in June, the only time of year you can see traditional dances performed by all five of Kyoto's traditional geisha districts; Gion Odori dances in October featuring *geiko* and *maiko* (geisha and apprentice geisha in Kyoto) dressed in elaborate costume; and Kabuki at the Minamiza Theater in December. To find out what's happening while you're in Kyoto, pick up the monthly magazine *Kansai Time Out,* available in Kyoto at the Junkudo Kyoto BAL bookstore on Kawaramachi Dori for ¥300 ($2.85). Although major concerts are infrequent in Kyoto (they're usually held in nearby Osaka), the magazine is the best source for finding out what's going on in the classical and contemporary music scene. In addition, the *Kyoto Visitor's Guide,* a monthly tabloid distributed free at tourist offices, hotels, and restaurants, contains a calendar of events and performances for the month.

## THE MAJOR NIGHTLIFE DISTRICTS
### GION  ��

A small neighborhood of plain wooden buildings in Higashiyama-ku on the eastern side of the Kamo River, Gion doesn't look anything like what you've probably come to expect from an urban Japanese nightlife district; in fact, there's hardly any neon in sight. There's something almost austere and solemn about Kyoto's most famous geisha district, as though its raison d'être were infinitely more important and sacred than mere entertainment. Gion is a shrine to Kyoto's past, an era when geisha numbered in the thousands.

Contrary to popular Western misconceptions, geisha are not prostitutes. Rather, they're trained experts in the traditional arts, conversation, and coquettishness, and their primary role is to make men feel like kings when they're in the soothing enclave of the geisha house. There are now only a mere 200 geisha in Gion; after all, in today's high-tech world, few women are willing to undergo the years of rigorous training to learn how to conduct the tea ceremony, to play the *samisen* (a three-stringed instrument), or to perform ancient court dances.

Gion is about a 5-minute walk from the Shijo-Kawaramachi intersection; to reach it, walk east on Shijo Dori and then take a right on Hanamikoji Dori. Its narrow streets are great for strolling; a good time to take a walk through the neighborhood is around dusk when geisha are on their way to their evening appointments. Perhaps you'll see one—or a *maiko* (a young woman training to be a geisha)—clattering in her high wooden shoes (called *geta*). She'll be dressed in a brilliant kimono, her face a chalky white, and her hair adorned with hairpins and ornaments. From geisha houses, music and laughter lilt from behind paper screens, sounding all the more inviting because you can't enter. Don't take it personally; not even Japanese will venture inside without the proper introductions. There are, however, an increasing number of bars and restaurants in Gion that are open to outsiders; it's not hard to imagine that in another 100 years, Gion will look no different from Tokyo's Ginza.

**Gion Corner**    After strolling around Gion, visit Gion Corner, which stages special variety programs in the ancient cultural arts. You'll see short demonstrations of the tea ceremony, *ikebana* (flower arranging), *koto* (Japanese harp) music, *gagaku* (ancient court music and dance), *kyogen* (Noh comic play), *kyomai* (Kyoto-style dance) performed by maiko, and *bunraku* (puppetry). The shows cater to tourists, and none of the individual performances beat a full-scale production of the real thing, but this is a convenient and quick introduction to the traditional forms of Japanese entertainment. If you wish, you can also partake in a 30-minute tea ceremony following each performance. March 1 to November 29, programs are held daily (except Aug 16) at 7pm and 8pm. Reservations are not necessary, but arrive early (no credit cards accepted), or purchase in advance at most hotels or Gion Corner box office. Yasaka Hall, Hanamikoji Dori, Shijo-sagaru, Gion. ✆ 075/561-1119. Tickets ¥2,800 ($27); ¥4,000 ($38) including tea ceremony. Bus: 4, 5, 17, or 205 to Shijo Kawaramachi (8 min.); or from other than Kyoto Station, 11, 12, 46, 201, 203, or 207 to Shijo Keihan-mae (4 min.). Located on Hanamikoji Dori south of Shijo Dori.

## PONTOCHO

Pontocho is a narrow alley that parallels the Kamo River's western bank, stretching from Shijo Dori north to Sanjo Dori. Once riddled with geisha houses and other members-only establishments, it is now lined with bars, clubs, restaurants, and hostess bars that fill every nook and cranny. Pontocho makes for a fascinating walk as you watch groups of Japanese enjoying themselves.

Another good place to look for nightlife is **Kiyamachi,** a small street that parallels Pontocho to the west and runs beside a small canal.

## THE CLUB & LIVE MUSIC SCENE

**Hello Dolly**    With an unlikely location on Pontocho, this dark, tiny club with velvet-upholstered chairs looks like a holdout from the '50s. It has live jazz Friday and Saturday, with classic jazz recordings the rest of the week. To find it, look for an album cover of Doris Day in the window; it's that kind of place. East side of Pontocho. ✆ 075/241-1728. Live music cover ¥1,000–¥1,100 ($9.50–$10); table charge an additional ¥900 ($8.55). Bus: 4, 5, 17, or 205 to Shijo Kawaramachi (3 min.).

**Live Spot Rag**    Depending on who's playing, the crowd at one of Kyoto's longest-standing live clubs, established in 1981, ranges from an older, more mellow audience to a younger, rowdier bunch. Mostly, however, it's a college-age crowd that comes here to listen to rock, jazz, acoustic, and fusion. Open nightly from 6pm to 3am, with live music 7:30 to 10:30pm. Empire Building, 5th floor, Kiyamachi Dori, Sanjo Agaru. ✆ 075/241-0446 (or 075/255-7273 10am–7pm). www.ragnet.co.jp. Live music cover ¥1,000–¥5,000 ($9.50–$48) depending on the band plus a 1-drink, 1-dish minimum. Discounts for advance purchases and usually for students. Subway: Kyoto Shiyakusho-mae (3 min.). Bus: 5, 17, or 205 to Kawaramachi Sanjo (2 min.). On the east side of Kiyamachi (beside a small stream) north of Sanjo Dori.

## THE BAR SCENE

**The Hill of Tara**    Live traditional Irish music is the main draw here Friday and Saturday evenings and Sunday from 6pm, but it's lively any day of the week at this popular pub. Happy hour is from 5 to 8pm daily, and the menu lists Irish stew, fish and chips, and other pub grub. Open daily 5pm to midnight (to 1am Fri–Sat). Oike Dori, Kawaramachi-higashiiru. ✆ 075/213-3330. Subway: Kyoto Shiyakusho-mae (2 min). Bus: 17 or 205 to Kawaramachi shiyakusho-mae (3 min.). On Oike Dori, beside the Kyoto Hotel.

**Pig & Whistle**   Here's a traditional, noisy, and fun English-style pub where you can play darts, stand at the bar, or sit at a table with your mum. It attracts an older, mixed crowd of both foreigners and Japanese, including foreigners who are networking for employment or business opportunities. Happy hour is from 5 to 8pm nightly. Open daily 5pm to midnight (to 1am Fri and Sat). Shobi Building, 2nd floor, 115 Ohashi-cho, Ohashi, Higashi Iru, Sanjo Dori. ✆ 075/761-6022. Subway: Sanjo Keihan (2 min.). On the north side of Sanjo Dori, east of the Kamo River.

**Rub-A-Dub**   This tiny basement bar has been Kyoto's premier Reggae spot for 20 years, a laid-back place that plays all genres of Jamaican music. Open Monday to Thursday 7pm to 2am and Friday and Saturday 7pm to 4am. Tsujita Building, 115 Ishiya-cho. ✆ 075/256-3122. Bus: 4, 5, 17, or 205 to Kawaramachi Sanjo. On Kiyamachi Dori, south of Sanjo Dori.

## 9  A Side Trip to Nara ★★

42km (26 miles) S of Kyoto

In early Japanese history, the nation's capital was moved to a new site each time a new emperor came to the throne. In 710, however, the first permanent Japanese capital was set up at **Nara.** Not that it turned out to be so permanent—after only 74 years, the capital was moved first to Nagaoka and shortly thereafter to Kyoto, where it remained for more than 1,000 years. What's important about those 74 years, however, is that they witnessed the birth of Japan's arts, crafts, and literature, as Nara imported everything from religion to art and architecture from China. Even the city itself, laid out in a rectangular grid pattern, was modeled after Chinese concepts. It was during the Nara Period that Japan's first historical account, first mythological chronicle, and first poetry anthology (with 4,173 poems) were written. Buddhism also flourished, and Nara grew as the political and cultural center of the land with numerous temples, shrines, pagodas, and palaces.

Japanese flock to Nara because it gives them the feeling that they're communing with ancestors. Foreigners come here because Nara offers them a glimpse of a Japan that was. Remarkably enough, many of Nara's historic buildings and temples remain intact, and long ago someone had enough foresight to enclose many of these historical structures in the quiet and peaceful confines of a large and spacious park, which has the added attraction of free-roaming deer.

## ESSENTIALS

**GETTING THERE**   Nara is easily reached from Kyoto Station on two lines: the JR Nara Line and the Kintetsu Limited Express. If you have a Japan Rail Pass, you'll probably want to take the commuter **JR Nara Line,** which departs about four times an hour and takes 43 to 57 minutes depending on the train; if you don't have a pass, the trip costs ¥690 ($6.50) one-way. If speed or luxury is of the utmost importance, the deluxe **Kintetsu Limited Express** whisks you to Nara in 34 minutes, guarantees you a seat (all seats are reserved), and costs ¥1,110 ($11) one-way; departures are every 30 minutes (if it's peak season, it's a good idea to buy your ticket in advance). A slower **Kintetsu ordinary express** takes 45 minutes and costs ¥610 ($5.80).

You can also reach Nara from Osaka in about 30 to 50 minutes, depending on the train and the station from which you leave. The **Kintetsu Nara Line,** departing from Namba Station, takes 40 minutes and costs ¥540 ($4.50) one-way.

*Moments* **Your Own Personal Guide**

**Nara YMCA Goodwill Guides** will be glad to show you the sights in exchange for the chance to practice their English. A national organization of volunteers, Goodwill Guides range from students and housewives to retired people. One guide each is often posted at both the JR and Kintetsu Station tourist offices and is available to the first tourists who show up any day except Sunday. But if you want to be assured of having a guide, make reservations in advance by calling ℂ **0742/45-5920** at least the day before to arrange a time. Guides are available daily from 9am to 5pm. There's no charge for these personal guides, but you are requested to pay their transportation to meet you, and I suggest you also pay for the guide's lunch (guides do not have to pay admission fares to attractions). A similar service is provided by **Nara Student Guides** by calling ℂ **0742/26-4753.**

**VISITOR INFORMATION**   There are tourist information offices at both **JR Nara Station** (ℂ **0742/22-9821;** open daily 9am–5pm) and **Kintetsu Nara Station** (ℂ **0742/24-4858;** open daily 9am–5pm). Both have good brochures and maps with useful information on how to get around Nara by foot and bus. For more detailed information on Nara, visit the **Nara City Tourist Center,** 23–4 Kami-sanjo-cho (ℂ **0742/22-3900;** open daily 9am–9pm), located in the heart of the city on Sanjo Dori between both stations and about a 5-minute walk from each. Finally, there's **Sarusawa Information Center** (ℂ **0742/26-1991;** open daily 9am–5pm), located at Sarusawa-ike Pond, south of Nara Park and not far from Nara's many attractions.

**GETTING AROUND**   If you take the Kintetsu Line, you'll arrive at **Kintetsu Nara Station;** if you take the JR train, you'll arrive at **JR Nara Station.** Both stations are about a 10-minute walk from each other and are within walking distance of Nara Park and its attractions. Kintetsu Station is slightly closer, about a 5-minute walk to the entrance of the park, while the JR Station is about a 10-minute walk to the park. Keep in mind, however, that Nara Park is quite large and its major attractions are far-flung; it takes about 20 minutes to walk from Kintetsu Nara Station to Todaiji Temple. Around the stations themselves is Nara's small downtown area, with Sanjo Dori serving as the main shopping street and running from JR Nara Station to Nara Park.

**IF YOU'RE HEADING TO HORYUJI**   If you plan to visit the Horyuji Temple Area (see below), the cheapest and fastest way to get there is from JR Nara Station on the JR Kansai Yamatoji Line going in the direction of Namba (in Osaka); departures are every 10 minutes or so and bring you to Horyuji Station in 12 minutes (fare: ¥210/$2). From there, you can either walk to the temple area in about 20 minutes or take the bus (¥170/$1.60), which departs two to three times an hour. Obviously, since it takes quite a bit of time getting to and from Horyuji, you must limit your sightseeing to only the major attractions if you plan on visiting both Nara Park and Horyuji in 1 day.

## SEEING THE SIGHTS

The best way to enjoy Nara is to arrive early in the morning before the first tour buses start pulling in. If you don't have much time, the most important sites to see are **Todaiji Temple, Kasuga Shrine,** and **Kofukuji Temple's Treasure House,** which you can view in about 3 hours. If you have more time, add **Horyuji Temple.**

# Nara

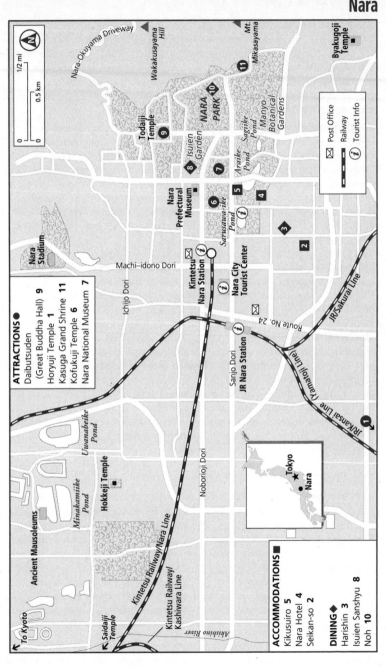

**ATTRACTIONS ●**
Daibutsuden
(Great Buddha Hall) **9**
Horyuji Temple **1**
Kasuga Grand Shrine **11**
Kofukuji Temple **6**
Nara National Museum **7**

**ACCOMMODATIONS ■**
Kikusuiro **5**
Nara Hotel **4**
Seikan-so **2**

**DINING ◆**
Harishin **3**
Isuien Sanshyu **8**
Noh **10**

☒ Post Office
━━ Railway
🛈 Tourist Info

Byakugoji Temple

Nara-Okuyama Driveway
Wakakusayama Hill
Mt. Mikasayama

NARA PARK

Manyo Botanical Gardens

Todaiji Temple

Isuien Garden

Sagiike Pond
Araike Pond

Nara Prefectural Museum

Sarusawa-ike Pond

Nara Stadium

Machi–idono Dori

Kintetsu Nara Station
Nara City Tourist Center

Ichijo Dori

JR/Sakurai Line

Route No. 24

Sanjo Dori
JR Nara Station

JR/Kansai Line (Yamatoji Line)

To Kyoto

Ancient Mausoleums

Uwanabeike Pond
Minakamiike Pond

Hokkeji Temple

Noborioji Dori

Kintetsu Railway/Nara Line

Kintetsu Railway/
Kashiwara Line

Saidaiji Temple

Akishino River

Tokyo
Nara

1/2 mi
0.5 km

## AROUND NARA PARK

With its ponds, grassy lawns, trees, and temples, Nara Park covers about 520 hectares (1,300 acres) and is home to more than 1,000 deer, which are considered divine messengers and are therefore allowed to roam freely through the park. The deer are generally quite friendly; throughout the park you can buy "deer cookies," which all but the shyest fawns will usually take right out of your hand. All of the below listings are within Nara Park.

**Kofukuji Temple**  As you walk east from either the JR or Kintetsu Station, this is the first temple you reach. It was established in 710 as the family temple of the Fujiwaras, the second-most powerful clan after the imperial family from the 8th to 12th centuries. At one time as many as 175 buildings were erected on the Kofukuji Temple grounds, giving it significant religious and political power up until the 16th century; through centuries of civil wars and fires, however, most of the structures were destroyed. Only a handful of buildings remain, but even these were rebuilt after the 13th century. The **five-story pagoda,** first erected in 730, was burned down five times. The present pagoda dates from 1426 and is an exact replica of the original; at 49m (164 ft.) tall, it's the second-tallest pagoda in Japan (the tallest is at Toji Temple in Kyoto). Also of historical importance is the **Eastern Golden Hall (Tokondo),** originally constructed in 726 by Emperor Shomu to speed the recovery of the ailing Empress Gensho. Rebuilt in 1415, it houses several priceless images, including a bronze statue of Yakushi Nyorai, a Buddha believed to cure illnesses, which was installed by Emperor Shomu on behalf of his sick wife; a 12th-century wooden bodhisattva of wisdom, long worshipped by scholar monks and today by pupils hopeful of passing university entrance exams; and guardians and assistants of Yakushi. But the best thing to see here is the temple's **Treasure House (Kokuhokan)** , which displays many statues and works of art originally contained in the temple's buildings, many of them National Treasures. Most famous are a statue of Ashura carved in the 8th century and a bronze head of Yakushi Nyorai, but my favorites are the 12th-century carved wooden statues representing priests of the Kamakura Period with fascinating facial features that render them strikingly human.

*0742/22-7755.* Treasure House ¥500 ($4.75) adults, ¥400 ($3.80) junior-high and high-school students, ¥150 ($1.45) elementary-school students; Eastern Golden Hall ¥300 ($2.85) adults, ¥200 ($1.90) junior-high and high-school students, ¥100 (95¢) elementary-school students. Daily 9am–5pm.

**Nara National Museum (Nara Kokuritsu Hakubutsukan)**  To the east of Kofukuji, this museum opened in 1895 to house invaluable Buddhist art and archaeological relics and has since expanded into a second building, used for special exhibits. Many masterpieces originally contained in Nara's temples are now housed here, including Buddhist sculptures from various periods in Japan's history, paintings, masks, scrolls, calligraphy, and archaeological objects obtained from temple ruins, tombs, and sutra mounds. Unfortunately, although items are identified in English, explanations of their historical significance are not. You'll spend 20 to 30 minutes here.

*0742/22-7771.* Admission ¥420 ($4) adults, ¥130 ($1.25) high-school and college students, free for junior-high and elementary students and seniors 70 and older. Higher admission during special exhibitions. Tues–Sun 9am–5pm.

**Todaiji Temple**  Nara's premier attraction is Todaiji Temple and its **Daibutsu (Great Buddha),** Japan's largest bronze Buddha. When Emperor Shomu ordered construction of both the temple and Daibutsu in the mid-700s, he intended to make Todaiji the headquarters of all Buddhist temples in the land. As part of his plans for a

Buddhist utopia, he commissioned work for this huge bronze statue of Buddha; it took eight castings to complete this remarkable work of art. At a height of more than 15m (50 ft.), the Daibutsu is made of 437 tons of bronze, 286 pounds of pure gold, 165 pounds of mercury, and 7 tons of vegetable wax. However, thanks to Japan's frequent natural calamities, the Buddha of today isn't quite what it used to be. In 855, in what must have been a whopper of an earthquake, the statue lost its head. It was repaired in 861, but alas, the huge wooden building housing the Buddha was burned twice during wars, melting the Buddha's head. The present head dates from 1692.

The wooden structure housing the Great Buddha, called **Daibutsuden,** was destroyed several times through the centuries; the present structure dates from 1709. Measuring 48m (161 ft.) tall, 56m (187 ft.) long, and 49m (164 ft.) wide, it's the largest wooden structure in the world—but is only two-thirds its original size. Be sure to walk in a circle around the Great Buddha to see it from all angles. Behind the statue is a model of how the Daibutsuden used to look, flanked by two massive pagodas as well as a huge wooden column with a small hole in it near the ground. According to popular belief, if you can manage to crawl through this opening, you'll be sure to reach enlightenment (seemingly a snap for children). You can also get your English-language fortune for ¥150 ($1.25) by shaking a bamboo canister until a wooden stick with a number comes out; the number corresponds to a piece of paper. Mine told me that though I will win, it will be of no use, an illness will be serious, and the person for whom I am waiting will not come. And the monk who gave me the fortune said mine was a good one!

*©* **0742/22-5511.** Admission ¥500 ($4.75) adults, ¥300 ($2.85) children. Mar daily 8am–5pm; Apr–Sept daily 7:30am–5:30pm; Oct daily 7:30am–5pm; Nov–Feb daily 8am–4:30pm.

**Kasuga Grand Shrine** *✿*   A stroll through the park will bring you to one of my favorite Shinto shrines in the Kyoto area. Originally the tutelary shrine of the powerful Fujiwara family, it was founded in 768 and, according to Shinto concepts of purity, was torn down and rebuilt every 20 years in its original form until 1863. Since virtually all empresses hailed from the Fujiwara family, the shrine enjoyed a privileged status with the imperial family. Nestled in the midst of verdant woods, it's a shrine of vermilion-colored pillars and an astounding 3,000 stone and bronze lanterns. The most spectacular time to visit is mid-August or the beginning of February, when all 3,000 lanterns are lit. Here, too, you can pay ¥200 ($1.90) for an *onikuji,* a slip of paper on which your fortune is written in English. If the fortune is unfavorable, you can conveniently negate it by tying the piece of paper to the twig of a tree. Although admission to the grounds is free, admission to the inner grounds is expensive—and not worth it in my opinion.

*©* **0742/22-7788.** Free admission to grounds; inner grounds ¥500 ($4.75) adults, free for children. Daily 9am–4:30pm (4pm in winter).

## THE HORYUJI TEMPLE AREA *✿✿✿*

Founded in 607 by Prince Shotoku as a center for Buddhism in Japan, **Horyuji Temple** (*©* **07457/5-2555**) is one of Japan's most significant gems for historic architecture, art, and religion. It was from here that Buddhism blossomed and spread throughout the land. Today about 45 buildings remain, some of them dating from the end of the 7th century and comprising what are probably the oldest wooden structures in the world. Although they are the main reason people come here, it's the

atmosphere of the compound itself that I love—serene, ancient, and a fitting tribute to Prince Shotoku, founder of Buddhism in Japan and much revered still today. Little wonder Horyuji was selected as Japan's first UNESCO World Cultural Heritage Site, in 1993 (for details on reaching Horyuji, see "Essentials," above).

At the western end of the grounds is the two-story, 17m-high (58-ft.) **Kondo,** or main hall, which is considered the oldest building at Horyuji Temple, erected sometime between the 6th and 8th centuries. It contains Buddhas commemorating Prince Shotoku's parents, protected by Japan's oldest set of four heavenly guardians (from the late 7th or early 8th c.). Next to the main hall is Japan's oldest **five-story pagoda,** dating from the foundation of the temple and considered the most important structure of Buddhist temples, since it is here that relics of the Buddha are enshrined; it contains four scenes from the life of Buddha. The **Gallery of Temple Treasures,** or Daihozoden, constructed in 1998, contains statues, tabernacles, and other works of art from the 7th and 8th centuries, many of them National Treasures. On the eastern precincts of Horyuji Temple is an octagonal building called **Yumedono Hall,** or the Hall of Visions, built in 739 as a sanctuary to pray for the repose of Prince Shotoku.

Admission to Kondo, Gallery of Temple Treasures, and Yumedono Hall is ¥1,000 ($9.50) for adults and ¥500 ($4.75) for children. The grounds are open daily from 8am to 5pm (to 4:30pm Nov 4–Feb 21).

Just behind Yumedono is ⑩⑪ **Chuguji Temple** (© 07457/5-2106), once part of a large nunnery built for members of the imperial family. It contains two outstanding National Treasures. The wooden statue of **Nyoirin Kannon Bosatsu,** dating from the 7th century, is noted for the serene and compassionate expression on her face. The **Tenjukoku Mandala,** the oldest piece of embroidery in Japan, was originally 4.8m (16 ft.) long and was created by Shotoku's consort and her female companions after Shotoku's death at the age of 48. It shows scenes from the Land of Heavenly Longevity, where only those with good karma are invited by the Buddha in the afterlife and where Shotoku surely resides. Only a replica of the fragile embroidery is now on display. Open daily from 9am to 4:30pm (to 4pm Oct 1–Mar 20); admission is ¥500 ($4.75) for adults, ¥250 ($2.40) for children.

## WHERE TO STAY

Although you can see Nara in a day trip from Kyoto or Osaka, I've included some recommendations for an overnight stay for more leisurely sightseeing. An extra incentive for staying overnight is provided July through October, when a dozen of Nara's most famous temples, shrines, and pagodas and other historic structures are lit at night, making for a romantic nighttime stroll.

⑩⑫ **Kikusuiro** ✿✿✿    You can't find a more beautiful example of a Japanese-style ryokan than this lovely 130-year-old inn, an imposing structure with an ornate Japanese-style roof surrounded by a white wall. The ryokan has been designated a private cultural asset by the Ministry of Culture. Rooms, some of which face Ara-ike Pond, are outfitted with scrolls and antiques and are connected to one another with rambling wooden corridors. There's also a beautiful garden. The manager, Mr. Itoh, speaks English.

1130 Takahata-cho Bodaimachi, Nara 630-8301. © **0742/23-2001.** Fax 0742/26-0025. 14 units (8 with bathroom). ¥31,500–¥40,000 ($300–$381) per person. Rates include 2 meals. DC, MC, V. South of Nara Park's Kofukuji 5-story pagoda on Sanjo Dori (corner of Rte. 308 and 369); a 10-min. walk from Kintetsu Nara Station, 15 min. from JR Nara Station. **Amenities:** 2 restaurants (Western, Japanese); in-room massage. *In room:* A/C, TV, fridge, hot-water pot w/tea.

**Nara Hotel** ★★★    One of the most famous places to stay in Nara (and with a front-desk staff eager to please), the Nara Hotel sits like a palace atop a hill overlooking several ponds. Built in 1909 in the Momoyama Period style of architecture and similar to Japan's other hotels built around the turn of the 20th century to accommodate the foreigners who poured into the country following the Meiji Restoration, it's constructed as a Western-style hotel but has many Japanese features. Photographs of visiting imperial family members adorn the walls. You have your choice of accommodations in the old section of the hotel with its wide corridors, high ceilings, antique light fixtures, fireplaces (no longer in use), and comfortable old-fashioned decor, or in the new addition, which opened in 1984 and offers larger modern rooms with dataports and verandas overlooking the old town. I personally prefer the atmosphere of the older rooms—those facing the city are less expensive than those in the new wing, while the higher-priced ones have a view of the pond or park.

Nara-Koennai, Nara 630-8301. ✆ **0742/26-3300.** Fax 0742/23-5252. www.miyakohotels.ne.jp. 132 units. ¥16,170 ($154) single; ¥26,565–¥31,185 ($253–$297) double; ¥25,410–¥57,750 ($242–$550) twin. Prices include service charge. 10% discount for holders of Japan Rail Pass. AE, DC, MC, V. About a 4-min. walk south of Nara Park; an 8-min. taxi ride from the train station. **Amenities:** 2 restaurants (Japanese, Western); 1 bar; 1 lounge; souvenir shop; room service (4–10:30pm); in-room massage; same-day laundry/dry-cleaning service. *In room:* A/C, satellite TV, dataport, minibar, hot-water pot w/tea, hair dryer, Washlet toilet.

**Seikan-so** ★★ ⒱ᵥₐₗᵤₑ    This is a lovely choice in inexpensive Japanese-style accommodations. It boasts the most beautiful garden of any Japanese Inn Group member I've seen, complete with azalea bushes and manicured trees—the kind of garden usually found only at ryokan costing twice as much. Located in a quiet neighborhood about a 10-minute walk south of Nara Park, it dates from 1916 and is owned by a friendly couple who speak English. The traditional Japanese building wraps around the inner garden. Unfortunately, the rooms are beginning to show their age, but all is forgiven if you can get one of the six facing the garden—be sure to request one when making your reservation. A Japanese or Western breakfast is available.

29 Higashi-Kitsuji-cho, Nara 630-8327. ✆ **0742/22-2670.** Fax 0742/22-2670. seikanso@chive.ocn.ne.jp. 9 units (none with bathroom). ¥4,200 ($40) per person. Discounts available for children under 10. Breakfast ¥472–¥735 ($4.50–$7) extra. AE, MC, V. Loop bus 1 to Kitayobate stop (1 min.), or a 12-min. walk from Kintetsu Nara Station, 25 min. from JR Nara Station. *In room:* A/C, TV, hot-water pot w/tea, no phone.

## WHERE TO DINE

⑩③ **Harishin** ★★★ Ⓕⁱⁿᵈˢ OBENTO    Many tourists never see this lovely part of old Nara near Gangoji Temple, which consists of narrow lanes and traditional wooden homes and shops. The restaurant itself is a 200-year-old house of ocher-colored walls and a wood-slat facade, and dining is on tatami with a view of a garden. Only an obento that changes with the season, the creation of chef-owner Nakagawa-san, is served (a mini-kaiseki meal is also available for ¥3,675/$35, but only if you make a reservation). My obento included an aperitif wine, light tofu flavored with sesame, soup, rice, pickled vegetables, tempura, and various exquisitely prepared bite-size morsels of shrimp, chicken, potatoes wrapped in bacon, and scallops. A meal here is highly recommended.

15 Nakashinya-cho. ✆ 0742/22-2669. Reservations required for dinner 2 days in advance. Obento ¥2,625 ($25). AE, DC, MC, V. Tues–Sun 11:30am–2:30pm and 6–8pm (last order); if Mon is a national holiday, open Mon and closed Tues. A 5-min. walk south of Sarusawa-ike Pond on the road that leads south from the west edge of the pond (stop at the tourist office for directions).

**Isuien Sanshyu** *🍸🍸* EEL   Isuien Garden, established during the Edo Period and enlarged a century ago by a Nara merchant, is a strolling garden that uses the principles of borrowed landscape, incorporating the hills of Kasuga and Wakayama in its design. While nothing spectacular, it does have a wonderful thatched-roof restaurant overlooking part of the garden and a pond—a great, traditional place for a meal. It serves only one thing, a set meal of eel *(unagi)* basted with a yam paste, soup, rice, and pickled vegetables—considered very healthy. If you wish, you can pay the extra admission to see the entire garden (¥600/$5.70 for adults), but there are better gardens in Kyoto.

Isuien Garden, 74 Suimoncho. *📞* **0742/22-2173.** Eel set meal ¥2,520 ($24). No credit cards. Wed–Mon 11:30am–1:30pm. North of Nara Park. Take the road between Kofukuji Temple and Nara National Museum (Rte. 369) north in the direction of Kyoto; after passing the busy street, take the 1st right. Isuien is at the end of this street.

**Noh** *🍸* JAPANESE/WESTERN   This looks like an unlikely place for a meal. Housed in the Nara Prefecture Public Hall, which looks like some kind of modern temple building at the east end of Nara Park, this restaurant would be rather ordinary if it weren't for one thing: a glass wall overlooking an expanse of lawn and a manicured garden. It offers both Western and Japanese food from an English-language menu, including main courses like fried prawns with tartar sauce and veal cutlet rosemary, lighter fare like spaghetti and curry rice, and obento box lunches. Both Japanese and Western set lunches are also available.

Nara Park. *📞* **0742/27-0620.** Main dishes ¥840–¥3,675 ($8–$35); Western set meals ¥2,625–¥6,300 ($25); Japanese teishoku ¥1,575 ($15); obento ¥2,730 ($26). AE, DC, MC, V. Tues–Sun 10:30am–7pm (to 5pm Dec–Feb). Closed national holidays.

# The Rest of Western Honshu

In addition to Tokyo, Kyoto, and the Japan Alps, the island of Honshu has numerous other cities, towns, and attractions in its western half that are well worth a visit. As the largest of Japan's islands and home to 80% of the country's population, Honshu is where most of the country's important historical events took place; you'll find many castles, gardens, temples, shrines, and other famous sights linked to the past here. Honshu's climate ranges from snowy winters in the north and in its mountain ranges to subtropical weather in the south. The middle of the island is traversed by Japan's longest river, the Shinano. With all this to offer, it's little wonder that many travelers to Japan never make it off this central island.

## 1 Nagoya

366km (227 miles) W of Tokyo; 147km (92 miles) E of Kyoto; 186km (116 miles) E of Osaka

**Nagoya** was founded as a castle town more than 390 years ago on orders of Tokugawa Ieyasu, who considered its strategic position on the Tokaido Highway useful for controlling Osaka and other points west. Today, Nagoya is Japan's fourth-largest city with a population of 2.19 million—yet it's a place most foreigners never stop to see. True, it doesn't have the attractions of many of the nation's other cities, but it does have a castle originally built by the first Tokugawa shogun, as well as one of Japan's most important Shinto shrines. You can also stroll through an aquarium famous for its penguins and sea turtles, visit the world-famous Noritake chinaware display rooms, spend hours at an open-air architectural museum (one of my favorites in Japan), and watch cormorant fishing in summer. Nagoya, capital of Aichi Prefecture, is also home to Japan's newest international airport and has long served as the gateway to Takayama in the Japan Alps (see the "Takayama, Little Kyoto of the Mountains" section in chapter 7) and Ise-Shima National Park (covered later in this chapter).

### ESSENTIALS

**GETTING THERE  By Plane**  Known formally as the Central Japan International Airport but dubbed **Centrair** (② **0569/38-1195;** www.centrair.jp/en), Japan's newest international airport occupies 22 hectares (54 acres) of a man-made island in Ise Bay. It boasts two hotels, 130 shops and restaurants (including Japan's largest duty-free store), a 24-hour ATM that accepts foreign credit cards, health and dental clinics, a post office, and even a hot-spring bath, the **Kutsurogi-dokoro** (② **0569/38-8282**), with Jacuzzi, sauna, and observatory baths with views of planes landing and taking off (fee: ¥900/$8.55). There's also a Tourist Information Center (② **0569/38-1050**), located past the arrivals hall, open daily 6:40am to 9:50pm. JAL's one-way fare from Tokyo to Nagoya is ¥15,700 ($150).

Trains connect Centrair with Nagoya Station in 40 minutes by regular train (¥850/$8.10) or in 30 minutes by express (¥1,200/$11). If you have luggage you might opt for the JR Airport Bus with direct service to downtown hotels for ¥1,000 ($9.50), with most trips taking about an hour (JR Rail Pass not valid). A taxi from Centrair to downtown Nagoya will run about ¥15,000 ($143).

**By JR Train**    The Shinkansen bullet train to **JR Nagoya Station** takes approximately 2 hours from Tokyo, 40 minutes from Kyoto, and 1 hour from Shin-Osaka Station. The fare from Tokyo Station is ¥10,070 ($96) for an unreserved seat.

**By Bus**    From Shinjuku Station in Tokyo, the Chuo Line bus charges ¥5,100 ($48) one-way for the 6-hour trip, with several departures daily. From Kyoto, the Meishin Highway Bus costs ¥2,500 ($24) and takes 2¾ hours; from Osaka, the trip takes just over 3 hours and costs ¥2,900 ($28).

**VISITOR INFORMATION**    Before departing Tokyo or Narita or Kansai international airports, stop by the Tourist Information Center for the leaflet "Nagoya and Vicinity," which contains a city map and transportation and sightseeing information (you can also download it from the Japan National Tourist Organization's website at www.jnto.go.jp by looking under *Regional Tourist Guides*). In Nagoya Station, you can pick up a map and the *Nagoya Visitors Guide* at the **Nagoya Tourist Information Center** (✆ **052/541-4301;** open daily 9am–7pm) in the central concourse, opposite the Central exit wickets of the JR Line; look for the ? and JR signs.

For more detailed information about Nagoya, walk 8 minutes from Nagoya Station's Central exit straight down Sakura Dori (or take the subway one stop to Kokusai Center Station) to the **Nagoya International Center** on the third floor of the Nagoya International Center Building, 1–47–1 Nagono (✆ **052/581-0100;** open Tues–Sat 9am–8:30pm, Sun and holidays 9am–5pm; closed second Sun in Feb and Aug). It's one of Japan's best facilities for foreign visitors and residents, with an English-speaking staff, a lounge area with a TV featuring CNN newscasts, Internet access, and lots of information on the city, including the free monthly publications *Nagoya Calendar* and *Avenues.* The center also advises foreign residents on how to get a visa, where to find an apartment, and which doctors speak English. On the fourth floor, you can apply to visit a Japanese family in their home in the local **Home Visit** system. You must apply in person no later than 5pm the day before you wish to visit; be sure to bring your passport. Call ✆ **052/581-5689** for details.

For recorded English-language information on events, concerts, festivals, and the arts, call ✆ **052/581-0400.** You can check the city's website at www.ncvb.or.jp.

**INTERNET ACCESS**    The Nagoya International Center (see "Visitor Information," above) provides Internet access for ¥200 ($1.90) per 30 minutes.

**MONEY/MAIL**    Nagoya's Central Post Office (✆ **052/564-2106**), located to the left of the Sakura exit of JR Nagoya Station, is open for mail and money exchange Monday to Friday 9am to 6pm. In addition to a counter open 24 hours for mail, it has ATMs open Monday to Saturday 7am to 11:55pm and Sunday and holidays 12:05am to 8pm.

**ORIENTATION**    Almost completely destroyed during World War II, Nagoya was rebuilt with wide, straight streets, many of which are named.

The ultramodern, twin-towered **JR Nagoya Station,** with its many train lines (including the Shinkansen), soars more than 50 stories above the skyline and contains

# Nagoya

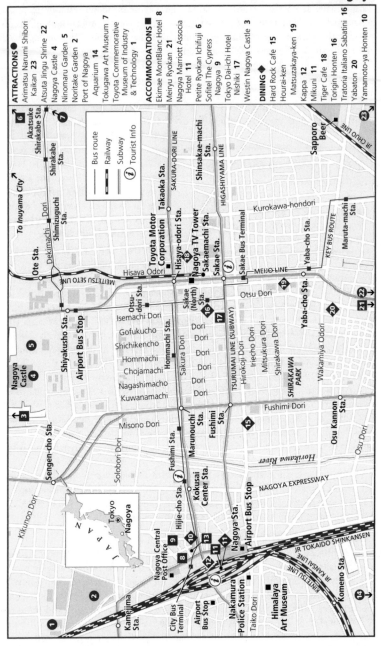

## ATTRACTIONS ●
Arimatsu Narumi Shibori Kaikan **23**
Atsuta Jingu Shrine **22**
Nagoya Castle **4**
Ninomaru Garden **5**
Noritake Garden **2**
Port of Nagoya Aquarium **14**
Tokugawa Art Museum **7**
Toyota Commemorative Museum of Industry & Technology **1**

## ACCOMMODATIONS ■
Ekimae MontBlanc Hotel **8**
Meiryu Ryokan **21**
Nagoya Marriott Associa Hotel **11**
Petite Ryokan Ichifuji **6**
Sofitel The Cypress Nagoya **9**
Tokyo Dai-ichi Hotel Nishiki **17**
Westin Nagoya Castle **3**

## DINING ◆
Hard Rock Cafe **15**
Hourai-ken
Kappa **12**
Mikuni **11**
Matsuzakaya-ken **19**
Tiger Cafe **18**
Torigin Honten **16**
Tratoria Italiano Sabatini **16**
Yabaton **20**
Yamamoto-ya Honten **10**

Takashimaya department store, offices, a Marriott hotel, many restaurants, and an observatory. Built in 1999, it has been recognized by the Guinness Book of Records as being the world's largest building containing a railway station. Clustered nearby are the Meitetsu Bus Terminal, Meitetsu Shin-Nagoya Station, the city bus terminal, Kintetsu Station, and a subway station for the Sakura Dori and Higashiyama lines, as well as many hotels and a huge underground shopping arcade that stretches 6km (3¾ miles) and includes about 600 shops.

Most of the city's attractions spread out east of Nagoya Station (take the Central/Sakuradori exit), including the city's downtown area, **Sakae,** two subway stops from Nagoya Station and with many shops, restaurants, and department stores. Also in Sakae is **Hisaya Odori,** a wide boulevard that stretches north and south with a park and a TV tower in its green meridian. North of Hisaya Odori is **Nagoya Castle,** while south is **Atsuta Jingu Shrine.**

> **⎛Tips⎞  A Note on Directions**
>
> All directions in the listings below are from Nagoya Station unless otherwise noted; the time indicates walking time from the subway or bus stop indicated.

**GETTING AROUND**   The easiest way to get around is via the city's four-line **subway** system, which is simple to use because station names are written in both English and Japanese, and there are English-language announcements and digital signs in trains. Probably the most important line for tourists is the **Meijo Line,** which runs through Sakae underneath Hisaya Odori and takes you to both Nagoya Castle (stop: Shiyakusho) and Atsuta Jingu Shrine (stop: Jingu-Nishi), with one branch terminating at Nagoya Port with its aquarium; if you take this line in the opposite direction, you'll eventually end up at the—I like this—Ozone stop. Individual tickets for the subway are ¥200 to ¥320 ($1.90–$3.05), depending on the distance.

To go where subway lines don't, such as the Tokugawa Art Museum, you'll find it convenient to take one of the **city buses,** for which you'll pay a flat fare of ¥200 ($1.90). City buses depart from Nagoya Station and the Sakae Bus Terminal. There's also the private **Meitetsu Bus Line** with a terminal located at Nagoya Station; for these buses, take a ticket and pay the exact fare according to the digital panel display at the front when you get off.

There are several **transportation passes** worth considering if you'll be traveling a lot within a single day. For subways, there's a 1-day pass **(Ichinichi Jo-sha)** for ¥740 ($7.05) that allows you to ride as much as you want for a full day; for ¥850 ($8.10), you can ride as much as you want on both subways and city buses.

## SEEING THE SIGHTS

⑩④ **Arimatsu Narumi Shibori Kaikan**   During the days of the shogun, Arimatsu was a small village on the old Tokaido Highway. Its inhabitants made a living producing tie-dyed cotton cloth *(shibori),* which they then sold as towels to passing travelers. Today, Arimatsu is a suburb of Nagoya on its southeastern edge, yet it still retains its historic core, with several buildings remaining from the Edo Period and more than 2,500 people still involved in the cottage industry. This small museum pays tribute to the painstaking tie-dying process; more than 100 patterns are possible, with a single kimono requiring between 50,000 and 200,000 handmade stitches and taking 4 to 6 months to complete. A 15-minute film tells the history of Arimatsu tie-dying and the

lengthy process involved in the craft: engraving a pattern, transferring the pattern to the cloth, tying the cloth, dying it, and then taking the stitches out. Several women are usually on hand practicing their trade; a small shop sells their wares.

Hashi-higashiminami 60–1, Arimatsu-cho, Midori-ku. © 052/621-0111. www.shibori-kaikan.com. Admission ¥300 ($2.85) adults, ¥100 (95¢) children. Thurs–Tues 9:30am–5pm. From Shin-Nagoya Station (next to Nagoya Station), take the Meitetsu train line (the local, not express) 30 min. to Arimatsu Station, walk straight out of the station, turn left at the bottom of the stairs, and then turn left at the sign for HATTORI RESIDENCE; the museum will be on the right (5 min.).

**Atsuta Jingu Shrine**    Because it contains one of the emperor's Three Sacred Treasures, this is revered as one of the three most important shrines in Japan. Founded in the 2nd century and last rebuilt in 1935, it enshrines the Kusanagi-no-Tsurugi (Grass-Mowing Sword), which is one of the Three Regalia of the Emperor. The other two sacred treasures are the Sacred Mirror (in the Ise Grand Shrines; see p. 359) and the Jewels (in the Imperial Palace in Tokyo; see p. 173). According to legend, the Grass-Mowing Sword was presented to a prince named Yamato-Takeru, who used it during a campaign against rebels in eastern Japan; the rebels set a field of grass on fire, and the prince used the sword to mow down the grass, thereby quelling the fire. (*Atsuta* means "hot field" in Japanese.) Actually, there isn't much to see here—the sword is never on public display—yet this remains one of Nagoya's top attractions, and Japanese make pilgrimages here to pay their respects, first purifying their hands or mouths with water, then throwing coins into the money box, clapping to gain the attention of the gods, and bowing as they pray. Surrounded by stately, ancient cypress trees, the shrine provides a nice respite from city life.

1–1–1 Jingu, Atsuta-ku. © 052/671-4151. Free admission to the grounds. Open 24 hr. Station: Jingu-mae (4 min.) via the Meitetsu train line from Shin-Nagoya Station or Jingu-Nishi via subway (5 min.).

**Nagoya Castle**  ⊛    Built for his ninth son by Tokugawa Ieyasu, the first Tokugawa shogun, Nagoya Castle was completed in 1612 and served as both a strategic strong-hold and a residence for members of the Owari branch of the Tokugawa family for almost 250 years, until the Meiji Restoration ended their rule in 1868. A shrewd and calculating shogun, Tokugawa forced feudal lords throughout Japan to contribute to the castle's construction, thereby depleting their resources and making it harder for them to rebel. Although Nagoya Castle was largely destroyed in World War II (only three turrets and three gates escaped destruction), the main donjon and other structures, rebuilt in 1959, are almost carbon copies of the original. Like most recon-structed castles in Japan, this replica is made of ferroconcrete, yet it's still impressive from afar. Inside, the 96m-high (154-ft.) donjon is thoroughly modern and even has an elevator up to the fifth floor, where you have fine views of Nagoya and beyond. The castle houses treasures that escaped the bombing during World War II, including beautiful paintings on sliding doors and screens. There's also a model of Honmaru Palace (destroyed during World War II), the living quarters of the shogun when he vis-ited Nagoya, flintlocks, swords, and helmets, as well as displays that explore Nagoya Castle's construction and what life was like during the Edo Period.

Atop the donjon roof are two **golden dolphins,** replicas of those that perished dur-ing World War II and long thought to protect the castle from dreaded fires. The dol-phins each weigh about 1,193 kilograms (2,650 lb.) and are made of cast bronze covered with 18-karat-gold scales. Incidentally, the dolphin on the south end—the favored, warmer side—is considered male, while the one relegated to the colder north-ern side is female.

East of the castle is **Ninomaru Garden,** laid out at the time of the castle's construction, converted to a dry Japanese landscape garden in 1716 and today one of the few remaining castle gardens in Japan. Besides providing a beautiful setting, it served as an emergency shelter for the lord in case of enemy attack. Stop by the **Ninomaru Tea House**—it's said that if you drink tea here, 5 years will be added to your life. That should allow you ample time to linger, but otherwise you can tour the castle and grounds in less than 1½ hours.

1–1 Honmaru, Naka-ku. ⓒ 052/231-1700. Admission ¥500 ($4.75) adults, ¥100 (95¢) junior-high and elementary-school students. Daily 9am–4:30pm. Station: Shiyakusho (5 min.).

**Noritake Garden** 𝘈𝘈 Nagoya has been a pottery and porcelain production center for centuries; today, the city and its vicinity manufacture 90% of Japan's total export chinaware. The largest chinaware company in Japan is Noritake, founded in 1904 and known the world over for its fine tableware. You can learn more about Noritake by spending about an hour at the site of its former factory, beginning with the Welcome Center's short film depicting the history of Noritake. At the Craft Center, you can see displays explaining the manufacturing and decorating processes involved in making porcelain, as well as watch artisans at work. Unlike most modern-day factories, where work is largely automated, almost all the work done at Noritake is still done by hand. Other highlights include a great museum with examples of all the Noritake chinaware ever produced (including a great Art Deco collection), and a shop selling Noritake (including an outlet corner for discounted products).

3–1–36 Noritake Shinmachi, Nishi-ku. ⓒ 052/561-7114. www.noritake.co.jp. Admission ¥500 ($4.75) adults, ¥300 ($2.85) high-school students, free for children and seniors. Tues–Sun 10am–5pm (you must enter the Craft Center by 4pm); shop open until 6pm. Subway: Kamejima (5 min.), or a 10-min. walk north of Nagoya Station.

**Port of Nagoya Public Aquarium** 𝘈𝘈 𝘒𝘪𝘥𝘴 Young Japanese flock to Nagoya's port area on weekends, drawn by a small amusement park, a maritime museum, a shopping complex, and sightseeing boats. But the Public Aquarium, one of Japan's largest, is the major draw for kids of all ages, with displays that concentrate on marine life from the seas around Japan. There's a 15-minute hologram show that transports you to the deep sea in a "submarine"; a touch tank with sea urchins, starfish, and other animals; and an IMAX theater with shows on the hour (included in the entry price). The aquarium is best known, however, for the penguin tank, which copies the environment of the Antarctic with artificial falling snow and cold temperatures to maintain the penguins' reproductive cycle; the loggerhead and green turtles with a sand beach to encourage them to lay eggs; and the half-dozen Beluga whales. There are also dolphin performances and Beluga training sessions (apparently, to keep the Belugas from getting bored). You'll probably spend about 3 hours here, including the IMAX film.

1–3 Minato-machi, Minato-ku. ⓒ 052/654-7080. www.nagoyaaqua.or.jp. Admission ¥2,000 ($19) adults, ¥1,000 ($9.50) junior-high and elementary students, ¥500 ($4.75) children. Tues–Sun 9:30am–5:30pm (to 5pm Dec–Mar, to 8pm July 21–Aug). Station: Nagoyako (exit 3, 7 min.).

**Tokugawa Art Museum** 𝘈𝘈𝘈 𝘍𝘪𝘯𝘥𝘴 Located on the grounds of a former mansion owned by the Owari branch of the Tokugawa family—with the original entry gate and a guardhouse still intact—this worthwhile museum houses thousands of documents, samurai armor, swords, matchlocks, helmets, pottery, lacquerware, Noh costumes and masks, and paintings that once belonged to the Tokugawa family, including objects inherited from the first Tokugawa shogun, Ieyasu. There are also replicas of structures and items that once adorned Nagoya Castle, including decorative alcoves, a teahouse,

and a Noh stage. The museum's most famous exhibit is the 12th-century picture scrolls of *The Tale of Genji (Genji Emaki)*, but they're displayed only 1 week a year in autumn (check with the tourist office); otherwise, replicas are on display. Excellent English-language explanations throughout the museum put the displays in historical context. You can easily spend an hour here and in the museum's newly restored garden.

1017 Tokugawa-cho, Higashi-ku. ℂ 052/935-6262. www.tokugawa-art-museum.jp. Admission ¥1,200 ($11) adults, ¥1,000 ($9.50) seniors, ¥700 ($6.65) university and high-school students, ¥500 ($4.75) children. Tues–Sun 10am–5pm. City bus: From platform no. 7 at Nagoya Station bus terminal, take a bus bound for JIYUGAOKA or IDAKA SHAKO. Or from Sakae, take bus no. 2 to the Shindeki stop (3 min.). Station: JR Ozone (south exit, 10 min.).

## Toyota Commemorative Museum of Industry and Technology ⭐ (Kids) This
museum seems an odd marriage—it's devoted to both textile machinery and automobile production and technology. That's because the Toyota Group, founded by Toyoda Sakichi, the inventor of automatic looms, has a long history of producing both. Housed in an attractive brick building dating from the Taisho Period (1912–25), the museum displays approximately 80 looms and textile machinery, from wooden hand looms to air-jet looms that utilize computer graphics. The automobile pavilion provides a historical chronology of automobile production, beginning with a replica of the first Toyota car (1936), early assembly lines using manpower, and automated assembly lines using industrial robots for everything from engine mounting to painting. There's also a display of both old and new Toyota cars and a film of how Toyota makes its cars. Frequent demonstrations of looms (they're loud!) and auto-making equipment (including robotics) make this a fun destination for adults and kids alike. There's also a hands-on discovery room for kids. Expect to spend 90 minutes here.

4-1-35 Noritake Shinmachi, Nishi-ku. ℂ 052/551-6115. www.tcmit.org. Admission ¥500 ($4.75) adults, ¥300 ($2.85) junior-high and high-school students, ¥200 ($1.90) children, free for seniors. Tues–Sun 9:30am–5pm. Train: Meitetsu Line to Sakou (3 min.). Subway: Kamejima (10 min.). Just north of the Noritake Craft Center, about a 15-min. walk from Nagoya Station.

## IN NEARBY INUYAMA CITY

Inuyama City has several worthwhile attractions, so I suggest coming here for a day of sightseeing and, in summer, topping it off with some cormorant fishing (see below). The **Inuyama Tourist Information Center** (ℂ 0568/61-6000) is located in Inuyama Station (open daily 9am–5pm), but for information by phone, call the **Inuyama Tourist Center** (ℂ 0568/61-1000). Or, check the website www.city.inuyama.aichi.jp. *Note:* There are no specific addresses in this section, since addresses in smaller Japanese cities are of a region rather than an exact street address. However, everyone will know where these attractions are.

**Inuyama Castle** ⭐ Constructed in 1537 atop a bluff overlooking the Kiso River, miraculously surviving centuries of war and earthquake (part of it was damaged by an 1891 earthquake but then repaired), Japan's oldest castle is a designated National Treasure. The four-story keep—much smaller than most of Japan's castles—is the nation's only privately owned castle, owned by the Naruse family since 1618. In addition to displaying a few samurai outfits, it offers a nice, expansive view over the river that's especially worth a look if you intend to join the nearby cormorant fishing. The castle is so diminutive you can see everything in 15 minutes.

ℂ 0568/61-1711. Admission ¥500 ($4.75) adults, ¥100 (95¢) children. Daily 9am–5pm. From Meitetsu Shin-Nagoya Station, take the Inuyama Line 23 min. to Inuyama Yuen Station; from there it's about a 15-min. walk.

**Museum Meiji Mura** ✿✿✿    Inuyama City's most important attraction is one of my favorite museums in Japan. In fact, it may well be the main reason for a Nagoya stopover. A 100-hectare (250-acre) open-air architectural museum, it features more than 65 buildings and structures dating from the Meiji Period (1868–1912), all beautifully situated on landscaped grounds on the shores of a lake. Before Japan opened its doors in the mid-1800s, unpainted wooden structures dominated Japanese architecture; after Western influences began infiltrating Japan, however, stone, brick, painted wood, towers, turrets, and Victorian features came into play. Unfortunately, earthquakes, war, fire, and developer greed have destroyed most of Japan's Meiji-Era buildings, making this a priceless collection.

On the grounds are Western homes that once belonged to foreigners living in Nagasaki and Kobe, official government buildings and schools, two Christian churches, a post office, a bathhouse, a Kabuki theater, a brewery, bridges, Japanese-style homes, a martial-arts hall, and even a prison. Don't miss the front facade and lobby of the original Imperial Hotel in Tokyo, designed by Frank Lloyd Wright and containing some of the hotel's original Wright-designed furniture. In fact, most of the buildings display furniture and other items related to the building in which they're housed. You can mail a postcard from the post office, buy candy at the old candy shop, have coffee or tea in the Imperial Hotel lobby sitting on original Wright-designed chairs, or stop for a drink at the brewery. Plan on spending at least 3 hours here. *Tip:* Save money by purchasing a "Bikkuri coupon" at the Meitetsu ticket counter at Shin-Nagoya Station, which includes round-trip bus/train fare and admission to Meiji Mura for ¥2,140 ($20).

*(f)* **0568/67-0314.** www.meijimura.com. Admission ¥1,600 ($15) adults, ¥1,000 ($9.50) high-school students, ¥600 ($5.70) children. Daily 9:30am–5pm (to 4pm Nov–Feb). Take the Meitetsu Line from Meitetsu Shin-Nagoya Station to Inuyama Station (¥540/$4.50 one-way), which takes about 30 min. by express; change there for a 20-min. direct bus to Meiji Mura (¥410/$3.40 one-way).

## WATCHING CORMORANT FISHING ✿✿✿

There are two places near Nagoya where you can watch **cormorant fishing** every night in summer (except during a full moon or the 2 or 3 days following a heavy rain). In this ancient, 300-year-old Japanese fishing method, trained *ukai* (seabirds) dive into the water in search of *ayu*, a small Japanese trout. At nightfall, wooden fires are lit in suspended cages at the fronts of long wooden boats to attract the ayu, whereupon leashed cormorants are released into the water. To ensure that the cormorants don't swallow the fish, the birds are fitted with neck rings.

In **Inuyama,** cormorant fishing takes place from June 1 to September 30 on the Kiso River. Spectators can board boats beginning at around 6pm to observe the spectacle firsthand. While waiting for the full darkness that must descend before the fishing takes place (usually around 7:30pm), you can dine on set meals (¥2,000–¥7,000/$19–$66) that you order when you make your reservations. You can also purchase drinks from boat vendors and can even buy and set off Japanese fireworks, which give the evening a celebratory atmosphere. The actual fishing itself occupies only 20 minutes. To partic-ipate, take the Inuyama Line of the Meitetsu Railways from Meitetsu Shin-Nagoya Station 23 minutes to Inuyama Yuen Station (¥590/$5.60); from there, it's a 5-minute walk. Call ahead to make reservations (*(f)* **0568/61-0057**); upon arrival, stop by the ticket office near the bridge. Tickets for boarding the boats and watching the fishing (meal prices are listed above) cost ¥2,500 ($24) for adults and ¥1,250 ($12) for

children in June and September, ¥2,800 ($27) and ¥1,400 ($13) respectively in July and August.

The city of **Gifu** features cormorant fishing from May 11 to October 15 on the Nagaragawa River, where you can also dine and view the whole spectacle aboard a small wooden boat. To reach Gifu, take the Meitetsu Main Line train from Meitetsu Shin-Nagoya Station to Shin-Gifu Station (¥540/$5.15). From there, switch to a local train or bus (¥200/$1.90) heading for Nagarabashi Station. You'll see the ticket office (Gifu-shi Ukai Kanransen Jimusho) after exiting the station. You can call ahead to reserve your ticket (© **058/262-0104**) beginning in mid-April, daily between 8:45am and 8pm. Tickets cost ¥3,300 ($31) for adults and ¥2,900 ($28) for children. Boats depart at 6:15pm, 6:45pm, and 7:15pm.

## WHERE TO STAY
### EXPENSIVE

In addition to the hotels listed below, the **Nagoya Hilton,** 1–3–3 Sakae, Naka-ku, Nagoya 460-0008 (© **800/HILTONS** or 052/212-1111; fax 052/212-1225; www. hilton.com), offers 438 units to mostly foreign business travelers.

**Nagoya Marriott Associa Hotel** 🕭🕭    A location right over Nagoya Station makes this Nagoya's most convenient hotel. Occupying the 15th to 52nd floors of one of the twin towers that straddles the station, Nagoya's tallest building also offers the city's best views (ask for a room facing the castle and downtown; higher floors cost more), not to mention quick access to the many restaurants and shops on the lower floors of this "vertical city." Despite its central location, it doesn't skimp on facilities, offering a wide range of in-house dining possibilities (to eat at French restaurant Mikuni, considered Nagoya's top restaurant, you must make reservations months in advance) and a health club, as well as good-size, up-to-date guest rooms. Don't miss having a drink at the 52nd-floor Sky Lounge Zenith (open daily 11:30am–midnight)—but all this is assuming you can even find the hotel. Guests arriving by train not only have to search for the obscure ground-floor entryway, but have to battle the crowds taking elevators to the many restaurants. Luckily, it's worth it.

1–1–4 Meieki, Nakamura-ku, Nagoya 450-6002. © **800/228-9290** in the U.S. and Canada, or 052/584-1113. Fax 052/584-1114. www.associa.com/nma. 780 units. ¥20,000–¥34,000 ($190–$323) single; ¥28,000–¥42,000 ($266–$399) double or twin; from ¥35,000 ($333) executive-floor double. Rates include service charge. AE, DC, MC, V. Station: Nagoya/Shin-Nagoya (below the hotel). **Amenities:** 8 restaurants; 1 bar; 2 lounges; 20m (66-ft.) 4-lane pool, Jacuzzi, and fitness gym (fee: ¥3,150/$30); concierge; business center; salon; 24-hr. room service; in-room massage; same-day laundry/dry-cleaning service; nonsmoking rooms; executive-level rooms. In room: A/C, cable TV w/on-demand pay movies, free high-speed dataport, minibar, hot-water pot w/tea, hair dryer, safe, Washlet toilet, trouser press.

**Westin Nagoya Castle** 🕭🕭    Situated just west of Nagoya Castle, the chief attraction of this 30-some-year-old hotel—a local favorite for special occasions and meetings—is the wonderful views of the moat and castle from its rooms, especially at night when the castle is illuminated. Rooms are spacious enough, but it's worth staying here only if you get a room with a view (note that the cheapest singles do not face the castle); otherwise, the location is rather inconvenient, though courtesy shuttle buses to Nagoya Station once an hour are a big plus.

3–19 Hinokuchi-cho, Nishi-ku, Nagoya 451-8551. © **800/Westin-1** in the U.S. and Canada, or 052/521-2121. Fax 052/531-3313. www.castle.co.jp. 229 units. ¥16,000–¥35,000 ($152–$336) single; ¥33,000–¥42,000 ($314–$400) double or twin; from ¥26,000 ($277) executive single, from ¥33,000 ($314) executive double. Rates include service charge. AE, DC, MC, V. Subway: Tsurumai Line to Sengencho (10 min.). Bus: Free shuttle from Nagoya Station every hour on the hour 10am–8pm (15-min ride). **Amenities:** 5 restaurants; 1 bar; 1 lounge; indoor 5-lane 25m (82-ft.) pool and

Jacuzzi (fee: ¥1,575/$15) w/exercise room and sauna (fee: ¥3,150/$30 for everything); concierge; salon; 24-hr. room service; in-room massage; babysitting; same-day laundry/dry-cleaning service; nonsmoking rooms; executive-level rooms. *In room:* A/C, cable TV w/pay movies, minibar, hot-water pot w/tea, hair dryer, Washlet toilet.

## MODERATE

**Ekimae MontBlanc Hotel** *Value*    There isn't a lot to say about this simple hotel except that it's close to the station and offers mostly single functional rooms at reasonable rates. Its corner location frees it from close proximity to taller buildings, which means you can actually look outside rather than face another building (ask for a room on a higher floor). Otherwise, there's not much to crow about; this is strictly a sleeping machine with a fancy name.

3-14-1 Meieki, Nakamura-ku, Nagoya 450-0002. (C) **052/541-1121.** Fax 052/541-1140. www.montblanc-hotel.jp. 277 units. ¥7,560–¥8,610 ($72–$82) single; ¥12,075–¥13,125 ($115–$125) twin; ¥12,075 ($115) double. AE, MC, V. Station: Nagoya (2 min.). Turn left out of the Sakura Dori/Central exit and then right just before the post office. **Amenities:** 2 restaurants (Japanese, Continental); same-day laundry/dry-cleaning service. *In room:* A/C, TV w/pay movies, fridge, hair dryer, Washlet toilet.

**Sofitel The Cypress Nagoya** *Value*    Sofitel took over the former Century Hyatt in 2002, and though standards have not yet reached those of its Tokyo property, it has updated its look with contemporary yet comfortable furnishings and offers the same boutiquelike atmosphere and friendly service. Its location near Nagoya Station is also a huge plus. Standard rooms are fairly small, and since some face other buildings, ask for a room on a higher floor, where you might have an urban view. Deluxe rooms add space, larger windows, and sink and vanity areas separate from the bathrooms. In short, you won't go wrong staying here, especially at these prices.

2-43-6 Meieki, Nakamura-ku, Nagoya 450-0002. (C) **052/571-0111.** Fax 052/569-1717. www.accorhotels-asia. com. 115 units. ¥15,300–¥18,000 ($145–$171) single; ¥19,000–¥25,000 ($181–$238) twin or double. Rates include service charge. AE, DC, MC, V. Station: Nagoya (4 min.). Turn left out of the Sakura Dori/Central exit and then right just before the post office. **Amenities:** 2 restaurants (Continental, coffee shop); 1 bar; 24-hr. room service; in-room massage; same-day laundry/dry cleaning; nonsmoking rooms. *In room:* A/C, cable TV w/pay movies, dataport, minibar, hot-water pot w/tea, hair dryer, safe, Washlet toilet.

**Tokyo Dai-Ichi Hotel Nishiki** *Finds*    This smart-looking hotel is my top pick among Nagoya's moderately priced hotels in the city center. Located in the heart of Nagoya's nightlife and business district on Nishiki Dori, it opened in 1997 with prices comparable to those of a business hotel but with a much classier atmosphere and decor. Targeting female travelers as well as businesspeople, it offers smartly decorated rooms with large desks and larger-than-usual bath towels; all but the cheapest singles, which are located next to elevator shafts, have dataports as well. Some of the standard twins have two sinks (good for two people trying to get ready at the same time), while deluxe twins are separated into living and sleeping areas and even have two TVs and broadband access. Rooms facing another building have glazed windows, so if seeing out is important to you, be sure to say so.

3-18-21 Nishiki, Naka-ku, Nagoya 460-0003. (C) **052/955-1001.** Fax 052/953-6783. www.daiichihotels.com/ hotel/nishiki. 233 units. ¥9,240–¥11,500 ($67–$109) single; ¥15,015 ($108) double; ¥17,325–¥23,300 ($165–$221) twin. Rates include service charge. AE, DC, MC, V. Station: Sakae (exit 1, 3 min.). **Amenities:** 3 restaurants (Chinese, coffee shop, Japanese seafood); in-room massage; same-day laundry/dry-cleaning service; nonsmoking rooms. *In room:* A/C, cable TV w/pay movies, minibar, hot-water pot w/tea, hair dryer, safe, Washlet toilet, trouser press.

## INEXPENSIVE

**Meiryu Ryokan**    A Japanese Inn Group member and family-owned for more than 50 years, this is a no-nonsense place. Most customers are Japanese businessmen, some

of whom have lived here during the week for years, commuting home to families on weekends. Tatami rooms are spotless and cozy, with more space and features than most other hotel rooms in this price category, including a closet and free coffee. The men's public bathroom has a sauna (they don't have many female guests at this ryokan—fewer than 5%—but there's a separate bathroom in case a lone female makes an appearance). The owners' son, who often clerks the front desk, speaks English well and is very helpful. In short, this place is okay for males and couples, but single females may feel uncomfortable.

2–4–21 Kamimaezu, Naka-ku, Nagoya 463-0013. © 052/331-8686. Fax 052/321-6119. www.japan-net. ne.jp/~meiryu. 23 units (none with bathroom). ¥5,250 ($50) single; ¥8,400 ($80) twin; ¥11,025 ($105) triple. Japanese breakfast ¥630 ($6) extra; Japanese dinner ¥2,310 ($22) extra. AE, V. Station: Kamimaezu (exit 3, 4 min.). Walk straight out of the station 1 block and turn left; it's on the 2nd block, on the left. **Amenities:** Coin-operated laundry. *In room:* A/C, TV, hot-water pot w/tea.

### Petit Ryokan Ichifuji  *Finds* *(Kids)*    Although this place is way out there in Ozone (pronounced *Ozon-ay* in Japanese), the couple running this Japanese Inn Group ryokan has put so much heart and soul into the accommodations that it's well worth the subway ride. Ishida Tomiyasu, who speaks a little English, inherited the 45-year-old ryokan from his father and grandfather, and together with his wife, Yoko, has remodeled it to fit younger Japanese taste and has put in a cypress public bath (open 24 hr.). While the house's bright pink exterior and its collection of bears and rabbits may be too cutesy for some, the youthful staff and the owners' two children make this a welcoming, family-oriented retreat. Best of all, children under 7 years of age stay for free, while those under 13 are half price. Even dogs and cats are welcome here (the owners have two dogs of their own). All except one of the rooms is tatami, and both Japanese and Western breakfasts and dinners are available. You'll feel right at home.

1–7 Saikobashi-dori, Kita-ku, Nagoya 462-0818. © 052/914-2867. Fax 052/981-6836. www.jin.ne.jp/ichifuji. 10 units (none w/bathroom). ¥5,880–¥6,300 ($56–$60) single; ¥11,130–¥11,970 ($106–$114) double; ¥15,750–¥17,010 ($150–$162) triple. Rates include breakfast. Dinner ¥2,100 ($20) extra. AE, MC, V. Station: Heiandori (exit 2, 3 min.); Ozone (8 min.). **Amenities:** Coin-operated washer and dryer. *In room:* A/C, TV, hot-water pot w/tea.

## WHERE TO DINE

One of Nagoya's specialties is *kishimen,* fettuccine-like broad and flat white noodles usually served in a soup stock with soy sauce, tofu, dried bonito shavings, and chopped green onions. Nagoya is also famous for *miso nikomi udon*—udon noodles served in a bean-paste soup and flavored with such ingredients as chicken and green onions. *Cochin* (free-range) chicken and breaded pork cutlets *(tonkatsu)* are also Nagoya favorites.

### AROUND NAGOYA STATION

The best place for one-stop dining is Nagoya Station itself, on the 12th and 13th floors of one of the twin towers atop the station. Called **Towers Plaza,** it offers more than 30 food-and-beverage outlets (in addition to Kappa; see below) serving noodles, sushi, tempura, Chinese food, Italian fare, and more, most with glass-window displays.

If you reserve early enough (at least 2 months in advance), you might also get one of the coveted tables at French restaurant **Mikuni** on the 52nd floor of the Nagoya Marriott Associa Hotel (© **052/584-1111**). Decorated in Art Nouveau style and considered by some to be the city's finest restaurant due to its celebrated chef Kiyomi Mikuni (who has restaurants also in Tokyo and Sapporo), it offers set lunches for ¥6,000 to ¥12,000 ($57–$114) from 11:30am to 2:30pm and set dinners for ¥14,000 to ¥21,000 ($133–$200) from 5:30 to 10pm, with a menu that changes daily.

---

**Tips  A Note on Japanese Symbols**

Many establishments and attractions in Japan do not have signs in Roman (English-language) letters. Those that don't are indicated in this guide with an oval with a number that corresponds to a number in appendix C showing the Japanese symbols. Thus, to find the Japanese symbol for, say, **Yamamoto-ya Honten** (below), refer to no. 105 in appendix C.

---

**Kappa**  *Finds*  SUSHI/VARIED JAPANESE   This friendly establishment, easily found because of its castlelike exterior, is actually two restaurants, one serving varied Japanese cuisine, and the other, to the right, serving sushi. Since the sushi is delivered via a conveyor belt, choosing is no more difficult than reaching out for a passing plate, which is color-coded according to price. Set sushi meals are also available. The dining room to the left, decorated with bamboo-slatted screens for added privacy and Frank Lloyd Wright–inspired grillwork and stained glass, offers both a menu with photographs and a display case for meals that include tempura, noodles, fish, tonkatsu, and other fare. Seating here is at tables and chairs or on the floor at low tables with leg wells, some with nice city views. Both restaurants offer weekday set lunches for ¥900 ($8.55) until 3pm. To find Kappa in the "city" that Nagoya Station has become, take the elevators next to the Takashimaya cloakroom.

12th floor, Towers Plaza, Nagoya Station, 1–1–4 Meieki, Nakamura-ku. © 052/541-7888. 2 pieces sushi ¥126– ¥630 ($1.20–$6); set meals ¥980–¥2,000 ($9.30–$19). AE, DC, MC, V. Daily 11am–10:30pm (last order).

(105)  **Yamamoto-ya Honten** UDON NOODLES   This chain noodle shop, a 2-minute walk from Nagoya Station, specializes in miso nikomi udon. Its noodles, all handmade, are thick, hard, and chewy and are served in a type of bean paste that's special to Nagoya. If you like your noodles spicy, add spices to your food from the large bamboo container on your table. An English-language menu with explanations makes ordering easy.

25–9 Meieki, basement of the Horiuchi Building, Sakura Dori, Nakamura-ku. © 052/565-0278. Udon dishes ¥1,200– ¥1,950 ($11–$19); set meal ¥1,900 ($18). AE, DC, MC, V. Daily 11am–10pm. Station: Nagoya (exit 6, 2 min.); on Sakura Dori's north side.

**IN SAKAE**

If you are collecting T-shirts or are hungry for a hamburger, there's a **Hard Rock Cafe** on the third floor of the ZXY Building on Hirokoji Street not far from the Hilton, at 1–4–5 Sakae, Naka-ku (© **052/218-3220;** open Sun–Thurs 11:30am–11pm, Fri 11:30am–midnight, Sat 11:30am–3am).

**Hourai-ken Matsuzakaya-ken** EEL   This eel restaurant is a branch of two famous restaurants near Atsuta Shrine. There's no English-language menu, but you can't go wrong ordering one of the various *unagi donburi* (rice casserole with eel on top). Most famous is the Hitsumabushi, a set meal for ¥2,300 ($22) that includes unagi donburi, various condiments, miso soup, and Japanese pickles. Eating it is a ritual: First, dish out some of the eel casserole into the smaller wooden bowl and eat it plain. For the next course, try it with some of the seaweed and green onions that come with it. Finally, add some of the soup and wasabi to the last mixture you tried.

The other, more elegant branches are both south of Atsuta Shrine at 2–10–26 Jingu, Atsuta-ku (© **052/682-5598;** open Wed–Mon 11:30am–2:30pm and 4:30–8:30pm);

and at 503 Goudo-cho, Atsuta-ku (☎ **052/671-8686;** open Tues–Sun 11:30am–2pm and 4:30–8:30pm).

In the south building of Matsuzakaya department store, in the back on the 10th floor (look for the sign that says UNAGI HORAIKEN), 3–16–1 Sakae, Naka-ku. ☎ **052/264-3825.** *Unagi teishoku* (set meal) ¥1,500–¥2,300 ($14–$22). AE, V. Daily 11am–9pm (last order). Station: Yabacho (1 min.).

**Tiger Cafe** FRENCH   With its antique-looking advertisements for Pernod, tiled floor, small tables, and rattan chairs facing the open facade, this coffee shop is the closest thing in Nagoya to a Parisian cafe. Stop for a drink, a snack of quiche, *escargots et champignon,* or an omelet, or dine on more substantial fare like the fish of the day, pan-fried duck, or steak, and be glad you're not part of the traffic whizzing by.

1–9–22 Higashi-sakura, Higashi-ku. ☎ **052/971-1031.** Main dishes ¥1,500–¥2,000 ($14–$19). No credit cards. Mon–Sat 11am–3am; Sun 11am–midnight. Station: Sakae (6 min.); across from the NHK building (which you won't be able to miss).

⑩ **Torigin Honten** 𝆄 COCHIN CHICKEN   In the heart of Nagoya, next to Sabatini (below), this 30-year-old casual restaurant with counter, tatami, or table seating is known for its *Nagoya cochin* (free-range chicken). It also serves yakitori, with a set menu of eight different skewers costing ¥1,900 ($18), as well as *miso-nabe* (rice cake, tofu, chicken, and vegetable stew) and *kamameshi* set meals (rice casseroles). An amiable staff makes it diner-friendly; a black-and-white kura-style facade makes it easy to identify.

3–14–22 Nishiki, Naka-ku. ☎ **052/973-3000.** Set meals ¥3,000–¥5,200 ($29–$50). AE, DC, MC, V. Daily 5–11pm (last order). Closed irregularly. Station: Sakae (2 min.).

**Trattoria Italiano Sabatini** 𝆄𝆄𝆄 ITALIAN   Boasting an airy atrium with large mural "windows" opening onto an Italian town, this branch of the famous Tokyo restaurants run by brothers from Rome is a welcome addition to the Nagoya dining scene. With staff and chef trained in the Tokyo store, it serves the same excellent, very Italian cuisine with many ingredients imported from Italy. Lunches change daily and dinners weekly, with a wide variety of antipasto and pasta always available. *Pollo alla cacciatorae* (chicken in a tomato and olive sauce) and *filetto al carpaccio* (thin slices of beef) are on the a la carte menu. My lunch menu consisted of antipasto; linguine with spicy tomato and mushroom sauce; grilled garlic, potatoes, spinach, and broccoli; two kinds of homemade gelato; pie; and coffee, after which I was ready to climb through that "window" in search of my siesta.

3–14–22 Nishiki, Naka-ku. ☎ **052/973-4560.** Main dishes ¥1,900–¥4,400 ($18–$42); pasta ¥1,200–¥1,900 ($11–$18); set lunch ¥2,500–¥5,000 ($24–$48); set dinner ¥6,000–¥10,000 ($57–$95). AE, DC, MC, V. Daily 11:30am–2pm and 5:30–10pm (last order). Station: Sakae (4 min.).

⑩ **Yabaton** 𝆄𝆄 *Finds* TONKATSU   You'll recognize this Everyman's eatery in Nagoya's old downtown district immediately by its curtains displaying comical pigs dressed like sumo wrestlers. It's light-years from being fancy, with a very local, lively atmosphere. The only thing served is *tonkatsu* (pork cutlet), and Yabaton is famous for it. You'll be asked whether you want yours with *sa-u-zu* (sauce) or *miso katsudon;* the former is thicker and sweeter, but the latter is the specialty here (if you can't decide, ask for a little of both). *Donburi,* a breaded and fried pork cutlet on rice, is the cheapest, but recommended is *hire,* a tender cut with less fat. Main dishes all come with cabbage; rice or miso soup are ¥100 (95¢) extra.

3–6–23 Osu. ☎ **052/241-2409.** Main dishes ¥700–¥1,300 ($6.65–$12); set meal ¥1,000–¥1,900 ($9.50–$18). AE, DC, MC, V. Tues–Sun 11am–9pm. Station: Yabacho (3 min.). From Wakamiya-Otsu Dori intersection, walk 1 short block south on Otsu Dori and turn right.

## 2 Ise-Shima National Park ★★

465km (289 miles) W of Tokyo; 100km (62 miles) S of Nagoya

Blessed with subtropical vegetation, small islands dotting its shoreline, and the most revered Shinto shrine in Japan, **Ise-Shima National Park** merits a 1- or 2-night stopover if you're anywhere near Nagoya. Located on and around Shima Peninsula and covering 518 sq. km (200 sq. miles), this national park has bays and inlets that make up the home of the Mikimoto pearl and thousands of pearl-cultivating rafts. Although you could conceivably cover the major attractions on a day's outing from Nagoya, I've recommended accommodations in case you'd like to take in the sights at a more leisurely pace.

Ise-Shima's major attractions are concentrated in the small towns of Ise, Futami-no-ura, Toba, and Kashikojima, all in Mie Prefecture. **Ise** (also called Ise-Shi, which translates as Ise City) is where you'll find the Ise Grand Shrines. **Futami-no-ura** (also called simply Futami) is famous for a theme park based on Japan's history from 1477 to 1598. **Toba** contains Mikimoto Pearl Island, which offers a pearl museum and demonstrations by its famous women divers, as well as the Toba Aquarium. Near **Kashikojima,** you can visit an amusement park with a Spanish theme or take boat trips around Ago Bay which, with its islets and pearl-cultivating oyster rafts, is one of the most scenic spots in the park.

### ESSENTIALS

**GETTING THERE    By Train**    The easiest way to get to Ise-Shima is from Nagoya on the private **Kintetsu Nagoya Line** (Kinki Nippon Railway; © **052/561-1604**), which departs about every 30 minutes or so from Kintetsu Station, next to the JR Nagoya Station. It takes about 1 hour and 20 minutes via limited express to reach Ise (with stops at both Ise-Shi and Ujiyamada stations), about 1 hour and 35 minutes to reach Toba, and 2 hours to reach Kashikojima. *Note:* Kintetsu trains do not go to Futami-no-ura. A ticket from Nagoya to the end of the line in Kashikojima costs ¥3,480 ($33) one-way. There are also Kintetsu lines to Shima Peninsula both from Kyoto (2 hr. and 15 min. to Toba; fare: ¥3,780/$36) and from Osaka's Kintetsu stations in Uehonmachi and Tsuruhashi (2 hr. to Toba; fare: ¥3,550/$34 and ¥3,450/$33 respectively). Most economical, however, is to purchase a Kintetsu Rail Pass, which costs ¥3,550 ($34), is valid for 5 days (but only three journeys can be aboard a limited express train) and includes travel to and from Nagoya, Osaka/Kyoto, and Ise.

If you're traveling on a **Japan Rail Pass,** you can also reach Ise-Shima by **JR Kaisoku (Rapid) Mie** trains, which depart hourly from Nagoya Station, but you'll be charged an extra ¥490 ($4.65). JR trains stop at Ise-Shi and Futami-no-ura before terminating at Toba where, if you're heading to Kashikojima, you'll have to transfer to the Kintetsu Line.

**By Bus**    Buses depart nightly from Tokyo's Ikebukuro Station's east exit at 10:20 and 11:20pm, arriving at Ise-Shi Station at 7:10 and 8:10am respectively. The fare is ¥7,850 ($75) one-way.

**VISITOR INFORMATION**    Be sure to drop by the Tourist Information Centers in Tokyo or the international airports at Narita or Osaka to pick up the free leaflet, "Ise-Shima," which lists train schedules from Osaka, Kyoto, and Nagoya and gives information on the park's main attractions (you can also download it from the Japan National Tourist Organization's website at www.jnto.go.jp by looking under *Regional*

*Tourist Guides*). Otherwise, drop by the **Ise-Shi City Tourist Information Center** located at Kintetsu Ujiyamada Station in Ise City (© **0596/23-9655**), or the **Toba Tourist Office** at Toba Station (© **0599/25-2844**), both open daily 9am to 5:30pm.

**GETTING AROUND**    Transportation within Ise-Shima National Park is either by train or by bus. **Trains** are convenient if your destinations are Ise City, Toba, Futami-no-ura, and Kashikojima (see "Getting There," above). Some major sites, however, including the Outer and Inner Shrines and Edo Wonderland Ise, are best reached by bus. For sightseers, there's the **CAN-Bus,** which you can board in front of the JR stations in Ise City and Toba. Buses, departing hourly on weekdays and twice an hour on weekends, travel from Ujiyamada and Ise-Shi stations to both Outer and Inner Shrines of the Ise Grand Shrines and Edo wonderland Ise before continuing onward to Toba. One-day passes for ¥1,000 ($9.50) and 2-day passes for ¥1,600 ($15) can be bought aboard the buses. There are also local city buses that run between the Outer and Inner Shrine of the Ise Grand Shrines; you must take a bus to reach Parque España.

## EXPLORING ISE-SHIMA NATIONAL PARK

The easiest way to see the park's sights is to start in Ise City, the northern gateway to Ise-Shima National Park, and work your way down the peninsula to Kashikojima.

### ISE CITY (ISE-SHI)

**THE ISE GRAND SHRINES** 🐟🐟    Tied historically to the imperial family and considered the most venerable Shinto shrines in the nation, the Ise Grand Shrines (Ise Jingu; © **0596/24-111**) consist of the Outer Shrine and the Inner Shrine, plus more than 100 minor shrines spread through a dense forest of Japanese cypress. Since the Outer and Inner shrines are about 6.4km (4 miles) apart, your best bet is to first visit the Outer Shrine, which is a 5-minute walk from Ise-Shi Station, and then take a bus to the Inner Shrine. In addition to the CAN-Bus (described above in "Getting Around"), local bus nos. 51 and 55 run between the two shrines every 10 to 15 minutes and cost ¥410 ($3.90) one-way. Because of the distance between the shrines and their large grounds, plan on spending at least 2 hours exploring Ise. If you have luggage but the biggest lockers are already taken, you can leave your bags at the left-luggage counter (look for the sign that says CLOAK ROOM) at Ise-Shi Station, open daily. Ise-Shi and Ujiyamada stations are a 7-minute walk apart.

The **Outer Shrine (Geku)** was founded in 477 and is dedicated to the Shinto goddess of harvest, agriculture, clothing, and housing. The **Inner Shrine (Naiku)** was founded a few centuries earlier and is dedicated to Amaterasu, the sun goddess. Both are among the few Shinto shrines in Japan without any Chinese Buddhist influences. Constructed of plain cypress wood with thick thatched roofs in the oldest style of architecture in Japan, they're starkly simple and have no ornamentation except for gold and copper facing on their beams and doors. In fact, if you've come all the way to Shima Peninsula just to see the shrines, you may be disappointed—there's nothing much to see. The shrines are so sacred that no one is allowed near them except members of the imperial family and high-ranking Shinto priests. Both shrines are surrounded by four wooden fences, and lesser mortals are allowed only as far as the third gate.

The fences don't allow you to see much, but that doesn't stop the estimated six million Japanese who come here annually. They come because of what the shrines represent, which is an embodiment of Japanese Shinto itself. The Inner Shrine is by far the more important because it's dedicated to the sun goddess, considered to be the

legendary ancestress of the imperial family. It contains the Sacred Mirror (Yata-no-Kagami), one of the Three Sacred Treasures of the emperor.

According to legend, the sun goddess sent her grandson to Japan so that he and his descendants could rule over the country. Before he left, she gave him three insignia—a mirror, a sword, and a set of jewels. As she handed him the mirror, she is said to have remarked, "When you look upon this mirror, let it be as if you look upon me." The mirror, therefore, is said to embody the sun goddess herself and is regarded as the most sacred object in the Shinto religion. It's kept in the deep recesses of the Inner Shrine in a special casket and is never shown to the public. (The sword is in the Atsuta Shrine in Nagoya, and the jewels are in the Imperial Palace in Tokyo.)

Perhaps the most amazing thing about the Outer and Inner shrines is that, even though they were founded centuries ago, the buildings themselves have never been more than 20 years old—every 20 years they're completely torn down and rebuilt exactly as they were on neighboring sites. The present buildings were built in 1993 for the 61st time. No photos of the shrines are allowed.

Even though you can't see much of the shrines, they're still the most important stops in Ise-Shima. The Inner Shrine is approached by crossing the elegant Uji Bridge of the Isuzu River, passing through a manicured garden, and then entering a dark forest of 800-year-old cypress trees. Watch how Japanese stop after crossing the second small bridge on the approach to the shrine to wash and purify their hands and mouths with water from the Isuzu River. Its source lies on the Inner Shrine, and it's considered sacred. You may also see a couple of royal horses, one white and one brown, kept in stables near the shrine for the use of the sun goddess.

**ISE'S HISTORIC DISTRICTS** 🏵🏵🏵    After visiting the Inner Shrine (a 45-min. walk round-trip), turn right after recrossing Uji Bridge for the nearby historic district of **Oharai-machi,** whose main street is lined with beautiful wooden buildings and *kura* (storehouses), some dating from the Edo Period and others newly constructed but faithful to traditional architecture. It once served as the main pilgrimage road leading to the Grand Shrines of Ise. During the Edo Period, when travel was strictly controlled, joining a mass pilgrimage to Ise was for many Japanese a once-in-a-lifetime opportunity to venture beyond their homes; they took full advantage of it here. Today it's an interesting area for a stroll, shopping, or a meal.

About halfway down is **Okage-yokocho,** a re-created Meiji Era village with teahouses, restaurants, and shops selling Japanese candies, traditional toys, folk crafts, and candles. If you have time, stop by the ⑧ **Okageza** 🏵 (© 0596/23-8838; open daily 10am–6pm, to 5pm in winter), a museum housed in an authentic Edo-Era building that captures the spirit of Oharai-machi during the Edo Period; dioramas of half-scale models and street scenes vividly convey what life was like for both the residents and the pilgrims passing through. It's the next best thing to a time machine. Admission is ¥300 ($2.85) for adults and ¥100 (95¢) for children. You'll spend about 15 minutes here.

Across from Okage-yokocho is ⑨ **Akafuku** (© 0596/22-2154; open daily 5am–5pm), the original makers (opened in 1707) of the sticky rice cakes for which Ise-Shima is famous. You'll recognize the shop by the *kamado* (huge, red, ginger jar–shaped ceramic cooking stoves) used to heat water for tea in the open entryway. It has been a tradition to serve complimentary tea to shrinegoers for centuries, and this shop, built in 1887, still does. You pay only for the cakes—¥280 ($2.65) for three cakes with tea. First pay at the old cash register on the dark-wood counter; the staff, in traditional dark-blue outfits, will then serve you on tatami mats around braziers or on benches in

the back overlooking the river. You can watch cakes being made and, May through August, you can also watch swallows fly in and out to their nests in the eaves.

Off the beaten tourist track is **Kawasaki,** which served as Ise City's business district during the Edo Period, when boats traversing the Setagawa River delivered goods to storehouses along the river's banks. A grass-roots movement has restored four of these storehouses along with an Edo-Era house, grouped together in the ⑩ **Ise-Kawasaki Shonin-Kan,** 2–25–32 Kawasaki (**© 0596/22-4810;** open Wed–Mon 9:30am–5pm), which you can tour for ¥300 ($2.85). Surrounding buildings have been turned into restaurants and shops selling crafts, food, antiques, and pottery. In a country where old neighborhoods are disappearing by the minute, the local people who have fought to preserve this historic district deserve medals. It's a 10-minute walk from Ujiyamada Station.

## FUTAMI-NO-URA

### Edo Wonderland Ise (Ise Azuchi Momoyama Bunka-Mura) 🎎🎎🎎 (Kids   The castle you see on the hill from Futami-no-ura Station (which, by the way, is a mirrored building shaped like the Wedded Rocks) is not the former residence of a famous shogun but a replica of Azuchi Castle in Edo Wonderland, one of Japan's many theme parks. If you have youngsters in tow or if you haven't seen one of these period theme parks elsewhere in Japan, go to one—they're fun! This one is among my favorites because, rather than try to re-create a village in Holland or Spain, it's centered on a specific time in Japan's history, the Age of the Warring States—the Sengoku Era (1477–1573), when local warlords struggled for supremacy, and the Azuchi-Momoyama Era (1573–98), when Oda Nobunaga gained control of the land and finally put an end to civil war. In keeping with the theme of this Japanese equivalent of Dodge City, all the staff are dressed in 16th-century costumes, and attractions reflect the pre–Edo Era; visually, it looks just like a movie set. You can watch period dramas and theater ranging from a courtesan performance that includes singing and dancing to the action-charged antics of a Ninja troupe. A 3-D movie captures the destruction of Toyotomi Hideyoshi's Osaka Castle by Tokugawa forces, while in the Ninja Labyrinth you can try to negotiate 11 challenging obstacles. There are no thrill rides here, but there are old-fashioned game centers, including shooting ranges using bows and arrows and other weaponry of the era. That gold-roofed castle is dedicated to Nobunaga—who built Azuchi Castle—and is filled with high-tech giant screens, dioramas, and lasers that depict famous attacks he staged to gain control; plenty of visual and audio effects will make you feel you're in the midst of war. The top-floor Gold Room, lined with real gold, has a great view of Ise-Shima. You'll probably spend 2 to 3 hours here.

© **0596/43-2300.** Admission ¥4,900 ($47) adults, ¥2,500 ($24) children 4–12. Daily 9am–5pm (9:30am–4pm Dec–Mar 19). A 15-min. walk from Futami-no-ura Station or a 2-min. walk from the CAN-Bus Ise Sengoku Jidaimura/Edo Wonderland bus stop.

## TOBA

### Mikimoto Pearl Island 🎎🎎   Toba's best-known attraction is touristy but still quite enjoyable, especially if you have a weakness for pearls or have ever wondered how they're cultivated.

To learn about the man who toiled through years of adversity to produce the world's first cultured pearl, visit **Kokichi Mikimoto Memorial Hall,** built in 1993 to commemorate the 100th anniversary of Mikimoto's success. Born in Toba in 1858 as the eldest son of a noodle-shop owner, Kokichi Mikimoto went to Yokohama as a young man and was surprised to see stalls selling pearls with great success. He reasoned that if

oysters produced pearls as the result of an irritant inside the shell, why couldn't humans introduce the irritant themselves and induce oysters to make pearls? It turned out to be harder than it sounded. It wasn't until 5 years after he started his research that Mikimoto finally succeeded in cultivating his first pearl, here on what is today called Mikimoto Pearl Island. In 1905, Mikimoto cultivated his first perfectly round pearl, after which he built what is probably the most successful pearl empire in the world.

Mikimoto, who died at the age of 93, was a remarkable man and a real character. In addition to chronicling his life, the Memorial Hall contains some of his earliest jewelry and models made with pearls, many of which were only recently re-acquired by Mikimoto & Co. Ltd. through auctions. My favorite is the brooch made for the 1937 Paris International Exhibition, which can be worn a dozen different ways by employing various clasps. The Pearl Pagoda has 12,760 Mikimoto pearls and took 750 artisans 6 months to complete, after which it was exhibited at the Philadelphia World Exhibition in 1926. The Liberty Bell, a third the size of the original, has 12,250 pearls and was displayed at the New York World's Fair in 1939.

The **Pearl Museum** tells all you'd probably ever want to know about the creation of pearls, with live demonstrations that show the insertion of the round nucleus into the shell, a video of the harvesting of the pearls 2 years later, and more live demonstrations that explain the process of making a pearl necklace by hand, from the selection and sorting of pearls to the drilling and stringing. You can learn about the criteria used for pricing pearls (luster is the most important) and can see an exhibit that examines the relationship between people and pearls since ancient times. There are also more Mikimoto pearl creations like the Pearl Pavilion, which contains a pearl 4 centimeters (1⅗ inches) in diameter and resembles Nara's Hall of Dreams.

In addition, **women divers** *(ama)* in traditional white outfits demonstrate how women of the Shima Peninsula have dived through the ages in search of abalone, seaweed, and other edibles. They were also essential to the pearl industry, diving to collect the oysters and then returning them to the seabed following insertion of the nuclei. At one time, there were thousands of ama, known for their skill in diving to great depths for extended periods of time. It is said that there are still more than 1,000 of these women divers left, but I've seen them only at demonstrations given for tourists. If you happen to see ama working in earnest (diving for abalone and other food, not pearls), consider yourself lucky. Here you can watch them from the airconditioned comfort of a viewing room built especially for overseas guests.

There's also, of course, a shop selling Mikimoto pearl jewelry and a restaurant. You can easily spend 1½ hours on Pearl Island.

1–7–1 Toba, ⓒ **0599/25-2028.** www.mikimoto-pearl-museum.co.jp. Admission ¥1,500 ($14) adults, ¥750 ($7.15) children 7–15. Mid-Mar through May, mid-July through Aug, and Oct to mid-Nov, daily 8:30am–5:30pm; Jan to mid-Mar, June to mid-July, Sept, and mid-Nov through Nov, daily 8:30am–5pm; Dec, daily 9am–4:30pm. Closed 2nd Tues, Wed, and Thurs of Dec. Station: Toba (a few minutes' walk), connected to the mainland via a short pedestrian bridge.

**Toba Aquarium**  �’ 🄺ⁱᵈˢ    Next to Pearl Island is one of Japan's largest aquariums, containing more than 850 species of aquatic plants and animals. Various zones and themes make it easy to navigate. The display of marine animals around Ise-Shima and Japan includes giant spider crabs and the finless porpoise, the world's smallest whale. The exhibit of "living fossils"—creatures that have remained relatively unchanged since ancient times—includes sharks, horseshoe crabs, and the nautilus (which are bred here; babies are often on display), while the marine mammal kingdom includes Commerson's dolphins, seals, and sea lions, with sea-lion shows several times a day.

The aquarium also boasts exotic and rare creatures such as dugongs, African manatees, and Amazonian turtles and frogs. My only complaint is that some of the tanks look rather bare and outdated in today's world of ever-more-sophisticated aquariums; maybe the animals don't mind, but spectators sure do. Plan on spending at least 90 minutes here, longer if you have kids.

3–3–6 Toba, (© 0599/25-2555. www.aquarium.co.jp/english. Admission ¥2,400 ($23) adults, ¥1,200 ($11) children. Nov to mid-Mar daily 9am–4:30pm; mid-Mar to mid-July and Sept–Oct daily 9am–5pm; mid-July to Aug daily 8:30am–5:30pm. Station: Toba (a few minutes' walk).

## KASHIKOJIMA

At the southern end of the Shima Peninsula, the last stop on the Kintetsu Line is Kashikojima.

One of the main attractions of Kashikojima for Japanese is the **boat cruises of Ago Bay.** Vessels, built to resemble Spanish galleons or with other Spanish-based themes, depart from the town's boat dock, about a 2-minute walk from the tiny train station. The cost of the cruise is ¥1,500 ($14) for adults, half price for children. You'll pass pearl-cultivating rafts, fishing boats, and many small islands along the way. The trip lasts almost an hour, with boats departing every half-hour or so between 9:30am and 4:30pm March 21 through October, less frequently in winter. For more information or inquiries about the winter schedule, call the **Shima Marine Leisure Co.** (© **0599/43-1023**).

**Parque España** *Kids*    You may wonder what this Spanish village, called Shima Spain Mura by the locals, is doing in southern Ise Shima. Mie Prefecture has a sister relationship with Valencia in Spain, a relationship that is exploited to the hilt in this ambitious theme park. A huge facility that employs about 40 Spanish-speaking natives, the Spanish-themed amusement park includes a shopping area specializing in products from Spain; a plaza that stages dances, festivals, and other outdoor entertainment; a coliseum that features folk dancing and singing; a live theater production called *Lost Legend* that features a fire-and-flood extravaganza (summers only); and amusement rides that range from an adventure lagoon ride through a world of fantasy to the fastest roller coaster I'll ever care to ride (and one of the longest, lasting more than 3 hair-raising min.). Although the park opened to much fanfare in 1994, it has suffered declining attendance ever since, which is bad for business but means there's virtually no waiting time for rides, except during school holidays.

Most educational is the Museo Castillo de Xavier, a reproduction of the castle where Francis Xavier was born (Xavier later brought Christianity to Japan); it presents a brief overlook of highlights in Spanish history, though in Japanese. Still, there's no mistaking the replica of prehistoric drawings from the Altamira caves, the model of the *Santa Maria* that Columbus sailed to America, and replicas of the Prado's most famous works. There are amusements geared to all ages, as well as numerous restaurants. Plan on spending about 3 hours here.

© 0599/57-3333. Passport admission to all attractions ¥4,800 ($46) adults, ¥3,800 ($36) seniors and children 12–17, ¥3,200 ($30) children 4–11; extra charges for gaming houses and flamenco show. Admission only, which includes the museum and most shows but no rides (which you can purchase separately for ¥200–¥600/$1.90–$5.70 per ride) ¥2,800 ($27) adults, ¥1,800 ($17) children 12–17, ¥1,200 ($11) children 4–11. July 19–Aug daily 9am–9pm; rest of the year, Mon–Fri 9:30am–5pm, Sat–Sun and holidays 9:30am–6pm. Closed last 2 weeks of Feb. Station: Isobe (Kintetsu Line), then a bus that runs 3 times per hour and costs ¥360 ($3) for the 15-min. ride. There are also 3 buses a day from Kashikojima.

## WHERE TO STAY

Kashikojima is the best place to go if you want to escape the crowds and relax in a rural setting, while Toba and Ise have the greatest number of attractions.

### ISE

⑪ **Asakichi** ✿ Since a pilgrimage to the Ise Grand Shrines during the Edo Period was often the only trip a commoner might make in his lifetime, he often lived it up to the hilt in Furuichi, Ise's former red-light district. Located between the Inner and Outer shrines, it was filled with many ryokan, brothels, and restaurants. Now only Asakichi remains, founded more than 200 years ago by the present owner's family, on an impossibly narrow street. The ryokan takes its name from the family name Asa, which means "hemp" and which was probably supplied to commoners seeking offerings for the shrines. In any case, the ryokan seems little changed since then, built on a slope and even containing a museum of sorts filled with dusty, Edo-Era memorabilia which you can request to see. The tatami rooms are simple. Meals are served in the privacy of your room, except during peak times when they're served in a dining room. Western breakfasts are available. The proprietor doesn't speak much English but understands the basics.

109 Nakanocho, Ise-Shi, Mie 516-0034. © **0596/22-4101.** Fax 0596/22-4102. 15 units (3 with bathroom). ¥11,500 ($109) per person. Rates include 2 meals. No credit cards. Station: Ise-Shi, then bus no. 1 or 2 from platform 7 another 9 min. to the Nakanocho stop (1 min.). **Amenities:** Museum. *In room:* A/C, TV.

⑫ **Hoshidekan** ✿✿ (Finds) Catering to the health conscious, this inexpensive 80-year-old wooden Japanese Inn Group ryokan has several tatami rooms with windows framed with gnarled roots and bamboo (they simply don't make windows like this anymore) encircling an inner courtyard. It's nothing fancy, but it's run by a friendly, grandmotherly woman who is a strong advocate of macrobiotic vegetarian meals, which are served in your simple tatami room. (Both Japanese and Western meals are available, but we prefer the ¥1,000/$9.50 *Genmai teishoku* vegetarian course for dinner; be sure to reserve it by 3pm.) The food, however, is only one of the reasons to stay here. We also like the bicycles, which you can use to visit the Ise Grand Shrines and the nearby Kawasaki historic district; your ¥100 (95¢) donation for the day goes to a local organization that fights pollution.

2–15–2 Kawasaki, Ise-Shi, Mie 516-0009. © **0596/28-2377.** Fax 0596/27-2830. www.hoshidekan.jp. 12 units (none with bathroom). ¥4,800 ($46) single; ¥9,000 ($86) double; ¥13,500 ($128) triple. Breakfast ¥800 ($7.60) extra; dinner ¥1,000 ($9.50) extra. AE, MC, V. Station: Ise-Shi, then a 7-min. walk in the opposite direction from the shrine; look for the sign on the right that says HOSHIDE. **Amenities:** Macrobiotic restaurant (reservations required); in-room massage; coin-op washer and dryer; nonsmoking rooms. *In room:* A/C, TV, hot-water pot w/organic tea, no phone.

### TOBA

**Thalassa Shima** ✿✿✿ (Value) Although the approach to this luxury hotel doesn't seem to promise much, inside it's another story. Everything about this sophisticated seaside luxury hotel is focused on its stunningly beautiful setting on the sea, with nary another building in sight. It has a soothing, subdued atmosphere, fitting for a resort dedicated to healing. Thalassa Shima is a French-Japanese joint venture into thalasso therapy, which uses seawater, seaweed, and sea-mud treatments to combat stress, fatigue, and excess weight. Although thalasso therapy has long been popular in France, this modern, striking, and elegant hotel is the first such resort in Japan and attracts mostly Japanese and French living in Japan. My coauthor was skeptical that a 1-night

stay involving a seaweed bath, an underwater-jet treatment, a massage bath, and pressure therapy could make much difference, but she has to admit she left the hotel much more relaxed and feeling beautiful! Rooms—all of which have small balconies facing the sea—are large, well appointed, and full of amenities. Ask for a room on a higher floor for more expansive sea views, and at check-in, reserve a dinner table at either the **Lumiere** with its nouvelle French cuisine or the classic Japanese restaurant, both with views of the sea. There's a glass-enclosed swimming pool, as well as a public beach just a short walk away.

1826-1 Shirahama, Uramura-cho, Toba-shi, Mie 517-0025. (C) **0599/32-1111.** Fax 0599/32-1109. reservation@ thalasso.co.jp. 114 units. ¥21,000–¥34,700 ($200–$330) per person double occupancy, including dinner; more on Sat and holidays. Thalasso therapy treatment ¥14,700 ($140). 2-night Resort Plan packages from ¥63,000 ($599) per person, including 4 meals and thalasso therapy. AE, DC, MC, V. Free 25-min. shuttle bus every hour from JR or Kintetsu Toba Station. **Amenities:** 2 restaurants (French, Japanese); 1 bar; thalasso therapy center w/pool overlooking the bay, exercise room, full French thalasso therapy equipment, massage room, sauna, and Jacuzzi; sundries shop; aesthetic salon; room service (8–10am, noon–5pm, 9:15–10:15pm); in-room massage; dry-cleaning/laundry service; nonsmoking rooms. *In room:* A/C, TV w/free video movies, minibar w/free drinks, hot-water pot w/herb tea, hair dryer, safe, bathroom scale.

## KASHIKOJIMA

(113) **Ishiyama-So** *Finds*    If you're looking for an inexpensive, unusual place to stay, a good choice is this family-run *minshuku* located on a small island just a stone's throw from the Kashikojima pier. It can be reached only via the hotel's own private boat—call to let them know you've arrived at Kashikojima; the boat will arrive shortly, and you'll be delivered right to the ryokan's front door. Although the building itself is concrete, its location on the water gives it a slightly exotic atmosphere, right up to the small crabs that scurry in through the front door. There's a sun deck overlooking the bay (a good place to eat breakfast), you can swim off the dock (because of boat traffic, though, you shouldn't go farther out than the dock), and footpaths crisscross the small island. While the owner speaks English, all rooms are Japanese style and face the bay; meals, which can only be paid for in cash, are also Japanese.

Yokoyama-jima, Kashikojima, Ago-cho, Mie 517-0502. (C) **0599/52-1527.** Fax 0599/52-1240. 6 units (3 with bathroom, 3 with toilet only). ¥5,500 ($52) single with toilet only, ¥6,000 ($57) single with bathroom; ¥8,500 ($81) double with toilet only, ¥9,500 ($90) double with bathroom. Breakfast ¥600 ($5.70) extra. Dinner ¥1,600 ($15) extra. AE, MC, V. A 2-min. walk from the station to Kashikojima pier, then a 2-min. boat trip. *In room:* A/C, coin-op TV, hot-water pot w/tea, no phone.

**Shima Kanko Hotel**    Sitting on a hill above Ago Bay, this is a resort hotel in the old tradition, established in 1951 and boasting impeccable service and great views. It was the hotel of choice of the Showa Emperor; he stayed here five times. The present emperor stayed here in 2001. Most rooms have views of the bay and are spacious, and despite periodic updating, they retain an old-fashioned, '50s atmosphere with their shoji screens and wooden furniture. The highest-priced twins facing the bay in the main building are the best; they offer splendid views, large bathrooms with two sinks, and separate Washlet toilets. The hotel boasts its own garden (cared for by three gardeners), at the edge of which is the lovely outdoor pool. I especially like the pathway leading down to a private dock where you can sit and watch pearl cultivators at work on their rafts. On the hotel's roof is an observatory, great for watching the beautiful sunsets; the coffee shop's outdoor terrace is another wonderful place to soak up the view. Restaurant standouts include the Japanese seafood restaurant with its airy, old-fashioned ambience; and the French restaurant La Mer, famous for its abalone.

Note that at press time, a reduced "foreigner rate" for a twin room was offered; ask whether it's still available.

Kashikojima, Ago-cho, Shima, Mie 517-0593. ✆ **0599/43-1211.** Fax 0599/43-3538. www.miyakohotels.ne.jp/shima. 152 units. ¥19,058 – ¥32,918 ($181–$313) single; ¥20,790 – ¥34,650 ($198–$329) twin; ¥20,790 – ¥25,410 ($198–$241) double. Peak season ¥5,775 ($55) extra; Sat and evenings before holidays ¥3,465 ($33) extra. Rates include service charge. AE, DC, MC, V. Station: Kashikojima (then free shuttle to hotel or a 5-min. walk). **Amenities:** 3 restaurants (Japanese, French, coffee shop); 1 lounge; outdoor pool w/children's slides (free for hotel guests); games arcade; concierge; souvenir shop; room service (8–9:30pm); in-room massage; next-day laundry/dry-cleaning service. *In room:* A/C, TV, dataport, minibar, hot-water pot w/tea, hair dryer, Washlet toilet.

## WHERE TO DINE

Shima Peninsula is understandably famous for its seafood. In addition to the choices below, resorts and hotels throughout the Shima Peninsula offer wonderful seafood dining. For a splurge, I recommend **La Mer** 🐟🐟 in the Shima Kanko Hotel (see above), which serves its own delightful French cuisine with a decidedly Japanese twist. Matsuzaka beef, lobster, and abalone are house specialties, with set lunches starting at ¥7,000 ($67) and set dinners at ¥17,500 ($166). Reserve a window seat and get there before sunset. It's open daily from 11:30am to 2pm and 5:30 to 8:30pm.

### ISE

⑭ **Sushi Kyu** 🐟🐟 *Kids* SUSHI/LOCAL SPECIALTIES  Located on the main street of Oharai-machi in a 130-year-old former ryokan, this traditional restaurant offers tatami seating at low tables with a view out over the river. Even the cashier sits on tatami behind an enclosure, just like the old days. Kimono-clad waitresses serve sushi and local cuisine from a Japanese menu. Try the tekoni sushi (raw bonito marinated with soy sauce and mixed with vinegared rice in a bowl) or the obento of various delicacies. Like many family-type restaurants, there's also a child's plate with rice, soup, fried shrimp, salad, dessert, and drink for ¥630 ($6).

20 Uji Nakanokiri-machi, Ise. ✆ **0596/27-0229.** Set meals ¥950 – ¥2,500 ($9.05–$24). No credit cards. Tues–Sun 11am–8pm; Mon 11am–5pm. Closed the 1st and last day of every month. Station: Ise-Shi, then bus no. 51 or 55 or the CAN-Bus to the Inner Shrine stop, from which it's a 5-min. walk to Oharai-machi historic district.

### TOBA

⑮ **Osakaya** SUSHI  Located 2 blocks inland from Mikimoto Pearl Island on the other side of the train tracks, this simple local eatery with tatami, table, and counter seating offers assorted sushi platters *(nigiri-zushi)* and sushi rolls *(maki-sushi)*, but the specialty is *ebi* fry, humungous shrimp deep-fried in batter. I recommend the set meal for ¥3,460 ($33), which includes ebi fry, sashimi, rice, soup, and vegetables.

4164 1-chome, Toba. ✆ **0599/25-2336.** Maki-sushi ¥630 – ¥1,900 ($6–$18); sushi platter ¥1,050 – ¥3,700 ($10–$35); set meal ¥3,460 ($33). AE, MC, V. Fri–Wed 11am–2pm and 4–8:30pm (last order). Station: Toba. Walking in the direction of Mikimoto Pearl Island, turn right on Iwasaki Dori; Osakaya will be on the right (look for the fish tank).

## 3 More of Old Japan: Kanazawa 🌟🌟

622km (386 miles) NW of Tokyo; 224km (140 miles) NE of Kyoto

On the northwest coast of Honshu on the Sea of Japan, Kanazawa is the gateway to the rugged, sea-swept Noto Peninsula. It was the second-largest city (after Kyoto) to escape bombing during World War II, and some of the old city has been left intact, including a district of former samurai mansions, old geisha quarters, Edo-Era canals, and tiny narrow streets that run crookedly without rhyme or reason (apparently to confuse any enemies foolish enough to attack). Kanazawa is most famous for its

**Kenrokuen Garden,** one of the most celebrated gardens in all of Japan. It's the main reason people come here, though several fine museums nearby are worth a visit, too. Kanazawa is also renowned for its crafts.

Kanazawa first gained notoriety about 500 years ago, when a militant Buddhist sect joined with peasant fanatics to overthrow the feudal lord and establish its own autonomous government, an event unprecedented in Japanese history. The independent republic survived almost 100 years before it was attacked by an army of Oda Nobunaga, who was trying to unite Japan at a time when civil wars wracked the nation. Kanazawa was subsequently granted to one of Nobunaga's retainers, Maeda Toshiie, who constructed a castle and transformed the small community into a thriving castle town. The Maeda clan continued to rule over Kanazawa for the next 300 years, amassing wealth in the form of land and rice and encouraging development of the arts. Throughout the Tokugawa shogunate, the Maedas remained the second-most powerful family in Japan and controlled the largest domain in the country. The arts of Kutani ware, Yuzen silk dyeing, lacquerware, and Noh theater flourished—and enjoy success and popularity in Kanazawa even today. Japan's fourth-largest city at the end of the Feudal Era, Kanazawa now has a population of 457,400 and is capital of Ishikawa Prefecture.

## ESSENTIALS

**GETTING THERE   By JR Train**   Direct trains from Osaka (via Kyoto) depart half-hourly or hourly; the ride takes less than 3 hours and costs ¥6,930 ($66) for an unreserved seat. From Nagoya, direct trains depart for Kanazawa every 2 hours and take about 3 hours; the cost is ¥6,620 ($63) for an unreserved seat.

From Tokyo, take the Joetsu Shinkansen to Echigoyuzawa and switch there for the limited express Hakutaka train to Kanazawa. The trip takes about 4½ hours and costs ¥11,690 ($111).

**By Bus**   Buses depart four times a day from Ikebukuro Station's east exit in Tokyo, arrive in Kanazawa 7½ hours later, and cost ¥7,840 ($74). Buses also depart several times daily from Nagoya and Kyoto stations; both trips take about 4 hours and cost ¥4,060 ($39).

**VISITOR INFORMATION**   Be sure to pick up the flyer "Kanazawa" at the Tourist Information Centers in Tokyo, at the Narita or Kansai international airports, or at the local **Tourist Information Center (© 076/232-6200)** inside Kanazawa Station (you can also download it from the Japan National Tourist Organization's website at www.jnto.go.jp by looking under *Regional Tourist Guides*). To find the center, turn right after passing through the wicket (you'll be heading toward the East Gate exit); it will soon be on your left beside a shopping arcade. Open daily 9am to 7pm (with English-speaking volunteers on duty 10am–6pm), it distributes an excellent English-language map and brochure. You can also book hotel rooms here. Visit the city's home page at www.city.kanazawa.ishikawa.jp.

**INTERNET ACCESS**   The **Ishikawa Foundation for International Exchange,** a 5-minute walk from the east exit of Kanazawa Station (on the road running between the Miyako and Nikko hotels), on the third floor of the Rifare building at 1–5–3 Honmachi (© **076/262-5931**), has four computers you can use free of charge Monday to Friday 9am to 6pm and Saturday and Sunday 9am to 5pm. There's a sign-up sheet and users are limited to 30 minutes, but the turnover is pretty fast. In the heart of the city, head to **Biz Café,** north of Chuo Dori above Asian Café Cha Cha, 2–2–9

Katamachi (© **076/233-1008**), where you can log onto the Internet Thursday to Tuesday from 10am to 9pm for the price of a cup of coffee (¥300/$2.85).

**GETTING AROUND** Kanazawa's attractions spread south and southeast from the station (take the East Gate exit). Katamachi, 3.2km (2 miles) southeast of the station, is Kanazawa's downtown. Sights are too far-flung to see everything on foot, so the easiest way to get around Kanazawa is by **bus.** All major lines depart from Kanazawa Station, and as many as 15 lines pass Kenrokuen Garden. Take a ticket when boarding the bus and pay when you get off; the fare is ¥200 ($1.85) to most sights in the city.

Easiest for tourists, however, is the **Kanazawa Loop Bus (Shu-yu Bus),** which departs from platform 0 at Kanazawa Station's east exit every 15 minutes and travels to all the tourist sights making 19 stops in a circular route. Stops are announced in English and displayed on a digital board at the front of the bus. A single ride costs ¥200 ($1.85) and a 1-day pass costs ¥500 ($4.75). The bus runs daily from 8:30am to 6pm.

You can also travel around Kanazawa by **bicycle. JR Rental Cycle** (© **076/ 261-1721;** open daily 8am–6pm), at the west exit of Kanazawa Station, rents bicycles for ¥1,200 ($11) per day.

## EXPLORING KANAZAWA

Much of Kanazawa's charm lies in the atmosphere of its old neighborhoods. Be sure to wear your good walking shoes, since the best way to explore various parts of the city is on your own two feet. One suggested itinerary for tackling the city's sights is to take the Loop Bus to the Higashi Chaya district, then another Loop bus onward to Kenrokuen and the sights in its vicinity, and then reboard the bus or walk the 15 minutes to the Nagamachi Samurai district. Directional English-language signs to major sights are posted throughout the city. *Note:* What is identified as Saigawa Odori Avenue on the map issued by the tourist office is called Chuo Dori by the locals.

### THE TOP ATTRACTION

**Kenrokuen Garden** ***&&&*** At one time, Kanazawa possessed an impressive castle belonging to the powerful Maeda clan, but it was destroyed by fire several times, the last time in 1881. Near the garden entrance is one of the few original structures remaining, the handsome **Ishikawamon (Ishikawa Gate),** which used to be the south entrance to the castle. Observing how big and grand the gate is, you can appreciate the size of the original Maeda castle. Remarkably, its roof tiles are actually lead, in case emergency dictated they be melted down for musket balls. The area just beyond the gate is the newly created **Kanazawa Castle Park** (© **076/234-3800;** open Mar–Oct 15 daily 7am–6pm; Oct 16–Feb daily 8am–4:30pm), which contains a botanical garden and a reconstructed castle building. Skip the empty reconstruction (admission: ¥300/$2.85) unless you're especially interested in building techniques, but the botanical garden with its contemporary layout is worth a stroll.

Just southeast of Kanazawa Castle Park is Kanazawa's main attraction, the 10-hectare (25-acre) **Kenrokuen Garden** ***&&&***. The largest of what are considered to be the three best landscape gardens in Japan—the other two are Kairakuen Garden in Mito and Korakuen Garden in Okayama—it's considered by some to be the grandest. Its name can be translated as "a refined garden incorporating six attributes"—spaciousness, careful arrangement, seclusion, antiquity, elaborate use of water, and scenic charm. Ponds, trees, streams, rocks, mounds, and footpaths have all been combined so aesthetically that the effect is spellbinding. Best of all, unlike most other gardens in Japan, there are no surrounding skyscrapers to detract from the splendid views.

Altogether, it took about 150 years to complete the garden, which served as the outer garden of Kanazawa Castle. The fifth Maeda lord started construction in the 1670s, and successive lords added to it according to their individual tastes. The garden as you now see it was finished by the 12th Maeda lord in 1822; only after the Meiji Restoration was it opened to the public. In addition to cherry trees, irises, ponds, and other elements of natural beauty, there are several historic structures here, including a tea-ceremony house, a former samurai house and, most important, Seisonkaku Villa (see below). Plan on 1½ hours of blissful wanderings.

*Tip:* You may want to arrive at dawn or near the end of the day, since Kenrokuen Garden is a favorite destination of Japanese tour groups, led by guides who explain everything in detail—through loudspeakers.

1–4 Kenroku-machi. ✆ **076/234-3800.** Admission ¥300 ($2.85) adults, free for seniors over 65, ¥100 (95¢) children 6–18. Mar to mid-Oct daily 7am–6pm; mid-Oct to Feb daily 8am–4:30pm. Loop Bus: Kenrokuenshita (stop no. 9, 3 min.).

## IN THE VICINITY OF KENROKUEN GARDEN

116 **Ishikawa Prefectural Art Museum (Ishikawa Kenritsu Bijutsukan)** ✦✦ *Finds*
One of the Maeda clan's lasting contributions was its encouragement of the arts, in full evidence here. Founded to preserve Ishikawa Prefecture's most important cultural resources, this museum houses scrolls, paintings, Kutani ware, and items that may range from samurai costumes belonging to the Maeda family to kimono, as well as contemporary oil paintings and decorative art by artists who were born in Ishikawa, lived here, or had some connection to the prefecture, many of them National Living Treasures. One room is reserved solely for a pair of pheasant-shaped incense burners (by a 17th-c. Kyoto potter), National Treasures and among the most valuable pieces in the collection. Otherwise, exhibits change monthly; be sure to take advantage of the English-spoken audio guides included in the admission fee, which provide commentary on the individual works of art and their significance. You'll need 45 minutes here.

2–1 Dewa-machi. ✆ **076/231-7580.** www.ishibi.pref.ishikawa.jp. Admission ¥350 ($3.35) adults, ¥280 ($2.65) students, free for children under 18; more for special exhibits. Daily 9:30am–5pm. Closed 3–4 days monthly during exhibit changes. Loop Bus: Hirosaka (stop no. 10, 4 min.). Just south of Kenrokuen Park, not far from Ishikawa Prefectural Museum for Traditional Products and Crafts.

**Ishikawa Prefectural Museum for Traditional Products and Crafts (Ishikawa Kenritsu Dento Sangyo Kogeikan)** ✦✦✦   If you have time to visit only one museum in Kanazawa, this is the one to choose. It's by far the best place in town to view and learn about all the beautiful handcrafted items for which Kanazawa has long been famous. There are English-language explanations, a detailed English-language pamphlet, and an audio guide that describes how the crafts are made. You can see the famous Kutani pottery, first produced under the patronage of the Maeda clan in the 1600s and known for its hues of green, red, purple, navy blue, and yellow, as well as displays of Kaga Yuzen dyeing and hand-painting on silk (Kanazawa is known for its bold and clear picturesque designs). Also on display are Kanazawa lacquerware (which uses raised lacquer painting), paulownia woodcrafts, metalwork, family Buddhist altars, Kanazawa gold leaf, wooden molds for sweets, koto and *shamisen* stringed instruments, drums, lion masks, bambooware, fishing hooks, flies, rods, folk toys, Japanese paper *(washi),* umbrellas, and even fireworks. Schedule about an hour to appreciate everything.

1–1 Kenroku-machi. ✆ **076/262-2020.** Admission ¥250 ($2.40) adults, ¥200 ($1.85) seniors, ¥100 (95¢) children. Apr–Nov daily 9am–5pm (closed 3rd Thurs of every month); Dec–Mar Fri–Wed 9am–5pm. Loop Bus: Hirosaka (stop no. 10, 6 min.). Next to Seisonkaku Villa.

(117) **Seisonkaku Villa** 🐟🐟 Just outside the Kodatsuno (southeast) exit of Kenrokuen Garden is this must-see villa, built in 1863 by the 13th Maeda lord as a retirement home for his widowed mother. Elegant and graceful, it has a distinctly feminine atmosphere with delicately carved, brightly painted wood transoms and painted shoji screens. The bedroom is decorated with tortoises painted on the shoji wainscoting; tortoises were associated with long life, and it must have worked—the mother lived to be 84. Expect to linger about 20 minutes here.

1–2 Kenroku-machi. 📞 076/221-0580. Admission ¥600 ($5.70) adults, ¥300 ($2.85) junior-high and high-school students, ¥250 ($2.40) children. Thurs–Tues 9am–5pm. Loop Bus: Hirosaka (stop no. 10, 5 min.). Next to the Ishikawa Prefectural Museum for Traditional Products and Crafts.

**21st Century Museum of Contemporary Art** Kanazawa's newest museum, centrally located between Kenrokuen Garden and the Katamachi shopping district, is ensconced in a striking circular building that has no front or back, allowing visitors to explore it from all directions. Galleries, which range from bright spaces with sunlight pouring through glass ceilings to darkened rooms with no natural light, display a collection that concentrates on works of the past 15 years, particularly of Japanese artists born after 1965, along with contemporary works from around the world shown in changing exhibitions.

1–2–1 Hirosaka. 📞 076/220-2800. www.kanazawa21.jp. Admission prices vary according to the exhibition. Sun and Tues–Thurs 10am–6pm; Fri–Sat 10am–8pm. Loop Bus: Hirosaka (stop no. 10, 2 min.).

### THE NAGAMACHI SAMURAI (BUKE YASHIKI) DISTRICT

About a 15-minute walk west of Kenrokuen Garden and just a couple minutes' walk west of Katamachi (Kanazawa's main shopping district), the Nagamachi Samurai District is basically a few streets lined with beautiful wooden homes hidden behind gold-colored mud walls and bordered by canals left over from the Edo Period. An unhurried stroll in the neighborhood will give you an idea of what a feudal castle town might have looked like. But only fleetingly—Lord Maeda had as many as 8,000 samurai retainers, who in turn had their own retainers, making the samurai population here very large indeed. To reach the district from Katamachi, take the side street to the right of the Excel Hotel Tokyu.

**Nomura Samurai House** 🐟 Stop 20 minutes here to see how samurai lived back in the Edo Period. Occupied by members of the Nomura family for 10 generations, this traditional Japanese home boasts a drawing room made of Japanese cypress, with elaborate designs in rosewood and shoji screens painted with landscapes, and a tea-ceremony room upstairs (tea costs ¥300/$2.85). Rooms overlook a small, charming garden with a miniature waterfall, a winding stream, and stone lanterns. Personal effects of the Nomura family and other objects from the Edo Period are on display, including a samurai outfit, the family altar, and a nightingale box (deliberately dark so the nightingale would sing).

1–3–32 Nagamachi. 📞 076/221-3553. Admission ¥500 ($4.75) adults, ¥400 ($3.80) high-school students, ¥250 ($2.40) children. Apr–Sept daily 8:30am–5:30pm; Oct–Mar daily 8:30am–4:30pm. Loop Bus: Kohrinbo (stop no. 15, 5 min.). Take the side street to the right of the Excel Hotel Tokyu, turn right, and then turn left; look for the samurai outfit at the entrance.

### OTHER SIGHTS

**HIGASHI CHAYA DISTRICT** There are approximately 50 geisha practicing their trade in three old entertainment quarters in Kanazawa, including this one. A walk here reveals rather solemn-looking, wood-slatted facades of geisha houses dating from

the 1820s, where men of means have long come to be entertained with music, dancing, songs, the tea ceremony, poem recitals, and other pleasurable pursuits. Geisha still perform at seven houses in the Higashi Chaya District, but most of the other former geisha homes have been turned into shops and restaurants. For an inside peek at the geisha world, visit the 185-year-old ⑪⑧ **Shima Geisha House,** 1–13–21 Higashiyama (☏ **076/252-5675;** open daily 9am–6pm), a former tearoom where merchants as well as men of letters came to watch geisha perform. Inside, you'll find rooms that were allotted to personal use, as well as to performing, along with displays of ordinary artifacts from combs, pipes, and game boards to cooking utensils. Architectural details worth noting include: several stairways (so that customers could come and go without being seen); a small Shinto shrine at the entrance to the home; a more elaborate family Buddhist altar in a place of honor in a front room; the gleaming wood-lacquered surfaces of furniture; and the cloisonné door pulls on sliding doors. Admission is ¥400 ($3.80) for adults, ¥300 ($2.85) for children; but you'll probably want to stop for tea in the new addition facing a garden, which costs ¥500 to ¥700 ($4.75–$6.65) more. It takes only 10 minutes or so to tour the house. To reach it, take the Loop Bus to Hashibacho (stop no. 6); then look for the *koban* police box with a map of the area.

⑪⑨ **MYORYUJI TEMPLE** ✿✿    Myoryuji Temple (1–2–12 Nomachi; ☏ **076/ 241-2877**) is popularly known as Ninja-dera (Temple of the Secret Agents) because of its secret chambers, hidden stairways, tunnels, and trick doors. Built by the Maeda clan for family prayer in 1643, it looks rather small from the outside, just two stories high to comply with height restrictions during the Edo Period. Inside, four stories are evident, but even this is false—three more levels are concealed. The fortresslike structure contains an amazing 29 stairways and a labyrinth of corridors, along with such trick devices as pitfalls to trap unsuspecting intruders, slatted stairs where lances could make stabs at passing legs, escape hatches, hidden stairways, and rooms that could be opened only from the outside—just one more example of how deep paranoia ran during the Edo Period. Although rumor has it that a tunnel once connected the temple to the castle, a river running between them makes it unlikely.

Myoryuji Temple can be seen only by phoning ahead for a reservation; chances are good that you'll be able to see it the same day you call. To ensure that you don't get lost (which would be quite easy because of all the trick doors), you'll be grouped with other visitors and led by a guide who, unfortunately, describes everything in Japanese only. However, demonstrations of the various trick devices are fairly self-explanatory and there's an English-language pamphlet. Tours, given daily from 9am to 4:30pm (to 4pm in winter), last 30 minutes and cost ¥800 ($7.60) for adults and ¥600 ($5.70) for children (only children over 6 are admitted). To reach it, take the Loop Bus to Jusangenmachi (stop no. 13), cross the bridge you see straight ahead of you, take the second left (Teramachi), and then take the first right. It will be on your right.

## SHOPPING

Kanazawa's most famous products are its **Kutani pottery,** with its bright five-color overglaze patterns, and its hand-painted **Yuzen silk.** Kanazawa also produces maki-e lacquerware, sweets, toys, wooden products, and almost all of Japan's gold leaf. For convenient shopping for these and other souvenirs, try the **Omiyage Kan shopping arcade** right in Kanazawa Station.

For department stores, boutiques, and contemporary shops, visit the **Katamachi and Tatemachi shopping streets,** within walking distance of Kenrokuen Garden and

the Nagamachi Samurai district. **Omicho Market,** just off Hyakumangoku Dori between the station and Kenrokuen Garden, is the city market with more than 200 stalls selling seafood, vegetables, and fruit.

**Ishikawa Prefectural Products Center (Kanko Bussankan)**   Located just north of Kenrokuen Garden, this is the place to come for one-stop shopping of all the products Ishikawa Prefecture is famous for. The ground floor sells crafts ranging from lacquerware and pottery to glassware and toys, while the second floor houses a restaurant. Open daily 10am to 6pm (closed some Tues Nov–Mar). 2–20 Kenroku-machi. ✆ 076/ 222-7788. Loop Bus: Kenrokushita (stop no. 9, 2 min). Backtrack to Hyakumangoku Dori and turn right.

120 **Kaga Yuzen Dento Sangyo Kaikan**   Skip the ground-floor museum with its explanations in Japanese and instead take the stairs to the left of the entryway to the basement shop, where you can purchase scarves, purses, fans, ties, clothing, *furoshiki* (traditionally used for wrapping presents), and other items made from hand-dyed Yuzen cloth, which borrows heavily from nature for its designs—mainly flowers, animals, and landscapes. Open Thursday to Tuesday 9am to 5pm. 8–8 Kosho-machi. ✆ 076/ 224-5511. Loop Bus: Kenrokushita (stop no. 9, 2 min.). Cross Hyakumangoku Dori and turn right, then left after the parking lot.

**Kutani Kosen Pottery Kiln (Kutani Kosengama)**   If your interest lies in pottery, it's worth a visit to this Kutani-ware kiln and shop, open since 1870 and about a 10-minute walk from Myoruyji Temple. In addition to browsing its showroom, you can also see the entire process of producing handmade Kutani ware, including the kilns heated by pine and the painting, on a 15-minute tour led by a guide who speaks some English. Open daily 9am to noon and 1 to 5pm. 5–3–3 Nomachi. ✆ 076/241-0902. City Bus: 20 min. from Kanazawa Station to the Nomachi Eki stop (1 min).

121 **Sakuda**   Thinking about wallpapering a room in gold leaf? Then you'll certainly want to pay a visit to Sakuda, located in a modern building in the Higashi Chaya district. (As much as 98% of Japan's entire national output of gold leaf is produced in Kanazawa.) Here you can watch artisans at work, pounding the gold leaf and spreading it until it's paper-thin and translucent; it's the equivalent of pounding a ¥10 coin into the size of a tatami mat. But most people come here to shop for gold-leafed vases, boxes, chopsticks, bowls, trays, screens, furniture, and—this being Japan—golf balls and clubs. You can even buy gold flakes to add to your coffee or sake. Don't miss the second-floor bathrooms; the women's is done entirely in gold leaf, the men's in platinum. The staff was serving complimentary tea spiked with gold leaf to everyone who dropped by during my last visit. Open daily 9am to 6pm. 1–3–27 Higashiyama. ✆ 076/251-6777. Loop Bus: Hashibacho (stop no. 6, 4 min.).

122 **Shamisen no Fukushima** *(Finds)*   There used to be other makers of the three-stringed *shamisen* instrument in Kanazawa to keep the geisha supplied with one of the tools of their trade, but this shop in the Higashi Chaya District is the only one remaining. While you may not be in the market for a shamisen, you can have a 30-minute lesson in English (¥300/$2.85; reservations required) between 10am and 4pm, followed by a cup of tea. You can also visit the small showroom upstairs where you can see how these instruments are made, including the cat and dog skin used to cover the sound box (cat skin is more expensive). Open Monday to Saturday 10am to 5:30pm; closed the second and fourth Saturdays of the month and holidays. 1–1–8 Higashiyama. ✆ 076/252-3703. Loop Bus: Hashibacho (stop no. 6, 2 min.). On Kannon-machi street.

⑫ **Tawaraya Ame**    They've been selling Japanese confectionery from this traditional wood-slatted building for more than 170 years. Tawaraya makes two types of candy from rice and barley, using malt instead of sugar, and now touts the candy as health food. One of the candies is soft like honey, purportedly developed for babies who, for one reason or another, could not be breast fed. The other is hard and comes in a wooden bucket; the staff recommends breaking the hard candy with a hammer (kids love this) and putting it in a refrigerator. Soft lollipops and hard candy (true jawbreakers!) are also available. Open Monday to Saturday 9am to 6pm; Sunday 9am to 5pm. 2–4 Kobashi-machi. ℂ **076/252-2079.** Loop Bus: Kobashi (stop no. 3, 2 min.). Cross the bridge and turn left.

# WHERE TO STAY
## EXPENSIVE

Most of the expensive accommodations and some of the moderately priced hotels add a surcharge averaging ¥1,000 ($9.50) per person during peak season—New Year's, Golden Week (Apr 29–May 5), and mid-July through mid-November. We've indicated those that do in the listings below.

Directions are from Kanazawa Station; minutes indicate the walking time required from the bus stop.

**ANA Hotel Kanazawa**    This sleek, curved, white building soaring next to Kanazawa Station is part of the ANA conglomerate that includes All Nippon Airways. It offers convenient access to the station, good service, and varied dining choices (including a summertime beer garden and a 19th-floor teppanyaki restaurant with good views). The marbled lobby is filled with the sounds of a cascading waterfall, and a river of chandeliers shimmers from the atrium above. Rooms are simple, comfortable, and uncluttered, with everything you'd expect from one of Kanazawa's best hotels. Since the cheapest rooms are on lower floors facing another building, consider spending a bit more for a higher room overlooking the station.

16–3 Showa-machi, Kanazawa, Ishikawa 920-8518. ℂ **800/ANA-HOTELS** in the U.S. and Canada, or 076/224-6111. Fax 076/224-6100. www.anahotels.com. 254 units. ¥12,600 –¥14,700 ($120–$140) single; ¥19,950 –¥26,250 ($190–$249) double; ¥24,150 –¥48,300 ($229–$459) twin. Peak season ¥1,000 ($9.50) extra per person. AE, DC, MC, V. Station: Kanazawa (east exit, 1 min.). **Amenities:** 4 restaurants (Japanese, teppanyaki, Chinese, coffee shop); 1 bar; 1 lounge; salon; room service (7am–11pm); in-room massage; same-day laundry/dry-cleaning service; nonsmoking rooms. *In room:* A/C, cable TV w/pay movies, minibar, hot-water pot w/tea, hair dryer, Washlet toilet.

**Hotel Nikko Kanazawa**    Owned by rival Japan Airlines and giving the ANA Hotel across the street a run for its money, this 29-story high-rise was designed by a Japanese-French team, who succeeded in giving it a boutique-hotel ambience despite its size. Its lobby exudes an exotic, French-colonial atmosphere, adorned with a bubbling fountain, rattan chairs stuffed with pillows, fake trees, antiques, and Asian decorative art ranging from ginger jars to Japanese lacquered boxes. The English-speaking concierge staff receives high marks. Rooms are spacious, all with double-size or larger beds and decent-size bathrooms. Sink areas are separated from the bathrooms in doubles and twins, the most expensive of which add vanities. Higher-priced rooms offer great views from Kanazawa's tallest building.

2–15–1 Hon-machi, Kanazawa, Ishikawa 920-0853. ℂ **800/NIKKO-US** (800/645-5687) in the U.S. and Canada, or 076/234-1111. Fax 076/234-8802. www.hnkanazawa.co.jp. 260 units. ¥15,225 ($145) single; ¥26,250 ($249) double; ¥28,350 –¥30,450 ($269–$289) twin. Executive floor from ¥16,800 ($160) single; ¥31,500 ($299) twin. ¥1,050 ($10) added Sat and nights before holidays. AE, DC, MC, V. Station: Kanazawa (east exit, 1 min.). **Amenities:** 5 restaurants; 1 bar; 1 lounge; access to next-door health club with indoor pool (fee: ¥2,100/$18); concierge; shopping arcade; salon;

room service (7am–10pm); in-room massage; babysitting; same-day laundry/dry-cleaning service; nonsmoking rooms; executive-level rooms. *In room:* A/C, satellite TV w/pay movies, minibar, hot-water pot w/tea, hair dryer, Washlet toilet.

## MODERATE

**APA Hotel Kanazawa-Ekimae** Although just a business hotel, this place does have a special feature that sets it apart—large public baths complete with sauna and a rooftop outdoor bath, all free to hotel guests. Other pluses: a convenient location just steps away from Kanazawa Station; bold use of bright colors that are a welcome relief from the usual bland white of most business hotels; and a Seattle's Best cafe (a Starbucks wannabe). If you're not a fan of public baths, however, you might choose to stay elsewhere; the hotel is not geared toward tourists, little English is spoken, and rooms are so minuscule that if you open your luggage you may have to leap to reach your bed. Even the deluxe corner rooms would be considered small in a regular hotel. But rooms are clean and have basic necessities, including small windows that open.

If you'd rather be in the heart of the city, the newly opened **APA Hotel Kanazawa-Chuo,** 1–5–24 Katamachi (② **076/235-2111;** fax 076/235-2112), offers similar-size rooms at the same rates, except the water tapped for its public bath is from hot springs.

1–9–28 Hirooka, Kanazawa, Ishikawa 920-0031. ② **076/231-8111.** Fax 076/231-8112. 456 units. ¥8,000 ($76) single; ¥12,500 ($119) double; ¥13,500–¥18,000 ($128–$171) twin. AE, MC, V. Station: Kanazawa (west exit, 2 min.). **Amenities:** 4 restaurants (French, Japanese, Western, coffee shop); 1 bar; public baths with sauna (free for hotel guests); in-room massage; coin-op washer and dryer; nonsmoking rooms. *In room:* A/C, TV, fridge, hot-water pot w/tea, hair dryer, Washlet toilet.

**Kanazawa Manten** *Value* A fountain at the entrance, a front desk backed by trees, jazz playing in the hotel restaurant, and attentive service all conspire to make this business hotel seem like it's more expensive than it is. Alas, the overwhelmingly single rooms are no different or larger than those of any other business hotel, with semi-double-size beds that take up most of the floor space. On the bright side, the windows can be opened or covered by panels for complete darkness. There are 72 twin rooms and 10 doubles. There's no hot-water pot with tea in the rooms, but on each floor there's a convenience corner with hot water and cups, as well as a microwave, trouser press, and vending machines. In short, the cramped quarters and self-serve philosophy of the upper floors reinforce the business-hotel status, but at least in the lobby you can feel grand.

1–6–1 Kita-yasue, Kanazawa, Ishikawa 920-0022. ② **076/265-0100.** Fax 076/265-0120. 551 units. ¥5,800 ($55) single; ¥11,600 ($110) twin or double. AE, MC, V. Station: Kanazawa (west exit, 3 min). Turn right out of the station's west exit. **Amenities:** Restaurant (Western); lounge; in-room massage; coin-op washers and dryers; nonsmoking rooms. *In room:* A/C, TV, fridge, hair dryer, Washlet toilet.

**Kanazawa Miyako Hotel** Don't be turned off by the hotel's cheerless, aging exterior and functional lobby—all of the rooms have been nicely updated and, except for the singles, are among the largest for their price in Kanazawa. Add to that the Miyako name (synonymous with friendly service), free breakfasts for Frommer's readers, discounts for ladies, nonsmoking restaurants (a rarity in Japan), and a convenient location (linked to the station via an underground passage), and you'll see why I like this lodging. There's even a floor for ladies, decorated in pastel colors and with a vanity and toiletry bag that includes a pedicure kit, bath gel, and other female-oriented amenities. I also like rooms facing the station's bus terminal; when a Loop Bus pulls out, I know I have 15 minutes to make the next one. Be sure to mention Frommer's when you make a reservation.

6–10 Konohanacho, Kanazawa, Ishikawa 920-0852. ② **076/261-2111.** Fax 076/261-2113. www.miyakohotels. ne.jp/kanazawa. 193 units. ¥10,500–¥12,6000 ($100–$120) single; ¥16,800–¥25,200 ($160–$239) double; ¥18,900–¥29,400 ($180–$279) twin. 20% discount for ladies; complimentary breakfast for Frommer's readers. AE, MC, V. Station:

Kanazawa (east exit, 1 min). **Amenities:** 2 restaurants (Japanese, Western); 1 bar/lounge; 1 summertime beer garden; tour desk; salon; room service (7–10am and 5pm–9:30pm); in-room massage; same-day laundry/dry-cleaning service; nonsmoking rooms. *In room:* A/C, TV w/pay movies, minibar, hot-water pot w/tea, hair dryer, Washlet toilet.

## INEXPENSIVE

**Ryokan Murataya**    This Japanese Inn Group ryokan is in the heart of Kanazawa, not far from Katamachi and Tatemachi shopping streets and within walking distance of Kenrokuen. It's modern and rather uninteresting from the outside but comfortable and pleasant inside. All rooms are clean and are Japanese-style without bathrooms. The inn has its own map of the Katamachi area, showing the locations of banks, post offices, stores, and restaurants.

1–5–2 Katamachi, Kanazawa, Ishikawa 920-0981. ⓒ 076/263-0455. Fax 076/263-0456. murataya@spacelan.ne.jp. 11 units (none with bathroom). ¥4,700 ($45) single; ¥9,000 ($86) twin; ¥12,600 ($120) triple. Continental breakfast ¥500 ($4.75) extra; Japanese breakfast ¥800 ($7.60) extra. AE, MC, V. Bus: From platform 6, 7, or 8 to Katamachi, take a 3-min. walk. Take the small pedestrian lane on the right side of the APA Hotel and then turn left. **Amenities:** Coin-operated washer and dryer. *In room:* A/C, TV, hot-water pot w/tea, no phone.

## WHERE TO DINE

Kanazawa's local specialties, known collectively as **Kaga Ryori,** consist of seafood, such as tiny shrimp and winter crabs, as well as freshwater fish, duck, and mountain vegetables.

All directions are from Kanazawa Station.

### AROUND KANAZAWA STATION

**Le Grand Chariot** 🕈🕈 FRENCH    This combination lounge and restaurant is decorated in such a riot of colors that it looks like a kaleidoscope gone awry. The hotel describes it as "Arabic imagination"—whatever. The sophisticated lounge occupies the center of the room, while dining tables line windows at either side with the best ringside views. Since this is the highest spot in Kanazawa, the views are great, particularly at sunset, making this a good romantic splurge. From the west windows you can even see the Japan Sea in the distance. The menu has only a few a la carte choices and is mostly for fixed-price meals that change but have included options like snapper with sauce Provençale or lobster with rice in a truffle sauce, all artfully presented though portions can be small. Live music serenades you from 8:30 to 11pm, but the ¥840 ($8) cover charge is waived for diners.

Hotel Nikko Kanazawa, 30th floor, 2–15–1 Hon-machi. ⓒ 076/234-1111. www.hnkanazawa.co.jp. Set lunches ¥2,310–¥4,620 ($22–$44); set dinner ¥6,000–¥12,000 ($57–$114). AE, DC, MC, V. Daily 11:30am–2pm and 5–9:30pm (last order). Station: Kanazawa (east exit, 1 min.).

### AROUND KENROKUEN GARDEN

⟨124⟩ **Miyoshian** 🕈🕈 *Finds* KAGA KAISEKI    A great place to try the local Kaga cuisine right in Kenrokuen Garden, this 100-year-old restaurant consists of three separate wooden buildings, the best of which is a traditional room extending over a large pond. This is where you'll probably dine, seated on tatami with a view of an ancient pond (giant carp swim in the murky waters). Only set meals of Kaga cuisine are served, all featuring *jibuni* (a duck-and-vegetable stew eaten primarily in winter). The more expensive the meal, the more dishes it adds. The ¥1,575 ($15) meal includes soup, jibuni, sashimi, a seasonal dish like eel on rice, pickles, a Japanese sweet, and thick green tea. The ¥3,150 ($30) meal adds dishes like salmon, crab, tofu, and various small delicacies. You can also come just for green tea and sweets for ¥525 to ¥630 ($5–$6).

Kenrokuen Garden, 1–11 Kenrokumachi. ✆ **076/221-0127.** Kaga teishoku ¥1,575–¥3,150 ($15–$30). MC, V. Thurs–Tues 10:30am–2pm (last order). Loop Bus: Kenrokuenshita (stop no. 9), then turn right after entering the park (5 min.).

## KATAMACHI & THE NAGAMACHI SAMURAI DISTRICT

Just north of the Saigawa Ohashi Bridge is an area full of restaurants and drinking establishments, radiating from Katamachi Shopping Street and Saigawa Odori (called Chuo Dori by the locals).

**Aglio Olio** PASTA   Located beside a flowing canal between Katamachi and the Nagamachi Samurai District, this simple eatery with only a few tables and a counter is owned by a *nisei* (second-generation Japanese) from Brazil who offers a few pasta dishes like lasagna or spaghetti with a beef tomato sauce. The lunch special, which changes daily, includes pasta, salad, and bread.

1–12–10 Kohrinbo. ✆ **076/260-8223.** Pasta ¥850–¥1,100 ($8.10–$10); set lunches ¥900 ($8.55). No credit cards. Mon–Sat 11:30am–2pm and 6–10pm. Loop Bus: Kohrinbo (stop no. 15, 3 min.). Take the side street to the right of the Excel Hotel Tokyu and turn right; it will be on the right, across the small canal.

⑫⑤ **Hamacho** ✿ JAPANESE SEAFOOD   Hamacho offers seafood and vegetables in season; the menu, written on a blackboard but in Japanese only, changes according to what's fresh and available and may include *imo* (Japanese potatoes), freshly picked mushrooms, vegetables, various seafood selections, and sashimi. Just tell Mr. Ishigami, the owner and chief chef, how much you want to spend and he'll do the rest. If there's anything you don't like, be sure to tell him that, too. Sit at the counter where you can watch the preparation of your set meal, which may include grilled fish or shrimp, noodles, tofu, sashimi, soup, and vegetables.

2–27–24 Katamachi. ✆ **076/233-3390.** Reservations recommended. Set meals ¥6,000–¥10,000 ($57–$95). AE, DC, MC, V. Mon–Sat 5pm–midnight. Closed holidays. Loop Bus: Katamachi (stop no. 14, 2 min.). From the bus stop, backtrack to Saigawa Dori and turn right (west); it's set back from the road on the left, beside a small canal.

**Kincharyo** VARIED JAPANESE   This, without a doubt, is Katamachi's easiest restaurant to find: It's located on the third floor of the very visible Excel Hotel Tokyu. Sister restaurant to a famous 80-year-old restaurant in the Teramachi Temple district (near Myoryuji Temple), this one is popular with Japanese women. For lunch there's tempura, mini-kaiseki (¥4,515/$43), sushi, and more, but most popular is the obento for ¥1,890 to ¥3,675 ($18–$35)—so popular, in fact, that it sometimes runs out. Set dinners include tempura, Kaga kaiseki, sushi, shabu-shabu, and more.

Excel Hotel Tokyu, 2–1–1 Kohrinbo. ✆ **076/263-5511.** Set lunch ¥1,890–¥6,300 ($18–$60); set dinner ¥3,675–¥10,500 ($35–$100). AE, DC, MC, V. Daily 11:30am–2pm and 5–9pm (last order). Loop Bus: Kohrinbo (stop no. 15, 1 min.).

⑫⑥ **Kitama** ✿✿ VARIED JAPANESE/KAGA   Sitting on tatami mats, you'll have a pleasant view of moss-covered greenery at this modern restaurant with a 140-year-old history. The Kojitsu obento (¥2,100/$20), served in an upright lunch box, features sashimi, small pieces of pork and fish, fried shrimp, a soybean patty, and various seasonal vegetables. The jibuni teishoku (¥1,575/$15), with duck stew, clear soup, pickled vegetables, rice, and hors d'oeuvres, is also quite satisfying. The restaurant is also known for its tempura and (by reservation only) kaiseki meals starting at ¥5,250 ($50).

2–3–3 Katamachi. ✆ **076/261-7176.** Set meal ¥1,050–¥3,990 ($10–$38). MC, V. Daily 11:30am–8:30pm (last order). Closed irregularly. Loop Bus: Katamachi (stop no. 14, 2 min.). From the intersection of Katamachi and Saigawa

Dori, walk 1 block west on Chuo Dori and turn right; the restaurant will be on your left with a display case and bamboo fence at its entrance.

## HIGASHI CHAYA DISTRICT

(127) **To Mu** *Finds* VARIED JAPANESE  To Mu translates roughly as "rabbit dream," and maybe that's what that rabbit on the shoji screen is doing as it contemplates the moon. Otherwise, there's no rhyme or reason to this restaurant's name, but no doubt the geisha and their patrons who used to frequent this former teahouse had dreams of their own, none of which involved rabbits. Ground-floor dining is at a huge wooden slab of a counter, with leg wells for those errant appendages and a small outdoor garden to look at beyond the open kitchen. Upstairs it's tables and chairs on tatami, which Japanese find very weird. At any rate, this is one of the most popular restaurants of the moment, good for a light lunch (served 11:30am–2:30pm) that might include minced pork with tofu, udon noodles, or seasonal specials along with rice, salad, pickled vegetables, soup, and coffee or dessert. You can also come just for dessert; if you've never had ice cream made from green tea or sweet red beans, order it here.

1–26–16 Higashiyama. (© 076/253-3112. Set lunch ¥1,260–¥1,575 ($12–$15). No credit cards. Tues–Sun 10am–4pm. Loop Bus: Hashibacho (stop no. 6, 4 min.).

## ELSEWHERE

(128) **Kotobuki-Ya** *Finds* VEGETARIAN  Specializing in *shojin ryori* (Buddhist vegetarian cooking), Kotobuki-ya is in a beautiful 160-year-old merchant's house with a two-story airy entryway. Dining here, on beautiful lacquer and pottery tableware, is a wonderful experience—not surprisingly, they have had many fine reviews. For lunch, you can dine for ¥2,625 ($25) on the shojin ryori obento (not available Sun); for ¥300 ($2.85) more per person, you can have your own private tatami room. Lunch kaiseki costs ¥5,500 ($52), and the price already includes your private room. Kaiseki dinners are vegetarian or with fish, with private rooms costing ¥800 ($7.60) more per person. Two of the rooms have views of the garden.

2–4–13 Owari-cho. (© 076/231-6245. Reservations required by 3pm for dinner. Set lunch ¥2,625–¥5,500 ($25–$52); kaiseki dinner ¥7,350–¥12,600 ($70–$120). No credit cards. Daily 11:30am–2pm and 5–7pm (last order). Loop Bus: Musashigatsuji (stop no. 18, 3 min.). On a side street north of Hyakumangoku Dori, behind Eneos gas station.

## 4 Osaka

553km (343 miles) W of Tokyo; 42km (26 miles) SW of Kyoto; 339km (212 miles) E of Hiroshima

Although its history stretches back almost 1,500 years, Osaka first gained prominence when Hideyoshi Toyotomi, the most powerful lord in the land, built Japan's most magnificent castle here in the 16th century. To develop resources for his castle town, he persuaded merchants from other parts of the nation to resettle in Osaka. During the Edo Period, the city became an important distribution center as feudal lords from the surrounding region sent their rice to merchants in Osaka, who in turn sent the rice onward to Tokyo and other cities. As the merchants prospered, the town grew and such arts as Kabuki and Bunraku flourished. With money and leisure to spare, the merchants also developed a refined taste for food.

Nowadays, Osaka, capital of Osaka Prefecture on the southern coast of western Honshu, is the mover and shaker of this region of Japan, known as Kansai. An industrial city with a population of about 2.6 million, it's the third-most populated city in Japan (after Tokyo and Yokohama). The legacy of the city's commercial beginnings is

# Osaka

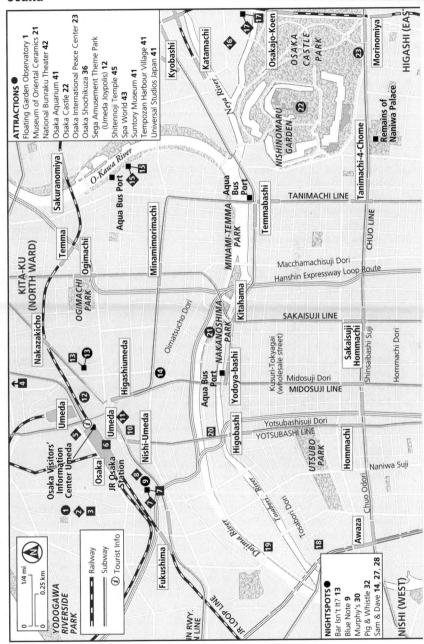

ATTRACTIONS ●
Floating Garden Observatory 1
Museum of Oriental Ceramics 21
National Bunraku Theater 42
Osaka Aquarium 41
Osaka Castle 22
Osaka International Peace Center 23
Osaka Shochikuza 36
Sega Amusement Theme Park
  (Umeda Joypolis) 12
Shitennoji Temple 45
Spa World 43
Suntory Museum 41
Tempozan Harbour Village 41
Universal Studios Japan 41

NIGHTSPOTS ●
Bar Isn't It? 13
Blue Note 9
Murphy's 30
Pig & Whistle 32
Sam & Dave 14, 27, 28

378

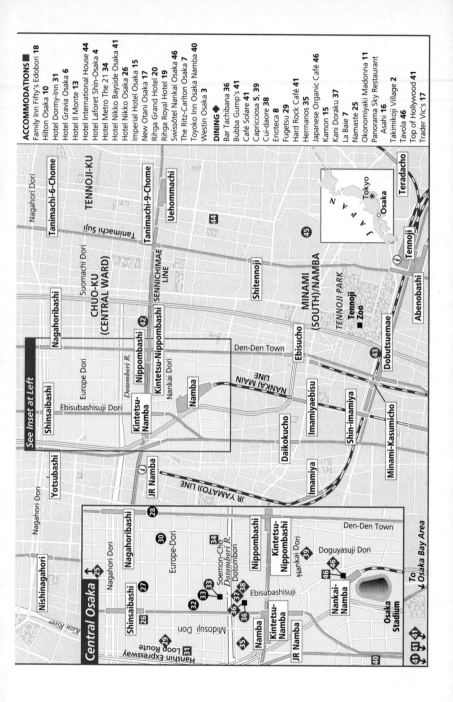

## ACCOMMODATIONS

Family Inn Fifty's Edobori **18**
Hilton Osaka **10**
Hotel Dormy-Inn **31**
Hotel Gravia Osaka **6**
Hotel Il Monte **13**
Hotel International House **44**
Hotel Laforet Shin-Osaka **4**
Hotel Metro The 21 **34**
Hotel Nikko Bayside Osaka **41**
Hotel Nikko Osaka **26**
Imperial Hotel Osaka **15**
New Otani Osaka **17**
Rihga Grand Hotel **20**
Rihga Royal Hotel **19**
Swissôtel Nankai Osaka **46**
The Ritz-Carlton Osaka **7**
Toyoko Inn Osaka Namba **40**
Westin Osaka **3**

## DINING ◆

Bar Tachibana **36**
Bubba Gump's **41**
Café Solare **41**
Capricciosa **5, 39**
Cui-daore **38**
Enoteca **8**
Fugetsu **29**
Hard Rock Café **41**
Hermanos **35**
Japanese Organic Café **46**
Kamon **15**
Kani Doraku **37**
La Baie **7**
Namaste **25**
Okonomiyaki Madonna **11**
Panorama Sky Restaurant Asahi **16**
Takimikoji Village **2**
Tavola **46**
Top of Hollywood **41**
Trader Vic's **17**

## Central Osaka

## TENNOJI-KU

## CHUO-KU (CENTRAL WARD)

## MINAMI (SOUTH)/NAMBA

379

still present—Osakans are usually characterized as being outgoing and clever at money affairs: One Osakan greeting is "Are you making any money?" Osaka has a reputation throughout Japan as an international and progressive business center and is known for its food, castle, port, underground shopping arcades, and Bunraku puppet theater. It also boasts the oldest state temple in Japan, one of nation's best aquariums, and the only Universal Studios outside the United States. Because of its international airport, it also serves as a major gateway to the rest of Japan. Indeed, some travelers base themselves in Osaka, taking day trips to Kyoto, Nara, Kobe, and Mount Koya.

## ESSENTIALS
### GETTING THERE

**BY PLANE**   Osaka's **Kansai International Airport** (**KIX**; ✆ **0724/55-2500;** www.kansai-airport.or.jp) receives both domestic and international flights; for details on the international carriers that fly here, see "Getting There" in chapter 2.

The two major domestic airlines that fly into KIX are **Japan Airlines** (✆ **800/ 525-3663** in the U.S. and Canada, or 0120/25-5971 toll-free in Japan; www.jal.com) and **All Nippon Airways** (**ANA;** ✆ **800/235-9262** in the U.S. and Canada, or 0120/029-222 toll-free in Japan; www.anaskyweb.com). From Tokyo's Haneda and Narita airports, flight time is about 1¼ hours. A **JAL** fare is ¥19,200 ($183) one-way.

**Arriving at KIX**   Arriving at KIX, you experience Japan at its modern best. Constructed on a huge synthetic island 4.8km (3 miles) off the mainland in Osaka Bay and connected to the city by a six-lane highway and two-rail line bridge, this 24-hour airport boasts the latest in technology—glass elevators ferry passengers to the four floors of the complex in an atrium setting, 25 computers spread throughout the terminal provide Internet access for ¥200 (95¢) per 10 minutes, and touch screens provide information in many languages. And, like the city itself, it's traveler-friendly: Signs are clear and abundant, and facilities—which range from restaurants and shops to a **post office** (second floor south, near JAL counter; open daily 8am–7pm), **ATMs** that accept foreign credit cards, a children's **playroom** in the international departure area (free of charge), and **dental and medical clinics**—are seemingly endless.

**Getting from KIX to Osaka**   Taxis are prohibitively expensive: expect to spend at least ¥26,000 ($248) for a cab to the city center. Easiest, especially if you have luggage, is the **Kansai Airport Transportation Enterprise** (✆ **0724/61-1374;** www. kate.co.jp), which provides bus service to major stations and hotels in Osaka. Most fares cost ¥1,300 ($12), and tickets can be purchased at counters in the arrival lobby. Another bus service, the **OCAT Shuttle 880** (✆ **06/6635-3030**), travels from KIX to the Osaka City Air Terminal (a downtown bus station for shuttle buses going to the airport), next to JR Namba Station (the major train station in Namba) in the heart of Osaka, every 30 minutes for ¥880 ($8.35).

If you're taking the **train** into Osaka (stations: Osaka, Tennoji, or Shin-Osaka) or even farther to Kyoto, simply walk through KIX's second-floor connecting concourse (baggage carts are designed to go on escalators and as far as train ticket gates) and board the limited express **JR Haruka,** which travels to Tennoji and Shin-Osaka stations before continuing to Kyoto. The fare to Shin-Osaka is ¥2,470 ($24) for the 45-minute trip, with departures generally twice an hour. Slower is the **JR rapid (JR Kanku Kaisoku),** which travels from the airport to Tennoji and Osaka stations before continuing to Kobe. The 65-minute trip to Osaka Station costs ¥1,160 ($11).

If you a have a **Japan Rail Pass,** you can ride these trains for free. Exchange your voucher at the Kansai Airport (rail) Station on the third floor (open daily 6am–11:30pm).

Next to the JR trains in the same station at the airport is the private **Nankai Line,** which has three types of trains to Namba Nankai Station. The sleek **rapi:t a** (pronounced *rapito alpha*) train reaches Namba in 30 minutes. There's one train an hour, and ordinary reserved seats cost ¥1,390 ($13). The **rapi:t b** *(rapito beta)* at the same price stops at more stations, including Sakai, and takes 35 minutes. You can also take an ordinary **Nankai Express Line** for ¥890 ($8.45) and reach Namba in 42 minutes.

**Itami Airport**    If you're arriving on a domestic flight, chances are you'll arrive at Itami Airport (© 06/6856-6781), north of the city. Buses connect to various parts of Osaka; to Osaka Station, the ride takes 25 minutes and costs ¥620 ($5.90).

**BY TRAIN**    Osaka is 3 hours from Tokyo by Shinkansen bullet train; tickets are ¥13,750 ($131) for a reserved seat (the Nozomi Shinkansen, which is not valid with a Japan Rail Pass, is faster and more expensive). All Shinkansen bullet trains arrive at **Shin-Osaka Station** at the city's northern edge. To get from Shin-Osaka Station to Osaka Station and other points south, use the most convenient public transportation, the **Midosuji Line** subway; the subway stop at Osaka Station is called **Umeda Station. JR trains** also make runs between Shin-Osaka and Osaka stations.

If you haven't turned in your voucher for your **Japan Rail Pass** yet, you can do so at Osaka Station's or Shin-Osaka Station's Green Windows (open daily 5:30am–11pm).

**If you're arriving in Osaka from Kobe or Kyoto,** the commuter lines, which will deliver you directly to Osaka Station in the heart of the city, are more convenient than the Shinkansen, which will deposit you at out-of-the-way Shin-Osaka Station.

**BY BUS**    JR night buses depart from both Tokyo (Yaesu exit; © 03/3215-1468) and Shinjuku (new south exit; © 03/5379-0874) stations several times nightly, arriving at Osaka Station the next morning. The trip from Tokyo takes about 8 hours and costs ¥8,610 ($82). Cheaper yet are **JR day buses** from Tokyo Station to Osaka Station costing ¥6,000 ($57), and a twice-a-night JR bus from Tokyo station and once a night from Shinjuku station costing only ¥5,000 ($48). Tickets can be bought at any major JR station or at a travel agency.

## VISITOR INFORMATION

**AT THE AIRPORT**    The **Kansai Tourist Information Center** (© 0724/56-6025; open daily 9am–9pm) is near the south end of the International Arrivals Lobby. The multilingual staff can help with general travel information about Japan and hotel reservations, and they offer brochures and maps.

**IN TOWN**    At **Osaka Station,** the **Visitors Information Center Umeda** (© 06/ 6345-2189; open daily 8am–8pm) is at the east (Midosuji) exit of JR Osaka Station in a kiosk beside the bus terminal; the English-speaking staff gives out good maps of the city and can assist in securing a hotel room. Another center is just east of the central exit of **Shin-Osaka Station** on the third floor (© 06/6305-3311; open daily 8am–8pm). Note that if you're arriving by Shinkansen, you'll be up on the fourth floor, so simply go down one flight to the tourist office. At **JR Namba Station,** you'll

find the **Visitors Information Center Namba** (© **06/6643-2125;** open daily 8am–8pm) in the basement of the Osaka City Air Terminal (OCAT) Building. Other tourist information centers are located just outside **Universal City Station** (© **06/ 4804-3824;** open daily 9am–8pm) and at **JR Tennoji Station** (© **06/6774-3077;** open daily 8am–8pm).

To find out what's going on in Osaka, pick up a copy of *Kansai Time Out,* a monthly magazine sold at bookstores for ¥300 ($2.85) with information on sightseeing, festivals, restaurants, and other items of interest pertaining to Osaka, Kobe, and Kyoto. *Kansai Scene* (www.kansaiscene.com) is a free bilingual magazine also available online with articles, reviews, listings, and information on the Kansai area. **Osaka InfoGuide** is a free giveaway at popular foreigner hangouts with maps and information on tourist spots and restaurants.

Another source of information available free at tourist offices and at many hotels is *Meet Osaka,* a quarterly pamphlet with maps and information on sightseeing, Bunraku, festivals, concerts, and special exhibits and events. Look, too, for the free *Osaka Event and Tourist Guide,* published every 2 months by the Osaka Convention and Tourism Bureau with information on special events, museum exhibitions, concert information, and even which nearby beaches are open in summer.

Finally, information on Osaka is available on the Web at **www.tourism.city.osaka.jp** and at **www.kansai.gr.jp,** which gives information on the Kansai region.

**CONSULATES** Several embassies maintain consulates in Osaka, including **Australia** (© **06/6941-9271** or 06/6941-9448); **Canada** (© **06/6212-4910**); **Great Britain** (© **06/6120-5600**); and the **United States** (© **06/6315-5900**).

**INTERNET ACCESS** Internet access is available at two locations inside Osaka Station, though they're difficult to find. **Kinko's,** on the north concourse, between the east and central passages and across from JTB (© **06/6442-3700**), is open daily 7am to 10:30pm and charges ¥210 ($2) for 10 minutes of computer use. Nearby, up a narrow flight of stairs, is the **complex café [X-Time]** Internet cafe (© **06/6341-8222**), which charges ¥250 ($2.40) for 30 minutes on the computer. Easier to find is **Yahoo BB** (© **06/6630-1611**), across the street on the north side of Osaka station in the Yodobashi Camera building, which charges ¥100 (95¢) per hour and is open from 10am to 8pm.

**MAIL** The Central Post Office, or Osaka Chuo Yubinkyoku (© **06/6347-8006**), a minute's walk west of Osaka Station, is open 24 hours for mail and has ATMs for international credit cards. For postal service information in English, call © **06/6944-6245** Monday to Friday 9:30am to 4:30pm.

## ORIENTATION

Osaka is divided into various wards, or *ku,* the most important of which for visitors are Kita-ku (North Ward), which encompasses the area around Osaka Station; and Chuo-ku (Central Ward), where you'll find Osaka Castle and Namba, the heart of the city. Some city maps divide Osaka by location: Kita (North), around Osaka Station; Minami (South), around Namba and Shinsaibashi; Higashi (East), around Osaka Castle; and Nishi (West) which is Osaska's bay area. Shin-Osaka Station, three subway stations north of Osaka (Umeda) Station, is a tourist wasteland, though it does have a few hotels.

**AROUND OSAKA STATION**    Kita-ku embraces the area around Osaka and Umeda stations and includes many of the city's top hotels, the city's tallest buildings, lots of restaurants, and several shopping complexes, mostly underground.

**AROUND OSAKA CASTLE**    Osaka Castle, which lies to the east, is the historic center of the city. It's in **Chuo-ku,** the Central Ward, which stretches through the city center.

**MINAMI/NAMBA**    Four subway stops south of Umeda Station is Namba (also referred to as **Minami,** or South Osaka), with a cluster of stations serving subways, JR trains, and Kintetsu and Nankai lines, all of which are connected to one another via underground passageways. This is the heart of the city, bustling with the spirit of old Osaka, where you'll find more hotels, Osaka's liveliest eating and entertainment district centered on a narrow street called **Dotombori** (also written Dotonbori), and major shopping areas like the enclosed pedestrian streets **Shinsaibashi-Suji** and **America-Mura** with imported goods from America. Farther south is **Den Den Town,** Osaka's electronics district; and **Dogayasuji,** famous for restaurant supplies. Connecting Kita-ku with Namba is Osaka's main street, **Midosuji Dori,** a wide boulevard lined with gingko trees and name-brand shops.

**AROUND TENNOJI PARK**    At the south end of the JR Loop Line is **Tennoji-ku,** which was once a thriving temple town with **Shitennoji Temple** at its center. In addition to a park with a zoo, it boasts **Spa World,** Japan's biggest and most luxurious public bathhouse.

**OSAKA BAY & PORT**    West of the city around Osaka Bay is where you will find **Universal Studios Japan** and Universal CityWalk shopping and dining complex; **Tempozan Harbour Village** with its first-class aquarium, shopping complex, and Suntory Museum; and domestic and international ferry terminals.

## GETTING AROUND

Despite its size, I find Osaka easier to get around than other large Japanese cities because there are lots of English-language signs and information. The exception is Osaka Station, used for JR trains, and its adjoining Umeda Station, used by subway lines and private railway lines Hankyu and Hanshin. Underground passages and shopping arcades complicate navigation; there's no escaping—you will get lost.

When exploring by foot, it helps to know that most roads running east and west end in *"dori,"* while roads running north and south end in *"suji,"* which means "avenue."

**BY SUBWAY**    Osaka's user-friendly subway network is easy to use because all lines are color-coded and the station names are in English (even English-language announcements are on many lines). The red **Midosuji Line** is the most important one for visitors; it passes through Shin-Osaka Station and on to Umeda (the subway station next

---

*Tips*  **A Note on Directions**

For all the attractions, accommodations, and restaurants listed below, I've included the nearest subway or JR station followed by the walking time to the establishment once you reach the indicated station.

to Osaka Station), Shinsaibashi, Namba, and Tennoji. Fares begin at ¥200 ($1.90) and increase according to the distance traveled.

**TRANSPORTATION PASSES**    If you think you'll be traveling a lot by subway on a given day, consider purchasing a **1-Day Pass (Ichinichi-Joshaken)** for ¥850 ($8.10), which allows unlimited rides on subways and buses all day. On the 20th of each month (or on the following day if the 20th falls on a Sun or holiday) and every Friday, this pass (nicknamed No-My-Car-Day) costs just ¥600 ($5.70) and offers slight discounts to several attractions. There's also a prepaid card for ¥3,000 ($29) that gives you ¥3,300 ($32) worth of travel on subways and buses in Osaka.

For trips outside Osaka, the **Surutto Kansai Card (Kansai Thru Pass)** allows you to ride subways, private railways (no JR trains), and buses in Osaka, Kyoto, Nara, and Kobe, with a 2-day pass costing ¥3,800 ($36) and a 3-day pass costing ¥5,000 ($48). Children pay half price. It can be purchased at KIX KAA Travel Desk (first floor international arrivals) or at the Visitor Information Centers in Namba or Shin Osaka. For JR trains, there's the **Kansai Area Pass** available for 1 day (¥2,000/$19) to 4 days (¥6,000/$57), available at major JR stations in the Kansai area.

**BY JR TRAIN**    A Japan Railways train called the Osaka Kanjo Line, or **JR Loop Line,** passes through Osaka Station and makes a loop around the central part of the city (similar to the Yamanote Line in Tokyo); take it to visit Osaka Castle. Fares begin at ¥120 ($1.15).

## SEEING THE SIGHTS
### NEAR OSAKA STATION
**Floating Garden Observatory (Kuchu Teien Tenbodai)**    This futuristic observatory 167m (557 ft.) in the air looks like a space ship floating between the two towers of the Umeda Sky Building. Take the superfast glass elevator from the East Tower building's third floor; you'll then take a glass-enclosed escalator that also bridges the two towers before depositing you on the 39th floor. I'm not afraid of heights, but taking an escalator over thin air in an earthquake-plagued nation certainly caught my attention; it made the "floating" observatory feel safe in comparison. From here, you have an unparalleled view of Osaka, making it a popular nightspot for couples on dates. My own interest in the place, however, has waned since the female attendants stopped wearing cone head–shaped hats.

Umeda Sky Building, 1–1–88 Oyodo-naka, Kita-ku. ✆ 06/6440-3901. www.skybldg.co.jp. Admission ¥700 ($6.65) adults, ¥500 ($4.75) junior-high and high-school students, ¥300 ($2.85) children. Daily 10am–10:30pm. Station: JR Osaka or Umeda (Central North exit of JR Osaka Station, 9 min.).

**Museum of Oriental Ceramics (Toyotoji Bijutsukan)** *★★* *(Finds*    This modern facility, about a 15-minute walk south of Osaka Station on Nakanoshima Island in the Dojima River, is my favorite museum in Osaka. Indeed, its 2,700-piece collection of Chinese, Korean, and Japanese ceramics—of which 300 are on display at any one time on a rotating basis—ranks as one of the finest in the world. Built specifically for the collection, the museum does a superb job showcasing the exquisite pieces as the masterpieces they truly are, in darkened rooms that utilize natural light and computerized natural-light simulation. Korean celadon, Chinese ceramics from the Song and Ming dynasties, Arita ware from the Edo Period, and much more are on display. Even if you've never given ceramics more than a passing glance, you're likely to come away with a heightened sense of appreciation. You'll want to spend 30 minutes or more here.

1–1–26 Nakanoshima, Kita-ku. © 06/6223-0055. Admission ¥500 ($4.75) adults, ¥300 ($2.85) students, free for children. Tues–Sun 9:30am–5pm. Closed during exhibition changes. Station: Yodoyabashi or Kitahama (5 min.).

## Sega Amusement Theme Park (Umeda Joypolis) ✿ *Kids*

I suppose it could be argued that you haven't experienced today's Japan unless you've visited at least one Joypolis, the reigning king of amusement arcades. This one, on the eighth and ninth floors of a shopping arcade complete with a Ferris wheel on top, overloads the senses with lots of flashing lights, bells and whistles, and throngs of squealing kids and teenagers. In addition to arcade games, virtual rides simulate gliding through the air or shooting the rapids of a wild river. ***Note:*** Children under the age of 17 aren't allowed here after 7pm and some "rides" carry height restrictions, with rules enforced by what—the joy police?

HEP FIVE, Umeda Kita-ku. © 06/6366-3647. Free admission; attractions ¥500–¥600 ($4.75–$5.70). Daily 11am–11pm (you must enter by 10:15pm). Station: JR Osaka or Umeda (5 min.).

## AROUND OSAKA CASTLE

### Osaka Castle (Osaka-jo) ✿✿

First built in the 1580s on the order of Toyotomi Hideyoshi, Osaka Castle was the largest castle in Japan, a magnificent structure used by Toyotomi as a military stronghold from which to wage war against rebellious feudal lords in far-flung provinces. By the time he died in 1598, Toyotomi had accomplished what no man had done before: crushed his enemies and unified all of Japan under his command.

After Toyotomi's death, Tokugawa Ieyasu seized power and established his shogunate government in Edo. But Toyotomi's heirs had ideas of their own: Considering Osaka Castle impregnable, they plotted to overthrow the Tokugawa government. In 1615, Tokugawa sent troops to Osaka where they not only annihilated the Toyotomi insurrectionists but destroyed Osaka Castle. The Tokugawas rebuilt the castle in 1629, but the main tower was destroyed by lightning 36 years later, and the rest burned in 1868 as the shogunate made their last stand against imperial forces and what later became known as the Meiji Restoration.

The present Osaka Castle dates from 1931 and was extensively renovated in 1997. Built of ferroconcrete, it's not as massive as the original but is still one of Japan's most famous castles and is impressive with its massive stone walls, black and gold-leaf trim, and copper roof. Its eight-story *donjon* (keep) rises 39m (130 ft.), with an observation platform on the top floor offering bird's-eye views of the city. The rest of the donjon houses a museum that uses videos, holograms, models, and artifacts to describe the life and times of Toyotomi Hideyoshi and the history of the castle. Unfortunately, most explanations are in Japanese only, but there's plenty to see, including a folding screen with scenes of the intense fighting that took place between Toyotomi and Tokugawa forces, samurai armor and gear, a full-scale reproduction of Toyotomi's Gold Tea Room, and a model of Osaka Castle during the Toyotomi Era. If you want, you can have your photo taken in period clothing for ¥300 ($2.85). You'll probably spend about 45 minutes here.

1–1 Osakajo, Chuo-ku. © 06/6941-3044. www.osakacastle.net. Admission ¥600 ($5.70) adults, free for junior-high-age children and younger. Daily 9am–5pm. Station: Osakajo-Koen on the JR Loop Line or Morinomiya (15 min.); or Temmabashi or Osaka Business Park (10 min.).

### Osaka International Peace Center ✿

Located on the southern edge of Osaka Castle Park, this museum strives for global peace by educating present and future

generations about the horrors of war, related by those who survived it. Unlike other museums in Japan dedicated to peace—including those in Hiroshima and Nagasaki—this one does not shy away from Japan's role in the Asian conflict, including its war campaign in China, the abduction of Koreans to work in dangerous areas, and massacres committed by Japanese in Singapore, Malaysia, and elsewhere. But its main focus is on wartime death and destruction, with personal testimonies of air raid survivors (15,000 people died during World War II air raids on Osaka), displays centering on the suicide attacks by *kamikaze* pilots at the end of the war, graphic photographs of Hiroshima and Nagasaki after the atomic bombs were dropped, and a section devoted to the horrors of the Auschwitz concentration camp. You'll probably spend 45 sobering minutes here.

2–1 Osakajo, Chuo-ku. Ⓒ **06/6947-7208**. Admission ¥250 ($2.38) adults, ¥150 ($1.40) high-school students, free for children. Tues–Sun 9:30am–5pm. Closed on days following national holidays and last day of each month. Station: Morinomiya (3 min.) or Osakajo-Koen (8 min.).

## AROUND TENNOJI

**Shitennoji Temple**   Founded 1,400 years ago as the first—and therefore oldest—officially established temple in Japan, Shitennoji Temple is the spiritual heart of Osaka. It was constructed in 593 by Prince Shotoku, who is credited with introducing Buddhism to Japan. However, like most wooden structures in Japan, its buildings have been destroyed repeatedly through the centuries by fire and war, including the 1615 Tokugawa raid on Osaka Castle, and World War II. And through the centuries, the buildings have been faithfully reconstructed exactly as they were in the 6th century, with the Main Gate, the five-story Buddhist Pagoda, the Main Golden Hall, and the Lecture Hall all on a north-south axis. Japanese flock to Shitennoji to pay respects to Prince Shotoku, who remains a revered, popular figure even today. There's also a turtle sanctuary. But the best thing to do here is wander the temple's newly restored Japanese landscape garden, first laid out during the Tokugawa regime and a lovely oasis with its manicured bushes, meandering streams, and waterfall.

Shitennoji 1-11-18, Tennoji-ku. Ⓒ **06/6771-0066**. Admission to either temple buildings or garden ¥300 ($2.85) adults, ¥200 ($1.90) children. Temple grounds open 24 hr.; garden daily 10am–4pm. Station: Shitennoji-mae Yuhigaoka (exit 4, 5 min.); or JR Tennoji (north exit, 10 min.).

**Spa World** ⚔   This is one of the most luxurious and ambitious bathhouses I've seen. It can accommodate up to 5,000 people and draws upon hot springs brought up from 891m (2,970 ft.) below the earth's surface. On its roof, in a large hangarlike room, is a covered swimming complex that includes a pool, a slide, a wave pool, a sunning terrace, and a wading pool (rental bathing suits available). The rest of the large complex is divided into themed, geographical bathing zones, which are rotated between the sexes and include luxurious locker rooms. At the Asian Zone, for example, Middle Eastern music and tiled mosaics set the tone for the Turkish bath, while China is represented by a medicinal bath. Massage is also available. If you're timid about going to a public bath, this one will convert you. If you're already a fan, you'll want to move in—note, however, that at 5am you're charged for a new day. And sorry, people with tattoos—associated with the Japanese mafia—are not allowed.

3-2-24 Ebisu-higashi, Naniwa-ku. Ⓒ **06/6631-0001**. Admission weekdays ¥2,700 ($26) adults, ¥1,500 ($14) children; weekends and holidays ¥3,000 ($29) adults, ¥1,700 ($16) children. Daily 10am–9pm. Station: Shin-Imamiya or Dobutsuenmae (2 min.). Next to festival gate.

## OSAKA BAY AREA

Osaka's well-developed waterfront offers a quick getaway for Osakans wishing to escape urban life. In addition to shopping malls, an aquarium, and other attractions, it boasts **Universal Studios Japan,** one of Japan's major draws.

**Osaka Aquarium (Kaiyukan)** ✿✿✿ (Kids) Of all the aquariums in Japan, this is probably my favorite. One of the world's largest—encompassing 26,570 sq. m (286,000 sq. ft.) and containing 2.9 million gallons of water—it's constructed around the theme "Ring of Fire," which refers to the volcanic perimeter encircling the Pacific Ocean. Tours begin through a tunnel filled with reef fish, followed by an escalator ride to the eighth floor; from there, you'll pass through 16 different habitats ranging from arctic to tropical as you follow a spiraling corridor back to the ground floor, starting with the daylight world—a Japanese forest—above the ocean's surface and proceeding past Antarctica, Monterey Bay, the Great Barrier Reef, and other ecosystems as you travel to the depths of the ocean floor. The walls of the aquarium tank are constructed of huge acrylic glass sheets, making you feel like you're immersed in the ocean. You'll see 30,000 specimens representing 580 species; stars of the show include whale sharks (the largest fish in captivity), Antarctic penguins, the odd-looking ocean sunfish (which has the circumference of a truck tire but is as flat as a pancake), and the Japan giant spider crab with its incredible 3m (9¾-ft.) span. English-spoken audio guides are available for rent for ¥300 ($2.85). Allow about 1½ hours to tour the aquarium, avoiding weekends.

1–1–10 Kaigan-dori, Minato-ku. © 06/6576-5501. www.kaiyukan.com. Admission ¥2,000 ($19) adults, ¥900 ($8.55) children 7–15, ¥400 ($3.80) children 4–6. Daily 10am–8pm. Closed 7 days a year (in June and in winter). Station: Osakako (5 min.).

**Suntory Museum** ✿ The Suntory Museum, which you can tour in about 30 minutes, is that fantastically modern-looking structure you see near the aquarium, designed by well-known architect Tadao Ando. It stages changing exhibitions in airy rooms against a dramatic background of the sea beyond its glass walls. Past exhibits have included Art Deco, posters by Toulouse-Lautrec, paintings by German expressionists, and glass by Emile Gallé; call or check the *Meet Osaka* quarterly for current information. There's also a 3-D IMAX theater with scenes so real you'll think you are part of the film, a good museum shop, the Sky Lounge (perfect for taking a break), and a restaurant, Café Solare (p. 399).

1–5–10 Kaigan-dori, Minato-ku. © 06/6577-0001. www.suntory.co.jp/culture-sports/smt. Admission to either museum or IMAX theater ¥1,000 ($9.50) adults; ¥700 ($6.65) seniors, high-school, and university students; ¥500 ($4.75) children. Museum Tues–Sun 10:30am–7:30pm; IMAX Tues–Sun 11am–7pm (last show). Station: Osakako (5 min.).

---

### ⌜Tips⌝ Mutineers Need Not Apply

The quickest—and most scenic—way to travel between Suntory Museum/aquarium and Universal Studios is via the **Captain Cook** shuttle boat (© 06/6573-8222), which departs every 30 minutes and charges ¥600 ($5.70) for the 10-minute ride. At our last boarding, the crew—from captain to wharf assistants—were all females. You've come a long way, Captain Cook! A bonus: The boat ticket includes a ¥200 ($1.90) discount for the aquarium.

---

**Universal Studios Japan** ★★★ *Kids*    Following the tradition of Universal's Hollywood and Orlando theme parks, USJ takes guests on a fantasy trip through the world of American blockbuster movies, with thrill rides, live entertainment, back-lot streets, restaurants, shops, and other attractions based on actual movies. Board a boat for a harrowing encounter with a great white straight out of *Jaws,* escape a T-Rex as you roller-coaster your way through a setting of *Jurassic Park,* fly and leap at high speed among skyscrapers in the *Amazing Adventures of Spider Man—The Ride,* and see, feel, and smell *Sesame Street 4-D Movie Magic* or *Shrek's 4-D Adventure* (4-D in movie lingo means there are smells and other sensations). Unfortunately, most of the attractions have been dubbed into Japanese (I wonder why the original English isn't available on audio guide), so it helps to know the movies beforehand. Plan for a whole day here, but note that it is immensely popular: Avoid weekends, arrive early, and buy a Universal Express Pass Booklet 4 (¥2,800/$27) or Universal Express Pass Booklet 7 (¥4,200/$40), which allows priority entry into four or seven designated rides.

2–1–33 Sakurajima, Konohana. ✆ 06/4790-7000. www.usj.co.jp. Studio Pass to all attractions ¥5,500 ($52) adults, ¥4,800 ($46) seniors, ¥3,700 ($35) children 4–11. Daily, generally 9am–7pm (to 9pm in peak season), but hours vary so check the website. Station: Universal City (5 min.).

## IN NEARBY TAKARAZUKA

Northwest of Osaka, the town of Takarazuka is synonymous with the all-female **Takarazuka Troupe.** Founded in 1914 to attract vacationers to Takarazuka, the troupe proved instantly popular with the general public, whose taste turned from traditional Japanese drama to lively Western musicals and entertainment. Performances are held at the **Takarazuka Revue Hall** (✆ 0797/85-6770) most days throughout the year (closed Wed), usually at 1pm on weekdays and at 11am and 3pm on weekends and holidays. Tickets range from about ¥3,500 to ¥7,500 ($33–$71). For more information on the troupe, see the "Takarazuka Kagekidan" section on p. 212.

## SHOPPING

Osaka is famous in Japan for shopping, in no small part because of the discerning nature of the Osakans themselves. Osaka, after all, developed as a commercial town of merchants—and who knows merchandise better than the merchants themselves?

Osaka must rank as one of the world's leading cities in underground shopping arcades. Enter the vast underground arcades in Umeda (where the JR, Hanshin, subway, and Hankyu train lines intersect) with names like **Whity Umeda, Hankyu Sanbangai, Diamor Osaka,** and **Dojima Underground Shopping Center,** and you may never emerge in this lifetime. **Crysta Nagahori,** connecting Nagahoribashi Station to Yotsubashi-suji, has a glass atrium ceiling, flowing streams of water, and 100 shops, making it one of the largest—if not the largest—shopping malls in Japan. Nearby are **Namba Walk, Nan-nan Town,** and **Namba City,** all interconnected by underground passageways.

There are plenty of aboveground shopping options as well. **Den Den Town** (station: Nipponbashi or Ebisucho) is Osaka's electronics shopping region (*Den* is short for "electric"), similar to Tokyo's Akihabara and just as good. Some 200 open-fronted shops here deal in electrical and electronic equipment, from rice cookers and refrigerators to DVD players, MP3 players, calculators, cameras, and computers. Most stores here are open daily 10am to 8pm.

Running north to south and a few blocks east of Nankai Namba Station is **Sennichimae Doguya-suji,** a covered shopping lane with about 45 open-fronted

shops selling all the pots, pans, dishes, and implements you'd ever need to prepare and serve Japanese food. Chopsticks, chopstick rests, pottery, lacquerware, frying pans, trays, kitchen knives, rice bowls, plastic food, and lots of gift ideas are here at very inexpensive prices—not surprising since Osaka is known as the food capital of Japan.

**Midosuji Dori,** a wide boulevard lined with gingko trees running north and south in the heart of the city, is the city's calling card for name-brand boutiques. Just to the east is **Shinsaibashi-suji,** a covered promenade with many long-established shops, some dating back to the Edo Period. On the other side of Midosuji Dori is **America-Mura,** a popular spot for young Japanese shopping for T-shirts, Hawaiian shirts, ripped jeans, and other American fashions at inflated prices; its biggest marketplace is **Big Step.** Teens also flock to **HEP FIVE,** a huge shopping complex near Umeda with a Joypolis amusement arcade and a Ferris wheel on top.

**Universal CityWalk,** near Universal Studios, offers everything from Hello Kitty goods to Italian imports. In Rinkan Town near KIX airport is **Rinku Premium Outlets,** one of the largest outlet malls in Japan, with 153 shops.

## WHERE TO STAY

Most of Osaka's hotels are clustered around Osaka Station. In the listings below, the nearest subway or JR station is indicated followed by the number of minutes it takes to walk from the station to the hotel. Also, note that service charge is included in all room rates given below.

### AROUND OSAKA & SHIN-OSAKA STATIONS
### VERY EXPENSIVE

**The Ritz-Carlton, Osaka** 🌸🌸🌸    Opened in 1997, The Ritz-Carlton's first Japanese venture immediately gained a reputation as one of the nation's top hotels. Instead of the grandiose marble lobby most Japanese hotels favored at the time, the lobby here is small and intimate, done in old-world style with overstuffed sofas, 100-year-old Persian carpets, Italian marble fireplaces, stunning flower arrangements, crystal chandeliers, antiques, and museum-grade landscape paintings and portraits from the 18th and 19th centuries. Unique standouts include The Bar with its single-malt whiskey, cigars, and live music nightly; La Baie (see "Where to Dine," later in this chapter), rated by many as Osaka's best French restaurant; an outdoor garden serving champagne in summer; afternoon tea served in the lobby lounge with live classical music; and a health club free to hotel guests. Stylish rooms—located from the 24th through 37th floors and among the largest in the city—offer panoramic views, especially from deluxe corner rooms, as well as goose-down pillows and comforters; terry robes; and spacious marble bathrooms with magnifying mirrors, separate areas for the shower stall, tub, and toilet, and two sinks.

2–5–25 Umeda, Kita-ku, Osaka 530-0001. ⓒ 800/241-3333 in the U.S. and Canada, or 06/6343-7000. Fax 06/6343-7001. www.ritzcarlton.com. 292 units. ¥46,273 – ¥64,071 ($440–$610) single; ¥58,138 – ¥75,936 ($554–$723) twin or double. Club floors ¥58,138 – ¥70,003 ($554–$667) single, ¥70,003 – ¥81,868 ($667–$780) double. ¥5,000 ($48) extra on Sat and nights before holidays. AE, DC, MC, V. Station: Osaka, Umeda, or Nishi-Umeda (7 min.). **Amenities:** 4 restaurants (Japanese, Italian, French, Cantonese); 2 bars; 1 lounge; state-of-the-art health club w/gym, 20m (66-ft.) indoor lap pool, and indoor/outdoor whirlpools (free to hotel guests); spa w/dry and wet saunas and baths (fee: ¥1,000/$9.50); aesthetic salon; concierge; small business center; shopping arcade; 24-hr. room service; in-room massage; same-day laundry/dry-cleaning service; nonsmoking rooms; executive-level rooms. *In room:* A/C, cable TV w/pay movies on demand, high-speed dataport, minibar, hot-water pot w/tea, hair dryer, safe, bathroom scale, Washlet toilet.

## EXPENSIVE

In addition to the choices listed below, consider the **Hilton Osaka,** 1–8–8 Umeda, Kita-ku, Osaka 530-0001 (© **800/HILTONS** or 06/6347-7111; fax 06/6347-7001; www.hilton.com), a well-established branch of the Hilton chain with a wide range of services and facilities, including an adjacent shopping and dining complex.

**Rihga Royal Hotel**     Osaka's oldest hotel opened in 1935, later expanding and becoming part of the Rihga chain. Located on Nakanoshima, an island in the middle of the Dojima River in the heart of Osaka (a 10-min. ride from Osaka Station), it enjoys a good reputation among Japanese and a high occupancy rate on weekends, due in no small part to the convention center next door. It offers a wide range of facilities, including a 60-store shopping arcade, a deli with health-conscious choices and—at the other end of the extreme—the best-stocked hotel gourmet foods shop I've seen, with 700 eye-popping pastries and delicacies. It also has one of my favorite lobby lounges in the city—a restful oasis where you can sip your drink and watch a cascading waterfall against a backdrop of cliffs and foliage. Comfortable guest rooms sport a variety of interior designs, from modern to classical drawing-room style. Of the hotel's many restaurants, most renowned is the Chambord, offering French cuisine and views from the 29th floor. In short, you could do much worse than this hotel despite the crowds, and a new subway line running near the hotel, due for completion in 2007, is sure to boost its rating.

5–3–68 Nakanoshima, Kita-ku, Osaka 530-0005. © **06/6448-1121.** Fax 06/6448-4414. www.rihga.com. 985 units. ¥14,000–¥19,000 ($133–$180) single; ¥28,000–¥49,000 ($267–$467) double or twin. Presidential Towers executive floor from ¥44,000 ($419) single, ¥47,000 ($448) double. AE, DC, MC, V. Station: Yodoyabashi, then free shuttle bus from exit 4 (turn left) with departures every 15 min.; or JR Osaka Station north exit, free shuttle every 6 min. **Amenities:** 18 restaurants; 3 bars; 2 lounges; indoor circular "shape-up" pool, 25m (82-ft.) lap pool, Jacuzzi, and sauna (fee: ¥2,100/$20); concierge; tour desk; business center; shopping arcade; salon; 24-hr. room service; in-room massage; babysitting; same-day laundry/dry-cleaning service; nonsmoking rooms; executive-level rooms. In room: A/C, cable TV w/pay movies, dataport, minibar, hot-water pot w/tea, hair dryer, Washlet toilet.

**Westin Osaka**     Located next to the futuristic-looking Umeda Sky Building (with its Floating Garden Observatory), the Westin has generously sized guest rooms with expansive city views and a laid-back yet chic interior that make it a top choice for business travelers and tourists alike. A sun-drenched lobby lounge with a three-story glass facade overlooking greenery and a dome bathed in colored lights greet guests arriving from Osaka Station via the free shuttle. Guest rooms, which increase in price the higher they are, come with all you might expect, including shower stalls separated from tubs and, on higher floors, two basins instead of one. L-shaped corner rooms are especially good, with separate sleeping and lounging areas. Joggers take note: There's a map featuring 3- and 5-mile runs from the hotel.

1–1–20 Oyodo Naka, Kita-ku, Osaka 531-0076. © **800/WESTIN-1** in the U.S. and Canada, or 06/6440-1111. Fax 06/6440-1100. www.westin-osaka.co.jp. 304 units. ¥33,495–¥43,890 ($319–$418) single; ¥40,425–¥50,820 ($385–$484) double or twin. Executive Club Floors ¥48,510 ($462) single, ¥57,750 ($550) double. AE, DC, MC, V. Station: JR Osaka, then free shuttle bus every 15 min.; or a 15-min. walk. **Amenities:** 5 restaurants; 1 bar; 1 lounge; 20m (82-ft.) indoor lap pool, fitness room, and sauna (fee: ¥4,000/$38); children's day-care center (¥5,000/$48 for 2 hr.); concierge; salon; 24-hr. room service; in-room massage; babysitting; same-day laundry/dry-cleaning service; nonsmoking rooms; executive-level rooms. In room: A/C, cable TV w/pay movies, dataport, minibar, hot-water pot w/tea, hair dryer, Washlet toilet.

## MODERATE

**Hotel Granvia Osaka** *(Kids)*     You can't get any closer to Osaka Station than this hotel, with discounts for holders of Japan Rail Passes making it even more attractive

for train travelers. Parents might also rejoice at discounts offered for Universal Studios. But there are prices to pay: a lobby that's hard to find in the maze that is Osaka Station, and elevators that are crowded with hungry masses on their way to the hotel's many 19th-floor restaurants. Guest rooms, on floors 22 to 26, are cramped but clean. Families may want to opt for one of the "Corner Family" rooms, larger "Deluxe Family" rooms, or largest "Excellent Family" rooms, which cost ¥54,285 ($517), ¥62,370 ($594), and ¥92,400 ($880) respectively for a family of four. The hotel provides direct access to the Daimaru department store in the basement.

3–1–1 Umeda, Kita-ku, Osaka 530-0001. ℂ 06/6344-1235. Fax 06/6344-1130. www.granvia-osaka.jp. 652 units. ¥15,592–¥20,212 ($148–$192) single; ¥24,832 ($236) double; ¥24,832–¥31,185 ($236–$297) twin. Discounts available for holders of Japan Rail Pass. AE, DC, MC, V. Station: Osaka or Umeda (1 min.; above the station). **Amenities:** 8 restaurants; 1 bar; 2 lounges; salon; room service (10pm–1am); same-day laundry/dry-cleaning service; nonsmoking rooms. *In room:* A/C, TV, dataport, minibar, hot-water pot w/tea, hair dryer, Washlet toilet.

## Hotel Laforet Shin-Osaka
I can't think of any reason to stay near Shin-Osaka Station except for the sheer convenience of nearby bullet trains, since there are no attractions there and the rest of Osaka is just a short subway ride away. If you're unconvinced, this modern hotel is your best bet, just a minute's walk from the station and offering comfortable rooms with contemporary decor. Deluxe rooms are swankier, with massage chairs and round desks.

1–2–70 Miyahara, Yodogawa-ku, Osaka 532-0003. ℂ 06/6350-4444. Fax 06/6350-4460. 332 units. ¥20,790–¥23,100 ($198–$220) single; ¥25,410–¥30,030 ($242–$286) twin; ¥30,030 ($286) double. AE, DC, MC, V. Station: Shin-Osaka (1 min.); take the west exit and turn right. **Amenities:** 2 restaurants (coffee shop, teppanyaki); 1 bar; room service (7am–11pm); in-room massage; same-day laundry/dry-cleaning service; nonsmoking rooms. *In room:* A/C, cable TV w/pay movies, minibar, hot-water pot w/tea, hair dryer, Washlet toilet, trouser press.

## Rihga Grand Hotel
This is a fine small hotel on the island of Nakanoshima in the heart of Osaka, about a 12-minute walk from Osaka Station. Its location, next to Osaka's Festival Hall, makes it a favorite among concertgoers and musicians, though business travelers favor it as well. Dating from 1960, it's also one of Osaka's older hotels, and it has aged gracefully. Rooms, with contemporary furnishings, include very small singles with no closets, though the standard doubles and twins are of average size for its price category. Deluxe rooms add love seats and vanities. I prefer rooms that face the river—although there's little boat traffic and nothing really to see, the view helps convey a sense of spaciousness.

2–3–18 Nakanoshima, Kita-ku, Osaka 530-0005. ℂ 06/6202-1212. Fax 06/6227-5054. www.rihga.com. 310 units. ¥13,860–¥17,325 ($132–$165) single; ¥25,410–¥32,340 ($242–$308) double; ¥27,720–¥34,650 ($264–$330) twin. AE, DC, MC, V. Station: Higobashi (3 min.). **Amenities:** 4 restaurants (Japanese, Western, buffet, coffee shop); 1 bar; 1 lounge; barbershop; in-room massage; same-day laundry/dry-cleaning service; nonsmoking rooms. *In room:* A/C, TV w/pay movies, dataports (in some rooms), fridge, hot-water pot w/tea, hair dryer, Washlet toilet, trouser press.

## INEXPENSIVE

### Family Inn Fifty's Edobori  ✿ *Value*
This motel-like facility, south of Nakanoshima island, offers low prices and no-nonsense clean but small rooms, outfitted with double bed, sofa bed, wall-mounted TV, and tiled bathroom (but no closet). Check-in is automated, but humans behind the front desk can help with the process (you'll need a credit card). You pay extra for toothbrushes and slippers here. The catch is that the place is a bit of a chore to reach from Osaka Station (you have to change subway lines) or take JR bus no. 88 from Osaka Station 15 minutes to Tosabori Ni Chome stop, then a 2-minute walk. Once you're settled, you'll find its location fine.

2–6–18 Edobori, Nishi-ku, Osaka 550-0002. © **06/6225-2636.** www.fiftys.com. 90 units. ¥5,250 ($50) single; ¥8,400 ($80) double; ¥9,450 ($90) triple. More for phone reservations. Rates include continental breakfast. AE, MC, V. Station: Awaza (exit 1, 8 min.). **Amenities:** Coffee shop; free use of computers w/Internet access; nonsmoking rooms. *In room:* A/C, TV.

**Hotel Il Monte** *(Finds)*  Open since 1997, this smart-looking hotel has a convenient location that brings in both business and leisure travelers and is my top choice for budget accommodations near the station. A small reception on the third floor has a helpful staff. Breakfast is the only meal available, and in the lobby you'll find coffee and computers with Internet connection available free to guests. Simple, modern rooms have a desk with dataport, 200-channel music system, LCD TVs, and double-paned windows to shut out noise.

7–13 Doyama-cho, Kita-ku, Osaka 530-0027. © **06/6361-2828.** Fax 06/6361-3525. www.ilmonte.co.jp. 122 units. ¥7,500–¥9,000 ($71–$85) single; ¥13,000 ($124) double; ¥13,000–¥16,000 ($124–$152) twin. AE, DC, MC, V. Station: Osaka, Umeda, or Higasahi Umeda (10 min.). East of Osaka Station on Shin-Midosuji Ave. beside the Hankyu-Higashi Dori shopping street. **Amenities:** Same-day laundry/dry-cleaning service; nonsmoking rooms. *In room:* A/C, TV w/pay movies, dataport, minibar, hot-water pot w/tea, hair dryer, Washlet toilet, trouser press.

## AROUND OSAKA CASTLE
### EXPENSIVE

**New Otani Osaka**  In a business park that's home to corporate headquarters for KDD, NEC, Sumitomo, and other big companies, this Leading Hotel of the World member attracts both business and tourist clientele. Its proximity to Osaka Castle Park, popular with joggers, families, and young Japanese, and its varied public facilities, ranging from a multitude of restaurants to a fitness club (free to hotel guests in the morning), give the property something of an "urban resort" atmosphere. Everything about the hotel's public spaces is visually pleasing, from the airy, four-story atrium lobby with a sunken lounge in its center to the indoor pool with its glass-vaulted ceiling. Rooms, however, are rather standard, with rates based on size, height, and view. The best rooms provide the city's most dramatic views of Osaka Castle, which is lit at night, but at fairly hefty prices.

1–4–1 Shiromi, Chuo-ku, Osaka 540-8578. © **800/223-6800** in the U.S. and Canada, or 06/6941-1111. Fax 06/6941-9769. www.osaka.newotani.co.jp/english. 525 units. ¥24,255–¥30,030 ($231–$286) single; ¥33,033–¥55,440 ($315–$528) double; ¥39,270–¥55,440 ($374–$528) twin. ¥3,150 ($30) extra Sat and nights before holidays. AE, DC, MC, V. Station: JR Loop Line to Osakajo-Koen (3 min.) or Osaka Business Park Station (3 min.). Across the moat from Osaka Castle. **Amenities:** 11 restaurants; 2 bars; 1 lounge; fitness club w/indoor and outdoor pools and sauna (fee: ¥2,500/$24; fitness room and indoor pool free 7–10am); 2 outdoor tennis courts; children's day-care center (¥5,000/$48 for 2 hr.); concierge; tour desk; business center; shopping arcade; salon; room service (6am–1am); in-room massage; same-day laundry/dry-cleaning service; nonsmoking rooms. *In room:* A/C, cable TV w/pay movies on demand, high-speed dataport, minibar, hot-water pot w/tea, hair dryer, Washlet toilet.

## NAMBA & SHINSAIBASHI
### EXPENSIVE

**Hotel Nikko Osaka**  A white monolith soaring 32 stories aboveground (and with four stories of shopping and parking underground), the Nikko has a great location above a subway station and is right on Osaka's most fashionable boulevard, Midosuji Dori, making its lobby lounge a popular spot for locals meeting friends. In fact, location is mainly what you're paying for here: There is no health club, and guests are overwhelmingly business travelers. Rooms are small but pleasing, and since there are no high buildings to obstruct views, city panoramas are a plus from most floors.

Still, you'll pay more for rooms on higher floors and for more space. This is a good choice if you want to be in the midst of Osaka's shopping and nightlife.

1–3–3 Nishi-Shinsaibashi, Chuo-ku, Osaka 542-0086. © 06/6244-1111. Fax 06/6245-2432. www.hno.co.jp. 640 units. ¥21,367–¥23,677 ($203–$225) single; ¥32,917–¥43,890 ($313–$418) double; ¥32,917–¥38,692 ($313–$368) twin; Nikko executive floors from ¥35,800 ($340) double or twin. ¥1,155 ($11) extra per person Sat and nights before holidays. AE, DC, MC, V. Station: Shinsaibashi (exit 8 underneath the hotel, 1 min.). **Amenities:** 5 restaurants; 1 bar; 2 lounges; concierge; large underground shopping arcade; salon; room service (7am–midnight); in-room massage; same-day laundry/dry-cleaning service; nonsmoking rooms; executive-level rooms. *In room:* A/C, cable TV w/pay movies, minibar, hot-water pot w/tea, hair dryer, Washlet toilet.

**Swissôtel Nankai Osaka** 🐟🐟🐟   This Raffles International property exudes luxury, from its sophisticated, four-story lobby to its spacious, well-appointed rooms. Located in the vibrant Namba area and connected to Nankai Namba Station, which offers the most rapid service to KIX airport as well as tourist destinations like Kyoto and Mount Koya, the Swissôtel could well be the most conveniently located hotel in Osaka. Not surprisingly, guests include flight crews in addition to tourists and business executives. Rooms, while comfortable, are rather generic, with wide windows providing city views. For business travelers, Business Advantage rooms offer ergonomic chairs, larger desks, and office supplies.

5–1–60 Namba, Chuo-ku, Osaka 542-0076. © 1-800/637-9477 or 06/6646-1111. Fax 06/6648-0331. www. swissotel-osaka.com. 548 units. ¥25,000–¥60,000 ($238–$571) single; ¥35,000–¥60,000 ($333–$571) double or twin; Swiss Executive Club ¥43,000–¥58,000 ($410–$552) double or twin. ¥3,000 ($29) extra per person Sat and nights before holidays. AE, DC, MC, V. Station: Nankai Namba (1 min.). **Amenities:** 8 restaurants; 1 bar; 1 lounge; concierge; business center; shopping arcade; health club w/gym, sauna, and atrium lap pool (¥2,000/$19 for each); spa; 24-hr. room service; in-room massage; same-day laundry/dry-cleaning service; nonsmoking rooms; executive-level rooms. *In room:* A/C, satellite TV w/pay movies, minibar, hot-water pot w/tea, hair dryer, Washlet toilet.

## MODERATE

**Hotel Metro The 21** *Value*   Opened in 1996, this hotel has a great location for night owls, just a few minutes' walk from Dotombori, Osaka's main nightlife district. Its mostly single rooms, along with 100 twins and doubles, are very small but clean and modern, with higher rates charged for higher floors. There's also a ladies' floor for extra security, decorated with a more feminine touch and adding women's toiletries. All rooms have dataports. Stock your empty fridge with purchases from the ground-floor 7-Eleven.

2–13 Soemon-cho, Chuo-ku, Osaka 542-0084. © 06/6211-3555. Fax 06/6211-3586. 339 units. ¥8,400–¥9,975 ($80–$95) single; ¥12,600–¥14,700 ($120–$140) double; ¥14,700–¥16,800 ($140–$160) twin. AE, DC, MC, V. Station: Nipponbashi (exit 2, 5 min.); cross Dotombori canal and turn left. Or Namba (exit 14, 10 min.); cross Dotombori Canal and turn right. **Amenities:** 2 restaurants (Chinese, Western); 1 bar; 1 convenience store, room service (7am–11:30pm), same-day laundry/dry-cleaning service, nonsmoking rooms. *In room:* A/C, TV w/pay movies, dataport, fridge, hot-water pot w/tea, hair dryer, Washlet toilet.

## INEXPENSIVE

**Hotel Dormy-Inn**   One of the few inexpensive hotels in the shopping and nightlife area of Shinsaibashi, and the only one in America-mura, this 2005 chain entry offers standard business-type rooms, spotlessly clean with two kinds of pillows and sliding window panels to cut out light and highway noises, as well as 10 combination rooms with tatami areas and twin beds. Public baths made of cedar are a plus, but alas, little English is spoken.

2–17–3 Nishishinsaibashi, Chuo-ku, Osaka 542-0086. © 06/6211-5767. Fax 06/6211-5773. 134 units. ¥7,800 ($74) single; ¥10,300 ($98) double; ¥12,300 ($117) twin. AE, DC, MC, V. Station: Yotusbashi (exit 5, 5 min.) or Shinsaibashi (exit 7, 7 min.). 1 block south of Europa Dori and 3 blocks west of Midosuji Ave. **Amenities:** Restaurant; coin-op washers and dryers; nonsmoking rooms. *In room:* A/C, TV, dataport, fridge, hot-water pot w/tea, hair dryer, bathroom scale, Washlet toilet.

**Toyoko Inn Osaka Namba** ⚘ (Value)   This chain is smart to offer perks that set it apart from other business hotels, including computers with free Internet access in the lobby, free Japanese breakfasts, free 3-minute telephone calls within Japan from the lobby, free movie channels, and semi-double-size beds in the mostly single rooms. Of course, at these rates, you can't expect accommodations much larger than shoeboxes. There are no views to speak of, though those rooms facing Yasaka Jinja shrine are quieter.

2–8–7 Motomachi, Naniwa-ku, Osaka 556-0016. ℂ 06/4397-1045. Fax 06/4397-1046. www.toyoko-inn.com. 143 units. ¥6,510 ($62) single; ¥7,560 ($72) double; ¥8,610 ($82) twin. Rates include free Japanese breakfast. AE, DC, MC, V. Station: Namba on the Midosuji Line (exit 5, 4 min.) or Namba of the JR and Kintetsu lines (10 min.). On Yotsubashisuji Dori Ave. **Amenities:** Free Internet access at lobby computers; coin-op washers and dryers; laundry service; nonsmoking rooms. *In room:* A/C, TV, fridge, hot-water pot w/tea, hair dryer, Washlet toilet.

## ELSEWHERE IN THE CITY
## EXPENSIVE
**Imperial Hotel Osaka (Teikoku Hotel)** ⚘⚘⚘   Although a bit off the beaten track, this luxury hotel's location on the cherry tree–lined Okawa River is great for jogging and imparts a relaxing, resortlike setting despite the adjoining OAP, a large office building that attracts business travelers but also contains shops and restaurants. To help offset its location, the hotel provides free shuttle service to Osaka Station. Like its Tokyo namesake, its bold interior designs show the same Frank Lloyd Wright inspirations, including an Old Imperial Bar that pays homage to the American architect. The hotel's fitness center is the largest and best equipped in the city, while restaurants take advantage of the river and city views. It goes without saying that this Osaka property offers the same faultless service as the famed Tokyo Imperial. The high-ceilinged guest rooms offer large windows with remote-control drapes and great views (request rooms facing the river), good working desks, down pillows and comforters, fluffy bathrobes, aromatherapy cosmetics, magnifying mirrors, and marble bathrooms.

1–8–50 Temmabashi, Kita-ku Osaka 530-0042. ℂ 800/223-6800 in the U.S. and Canada, or 06/6881-1111. Fax 06/6881-1200. 390 units. www.imperialhotel.co.jp. ¥28,350 – ¥37,800 ($270–360) single; ¥33,600 – ¥43,050 ($320–$410) double or twin; Imperial executive floor from ¥32,550 ($310) single, ¥37,800 ($360) double. ¥2,000 – ¥3,000 ($19–$29) more Sat and nights before holidays. AE, DC, MC, V. Station: JR Sakuranomiya west exit (5 min.); or Osaka Station north exit, free shuttle every 20 min. (more on weekends). **Amenities:** 6 restaurants; 1 bar; 2 lounges; golf driving range (¥5,000/$48); Osaka's largest state-of-the-art health club w/3 lit outdoor tennis courts, 25m (82-ft.) indoor pool, spa, Jacuzzi, and sauna (fee: ¥2,000/$19 morning, ¥5,000/$48 afternoon); children's day-care center; concierge; business center; shopping arcade; salon; barbershop; 24-hr. room service; in-room massage; same-day laundry/dry-cleaning service; nonsmoking rooms; executive-level rooms; medical clinic; free bicycles (the castle is a 10-min. ride away). *In room:* A/C, cable TV w/pay movies, fax, dataport, minibar, hot-water pot w/tea, hair dryer, safe, bathroom scale, Washlet toilet.

## MODERATE
**Hotel International House Osaka** (Value)   The International House is a modern facility used for international seminars, conventions, and meetings. It includes this hotel, used mainly by those attending seminars but also open to the public—try to book well in advance. Rooms are spartan with about as much personality as those in a business hotel, but they have everything you need, including tiny tiled bathrooms, *yukata*, and a small desk. Some 40 of the 50 rooms are singles, making this a great choice for the single traveler, but note that they don't have closets and are fairly small. The twins, however, are of adequate size. There are computers in International House with Internet access you can use for free.

8–2–6 Uehommachi, Tennoji-ku, Osaka 543-0001. ℂ 06/6773-8181. Fax 06/6773-0777. 50 units. ¥7,600 ($72) single; ¥13,900 ($132) twin; ¥17,800 ($170) triple. Rates include breakfast. AE, DC, MC, V. Station: Uehommachi on the

Kintetsu Line (5 min.); or the Tanimachi 9-chome (8 min.) or Shitennoji-mae subway station (5 min.). **Amenities:** 2 restaurants (Western, coffee shop); same-day laundry/dry-cleaning service. *In room:* A/C, cable TV w/pay movies (¥1,000/$9.50), dataport, fridge, hot-water pot w/tea, hair dryer.

## WHERE TO DINE

There's a saying among Japanese that whereas a Kyotoite will spend his last yen on a fine kimono, an Osakan will spend it on food. You don't have to spend a lot of money, however, to enjoy good food in Osaka. Local specialties include *Oshi-zushi* (pressed square-shaped sushi), **udon** noodles with white soy sauce, and *takoyaki* (wheat-flour dumplings with octopus).

Osaka is probably best known, however, for *okonomiyaki,* which literally means "as you like it." Its origins date from about 1700, when a type of thin flour pancake cooked on a hot plate and filled with miso paste was served during Buddhist ceremonies. It wasn't until this century that it became popular, primarily during food shortages, and gradually, other ingredients such as pork, egg, and cabbage were added. Today, Osaka is literally riddled with inexpensive okonomiyaki restaurants—more than 4,000 of them.

### AROUND OSAKA STATION
### VERY EXPENSIVE

**La Baie** ✿✿✿ FRENCH NOUVELLE    It's easy to pretend you're the honored guest in a nobleman's house when dining at The Ritz-Carlton's premier restaurant, decorated in elegant drawing-room style with a fireplace, landscape paintings, still lifes, and other objets d'art. The menu of fresh seafood and seasonal dishes is French, very nouvelle cuisine meant to please all the senses. My mushroom soup looked to be a perfect, frothy café au lait served in a tiny liqueur glass. If marinated striped jack served with caviar and crunchy celery doesn't fit into your budget, come for the set lunch, which gives choices of appetizers and main dishes, along with recommended wines. Weekdays, there's even a special ladies' lunch for ¥3,800 ($36). Many consider this to be Osaka's finest restaurant, with a reputation that extends far beyond Osaka's borders.

The Ritz-Carlton, 5th floor, 2–5–25 Umeda. ✆ **06/6343-7000.** Reservations recommended. Main dishes ¥4,900–¥9,800 ($47–$93); set dinners ¥12,000–¥23,800 ($114–$227); set lunches ¥5,800–¥9,800 ($55–$93). AE, DC, MC, V. Daily 11:30am–2:30pm and 5:30–9:30pm. Station: Osaka, Umeda, or Nishi-Umeda (7 min.).

### MODERATE

**Enoteca** ✿ CONTINENTAL    Shelves filled with wine bottles line the walls of this upscale shop, in the back of which is a casual restaurant specializing in meals that complement our favorite form of the grape. The relaxed ambience and reasonably priced food drew us in (okay, so the wine had something to do with it), but what better way to imbibe a celebratory glass or two than with selections of cheese, smoked salmon, a classic croque-monsieur, or the day's lunch? The menu is limited, but the fun part is selecting a bottle of wine from the shop (corkage fee is ¥1,000/$9.50) to accompany your meal.

Herbis Plaza, 2nd floor, 2–5–25 Umeda. ✆ **06/6343-7175.** Main dishes ¥850–¥1,050 ($8.10–$10); set lunch ¥840 and ¥1,000 ($8 and $9.50). AE, DC, MC, V. Daily 11am–8pm (last order). Station: Nishi-Umeda (3 min.). South of Osaka Station in the Herbis Plaza complex adjacent to The Ritz-Carlton.

### INEXPENSIVE

In addition to the choices here, a fun place for a meal is **Takimikoji Village,** located in the basement of the same building as the Floating Garden Observatory (p. 384). It's a re-created Showa-Era 1920s and 1930s Japanese village, boasting everything

from an old-fashioned sweets shop and a barbershop to a post office and a miniature shrine. There are about a dozen restaurants here—branches of well-known Osaka establishments—serving okonomiyaki, kushikatsu, teppanyaki, noodles, yakitori, and more. Most lunches cost less than ¥1,000 ($9.50) and dinners less than ¥2,000 ($19), making it very popular with those who work in the area. It's open daily, with lunch served from about 11:30am to 2pm and dinner from 5 to 10:30pm.

**Capricciosa** (Kids) PIZZA/PASTA   This chain restaurant is very popular with students and families for its pizza and pasta, available in regular size (good for one person) or large size for hearty appetites or two diners. The English-language menu lists everything from pizza capricciosa (with bacon, salami, onion, and more) to spaghetti with eggplant and spinach in meat sauce. The salads are big enough for two to share. While the cheesy decor and fake plants just don't do it for me, a walk through Yodobashi Camera shop with its endless stock is a trip.

There's a branch in the Namba Oriental Hotel Building, 2–8–17 Sennichimae (📞 **06/6644-8330;** station: Midosuji), open daily 11am to 10:30pm.

Yodobashi Camera, 8th floor, 1–1 Obukacho. 📞 **06/6488-2271.** Pizza and pasta ¥870–¥1,180 ($8.30–$11) for small sizes, ¥980–¥1,790 ($9.35–$17) for large sizes. AE, DC, MC, V. Daily 11am–10pm. Station: JR Osaka or Umeda (1 min.). Just north of the station.

(129) **Okonomiyaki Madonna** OKONOMIYAKI   At this modern okonomiyaki restaurant with a young and friendly staff, ingredients change with the seasons but may include pork, beef, squid, octopus, shrimp, potato, mushroom, or oyster. Fried noodles are also available. Single diners will feel comfortable at this very casual establishment, sitting around a counter watching food being prepared.

Hilton Plaza, 2nd basement, 1–8–8 Umeda. 📞 **06/6347-7371.** Okonomiyaki ¥1,050–¥1,600 ($10–$15); set meal ¥1,260–¥2,940 ($12–$28). AE, DC, MC, V. Daily 11am–9:30pm (last order). Station: Umeda or Nishi-Umeda (2 min.), Osaka (4 min.). In the basement of Hilton Plaza (next to the Osaka Hilton hotel).

## AROUND OSAKA CASTLE
### MODERATE
**Trader Vic's** INTERNATIONAL   This is a great lunch choice for Osaka Castle sightseers. Decorated in Polynesian style typical of Trader Vic's branches around the world, it offers dining with a view of the castle, the park, and the river. In addition to lunch specials (available Mon–Fri), there are a la carte lunch selections that include club sandwiches, pasta, and other international fare. On weekends and holidays, there's a lunch buffet (served 11:30am–3pm), when for ¥1,050 ($10) extra you can drink unlimited sparkling wine. Dinners offer a wider, and more expensive, selection, including salads, a good range of vegetable side dishes, curries, steaks, seafood, barbecued chicken, and Chinese dishes. There's also an extensive cocktail menu.

New Otani Hotel, 1–4 Shiromi. 📞 **06/6949-3210.** Main dinner courses ¥2,625–¥11,525 ($25–$110); set lunches ¥1,470–¥3,780 ($14–$36); Sun brunch ¥3,675 ($35). AE, DC, MC, V. Mon–Fri 11:30am–2:30pm; Sat–Sun 11:30am–3pm; daily 5–11pm. Subway: Osaka Business Park (1 min.). JR train: Osakajo-Koen (3 min.).

### INEXPENSIVE
**Panorama Sky Restaurant Asahi** VARIED WESTERN   Views and the beer are the best reasons to pay a visit to this Asahi beer hall, which does provide panoramic city views but none of the castle. Popular with area office workers, it offers pizza, pasta, beefsteak, and rather mundane choices from an English-language menu. The set lunches are a bargain and come with salad, rice, vegetables, and all-you-can-drink

tea, coffee, or juice. Or, come for a snack and wash it down with a mug or two of Asahi beer.

IMP Building, 26th floor, 1–3–7 Shiromi Chuo-ku. © 06/6946-2595. Main dishes ¥980–¥2,500 ($9.35–$24); set lunches ¥850–¥1,500 ($8.10–$14). AE, DC, MC, V. Mon–Fri 11:30am–2pm and 4:30–10pm; Sat–Sun and holidays 11:30am–10pm. Subway: Osaka Business Park (1 min.). JR train: Osakajo-Koen (4 min.). In Osaka Business Park, across from the New Otani Hotel.

## NAMBA

**Dotombori** (or Dotonbori), a narrow pedestrian lane just off Midosuji Dori that flanks the south bank of the Dotombori River Walk, is the center of Osaka's most famous nightlife district, which radiates from Dotombori on both sides of the canal; you'll find lots of restaurants and bars in this area. A healthy choice in Namba Station (just outside the south exit near Namba Park) is **Japanese Organic Café (© 06/ 6644-2782)** serving inexpensive soups, brown rice balls, curry, and organically grown coffee, with main dishes priced below ¥700 ($6.65). It's open Monday to Friday 7:30am to 10pm and Saturday and Sunday 10am to 10pm.

## MODERATE

⑬ **Kani Doraku** CRAB    Specializing in *kani* (crab), this restaurant is difficult to miss—it has a huge model crab on its facade, moving its legs and claws. Part of a chain originating in Osaka a couple of decades ago, this is the main shop of more than 50 locations throughout Japan, including another one just down the street at 1–6–2 Dotonbori (© **06/6211-1633**). Dishes range from crab-suki, crab-chiri (a kind of crab sukiyaki), and fried crab dishes to crab croquette, roasted crab with salt, crab salad, crab sushi, and boiled king crab. The easiest thing to do, however, is to order a set meal from the display case outside or from the menu with its photos. This main location occupies several floors, with some tables offering a view of the water.

1–6–18 Dotonbori. © 06/6211-8975. Set dinners ¥4,515–¥10,500 ($43–$100); set lunches ¥1,050–¥3,675 ($10–$35). AE, DC, MC, V. Daily 11am–11pm. Station: Namba (exit 14, 2 min.). On Dotonbori beside the Ebisu-bashi Bridge.

**Tavola** ITALIAN    Panoramic city views and expertly prepared Italian cuisine marry here for a fine dining experience. The spacious dining room is dotted with tables draped in white tablecloths, with bar seating a good option for lone diners. Lunch buffets offer so many choices, it's hard to know where to begin and when to say enough, though wills may falter at the gelatti counter. A la carte dishes include grilled lamb with rosemary and Mediterranean vegetables and breast of chicken filled with Fontina cheese and sun-dried tomatoes. On weekends and holidays, you can come for High Tea in the Sky (¥2,194/$21) from 3 to 4:30pm.

Swissôtel 36F, 5–1–60 Namba, Chuo-ku, Osaka 542-0076. © 06/6646-1111. Main dishes ¥3,003–¥4,735 ($29–$45); pizza and pasta ¥1,732–¥2,541 ($16–$24); set dinners ¥5,917–¥16,170 ($56–$154); weekday lunch buffet ¥3,349 ($32); weekend brunch buffet ¥4,042 ($38). AE, DC, MC, V. Mon–Thurs 11:30am–11:30pm; Fri and night before holidays 11:30am–midnight; Sat 11am–midnight; Sun 11am–11:30pm. Station: Nankai Namba (1 min.).

## INEXPENSIVE

⑬ **Bar Tachibana** TOFU/VARIED JAPANESE    Whether you are sightseeing in Dotombori or viewing Kabuki, this restaurant, in a lovely, typical Japanese setting in the basement of the Shochikuza Theater, is a good pick. A microbrewery (¥450/$4.30 for a glass of light or dark beer), Tachibana specializes in tofu, with tofu included in most of the set meals. There's no English-language menu, but a changing daily lunch and the tempura teishoku are affordable and delicious. You can see famous Kabuki actors dining here, but how could you recognize them without their makeup?

Osaka Shochikuza Theater, 2nd basement, 1–9–19 Dotombori. ℂ **06/6212-6074.** Main dishes ¥680–¥1,700 ($6.45–$16); set dinners ¥2,730–¥6,090 ($26–$58); set lunches ¥850–¥2,940 ($8.10–$28). AE, DC, MC, V. Daily 11am–11pm. Station: Namba (exit 14, 2 min.). Look for its improbable entrance, on Dotombori near the bridge.

**Cui-daore** 🐾🐾 (Kids) VARIED JAPANESE   Cui-daore is famous for its clown model outside the front door, which began beating a drum and wiggling its eyebrows shortly after the place first opened in 1950. The restaurant's name means to "eat your way to bankruptcy" in reference to the Osakan joy of eating, but a look at the prices in the extensive plastic-food display case shows you can dine very reasonably here on a great variety of food ranging from tempura and yakitori to sushi, shabu-shabu, kaiseki, and even Western food. What's more, the restaurant is very user-friendly; items in the display cases are identified in English and by number for easy ordering, and there's also an English-language menu.

Altogether, there are eight floors of dining, and prices increase the higher you go. On the ground floor is a modern, family-style dining area, serving everything from chicken curry and rice to a mixed seafood set. If you want to try Osaka's version of sushi, try the ¥1,050 ($10) combo. From the clown outside to the food inside, this is a great place to bring youngsters; a child's set meal (¥840/$8) includes a pair of black glasses just like the clown's. On the second floor is an *izakaya,* or Japanese-style pub, open from 5pm, where you can order a beer, yakitori, and snacks. In winter, the third floor serves *nabe* (one-pot stews) in a quiet and comfortable setting, while the top floors have sukiyaki, shabu-shabu, and kaiseki meals that change monthly (kaiseki courses begin at ¥3,150/$30).

1–8–25 Dotonbori. ℂ **06/6211-5300.** Set meals ¥650–¥5,000 ($6.20–$48). AE, DC, MC, V. Daily 11am–10pm. Station: Namba (exit 14, 2 min.).

⑬ **Fugetsu** OKONOMIYAKI   Big Step is the biggest shopping complex in America-Mura, young Osakans' favorite place to shop for American clothing. As such, this branch of a famous okonomiyaki restaurant appeals to young diners with its hip, modern interior, pop music, and individual booths for dining. I recommend the squid, octopus, and pork *yakisoba* (fried noodles) or the *butatama,* an okonomiyaki with pork and egg from the English-language menu.

Big Step, 3rd floor, 1–6–14 Nishi Shinsaibashi. ℂ **06/6258-5189.** Okonomiyaki ¥580–¥980 ($5.50–$9.35); yakisoba ¥620–¥1,020 ($5.90–$9.70). AE, MC, V. Daily 11am–9:30pm (last order). Station: Shinsaibashi (2 min.).

**Hermanos** MEXICAN   Good for a quick fix if you're craving Mexican food, this tiny, brightly colored restaurant offers all the classics, from enchiladas to burritos, tostadas, and tacos. A basket of small chips and sauce arrive at your table free if you order food and show them this book. Hot salsa music adds to the atmosphere. Strawberry margaritas, anyone?

2–3–23 Dotombori. ℂ **06/6213-9612.** Combination plates ¥1,100–¥1,900 ($10–$18). AE, MC, V. Tues–Sun 4pm–midnight. Station: Namba (5 min.). On the west end of Dotombori (west of Midosuji Dori) just past the Dotombori Hotel.

**Namaste** 🐾🐾 INDIAN   This is a good place for hot and spicy Indian food, including tandoori and chicken, mutton, prawn, fish, and vegetable curries. The owner, who will wait on you, is so friendly and happy, you might think he's reached nirvana. You can reach yours by telling him how hot to make your food. The set lunches are a particularly great deal.

A second Namaste, located near the west exit of Juso station (3–7–46 Juso Hommachi Yadogawa-ku; ℂ **06/6886-6609**) has the same great food at cheaper prices—the owner passes the lower rent savings on to his customers.

Rose Building, 3–7–28 Minami Semba. ℂ **06/6241-6515**. Main dishes ¥750–¥1,500 ($7.15–$14); set dinners ¥1,980–¥4,300 ($19–$41); set lunches ¥785–¥1,980 ($7.45–$19). 10% discount for Frommer's readers. AE, DC, MC, V. Daily 11:30am–3pm and 5:30–11pm. Station: Shinsaibashi (exit 1, 3 min.). 3 blocks north of the Sony Tower Building; walk north on Midosuji Dori, turn east (right) at the Rolex shop and walk past the Shinsaibashi-Suji covered pedestrian shopping street; it will be on the right.

## OSAKA BAY AREA

In addition to the choices below, Universal CityWalk has lots of restaurants, most of which are open daily from 11am to 10pm, including **Bubba Gump's** (ℂ **06/4804-3880**) for shrimp and **Hard Rock Cafe** (ℂ **06/4804-3870**) with its T-shirts for sale and a menu of burgers, steaks, sandwiches, and barbecued ribs.

### EXPENSIVE

**Top of Hollywood** 𝓕𝓕    Original California cuisine, 32nd-floor views, and soft jazz set the tone for this upbeat, chic restaurant with an outstanding wine cellar. After a day spent at the Hollywood-themed Universal Studios Japan, what better way to top it off than with a meal here? Dishes include melt-in-your-mouth grilled free-range chicken with crispy bacon, sole meunière with piquant sauce and filet of beef steak with a red-wine sauce.

Hotel Nikko Bayside, 6–2–45 Shimaya, Konohana-ku. ℂ **06/6460-3111**. Set dinners ¥5,198–¥11,550 ($50–$110). AE, DC, MC, V. Daily 5–11pm. Station: Universal City (1 min.).

### INEXPENSIVE

**Café Solare** PASTA    This casual, airy, and down-to-earth restaurant, with some tables offering a view of the harbor, is convenient if you're visiting the Suntory Museum or nearby Osaka Aquarium (you don't have to buy museum admission to eat here). The pasta is freshly made, and there are also salads, soups, and other items at the self-service counter. After eating, you might want to retire to the museum's ninth-floor Sky Lounge (open Tues–Sun 11:30am–9pm), offering cocktails and other drinks, a limited menu and daily set lunches, and views of the harbor and port.

Suntory Museum, Tempozan Harbour Village, 1–5–10 Kaigandori. ℂ **06/6577-0009**. Main dishes ¥680–¥900 ($6.45–$8.55); set lunch ¥800 ($7.60). AE, DC, MC, V. Tues–Sun 11am–9pm. Closed when the museum is closed. Station: Osakako (5 min.).

### ELSEWHERE IN OSAKA
### EXPENSIVE

**Kamon** 𝓕𝓕𝓕 TEPPANYAKI    Kamon, or Gate of Celebration, is just that—a celebratory feast. Chefs weld their knives just as samurai must have once wielded their swords, as you sit at a counter and watch your dinner being prepared and grilled according to your specifications. Tender Japanese sirloin steak and seafood ranging from fresh prawns and scallops to crab and fish are served along seasonal vegetables. After your meal, retire to armchairs in a quiet corner for dessert and coffee, where you can relax in a more intimate setting and spend as much time as you like.

Imperial Hotel, 1-8-50 Temmabashi. ℂ **06/6881-1111**. Set lunches ¥3,150–¥5,250 ($30–$50); set dinners ¥10,290–¥15,750 ($98–$150). AE, DC, MC, V. Daily 11:30am–2:30pm and 5:30–9:30pm. Station: JR Sakuranomiya west exit (5 min.); or free shuttle from Osaka Station's north exit every 20 min. (more frequently on weekends).

## OSAKA AFTER DARK
### PERFORMING ARTS

**BUNRAKU** The **National Bunraku Theater,** 1–12–10 Nipponbashi, Chuo-ku (*C* **06/6212-2531** for information, or 06/6212-1122 for reservations), was completed in 1984 as the only theater in Japan dedicated to Japanese traditional puppet theater. Productions are staged five times a year, with most productions running for 2 to 3 weeks at a time and held daily at 11am for Part 1 and at 4pm for Part 2. When Bunraku is not being performed, other traditional performing arts are often shown, including classical Japanese music. English-language programs are available. To find out whether a performance is being held, check *Meet Osaka* or contact one of the visitor information centers (see "Essentials" on p. 380). Tickets usually run ¥2,300 to ¥5,800 ($22–$55). The National Bunraku Theater is located east of Namba and the Dotombori entertainment district, a 1-minute walk from exit 7 of Nipponbashi Station.

**KABUKI** The **Osaka Shochikuza,** 1–9–19 Dotombori, Chuo-ku (*C* **06/6214-2211;** station: Namba), was built more than 50 years ago but was remodeled in 1997 as part of a revival of interest in Kabuki. Traditional kabuki is performed in January, July, and some other months of the year (the schedule changes yearly), and performances start usually at 11am and 4:30pm, with tickets ranging from ¥4,200 to ¥13,650 ($40–$130) for major performances. Performance information is also listed in *Meet Osaka.* The theater is located on Dotombori, just west of the Ebisu-bashi Bridge.

**JAZZ** **Blue Note,** Basement 2 of the Herbis Plaza Building, 2-2-22 Umeda (*C* **06/6342-7788,** reservations required; station: Nishi-Umeda), serves up great music in a chic new theater consisting of several levels surrounding the stage. Many jazz greats—Oscar Peterson, Herbie Hancock, Vanessa Williams, Art Blakie, and George Benson—have played here. Tickets range from ¥5,400 to ¥7,400 ($51–$70) for regular acts, with popular artists costing more.

### THE BAR SCENE

Osaka's liveliest—and most economical—nightlife district radiates from a narrow pedestrian lane called **Dotombori** (or Dotonbori), which flanks the south bank of the Dotombori Canal. About a 2-minute walk from exit 14 of Namba Station or less than a 10-minute walk from Shinsaibashi Station, it's lined with restaurants and drinking establishments and is good for a lively evening stroll even if you don't wish to stop anywhere.

**Bar Isn't It?** Part of a chain, Bar Isn't It? attracts a mainly young Japanese clientele with its low prices—all food and drinks cost ¥500 ($4.75). No money is wasted on decor, and seating is at bar stools around dozens of high tables, but after midnight, it's standing room only. Live DJ sounds range from reggae to rock, and although there's no cover charge per se, on weekends there's a door charge of ¥1,000 ($9.50), which includes two drink tickets on Friday and one drink ticket on Saturday, apparently to keep out those who want to join in the fun but don't want to drink. Daily 6pm to 2am, Friday to Saturday to 5am. Kakusho Building, 5th floor, 7–7 Doyamacho. *C* **06/6363-4001.** Station: Osaka, Umeda, or Higashi Umeda (10 min.). East of Osaka Station on Shin-Midosuji Ave. beside the Hankyu-Higashi Dori shopping street.

**Murphy's** Of Osaka's several Irish pubs, this is probably the most popular (and our favorite), drawing a mixed crowd of both Japanese and foreigners and offering live Irish music most Wednesdays. Fish and chips or shepherd's pie are reasonable and

surprisingly good, but you can also make a meal of the Guinness or Killkenny Ale. Monday through Thursday 5pm to 1am; Friday to Saturday 5pm to about 3am. Lead Plaza Building, 6th floor, 1–6–31 Higashi Shinsaibashi. ✆ 06/6282-0677. Station: Nagahoribashi (1 min.) or Shinsaibashi (4 min.). On Suzuki St. (1 block north of Europa Dori/Shimizu Dori), the road to the south of the Daimaru department store, several blocks east of the Shinsaibashi-suji covered arcade, on the right in a small building with lots of tiny bars.

**Pig and Whistle**   This is probably the best-known and one of the oldest expatriate bars in Osaka, as well as one of the easiest to find. Through the years, the number of foreign customers has fallen to less than 25% (I remember when it was almost exclusively foreign), but remaining are its dartboards for entertainment, happy hour until 7:30pm, and munchies that include, of course, fish and chips. Hours are Sunday through Thursday 5pm to midnight, Friday to Saturday 5pm to 1am. Across Building, 2nd floor, 2–6–14 Shinsaibashi-Suji. ✆ 06/6213-6911. Station: Namba or Shinsaibashi (4 min.). On the east side of Midosuji St., 2 blocks north of Dotombori Canal.

**Sam & Dave Four**   With exposed, wrapped pipes and fluorescent lighting, this bar with a dance floor and pool table stages events several times a month, including salsa lessons every Tuesday. Happy hour is until 9pm. It attracts both a Japanese and gaijin crowd.

Attracting a larger foreign clientele is **Sam & Dave Five** in Nagahoribashi, across from the post office (✆ 06/6251-5333), which has an even bigger dance floor and holds salsa nights on Thursdays; upscale **Sam & Dave Two Shinsaibashi**, 1 block east of Midosuji St. near Shakey's (✆ 06/6243-6848), is the hot spot for hip-hop, soul, and R&B. Hours are Sunday through Thursday 7pm to 5am, Friday to Saturday 7pm to 6am. Plaza Umeshin Building, 4–15–19 Nishi-tenma. ✆ 06/6365-1688. Fri–Sat ¥1,000 ($9.50) cover, which includes 1 drink. Station: JR Kitashinchi (2 min.), Umeda (5 min.), Osaka (7 min.). Southeast of Osaka Station on a triangle-shaped parcel of land where Midosuji Dori curves southward before crossing the river and Nakanoshima Island.

# 5 Kobe

589km (366 miles) W of Tokyo; 75km (47 miles) W of Kyoto; 31km (19 miles) W of Osaka

In January 1995, the world was riveted by news of one of the worst natural disasters of that decade: the Great Hanshin Earthquake that struck Kobe, killing more than 6,400 people and destroying much of the city. In the years since, Kobe has risen from the ashes with more attractions, hotels, and urban redevelopment than ever before and with only a few telltale signs of the city's grimmest hours. Indeed, if it weren't for several earthquake memorials and a museum dedicated to the event, visitors would never guess at the devastation of just 10 years ago.

Blessed with the calm waters of the Seto Inland Sea, Kobe (the capital of Hyogo Prefecture) has served Japan as an important port town for centuries. Even today its port is the heart of the city, its raison d'être. I find Kobe's port fascinating. Unlike many harbor cities where the port is located far from the center of town, Kobe's is right there, demanding attention and getting it. One of the first ports to begin accepting foreign traders in 1868 following Japan's 2 centuries of isolation, this vibrant city of 1.5 million inhabitants is quite multicultural, with foreigners from more than 110 different nations residing here. Each group of immigrants has brought with it a rich heritage, and there are a number of fine restaurants serving every kind of cuisine—Western, Chinese, Korean, and Indian—as well as many steakhouses offering that famous local delicacy, Kobe beef.

Equally famous is Kobe's wonderful nightlife, crammed into a small, navigable, and rather intimate quarter of neon lights, cozy bars, brawling pubs, and sophisticated nightclubs. As one resident of Kobe told me, "We don't have a lot of tourist sights in Kobe, so we make up for it in nightlife." Yet the attractions Kobe does offer are unique to Japan, including a neighborhood of Western-style residences built around the turn of the 20th century, and a museum devoted to fashion. The people of Kobe are also proud of the 1998 opening of the world's longest suspension bridge, Akashi Kaikyo, one of a series of bridges linking Honshu with Shikoku.

## ESSENTIALS

**GETTING THERE   By Plane**   If you're arriving at Kansai International Airport (KIX; see "Getting There," under Osaka, on p. 380), there are a couple options for travel onward to Kobe. Easiest are the **limousine buses** departing KIX every 15 minutes for Sannomiya Station, costing ¥1,800 ($17) one-way and taking about 75 minutes. If you want to use your **Japan Rail Pass,** take a *kaisoku* (rapid train making only major stops) to Osaka Station and change there for the JR Kobe Line's 20-minute ride to Sannomiya Station (considered the heart of the city). If you're staying in a hotel closer to Shin-Kobe Station, take the JR Haruka train from the airport to Shin-Osaka Station and transfer there for a speedy Shinkansen connection to Shin-Kobe Station (see the Osaka section on p. 381 for detailed information).

If you're arriving at Kobe Airport, which opened in 2006 on Port Island to serve domestic flights, you can take the new transit system to Sannomiya Station in 16 minutes.

**By Train**   The **Shinkansen** bullet train takes 3¼ hours from Tokyo, 31 minutes from Kyoto, and about 14 minutes from Osaka; the fare from Tokyo for an unreserved seat is ¥13,760 ($131). All Shinkansen trains arrive at **Shin-Kobe Station,** which is linked to **Sannomiya Station** (considered the heart of the city) via a 3-minute subway ride (or a 20-min. walk). If you're arriving from nearby Osaka, Kyoto, Himeji, or Okayama, it may be easiest to take a local train stopping at Sannomiya Station if you're staying in one of the area's hotels.

**By Bus**   Buses depart from Tokyo Station's Yaesu south exit for Kobe every night at 10:40pm, arriving in Kobe at 7:30am. They also depart nightly from Shinjuku Station's New South Exit at 11pm, arriving in Kobe at 7:42am. The one-way fare is ¥8,690 ($83).

**VISITOR INFORMATION**   There are tourist information offices at **Shin-Kobe Station** (© 078/241-9550; open daily 9am–5pm) and near **Sannomiya Station,** across the street and to the right from the south exit, on Flower Road in the Kotsu Center Building (© 078/322-0220; open daily 9am–7pm). The English-speaking staff can provide maps and sightseeing information and make hotel reservations. Tourist information is available online at http://feel-kobe.jp.

Information on Kobe's sights, festivals, and attractions appears in the monthly *Kansai Time Out,* available at bookstores, restaurants, and tourist-oriented locations for ¥315 ($3).

**INTERNET ACCESS**   The **Comic Café,** on the third floor of the Heiwa Building just north of Sannomiya Station (© 078/241-8815), is open 24 hours and charges ¥380 ($3.60) for the first hour and then ¥150 ($1.45) for each subsequent 30 minutes. The **Hyogo International Plaza,** located a 10-minute walk south of Nada Station in the new HAT urban renewal development at 1–5–1 Kaigandori, Wakinohama,

Chuo-ku (© **078/230-3060;** open Mon–Fri 9am–8pm, Sat 9am–5pm), offers free Internet access.

**ORIENTATION & GETTING AROUND**    Squeezed between Mount Rokko rising in the north and the shores of the Seto Inland Sea to the south, Kobe stretches some 29km (18 miles) along the coastline but in many places is less than 3.2km (2 miles) wide. It's made up of many wards *(ku)* such as Nada-ku, Chuo-ku, and Hyogo-ku. The heart of the city lies around Sannomiya, Motomachi, and Kobe stations in the **Chuo-ku (Central Ward).** It's here you'll find the city's nightlife, its port, its restaurants, its shopping centers, and most of its hotels. Unlike most other Japanese cities, many of the major streets in Kobe have names with English-language signs posted, so it's easier to get around here than elsewhere. Additionally, the maps provided by the tourist office are good.

Because the city isn't very wide, you can walk to most points north and south of Sannomiya Station. South of Sannomiya Station is the **Sannomiya Center Gai** covered-arcade shopping, beyond which lies Kobe's business and administrative district. North of Sannomiya Station are bars and restaurants clustered around narrow streets like **Higashimon Street.** Kitano-zaka leads to **Kitano-cho** (usually shortened to Kitano) with its Western-style houses, about a 15-minute walk north of Sannomiya Station. **Shin-Kobe Station** is a 20-minute walk north of Sannomiya. Running from Shin-Kobe Station south through Sannomiya all the way to the port is a flower-lined road—called, appropriately enough, **Flower Road.**

About a 10-minute walk west of Sannomiya Station is **Motomachi Station,** south of which lies the fashionable Motomachi covered-arcade shopping street, **Chinatown,** and **Meriken Park**, established to commemorate the birthplace of Kobe's port. The next stop on the JR line from Motomachi Station is **Kobe Station,** just south of which is **Harborland,** a waterfront development with hotels, restaurants, and the colorful Mosaic outdoor restaurant and shopping complex.

Two train stops east of Sannomiya Station is **Nada Ward,** home of several renowned breweries, as well as one of the city's most ambitious urban renewal projects. Called **HAT Kobe** (an abbreviation of Happy Active Town), it's a mixed-use neighborhood of apartment complexes, research facilities, schools, and museums, including the new Disaster Reduction and Human Renovation Institution, which chronicles the Great Hanshin Earthquake.

Because of restricted space, Kobe has also constructed two artificial islands in its harbor, Port Island and Rokko Island. Farther afield, on Mount Rokko, is the Arima Onsen Spa.

A 13km (8-mile) **City Loop Line** bus, distinguished by its old-fashioned appearance, passes all major attractions, including Kitano, Chinatown, Meriken Park, and Harborland. Buses run every 15 to 20 minutes from about 9am to 5 or 6pm, with the route marked on the map distributed by the tourist office. It costs ¥250 ($2.40) for adults and ¥130 ($1.25) for children per ticket. A 1-day pass, allowing you to get off and reboard as often as you like, costs ¥650 ($6.20) for adults and ¥330 ($3.15) for children.

You can also use the **JR Local Commuter train,** which includes stops at Sannomiya, Motomachi, and Kobe stations, if you don't mind walking to destinations north and south of its stations (the City Loop Line buses will get you closer to major attractions). The subway is useful only for transportation between Shin-Kobe and Sannomiya stations. The **Portliner Monorail** connects Sannomiya with Port Island, while the Rokko Liner travels between JR Sumiyoshi Station and Rokko Island.

## EXPLORING THE CITY

In addition to the sights below, you might wish to drop by **City Hall** on Flower Road, where on the 24th floor there's an **observatory** open free to the public daily from 9am to 9pm (8:15am–10pm weekends and holidays). Farther south on Flower Road, at the southern end of Higashi Yuenchi Park, is the **Memorial Zone,** where the Flame of Hope created by flames gathered from cities all over Japan burns in memory of those lost in the earthquake. Nearby, an underground passageway leads to a meditation rotunda inscribed with the names of the quake's victims. Further evidence of Kobe's horrific disaster can be found at **Meriken Park,** a 10-minute walk south of Motomachi Station or a minute's walk from the Meriken Park stop on the City Loop Line bus. On its eastern edge is the **Port of Kobe Earthquake Memorial,** dedicated to the thousands of people who lost their lives in the tragic 1995 earthquake. Established with the intent of preserving some of the quake's horrific force (250,000 buildings and homes were destroyed), it shows unrepaired damage, including tilted lampposts and a submerged and broken pier.

### KITANO

When Kobe was chosen as one of five international ports following the Meiji Restoration, foreign traders and diplomats who settled here built homes in much the same style as those they left behind in their native lands. Approximately 30 of these Western-style homes, called *ijinkan,* remain on a hill north of Sannomiya Station called Kitano-cho. Because the area seems so exotic to young Japanese, this is the number-one draw for domestic visitors, who come also to shop the area's many boutiques.

Approximately 20 Victorian- and Gothic-style homes are open to the public, many with lovely views of the sea from verandas and bay windows. Although you may not be interested in visiting all of them, Kitano is very pleasant for an hour's stroll. It's located about a 15-minute walk north of Sannomiya Station or a 10-minute walk west from Shin-Kobe Station. Or take the City Loop Line to Kitano Ijinkan.

Two of the more interesting homes open to the public are the **Moegi no Yakata,** 3–10–11 Kitano-cho (© 078/222-3310; open daily 9am–6pm), a pale-green, 100-year-old home built for a former American consul general, Hunter Sharp, and filled with antiques; and **Kasamidori-no-Yakata** ⚑, 3–13–3 Kitano-cho (© 078/242-3223; open daily 9am–6pm; closed first Tues in June, Sept, Dec, and Mar), popularly referred to as the Weathercock House because of its cock weathervane. This 1909 brick residence was built by a German merchant and is probably Kobe's most famous home if not its most elaborate. Admission to either home, located across from one another, is ¥300 ($2.85), or purchase a combination ticket for ¥500 ($4.75).

Another home of note (because it contains porcelain, glass, and art, not because of its historical value) is **Uroko no Ie,** 2–20–4 Kitano-cho (© 078/242-6530; open daily 9am–6pm in summer, to 5pm in winter), which has a castlelike exterior and is nicknamed the Fish-scale House because of its slate walls. It contains lovely antiques, including Meissen porcelain and Tiffany glass, as well as a small private museum of Western 18th- to 20th-century art, with a few works by Andrew Wyeth, Utrillo, and others. Admission is ¥1,000 ($9.50) for adults, ¥300 ($2.85) for children.

**A GARDEN RETREAT**   If you're a gardener, want a respite from city life, or simply want to spend an hour in a cooler climate, take the Shin-Kobe ropeway located next to Shin-Kobe Station for a 10-minute ride to the **Nunobiki Herb Garden** ⚑ (© 078/271-1131), with its lovely, meandering, fragrant gardens planted with

various flowering shrubs and herbs and offering great views over Kobe. Be sure to take the ropeway to the end (don't get off at the first stop) and then walk downhill. The garden opens daily at 10am, closing at 5pm on weekdays and 8:30pm on weekends, holidays, and peak season (mid-July to Aug). From December through March it closes daily at 5pm. It's closed for 2 weeks in January. Admission, including round-trip by ropeway, is ¥1,200 ($11) for adults, half price for children.

## CHINATOWN &

Like the Kitano-cho area, **Chinatown** (called Nankin-machi), a 3-minute walk south of Motomachi Station (or to the Sakaemachi 1-chome stop on the City Loop Line bus), is worth a walk-through for its lively street scene, with sidewalk vendors selling snacks and with open-fronted souvenir shops and produce stands. If the sidewalk vendors tempt you, eat your snack in the central square called **Nankin Park,** adorned with statues representing the animals of the 12-year Chinese astrological calendar. Chinatown's public restroom, called **Garyoden,** which means "palace of a secluded wise man," is certainly one of Japan's most colorful—its outer wall is decorated with five-clawed dragons and is based on a famous Chinese epic about a dragonlike hero; it's located a block off the main street. You may also want to come to Chinatown for a meal (see "Where to Dine," beginning on p. 410).

## KOBE HARBORLAND

Kobe Harborland is a leisure center that's fun to stroll and browse. It's a few minutes' walk from either Kobe Station or Meriken Park, or you can take the City Loop Line to Harborland. For shopping, stop by Harbor Circus with its many boutiques or Kobe Hankyu department store, but best is **Mosaic,** an outdoor restaurant and shopping complex designed to resemble a Mediterranean village. Through the use of varying architectural and color schemes, it avoids the generic mall atmosphere, and by offering a diversity of ethnic goods and foods, it mirrors Kobe's international roots. Shops here are open daily from 11am to 8pm.

Beside it is **Mosaic Garden,** a small amusement park for younger children complete with kiddie rides, carousel, roller coaster, enclosed Ferris wheel, and games arcade. It's open from 11am to 10pm daily, with rides costing ¥300 to ¥600 ($2.85–$5.70).

## MUSEUMS WORTH CHECKING OUT

If you're on your way to the Disaster Reduction and Human Renovation Institution, below, it might be worthwhile to check out what's being shown at the **Hyogo Prefectural Museum of Art** practically next door (© **078/262-0901;** www.artm.pref.hyogo. jp). Designed by renowned Japanese architect Tadao Ando, it displays contemporary art, prints, sculpture, and other works produced by artists with connections to Hyogo Prefecture, as well as temporary exhibits from around the world. It's open Tuesday to Sunday from 10am to 6pm and charges ¥500 ($4.75) for adults, ¥400 ($3.80) for high-school and college students, and ¥250 ($2.40) for children; temporary exhibits cost more.

**Disaster Reduction and Human Renovation Institution** &&&    Despite its rather official-sounding name, this museum gives a human dimension to the Great Hanshin Earthquake, which measured 7.3 on the Richter scale. Sheathed in glass and built to withstand both vertical and horizontal earthquakes, the museum vividly conveys what happened during the first moments of the earthquake and the weeks, months, and years that followed. English-speaking volunteers are on hand to help explain some of the museum's more technical displays.

A visit to the museum begins with a powerful 7-minute film that re-creates the exact moment the earthquake struck, with computer-generated scenes that show buildings imploding or bursting into flames and highways collapsing. From the movie theater, visitors emerge into a life-size diorama depicting a typical Kobe neighborhood destroyed by the quake. They then enter another movie theater where a 13-minute documentary shows actual footage shot shortly after the quake and during the weeks that followed, presented through the eyes of a teenage survivor. Other displays in the museum concentrate on the individual experiences of survivors, emergency relief, and reconstruction. A hands-on section helps visitors learn how construction techniques can minimize and even prevent earthquake damage and dispenses information on disaster management. There is no other museum in Japan quite like this one; you'll probably spend an hour here.

1–5–2 Wakinohama Kaigan-Dori, Chuo-ku. ⓒ 078/262-5050. www.dri.ne.jp. Admission ¥500 ($4.75) adults, ¥400 ($3.80) high-school and college students, ¥250 ($2.40) children. Tues–Sun 9:30am–5:30pm (to 7pm Fri–Sat). You must enter 1 hr. before closing. Station: JR Nada (10 min. south).

**Hakutsuru Sake Brewery Museum** *⚛*  Everything you ever wanted to know about sake production is available at this former brewery, with English-language videos and pamphlets describing the various painstaking steps and comparing the old techniques to those used today. Hakutsuru, established in 1743, is one of many sake breweries in this part of Kobe; its actual brewery is now across the street (closed to the public). Plan on spending 30 minutes on your self-guided tour, which ends with hints on how to enjoy sake and—what would a brewery tour be without this?—free tastings.

4–5–5 Sumiyoshi-minami-machi, Higashinada-ku. ⓒ 078/822-8907. Free admission. Tues–Sun 9:30am–4:30pm. Station: Hanshin Sumiyoshi (5 min.); JR Sumiyoshi (15 min.).

**Kobe Fashion Museum** *⚛ (Finds*  Opened in 1997 and located on artificial Rokko Island, this is Japan's first museum devoted to fashion, housed in a contemporary, sophisticated setting that does justice to the highbrow costumes it contains. Temporary displays devoted to individual designers (there was a great show by John Galliano on one of my visits, in a setting designed by Japanese architect Tadao Ando) allow closer inspection than you could ever get at a fashion show. Other displays, which are imaginative tableaux complete with visual images, music, and lighting, may feature anything from 20th-century gowns by Christian Dior and Nina Ricci to extravagant Kabuki costumes or ethnic clothing worn by indigenous peoples from around the world. Displays change four or five times a year, rotating the many costumes owned by the museum. In all, a very entertaining, unique museum, and a must-see if you're addicted to fashion and have an extra hour.

2–9 Koyocho-naka, Rokko Island. ⓒ 078/858-0050. Admission ¥500 ($4.75) adults, ¥250 ($2.40) children and seniors. Thurs–Tues 10am–6pm. Closed 1 week during exhibit changes. Take the local JR train to Sumiyoshi Station, transferring there for the Rokkoliner monorail to Island Center.

## WHERE TO STAY

*Note:* Some hotels charge more for Saturday nights and nights before holidays, as well as during peak season (Golden Week, summer holidays, and New Year's).

### EXPENSIVE

**Hotel Okura Kobe** *⚛⚛ (Kids*  This majestic 35-story hotel has the prestige of the Okura name, as well as a grand location right beside Meriken Park; it's within easy walking distance of the Motomachi covered shopping arcade and Chinatown. Its

## (Finds) Silver & Gold

On the opposite side of Mount Rokko is **Arima Onsen,** one of Japan's oldest hot-spring spas. There are two public baths here: the ⑬ **Kin-no-Yu** (*C* **078/ 904-0680**), or Gold Spring, with copper-colored waters that have twice the salinity and iron of seawater; and the ⑭ **Gin-no-Yu** (*C* **078/904-0256**), or Silver Spring, with transparent water rich in carbonic acid. It's said that if you bathe in both these waters and drink carbonated water, you'll be cured of all ailments. The Kin-no-yu, open daily 8am to 10pm (closed the second and fourth Tues of every month), charges ¥650 ($6.20), while the Gin-no-yu, open daily 9am to 9pm (closed the first and third Tues of every month), charges ¥550 ($5.25). Buses from Sannomiya Station reach Arima Onsen in 40 minutes and cost ¥680 ($6.45) one-way. You can also travel by train to Rokko Station, followed by a trip by bus, cable car, and ropeway. Contact the Kobe Tourist Information office for more information.

inviting lobby has views of a small garden (the only hotel garden in downtown Kobe) against a backdrop formed by the port. Each elegantly appointed room has all the comforts you'd expect of a first-class hotel, plus the bonus of great views from its more expensive rooms, which are on higher floors facing the harbor or the city with Mount Rokko rising behind it. Rooms on the 27th floor also offer high-speed Internet connection. In short, this hotel appeals to everyone from families—its target customer— to business travelers. Even the imperial family makes this their home base when in Kobe. *Tip:* Upon check-in, ask for immediate free membership in the Okura Club International, which allows late checkout, free use of the health club and both outdoor and indoor pools, and other privileges.

2–1 Hatoba-cho, Chuo-ku, Kobe 650-8560. *C* **800/526-2281** in the U.S., or 078/333-0111. Fax 078/333-6673. www.kobe.hotelokura.co.jp. 489 units. ¥16,800–¥22,500 ($160–$214) single; ¥26,250–¥37,800 ($250–$351) double or twin. AE, DC, MC, V. Station: Motomachi (10 min. south). Loop Line bus: Meriken Park (1 min.). **Amenities:** 5 restaurants; 1 bar; 2 lounges; outdoor pool (free w/membership); health club w/gym, sauna, and heated indoor lap pool (free w/membership); 2 lit outdoor tennis courts; children's day-care center (fee: ¥5,000/$48 for 2 hr.; reservations necessary 2 days in advance); concierge; tour desk; business center; shopping arcade; salon; room service (6am–midnight); in-room massage; same-day laundry/dry-cleaning service; nonsmoking rooms. *In room:* A/C, cable TV w/pay movies, dataport, minibar, hot-water pot w/tea, hair dryer, bathroom scale, Washlet toilet.

**Shinkobe Oriental Hotel** This hotel is directly connected to Shin-Kobe Station— very convenient if you're arriving by Shinkansen train (though the hotel's entrance is a bit hard to find). Rising 37 stories, with rooms on the 14th to 33rd floors, it offers great views of Kobe and the bay or the mountains from fully equipped but rather plain rooms. Rates are based on room size and floor, with top floors commanding the grandest views at the highest prices. A plus is the large mall occupying the first four floors, with many additional choices in dining.

1 Kitano-cho, Chuo-ku, Kobe 650-0002. *C* **078/291-1121.** Fax 078/291-1151. www.orientalhotel.co.jp. 600 units. ¥13,650–¥19,950 ($130–$190) single; ¥24,150–¥35,700 ($229–$339) twin; ¥24,150–¥31,500 ($229–$299) double. AE, DC, MC, V. Station: Shin-Kobe (1 min.). **Amenities:** 7 restaurants; 1 bar; 2 lounges; health club w/gym, indoor pool, and sauna (fee: ¥5,000/$48); shopping arcade; salon; room service (6am–midnight); in-room massage; same-day laundry/dry-cleaning service; nonsmoking rooms. *In room:* A/C, satellite TV w/pay movies, free high-speed dataport, hot-water pot w/tea, hair dryer, Washlet toilet.

## MODERATE

**Hotel Monterey Amalie** 🍴  Taking its name from a long-ago Dutch sailing vessel and decorated with a nautical theme, this property is part of a smart chain of boutique hotels that targets mostly female Japanese travelers with old-world European decor and atmosphere. From its ivy-covered facade to whitewashed walls (some of which could use a fresh coat) and heavy-beamed ceilings, it looks much older than its 1992 construction date. Wood-floored guest rooms feature natural wooden furniture, sheer curtains and heavy wooden shutters, tiled bathrooms, and free-standing wardrobes. Ask for a room overlooking Ikuta Shrine, but since occupancy is an enviable 85%, book early. Otherwise, try nearby sister hotel Monterey Kobe (𝄞 **078/392-7111**), with similar prices and a cloisterlike atmosphere.

2–2–28 Nakayamate Dori, Chuo-ku, Kobe 650-0004. 𝄞 **078/334-1711.** Fax 078/334-1788. 69 units. ¥8,400–¥10,500 ($80–$100) single; ¥18,900–¥22,050 ($180–$209) double; ¥19,950–¥26,250 ($190–$250) twin. AE, DC, MC, V. Station: Sannomiya (10 min). Just west of Ikuta Shrine. **Amenities:** Restaurant (French); in-room massage; same-day laundry/dry-cleaning service; nonsmoking rooms. *In room:* A/C, TV w/pay movies, minibar, hot-water pot w/tea, hair dryer, Washlet toilet.

**Hotel Tor Road** 🍴  An imitation fireplace, knickknacks on the mantle, antiques, a drop-leaf desk, and dark-wood wainscoting lend an English country atmosphere to this tourist hotel's lobby. The decent-size rooms are clean and tastefully decorated with double-size beds and larger-than-usual bathrooms, with twins and doubles even providing a separate sink area. The most expensive rooms are so-called "designer theme rooms" on the ninth floor. The "cat" room, for example, has the logo of a cat repeated on the drapes, pillows, sheets, and elsewhere, but I fail to see why anyone would pay more for it.

3–1–19 Nakayamate Dori, Chuo-ku, Kobe 650-0004. 𝄞 **078/391-6691.** Fax 078/391-6570. htorroad@oak. ocn.ne.jp. 78 units. ¥7,875–¥9,450 ($75–$90) single; ¥15,750–¥19,950 ($150–$190) double or twin. ¥1,050 ($10) more per room Sat, days before holidays, and peak season. Rates include buffet breakfast. AE, DC, MC, V. Station: Sannomiya or Motomachi (10 min.). On Tor Rd. just north of Ikuta Shinmichi Dori. **Amenities:** Restaurant (Italian); in-room massage; same-day laundry service; nonsmoking rooms. *In room:* A/C, TV w/pay movies, minibar, hot-water pot w/tea, hair dryer.

**Kobe Meriken Park Oriental Hotel** 🍴🍴  An outstanding location on a spit of land jutting seaward from the edge of Meriken Park (it's practically on the water and surrounded by a park) makes this Kobe's best hotel with a view—which it capitalizes on by providing each room with a balcony with views of Kobe's harbor and of the city as it rises up the hills. Popular with couples (weddings are big here) and women, the hotel looks like one of the many cruise ships that dock nearby, rising 14 stories in a lopsided half circle. Its center is hollow, an airy atrium filled with palm trees and bubbling fountains. Rooms, which vary in size and view, come with all the basics, with the best views considered those that overlook Harborland and its amusement park. Don't be alarmed by the encampment of homeless just outside the hotel—they're harmless. (Parks have become popular sites for Japan's ever-growing number of homeless, who happen to be very orderly and organized, with encampments that consist of homemade shelters—made primarily of blue plastic—washed clothing hanging on clotheslines, and even locks on the makeshift homes.) But in case you don't want to walk, a free shuttle provides service to both Sannomiya and Kobe stations every 20 or 30 minutes.

5–6 Hatoba-cho, Chuo-ku, Kobe 650-0042. 𝄞 **078/325-8111.** Fax 078/325-8106. www.meriken-oh.co.jp. 331 units. ¥10,500 ($100) single; ¥16,800–¥36,750 ($160–$350) double; ¥24,150–¥29,400 ($229–$279) twin. ¥4,200 ($40) more per room Sat., days before holidays, and Aug. AE, DC, MC, V. Free shuttle service every 20–30 min. from Sannomiya Station (east exit, from Rte. 2 Hwy.) and Kobe Station. (If you arrive at Shin-Kobe Station, take the

subway to Sannomiya Station to catch the free shuttle.) Loop Line bus: Nakatottei Pier (5 min.). **Amenities:** 4 restaurants (Japanese, teppanyaki with Kobe beef, Cantonese, Western buffet); 2 lounges; indoor swimming pool (fee: ¥1,000/$9.50); children's day-care center (¥5,000/$48 for 2 hr.); salon; room service (7am–10:45pm); in-room massage; same-day laundry/dry-cleaning service; nonsmoking rooms. *In room:* A/C, cable TV w/pay movies, minibar, hot-water pot w/tea, hair dryer, Washlet toilet.

**Seaside Hotel Maiko Villa Kobe** *(Kids)*   Located on a hill in West Kobe beside the world's longest suspension bridge, about a 20-minute train ride from Sannomiya Station, Maiko Villa is a bit far from the town center but its inconvenient location does offer some advantages, including cheaper prices than those of hotels in the center. Situated near the sea with the sound of seagulls and the faint scent of saltwater, it exudes a resortlike atmosphere, making it a good place to relax in a more leisurely setting—at the man-made sandy beach nearby or the hotel outdoor pool (open July and Aug). Its grounds are lovely, with ancient dwarf pines that date from the early 1900s, when Emperor Meiji once had a second home here. Popular with vacationing Japanese and for marriage ceremonies (more than 700 a year), the modern hotel offers a variety of rooms, most with views of the sea, fishing boats, and the bridge (which changes color at night). Best are the deluxe twins—corner rooms, they boast heart-shaped tubs where you can bathe looking out at the sea. Avoid the 26 singles and doubles; facing inland, they are used mainly by bus drivers and tour guides. Better and almost as reasonable are the Japanese-style and combination (with both tatami rooms and twin beds) rooms in the annex, almost all with balconies facing the sea. In addition to the outdoor pool and nearby beach, kids will like the playground across the street.

18–11 Higashi Maiko-cho, Tarumi-ku, Kobe 655-0047. ✆ **078/706-3711.** Fax 078/706-2212. 251 units. ¥7,875 ($75) single; ¥11,550 ($110) double; ¥15,750–¥21,000 ($150–$200) twin. Japanese-style rooms ¥13,440 ($128) double. Combination rooms ¥15,330–¥25,200 ($146–$239). ¥1,575 ($15) more per person in peak season. AE, DC, MC, V. Station: From Sannomiya Station, take the JR Kobe Line rapid express (Kaisoku) 20 min. to JR Maiko (5 min.). Follow signs and then take the hillside elevator. **Amenities:** 4 restaurants (Chinese, Japanese, French/Italian, coffee shop); 1 bar; outdoor pool (free to hotel guests); 300-seat concert hall with piano recitals twice a week; salon; in-room massage; same-day laundry/dry-cleaning service; nonsmoking rooms. *In room:* A/C, TV w/pay movies, fridge, hot-water pot w/tea, hair dryer, Washlet toilet (main building only).

## INEXPENSIVE

**Green Hill Hotel Urban**   Between Sannomiya and Shin-Kobe stations, this simple business hotel with mostly single rooms in a dormitory-like setting is primarily a place to park your head at night. Clean rooms are about as small as they come, most without closets and with glazed windows and minuscule plastic-unit bathrooms. Free tea is dispensed from machines on each floor. About the only thing setting this hotel apart from thousands of other business hotels across the country is its automatic check-in via machine (you need a credit card); you can ask for assistance from the front desk, but English is limited. Don't confuse this with the older Green Hill Hotel around the corner.

2–5–16 Kano-cho, Chuo-ku, Kobe 650-0001. ✆ **078/222-1221.** Fax 078/242-1194. 102 units. ¥6,500 ($62) single; ¥13,000 ($123) twin or double. AE, DC, MC, V. Station: Shin-Kobe or Sannomiya (10 min.); between the stations, on Flower Rd. **Amenities:** Coffee shop; in-room massage; coin-op washers and dryers; nonsmoking rooms (singles only). *In room:* A/C, TV, fridge (singles and twins only), hair dryer.

**Toyoko Inn Kobe-Sannomiya** *(Value)*   Opened in 2003, this Kobe addition to one of Japan's fastest-growing business hotel chains surpasses others for such perks as free Internet access in rooms and from computers in the lobby, free domestic phone calls, free movies (but in Japanese only), and free breakfasts. Rooms are small but clean, and female travelers even get a cosmetic set geared just for them.

2–2–2 Gokodori, Chuo-ku, Kobe 651-0087. ✆ **078/271-1045.** Fax 078/271-1046. www.toyoko-inn.com. 135 units. ¥6,090 ($58) single; ¥8,190 ($78) twin or double. Rates include breakfast and tax. MC, V. Station: Sannomiya (8 min.); southeast of the station. **Amenities:** In-room massage; coin-op washers and dryers; nonsmoking rooms. *In room:* A/C, TV w/free movies, fridge, hot-water pot w/tea, hair dryer, safe, trouser press.

## WHERE TO DINE

With its sizable foreign population, Kobe is a good place to dine on international cuisine, including Indian and Chinese food. The greatest concentration of Chinese restaurants is along a pedestrian lane in Chinatown, called **Nankin-machi** by the locals, just a 2-minute walk south of Motomachi Station. If you're on a budget, you may just want to wander through and buy sticky buns or other inexpensive fare from street stalls.

### EXPENSIVE

**Alain Chapel** �466 FRENCH   For elegant French dining, Alain Chapel is one of the city's top choices. In a stately drawing-room setting with great panoramic views of either Kobe city or the sea, this restaurant serves the creations of French chef Alain Chapel, whose set meals are popular with his Japanese clientele. If you decide to dine a la carte, you might start with lobster salad and then try Kobe beef, lamb, pigeon, or duck. Average dinner checks, including wine, tax, and service, are generally around ¥18,000 ($171) per person. Clearly, recession is a foreign word here, though set lunches are reasonable.

Kobe Portopia Hotel, 31st floor, 6–10–2 Minatojima, Port Island. ✆ **078/302-1111.** Reservations recommended. Main dishes ¥3,400–¥9,000 ($32–$86); set dinners ¥7,800–¥18,000 ($74–$171); set lunches ¥2,940–¥6,300 ($28–$60). AE, DC, MC, V. Daily 11:30am–2pm and 5–9pm (last order). Portliner Monorail from Sannomiya Station to Shimin Hiroba Station (2 min.); or free shuttle service every 20 min. from Sannomiya and Shin-Kobe stations.

**Kitano Club** ✎ FRENCH   Located on a hill overlooking the city, this well-known restaurant with a country-club setting has been offering meals with a view for more than 25 years. It's especially popular with middle-aged Japanese women, who come to take advantage of the daily lunch special, called Queen's Lunch, for ¥3,150 ($30)— and, yes, guys can order it, too. There are also set steak lunches and dinners. The dinner menu also includes fish of the day, lamb, and duck.

1–5–7 Kitano-cho. ✆ **078/222-5123.** Reservations recommended. Main dishes ¥2,900–¥7,500 ($28–$71); set dinner ¥8,400–¥10,500 ($80–$100); set lunch ¥3,150–¥7,350 ($30–$70). AE, DC, MC, V. Daily 11:30am–2pm and 5:50–9pm (last order). Station: Shin-Kobe (7 min.). Go west on Kitano Rd. from Shinkobe Oriental Hotel, taking the 1st street on the right (when you see the Kitano Chapel); it will be on your left.

**Wakkoqu** ✎ TEPPANYAKI STEAKS   This tiny, second-floor restaurant has room for only 30 diners at two counters, where expert chefs cook sirloin, tenderloin, or other cuts of tender Kobe beef on the grill in front of them. Fixed-course meals come with side dishes like soup and fried vegetables. This is a good place to try Kobe's most famous product.

Hillside Terrace, 1–22–13 Nakayamate Dori. ✆ **078/222-0678.** Reservations recommended. Set dinner ¥7,140–¥13,650 ($68–$130); set lunch ¥2,625–¥4,725 ($25–$45). AE, DC, MC, V. Daily noon–9:30pm (last order). Station: Sannomiya (7 min.). On Pearl St. just east of Kitano-zaka.

### MODERATE

⑬⑤ **Steakland Kobe** STEAKS   If you want to eat teppanyaki steak but can't afford the high prices of Kobe beef, one of the cheapest places to go is Steakland Kobe, which is used to tourists and offers an English-language menu. Lunch specials, served from

11am to 3pm, feature steak (cooked on a hot plate in front of you), miso soup, rice, Japanese pickles, and a vegetable. More expensive Kobe beef is also available, with the least expensive fixed-price dinner offering Kobe sirloin costing ¥4,100 ($39).

1–8–2 Kitanagasa Dori. ☎ 078/332-1787. Steaks ¥1,980–¥5,280 ($93–$50); set steak dinner ¥2,680–¥5,980 ($25–$57); set lunch ¥980–¥2,980 ($9.30–$28). AE, DC, MC, V. Daily 11:30am–10pm (last order). Station: Sannomiya (2 min.). On the north side of Sankita, the street that runs along the north side of Hankyu Sannomiya Station, diagonally across from McDonald's; look for the sign with the plaid ribbon.

## INEXPENSIVE

⑬⑥ **Hyotan** *(Value* GYOZA   Roll up your sleeves and join the working class at this greasy hole-in-the-wall eatery underneath the tracks of Hanshin Sannomiya Station. It must be doing something right, since it's been selling nothing but gyoza for more than 40 years, favored for the light texture of its dumpling skin and stuffed with minced pork, leek, and cabbage. At your table will be soy sauce, vinegar, and chile sauce, which you should mix in the little bowl provided; gyoza come eight to a serving. Avoid the noontime rush, when this tiny place is like an assembly line for speed eating.

1–31–37 Kitanagasadori. ☎ 078/331-1354. Gyoza ¥370 ($3.50). No credit cards. Daily 11:30am–10pm (last order). Closed the 2nd and 4th Mon of each month. Station: Sannomiya (2 min.). Underneath the tracks of Hanshin Sannomiya Station in a small passageway at the west end; look for the red curtains.

**Nishimura** COFFEE SHOP   In business for some 50 years, Nishimura is a Kobe landmark. It's on the north side of Yamate Kansen Dori (also called Nakayamate Dori), across from Higashimon Street, but if you can't find it, just follow your nose; the smell of roasting coffee broadcasts its location. At least 10 types of coffee are available, as well as snacks and desserts. *Note:* Renovation was scheduled to end in May 2006.

1–26–1 Nakayamate Dori. ☎ 078/221-1872. Coffee from ¥450 ($4.30). No credit cards. Daily 8:30am–11pm. Station: Sannomiya (10 min.).

**Old Spaghetti Factory** *(Kids* *(Value* SPAGHETTI   A branch of a U.S. chain founded in Portland in 1969, the Old Spaghetti Factory gets kudos for its renovation of an 1898 warehouse in Harborland next to Mosaic, complete with antiques and an airy setting. It offers inexpensive spaghetti with a choice of more than a dozen sauces, from the usual meat sauce to sautéed bacon and spinach. Set lunches (spaghetti, soup or salad, drink, and bread) are available on weekdays. Set dinners let you compose your meal according to appetite, adding just bread and a drink to your pasta or going all out with an appetizer, bread, soup or salad, drink, and dessert. A kids' menu is also available.

Harborland, 1–5–5 Higashi Kawasaki-cho. ☎ 078/360-3911. Set lunch ¥800–¥1,100 ($7.60–$10); set dinner ¥900–¥2,000 ($8.55–$19). No credit cards. Mon–Fri 11am–2:30pm and 5–10pm; Sat–Sun 11am–10pm (last order). Loop Line bus: Harborland. Station: Kobe (8 min.). From JR Kobe Station, take the C exit of DuoKobe and walk straight down Kobe Gas Light St. past Hankyu, following signs for BRICK WAREHOUSE RESTAURANT until you see the brick warehouse on your right.

**Pinocchio** PIZZA/PASTA   This small and cozy corner establishment opened in 1962 and proudly claims to have never fallen victim to the many fads that have come and gone since then. Instead, it still produces handmade pizza, which you can order from the menu or create yourself by ordering the basic pizza for ¥840 ($8) and adding ingredients like garlic, asparagus, mushroom, pineapple, chicken, or bacon, all priced at ¥100 (95¢) each. Pasta, pilaf, and gratin are also available.

2–3–13 Nakayamate Dori. ☎ 078/331-3330. Pizza and pasta ¥1,050–¥1,575 ($10–$15). DC, MC, V. Daily 11:30am–midnight. Station: Sannomiya (12 min.). On the south side of Yamate Kansen Dori (also called Nakayamate Dori), west of Ikuta Shrine.

## KOBE AFTER DARK

Kobe has a wide selection of English-style pubs, bars, expatriate hangouts, and night-clubs. All the establishments below are easily accessible to foreigners, and most are within walking distance of Sannomiya Station.

### THE CLUB & MUSIC SCENE

**Chicken George**　This place is one of Kobe's most popular for 20-somethings in search of well-known Japanese music acts, including pop, jazz, and alternative. It's easy to spot with its grungy, graffiti-filled exterior; the inside is dark and cavernous. Though there's table seating for more mellow acts, sold-out sets mean everyone stands. Check *Kansai Time Out* for concert listings and times. 2–17–15 Shimo-Yamate Dori. ℂ 078/392-0146. www.chicken-george.co.jp. Cover ¥2,500–¥6,000 ($24–$57). Station: Sannomiya (5 min.). Just west of Ikuta Shrine.

**Garage Paradise**　Candlelight, gauzy curtains draped from the high ceiling, Roman statues, a copper and stone bar, and stone walls set the scene at this basement with five sets of good, live music Friday through Sunday nights and DJs the rest of the week. The interesting setting attracts the local foreigner clientele. Open daily 6pm to 3am (Sun and holidays to 1am). Kobe Yamashita Building, basement, 1–13–7 Nakayamate Dori. ℂ 078/391-6640. Cover Sun–Thurs ¥520 ($4.95); Fri–Sun ¥520 ($4.95 for women, ¥730 ($6.95) for men. Station: Sannomiya (10 min.). On Yamate Kansen Dori east of Higashimon, catty-corner from Nishimura coffee shop.

**Satin Doll**　This traditional jazz club first opened in 1972 and remains one of the city's top venues. Its sophisticated interior offers table and bar seating with some city views. There are three live music sets nightly (7, 8:30, and 10pm), an English-language menu offering mainly snacks, and a wine list. *Note:* A 10% service charge will be added to your bill. Open daily 6pm to midnight. Bacchus Building, 1–26–1 Nakayama Dori. ℂ 078/242-0100. Cover from ¥500 ($4.75), more for international acts, plus ¥500 ($4.75) table charge. Station: Sannomiya (10 min.). On Yamate Kansen Dori opposite Higashimon Dori.

**Sone**　Kobe's oldest and best-known jazz club has changed little since its 1969 opening, offering the same traditional jazz, including Dixieland ensembles and piano-vocalist duos, in a clubby, dated atmosphere. There are four stages nightly, and most people come to eat; the Japanese-language menu lists pasta, pizza, fish, and Kobe steaks, with set meals starting at ¥2,000 ($19). Open daily 5pm to 12:30am (Sun to midnight). 1–24–10 Nakayamate Dori. ℂ 078/221-2055. Cover usually ¥900 ($8.55). Station: Sannomiya (5 min.). North of the station on the left side of Kitano-zaka.

### THE BAR SCENE

**Ryan's Irish Pub**　Alan Ryan is the ever-present owner and host at this very popular expatriate bar, the only Irish-owned pub in Kansai. Tuesday through Sunday features live music—everything from blues, country-and-western, and Irish—for which there's never a cover charge. There's Guinness on tap and food items like Irish stew and fish and chips to wash it all down. A good place to relax after a hard day of sightseeing; happy hour is till 8pm. Open daily 5pm to midnight (Fri to 1am, Sat to 2am). Kondo Building, 7th floor, 4–3–2 Kano-cho. ℂ 078/391-6902. Station: Sannomiya (1 min.). Across the north side of Sannomiya Station on the corner of Ikuta Shinmichi St. and Flower Rd., above a McDonald's.

**Second Chance**　This all-nighter, in business an astonishing 30 years (which makes it older than most of its customers), is a small, one-room bar favored by night owls who don't mind the rather sparse furnishings with Hawaiian touches. Decorated with surfboards and mock thatched roofs, it's where people congregate when the other bars

have had the good sense to close down for the night. Open daily 6pm to 5am. Takashima Building, 2nd floor, 2–1–12 Nakayamate Dori. ✆ 078/391-3544. Station: Sannomiya (10 min.). On Yamate Kansen Dori west of Higashimon and catty-corner from Nishimura coffee shop.

**Smokey**    This place is one of a kind—a tiny bar with only eight seats at the counter, all under the watchful eye of 80-something bartender Kamogawa-san, who worked at several hotels (he even served Marilyn Monroe and Joe DiMaggio at the old Kobe Oriental Hotel) before opening his own bar in 1955. Now the oldest bar in Kobe, it's filled with memorabilia of a lifetime, and if you ask, Kamogawa-san will drag out his photographs of actors, actresses, comedians, baseball players, sumo wrestlers, and politicians who have sat here. He's also likely to show you a few of his magic tricks when he's not busy changing records on his old player. There's no cover or table charge, but the average bill is about ¥4,500 ($43). (There are never prices posted in these kinds of bars and there are no menus; most customers are regulars and they don't come just for one drink—they come for the evening. The price above includes snacks like nuts and whatever other dishes are offered that day.) Since this place is tiny, even regular clientele often call to reserve a seat. Open Monday to Saturday 5 to 11:30pm. 1–9–1 Nakayamate Dori. ✆ 078/391-0257. Station: Sannomiya (4 min.). North of the station on the left side of Kitano-zaka.

**Starlight Lounge**    For cocktails with a view, head to this sophisticated lounge on the 35th floor of Hotel Okura Kobe in Meriken Park, with two-tiered seating for optimal views. *Note:* No children are allowed after 5pm, and on Saturday nights there's live music, for which there's a ¥1,000 ($9.50) charge. Open Monday to Friday 6pm to midnight and Saturday and Sunday from 1pm to midnight. 2–1 Hatoba-cho. ✆ 078/333-3521. Station: Motomachi (10 min. south). Loop Line bus: Meriken Park (1 min.).

## 6 The Temples of Mount Koya ★ ★ ★

730km (465 miles) W of Tokyo; 199km (124 miles) S of Osaka

If you've harbored visions of wooden temples nestled in among trees whenever you've thought of Japan, the sacred mountain of **Mount Koya** is the place to go. It's all here—head-shaven monks, religious chanting at the crack of dawn, the wafting of incense, temples, towering cypress trees, tombs, and early-morning mist rising above the treetops. Mount Koya—called Koyasan by Japanese—is one of Japan's most sacred places and the mecca of the Shingon Esoteric sect of Buddhism. Standing almost 900m (3,000 ft.) above the world, the top of Mount Koya is home to more than 115 Shingon Buddhist temples scattered through the mountain forests. Some 50 of these temples offer accommodations, making this one of the best places in Japan to observe temple life firsthand.

A World Heritage Site, Koyasan first became a place of meditation and religious learning more than 1,180 years ago when Kukai, known posthumously as Kobo Daishi, was granted the mountaintop by the imperial court in 816 as a place to establish his Shingon sect of Buddhism. Kobo Daishi was a charismatic priest who had spent 2 years in China studying Esoteric Buddhism before returning to his native land to spread his teachings among Japanese. Revered for his excellent calligraphy, his humanitarianism, and his teachings, Kobo Daishi remains one of the most beloved figures in Japanese Buddhist history. When he died in the 9th century, he was laid to rest in a mausoleum on Mount Koya. His followers believe Kobo Daishi is not dead but simply in a deep state of meditation, awaiting the arrival of the last bodhisattva

(Buddha messiah). According to popular belief, priests opening his mausoleum decades after his death found his body still warm.

Through the centuries, many of Kobo Daishi's followers, wishing to be close at hand when the great priest awakens, have had huge tombs or tablets constructed close to Kobo Daishi's mausoleum, and many have had their ashes interred here. Pilgrims over the last thousand years have included emperors, feudal lords, samurai, and common people, all climbing to the top of the mountain to pay their respects. Women, however, were barred from entering the sacred grounds of Koyasan until 1872.

## ESSENTIALS

**GETTING THERE** The easiest way to get to Koyasan is from Osaka. Ordinary express *(kyuko)* trains of the **Nankai Line** depart from Osaka's Namba Station every half-hour or hour bound for Gokurakubashi, and the trip south takes about 1 hour and 40 minutes. If you want to ride in luxury, use one of the limited-express cars with reserved seats that take about 1 hour and 20 minutes. After arriving at the last stop, Gokurakubashi, you continue your trip to the top of Mount Koya via a 5-minute ride in a cable car. The entire journey from Namba Station to Mount Koya costs ¥1,230 ($12) one-way, including the cable car; if you take the faster limited express, it'll cost ¥760 ($7.25) extra. Otherwise, Nankai offers a **discount ticket** called **Koyasan Free Servic** for ¥2,780 ($26) which includes round-trip travel by regular train from Osaka's Namba Station and the cable car, plus unlimited rides on Koya's buses for 24 hours and slight discounts to the attractions listed below.

**VISITOR INFORMATION** At the top of Mount Koya is Koyasan Station, where you'll find a booth of the local tourist office, the main office of which is located approximately in the center of Koyasan village near Kongobuji Temple. You can pick up a map of Koyasan and book a room in a temple at either office, but it is recommended that you fax ahead for a reservation (see "Where to Stay," below). Both offices are open daily from 8:30am to 4:30pm in winter (Nov–Feb), to 5pm the rest of the year. For more information, contact the **Koyasan Tourist Association** (© **0736/56-2616**) or check the websites www.koyasan.org or www.shukubo.jp/eng.

**GETTING AROUND** Outside the cable car station, you must board a **bus** that travels 2km (1¼ miles) along a narrow, winding road to the village of Koyasan and then continues along the main street all the way through town to the Okunoin-mae or Ichinohashi (also called Ichinohashi-guchi) bus stop, the location of Kobo Daishi's mausoleum. The bus passes almost all the sights along the way, as well as most temples accommodating visitors and the Koyasan Tourist Association's main office. Buses depart every 30 minutes between 6:20am and 7pm, and the trip to Okunoin-mae takes 20 minutes and costs ¥400 ($3.80). Otherwise, once you're settled in at your temple accommodations, you can probably walk to Okunoin and other locations mentioned below, but daylong bus passes, called Free Passes, are available for ¥800 ($7.60).

## EXPLORING MOUNT KOYA

**THE TOP ATTRACTION** The most awe-inspiring and magnificent of Koyasan's many structures and temples, **Okunoin** ✿✿✿ contains the mausoleum of Kobo Daishi. The most dramatic way to approach Okunoin is from the Ichinohashi bus stop, where a pathway leads 1.6km (1 mile) to the mausoleum. Swathed in a respectful darkness of huge cypress trees forming a canopy overhead are monument after

monument, tomb after tomb—approximately 200,000 of them, all belonging to faithful followers from past centuries.

I don't know whether being here will affect you the same way, but I was awestruck by the sheer density of tombstones, the iridescent green moss, the shafts of light streaking through the treetops, the stone lanterns, and the gnarled bark of the old cypress trees. Together, they present a dramatic picture representing a thousand years of Japanese Buddhist history. If you're lucky, you won't meet many people along this pathway. Tour buses fortunately park at a newer entrance to the mausoleum at the bus stop called Okunoin-mae. I absolutely forbid you to take this newer and shorter route; its crowds lessen the impact of this place considerably. Rather, make sure you take the path farthest to the left, which begins near the Ichinohashi stop. Much less traveled, it's also much more impressive and is one of the main reasons for coming to Koyasan in the first place. And be sure to return to the mausoleum at night—the stone lanterns (now lit electrically) create a mysterious and powerful effect.

At the end of the pathway, about a 30-minute walk away, is the **Lantern Hall,** or Torodo, which houses about 21,000 lanterns, donated by prime ministers, emperors, and others. If you'd like to buy a lantern to dedicate to someone, it costs ¥500,000 to ¥1,000,000 ($4,762–$9,523). Two sacred fires, which reportedly have been burning since the 11th century, are kept safely inside. The mausoleum itself is behind the Lantern Hall. Buy a white candle, light it, and wish for anything you want. Then sit back and watch respectfully as Buddhists come to chant and pay respects to one of Japan's greatest Buddhist leaders.

**MORE TO SEE & DO**    ⑬⑦ **Kongobuji Temple** ✱, located near the main Koyasan Tourist Association office in the center of town (✆ **0736/56-2328;** open daily 8:30am–4:30pm), is the central monastery headquarters of the Shingon sect in Japan. Although Kongobuji was originally built in the 16th century by Toyotomi Hideyoshi to commemorate his mother's death, the present building is 150 years old, reconstructed following a fire. Pictures by famous artists from long ago decorate the rooms, and the huge kitchen, big enough to feed multitudes of monks, is also on view. The most important thing to see, however, is the temple's magnificent rock garden, reputedly the largest in Japan and said to represent a pair of dragons in a sea of clouds. If it's raining, consider yourself lucky—the wetness adds sheen and color to the rocks. Admission is ¥500 ($4.75).

Another important site is the **Garan** ✱ (✆ **0736/56-3215;** open daily 8:30am–4:30pm), the first buildings constructed on Koyasan and still considered the center of religious life in the community. It's an impressive sight with a huge main hall *(kondo);* a large vermilion-colored pagoda *(daito),* which many consider to be Koyasan's most magnificent structure and which is very much worth entering (¥200/$1.90 each for the kondo and daito); and the oldest building on Mount Koya, the Fudodo, which was built in 1197. Next to the complex is the ⑬⑧ **Reihokan Museum** (✆ **0736/56-2029;** open daily 8:30am–4:30pm), displaying such treasures of Koyasan as wooden Buddha sculptures, scrolls, art, and implements spread through two buildings. Admission is ¥600 ($5.70).

All of the sites above half price for children's admission.

## WHERE TO STAY
Although this community of 4,000 residents has the usual stores, schools, and offices of any small town, there are no hotels here—the only place you can stay is at a temple, and I strongly urge you to do so.

Japanese who come here have almost always made reservations beforehand, and you should do the same. You can make reservations by calling the temple directly or through travel agencies such as JTB. You can also make reservations upon arrival in Koyasan at either Tourist Association office (see "Essentials," above); I suggest faxing in advance to be sure you can get a space (fax **0736/56-2889**), especially during peak travel seasons.

**WHAT IT'S LIKE TO STAY AT A KOYASAN TEMPLE**   Prices for an overnight stay in one of the temples, including two vegetarian meals, range from ¥9,500 to ¥15,000 ($90–$143) per person, depending on the room. You should bring your own towel and toiletries and check-in is around 3pm; checkout is at 9am.

Your room will be tatami and may include a nice view of a garden. High-school and college students attending Koyasan's Buddhist university live at the temple; they'll bring your meals to your room, make up your futon, and clean your room. The Buddhist vegetarian meals served *(shojin ryori)* are generally quite good, and since Buddhist monks are vegetarians but not teetotalers (beer and sake are made of rice and grain), alcoholic drinks are readily available at the temples for an extra charge. The morning religious service is at 6am; you don't have to attend, but I strongly recommend that you do. There's something uplifting about early-morning meditative chanting, even for nonbelievers. Both baths and toilets are communal, and meals are at set times. Because the students must leave for school, breakfast is usually served by 7:30am.

Below are just a few of the dozens of area temples open to overnight guests. They're all located very near the indicated bus stop. All of them have public baths, but none offer rooms with bathrooms.

⑬⑨ **Ekoin**   This 100-year-old temple, with origins stretching back almost 1,200 years when Kukai was said to have erected a stupa on this site, has nice grounds and is nestled in a wooded slope. For centuries it enjoyed support of the Shimazu clan of southern Kyushu. It's known for its excellent Buddhist cuisine, and the master priest will give zazen meditation lessons if his schedule permits. More than half the rooms have TVs and telephones; most also have nice sitting alcoves. There's always someone here who speaks a little English. Reservations should be made in advance, especially for peak season.

Koyasan 497, Koya-cho, Ito-gun, Wakayama-ken 648-0211. ℂ **0736/56-2514.** Fax 0736/56-2891. ekoin@mbox.co.jp. 36 units (none with bathroom). ¥10,000–¥13,000 ($95–$124) per person. Rates include 2 meals. AE, MC, V. Bus: Karukaya-do or Ichinohashi. *In room:* TV (some rooms), hot-water pot w/tea, no phone in some rooms.

⑭⓪ **Fudoin Temple**   Founded in 906, this temple's oldest existing building is 400 years old. Rooms, in new, modern buildings, look out on a garden and a carp pond. The young head priest speaks English and offers towels and yukata to foreigners.

Koyasan, Koya-cho, Ito-gun, Wakayama-ken 648-0211. ℂ **0736/56-2414.** Fax 0736/56-4700. 20 units (none with bathroom, 7 with toilet). ¥10,500 ($100) without toilet; ¥12,600 ($120) with toilet. Rates are per person, including 2 meals. MC, V. Bus: Rengedani. *In room:* TV (most rooms), hot-water pot w/tea, safe.

⑭① **Muryokoin Temple**   Kakuho Shinno, son of Emperor Shirakawa, founded Muryokoin in the Heian Period around 1100. Because the emphasis here is on monastic life, facilities are very simple. One of the monks, however, speaks English and can impart information on Buddhism, as well as provide guidance around Mount Koya. Towels and yukata are provided.

Koyasan, Koya-cho, Ito-gun, Wakayama-ken 648-0211. ℂ **0736/56-2104.** Fax 0736/56-4555. muryoko@ cypress.ne.jp. 24 units (none with bathroom). ¥10,500–¥13,500 ($100–$129). Rates are per person, including 2 meals. No credit cards. Bus: Keisatsu-no-mae. *In room:* Hot-water pot w/tea.

⑭ **Rengejoin Temple**    This temple's head priest speaks English, so a lot of foreigners are directed here—it's a good place to meet people and to find out about Buddhism. It's also one of the few temples that may take you in without a reservation. Established 900 years ago, it was rebuilt 150 years ago after a fire. Rooms have views of a nice garden with a pond; a plus are the English-language videos placed in some rooms that explore the history and significance of Mount Koya and Kongobuji Temple and the new baths. The disadvantage is that it's on the opposite end of town from Okunoin, about a 50-minute walk away.

Koyasan 700, Koya-cho, Ito-gun, Wakayama-ken 648-0211. ℂ **0736/56-2233.** Fax 0736/56-4743. 48 units (none with bathroom). ¥9,500–¥15,750 ($90–$150) per person. Rates include 2 meals. No credit cards. Bus: Ishinguchi stop. *In room:* TV, hot-water pot w/tea, no phone.

⑭ **Shojoshinin**    This temple has a great location at the beginning of the tomb-lined pathway to Okunoin, making it convenient for your late-night stroll to the mausoleum. Originating as a thatched hut built by Kukai more than 1,150 years ago and once the second-largest temple in Koyasan after Kongobuji, today it boasts attractive 150-year-old buildings, including a large wooden structure with rooms overlooking a small garden and pond. It's usually full in August and peak seasons, so make reservations early.

Koyasan 566, Koya-cho, Ito-gun, Wakayama-ken 648-0211. ℂ **0736/56-2006.** Fax 0736/56-4770. 20 units (none with bathroom). ¥9,500–¥12,000 ($90–$114) per person. Rates include 2 meals. No credit cards. Bus: Ichinohashi. *In room:* TV (most rooms), hot-water pot w/tea, no phone in most rooms.

⑭ **Tentokuin**    The rooms of this temple, which dates from 1622, are located in a new annex. Most look out onto the garden, which in the 1930s was described as one of the most beautiful places in Japan. With a natural mountain background, the garden is of the "borrowed landscaping" style and retains its layout design dating from the Momoyama Period. Rates depend on room size and garden view. One priest speaks English.

Koyasan 370, Koya-cho, Ito-gun, Wakayama-ken 648-0211. ℂ **0736/56-2714.** Fax 0736/56-4725. 55 units (none with bathroom). ¥8,000–¥15,000 ($76–$143) per person. Rates include 2 meals. AE, V. Bus: Honzanmae or Senjuin-bashi. *In room:* TV, hot-water pot w/tea, no phone.

## 7 Himeji, A Castle Town ⭐

640km (400 miles) W of Tokyo; 130km (81 miles) W of Kyoto; 87km (54 miles) E of Okayama

The main reason tourists come to Himeji, in Hyogo Prefecture, is to see its 400-year-old beautiful **castle,** which embodies better than any other castle the best in Japan's military architecture. If you were to see only one castle in Japan, this is my pick.

Because of the castle's close proximity to Himeji Station on the Shinkansen line, many tourists stop only long enough to see the castle and a few other sites before continuing onward. I've included a few recommendations, however, for those wishing to make an overnight stop.

### ESSENTIALS

**GETTING THERE**    A stop on the **Tokaido/Sanyo Shinkansen** bullet train, which runs between Tokyo and Kyushu, Himeji is about 3½ hours from Tokyo, 1 hour from Kyoto, and a half-hour from Okayama. The fare from Tokyo is ¥14,700 ($140) for a nonreserved seat.

**VISITOR INFORMATION** The **Himeji City Tourist Information Center** (© **0792/85-3792**) is located at the central exit of the station's north (castle) side, to the left after you exit from the ticket gate. It's open daily from 9am to 5pm, but foreigners are asked to visit the center between 10am and 3:30pm when an English-speaking volunteer is on hand to answer questions. Another tourist office, **Himeji Kanko Navi Port** (© **0792/87-3658**), is located on Otemae Dori, Himeji's main road, on the right side just before the castle and is open daily from 9am to 5pm. Some tourist information is also available online at www.city.himeji.hyogo.jp and www.himeji-kanko.jp/english.

If you're stopping in Himeji only for a few hours to see the castle, deposit your luggage in the coin lockers just beside the tourist office or underneath the Shinkansen tracks.

**INTERNET ACCESS** **Jyukukan Himeji,** beside the Himeji Washington Hotel Plaza, Higashi Ekimai-cho 98 (© **0792/86-6006**), is open 24 hours and charges ¥290 ($2.75) for the first 30 minutes and then ¥100 (95¢) for each subsequent 15 minutes.

**ORIENTATION & GETTING AROUND** You can **walk** to Himeji's attractions. The main road in town is Otemae Dori, a wide boulevard that stretches from Himeji Station north to Himeji Castle (you can walk the distance in about 15 min.). To the east (right) of Otemae Dori are two parallel streets, Miyukidori and Omizusuji, both covered shopping arcades. If you want, you can use a **bicycle** free of charge from 9am to 6pm. Just fill out an application form (before 4pm) at either the station's tourist information counter or Himeji Kanko Navi Port and then exchange the ticket for a bicycle. Finally, red-painted **tourist buses** make runs on weekends and holidays 9am to 5pm every 15 to 30 minutes from Himeji Station to the castle and beyond and cost ¥100 (90¢) per ride or ¥300 ($2.85) all day.

## SEEING THE SIGHTS

**Himeji Castle** 𝕬𝕬𝕬 As soon as you exit from Himeji Station, you'll see Himeji Castle straight ahead at the end of a wide boulevard called Otemae Dori. Perhaps the most beautiful castle in all of Japan, Himeji Castle is nicknamed "White Heron Castle" in reference to its white walls, which stretch out on either side of the main donjon and resemble a white heron poised in flight over the plain. Whether it looks to you like a heron or a castle, the view of the white five-story donjon under a blue sky is striking, especially when the area's 1,000 cherry trees are in bloom. This is also one of the few castles in Japan that has remained virtually as it was since its completion in 1618, surviving even the World War II bombings that laid Himeji city in ruins. From 1956 to 1964, the castle underwent massive restoration, during which parts were totally disassembled and then rebuilt using traditional methods. In 1993 it became Japan's first listing in UNESCO's World Heritage List.

Originating as a fort in the 14th century, Himeji Castle took a more majestic form in 1581 when a three-story donjon was built by Toyotomi Hideyoshi during one of his military campaigns in the district. In the early 1600s, the castle became the residence of Ikeda Terumasa, one of Hideyoshi's generals and a son-in-law of Tokugawa Ieyasu. He remodeled the castle into its present five-story structure. With its extensive gates, three moats, turrets, and a secret entrance, it had one of the most sophisticated defense systems in Japan. The maze of passageways leading to the donjon was so complicated that intruders would find themselves trapped in dead ends. The castle walls were constructed with square or circular holes through which gun muzzles could poke;

the rectangular holes were for archers. There were also drop chutes where stones or boiling water could be dumped on enemies trying to scale the walls.

On weekends (and sometimes weekdays), volunteer guides hang around the castle ticket office who are willing to give guided tours of the castle for free. It gives them an opportunity to practice their English while you learn about the history of the castle and even old castle gossip. But even if you go on your own, you won't have any problems learning about the history of the castle since there are good English-language explanations throughout the castle grounds. With or without a guide, you'll spend at least 2 hours here. But beware, there are lots of stairs. *Tip:* A combination ticket, allowing discounted admission to both the castle and Koko-en (see below), is available at either entrance.

68 Honmachi. ✆ **0792/85-1146.** Admission ¥600 ($5.70) adults, ¥200 ($1.90) children. Combination ticket to both Himeji Castle and Koko-en ¥720 ($6.85) adults, ¥280 ($2.65) children. June–Aug daily 9am–6pm; Sept–May daily 9am–5pm. You must enter 1 hr. before closing time. A 15-min. walk straight north of Himeji Station via Otemae Dori.

(145) **Koko-en** ✿✿✿ *Finds*    Although laid out only in 1992, this is a wonderful garden, occupying land where samurai mansions once stood at the base of Himeji Castle, about a 5-minute walk away. Actually it's composed of nine separate small gardens, each one different and enclosed by traditional walls, with lots of rest areas to soak in the wonderful views. The gardens, typical of those in the Edo Period, include a garden of deciduous trees, a garden of pine trees, a garden of flowers popular during the Edo Period, tea-ceremony gardens, and traditional Japanese gardens with ponds, waterfalls, and running streams. If you wish, relax at the Souju-an teahouse in the Cha-no-niwa (tea-ceremony garden) with tea and a sweet (¥500/$4.75; open 10am–4pm) or dine at a restaurant overlooking a carp pond (see "Where to Dine," below). In any case, I wouldn't miss this special place. If you don't stop (but how could you resist?), you can stroll through all the gardens in about 45 minutes.

68 Honmachi. ✆ **0792/89-4120.** Admission ¥300 ($2.85) adults, ¥150 ($1.45) children. Combination ticket to both Himeji Castle and Koko-en ¥720 ($6.85) adults, ¥280 ($2.65) children. Daily 9am–5pm (to 6pm June–Aug). A 15-min. walk north of Himeji Station; turn left in front of Himeji Castle (the entrance will be on your right).

## A PILGRIMAGE TO MOUNT SHOSHA & ENGYOJI TEMPLE

If you're staying overnight, you might consider a half-day trip to **Mount Shosha** (called Shoshazan in Japanese; ✆ **0792/66-3327**), the 360m-high (1,200-ft.) mountain retreat of Engyoji Temple, founded more than 1,000 years ago by a holy man who received enlightenment from the God of Wisdom and Intellect. Since then, Japanese have flocked to the mountain to seek purification of both body and spirit. Many make it a fun day's outing as well, bringing obento lunch boxes with them to enjoy under the wooded trees. No doubt, the fact that scenes from *The Last Samurai* starring Tom Cruise were shot here boosted its popularity. But I like this 3- to 4-hour excursion mainly for the lovely hike. The temple buildings spread along the mountaintop are a bonus.

To reach Shoshazan, take bus no. 8 from in front of Himeji Station or Himeji Castle 25 minutes to the last stop (fare: ¥260/$2.45). From there, board a ropeway (cable car) that departs every 15 minutes and costs ¥900 ($8.55) round-trip (half price for children). Make sure to check when the last ropeway departs the mountain (5pm in winter; 6 or 7pm in summer).

After paying an admission of ¥300 ($2.85) for admission to temple grounds (children get in free), you'll walk 20 minutes to reach the Maniden, the main temple building. An impressive, cliff-side wooden structure dedicated to the Goddess of Mercy,

it was first constructed in 970, burned to the ground almost 1,000 years later, and was reconstructed in 1932. Other highlights among the many other structures spread along the mountaintop are the Jikido, a former dormitory for priests-in-training (this, together with Jogyodo and Daikodo, make up the Three Temples, where *The Last Samurai* was filmed) and the five mausolea of the Honda clan, rulers of Himeji Castle in the 17th century.

## WHERE TO STAY
### EXPENSIVE

**Hotel Nikko Himeji** ✿✿    The Nikko chain took over this existing hotel in 2005, already considered Himeji's best but now a notch higher due to renovated rooms (redone in subdued natural colors and with duvets) and better service. Of course, rates are also higher. Its location (only a 1-min. walk from Himeji Station's Shinkansen side) is a definite plus, as are its many restaurants, its top-floor lounge with a view of the castle, and its health club. In addition, some of its double rooms offer views of the castle in the distance; ask for a room on a higher floor facing north.

100 Minami-ekimai-cho, Himeji 670-0962. ✆ **0792/22-2231.** Fax 0792/24-3731. www.hotelnikkohimeji.co.jp. 257 units. ¥10,925–¥11,200 ($104–$107) single; ¥20,700–¥26,850 ($197–$256) twin; ¥20,700 ($197) double. Rates include service charge. AE, DC, MC, V. A 1-min. walk from the south (Shinkansen) exit of Himeji Station. **Amenities:** 4 restaurants (2 Japanese, 1 Chinese, 1 Western); 1 bar; 1 lounge; health club w/20m (66-ft.) indoor lane pool, sauna, whirlpool, and exercise room (fee: ¥2,000/$19); salon; in-room massage; same-day laundry/dry-cleaning service; nonsmoking rooms. *In room:* A/C, satellite TV w/pay movies, minibar, hot-water pot w/tea, hair dryer, Washlet toilet.

### MODERATE

**Claire Higasa**    This family-owned hotel is a good bet. Although distinctly a business hotel with its 50 single rooms, coin-operated fax and photocopy machine in the lobby, and soda and noodle vending machines, several pluses—like soothing music and flower arrangements in the lobby and an accommodating, English-speaking staff—take it out of the ordinary. Ask for a room with castle view on the sixth or seventh floor for the same price. The bathrooms are tiny and the shower/sink combination faucet a bit mind-boggling for the technically challenged, but who cares when the large seventh-floor public baths with Jacuzzi jets have castle views?

22 Junishomae-cho, Himeji 670-0911. ✆ **0792/24-3421.** Fax 0792/89-3729. www.hotel-higasa.com. 60 units. ¥6,720–¥7,350 ($64–$70) single; ¥13,650 ($130) twin; ¥14,700 ($140) double; ¥12,000 ($114) Japanese-style double. MC, V. Station: Himeji (north exit, 5 min.). Walk north on Otemae-Dori toward the castle and after the Shirogane intersection (the one with a large, one-way street named Junishomae Dori and a traffic light) take the next left; it's 4 short blocks farther, on the left across from a small park. **Amenities:** Restaurant (Japanese); in-room massage; coin-operated washer/dryer; same-day laundry/dry-cleaning service; nonsmoking rooms. *In room:* A/C, TV, fridge, hot-water pot w/tea, hair dryer, Washlet toilet (except in the cheapest singles).

**Himeji Washington Hotel Plaza**    The Washington is part of a chain of business hotels. Some of the staff speak a little English, and everyone is extremely helpful. Rooms are tiny but cheerful (the cheapest doubles couldn't get much tinier), with windows that open (though some face another building), panels that close for complete darkness, and slippers that, so the hotel claims, are washed after every guest's use (my goodness, what do the other hotels do?). The lobby is on the second floor, above an Internet cafe.

98 Higashi Ekimae-cho, Himeji 670-0926. ✆ **0792/25-0111.** Fax 0792/25-0133. 149 units. ¥7,800–¥8,900 ($74–$85) single; ¥15,600 ($149) twin; ¥10,500–¥15,600 ($100–$149) double. AE, DC, MC, V. A 5-min. walk from Himeji Station's north exit. Walk north from the station on Otemae Dori toward the castle; turn right at the 1st large intersection, Shirogane, on a street called Junishomae (a one-way street with a traffic light) and walk past 2 covered

shopping arcades and Starbucks; it will be on the left. **Amenities:** Restaurant (Japanese); Internet cafe; in-room massage; same-day laundry/dry-cleaning service; nonsmoking rooms. *In room:* A/C, TV w/pay movies, minibar, hot-water pot w/tea, hair dryer, Washlet toilet.

## INEXPENSIVE

**Toyoko Inn** ⏱ *Value*   This budget hotel chain beats all the rest with free use of computers in the lobby with Internet access, free domestic phone calls from lobby phones, a choice of two free movie channels nightly, and low prices. Opened in 2004 next to Himeji Station's south (Shinkansen) exit, it offers tiny rooms, with singles from the ninth floor boasting views of the castle in the distance.

97 Minami-ekimae-cho, Himeji 670-0962. ⏱ 0792/84-1045. Fax 0792/84-1046. www.toyoko-inn.com. 210 units. ¥5,880 single; ¥7,980 ($76) double or twin. Rates include free Japanese breakfast. AE, DC, MC, V. A 1-min. walk from the south (Shinkansen) exit of Himeji Station, to the left. **Amenities:** Computers w/free Internet access in the lobby; nonsmoking rooms. *In room:* A/C, TV, dataport, fridge, hot-water pot w/tea, hair dryer, safe, trouser press.

## WHERE TO DINE

Just east of Otemae Dori, the main drag from Himeji Station to the castle, is a parallel street called **Miyukidori,** a covered shopping arcade with lots of restaurants and coffee shops.

In the listings below, directions are from Himeji Station.

⑭⑥ **Asaka Sushi** SUSHI   This is sushi Himeji-style—you order by the plate, and then, using cups of sauce and brushes at your table, you brush on your sauce yourself. There's no menu at this small neighborhood eatery, very much a local place with room for only 10 patrons, but there's a display case outside. The *nigiri* will give you one sushi each of octopus, squid, shrimp, tuna, and whitefish; the *anago* is five pieces of grilled conger eel on rice; the *tekka* is eight pieces of tuna and rice rolled in nori seaweed. Each plate costs ¥400 ($4).

106 Shiroganemachi. ⏱ 0792/22-3835. Sushi ¥400 ($3.80) a plate. No credit cards. Mon–Sat 10:30am–6pm. Walk north on Otemae Dori toward the castle until you come to the 1st one-way street with a traffic light (Junishomae Dori; the intersection is called Shirogane); turn left and then right. It'll be on your left (3 min.).

⑭⑦ **Kassui-ken** ⏱ EEL/NOODLES   This charmless restaurant would not have much to recommend it except for one overwhelming feature: It overlooks a waterfall and koi pond in lovely Koko-en Garden. It's certainly the most picturesque place in town to try Himeji's specialty, conger eel. If that's too exotic, however, it also serves a few noodle dishes, spaghetti, curry rice, and fried rice. Or you can stop just for dessert or a refreshing drink of beer, soda, or coffee; but avoid the busy lunchtime crowd.

Koko-en Garden, 68 Honmachi. ⏱ 0792/89-4131. Main dishes ¥840–¥1,050 ($8–$10); set meal ¥1,575–¥2,100 ($15–$20). No credit cards. Daily 9:30am–4:30pm (10am–5:30pm June–Aug). Inside Koko-en (see "Seeing the Sights," above, for directions).

**Sainte Vierge** ⏱⏱ FRENCH   This is Himeji's fanciest place for French cuisine, with an elegant drawing-room ambience and white table-clothed tables spaced far apart for privacy. Only set meals are served, giving choices of fish, meat, or both as main courses, along with side dishes. Since this is a popular wedding venue, especially on weekends, be sure to call first to see whether it's open to the public.

Konyamachi 23. ⏱ 0792/23-1122. Set dinners ¥2,310–¥11,550 ($22–$110); set lunches ¥2,000–¥3,800 ($19–$36). AE, DC, MC, V. Wed–Mon 11:30am–2pm and 5–8pm (last order). Walk north on Otemae Dori toward the castle and take the 2nd right after the Shirogane intersection (there's a Tokyo-Mitsubishi bank here); it's past the 2 covered shopping arcades, on the right.

## 8 Okayama: Gateway to Shikoku

733km (455 miles) W of Tokyo; 218km (136 miles) W of Kyoto; 160km (100 miles) E of Hiroshima

Okayama is a major gateway to the island of Shikoku (see chapter 10), thanks to the Seto Ohashi Bridge, which measures almost 9.5km (6 miles) in length and connects Okayama Prefecture on Honshu island with Sakaide on Shikoku. Before the bridge was built in 1988, it took an hour by ferry to reach Shikoku, whereas traveling by train or car along the double-decker bridge cuts travel time down to just 15 minutes. Now there are two other bridges linking Honshu with Shikoku (one near Kobe and the other in Hiroshima Prefecture), but they're for vehicular travel only (no train service).

For those of you less interested in bridges, Okayama and its environs are important for other reasons as well. Okayama city, with a population of 1.9 million, boasts one of the most beautiful gardens in Japan. In nearby Kurashiki (see "Kurashiki, Market Town of Many Charms," beginning on p. 429), a historic quarter ranks as one of the most picturesque neighborhoods in Japan. And scattered through Okayama Prefecture are so-called **International Villas,** built by the prefecture especially for foreigners and located primarily in rural areas, with amazingly low rates.

### ESSENTIALS

**GETTING THERE**    Okayama is a major stop on the **Shinkansen** Tokaido/Sanyo Line, about 4 hours from Tokyo (fare: ¥15,850/$151 for an unreserved seat), 1 hour and 15 minutes from Kyoto (fare: ¥6,820/$65), and 50 minutes from Hiroshima (fare: ¥5,350/$51).

**Buses** (Ryobi Bus Co.; 𝄐 03/3743-0022) depart nightly from Shinjuku Station's west exit in Tokyo at 9:30pm and arrive at Okayama Station the next day at 7:50am. The fare is ¥9,800 ($93) one-way. For the same fare, you can depart from Tokyo's Shinagawa Station (Shimoden Bus Co.; 𝄐 03/5438-8511) at 9:15pm and arrive at 7:35am.

**VISITOR INFORMATION**    Before you depart Tokyo or Narita or Kansai airports, stop by the Tourist Information Center for the leaflet "Okayama, Kurashiki and Seto Ohashi Bridge," which contains useful information on train transportation to Okayama and important sights in the prefecture (you can also download it from the Japan National Tourist Organization's website at www.jnto.go.jp by looking under *Regional Tourist Guides*). In Okayama, the **Okayama City Tourist Information Office** (𝄐 086/222-2912; open daily 9am–6pm) is inside Okayama Station near the central exit of the east side (look for the sign displaying a question mark). The office is well prepared for foreign visitors, supplying English-language maps of Okayama and Kurashiki as well as brochures.

Just a 4-minute walk from Okayama Station is the **Okayama International Center,** 2–2–1 Hokancho (𝄐 086/256-2000; open Tues–Sun 9am–5pm), where you can get more detailed information, obtain a better map of Okayama than those available at the station, take classes, and log onto the Internet. Although geared mainly toward foreign residents, classes that accept one-timers include instruction in tea ceremony, Japanese cooking, Japanese language, ikebana, and aikido. Check with the International Center for availability, times, and prices. The multilingual staff here is very helpful and is happy to steer you to Okayama Prefecture's International Villas, your hotel, or your next destination. To find the center, take the west exit of the station and turn right (north) onto the main street running in front of the station until you come to a 7-Eleven, where you should turn left; the center is the big building on your right.

More information on Okayama is available on the Internet at **www.pref.okayama.jp** and **www.city.okayama.okayama.jp**.

**INTERNET ACCESS**    You can check and send e-mail at the Okayama International Center (see "Visitor Information," above) free of charge, but you're limited to 30 minutes of usage. Be aware, too, that you may have to reserve the center's two computers in advance for busy times, or be prepared to wait.

**GETTING AROUND**    Okayama's sights are all clustered within walking distance of each other, due east of Okayama Station. The easiest way to sightsee is to board a **streetcar** from Okayama Station's east side bound for Higashiyama (platform 1) and disembark about 8 minutes later at the Shiroshita streetcar stop (the third stop; to your right will be the very noticeable Okayama Symphony Hall building). Pay the ¥100 (95¢) fare when you get off. From here you can continue walking straight ahead (east) 8 minutes to Okayama Castle and then visit nearby Korakuen Garden and the Yumeji Art Museum.

## SEEING THE SIGHTS

**Korakuen Garden** ✿✿✿    Okayama's claim to fame is this garden, considered one of Japan's three most beautiful landscaped gardens (the other two are in Kanazawa and Mito). Completed in 1700 by the Ikeda ruling clan after 14 years of work, its 11 hectares (28 acres) are graced with a pond, running streams, pine trees, plum and cherry trees, flowering bushes like azaleas and hydrangeas, bamboo groves, teahouses, and tea plantations. The surrounding hills, as well as Okayama's famous black castle, are incorporated into the garden's design. Its name, Korakuen, means "the garden for taking pleasure later," which has its origins in an old saying: "Bear sorrow before the people; take pleasure after them." This garden differs from most Japanese gardens in that it has large expanses of grassy open areas—the first Japanese garden to do so and still a rarity in crowded Japan. Other unusual features worth seeking out are the Ryuten, a wooden pavilion that straddles a stream where poem-composing parties were held (participants had to complete poems before a cup of sake floated by), and an enclosure of red-crested cranes. You can easily spend an hour here.

1–5 Korakuen. ✆ **086/272-1148**. Admission ¥350 ($3.35) adults, ¥140 ($1.35) children, free for seniors. Combination ticket to Okayama Castle and Korakuen Garden ¥520 ($4.95) adults, ¥260 ($2.45) children. Apr–Sept daily 7:30am–6pm; Oct–Mar daily 8am–5pm. Streetcar stop: Shiroshita (11 min.). Continue walking straight east and then turn left for the footbridge.

**Okayama Castle** *(Overrated*    Originally built in the 16th century, Okayamajo was destroyed in World War II and rebuilt in 1966. Thanks to its black exterior, it has earned the nickname "Crow Castle"; it was painted black to contrast with neighboring Himeji's famous White Heron castle. Unlike castles of yore, an elevator whisks you up to the fourth floor of the donjon. The top floor affords a good view of the park and the city beyond, while the other floors contain a few swords, samurai outfits, lacquerware, and other Edo-Period items, most identified in Japanese only and quickly seen in 15 minutes or so. There's also a children's play area with old-fashioned toys, but probably the most rewarding thing to do here is to try on a kimono and have someone snap a picture of you with your own camera. Donning costumes is free, but only five participants are accepted at 10am, 11am, 1pm, 2pm, and 3pm. Frankly, if you've seen other Japanese castles, you might just want to photograph this one from the outside and move on. For a fairy-tale fantasy indulgence, you can rent swan-shaped paddle boats on the river below the castle (just be glad your neighbors aren't here to see you).

## Kids  Joypolis

If you have children in tow, you might want to temper Okayama's cultural offerings with some good old-fashioned fun at **Joypolis,** 2–10–1 Shimoishii (© **086/232-8790;** open daily 10am–midnight), a chain of Japan's most sophisticated and largest video-game arcades. In addition to a toddler's play area, pachinko, video games, virtual horse races, and simulators (how good are you at skateboarding or racing cars?), there are 3-D motion rides and other amusements. Entry is free, with most attractions individually priced between ¥300 and ¥600 ($2.85–$5.70). With or without kids, it's worth at least visiting one of these eye-opening arcades while you're in Japan. *Note:* You must be 17 or older to stay after 6pm and 19 or older to stay after 10pm.

2–3–1 Marunouchi. © 086/225-2096. Admission ¥300 ($2.85) adults, ¥120 ($1.15) children. Combination ticket to Okayama Castle and Korakuen Garden ¥520 ($4.95) adults, ¥260 ($2.45) children. Special exhibits cost more. Daily 9am–5pm. Streetcar: Shiroshita stop (8 min.). Continue walking east; it will be on your right.

(148) **Yumeji Art Museum (Yumeji-Kyodo Bijutsukan)**    This museum, in a brick building topped by a cock weathervane just a few minutes' walk north of Korakuen, is dedicated to the works of Yumej Takehisa. Born in Okayama Prefecture in 1884, Yumeji is sometimes referred to as Japan's Toulouse-Lautrec and is credited with developing the *fin de siècle* Art Nouveau movement in Japan. This collection includes some of his most famous works, mostly in the sparse, Nihonga style of painting. Beautiful women were his favorite subjects. The small three-room exhibition can be toured in about 15 minutes.

2–1–32 Hama. © 086/271-1000. Admission ¥700 ($6.65) adults, ¥400 ($3.80) students, ¥300 ($2.85) children. Tues–Sun 9am–5pm. Streetcar: Shiroshita stop (15 min.). Just north of Korakuen Park, a short walk across Horai-bashi Bridge.

## SHOPPING

You can choose from a sampling of products and crafts made in Okayama Prefecture at the (149) **Okayama Prefectural Product Center (Okayama-ken Kanko Bussan Sen-ta),** 1–5–1 Omotecho (© **086/234-2270;** open daily 10am–8pm, closed second Tues each month), conveniently located beside (south of) the Shiroshita streetcar stop on the first floor of Okayama Symphony Hall (a round purple building). Bizen pottery (unglazed pottery with a history stretching back 1,000 years), rush-grass mats *(igusa),* wooden trays, spirits, papier-mâché toys, and more are all for sale here. There is also an information counter and videos (in Japanese only) about Okayama Prefecture here.

For general shopping, there's a large underground shopping arcade called **Ichibangai** at Okayama Station, with boutiques selling clothing, shoes, and accessories. Across from the station and connected to Ichibangai is **Takashimaya** department store. In the heart of the city, just south of Shiroshita streetcar stop, is the 1km (½-mile) **Omotecho** covered shopping arcade, where you'll find **Tenmaya,** Okayama's largest department store.

## WHERE TO STAY
### EXPENSIVE
**Hotel Granvia Okayama** 🐾🐾    Owned by the East JR Railway Group and offering a discount for holders of a Japan Rail Pass, this is Okayama's best hotel in terms of luxury and location. Although connected to Okayama Station and the Ichibangai shopping center, it's probably easier to find if you go out the Central exit and look for

it on your right. Rooms are large, with the best city views offered by the more expensive twins and doubles. Most singles face another building. Some 18 rooms are for women only and offer special amenities. Among the hotel's several food-and-beverage outlets, best are those on the 19th floor with great views; among these, Applause, a classy cocktail lounge with a curved window facade, is a favorite for evening drinks (but note that there's a ¥1,050/$10 music cover charge after 8pm).

1–5 Ekimoto-cho, Okayama 700-8515. © 086/234-7000. Fax 086/234-7099. www.hotels.westjr.co.jp. 328 units. ¥8,925–¥15,750 ($85–$150) single; ¥23,100–¥24,150 ($220–$230) double; ¥17,850–¥31,500 ($170–$300) twin. 10% discount for JR Pass holders. AE, DC, MC, V. Connected to Okayama Station's east side by direct walkway (1 min.). **Amenities:** 5 restaurants; 1 bar; 2 lounges; 20m (66-ft.) indoor pool, sauna, and Jacuzzi (fee: ¥1,600/$15); concierge; shopping arcade; florist; salon; room service (6:30am–11:30pm); in-room massage; same-day laundry/dry-cleaning service; nonsmoking rooms. *In room:* A/C, satellite TV, dataport, minibar, hot-water pot w/tea, hair dryer, Washlet toilet.

## MODERATE

**Ark**    Although this hotel with a good location near Okayama Station has a mostly business clientele, its spacious lobby is classier than in most business hotels and the staff is used to foreign guests. Rooms, however, are small, with only a tiny recessed alcove for the closet. The cheapest singles have a semi-double-size bed, while the more expensive ones have a double bed. Ask for a room on a higher floor with its better night view.

2–6–1 Shimoishii, Okayama 700-0907. © 086/233-2200. Fax 086/225-1663. http://okayama.ark-hotel.co.jp. 183 units. ¥8,100–¥8,700 ($77–$83) single; ¥15,100–¥16,200 ($144–$154) twin; ¥15,100 ($144) double. AE, DC, MC, V. A 7-min. walk southeast of Okayama Station (behind Hotel Granvia). Take the central (east) exit and then turn right (south) onto Shiyakusho-suji until you come to a gas station, where you should turn right; the Ark will be on your left. **Amenities:** 2 restaurants (Japanese, Continental); 1 bar; 1 lounge; in-room massage; same-day laundry/dry-cleaning service; nonsmoking rooms. *In room:* A/C, TV, fridge, hot-water pot w/tea, hair dryer, Washlet toilet.

**Mitsui Garden** ⚘    Opened in 2000 near Okayama Station, this smart-looking business hotel distinguishes itself from most in this category with handsome public baths and rooms that are small but with an upbeat color scheme and modern decor. There are mostly singles and a few twins; since most face another building, you might want to request one that doesn't. There's a coin-operated fax, copy machine, and computer with free Internet connections off the lobby.

1–7 Ekimoto-cho, Okayama 70-0024. © 086/235-1131. Fax 086/225-8831. 352 units. ¥6,900–¥8,500 ($66–$81) single; ¥15,200–¥16,800 ($145–$160) twin. AE, DC, MC, V. A 2-min. walk southeast of Okayama Station. Take the central (east) exit and turn right; it's behind Hotel Granvia. **Amenities:** Buffet restaurant open only for breakfast (Japanese/Western); in-room massage; same-day laundry/dry-cleaning service; nonsmoking rooms. *In room:* A/C, TV w/pay movies, dataports, fridge, hot-water pot w/tea, hair dryer, Washlet toilet.

**Okayama International Hotel** ⚘⚘ *(Value)*    This Western-style hotel (called the "Kokusai Hotel" in Japanese) is located on a hill above the city and has a resortlike holiday atmosphere. It's surrounded by greenery, and the lobby has a restful view of wooded hills and a waterfall. The lobby also boasts an impressive four-story wall made of Bizen-yaki ceramic tiles, for which Okayama Prefecture is famous. Comfortable, larger-than-average rooms face either the city or woods. City views are more dramatic; these rooms come with a map to help you pick out the speck of the castle, which you can just barely see if you squint. No matter—the night views are even better. Restaurants also take advantage of the hotel's location with views of either greenery or city panoramas; best is the French L'Arc en Ciel (see "Where to Dine," below). The main drawback to staying here is one of access—there are free shuttle buses from the station but only in the evenings (at 6:30pm, 7:30pm, and 8:40pm) and the no. 12 bus from Okayama Station's no. 9 platform to the hotel departs only nine times a day.

4–1–16 Kadota Honmachi, Okayama 703-8274. © **086/273-7311**. Fax 086/271-0292. www.oih.co.jp. 175 units. ¥7,500–¥14,000 ($71–$133) single; ¥16,500–¥25,000 ($157–$238) twin; ¥16,500–¥21,000 ($157–$200) double. Rates include service charge. AE, DC, MC, V. Taxi: 15 min. **Amenities:** 4 restaurants (French, Japanese, Chinese, coffee shop); 1 bar; salon; room service (6:30pm–9pm); in-room massage; same-day laundry/dry-cleaning service. *In room:* A/C, TV, minibar, hot-water pot w/tea, hair dryer.

## INEXPENSIVE

⑮ **Abis Inn** *Value*   Spotlessly clean and newly opened in 2005, this personable, small business hotel goes out of its way to make you feel welcome, despite the fact that not much English is spoken. Because it's off the beaten tourist track (10 min. by streetcar from Okayama Station), it's more reasonably priced than more conveniently located lodging and offers rooms with fluffy quilts and free Internet connections. All the singles offer semi-double beds and twin rooms have a double bed and a semi-double, making them practical for families. However, tiny bathrooms have no counter space and desk space is also limited, which is okay if you don't plan to unpack.

1–3–10 Daiku, Okayama 700-0913. © **086/234-6000**. Fax 086/234-6001. 104 units. ¥4,980 ($47) single; ¥7,980 ($76) twin; ¥9,480 ($90) triple. Rates include continental breakfast. No credit cards. Streetcar: Daiunji (2 min. west). Or a 15-min walk southeast of the station (walk south on Shiyakusho-suji past Joypolis, cross the 6-lane intersection and turn left; it's 2 blocks down, on the right before the river). **Amenities:** Coin-operated laundry; same-day laundry/dry-cleaning service; nonsmoking rooms. *In room:* A/C, TV w/pay movies, dataport, fridge, hot-water pot w/tea, hair dryer, Washlet toilet.

⑮ **Matsunoki Ryokan** *Finds*   This family-owned enterprise welcomes foreigners and gives them (to my mind) special treatment. Although it offers rooms with and without bathrooms in a cluster of three buildings, foreigners are automatically given rooms in the newer, main building, all with bathrooms at a price normally given to bathroomless units (only if accommodations in the main building are full, which rarely happens, are foreigners shunted to the older buildings). Spotless rooms are mostly Japanese style, though three Western-style rooms are available, with glazed windows that open. The owners are earnestly learning English and offer a small gift to those who make reservations through Matsunoki's Web home page. Meals are served in a cheerful communal dining hall (Western breakfasts are available), but even better is the ryokan's nearby Matsunoki-Tei (see "Where to Dine," below). You'll like this place, especially since they will do your laundry for free.

19–1 Ekimoto-machi, Okayama 700-0024. © **086/253-4111**. Fax 086/253-4110. ww3.tiki.ne.jp/~matunoki. 58 units (24 with bathroom). ¥5,000 ($48) single with bathroom; ¥8,000 ($76) twin with bathroom (foreigners are only put in rooms with bathrooms). Breakfast ¥600 ($5.70) extra; dinner ¥1,300 ($12) extra. No credit cards. Station: Okayama (west exit, 2 min.). Walk west on the street to the north of NHK; it's just past the New Station Hotel, on the right. **Amenities:** Restaurant (Japanese); room service (3pm–10:50pm); coin-op washer and dryer; free same-day laundry service for clothes that do not need ironing. *In room:* A/C, TV w/free videos, hot-water pot w/tea, hair dryer.

## WHERE TO DINE

Okayama's most famous dish is Okayama *barazushi,* which features Seto Inland Sea delicacies and fresh mountain vegetables. Traditionally served during festive occasions, it consists of a rice casserole laced with shredded ginger and cooked egg yolk and is topped with a variety of goodies, including conger eel, shrimp, fish, lotus root, and bamboo.

## EXPENSIVE

**L'Arc en Ciel** *FRENCH*   For a memorable meal in a romantic, intimate setting, head for L'Arc en Ciel, which sits atop a hill in the Okayama International Hotel (see "Where to Stay," above) with sweeping views of the city—beautiful at sunset.

## *Value*  Countryside Delights: Okayama Prefecture's International Villas

If you're not on a tight schedule and you don't mind roughing it a bit, you might consider treating yourself to a few days in the countryside around Okayama at one of the prefecture's **International Villas**. Financed and maintained by the Okayama Prefectural Government, these small country inns are the brainstorm of a former Okayama governor, who wished to repay the kindness he received from foreigners during his trips abroad as a youth. Thus, these villas are open only to foreigners, though accompanying Japanese guests are welcome.

Altogether, there are five International Villas, most in small villages or in rural settings 1 to 2 hours by train or bus from Okayama city. One, modeled after a traditional soy-sauce warehouse, is located in a mountain village named **Fukiya,** an old copper-mining town that has changed little since the mid–19th century. In **Hattoji,** accommodations are in a 19th-century renovated thatched farmhouse. In **Ushimado,** you'll stay in a modern exposed-beam villa with sweeping views of the Seto Inland Sea—this one's probably the most popular among young backpackers craving isolation (though beware; it's a long, steep hike from the bus stop). Also offering great views is the villa on **Shiraishi Island** in the Seto Inland Sea, which features beaches, shrines, hiking trails, and accommodations in an airy glass-and-wooden building. In **Takebe,** known for its adjoining hot-springs bathhouse, you'll stay in an innovative wooden building designed to resemble a traditional wooden barge. All of these villas are remarkable; how wonderful it would be if other prefectures took a cue from Okayama and started building similar affordable lodgings!

Each villa is small, with only a half-dozen or so simply furnished guest rooms (only those in Ushimado and Takebe have private bathroom), and is outfitted with kitchen facilities so you can cook your own meals if you'd like a break from eating out (no meals are served), though you should do your grocery shopping before arriving at the villa, since stores may not be close at hand.

If these villas were privately owned, you'd easily pay more than twice what you'll be charged. The cost of staying at an International Villa is only ¥3,000 ($29) per person for nonmembers, ¥2,500 ($24) for members (add ¥500/$4.75 for single occupancy). Children under 7 stay for free. Membership cards are easily available for ¥500 ($4.75) upon check-in at any villa—certainly worth it if you're staying more than 1 night. Reservations can be made up to 2 months in advance by contacting the **Okayama International Center,** 2-2-1 Hokancho, Okayama 700-0026; or by calling © **086/256-2535** from 9am to noon and 1 to 5pm (Japan time) Tuesday through Sunday (if Mon is a public holiday, it remains open but closes Tues instead); you can also fax the center at 086/256-2576. More information is available via the Internet at www.harenet.ne.jp/villa.

Chef Yuasa Shigeo, who learned his craft in France, creates imaginative seasonal menus. Dishes are works of art, creative and fun; I was surprised to see the filet of sole in white-cream sauce arrive with a small squid and a shrimp and topped with shredded crab and carrots. Another time, I opted for steak in a red-wine sauce, cooked to perfection and served with tomato stuffed with ratatouille—with a clean, hollow beef bone serving as a cup for chives and other condiments. If you can't decide, the Chef's Menu for ¥4,500 ($43) offers very good value. This restaurant is a bit out-of-the-way, but it's worth it.

Okayama International (Kokusai) Hotel, 13th floor, 4–1–16 Kadota Honmachi. ✆ **086/273-7311.** Reservations recommended. Main dishes ¥3,500–¥5,800 ($33–$55); set dinner ¥9,000–¥12,000 ($86–$114); set lunch ¥4,500–¥7,000 ($43–$67). Rates include service charge. AE, DC, MC, V. Tues–Sun 11:30am–2pm and 6–10pm. Free shuttle at 6:30pm, 7:30pm, and 8:40pm from Okayama Station, or a 15-min. taxi ride.

## MODERATE

⑮ **Matsunoki-Tei** 🎔🎔 (Value) KAISEKI/SHABU-SHABU  The family who has long run the inexpensive Matsunoki ryokan (see "Where to Stay," above) also owns this very refined Japanese restaurant, located in an older house in a beautiful traditional setting. Dining here is a luxurious experience, as you sit in a private tatami room (some with leg wells under the table) and enjoy well-prepared dishes brought by an efficient and courteous staff. Although kaiseki is one of the most expensive meals you can have in Japan, it's quite reasonable here, and the all-you-can-eat shabu-shabu has a 2-hour time limit (indicate whether you want kaiseki or shabu-shabu when making your reservation). Even more economical are the obento lunch boxes for ¥1,700 ($16) and more elaborate mini-kaiseki lunches.

20–1 Ekimotomachi. ✆ **086/253-5410.** Reservations required by noon for evening meals. Kaiseki ¥3,500–¥10,000 ($33–$95); all-you-can-eat shabu-shabu ¥3,400 ($32); set lunches ¥1,700–¥4,000 ($16–$38). No credit cards. Daily 11am–2pm and 5–10pm. See Matsunoki (under "Where to Stay," above) for directions.

**Okayama Plaza** WESTERN/JAPANESE  For Western fare near the castle and Korakuen, head for the Okayama Plaza Hotel's ninth-floor restaurant, which has the added benefit of castle views. Steak and sole are on the menu, as well as less expensive pasta dishes and sandwiches. Some Japanese set meals are also available, including a tempura set and an obento lunch box (Makunouchi Bento; ¥2,500/$24). Or, if it's not crowded, you can come just for a drink. This is a nice place to relax after a day of sightseeing.

Okayama Plaza Hotel, 2–3–12 Hama. ✆ **086/272-1201.** Main dishes ¥850–¥1,500 ($8–$14); set lunches ¥1,800–¥2,500 ($17–$24); set dinners ¥1,800–¥5,500 ($17–$52). AE, DC, MC, V. Daily 7am–8:30pm. Bus: Okaden bus from gate 5 to Yumeiji-kyodo Bijutsukan-mae (1 min.). Streetcar stop: Shiroshita (15 min.). Just north of Korakuen Park, a short walk across Horai-bashi Bridge.

**Petite Mariée** 🎔 FRENCH  Brick walls, a beamed ceiling, French music, a large bouquet of flowers, and numerous European knickknacks set the mood at the tiny Petite Mariée, which serves inexpensive yet good French food. The set meals change monthly, but my ¥1,050 ($10) set lunch consisted of creamy mushroom potage, bread, seafood soufflé, vegetables, and coffee or tea. A glass of wine with lunch costs only ¥105 ($1) extra. Unfortunately, set meals are written in Japanese only (though the main dishes of set meals are displayed outside), while the a la carte menu, which may include roast lamb or scallops, is in French. Nevertheless, this is a civilized place for a meal.

1–3–8 Yanagimachi. ✆ **086/222-9066.** Main dishes ¥1,700–¥4,500 ($16–$43); set lunches ¥1,050–¥2,100 ($10–$20); set dinners ¥2,650–¥8,950 ($25–$85). MC, V. Thurs–Tues 11:30am–2pm and 5–9pm (last order). Station:

Okayama (a 5-min. walk southeast). Take the central (east) exit, turning right (south) onto Shiyakusho-suji; go 1 block past the gas station (it will be on your right) and turn left onto Akura Dori. It's 2 blocks farther on your right.

## INEXPENSIVE

In addition to the choices below, there are some inexpensive, rustic snack houses along the moat that separates Okayama Castle and Korakuen Garden, at Tsukimi Bridge, where you can order a drink, noodles, or ice cream and relax with a view of the castle. Most are open daily 8:30am to 5pm (to 4:30pm in winter).

(153) **Okabe** *(Finds)* TOFU    This informal eatery in the heart of Okayama is a local institution, popular for its specialty, homemade tofu. There's no problem ordering since it serves only two teishoku: one with two kinds of tofu along with soup, rice, and pickled vegetables, the other a *donburi* (rice bowl) topped with *namayuba*, a kind of tofu. Seating is along one long counter, behind which an army of women scurry to get out orders. It's simple but atmospheric.

1–10–1 Omotecho. (C) **086/222-1404.** Tofu teishoku ¥700 ($6.65), donburi ¥750 ($7.15). No credit cards. Mon–Sat 11:30am–2pm. Closed national holidays. Streetcar: Shiroshita (2 min.). Walk south through the Omotecho covered shopping arcade to the stoplight and turn right (west); it's on the left, on a corner.

(154) **Shikisai** VARIED JAPANESE    Located just outside the entrance to Korakuen Garden (its name translates as Four Seasons of Color), this modern restaurant is decorated with Bizen pottery and Japanese ikebana and is a good place to try Okayama specialties, including *barazushi* (¥1,575/$15) and seasonal dishes like *nabe* (a one-pot stew eaten in winter), *anago* (sea eel), and mountain vegetables, as well as soba and udon noodles. Minikaiseki are available for lunch. The menu is written in Japanese only, so look at what others are eating. Top it off with Doppo, a locally brewed beer.

1–5 Korakuen-gaien. (C) **086/273-3221.** Reservations required for dinner. Main dishes ¥1,000–¥1,900 ($9.50–$18); set lunches ¥1,155–¥1,890 ($11–$18); set dinners from ¥5,000 ($48). No credit cards. Daily 11am–2pm and 6–10pm. Streetcar: Shiroshita (11 min.). Located just north of the main entrance gate, next to a souvenir shop.

(155) **Yamadome** *(Finds)* KUSHIKATSU    This 35-year-old restaurant was recently renovated and now sports a classy modern interior, classical music, and local artist's work on the walls. It serves fried foods on a stick, from beef to fish to vegetables. The menu is in Japanese only, but the owner speaks English. A 10-stick kushikatsu course will set you back ¥1,350 ($13).

1–22 Tenjincho. (C) **086/224-6886.** Kushikatsu sticks ¥110–¥170 ($1.05–$1.60); set lunches ¥630–¥1,270 ($6–$12); kushikatsu sets ¥1,350–¥2,290 ($13–$22). No credit cards. Mon–Sat 11am–2:30pm and 5–9pm. Closed 1 week in mid-Aug. Streetcar: Shiroshita (1 min.). Just north of the streetcar stop, across the small street from the gas station (which you can see from the stop).

## 9 Kurashiki, Market Town of Many Charms ★★★

26km (16 miles) W of Okayama

If I were to select the most picturesque town in Japan, **Kurashiki** would certainly be a top contender. Here, in the heart of the city, clustered around a willow-fringed canal, is a delightful area of old buildings and ryokan perfect for camera buffs.

As an administrative center of the shogunate in the 17th century, Kurashiki blossomed into a prosperous market town where rice, sake, and cotton were collected from the surrounding region and shipped off to Osaka and beyond. Back in those days, wealth was measured in rice; large granaries were built to store the mountains of granules passing through the town, and canals were dug so that barges laden with grain

could work their way to ships anchored in the Seto Inland Sea. Kurashiki, in fact, means "Warehouse Village."

It's these warehouses, still standing, that give Kurashiki its distinctive charm. Kurashiki is also known throughout Japan for its art museums, including the prestigious Ohara Museum of Art with its collection of European and Japanese art. For these reasons, Kurashiki is hardly undiscovered, and Japanese flock here in droves, especially in summer months. Yet despite its overcrowdedness, Kurashiki still rates high on my list of places to see in Japan.

## ESSENTIALS

**GETTING THERE  By Train**   If you're arriving in Kurashiki by **Shinkansen** (which takes about 4½ hr. from Tokyo, excluding transfers, and almost 2 hr. from Kyoto), you'll arrive at **Shin-Kurashiki Station,** about 9.5km (6 miles) west of **Kurashiki Station** and the heart of the city; the **local train** that runs between the two stations departs about every 15 minutes and takes 9 minutes. However, because there are no through Shinkansen trains from Tokyo directly to Shin-Kurashiki Station (except for the Nozomi, which does not accept the JR Rail Pass; all others require a change of trains in Okayama), because not all Shinkansen trains stop in Kurashiki, and because Shin-Kurashiki Station is not the town's most convenient station for sightseeing, if you're coming from the east it's much easier to disembark from the Shinkansen in Okayama and transfer to a local train for the 12-minute ride directly to Kurashiki Station.

**By Bus**   The same buses that depart from Tokyo's Shinjuku and Shinagawa stations for Okayama (see "Okayama: Gateway to Shikoku" on p. 422) continue onward to Kurashiki, arriving in Kurashiki about 40 minutes after their Okayama stop and costing ¥10,000 ($95) one-way.

**VISITOR INFORMATION**   There's a tourist information office on the second floor of **Kurashiki Station** (© 086/426-8681) near the ticket wicket, with English-language maps and a leaflet, "Stroll around Kurashiki." Another information office, called the **Kurashiki-Kan** (© 086/422-0542), is right on the canal in the historic district; ironically the only Western-looking wooden building in the area (built in 1916), it also distributes a map and brochure and has a rest area with tables and vending machines. Both offices are open daily from 9am to 6pm (to 5pm in winter).

**ORIENTATION**   The willow-lined canal, called the **Bikan Historical Area,** is only a 10-minute walk from Kurashiki Station; take the south exit and walk south on Chuo Dori, turning left just before the Kurashiki Kokusai Hotel. In fact, you can walk virtually everywhere of interest in Kurashiki; the Bikan Historical Area is zoned mostly for pedestrians.

## EXPLORING THE BIKAN HISTORICAL AREA & ENVIRONS

Kurashiki's **historic old town** is centered on a canal lined with graceful willows and 200-year-old granaries made of black-tile walls topped with white mortar. Many of the granaries have been turned into museums, ryokan, restaurants, and boutiques selling hand-blown glass, Bizen pottery, papier-mâché toys, women's ethnic clothing imported from Bali and India, and mats and handbags made of *igusa* (rush grass), a local specialty. Street vendors sell jewelry, their wares laid out beside the canal, and healthy young boys stand ready to give visitors rides in rickshaws.

A resident advised me that, because of the crowds that descend upon Kurashiki during the day (about four million tourists come here a year), I should get up early in the

morning before the shops and museums open and explore this tiny area while it's still under the magic spell of the early-morning glow. "Real lovers of Kurashiki come on Monday," he added. "Because that's when most everything is closed, and there are fewer people." I've found that early evening is also a magical time to walk the streets.

Do try to avoid weekends, but no matter when you come, you're likely to fall under the city's spell. One of the most rewarding things to do in Kurashiki is simply explore; even rain only enhances the contrasting black and white of the buildings.

## THE MUSEUMS & OTHER SIGHTS

**Kurashiki Folkcraft Museum (Kurashiki Mingei-Kan)**    Under the slogan USABILITY EQUALS BEAUTY, this museum contains folkcrafts not only from Japan but from various other countries as well, giving unique insight into their cultural similarities and differences as reflected in the items they make and use in daily life. Spread through three old rice granaries, displays include baskets made of straw, bamboo, and willow, as well as ceramics, glass, textiles, and woodwork from China, Korea, Taiwan, Indonesia, India, Mexico, Sweden, England, Portugal, Spain, Greece, Germany, and Japan. Even though not all items are identified in English, you'll appreciate their beauty. Plan on spending about 30 minutes here.

1–4–11 Chuo. ✆ **086/422-1637.** Admission ¥700 ($6.65) adults, ¥400 ($3.80) university and high-school students, ¥300 ($2.85) children. Tues–Sun 9am–5pm (to 4:15pm Dec–Feb). On the canal, beside the Kurashiki-Kan tourist office.

**Japan Rural Toy Museum (Nihon Kyodogangu-Kan)** ⚐★★ ⚐Kids    Almost next to the Folkcraft Museum is this museum with its delightful and colorful display of traditional and antique toys, mostly from Japan but from other countries as well (the United States is represented by a cornhusk doll and a Raggedy Ann, among others). Opened in 1967, it has an astounding 12,000 items crammed into six rooms, including kites (200 of them!), miniature floats, antique Japanese dolls, masks, and spinning tops. Incidentally, the huge top in the corner helped the owner of the museum gain entry into the *Guinness World Book of Records*—by spinning 1 hour, 8 minutes, and 57 seconds. You can tour the museum in much less time than that—30 or 40 minutes. A large store at the entrance sells great traditional Japanese toys.

1–4–16 Chuo. ✆ **086/422-8058.** Admission ¥500 ($4.75) adults, ¥300 ($2.85) junior-high and high-school students, ¥200 ($1.90) children. Daily 9am–5pm. On the canal.

**Ohara Museum of Art (Ohara Bijutsukan)** ⚐★★★    This is by far Kurashiki's most impressive museum, a must-see even on a short list of sightseeing. Ohara Magosaburo, who believed that even people in remote Kurashiki should have the opportunity to view great works of art, founded it in 1930 as Japan's first museum of Western art. The main building, a two-story stone structure resembling a Greek temple, is small but manages to contain the works of such greats as Picasso, Matisse, Vlaminck, Chagall, Manet, Monet, Degas, Pissarro, Sisley, Toulouse-Lautrec, Gauguin, Cézanne, El Greco, Renoir, Kandinsky, Klee, Pollack, Jasper Johns, Oldenburg, Frank Stella, Rothko, De Kooning, and Hundertwasser. The museum has expanded so much since its founding that several annexes have been added over the years. A crafts gallery housed in a renovated granary contains works by some of my favorites, including ceramics by Hamada Shoji, Bernard Leach, and Kawai Kanjiro; and woodblock prints by Munakata Shiko, who lived in Kurashiki 3 years. Another building is devoted to Japanese artists painting in the Western style and to contemporary Japanese artists, which makes for a fascinating comparison. Yet another building displays ancient

Chinese art, primarily from prehistoric times to the Tang Dynasty (A.D. 618–907). Allow 1½ hours to see everything, but since your ticket is good all day, you don't have to see it all at once. An audio guide, which will direct you to the most important works in the main gallery, is available for ¥510 ($4.85).

1–1–15 Chuo. (📞 **086/422-0005.** Admission ¥1,000 ($9.50) adults, ¥600 ($5.70) university and senior-high students, and ¥500 ($4.75) children. Tues–Sun 9am–5pm. On the canal.

⑮⑥ **Ohashi House (Ohashi-tei)**   Built in 1796 by a wealthy rice merchant, this traditional mansion is typical of the era, with front rooms used for business and the entertaining of guests, and the rear used as family living quarters. On display are Ohashi family heirlooms, but otherwise the rooms are fairly empty. It's the only merchant's house open to the public, but come for a 15-minute spin through if you've never seen the inside of a traditional Japanese home.

3–21–31 Achi. (📞 **086/422-0007.** Admission ¥500 ($4.75) adults, ¥300 ($2.85) seniors and children. Tues–Sun 9am–5pm. Across Chuo Dori from the Bikan Historical Area, behind the Nikko Hotel.

## IVY SQUARE

A few minutes' walk from the canal and museums is a complex called **Kurashiki Ivy Square,** 7–1 Honmachi. Built as a cotton mill by a local spinning company in 1888, this handsome redbrick complex shrouded in ivy has been renovated into a hotel, restaurants, museums, and a few boutiques and galleries selling crafts. It's especially romantic in the evening when, from mid-June to the end of August, there's a beer garden in the inner courtyard (open daily 6–9:30pm) and classical music wafts from loudspeakers built into the courtyard's brick floors.

Museums at Ivy Square include **Kurabo Memorial Hall** (📞 086/422-0011), which depicts the history of the old spinning company, Kurashiki's biggest employer for decades and providing jobs for many young women in the area; and **Kojima Torajiro Memorial Hall** (📞 086/422-0010), named for and displaying paintings by the local artist who went to Europe to purchase most of the pieces in the Ohara museum. Both are open Tuesday to Sunday from 9am to 5pm and admission to each is ¥350 ($3.35) for adults and ¥200 ($1.90) for students; a joint ticket costs ¥600 ($5.70) and ¥400 ($3.80) respectively. Most unique, however, in my opinion, is the ⑮⑦ **Orgel Musée** (📞 086/427-3904), where 30-minute concerts on 30 antique organs, player pianos, and music boxes from Europe, the United States, and Japan take place. You must enter on the hour, at 10am, 11am, 1pm, 2pm, 3pm, 4pm, and 5pm. Admission is ¥500 ($4.75) for adults and ¥300 ($2.85) for children.

## ESPECIALLY FOR KIDS

**Tivoli Park** (Kids)   This branch of Copenhagen's Tivoli Park imitates the real thing with reproduction 19th-century buildings, flower beds, shows, and rides, including a Ferris wheel, carousel, roller coaster, kiddie rides, 3-D motion theater, and water slide. Even a copy of the Little Mermaid herself is here. What makes it particularly attractive is that it's only a minute's walk from Kurashiki Station and, except during Golden Week and mid-August, is hardly ever crowded. Young Japanese come here on dates, when it's all lit up at night.

12–1 Kotobuki Cho. (📞 **086/434-1111.** Admission for everything ¥3,900 ($37) adults, ¥3,600 ($34) high-school students, ¥2,700 ($26) junior-high and primary students, ¥800 ($7.60) children 4–5 years. Generally daily 10am–8pm, but varies with the season. Closed end of Jan/beginning of Feb. Station: Kurashiki (north exit, 1 min.).

# WHERE TO STAY

## EXPENSIVE

**Hotel Nikko Kurashiki** ✿✿   Although thoroughly modern, this hotel manages to convey the traditional kura style with its gray stone facade. Inside, however, it's a different story, with disco lights highlighting the 11-story atrium's elevator. Still, this is the most sophisticated, full-service hotel in town, and the staff is very helpful. We also like the hotel's unique Hachikengura restaurant (see "Where to Dine," below), serving French cuisine in an adjacent converted rice granary that once belonging to the Ohashi family (the museum is directly behind the hotel). Rooms are spacious, with large closets, TVs hidden in armoires (where they should be) and vanity tables in addition to desks. Marble bathrooms have full-size tubs that are separated from showers.

3–21–19 Achi, Kurashiki 710-0055. ✆ **800/NIKKO-US** or 086/423-2400. Fax 086/423-2401. www.nikko-kurashiki. com. 70 units. ¥19,000–¥22,000 ($181–$210) single; ¥30,000 ($286) double; ¥27,000 ($257) twin. Rates include service charge. AE, DC, MC, V. Across from the Bikan Historical Area. **Amenities:** 3 restaurants (Japanese, French, coffee shop); 1 bar; concierge; tour desk; in-room massage; same-day laundry/dry-cleaning service; nonsmoking rooms. *In room:* A/C, TV w/pay movies, dataport, hot-water pot w/tea, Washlet toilets.

⑮⑧ **Ryokan Kurashiki** ✿✿✿ *Finds*   The best place to stay to get a feeling for old Kurashiki is right in the heart of it—in one of the old warehouses on Kurashiki's picturesque willow-lined canal. This venerable ryokan consists of an old mansion and three converted rice-and-sugar warehouses more than 250 years old. Filled with antiques and curios, it has long, narrow corridors, nooks and crannies, and the peaceful sanctuary of an inner garden. There's no other ryokan in Japan quite like this one—it's fun simply walking through the corridors and looking at all the antiques, including camera and clock collections. No two rooms are alike; some have views of the canal, while others look out over rooftops or the hotel garden. Western-style breakfasts are available, and at the adjoining Terrace de Ryokan Kurashiki, you can sip ceremonial green tea while looking out over a small garden. Even if you don't stay here, you may wish to stop by for tea or coffee (look for the sign that reads ALBERGO DEL GIGLIO D'ORO around the corner from the main entrance).

4-1 Honmachi, Kurashiki 710-0054. ✆ 086/422-0730. Fax 086/422-0990. www.ryokan-kurashiki.jp. 17 units (9 with bathroom). ¥15,000 ($143) per person without bathroom, ¥18,000–¥23,000 ($171–$219) per person with bathroom. Rates include 2 meals and service charge. AE, DC, MC, V. In the Bikan Historical Area, on the canal. **Amenities:** Tea lounge; in-room massage; nonsmoking rooms. *In room:* A/C, TV, hot water pot w/tea.

⑮⑨ **Tsurugata** ✿✿   Rustic furniture, gleaming wood, and high ceilings are trademarks of this ryokan, housed in a 250-year-old building on the canal that was once a merchant's house and shop selling rice, cotton, seafood, and cooking oil. The most expensive rooms have a view of the garden with its 400-year-old pine trees and stone lanterns, while the least expensive rooms are on the second floor without a view. All rooms, however, have private toilets, and there are public baths with English-language instructions on how to use them, indicating that they're accustomed to foreign guests here. In fact, it's owned by the Kurashiki Kokusai Hotel, which has long been the most popular hotel for foreign visitors (see below).

1–3–15 Chuo, Kurashiki 710-0046. ✆ 086/424-1635. Fax 086/424-1650. 12 units (all with toilet, 3 with bathroom). ¥12,600–¥34,650 ($120–$330) per person. Rates include 2 meals and service charge. AE, DC, MC, V. In the Bikan Historical Area, on the canal. **Amenities:** Restaurant (Japanese); in-room massage; nonsmoking rooms. *In room:* A/C, TV, hot-water pot w/tea, Washlet toilet.

## MODERATE

**Hotel Kurashiki**  If you prefer a place near Kurashiki Station, you can't get any closer than this Japan Railways Group combination business-tourist hotel above the station. It also offers the advantage of discounts for Japan Rail Pass holders. The rooms in this modern, spotless hotel are pleasantly decorated and have double-paned windows to shut out noise and nicely tiled bathrooms instead of the usual one-unit cubbyholes of most business hotels. The most expensive singles have double-size beds and sofas, making them quite roomy for Japan, though the cheapest rooms in all categories are quite small. Personally, I think it's a shame to come all this way and miss out staying in the Bikan Historical Area, but if it's convenience you want, this is your best bet.

1–1–1 Achi, Kurashiki 710-0055. Ⓒ **086/426-6111.** Fax 086/426-6163. www.hotels.westjr.co.jp. 133 units. ¥8,500–¥13,000 ($81–$124) single; ¥16,000–¥20,000 ($152–$190) twin; ¥12,000–¥18,000 ($114–$171) double. Rates include service charge. 10% discount for holders of Japan Rail Pass. AE, DC, MC, V. Above Kurashiki Station's south exit. **Amenities:** 2 restaurants (Japanese, Western); shopping arcade; salon; in-room massage; same-day laundry/dry-cleaning service. *In room:* A/C, TV, minibar, hot-water pot w/tea, hair dryer, Washlet toilet.

**Kurashiki Ivy Square Hotel** �  An interesting place to stay and a good choice in this price category, this hotel is located in a brick converted cotton mill on Ivy Square. Much of the architectural style of the old mill has been left intact, and rooms have a rural, country atmosphere. Some rooms face a tiny expanse of green grass and an ivy-covered wall or a canal with koi fish (much better than those facing a parking lot). The Bikan Historical Area is just a few minutes' walk away, but the train station is a 25-minute hike away.

7–2 Honmachi, Kurashiki 710-0054. Ⓒ **086/422-0011.** Fax 086/424-0515. info@ivysquare.co.jp. 161 units (all with toilet, 67 with bathroom). ¥7,875 ($75) single with toilet, ¥10,500 ($100) single with bathroom; ¥13,125 ($125) twin with toilet, ¥16,800–¥28,350 ($160–$270) twin with bathroom; ¥18,900 ($180) double with bathroom. Rates include service charge. ¥1,050 ($10) extra per person on nights before holidays; ¥2,100 ($20) extra per person during peak holidays. AE, DC, MC, V. A few minutes' walk south of the Bikan Historical Area. **Amenities:** Restaurant (Japanese/Western); summer beer garden; shopping arcade; in-room massage. *In room:* A/C, TV, fridge, hot-water pot w/tea, hair dryer, Washlet toilet.

**Kurashiki Kokusai Hotel** ⚑⚑  This has long been Kurashiki's most popular Western-style hotel—and it's easy to see why. This delightful hotel, built in 1963, blends into its surroundings with black-tile walls set in white mortar. Its atmosphere is decidedly old-fashioned, which only adds to the charm. Look for the two huge woodblock prints in the lobby, *Great Barriers of the Universe,* by Japanese artist Munakata Shiko (you can see more of his work at the Ohara Museum). Rooms have nice touches of locally made crafts that lift them out of the ordinary, including woven place mats, Kurashiki glass lampshades, and woodblock prints by a local artist. Female travelers receive a flower in their room. A newer annex offers slightly larger (mostly) twin rooms with larger bathrooms and Washlet toilets, but best are the rooms facing the back with a pleasant view of the Ohara Museum, garden greenery, and the black-tile roofs of the old granaries.

1–1–44 Chuo, Kurashiki 710-0046. Ⓒ **086/422-5141.** Fax 086/422-5192. www.kurashiki-kokusai-hotel.co.jp. 106 units. ¥9,450 ($90) single; ¥14,700–¥17,850 ($40–$170) double; ¥15,750–¥31,500 ($150–$300) twin. AE, DC, V. A 10-min. walk south of Kurashiki Station, on Chuo Dori next to the Bikan Historical Area. **Amenities:** Restaurant (Western); bar; lounge; summer beer garden; business center (no charge); in-room massage; same-day laundry/dry-cleaning service. *In room:* A/C, cable TV, dataport, minibar, hot-water pot w/tea, hair dryer, Washlet toilet.

## INEXPENSIVE

⑯⓪ **Kamoi** ⚑  This minshuku, popular among young people, is located on the edge of the Bikan Historical Area, on a slope leading toward Tsurugatayama Park and Aichi Shrine. There's a small, front-yard garden, and although built only a dozen years

ago, the minshuku follows an architectural style befitting old Kurashiki, with a collection of Edo-Period firearms and chests graces the front entrance. Tatami rooms, where you're expected to lay out your own bedding at night, are simple. Fourth-floor rooms have good views of the city and have Western-style communal toilets, but be aware that the hike up the many stairs can be cumbersome with heavy bags. Western-style breakfast is available if ordered the day before, and since the owner is also owner and chef of a restaurant with the same name (see "Where to Dine," below), the food served here is especially good. Not much English is spoken, but they're used to foreign guests. *Note:* There's a 10pm curfew.

1–24 Honmachi, Kurashiki 710-0054. ⓒ 086/422-4898. Fax 086/427-7615. 15 units (none with bathroom). ¥4,720 ($45) per person without meals; ¥7,350 ($70) per person with breakfast and dinner. No credit cards. A 15-min. walk southeast of Kurashiki Station; walk south on Chuo Dori, turning left just before the Kurashiki Kokusai Hotel and left again when you reach the Ohara Museum; then turn right at Chugoku Bank and look for signs to Aichi Shrine. *In room:* A/C, coin-op TV, hot-water pot w/tea, no phone.

**Toyoko Inn Kurashikieki Minamiguchi** *(Value* Opened in 2000, this inexpensive business hotel has a good location between Kurashiki Station and the Bikan Historical Area, above a convenience store. It also tries harder than most business hotels to draw in customers, offering free Internet access from two computers in the lobby, free domestic calls from lobby phones, free Internet access in guest rooms for those traveling with laptops, free movies, and free breakfast. Rooms are tiny, with most of the room taken up by double- or queen-size beds, but the price is right. Ask for a room on a top floor for unobstructed city views.

2–10–20 Achi, Kurashiki 710-0055. ⓒ 086/430-1045. Fax 086/430-1046. www.toyoko-inn.co.jp. 154 units. ¥5,250 ($50) single; ¥6,300–¥7,350 ($60–$70) double. Rates include continental breakfast. MC, V. A 3-min. walk south of Kurashiki Station, on Chuo Dori on the left side. **Amenities:** Free computer/Internet access in the lobby; in-room massage; coin-op washer/dryer; same-day laundry/dry-cleaning service; nonsmoking rooms. *In room:* A/C, TV w/free movies, dataport, fridge, hot-water pot w/tea, hair dryer, trouser press.

**Young Inn Kurashiki** For inexpensive rooms close to the station, you might try this rather different kind of place (at least for Japan). A redbrick building, it has an informal youth-hostel feel and seems more European than Japanese. Painted in bright colors, it looks as though it might have been rather chic at one time but has faded over the years. It caters mainly to young people and has two to three beds per room (all with sink); the beds are arranged on different levels in bunk-bed style. In fact, the three bed rooms on the fifth floor have to be seen to be believed—the third bed (which is actually a semi-double, so four can stay here) is about 3m (10 ft.) off the floor, and you have to climb a ladder to reach it. Definitely for the nimble who are unafraid of heights. The English-speaking owner also dabbles on the Internet; ask to check your e-mail on the computer in the coffee shop. Cinderella wannabes take note: there's a midnight curfew.

1–14–8 Achi, Kurashiki 710-0055. ⓒ 086/425-3411. Fax 086/427-8388. www.kurashiki.jp/English.htm. 37 units (4 with bathroom). ¥4,200 ($40) single without bathroom, ¥6,300 ($60) single with bathroom; ¥7,350 ($70) twin without bathroom, ¥11,550 ($110) twin with bathroom; ¥12,600 ($120) triple without bathroom; ¥14,700 ($140) quad without bathroom. No credit cards. Station: Kurashi (a 2-min. walk to the right [west] behind the Terminal Hotel). **Amenities:** Coffee shop; nonsmoking rooms. *In room:* A/C, coin-op TV, no phone in rooms without bathroom.

## WHERE TO DINE
### EXPENSIVE

**Hachikengura** *(★★* FRENCH  Gray-tiled walls, wooden floors, and enormous ceiling beams set the stage for sophisticated dining in this historic converted rice granary. Traditional French cuisine, like duck confit or quail stuffed with foie gras, is served in

a nouvelle style. The set lunch offers very good value and includes an appetizer, main dish (like pork confit with beans in tomato sauce), salad, dessert, bread, and coffee for ¥2,400 ($23).

Hotel Nikko Kurashiki 3–21–19 Achi. © 086/423-2400. Main dishes ¥2,000–¥4,500 ($19–$43); set lunches ¥2,400 and ¥5,000 ($23 and $48); set dinners ¥4,000–¥10,000 ($38–$95). AE, DC, MC, V. Daily 11:30am–3pm and 5:30–10pm. Across from the Bikan Historical Area.

## MODERATE

**Kiyutei** STEAKS   Enter through the front gate just off the canal, pass through the small courtyard, and go into a small room dominated by a counter with cooks grilling steaks, the specialty of the house. There's an English-language menu; you're probably best off ordering one of the set meals.

1–2–20 Chuo. © 086/422-5140. Main dishes ¥870–¥1,050 ($8.30–$10); steak dinners ¥2,625–¥5,800 ($25–$55); set weekday lunch ¥1,000 ($9.50); set weekend lunch ¥1,200 ($11). AE, DC, MC, V. Tues–Sun 11am–9pm (Dec–Feb Tues–Sun 11:30am–8:30pm). On the canal, across from the main entrance of the Ohara Museum of Art.

**Tsuta** VARIED JAPANESE/WESTERN   Tsuta means "ivy" in Japanese, a reference to the fact that this restaurant is in Ivy Square. Set in the converted spinning factory, it has high ceilings and is airy and bright. Half of the restaurant serves local Kurashiki specialties, including special rice dishes, fish, obento, dishes that change with the season and, for dinner, kaiseki and shabu-shabu. The other half of the restaurant, called Ivy, offers sandwiches, spaghetti, and other generic Western fare.

Ivy Sq., 7–2 Honmachi. © 086/422-0011. Set lunches ¥1,365–¥3,675 ($13–$35); set dinners ¥2,940–¥5,250 ($28–$50). AE, DC, V. Daily 11am–9pm.

## INEXPENSIVE

**El Greco Coffeehouse** COFFEE SHOP   El Greco is Kurashiki's most famous coffee shop, open since 1959 and simply decorated with a wooden floor, wooden tables and benches, vases of fresh flowers, and El Greco prints. It serves coffee, fruit juice, milkshakes, ice cream, and cake from an English-language menu.

1–1–11 Chuo. © 086/422-0297. Coffee ¥450 ($4.30). No credit cards. Tues–Sun 10am–5pm. Next door to the Ohara Museum in an ivy-covered stone building.

**Kamoi** *&* SUSHI   This sushi restaurant, occupying a 200-year-old rice granary on Kurashiki's willow-fringed canal, is run by the man who has a minshuku of the same name (see above). Its interior, with stark-white walls and dark wooden beams, is decorated with such antiques as cast-iron teapots, old rifles, gourds, and samurai hats. Since the menu is in Japanese, select from the plastic-food display outside the front door. In addition to sushi set meals, other set meals include a tempura teishoku, the Kamoi Teishoku (featuring sashimi and *barazushi*—a rice dish covered with vegetables and seafood and commonly served during festivals), and—my favorite—the Kurashiki Obento with tempura, tofu, vegetables, rice, and soup.

1–3–17 Chuo. © 086/422-0606. Main dishes ¥850–¥1,575 ($8.10–$15); set meals ¥1,200–¥2,100 ($11–$20). No credit cards. Thurs–Tues 10am–6pm (closed day may vary). Catty-corner across the canal from the Ohara Museum of Art.

161 **Kanaizumi** UDON   Kanaizumi, housed in a warehouse-style building with tall ceilings, is easy to spot—just look for its chef rolling out udon behind a large window open to the street (though he's on duty only from 11am–1pm daily). In addition to the thick, handmade wheat udon noodles, local cuisine is served, but all fixed-price meals come with udon. As the menu is in Japanese only, make your selection from the display case.

8–33 Honmachi. ℂ **086/421-7254.** Udon ¥578–¥893 ($5.50–$8.50); set meals ¥715–¥1,575 ($6.80–$15). No credit cards. Tues–Sun 11am–8pm. Behind (east of) Ryokan Kurashiki.

**Ristorante Rentenchi** PIZZA/PASTA   This simple, tiny restaurant (with an English-language menu), run by a kind husband-and-wife team, is a good choice for inexpensive dining between Kurashiki Station and the Bikan Historical Area. Neapolitan-style, thick-crusted pizza from a wood-burning oven is the specialty, most with one topping, though several more can be added upon request.

2–19–18 Achi. ℂ **086/421-7858.** Reservations recommended. Pizza and pasta ¥950–¥2,000 ($9.05–$19); set lunches ¥1,050–¥2,500 ($10–$24). AE, MC, V. Wed–Mon 11:45am–2pm and 6–11pm. A 7-min. walk south of Kurashiki Station on Chuo Dori, on the left side (look for the Italian flag).

---

## 10 Off the Beaten Path: Matsue ⓒ

921km (578 miles) W of Tokyo; 186km (116 miles) NW of Okayama; 402km (251 miles) NE of Hakata (Fukuoka)

Capital of Shimane Prefecture and with a population of about 150,000, **Matsue** lies near the northern coast of western Honshu. It's off the beaten track for most foreign tourists, who tend to keep to a southerly route in their travels toward Hiroshima and Kyushu. Japanese, however, are quite fond of Matsue, and a fair number of them choose to spend their summer vacation in and around this pleasant small town, visiting its castle and other sights, including two outstanding museums—one devoted to Tiffany glass and the other highlighting contemporary Japanese art in a fantastic garden setting. Hugging the shores of Lake Shinji and Nakaumi Lagoon, cut in half by the Ohashi River, and crisscrossed by a network of canals, Matsue is a pretty castle town blessed with Edo-Era architecture, particularly along the castle moat where many samurai settled. All these things conspire to make a trip to Matsue—despite its out-of-the-way location—very worthwhile.

### ESSENTIALS

**GETTING THERE   By Train**   The easiest way to reach Matsue is from Okayama via a 2½-hour **JR limited express train** ride that costs ¥4,850 ($46) for an unreserved seat. There's also one train a day, the **Isokaze,** that travels between Kokura in eastern Kyushu and Matsue in about 6 hours, costing ¥4,000 ($38) for an unreserved seat.

**By Bus**   A bus departs from Tokyo's Shibuya Station (in front of Mark City) nightly at 8pm, arriving at Matsue Station at 6:35am and costing ¥11,550 ($110) one-way. From Hiroshima, 14 buses depart daily, taking 3½ hours and costing ¥4,000 ($38) one-way.

**VISITOR INFORMATION**   At the Tokyo or Narita or Kansai airport Tourist Information Centers, be sure to pick up the leaflet "Matsue and Izumo Taisha Shrine" (you can also download it from the Japan National Tourist Organization's website at www.jnto.go.jp by looking under *Regional Tourist Guides*). Upon arrival at **Matsue Station,** stop off at the **Matsue International Tourist Information Office** (ℂ **0852/ 21-4034;** open daily 9am–6pm), located in a contemporary-looking kiosk in front of the station's north exit, where you can pick up English-language brochures on Matsue and Shimane Prefecture and a good map of the city. More information is available online at www.kankou.pref.shimane.jp.

**INTERNET ACCESS   Kunibiki Messe,** Matsue's convention center a 10-minute walk north of Matsue Station, has computers with free Internet connections at its International Center on the third floor (ℂ **0852/31-5056**). It's open Monday to Saturday from 9am to 7pm.

**MAIL**    The main post office, where you can obtain cash from an ATM, is a 5-minute walk from the north exit of Matsue Station, on the street that runs in front of the station to your right (east).

**ORIENTATION & GETTING AROUND**    Matsue's attractions lie to the northwest of the station and across the Ohashi River, and although buses run virtually everywhere, you can easily cover most distances **on foot.** Matsue Castle is about a 30-minute walk from Matsue Station, with most attractions located just north of the castle along a picturesque moat on a street called Shiomi Nawate. To the west of Matsue Station, about a 10-minute walk away, is Lake Shinji, famous for its sunsets.

If you prefer to ride, ¥500 ($4.15) buys you an all-day pass for the **Lake Line,** which features red, old-fashioned buses running every 20 minutes in a 1-hour loop through the city beginning at Matsue Station and stopping at most tourist sights daily between 8:40am and 5:40pm. Single trips cost ¥200 ($1.90). Note that only major stops are flashed in Roman letters inside the bus. Another bus, the **Matsue Walker,** runs every 30 minutes from Matue Station to major inner-city stops and costs ¥100 (95¢) for one trip or ¥300 ($2.85) for the whole day.

**GOODWILL GUIDES**    Although Matsue's sights are concentrated in one area of town and are easy to find on your own, you may want a "goodwill guide" to show you around, especially if you're going to Izumo Taisha Shrine. Established by the Japan National Tourist Organization, the goodwill guide network is composed of volunteers with foreign-language abilities who act as guides in their city. All you have to do is pay their transportation costs and entrance fees into museums and sights—and it's nice if you buy them lunch, too. If you wish to have a guide, apply at the tourist information office 2 or 3 days in advance (by phone ✆ **0852/21-4034;** by fax 0852/27-2598).

## SEEING THE SIGHTS

International visitors are entitled to 50% discounts at Matsue Castle, Buke Yashiki, Lafcardio Hearn Memorial Museum, Adachi Museum of Art, Louis C. Tiffany Museum and Gardens, and a few other attractions by showing their passport at attraction entrances. The prices below are the regular fare, without the discount.

**Matsue Castle** 🚶🚶    First built in 1611 and partly reconstructed in 1642 and again in the 1950s, Matsue Castle is the only castle along this northern stretch of coast built for warfare as opposed to serving merely as a residence. It's also one of Japan's few remaining original castles—that is, it's not a ferroconcrete reconstruction. Rising up from a hill about 1.6km (1 mile) northwest of Matsue Station with a good view of the city, the five-story donjon (which actually conceals six floors to give its warriors a fighting advantage) houses the usual daimyo and samurai gear, including armor, swords, helmets, and lacquerware that belonged to the Matsudaira clan, who ruled for 10 generations.

Lafcadio Hearn (a European who lived in Matsue in the 1890s, adopted Japanese citizenship, and wrote extensively about Japan and Japanese) said of Matsue Castle: "Crested at its summit, like a feudal helmet . . . the creation is a veritable architectural dragon, made up of magnificent monstrosities." As you walk through the castle up to the top floor, notice the staircase. Although it looks sturdy, it's light enough to be pulled up to halt enemy intrusions. Concealed holes on the second floor could serve as drop chutes for raining stones down on invaders. The top floor, with windows on all four sides from which the feudal lord could command his army, is one of the few watchtowers remaining in Japan. And to think the castle almost met its demise during the Meiji

Restoration when the ministry of armed forces auctioned it off, hoping to rid the city of its Feudal-Era landmark. Luckily, former vassals of the clan pooled their resources and bought the castle keep. In 1927, the grounds were donated to the city.

Also on castle grounds is the **Matsue Kyodo Kan,** a Western-style, Meiji-Era building built in 1903 to accommodate Emperor Meiji should he ever turn up (he never did). Today it houses the Matsue Historical Museum, with free admission to its changing exhibits. You can tour this and the castle in less than an hour.

1–5 Tonomachi. © 0852/21-4030. Daily 8:30am–5pm (to 6:30pm Apr–Sept). Admission ¥550 ($5.25) adults, ¥280 ($2.65) children. Lake Line bus: Stop No.7, Matsue-jo Otemae (1 min.), or a 30-min. walk northwest of Matsue Station.

## ATTRACTIONS NEAR THE CASTLE

Most of these attractions are located on Shiomi Nawate, a small, picturesque street beside the castle's north moat. I've listed them in geographic order, walking from east to west.

(162) **Teahouse Meimei-an**    This is one of Japan's most renowned and well-preserved thatch-roofed teahouses, built in 1779 upon orders of a 29-year-old lord of the Matsudaira clan. It's located at the top of a flight of stairs, from which you have a good view of Matsue Castle (read: photo op). Note the waiting room (and its ancient toilet), for guests awaiting a summons to the teahouse. A separate building offers the bitter Japanese green tea and sweets for an additional ¥400 ($3.80), which you might find refreshing before you move on to your next destination.

278 Kitahori-cho. © 0852/21-9863. Admission ¥400 ($3.80) adults, ¥200 ($1.90) students, free for children. Daily 9am–5pm. Lake Line bus: Stop no. 9, Shiomi Nawate (4 min.), or a 5-min. walk northeast of Matsue Castle, back from Shiomi Nawate on a small side street and up a flight of stairs to the left.

(163) **Buke Yashiki** ⚸    This ancient samurai house, facing the castle moat, was built in 1730 and belonged to the Shiomi family, one of the chief retainers of the Matsudaira feudal clan residing in the castle. High-ranking samurai, the Shiomi family lived pretty much like kings themselves, having separate servants' quarters, a tearoom, and even a shed for their palanquin. Compared with samurai residences in wealthier regions of Japan, however, this samurai house is considered rather austere. As you walk around it, peering into rooms with their wooden walls slid open to the outside breeze, you'll see furniture and objects used in daily life by samurai during the Edo Period. You can see it all in 10 minutes.

305 Kitahori-cho. © 0852/22-2243. Admission ¥300 ($2.85) adults, ¥150 ($1.45) children. Daily 8:30am–5pm (to 6:30pm Apr–Sept). Lake Line bus: Stop no. 10, Koizumi Yakumo Kinenkan-mae (3 min.). Northeast of Matsue Castle across the moat, on Shiomi Nawate.

## Lafcadio Hearn Memorial Museum (Koizumi Yakumo Kinenkan)    Here you'll

find memorabilia of writer Lafcadio Hearn (1850–1904) including his desk, manuscripts, photographs, and smoking pipes. Japanese are fascinated with this man who married the daughter of a Matsue high-ranking samurai, became a Japanese citizen, and adopted the name Koizumi Yakumo. He was one of the first writers to give Japanese the chance to see themselves through the eyes of a foreigner and to describe Japan to the outside world. His books still provide insight into Japanese life at the turn of the 20th century and are available at all bookstores in Japan with an English-language section.

Since most Japanese will assume it's out of respect for Hearn that you've come to Matsue, you may want to read one of his books before coming here. His volume *Glimpses of Unfamiliar Japan* contains an essay called "In a Japanese Garden," in which

he gives his impressions of Matsue, where he lived for 15 months before moving to Kumamoto to teach English.

For die-hard Hearn fans, next to the memorial is **Lafcadio Hearn's Old Residence** (✆ **0852/23-0714**), a Japanese-style house (and former samurai mansion) where Hearn lived in 1891. It has a pleasant, small garden immortalized in Hearn's essay "In a Japanese Garden." Admission here is ¥350 ($3.35) for adults, ¥180 ($1.70) for children. It's open daily 9am to 5pm (10am–4:40pm Dec–Feb). You can tour both the museum and the residence in 30 minutes.

322 Okudani-cho. ✆ 0852/21-2147. Admission ¥300 ($2.85) adults, ¥150 ($1.45) children. Daily 8:30am–5pm (to 6:30pm Apr–Sept). Lake Line bus: Stop no. 10, Koizumi Yakumo Kinenkan-mae (1 min.). On Shiome Nawate north of Matsue Castle.

⑯⑭ **Gesshoji Temple** 🐾 This is the family temple and burial ground of the Matsudaira clan, feudal lords of Matsue and the surrounding region. It was established back in 1664 by Matsudaira Naomasa, whose grandfather was the powerful Tokugawa Ieyasu. Nine generations of the Matsudaira clan are buried here, each in his own small compound spread throughout the solemn grounds (allow 20 min. to see all of them). What I like most about this cemetery is that it seems ancient and forgotten—you might find yourself the only living soul here. At the grave of the sixth lord is a stone turtle (described by Hearn as "the monster tortoise") famous for midnight strolls that terrorized residents; if you rub its head, you'll have good luck. Stop for ceremonial green tea (¥400/$3.80) in a room of a modern building facing a great little garden. And in June, temple grounds are famous for stunning hydrangeas—don't miss it.

Sotonakabara-cho. ✆ 0852/21-6056. Admission ¥500 ($4.75) adults, ¥300 ($2.85) university and high-school students, ¥150 ($1.45) children. Daily 8:30am–5:30pm (to 5pm Nov–Mar). Lake Line bus: Stop no. 15, Gesshoji-mae (4 min.). A 15-min. walk west of Matsue Castle.

## MUSEUMS ON THE SHORES OF LAKE SHINJI

**Louis C. Tiffany Museum and Gardens** 🐾🐾🐾 Quite simply, this museum ranks among the finest collections of Tiffany in the world, in a gorgeous setting that does justice to the works it contains. Opened in 2001 in a building constructed expressly for the world's largest Tiffany collection (Matsue was chosen because it has relatively few earthquakes), the museum chronicles the rich and varied history of Tiffany's nearly 60 years of prolific work in fine and decorative arts from the 1870s to the 1930s. Included are paintings, furniture, lamps, mosaics, ceramics, and the largest Tiffany jewelry collection in the world. The stained-glass works are in darkened rooms with natural lighting. Look for the museum's most valuable work, **Deer Window** 🐾🐾🐾, made in 1910 of 4,000 pieces of glass brilliantly depicting a deer drinking from a stream on an autumn day in late afternoon. Another exhibit shows *Japonisme* influence on Western artists from the Art Nouveau period onward, from van Gogh to Lalique, while outdoors, the Matsue English Garden is a profusion of plants, shrubs, trees, and flowers divided into various "rooms," typical of English-style gardens of the late 1800s. You can easily spend 1½ spellbound hours here seeing it all.

369 Nishihamasada-cho. ✆ 0852/36-3111. Admission ¥2,000 ($19) adults, ¥1,800 ($17) university and high-school students, ¥1,600 ($15) children, free for children under 7. Daily 9am–5:30pm (to 4:30pm Oct–Mar). Lake Line Bus: Stop no. 19, Louis C. Tiffany-Bijutsukan-mae (1 min.).

**Shimane Art Museum (Kenritsu Bijitsukan)** This modern museum with huge glass windows overlooking Lake Shinji showcases works by artists of Shimane Prefecture, as well as art that employs water as a theme. Most of the permanent collection

consists of works by Japanese artists, though there are also a few pieces by Monet, Courbet, and Rodin. In addition to its many paintings, woodblock prints, photography, crafts, and ceramics, there's a rooftop terrace and an outdoor sculpture garden (free of charge) along Lake Shinji, perfect for a sunset stroll. In fact, the museum is so attuned to sunsets that in summer it remains open 30 minutes past sunset. You can see the permanent exhibit in about 30 minutes.

1–5 Sodeshi-cho. ⓒ **0852/55-4700.** Admission ¥300 ($2.85) adults, ¥200 ($1.90) university and high-school students, free for children. Special exhibitions cost extra. Tues–Sun 10am–6:30pm (Mar–Sept closes 30 min. after sunset). Lake Line bus: Stop no. 27, Kenritsu Bijitsukan (in front of the museum). Or a 15-min. walk west of Matsue Station.

## BOAT TRIPS

The **Horikawa Pleasure Boat Tour (Horikawa Meguri;** ⓒ **0852/27-0417)** is a tour of the castle moat aboard flat-bottom boats (take off your shoes and sit on tatami) with a rooftop canopy that lowers for tight squeezes under bridges. It's a picturesque, relaxing way to see the city, with trips around the castle lasting about an hour. In winter, you can keep warm huddled under a *kotatsu* (a kind of heated blanket). Note, however, that commentary is in Japanese only. Boarding spots are at Karakoro Hiroba near the Kyobashi Bridge (Lake Line Bus stop no. 6) and Otemae near Matsue Castle (Lake Line Bus stop no. 8). Boats run every 15 minutes daily from 9am to 5pm (to 6pm in summer) March through October and in November from 9am to 4pm; every 20 minutes daily from 10am to 3pm December through February. Tickets cost ¥1,200 ($11) for adults and half price for children, but you can get a 30% discount if you're a foreigner by showing your passport.

## SHOPPING

For one-stop shopping for locally crafted goods, visit the **Shimane Prefectural Products and Tourist Center (Shimane-ken Bussankanko-kan),** 191 Tonomachi (ⓒ **0852/22-5758;** open daily 9:30am–6pm), just southeast of Matsue Castle (Lake Line bus to stop no. 8 to Otemae, then a 1-min. walk). In a modern building that resembles the black-and-white structures typical of the region, the center sells everything from ceramics and abacuses (one of the few prefectures in Japan that still produces them) to toys, jewelry, and foodstuffs, all products of Shimane Prefecture. On the second floor are displays showing how various local products are produced, as well as an English-language DVD about the prefecture (instructions for how to work the player, however, are in Japanese only, so ask someone to help you, since all the buttons are also in Japanese only).

Another interesting place to shop is the **Karakoro Art Studio,** Kyomise Karakoro Hiroba Square (ⓒ **0852/20-7000;** open Wed–Mon 9:30am–6:30pm), a handsome, century-old former bank renovated into studios and shops selling locally made sweets, tea, jewelry, glassware, woodworking, and other crafts. Changing exhibitions are held in the basement vaults. It's located south of the castle on the moat; both the Lake Line bus and Horikawa Pleasure Boat Tour stop here.

## EASY SIDE TRIPS

**IZUMO GRAND SHRINE (IZUMO TAISHA)** *Overrated* The most important religious structure in the vicinity of Matsue is easy to see on a half-day side trip, but come only if you have extra time. **Izumo Taisha,** 195 Kizuki Higashi, Taisha-cho (ⓒ **0853/53-3100;** open daily sunrise–sunset), is considered one of Japan's holiest shrines because, according to popular lore, all the gods in the Shinto pantheon gather

here for 1 month every autumn to determine the world's fate for the upcoming year. In Izumo this month is called the "Month with the Gods." Everywhere else in Japan it's referred to as the "Month without Gods," since they're all away performing their duty here, housed in those long buildings flanking both sides of the main shrine. Otherwise, like the Ise Grand Shrines, the main shrine here, reconstructed in 1744, is considered too sacred for mere mortals and is hidden away from close inspection. You'll have to content yourself with a picture showing how it looked 1,000 years ago, when it was reputedly 23m (78 ft.) higher to heaven on top of huge pilings. This makes it the oldest site of a Shinto Grand Shrine displaying the Taisha style of architecture. It's dedicated to Okuninushi-no-kami, the Shinto deity responsible for medicine, farming, and happiness. To the left of the main shrine is the marriage shrine, where you'll see people throwing coins up into the bristled ends of thick, twisted rice ropes adorning the entrance—legend has it that if a coin gets stuck in the bushy end, the thrower will have good luck in marriage.

It's a 30- to 40-minute JR train ride from Matsue Station to Izumoshi Station (¥570/$5.15), followed by a 30-minute bus ride (¥460/$4.40) bound for Izumo Taisha ("Taisha-yuki"; get off at the last stop). Or, for a more atmospheric journey, you can also reach Izumo Taisha Shrine by taking the private Ichibata train from Matsue Shinjiko Onsen Station (departures are once or twice an hour) 55 minutes to Izumo Taisha-mae Station (only a couple of trains a day travel directly; otherwise you'll have to change trains in Kawato). The train stops at stations no larger than American closets and costs ¥790 ($7.50). From Izumo Taisha-mae Station it's a 15-minute walk to the shrine. Admission to the shrine is free.

**ADACHI MUSEUM** ✦✦✦ *(Finds)* I was blown away the first time I laid eyes on the Adachi Museum, 320 Furukawa-cho, Yasugi (© **0854/28-7111;** www.adachi-museum.or.jp; open daily 9am–5:30pm, to 5pm Oct–Mar), which houses one of Japan's premier collections of Japanese modern art (from the Meiji, Taisho, and Showa periods) amid a meticulously sculpted garden that I consider one of Japan's finest. Exhibitions, which are changed four times a year to reflect the seasons, are comprised of 200 works and include the largest collection of distinguished painter Yokoyama Taikan, with at least 20 of his 130 works here always on display. A Ceramics Hall displays works by Kawai Kanjiro and Kitaoji Rasanjin.

But what makes this museum truly unique is its perfectly landscaped garden, crafted to complement Taikan's masterpieces and continually visible through cleverly crafted windows to incorporate it into the museum's artwork. The effect is surreal, as though the garden is a still picture, a scroll, a Taikan painting. There are several outdoor viewing spots, as well as a coffee shop overlooking a koi pond and two teahouses serving traditional cakes and powdered green tea (one with a nice view of a moss garden). You'll want to spend at least 1½ hours here, more if you opt for the audio guide, which costs ¥300 ($2.85) extra and describes 130 works of art.

Admission to the museum is ¥2,200 ($21) for adults, ¥1,700 ($16) for university students, ¥900 ($8.55) for high-school students, and ¥400 ($3.80) for children, but foreigners can get a 50% discount by showing their passport. To get there, take the JR train from Matsue Station 20 minutes to Yasugi, and then board one of the free shuttle buses that departs eight times a day for the 20-minute ride to the museum. (At last check, buses departed at 9:15, 10:15, and 11:05am and at 12:05, 1:05, 1:55, 3:05, and 3:55pm, but you'd be wise to verify this.) There are also city buses, but they're infrequent. In any case, since there are very few buses, it's best to work out a schedule

with the Matsue tourist office. A certain travel writer got stranded out here and had to hitchhike.

## WHERE TO STAY

Directions are from Matsue Station.

### EXPENSIVE

(165) **Minami-Kan** ⋆⋆ *(Finds)*   You'll be treated like royalty here at this ryokan, located right beside Lake Shinji. Although parts of the ryokan, including its lobby and rooms with private bathroom, are modern, the original building stems from 1888 and boasts several great tatami rooms with nice wood detailing (these have private toilets but no tubs). Most rooms have views of the lake, but if you really want to feel special, stay in the two-room garden cottage right beside the lake with views of the lake and a garden. Minami-Kan is also renowned for its cuisine, open to the public for lunch daily from 11:30am to 2:30pm, with set meals costing ¥2,200 to ¥5,000 ($21–$48).

14 Suetsugu Honmachi, Matsue, Shimane-ken 690-0843. © 0852/21-5131. Fax 0852/26-0351. 7 units (5 with bathroom, 2 with toilet only); 1 cottage with bathroom. ¥21,000–¥52,500 ($200–$500) per person. Cottage from ¥36,750 ($350) per person. Rates include 2 meals. AE, DC, MC, V. Taxi: 8 min. Lake Line bus: Stop no. 6, Kyobashi (2 min.). Off the Kyomise covered shopping arcade in the heart of Matsue. **Amenities:** Restaurant (Japanese); hot-spring baths; in-room massage. *In room:* A/C, TV, minibar, hot-water pot w/tea, safe.

### MODERATE

(166) **Horaiso** ⋆⋆ *(Value)*   Tucked away on a side street not far from Matsue Castle, this 50-year-old, family-run ryokan is guarded by a wall, an imposing wooden gateway, and an ancient pine tree. Each Japanese-style room is different, some with nice views of an inner courtyard garden. Although the ryokan is a bit worn, it has a certain charm missing in generic establishments. Unlike most ryokan, no dinners are served, making it also cheaper.

101 Tonomachi, Matsue, Shimane-ken 690-0877. © 0852/21-4337. Fax 0852/21-4338. 10 units (3 with bathroom). ¥5,250 ($50) per person; ¥6,300 ($60) per person Sat and nights before holidays. Rates include breakfast. No credit cards. Lake Line bus: Stop No. 7, Matsue-jo, Otemae (3 min.). *In room:* A/C, TV, hot-water pot w/tea.

**Hotel Ichibata** ⋆   Matsue's best-known tourist hotel is the Hotel Ichibata, which first opened its doors 40 years ago in a part of town called Matsue Shinjiko Onsen, a hot-spring spa. Pluses include the hotel's indoor and outdoor hot-spring public baths with views over Lake Shinji and a nearby jogging path that hugs the shores of the lake. Just behind the hotel is the private Ichibata Line train to Izumo Taisha. None of the singles or doubles has a view of the lake, but the more expensive twins and all the Japanese-style rooms do, including some combination-style rooms with both beds and tatami area.

30 Chidori-cho, Matsue, Shimane-ken 690-0852. © 0852/22-0188. Fax 0852/22-0230. hotel@ichibata.co.jp. 142 units. ¥9,390 ($89) single; ¥16,470–¥26,865 ($157–$256) twin; from ¥21,090 ($201) Japanese style for 2. ¥1,155 ($11) extra per person Sat and nights before holidays. AE, DC, MC, V. Lake Line bus: Stop no. 18, Chidori Minami Koen (1 min., in front of the hotel). **Amenities:** 3 restaurants (Japanese, Western, coffee shop); 1 bar; 1 lounge; outdoor beer garden (summer only); indoor/outdoor hot-spring baths; in-room massage; same-day laundry/dry-cleaning service. *In room:* A/C, TV, minibar, hot-water pot w/tea, hair dryer, Washlet toilet.

**Matsue New Urban Hotel**   Although it's a business hotel with the usual vending machines in the lobby, this property near Lake Shinji (with free morning shuttle service from the station) and within walking distance of Matsue Castle and other tourist sights offers large hot-spring baths and rooms with great views of the lake. Rooms facing away from the lake are slightly cheaper, though some of these on higher floors do have views of Matsue Castle in the distance. By the way, this is the newest of four Urban hotels in

Matsue. The original hotel, next door, and the two you can see from the station's north exit are more worn, with fewer amenities, but they are less expensive.

40–1 Nishi-chamachi, Matsue, Shimane-ken 690-0845. © 0852/23-0003. Fax 0852/23-0018. 76 units. ¥6,300–¥7,875 ($60–$75) single; ¥9,450 ($90) double; ¥12,600–¥13,650 ($120–$130) twin. AE, DC, MC, V. Free shuttle bus from Matsue Station every 30 min. 7–9am. Lake Line bus: Stop no. 23, Suetsugu Jinja-mae (3 min.). **Amenities:** Restaurant (Western/Japanese); rooftop beer garden (summer only); hot-spring baths; lobby computers with free Internet access; in-room massage; coin-op washers and dryers; rental bikes (free 1st hr., ¥315/$3 next 4 hr.), nonsmoking rooms. *In room:* A/C, TV, dataport, fridge, hot-water pot w/tea, hair dryer.

**Tokyu Inn**  Part of a national business hotel chain, the Tokyu Inn is a good choice for travelers who want to spend the night close to Matsue Station. Rooms are small and generic but have everything you need, including Tempur Comfort Pillows that mold to your head; bathrooms are a bit larger than in most business hotels. Paying slightly higher rates in each category will get you a larger bed in single rooms and a larger room in double and twin rooms. There are also Ladies' Rooms equipped with humidifiers, irons, and female-oriented toiletries. Twenty-two rooms have dataports.

590 Asahimachi, Matsue, Shimane-ken 690-0003. © **0852/27-0109.** Fax 0852/25-1327. www.tokyuhotels.co.jp. 181 units. ¥7,875–¥9,660 ($75–$92) single; ¥12,915–¥16,380 ($123–$156) double; ¥14,910–¥27,090 ($142–$258) twin. AE, DC, MC, V. Across the street from Matsue Station's north exit, behind a building to the right. **Amenities:** Restaurant (Western); lounge; salon; in-room massage; same-day laundry/dry-cleaning service; nonsmoking rooms. *In room:* A/C, TV w/pay movies, minibar, hot-water pot w/tea, hair dryer, Washlet toilet, trouser press.

## INEXPENSIVE

⟨167⟩ **Ryokan Terazuya** ★★ *(Value)*  Terazuya offers good value for your money, but it also offers something money can't buy: true hospitality. This Japanese inn has been in business since 1893, owned by the Terazu family, who has shown so much kindness to foreigners that many consider their stay here a highlight of their trip. The Terazus treat guests like family, teaching them the tea ceremony in the tearoom, showing them how to make sushi in the communal dining hall, giving calligraphy lessons, and singing traditional Noh songs in the tatami-matted party room. They've even been known to escort guests to the onsen. The postwar building, while nothing special on the outside, is spotless and colorfully decorated inside. Located across from a small shrine, it's also near the Shimane Art Museum and Lake Shinji, making it convenient for watching those famous sunsets. And although it's only a 7-minute walk from Matsue Station (head west along the north side of the railroad tracks), the Terazus will pick you up if you call ahead. If faxing, please do so during Japanese business hours so as not to wake them.

60–3 Tenjin-machi, Matsue, Shimane-ken 690-0064. © **0852/21-3480.** Fax 0852/21-3422. terazuya@mable.ne.jp. 9 units (none with bathroom). ¥4,000 ($38) per person with coffee and bread; ¥4,800 ($46) per person with breakfast; ¥7,000 ($67) per person with breakfast and dinner. No credit cards. Lake Line bus: Stop no. 27, Kenritsu Bijutsukan (3 min.). **Amenities:** Restaurant (Japanese); computer w/free Internet access. *In room:* A/C, TV, hot-water pot w/tea.

**Toyoko Inn Matsue Ekimae**  This budget chain offers tiny rooms with all the basics, along with free Internet access at lobby computers, free movie channels, and free domestic calls from lobby phones. A good choice if you don't need much personal attention.

498-10 Asahimachi, Matsue, Shimane-ken 690-0003. © **0852/60-1045.** Fax 0852/60-1046. www.toyoko-inn.com. 190 units. ¥6,090 ($58) single; ¥8,190 ($78) double or twin. Rates include Japanese breakfast. AE, DC, MC, V. From Matsue Station's north exit, walk past the buses to the main road and turn left (3 min.). **Amenities:** Computers w/free Internet access; nonsmoking rooms. *In room:* A/C, TV w/free movies, dataport, fridge, hot-water pot w/tea, hair dryer, safe, Washlet toilet, trouser press.

## WHERE TO DINE

Much of Matsue's regional cuisine comes from Lake Shinji, including sea bass, smelt, carp, freshwater eel, and a small black clam (*shijimi,* popular in soups). *Warigo soba,* which comes with stacked layers of noodles to which you add grated daikon radish, yam, fish flakes, seaweed, and other condiments, is also popular.

### MODERATE

**Ji Beer Kan** GRILLED MEAT    In a large, airy setting beside the castle moat west of the Hearn Memorial Hall, this is Matsue's microbrewery/restaurant (every town seems to have one now). You'll find it on the second floor above a souvenir shop. Three different kinds of beer are brewed: a pilsner, a fruity pale ale, and an herb-flavored ale; a sampler of all three costs ¥950 ($9.05). The fare is Genghis Khan, with strips of beef or pork that you cook on a grill at your table, with set meals including all the vegetables, rice, and salad you can eat. If all you want is a beer, buy one from a counter in the souvenir shop and take it outside to enjoy at the tables beside the moat.

509–1 Kuroda-cho. ✆ **0852/55-8877.** Set meals ¥2,100 – ¥7,500 ($20–$71); set lunches ¥800 – ¥1,300 ($7.60–$12). AE, MC, V. Daily 11am–5pm. Lake Line bus: Stop no. 11, Horikawa Yuransen Noribo (1 min.).

⑯⑧ **Kyoragi** LOCAL SPECIALTIES    Located across from Ji Beer Kan (above), this modern restaurant with an wood interior, lots of windows, and both tatami and table seating specializes in dishes based on original Izumo recipes, using organic meats and vegetables whenever possible. There are pictures of some of the set meals offered on the Japanese-language menu, including the very tasty Hanagoromo set meal for ¥1,680 ($16) with lots of local delicacies. Another set meal, served only for dinner for ¥2,625 ($25), allows you to choose from almost a dozen different kinds of fresh fish for your main course, along with side dishes that change weekly. From Tuesday to Friday, there's a daily set lunch for only ¥735 ($7).

512-5 Kuroda-cho. ✆ **0852/25-2233.** Set meals ¥1,260 –¥3,150 ($12–$30). DC, MC, V. Tues–Sun 11am–2pm and 5–9:30pm (open on holidays Mon, closing Tues instead). Lake Line bus: Stop no. 11, Horikawa Yuransen Noribo (1 min.).

**River View** CONTINENTAL    Decorated in white, with a large wooden terrace (open only in summer) overlooking a river and jazz background music, this restaurant turns out very good dishes that might include mustard steak, grilled fish, vegetable risotto, shoulder pork roast, or grilled chicken. Portions are small, so order several dishes if you're hungry, or go for one of the set meals such as the one for ¥3,150 ($30), which offers five dishes to be shared by two people. There's also a large cocktail menu, with drinks costing ¥580 to ¥750 ($5.50–$7.15).

562-1 Otesemba-cho. ✆ **0852/60-6122.** Main dishes ¥750–1,680 ($7.15–$16); set dinners ¥2,520 –¥3,150 ($24–$30); set lunches ¥900–¥1,800 ($8.55–$17). AE, MC, V. Wed–Mon 11am–2pm and 5:30–11pm. A 3-min. walk north of Matsue Station, 2 blocks behind Tokyu Inn.

### INEXPENSIVE

⑯⑨ **Daikichi** YAKITORI    Daikichi means "big happiness," and judging from the English-speaking owner's smiling face, that's the order of the day. Customers seem to be content, too, as they crowd into this small counter-seating restaurant. A branch of an Osaka yakitori-ya, Daikichi offers an English-language menu of various yakitori, including chicken, minced chicken meatballs, and chicken with leek or green pepper (which must be ordered in sets of three), as well as its own brand of sake and wine. There's a ¥150 ($1.45) snack charge.

491–1 Asahimachi. ✆ **0852/31-8308.** Yakitori ¥80–¥250 (75¢–$2.40) per stick. No credit cards. Daily 5pm–midnight. From Matsue Station's north exit, walk past the buses and turn left on the main street; it will be on your right, before Toyoko Inn (2 min.).

⑰ **Kaneyasu**   FISH/VARIED JAPANESE   This modest one-counter place with tatami rooms upstairs has good food and is run by grandmotherly, bustling women. It has been around for more than 40 years, and most of its customers are local working people, so avoid the noontime rush. It has a great lunch teishoku, which includes a piece of *yakizakana* (grilled fish), vegetable, soup, tofu, rice, and tea. In the evening, dishes like grilled fish, yam, bamboo, seasonal dishes, and various vegetables are available, but it's probably easier to order one of the two set meals, both of which feature locally caught seafood.

569-3 Otesemba-cho. ✆ **0852/21-0550.** Reservations recommended for dinner. Set dinners ¥1,500–¥2,000 ($14–$19); lunch teishoku ¥650–¥900 ($6.20–$8.55). No credit cards. Mon–Fri 11am–2pm; Mon–Sat 5–9pm. Closed holidays. 1 block north of the main street that runs in front of Matsue Station's north exit.

⑱ **Yakumoan** ★★ *Finds* SOBA NOODLES   A wonderful place to stop off for lunch if you're sightseeing along Shiomi Nawate north of Matsue Castle, this lovely soba shop with a teahouselike atmosphere is surrounded by a stone wall with a large wooden entryway, a grove of bamboo, bonsai, a Japanese garden, and a pond full of prize carp. Part of the restaurant, a former samurai residence, dates from 200 years ago. Its specialty is noodles, all handmade, including the local specialty Warigo soba and udon. You'll find a plastic-food display case to the left as you step through the entryway. Seating is at either tables or tatami.

308 Kitabori-cho. ✆ **0852/22-2400.** Noodles set meals ¥1,100–¥1,320 ($10–$13). No credit cards. Daily 9:15am–4pm (last order). Lake Line bus: Stop no. 10, Koizumi Yakumo Kinenkan-mae (1 min.). On Shiomi Nawate St., near the Buke Yashiki samurai house.

## 11 Hiroshima ★★

894km (554 miles) W of Tokyo; 376km (235 miles) W of Kyoto; 279km (174 miles) E of Hakata/Fukuoka

With a population of more than one million, Hiroshima looks just like any other up-and-coming city in Japan. With modern buildings and an industry that includes the manufacture of cars and ships, it's a city full of vitality and purpose with a steady flow of both Japanese and foreign business executives in and out.

But unlike other cities, Hiroshima's past is clouded: It has the unfortunate distinction of being the first city ever destroyed by an atomic bomb. (The second city—and it is hoped the last—was Nagasaki, on Kyushu island.)

It happened one clear summer morning, August 6, 1945, at 8:15am, when a B-29 approached Hiroshima from the northeast, passed over the central part of the city, dropped the bomb, and then took off at full speed. The bomb exploded 43 seconds later at an altitude of 600m (1,980 ft.) in a huge fireball, followed by a mushroom cloud of smoke that rose 8,910m (29,700 ft.) in the air.

There were approximately 350,000 people living in Hiroshima at the time of the bombing, and almost a third lost their lives on that day. The heat from the blast was so intense that it seared people's skin, while the pressure caused by the explosion tore clothes off bodies and caused the rupture and explosion of internal organs. Flying glass tore through flesh like bullets, and fires broke out all over the city. But that wasn't the end of it: Victims who survived the blast were subsequently exposed to huge doses of radioactivity. Even people who showed no outward signs of sickness suddenly died,

# Hiroshima

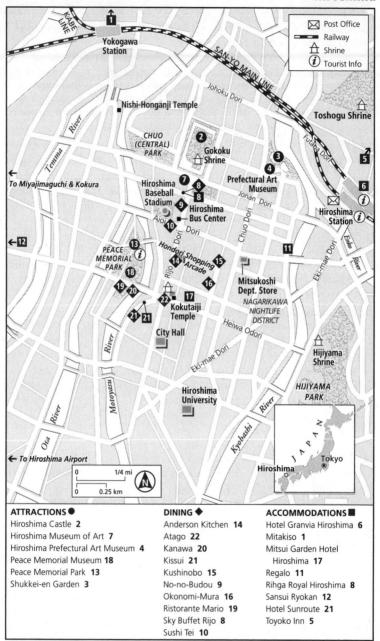

**Legend:**
- ⊠ Post Office
- ▬ Railway
- ⛩ Shrine
- ⓘ Tourist Info

Yokogawa Station
KABE LINE
SAN-YO MAIN LINE
Johoku Dori
Nishi-Honganji Temple
Toshogu Shrine
CHUO (CENTRAL) PARK
Gokoku Shrine
Futaba Dori
Temma River
To Miyajimaguchi & Kokura
Hiroshima Baseball Stadium
Prefectural Art Museum
Jonan Dori
Hiroshima Bus Center
Chuo Dori
Aioi Dori
Hiroshima Station
Enko River
Hondori Shopping Arcade
Rijo Dori
PEACE MEMORIAL PARK
Mitsukoshi Dept. Store
NAGARIKAWA NIGHTLIFE DISTRICT
Eki-mae Dori
Kokutaiji Temple
Heiwa Odori
City Hall
Eki-mae Dori
Hijiyama Shrine
HIJIYAMA PARK
Hiroshima University
Motoyasu River
River
Ota River
Kyobashi River
To Hiroshima Airport
0    1/4 mi
0    0.25 km
JAPAN
Tokyo
Hiroshima

**ATTRACTIONS** ●
Hiroshima Castle **2**
Hiroshima Museum of Art **7**
Hiroshima Prefectural Art Museum **4**
Peace Memorial Museum **18**
Peace Memorial Park **13**
Shukkei-en Garden **3**

**DINING** ◆
Anderson Kitchen **14**
Atago **22**
Kanawa **20**
Kissui **21**
Kushinobo **15**
No-no-Budou **9**
Okonomi-Mura **16**
Ristorante Mario **19**
Sky Buffet Rijo **8**
Sushi Tei **10**

**ACCOMMODATIONS** ■
Hotel Granvia Hiroshima **6**
Mitakiso **1**
Mitsui Garden Hotel Hiroshima **17**
Regalo **11**
Rihga Royal Hiroshima **8**
Sansui Ryokan **12**
Hotel Sunroute **21**
Toyoko Inn **5**

creating panic and helplessness among the survivors. Today, aging blast survivors still continue to suffer from the effects of the bomb, with a high incidence of cancer, disfigurement, scars, and keloid skin tissue.

Ironically, Hiroshima's tragedy is now the city's largest tourist draw, and visitors from around the world come to see Peace Memorial Park with its haunting museum. But Hiroshima, laced with rivers and wide, tree-lined boulevards, boasts other worthwhile attractions as well, including several excellent museums. Hiroshima is also the most popular gateway for trips to nearby Miyajima, a jewel of an island considered to be one of Japan's most scenic spots, covered later in this chapter.

## ESSENTIALS

**GETTING THERE   By Plane**   Flights from Tokyo's Haneda Airport take about 1 hour and 20 minutes and cost ¥26,300 ($250) to **Hiroshima Airport** (© 0848/86-8151; www.hij.airport.jp), which is also served by flights from Seoul, Beijing, Shanghai, Taipei, and Bangkok. Limousine Buses connect the airport with Hiroshima Station's Shinkansen (north) exit in 48 minutes, costing ¥1,300 ($12) one-way.

**By Train**   Hiroshima is about 6 hours from Tokyo by **Shinkansen** bullet train (you have to change trains in Okayama or Osaka if you have a Japan Rail Pass, since only the Nozomi, which is not covered by the pass, covers the entire distance in 4 hr.), 3 hours from Kyoto, and 1 hour and 20 minutes from Hakata Station on Kyushu. The fare from Tokyo is ¥17,540 ($167) for an unreserved seat on the Nozomi.

**By Bus**   Buses depart from Tokyo Station every night at 8 and 9pm, both reaching Hiroshima Station at 8am the next morning. The one-way fare is ¥11,600 ($110). From Osaka, buses depart six times a day, taking 5 hours to reach Hiroshima and costing ¥5,000 ($48).

**By Boat**   You can also reach Hiroshima by **high-speed boat** from Matsuyama on Shikoku in 1 hour and 17 minutes for ¥5,800 ($55), but slower ferries, which cover the distance in 2 hours and 40 minutes, are cheaper (¥2,700/$26) and provide better views of the Seto Inland Sea. Hiroshima Port, in Ujina, is connected to Hiroshima Station by streetcar in 43 minutes.

**VISITOR INFORMATION**   Before leaving Tokyo or the Narita or Kansai airports, pick up a copy of the leaflet "Hiroshima and Miyajima" at the Tourist Information Center (you can also download it from the Japan National Tourist Organization's website at www.jnto.go.jp by looking under *Regional Tourist Guides*).

In Hiroshima, you'll find two local tourist offices at **Hiroshima Station.** The main office (© 082/263-6822), at the north exit where Shinkansen bullet trains arrive, is open daily from 9am to 12:30pm and 1:30 to 5:30pm. The other tourist office (© 082/261-1877), at the station's south exit, is open daily from 9 to 11:30am and 12:30 to 5:30pm. A third tourist office is located in the center of **Peace Memorial Park** in the Rest House (© 082/247-6738; open daily 9:30am–6pm Apr–Sept, 8:30am–5pm Oct–Mar). All three facilities have English-language brochures of both Hiroshima and Miyajima with maps. Be sure, too, to ask for the **Setouchi Welcome brochure,** available free to visitors; it offers coupons with discounts on member hotels, restaurants, some attractions, and more. More information on the Setouchi Welcome Card is available at www.japansetouchi.jp. Information on Hiroshima is available at www.hiroshima-navi.or.jp and www.pref.hiroshima.jp

**INTERNET ACCESS** There are coin-operated computers at two locations in Hiroshima Station that cost ¥100 (95¢) for every 15 minutes. They're even equipped with headphones for all you Skype users. Otherwise, most convenient for longer navigation is **Media Café Popeye,** located in the Hondori covered shopping arcade (© **082/545-0369**) above a shop called Beams. It's open 24 hours and charges ¥250 ($2.40) for the first 30 minutes, then ¥63 (60¢) for each subsequent 10 minutes.

**MAIL** Hiroshima's main post office, 2–62 Matsubara-cho (© **082/261-6401**), is located to the right after exiting from Hiroshima Station's south side. You can get cash from international credit cards here Monday to Saturday 5am to 11:55pm and Sunday 5am to 10pm.

**ORIENTATION & GETTING AROUND** One legacy of Hiroshima's total destruction was its rebirth into one of Japan's most navigable cities, with wide, open boulevards instead of the usual cramped streets. Hiroshima's main attractions, including Peace Memorial Park, Hiroshima Castle, Shukkei-en Garden, Hiroshima Prefectural Art Museum, and Hiroshima Museum of Art, lie to the west and southwest of Hiroshima Station. The most convenient mode of transportation in the city is **streetcar,** which costs only ¥150 ($1.45) one-way; children pay half fare. If you need to transfer to another line, ask the driver for a transfer *(norikae)* card, which you then pass through the card machine upon alighting from the first streetcar and again when boarding the second streetcar. When you arrive at your destination, return the card to the streetcar driver. A 1-day pass, which you can buy from the conductor, costs ¥600 ($5.70). Be sure to pick up a streetcar map from the tourist office.

It's probably easiest to make the circuit to Hiroshima's centrally located attractions **on foot.** From Hiroshima Station you can walk to Shukkei-en Garden and the Prefectural Art Museum in about 15 minutes, from which it's another 10-minute walk to Hiroshima Castle. You can walk onward to Peace Memorial Park in about 15 minutes, passing the Hiroshima Museum of Art and the A-Bomb Dome on the way. Just east of Peace Park is the **Hondori** covered shopping arcade and its neighboring streets, considered the heart of the city with its many department stores, shops, and restaurants.

## SEEING THE SIGHTS

As you walk around Hiroshima today, you'll find it hard to imagine that the city was the scene of such widespread horror and destruction just a little more than 60 years ago. On the other hand, Hiroshima doesn't have the old buildings, temples, and historic structures that other cities have, yet it draws a steady flow of travelers who come to see Peace Memorial Park, the city's best-known landmark (Hiroshima draws 9.4 million tourists a year, 217,000 of them from other countries). Dedicated to peace, the city also seems committed to art—in addition to its fine art museums, you'll find statues, stone lanterns, memorials, and sculptures lining the streets.

Be sure to pick up a **Setouchi Welcome brochure,** available for free at city tourist offices, which gives slight discounts (up to 20%) on admission to Hiroshima Castle, Hiroshima City Museum of Contemporary Art, and Shukkei-en Garden.

## PEACE MEMORIAL PARK & ENVIRONS

**Peace Memorial Park (Heiwa Koen)** ✿✿✿ lies in the center of the city. English-language signs all over the city indicate how to reach it. From Hiroshima Station, take streetcar no. 2 or 6 to the Genbaku-Domu-mae (in front of the Atom Bomb Dome, which is just north of the park) stop. The first structure you'll see as you alight from the streetcar is the **A-Bomb Dome,** the skeletal ruins of the former Industrial Promotion

Hall, left as a visual reminder of the death and destruction caused by the atomic bomb. Across the river is the park; it takes about 10 minutes to walk from its northern end to the museum.

Along the way you'll see the park's most touching statue, the **Children's Peace Monument,** dedicated to the war's most innocent victims, not only those who died instantly in the blast but also those who died afterward from the effects of radiation. It's a statue of a girl with outstretched arms, and rising above her is a crane, a symbol of happiness and longevity in Japan. The statue is based on the true story of a young girl, Sadako, who suffered from the effects of radiation after the bombing in Hiroshima. She believed that if she could fold 1,000 paper cranes she would become well again. However, even though she folded more than 1,000 cranes, she still died of leukemia. Today, all Japanese children are familiar with her story, and around the memorial are streamers of paper cranes donated by schoolchildren from all over Japan. To the east of the statue is the **Rest House,** where you'll find a branch of the Hiroshima Tourist Office.

Also in Peace Memorial Park is a **Cenotaph for Korean Victims.** It's a little-publicized fact that 20,000 Koreans were killed that fateful summer day, most of them brought to Japan as forced laborers. The monument reads: "The Korean victims were given no funerals or memorial services and their spirits hovered for years unable to pass on to heaven." It's significant to note that for 29 years, the cenotaph remained outside the park. In 1999, Hiroshima's mayor, calling for an end to prejudice against Korean residents in Japan, gave the memorial a new home within Peace Memorial Park.

Between the statue and the museum is the **Memorial Cenotaph,** designed by Japan's famous architect Kenzo Tange (who also designed the Tokyo Metropolitan Government offices in Shinjuku; see p. 103). Shaped like a figurine clay saddle found in ancient tombs, it shelters a stone chest, which in turn holds the names of all of those killed by the bomb. An epitaph, written in Japanese, carries the hopeful phrase, "Let all the souls here rest in peace, for we shall not repeat the evil." If you stand in front of the cenotaph, you'll have a view through the hollow arch of the Peace Flame and the A-Bomb Dome. It is said that the **Peace Flame** will continue to burn until all atomic weapons vanish from the face of the earth and nuclear war is no longer a threat to humanity.

East of the Peace Flame is the **Hiroshima National Peace Memorial Hall for the Atomic Bomb Victims** (✆ 082/543-6271), dedicated to atomic bomb victims. Its Hall of Remembrance, a 360-degree panorama recreating the bombed city as seen from the hypocenter, is made of 140,000 tiles, the number of people estimated to have died by the end of 1945. The rest of the memorial is a vast, computerized audiovisual library with information on victims, their histories, and photos. The English-language leaflet not only provides excellent information but also gives access to the large-screen computers (insert it to activate them). Admission is free and it's open the same hours as the Peace Memorial Museum.

Just beyond is the main focus of the park, the **Peace Memorial Museum (Heiwa Kinen Shiryokan)** ✷✷✷, 1–2 Nakajima-cho, Naku-ku (✆ 082/241-4004; www.pcf.city.hiroshima.jp; daily 8:30am–6pm Mar–Nov [until 7pm in Aug], daily 8:30am–5pm Dec–Feb). It comprises two buildings: the East Building, which tells of Hiroshima before the bomb fell and what happened to the city in the following months and years, and the West Building, which concentrates on that fateful August day. Entrance to the museum is in the East Building; admission is ¥50 (45¢). Although an audio guide is available for an additional ¥300 ($2.85), you can learn just

as much by reading the excellent English-language descriptions throughout the museum. You must enter 30 minutes before closing time, but you'll need at least 1 hour here to do the museum justice.

The newer East Building addresses Hiroshima's militaristic past, challenging the city's former self-characterization as a blameless victim. In great detail, it explains why Hiroshima was selected as the blast site—as Imperial Headquarters, Hiroshima was home to Japan's military command center as well as a military supply base (Mitsubishi, which produced war ships, was based here). It also gives food for thought as to why the bomb was dropped, suggesting that the high cost to develop the bomb (called the Manhattan Project), coupled with the desire to establish U.S. supremacy over the Soviet Union and facilitate defeat in Japan, all played a role. TV screens show actual footage of the bomb being dropped and its aftermath. A 360-degree photograph shows Hiroshima's utter destruction. The museum also documents Hiroshima's current dedication to the abolition of nuclear weapons; a globe of the world provides a chilling map of nuclear proliferation. On the ground floor is the Video Theatre, where two English-language documentaries are shown throughout the day. One is an appeal for peace from a mother's point of view, with footage of the bombing, while the second film takes a more scientific look at the atomic bombs in both Hiroshima and Nagasaki.

The West Building concentrates on the suffering caused by the atomic bomb, beginning with panoramas of scorched earth and seared victims and photographs of the atomic bomb that destroyed the city and the intensity of the blast's epicenter. It then shows in graphic detail the effects of the blast on bodies, buildings, and materials. Most of the photographs in the exhibit are of burned and seared skin, charred remains of bodies, and people with open wounds, while displays explain the effects of radiation, including hair loss, keloid scars, leukemia, and cancer. There's a bronze Buddha that was half-melted in the blast and melted glass and ceramics. Tattered clothing and other personal effects are accompanied by short biographies of their owners, many of them children and teenagers and many of whom died in the blast.

Needless to say, visiting Peace Memorial Park is a sobering and depressing experience but perhaps a necessary one. And to think that what was dropped on Hiroshima is small compared to the bombs of today; by 1961, the Soviet Union had tested a hydrogen bomb 3,300 times more powerful than the atomic bomb dropped on Hiroshima. From the museum, the closest streetcar stop is Fukuro-machi, where you can catch streetcar no. 1 for Hiroshima Station.

## MORE SIGHTS & ATTRACTIONS

**Hiroshima Castle**    Completed in 1591 but destroyed in the atomic blast, Hiroshima Castle was reconstructed in 1958. Its five-story wooden donjon is a faithful reproduction of the original, but the main reason to come here is the very good museum housed in the castle's modern interior, which can be toured in about 30 minutes. The museum is devoted to Hiroshima's history as a flourishing castle town, with good English-language presentations. It also gives the best description I've seen on castles in Japan, including differences in architecture between those built on hills (for defense) and those built on plains (mainly administrative). Videos describe Hiroshima's founding and the construction of Hiroshima Castle, while displays explain the differences in lifestyle between samurai and townspeople, the hierarchy of the feudal administration system, and other aspects of Edo life. There's also samurai gear, models of old Hiroshima and the castle, and, for children, a kimono and samurai outfit they can try on. The top of the donjon provides a panoramic view of the city.

21–1 Moto-machi, Naka-ku. ⓒ 082/221-7512. Admission ¥360 ($3.45) adults, ¥180 ($1.70) children. Daily 9am–5:30pm (to 4:30pm Oct–Mar). A 15-min. walk north of Peace Memorial Park, or a 25-min. walk west of Hiroshima Station. Streetcar: 1, 2, or 6 to Kamiya-cho (10 min.).

### Hiroshima Museum of Art (Hiroshima Bijutsukan)   This gem of a private
museum, housed in a modern round building in a park in the heart of the city, has a permanent collection of some 200 paintings, half by French painters from Romanticism to Ecole de Paris and presented in chronological order in four rooms. Though small, virtually every piece is by a well-known artist, including Delacroix, Courbet, Corot, Manet, Monet, Renoir, Degas, Toulouse-Lautrec, Rousseau, Cézanne, Gauguin, van Gogh, Matisse, Picasso, Braque, Utrillo, Chagall, and Modigliani. Also on display are about 90 works by Japanese artists in the Western style from the Meiji Era to the present, including works by Kuroda Seiki and Kishida Ryusei. You'll spend an hour here.

3–2 Motomachi, Naka-ku. ⓒ 082/223-2530. www.hiroshima-museum.jp. Admission ¥1,000 ($9.50) adults, ¥500 ($4.15) university and high-school students, ¥200 ($1.65) junior-high and elementary students. Special exhibits cost more. Daily 9am–5pm. Streetcar: 1, 2, or 6 to Kamiya-cho (Kencho-mae exit, 3 min.). In Chuo Park, across from the Rihga Royal Hotel (Hiroshima's tallest building).

### Hiroshima Prefectural Art Museum (Hiroshima Kenritsu Bijutsukan)   The
main focus of this museum is art created by artists who have some kind of relationship to Hiroshima Prefecture, including Aimitsu (look for his self-portrait), Minami Kunzo, Kobayashi Senko, and Hirayama Ikuo (famous for his paintings of Hiroshima after the atomic bomb, especially *The Holocaust of Hiroshima*), as well as works from the 1920s and 1930s by non-Japanese artists who have influenced contemporary art in Japan such as Salvador Dalí, Lyonel Feininger, Picasso, and Thomas Hart Benton. Asian decorative arts, including ceramics and lacquerware, round out the permanent collection. If you purchase a combination ticket to Shukkei-en Garden, you can enter the garden directly from the museum. Plan on about 30 minutes here.

2–22 Kaminobori-cho, Naka-ku. ⓒ 082/221-6246. www1.hpam-unet.ocn.ne.jp. Admission ¥500 ($4.75) adults; ¥300 ($2.85) university students; free to high-school, junior-high, and elementary students. Combination ticket for museum and Shukkei-en Garden ¥600 ($5.70) for adults and ¥380 ($3.60) for students. Tues–Fri and Sun 9am–5pm; Sat 9am–7pm. Streetcar: 9 to Shukkeien-mae (1 min.). Adjacent to Shukkei-en Garden; a 15-min. walk from Hiroshima Station.

### Shukkei-en Garden   Shukkei-en Garden, which means "landscape garden in
miniature," was first laid out in 1620 by a master of the tea ceremony, with a pond constructed in imitation of famous Lake Xi Hu in Hangzhou, China. Using streams, ponds, islets, and bridges, it was designed to appear much larger than it actually is and is best viewed on a 30-minute circular stroll. Like everything else in Hiroshima, it was destroyed in 1945, but amazingly, it looks like it's been here forever. Unfortunately, like most gardens in Japan, tall neighboring buildings detract from the garden's beauty (there ought to be a law), but it's still a pleasant respite from city traffic.

2–11 Kaminobori-cho, Naka-ku. ⓒ 082/221-3620. Admission ¥250 ($2.40) adults, ¥180 ($1.70) university and high-school students, ¥120 ($1.15) children. Combination ticket for Hiroshima Prefectural Art Museum and the garden ¥600 ($5.70) for adults and ¥380 ($3.60) for university students. Daily 9am–6pm (to 5pm Oct–Mar). Adjacent to Hiroshima Prefectural Art Museum.

## EXPLORING SIGHTS OF THE SETO INLAND SEA
**BY BOAT**   Stretching between Honshu and the islands of Shikoku and Kyushu, the Inland Sea is dotted with more than 3,000 pine-covered islands and islets, part of which is protected as Seto-Nakai (Seto Inland Sea) National Park. Hiroshima Prefecture serves as a departure point for boats traveling to islands throughout the Seto

Inland Sea and to Shikoku. For an interesting day's excursion, I suggest taking the Shinkansen 30 minutes to Mihara (fare: ¥2,220/$21), from which you can take a **high-speed boat** operated by Mihara-Setoda Kyodo Line (© **0848/64-0564**) 30 minutes to Setoda on Ikuchijima island. Ferries depart approximately once an hour, with one-way fares costing ¥670 ($6.40).

From Setoda's ferry pier, it's about a 10-minute walk to **Choseizan Kosanji Temple** ✿✿ 553–2 Setoda (© **0845/27-0800;** www.kousanji.or.jp). This place is like no other, a re-creation of famous historic buildings from throughout Japan, erected by a former businessman-turned-Buddhist-priest over a 30-year period beginning in 1936 in honor of his mother. Occupying a picturesque, hillside setting with many flowering trees, the grounds contain remakes of Byodoin Temple outside Kyoto, Nikko's Yomeimon Gate, Horyuji's Hall of Visions in Nara, and other important buildings, all expertly crafted. Be sure to tour Choseikaku Villa, built in 1927 as the home of the priest's beloved mother and employing an amazing variety of woods for its intricately carved transoms, paneling, and other traditional features. Another highlight is the grotto cave (beside Byodoin Temple). Stretching 350m (1,155 ft.), it depicts unfortunate souls in hell being burned, chopped to pieces, eaten by animals, and suffering other gruesome forms of torture for crimes ranging from murder and thievery to drinking too much or having sex with a nun. After passing through caves and Buddhist statues, you then emerge to see a 15m (50-ft.) statue of the Goddess of Mercy, hoping by now that she is, indeed, merciful. On the crest of the hill is the Heights of Eternal Hope for the Future, a huge white-marble installation by a Hiroshima sculptor; its jagged edges resemble a glacier and there's a coffee shop here in what looks like an igloo. Other things to see include museums showcasing art relating to Buddhism, the tea ceremony, and modern Japanese art.

Admission to Kosanji Temple, open daily 9am to 5pm, is ¥1,200 ($11) for adults, ¥700 ($6.65) for high-school students, and free for children. By the way, near the front gate to Kosanji is a branch of a famous ice-cream shop, ⑫ **Dolce**, Kosanji-mae Ten (© **0845/26-4036**), renowned for its *Hakata-no-shio,* an ice cream that contains salt obtained from seawater (and tastes much better than it sounds). Ikuchijima is also known for its many outdoor sculptures placed around the island and for its 800m (2,640-ft.) Sunset Beach, a popular swimming destination.

**BY BICYCLE**    A more active way to see the Seto Inland Sea is to cycle across on the **Shimanami Kaido** (also referred to as the Nishi Seto Expwy. and the Setouchi Shimanami Seaway), an 80km (50-mile) route between Onomichi in Hiroshima Prefecture and Imabari on Shikoku Island. The route travels over six islands connected by seven bridges, with numerous temples (including Kosanji, above), sightseeing spots, restaurants, and inns along the way. Rental bikes are available at ⑬ **Onomichi Ekimae Kowan Chushajo,** 9 Higashi Goshocho, Onomichi City (© **0848/22-5332**), open daily 7am to 6pm. Bikes cost ¥500 ($4.75) for a day, plus a deposit of ¥1,000 ($9.50). If you wish to make a one-way trip and leave your bike in Imabari or at one of the 14 cycle rental stops along the way, you forfeit your deposit. The bridges along the route charge a toll, which you deposit into a box on the honor system, for a total of ¥510 ($4.25) if you go all the way to Shikoku (you can buy prepaid toll tickets at the Onomichi cycling shop so you don't have to fish for change). To reach Onomichi from Hiroshima, take the JR Sanyo Honsen line 1½ hours to Onomichi Station (fare: ¥1,450/$14), from which it's a 3-minute walk to the port where the cycling company is

located. If you have a Japan Rail Pass, it's quicker to take the Shinkansen 30 minutes to Mihara, followed by a 10-minute local train (fare: ¥230/$2.20) to Onomichi Station.

If you wish to cycle but have no interest in going all the way to Shikoku (truth be told, the beginning of the biking trail, from Onomichi, is not that interesting), I suggest taking the ferry from Mihara to Setoda (described above) and renting a bike at the Setoda-cho Kanko Annaisho (in front of the **Hirayama Ikuo Museum;** *C* **0845/ 27-0051;** open daily 9am–5pm). You can cycle around Ikuchijima in a couple of hours. Or, you can bike from Kosanji over the Tatara Ohashi bridge to **Oyamazumi Shrine** (with a fantastic collection of samurai weaponry; see p. 480), on Omishima island, in about 2 hours. You can drop off your bike at the rental shop there, take a bus 9 minutes to Inokuchi-ko (buses depart approximately twice an hour; fare: ¥200/$1.90), and from there take a high-speed boat for ¥1,070 ($10) back to Mihara for the Shinkansen to Hiroshima (at last check, afternoon boat departures were at 3:36 and 4:55pm but you should confirm this).

For more information on cycling the Shimanami Kaido, see the section on Matsuyama in chapter 10.

## WHERE TO STAY

The **Setouchi Welcome booklet,** available free at local tourist offices, provides a 10% discount for several hotels, including the Granvia, Sunroute, and Regalo.

### EXPENSIVE

**Rihga Royal Hiroshima** ✦✦✦   Opened in 1994, the 33-story Rihga Royal stands out as Hiroshima's tallest hotel and has a convenient location in the heart of the city between Hiroshima Castle and Peace Park. It's connected to a large complex called Motomachi CRED, which includes the Pacela shopping mall and Sogo department store. A sophisticated, European atmosphere and polished service make it a favorite among foreign travelers; even the lobby lounge—with its tall ceiling and circular glass facade—makes for a cheerful meeting place. Large rooms with luxurious furnishings come with plenty of features, including semi-double beds in the singles and twins, and magnifying mirrors and lots of counter space in the bathrooms. Rates are based on floor height and room size, but even some of the cheapest twins have views of the castle or Peace Park. The best views, however, are from top floors with panoramas of the Seto Inland Sea (you can even see Miyajima). A nice touch are the pictorial maps in each room describing the view, but the best view of all is afforded from the 33rd floor, where the Sky Buffet Rijo serves all-you-can-eat buffet lunches and dinners (see "Where to Dine," below) and the Rihga Top provides a sophisticated setting for afternoon tea, French dinners, or evening cocktails.

6–78 Motomachi, Naka-ku, Hiroshima 730-0011. *C* 082/502-1121. Fax 082/228-5415. www.rihga.com. 490 units. ¥15,015–¥17,325 ($143–$165) single; ¥21,945–¥31,185 ($219–$297) double; ¥23,100–¥35,805 ($220–$341) twin; from ¥38,115 ($363) executive twin. Rates include service charge. AE, DC, MC, V. Streetcar: 1, 2, or 6 to Kamiya-cho (1 min.). **Amenities:** 7 restaurants; 1 bar; 2 lounges; atrium-style pool w/Jacuzzi and sauna (¥3,150/$30); health club (¥3,150/$30); concierge; shopping arcade; health and dental clinic; salon; barber; room service (7am–11:30pm); in-room massage; babysitting; same-day laundry/dry-cleaning service; nonsmoking rooms; executive-level rooms. *In room:* A/C, cable TV w/pay movies, minibar, hot-water pot w/tea, hair dryer, bathroom scale, Washlet toilet, trouser press.

### MODERATE

**Hotel Granvia Hiroshima** ✦   Owned by JR West (and offering discounts to holders of the Japan Rail Pass), this hotel is convenient for short stays because it's connected to the Shinkansen (north) side of the station. Inconvenient, however, is that to get to

Hiroshima's sights and streetcars, which are on the other side of the station, you have to navigate a confusing underground passage (if you have a rail pass, you can pass through the station, which is much quicker). Rooms are comfortable but are small and have no view, unless you count views of the Shinkansen pulling into the station. A plus are the hotel's many dining options, including one serving Hiroshima-style okonomiyaki.

1–5 Matsubara-cho, Minami-ku, Hiroshima 732-0822. ℂ 082/262-1111. Fax 082/262-4050. www.hgh.co.jp. 410 units. ¥11,319–¥16,747 ($108–$159) single; ¥17,902–¥21,945 ($170–$209) double; ¥21,945–¥34,650 ($209–$330) twin. 10% discount for holders of Japan Rail Pass. AE, DC, MC, V. Attached to Hiroshima Station. **Amenities:** 9 restaurants; 2 bars; 1 lounge; 1 outdoor beer terrace (summer only); access to health club in Hiroshima Station w/gym, indoor pool, and sauna (discount ticket at concierge desk ¥2,620/$25); concierge; tour desk; business center; shopping arcade; salon; room service (7–10am and 5–11pm); in-room massage; same-day laundry/dry-cleaning service; nonsmoking rooms. *In room:* A/C, cable TV, dataport, minibar, hot-water pot w/tea, hair dryer, Washlet toilet.

## Mitsui Garden Hotel Hiroshima 𝔊

Located on Heiwa Odori (Peace Boulevard), about an 8-minute walk east of Peace Memorial Park, this is a smart-looking business hotel. Although not as convenient as the Sunroute (below), it's classier, with a chic lobby outfitted in warm, dark browns and small rooms with a contemporary edge. I especially like the rooms on the Ladies' Floor, which are cheerfully done in yellow instead of the usual white. Room air conditioners can be set for either Celsius or Fahrenheit, taking away the guessing for most of us.

9–12 Naka-machi, Naka-ku, Hiroshima 730-0037. ℂ **082/240-1131.** Fax 082/242-3001. 280 units. ¥8,500–¥10,500 ($81–$100) single; ¥16,800–¥21,000 ($160–$200) double; ¥16,800–¥26,000 ($160–$248) twin. AE, DC, MC, V. Streetcar: 1 to Fukuro-machi (5 min.). Walk south (the same direction as your streetcar) on Rijo Dori to Heiwa Odori (there's a small shrine on the corner) and turn left; it will be on your left. **Amenities:** 3 restaurants (Japanese, Continental, coffee shop); 1 bar; salon; in-room massage; same-day laundry/dry-cleaning service; nonsmoking rooms. *In room:* A/C, TV w/pay movies, dataport, fridge, hot-water pot w/tea, hair dryer, Washlet toilet.

## Hotel Sunroute 𝔊𝔊

Although most hotels in this chain are strictly business hotels, this hotel's excellent location, next to the river and catty-corner from the museum in Peace Memorial Park, plus two very good restaurants with great views, makes it a popular choice for tourists as well (see Kissui, below, in the dining section). The highest-priced rooms have the additional advantage of views of the park and river; the cheapest rooms, however, are on low floors and have no views whatsoever. Nice touches are bedside reading lights that can be dimmed and chilled glasses in the fridge.

3–3–1 Otemachi, Naka-ku, Hiroshima 730-0051. ℂ **082/249-3600.** Fax 082/249-3677. www.sunroute.jp. 284 units. ¥8,925–¥9,975 ($85–$95) single; ¥15,750–¥18,900 ($150–$180) double; ¥16,800–¥26,250 ($160–$250) twin. AE, DC, MC, V. Streetcar: 1 to Chuden-mae (3 min.). Backtrack north to Heiwa Odori and turn left; it's on your left before the river. **Amenities:** 2 restaurants (Japanese, Italian); 1 bar; in-room massage; same-day laundry/dry-cleaning service; nonsmoking rooms. *In room:* A/C, satellite TV w/pay movies, dataport (most rooms), minibar, hot-water pot w/tea, hair dryer, Washlet toilet, trouser press.

## INEXPENSIVE

**Regalo** 𝔊𝔊 *Finds* Opened in 1998 on one of Hiroshima's many rivers, this small, personable hotel, located about halfway between Hiroshima Station and downtown, offers great value and is a true find—nicely decorated with an Italian flair and managed by a very friendly staff, some of whom speak English. The cheapest rooms have glazed windows facing the back, while rooms only slightly more expensive have refreshing views of the river. A very atmospheric Italian restaurant also capitalizes on the river view, while across the street, right beside the river, is the hotel's open-air pavilion cafe. There's a computer in the lobby you can use for free, as well as telephones with free domestic calls to land lines (in-room phones are only for receiving

calls, not for making calls). In short, this establishment is a pleasant surprise compared to most inexpensive lodgings and has more personality than the Toyoko Inn chain.

9–2 Hashimoto-cho, Naka-ku, Hiroshima 730-0015. ☎ **082/224-6300.** Fax 082/224-6301. info@regalo-h.com. 63 units. ¥6,500–¥7,000 ($62–$67) single; ¥9,500–¥10,000 ($90–$95) double; ¥9,800–¥10,000 ($93–$95) twin. Rates include breakfast. AE, DC, MC, V. Streetcar: 1, 2, or 6 to Kanayama-cho (2 min.). Walk back toward the bridge but don't cross it; turn left at the river. Or a 13-min. walk from Hiroshima Station. **Amenities:** Restaurant (Italian); cafe; tea lounge; computer in lobby w/free Internet access; in-room massage; coin-op washer and dryer; same-day laundry/dry-cleaning service; nonsmoking rooms (only 4 twin rooms). *In room:* A/C, TV w/pay movies, dataport, fridge, hot-water pot w/tea, hair dryer, Washlet toilet, no phone.

**Sansui Ryokan** 🐕 This is a good choice for travelers who like meeting locals rather than staying in impersonal hotels. It's run by motherly Katou-san, who cheerfully oversees operations, has kimono you can try on for free, and can even arrange lessons in calligraphy, the tea ceremony, and Japanese dance with local teachers (fees ¥1,000–¥2,500/$9.50–$24 and reservations must be made 3 weeks in advance). It has a cozy communal room, but note that tatami rooms on the second floor are reached by steep stairs. Best of all, it's only a few minutes' walk west of Peace Memorial Park.

4–16 Koami-cho, Naka-ku, Hiroshima 730-0855. ☎ **082/293-9051.** Fax 082/233-2377. sansui@ccv.ne.jp. 6 units (none with bathroom). ¥4,200 ($40) single; ¥7,500 ($71) twin; ¥10,500 ($100) triple. Breakfast ¥600 ($5.70) extra. MC, V. Streetcar: 2 or 3 to Kaomi-cho (1 min.). Walk toward the river and turn left, then left again. **Amenities:** Rental bikes (¥300/$2.70 per day); free coffee. *In room:* A/C, TV, hot-water pot w/tea, no phone.

**Toyoko Inn Hiroshima-Eki Shinkansen-Guchi** *Value* Although convenient if you're arriving by Shinkansen, this chain business hotel is inconvenient to the rest of the city, since streetcars depart from the other side of Hiroshima Station, reached only by underground passage unless you have a Japan Rail Pass. Still, it has the usual two computers in the lobby with free Internet access, two free movie channels, and free domestic calls from lobby phones.

There's another branch, Toyoko Inn Hiroshima Heiwa-Odori, 5–15 Tanaka-machi (☎ **082/504-1045**), which is closer to downtown, but it's a 7-minute walk from the nearest streetcar station, past the nightlife district.

2–6–25 Hikari-machi, Higashi-ku, Hiroshima 732-0052. ☎ **082/506-1045.** Fax 082/506-1052. www.toyoko-inn. com. 190 units. ¥6,300 ($60) single; ¥8,400 ($80) double or twin. Rates include Japanese breakfast. AE, DC, MC, V. A 3-min. walk from Hiroshima Station's North Shinkansen exit, straight ahead. **Amenities:** Computers w/free Internet access; nonsmoking rooms. *In room:* A/C, TV w/free movies, fridge, hot-water pot w/tea, hair dryer, safe, Washlet toilet.

## WHERE TO DINE
### EXPENSIVE

**Atago** 🐕🐕 TEPPANYAKI This teppanyaki steak restaurant, on the ground floor of an office building on Heiwa (Peace) Odori just east of Rijo Dori, is good and convenient if you're visiting the Peace Memorial Museum just across the river. It's strikingly modern with its marble tables and geometric lines, and chefs prepare steak and seafood before your eyes. The ¥2,888 ($28) set steak lunch from the English-language menu includes salad, steak, a vegetable, miso soup, rice, and dessert.

7–20 Nakamachi. ☎ 082/241-9129. Reservations recommended. Set dinners ¥7,000–¥18,000 ($67–$171); set lunches ¥2,888–¥10,395 ($28–$99). AE, DC, MC, V. Daily 11:30am–2pm and 5–9:30pm (last order). Streetcar: 1 to Fukuro-machi (2 min.). Between Shirakami-sha Shrine and ANA Hotel on Heiwa (Peace) Odori.

⑦⑦④ **Kanawa** 🐕🐕 *Finds* OYSTERS There are 10,000 rafts cultivating oysters in Hiroshima Bay, with a yearly output of 30,000 tons of shelled oysters. Needless to say, oysters are a Hiroshima specialty, and this houseboat, moored east of Peace Memorial Park on the Motoyasu River at the Heiwa Odori Bridge, is one of the best places to

enjoy them. Although winter is the optimal time for fresh oysters, the owner has his own oyster rafts and can harvest them also in summer, as well as freeze his best stock in January so he's able to serve excellent oysters year-round. This floating restaurant has been here more than 45 years, and dining is in tatami rooms with views of the river. The English-language menu lists set meals that feature oysters prepared various ways, including in the shell, fried, baked, steamed in soy broth, and marinated in vinegar. In addition to oysters, flounder, eel, and a few other dishes are available as well.

On the Motoyasu River, at Heiwa-Ohashi Bridge. © 082/241-7416. Reservations required. Main dishes ¥1,000–¥2,800 ($9.50–$28); set dinners ¥8,500–¥11,000 ($81–$105); set lunches ¥3,100–¥6,500 ($30–$62). AE, DC, MC, V. Daily 11am–2pm and 5–9pm (last order). Streetcar: 1 to Chuden-mae (3 min.). Backtrack north to Heiwa Odori and turn left; it's just past the Sunroute Hotel.

## MODERATE

**Sky Buffet Rijo** ✿ VARIED BUFFET   This pleasant restaurant, serving inexpensive all-you-can-eat buffets, has a drawing-room ambience, but the main reason to dine here is that it's the city's highest restaurant, with a view of Hiroshima Castle. Buffets center on changing monthly themes (perhaps Italian one month, curries or regional Japanese cuisine the next) but always have Japanese and Western selections as well, plus one of the largest dessert and ice-cream buffets we've ever seen. After your meal, retire to the classy Rihga Top bar with great views of the Seto Inland Sea, but note that there's a ¥1,050 ($10) table charge for the live music in the evenings.

Rihga Royal Hiroshima, 33rd floor, 6–78 Motomachi. © 082/228-5473. Lunch buffet ¥3,003 ($29); dinner buffet ¥4,158 ($40) weekdays, ¥4,620 ($44) weekends and holidays. AE, DC, MC, V. Daily 11am–2pm and 5:30–9pm (last order). Streetcar: 1, 2, or 6 to Kamiya-cho (1 min.).

**Kissui** ✿✿ KAISEKI   Convenience to Peace Memorial Park, great 15th-floor views, and beautifully prepared kaiseki meals make this an optimal choice for tourists. Though the menu is in Japanese only, choose from the various seasonal kaiseki and shabu-shabu set meals according to your budget, but no matter what you choose, you can't go wrong here.

Hotel Sunroute, 15th floor, 3–3–1 Otemachi. © 082/249-5657. Kaiseki set meals ¥5,775–¥12,600 ($55–$120); shabu-shabu set meals ¥4,725–¥7,875 ($45–$75); set lunches ¥2,100–¥4,725 ($20 and $45). AE, DC, MC, V. Daily 11:30am–2pm and 5–8:30pm (last order). Streetcar: 1 to Chuden-mae (see directions to hotel, above).

## INEXPENSIVE

In addition to the choices here, the Pacela building, part of the fancy Motomachi CRED (pronounced *Kuredo* in Japanese) complex next to the Rihga Royal hotel, offers several ethnic choices, including restaurants serving Vietnamese, Korean, Chinese, Italian, and Indian cuisine.

**Anderson Kitchen** INTERNATIONAL   Occupying an old, renovated bank building in the Hondori covered shopping arcade, this popular place not far from Peace Memorial Park has a gourmet food department on its ground floor offering baked goods, wine, and imported delicacies, while the second floor has a cafeteria with various counters specializing in different types of food—salads, sandwiches, pizza, pasta, steaks, Chinese dishes, desserts, or drinks: Just pick up a tray and select the items you want. You pay at the end of each counter.

7–1 Hondori. © 082/247-2403. Dishes ¥600–¥1,360 ($5.70–$13). No credit cards. Daily 11am–9pm (last order). Closed some Wed. Streetcar: 1 to Hondori (1 min.); in the Hondori covered shopping arcade 1 block to the east.

(175) **Kushinobo** ✿✿ KUSHIYAKI   This is a friendly, rub-elbows-with-the-locals kind of place, lively and crowded and decorated with Japanese knickknacks. It's

located due east of the Hondori covered shopping arcade. Although kushiyaki connoisseurs like ordering skewers a la carte, you'll probably be better off ordering from the English-language menu, which lists only set meals. I always enjoy the Kushinobo-gozen with 10 skewers of vegetables, meat, and seafood plus fresh vegetables, rice, soup, and dessert, but what I like the most is watching skewers being prepared behind the counter and the friendly interactions between customers. The chef is a serious fellow, but he speaks English and somehow manages to keep all the orders straight.

Parco-mae, 7–4 Horikawa-cho. ℂ 082/245-9300. Reservations recommended. Set dinners ¥2,310 – ¥4,200 ($22–$40); set lunches ¥1,150–¥1,378 ($11–$13). AE, DC, MC, V. Daily 11:30am–1:30pm and 5–9:30pm (last order). Streetcar: 1, 2, or 6 to Hatchobori (2 min.). Walk south on Chuo Dori 2 blocks to Parco department store and turn right into a covered shopping arcade; take the 1st left and then the 1st right. Look for its bright red facade.

(176) **No-no-Budou** ✦ *Value* JAPANESE BUFFET   This popular buffet restaurant in the Pacela shopping complex specializes in healthy, organic foods, with some 50 choices that change daily but always include choices of Chinese and Japanese dishes, from noodles and fried vegetables to soups and salads. Some seats beside windows provide city views, but avoid the lunchtime rush.

Motomachi CRED complex, 7th floor of Pacela, 78–6 Motomachi. ℂ 082/502-3340. Buffet lunch ¥1,575 ($15) weekdays, ¥1,680 ($16) weekends and holidays; buffet dinner ¥2,100 ($20) weekdays, ¥2,310 ($22) weekends and holidays. AE, DC, MC, V. Daily 11am–3pm and 5–9:30pm (last order). Streetcar: 1, 2, or 6 to Kamiya-cho (1 min.); follow the underground signs toward the Astram Line and take the exit on your left.

(177) **Okonomi-Mura** ✦✦ *Finds* OKONOMIYAKI   Although the people of Osaka claim to have made okonomiyaki popular among the masses, the people of Hiroshima claim to have made it an art. Okonomiyaki is a kind of Japanese pancake filled with cabbage, meat, and other fillings. Whereas in Osaka the ingredients are mixed together, in Hiroshima each layer is prepared separately, which means the chefs have to be quite skilled at keeping the whole thing together. This is the best place in town to witness these short-order cooks at their trade, although the building doesn't look as though it contains restaurants. Its name means "okonomiyaki village," and that's what it is—floors of individual stalls, dishing out okonomiyaki (the food still remains a dish for the masses). All okonomiyaki stalls offer basically the same menu—sit down at one of the counters and watch how the chef first spreads pancake mix on a hot griddle; follows it with a layer of cabbage, bean sprouts, and bacon; and then adds an egg on top. If you want, you can have yours with *udon* (thick wheat noodles) or *soba* (thin buckwheat noodles). The portion sizes are enormous; this is one of Hiroshima's most beloved establishments.

Wander through the area and stop at a stall that catches your fancy. Or, for a specific recommendation, try (178) **Chii-chan** (ℂ 082/249-8102), on the second floor. It serves food until midnight (closed on Tues) and has an English-language menu. Chii-chan and his female staff sell between 200 and 500 okonomiyaki a day.

5–13 Shintenchi. ℂ 082/241-8758. Set meals ¥730–¥1,365 ($6.95–$13). No credit cards. Daily 11am–9pm, but some stalls stay open later. Streetcar: 1, 2, or 6 to Hatchobori (2 min.). Walk south on Chuo Dori 4 blocks (you'll see Yamada on the corner) and turn right.

**Ristorante Mario** ✦✦ *Value* ITALIAN   Located south across Heiwa Odori from the Peace Memorial Museum, this casual restaurant beckons with a cozy, terra-cotta-hued interior, a glass facade open wide in nice weather, and a kind, welcoming staff. The food is good, too, with about a dozen kinds of pasta on the English-language menu, like spinach and sweet-potato gnocchi with a cheese sauce. There are also a few main dishes of the day.

4–11 Nakashima-cho. ✆ **082/248-4956**. Reservations recommended. Pasta ¥900–¥1,500 ($8.55–$14); set dinner ¥3,000 ($29); set lunches ¥1,200–¥2,400 ($11–$23). AE, DC, MC, V. Daily 11:30am–2:30pm and 5–11:30pm. Streetcar: 1 to Chuden-mae (4 min.). Backtrack north to Heiwa Odori and turn left; it's beyond the river to the left.

⑰⑨ **Sushi Tei** ⋇ 𝒱𝒶𝓁𝓊𝑒 SUSHI    Excellent sushi at reasonable prices is the reason this establishment is so popular. You'll be seated at the counters, as cooks shout greetings and orders back and forth. Ordering is made easy by an English-language menu. There are many other Sushi Tei restaurants in town, but this is perhaps the most convenient, since it is near the A-Bomb Dome, 1 block south of Aioi Dori, between the Kamiyacho and Genbaku-Dome-mae stops.

1-4-31 Otemachi. ✆ **082/545-1333**. 1 piece sushi ¥105–¥525 ($1–$5); sushi sets ¥525–¥2,100 ($5–$20). No credit cards. Mon–Sat 5pm–midnight; Sun and holidays noon–10pm. Streetcar: 1, 2, or 6 to Kamiyacho (1 min.).

## 12  Miyajima, Scenic Island in the Seto Sea ⋇⋇⋇

13km (8 miles) SW of Hiroshima

Easily reached in about 30 minutes from Hiroshima, **Miyajima** is a treasure of an island only 2km (1¼ miles) off the mainland in the Seto Inland Sea. No doubt you've seen pictures of its most famous landmark—a huge red *torii*, or shrine gate, rising out of the water. Erected in 1875 and made of camphor wood, it's one of the largest torii in Japan, measuring more than 16m (53 ft.) tall. It guards Miyajima's main attraction, Itsukushima Shrine.

With the Japanese penchant for categorizing the "three best" of virtually everything in their country—the three best gardens, the three best waterfalls, and so on—it's no surprise that Miyajima is ranked as one of the three most scenic spots in Japan (the other two are Matsushima in Tohoku; and Amanohashidate, a remote sand spit, on the Japan Sea coast). Only 31 sq. km (12 sq. miles) in area and consisting mostly of steep, wooded hills, it's an exceptionally beautiful island, part of the Seto-Naikai (Inland Sea) National Park that is mostly water, islands, and islets. Of course, this distinction means it can be quite crowded with visitors, particularly in summer.

Miyajima has been held sacred since ancient times. In the olden days, no one was allowed to do anything so human as to give birth or die on the island, so both the pregnant and the ill were quickly ferried across to the mainland. Even today there's no cemetery on Miyajima. Covered with cherry trees that illuminate the island with snowy petals in spring, and with maple trees that emblazon it in reds and golds in autumn, Miyajima is home to tame deer that roam freely through the village, and to monkeys that swing through the woods. It's a delightful island for strolls and hikes—but avoid coming on a weekend.

## ESSENTIALS

**GETTING THERE**    The easiest way to reach Miyajima is from Hiroshima. You can travel from Hiroshima by JR train, streetcar, bus, or boat, but the fastest and most reliable method is the **train,** which departs from Hiroshima Station approximately every 5 to 15 minutes, depending on the time of the day, and costs ¥400 ($3.80; free for JR Rail Pass holders) for the 26-minute ride to Miyajimaguchi (if you're downtown or in Peace Memorial Park, you might find it easier to catch the train at Nishi-Hiroshima Station). Otherwise, a **streetcar** takes about an hour from Hiroshima Station to Hiroden Miyajima, the last stop, and costs ¥270 ($2.55). All modes of transportation deposit you at Miyajima-guchi, from which it's just a couple minutes' walk to the **ferry** bound for Miyajima. There are two ferry companies offering the 10-minute ride

to Miyajima for ¥170 ($1.60), but if you have a **Japan Rail Pass,** you can ride on the JR ferry for free.

Alternatively, there's a boat that travels from downtown Hiroshima directly to Miyajima in 45 minutes. Operated by Aqua Net Hiroshima (© 082/240-5955), the **Sekai Isan Koro** boat departs from Motoyasu-bashi Bridge, near the A-Bomb Dome, five times daily (at last check, at 9am, 10:50am, 1:25pm, 3:15pm, and 5:05pm, but you'd be wise to confirm this). Fare is ¥1,900 ($18) one-way or ¥3,000 ($29) round-trip; children pay half fare. Note that service is suspended during inclement weather and when the tide is low. From mid-January through February, it operates only Friday to Sunday and holidays.

**VISITOR INFORMATION**   On Miyajima island, stop off at the **Tourist Information Office** (© 0829/44-2011), located in the Miyajima ferry terminal and open daily 9am to 7pm (to 6pm Dec to mid-Mar). It has an English-language flyer with a map, and the helpful staff can show where restaurants and accommodations are on the map or even make accommodations reservations for you. For ¥300 ($2.85) you can rent an English-spoken audio guide that describes the 20 places of interest noted on a companion map with a recommended walking tour—a great convenience. For more information, visit www.miyajima.or.jp.

**GETTING AROUND**   You can **walk** to all the sights, accommodations, and restaurants listed below. If you wish to visit one of the island's beaches or explore more of the island, rental **bicycles** are available at the JR ferry pier 8am to 5pm costing ¥320 ($3.05) for 2 hours or ¥1,050 ($10) for the whole day. Inquire at the JR ticket window. Otherwise, shuttle **buses** travel to the beaches twice an hour in July and every 15 minutes in August for ¥300 ($2.85). Ask the Tourist Information Office for a schedule.

## EXPLORING THE ISLAND
### SEEING THE SIGHTS

Miyajima's major attraction, **Itsukushima Shrine** ✿✿, 1-1 Miyajima-cho (© 0829/44-2020), is less than a 10-minute walk from the ferry pier (turn right from the terminal), at the end of a long a narrow pedestrian street called Omotesando Dori that is lined with souvenir shops and restaurants. Founded in 593 to honor three female deities, the wooden shrine is built over the water so that, when the tide is in, it appears as though the shrine is floating. A brilliant vermilion, it contrasts starkly with the wooded hills in the background and the blue of the sky above, casting its reflection in the waters below. If you do happen to see Itsukushima Shrine when the tide is in and it's seemingly floating on water, you should consider yourself very lucky indeed—most of the time the lovely shrine floats above a surface that's only a little more glamorous than mud. That's when imagination comes in handy (the Hiroshima tourist offices may have a tide calendar).

The majority of the shrine buildings are thought to date from the 16th century, preserving the original style of 12th-century architecture, but they have been repaired repeatedly through the centuries. Most of the shrine buildings are closed, but from sunrise to sunset daily (usually 6:30am–6pm in summer, to 5pm in winter), you can walk along the 231m (770-ft.) covered **dock,** which threads its way past the outer part of the main shrine and the oldest Noh stage in Japan. From the shrine, you'll have a good view of the red torii standing in the water. **Bugaku** (festival dances) are staged here 10 times a year (expect those days to be crowded with tour groups). An ancient dance performed to the accompaniment of court music, Bugaku was introduced to Japan centuries ago from India through China and Korea. The performer's costume is

orange, matching the shrine around him. Admission to the shrine is ¥300 ($2.85) for adults, ¥200 ($1.90) for college and high-school students, ¥100 (95¢) for children.

Turn right upon exiting the shrine. After a few minutes, you'll come to the island's most interesting museum, the **Miyajima Municipal History and Folklore Museum (Rekishi Minzoku Shiryokan)** 🎌🎌, 57 Miyajima-cho (© **0829/44-2019**; open Tues–Sun 8:30am–5pm). It has a colorful, English-language brochure to guide you through the 170-year-old house (which once belonged to a wealthy soy-sauce merchant and is built around a small Japanese garden), as well as through several other buildings. Packed with items donated by the people of Miyajima, the museum is a window into commoners' daily lives in ages past, with farm tools, water jars, cooking objects, carved-wood boxes, furniture, lacquerware, combs, and much more. Be sure to see the narrow, three-room dwelling in the back of the museum complex, typical of the island. Admission is ¥300 ($2.85) for adults, ¥170 ($1.60) for high-school students, and ¥150 ($1.45) for junior-high and elementary students. It will take about 30 minutes to see everything.

Another sight worth exploring is **Daisho-in Temple,** on the slope of Mount Misen, 210 Miyajima-cho (© **0829/44-0111**; open daily 8am–5pm). One of the most famous Shingon temples in western Japan, it has numerous worthwhile sights spread on its leafy grounds, including a mandala made of colored sand that was created by Tibetan priests, a main hall where worshippers pray for health and contentment, and a hall dedicated to Kobo Daishi, founder of the Shingon sect (his remains are interred on Mount Koya). In Henshokutsu Cave are Buddhist icons and sand gathered from all 88 pilgrimage temples on Shikoku; making a round here is considered as auspicious as visiting the temples themselves. Other halls contain deities thought to bring good health and to save humans from earthly sexual desires. Every year there are fire-walking festivals here, in which worshippers walk over hot coals. An excellent brochure at the entrance describes the various sights, free to the public.

## ENJOYING MIYAJIMA'S NATURAL WORLD

The other popular thing to do on Miyajima is to visit its highest peak, 525m (1,750-ft.) **Mount Misen.** Signs direct you to Momijidani Park, a pleasant hillside park covered with maple trees (spectacular in autumn) and cherry trees (heavenly in spring) and marked by a picturesque stream. From here, you can take cable cars to Mount Misen; round-trip tickets cost ¥1,800 ($17) for adults and ¥900 ($8.55) for children. However, you might wish to enjoy some of the scenery by walking back down (it takes about an hour), in which case one-way tickets cost ¥1,000 ($9.50) and ¥500 ($4.75) respectively. In any case, the summit of Mount Misen, a 30-minute walk from the cable car station, offers splendid views of the Seto-Naikai (Inland Sea) National Park, and Mount Misen itself is home to much of the island's wild monkey population. But it is best known for Kobo Daishi's visit in 806, when he spent a 100-day retreat here and is said to have lit the Eternal Fire, which has reputedly been burning for more than 1,200 years and was used to light the Peace Flame in Hiroshima's Peace Memorial Park.

Miyajima is also known for its beaches. If you're looking to swim, there are two beaches west of the town and shrine: **Suginoura** and **Tsutsumigaura Natural Park** (you can also camp here). Ask at the tourist office for a schedule of shuttle buses that will bring you to the beaches.

## WHERE TO STAY

You can see Miyajima easily on a day's trip from Hiroshima, but because it's such a beautiful respite from city life and because most tourists are day-trippers, you'll enjoy

the island much more if you stay behind after the last ferry leaves. An added benefit of a longer stay: Itsukushima Shrine is illuminated at night, a gorgeous sight overnighters should not miss. I've therefore included a few recommendations on where to stay, but avoid Golden Week and weekends in July, August, October, and November (when maple leaves are in full color), since accommodations are usually full.

180 **Guest House Kikugawa** ★★ *Value*   Located in a quiet residential neighborhood an easy walk from the ferry pier, this guesthouse is modern yet adheres to traditional Japanese design with its whitewashed walls, dark timber framing, white paper lanterns, and simple elegance. The owner, Kikugawa-san, speaks English and is an accomplished chef, serving French food with a Japanese twist in his pleasant restaurant with a restful view of a maple tree (advance reservations required). Six of the guest rooms are Western style and are rather ordinary, reflected in the cheaper room rates below. The two other more expensive rooms face the front and boast flowers, bilingual TV, and Washlet toilet; the smaller is a tatami room, while the larger has a tatami area and a loft with Western-style beds. Since this place is small, make reservations 6 months in advance if you want to stay here in July, August, October, or November.

66615–796 Miyajima-cho, Hatsukaichi-shi, Hiroshima-ken 739-0511. © 0829/44-0039. Fax 0829/44-2773. www. kikugawa.ne.jp. 8 units. ¥6,615 ($63) single; ¥11,550–¥17,850 ($110–$170) twin/double. ¥1,050 ($10) more per person in peak season. Breakfast ¥1,050 ($10) extra; dinner ¥3,675 and ¥5,250 ($35 and $50) extra. AE, DC, MC, V. A 3-min. walk from the ferry terminal; walk through the short tunnel in front of the terminal toward the right and then turn right. **Amenities:** Restaurant (Japanese/French). *In room:* A/C, TV, hot-water pot w/tea, hair dryer.

181 **Iwaso Ryokan** ★★★ *Finds*   This is the most famous ryokan on the island, and with a history spanning more than 150 years, it was also the first ryokan to open on Miyajima, which explains its idyllic location in Momijidani Park. It's highly recommended for a splurge, with the price dependent on the room, its view, and the meals you select (when booking your room, be sure to specify any dietary needs such as vegetarian food only, whether you want a Western breakfast, or whether there are Japanese foods you cannot eat). The newest part of the ryokan was built in 1981, and though some of its newer rooms have very peaceful and relaxing views of a stream and woods, I prefer the rooms dating from about 70 years ago; they have more individuality. If you really want to go all out and live in style, there are also a couple of separate cottages *(hanare)* that are more than 80 years old, all exquisitely decorated. Open your shoji screens to see maples, a gurgling brook, and woods, all in utter privacy. You'll be treated like royalty here, but of course you have to pay for it.

Momijidani, 345 Miyajima-cho, Hatsukaichi-shi, Hiroshima-ken 739-0522. © 0829/44-2233. Fax 0829/44-2230. www.iwaso.com. 44 units (36 with bathroom). ¥21,050–¥42,000 ($200–$400) per person. Cottages ¥36,750– ¥42,000 ($350–$400) per person. Rates are higher during peak season and nights before holidays. Rates include 2 meals and service charge. AE, V. A 15-min. walk from the ferry pier in Momijidani Park. Pickup service available. **Amenities:** Hot-spring baths; in-room massage. *In room:* A/C, TV, minibar, hot-water pot w/tea, hair dryer, safe.

182 **Miyajima Morinoyado** ★★ *Value*   You're forgiven if you pass this place by, thinking it must be an exclusive ryokan. Indeed, if it weren't a municipally owned Kokumin Shukusha (People's Lodge), rates here would easily be three times as much as they are. Though modern, it has a lovely Japanese design with a lobby overlooking a carp pond. On the other hand, the many school groups and families staying here leave no doubt that it's a public lodge, and it's quite a hike from the ferry pier. Both tatami rooms and Western-style twins—simple but spacious and spotless—are available, some with views of the bay. The public baths look onto rock gardens. Reservations should be made 1 year in advance, especially for August, but sometimes there are

cancellations; when I dropped by on a weekday in June, rooms were available. Both Western and Japanese breakfasts are available; dinners are Japanese.

Miyajima-cho, Hatsukaichi-shi, Hiroshima-ken 739-0500. ℂ 0829/44-0430. Fax 0829/44-2248. 30 units (26 with bathroom, 4 with toilet only). ¥8,400–¥11,865 ($80–$113) per person. ¥735 ($7) more per person on Sat, nights before holidays, and during peak season (Apr–May and July–Aug). Discounts given for children. Rates include 2 meals. No credit cards. A 25-min. walk from the ferry pier, across from the aquarium and just before the tunnel. **Amenities:** Restaurant (Japanese). *In room:* A/C, TV, hot-water pot w/tea.

**Momiji-so** ⭐⭐    This small, Japanese-style house has a great location in Momijidani Park, not far from the ropeway to Mount Misen, and has been in business for 90 years. Tatami rooms vary in size, though all have artwork, flowers, and views of the surrounding park; the best looks out over a koi pond. A plus is the nice outdoor Japanese restaurant serving noodles, barbecued conger eel on rice, and other dishes—weather permitting, you'll dine outside. Not much English is spoken, but they're used to foreigners and are very kind.

Momijidani-koennai, Miyajima-cho, Hatsukaichi-shi, Hiroshima-ken 739-0500. ℂ 0829/44-0077. Fax 0829/44-0076. www.gambo-ad.com. 7 units (3 with bathroom). ¥7,350 ($70) per person without meals, ¥8,925 ($85) per person with breakfast, ¥12,075–¥16,800 ($115–$160) per person with 2 meals. No credit cards. A 25-min. walk from the ferry pier in Momijidani Park. Pickup service available. *In room:* A/C, TV, minibar, hot-water pot w/tea, no phone.

## WHERE TO DINE

*Note:* There are no addresses in this section, because the village is small, and the address would only be meaningful to the postman.

(183) **Fujitaya** ⭐⭐ *(Finds)* ANAGOMESHI    Although the building itself is not old, this pleasant restaurant has a history of more than 80 years and preserves a traditional atmosphere with its wooden ceiling, shoji lamps, and a back courtyard with a maple tree, moss-covered rocks, and water running from a bamboo pipe into a pool carved into a flat rock. Fujitaya serves only *anagomeshi* (barbecued conger eel on rice), which comes with side dishes (such as pickled vegetables), soup, and tea. It closes when it runs out of anago.

ℂ 0829/44-0151. Anagomeshi teishoku ¥2,300 ($22). No credit cards. Mon–Fri 11am–3pm; Sat–Sun 11am–5pm. A 20-min. walk from the ferry pier, on the right side of the road leading toward Daishoin after exiting from Itsukushima Shrine. Look for its name written on an oversize paddle on its facade.

(184) **Koumitei** ⭐ OKONOMIYAKI    Convenient to the ferry pier, this simple restaurant with counter, table, and tatami dining stays open later than most restaurants on the island and is one of the cleanest okonomiyaki restaurants we've seen. Both Hiroshima-style (which is prepared for you) and Kansai-style (which you prepare yourself) okonomiyaki are available from the English-language menu.

ℂ 0829/44-0177. Okonomiyaki ¥735–¥945 ($7–$9); set meals ¥1,050–¥1,260 ($10–$12). No credit cards. Thurs–Tues 11am–2:30pm and 5–9pm. A 1-min. walk from the ferry pier, catty-corner to the right.

(185) **Tonookajaya** NOODLES    Dine inside or out at this tiny teahouselike shop next to the five-story pagoda. The shop serves mostly *udon* (thick wheat noodles), including udon with tempura, but it also offers a few other choices on its English-language menu, including a sweet rice porridge *(amazake,* served Oct–May). What makes this place especially interesting is the 200-year-old pine tree out front that has been guided through the centuries to attain its unique, horizontal shape. You can also come here just for drinks.

ℂ 0829/44-2455. Main dishes ¥580–¥750 ($5.50–$7.15). No credit cards. Daily 10am–5pm. A 10-min. walk from the ferry pier on the hill with the 5-story pagoda, down steps leading toward the bay.

# Shikoku

The smallest of Japan's four main islands, Shikoku is also the one least visited by foreigners. That's surprising considering the natural beauty of its rugged mountains, its mild climate, and its most famous monuments—88 sacred Buddhist temples. Many Japanese wish to make a pilgrimage to all 88 temples at least once in their lifetime as a tribute to the great Buddhist priest Kobo Daishi, who was born on Shikoku in 774 and who founded the Shingon sect of Buddhism.

This pilgrimage has been popular since the Edo Period in the belief that a successful completion of the tour exonerates Buddhist followers from rebirth. It used to take a couple months to visit all 88 temples on foot. Even today, you can see pilgrims making their rounds dressed in white—only now they go mostly by organized tour buses, which cut travel time down to 2 weeks.

**GETTING TO SHIKOKU** For centuries, the only way to reach Shikoku was by boat. However, the 1988 completion of the Seto Ohashi Bridge, which links Shikoku with Okayama Prefecture and accommodates both cars and trains, changed Shikoku forever. And in 1999, a series of bridges connecting Shikoku with Hiroshima Prefecture and spanning six scenic islands in the Seto Inland Sea opened with fanfare. Complete with cycling paths offering views of the islands and the Seto Inland Sea, the 1999 bridges have since become one of Shikoku's hottest attractions. A third bridge, for cars only, connects Shikoku with Kobe.

In any case, Shikoku is no longer as far off the beaten track as it used to be, simply because access is so easy. Shinkansen travelers can simply transfer in Okayama to trains bound for either Takamatsu or Matsuyama. The energetic can even cycle from Honshu to Shikoku, from Hiroshima Prefecture to Ehime Prefecture.

## 1 Takamatsu ✶

805km (500 miles) W of Tokyo; 71km (44 miles) S of Okayama

The second-largest town on Shikoku, with a population of 330,000, Takamatsu, the capital of Kagawa Prefecture, is on the northeastern coast of the island, overlooking the Seto Inland Sea. Takamatsu means "high pine," and the city served as the feudal capital of the powerful Matsudaira clan from 1642 until the Meiji Restoration in 1868. The Matsudairas are responsible for Takamatsu's most famous site, Ritsurin Park, one of the most outstanding gardens in Japan. Takamatsu also boasts more bonsai nurseries than anywhere else in Japan, while nearby is Kotohiragu Shrine, a popular mountaintop destination that requires a real workout just to see.

# Shikoku

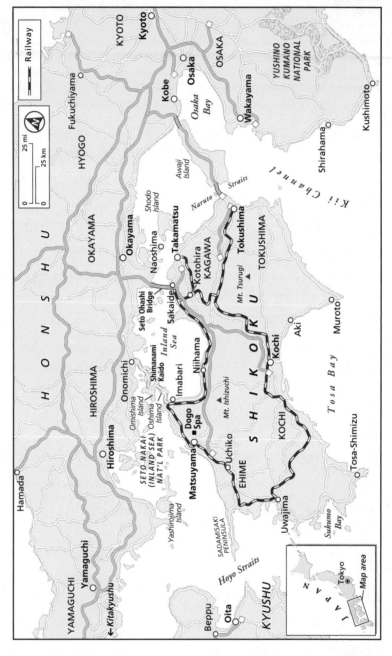

## ESSENTIALS

**GETTING THERE   By Plane**   JAL flies from Tokyo's Haneda Airport (¥25,700/$245 for a one-way ticket) in 1 hour and 20 minutes. There is also air service from Osaka, Sapporo, Nagoya, and Fukuoka. An airport bus delivers passengers downtown in about 45 minutes for ¥740 ($7.05).

**By Train   JR's Marine Liner** trains depart from Okayama Station approximately once an hour, reaching Takamatsu in an hour; the fare is ¥1,470 ($14). From Matsuyama, trains take less than 2½ hours and cost ¥5,500 ($52).

**By Bus**   Buses depart from Tokyo Station nightly at 8:20pm, reaching Takamatsu at 5:55am the next day. One-way fare is ¥10,000 ($95). There are also night buses from Shinjuku.

**VISITOR INFORMATION**   The **Takamatsu Information Plaza** (© 087/851-2009; open daily 9am–6pm), located outside the main exit of the train station in a small building on the left side of the circular plaza, offers an English-language map of the city and the Kagawa Welcome Card, a free miniguide complete with a discount card offering reduced rates for participating hotels, shops, restaurants, and attractions. The Shikoku Passport—also available here—also gives discounts to some of the listings below. Information is also available online at www.city.takamatsu.kagawa.jp/english.

If you crave a bit of news from home or plan to remain in the area, head for **I-Pal Kagawa,** 1–11–63 Bancho (© 087/837-5908; open Tues–Sun 9am–6pm), located about a 15-minute walk south of Takamatsu Station on Chuo Dori in the northwest corner of Central (Chuo) Park. Here you'll find magazines and newspapers in many languages, CNN on the tube, and three computers you can use free of charge for 30 minutes. This is also a good place to find out what's going on in the area.

**INTERNET ACCESS**   Since I-Pal Kagawa, above, has only three computers, you might be better off going to Queensberry@Café, on the third floor of the Maritime Plaza in the Hall Building of Takamatsu Symbol Tower, just outside Takamatsu Station (© 087/811-2040). It's open daily 11am to midnight, charging ¥100 (95¢) for 30 minutes, plus a one-drink minimum.

**ORIENTATION & GETTING AROUND**   Takamatsu Station, Takamatsu Port, and the local streetcar terminus are clustered at the north edge of the city on the coast of the Seto Inland Sea, in a new urban development called Sunport Takamatsu, which also includes the 30-story Takamatsu Symbol Tower, convention halls, exhibition and concert facilities, restaurants, shops, and offices. Office workers take respite along the Waterfront Harbor Walk and Tamamo Park, site of Takamatsu Castle's remains.

Most of the hotels and restaurants listed below, as well as Ritsurin Park, are located south and southeast of Sunport Takamatsu. **Chuo Dori** is the town's main avenue, running south from Sunport to Ritsurin Park and beyond. Bisecting Chuo Dori and paralleling it to the east are 2.5km (1½ miles) of shopping arcade.

Although the main attractions of Takamatsu are spread out, they're easily reached from Takamatsu Station by **JR train** or by a commuter streetcar called the **Kotoden Line.** The Kotoden streetcar terminus, called **Kotoden Chikko Station,** is a 2-minute walk from Takamatsu Station's main exit, past the ANA hotel and to the right. Two stops south on the Kotoden streetcar (or a 25-min. walk from Takamatsu Station) is **Kawaramachi Station,** where you'll find many department stores, restaurants, and nightspots.

# SEEING THE SIGHTS

**Ritsurin Park** 🐝🐝🐝  Ritsurin Park was once the summer retreat of the Matsudaira family. Work on the park began in the 1600s and took about 100 years to complete. Using the backdrop of adjacent Mount Shiun in a principle known as "borrowed landscaping," the 54-hectare (134-acre) park incorporates the mountain into its overall design. Basically, the garden can be divided into two parts: a traditional, classical, southern garden; and a modern, northern garden, once a lord's private hunting grounds and with wide grassy lawns and huge lotus ponds.

The **southern garden** is the more interesting. Arranged around the prescribed six ponds and 13 scenic mounds, it represents what's called a strolling garden, in which each bend of the footpath brings another perspective into view, another combination of rock, tree, and mountain. The garden is absolutely exquisite, and what sets it apart are its twisted, contorted pines. On one of my visits, a mist was rolling off Mount Shiun, lending mystery to the landscape; what better fits the image of traditional Japan than mist and pine trees? Altogether, there are 1,400 pine trees and 350 cherry trees in Ritsurin Park, which you should tour in a counterclockwise fashion to fully appreciate the changing views. Although I consider this garden just as beautiful as those in Okayama and Kanazawa, tall buildings on its eastern periphery detract from its overall effect; without them I would give this garden top rating.

There are a couple of things you can stop and see during your tour of the park. In the northern garden are the **Sanuki Folk Art Museum (Sanuki Mingei Kan),** which is included in the park's admission fee and displays local folk art and handicrafts such as ceramics, lacquerware, furniture, and items used in daily Edo life (regrettably, there are no English-language descriptions); and the **Commerce and Industry Hall (ShokoShorei-kan),** which sells local products, including kites, masks, woodcarvings, umbrellas, fans, and food items. But my favorite thing to do is drop by **Kikugetsu-tei (Scooping the Moon House)** in the southern garden, with its teahouse dating from feudal days overlooking a pond. Powdered tea, used in tea ceremonies, costs ¥710 ($6.75) for adults and ¥550 ($5.25) for children. It takes about an hour to see the southern garden; add another half-hour if you also take in the northern garden.

1–20–16 Ritsurin-cho. Ⓒ 087/833-7411. Admission ¥400 ($3.80) adults, ¥170 ($1.60) children. 20% discount available with the Kagawa Welcome Card or Shikoku Passport. Daily sunrise–sunset (approximately 7am–5pm in winter, 5:30am–7pm June–Aug). Kotoden streetcar: Ritsurin-koen Station (10 min.). JR train: If you have a Japan Rail Pass, go by JR train toward Tokushima; get off at Ritsurin-koen Kita Guchi, turn right out of the station, follow the tracks to the 1st street, and turn right (4 min.).

**Shikoku Mura Village** 🐝🐝  On the northeastern edge of town, this open-air museum boasts more than 30 traditional houses, sheds, and storehouses dating from the Edo Period and collected from all over Shikoku. The structures, picturesquely situated on the wooded slope of Yashima Hill, include thatch-roofed homes of farmers and fishermen, century-old cottages used by lighthouse keepers, a rustic tea-ceremony house, a 250-year-old rural Kabuki stage, rice and soy-sauce storehouses, and sheds for pressing sugar and for producing paper out of mulberry bark. There's also a suspended bridge made of vines, once a familiar sight in Shikoku as a means for crossing the island's many gorges and ravines—if you look closely, however, you'll see that this one is reinforced by cables.

It takes at least an hour to stroll through the village (and there are lots of stairs). I heartily recommend a visit if you haven't had the opportunity to see similar villages in

---

**Finds  Bonsai Is Big in Kinashi**

If you've long admired the art of **bonsai**—the crafting of miniature pines and other trees through skillful manipulation—you might wish to take a stroll through **Kinashi**, a western suburb of Takamatsu. With more than 100 nurseries, most of them cultivating bonsai, Kinashi has been a center of bonsai since the Edo Period and remains the largest bonsai-growing region in Japan. To reach it, take a local JR train from Takamatsu Station two stations to Kinashi, walk north a few minutes, and then turn right onto Bonsai Street. One of the largest nurseries, ⑱⑥ **Kandaka-Shoju-en** (© **087/881-2852**), will soon be on your right. It's owned by a fourth-generation bonsai cultivator; some of the larger pines here were started by his ancestors. You're welcome to walk through this and other nearby nurseries. This is the only place I've ever seen bonsai groves, with hundreds of tiny pine trees planted in rows. On the 5th, 15th, and 20th of each month from 9am to 5pm, there's a Bonsai Auction on Bonsai Street, where serious bidding takes place.

---

Takayama, Shirakawago, or Kawasaki, since they convey better than anything else rural life in Japan in centuries past. Also in Shikoku Mura is the **Shikoku Mura Gallery,** designed by famed Japanese architect Tadao Ando and displaying mostly 19th- and 20th-century French paintings (works by Renoir and Bonnard are especially significant), calligraphy, Chinese Buddhist images, and ancient glassware, earthenware, and bronze mirrors. It's open daily 9am to 5:30pm (to 6pm in summer). Admission here is an extra ¥500 ($4.75) for adults, ¥300 ($2.85) for children.

91 Yashima-naka-machi. © **087/843-3111.** Admission ¥800 ($7.60) adults, ¥500 ($4.75) high-school students, ¥400 ($3.80) junior-high students, ¥300 ($2.85) children. Daily 8:30am–5pm (to 4:30pm in winter). 20% discount with Kagawa Welcome Card. Kotoden streetcar: To Kotoden Yashima Station, about a 20-min. ride and then a 5-min. walk. JR train: Take a JR train bound for Tokushima and get off at Yashima Station (15-min.).

## EASY SIDE TRIPS FROM TAKAMATSU

If you're spending more than a day in Takamatsu, these major attractions are worth the trek.

**KOTOHIRA** 🎏🎏  If you have 4 hours to spare, one of the best historical side trips you can take is to Kotohira, home of Japan's oldest Kabuki theater and of **Kotohiragu Shrine** 🎏🎏, 892 Kotohira-cho (© **0877/75-2121**), one of Japan's oldest and most popular shrines. It takes about an hour to reach Kotohira by JR train from Takamatsu, but that isn't the end of it—the shrine itself is at the top of 785 granite steps, which on average take 40 minutes to ascend. If that's too much for you, you can hire one of the porters who wait at the bottom of the steps; they'll take you only to the main gate (called *Omon* in Japanese), which is reached after climbing 365 steps. The cost of riding in one of these palanquins is ¥5,300 ($50) one-way and ¥6,500 ($62) if you're carried back down. What decadence.

Otherwise, begin the long trek up to Kotohiragu Shrine by taking the JR Kotohira Station's only exit. Walk straight past a small park (with a wooden tower that served as a beacon for traveling pilgrims in the Edo Period), and pass the Kotoden Station. (You can also travel from Takamatsu in 1 hr. by Kotoden streetcar.) Turn left at the T-junction with a post office. You'll soon see, to the right, a sloping, narrow street lined

with souvenir shops (though I wouldn't buy anything on the way up). Eventually, you'll reach the first flight of stairs. If you're making a detour to the Kabuki theater (described below), turn left after the 22nd step, from which the theater is only a 3-minute walk.

At about the 475th step (in case you're counting), just past the stables to the right, you'll find **Shoin,** built in 1659 to receive important visitors. Its doors and alcoves contain paintings by Maruyama Oukyo, a famous 18th-century landscape artist, making the building an Important Cultural Property. Especially famous is the painting of two tigers drinking from a stream. It's open daily from 8:30am to 4:30pm; admission is ¥500 ($4.75) for adults, ¥200 ($1.90) for students, and free for children. After another 15-minute workout, you'll reach **Hongu,** the main shrine, where you'll be rewarded with a sweeping view of the surrounding countryside as well as of the shrine itself. Popularly known as Kompira-San, Kotohiragu Shrine was originally founded in the 11th century but has been rebuilt many times, with the main shrine buildings re-erected about 100 years ago. It's dedicated to the Shinto god of seafarers and voyagers (look for the Votive Picture Pavilion with photos of ships and other vessels that have asked for blessings) and, in recent years, has even become revered as the protector of foreign travelers. For my part, I was just thankful for having successfully traveled the stairs to the shrine. And to be honest, the shrine itself is not the main draw; most of the four million annual hikers, it seems, come for the hike itself and the comradeship it inspires. If you're still game (and want to say you went the whole distance), you can continue another 583 steps to **Okunoyashiro.** You can say your prayers here, but the inner shrine is closed to the public.

Since you're in the vicinity, you should make every effort to see the highly recommended (187) **Kompira Grand Playhouse (Kompira O-Shibai** or Kanamaruza) ✵, 241 Otsu, Kotohira-cho (✆ **0877/73-3846**), which was built to entertain the masses flocking to Kotohiragu Shrine. Located 300m (984 ft.) to the left of the 22nd step as you ascend and then up the hill to the right, it's the oldest existing Kabuki stage in Japan, stunning in its simplicity and delightful in its construction. Since there was no electricity when it was built in 1835, the sides of the hall are rows of shoji screens and wooden coverings, which can be opened and closed to control the amount of light reaching the stage. Notice the tatami seating, the paper lanterns, and the revolving stage, which was turned by four men in the basement. You can also tour the various makeup and dressing rooms behind the stage and watch a video in Japanese. It's open daily from 9am to 5pm and charges an admission of ¥500 ($4.75) for adults, ¥300 ($2.85) for junior-high and high-school students, and ¥100 (95¢) for children (the Shikoku Passport offers a 20% discount). Ask for the English-language handout.

---

### ⌢ Fun Fact  Doggedly Faithful

In the olden days, faithful who could not manage a trip to Kotohiragu Shrine in person would set a barrel adrift at sea, along with an offering and a plea for passing fishermen to take the offering to the shrine on their next pilgrimage. The more resourceful would even send dogs on the pilgrimage, with a tag that read "Kotohira Pilgrimage" and a pouch of money around their necks. Travelers who encountered the dogs used the money to buy the animals food and passage on boats until the dogs reached their destination.

**BENESSE ART SITE NAOSHIMA** ✦✦✦   Naoshima, a small island in the Seto Inland Sea, is devoted to contemporary art in a big way, with two striking museums, interactive installations housed in traditional buildings, and outdoor sculptures spread throughout the island, making it the nation's major destination for cutting-edge art in Japan. But more than that, Naoshima is a place of discovery, with a unique symbiotic relationship between natural scenic beauty and art. Plan on at least 6 hours for the experience, including the 50-minute ferry from Takamatsu. Note that for art venues closed on Monday, if Monday is a national holiday, they stay open but will close the next day, on Tuesday, instead.

**Shikoku Kisen ferries** (© **087/821-6798**) depart Takamatsu Port six times daily (¥970/$9.25 for a round-trip ticket) for Miyanoura Port on Naoshima. At Miyanoura, if you turn left from the ferry pier and then right, you'll see the Tourist Information Center beside the fire station, open daily 8:30am to 6pm and offering an English-language map of the island, rental bikes (¥500/$4.75 for the day), and schedules for buses that travel to all art sites (fare: ¥100/95¢).

From Miyanoura Port, you can take the bus 5 minutes (stop: Nokyo-mae, in front of JA Bank) or walk 30 minutes to Honmura, where you'll find **Art House Projects**, old buildings that have been remodeled by artists into interactive art installations. At Kadoya (by Miyajima Tatsuo), you'll see a 200-year-old farmhouse that contains a darkened room with a shallow pool of water and submerged colored numbers that blink on and off at varying frequencies, with the speed of each number controlled by an islander and each number representing a human life. Go'o Jinja is an Edo-Era shrine that has been transformed by Sugimoto Hiroshi, with glass stairs, white rocks, and a narrow underground passageway that leads to a tomblike space. But my favorite is Minamidera, a stark wooden building designed by famed architect Tadao Ando, with an installation by James Turrell called *Backside of the Moon*. After being led into a pitch-black room by staff, you wait about 10 minutes until your eyes adjust, when you see a faint glow ahead. You're told you can walk to the light to touch it, only to find—well, you'll have to "see" for yourself. Art House Projects are open Tuesday to Sunday 9:30am to 4:30pm and cost ¥500 ($2.85) for a combination ticket for all three. Buy your ticket at the projects themselves, at the tourist office above, or at Ueda's Tobacconist, across from the bus stop.

From Honmaru, it's a 10-minue bus ride and a walk uphill to **Benesse House,** a museum designed by Tadao Ando and containing an expensive hotel (© **087/892-2030;** rates begin at ¥30,030/$285 for a twin), cafe, restaurant, and art by Jasper Johns, Robert Rauschenberg, Frank Stella, Pollock, Warhol, and others who created site-specific art that takes Ando's architecture and Naoshima's natural beauty into consideration. It's open daily 8am to 9pm, with admission costing ¥1,000 ($9.50) for adults and ¥500 ($4.75) for children.

The nearby **Chichu Art Museum,** 3 minutes away by bus (there's a free shuttle bus between the two museums weekends and holidays) or a 30-minute walk, was also designed by Ando. It's a striking concrete structure with sharp angles, contemplative spaces, and only a few works of art, including light installations by James Turrell and a room by Walter De Maria containing a huge granite ball and gold-leaf-covered bars. This museum is open Tuesday to Sunday 10am to 6pm (to 5pm Oct–Feb) and costs ¥2,000 ($19) for adults and ¥1,000 ($9.50) for children. From here, the bus back to Miyanoura Port takes 20 minutes.

For more information on Benesse Art Site Naoshima and its museums, call
℗ 087/892-2887 or go online at www.naoshima-is.co.jp.

## WHERE TO STAY

All hotel rates below include service charge.

### EXPENSIVE

**ANA Hotel Clement Takamatsu** ✿✿    Opened in 2001 in Sunport across from
Takamatsu Station (and offering a discount to holders of a Japan Rail Pass), the city's
most expensive hotel is also its most conspicuous—sleek, 21 stories high, cutting across
the landscape like a white sail, and by far the best place in town. It's designed with an
aquatic theme, with a cascading fountain in the sunlit lobby lounge, carpets with wavy
patterns, bubbled or crackled glass in public places, and curving, seductive lines everywhere, even in corridors. It's the kind of place sightseers happily return to after a hard
day's work. Room rates are based on size, view, and amenities, with the best twin and
double rooms offering views of the sea or nearby Tamamo Park, even from windows in
the bathroom. But the least expensive rooms are also recommendable—spacious and
chic with contemporary furnishings and good bedside reading lamps; ask for a room
on the highest available floor. Note that the cheapest double has a semi-double bed.

1–1 Hamano-cho, Takamatsu 760-0011. ℗ **087/811-1111.** Fax 087/811-1100. www.anahotels.com. 300 units.
¥12,474–¥18,480 ($119–$176) single; ¥20,790–¥32,340 ($294–$308) double; ¥24,255–¥40,425 ($231–$385)
twin. 10% discount with Japan Rail Pass. AE, DC, MC, V. Station: Takamatsu (1 min.). **Amenities:** 4 restaurants (Japanese, Chinese, Italian, coffee shop); 1 bar; 1 lounge; 1 beer garden; concierge; business center; room service
(7–10:30am and 5–11pm); in-room massage; same-day laundry and dry-cleaning service; nonsmoking rooms.
*In room:* A/C, cable TV w/pay movies, dataport, minibar, hot-water pot w/tea, hair dryer, Washlet toilet, trouser press.

### MODERATE

**Rihga Hotel Zest**    This beige-brick hotel, first opened in 1980 and adding an
annex with more luxurious accommodations 10 years later, appeals to both business
and leisure travelers with its convenient location on Chuo Dori next to Hyogo-machi
shopping arcade. It has an accommodating staff and offers a variety of rooms at different price ranges. The cheapest rooms, including all singles, are located in the main
building and are narrow with tiny bathrooms. More expensive and spacious annex
rooms sport shoji screens and window panels that close for complete darkness. There
are also combination rooms with both tatami areas and beds.

9–1 Furujinmachi, Takamatsu 760-0025. ℗ **087/822-3555.** Fax 087/822-7516. www.rihga.com. 122 units.
¥7,854–¥9,471 ($75–$90) single; ¥15,015–¥25,410 ($143–$242) double; ¥17,325–¥25,410 ($165–$242) twin.
10% discounts with the Kagawa Welcome Card; be sure to mention the card when making your reservation and show
it when you check in. AE, DC, MC, V. Station: Takamatsu (a 10-min. walk south of the station, on Chuo Dori just past
Hyogo-machi arcade). **Amenities:** 4 restaurants (Japanese, Chinese, French, coffee shop); 1 lounge; in-room massage;
same-day laundry/dry-cleaning service; nonsmoking rooms. *In room:* A/C, TV, minibar, hot-water pot w/tea, hair dryer,
Washlet toilets.

**Royal Park Hotel Annex**    This business hotel, with imitation Art Deco decor in
its lobby and hallways, offers mostly single rooms in a convenient location near
Kawaramachi Station in the heart of the city's shopping and nightlife district. Rooms,
though small, are pleasantly decorated, but it's been a while since I've seen pink tiled
bathrooms like those here. The cheapest singles are on lower floors where traffic is
noisiest. The hotel's seven twins are all corner rooms, bright and large for the price
with vanity/sink separate from the—you guessed it—pink bathrooms (which also
have a sink). Little English is spoken.

11–1 Fukuda, Takamatsu 760-0048. ℂ **087/823-1111.** Fax 087/823-1123. 117 units. ¥6,352–¥9,066 ($60–$86) single; ¥16,008 ($152) double; ¥18,711 ($178) twin. AE, DC, MC, V. Kotoden streetcar: Kawaramachi (5 min.). Take the west exit (in the direction of the bus stop) and walk north on Ferry Dori, turning right at the 1st traffic signal and crossing the tracks; you'll see the hotel on the left. **Amenities:** Restaurant (Chinese); in-room massage; lobby computer with free Internet access; free rental bikes; coin-operated laundry; same-day laundry/dry-cleaning service; nonsmoking rooms. *In room:* A/C, TV, minibar, hot-water pot w/tea, Washlet toilet, trouser press.

## INEXPENSIVE

**Business Hotel Parkside Takamatsu** ⭐ *Value*    Although a business hotel, this small, boutiquelike hotel has a great location across from Ritsurin Park. Rooms are small, but who cares when you can open the window and look out over the fabled garden? Some rooms have only a partial view, so be sure to request a ringside seat on an upper floor.

1–3–1 Ritsurin-cho, Takamatsu 760-0073. ℂ **087/837-5555.** Fax 087/837-3000. 116 units. ¥4,950–¥5,400 ($47–$51) single; ¥7,950 ($76) double; ¥7,950–¥8,400 ($76–$80) twin; ¥11,900 ($113) triple. AE, DC, MC, V. Kotoden streetcar: Ritsurin Koen (10 min.). Walk straight from the west exit and turn right on Chuo Dori; the hotel will be on the right. **Amenities:** Restaurant (Japanese); lobby computers with free Internet access; coin-operated laundry; in-room massage; same-day laundry/dry-cleaning service. *In room:* A/C, TV, high-speed dataport, minibar, hot-water pot w/tea, humidifier, hair dryer, Washlet toilet, trouser press.

# WHERE TO DINE

Takamatsu is known throughout Japan for its ***sanuki udon***—thick white noodles made from wheat flour. Takamatsu also has a fresh supply of fish from the Seto Inland Sea.

## EXPENSIVE

**Szechwan** ⭐⭐⭐ CHINESE    Classic standards, like bird's-nest soup, sweet-and-sour pork, and chicken with cashew nuts, receive innovative makeovers at this elegant 29th-floor restaurant. Add panoramic views of the Seto Inland Sea and excellent service, and you're in for a memorable dining experience.

29th floor, Takamatsu Symbol Tower, 2–1 Sunport. ℂ **087/811-0477.** Main dishes ¥1,600–¥3,500 ($15–$33); set lunches ¥1,500–¥4,000 ($14–$38); set dinners ¥5,250–¥16,800 ($50–$160). AE, DC, MC, V. Daily 11am–3pm and 5–10pm. Station: Takamatsu (1 min.).

## MODERATE

(188) **Tenkatsu** TEMPURA/SUSHI    This well-known tempura and sushi restaurant is in a modern-looking building with a plastic-food display case and a window where passersby can watch a chef prepare sushi. Inside the restaurant are tatami mats and tables, but I suggest sitting at the counter, which encircles a large pool filled with fish. As customers order, fish are swept out of the tanks with nets—they certainly couldn't

---

## *Tips*  A Note on Japanese Symbols

Many hotels, restaurants, attractions, and other establishments in Japan do not have signs giving their names in Roman (English-language) letters. Appendix C lists the Japanese symbols for all such places described in this guide. Each set of characters representing an establishment name has a number in the appendix that corresponds to the number that appears inside the oval before the establishment's name in the text. Thus, to find the Japanese symbol for, say, **Tenkatsu** (above) refer to no. 188 in appendix C.

be fresher. A photo menu and a display case help you choose. For a splurge, order a kaiseki course, beginning at ¥5,000 ($48).

7–8 Hyogo-machi. ✆ 087/821-5380. Reservations recommended; required for kaiseki. Dishes ¥1,050–¥2,940 ($10–$28); set lunches ¥1,050–¥3,990 ($10–$38); set dinners ¥1,500–¥10,000 ($14–$95). AE, DC, MC, V. Mon–Fri 11am–2pm and 4–10pm; Sat–Sun 11am–9pm. Station: Takamatsu (a 5-min. walk south from the station). Walk south on Chuo Dori until it intersects with a large covered pedestrian shopping arcade called Hyogo-machi. Turn right and walk all the way through the arcade; upon emerging, you'll find the restaurant on your left.

189 **Tokiwa Saryo** 🍴🍴 *Finds* VARIED JAPANESE   This restaurant, easily spotted with its castlelike roof, occupies what was once a traditional Japanese inn and retains many of its original traditional features, including a delightful inner courtyard complete with a pond, dwarf pine trees, carp, and some lanterns. You'll probably want to order one of the set meals like obento lunch boxes or tempura and sashimi teishoku, made easy to choose from by photos in the Japanese-language menu. For dinner, minikaiseki meals are also available for ¥2,000 to ¥4,000 ($19–$38), though no photos are available for these, as they change with the season. At any rate, the food is delicious and very reasonably priced; you can't go wrong.

1–8–2 Tokiwa-cho. ✆ 087/861-5577. Reservations required. Set meals ¥1,380–¥5,000 ($13–$48); set lunches ¥1,050–¥3,150 ($10–$30). AE, DC, MC, V. Daily 11am–2:30pm and 5–9:30pm (last order). Kotoden streetcar: Kawaramachi Station (2 min.). From the west exit (with its BUS STOP sign), take the side street south (to the left) parallel to Tokiwa-cho (a covered arcade); the restaurant will be on your right, on the corner.

## INEXPENSIVE

190 **Kanaizumi** SANUKI UDON   This modern cafeteria is about as casual as you can get—your noodles are scooped for you as you go through the line and you choose your ingredients, including tempura (¥80–¥120/75¢–$1.15 per piece). Be prepared for slippery noodles and the good-natured slurping sounds of a noodle shop.

9–3 Konyamachi. ✆ 087/822-0123. Sanuki udon ¥160–¥490 ($1.50–$4.65). No credit cards. Daily 9:30am–5:30pm. Station: Takamatsu (a 15-min. walk south of the station, off Chuo Dori to the right just before the city art museum).

191 **Maruichi** 🍴 YAKITORI   Although a cozy and friendly drinking establishment, this is also a great place for an inexpensive meal. An English-language menu lists sashimi, Korean spiced cabbage *(kimchi)*, pork, tofu, deep-fried prawns and, of course, a variety of yakitori costing ¥100 to ¥350 (95¢–$3.35) per skewer. An evening of eating, drinking, and merriment here should cost about ¥2,000 ($19) per person, including the obligatory ¥280 ($2.65) snack charge.

1–4–13 Tokiwa-cho. ✆ 087/861-7623. Main dishes ¥450–¥650 ($4.30–$6.20); set meals ¥2,500–¥3,500 ($24–$33). AE, MC, V. Mon–Fri 5pm–1am. Kotoden streetcar: Kawaramachi Station (1 min.). Take the west exit (with the BUS STOP signs), use the promenade deck to cross the street, take the elevator to street level; the small street is in front of you with Maruichi on the left, under a white lantern with a circle *(maru)* and horizontal line *(ichi)* through it.

**Milano No Okazuyasan** 🍴 NORTHERN ITALIAN   Beneath an Italian flag is the recessed entrance to this second-floor restaurant. Hospitable chef-owner Mr. Takeda, who speaks some English and has an English-language menu, serves mainly homemade pastas, from the usual spaghetti Bolognese with meat sauce to spaghetti with squid in black sauce, as well as a handful of pizzas and main dishes that might include seafood saffron risotto. Set lunches include all the salad and fresh-baked bread you can eat, plus a choice of soup, dessert, or coffee. Don't miss the homemade bread, and top it all off with a cappuccino and dessert.

Egou Building, 11–14 Kamei-cho. ⓒ 087/837-1782. Main dishes and pasta ¥840–¥1,350 ($8–$13); set lunch ¥840 ($8); set meals ¥1,780–¥8,980 ($17–$86). MC, V. Daily 11am–10pm. Kotoden streetcar: Kawaramachi (4 min.). Take the west exit (with the BUS STOP sign) and walk through the covered walking arcade (Tokiwa-cho) until the awning ends; then start looking carefully for Milano on your left, opposite a bookstore.

⑲⑫ **Shabutei Maru** *Value* SHABU-SHABU  This casual, small, second-floor eatery has inexpensive lunches of chicken, pork, and beef, with second helpings of rice and vegetables included in the price. From 5pm, it offers all-you-can-eat shabu-shabu (and in winter, sukiyaki) with a 90-minute time limit—kind of like an "on-your-mark, get-set, go" spree of uninhibited gorging. Ditto with all you can drink if you pay ¥1,300 ($12) more. Seating is at counters or tables and, as you might have guessed, the place is usually very crowded.

8–8 Kamei-cho. ⓒ 087/835-9842. Set lunches ¥475–¥1,800 ($4.50–$17); all-you-can-eat shabu-shabu ¥2,200 ($21) men, ¥2,000 ($19) women. MC, V. Daily 11am–2pm and 5–11pm. Kotoden streetcar: Kawaramachi (5 min.). Catty-corner from the southeast corner of Chuo Park, just off Chuo Dori on Kikuchikan-dori, next to the Japanese Tourist Board office.

## 2 Matsuyama Castle & Dogo Spa ✦✦

947km (588 miles) W of Tokyo; 192km (120 miles) E of Takamatsu; 211km (132 miles) SW of Okayama

Although Matsuyama is Shikoku's largest town and the capital of Ehime Prefecture with a population of more than 510,000, it has the relaxed atmosphere of a small town. Located on the island's northwest coast, Matsuyama features one of Japan's best-preserved feudal castles and what I consider to be the most delightful, historic public bathhouse in the country, located in Dogo Onsen. The nearby Shimanami Kaido, a series of bridges connecting Ehime and Hiroshima prefectures, has a dedicated cycling lane, with fantastic views of the Seto Inland Sea.

## ESSENTIALS

**GETTING THERE  By Plane**  Flights connect Matsuyama with Tokyo, Osaka, Nagoya, Fukuoka, Sapporo, Kagoshima and Okinawa. The flight from Tokyo takes 1 hour and 25 minutes and costs ¥27,700 ($264). Buses connect the airport to downtown in 30 minutes for ¥400 ($3.80).

**By Train**  The easiest way to reach Matsuyama is by **JR train** from Okayama (on Honshu island), with 15 departures daily; the trip takes 2 hours and 40 minutes, and the fare is ¥6,120 ($58). There are also hourly departures from Takamatsu, taking less than 2½ hours and costing ¥5,500 ($52).

**By Bus**  Buses depart nightly from Tokyo Station at 8:20pm and from Shinjuku Station at 7:10pm, arriving at Matsuyama Station the next day at 8:32am and 7:10am respectively. Either fare is ¥12,000 ($114) one-way.

**By Boat**  Matsuyama is also linked by ferry to various ports on Honshu and Kyushu islands, including Kobe (overnight trip time: 9 hr.), Osaka (overnight: 9½ hr.), Oita (near Beppu; 3½ hr.), and Hiroshima (70 min. by hydrofoil). The fare to Matsuyama is ¥5,500 ($52) from Osaka, ¥2,800 ($27) from Beppu, and ¥5,800 ($55) from Hiroshima. Boats dock at **Matsuyama Port (Matsuyama Kanko Ko),** where buses transport passengers to Matsuyama Station in about 20 minutes for ¥450 ($4.30).

**VISITOR INFORMATION**  The **Matsuyama City Tourist Information Office** (ⓒ **089/931-3914;** open daily 8:30am–8:30pm) is inside JR Matsuyama Station to

the left as you leave the wicket. The Dogo Tourist Information Center (© 089/ 921-3708; open 8am–8pm) is across the street from the streetcar stop. The **Ehime Prefectural International Center (EPIC),** located between Matsuyama Castle and Dogo Onsen (© 089/917-5678; open Mon–Fri 8:30am–5pm), provides information on Ehime Prefecture, including Uchiko, Tobe, and the Shimanami Kaido cycling path. You'll also find a TV with CNN, English-language newspapers, and three computers you can use for free. Be sure to pick up the useful *What's Going On* (an excellent, free, English-language guide to Matsuyama's events and points of interest), your free **Setouchi Welcome booklet** (with coupons for discounts on hotels, sights, and restaurants in Ehime, Yamaguchi, and Hiroshima Prefectures) and the **Shikoku Passport** (discount coupons for all of Shikoku). To reach EPIC, take streetcar no. 3, 5, or 6 heading toward Dogo Onsen to the Minami-machi stop. Backtrack and look to the right for the INFORMATION sign; the office is in a barrack partially hidden behind another building. More information is available online at www.city.matsuyama.ehime.jp.

**INTERNET ACCESS**    In addition to EPIC, above, you can also check e-mail (and get information about the area) at COMS on the second floor of the Matsuyama International Center, 6–4–20 Sanbancho (© **089/943-2025;** open Tues–Sun 9am–5:30pm) for ¥100 (95¢) an hour. It's a 7-minute walk from either Matsuyama Station or Matsuyama Shieki; or take the streetcar to the Minami-horibata-cho stop.

**ORIENTATION & GETTING AROUND**    JR **Matsuyama Station,** which serves long-distance trains, is on the west edge of town, with most attractions, hotels, shopping, and restaurants spreading to the east. **Matsuyama Castle** lies less than 2.5km (1½ miles) due east of the station. Just southwest of the castle is the **Okaido** shopping arcade, a covered pedestrian passageway lined with restaurants and shops and considered to be the heart of the city. **Dogo Onsen,** Japan's oldest hot-spring spa, is on the eastern edge of the city.

The easiest and most convenient form of transportation in Matsuyama is **streetcar.** The no. 5 line runs from Matsuyama Station to the Okaido arcade (**Note:** the Okaido stop is marked "Ichibancho" on some tourist maps), Matsuyama Castle, and Dogo Onsen. The fare is ¥150 ($1.40) per trip or only ¥300 ($2.85) for a **1-day pass (Ichinichi Joshaken).** An old-fashioned locomotive-style streetcar nicknamed "Bochan" (after a novel by Natsume Soseki set in Matsuyama) runs between Matsuyama Station and Dogo Onsen. It costs ¥300 ($2.85) per ride but only ¥200/$1.90 if you have the 1-day pass.

## SEEING THE SIGHTS

Setouchi Welcome coupons and the Shikoku Passport give discounts for both Matsuyama Castle and Dogo Onsen.

**Matsuyama Castle** 🎏🎏    Right in the heart of the city, Matsuyama Castle crowns the top of a 131m (435-ft.) hill, commanding an impressive view. It was built by feudal lord Kato Yoshiakira more than 400 years ago, later falling into the hands of the powerful Matsudaira family that ruled the surrounding region from here during the Edo Period. Like most structures in Japan, Matsuyama Castle has suffered fire and destruction through the ages, but unlike many other castles (such as those in Osaka and Nagoya), this one was renovated with original materials. There's only one entrance, a pathway leading through a series of gates that could be swung shut to trap attacking enemies. A secret gate allowed a surprise rear attack, while drop chutes could

be used to rain stones onto the enemy. The three-story donjon houses some samurai gear, swords, screens, and scrolls from the Matsudaira family, as well as photographs of Japan's other castles. Allow yourself 30 minutes to tour the inside.

Surrounding the castle is a park; if you're feeling energetic, you can walk through the park to the castle in about 15 minutes. Otherwise, the easiest way to reach the castle is to take the streetcar to the Okaido stop, walk 5 minutes along the street with the arch marked WELCOME TO MATSUYAMA CASTLE, and then take a cable car or chairlift (more fun) from the east side of Katsuyama Hill. A round-trip ticket for either the cable car or the chairlift, and including admission to the castle, costs ¥1,000 ($9.50) for adults and ¥400 ($3.80) for children.

*©* **089/921-4873.** Admission ¥500 ($4.75) adults, ¥150 ($1.40) children. Daily 9am–5pm (to 4:30pm in Jan and 5:30pm in Aug.). Streetcar: Okaido stop, then chairlift.

## DOGO ONSEN (DOGO SPA) 𝕲𝕲𝕲

Dogo Onsen boasts a 3,000-year history and claims to be the oldest hot-spring spa in Japan. According to legend, the hot springs were discovered after a white heron healed an injured leg by soaking it in the thermal mineral waters. Located in the city's northeast, about a 20-minute streetcar ride from Matsuyama Station (take streetcar no. 5 to Dogo Onsen, the last stop), Dogo Spa can accommodate about 7,200 people in 38 hotels and ryokan, which means the narrow streets resound at night with the slap of thonged slippers and the occasional clatter of wooden platform sandals *(geta)* as vacationers go to the various bathhouses dressed in cotton robes *(yukata)*. Friendly conversations start as tourists come on the hour to see the Bochan clock (across from the Dogo Onsen streetcar stop), an animated clock featuring characters from Natsume Soseki's novel, and soak their feet in the nearby foot bath, which features the original water spout from Dogo Onsen Honkan.

Most of the hotels and ryokan in Dogo have their own hot-spring bath *(onsen)*, but I suggest that no matter where you stay, you make at least one trip to **Dogo Onsen Honkan** 𝕲𝕲𝕲, 5–6 Yunomachi, Dogo (*©* **089/921-5141**), a wonderful three-story public bathhouse built in 1894. A wooden structure with shoji screens, tatami rooms, creaking wooden stairways, and the legendary white heron topping the crest of its castle-like roof, this Momoyama-style building is as much a social institution as it is a place to soak and scrub. On busy days, as many as 4,000 people pass through its front doors. The water here is transparent, colorless, tasteless, and alkaline, helpful for rheumatism and neuralgia. At the very least, it makes your skin feel great—soft and smooth. The hottest spring water coming into the spa is 120°F (49°C); the coolest, 70°F (21°C). But don't worry—the waters are mixed to achieve a comfortable 108°F (42°C).

Bathing in the ground-floor granite bath, however, is just a small part of the experience here. Most people come to relax, socialize, and while away an hour or more, and I suggest you do the same. Although you can bathe for as little as ¥400 ($3.80) for adults and ¥150 ($1.40) for children 2 to 11, it's worth it to pay extra for the privilege of relaxing on tatami mats in a communal room on the second floor, dressed in a rented yukata, drinking tea from a lacquered tea set, and eating Japanese rice crackers. If the weather is fine, all the shoji screens are pushed open to let in a breeze, and as you sprawl on the tatami, drinking your tea and listening to the clang of the streetcar and voices of people coming and going, you can imagine that you've landed in ancient Japan. To my mind, the whole scene resembles an old woodblock print suddenly come to life.

The cost of the bath, yukata, crackers, and tea for 1 hour is ¥800 ($7.60) for adults, half price for children 2 to 11. Use of a smaller, more private bath and lounging area for an hour where tea and sweets are also served costs ¥1,200 ($11) for adults and half price for children and includes a visit to Yushinden (see below). And if you really want to splurge for 1 hour and 20 minutes, you can rent a private tatami room on the third floor, which also comes with tea, sweets, and yukata, for ¥1,500 ($14) for adults, half price for children. This differentiation in luxury probably dates from the early days when there were separate baths for the upper class, priests, commoners, and even animals.

While at the spa, be sure to see the **Yushinden,** the imperial rooms built for the imperial family in 1899 for their visits to the spa and last used in 1952. You can take a tour of its rooms for ¥250 ($2.40) for adults and ¥120 ($1.15) for children.

The spa is open from 6am (the arrival time of the first streetcar) until 11pm, but you must enter by 10:30pm. The second floor closes at 10pm (you must enter by 9pm) and the Yushinden at 9pm.

**A NEARBY TEMPLE**   After your bath, you may want to visit **Ishiteji Temple** ✿, 2–9–21 Ishite (© **089/977-0870**), about a 15-minute walk east of Dogo Onsen Station; from the station, walk under the neon archway and keep going straight east. Built in 1318, it's the 51st of Shikoku's 88 sacred temples; with its blend of Chinese and Japanese styles, it is a good example of architecture of the Kamakura Period. Notice the huge straw sandals at the main gate; those with feet or leg ailments are thought to regain their health by touching them. You'll also see regular-size sandals at the temple, donated by older Japanese in hopes of regaining new strength in their legs (who knows, maybe they've been walking the pilgrimage). The most interesting site, however, is the lit tunnel to the left behind the main temple. It contains stone statues representing the 88 temples of Shikoku; in front of each is sand from each temple location. If you pause in front of each statue, you'll make a short circuit to the actual pilgrimage, convenient for those who don't have time for the real thing but still hope for the pilgrimage's blessings. The temple is open daily from 7:30am to 6pm, but the tunnel (¥100/95¢) closes at 5pm.

## AN EASY SIDE TRIP

**UCHIKO** ✿✿   If you have time for a side trip around Ehime Prefecture, I strongly recommend an excursion to the village of **Uchiko,** which has some fine old homes and buildings dating back to the Edo Period and the turn of the 20th century. Whereas about 70% of Matsuyama was destroyed during World War II, Uchiko was left intact, and a tiny part of the old historic district is a living memorial to the days of yore, when it prospered as a production center for wax. Even the 25-minute express train ride from JR Matsuyama Station (departing every hour or so) is enjoyable as you weave through valleys of wooded hills past grape, mikan orange, persimmon, rice, and tobacco farms. At Uchiko Station, ask for the "Uchiko Visitor's Guide" at the train station ticket window; it contains a map showing the 5-minute walk to Yokaichi, the historic part of town.

Your first stop is ⑲③ **Uchikoza,** 1152–2 Kou, Uchiko-cho (© **0893/44-2840**), a Kabuki theater built in 1916 (look for the sign post on the left after you pass the creek). Though not as grand as the one near Takamatsu (p. 470), it's a good example of how townspeople used to enjoy themselves years ago. It features a revolving stage, many windows that can be opened and closed to control the amount of light reaching the stage, and a small display of memorabilia (note the ultimate platform shoes, *geta,*

used by Bunraku puppeteers). Uchikoza is open daily 9am to 4:30pm. A combination ticket for ¥700 ($6.65) for adults and ¥370 ($3.50) for children allows admission to the theater, Museum of Commercial and Domestic Life, and Kami-Haga Residence listed below, but you'll get cheaper admission by using the Shikoku Passport.

A 5-minute walk farther along the main street, on the right, is the **Museum of Commercial and Domestic Life (Akinai to Kurashi Hakubutsukan),** 1082–1 Kou, Uchiko-cho (✆ **0893/44-5220**). This museum—once housing a pharmacy and built in typical Uchiko style—uses life-size figures, recordings, and authentic artifacts in its dioramas depicting various professions and scenes from daily life, from shop owner to restaurant owner. One of the dioramas, for example, is of a Taisho-Era pharmacy, with two figures kneeling on a tatami floor as they discuss the business at hand (in Japanese). Other places of interest in Yokaichi include two restored homes, **Machi-ya Shiryokan,** 1579–1 Kou, Uchiko-cho (✆ **0893/44-2111**), open free to the public (as an empty house, it wouldn't be of much interest if it weren't free); and **Kami-Haga Residence,** 1519 Kou, Uchiko-cho (✆ **0893/44-2771;** admission price included in the combination ticket described earlier). Built in 1894, the Kami-Haga Residence is especially grand, having once belonged to a merchant who made his fortune exporting wax. During the Edo and Meiji periods, Uchiko gained fame as a center of candlemaking and wax production, producing about 30% of the country's wax, used for lighting, umbrellas and for the styling of elaborate Feudal-Era hairdos. You can see the traditional methods for wax production, as well as tour the house. There's also a cafe, down a long covered passage, where you might have to rouse someone to be served. All sites are open daily from 9am to 4:30pm.

Today, only one person carries on the wax-making tradition—a man named ⑲④ **Omori,** who represents the sixth generation of candlemakers. Following the same techniques as those developed by his ancestors 200 years ago, he collects his own haze berries (a kind of sumac) and makes his candles by hand. You can observe him at his workshop at 1587 Sakamachi-ko, Uchiko-cho (✆ **0893/43-0385;** open Tues–Thurs and Sat–Sun 9am–5pm).

**Where to Dine** ⑲⑤ **Shimohagatei,** 1946 Uchiko-ko (✆ **0893/44-6171;** open Thurs–Tues 11am–5pm), is housed in a 130-year-old former residence/shop on the historic area's main street, near the Museum of Commercial and Domestic Life. With an inner garden courtyard typical of Uchiko architecture, it offers noodles, tempura, and set meals costing ¥1,300 and ¥2,000 ($12–$19). No credit cards are accepted.

## CYCLING THE SHIMANAMI KAIDO ★★★

If you're a bicyclist—and even if you're not—you owe it to yourself to ride one of Japan's most rewarding cycling routes: a dedicated biking and pedestrian lane that connects Ehime Prefecture on Shikoku with Onomichi in Hiroshima Prefecture on Honshu (Japan's main island). Part of the Shimanami Kaido route (also called the Setouchi Shimanami Seaway and Nishi Seto Expwy.), which is actually a series of seven bridges that hopscotch across the Seto Inland Sea via six islands, the cycling path runs beside vehicular traffic on the bridges but often diverges from the highway on the islands. Needless to say, views of the sea and surrounding countryside are great, and the pathway, clearly marked in green, is easy to follow (though steep in some areas). If you want, you can cycle the entire 80km (50-mile) distance between Shikoku and Honshu in less than 7 hours and then return by bus. Alternatively, you can cycle for a few hours and then head back; or you can go as far as you wish, leave your rental

bike at one of 14 bike drop-off sites along the cycling path, and then catch a bus back. In my opinion, of the entire cycling path, the stretch from Shikoku is more scenic and easier to follow than the stretch closer to Hiroshima.

For a fun day's outing, I suggest bicycling to Omishima, an island you'll reach in about 2 hours, where another 30 minutes of cycling will bring you to **Oyamazumi Shrine.** Worshipped through the years by samurai, the shrine is home to the **Shiyoden Treasure Museum** ✿✿ (© **0897-82-0032**), with an astounding collection of helmets, armor, and swords, all donated to the shrine by warriors who wished to express thanks for victories in battle. About 80% of Japanese samurai gear designated National Treasures (look for the red mark) or National Important Cultural Assets are housed here, including items once worn by Minamoto Yoshitsune and Minamoto Yoritomo. The museum is open daily 8:30am to 5pm; admission is ¥1,000 ($9.50) for adults, ¥800 ($7.60) for students, and ¥400 ($3.80) for children. By the way, there's a bike drop-off center just before the shrine, where you can leave your bike and catch a bus to Omishima BS stop and transfer there for the Shimanami Liner to Imabari (check bus schedules beforehand).

Rental bikes are available at the foot of the first bridge at **Sunrise Itoyama** (© **0898-41-3196**), which also offers showers and a restaurant. Bikes rent for ¥500 ($4.75) a day, plus a ¥1,000 ($9.50) deposit which you forfeit if you decide to ditch your bike at one of the drop-off sites; be sure to ask the folks at Sunrise Itoyama for a bus schedule back. You'll also have the annoyance of bridge toll fees at varying distances, which you deposit into boxes on the honor system. There are also power-assisted bikes for ¥800 ($7.60); I rented one (in the interest of research, of course) and found it helpful on the circular ramp that climbs 65m (213 ft.) just to meet the first bridge. However, power-assisted bikes must be returned to Sunrise Itoyama and have enough juice to run only 4 hours or so. Sunrise Itoyama is open daily 8am to 8pm (to 5pm Oct–Mar).

To reach Sunrise Itoyama, take an express train from Matsuyama Station 30 minutes to Imabari, from where there are three to five buses a day to the Sunrise Itoyama cycling center. You'll probably find it easier, therefore, to take a local train 5 minutes onward from Imabari to Hashihama, from which the cycling center is a 20-minute walk. For information on cycling the Shimanami Kaido from Hiroshima Prefecture, see p. 479).

## SHOPPING

**TOBE** Ehime Prefecture is famous for its Tobe pottery, called *Tobe-yaki* in Japanese. About 100 families in the town of Tobe are still engaged in the craft. An excellent way to see this pottery, noted for its thick white porcelain painted with cobalt-blue designs, is to visit ⑲⑥ **Tobe Pottery Traditional Industry Hall (Tobeyaki Dento Sangyo Kaikan)** at 335 Ohminami, Tobe-cho (© **089/962-6600;** open Fri–Wed 9am–5pm). In addition to displays of Tobe ware from the Edo Period to the present and a video showing the creative process, it also sells contemporary ware from local producers, making it a good place to shop for a variety of styles. Admission is ¥200 ($1.90) for adults, ¥150 ($1.40) for high-school and university students, and ¥100 (95¢) for children. To get there, take a bus bound for Danso-guchi, Toyama, or Oiwabashi from platform no. 3 at Matsuyama Shi-eki; it takes 30 minutes to reach the Dento Sangyo Kaikan-mae stop (fare: ¥600/$5.70), from which it's a 2-minute walk (continue straight on and take the first right; it's at the T-intersection). A 30-minute taxi ride

costs about ¥4,000 ($38). There are also several kilns open to the public; the largest and best known of these is ⑲⑦ **Umeno-Seito-Sho** at 1441 Ohminami, Tobe-cho (𝓒 **089/962-2311;** open Tues–Sun 10am–4:50pm, closed second and third Sun of each month and a few days in mid-Aug). Founded in 1882 and now in its fifth generation of ownership by the Umeno family, it employs more than 50 people. You can watch all the artisans except those who do the color glazing—the technique is a closely guarded secret. Inside the shop, be sure to check out the backroom, where pieces with slight imperfections go for about half price. Get a map from the Tobe Pottery Traditional Industry Hall that shows the 20-minute walk to Umeno-Seito-Sho.

## WHERE TO STAY

For more suggestions of where to stay in the Dogo Onsen area, or to make a reservation in a ryokan there, contact the **Dogo Onsen Ryokan-Kumiai** (𝓒 **089/943-8342;** fax 089/943-8343), located near the Dogo Onsen streetcar stop at the entrance to the shopping arcade (on the right). It's open daily 8am to 8pm.

Your Setouchi Welcome coupons and Shikoku Passport provide a 5% to 20% discount on some of the accommodations below; mention the discount when making your reservation and upon check-in.

### VERY EXPENSIVE

⑲⑧ **Yamatoya Besso** ⋆⋆⋆    The ultimate ryokan experience awaits you at this famous ryokan in Dogo Onsen. It's the little things that make it special—the rustle of kimono as you're met by bowing, smiling women in the front courtyard; pillars of salt at the front door in good Shinto fashion; lit shoji lanterns guiding the way through hushed hallways; scrolls of haiku poems, in beautiful calligraphy, decorating all the rooms and changed seven times a year to fit the season. With a history dating back 140 years—it was rebuilt in 1988 as a refined, luxurious inn—it offers rooms that preserve the integrity of the past with TVs hidden behind shoji screens and old-fashioned cypress tubs that use water from the hot springs. Lavish kaiseki meals feature seafood of the Seto Inland Sea. The only thing lacking at this superb ryokan is the requisite garden.

2–27 Dogo Sagidani-cho, Matsuyama 790-0836. 𝓒 089/931-7771. Fax 089/931-7775. 19 units. ¥46,350–¥78,690 ($441–$749) per person. Rates include 2 meals and service charge. Weekday and off-season discount available. AE, DC, MC, V. Streetcar: Dogo Onsen (5 min). **Amenities:** Public indoor and outdoor hot-spring baths; in-room massage; same-day laundry/dry-cleaning service. *In room:* A/C, cable TV, hot-water pot w/tea, hair dryer, Washlet toilet.

### EXPENSIVE

**ANA Hotel** ⋆    Matsuyama's premier hotel (called Zenniku Hotel in Japanese) has a great location in the heart of the city, just a few minutes' walk to the Matsuyama Castle ropeway and the Okaido covered shopping arcade; streetcars heading for Dogo Onsen pass right in front of the hotel. Built in 1979 but constantly updated, it offers business hotel–like inexpensive singles (the cheapest listed here), as well as larger and well-appointed singles, twins, and doubles; ask for a double or a twin with a castle view.

3–2–1 Ichiban-cho, Matsuyama 790-8520. 𝓒 800/262-4683 in the U.S. and Canada, or 089/933-5511. Fax 089/921-6053. www.anahotels.com. 327 units. ¥6,930–¥19,635 ($66–$187) single; ¥19,635–¥36,960 ($187–$380) double; ¥20,213–¥28,875 ($192–$275) twin. Rates include service charge. AE, DC, MC, V. Streetcar: Okaido (1 min.). **Amenities:** 3 restaurants (Japanese, Chinese, Western); 1 bar; 1 tea lounge; 1 rooftop beer garden (summer only); large shopping arcade; room service (6:30am–11pm); in-room massage; same-day laundry/dry cleaning (weekdays only); nonsmoking rooms. *In room:* A/C, cable TV, dataport, minibar, hot-water pot w/tea, humidifier, hair dryer, Washlet toilet, trouser press.

(199) **Umenoya** 👍👍👍   Small, intimate, and secluded from the world behind a wall, this wonderful, 60-something-year-old inn boasts a beautiful small garden, beyond which are a canal, a park, and a wooded hill in the distance (a good example of borrowed landscape). Rooms, which are graced with such architectural details as bamboo weavings and wood-carved transoms, vary in price according to amenities and view; the best have cypress tubs, toilets with heated seats, and views of the garden. One of the public baths is in a hut with a conical-shaped roof in the garden.

2–8–9 Kami-ichi, Matsuyama 790-0853. ✆ 089/941-2570. Fax 089/941-1025. umenoya@sgr.e-catv.ne.jp. 10 units (2 with bathroom, 8 with toilet only). ¥23,250 ($221) per person in room with toilet only; ¥29,250 ($279) per person in room with bathroom. Rates include 2 meals and service. AE, DC, MC, V. Streetcar: Dogo Onsen (5 min.). **Amenities:** Public indoor and outdoor hot-spring baths; in-room massage. *In room:* A/C, TV, minibar, hot-water pot w/tea, safe.

## MODERATE

**Hotel Patio Dogo** 👍   With a great location just across the street from the delightful Dogo Onsen Honkan spa, this smart-looking medium-class hotel offers semi-double beds in singles, and queens in the more expensive double rooms. Ah, space at last! Some rooms (on the eighth and ninth floors) have a view of Matsuyama Castle far in the distance (binoculars would come in handy), but best are rooms on the second through fourth floors whose windows overlook the historic spa. The most expensive accommodations in each category are larger, corner rooms. In the evening, be sure to join all the other tourists staying in Dogo and wear your yukata across the street for a nighttime soak in the historic spa.

20–12 Yuno-machi, Dogo, Matsuyama 790-0842. ✆ 089/941-4128. Fax 089/941-4129. www.patio-dogo.co.jp. 101 units. ¥6,825–¥9,030 ($65–$86) single; ¥11,025–¥13,125 ($105–$125) double; ¥14,175–¥21,000 ($135–$200) twin. AE, DC, MC, V. Streetcar: Dogo Onsen (5 min.). Walk though the covered shopping arcade and turn left. **Amenities:** Restaurant (a branch of Sushimaru; see "Where to Dine," below); in-room massage; same-day laundry/dry-cleaning service (weekdays only). *In room:* A/C, TV, fridge, hair dryer, Washlet toilet.

**International Hotel Matsuyama (Kokusai Hotel)**   Opened in 1981 but updated, this medium-priced hotel is comfortable enough and, centrally located near the Okaido shopping arcade and Matsuyama Castle ropeway, is a good base for exploring the city. It caters almost exclusively to Japanese, with single rooms boasting double-size beds and good-size desks. Some of the twins have castle views, and there are also "corner" doubles and twins that are spacious with lots of windows that open and let in lots of light. Frommer's readers receive a special 20% discount; show this book when you check in.

1–13 Ichiban-cho, Matsuyama 790-0001. ✆ 089/932-5111. Fax 089/945-2055. k-hotelm@cello.ocn.ne.jp. 78 units. ¥7,068–¥7,854 ($67–$75) single; ¥12,705–¥23,100 ($121–$220) twin; ¥12,127–¥23,100 ($115–$220) double. AE, DC, MC, V. Streetcar: Okaido—marked "Ichibancho" on some tourist maps (3 min.). Continue east on Densha Dori to the 1st gas station and turn left; the hotel is on your right. **Amenities:** 3 restaurants (Japanese, Western, Chinese); rental bikes (¥500/$4.75 per day); room service (11:30am–10pm); in-room massage; same-day laundry/dry-cleaning service; nonsmoking rooms. *In room:* A/C, TV, dataports, minibar (twins only), fridge (singles and doubles), hot-water pot w/tea, hair dryer, Washlet toilet.

## INEXPENSIVE

(200) **Minshuku Miyoshi**   This simple establishment is located in Dogo Onsen near Ishiteji Temple; if you call ahead, someone can pick you up at the Dogo Onsen streetcar stop. Although not much English is spoken, they're used to foreigners here. Clean but simple tatami rooms, all with sink and toilet, make it a good choice for young budget travelers.

3–7–23 Ishite, Matsuyama 790-0852. ✆ **089/977-2581**. Fax 089/977-2581. 6 units (none with bathroom, all with toilet). ¥4,000 ($38) without meals; ¥5,000 ($48) with breakfast; ¥7,350 ($70) with breakfast and dinner. All rates are per person. No credit cards. Streetcar: Dogo Onsen (10 min.). Bus: no. 52 to Ishiteji. Across from Ishiteji Temple, set back from the road behind Cosmo gas station and parking lot. **Amenities:** Washer/dryer (free of charge). *In room:* A/C, TV, no phone.

**Toyoko Inn Matsuyama Ichibancho** *Value*    It's hard to beat this chain business hotel for its handy location in front of Katsuyama-cho streetcar stop near the castle and nightlife area, free lobby computers, and free movie channels. Of course, rooms are cookie-cutter identical and tiny, but otherwise provide all you need for a night's rest.

1–10–8 Ichiban-cho, Matsuyama 790-0001. ✆ **089/941-1045**. Fax 089/941-2046. www.toyoko-inn.com. 216 units. ¥5,460–¥6,090 ($52–$58) single; ¥8,190 ($78) double or twin. Rates include Japanese breakfast. AE, DC, MC, V. Streetcar: Katsuyama-cho (1 min.). **Amenities:** Restaurant (Japanese); in-room massage; same-day laundry/dry-cleaning service; coin-operated washer/dryer; nonsmoking rooms. *In room:* A/C, TV, dataport, fridge, hot-water pot w/tea, hair dryer, trouser press.

# WHERE TO DINE
## EXPENSIVE
**Kadota** ✿ FRENCH    Chef Kadota worked 9 years at the venerable Okura Hotel and then at the ANA Hotel Matsuyama before opening his own restaurant here in 1993. Small and cozy, with classical music playing in the background, flowers on every table, and French cuisine served on elegant tableware, it offers homemade appetizers, organic vegetables whenever possible, and—the house specialty—steaks and seafood in season. It offers only fixed-price meals; your dinner may start with yellowtail sashimi in mandarin orange sauce, followed by Seto Inland Sea sea bream served in a white-wine sauce, or steak in red-wine sauce with sweet-potato gratin.

3–4–25 Sanban-cho. ✆ **089/931-3511**. Reservations recommended. Set dinner ¥5,250–¥15,750 ($50–$150); set lunch ¥2,100–¥3,150 ($20–$30). AE, DC, MC, V. Daily 11am–2pm and 5–9pm (last order). Closed 2 days in Aug. Streetcar: Kencho-mae (5 min.). Take the side road to the east of the ANA hotel, continue straight 7 blocks, turn right where you'll see the restaurant with a tree lit in tiny white lights.

## MODERATE
㉑ **Kushihide** YAKITORI/GRILLED FOODS    Behind the counter of this 40-year-old-eatery are some 400 individual sake cups inscribed with the names of regular customers—the cook joked that this way, the cups didn't have to be washed. Washed or unwashed, they're testimony to the popularity of this simple eating and drinking venue. As soon as you sit down, a large bowl of cabbage with a dip and an appetizer will be placed in front of you. The restaurant is most famous for its boiled chicken leg and thigh for ¥800 ($7.60), included in some of the set meals. It also offers chicken sashimi; the restaurant claims to be one of the few places you can eat it safely, as the restaurant raises its own chickens and serves them the day of their demise.

3–2–8 Nibancho. ✆ **089/921-1587**. Sticks ¥150–¥200 ($1.40–$1.90); set meals ¥1,500–¥4,000 ($14–$38). AE, MC, V. Daily 4:30–10:30pm. Streetcar: Okaido—marked "Ichibancho" on some tourist maps (2 min.). Walk down Okaido Arcade and take the 1st right after the stoplights; it's 1 block farther on your left.

㉒ **Sushimaru** SUSHI    Located just east of the Okaido shopping arcade, Sushimaru has Japanese *noren* (shop curtains), a display case outside, and old-fashioned architecture. The popular *higawari* (today's lunch), served Monday through Saturday until 2pm and displayed outside the front door, consists of sushi, *nigiri* sushi (sushi rolls), salad, and soup for ¥800 ($7.60). A Japanese-language menu with photos shows other set meals. In the evening, kaiseki featuring sashimi are also available.

Another Sushimaru with the same menu (except the daily lunch is ¥1,050/$10 here) and same hours is located across the street from Dogo Onsen in the Hotel Patio Dogo at 20–12 Yunomachi (© **089/932-6157**).

2-3-2 Nibancho. © **089/941-0447**. Set meals ¥1,365–¥3,675 ($13–$35); kaiseki ¥3,675–¥10,000 ($35–$95). AE, DC, MC, V. Mon–Fri 11am–2pm and 4:30–10:30pm; Sat–Sun and holidays 11am–10:30pm. Streetcar: Okaido—marked "Ichibancho" on some tourist maps (2 min.). Walk south along the Okaido shopping arcade. After you cross Nichiban-cho (the 1st light), take the 1st small street on your left; it will be on your right a few shops down.

㉒⑬ **Tokuhiro** SHABU-SHABU/YAKINIKU    Located near the castle ropeway, this modern restaurant has tables with views of a waterfall and a pond in which more than 300 koi swim happily about, as well as quiet tatami rooms. It offers all-you-can-eat yakiniku and shabu-shabu with a 90-minute time limit. Prices are ¥3,000 ($29) for men and ¥2,600 ($25) for women. The cheapest lunch, costing ¥710 ($6.75), is served until 2pm.

3-7-10 Okaido. © **089/934-0880**. Set lunches ¥710–¥2,000 ($6.75–$19); set dinners ¥1,680–¥5,500 ($16–$52). MC, V. Daily 11am–3pm and 5–11pm (last order 10pm). Streetcar: Okaido—marked "Ichibancho" on some maps (5 min.). Walk up the street with the WECOME TO MATSUYAMA CASTLE arch; the restaurant will be on your right.

## INEXPENSIVE

**Dogo Beer** *Finds*    If you agree that "One gulp of beer taken just after a bath is the time when you feel most refreshed," as proclaimed in this microbrewery's pamphlet, then after bathing at Dogo Onsen Honkan head straight across the street for some sake or beer. (The parent company has been a sake producer for more than a century; it opened a brewery in 1996 following deregulation that had long assured a beer monopoly by the major players.) An upbeat establishment with an eclectic decor mixing the traditional (bamboo ceilings) and the modern (artwork), and with jazz the background music of choice, it offers German-style beers, a stout, and sake. Although a sign outside its doors reads BREWERY RESTAURANT, its Japanese-language menu with pictures is limited to yakitori (¥400/$3.80 for three sticks), fried chicken *(senzanki)*, deep-fried fish paste *(jyakoten)*, and other pub foods, with most dishes priced below ¥700 ($6.65). Your best bet is to order one of the set meals.

20–13 Yuno-machi, Dogo. © **089/945-6866**. Set lunch ¥740 ($7.05); set dinners ¥1,030–¥1,580 ($9.80–$15). No credit cards. Daily 11am–10pm. Streetcar: Dogo Onsen. On the north side of the Dogo Onsen Honkan.

# 11

# Kyushu

The southernmost of Japan's four main islands, Kyushu offers a mild climate, famous hot-spring spas, beautiful countryside, national parks, and warm, friendly people. It also boasts a couple of high-tech theme parks that make it Japan's number-one destination for visitors from Korea, Taiwan, Hong Kong, and other Asian cities.

Historians believe that Japan's earliest inhabitants lived on Kyushu before gradually pushing northward. According to Japanese legend, it was from Kyushu that the first emperor, Jimmu, began his campaign to unify Japan. Kyushu is therefore considered to be the cradle of Japanese civilization. And because Kyushu is the island closest to Korea and China, it has served through the centuries as a point of influx for both people and ideas from abroad, including those from the West.

## 1 Fukuoka

1,174km (730 miles) W of Tokyo; 450km (281 miles) W of Hiroshima

With a population of 1.38 million, **Fukuoka** is Kyushu's largest city and serves as a major international and domestic gateway to the island. On the northern coast of Kyushu, it lies closer to Seoul, Korea, than to Tokyo.

During Japan's feudal days, Fukuoka was divided into two distinct towns separated by the Nakagawa River. Fukuoka was where the samurai lived since it was the castle town of the local feudal lord. Merchants lived across the river in Hakata, the commercial center of the area. Both cities were joined in 1889 under the common name of Fukuoka. Fukuoka's main train station, however, is in Hakata and is therefore called Hakata Station. Hakata Station serves as the terminus of the Tokaido-Sanyo Shinkansen Line from Tokyo (though only Nozomi bullet trains, which are not covered in the Japan Rail Pass, travel the entire distance).

In the 13th century, Fukuoka was selected by Mongol forces under Kublai Khan as the best place to invade Japan. The first attack came in 1274, but Japanese were able to repel the invasion. Convinced the Mongols would attack again, Japanese built a 3m-high (10-ft.) stone wall along the coast. The second invasion came in 1281. Not only did the Mongols find the wall impossible to scale, but a typhoon blew in and destroyed the entire Mongol fleet. Japanese called this gift from heaven "divine wind," or *kamikaze,* a word that took on a different meaning during World War II when young Japanese pilots crashed their planes into American ships in a last-ditch attempt to win the war.

Today, Fukuoka is a modern, internationally oriented commercial and business center with a highly developed port and coastal area. Although it's not a must-see tourist destination, there are some interesting museums, shrines, and a temple worth seeing if you've arrived in Fukuoka on the Shinkansen.

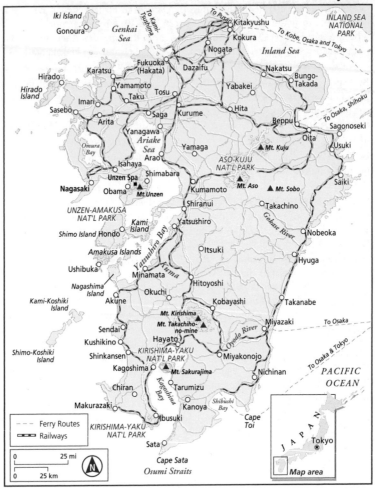

# Kyushu

Iki Island
Gonoura
*Genkai
Sea*
To Kami-Tsushima
To Pusan
Kitakyushu
Kokura
To Kobe, Osaka and Tokyo
INLAND SEA NATIONAL PARK
*Inland Sea*
Nogata
Fukuoka (Hakata)
Dazaifu
Nakatsu
Bungo-Takada
Karatsu
Hirado
Yamamoto
Taku
Tosu
Yabakei
To Osaka, Shikoku
Hirado Island
Imari
Sasebo
Arita
Saga
Kurume
Hita
Beppu
Sagonoseki
Yanagawa
*Ariake Sea*
Yamaga
Oita
Usuki
Isahaya
Arao
Mt. Kuju
ASO-KUJU NAT'L PARK
Saiki
*Omura Bay*
Unzen Spa
Shimabara
Nagasaki
Obama
Mt.Unzen
Kumamoto
Mt. Aso
Mt. Sobo
UNZEN-AMAKUSA NAT'L PARK
Shiranui
Takachino
*Gokase River*
Kami Island
Yatsushiro
Nobeoka
Shimo Island Hondo
*Amakusa Islands*
Itsuki
*Yatsushiro Bay*
*Kuma*
Hyuga
Ushibuka
Minamata
Nagashima Island
Okuchi
Hitoyoshi
Kami-Koshiki Island
Akune
Kobayashi
Takanabe
Sendai
Mt. Kirishima
Mt. Takachiho-no-mine
Miyazaki
To Osaka
Shimo-Koshiki Island
Kushikino
Hayato
*Oyodo River*
Shinkansen
KIRISHIMA-YAKU NAT'L PARK
Miyakonojo
To Osaka & Tokyo
Kagoshima
Mt. Sakurajima
Nichinan
PACIFIC OCEAN
Chiran
Tarumizu
*Kagoshima Bay*
Makurazaki
Kanoya
*Shibushi Bay*
Cape Toi
Ibusuki
KIRISHIMA-YAKU NAT'L PARK
JAPAN
Tokyo
Sata
Cape Sata
*Osumi Straits*
Map area

- - - Ferry Routes
▭▭▭ Railways

0    25 mi
0    25 km

## ESSENTIALS

**GETTING THERE   By Plane**   Direct flights connect **Fukuoka Airport** (☎ 092/ 621-6059; www.fuk-ab.co.jp) to a variety of international cities, including Beijing, Hong Kong, and Bangkok, as well as numerous domestic cities. Flying time from Tokyo's Haneda Airport is 1½ hours; the regular, one-way fare costs ¥31,000 ($295) on Japan Airlines. However, because of fierce competition on the Fukuoka–Haneda route, bargains do exist. **Skymark** (☎ 03/3433-7670 in Tokyo, or 092/736-3131 in Fukuoka), for example, a small airline serving Fukuoka, offers nine flights daily from Haneda to Fukuoka for as low as ¥15,000 ($143) one-way, while even major airlines sometimes offer special rates of ¥15,500 ($148), depending on the time of day and season. To get into town, there's a subway station located directly under the domestic terminal of **Fukuoka Airport** (if you've arrived at the international terminal, take the

free shuttle bus to the domestic terminal). The trip to Hakata Station takes only 5 minutes and to Tenjin takes 11; the fare is ¥250 ($2.40), or you can purchase a 1-day subway pass for ¥600 ($5.70) if you plan to sightsee the same day. Alternatively, there's Nishitetsu bus service directly from the international terminal to Hakata Station's bus terminal; departures are every 20 to 30 minutes and cost ¥250 ($2.40).

**By Train**    Fukuoka's **Hakata Station** is the last stop on the Nozomi Shinkansen bullet train from Tokyo (if you have a Japan Rail Pass, which doesn't cover Nozomi trains, you'll have to change trains in Osaka or Okayama). The trip takes almost 6 hours not including transfers and costs ¥21,210 ($202) for an unreserved seat. Hiroshima is 1 hour and 10 minutes away; Kyoto is 2 hours and 45 minutes away.

**By Bus**    Buses depart from Tokyo's Shinjuku Station nightly at 9pm, arriving at Tenjin Station in the heart of the city at 11:20am the next morning. The fare is ¥15,000 ($143) one-way.

**VISITOR INFORMATION**    Before leaving Tokyo or the Narita or Kansai airports, pick up a copy of the leaflet "Fukuoka" at the Tourist Information Center (you can also download it from JNTO's website at www.jnto.go.jp by looking under *Regional Tourist Guides*).

Fukuoka **Tourist Information Office** (© 092/431-3003; open daily 8am–8pm) is in Hakata Station near the East Gate. It has maps and sightseeing pamphlets. Ask, too, for *Rainbow,* a free monthly with concert, exhibition, events, and festival information; and *Fukuoka Now,* good for restaurant and nightlife listings. Be sure to pick up the free **Welcome Card** and accompanying guide, which gives overseas visitors discounts for selected hotels, restaurants, attractions, and shops (the card must be presented at check-in to receive hotel discount). On the Internet, sightseeing information is available at www.yokanavi.com. Other useful sites include www.fukuoka-now.com (good for restaurants and nightlife) and www.acros.or.jp (with information on Fukuoka City and Fukuoka Prefecture, including Daizafu and Space World).

**INTERNET ACCESS**    You can check e-mail 24 hours a day at **Media Café Popeye,** located on the eighth floor of the Kotsu Center, next to Hakata Station (© 092/432-8788). It charges ¥390 ($3.70) for 1 hour.

**MAIL & ATMs**    An international post office, with a counter for stamps and mail that is open 24 hours, as well as an ATM that accepts international credit cards, is located next to the Hakata (west) exit of Hakata Station.

**ORIENTATION**    Although Hakata Station is the terminus for the Shinkansen bullet train and trains departing for the rest of Kyushu, with most of Fukuoka's hotels clustered nearby, the heart and business center of Fukuoka is an area to the west called **Tenjin.** It's home to several department stores, its own train station and bus center, a large underground shopping arcade, and restaurants. Just a few minutes' walk from Tenjin is **Nakasu,** one of Japan's most famous nightlife districts, with more than 2,000 bars, restaurants, and small clubs clustered on what's actually an islet bounded by the Nakagawa River.

Across the river from Nakasu (and a 10-min. walk west of Hakata Station) is **Canal City Hakata,** an intriguingly designed (by award-winning American architect Jon Jerde) entertainment, hotel, and shopping complex with 125 shops and restaurants. Also nearby and within walking distance are Tochiji Temple, Hakata Machiya Folk Museum, Kushida Shrine, and the Fukuoka Asian Art Museum.

**GETTING AROUND**    You can **walk** from Hakata Station to most of the attractions recommended below.

**By Subway**    This is the easiest method of transportation because there are only two major lines. One line runs from Hakata Station to Tenjin (the third stop), passing Nakasu-Kawabata on the way, the stop for the Nakasu nightlife district. This same line will also take you to Fukuoka Airport. Stops are announced in English. Fares start at ¥200 ($1.90), but if you think you'll be riding a lot, purchase a 1-day subway pass for ¥600 ($5.70).

**By Train**    Whereas Hakata Station serves as the terminus for the Shinkansen and Japan Railways trains departing for the rest of Kyushu, Tenjin has its own station, called **Nishitetsu Fukuoka Station,** located inside the Mitsukoshi department store building and useful for trips to Dazaifu.

**By Bus**    The city's two bus terminals are located near Hakata Station at the Kotsu Center and in Tenjin near Nishitetsu Fukuoka Station and Mitsukoshi department store; both are clearly marked in English. Buses running inside the central Hakata-Tenjin District charge a flat fare of ¥100 (95¢). Most useful for tourists is the so-called "¥100 Bus," which sports a big, ¥100 coin on its side and travels a circular route going both directions from Haktaka Station to 18 stops in the downtown area, including Tenjin, Canal City, and the Hakata Riverain shopping/cultural complex.

## EXPLORING THE CITY

About an 8-minute walk northwest of Hakata Station and located on the right side of Taihaku-dori is ⑳④ **Tochoji Temple,** 2–4 Gokushomachi (© **092/291-4459;** daily 9am–5pm; subway: one stop from Hakata Station to Gion, exit 1, 1 min; ¥100 Bus: Gion-machi, stop no. 16; look for a picture of a Buddha at the front gate). This modern reconstruction of a long-established temple may not look like much, but up on the second floor is Japan's largest seated wooden Buddha, measuring 9.9m (33 ft.) tall. Admission is free, but refrain from taking photographs. Particularly interesting is the trip through the Hells of Buddhism, upon which you can embark by entering the small room to the left of the Buddha. After viewing colored reliefs of unfortunate souls burning in hell, being boiled alive, and suffering other tortures, enter the darkened, twisting passageway and walk through it guided by a rail, whereupon you'll reach the end—enlightenment! It's fun for older kids.

On the other side of Taihaku-dori Avenue, down the side street with a 7-Eleven and marked by a large cement gate (*torii*), is the ⑳⑤ **Hakata Machiya Folk Museum (Hakata Machiya Furusato-Kan)** ⚘, 6–10 Reisen-machi (© **092/281-7761;** daily 10am–6pm; subway: Gion, exit 2, 4 min.; ¥100 Bus: Gion-machi, stop no. 16). This museum celebrates the history and cultural heritage of Hakata, the old merchants'

---

### *Tips*  A Note on Japanese Symbols

Many establishments and attractions in Japan do not have signs in Roman (English-language) letters. Those that don't are indicated in this guide with an oval with a number that corresponds to a number in appendix C showing the Japanese symbols. Thus, to find the Japanese symbol for, say, the **Hakata Machiya Folk Museum** (above), refer to no. 205 in appendix C.

town, concentrating primarily on the Meiji and Taisho eras. It occupies three build-ings, two of which are Meiji-Era replicas; the third is an authentic, 150-year-old house of a weaver. On display are items used in everyday life, as well as dioramas depicting festivals, everyday street scenes, and a home typical of a Hakata merchant family. On a telephone, you can listen to Hakata-ben, the local dialect, which is quite difficult even for native Japanese speakers to understand. You can also watch artisans at work on Hakata's most famous wares, including the highly refined Hakata dolls, tops, wooden containers, and Hakata-ori cloth, used for *obi* sashes and famous for loin-cloths worn by sumo wrestlers. Be sure to see the 22-minute film of the Yamakasa Fes-tival, Fukuoka's most famous festival, featuring races of men carrying enormous floats. Add another 30 minutes to see the museum itself and its crafts shop. Admission is ¥200 ($1.90) for adults and free for children.

Beyond the Hakata Machiya Folk Museum is **Kushida Shrine,** 1 Kamikawabata-machi (© **092/291-2951;** shrine grounds open 24 hr.), Fukuoka's oldest shrine. Site of the Yamakasa Festival, it has long been the shrine for merchants praying for good health and prosperity. Most interesting is a tall, towering float on view year-round that is used in the Yamakasa Festival held in mid-July and decorated with dolls made by Hakata doll makers. Incredibly, the elaborate floats are made anew every year.

Walk through Kushida Shrine and turn right into the **Kawabata-dori covered shopping arcade.** Linking Canal City Hakata and Hakata Riverain, it was once the city's main shopping street but has been overtaken by the two complexes it connects. Halfway down is another float on view year-round that's used in the Yamakasa Festi-val. At the end of the arcade, across the street, is Riverain, where up on the seventh and eighth floors is the **Fukuoka Asian Art Museum** ✦✦✦, 3–1 Shimo-Kawabata-machi (© **092/263-1100;** http://faam.city.fukuoka.jp; Thurs–Tues 10am–8pm), the only museum I've seen in Japan devoted to contemporary and modern art from around Asia. From folk pop art to political art, the permanent exhibition presents the cutting edge of art from the Philippines, Indonesia, Malaysia, Singapore, Thailand, China, Mongolia, Korea, India, and other Asian countries, with changing displays culled from the museum's own collection. It's very much worth the hour you'll spend here and the ¥200 ($1.90) admission for adults, ¥150 ($1.45) for college and high-school students, and ¥100 (95¢) for junior-high students and younger (special exhibits cost more). The closest subway station is Nakasu-Kawabata Station (exit 6) in front of Riverain; or take the ¥100 Bus to Kawabata-machi (stop no. 12).

If you're ready for dining or shopping, retrace your steps through Kawabata-dori arcade and take the escalator leading to **Canal City Hakata,** a virtual city-within-a-city complete with hotels, shops, restaurants, the Club Sega amusement arcade, and a 177m-long (590-ft.) canal that runs through its center.

## EASY SIDE TRIPS FROM FUKUOKA
### DAZAIFU
If you have 4 or more hours to spare, I heartily recommend taking a side trip to **Daza-ifu,** a pleasant village that is home to a shrine that is immensely popular with Japan-ese and the new Kyushu National Museum. Daizafu has a festive atmosphere, and one of the main reasons to visit, in my opinion, is to see everyone else.

The best way to reach Dazaifu is from Nishitetsu Fukuoka Station in Tenjin (located in the Mitsukoshi department store building). Take a limited express *(tokyu)* of the Nishitetsu Omuta Line (there are departures every 30 min.) 12 minutes to Fut-sukaichi (the second stop); transfer there (across the platform) for the 8-minute train

ride on the Nichitetsu Daisafu Line (two stops) to Dazaifu Station, the last stop (though there are a few trains that go directly from Fukuoka Station to Dazaifu). If you don't catch a limited express, the trip to Dazaifu can take about 50 minutes. In any case, the fare is ¥390 ($3.70) one-way. The **Dazaifu Tourist Office** (© 092/733-2220; daily 8:30am–5pm), located to the right outside Dazaifu Station, has an English-language pamphlet.

**Dazaifu Tenmangu Shrine** ✿✿✿, 4–7–1 Saifu Dazaifu (© 092/922-8225), is a 5-minute walk from the station, reached by taking a right onto a pedestrian lane lined with shops selling souvenirs, sweets, and crafts, followed by a three bridges (representing the past, present and future) spanning a turtle-filled pond in the kanji for "heart." The shrine itself was established in 905, soon after the death of Sugawara Michizane, who was demoted from his position as Minister of the Right in Kyoto and exiled to Daizafu, where he continued his scholarly studies despite extreme hardship. Today, Michizane is deified as the god of literature and calligraphy, which explains why this shrine is so popular—as the head office of 12,000 Tenmangu shrines spread throughout Japan and presided over by the 39th-generation Michizane descendant, it draws six million visitors a year, many of them high-school students praying to pass tough entrance exams into universities. Behind the main hall, which dates from 1591, hang wooden tablets, written with the wishes of visitors—mostly for successful examination scores. Also behind the main hall is an extensive plum grove with 6,000 trees; the plum blossom, in bloom from late January to March, is considered the symbol of scholarship.

Whatever you do, don't miss **Komyozenji Temple** ✿, just a 2-minute walk from the shrine. This Zen temple boasts Kyushu's sole rock garden, arranged to form the Chinese character for "light." In the back is also a combination moss-rock garden, representing the sea and land and shaded by maple trees. It's a glorious sight and is almost never crowded, except in autumn when changing maple leaves make it even more spectacular. To see it, take your shoes off, throw ¥200 ($1.90) into the donation box, and walk to the wooden veranda in back where you can sit and meditate. It's open daily from 8am to 5pm.

Behind Daizafu Tenmangu Shrine, to the right, is an escalator that will take you to the **Kyushu National Museum,** 4–7–2 Ishizaka (© 092/918-2807; www.kyuhaku.jp), which in 2005 opened as Japan's first new national museum in 100 years. Perched on a hillside, it's a strikingly modern structure that undulates down the slope in mimicry of the hills around it, with surrounding woods reflected on its facade. Through permanent and special exhibits, it focuses on Japan's cultural heritage, how that heritage has been influenced by other Asian cultures through the ages, and the role Kyushu has played in cultural exchange. Religious objects, musical instruments, ceramics, lacquerware, art, and other items from ancient to modern times from a number of nations are on display in permanent and special exhibits. It's open Tuesday to Sunday from 9:30am to 5pm and costs ¥400 ($3.80) for adults, ¥210 ($2) for university and high-school students, and free for children. Special exhibits cost more.

## SPACE WORLD

**Space World,** 4–1–1 Higashida (© 093/672-3600; www.spaceworld.co.jp), in the town of Kitakyushu, is a space travel–theme amusement park with features various thrill rides, including roller coasters, splash rides, a 98m-high (328-ft.) Ferris wheel, a movie theater with seats that move in sync with the action, an IMAX theater, kiddie

## Take Me Out to the Ballgame

If you're in town March through September, consider seeing the **Fukuoka Softbank Hawks** baseball team play one of its 70-some home games in Fukuoka Dome, the first retractable-roof stadium in Japan. Tickets start at ¥1,000 ($9.50) for an unreserved seat in the outfield and are available at any Lawson convenience store up to 2 hours before the start of the game or at the box office. Personally, I find watching the spectators as much fun as watching the game, with their coordinated cheering, flag waving, trumpet blowing, and more. Oddly enough, the roof is kept closed (in case it rains and so that players aren't distracted by their shadows) except for occasional night games and during the last 15 minutes of a game if it looks like the Hawks are going to win. And this being Japan, the dome is part of a larger **Hawks Town** complex with restaurants and other amusements. To reach Hawks Town, take the subway to the Tojinmachi stop, from which it's about a 15-minute walk. Or take bus no. 39 or 306 from gate 5 of the Kotsu Bus Center in front of Hakata Station to the Fukuoka-Dome Mae. On game days, there are also special shuttle buses departing from the bus centers in Tenjin and Kotsu Center near Hakata Station.

rides, and Space Dome, in which visitors take a "shuttle" to a space station and from there embark on roller-coaster journeys around the solar system or through a black hole. You'll probably spend a minimum of 4 hours here. An all-inclusive pass costs ¥3,800 ($36) for adults (12 and older), ¥2,800 ($27) for children ages 4 to 11, and free for seniors (proof of age required). Minimum daily open hours are November through March 10am to 5pm, and April through October 9:30am to 5pm, with extended hours many holidays and weekends. To reach Space World, take a JR Kaisoku (express) train from Fukuoka's Hakata Station directly to Space World Station. The trip time is about 60 minutes, and the park is a 5-minute walk from the station. If you have a JR Rail Pass, it's quicker to take the Shinkansen bullet train 20 minutes from Hakata Station to Kokura Station, transferring there to a local line for the 10-minute ride to Space World. Likewise, if you're coming from Honshu via Shinkansen, transfer in Kokura. If you have luggage to stow, there are lockers at Kokura Station and at Space World's entrance.

## WHERE TO STAY
### EXPENSIVE

**Grand Hyatt Fukuoka** ✿✿✿    Opened in 1996, Fukuoka's top hotel commands a grand setting in the innovative Canal City Hakata, with easy pedestrian access to the city's main sights. Its black-marbled lobby has a curved facade that overlooks the shopping complex, but for guests who desire solitude, the hotel also has its private roof garden. Service throughout the hotel is superb—along the order of "Your wish is our command." Small but stylish rooms provide views of the private garden or the river and its night scenes. Besides all the luxury, a stay at the Grand Hyatt is fun, with Canal City's many shops and restaurants right outside the door.

1–2–82 Sumiyoshi, Hakata-ku, Fukuoka 812-0018. Ⓒ **800/591-1234** in the U.S., or 092/282-1234. Fax 092/282-2817. http://fukuoka.grand.hyatt.com.   370 units.   ¥20,790 – ¥34,650 ($198–$330) single;   ¥26,565 – ¥40,425 ($253–$385) double or twin. Grand Club ¥6,930 ($66) extra per room. Rates include service charge. AE, DC, MC, V. A 12-min. walk west of Hakata Station. ¥100 Bus: Canal City Hakata-mae (stop no. 4; 2 min). **Amenities:** 3 restaurants (Continental, Cantonese, Japanese); 2 bars; 1 lounge; fitness center and spa with 25m (82-ft.) indoor pool (fee: ¥3,000/$29;   free for Grand Club guests); 24-hr. concierge; Canal City shopping arcade; salon; room service (6:30am–midnight, Fri–Sat until 2am); in-room massage; same-day laundry/dry-cleaning service; nonsmoking rooms, executive-level rooms. *In room:* A/C, satellite TV w/pay movies, dataport, minibar, hot-water pot w/tea, hair dryer, safe, bathroom scale, Washlet toilet.

**Il Palazzo** 🐦🐦   Eye-catching with its brick-warehouse-meets-Art-Deco-temple architecture, this uniquely designed boutique hotel is the hotel of choice for artists, designers, and other creative folks. Jazz plays in the lobby with its soaring ceiling and wood and marble design. Contemporary rooms, innovative when they debuted in 1989, seem rather ordinary now, with marbled bathrooms thoughtfully divided by a large glass plate into "wet" areas (shower/bathtub) and "dry" areas (sink and toilet). Unfortunately, even though Canal City Hakata is just across the river, none of the rooms face the river or provide a view. The highest rates in each category below are those charged on Saturdays and evenings before holidays.

3–13–1 Haruyoshi, Chuo-ku, Fukuoka 810-0003. Ⓒ **092/716-3333.** Fax 092/724-3330. www.ilpalazo.jp. 62 units. ¥15,015–¥17,325 ($43–$165) single; ¥25,410–¥28,875 ($242–$275) double; ¥24,255–¥27,720 ($231–$264) twin. Rates include service charge. AE, DC, MC, V. ¥100 Bus: Minami Shinchi (stop no. 5; 4 min.). **Amenities:** 2 restaurants (Italian, coffee shop); 1 bar; room service (4–10pm); in-room massage; same-day laundry/dry cleaning service. *In room:* A/C, TV, dataport, minibar, hot-water pot w/tea, hair dryer.

## MODERATE

**Canal City Fukuoka Washington Hotel** *(Value)*   Though part of a nationwide business-hotel chain, this Washington is different—it has more style and lots of pluses. For one thing, it's located in Canal City Hakata, Fukuoka's number-one shopping and entertainment complex, offering convenience right outside the front door. In addition, its rooms come with extras not usually found in business hotels, including LCD TVs. The cheapest singles face the Grand Hyatt above the Canal City complex, while higher-priced, larger singles and all twins and triples have better views outward toward the city. Lobby computers connect you to the Internet for ¥100 (95¢) for 10 minutes. The downside: Its good location makes it popular; you'll find the lobby crowded at check-in and checkout times.

1–2–20 Sumiyoshi, Hakata-ku, Fukuoka 812-0018. Ⓒ **092/282-8800.** Fax 092/282-0757. 423 units. ¥9,200 – ¥11,000 ($88–$105) single; ¥18,500 ($176) double; ¥17,500–¥19,000 ($167–$181) twin. ¥1,000 ($9.50) extra per person Sat and evenings before holidays. AE, DC, MC, V. A 10-min. walk west of Hakata Station. ¥100 Bus: Canal City Hakata-mae (stop no. 4; 1 min.). **Amenities:** Restaurant (coffee shop); Canal City shopping arcade; in-room massage; same-day laundry/dry cleaning service; nonsmoking rooms. *In room:* A/C, satellite TV, minibar, hot-water pot w/tea, hair dryer, Washlet toilet.

**Dukes Hotel** 🐦   Flower boxes, plants, and evergreens outside the front door hint that this is no ordinary hotel. Indeed, it's an inexpensive hotel with class, with a small but very civilized lobby that exudes charm and invites you to linger with its Chinese vases, palm trees, antiques, and classical music. Most of the rooms, tiny but comfy with a simple decor that suggests an English-style countryside manor, are singles, with only nine twins and nine doubles. In the world of cloned business hotels, this establishment, a short walk from Hakata Station in the direction of Canal City, is a welcome relief.

Farther from the station but in the heart of the city (4 min. from the Nakasukawa-bata subway stop or Higashi-Nakasu/stop no. 11 of the ¥100 Bus), **Dukes Hotel Nakasu,** 1–1 Nakasunakashima-machi, Hakataku (© **092/283-2800**), offers the same amenities and style at a cheaper price.

2–3–9 Hakataeki-mae, Hakata-ku, Fukuoka 812-0011. © **092/472-1800**. Fax 092/472-1900. www.dukes-hotel. com. 153 units. ¥8,190–¥9,450 ($78–$90) single; ¥12,600 ($120) double; ¥13,650 ($130) twin. AE, DC, MC, V. Station: Hakata (2 min.). From the west (Hakata) exit, take the road straight ahead (the one to between Fukuoka City Bank and the red stone Center Building); it's down this street on your right in the 2nd block. **Amenities:** Restaurant (coffee shop); souvenir/convenience shop; in-room massage; same-day laundry/dry cleaning service; nonsmoking rooms. *In room:* A/C, TV, high-speed dataport (8th floor only), fridge, hot-water pot w/tea, hair dryer, Washlet toilet.

## JR Kyushu Hotel Fukuoka
One block east of Hakata Station, this hotel beckons with a flower-lined entryway, a European-style lobby, and rooms that are larger than those in most business hotels. Though there are no doubles per se, two can tough it out in a single room with a semi-double-size bed for ¥13,800 ($131). A ladies' floor offers specialized amenities. But the best reasons to stay here are its convenient location and the discount extended to those with Japan Rail Passes.

2–2–4 Hakataeki-Higashi, Hakata-ku, Fukuoka 812-0013. © **092/413-8787**. Fax 092/413-9746. www.jrhotelgroup. com. 90 units. ¥7,500–¥8,800 ($71–$84) single; ¥14,600 ($140) twin. 10% discount with Japan Rail Pass. AE, DC, MC, V. Station: Hakata (a 2-min. walk from the east Shinkansen exit, past the Miyako Hotel). **Amenities:** Restaurant (Japanese); concierge; in-room massage; coin-op washers and dryers; same-day laundry/dry cleaning; nonsmoking rooms. *In room:* A/C, TV, fridge, hot-water pot w/tea, hair dryer, Washlet toilet.

## INEXPENSIVE
In addition to the choices here, the budget chain Toyoko Inn (www.toyoko-inn.com) has two locations within walking distance of Hakata Station. **Toyoko Inn Hakataguchi Ekimae,** 1–15–5 Hakataekimae (© **092/451-1045**), a 2-minute walk northwest of the station, has singles starting at ¥5,880 ($56) and doubles at ¥7,560 ($72), while **Toyoko Inn Hakata Gion,** 1–38 Gion-cho (© **092/281-1045**), a 5-minute walk northwest of the station, offers slightly cheaper singles and doubles. As with all Toyoko Inns, they offer two computers in the lobby providing free Internet access, free nightly movies, and complimentary Japanese breakfast.

## Hakata JBB Hotel
In the heart of the city, beside the Hakata Machiya Folk Museum and within easy walking distance of Canal City Hakata, the Asian Art Museum, and other attractions, this is a simple but well-managed establishment under the watchful eye of friendly Yamada-san, who speaks English and offers coffee free of charge mornings in the lobby. Open-air passageways lead to tiny but well-kept rooms complete with toothbrush, shampoo, and pajamas. Beds are semi-double in size and are for single use, but married couples or two women can room together for ¥6,000 ($57). You won't find anything in the city center cheaper than this.

6–5–1 Reisen-machi, Hakata-ku, Fukuoka 812-0039. © **092/263-8300**. Fax 092/263-8301. 59 units. ¥4,725 ($45) single; ¥6,000 ($57) double. No credit cards. A 10-min. walk west of Hakata Station. Subway: Gion (exit 2, 4 min.). ¥100 Bus: Okunodo (stop no. 15, 3 min.). *In room:* A/C, TV, hot-water pot w/tea, hair dryer, no phone.

## Ryokan Kashima Honkan 🔎 *Finds*
It comes as something of a surprise to find a traditional Japanese inn in the heart of Kyushu's largest city, and an inexpensive one to boot. Housed in a 100-year-old building with a homey atmosphere, an enclosed garden, and rambling hallways leading to simple tatami rooms, each one different, it's a good choice for budget-seeking traditionalists. Its convenient location, down the street from the Hakata Machiya Folk Museum, is another plus.

3–11 Reisen-machi, Hakata-ku, Fukuoka 812-0039. ✆ **092/291-0746.** Fax 092/271-7995. kashima-co@mx7.tiki.
ne.jp. 17 units (none with bathroom). ¥8,400 ($80) for 2 persons weekdays, ¥10,500 ($100) for 2 persons weekends
and nights before holidays. Breakfast ¥1,050 ($10) extra. Dinner ¥3,675 ($35) extra. MC, V. A 9-min. walk west of
Hakata Station. Subway: Gion (exit 2, 3 min.). ¥100 Bus: Okunodo (stop no. 15, 2 min.). **Amenities:** Computer w/free
Internet access in lobby. *In room:* A/C, TV, fridge, hot-water pot w/tea.

## WHERE TO DINE

For one-stop dining, head to **Canal City Hakata** (✆ **092/282-2525**), a 10-minute
walk west of Hakata Station or a 1-minute walk from Canal City Hakata-mae bus
stop no. 4. You'll find dozens of restaurants in this shopping complex, situated around
a canal and water fountains and offering everything from Chinese, Italian, and Japanese cuisine to fast food and bar snacks. On the fifth floor is **Ramen Stadium,** with
eight ramen (Chinese noodle) shops offering noodles, gyoza, and other fare from different regions of Japan, including Tokyo, Katoshima, Fukuoka, and Okinawa. Pick
your meal from the ticket vending machine outside each shop; there are photos of
most selections, priced from ¥700 to ¥900 ($6.65–$8.55). Like most restaurants in
Canal City, they're open from 11am to 11pm daily.

For a bit more local flavor, head to one of Fukuoka's famous 200 *yatai* stalls (street-
side food stalls). Most are located in Tenjin and along the Nakagawa River, on Nakasu
Island south of Kokutai-Doro Avenue. Most stalls sell *ramen,* though some also serve
oden, yakitori, tempura, and other simple fare. They're open from about 6pm to 2am.
Many nighttime revelers stop here before or after a cruise through the Nakasu entertainment district. Choose a stall and sit down, and you'll be served a steaming bowl
of ramen, most of which average about ¥800 ($7.60).

**Aroma's** EUROPEAN   Located on the lobby floor of the Grand Hyatt, which has
a great location in Canal City, this upbeat, modern restaurant has a great lunch buffet serving mostly Mediterranean-inspired cuisine, including salads, antipasto, soup,
and fish and meat entrees. In the evening, you can choose a set meal, or opt for a combination buffet/set meal that allows you to help yourself to an appetizer and dessert
buffet and order your soup and main dish from a menu.

Grand Hyatt Fukuoka, 1–2–82 Sumiyoshi. ✆ **092/282-1234.** Buffet lunch ¥2,100 ($20) weekdays, ¥2,300 ($22)
weekends and holidays; buffet/set meal ¥4,000 ($38); set dinner ¥5,000 ($48). AE, DC, MC, V. Daily 11:30am–2:30pm
and 5:30–10pm. A 12-min. walk west of Hakata Station. ¥100 Bus: Canal City Hakata-mae (stop no. 4; 2 min.).

⑳⑥ **Kazaguruma** LOCAL SPECIALTIES   In a relocated 200-year-old farmhouse
accented with heavy wooden beams, this lively and tasty izakaya-style Japanese pub
specializes in locally brewed shochu. (An *izakaya* is a Japanese-style bar with beer, sake,
and Japanese food, generally open only from 5 or 6pm.) It offers a fish of the day
(since it's written in Japanese only, you might try asking a neighboring diner for help
with translations; this is a friendly place), yakitori, sashimi, and other local favorites.
Or order one of the set meals (for which you must make a reservation the day before).

Dangam Building 1F, 1–13–1 Hakata-eki Higashi. ✆ **092/481-3456.** Main dishes ¥420–¥700 ($4–$6.65); set lunch
¥680 ($6.50); set dinners ¥3,000 and ¥3,500 ($29 and $33). AE, DC, MC, V. Mon–Fri 11:30am–2pm; Mon–Sat
5pm–midnight. Station: Hakata (1-min. walk from the east exit). Walk straight ahead, cross the main street, and take
the 1st alley left.

⑳⑦ **Ume no Hana** VEGETARIAN/TOFU   Located along the Naka River on
Nakasu island, this restful and low-key chain is known for its appetizing low-calorie,
light vegetarian cuisine. It offers a variety of meals centered on tofu and vegetables,

though some set meals may include fish and seafood. It's simply decorated in that sparse yet elegant Japanese way, with seating at low tables with leg wells. There's a branch nearby in the second basement of the ACROS building, 1–1–1 Tenjin (② **0120-20-9022**).

Hakata Excel Tokyu Hotel, 2nd floor, 4–6–7 Nakasu. ② **092/262-3777**. Set dinners ¥3,700–¥6,000 ($35–$57); set lunches ¥1,300–¥2,800 ($12–$27). AE, MC, V. Daily 11am–3pm and 5–10pm. Subway: Nakasu-Kawabata (2 min.). ¥100 Bus: Higashi-Nakasu (stop no. 11, 1 min).

## 2 Nagasaki ⋆⋆

1,329km (826 miles) W of Tokyo; 152km (95 miles) SW of Fukuoka

Unlike Kumamoto, Kagoshima, Beppu, and other well-known Kyushu destinations, **Nagasaki** doesn't have a castle, a famous landscaped garden, or hot-spring spas. Rather, its charm is much more subtle. Many people in Japan—including foreign residents—consider this city one of the country's most beautiful. It's a place of hills rising from the deep, U-shaped harbor with boats and ferries chugging back and forth, of houses perched on terraced slopes, of small streets and distinctive neighborhoods, and of people extremely proud of their hometown. Without a doubt, Nagasaki is one of Japan's most livable cities, despite its population of 410,000 residents. Capital of Nagasaki Prefecture, Nagasaki is also perhaps Japan's most cosmopolitan city, with a unique blend of outside cultures interwoven into its history, architecture, food, and festivals.

Nagasaki, which is located on the northwest coast of Kyushu, opened its harbor to European vessels in 1571 and became a port of call for Portuguese and Dutch ships; Chinese merchants soon followed and set up their own community. Along with traders came St. Francis Xavier and other Christian missionaries, primarily from Portugal and Spain, who found many converts among the local Japanese. During Japan's more than 200 years of isolation, only Nagasaki was allowed to conduct trade with outsiders and thus served as the nation's window on the rest of the world. Even today, Japanese come to Nagasaki for a dose of the city's intermingled cultures. Its harbor remains one of Japan's most active, home to the Mitsubishi shipyards.

All the city's major attractions are connected to its diversified, and sometimes tragic, past. Nagasaki is perhaps best known as the second city—and, I hope, the last city—to be destroyed by an atomic bomb.

### ESSENTIALS

**GETTING THERE** **By Plane** ANA and JAL serve Nagasaki Airport (② **095/752-5555;** www.nabic.co.jp/English) from Tokyo's Haneda Airport. Flight time is 1 hour and 50 minutes, and the fare is around ¥33,000 ($314). Cheaper is **Skynet Asia Airways** (SNA; ② **0120/737-283** toll-free), a local airline connecting a few cities in Kyushu with Tokyo, with the regular Nagasaki-Tokyo fare of ¥25,300 ($241) reduced to ¥9,800 ($93) if you book 2 months in advance for selected days. Airport **buses** travel to the Ken-ei Bus Terminal across from Nagasaki Station in less than 1 hour for ¥800 ($7.60).

**By Train** Trains depart Hakata Station in **Fukuoka** approximately twice an hour, arriving at Nagasaki Station about 2 hours later at a cost of ¥4,710 ($45). From **Tokyo,** take the Shinkansen bullet train to Hakata Station and transfer there for a

# Nagasaki

| | |
|---|---|
| † Church | Ⓟ Police Box |
| ⊠ Post Office | ⌂ Shrine |
| ▭▭ Railway | ⓘ Tourist Info |

0    1/10 mile
0    100 meters

**1** **2** **4**

**3**

*NAGASAKI PARK* **6**

Honrenji Temple

ⓘ **5**
Ken-ei Bus Station

Shofukuji Temple

Museum of Art

ⓘ **7**
Nagasaki Station **8**

Central Post Office ⊠

Nishi Nakamachi
City Hall
Umamachi Dori

Dori

Chamber of Commerce

Imauomachi

**10** **9**
GOTO MACHI

Dori

Fukuromachi Dori

Kofukuji Temple

KOZEN MACHI

City Hall Street

Manzaimachi Dori

Ohato Dori

**11**

Megane-bashi

Nagaski Port Terminal

Nakajima Gowa

**12**
Kanko Dori

Teramachi Dori

Prefecture

**14**

Hamanomachi Arcade

**16**

Dejima Wharf **13**
DEJIMA MACHI

**15**
CHINA TOWN

**17** Sofukuji Temple

**18**

Nagasaki Bus Station

Shianbashi Dori

*JAPAN*
Tokyo
●Nagasaki

**19**

**20** Ⓟ

*MARUYAMA PARK*

MOTOKAGO MACHI

**21**

**ACCOMMODATIONS** ■
Best Western Premier Hotel
Nagasaki **1**

**22**

**23**

**24**

**DINING** ◆
Cancun **13**
Gohan **18**
Harbin **12**
Hortensia **4**
Kagetsu **20**
Obinata **19**
Shikairo **26**
Shippoku
Hamakatsu **17**
Tokiwa **24**

Holiday Inn Nagasaki **15**
Hotel Majestic **27**
Hotel New Nagasaki **8**
Hotel Wingport Nagasaki **5**
JR Kyushu Hotel Nagasaki **7**
Nagasaki Hotel Monterey **23**
Nishikiso **21**
Sakamoto-ya **9**
Tokyo Inn Nagasaki
Ekimae **10**

**26**

**25**

Oura Gawa

**27**

**28**

**ATTRACTIONS** ●
Confucius Shrine and
Museum of Chinese
History (Koshibyo) **25**
Dejima **14**
Dutch Slope **22**
Glover Garden **28**
Hollanders Slope **22**
Nagasaki Atomic Bomb
Museum **2**
Nishizaka Hill **3**
Peace Park
(Hirano-machi) **2**
Sofukuji Temple **16**
Spectacles Bridge **11**
Suwa Shrine **6**

495

train to Nagasaki; travel time is about 8½ hours, depending on connections and the fare is ¥23,420 ($223) for an unreserved seat.

**VISITOR INFORMATION** Pick up the "Nagasaki and Unzen" leaflet from the Tourist Information Center in Tokyo or Kansai or Narita international airports. or download it from JNTO's website at www.jnto.go.jp. In Nagasaki, the **Nagasaki City Tourist Information Office** (*©* 095/823-3631; open daily 8am–8pm) is located just outside the main ticket gates of Nagasaki Station, to the right in the Seattle's Best coffee shop. Information on all of Nagasaki Prefecture (including Huis Ten Bosch and Unzen, described later in this chapter), as well as souvenirs and goods from around the prefecture, is available across the street from the train station at the **Nagasaki Prefectural Tourist Federation** (*©* 095/826-9407; open daily 9am–5:30pm), on the second floor of the Ken-ei Bus Terminal.

Information on Nagasaki is available on the Internet at www1.city.nagasaki.nagaski.jp. See www.ngs-kenkanren.com for information on Nagasaki Prefecture, including Unzen.

**INTERNET ACCESS** Located in the Hamano-machi covered shopping arcade in the heart of downtown Nagasaki, **Internet Café Cybac,** 2–46 Aburaya-machi (*©* **0120-24-3189**) is open 24 hours and charges ¥300 ($2.85) for the first 30 minutes, then ¥100 (95¢) for each additional 15 minutes. Although it also charges a one-time ¥300 ($2.85) membership fee, you can pick up a brochure at the tourist office with a coupon offering free membership.

**ORIENTATION** Along with Kobe and Sapporo, Nagasaki is one of Japan's most navigable cities, with lots of English-language signs pointing the way to attractions. City layout follows natural boundaries set by the Urakami River, the long and narrow Nagasaki Bay, and the many steep-sloped hills. **Nagasaki Station,** along with AMU Plaza next door offering shopping and dining options, isn't located in the downtown part of the city; rather, most nightspots, shops, and restaurants are located southeast of the station, clustered around an area that contains **Shianbashi Dori** and **Kanko Dori streets,** the **Hamano-machi** covered shopping arcade, and a newly developed waterfront area called **Dejima Wharf** that includes the You-Me-Shopping Mall, restaurants, the Nagasaki Prefectural Art Museum with Spanish art and art related to Nagasaki, and Seaside Park. Nearby is **Chinatown,** with Chinese restaurants and shops selling Chinese-made souvenirs and clothing. Farther south is **Glover Garden,** where many foreigners settled in the 19th century. Nearby is **Hollanders Slope** (**Oranda-zaka,** also referred to as Dutch Slope), undoubtedly Nagasaki's prettiest street, a cobbled lane lined with wooden houses built by former European residents (a century ago, the people of Nagasaki referred to all Europeans as Hollanders). **Peace Park** and its atomic-bomb museum are located north of Nagasaki Station on the other end of town.

**GETTING AROUND** **By Streetcar** Streetcars have been hauling passengers in Nagasaki since 1915 and, from the looks of things, have changed little in the ensuing years; they're still the easiest—and most charming—way to get around. Four lines run through the heart of the city, with most stops written in English. The streetcars are ancient one-wagon affairs, retired to Nagasaki from other cities that considered them too slow and old-fashioned—and yet, since streetcars have their own lanes of traffic here, during rush hour they're usually the fastest on the road. It costs a mere ¥100

(95¢) to ride one no matter how far you go; pay at the front when you get off. You are allowed to transfer to another line only at **Tsukimachi Station** (ask the driver for a *noritsugi,* a transfer ticket, when you disembark from the first streetcar); otherwise, you must buy a separate ticket each time you board. If you need change for, say, a ¥500 coin or ¥1,000 bill, you may ask the driver when he's waiting at a red light and isn't busy, an endearing anachronism in high-tech Japan. To avoid the hassle of individual tickets, you can also buy a ¥500 ($4.75) **pass** at both tourist offices mentioned above and at major hotels; the pass allows unlimited rides for 1 day. Streetcars run from about 6:15am to 11:30pm.

**On Foot**    With the exception of Peace Park, you can also get around Nagasaki easily on foot, which is certainly the most intimate way to experience the city and its atmosphere. You can walk from the Hamano-machi downtown shopping district to Glover Garden, for example, in 20 minutes, passing Chinatown, Dejima, and the Dutch Slope on the way. Shianbashi Dori, located just off the streetcar stop of the same name and center of Nagasaki nightlife, is just a minute's walk from the Hamano-machi shopping arcade.

**By Bus**    Nagasaki has buses, but destinations are in Japanese only—stick to the streetcars.

## EXPLORING THE CITY
### NISHIZAKA HILL

After Nagasaki opened its port to European vessels, missionaries came to the city to convert Japanese to Christianity. Gradually, however, the Japanese rulers began to fear that these Christian missionaries would try to exert political and financial influence through their converts. Who was to say that conversion to Christianity wasn't the first step toward colonization? So in 1587, the shogun Toyotomi Hideyoshi officially banned Christianity. In 1597, 26 male Christians (20 Japanese and six foreigners) were arrested in Kyoto and Osaka, marched through the snow to Nagasaki, and crucified on **Nishizaka Hill** as examples of what would happen to offenders. Through the ensuing decades, there were more than 600 documented cases of Japanese, Portuguese, and Spanish Christians being put to death in the Nishizaka area. In 1862, the 26 martyrs were sainted by the pope.

Today, on Nishizaka Hill, about a 4-minute walk north of Nagasaki Station up a steep slope, there's the Monument to the 26 Saints, with statues of the martyrs carved in stone relief. Immediately striking is that three of them look very young; indeed, the youngest was only 12. Behind the relief is a small **museum** (© **095/822-6000;** www.26martyrs.com; open daily 9am–5pm) housing artifacts relating to the history of Christianity in Japan, including paintings and drawings of the 26 saints, reward notices for those turning in Christians to authorities, and religious objects, as well as remains of Japanese martyrs returned to Nagasaki in 1995 after more than 380 years of interment in Macau. Perhaps most amazing about the history of Christianity in Japan is that the religion was practiced secretly by the faithful throughout Japan's isolation policy, surviving more than 200 years underground without the benefits of a church or clergy. Admission to the museum, which can be toured in 15 minutes, is ¥250 ($2.40) for adults, ¥150 ($1.45) for junior-high and high-school students, and ¥100 (95¢) for children.

## PEACE PARK (HIRANO-MACHI) ⭐⭐

On August 9, 1945, at 11:02am, American forces dropped an atomic bomb over Nagasaki, 3 days after they had dropped one on Hiroshima. The bomb, which exploded 480m (1,600 ft.) aboveground, destroyed about a third of the city, killed an estimated 74,000 people, and injured 75,000 more. Today, Peace Park, located north of Nagasaki Station, serves as a reminder of that day of destruction with a museum, memorials, and statues. Nagasaki's citizens are among the most vigorous peace activists in the world; a peace demonstration is held in Peace Park every year on the anniversary of the bombing.

Near the Nagasaki Atomic Bomb Museum (see below), a black pillar marks the exact epicenter of the atomic blast; a black casket contains names of the bomb's victims. Ironically, the bomb exploded almost directly over the Urakami Catholic Church, built after centuries of persecution in Japan and of which only a fragmented wall remains. A few minutes' walk farther north, separated by several streets, is the largest part of Peace Park (the nearest streetcar station to this section is Matsuyama). It occupies the site of a former prison; all 134 inmates died in the blast. A fountain is dedicated to the wounded who begged for water; many of them died thirsty. Statues donated by countries from around the world line a pathway leading to Peace Statue, a 9m-high (30-ft.) statue of a male deity. One hand points to the sky from where the bomb came (meant as a warning?), and the other hand points to the horizon (representing hope? the future?).

**Nagasaki Atomic Bomb Museum** ⭐⭐⭐   Visiting this museum, with English-language displays, is by far the most important thing to do in Peace Park. Upon entering, guests circle an empty, glass-dome foyer via a spiraling ramp—bringing to mind, perhaps, the atomic mushroom cloud? This is followed by photographs of the city as it looked before the bomb, accompanied by the ominous, loud ticking of a clock. Displays illustrate events leading up to the bombing, the devastation afterward, Nagasaki's postwar restoration, the history of nuclear weapons, and the subsequent peace movement. Objects, photos, and artifacts graphically depict the bomb's devastation, including a clock stopped precisely at 11:02am, personal belongings ranging from mangled spectacles to a student's singed trousers, hand bones encased in a clump of melted glass, and photographs of victims, including a dead mother and her baby and a 14-year-old whose face has been hideously burned. On video, survivors describe their personal experiences on that fateful day. The adjoining Peace Memorial Hall for Atomic Bomb Victims contains a Remembrance Hall, with portraits of those who lost their lives. The museum is by no means pleasant, but something every concerned individual should see—plan on at least an hour here. (If, however, you've already seen the much larger and far more comprehensive Peace Memorial Museum in Hiroshima, this one will be largely repetitive.)

7–8 Hirano-machi. ☏ **095/844-1231.** www1.city.nagasaki.nagasaki.jp/na-bomb/museum. Admission ¥200 ($1.90) adults, ¥100 (95¢) children. Daily 8:30am–5:30pm (until 6:30pm May–Aug). Streetcar: 1 or 3 to Hamaguchi-machi (5 min.).

## DEJIMA

When the Tokugawa shogunate adopted a national policy of isolation in the 1630s, only Nagasaki was allowed to remain open as a port of trade with foreigners. Since the Portuguese and Spaniards were associated with the outlawed Christian religion, they were expelled in 1639; only the Dutch and the Chinese were allowed to remain and

continue trading. In 1641, all the Dutch were confined to a tiny, fan-shaped artificial island called Dejima, where they remained for 218 years (at any given time, about 15 Dutchmen were in residence; no wives were allowed). This was Japan's only official contact with the outside world; the director of Dejima was required to travel to Edo every 1 to 4 years to report to the shogun. Otherwise, the only people allowed to cross the bridge into the Dutch community were Japanese prostitutes and traders.

Today, after having long become part of the mainland through land reclamation and after decades of languishing as little more than a streetcar stop, Dejima has been reborn through an ambitious project that is re-creating the island as it was in the early 19th century (a total of 25 buildings are planned by 2010). After you alight at the Dejima streetcar stop and pay the admission of ¥500 ($4.75) for adults, ¥200 ($1.90) for high-school students or ¥100 (95¢) for children, go to the **Head Clerks Quarter's** (6–3 Dejima-machi; © 095/821-7200), where you can pick up a map and information in English. From there you will be directed to a re-created kitchen, an excavated west-side embankment, the First Ship Captain's Quarters with furnishings of the period, the No. 1 Warehouse documenting the painstaking restoration of Dejima's historic buildings, and the No. 2 Warehouse describing Dejima's role in the introduction of Western science and culture to Japan. At the Dejima Theatre, a 12-minute video recaptures daily life in a former Dejima Dutch factory. In your wanderings you will also see a large outdoor model showing how the island looked when the Dutch lived here. But the most important thing to see in Dejima is the **Dejima Museum of History,** which is housed in a blue, colonial-style wooden building constructed in 1877 as Japan's first Protestant seminary. It gives an excellent account of the historical development of the island, what life was like for the Dutch who lived here, and how the trading system worked. Nearby, in a replica of an old stone warehouse, is the museum's annex with folk objects from Holland and artifacts unearthed during excavations on Dejima. Dejima is open daily 8am to 6pm. You'll probably spend about an hour here.

## GLOVER GARDEN
**Glover Garden** 🐾🐾    After Japan opened its doors to the rest of the world and established Nagasaki as one of a handful of international ports, Nagasaki emerged as one of the most progressive cities in the country, with many foreign residents. A number of Western-style houses were built during the Meiji Period (1868–1912), many of them on a hill overlooking Nagasaki and the harbor. Today, that hill has been developed into Glover Garden, which showcases nine Meiji-Era buildings and homes on lushly landscaped grounds. Some of the structures stand on their original site; others have been moved here and given new life. The stone-and-clapboard houses have sweeping verandas, Western parlors, the most modern conveniences of the time, and Japanese-style roofs. Most famous is **Glover Mansion,** Japan's oldest Western-style house, built in this location in 1863 and romanticized as the home of Madame Butterfly, the fictitious, tragic heroine of Puccini's opera. Married to a Japanese woman (and much more faithful than his Puccini counterpart), Thomas Glover was a remarkable Scotsman who, among other things, financially backed and managed ship-repair yards in Nagasaki, brought the first steam locomotive to Japan, sold guns and ships, and exported tea. The **Ringer House,** dating from the early Meiji Period, contains a display of photos, clothes, and artifacts of Kiba Teiko, a Japanese opera singer who played Madame Butterfly.

Among the other buildings, a former boys' academy houses photographs of old Nagasaki, including portraits of foreigners who used to live here. The Mitsubishi

Dock House, built in 1896 to serve as a rest house for ship crews, offers great views of the harbor. One of Nagasaki's first Western restaurants is now a quaint cafe. And don't miss the **Nagasaki Traditional Performing Arts Museum,** which displays floats and dragons used in Nagasaki's most famous festival, the Okunchi Festival, held in October. The museum's highlight is an excellent film of the colorful parade, featuring massive ships deftly maneuvered on wheels and Chinese dragon dances. At any rate, the views from Glover Garden are among the best in the city. Plan on spending about 1 hour here.

8–1 Minami Yamate-machi. ✆ 095/822-8223. Admission ¥600 ($5.70) adults, ¥300 ($2.85) high-school students, ¥180 ($1.70) junior-high and elementary students. Daily 8am–6pm (to 9:30pm mid-July to mid-Oct). Streetcar: Oura Tenshudoshita (7 min.); cross the bridge, turn left after the Tokyu Hotel, and walk uphill, following the signs.

## TEMPLES, SHRINES & BRIDGES

### Confucius Shrine and Museum of Chinese History (Koshibyo) ✿   Chinese residents living in Nagasaki built this colorful, red-and-yellow shrine in 1893, aided by the Ch'ing Dynasty in China. This is the only Confucian shrine outside China built by the Chinese. In fact, the land upon which it stands belongs to China and is administered by the Chinese embassy in Tokyo. The main hall contains a statue of Confucius, attended by courtyard statues representing his 72 disciples. More fascinating, however, is the small Museum of Chinese History located behind the main hall with bronze jars, ceramics, jade carvings, painted enamel vases, and other treasures on loan from Beijing's National Museum of Chinese History and Beijing Palace's Museum of Historical Treasures. You can see everything in about 30 minutes.

10–36 Oura-machi. ✆ 095/824-4022. Admission ¥525 ($5) adults, ¥420 ($4) students, ¥315 ($3) children. Daily 8:30am–5pm. Streetcar: Oura Tenshudoshita (3 min.). Walk inland (continuing in the same direction of your streetcar if you're coming from downtown), and turn left when you reach a small playground on your right. Near the Dutch Slope.

### Sofukuji Temple ✿   Sofukuji is Nagasaki's most famous temple. Distinctly Chinese with its Ming architecture, it dates back to 1629, when it was founded by Chinese residents. Its Buddha Hall, painted a brilliant red and decorated with Chinese lanterns, was designed and cut in China before transportation to Nagasaki. Erected in 1646, it's the oldest building in Nagasaki and is a National Treasure. Another National Treasure is the temple's beautiful gate, which employs a complex jointing system and features brightly painted detailing. But most fascinating, in my opinion, is the temple's gigantic cauldron, built by a priest during a terrible famine in the 1680s to cook enough porridge to feed more than 3,000 people a day.

Kayjiya-machi. ✆ 095/823-2645. Admission ¥300 ($2.85) adults, ¥200 ($1.90) students, ¥100 (95¢) children. Daily 8am–5pm. A 7-min. walk from the Hamano-machi downtown shopping district. Streetcar: Shokakuji-shita (4 min.); head back toward the bay, turning right at Sofukuji St.

### Spectacles Bridge (Megane-bashi)   In addition to the temples described above, the Chinese also left their mark on Nagasaki with several bridges. Most famous is the so-called Spectacles Bridge, built in 1634 by a Chinese Zen priest. One of Nagasaki's most photographed objects, it's the oldest stone-arched bridge in Japan and is named after the reflection its two arches cast in the water; I wouldn't know, however, because I've never seen the Nakashima River larger than a trickle except once, when it rushed angrily after a heavy rain. There's a promenade along the river, complete with benches and children's playgrounds. It's just a 5-minute walk from the Hamano-machi shopping arcade.

Streetcar: Nigiwai-bashi or Kokaidomae.

**Suwa Shrine** Although Nagasaki's famous Okunchi Festival has Chinese roots, it's celebrated at this Shinto shrine, built to promote Shintoism at a time when the feudal government was trying to stamp out Christianity. Today, with a good location on top of a hill with views over the city, the shrine symbolizes better than anything else the spiritual heart of the Japanese community. When Japanese women turn 33 and men turn 40, they come here to pray for good health and a long life. Newborns are brought 30 days after their birth to receive special blessings and then again for their third, fifth, and seventh birthdays. On New Year's, the grounds are packed with those seeking good fortune in the coming year. People also visit to ask the shrine's many deities for favors—good marriage, safe childbirth, good health, and more. You can even have your automobile blessed here. The shrine sells English-language fortunes. If you're satisfied with your fortune, keep it; if you're not, tie it to the branch of a tree and the fortune is conveniently negated.

18–15 Kami-Nishiyama. © 095/824-0445. Free admission. Open 24 hr. Streetcar: Suwa Jinja-mae (4 min.); take the underground passage and follow the signs up many stone stairs.

## A SIDE TRIP TO HUIS TEN BOSCH ★★★

If you're ready for some R & R from your travels in Japan but have only 1 day to spare, perhaps **Huis Ten Bosch,** in Sasebo (© **0956/27-0001;** www.huistenbosch.co.jp), will do the trick. This replica of a 17th-century Dutch village boasts tree-lined canals, brick houses, city squares, brick-paved roads, churches, museums, shops, restaurants, hotels, and even stately private homes—proof at how adept Japanese are at imitation. Most of the buildings are faithful reproductions of originals back in the Netherlands; even the bricks were imported from Holland. Although I was a bit skeptical about visiting an imitation Dutch village in Japan, I must admit that the grounds and craftsmanship are beautifully done (Huis Ten Bosch is also environmentally correct, with its own desalination and sewage treatment plants; it even generates much of its own energy). Even Holland itself isn't this pristine. In fact, I consider this the country's premier theme park designed for adults. But although there are some rides and attractions, this is not an amusement park in disguise.

Highlights include **Paleis Huis Ten Bosch,** a replica of the formal residence of Queen Beatrix of the Netherlands, which contains an art gallery, period rooms showing how upper-class Dutch lived; baroque and flower **gardens; museums** with collections of porcelain, ornamental glass, teddy bears, carillons, and music boxes; and **theaters** that re-create a ship's voyage from Holland to Japan in the 17th century, the flooding of a Dutch town, and M. C. Escher's works with a 3-D film. There are also cruises of Omura Bay and the village's canals; parades, dances, concerts, and other events daily; more than 50 shops; and more than 40 restaurants (including open-air beer and wine gardens). The park is so vast that there are shuttle buses and other forms of transportation, but to really feel like you're in Holland, rent one of the park's bicycles.

A 1-day pass to Huis Ten Bosch costs ¥4,800 ($46) for adults, ¥3,600 ($34) for children 12 to 17, and ¥2,600 ($25) for children 4 to 11 (under 3 go free). The best time to visit is spring, during—what else?—tulip season. Open March through Christmas, daily 9am to 9:30pm (last entrance 8pm); December 26 through February, 9am to 8:30pm (last entrance 7pm).

To reach Huis Ten Bosch, take the **JR Sea Side Liner Express** from Nagasaki Station to Huis Ten Bosch Station (1 hr. and 15 min.); the train departs approximately every hour and costs ¥1,430 ($14) one-way.

## WHERE TO STAY

Nagasaki has reasonably priced hotels, but keep in mind that some accommodations may raise their rates during peak times, which are Golden Week (Apr 29–May 5), Obon (mid-Aug), and the Okunchi Festival (Oct 7–9).

### EXPENSIVE

**Best Western Premier Hotel Nagasaki** ✰✰✰    One of Nagasaki's finest hotels, the Best Western's marbled lobby, decorated with large Oriental vases, has a distinct Asian flair. Rooms, which combine colonial-style decor with Chinese accents, offer the usual comforts, with one wing reserved for ladies offering amenities geared toward female travelers. There are only three single rooms in the hotel, though discounts are given for single use of twins and doubles. Regrettably, none of the rooms boast much of a view; for that you'll need to visit the 15th-floor buffet restaurant or bar with their panoramic vistas.

2–26 Takara-machi, Nagasaki 850-0045. © 800/528-1234 in the U.S. and Canada, or 095/821-1111. Fax 095/823-4309. www.bestwestern.co.jp. 183 units. ¥15,000–¥18,000 ($143–$171) single; ¥23,000–¥28,000 ($219–$267) double; ¥26,000–¥35,000 ($248–$333) twin; from ¥33,000 ($314) executive twin. AE, DC, MC, V. Streetcar: Takara-machi (1 min.). Or an 8-min. walk north of Nagasaki Station in the direction of Peace Park. **Amenities:** 4 restaurants (Japanese, Chinese, steak/seafood, coffee shop); 1 bar; 1 lounge; 1 beer hall (summer only); spa; Japanese roof garden; concierge; salon; room service (7am–midnight); in-room massage; babysitting; same-day laundry/dry-cleaning service; nonsmoking rooms; executive-level rooms. In room: A/C, cable TV w/pay movies on demand, dataport, minibar, hot-water pot w/tea, hair dryer, large safe, Washlet toilets.

**Hotel New Nagasaki** ✰✰✰    One of Nagasaki's deluxe hotels, the Hotel New Nagasaki beats Best Western in location, right next to the train station. Its large, marbled lobby is light and airy, and its rooms are among the city's largest, with some even offering a view of Nagasaki's busy port. Add the hotel's wide range of facilities (including a fitness club), and you have what amounts to one of Nagasaki's best choices.

14–5 Daikoku-machi, Nagasaki 850-0057. © 095/826-8000. Fax 095/823-2000. www.newnaga.com. 149 units. ¥25,200 ($240) double; ¥25,200–¥47,250 ($240–$450) twin; ¥27,300 ($260) executive double/twin. AE, DC, MC, V. A 1-min. walk from Nagasaki Station, to the right. **Amenities:** 3 restaurants (Western, Japanese, Chinese); 1 bar; 1 lounge; well-equipped fitness club w/indoor lap pool (and retractable roof) and sauna (fee: ¥2,100/$20); concierge; art gallery; salon; room service (7am–10pm); in-room massage; same-day laundry/dry-cleaning service; executive-level rooms. In room: A/C, cable TV w/40 channels for music and radio, minibar, hot-water pot w/tea, hair dryer.

(208) **Sakamoto-ya** ✰✰✰ (Finds    This beautiful 112-year-old ryokan (Nagasaki's oldest) right in the heart of the city is a wonderful place, especially when you consider how rare traditional ryokan are nowadays in major Japanese cities. Most of the rooms, which are named after plants, flowers, and trees, have a Japanese-style bathtub made of wood, as well as traditional artwork on the walls. The best room is the Pine Room (Matsu No Ma), which even has its own miniature garden with a tiny shrine. Rates vary according to the room and the meals served; you may order a *shippoku* dinner, a Nagasaki specialty consisting of a variety of dishes showing European and Chinese influences, for ¥3,150 ($30) more. Western breakfasts are also served on request.

2–13 Kanaya-machi, Nagasaki 850-0037. © 095/826-8211. Fax 095/825-5944. 23 units (17 with bathroom). ¥15,750–¥30,500 ($150–$290) per person. Rates include breakfast, dinner, and service charge. AE, DC, MC, V. A 10-min. walk southeast of Nagasaki Station. Take the streetcar or turn right out of the station and follow the streetcar tracks south to the 1st streetcar stop (Goto-machi); turn left on the street between Shinwa Bank and a travel agency, and walk up a slight incline to an old building, where you turn right. **Amenities:** In-room massage. In room: A/C, TV, minibar, hot-water pot w/tea.

## MODERATE

**Holiday Inn Nagasaki** ⭐⭐ *Value*    This hotel offers standard American convenience but with a rich mix of Asian and European design. Unlike most Holiday Inns, it keeps a low profile; it's hidden in the middle of a block and has a small, intimate lobby that resembles a rich merchant's home in old Nagasaki rather than a place to check in. As with all Holiday Inns, beds are at least double-size (some are even queen-size or king-size). Note, however, that the cheapest singles face a wall .3m (1 ft.) away; if you're claustrophobic, specify a room with an outside view. One of the best things about this hotel is its convenient location, in the heart of the city near Chinatown and just a stone's throw from the Hamano-machi shopping arcade. You can walk from the hotel to most sites, including Glover Mansion and Sofukuji and Kofukuji temples. We also like its buffet restaurant specializing in seasonal organic dishes.

6–24 Doza-machi, Nagasaki 850-0841. ⓒ 800/HOLIDAY in the U.S., or 095/828-1234. Fax 095/828-0178. www.ic hotelsgroup.com. 87 units. ¥8,950–¥12,600 ($85–$120) single; ¥15,750 ($150) double; ¥16,800–¥42,000 ($160–$400) twin. Children under 12 stay free in parent's room. AE, DC, MC, V. Streetcar: no. 1 to Kanko Dori (1 min.). The hotel is across from the streetcar stop, behind a building; look for its sign. **Amenities:** Restaurant (international buffet); bar; concierge; in-room massage; same-day laundry/dry-cleaning service; nonsmoking rooms. *In room:* A/C, cable TV, dataport, minibar, hot-water pot w/tea, hair dryer.

**Hotel Majestic** ⭐⭐    The Majestic is a small, charming, quiet hotel. The beautifully appointed rooms are decorated in one of several themes—the country-living theme, for example, sports wooden floors, light-oak furnishings, and claw-foot bathtubs. All rooms have small balconies and larger-than-average bathrooms. There are no singles; the cheapest twins offer no views, and even more expensive rooms overlook a parking lot toward views of the harbor, glimpsed between buildings (best views are from the fourth floor). No matter. The best things about this getaway are its small size—which means no tour-bus groups in the lobby—and its great location near Glover Garden. Its tiny, cozy, European-style restaurant/bar will make you feel right at home.

2–28 Minami Yamate-machi, Nagasaki 850-0931. ⓒ **095/827-7777.** Fax 095/827-6112. 23 units. ¥24,150 ($230) double; ¥19,850–¥28,350 ($189–$270) twin. AE, DC, MC, V. Streetcar: no. 1 to Tsuki-machi, then no. 5 to Oura Ten-shudoshita (2 min.); cross the bridge and walk straight past the ANA Hotel Nagasaki Glover Hill. **Amenities:** Restaurant (Western); in-room massage; same-day laundry/dry-cleaning service; nonsmoking rooms. *In room:* A/C, TV, minibar, hot-water pot w/tea, hair dryer, Washlet toilet.

**JR Kyushu Hotel Nagasaki**    You can't get closer to Nagasaki Station than this new business hotel on the station's second floor; those traveling with a Japan Rail Pass will also profit from a discount. Otherwise, rooms are your basic boxes, with alcoves serving as closets, small bathrooms, and no views. Those wishing to avoid any quality time in their rooms might take advantage of adjoining Amu Plaza's many shops and restaurants (the hotel's Royal Host coffee shop is also a good bet for breakfast).

1–1 Onoue-machi, Nagasaki 850-0058. ⓒ **095/832-8000.** Fax 095/832-8001. www.jrhotelgroup.com. 144 units. ¥6,900 ($66) single; ¥12,600 ($120) twin. 10% discount with Japan Rail Pass. AE, DC, MC, V. **Amenities:** Restaurant (coffee shop); in-room massage; nonsmoking rooms. *In room:* A/C, TV, fridge, hot-water pot w/tea, hair dryer, Washlet toilet.

**Nagasaki Hotel Monterey** ⭐    Step into old Portugal in this whimsical place complete with whitewashed walls, imported tiles, a small chapel with decorations imported from Portugal, and hand-painted furnishings. There's even a kerosene lamp museum on hotel premises, free to hotel guests. Popular with young women, the hotel fits the historic past of Nagasaki and is conveniently located at the bottom of Hollander Slope.

Rooms, too, give hints of Portugal with their terra-cotta-colored floor tiles, dark-wood or painted furniture, and shuttered windows.

1–22 Oura-machi, Nagasaki 850-0918. © **095/827-7111.** Fax 095/820-7017. 123 units. ¥9,818 – ¥13,860 ($94–$132) single; ¥20,790 –¥25,410 ($198–$242) twin. AE, DC, MC, V. Streetcar: no. 1 to Tsuki-machi, then no. 5 to Oura Kaigan Dori (1 min.); walk inland. **Amenities:** 2 restaurants (Italian, coffee shop); in-room massage; same-day laundry/dry-cleaning service, nonsmoking rooms (singles only). *In room:* A/C, TV, fridge, hot-water pot w/tea, hair dryer, Washlet toilet.

## INEXPENSIVE

**Hotel Wingport Nagasaki**   This clean business hotel is closer to Nagasaki Station than Toyoko Inn but can't compete when it comes to services and amenities. Still, you might find room here if other places are full. It offers mostly singles that couldn't get much smaller. However, the fact that they're spotless, with white walls and cheerful bedspreads, helps alleviate claustrophobia, as do good bed lights and windows that can be opened. Panels close for complete darkness; note that some rooms face another building. The deluxe twins are actually quite roomy for a business hotel, with a sofa, a semi-double-size bed and a single bed.

9–2 Daikoku-machi, Nagasaki 850-0057. © **095/833-2800.** Fax 095/833-2801. 200 units. ¥5,800 ($55) single; ¥8,000 ($76) double; ¥7,000 –¥12,000 ($67–$114) twin. AE, DC, MC, V. Station: A 2-min. walk from Nagasaki Station. Cross both sets of streetcar tracks in front of the station and take the small side street beside Family Mart.

**Nishikiso**   This Japanese inn has a comfortable, lived-in atmosphere and friendly owners. Its simple tatami rooms vary in price depending on size and view, with the best views over rooftops from the ryokan's hilltop location. It's located near the Hamano-machi shopping arcade in the heart of the city.

1–2–7 Nishikoshima, Nagasaki 850-0837. © **095/826-6371.** Fax 095/828-0782. 11 units (6 with bathroom). ¥4,200– ¥5,250 ($40–$50) per person. Breakfast ¥600 –¥800 ($5.70–$7.60) extra. Dinner ¥3,000 ($29) extra. AE, DC, MC, V. Streetcar: no. 1 to Tsuki-machi, then no. 4 to Shianbashi. Head under the neon arch on the right onto Shianbashi Dori, turn right at the cute *koban* police box, walk 1 block past Maruyama Park and turn left; it will be on your right up the hill. **Amenities:** Coin-op washer/dryer. *In room:* A/C, TV, minibar, hot-water pot w/tea.

**Toyoko Inn Nagasaki Ekimae** *Value*   A good location near Nagasaki Station, cheap prices, and such freebies as Internet access from lobby computers, domestic calls from lobby phones, and evening movies make this chain hard to beat. Rooms are compact but practical, with flip-down bedside tables and everything else you need within easy reach.

5–45 Goto-machi, Nagasaki 850-0036. © **095/825-1045.** Fax 095/825-1046. www.toyoko-inn.com. 220 units. ¥5,460 ($52) single; ¥7,560 ($72) double or twin. Rates include Japanese breakfast. DC, MC, V. Streetcar: no. 1 to 1st stop (Goto-machi) or a 5-min. walk from Nagasaki Station (take a right out of the station and follow the streetcar tracks south). **Amenities:** Lobby computer w/free Internet access; coin-op washer/dryer; nonsmoking rooms. *In room:* A/C, TV w/free movies, dataport, fridge, hot-water pot w/tea, hair dryer, Washlet toilet, trouser press.

## WHERE TO DINE

Nagasaki's most famous food, called *shippoku,* is actually a whole meal of various courses with Chinese, European, and Japanese influences. It's a feast generally shared by a group of four or more people and includes such dishes as fish soup, sashimi, and fried, boiled, and vinegared seasonal delicacies from land and sea. Another Nagasaki specialty is *champon,* a thick Chinese noodle usually served in soup with meat, seafood, and vegetables.

Nagasaki's nightlife district centers on a small area south of Hamano-machi known as **Shianbashi,** which begins just off the streetcar stop of the same name and is easily

recognizable by the neon arch that stretches over the entrance of a street called Shian-bashi Dori. Shianbashi shimmers with the lights of various drinking establishments and yakitori-ya, which are often the cheapest places to go for a light dinner. Another good hunting ground for restaurants is **China Town.**

## EXPENSIVE

209 **Kagetsu** *(Finds)* SHIPPOKU/KAISEKI    If I were a woman of boundless means, this wonderful but expensive traditional restaurant is where I'd entertain all my friends—it's the ultimate Japanese dining experience, serving constantly changing exquisite dishes. First established in 1642, Kagetsu is one of Japan's longest-running restaurants; the oldest part of the present wooden building is about 360 years old. This is an oasis of dignified old Japan, where kimono-clad waitresses shuffle down wooden corridors and serve guests sublime food in tatami rooms. Formerly a geisha house, it has separate stairways for patrons and hostesses. It even has a stone-floored room designed for a table and chairs where foreign patrons could be entertained. Display cases exhibit treasures related to Kagetsu's history.

Behind the restaurant, which is set back from the road, is a beautiful 300-year-old garden. I'll never forget my evening stroll here as a half-moon rose above gnarled, stunted pines. The back of the restaurant, consisting mainly of glass, was lit up, so I could see into a multitude of private tatami rooms all on different levels. It was like a woodblock print suddenly sprung to life. Needless to say, this restaurant is very popular and is sometimes entirely booked a full month in advance. There must be at least two of you if you want to feast on shippoku or kaiseki.

2–1 Maruyama-machi. C 095/822-0191. Reservations required at least a day (a week is better) in advance. Lunch obento (available only weekdays) ¥5,200 ($50); shippoku set lunch ¥8,000 ($76); shippoku or kaiseki set meal ¥11,000–¥20,000 ($105–$190). AE, DC, MC, V. Daily noon–2pm and 5:30–8pm (last order). Closed irregularly. Streetcar: Shianbashi (3 min.). Head under the neon arch of a bridge onto Shianbashi Dori, continue straight, and then take the road between the cute koban police box and the small park; it's straight ahead where the street ends, with the traditional gate.

## MODERATE

210 **Gohan** *(★★)* ORIGINAL JAPANESE    Gohan's English-speaking owner-chef, Tsunehiro Yoshimura, is also a musician, so you'll hear interesting music as you dine on creative, original meals here. The interior of this restaurant is authentically old; salvaged beams and pieces from five different houses were given new lives here. The handwritten menu changes daily, but the set dinner more than satisfies. Included may be sashimi, new potato with sesame seed, whole snapper, crayfish, tofu, soup, and rice. The dishes themselves are by Keisuke Iwata, a talented local potter of some renown. Hip waiters bring the food from an open kitchen. The whole experience is very highly recommended.

2–32 Aburayamachi. C 095/825-3600. Lunch teishoku ¥840–¥1,575 ($8–$15); set dinners ¥3,150–¥6,300 ($30–$60). AE, MC, V. Mon–Sat noon–2pm and 5–10pm (last order 9:30pm). Streetcar: Shokakujishita (1 min.). Walk 1 block down Sofukuji-dori toward the temple and take the 1st left; it's the 2nd building on your right with the name on the *noren* (short curtains hung outside a shop or restaurant signify it is open)—look carefully, it's easy to miss.

**Harbin** *(★★★)* FRENCH/RUSSIAN    Established in 1959, Harbin is a Nagasaki tradition, one of those places you don't want to miss. Its owner was born in Manchuria and named his restaurant after Harbin, a town close to his birthplace that was once an international city of Russian, Chinese, and Japanese residents. His family-run restaurant serves a unique blend of French and Russian cuisine; in recent years, his

French-trained chef son has brought his own interpretations to the menu. A small, unpretentious-looking establishment, it offers a changing menu, written in Japanese, English, and Russian languages, which may include fried chicken Kiev style, Georgian spicy lamb pot, and roasted French duck in a red currant sauce, along with homemade sausages and bread. The *coulibiac* (traditional Russian salmon pie), when available, is perhaps the best thing on the menu. The ¥997 ($9.50) set lunch (served to 5pm) consists of *borsch* (beet soup), three kinds of *piroshki* (stuffed, savory pastries), salad, and coffee or tea.

Kanko Dori covered shopping arcade (which bisects Hamano-machi). ✆ 095/824-6650. Main dishes ¥1,575–¥3,675 ($15–$35); set meals ¥3,675–¥5,250 ($35–$50); set lunches ¥997–¥2,940 ($9.50–$28). AE, DC, MC, V. Daily 11:30am–10pm (last order). Closed every other Wed. Streetcar: Kanko Dori. Walk straight through the covered shopping arcade to the 3rd block; it's on the left, above a Doutour coffee shop.

**Hortensia** INTERNATIONAL This buffet restaurant is located on the second floor of the Park Side Hotel in the leafy green area of Peace Park, next to the Atomic Bomb Museum, making it a good choice if you're in the area. Lunch (available until 2pm) features an all-you-can-eat buffet of Chinese, Western, and Japanese fare, as well as set meals. In the evenings, both set meals and a buffet are offered, except during the summer months (June–Aug) when the restaurant transforms itself into a beer garden (in spirit only, as it's indoors), with buffet spreads costing ¥2,000 ($19), or all you can eat and drink for ¥3,500 ($33) within a 2-hour time limit.

Park Side Hotel, 14–1 Heiwa-machi. ✆ 095/845-3191. Buffet lunch ¥1,300 ($12); buffet dinner ¥3,500 ($33); set meals ¥1,050–¥8,400 ($10–$80). AE, DC, MC, V. Daily 11:30am–2pm and 5–9pm. Streetcar: Hamaguchi-machi (3 min.).

**Obinata** 🐸🐸 *Finds* ITALIAN One of my favorite restaurants, Obinata is an oasis of old Europe in the heart of Kyushu. The place has a warm, earthy feel to it, due perhaps to its heavy wooden beams, large bouquets of flowers, oil wick lamps on each table, scattered antiques, and classical music playing softly in the background. The atmosphere is cozy and the service is a delight. The menu, in Italian, lists such dishes as beef filet grilled with crushed black pepper with cream sauce; veal and ham served with wine sauce; risotto; spaghetti; lasagna; and pizza, all served with fresh, homemade bread. Dishes are creative and fun, and there's a wide selection of Bordeaux, Moselle, and Rhine wines—the owner is a wine buff.

3–19 Funadaiku-machi. ✆ 095/826-1437. Main dishes ¥2,000–¥6,000 ($19–$57); pizza and pasta ¥1,200–¥2,200 ($11–$21). AE. Mon–Sat 6–11pm (last order). Streetcar: Shianbashi (3 min.). Walk under the neon-lit arch onto Shianbashi Dori and turn right at the Fukusaya castella cake shop (an old traditional building); it will be almost immediately on your left—look for the sign.

㉑ **Shikairo** 🐸🐸 CHAMPON If you're interested in eating champon (a thick Chinese noodle usually served in soup with meat, seafood, and vegetables), this is the Chinese restaurant that claims to have invented them. First opened in 1899, it occupies a five-story modern building, with two red pillars and other hints of Chinese-influenced architecture, not far from Glover Garden. Unless you've made a reservation for a private room, take the elevator to the fifth floor, where you'll be treated to great harbor views and delicious food (be sure to dine at off-peak hours to snag a table with the best views). The English-language menu, complete with pictures, offers several champon set meals, including one for ¥1,470 ($14) that also includes gyoza (fried dumplings), rice, and pickled vegetables, available all day. After eating, be sure to see

the restaurant's free museum on the second floor, where displays depict the history of the restaurant and objects relating to champon.

4–5 Matsugae-machi. © **095/822-1296.** Main dishes ¥892–¥1,360 ($8.50–$13); set meals ¥1,470–¥3,150 ($25–$30). AE, DC, MC, V. Daily 11:30am–3pm and 5–8pm (last order). Streetcar: Oura Tenshudoshita (1 min.).

**(212) Shippoku Hamakatsu** SHIPPOKU   This modern restaurant, just a minute's walk from the Hamano-machi covered shopping arcade (and behind Internet Café Cybac) is one of Nagasaki's best-known shippoku restaurants. The ground floor, with Western-style table seating, is made private with alcoves and bamboo screens; upstairs is a large tatami room with individual low tables and seat cushions. It offers shippoku set meals for lone diners for both lunch (¥2,100/$20) and dinner (from ¥3,045/$29), making it a good place to try this unique cuisine if you're alone. More extensive set meals are for parties of two or more.

6–50 Kajiya-machi. © **095/826-8321.** Set lunch ¥2,100 ($20); dinner shippoku set meals ¥3,045–¥12,600 ($29–$120). AE, DC, MC, V. Daily 11:30am–8:30pm (last order). Streetcar: Shianbashi (4 min.). Walk under the arch with the clock and take the 2nd right (Lawson is on the corner); it's in the middle of the block on the left (look for a black facade and a lattice door).

**Tokiwa** SASHIMI/TEMPURA/KAISEKI   Raw fish doesn't come any fresher than at this conveniently located restaurant between Hamano-machi and Glover Garden. Tokiwa features a wooden counter surrounding a large pool filled with live fish; when its number is up, the fish is scooped out of the water and then prepared right before your very eyes. Sometimes the fish is gutted and filleted with only the head, heart, and skeleton left intact, so that the sashimi can be arranged around the alive and still-quivering creature and be delivered to your table. Barring that, you might opt for one of the lunch *teishoku* (set meals), which range from sashimi to tempura.

Nagasaki View Hotel, 2–33 Oura-machi. © **095/824-2211.** Set lunches ¥980–¥2,500 ($9.35–$24); set dinners ¥2,625–¥8,400 ($25–$80). AE, DC, MC, V. Daily 11:30am–2pm and 5–9:30pm (last order). Streetcar: Ourakaigan Dori (1 min.); across the street from the stop.

## INEXPENSIVE

**Cancun** INTERNATIONAL   On a fine summer's evening, one of the most picturesque places for a meal is at an outside table at Dejima Wharf, a complex of restaurants, bars, and shops strung along a boardwalk near the Dejima historic district. Cancun, with thatched-roof accents and a dining room open to the elements, has a relaxed island atmosphere and serves a variety of Mexican, Spanish, and Italian fare, including paella, tacos, pasta, nachos, salads, and risotto. I've had better food, but there are few places in Japan with this kind of boardwalk atmosphere, and it's fun watching boats and ferries come and go in the harbor, not to mention the crowds of people who pass by. There's live music (mostly hits of the '70s and '80s) from 7:30pm, with a ¥300 ($2.85) music charge.

Dejima Wharf, 1–1 Dejima. © **095/832-6210.** Main dishes ¥800–¥2,750 ($7.60–$26); set lunch ¥800 ($7.60) weekdays, ¥950 ($9.05) weekends. No credit cards. Tues–Sun 11:30am–2:30pm and 5:30–midnight. Streetcar: Dejima (2 min.).

**(213) Dai-ichi-no Taberu** INTERNATIONAL   Organic veggies, fish, stir fries, soups, noodles, and other healthy dishes are the focus of this all-you-can-eat buffet restaurant next to Nagasaki Station in Amu Plaza (which has many other restaurants; look for the sign THANKS GIVING! WE LOVE NATURE). Avoid the noontime rush, since hungry crowds make it a challenge to reach the food (from 3–5pm weekdays, buffet

meals cost only ¥1,000/$9.50). Fortunately, dishes are replenished quickly, and something new is added frequently, making a second perusal of offerings almost mandatory. For ¥1,000 ($9.50) extra, you can add all the beer you can drink in 90 minutes.

5th floor, Amu Plaza, 1–1 Onoue-machi. (© 095/8182388. Buffet lunch ¥1,200 ($11) weekdays, ¥1,500 ($14) weekends; buffet dinner ¥1,500 ($14). AE, DC, MC, V. Daily 11am–10pm (last order). Beside Nagasaki Station, in Amu Plaza.

## 3 Unzen Spa & Its Hells ★/★

66km (41 miles) SE of Nagasaki

**Unzen Spa** is a small hot-spring resort town located 700m (2,310 ft.) above sea level in the pine-covered hills of the Shimabara Peninsula. Thanks to its high altitude, cool mountain air, great scenery, and hot sulfur springs, Unzen became popular in the 1890s as a summer resort for American and European visitors, who came from as far away as Shanghai, Hong Kong, Harbin, and Singapore to escape the oppressively humid summers. They arrived in Unzen by bamboo palanquin from Obama, 11km (6¾ miles) away. In 1911, Unzen became the first prefectural park in Japan. In 1934, the area became **Unzen-Amakusa National Park** ★★, one of the nation's first national parks; it covers 282 sq. km (113 sq. miles).

I like Unzen Spa because it's small and navigable. It consists basically of just a few streets with hotels and ryokan spread along them, a welcome relief if you've been spending hectic weeks rushing through big cities and catching buses and trains. Only 1,230 people live here, and from the town a number of hiking paths wind into the tree-covered hills. Dense clouds of steam arise from solfataras (vents) and fumaroles, evidence of volcanic activity. For visitors, the best result of all that thermal activity is the abundance of hot springs: Unzen's name derives from "Onsen," meaning "hot spring."

## ESSENTIALS

**GETTING THERE**   The only way to get to Unzen via public transportation is by bus. From Nagasaki, buses depart nine times a day from the Ken-ei Bus Terminal (© 095/826-6221) across the street from Nagasaki Station (sit on the right side of the bus for the most panoramic views). The ride takes about 1 hour and 40 minutes and costs ¥1,900 ($18) one-way or ¥3,422 ($33) round-trip. For bus and train schedules, drop by the Nagasaki Prefecture Tourist Federation on the second floor of the Ken-ei Bus Terminal.

You can also reach Unzen from Kumamoto. From Kumamoto Port (which you can reach in 20 min. by bus from Kumamoto Station for ¥420/$4), take the 1-hour ferry for ¥590 ($5.60) or the faster 30-minute Ocean Arrow for ¥800 ($7.60) to Shimabara Port, where you can catch a bus bound for Unzen, which takes an additional 35 minutes and costs ¥730 ($6.95) one-way.

**VISITOR INFORMATION**   Before leaving Tokyo or Narita or Kansai international airports, be sure to stop by the Tourist Information Center to pick up the free leaflet "Nagasaki and Unzen," which describes places of interest in Unzen and the Shimabara Peninsula, or download it from JNTO's website at www.jnto.go.jp. In Nagasaki, stop by the **Nagasaki Prefectural Tourist Federation,** across from Nagasaki Station on the second floor of the Ken-ei Bus Terminal.

In Unzen, the **Tourist Information Center** (© 0957/73-3434; open daily 9am–5pm), is located in the heart of Unzen Spa next to the Unzen Spa House and

across from the police station (between the Nishi-Iriguchi and Oyama-no-Johokan bus stops). It has a good English-language map of Unzen and the surrounding area and a hiking map, but not much English is spoken. Nearby is the park's **Mount Unzen Visitor Center** (© **0957/73-3636;** open daily 9am–6pm, to 5pm in winter), with displays and information on the entire national park.

**GETTING AROUND**   Buses from Nagasaki make four stops in Unzen Spa, terminating at Unzen's Ken-ei Bus Center. I've provided the bus-stop name for accommodations so you can alight at the nearest stop. Otherwise, Unzen is so small you can walk from one end to the other in about 20 minutes.

## WHAT TO SEE & DO

When the area around Unzen Spa was designated a national park in 1934, it was named after what was thought to be an extinct volcanic chain, collectively called Mount Unzen. In 1990, however, a peak in Mount Unzen—Mount Fugen—erupted for the first time in almost 200 years, killing several dozen people on its eastern slope and leaving behind a huge lava dome. Unzen Spa, on the opposite side, was untouched and remains the area's most popular resort town.

**THE HELLS (JIGOKU)**   Unzen Spa literally bubbles with activity, as sulfurous hot springs erupt into surface cauldrons of scalding water in an area known as the Hells (Jigoku). Indeed, in the 1600s, these cauldrons were used for hellish punishment, as some 30 Christians were boiled alive here after Christianity was outlawed in Japan. Today, Unzen Spa has more than 30 solfataras and fumaroles, with the Hells providing the greatest show of geothermal activity, making this spot Unzen's number-one attraction. It's a favorite hangout of huge black ravens, and the barren land has been baked a chalky white through the centuries. Pathways lead through the hot-spring Hells, where sulfur vapors rise thickly to veil pine trees on surrounding hills. A simple cross erected on stones serves as a memorial to the Christians killed here.

**CLIMBING MOUNT FUGEN**  ⚘   If you feel like taking an excursion, head for Mount Fugen, Unzen's most popular destination outside Unzen Spa. Buses depart about six times a day for **Nitta Pass,** about a 23-minute ride away (round-trip fare: ¥740/$7.05). From Nitta Pass, board the 3-minute ropeway for ¥1,220 ($12) round-trip to go up higher to **Mount Myoken,** which at 1,333m (4,399 ft.) offers spectacular panoramic views. If you're ready for some real climbing, however, continue along a marked path for another hour or so; it leads starkly uphill to the summit of **Mount Fugen,** once Unzen's highest peak at 1,359m (4,485 ft.) above sea level—this is the peak that erupted in 1990. Here, on a clear day, you'll be rewarded with splendid views of other volcanic peaks as far away as Mount Aso in the middle of Kyushu. You can also see Mount Heisei Shinzan (a lava dome), born during Mount Fugen's last eruption and now Unzen's loftiest peak at 1,483m (4,894 ft.). Allow at least 2½ hours for the hike to Mount Fugen and back so you don't miss the last bus.

**TAKING THE WATERS**   On the main street of Unzen are the Finger Spa and the Foot Spa, where you can soak the appropriate appendages in outdoor baths for free. If you'd like to get more than your feet wet (though all accommodations below offer hot-spring baths), the **Unzen Spa House,** across from the Unzen Kanko Hotel (© **0957/73-3131**), is open Monday to Saturday 10am to 6pm and Sunday and holidays 10am to 7pm. Indoor cypress baths and *rotenburo* (outdoor hot-spring baths) cost ¥800 ($7.60); pay ¥1,700 ($16) if you also want a sand bath. In the Spa House

## *Moments*  Fertile Grounds

I was looking for an easy hike, somewhere quiet to write in my journal, and set-tled for Konohanasakuya-Hime Jinja, a hillside shrine established 300 years ago above the Gensei-Numa Marsh on the edge of Unzen Spa. Unknowingly, I had picked a shrine dedicated to the deity of flowers, where people come to pray for fertility, safe childbirth, and family harmony. So imagine my delight when I reached the shrine's small clearing to discover two unmistakable statues of—well, you'll just have to see for yourself. Benches provide views over Unzen to Mount Myoken and the ropeway. You won't find anything like this in Topeka, Kansas.

is also the **Vidro Museum** (open daily 9am–6pm), with Edo-Era Nagasaki glass and Bohemian, Italian, French, and other glassware. Admission here is ¥700 ($6.65) extra.

## WHERE TO STAY

Keep in mind that, as with most resort areas in Japan, Unzen tends to be crowded and sometimes even fully booked during Golden Week, during New Year's, and from mid-July to August. The best times of year are late April to June, when the azalea bushes are in glorious bloom, and late October and early November, when the maple leaves turn brilliant reds.

With the exception of one inexpensive accommodation at the end of this section, all the ryokan and hotels listed here are within an easy walk of bus stops along the route traversed by the bus from Nagasaki, so I've included the bus stops for each estab-lishment below. You can also tell the bus driver where you're staying, and he'll drop you off at the nearest stop (if you're arriving from Kumamoto, buses go only to the bus terminal).

### EXPENSIVE

**Kyushu Hotel** 𝔊𝔊𝔊    Despite its name, the Kyushu Hotel, built in 1917, is a lovely, old-style ryokan in an updated building with a view of a lovely traditional garden from its luxurious lobby. Yet it remains in step with the times, attracting young Japanese with a gracious and accommodating staff (the third-generation owners speak English), soft jazz playing in public places, and fusion cuisine in the dining hall that successfully blends Western and Japanese styles. If you prefer, you can opt for Japanese cuisine served in your room. But best of all, the Kyushu Hotel offers some of the most scenic views in town—many of its rooms boast great views of the hills as well as the Hells. Tatami rooms feature alcoves with Western-style chairs next to large windows, afford-ing relaxing places to take in the view. There are also five Western-style rooms and five combination rooms with tatami areas and beds. The communal baths are spacious and inviting with both indoor and outdoor bathing, but if you don't care to bathe with everyone, reserve the private family bath, also with outdoor bath, for ¥2,100 ($20; there's a 40-min. time limit).

Obamacho, Unzen-shi 320, Nagasaki-ken 854-0697. (𝒞 **0957/73-3234.** Fax 0957/73-3733. qshuhtl@alpha.ocn. ne.jp. 97 units. ¥15,000–¥40,000 ($125–$360) per person. Rates include breakfast, dinner, and service. AE, DC, MC, V. Bus: Oyama-no-Johokan (2 min.). **Amenities:** Restaurant (Japanese/Western fusion); bar; lounge; indoor/outdoor hot-spring baths; massage/treatment room; souvenir shop; in-room massage; same-day laundry/dry-cleaning service. *In room:* A/C, satellite TV, minibar, hot-water pot w/tea, hair dryer.

㉔ **Miyazaki Ryokan** 🕭🕭   One of the largest Japanese inns in Unzen, this modern ryokan first opened 75 years ago and overlooks a beautiful, gracefully manicured garden with hills and sulfur vapors rising in the background—absolutely exquisite when the azaleas are in bloom. Upon arrival, you'll be served green tea and sweets by graceful women in kimono. Afterward, you'll want to ease into the large, marble hotspring bath overlooking a rock-lined outdoor bath, separated for men and women. Or, if you're shy about bathing with others or want to make it a family affair, make a reservation at no extra charge for the private family bath (40-min. time limit). After bathing, relax in the peaceful tatami area with Go (a Japanese board game) tables, huge flower arrangements, and a dispenser of cool *mugi cha* (wheat tea). Next comes one of the best reasons to stay here—the kaiseki meal. Although breakfast (Western style, if desired) is served in a communal dining area, an excellent dinner is served in your guest room in true ryokan fashion. In addition to Japanese-style tatami rooms, there are combination rooms with twin beds and a separate tatami area. Since rates are the same regardless of which direction the rooms face, I advise securing one that looks out over the garden or, barring that, the Hells (views from here are not as good, however, as from the Kyushu Hotel above).

Obamacho, Unzen-shi 320, Nagasaki-ken 854-0692. ✆ **0957/73-3331.** Fax 0957/73-2313. www.miyazaki-ryokan. co.jp/miyazaki/English/top/index.html. 96 units. ¥18,900–¥34,650 ($180–$330) per person. ¥2,000 ($19) extra per person Sat, nights before holidays, and peak season. Rates include breakfast, dinner, and service charge. AE, DC, MC, V. Bus: Oyama-no-Johokan. (2 min.). **Amenities:** Lounge; indoor/outdoor hot-spring baths; Jacuzzi; sauna; in-room massage; shopping arcade; same-day laundry/dry-cleaning service. *In room:* A/C, TV, hot-water pot w/tea, hair dryer, tiny safe, Washlet toilet.

## MODERATE

**Unzen Kanko Hotel** 🕭🕭🕭 *Finds*   If you're the least bit romantic, you won't be able to resist staying at this old-fashioned mountain lodge, built in 1935 of stone and wood, covered in ivy, and resembling a Swiss chalet (even the female staff is donned in dirndl-like dresses). No wonder it's been designated an Important Tangible Cultural Heritage Site. The lobby, main dining hall, and public spaces have changed little over the decades, with their whitewashed walls, dark-beamed ceilings, and inviting sofas and chairs. The rooms are rustic and old-fashioned, too, with heavy ceiling-to-floor curtains tied back to reveal a balcony (ask for a room facing the front), brass doorsills, a high ceiling, and wooden beams. There are 48 Western-style rooms, eight Japanese-style tatami rooms, and two combination rooms that come with both a bed and tatami area.

Obamacho, Unzen-shi 320, Nagasaki-ken 854-0621. ✆ **0957/73-3263.** Fax 0957/73-3419. info@unzenkankohotel. com. 58 units. ¥9,240–¥9,817 ($88–$93) single; ¥18,480 ($176) double; ¥13,860–¥42,735 ($132–$407) twin; ¥28,875 ($275) Japanese-style rooms; ¥25,410 ($242) combination rooms. Rates include service charge. AE, DC, MC, V. Bus: Nishi-Iriguchi (1 min.). **Amenities:** Restaurant (Japanese/Western); bar; hot-spring baths (including a family bath; get the key at reception); billiard room; in-room massage; same-day laundry/dry cleaning service; nonsmoking rooms. *In room:* A/C, TV, hot-water pot w/tea, hair dryer.

## INEXPENSIVE

㉕ **Kaseya Ryokan**   Located on the main street through town not far from the bus center (the last stop on buses into town from Nagasaki), this economically priced ryokan dates from 1909 but has been remodeled. The kind owners are fond of children; they have three of their own and remembered Janie's daughter many years later. All of the rooms are Japanese-style, simply decorated but with high ceilings and flower arrangements. Ask for a room in the back—they're quieter. A small shop in the lobby sells blue-and-white tie-dyed clothing, a massage chair is available free of charge, and

a computer provides high-speed Internet connection (¥100/95¢ for 10 min.). Coffee is free in the mornings, and Western-style breakfasts are available.

Obamacho, Unzen-shi 315, Nagasaki-ken 854-0621. ✆ 0957/73-3321. Fax 0957/73-3322. info@kaseya.jp. 13 units (none with bathroom). ¥7,290 ($69) per person Sun–Fri; ¥8,550 ($81) per person Sat and nights before holidays; more during Golden Week and New Year's. Rates include breakfast, dinner, and service charge. AE, MC, V. Bus: Jinja-mae (2 min.). **Amenities:** Hot-spring baths (including a private one for families); in-room massage. *In room:* A/C, TV, hot-water pot w/tea, safe.

216 **Seiunso Kokumin Shukusha** *Value*    Formerly a youth hostel, this public lodging underwent extensive remodeling and now offers as much comfort and as many facilities as a moderately priced resort hotel. Rooms are pleasant, Japanese style (you lay out your own futon here); most have a small balcony offering views of the surrounding woods, and all have sinks and toilets. There are also three combination rooms with both beds and tatami areas that are quite spacious, are accessible to travelers with disabilities, and have the best views; you can stay in these rooms for the same charge if they're not booked. In addition to public baths, there are two private family baths (¥1,050/$10 for 50 min.). Needless to say, you should reserve early to stay here. The main disadvantage is that the location is outside Unzen, about a 30-minute walk from the Hells, and check-in isn't until 4pm.

Obamacho, Unzen-shi 500–1, Nagasaki-ken 854-0621. ✆ 0957/73-3273. Fax 0957/73-2698. 63 units (none with bathroom). ¥4,875 ($46) per person without meals; ¥7,920 ($75) per person with 2 meals. No credit cards. Bus: Nishi-Iriguchi (20 min.). Pickup service available from Ken-ei Bus Center. **Amenities:** Restaurant (Japanese); indoor/outdoor hot-spring baths w/relaxation room; playground; game center; in-room massage; coin-op washer/dryer. *In room:* A/C, TV, hot-water pot w/tea, safe, Washlet toilet.

## WHERE TO DINE

Even if you don't stay at the **Unzen Kanko Hotel,** you may want to come here for lunch. Its old-fashioned dining hall is large with a high ceiling, wainscoting, wooden floors, white tablecloths, and flowers on each table. It serves both Japanese and Western selections, with set lunches beginning at ¥2,100 ($20) and Japanese obento priced at ¥2,000 ($19) and ¥3,000 ($29). A la carte items include steak and chicken or inexpensive pasta or sandwiches. Set dinners start at ¥6,000 ($57). The dining hall is open for lunch from 11:30 to 2pm and for dinner starting at 6pm, with last orders taken at 8pm.

**Unzen Tabi no Beer Kan** WESTERN    This microbrewery, light and airy with large windows overlooking wooded hills and a lake, brews three different kinds of beer. A half liter costs ¥735 ($7), or you can have a sampler of all three for ¥787 ($7.50). A limited English-language menu lists three kinds of pizza and three kinds of pasta, but the restaurant is most known for its beer curry for ¥945 ($9), which includes a small salad. On weekends and holidays there's a buffet lunch for ¥1,575 ($15).

Across from the Ken-ei Bus Center. ✆ 0957/73-3113. Main dishes ¥682–¥1,050 ($6.50–$10). AE, MC, V. Daily 11am–8pm. Bus: Ken-ei Bus Center (1 min.).

## 4 Kumamoto ★

1,293km (804 miles) W of Tokyo; 189km (118 miles) S of Fukuoka

Located roughly halfway down Kyushu's western side, Kumamoto boasts a fine castle and a landscaped garden, both with origins stretching from the first half of the 17th century. Once one of Japan's most important castle towns, Kumamoto today is the progressive capital of Kumamoto Prefecture, with a population of 660,000. Yet it retains a small-town atmosphere, which is precisely why I like it.

## ESSENTIALS

**GETTING THERE    By Plane    JAL** and **ANA** fly to Kumamoto from Tokyo in 1 hour and 40 minutes, with one-way fares ranging from ¥19,000 ($181) for a 21-day advance purchase to ¥31,000 ($295) for a regular ticket. Local airline **Skynet Asia Airways** (© 0120/737-283 toll-free) offers a regular one-way ticket for ¥22,300 ($212), a 6-day advance ticket for ¥18,300 ($174), and a bargain ticket for ¥9,800 ($93) if purchased 2 months in advance for certain dates. Airport shuttle buses operate from the airport to Kumamoto Station and the Kumamoto Kotsu (bus) Center downtown, taking about 50 minutes and costing ¥670 ($6.40).

**By Train**    It takes about 9 hours to reach Kumamoto from **Tokyo,** not including transfers, at a cost of ¥23,020 ($219) for an unreserved seat. From **Fukuoka's Hakata Station** (terminus of the bullet train from Tokyo), limited express trains depart three times an hour, reaching Kumamoto in about 1½ hours and costing ¥3,740 ($36) for a reserved seat. (In 2011, a new bullet train will connect Kumamoto and Fukuoka in 24 min.) There are also four express trains daily from **Beppu,** reaching Kumamoto in 3 hours.

**VISITOR INFORMATION**    The leaflet "Kumamoto and Mount Aso," distributed by the Tourist Information Centers in Tokyo and in Narita and Kansai international airports, contains information on how to get to Kumamoto and places of interest in the city (you can also download it from JNTO's website at www.jnto.go.jp). In Kumamoto, there's a **Kumamoto Tourist Office** inside Kumamoto Station near the main exit (© 096/352-3743; open daily 8:30am–7pm). It has a good English-language map and brochure and is staffed by helpful English speakers who can make lodging reservations. In the city center, there's another Kumamoto Tourist Information Center on the first floor of the **Sanbun Kaikan Building** (which is part of the Sangyo Bunka Kaikan complex; © 096/322-5060; open daily 10am–6pm, closed second and fourth Mon of the month), opposite the Sunroad Shinshigai covered shopping street and in front of the Karashimacho streetcar stop. If you're coming by plane, stop by the **Kumamoto Airport Information Office** (© 096/232-2810; open daily 6:50am–9pm).

More information is available on the city's website at www.city.kumamoto. kumamoto.jp, but a more comprehensive overview is provided by Kumamoto Prefecture's website at http://cyber.pref.kumamoto.jp.

**INTERNET ACCESS**    The Kumamoto City International Center, 4–8 Hanabatacho (© 096/359–2121; streetcar: Kumamotojo-mae), offers three computers with free Internet access on the second floor Monday to Friday 9am to 8pm and weekends 9am to 7pm (closed the second and fourth Mon of every month). Otherwise, **Media**

---

### *Tips*  Bus & Ferry from Unzen Spa

From Unzen Spa, the fastest way to reach Kumamoto is to take a bus (there are two bus companies, with 16 departures daily) 35 minutes to Shimabara Port (fare: ¥730/$7), where you can then board a 1-hour ferry (fare: ¥590/$5.60) or a 30-minute Ocean Arrow (fare: ¥800/$7.60) to Kumamoto Port. Buses connect Kumamoto Port with Kumamoto Station in 20 minutes for ¥420 ($4).

**Café Popeye,** located on the Kamitori covered shopping street (© **096/326-6767;** streetcar: Toricho-suji), is open 24 hours and charges ¥420 ($4) for an hour's use of its computers.

**MAIL**   Kumamoto's main post office, with ATMs that accept international credit cards, is located beside Kumamoto Station to the north and is open Monday to Friday 9am to 5:30pm and 9am to 5pm Saturday and Sunday.

**ORIENTATION & GETTING AROUND**   **Kumamoto Station** lies far south of the city's downtown area, but transportation between the two is easy via streetcar no. 2, which departs from in front of the station and reaches the downtown area in about 10 minutes. **Downtown** centers on three covered shopping streets called Shimotori, Kamitori, and Sunroad Shinshigai, with many department stores, shops, hotels, bars, Pachinko parlors, and restaurants in the area. Here, too, is the city's bus station, the **Kumamoto Kotsu Center,** from which all buses in the city depart. Just north of downtown, within walking distance, rises **Kumamoto Castle,** which is surrounded by moats, turrets, and expansive greenery, on the edge of which are several museums and historic sites. **Suizenji Garden** lies far to the east.

Getting around Kumamoto via old-fashioned **streetcar** is easy because there are only two lines. Streetcar no. 2 is most convenient for tourists; the only one departing from Kumamoto Station, it passes through downtown and near Kumamoto Castle (stop: Kumamotojo-mae) before going onward to Suizenji Garden (stop: Suizenji-Koen-mae). Take a ticket when you board; fares increase the farther you go, from ¥130 to ¥200 ($1.25–$1.90) and you pay when you get off.

Because the grounds surrounding Kumamoto Castle encompass 97 hectares (242 acres), with a circumference of 9km (5½ miles), many visitors opt to see sights via the **Shu-yu shuttle excursion bus,** which makes a circular route around the castle grounds every 30 minutes and stops at Hosokawa Mansion and other places of interest. On weekends and holidays, an additional bus, the **Kumamotojo shuttle bus,** makes runs between the train station and castle every 20 minutes. These buses charge ¥130 ($1.25) for a single journey, ¥300 ($2.85) for the whole day; as always, children pay half fare.

If you plan on taking public transportation at least four times in 1 day, you can save money by purchasing a **1-day pass,** which allows unlimited travel on all city buses (including the above shuttle buses) and streetcars for ¥500 ($4.75). It includes a 20% discount off admission to a few sights, including Kumamoto Castle.

## THE TOP ATTRACTIONS

**Kumamoto Castle** 𝕽𝕽   Completed in 1607, Kumamoto Castle is massive—it took 7 years to build. It was constructed under the direction of Kato Kiyomasa, a great warrior who fought alongside Tokugawa Ieyasu in battle and was rewarded for his loyalty with land. The castle was built atop a hill and had two main towers, 49 turrets, 29 gates, and 18 two-story gatehouses; to make the walls impossible for enemies to scale, they were built with curves at the bottom and nearly vertical at the top and were crowned with an overhang. More than 100 wells ensured water even during a siege, while camphor and gingko trees were planted for firewood and edible nuts. The castle passed into the possession of the Hosokawa family in 1632 and remained an important stronghold for the Tokugawa shogunate throughout its 250 years of rule, particularly in campaigns against the powerful and independent-minded lords of

southern Kyushu. During that time, 11 generations of the Hosokawa clan ruled over Kumamoto.

Much of the castle was destroyed in 1877 during the Seinan Rebellion led by Saigo Takamori, a samurai who was unhappy with the new policies of the Meiji government in which ancient samurai rights were rescinded. Saigo led a troop of samurai in an attack on the castle and its imperial troops, who remained under siege for 53 days before government reinforcements finally arrived and quelled the rebellion. When the smoke cleared, most of the castle lay in smoldering ruins.

The castle was reconstructed in 1960 of ferroconcrete, and although it's not nearly as massive as before, it's still quite impressive and remains Kumamoto's star attraction. The interior houses a museum with elaborately decorated palanquins, models of Kumamoto and the castle during the Edo Period, armor, swords, former possessions of both Kato Kiyomasa and the Hosokawa family, and rifles and other artifacts from the Seinan Rebellion. Behind the castle is one of 11 remaining turrets, which is three tiered and five stories. Because the castle grounds are large, you'll probably spend more than an hour here (in 2007, a replica of the Honmaru Goten, a 17th-c. palace that was destroyed in the Seinan Rebellion, will open beside the castle). If you intend to visit Hosokawa Mansion (see "More to See & Do," below), buy a joint ticket for entrance to both sights (¥640/$6.10 for adults and ¥240/$2.30 for children).

1–1 Honmaru. ℂ 096/352-5900. Admission ¥500 ($4.75) adults, ¥200 ($1.90) children. Apr–Oct daily 8:30am–5:30pm; Nov–Mar daily 8:30am–4:30pm. Streetcar: Kumamotojo-mae (10 min.) or Shiyakusho-mae (6 min.). Shuttle bus: Kumamotojo stop (5 min.).

**Suizenji Garden (Suizenji Jojuen)** ⋆    Laid out in the 1630s by Hosokawa Tadatoshi as a retreat for the tea ceremony and as the grounds of a nearby temple, Suizenji Garden took about 80 years to complete. The garden wraps itself around a cold spring–fed lake (considered particularly good for making tea). But what makes the place especially interesting is that its design incorporates famous scenes in miniature from the 53 stages of the ancient **Tokaido Highway,** which connected Kyoto and Tokyo. (The 53 stages were also immortalized in Hiroshige's famous woodblock prints.) Most recognizable are cone-shaped Mount Fuji and Lake Biwa; near the garden's entrance is Nihon Bashi (Bridge of Japan), Edo's starting point on the Tokaido Road. The park is small—almost disappointingly so—and for the life of me, I can't figure out more than a handful of the 53 stages. Maybe you'll have better luck. Pastoral views are also marred by—my pet peeve—surrounding buildings. Take solace by sipping tea in a traditional thatched-roof teahouse with views of the pond (¥600/$5.70). On garden grounds is also **Izumi Shrine,** built in 1878 and dedicated to the Hosokawa lords, as well as a Noh theater, where Noh is performed in spring and fall ceremonies. A stroll of the garden takes about 30 minutes.

8–1 Suizenji Koen. ℂ 096/383-0074. www.suizenji.or.jp. Admission ¥400 ($3.80) adults, ¥200 ($1.90) children. Mar–Nov daily 7:30am–6pm; Dec–Feb daily 8am–5pm. Streetcar: no. 2 from Kumamoto Station or the downtown area to Suizenji-Koen-mae (about a 20-min. ride), followed by a 3-min. walk.

## MORE TO SEE & DO

**Contemporary Art Museum, Kumamoto** ⋆ *(Finds*    Since it's free (except during special exhibitions) and centrally located in downtown Kumamoto, consider taking a 30-minute jaunt through this forerunner in contemporary art, in which art is treated as an experience rather than something to be viewed passively by the viewer. Showcasing works by local talent Ide Nobumichi, as well as commissioned installations by

Kusama Yayoi (look for her *Infinity Mirrored Room*) and Miyajima Tatsuo (with a pillar of flashing diodes) and special exhibits, it seems more like a community center than a museum, with a children's play corner and a Ping-Pong table designed by Ishii Hiroshi that responds digitally to the ball. My favorite is the library, with art, books, and comfortable sofas (a favorite place, apparently, for dozing off), where there's a free Friday jam session at 6:30pm, as well as nightly piano music from 7 to 7:30pm, followed by 10 minutes of darkness in which a ceiling light installation, by James Turrell, slowly transforms from blue to red.

2–3 Kamitori-cho. © 096/278-7500. www.camk.or.jp. Free admission, except for some special exhibits. Wed–Mon 10am–8pm (you must enter by 7:30pm). Streetcar: Toricho-suji (1 min.).

### Hosokawa Mansion (Kyu-Hosokawa Gyobutei) ✿

A 10-minute walk north of Kumamoto Castle, this 300-year-old samurai mansion was built by a subsidiary member of the Hosokawa clan, Lord Gyobu, and was enlarged in the 1800s. Guided tours (often available in English-language) lasting 15 minutes take visitors through 24 rooms, including the lord's study and reception room, teahouse, kitchen, and servants' quarters. You'll see Edo-Era furnishings and personal items including an Edo clock, a suitcase, clothing, games, a woman's cosmetic case, lacquerware, a kimono chest, and more, giving you a good idea of how feudal lords lived during the Edo Period.

3–1 Furukyo-machi. © 096/352-6522. Admission ¥300 ($2.85) adults, ¥100 (95¢) children. Combination ticket for Hoskoawa Mansion and Kumamoto Castle ¥640 ($6.10) adults, ¥240 ($2.30) children. Apr–Oct daily 8:30am–5:30pm; Nov–Mar daily 8:30am–4:30pm. Shuttle bus: Hakubutsukan-mae (1 min.).

## SHOOTING THE KUMAGAWA RAPIDS ✿✿

If you've had enough of shrines, castles, and gardens, consider shooting the **Kumagawa Rapids.** Compared to wild rivers in the United States, the Kumagawa seems pretty tame; people do the trip not so much for the thrill of the ride but for the scenery of a narrow river valley bordered by wooded hills and for the camaraderie afforded by sitting on tatami in a traditional wooden boat steered by boatmen fore and aft. You can also ride a modern raft guided by a staff of young professionals that goes through slightly rougher water. Reservations are a must for all rides.

The **Kumagawa Kudari Kabushiki Company,** Shimoshin-machi 333–1 (a 20-min. walk from Hitoyoshi Station; walk straight ahead to the third stoplight and turn left), Hitoyoshi City (© **0966/22-5555**), offers two different 90-minute routes in its wooden boats. The **Seiryu Course (Calm Course)** covers 8km (5 miles) of a gentle stretch of the river beginning in Hitoyoshi and ending in Watari. It's offered year-round; December through February, the boats have *kotatsu* (heated blankets). The cost is ¥2,835 ($27) for adults and ¥1,890 ($18) for children; winter trips with kotatsu cost ¥3,675 ($35) and ¥2,835 ($27) respectively.

The **Kyuryu Course (Rapids Course)** covers 10km (6¼ miles), beginning downriver in Watari (a 5-minute walk from Watari Station; turn left out of the station and left again over the tracks) and ending in Kyusendo, and is more exciting and required more skillful maneuvering, though the river is still only a grade 2. It's offered April through October and costs ¥3,675 ($35) for adults and ¥2,100 ($20) for children. During rainy season (mid-June to mid-July), this trip is sometimes canceled due to swollen rivers or high winds.

Kumagawa Kudari Kabushiki also offers rafting. The **Fighting Course** (90 min.) for ¥6,300 ($60) begins at Watari Station; from there you'll be taken to Ishochi, where you will put in and raft to Kyusendo. The **All Around** rafting course (3 hr.) runs from

Watari to Kyusendo and costs ¥7,875 ($75). Both of these run April through October, include a post-trip soak in an onsen in Kunagawa, and conclude with a return trip via minibus to Watari. Note, however, that children under 11 and adults over 60 are not allowed on these trips.

You can reach **Hitoyoshi** by bus from Kumamoto Kotsu Center in about 1½ hours, with fares costing ¥2,300 ($22) one-way. There are also six trains a day from Kumamoto Station to Hitoyoshi; the express train takes 1½ hours and costs ¥1,774 ($17). Trains and buses connect Watari and Kyusendo with Kumamoto. If you're going onward to **Kagoshima,** you can return to Hitoyoshi by local train for a bus that will deliver you to Kagoshima Chuo Station in 2 hours for ¥2,050 ($20). There is also a retro-fitted scenic sightseeing train, the **Isaburo-Shinpei,** which travels between Hitoyoshi and Yoshimatsu twice a day in a little over an hour, including switchbacks along the way and stops at scenic overlooks. The fare is ¥720 ($6.85), with surcharges of ¥300 to ¥500 ($2.85–$4.75) added during peak season (free for holders of Japan Rail Pass). From Yoshimatsu, it then takes 100 minutes by train onward to Kagoshima (fare: ¥1,430/$14). For timetables, contact the JR information office in Kumamoto Station.

## SHOPPING

One of Kumamoto's most famous products is its Higo Inlay or **damascene,** in which gold, silver, and copper are inlaid on an iron plate to form patterns of flowers, bamboo, and other designs. Originally used to adorn sword guards and armor, damascene today is used on such accessories as paperweights, jewelry, and tie clasps. Another Kumamoto product is the **Yamaga lantern,** made of gold paper and used during the Yamaga Lantern Festival held in August. Other local products include Amakusa pearls, pottery, knives, toys, and bamboo items.

One place to shop for Higo Inlay, knives, pottery, Yamaga paper lanterns, Amakusa pearls, toys, shochu, sake, and confections is the ㉑⑦ **Display Hall of Kumamoto Products (Kumamoto-ken Bussankan),** located on the third floor of the Sanbun Kaikan Building (which is part of the Sangyo Bunka Kaikan complex) at 7–10 Hanabata-cho (✆ **096/353-1168;** open daily 10am–6pm, closed second and fourth Mon each month). It's located south of Kumamoto Castle, opposite the Sunroad Shinshigai shopping arcade and in front of the Karashimacho streetcar stop (the Kumamoto Tourist Information Center is in the same building).

## WHERE TO STAY
### EXPENSIVE
**Hotel New Otani Kumamoto** 👍👍 *Value*    This hotel has everything: a convenient location next to the station, the respected New Otani name, a perceptive staff, and the latest in design and amenities—all at reasonable rates. Although with the opening of the Nikko (below) it is no longer the only game in town, this 1991 property is still a fine choice. Rooms are comfortable, with queen-size beds in both single and double rooms, and come with individual reading lights with dimmer switches, window blinds to block light, double-paned windows that block noise and can also be opened, massage showerheads, and such extras as hangers with nonslip pads and bathroom phones.

1–13–1 Kasuga, Kumamoto 860-0047. ✆ **800/421-8795** in the U.S. and Canada, or 096/326-1111. Fax 096/326-0800. www.newotani.co.jp. 130 units. ¥13,000 ($124) single; ¥21,000–¥35,000 ($200–$333) double or twin. Rates include service charge. AE, DC, MC, V. A 1-min. walk from Kumamoto Station, to the left. **Amenities:** 4 restaurants; 2 bars (1 with live piano music); men's sauna (fee: ¥1,000/$9.50); souvenir shop/convenience store; salon; room service (6am–10pm); lobby computer w/Internet access (¥100/95¢/10 min); in-room massage; same-day

laundry/dry-cleaning service; nonsmoking rooms. *In room:* A/C, satellite TV, dataport, minibar, hot-water pot w/tea, hair dryer, Washlet toilet.

**Hotel Nikko Kumamoto** 🕮🕮🕮   In the same building as the Contemporary Art Museum and an adjoining shopping complex in the heart of downtown, this 14-story hotel (opened in 2002) is the most luxurious in Kumamoto. An inviting fireplace and contemporary art serve as the focal points of its two-story lobby, pleasingly decorated in strong contrasts of dark wood and light-colored marble. Large, comfortable rooms, with views of either Kumamoto Castle or Mount Aso in the distance, offer sitting areas, closets that light up as soon as you open them, focused bedside reading lights so your partner can sleep, blackout curtains for total darkness, and excellent insulation from traffic noise. Singles sport double-size beds, doubles have queen-size beds, and twins have large bathrooms with separate tub/shower/toilet areas.

2–1 Kamitori-cho, Kumamoto 860-8536. ✆ 800/645-5687 in the U.S. and Canada, or 096/211-1111. Fax 096/211-1175. www.nikko-kumamoto.co.jp. 191 units. ¥16,170 ($154) single; ¥43,890 ($418) double; ¥30,030–¥43,890 ($286–$418) twin. Rates include service charge. AE, DC, MC, V. Streetcar: Toricho-suji (1 min.). **Amenities:** 4 restaurants (Japanese, Chinese, steakhouse, international); 1 lounge; concierge; room service (11am–midnight); in-room massage; same-day laundry/dry-cleaning service; nonsmoking rooms. *In room:* A/C, cable/satellite TV w/pay movies, dataport, minibar, hot-water pot w/tea, hair dryer, Washlet toilet.

## MODERATE

**JR Kyushu Hotel** 🕮 *Value*   This business hotel right next to Kumamoto Station offers convenience, reasonable prices, and 10% discounts for holders of the Japan Rail Pass. Since a whopping 140 of its 150 rooms are singles, make reservations in advance for its one double or eight twin rooms. (It also has one room for those with limited mobility.) Singles are small but have surprisingly roomy bathrooms, while twins are corner rooms with windows on two sides and a sofa.

3–15–15 Kasuga, Kumamoto 860-0047. ✆ 096/354-8000. Fax 096/354-8012. www.jrhotelgroup.com. 150 units. ¥6,900 ($66) single; ¥12,600 ($120) double or twin. AE, DC, MC, V. A 1-min. walk from Kumamoto Station, to the right. **Amenities:** Restaurant (Japanese); in-room massage; coin-op washer/dryer; laundry/dry-cleaning service; nonsmoking rooms. *In room:* A/C, TV, fridge, hot-water pot w/tea, hair dryer, trouser presser, Washlet toilet.

**KKR Hotel Kumamoto** *Finds*   Located north of Kumamoto Castle across the street, this trendy hotel buzzes with activity as a popular wedding and banquet venue (weekdays are quieter and also cheaper). The best reason to stay here is its up-close view of the castle, with the absolute best views provided by twin rooms above the hotel's rooftop garden (visible also from the hotel's Japanese restaurant). Unfortunately, none of the hotel's 11 single rooms have castle views (though solo travelers can stay in a twin with castle views for ¥10,000/$95), and there are no double rooms. Since this hotel is a 10-minute trek from the nearest streetcar stop, stay here only if you can get that view.

3–31 Chibajo-machi, Kumamoto 860-0001. ✆ 096/355-0121. Fax 096/355-7955. 54 units. ¥7,500 ($71) single; ¥14,400–¥15,000 ($137–$143) twin. ¥1,000 ($9.50) extra weekends and holidays. AE, DC, MC, V. Streetcar: Shiyakusho-mae (10 min). Follow the streetcar tracks north and then take the first left over the bridge; the hotel is straight ahead. **Amenities:** 2 restaurants (Chinese, coffee shop); salon; in-room massage; same-day laundry/dry cleaning service. *In room:* A/C, TV, fridge, hot-water pot w/tea, hair dryer, Washlet toilet.

**Kumamoto Hotel Castle**   This tall brick hotel is just east of Kumamoto Castle, with good views of the castle from some of its more expensive twin rooms. A subdued, quiet, and conservative hotel that's been a city mainstay for 45 years, it's popular with middle-aged Japanese, including locals who come for receptions or to dine in one of its restaurants, and it sports the most elaborate Yamaga lantern (in the shape of a

pagoda) I've ever seen in its lobby. Rooms are rather standard, with the cheapest singles no larger than those at the Toyoko Inn (see below), though deluxe doubles and twins face the castle in a more spacious setting with windows that open.

4–2 Joto-machi, Kumamoto 860-8565. ℂ 096/326-3311. Fax 096/326-3324. 185 units. ¥9,300–¥15,225 ($89–$145) single; ¥17,850–¥22,050 ($170–$210) double; ¥16,800–¥26,250 ($160–$250) twin. AE, DC, MC, V. Streetcar: Shiyakusho-mae (2 min.). **Amenities:** 4 restaurants (Japanese, French, Chinese, coffee shop); 1 bar; salon; room service (11:30am–midnight); in-room massage; laundry/dry-cleaning service; nonsmoking rooms. *In room:* A/C, cable TV, minibar, hot-water pot w/tea, hair dryer, Washlet toilet.

## INEXPENSIVE

**Kajita**   Two pug-nosed dogs (real) in a cage by the front door, and a mongoose, a cobra, and birds (stuffed) in the lobby greet you at this friendly, family-run establishment, a member of the Japanese Inn Group. It has a central location, just a 10-minute walk to the castle grounds and a 2-minute walk to the streetcar that will take you onward to Suizenji Garden. Tatami rooms, named after flowers, are simple but clean. If you call, you'll most likely be picked up at the station, though if no car is available, someone will wait for you at the bus stop. A cupboard in the hall has self-service coffee and tea free of charge. The dining room is so packed with stuff I don't think you could fit in another single item.

1–2–7 Shinmachi, Kumamoto 860-0004. ℂ 096/353-1546. Fax 096/353-1546. kajita@se.kcn-tv.ne.jp. 10 units (none with bathroom). ¥4,000 ($38) single; ¥7,200 ($69) double; ¥10,500 ($100) triple. Breakfast ¥600 ($5.70) extra; dinner ¥2,000 ($19) extra. AE, V. Bus: no. 1 from Kumamoto Station to Shinmachi stop, then a 2-min. walk. Take the narrow road between a bank and a big brick health center and then take the 1st left. It's on the left, on the corner. **Amenities:** Coin-op washer/dryer. *In room:* A/C, TV, hot-water pot w/tea, no phone.

**Toyoko Inn Kumamoto Shinshigai** ⟨Value⟩   Right in the middle of downtown near department stores and shopping, this business chain offers the usual tiny rooms and free perks that make it the number-one choice for budget travelers. Just a 2-minute walk away is Toyoko Inn Kumamoto Karashima Koen, 1–24 Koyaimamachi (ℂ **096/322-1045**), with an additional 153 rooms at the same price and with the same amenities.

3–25 Shinshigai, Kumamoto 860-0803. ℂ 096/324-1045. Fax 096/324-1046. www.toyoko-inn.com. 221 units. ¥6,090 ($58) single; ¥8,190 ($78) double or twin. Rates include Japanese breakfast. DC, MC, V. Streetcar: Karashima-cho (1 min.). Walk down Sunroad Shinshigai covered shopping arcade and take the 2nd left onto Sakae Dori. **Amenities:** Lobby computers w/free Internet access; nonsmoking rooms. *In room:* A/C, TV w/free movies, fridge, hot-water pot w/tea, hair dryer, safe, Washlet toilet, trouser press.

## WHERE TO DINE

Kumamoto's specialties include *dengaku* (tofu, and sometimes taro and fish, coated with bean paste and grilled on a fire), *karashi renkon* (lotus root that has been boiled, filled with a mixture of bean paste and mustard, and then deep-fried), and *basashi* (raw horse meat sliced thin and then dipped in soy sauce flavored with ginger or garlic).

## EXPENSIVE

**Tao-Li** ⟨★⟩ NOUVELLE CANTONESE   This sophisticated contemporary restaurant in the heart of downtown serves Cantonese cuisine, though with a nouvelle twist to such standards as sweet-and-sour pork and Peking duck. Set meals are the way to go with the English-language menu; the Yamucha (dim sum) set lunch (¥2,100/$20), for example, offers an appetizer, soup, sautéed vegetables, rice or noodles, and a dessert along with fried, steamed, and crispy-fried dumplings. There must be a minimum of two persons, however, for the set dinners.

Hotel Nikko Kumamoto, 2–1 Kamitori-cho. ℂ **096/211-1662.** Set lunches ¥1,600–¥2,100 ($15–$20); set dinners ¥4,410–¥15,750 ($42–$150). AE, DC, MC, V. Daily 11:30am–2:30pm and 5–9:30pm (last order). Streetcar: Toricho-suji (1 min.).

## MODERATE

⑧ **Aoyagi** 🎋 LOCAL SPECIALTIES   Everyone in Kumamoto knows this restaurant, located in the downtown area just off the Shimotori covered shopping arcade. The modern building has four floors of dining with seating on tatami or at low tables with leg wells. There are photos outside the front door and in the menu showing dishes of basashi, eel, *kamameshi* (rice casseroles), and other local specialties. There's a vegetarian set dinner for ¥2,000 ($19) that includes dengaku and renkon and is very tasty, while the ¥5,250 set dinner includes all the local favorites. There's also a Ladies Sushi Set (¥1,600/$15). Set lunches center on kamameshi and sushi.

1–2–10 Shimotori. ℂ **096/353-0311.** Set lunches ¥1,000–¥2,700 ($9.50–$26); set dinners ¥1,600–¥5,250 ($15–$50). AE, MC, V. Daily 11:30am–10pm. Streetcar: Toricho-suji (2 min.). Walk through the Shimotori shopping arcade 2 blocks to Sannenzakadori St. (just past Daiei) and turn right; it's in the 2nd block on the right.

⑨ **Senri** 🎋🎋 LOCAL SPECIALTIES/VARIED JAPANESE   You can try Kumamoto's local dishes at this restaurant right in Suizenji Garden, available from a Japanese menu featuring set meals. For lunch, you can choose main dishes like eel, river fish, or tempura, served with side dishes of vegetable, soup, rice, and tea. Or order the Kyodo-ryori Course, which includes local specialties such as fried lotus, basashi, and dengaku. Dinners include the same items as lunch plus extra dishes. For a splurge, order kaiseki at least 1 day in advance. Dining is in small tatami rooms; choice rooms face the garden.

Suizenji Garden. ℂ **096/381-1415.** Reservations recommended, a must for kaiseki. Set dinner ¥3,150 ($30); set lunches ¥2,100–¥3,150 ($20–$30); kaiseki set meals from ¥5,000 ($48). No credit cards. Daily 11am–2pm and 5–9pm. Streetcar: Suizenji-Koen-mae; Senri has its own entrance to the right of Suizenji Garden's main gate and also an entrance in Suizenji Garden.

## INEXPENSIVE

**Fontana di Otani** ITALIAN/CONTINENTAL   Kumamoto Station is a culinary wasteland (which is sure to change once the Shinkansen rolls in), so this casual coffee shop in one of Kumamoto's most well-known hotels is your best bet here. Its menu features lighter fare such as spaghetti, curry, and sandwiches, available all day, as well as a very reasonably priced set lunch (served to 2pm) that includes a trip through a salad bar. The set dinner (available 5–9pm) gives a choice of main dish, like sautéed salmon in a pine nut sauce or roasted beef filet and mushrooms in a red-wine sauce, along with side dishes.

Hotel New Otani Kumamoto, 1–13–1 Kasuga. ℂ **096/326-1111.** Main dishes ¥1,050–¥1,365 ($10–$13); set lunch ¥1,300 ($12); set dinner ¥2,500 ($24). AE, DC, MC, V. Daily 11:30am–10pm. A 1-min. walk from Kumamoto Station, to the left.

**Merry Wish** 🎋 *Finds* ORGANIC JAPANESE   Although its location is not convenient to either Kagoshima Station or downtown (it lies on the streetcar route between them), people who like healthy, organic meals go out of their way to dine at this restaurant, simply decorated with rough wooden floors, jazz background music, and tables overlooking a canal. It's located at the back of a complex of Edo-Era buildings, which also contain an organic health-food store and shops selling natural, environmentally friendly products. Although set lunches change daily, they always include a

vegetarian choice. Other set meals offer a choice of fish or chicken, along with bread, rice, or *genmai* (unpolished brown rice).

15 Nakatoji-machi. (✆ **096/323-1552**. Set lunches ¥1,260 – ¥1,575 ($12–$15); set dinners ¥3,675 – ¥5,250 ($35–$50). AE, MC, V. Daily 11am–2pm and 5–9:30pm (last order). Streetcar: Gofukumachi (1 min.). Head west on the street beside the fire station (if you're coming from Kagoshima Station, it's ahead around the bend), and take the 1st left at the stoplight; it will be on your right.

**220 Tateki** ⚘ KUSHIAGE Located on a street filled with striptease clubs (be sure to match the kanji in appendix C with the sign outside the door—otherwise you'll get more than skewered food), Tateki serves *kushiage,* or skewered meats and vegetables. Although kushiage isn't unusual cuisine in Japan, this restaurant's method of cooking and serving it is—instead of counter seating, behind which the cook prepares your food, here you sit on tatami while a waiter in a beret kneels at your personal hibachi and grills your meal right in front of you. The least-expensive set dinner comes with 10 sticks of meat and vegetables plus appetizer, salad, and soba; the other two set dinners add one or two sticks along with more side dishes. The set lunch consists of seven sticks, two sauces, rice, soup, appetizer, and salad.

Kaishika Building, 1–11–8 Shimotori. (✆ **096/325-4989**. Set lunch ¥1,050 ($10); set dinner ¥2,100 – ¥4,200 ($20–$40). No credit cards. Daily 11:30am–11pm. Streetcar: Kumamotojo-mae (5 min.). Walk east on Ginza Dori 3 blocks, turn right into the Shimotori shopping arcade, and after 1 block turn right onto an unmarked street called Korinjidori; Tateki will be on the left toward the back of the 2nd (brick) building with a statue of a dog outside.

## 5 Kagoshima ⟨★⟩

1,483km (927 miles) SW of Tokyo; 315km (197 miles) S of Fukuoka; 197km (123 miles) S of Kumamoto; 343km (214 miles) SW of Beppu

With a population of 600,000 residents and capital of Kagoshima Prefecture, Kagoshima is a city of palm trees, flowering trees and bushes, wide avenues, and people who are like the weather—warm, mild-tempered, and easygoing. The city spreads along Kinko Bay and boasts one of the most unusual bay vistas in the world—Sakurajima, an active volcano, rising from the waters. During summer vacation (July 21–Aug), there are nightly fireworks displays over the bay (with a huge one held the end of August). Kagoshima is also home to Sengan'en Garden, one of my favorite gardens in Japan.

Because of its relative isolation at the southern tip of Japan, far away from the capitals of Kyoto and Tokyo, Kagoshima has developed an independent spirit through the centuries that has fostered a number of great men and accomplishments. Foremost is the Shimadzu clan (also spelled Shimazu), a remarkable family that for 29 generations (almost 700 years) ruled over Kagoshima and its vicinity before the Meiji Restoration in 1868. Much of Japan's early contact with the outside world was via Kagoshima, first with China and then with the Western world. Japan's first contact with Christianity occurred in Kagoshima when St. Francis Xavier landed here in 1549; although he stayed only 10 months, he converted more than 600 Japanese to Christianity. Kagoshima is also where firearms were introduced to Japan.

By the mid–19th century, as the Tokugawa shogunate began losing strength and the confidence of the people, the Shimadzu family was already looking toward the future and the modernization of Japan. In the mid-1850s, the Shimadzus built the first Western-style factory in the country, employing 200 men to make cannons, glass, ceramics, land mines, ships, and farming tools. In 1865, while Japan's doors were still

officially closed to the outside world and all contact with foreigners was forbidden, the Shimadzus smuggled 19 young men to Britain so they could learn foreign languages and technology. After these men returned to Japan, they became a driving force in the Meiji Restoration and Japan's modernization.

Another historical figure who played a major role during the Meiji Restoration was Saigo Takamori, who was born in Kagoshima Prefecture. A philosopher, scholar, educator, and poet, he helped restore Emperor Meiji to power, but because he was also a samurai, he subsequently became disillusioned when the ancient rights of the samurai class were rescinded and the wearing of swords was forbidden. He led a force of samurai against the government in what is called the Seinan Rebellion but was defeated. He then withdrew to Shiroyama in Kagoshima, where he committed suicide in 1877. Today, Saigo has many fans among Japanese, who still visit the cave on Shiroyama Hill where he committed suicide.

## ESSENTIALS

**GETTING THERE    By Plane**    You can reach Kagoshima from Tokyo (flight time: 1 hr. 50 min.), Osaka (1 hr. 10 min.), and Sapporo (2 hr. 35 min.) in addition to several other cities in Japan. The regular **JAL** and **ANA** fare from Tokyo is ¥33,300 ($314), but Skymark Airlines (© **03/3433-7670** in Tokyo, or 099/223-2340 in Kagoshima), based in Fukuoka, offers four flights daily from Tokyo's Haneda Airport for ¥25,500 ($243). The airport is linked to Kagoshima Chuo Station in 1 hour by **limousine bus**, which departs every 10 to 15 minutes and costs ¥1,200 ($11).

**By JR Train**    Thanks to the new Kyushu Shinkansen Tsubame, which presently links Kagoshima with Shin-Yatsushiro but will eventually stretch the whole length between Kagoshima and Fukuoka, travel time is approximately 7½ hours from **Tokyo** (if you have a Rail Pass, travel time will be slower because you can't take the Nozomi), 5 hours from **Osaka,** 2 hours and 11 minutes from **Fukuoka,** 1 hour from **Kumamoto,** and 2 hours and 10 minutes from **Miyazaki.** Tickets from Tokyo cost ¥25,100 ($240) for an unreserved seat, ¥9,420 ($90) from Fukuoka, and ¥5,550 ($53) from Kumamoto. All trains travel to Kagoshima Chuo (Central) Station. Trains from Miyazaki also stop at Kagoshima Station.

**By Bus**    Buses connect Kyushu's cities more cheaply than the train. From Fukuoka's Tenjin Station, 24 buses depart daily and cost ¥5,300 ($50) one-way for the 4-hour trip; from Miyazaki it takes almost 3 hours and costs ¥2,700 ($26).

**VISITOR INFORMATION**    Before departing Tokyo or Narita or Kansai international airports, stop by the Tourist Information Center to pick up the leaflet called "Kagoshima and Vicinity," which includes information on Ibusuki and Chiran, or download it from JNTO's website at www.jnto.go.jp by looking under "Regional Tourist Guides."

In Kagoshima, there's a Tourist Information Center at **Kagoshima Chuo Station** (© **099/253-2500;** open daily 8:30am–7pm) near the East Exit, as well as at the airport (© **0995/58-2740;** open daily 7am–9pm). They have good English-language maps and a hefty guide that covers everything from public transportation to recommended sightseeing itineraries.

The **Kagoshima Prefectural Tourist Office** is located on the third floor of the Sangyo Kaikan Building, 9–1 Meizan-cho (© **099/223-5771;** open Mon–Fri 8:30am–5:15pm), where you can obtain information on the city as well as the prefecture, including Ibusuki and Chiran. To find the office, take the streetcar to the Asahi-Dori stop and

then walk southeast (toward the bay); the Sangyo Kaikan Building is on your left in the second block. More information is available at www.city.kagoshima.lg.jp/webguide/kago_kanko.nsf.

**INTERNET ACCESS**    **Comic Buster,** 3–1 Chuo-cho (© **099/250-6369**), is about a 1-minute walk to the left after exiting from Kagoshima Chuo Station's east exit, on the fourth floor next to Sunkus convenience store. Open 24 hours, it charges ¥60 (55¢) for 10 minutes.

**MAIL**    Kagoshima's main post office (© **099/254-0288**), where you can send letters and packages and obtain cash through ATMs, is located just north of Kagoshima Chu Station, past the Amu Plaza. Its ATMs are open Monday to Friday 7am to 11pm, Saturday 9am to 9pm, and Sunday 9am to 7pm.

**ORIENTATION & GETTING AROUND**    Downtown Kagoshima lies between Kagoshima Chuo Station and Kinko Bay, northeast of the station, with **Tenmonkan-Dori** (a covered shopping street) serving as the heart of the city.

You can walk from the station to downtown in about 20 minutes, but the city is also easy to get around by **streetcar** and **bus.** There are two streetcar lines (fare: ¥160/$1.50), as well as two types of buses—City View buses and Kagoshima City buses. The **Kagoshima City buses** are regular buses used as commuter transportation by the people living here, while the **City View buses** are geared toward visiting tourists. Running every 30 minutes from 9am to 5pm daily (to 5:30pm daily mid-July through Aug), the City View buses look like old-time streetcars, have English-language announcements, and travel a 14km (9-mile) circuit through the city, beginning at Kagoshima Chuo Station (with departures on the hour and half-hour). They stop at all tourist sights, including Sengan'en, Sakurajima Ferry Terminal and Kagoshima Aquarium, and Tenmonkan covered shopping street. The fare is ¥180 ($1.70), half fare for children, and you pay when you get off.

If you think you'll be doing a lot of traveling by streetcar and bus (including City View buses), invest in a 1-day pass for ¥600 ($5.70), half fare for children, allowing unlimited travel on Kagoshima's two streetcar lines and on City View and Kagoshima City buses. Passes can be purchased at the tourist office in Kagoshima Chuo Station and aboard buses and streetcars.

## WHAT TO SEE & DO
### THE TOP ATTRACTIONS

**MOUNT SAKURAJIMA** *&*    With ties to Naples, Italy, as its sister city, Kagoshima bills itself the "Naples of the Orient." That's perhaps stretching things a bit, but Kagoshima is balmy most of the year and even has its own Mount Vesuvius—Mount Sakurajima, an active volcano across Kinko Bay that has erupted 30 times through recorded history and continues to puff steam into the sky and occasionally cover the city with fine soot and ash. In 1914, Sakurajima had a whopper of an eruption and belched up three billion tons of lava. When the eruption was over, the townspeople were surprised to discover that the flow was so great it now blocked the 500m-wide (1,666-ft.) channel separating the volcano from a neighboring peninsula—Sakurajima, which had once been an island, was now part of the mainland.

Magnificent from far away and impressive if you're near the top, Sakurajima can be visited by **ferry,** which departs from the Sakurajima Ferry Terminal. The terminal is about an 8-minute walk from downtown Kagoshima or the Shiyakusho-mae streetcar

## ⌒Moments  Evening Cruises

One of the most popular ways to enjoy summer nights in Kagoshima is on a boat cruise of Kinko Bay, offered mid-July through August every evening from 7 to 9pm (except for a few days during Obon in mid-Aug), the highlight of which are fireworks over the water. Boats depart from the Kagoshima side of the Sakurajima Ferry Terminal and charge ¥1,000 ($9.50) for adults, half fare for children. Call ⓒ 099/293-2525 for more information.

---

stop, or a 2-minute walk from the Kagoshima Suizokukan-mae/Sakurajima-sanbashi City View bus stop. Ferries run 24 hours, departing every 10 to 15 minutes during the day and about once an hour through the night. The 15-minute trip to Sakurajima costs ¥150 ($1.45) for adults, ¥80 (75¢) for children. Upon reaching Sakurajima, stop off at the small **tourist counter** (ⓒ 099/293-4333; open daily 8:30am–noon and 1–5pm) in the ferry terminal for a map of the island and information about buses to Furusato Onsen and beyond.

There are lava fields with walking paths near Sakurajima's ferry pier. The **Nagisa Lava Trail** is a 3km (1.8-mile) trail that starts near the pier and travels past huge lava boulders and pine trees (many, unfortunately, dying of disease). From the nearby **Sakurajima Visitor Center** (ⓒ 099/293-2443), with displays relating the history and natural history of Sakurajima, longer trails lead to the **Karasujima Observation Point.**

Another fun thing to do on Sakurajima is visit **Furusato Onsen** 𝆑𝆑, at the Furusato Kanko Hotel (ⓒ 099/221-3111), with open-air hot-spring baths set amid lava rocks right beside the sea. It also has an outdoor seawater swimming pool with a sunning terrace (presently closed due to damage from a typhoon; management isn't sure if it will reopen), an indoor 25m (82-ft.) lap pool heated with hot-spring water, and indoor hot-spring baths with windows overlooking the bay. You wear your swimsuit in the pools but should completely disrobe and wear only the provided white *yukata* (cotton kimono) when using the outdoor bath (an English-language handout provides guidelines). Furosato Onsen is open from 6am to 9:30pm. Note, however, that various parts of the onsen are closed for cleaning on different days of the week: The outdoor bath is closed Monday and Thursday until 2:30pm; the indoor hot-spring bath is closed Wednesday to 1:30pm; and the indoor hot-spring pool is closed the whole day Wednesday. Admission is ¥1,050 ($10) including yukata; bring your own towel or buy one for another ¥210 ($2). You can reach Furusato Onsen by taking the **free Furusato Kanko Hotel shuttle bus** departing from the Sakurajima Ferry Terminal every 30 minutes from 8:45am to 5pm (no service 12:20–2:20pm). Otherwise, take the **Kagoshima Kotsu Bus** that departs once an hour from the ferry terminal, costing ¥290 ($2.75) for the 15-minute trip. For more information on the Furusato Kanko Hotel, see "Where to Stay," below.

**Guided Tours of Sakurajima**    Because Sakurajima is sparsely populated with only limited public transportation, you might want to join a 6-hour tour that visits lava fields, lookout points (including the Yunohira lookout point halfway up the volcano), a shrine half-buried in lava, and other sights. Tours depart daily from Kagoshima Chuo Station's bus stop no. 8 at 9:30am and cost ¥1,900 ($18) for adults, half price for children. Call ⓒ 099/247-2333 for more information.

**SENGAN'EN GARDEN** ✿✿✿    Whereas Sakurajima, rising dramatically out of the bay, is Kagoshima's best-known landmark, **Sengan'en,** 9700–1 Yoshino-cho (© **099/ 247-1551**), is its most widely visited attraction. The grounds of a countryside villa, it's a garden laid out more than 300 years ago by the Shimadzu clan, incorporating Sakurajima and Kinko Bay into its design scheme in a principle known as borrowed landscape. There's a lovely grove of bamboo, a waterfall located a 30-minute walk up a nature trail with good views over the bay, and the requisite pond, but my favorite is a particularly idyllic spot where the 21st lord of the Shimadzu family held famous poem-composing garden parties. Guests seated themselves on stones beside a gently meandering rivulet and were requested to have completed a poem by the time a cup filled with sake came drifting by on the tiny brook. Ah, those were the days! Today it remains Japan's only garden with its original poem-composing garden (called Kyokusui) still intact.

The good life is also apparent in the **Iso Residence,** which was built as a villa by the Shimadzu clan about 350 years ago and became the family's main residence when the Meiji Restoration made feudal lords obsolete. Now only one-third its original size, the stately manor can be viewed by joining a tour conducted every 20 minutes and given in Japanese only (but with an English-language information sheet). You'll see 11 of the villa's 25 rooms, including a bedroom, a bathroom, a dressing room, living quarters, and reception rooms; throughout are furnishings and artifacts that once belonged to the Shimadzu clan. Ceremonial green tea and a sweet are included with the tour, served in a room with a view of an inner pond and garden. The 32nd generation of the Shimadzu family, incidentally, now resides in Kagoshima.

A must after visiting the garden, and included in the admission price to Sengan'en, is the **Shoko Shuseikan Museum,** located next to the garden. Built in the mid-1850s as Japan's first industrial factory, it houses items relating to the almost 700-year history of the Shimadzu clan, including family heirlooms ranging from lacquerware to tea-ceremony objects, palanquins used to carry Shimadzu lords back and forth to Edo (present-day Tokyo; the trip from Kagoshima took 40–60 days), everyday items used by the family, and photographs. A new exhibit explores southern Kyushu's role in maritime trade and the scope of the Shuseikan Project in its manufacture of cannons, textiles, and other products. In all, you'll probably spend at least 2 hours seeing everything, especially if you stop off at souvenir shops selling Satsuma glassware, pongee silk, and other Kagoshima products.

Sengan'en and the Shoko Shuseikan Museum are open daily from 8:30am to 5:30pm (to 5:20pm in winter); Iso Residence is open daily from 9am to 4:40pm (last tour). Admission to Sengan'en and Shoko Shuseikan Museum is ¥1,000 ($9.50) for adults and ¥500 ($4.75) for children. Tours of the residence are an extra ¥500 ($4.75) for adults and ¥250 ($2.40) for children. To reach Sengan'en, which is on the edge of town to the north, take the City View bus (32 min. from Kagoshima Chuo Station) to the Sengan'en-mae bus stop.

---

### ⌜Fun Fact  Mount Sakurajima's Produce

Mount Sakurajima's rich soil grows the world's largest radishes, averaging about 17 kilograms (37 lb.) but sometimes weighing in at as much as 36 kilograms (80 lb.), and the world's smallest oranges, only 3 centimeters (1¼ in.) in diameter.

## MORE TO SEE & DO

**KAGOSHIMA CITY AQUARIUM (SUIZOKU-KAN IOWORLD)**    This aquarium, within walking distance of downtown and located beside the Sakurajima Ferry Terminal at 3–1 Honko-Shinmachi (© **099/226-2233;** open daily 9:30am–6pm; you must enter by 5pm), concentrates on sea life from waters surrounding Kagoshima Prefecture. The largest tank is home to stingrays, bluefin tuna, Japanese anchovy, a whale shark, and other creatures from the Kuroshio (Black Current), which flows from the East China Sea past Kagoshima to the Pacific Ocean. Another tank contains squid, octopuses, the Japanese giant crab (the world's largest crab), and fish that inhabit the Kagoshima seas. Other highlights include the world's only display of tube worms (which inhabit the deep sea by hydrothermal vents), a 3-D movie of the surrounding seas, the world's largest eel, and a children's touch pool. Dolphins, which have access to open waters, are used only for educational shows (conducted in Japanese only). Expect to spend at least an hour here, more if you have kids. Admission is ¥1,500 ($14) for adults, ¥750 ($7.15) for junior-high and high-school students, and ¥350 ($3.35) for children. It's an 8-minute walk from the Suizokukan-guchi streetcar stop, or take the City View bus to the Kagoshima Suizokukan-mae/Sakurajima-sanbashi bus stop.

**MUSEUMS**    For an overview of Japanese history in general and Kagoshima Prefecture in particular, visit the ㉒㉑ **Kagoshima Prefectural Museum of Culture (Reimeikan),** 7–2 Shiroyama-cho (© **099/222-5100;** open Tues–Sun 9am–5pm; closed 25th of each month unless it falls on Sat or Sun). It occupies the former site of Tsurumaru Castle, of which only the stone ramparts and moat remain. Upon entering the museum, you'll walk over a glass floor above a map of Kagoshima Prefecture (much of it is islands). The museum then traces the history of the people of Kagoshima over the last 30,000 years, including the rise of the Shimadzu clan in the 11th century and Kagoshima's preeminence as a pottery center after Korean potters were brought here in the late 1500s. There are models of an 18th-century samurai settlement, Tsurumaru Castle and, best of all, Tenmonkan-Dori as it might have looked 70 years ago. The second floor is devoted to folklore and everyday life with bambooware, festival objects, and farming and fishing implements. The third floor shows Satsuma swords, pottery, scrolls, and paintings and has a hands-on learning room for children with old-fashioned toys and samurai outfits that can be tried on. You'll spend about an hour here. Admission is ¥300 ($2.85) for adults, ¥190 ($1.80) for college and high-school students, and ¥120 ($1.15) for children. To reach it, take the City View bus to the Satsuma Gishihi-mae stop in front of the museum. Or take the streetcar to Shiyakusho-mae stop; it's a 4-minute walk inland.

Only a few minutes' walk away from the Reimeikan is the **Kagoshima City Museum of Art (Kagoshima Shiritsu Bijitsukan),** 4–36 Shiroyma-cho (© **099/ 224-3400;** open Tues–Sun 9:30am–6pm), which has a collection of Western-style works by artists from Kagoshima Prefecture. Look for the portrait of Saigo Takamori, painted by Masayoshi Tokonomi, to the left upon entering the permanent gallery. A small selection of paintings by Western artists is also displayed (Pissarro, Monet, Renoir, Matisse, Kandinsky, Picasso, Warhol), as well as decorative art including the famous Satsuma pottery and cut glass. You can see everything in about 20 minutes. Admission is ¥200 ($1.90) for adults, ¥150 ($1.45) for college and high-school students, and ¥100 (95¢) for children. To reach the museum, take the City View bus to

Saigo Douzou-mae; the museum is a minute's walk away to the right of the statue of Saigo. Or take the streetcar to Asahi-dori and take the street beside the Minami-Nippon bank; it's a 5-minute walk ahead.

Although it's not as conveniently located, the **Nagashima Museum** ⟨⟨⟨, 3–42–18 Take (© **099/250-5400**; open daily 9am–5pm), is a very worthwhile private museum on a hill high atop the city with great views of Sakurajima and Kagoshima. While its focus is mostly works by Kagoshima artists like Seiki Kuroda, it also contains some works by well-known Western artists like Picasso, Braque, Kandinsky, Renoir, and Chagall, as well as pottery from South America. But most impressive, in my opinion, is an outstanding collection of mainly 19th-century white Satsuma pottery, including many pieces that were originally imported to London, Paris, and New York, and the more utilitarian 17th- to 20th-century black Satsuma pottery. An hour is enough time to see everything, but try to time your visit so you can eat lunch in the museum's French restaurant **Camellia** (open 11am–3pm with set meals for ¥2,100 and ¥2,625/$20 and $25), which has great views over the city. Admission to the museum is ¥1,000 ($9.50) for adults, ¥800 ($7.60) for college and high-school students, and ¥400 ($3.80) for children. You'll have to take a taxi to get here; it's about a 10-minute ride from Kagoshima Chuo Station.

## A SIDE TRIP TO THE GARDENS OF CHIRAN

If you have an extra morning or afternoon, I suggest taking an excursion to **Chiran** ⟨⟨, a small village 31km (19 miles) south of Kagoshima. Surrounded by wooded hills and rows of neatly cultivated tea plantations, it's one of 102 castle towns that once bordered the Shimadzu kingdom during the Edo Period. Although the castle is no longer standing, seven old gardens and samurai houses have been carefully preserved.

Apparently, the village headman of Chiran had the opportunity to travel with his lord Shimadzu in the mid-1700s to Kyoto and Edo, taking with him some of his local samurai as retainers. The headman and his retainers were so impressed with the sophisticated culture of Kyoto and Edo that they invited gardeners to Chiran to construct a series of modestly sized gardens on the samurai estates surrounding the castle.

Some of these gardens remain and are located on a delightful road nicknamed **Samurai Lane,** which is lined with moss-covered stone walls and hedges. Since descendants of the samurai are still living in the houses, only the gardens are open to the public. There are two types of gardens represented: One, belonging to the Mori family, is of the miniature artificial-hill style, in which a central pond symbolizes the sea, and rocks represent the mountains; the others are "dry" gardens, in which the sea is symbolized not by water but by white sand that is raked to give it the effect of rippling water. The gardens are masterful demonstrations of the borrowed-landscape technique, in which surrounding mountains and scenery are incorporated into the general garden design. Although the gardens are small, they are exquisite and charming. Notice, for example, how the tops of hedges are cut to resemble rolling hills, blending with the shapes of mountains in the background.

The seven gardens open to the public are indicated by a white marker in front of each entry gate. All seven can be visited for ¥500 ($4.75) for adults, ¥300 ($2.85) for children, and they're open daily from 9am to 5pm. Plan on about an hour to see them. For more information on the samurai gardens, call © **0993/83-2511.**

I also recommend a visit to Chiran's **Peace Museum for Kamikaze Pilots (Heiwa Kaikan;** 1788 kori; © **0993/83-2525;** open daily 9am–5pm), dedicated to the mostly young pilots who trained in Chiran for World War II suicide missions, steering bomb-laden planes into Allied warships and other targets. In addition to kamikaze aircraft and uniforms, it displays photographs of 1,036 pilots just before their departures, along with farewell letters and personal memorabilia. A film shows actual footage of the kamikaze pilots in action. Although there isn't much in English, there's an English-language pamphlet, and volunteers are sometimes on hand to explain the museum (to be sure a guide is available, call for a reservation). You'll spend about an hour here. Admission is ¥500 ($4.75) for adults, ¥300 ($2.85) for children.

Chiran's samurai gardens can be reached in about 1 hour and 12 minutes by a bus that departs across the street from Kagoshima Chuo Station at stop no. 23 (the tourist office in the station has a timetable and a map showing bus departures). There are seven buses a day, including departures at 9:07am, 10:17am, and 11:27am, and the ride costs ¥860 ($8.10) to the Bukeyashiki-Iriguchi bus stop. The same bus then travels onward to the Peace Museum (bus stop: Tokkokannon-Iriguchi) in 7 minutes. There are also three buses a day between the samurai gardens and Ibusuki (see section 6, later in this chapter), with the fare costing ¥940 ($8.95).

## SHOPPING

Local Kagoshima products include *oshima tsumugi,* beautiful silk made into such items as clothing, handbags, and wallets; *shochu,* an alcoholic drink made from such ingredients as sweet potatoes and drunk either on the rocks or mixed with boiling water; furniture, statues, and chests made from **yaku cedar;** and **Satsuma pottery**— probably Kagoshima's most famous product. It has been produced in the Kagoshima area for more than 380 years. Satsuma pottery comes in two styles: black and white. White Satsuma pottery is more elegant and was used by former lords; the black pottery was used by the townspeople in everyday life.

A good place to shop for local items is the **Kagoshima Brands Shop,** downtown in the Sangyo Kaikan Building (the same building housing the Kagoshima Prefectural Tourist Office) at 9–1 Meizan-cho (© **099/225-6120;** open daily 9am–6pm, closed the first and third Sun of the month). This one-room shop offers tinware, handmade knives, Satsuma pottery, glassware, oshima tsumugi, yaku cedar, shochu, and other locally made items. To reach it, take the streetcar to the Asahi-Dori stop, from which the shop is a 1-minute walk away toward the bay.

The most famous cake of Kagoshima (the one all Japanese tourists must buy before returning home) is *karukan,* a delicious spongy white cake made from rice, with Chinese and Korean origins. The most famous maker of karukan today is ㉒㉒ **Akashiya,** 4–16 Kinseicho (© **099/226-0431;** open daily 9am–8pm), which began selling the cakes 150 years ago. It has the solemnity of a first-rate jewelry store and is just as refined. It's located on the side street to the right of Yamakataya department store, a 1-minute walk from the Asahi-Dori streetcar stop. Although cakes are now available made from beans and other ingredients, old-timers insist that only the plain white ones are the real thing. A small round one, good for a snack, costs ¥147 ($1.40).

## WHERE TO STAY
### EXPENSIVE
**Castle Park Hotel (Shiroyama Kanko Hotel)** ⭐⭐    Kagoshima's foremost hotel sits 106m (353 ft.) high atop the wood-covered Shiroyama Hill and commands a great

> **_Tips_  A Note on Japanese Symbols**
>
> Many establishments and attractions in Japan do not have signs in Roman (English-language) letters. Those that don't are indicated in this guide with an oval with a number that corresponds to a number in appendix C showing the Japanese symbols. Thus, to find the Japanese symbol for, say, **Furusato Kanko Hotel** (below), refer to no. 223 in appendix C.

view of the city below and Sakurajima across the bay. Opened more than 40 years ago but updated, it offers pleasant and comfortable rooms, the most recommended (and more expensive) of which face the volcano and city with the best views in town. Other pluses include hot-spring (including open-air) baths with views of Kinko Bay, a free English-language movie shown nightly on a screen off the lobby, and good restaurants that take advantage of the hotel's views and garden-like setting (I especially like the buffet restaurant with its outdoor terrace and the microbrewery with its summer beer garden). In short, this is a great respite from city life, and to offset the hotel's main drawback—an isolated location away from the city center—it offers free shuttle buses to Tenmonkan-Dori in the heart of the city and Kagoshima Chuo Station every hour or more frequently (it's also served by City View bus).

41–1 Shinshoin-cho, Kagoshima 890-8586. ✆ **099/224-2211.** Fax 099/224-2222. info@shiroyama-g.co.jp. 365 units. ¥10,000–¥12,000 ($95–$114) single; ¥20,000–¥32,000 ($190–$305) double or twin. Rates include service charge. AE, DC, MC, V. Taxi or free shuttle bus 12 min. from Kagoshima Chuo Station. City View Bus: Shiroyama (1 min.). **Amenities:** 4 restaurants (Japanese, Chinese, Western, Italian); 1 lounge; 1 bar; outdoor/indoor hot-spring baths; sauna; souvenir shop selling locally made crafts; salon; room service (10pm–midnight); in-room massage; same-day laundry/dry-cleaning service; nonsmoking rooms; bakery; movie theater. _In room:_ A/C, TV w/pay movies, dataport, minibar, hot-water pot w/tea and coffee, hair dryer, trouser press.

㉓ **Furusato Kanko Hotel** ✻ _(Finds_    Although this ryokan on Sakurajima is inconvenient for sightseeing, it's great for relaxation. It boasts open-air hot-spring baths set amid rocks right beside the sea, an indoor 25m (82-ft.) lap pool heated with hot springs, and indoor hot-spring baths overlooking the sea (see "What to See & Do," earlier in this chapter; hotel guests are charged a one-time rental fee of ¥210/$2 for the bathing yukata). Afterward, retire to the shrinelike Meditation Room for spiritual cleansing as well. Rooms are all Japanese-style, most with balconies overlooking great sea views. Some even boast views from their bathrooms, while the very best (and most expensive) have private terraces with outdoor hot-spring baths. Breakfast features _kamameshi_ (rice casseroles) made with hot-spring water; dinner consists mainly of seafood, _tonkotsu_ (boiled pork), and other local specialties. Movies (sometimes English-language) are shown nightly in a small theater. This is a great getaway.

1076 Furusato-cho, Kagoshima 891-1592. ✆ **099/221-3111.** Fax 099/221-2345. info@furukan.co.jp. 42 units. ¥13,800–¥21,150 ($131–$201) per person. ¥2,100 ($20) extra per person weekends and holidays; ¥5,000 ($48) extra per person Golden Week and New Year's. Rates include breakfast, dinner, and service charge. AE, DC, MC, V. For directions to Furusato Kanko Hotel, see "Mount Sakurajima," earlier in this chapter. **Amenities:** Restaurant (Japanese, serving lunch only); indoor pool; great indoor/outdoor hot-spring baths; game room; in-room massage; meditation room. _In room:_ A/C, TV, minibar, hot-water pot w/tea, hair dryer, safe.

## MODERATE

**JR Kyushu Hotel Kagoshima**    Convenient to Kagoshima Chuo Station (you can enter it right from the station), this business hotel offers clean, mostly single rooms

(there are only 12 twins), devoid of character but equipped with everything you might need, including larger than usual desks. The biggest plus besides convenience: Japan Rail Pass holders receive a 10% discount.

1–1–2 Take, Kagoshima 890-0045. ⓒ **099/213-8000.** Fax 099/213-8029. www.jrhotelgroup.com. 138 units. ¥6,900 ($66) single; ¥12,600 ($120) twin. AE, DC, MC, V. Station: Kagoshima Chuo Station (west exit, 1 min.). **Amenities:** In-room massage; same-day laundry/dry-cleaning service; nonsmoking rooms. *In room:* A/C, TV, dataport, fridge, hot-water pot w/tea, hair dryer, Washlet toilet, trouser press.

### Kagoshima Tokyu Hotel *(Kids)*

This first-rate medium-priced hotel is in a newer area of Kagoshima, smack-dab on the waterfront with a good view of the volcano, even from its lobby lounge. Its twins and doubles face the water with balconies—great for watching the sun rise over Sakurajima. Note that singles, however, all face inland. All feature tempurapedic pillows, focused bed lights, and LCD TVs. Outdoor pools, including a children's pool and an outdoor hot-spring pool and Jacuzzi open year-round (you wear your bathing suits here), are free to hotel guests, making this a good bet for families. In summer, take advantage of the outdoor, seaside beer terrace with its good view. The main disadvantage, however, is that it's a 15-minute bus ride from the station and downtown.

22–1 Kamoike Shinmachi, Kagoshima 890-0064. ⓒ **099/257-2411.** Fax 099/257-6083. www.tokyuhotels.co.jp. 206 units. ¥9,817–¥16,170 ($93–$154) single; ¥20,790 ($198) double; ¥17,325–¥26,565 ($165–$253) twin. Rates include service charge. AE, DC, MC, V. Bus: from platform 15 from Kagoshima Chuo Station to Nokyo-kaikan-mae (2 min.). **Amenities:** 2 restaurants (Japanese, Western); 1 bar; 1 summer beer garden; outdoor pool; children's pool; outdoor hot-spring bath; Jacuzzi; concierge; shopping arcade; salon; room service (noon–9pm); in-room massage; same-day laundry/dry-cleaning service; nonsmoking rooms. *In room:* A/C, TV w/pay movies, minibar, hot-water pot w/tea, hair dryer, Washlet toilet.

### Roynet Hotel Kagoshima

This business hotel, opened in 2004, is located in the heart of downtown, with easy access from Kagoshima Chuo Station via streetcar passing right outside the front door. Check-in and checkout is accomplished via automatic machines, though humans are on hand to help guide you through the process. Note that rates below are for Roynet Hotel members, which requires just a ¥500 ($4.75) one-time membership fee, thereby shaving at least ¥2,700 ($70) off the price of a single room per night and ¥3,500 ($33) off the price of a double. Otherwise, this is your standard business hotel, with small rooms, LCD TVs, large desks, and special single rooms for ladies (reservations required) featuring tempurapedic pillows, free bottled water, terry-cloth robes, and female-oriented toiletries. Note that the cheapest singles and doubles are actually the same room, fine for one person but cramped for two.

5–3 Kinseicho, Kagoshima 890-0828. ⓒ **099/219-6655.** Fax 099/219-6668. 220 units. ¥7,300–¥7,800 ($70–$74) single; ¥9,000–¥12,800 ($86–$122) double; ¥13,800 ($131) twin. AE, DC, MC, V. Streetcar: Asahi Dori (1 min.). **Amenities:** Restaurant (Japanese); lobby computer w/free Internet access; in-room massage; coin-op laundry/dry cleaning service; nonsmoking rooms. *In room:* A/C, TV, dataport, fridge, hot-water pot w/tea and coffee, hair dryer, Washlet toilet.

## INEXPENSIVE

In addition to the choices here, there are two Toyoko Inns near the Tenmonkan Dori covered shopping street. **Toyoko Inn Kagoshima Tenmonkan No. 2,** 1–43 Higashi Sengoku-cho, Kagoshima 892-0842 (ⓒ **099/224-1045;** www.toyoko-inn.com), offers 231 single, twin, and double rooms along with the usual lobby computers with free Internet access, free domestic calls from lobby phones, and free movie channels. It charges ¥6,090 ($58) for a single and ¥8,190 ($78) for a double or twin, including

a Japanese breakfast. The nearby **Toyoko Inn Kagoshima Tenmonkan No. 1,** 3–6 Yamanoguchi-cho (📞 **099/219-1045**), is smaller, with only 120 single and double rooms and similar prices.

**Gasthof Hotel** ⋒   After traveling to Europe, the owner of this inexpensive, 40-year-old hotel decided to re-create the coziness of a German bed-and-breakfast with a cafe in the lobby, antiques in the hallway, and rooms that vary in decor, furniture, and bedspreads, including four-poster beds in some. Although it falls short, the Gasthof has a lot more character than a regular business hotel. The location near Kagoshima Chuo Station is convenient, and there's free coffee and a computer with free Internet access in the lobby. If you are lucky, the owner may even take you on a personal tour of his private Asian art museum, overflowing with priceless treasures from pottery to Buddha statues. Another plus are the six restaurants and Japanese *izakaya* (restaurant/bars) in the same building.

7–1 Chuo-cho, Kagoshima 890-0053. 📞 **099/252-1401.** Fax 099/252-1405. info@gasthof.jp. 48 units. ¥5,250 ($50) single; ¥8,925 ($85) double or twin; ¥12,600 ($120) triple. Breakfast ¥630 ($6) extra. AE, DC, MC, V. A 3-min. walk from Kagoshima Chuo Station. Take the underground passageway to wide, tree-lined Napoli Dori (beside Daiei department store), walk 3 blocks and turn left at the Mobil gas station; it's at the end of the street on the left. **Amenities:** 6 restaurants/bars; lobby computer w/free Internet access; in-room massage; same-day laundry/dry-cleaning service. *In room:* A/C, TV, fridge, hot-water pot w/tea, Washlet toilet.

**Nakazono Ryokan**   A member of the Japanese Inn Group, this simple, laid-back ryokan with simple Japanese-style rooms is located near Kagoshima Station (not to be confused with Kagoshima Chuo Station; trains arriving from Miyazaki make stops at Kagoshima Station but trains from Kumamoto do not), about a 10-minute walk from the Tenmonkan-Dori covered shopping street and a 3-minute walk from the Sakurajima ferry pier. Its English-speaking owner is knowledgeable about area sightseeing—he has even prepared handouts on how to get to Ibusuki and Chiran. No meals are served, but there's a communal refrigerator, and the owner will direct you to nearby restaurants or, if you wish, help you order delivery pizza or sushi.

1–18 Yasui-cho, Kagoshima 892-0815. 📞 **099/226-5125.** Fax 099/226-5126. www.satsuma.ne.jp/myhome/shindon. 10 units (none with bathroom). ¥4,200 ($40) single; ¥8,400 ($80) twin; ¥11,970 ($114) triple. Closed Aug 13–15. AE, V. Streetcar: Shiyakusho-mae (3 min.). Take the small alley that runs on the south side of a temple with a big bell and then the 1st left. **Amenities:** Free washer/coin-op dryer. *In room:* A/C, coin-op TV, hot-water pot w/tea.

## WHERE TO DINE

While in Kagoshima, be sure to try its local dishes, known as **Satsuma cooking** (Satsuma was the original name of the Kagoshima area). This style of cooking supposedly has its origins in food cooked on battlefields centuries ago; if that's the case, it certainly has improved greatly since then. Popular Satsuma specialties include *Satsuma-age* (ground fish mixed with tofu and sake and then deep-fried), *tonkotsu* (black pork that has been boiled for several hours in miso, shochu, and brown sugar—absolutely delicious), *sakezushi* (a rice dish flavored with sake and mixed with vegetables and seafood), and *Satsuma-jiru* (miso soup with chicken and locally grown vegetables including Sakurajima radishes). *Kibinago* is a small fish belonging to the herring family that can be caught in the waters around Kagoshima; a silver color with brown stripes, it's often eaten raw and arranged on a dish to resemble a chrysanthemum.

### EXPENSIVE

**Kumasotei** ⋒⋒ SATSUMA SPECIALTIES   Located in the city center, this restaurant specializes in local Satsuma dishes but carries them one step further by featuring

them as part of kaiseki set meals. It reminds me more of a private home or ryokan since dining is in individual tatami rooms. If there isn't a crowd, you'll probably have your own private room; otherwise, you'll share. The main menu is in Japanese, but there's a smaller English-language menu with photos of the various set meals, which may include such local dishes as Satsuma-age, tonkotsu, Satsuma-jiru, kibinago, or sakezushi, as well as shabu-shabu.

6–10 Higashi Sengoku-cho. Ⓒ **099/222-6356.** Set dinners ¥3,150–¥10,500 ($30–$100); set lunches ¥1,890– ¥5,250 ($18–$50). AE, DC, MC, V. Daily 11am–2:30pm and 5–9:30pm (last order). Streetcar: Tenmonkan-Dori (4 min.). Walk through the Tenmonkan-Dori covered shopping street (the one with The Tenmonkan on it) 4 blocks and turn left; it will be on your right.

## MODERATE

(224) **Ajimori** ✿ BLACK PORK   This 30-year-old establishment specializes in pork from small black pigs, which the locals claim is more tender and succulent than regular pork. The restaurant is divided into two parts: the upper floors, with both table seating and private tatami rooms, serve Satsuma Kuroshabu, a Kagoshima specialty of black-pork shabu; the first floor is a casual dining room specializing in *tonkatsu,* breaded black-pork cutlet. If you order the Kuroshabu, you'll eat it just like the more common beef shabu-shabu, cooking it yourself at your table by dipping it into a boiling broth and then in raw egg or sauce. Portions are generous, but if you wish, you can also order tonkatsu as a side dish. Otherwise, go to the first floor for perhaps the lightest, best-tasting tonkatsu you'll ever have; the set lunches, available every day except Sundays and holidays, are a bargain.

13–21 Sennichi-cho. Ⓒ **099/224-7634.** Shabu set dinners ¥4,200–¥8,400 ($40–$80), shabu set lunch ¥3,150 ($30); tonkatsu set dinners ¥820–¥3,150 ($7.80–$30), tonkatsu set lunch ¥680 ($6.50). DC, MC, V accepted only for meals costing more than ¥10,000 ($95). Daily 11:30am–2:15pm (1:30pm last order for shabu) and 5:30–8:45pm (8pm last order for shabu). Streetcar: Tenmonkan-Dori (3 min.). Walk all the way through Tenmonkan-Dori (the one beside Takapla) and keep going past the koban police box onto Ginza St.; it's on the left just before the next arch with the eyeglasses motif.

**Iso Kuwahara-kan** CONTINENTAL   If you are sightseeing at Senang'en, have lunch in this pleasant, historic building constructed in a Western style and dating from 1904. Built for the Shimadzu clan to serve as an assay office, today it houses a Western restaurant specializing in set meals, with offerings that generally give a choice of a main dish—like seafood risotto, steak, and beef stew—along with side dishes.

9688–1 Yoshinocho. Ⓒ **099/248-5883.** Set dinners ¥3,500–¥5,000 ($33–$48); set lunches ¥1,600–¥3,000 ($15–$29). No credit cards. Wed–Mon 11am–2:30pm and 5:30–9pm (last order). City View Bus: Sengan'en-mae stop (1 min.).

## INEXPENSIVE

(225) **Aburi-Banya** KOREAN BARBECUE   Dolphin Port is a new shopping and dining complex just a few minutes' walk from the Sakurajima ferry pier and aquarium. More than a dozen restaurants on two levels here offer a wide variety of ethnic cuisine, including Japanese (conveyor-belt sushi, tempura, udon noodles), Chinese, Czech, and French. Aburi-Banya, on the second floor with exposed ceiling beams and bamboo shades separating tables, is a Korean barbecue restaurant, with individual charcoal grills at tables both inside and out (the latter with views of the harbor). Its set meals include various options of marinated meat, along with soup, *kimchi* (spicy cabbage), and rice.

5–4 Honko-Shinmachi. ⓒ 099/223-2915. Set dinners ¥1,800–¥2,660 ($17–$25); set lunches ¥1,280–¥2,180 ($12–$21). MC, V. Daily 11am–11:30pm (last order). Streetcar: Shiyakusho-mae (8 min.). City View Bus: Kagoshima Suizokukan-mae/Sakurajima-sanbashi (3 min.).

226 **Noboruya** *(Finds* RAMEN NOODLES    This popular, inexpensive restaurant in the center of town is Kagoshima's best-known *ramen* (noodle) shop, in business for 60 years. It's a simple place, occupying one room of a small, wooden home with one counter and an open kitchen. Since only one dish is served, there's no problem ordering. A big bowl of ramen comes with noodles (made fresh every day) and slices of pork, all seasoned with garlic (you can add extra garlic if you want). You also get as much pickled radish as you want (supposedly good for the stomach) and tea. As you eat your ramen at the counter, you can watch an army of women peeling garlic and cooking huge pots of noodles over gas flames—it's a great place to soak up local atmosphere.

2–15 Horie-cho. ⓒ 099/226-6697. Noodles ¥1,000 ($9.50). No credit cards. Mon–Sat 11am–7pm. Streetcar: Izuro-Dori (1 min.). Walk down the wide street marked by stone lanterns on each side (Miami Dori) and take the 1st right; Noboruya is at the end of the 2nd block on the left, with its entrance around the corner.

227 **No-no-Budou** *(Value* JAPANESE BUFFET    Of the dozen or so restaurants located on the fifth and sixth floors of Amu Plaza adjoining Kagoshima Chuo Station, this is one of the more interesting, featuring 70 dishes that change every few months, with various offerings of tempura, soups, salads, fish, noodles, vegetables, and much, much more. Evening buffets also include sashimi and sushi. There's a large nonsmoking section. Other choices in Amu Plaza run the gamut from pork shabu-shabu and tonkatsu to Italian and Chinese fare.

Amu Plaza, 5th floor; 1–1 Chuo-cho. ⓒ 099/206-7585. Dinner buffet ¥2,200 ($21); lunch buffet ¥1,600 ($15). AE, MC, V. Daily 11am–3pm and 5pm–9:30 (last order). Beside Kagoshima Chuo Station.

## 6 Southern Kyushu's Top Spa: Ibusuki ✦

50km (31 miles) S of Kagoshima

At the southern tip of the Satsuma Peninsula, **Ibusuki** is southern Kyushu's most famous hot-spring resort and is home to 30,000 residents. With a pleasant average temperature of 65°F (18°C), it's a region of lush vegetation, flowers, and palm trees. It also boasts Japan's best natural hot-sand bath and a good public beach, making it a good choice for a low-key vacation.

## ESSENTIALS

**GETTING THERE**    Ibusuki is approximately an hour from Kagoshima Chuo Station by **JR train,** with the fare costing ¥970 ($9.25) one-way. **Buses** depart from Kagoshima's Yamagataya Bus Center in the heart of the city (near the Asahi Dori streetcar stop) seven times a day (some make stops at Kagoshima Chuo Station before traveling onward), reaching Ibusuki's train station 1½ hours later and costing ¥850 ($8.10) one-way.

**VISITOR INFORMATION**    Ibusuki Tourist Information (ⓒ 0993/22-4114; open daily 9am–6pm) is located in Ibusuki Station. For online information, go to www.city.ibusuki.kagoshima.jp.

**GETTING AROUND**    The small town of Ibusuki is spread along the coast, and public **buses** run along the main streets. **Taxis** are also readily available. However,

probably the easiest way to get around is by **rental bike,** available at Ibusuki Station for ¥500 ($4.75) for 2 hours or ¥1,500 ($14) all day. With a valid Japan Rail Pass, rates are just ¥300 ($2.85) and ¥900 ($8.55) respectively. By bike it takes about 7 minutes to the Natural Sand Bath and about 25 minutes to public swimming beaches and Chiringashima.

## WHAT TO SEE & DO

**TAKING A HOT-SAND BATH**  The most popular thing to do in Ibusuki is to have yourself buried up to your neck in black sand at Yunohama Beach, heated naturally by hot springs that surface close to the ground before running into the sea. To take part, head to the **Natural Sand Bath (Suna Mushi Onsen)** ✦✦✦ (✆ 0993/ 23-3900; open daily 8:30am–noon and 1–9pm), a modern facility nicknamed Saraku by the locals (*saraku* has two meanings: to walk around and to enjoy the sand). Take the elevator up to the reception, pay ¥900 ($8.55) for the baths and rental yukata (add another ¥100/95¢ if you didn't bring a towel), change into the yukata in the dressing room, and then head down to the beach. One of the women there will dig you a shallow grave. Lie down, arrange your yukata so no vulnerable areas are exposed, and then lie still while she piles sand on top of you. It's quite a funny sight, actually, to see nothing but heads sticking out of the ground. The water, a hot 185°F (85°C), contains sodium chloride and is considered beneficial in alleviating rheumatism, arthritis, gastrointestinal troubles, neuralgia, and female disorders. It is also valued as a beauty treatment for the skin. After your 15-minute sand bath, go indoors for a relaxing, hot-spring bath and the sauna. The Natural Sand Bath is a 20-minute walk or 7-minute bike ride from Ibusuki Station; from the main exit, head straight down Chuo Dori to the beach and turn right. You can also take a bus to the Suna Mushi-kaikan stop.

**SWIMMING & HIKING**  Also on the beach, but on the opposite edge of town, is Ibusuki's popular public beach, Sun-Beach Ibusuki, as well as Chiringashima, a small, uninhabited island and national park. During low tide, you can walk to the island via sandbridge in about 10 minutes. Be sure to inquire beforehand what time the tide comes in, however, so you don't get stranded.

## WHERE TO STAY
### EXPENSIVE

㉘ **Hakusuikan Ryokan** ✦✦✦  A driveway lined with pine trees sets the mood for this modern, elegant, and resortlike ryokan right on the beach with landscaped lawns and one of the most impressive hot-spring baths I've ever seen. Established in 1960 and expanded over the years, the ryokan seems like a village, with corridors that stretch seemingly forever and serve as galleries for an extensive collection of antique Satsuma and Chinese pottery, calligraphy, and old photographs. The public bath—a reproduction of an Edo-Era hot-spring spa—is classy and refined, also designed like a small village with a large bathing area made of cypress wood and stone with pools of varying temperatures, a huge *rotenburo* (outdoor hot-spring pool), a sand bath, a steam room, and a replica Edo-Era sauna with a round dome. Even the dressing rooms are faithfully styled after the Edo Period, though naturally with all the latest conveniences.

Several room types are available. Least expensive are the 30 Western-style twins, all of which face inland and are rather ordinary looking. Better are the Japanese-style tatami rooms facing the sea, as well as the ryokan's 115 combination rooms, spacious with both beds and separate tatami areas and available in various price categories. Meals are served in a choice of restaurants. This place is the perfect getaway; you'll

want to change into your yukata as soon as you arrive. No wonder Prime Minister Koizumi chose this ryokan for a summit meeting with Korea.

Chirin-no-Sato, Ibusuki, Kagoshima-ken 891-0404. ☎ 0993/22-3131. Fax 0993/23-3860. www.hakusuikan.co.jp/en. 205 units. ¥15,750–¥36,750 ($150–$350) per person. ¥1,000–¥2,000 ($9.50–$19) extra on weekends. Rates include breakfast, dinner, and service charge. AE, DC, MC, V. Taxi: 5 min. from Ibusuki Station. (No public transportation.) **Amenities:** 4 restaurants (all Japanese); 1 coffee shop; 2 bars (including a shochu tasting bar); 2 lounges; 1 night-club; fantastic indoor/outdoor hot-spring baths; outdoor swimming pool; shopping arcade; in-room massage; same-day laundry/dry-cleaning service. *In room:* A/C, TV w/pay movies, dataport, minibar, hot-water pot w/tea, hair dryer, safe, Washlet toilet.

**Ibusuki Iwasaki Hotel** ⚐    This is Ibusuki's best-known spa hotel, a self-contained pink-colored resort on 50 hectares (125 acres) of lush tropical grounds with pleasant walking trails throughout. It's very popular with Japanese tour groups, both for its facilities that include huge public baths, outdoor swimming pools, a beach, and the Ibusuki Golf Club (hotel guests get discounts; or ask about golf packages), and for its evening entertainment. If you come during the off season, however, you have the hotel seemingly to yourself. Another plus is the resort's private, eclectic museum featuring Japanese artists painting in the Western style, some Western artists (Matisse, Gauguin), crafts from Papua New Guinea, and Satsuma pottery.

All rooms have either a full or partial view of the sea and a balcony; the best rooms also have views of the wonderful grounds, one of the resort's best features and well worth a stroll. The majority of rooms are twins (there are no singles) with rattan furniture. Not quite as nice are Japanese-style rooms, which are rather small and are located in an older building. In any case, nights here are nice, with the sound of waves and frogs croaking in the lotus pond.

3755 Juni-cho, Ibusuki, Kagoshima-ken 891-0493. ☎ 0993/22-2131. Fax 0993/24-3215. ibusuki@iwasakihotels. com. 390 units. ¥11,550–¥25,200 ($110–$240) twin, from ¥27,300 ($260) twin in peak season. AE, DC, MC, V. Taxi: 5 min. from Ibusuki Station. Bus (7 times daily): to Ibusuki Iwasaki Hotel. **Amenities:** 5 restaurants; 1 coffee shop; 1 casino/bar; 2 outdoor swimming pools (1 free; the other ¥1,000/$9.50); 1 children's pool; fitness room (fee: ¥500/$4.75); Ibusuki Golf Club; minigolf; outdoor lighted tennis court; indoor/outdoor hot-spring baths overlooking the sea; hot-sand baths (fee: ¥1,050/$10); Jacuzzi; bowling arcade; game center; rental bikes (¥525/$5 per 2 hr.); museum; shopping arcade; room service (7–9am and 6–10pm); in-room massage; same-day laundry/dry-cleaning service. *In room:* A/C, satellite TV w/pay movies, minibar, hot-water pot w/tea, hair dryer, safe, Washlet toilet.

## MODERATE

㉒㉙ **Kyuka-Mura Ibusuki** *Value*    This government-owned lodge is located right at the water's edge near the public beach (but a bit far from town) and offers reasonably priced, basic accommodations, making it a popular choice with Japanese families. During summer vacation months, on New Year's, in March during spring vacation, and in May during school trips, you should reserve 6 months in advance. At other times, it's relatively easy to get a room here. Rates are based on the type of room and meals you select. Cheapest are the eight Western-style rooms, which face inland and have toilets but no bathrooms, but I prefer the Japanese-style rooms for the same price (also with toilet only) that are the size of 7.5 tatami mats and have glass sliding doors opening seaside. Most expensive are roomy, 10-mat Japanese-style rooms facing the sea with bathroom (you can even see the water from the tub); some even have a balcony with chairs.

10445 Higashikata, Ibusuki, Kagoshima-ken 891-0404. ☎ 0993/22-3211. Fax 0993/22-3213. 65 units (7 with bath-room, 58 with toilet only). ¥4,200–¥5,775 ($40–$55) per person. Buffet breakfast ¥1,050 ($10) extra. Japanese din-ner ¥2,626–¥5,250 ($25–$50) extra. AE, MC, V. Free shuttle buses depart from in front of Ibusuki Station 6 times a day; look for a bus with QKAMURA written on it. **Amenities:** Restaurant (Japanese); lounge; outdoor pool a 5-min. walk

from the lodge (fee: ¥300/$2.85); tennis courts; indoor/outdoor hot-spring baths; sand baths (¥840/$8); Ping-Pong; rental bikes (¥210/$2 per hour); game center; in-room massage; coin-op washers/dryers. *In room:* A/C, TV, fridge, hot-water pot w/tea, safe, Washlet toilet.

## INEXPENSIVE

(230) **Marutomi** ⚐ Just a minute's walk from the Natural Sand Bath at Yunohama Beach, this inexpensive inn is a family-run affair. Following the ryokan tradition of naming rooms instead of assigning numbers, rooms are named after fish (the owner was a fisherman)—you can stay in the Tuna Room! All the rooms are Japanese-style—clean and with more character than many in this price range. Meals, which include fresh seafood, are served communally on tatami at low tables. Several blocks north is an annex, Marutomi2, with hot-springs baths, a communal kitchen, and three additional rooms. Guests can use facilities at both inns. If you call from the station, the owner may be able to pick you up.

5–24–15 Yunohama, Ibusuki, Kagoshima-ken 891-0406. ✆ 0993/22-5579. Fax 0993/22-3993. 7 units (none with bathroom). ¥4,000 ($38) per person without meals, ¥7,000 ($67) per person with dinner and breakfast. No credit cards. A 20-min. walk from Ibusuki Station. From the main exit, walk straight on Chuo Dori to the beach and turn right; just past the Natural Sand Bath turn right again. It's on the right. Bus: Going in the direction of the Ibusuki Iwasaki Hotel (ask for the Ibusuki Iwasaki Hotel *yuki* bus; the bus does not have a number), get off at the Suna Mushi-kaikan stop and walk inland. **Amenities:** Small hot-spring bath; free washing machine. *In room:* A/C, TV, no phone.

## WHERE TO DINE

(231) **Chozjuan** ⚐⚐ (finds) SOMEN NOODLES If you're adventurous, try this fun, open-air restaurant specializing in *somen* (cold noodles) in the countryside near Mount Kaimon. Seating is under a pavilion beside a man-made waterfall, so you eat to the accompaniment of running water with Japanese traditional music playing in the background. In the middle of your table will be a large round container with water swirling in a circle; when you get your basket of noodles, dump them into the cold water, fish them out with your chopsticks, dip them in soy sauce, and enjoy. Probably best is to order one of five set meals, which in addition to noodles come with such main dishes as grilled trout or carp sashimi, along with vegetables and soup. Hot noodles are available in winter, when you can also dine indoors.

Kaimon-cho, Tosenkyo. ✆ 0993/32-3156. Noodles ¥530 ($5.05); set meals ¥1,300–¥2,600 ($12–$25). No credit cards. May–Sept daily 10am–8pm; Oct–Apr daily 10am–5pm. Bus: 7 departures weekdays from Ibusuki Station (a 30-min. ride), including departures at 10:40am and 12:40pm; 4 weekend departures, including 11am. From the bus stop, the restaurant is ahead to the left and down the stairs (there are photos of food at its entrance).

(232) **Oshinagaki** VARIED JAPANESE This simple restaurant near Ibusuki Station offers a variety of teishoku set meals from its Japanese menu, including those featuring tempura, sashimi, sushi, hirekatsu (pork filet), and grilled eel, available all day. Another good choice is its Satsume Teishoku, featuring Kagoshima specialties like Satsuma-age, tonkotsu, chicken sashimi, and kibinago (see the dining section in the Kagoshima section for a description of local cuisine). Full kaiseki courses are also available.

1–2–11 Minato. ✆ 0993/22-3356. Teishoku set meals ¥1,280–¥2,000 ($12–$19); kaiseki ¥2,500–¥3,000 ($24–$29). No credit cards. Thurs–Tues 11am–3pm and 5:30–9:30pm. A 1-min. walk from Ibusuki Station. Turn left out of the station; it's on the main road to the left.

## 7 Sunny Resort Destination: Miyazaki

1,448km (900 miles) SW of Tokyo; 407km (254 miles) SE of Fukuoka; 126km (79 miles) W of Kagoshima

The capital of Miyazaki Prefecture, **Miyazaki City** is one of the largest (pop. 310,000) and most important cities in southern Kyushu. As all Japanese schoolchildren know,

it boasts several famous sites relating to Japan's first emperor, Jimmu. Yet it seems iso-lated, even somewhat neglected, by the rest of Japan. Tokyo is far away, and Japanese honeymooners, who only a few decades ago favored Miyazaki over most other domes-tic destinations, are now flocking to Hawaii and Australia.

To counter its downward spiral into touristic oblivion, in the 1990s Miyazaki devel-oped a large resort called **Seagaia** on its wooded outskirts, complete with hotels, golf courses, a zoo, the world's largest indoor water park, and other attractions. The plan worked: Miyazaki is now a major stop for Asian tour groups making the rounds of Kyushu's theme parks. But beyond that, Miyazaki is a perfect place to relax, swim in the Pacific Ocean, get in some rounds of golf, and savor local delicacies. Temperatures here are the third warmest in Japan after Okinawa's and Kagoshima's (it shares the same approximate latitude with Jerusalem and San Diego), and flowers bloom throughout the year. The natives are warm and kind, maybe because they still don't see many foreigners here, particularly Westerners.

## ESSENTIALS

**GETTING THERE  By Plane**   There are daily flights to Miyazaki from several Japanese cities. Flight time is 1½ hours from Tokyo (with a regular one-way ticket costing ¥31,000/$295 on JAL or ANA and ¥22,300/$212 on Skynet Asia Airways), 1 hour from Osaka, and 45 minutes from Fukuoka. From the airport, a bus travels to Miyazaki Station in 25 minutes and costs ¥400 ($3.80). Buses also travel from the air-port to Seagaia for ¥800 ($7.60). There's also JR train service from the airport to Miyazaki Station; if you don't have a Japan Rail Pass, it costs ¥340 ($2.85) for the 10-minute trip.

**By Train**   From Tokyo, take the Shinkansen bullet train to Kokura and transfer there to the Nichirin limited express; the entire trip takes approximately 11 hours (not includ-ing transfers) and costs ¥24,780 ($236) for an unreserved seat. There are also direct trains from Fukuoka's Hakata Station (6 hr.), Beppu (3½ hr.), and Kagoshima (2 hr.).

**By Bus**   Buses depart daily from Hakata Station in Fukuoka for Miyazaki (trip time: 4 hr.), costing ¥6,000 ($57) one-way. Buses also depart from Kagoshima Chuo Sta-tion; the fare is ¥2,700 ($26) for the 2¾-hour trip. Long-distance buses arrive at the bus station in front of Miyazaki Station.

**VISITOR INFORMATION**   Before departing Tokyo or Narita or Kansai airports, pick up the leaflet "Miyazaki and Vicinity" at the Tourist Information Center or download it from JNTO's website at www.jnto.go.jp by looking under *Regional Tourist Guides.*

In Miyazaki, stop off at the tourist information center at **Miyazaki Airport** (© **0985/51-5114;** open daily 7am–9pm) or the east exit of **JR Miyazaki Station** (© **0985/22-6469;** open daily 9am–7pm Mar–Nov, to 6:30pm Dec–Feb) to pick up *Discovering Miyazaki* (which covers the entire prefecture and has good bus informa-tion), *Miyazaki City Tourist Guidebook* (with a city map), and the **Miyazaki Welcome Card,** which provides discounts on specific hotels, restaurants, and attractions for holders of foreign passports. Information on Miyazaki Prefecture is available online at www.kanko-miyazaki.jp.

**MAIL**   The **Miyazaki Central Post Office,** 1–1–34 Takachiho-dori (© **0985/24-3425**), is located on the right side of Takachiho-dori Avenue if you're walking from Miyazaki Station, about an 8-minute walk away. It's open daily 24 hours a day for

mail. Its ATMs for foreign credit cards are open Monday to Friday 7am to 11pm, Saturday 9am to 9pm, and Sunday 9am to 7pm.

**INTERNET Top Player,** 2–12–20 Hiroshima (© **0985/83-3115**), is open 24 hours and charges ¥250 ($2.40) for 30 minutes of Internet use, plus a ¥100 (95¢) membership fee. It's a 2-minute walk from Miyazaki Station, across the street to the left in the Ekimae covered shopping street, on the right side.

**ORIENTATION & GETTING AROUND**    Downtown lies west of Miyazaki Station, about a 10-minute walk away. From Miyazaki Station, take Takachiho-dori Avenue west to **Tachibana-dori,** the main street in town, which is lined with shops, department stores, and restaurants. Almost all city buses serving other parts of town, as well as buses traveling to other cities in Miyazaki Prefecture, make stops along this main thoroughfare—at Depaato-mae bus stop at the intersection of Takachiho- and Tachibana-dori; and at Tachibana-dori 3-chome bus stop, which is farther south. Otherwise, there are two major bus terminals: The **Miyazaki Ekimae Bus Center** (also called Miyazaki Unko Center) is just outside the west exit of Miyazaki Station, and the **Miyako-City Bus Center** is a few minutes' walk from the JR Minami Miyazaki Station.

Miyazaki Shrine, Miyazaki prefectural museums, and Heiwadai Park are located northwest of Miyazaki Station, while the Seagaia resort area is located on the coast northeast of Miyazaki Station. All these attractions are easily reached by bus from Miyazaki Station or Tachibana-dori. Fares start at ¥140 ($1.35) and increase according to the distance. There is also local train service from Miyazaki Station to Miyazaki Jingu Eki Station near Miyazaki Shrine. For traveling farther afield, there's a 1-day bus pass for ¥2,000 ($19) that covers all of Miyazaki Prefecture and is sold at both bus centers above.

## WHAT TO SEE & DO
### MIYAZAKI SHRINE & ENVIRONS

The most important shrine in town is **Miyazaki Shrine (Miyazaki Jingu)** ⟨R, 2–4–1 Jingu (© **0985/27-4004**), located about a 10-minute walk west of JR Miyazaki Jingu Station. It's dedicated to the first emperor of Japan, Emperor Jimmu, a somewhat mythical figure who established the Yamato Court in 660 B.C. and is believed to be the ancestor of every reigning emperor since. Although the shrine is thought to have originated around the time of Emperor Jimmu's reign some 2,600 years ago, either on a mountaintop or near present-day Heiwadai Park, its ancient history remains shrouded in mystery, much like the emperor himself. Peacefully surrounded by natural woods and majestic cedar, the shrine is built from cedar and is austerely plain. The grounds of the shrine are always open and there's no charge for admission. If you don't want to walk to the shrine, you can take a bus bound for Miyazaki Jingu (the name of the stop for Miyazaki Shrine) from Tachibana-dori Avenue (in the center of town).

From the shrine, head back south and take a left after passing the first torii gate (there's a map of the area here) and walk around the shrine to the east. Four 150- to 200-year-old, thatched-roof Japanese homes have been moved to the park for preservation. You can walk around them and enter some. Admission is free. North of Miyazaki Shrine on shrine grounds is the **Miyazaki Prefectural Museum of Nature and History (Miyazaki-ken Sogo Hakubutsukan),** 2–4–4 Jingu (© **0985/24-2071;** open Tues–Sun 9am–5pm). It does an excellent job of presenting the prefecture's animal and plant life, its history, and its folklore with well-designed displays and

a wealth of information—what a shame explanations are in Japanese only. Those of you who studied Latin can put it to practice here, as plant and animal specimens are identified in Latin, but for the rest of us there's an English-language pamphlet. In any case, it's worth spending an hour here because there's plenty to look at, from dinosaur bones to replica burial tombs. Very enlightening is a replica of a home with a wood-burning stove and a bathtub heated with wood—the home dates from the 1950s. Admission is free. The closest bus stop is Hakubutsukan-mae in front of the museum; board any bus bound for Aya, Kunitomi, or Heiwagaoka from Tachibana-dori.

West of Miyazaki Shine, about a 10-minute walk away, is the **Miyazaki Prefectural Art Museum (Miyazaki-kenritsu Bijutsukan)** ✿, 3–210 Funatsuka (© **0985/20-3792;** open Tues–Sun 10am–6pm). This very modern building presents works of Miyazaki artists from the Edo Period onward, those who illustrate recent artistic trends in Japan, and artists from around the world. Most famous of the local artists is probably Ei-Kyu (1911–60), an avant-garde pioneer whose last works consisted of dots. Ai-O, a contemporary of Ei-Kyu, is known for his Rainbow series. Admission to the permanent exhibit (which nonetheless changes) is free. The closest bus stop is Bunka Koen Mae; board a bus bound for Aya, Heiwagaoka, Ikeuchi, Kunitomi, or Bunka Koen.

**HEIWADAI PARK**    About a 15-minute walk northwest of Miyazaki Shrine is Hei-wadai Park, where you'll find the **Peace Tower,** built in 1940 in celebration of the 2,600th anniversary of the mythological foundation of Japan; it purportedly contains artifacts that once belonged to the first emperor. Its pedestal is made with stones donated by Japanese expatriates from all over the world, while its copper door was cre-ated with coins donated by Japanese children. It may seem ironic that a peace tower was erected at a time when Japan was busy colonizing much of Asia; the intention was to show that the world could live peaceably, albeit with Japan as leader. Figures on the tower depict the guardians of fishery, agriculture, self-defense, and commerce.

## THE MANY AMUSEMENTS OF SEAGAIA ✿✿

Seagaia (www.seagaia.co.jp) is a convention and resort complex set in a vast national reserve of beautiful pine forest stretching 12km (7½ miles) along the coastline. In addition to hotels, it has amusements too numerous to list. **Miyazaki City Phoenix**

---

*Finds* **Haniwa Garden**

My favorite thing to see in Heiwadai Park (and a good photo op) is **Haniwa Garden** ✿. Archaeological digs in Miyazaki Prefecture have unearthed a multi-tude of ancient burial mounds and clay figures known as *haniwa;* replicas of these ancient mounds and haniwa clay figures can be seen in Haniwa Garden, where approximately 400 of the figures have been placed between trees on mounds covered with moss. There are warriors, horses, pigs, boats, and houses. I especially like the haniwa with the simple face and body and the O-shaped mouth; it's said to represent a dancing woman.

If you wish to take a bus here, board a bus from Depaato-mae bus stop on Tachibana-dori bound for Heiwadai; get off 12 minutes later at the last stop in front of the park.

**Zoo** (© **0985/39-1306;** open Thurs–Tues 9am–5pm) has more than 2,000 animals of 100 species from Asia and Africa; admission is ¥800 ($7.60) for adults, ¥400 ($3.80) for students, and ¥300 ($2.85) for children. Golfers can try out their swings at the private refurbished **Phoenix Country Club** (© **0985/39-1301**), a 27-hole course with visitor greens fees of ¥31,465 to ¥39,340 ($300–$375); or at the more proletarian public **Tom Watson Golf Course** (© **0985/39-1301**), which has 18 holes and charges a greens fee of ¥17,271 ($164) on weekdays and ¥20,946 ($199) on weekends and holidays. If you want to sharpen your golf game, the **David Duval Golf Academy** (© **0985/38-1210**) tailors instruction to individual needs through high-tech, state-of-the-art facilities and top-notch teachers. A 1-day program is ¥31,500 ($300) for adults and ¥20,000 ($190) for children. If golf isn't your game, there's also tennis, bowling at a 36-lane alley, scuba diving, jet-skiing, fishing, horse-back riding, and paragliding, as well as jogging, cycling, in-line skating along an 8km (5-mile) path, exercise classes, and art and craft lessons. For information about these, contact the **Recreation Center** on the second floor of the Sheraton Grande Ocean Resort (p. 542), open daily 8am to 8pm (© **0985/21-1324.**)

For swimming, there's an artificial beach (with free shuttle service from Seagaia hotels), as well as hotel pools. But for the ultimate aqua experience there's Miyazaki's most entertaining attraction, **Ocean Dome** 𝄞𝄞𝄞 (© **0985/21-1177**), certified by the *Guinness Book of Records* as the world's largest all-weather indoor water park; it has a high-tech retractable Teflon roof (Miyazaki is one of the sunniest places in Japan). You have to see this place to believe it; children will think they've landed in heaven. At this faux tropical paradise, you can lounge on a 140m-long (466-ft.) beach (covered by artificial white sand made of marble), ride waves created by the world's largest wave-making system, watch a surfing exhibition, careen down water slides, eat, and shop. Other pools include a 200m (666-ft.) flowing circular pool and children's pools. If you don't have your swimsuit, rental suits are available. Needless to say, your kids will spend the whole day here, unless you drag them away kicking and screaming. Admission is ¥2,000 ($19) for adults, ¥1,000 ($9.50) for children 4 to 15, and free for children under 4. (Seagaia hotel guests and holders of the Miyazaki Welcome Card pay ¥1,500/$14 and ¥800/$7.60 respectively.) Although kiddie slides are included in the admission, you have to pay ¥500 ($4.75) extra for a pass to more daring slides, which come with height restrictions. (You have to be 110cm/3½ ft. or taller to ride them.) Ocean Dome is open daily in summer (Oct–Mar closed Mon and Thurs) from 10am to 5pm (until 8pm mid-July through Aug) but closes once or twice a month for maintenance, so check before you go.

Access to all the Seagaia attractions and hotels (see "Where to Stay," below) is by city bus no. 18 from platform no. 3 at the west exit of **JR Miyazaki Station** (¥470/$4.50 for the 30-min. trip). Seagaia is so large that a **free shuttle bus** loops to all its facilities, including hotels, every hour from 7am to 9:26pm.

## FARTHER AFIELD

**AYA**   This is my kind of theme park! Called **Shusen no Mori (Spirits Forest),** 1800–19 Oaza Minamimata (© **0985/77-2222**), and located in the town of Aya, it bills itself as a "Fine Spirits Theme Park" and lives up to its promise with a variety of facilities open free to the public, including a shochu distillery (with free tours Mon–Fri 9:30am–noon and 1–4pm); a refined sake plant and a tasting table; a winery where visitors can observe the winemaking process (90% of the grapes are grown

in Miyazaki Prefecture; the rest come from elsewhere in Kyushu) and sample the results in a tasting room; and a microbrewery that produces three kinds of brews (samples cost ¥100/95¢ each). There is also a glass-blowing factory, ateliers where woodworkers and potters practice their trade, shops selling locally made crafts, and the delightful Kotto-no-Yakata Antique Pavilion (admission: ¥300/$2.85), crammed full with local folk art and antiques, including hair pins, mirrors, store signboards, tobacco pouches, glassware, lacquerware, tea pots, and much more; don't miss the nice garden out back. Top off your day at hot-spring indoor/outdoor baths, open daily 10:30am to 9pm (fee: ¥1,050/$10). Otherwise, most facilities are free and open daily 9am to 5pm, except for four restaurants—offering everything from Miyazaki beef and freshwater fish to organic vegetables—which remain open to 8 or 9pm.

To reach Shusen no Mori, take a bus from Tachibana 3-chome in downtown Miyazaki (*Discovering Miyazaki* has a map with bus stops) once an hour (at last check, 29 min. past each hour), with the trip to the Shusen no Mori stop taking about 54 minutes and costing ¥900 ($8.55). Incidentally, there are two other sights worth seeing in Aya if you want to make a day out of it: Aya Castle, a reconstruction of a 660-year-old castle with an adjoining craft center (a 15-min. walk from the Aya bus stop, the stop just before Shusen no Mori), and the Aya-Taruha Suspension Bridge, the world's longest suspended pedestrian bridge (you'll have to take a taxi here). Ask the tourist office for more information.

**NICHINAN COAST**    South of Miyazaki city is the Nichinan Coast, famous for its beautiful scenery, beaches, and a coastline of exposed and eroded rock sea floor, which is weirdly shaped like rippling waves. Known to Japanese as Oni-no-Sentaku Iwa, or The Ogre's Washboard, it resembles just that.

Here, too, is one of the most famous sights associated with Miyazaki—**Aoshima,** a tiny island less than a mile in circumference and connected to the mainland via a long walkway. Surrounded by rippled rock in low tide, it is covered with Betel palms and subtropical plants. It takes only 15 minutes to walk around the island. In its center is a small vermilion shrine, **Aoshima Jinja,** dedicated to first Emperor Jimmu's grandparents. According to legend, the grandfather, a hunter, was a young man when he and his brother, a fisherman, decided to trade chores. The grandfather, fishing here on Aoshima, lost his brother's hook and dove into the depths to retrieve it, only to end up on a turtle that delivered him to an undersea Dragon's Palace, where he met a fair princess. When he finally found the hook and returned to land, the princess came with him, later bearing him a son. Because of the legend, Aoshima Shrine is considered fortuitous in matchmaking; those wishing for marriage come here to be blessed. The shrine is open daily from dawn until dusk.

You can reach Aoshima in about 30 minutes from Miyazaki Station on the JR Nichinan Line; the fare is ¥360 ($3.45) and trains depart about every hour. Aoshima island is about a 5-minute walk from Aoshima Station. More frequent are buses departing from Miyazaki Station every 15 to 30 minutes, taking 49 minutes to reach Kodomo-no-Kuni/Aoshima and costing ¥670 ($6.40).

Farther south on the Nichinan Coast, about 24km (15 miles) south of Aoshima and 40km (25 miles) south of Miyazaki, is **Udo Shrine** ✿✿ (© **0987/29-1001**). Dedicated to the father of Emperor Jimmu, this vermilion-colored shrine is actually located in a cave beside the ocean—an unusual setting for a shrine, but one boasting an exhilarating view. According to legend, it was here that Emperor Jimmu's grandparents

## Kids  A Beach & an Amusement Park

Near Aoshima you'll find **Aoshima Beach,** Miyazaki Prefecture's most popular swimming and windsurfing beach, open July and August (jellyfish make it impractical other months of the year); and **Kodomo-no-Kuni** (© **0985/65-1111),** a small amusement park known also for its year-round flowers and nightly fireworks during summer vacation. The park's kiddie rides, Ferris wheel, roller coaster, water ride, and paddle boats are good for younger children. It's open Wednesday to Monday 9am to 5pm (but closed irregularly for cleaning) with varying extended hours on holidays (to 9pm during summer vacation). Admission is free (except during Flower Festival, mid-Mar to May, when admission is ¥800/$7.60 for adults and ¥400/$3.80 for children). Rides cost extra (¥300 – ¥400/$2.85–$3.80 for most).

came for the birth of their son. As delivery drew near, the soon-to-be mother asked her husband not to watch. Naturally, he couldn't resist, and to his surprise, his wife turned into a dragon. Ashamed, she fled back to sea, leaving breasts on the cave ceiling to feed her newborn son.

Throughout the ages, Udo Shrine has been famous among newlyweds, who come to pray for harmony in marriage and successful childbirth. In the cave behind the shrine are formations thought to resemble breasts; the water dripping from them is lucky "milk," considered beneficial for pregnancy, childbirth, and nursing mothers (milk candy is a specialty here). If you want to make a wish, purchase some clay pottery pieces at the shrine and try to toss them inside a rope circle that adorns a turtle-shaped rock—if you manage to land one inside the circle, you've got your wish. Women are supposed to throw right-handed, men left-handed.

You can reach Udo Shrine, open daily 7am to 6pm, by bus from Aoshima or Miyazaki (it takes 83 min. from Miyazaki Station). Get off at Udo Jingu Iriguchi, from which it's a 1-minute walk to the first torii gate, followed by a 20-minute walk along a narrow road to the shrine itself. *Note:* It takes a lot of time and effort to get to Udo Shrine; go only if you have time to spare.

## WHERE TO STAY
### VERY EXPENSIVE
**Sheraton Grande Ocean Resort** ✿✿✿    The most relaxing and luxurious place to stay in Miyazaki is Seagaia's crowning jewel, the Sheraton Grande Ocean Resort, Kyushu's tallest hotel with 43 floors. It is also the most convenient hotel to Ocean Dome, just a 5-minute walk away. Its marbled, elegant lobby stretches 11 stories high, emitting lots of light; in its center is the tropical-themed Pacifica Bar with palm trees, a circular aquarium, and live evening music. Rooms, all of which face the sea with magnificent views, are palatial by Japanese standards and are equipped with lots of extras, including vanity/sink areas separate from the bathroom (many also have separate shower stalls and tubs), and both soft and firm pillows (more deluxe rooms, starting from the 33rd floor, also boast Sheraton's trademark Sweet Sleeper Bed). Since you're a bit far from town, it's good to know there are plenty of dining options immediately on hand, including the highly recommendable Queen Alice Agape Italian restaurant on the 42nd floor with good views. Banyan Tree Spa, on the 39th floor,

boasts 10 treatment rooms (3 for couples) and 27 types of treatment, while Shosenkyu is a deluxe hot-spring spa, nestled in the pine forest with both indoor/outdoor baths. And in true resort fashion, daily activities run the gamut from horseback riding to art classes. If you're looking for a pampered getaway, this is the place.

Hamayama Yamazaki-cho, Miyazaki City 880-8545. © 800/325-3535 in the U.S. and Canada, or 0985/21-1133. Fax 0985/21-1144. www.sheraton.com/grandeocean. 744 units. ¥36,750–¥49,350 ($350–$470) twin; ¥42,000–¥47,250 ($400–$450) double. AE, DC, MC, V. Bus: From JR Miyazaki Station or Miyazaki Airport; see directions for Seagaia under "What to See & Do," above. **Amenities:** 7 restaurants; 2 bars; 1 lounge; 1 disco; outdoor pool and children's pool in lush tropical setting (free for hotel guests); health club w/25m (82-ft.) indoor lane pool, fitness room, sauna, and Jacuzzi (fee: ¥2,100/$20); spa; hot-spring baths (fee: from ¥1,500/$14); rental bikes (¥600/$5.70 for 2 hr.); children's day-care center; concierge; business center; shopping arcade; 24-hr. room service; in-room massage; same-day laundry/dry-cleaning service; nonsmoking rooms. *In room:* A/C, cable TV w/video games and pay movies, dataport (not all rooms), minibar, hot-water pot w/tea and coffee, hair dryer, safe, bathroom scale, Washlet toilet.

## EXPENSIVE

**Aoshima Palm Beach Hotel** *(kids)* *(Kids)*    Located right on Aoshima Beach (open July and Aug) and surrounded by lovely grounds and palm trees, this attractive Palm Beach–style hotel is a great place for a vacation, especially for families. Kodomo-no-Kuni, an amusement park for children, is located right beside the hotel (which has nightly fireworks displays during summer vacation, observable from some rooms). TVs offer pay video movies, including English-language films the whole family can watch. All Western-style rooms and most of the 72 Japanese-style rooms (which can sleep up to five persons) have huge windows facing the sea and views of Aoshima island. During summer vacation (mid-July and Aug), reserve at least 2 months in advance.

1–16–1 Aoshima, Miyazaki 889-2162. © 0985/65-2929. Fax 0985/65-2655. info@palmbeach-h.com. 214 units. ¥18,400–¥20,500 ($175–$195) per person. Extra charges during Golden Week, Bon Festival, and New Year's. Rates include 2 meals and service charge. 10% discount with Miyazaki Welcome Card. AE, DC, MC, V. Train: JR Nichinan Line to Kodomo-no-Kuni Station (3 min.). Bus: hourly from Miyazaki Station 25 min. to Kodomo-no-Kuni (2 min.). **Amenities:** 4 restaurants (Chinese, Japanese, Western, coffee shop); 1 lounge; hot-spring baths with sea views; health club w/exercise room, indoor lap pool, children's pool, and sauna (¥500/$4.75); Kodomo-no-Kuni amusement park; in-room massage; same-day laundry/dry cleaning. *In room:* A/C, TV w/pay movies, fridge, hot-water pot w/tea, hair dryer, safe, Washlet toilet.

## MODERATE

**Cottage Himuka** *(kids)*    Located in the Seagaia resort area, Cottage Himuka is geared toward families, groups, and longer stays with clean, bright, functional apartments complete with kitchenettes (hot plate, microwave, refrigerator, cookware); four single beds; a sofa and two chairs; a balcony; and separate sink, toilet, and tub areas. Larger, more expensive apartments sleep up to eight persons. Apartments are grouped together in free-standing concrete "cottages" on spacious grounds around a restaurant (serving breakfast, lunch, and dinner), a convenience store, and an outdoor pool open July to mid-September. All the Seagaia facilities are at hand. Check-in is in the adjacent Luxze Hitotsuba, with deluxe condominiums.

Hamayama, Yamazaki-cho, Miyazaki City 880-8545. © 800/325-3535 in the U.S. and Canada, or 0985/21-1355. Fax 0985/21-1356. www.seagaia.co.jp. 72 units. ¥22,000 ($210) for up to 4 persons; ¥44,000 ($419) for up to 8 persons. AE, DC, MC, V. Bus: From JR Miyazaki Station or Miyazaki Airport; see directions for Seagaia in "What to See & Do," above. **Amenities:** Restaurant (Western/Japanese); outdoor swimming pool (free for hotel guests); rental bikes (¥500/$4.75 for 2 hr.); convenience store. *In room:* A/C, TV, kitchenette, hair dryer.

**Miyazaki Kanko Hotel**    The Miyazaki Kanko Hotel is the best of a string of hotels along the Oyodo River, which has been developed into a small waterfront promenade

and park not far from Miyazaki Station. It consists of a newer east wing with higher-priced rooms, which are larger and have more amenities than those in the 50-year-old west wing, though bedside reading lamps are annoyingly dim. Rooms face either the river or town (favored for its night view) for the same price. A plus are the hot-spring baths, fed by water excavated from deep below the ground after much effort.

1–1–1 Matsuyama, Miyazaki City 880-8512. (✆ **0985/27-1212.** Fax 0985/25-8748. 375 units. ¥10,500–¥14,700 ($100–$140) single; ¥13,650–¥22,000 ($130–$210) double or twin. AE, DC, MC, V. Station: Miyazaki (a 15-min. walk); turn left from Miyazaki Station's west exit, walk south on Rte. (Kendo) 341 to the Oyodo River, and turn right. Bus: from platform no. 1 in front of Miyazaki Station going in the direction of Miyako City or the airport 5 min. to Tamayura-no-Yu stop. **Amenities:** 3 restaurants (Japanese, Western, Chinese); 1 bar; 2 lounges; indoor/outdoor hot-spring baths; Jacuzzi; sauna; lobby computers w/free Internet access; game arcade; shopping arcade; salon; same-day laundry/dry cleaning. *In room:* A/C, TV, minibar, hot-water pot w/tea, hair dryer, Washlet toilet.

## INEXPENSIVE

**Hotel Kensington**   The main reason most people come to Miyazaki is to relax at accommodations at Seagaia or Aoshima, but if you can't afford those prices (or didn't book soon enough), this is a good budget choice in the city center. Located on Tachibana-dori Avenue in the heart of the city near department stores and shopping, this inexpensive establishment resembles a business hotel in its simplicity but is also popular with young Japanese women because of its location and rates. Despite its name, the only hints of English-style are a knight of armor guarding the drawing-room-style lobby and the afternoon tea served in the Café London. The mostly single rooms are tiny, with windows that open and sliding panels for complete darkness; ask for a room that doesn't face another building. The cheapest doubles are actually single rooms with semi-double-size beds, which are comfortable for one but cramped for two. Otherwise, there are only three rooms with double beds and two twins.

3–4–4 Tachibana-dori-higashi, Miyazaki City 880-0805. (✆ **0985/20-5500.** Fax 0985/32-7700. www.Kensington.jp. ¥6,615 ($63) single; ¥8,190–¥10,500 ($78–$100) double; ¥11,235 ($107) twin. Discounts for single rooms Sun and holidays. 10% discount with Miyazaki Welcome Card. AE, MC, V. A 10-min. walk from Miyazaki Station's west exit. Walk straight ahead down Takachiho-dori to Tachibana-dori and turn left; the hotel will be on your left. **Amenities:** Restaurant (Western/Japanese); lobby computer with Internet access (¥100/95¢ per 10 min.); coin-op washer/dryer; nonsmoking rooms. *In room:* A/C, TV, dataport (some rooms), fridge (twins and doubles have minibar), hot-water pot w/tea, hair dryer, Washlet toilet.

**Toyoko Inn Miyazaki Ekimae** *Value*   While Hotel Kensington (above) has more character and a more interesting location, Toyoko Inn can't be beat when it comes to convenience (next to Miyazaki Station) and amenities, including lobby computers with free Internet access, free domestic calls from lobby phones, and free movie channels (this hotel has four channels instead of the usual two).

2–2–31 Oimatsu, Miyazaki City 880-0801. (✆ **0985/32-1045.** Fax 0985/32-1046. www.toyoko-inn.com. ¥6,090 ($58) single; ¥8,190 ($78) twin or double. Rates include free Japanese breakfast. AE, DC, MC, V. A 1-min. walk from Miyazaki Station's west exit (turn left). **Amenities:** Lobby computers w/free Internet access; nonsmoking rooms. *In room:* A/C, TV, fridge, hot-water pot w/tea, hair dryer, safe, Washlet toilet, trouser press.

## WHERE TO DINE

Miyazaki's subtropical climate is conducive to the growth of a number of vegetables and fruits, including sweet pumpkins, oranges, mangos, cucumbers, shiitake mushrooms, and chestnuts. In summer, a popular dish is *Hiyajiru*, a rice dish topped with soup made from fish, miso soybean paste, tofu, cucumbers, and other ingredients, while year-round dishes include **chicken** *namban* (deep-fried chicken breast served with a sweet-and-sour tartar sauce) and sushi rolls made with lettuce, shrimp, and

mayonnaise. Miyazaki is also known for its **beef** and *shochu*, an alcoholic drink made from sweet potatoes, buckwheat, or corn.

In addition to the choices below, a great restaurant for a splurge in Seagaia is **Queen Alice Agape,** located on the 42nd floor of the Sheraton Grande Ocean Resort (© **0985/21-1133**) with sweeping ocean views. Utilizing fresh Miyazaki ingredients, its Italian cuisine is a collaboration of resident Chef Manaka and Ishinabe Hiroshi (nicknamed the Iron Chef), with past dishes ranging from pepperoncini with tiger crab from Aoshima Port to grilled Miyazaki beef filet served with organic Aya vegetables. Set lunches, served daily 11:30am to 2pm, cost ¥3,000 and ¥5,000 ($29 and $48); set dinners, available 6 to 9pm, are ¥8,500 and ¥10,000 ($81 and $95).

(233) **Koutatsu** LOCAL SPECIALTIES   Located on Miyazaki's main downtown street, this restaurant offers four floors of dining, mostly in private tatami rooms with leg wells, and traditional Japanese dishes and regional specialties made with fresh, locally grown ingredients. Set meals make ordering from the Japanese-language menu easy, with obento and mini-kaiseki available for lunch and more elaborate choices for dinner, including the Omakase (chef's choice) for ¥3,000 ($29) and the ¥5,000 ($48) *Himukazen,* comprised of local specialties like black pork shabu-shabu that change according to what's in season.

3–3–37 Tachibana-dori-nishi. © 0985/27-6717. Reservations strongly recommended. Set lunches ¥1,050–¥2,100 ($10–$20); set dinners ¥3,000–¥5,000 ($29–$48). 5% discount with Miyazaki Welcome Card. AE, MC, V. Daily 11:30am–2pm and 5:30–11pm. Station: Miyazaki (12 min.). From the station's west exit, walk straight ahead down Takachiho-dori and turn left after crossing Tachibana-dori; it's on Tachibana-dori, on the right just past a parking lot.

**Organic Restaurant Sizen** JAPANESE/WESTERN BUFFET   This pleasant, glass-enclosed buffet restaurant, surrounded by greenery and with outdoor terrace dining, is a good choice for lunch if you're visiting adjoining Heiwadai Park. It offers a changing buffet of Japanese and Western organic dishes in a casual, relaxed setting.

6146 Koshigazako, Shimokitakata-cho. © 0985/31-3693. Buffet lunch ¥1,300 ($12). No credit cards. Wed–Mon 11am–2pm. Bus: Heiwadai (1 min.).

**Restaurant Paris 5** ⚕ FRENCH   Located to the right of the main entrance to Miyazaki Shrine and convenient if you've been visiting the many sights in the area, this delightful restaurant looks imported directly from sunny southern France. It beckons with a balcony overflowing with flowers and plants and a tall and airy dining room. Only set meals—most featuring seafood and Miyazaki beef—are available for both lunch and dinner. (This is the only French restaurant in Miyazaki authorized to serve Miyazaki beef, but don't ask me why authorization is necessary.) Its cheerful balcony is open year-round (weather permitting). Call beforehand, however, because its close proximity to Miyazaki Shrine makes it a popular venue for private wedding receptions.

1–8–8 Jingu-Higashi. © 0985/29-8039. Set lunches ¥2,000–¥4,800 ($19–$46); set dinners ¥4,000–¥6,800 ($38–$65). AE, MC, V (accepted only at dinner). Wed–Mon 11:30am–2:30pm and 6–10pm. Bus: From Tachibana-dori Ave. or Miyako Kotsu Bus Center to Miyazaki Jingu (1 min.).

## 8 Beppu, King of the Hot-Spring Spas ⚑⚑

1,228km (763 miles) SW of Tokyo; 186km (116 miles) SE of Fukuoka

**Beppu** gushes forth more hot-spring water than anywhere else in Japan. With approximately 2,850 hot springs spewing forth 130,000 kiloliters (34 million gal.) of water

daily (enough to fill 3,600 25m/82-ft. pools), it has long been one of the country's best-known spa resorts. Some 11 million people come to Beppu every year to relax and rejuvenate themselves in one of the city's 83 public bathhouses, and they do so in a number of unique ways: They sit in mud baths up to their necks, they bury themselves in hot black sand, they soak in hot springs, and on New Year's they bathe in water filled with floating orange peels. They even drink hot-spring water and eat food cooked by its steam.

Bathing reigns supreme here—and I suggest you join in the fun. After all, visiting Beppu without enjoying the baths would be like going to a world-class restaurant with your own TV dinner.

Not a very large town, with a population of 123,000, Beppu is situated on Kyushu's eastern coast in a curve of Beppu Bay, bounded on one side by the sea and on the other by steep hills and mountains. On cold days, steam rises everywhere throughout the city, escaping from springs and pipes and giving the town an otherworldly appearance. Indeed, nine of the hot springs look so much like hell that that's what they're called— Jigoku, the Hells. But rather than a place most people try to avoid, the Hells are a major tourist attraction. In fact, everything in Beppu is geared toward tourism, and if you're interested in rubbing elbows with Japanese on vacation—particularly the older generation—this is one of the best places to do so.

## ESSENTIALS

**GETTING THERE   By Plane**   The nearest airport is in Oita, a 45-minute bus ride away (bus fare: ¥1,450/$14); flights from Tokyo's Haneda airport (ANA, JAL) take about 1½ hours and cost ¥30,000 ($286).

**By Train**   From Tokyo, take the Shinkansen to Kokura and transfer there to a limited express bound for Beppu; the trip takes about 7 hours (not including transfers) and costs ¥23,180 ($221) for an unreserved seat. There are also direct trains daily from Hakata Station in Fukuoka (trip time: 2½ hours), Kumamoto (3 hours), and Miyazaki (3½ hours).

**By Ferry**   Ferries make nightly runs to Beppu from Osaka, with fares beginning at ¥7,900 ($75); at last check, ferries departed Osaka's South Pier at 6:50pm and 9pm, arriving the next morning at 6:20am and 10:10am respectively. Contact tourist offices in Osaka (see chapter 9) or the Kansai Kisen company in Osaka (© **06/6572-5181**) for more information.

From Shikoku, the most practical ferry is from Yawatahama, running six times daily and costing ¥1,770 ($17) one-way for the 2½-hour trip; contact the **Uwajima Unyu Co.** for information (© **0894/23-2536**). The ferry from Matsuyama, also on Shikoku, departs twice daily and costs ¥2,800 ($27) for the 2¼-hour trip; it's run by the **Soreyu Express Co.** (© **0892/505-0077**).

**VISITOR INFORMATION**   Before leaving Tokyo or the Narita or Kansai airports, pick up a copy of the leaflet "Beppu and Vicinity" at the Tourist Information Center, or download it at www.jnto.go.jp.

In Beppu, the **Beppu Tourist Information Office** (© **0977/23-1119;** open daily 8:30am–5:30pm) is located in Beppu Station at the east (main) exit, with English-speaking volunteers on duty daily 9am to 5pm. There's a computer with Internet access you can use here for free, but you're limited to 10 minutes and you have to stand up. (**Note:** there is discussion of moving the tourist office to Sol Paseo, an international

shopping arcade a 5-min. walk due east of the main exit). More information is available on the Web at www.beppu-navi.jp.

**ORIENTATION & GETTING AROUND**    **Beppu Station** is located near the center of the city. Its main exit is to the east and the sea, while to the west lie the Hells and the majority of hot-spring baths. Because most destinations are not within walking distance, the easiest ways to get around Beppu are by bus and by taxi. Of the two bus companies serving Beppu, the **Kamenoi Bus Company** (② **0977/23-0141**) is the largest and serves most of the city. Bus fares begin at ¥140 ($1.35) and increase according to the distance, but if you plan on doing a lot of sightseeing, there's a 1-day pass called **My Beppu Free**—which nonetheless costs ¥900 ($8.55) for adults, half price for children under 12. It allows unlimited travel on Kamenoi Company buses (which are blue) in the city as well as slight discounts on a few attractions. You can purchase the passes at the Tourist Information Office.

## TAKING THE WATERS

Beppu is divided into eight hot-spring areas, each with its own mineral content and natural characteristics. Although any hot-spring bath can help stimulate metabolism and blood circulation and create a general feeling of well-being, there are specific springs with various mineral contents that Japanese believe help relieve ailments ranging from rheumatism and diabetes to skin disease. The tourist office has a pamphlet so you can select the baths that will benefit you the most. And whatever you do, don't rinse off with plain water after taking your bath because this will wash away all those helpful minerals. You should bring your own towel and, for some places, a *yukata* (cotton kimono), though the latter is also available for sale or for rent.

### HOT-SPRING BATHS

**SUGINOI PALACE**    A 15-minute bus ride from Beppu Station via bus no. 10, **Suginoi Palace** ⏣⏣ (② **0977/24-1160**) is an amusement center with one of the best-known baths in all of Japan. Called **Tanayu** and built of natural woods and glass, it's refined and spacious, with different kinds of baths both inside and out that take advantage of its hillside perch with great views out over the town toward the sea. In addition to an indoor bath, Jacuzzi, and sauna, there are outdoor cypress tubs, waterfall massages (great for shoulders and backs), and even shallow pools with headrests so you can recline to gaze upon the view.

As if that weren't enough, Suginoi Palace itself also has bowling lanes, the attached Uzone complex with arcade games, and stage shows that range from music to dance.

Admission to Tanayu, open daily from 9am to 11pm, costs ¥2,000 ($19) for adults, ¥1,200 ($11) for junior-high and high-school students, and ¥700 ($6.65) for children. If, however, you're staying at the Suginoi Hotel (p. 550), you can use the baths for free.

If you're shy about disrobing in front of strangers or have kids in tow, you might want to visit Suginoi's **Aqua-Beat** (② **0977/26-7600**). It's a water park with water slides (great fun!), children's pools, a simulated wave pool, an artificial beach, outdoor hot springs, and a Jacuzzi. A bar-coded locker key on a wristband allows you to lock up your valuables, wear your bathing suit (rental suits available), and dine without having to worry about carrying money; upon exiting, you'll simply feed it into a machine to get your bill. Admission is ¥2,800 ($27) for adults, ¥1,600 ($15) for junior-high and high-school students, and 1,000 ($9.50) for children 4 to 12. In the off

season (Sept–June), it costs only ¥1,500 ($14), ¥1,000 ($9.50), and ¥500 ($4.75) respectively. Guests staying at the Suginoi Hotel can go for free. It's open Monday to Friday 10am to 7pm and Saturday, Sunday, and holidays from 10am to 8pm, with extended hours during major holidays. It's closed for maintenance December 5 to December 9.

**TERMAS SPA**   A new hot-spring public spa beside the sea, **Termas Spa (Kitahama Onsen),** Kyomachi 11–1 (© 0977/24-4126; open Fri–Wed 10am–10pm), offers indoor baths and a sauna, as well as a large outdoor hot-spring pool and Jacuzzi for both sexes overlooking the sea (you wear your swimsuit here). Admission is ¥500 ($4.75) for adults and ¥250 ($2.40) for children. It's a 20-minute walk from Beppu Station (take the east exit and turn left when you reach the sea; it will be on the right); or take bus no. 20, 21, 23, 25, or 26 to Matogahama Koen stop.

## HOT-SAND BATHS

One of the unique things you can do in Beppu is take a bath in hot sand, considered useful for treating muscle pain, arthritis, and indigestion. Although several public baths offer hot-sand baths, one of the most atmospheric places is the **Takegawara Bathhouse** ⚘⚘⚘, 16–23 Motomachi, Beppu 874 (© 0977/23-1585; open daily 8am–9:30pm, closed third Wed of each month), a 10-minute walk from Beppu Station. Built in 1879 in traditional, Meiji-Era architecture, this beautiful wooden structure is one of the oldest public baths in the city and has an interior that resembles an ancient gymnasium, dominated by a pit filled with black sand. The attendants are used to foreigners here; they'll instruct you to change into the provided yukata and lie down in a hollow they've dug in the sand. An attendant will then shovel sand on top of you and pack you in until only your head and feet are sticking out. I personally didn't find the sand all that hot, but it is relaxing as the heat soaks into your body. You stay buried for 10 minutes, contemplating the wooden ceiling high above and hoping you don't get an itch somewhere. When the time is up, the attendant will tell you to stand up, shower off the sand, and then jump into a bath of hot water. The cost is ¥1,000 ($9.50). To reach the bathhouse, take the main (east) exit from Beppu Station and walk toward the sea, turning right at the street just before the big intersection (across from Tokiwa). The bathhouse is a couple blocks down this street on the right, with its entrance around the corner.

## MORE TO SEE & DO

**THE HELLS (JIGOKU)**   You might as well join everyone else and go to the Hells, boiling ponds created by volcanic activity. Their Japanese name, Jigoku, refers to the burning hell of Buddhist sutras. Seven of the nine Hells are clustered close together in the Kannawa hot-spring area, within walking distance of each other, and they can be toured in about 90 minutes or so. Each hell has its own attraction, but since a few are kind of hokey, you might just want to visit a couple. **Umi Jigoku,** or Sea Hell, has a nice garden setting (spectacular in spring when azaleas are in bloom), a cobalt-blue pond, a greenhouse with giant lotus plants, and a foot bath where you can soak your feet in hot springs. **Oniishibozu Jigoku** features bubbling mud, a foot bath, and its own hot-spring baths (extra admission charged); **Kamado Jigoku,** the Oven Hell, was used for cooking and has a statue of a red devil (read: photo op); **Chinoike Jigoku,** the Blood-Pond Hell, is blood red in color because of the red clay dissolved in the hot water; **Tatsumaki Jigoku,** or Waterspout Hell, has one of the largest geysers in Japan.

**_Finds_   On the Road to Hell**

Smack dab in the midst of the Hells, across from Oniyama Jigoku, is the **Beppu Utamaro Gallery (Minzoku Shiryokan),** Kannawa Shibuya 338-3 (© **0977/66-8790;** open daily 9am–10pm), a museum devoted to sex. Fertility gods, erotic statues, pictures of zebras and lions in the act, replicas of penises from the animal kingdom ranging from tiny to humongous, Edo-Era erotic woodblock prints by Utamaro, kinky dioramas (including an adult version of Snow White and her seven little men), and a small theater with porn films are just some of the things on display here. Think of those unsuspecting visitors hoping to see a gallery devoted to famed ukiyo-e artist Utamaro's work! Admission is ¥1,000 ($9.50).

Skip **Yama Jigoku,** which features animals living in deplorable conditions, and **Oniyama Jigoku,** ditto for crocodiles. To reach Kannawa, take bus no. 2 from Beppu Station's west exit 25 minutes to Umijigoku-mae bus stop. After walking to the seven Hells, you can then take bus no. 16 from the Kannawa bus stop onward to the other two Hells.

The Hells are open daily 8am to 5pm. A combination ticket, costing ¥2,000 ($19) for adults, ¥1,300 ($12) for high-school students, ¥1,000 ($9.50) for junior-high students, and ¥900 ($8.55) for children, allows entrance to eight Hells. Separate entrance fee to each one is ¥400 ($3.80). A ninth Hell, the Golden Dragon Jigoku, is free (I like its sign, which announces matter-of-factly, IF YOU FALL IN THE POND, YOU WILL BE BOILED.) For more information, contact the **Beppu Tourist Information Office** (see above) or the **Beppu Jigoku Association** (© 0977/66-1577).

(234) **JAPAN BAMBOO MUSEUM**   Beppu is famous for its bamboo crafts, and the best place to shop for bambooware and to learn more about this amazingly durable material is this museum, called **Nihon Take-no-Hakubutsukan** (6–8–19 Ishigaki-higashi; © 0977/25-7776; open daily 8:30am–5pm). Exhibits explain how bamboo grows, the different varieties of bamboo (630 kinds are found in Japan), and the role bamboo has played in Japanese life. Bamboo products from all over Japan are on display, including palanquins, fish traps, lunch boxes, rakes, fans, hats, bows, and arrows. Even Edison's electric light bulb used a bamboo filament. You can see it in 15 minutes, but with your new appreciation for bamboo, you'll easily spend an additional 15 minutes in its shop. Admission is ¥300 ($2.85) for adults, ¥200 ($1.90) for junior-high and high-school students, and ¥100 (95¢) for children. To reach it, take Kamenoi bus no. 25 from Beppu Station's east exit to Takezaeku Densan Kaikan stop, in front of the museum's brown brick building.

**MONKEYS & AN AQUARIUM**   On Beppu's southern border rises **Mount Takasaki,** home to some 1,200 wild monkeys and one of Japan's largest monkey habitats (© 097/532-5010; open daily 8:30am–5pm). At the base of the mountain where they're fed, however (to keep them from raiding farmers' fields), it's nothing but concrete and they don't seem particularly wild or concerned about the humans walking among them. Admission is ¥500 ($4.75) for adults and ¥250 ($2.40) for children. Come here only if you have children, combining it with a trip to **Umitamago,** Kaigan, Takasakiyama-shita (© 097/534-1010; open daily 9am–6pm), across the

highway via pedestrian bridge. This aquarium, opened in 2004, features an 8m-high (26-ft.) circular tank with 3,000 fish and sea creatures, as well as seals, sea lions, dolphins, sea otters, sea turtles, a touch pool with harmless sharks and rays, a discovery room for small children, and shows. Admission is ¥1,890 ($18) for adults, ¥950 ($9.05) for junior-high and elementary students, and ¥630 ($6) for children (free for children 3 and younger). To reach Mount Takasaki and the aquarium, take an Oita Kotsu bus that departs from Beppu Station four times an hour (there is no bus number) for 10 minutes to Takasakiyama stop; unfortunately, your My Beppu Free pass isn't accepted on this bus, so you'll have to pay ¥230 ($2.20).

## WHERE TO STAY

As with most hot-spring spas, Beppu levies a hot-springs tax: ¥150 ($1.40) per person, per night. In addition, some places raise their rates during New Year's, Golden Week (Apr 29–May 5), Obon (mid-Aug), Saturdays, and the evenings before holidays.

### EXPENSIVE

(235) **Kannawaen** ✿★★   If it's peace and quiet you're searching for, here's the place for you: a wonderful, 65-year-old ryokan hidden away on a lushly landscaped hill just a stone's throw from the Hells. It actually consists of a main building (built as a private summer villa) and five separate houses spread around its grounds, and its tatami rooms with shoji screens look out onto carefully tended gardens, hot springs, bamboo, streams, bonsai, stone lanterns, flowers, and different kinds of cherry trees. This is the perfect place to escape the crowds and to relax in a meandering, open-air bath set among rocks and trees; its water is said to change color seven times a day depending on the intensity of the sunlight. Meals are served in a traditional communal room with leg wells. Even members of the imperial family and prime ministers have stayed here.

Kannawa, Beppu 874-0045. ✆ **0977/66-2111.** Fax 0977/66-2113. 12 units (10 with bathroom). ¥23,000–¥35,000 ($219–$333) per person. ¥5,000 ($48) extra on weekends. Rates include 2 meals and service charge. AE, MC, V. Bus: No. 2 from Beppu Station's west exit to Umijigoku-mae (3 min); look for its entrance between Umi Jigoku and Kamado Jigoku. **Amenities:** Indoor/outdoor hot-spring baths; in-room massage. *In room:* A/C, TV, fridge, hot-water pot w/tea, safe.

**Suginoi Hotel** ✿ *Kids*   Probably the best-known hotel in Beppu, Suginoi is famous for its adjoining Suginoi Palace, a huge bathing complex with hot-spring baths and a water park (both free to hotel guests). Situated on a wooded hill with a sweeping view of the city and sea below, it's a lively and noisy hotel, filled with good-natured vacationers. If you like being in the middle of the action, this is the place for you. The hotel is divided into two wings, each with its own check-in counter. The older main building (Honkan) is larger, catering primarily to families and groups with Japanese-style rooms and combination rooms with both beds and separate tatami areas. The newer Hana wing is more European in atmosphere with mostly Western-style rooms. Rates are based on the type of room; those facing inland are slightly cheaper than those with fantastic sea views. Both include two buffet-style meals of either Japanese or Western food in their price. With all the kiddie diversions—the water park, game room, cheap eats in Suginoi Palace (even a McDonald's)—this is a good choice for families.

Kankaiji, Beppu 874-0822. ✆ **0977/24-1141.** Fax 0977/21-0010. www.suginoi-hotel.com. 570 units. ¥15,900–¥22,200 ($151–$211) per person. Rates include 2 meals and service charge. Rates higher in peak season. AE, DC, MC, V. Bus: 10 from Beppu Station to Suginoi Palace. Taxi: 8 min. **Amenities:** 6 restaurants; 1 bar; 1 lounge; Suginoi Palace with hot-spring baths and Aqua-Beat (see "Taking the Waters," above); 2 24-hr. hot-spring baths for hotel guests

only; game room; shopping arcade; salon; room service (2pm–midnight); in-room massage; nonsmoking rooms. *In room:* A/C, TV, minibar, hot-water pot w/tea, hair dryer, safe, Washlet toilet.

## MODERATE

**Hotel Arthur**    I like the location of this hotel, just a 2-minute walk from Beppu Station but tucked away in a side street near restaurants and bars. A warmly decorated lobby sporting a medieval suit of armor leads to the usual small rooms, which have shades in addition to curtains for extra darkness. Some single rooms from the seventh floor have views of the sea at no extra charge. Other extras include a 10th-floor restaurant with good views from three sides and decent Western food, plus two small hot-spring baths, one with a sauna (and the first I've ever seen with a TV in it), with alternating open hours for men and women. The hotel does a good job explaining all its services in English.

1–2–5 Kitahama, Beppu 874-920. (©) **0977/25-2611.** Fax 0977/24-0073. www.hotel-arthur.co.jp. 123 units. ¥6,300–¥8,400 ($60–$80) single; ¥10,500–¥14,700 ($100–$140) twin; ¥9,240–¥10,500 ($88–$100) double. Rates higher on Sat for twin and double rooms only. AE, DC, MC, V. A 2-min. walk from Beppu Station's east exit; turn right just past the Ekimae Onsen. **Amenities:** Restaurant; indoor hot-spring bath; sauna; lobby computers w/free Internet access; coin-op washer/dryer; in-room massage; nonsmoking rooms. *In room:* A/C, TV, dataport, minibar, fridge, hot-water pot w/tea, hair dryer, Washlet toilet.

(236) **Sakaeya** ✦✦ *(Finds*    The oldest *minshuku* in the city, this is one of the best places to stay near the Hells. There are several interesting features here that have utilized the hot springs for decades. Old radiators, for example, are heated naturally from hot springs. Another relic is the stone oven *(jigokugama)* in the courtyard, which uses steam from hot springs for cooking (many older homes in Beppu still use such ovens). Use of the oven is free in case you want to cook your own meals, but there's also a modern kitchen you can use. I recommend, however, that you opt for rates that include meals. Most of your dinner will be steamed using the hot springs and then served in a Japanese dining room with whitewashed walls and a heavy timbered ceiling. In winter, the *kotatsu* (a table with a heating element and covered with a blanket to keep legs warm) in the dining room is steam heated. All rooms are Japanese-style, the oldest of which don't have bathrooms but are very nice and date from the Meiji Period (1868–1912), while those with private bathroom are in a newer addition that nonetheless maintains a traditional atmosphere with sitting alcoves.

Ida, Kannawa, Beppu 874-0043. (©) **0977/66-6234.** Fax 0977/66-6235. 12 units (7 with bathroom). Without meals, ¥3,500 ($33) per person without bathroom, ¥5,000 ($48) per person with bathroom. Rates with 2 meals, ¥13,000–¥20,000 ($124–$190) per person with bathroom. Rates higher on weekends and holidays. No credit cards. Bus: Jigokubara (2 min.); take the 1st left. **Amenities:** Indoor hot-spring baths. *In room:* A/C, TV, fridge, hot-water pot w/tea.

## INEXPENSIVE

**Kokage**    In operation for 40 years, this minshuku is a member of the Japanese Inn Group. There are both Japanese and twin rooms, simply furnished. Those with bathrooms have hot-spring water, while one room for three people has only a sink and toilet. There's also a public, rock-lined, hot-spring bath, and meals are served in a homey dining room with a cluttered but interesting collection of antique lamps, clocks, and other items. If you like, the owners will fit you out in a wedding kimono and take your picture with your camera. Note, however, that there's a midnight curfew and the inn is lax about answering faxes. If you don't get an answer by e-mail, try reserving by phone.

8–9 Ekimaecho, Beppu 874-0935. ℂ **0977/23-1753.** Fax 0977/23-3895. kokage@mx6.tiki.ne.jp. 11 units (10 with bathroom, 1 with toilet only). ¥4,350 ($41) single with bathroom; ¥7,650 ($73) twin with bathroom; ¥9,900 ($94) triple with toilet only, ¥11,475 ($109) triple with bathroom. Breakfast ¥840 ($8) extra; Japanese dinner ¥1,890 ($18) extra. AE, MC, V. Station: Beppu (2-min). From the station's main east exit, walk straight ahead for 2 blocks to a stop-light just past Ekimae Onsen, turn right, and then turn immediately right again into a small alley (it's easy to miss). **Amenities:** Lobby computer (¥100/95¢/30 min); free washer/dryer. *In room:* A/C, TV, hot-water pot w/tea.

237 **Yokoso**   Housed in a beige-colored, two-story building on Ideyuzaka, the main road between the group of Hells, Yokoso offers what are probably the cheapest rooms in all of Beppu. Run by English-speaking, third-generation innkeepers, it has clean Japanese-style rooms equipped with only the basics. Air-conditioning in summer is coin operated, but steam heating is free. No meals are served, but a communal open-air kitchen is available for do-it-yourselfers, complete with a hot-springs-powered oven and suggestions for how long to cook food in bamboo steamers (20 min. for potatoes; there's a grocery store across the street). Four public baths boast water from hot springs. In an annex are 25 more rooms, a *rotenburo* (outdoor bath; you wear your swimming suit here), and a carp pond in a garden. It also has one of the most interesting saunas I've ever seen, so tiny you have to crawl inside; heated naturally with hot springs, it even has a grass floor, as in the days of yore. Note that there's an 11pm curfew here.

Ida 3 Kumi, Kannawa, Beppu 874-0043. ℂ **0977/66-0440.** Fax 0977/66-0440. www.coara.or.jp/~hideharu/ EngSmry.html. 35 units. ¥3,400 ($32) per person. No credit cards. Bus: Jigokubara (3 min.). and then the first left; around the corner from Sakaeya, above. **Amenities:** Lobby computer w/Internet access (¥100/95¢/30 min.); in-room massage; coin-op washer/dryer. *In room:* Coin-op A/C, coin-op TV, hot-water pot w/tea, no phone.

## WHERE TO DINE

238 **Biliken** VARIED JAPANESE   It is easy to spot this casual restaurant on the main street halfway between the station and the sea because of the gold statue to the left of the doorway of Biliken—a curious-looking, bald-headed, round-tummied god who is said to bring good luck. Popular with shoppers, businessmen, and families, the place is managed by English-speaking Hideko-san and her husband. A display case outside and a picture menu make ordering easy for Japanese set meals that include tempura, broiled eel, sashimi, tonkatsu, and more, with seating on tatami or at dark lacquered tables.

2–1–18 Kitahama. ℂ **0977/21-2088.** Set meals ¥750–¥2,100 ($7.15–$20); set lunch ¥600 ($5.70). No credit cards. Fri–Wed 11:30am–9:30pm. A 4-min. walk from Beppu Station, on the left side of the main road leading to the sea.

239 **Mitsu Boshi**  ⌘⌘ FRENCH KAISEKI   This small, cozy restaurant on the main road leading south of the seven cluster of Hells serves French cuisine with a Japanese twist, presented in a kaiseki style with set meals consisting of many small dishes expertly executed by the owner-chef. Seasonal seafood, steaks with a choice of four sauces, and original creations round out the menu.

284 Kannawa. ℂ **0977/67-3536.** Main dishes ¥1,575–¥2,800 ($15–$27); set dinners ¥3,990–¥6,000 ($38–$57); set lunches ¥1,400–¥5,250 ($13–$50). No credit cards. Wed–Mon 11am–2:30pm and 5–9pm (last order). Bus: Kamenoi Bus no. 5, 41, or 43 from Beppu Station's west exit 16 min. to Kannawa (1 min.). In front of the bus stop, on Miyuki Zaka.

# Northeastern Honshu—Tohoku

Because so many of Japan's historic events took place in Kyoto, Tokyo, and other cities in southern Honshu, most visitors to Japan never venture farther north than Tokyo. True, northeastern Honshu (called the Tohoku District) does not have the famous temples, shrines, gardens, and castles of southern Japan, but it does have spectacular mountain scenery, national parks, hot springs in abundance, excellent ski resorts, and many hiking trails. Its rugged, mountainous terrain, coupled with cold, snowy winters, has also helped preserve the region's traditions. You won't find any of Tokyo's edgy flashiness here, but rather a down-to-earth practicality, warm hospitality, and a way of life that harks back generations.

**Matsushima,** about 3 hours north of Tokyo, is considered one of Japan's most scenic spots, with pine-covered islets dotting its bay. Farther north, near the middle of Tohoku, is the pleasant village of **Kakunodate,** once a thriving castle town and famous for its remaining samurai houses and cherry trees. Occupying 862 sq. km (333 sq. miles) of northern Tohoku is the resplendent **Towada-Hachimantai National Park,** best visited for its scenic lakes, rustic hot-spring spas that seem little changed over the decades, skiing, and hiking, including a trail that flanks the picture-perfect Oirase Stream. And after a day of trekking or skiing, what can be better than a soothing, hot-spring soak?

## TOHOKU ESSENTIALS

**GETTING THERE & AROUND** Northern Tohoku's major airports are in Aomori and Akita. JAL flies from Tokyo's Haneda Airport to Aomori (¥26,200/$250 one-way) as well as to Akita (¥21,200/$202 one-way). You can also travel to Tohoku via **Shinkansen** bullet train from Ueno or Tokyo Station in Tokyo as far as Akita, with stops at Kakunodate and Tazawako, a convenient springboard for travel onward to Towada-Hachimantai National Park.

Although there is bus service in the national park, buses to some of the more remote areas are infrequent or nonexistent. For that reason, Tohoku is one of the few regions in Japan where **rental cars** are a great convenience, if not a necessity. In addition to car-rental agencies at both Aomori and Akita airports, there are JR Eki Rent-A-Car offices at train stations throughout Japan, including Aomori, Morioka, Kakunodate, and Tazawako stations, which offer 20% discounts for train fares booked in conjunction with car rentals. You'll also find Toyota Rent-A-Car offices virtually everywhere. If you want to keep your driving to a minimum, I suggest taking a Shinkansen as far as Tazawako and renting a car there. You could then visit nearby Kakunodate, Lake Tazawa, and Nyuto Onsen before continuing northward to Lake Towada. A 2-day rental of a subcompact car costs about ¥19,270 ($184), including mileage and insurance. Drop-off

fees can add ¥4,000 ($38). Keep in mind that Tohoku's winter season, from November to March, can bring below-freezing temperatures and up to a foot of snowfall virtually overnight. Some mountain passes are occasionally closed due to snowfall, though access to major ski resorts is generally open.

See "Getting Around Japan" in chapter 2 for more information on renting a car in Japan. Contact information for rental agencies in Tohoku is provided under individual destination listings below.

## 1 The Pine-Clad Islands of Matsushima (★)

375km (234 miles) NE of Tokyo

Because the trip to northern Tohoku or onward to Hokkaido is such a long one, the most pleasant way to travel is to break up the journey with an overnight stay in **Matsushima** ★. Matsushima means "Pine-Clad Islands"—and that's exactly what this region is. More than 260 pine-covered islets and islands dot Matsushima Bay, giving it the appearance of a giant pond in a Japanese landscape garden where twisted and gnarled pines sweep upward from volcanic tuff and white sandstone, creating bizarre and beautiful shapes.

Matsushima is so dear to Japanese hearts that it's considered one of the three most scenic spots in Japan (the other two are Miyajima in Hiroshima Bay and Amanohashidate on the north coast of Honshu)—and was so designated about 270 years ago in a book written by a Confucian philosopher of the Edo government. Basho (1644–94), the famous Japanese haiku poet, was so struck by Matsushima's beauty that it's almost as though he were at a loss for words when he wrote: "Matsushima, Ah! Matsushima! Matsushima!"

Unfortunately, motorboats have been invented since Basho's time, detracting from the beauty that evoked such ecstasy in him long ago.

## ESSENTIALS

**GETTING THERE**    From Tokyo, take the **Tohoku Shinkansen** train from Ueno or Tokyo Station to Sendai, which will take from 1½ to 2¼ hours, depending on the number of stops. In Sendai, change to the **JR Senseki Line**—it's well marked in English and trains depart approximately every half-hour. From Sendai, the trip to **Matsushima Kaigan Station** takes about 25 minutes by express train and costs ¥400 ($3.80).

A more picturesque way to get to Matsushima, however, is to take the Senseki Line from Sendai only as far as **Hon-Shiogama** (about 18 min. by express), where you can catch a **sightseeing boat** operated by the Matsushima Backroads Co. (© **022/366-5111**) for a 50-minute trip to **Matsushima Kaigan Pier;** tickets cost ¥1,420 ($14) for adults and ¥710 ($6.75) for children. You'll pass the unsightly Tohoku Thermal Electric Power Station, which it is said, was built in such a way "as not to distract from Matsushima Bay's beauty, but rather harmonize with it." I don't even have to tell you my thoughts on this. Otherwise, it's a pleasant trip, despite the nonstop commentary in Japanese. Boats depart from both Hon-Shiogama and Matsushima Kaigan piers in both directions about every half-hour between 8am and 4pm, but only once an hour between 9am and 3pm December through March. From Hon-Shiogama Station, it's a 10-minute walk to the boat pier; take a right out of the station, cross the street, turn right at the first red light (crossing under the tracks), and continue straight on.

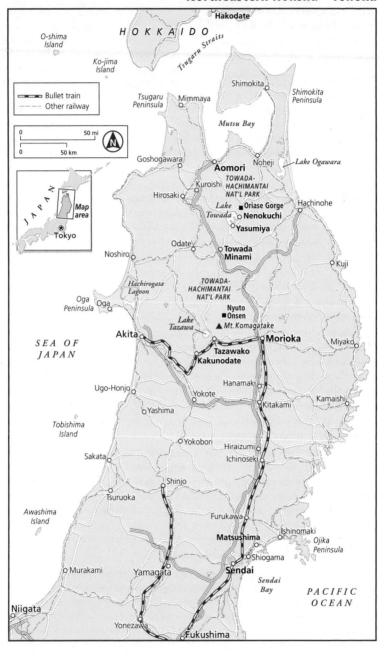

**VISITOR INFORMATION**    Upon your arrival in Matsushima, stop off at one of the two **Matsushima Tourist Association offices,** where you can pick up an English-language map with information on major sites and get directions to your hotel. One is located to the right as you exit **Matsushima Kaigan Station** (© **022/354-2263;** open weekdays 9am–4:30pm and weekends and holidays, 8:30am–5:30pm). The English-speaking staff here will also help reserve lodging. Adjoining the tourist office is a left-luggage counter, useful if you're making a quick stopover (there are also lockers in Sendai Station).

If you're arriving in Matsushima by boat, you'll find another information booth at **Matsushima Kaigan Pier** (© **022/354-2618;** open daily 8:30am–5pm, to 4:30pm in winter). *Note:* This office does not arrange accommodations.

Although information is limited, you can search for more on the Web at www.pref. miyagi.jp.

**ORIENTATION & GETTING AROUND**    **Matsushima Kaigan Station** lies to the west of the boat pier and Matsushima's main attractions; the train station and pier are about a 6-minute walk apart. All of Matsushima's major attractions are within walking distance of both the station and the pier (though the pier is more centrally located); you can cover the whole area on foot in a half-day of leisurely sightseeing. Otherwise, a Loop Line Bus passing many sights and most hotels runs daily twice an hour (7:50am–6:45pm) and costs ¥100 (95¢).

## SEEING THE SIGHTS

**CRUISING THE BAY**    Arriving in Matsushima by **sightseeing boat** is a good introduction to the bay because you'll pass pine-covered islands and oyster rafts along the way. Board the boat in Hon-Shiogama for the 50-minute trip to Matsushima Kaigan Pier (see "Getting There," above).

If you come by train or even if you arrive by boat, you might want to take a **boat trip** in the bay. Regular sightseeing boats depart from the pier once an hour between 9am and 4pm, making 50-minute trips around the bay; they charge ¥1,400 ($13) for adults, half price for children.

## TEMPLES & HISTORIC BUILDINGS

(240) **Zuiganji Temple** 𝒜𝒜𝒜    Matsushima's best-known structure is the most famous Zen temple in northern Japan. Located just a few minutes' walk from Matsushima Kaigan Pier and 7 minutes from the train station, its entrance is shaded by tall cedar trees. On the right side of the pathway leading to the temple are caves and grottoes dug out by priests long ago; adorned with Buddhist statues and memorial

---

### *Tips* A Note on Japanese Symbols

Many hotels, restaurants, attractions, and other establishments in Japan do not have signs giving their names in Roman (English-language) letters. Appendix C lists the Japanese symbols for all such places described in this guide. Each set of characters representing an establishment name has a number in the appendix that corresponds to the number that appears inside the oval before the establishment's name in the text. Thus, to find the Japanese symbol for, say, **Zuiganji Temple** (above), refer to no. 240 in appendix C.

tablets, they were used for practicing zazen (sitting meditation) and are an impressive sight. Here, too, you'll find what is probably Japan's only monument to—eels!

Now a National Treasure and the highlight of a stay in Matsushima, Zuiganji Temple was originally founded in the Heian Period (828) as a Tendai temple but became a Zen temple in the 13th century. After a period of decline, it was remodeled in 1604 by order of Date Masamune, the most powerful and important lord of northern Honshu. Unifying the region known as Tohoku, Date built his castle in nearby Sendai, and today almost all sites in and around Sendai and Matsushima are tied to the Date family. It took hundreds of workers 6 years to build the impressive main hall, a large wooden structure that was constructed in the shoin-zukuri style typical of the Momoyama Period; the hall originally served as the family temple of the Date clan. Be sure to walk around the temple for a better look at its gorgeous, gold-plated sliding doors.

The **Homotsuden** houses the **Zuiganji Art Museum (Seiryuden)** with its displays of temple and Date family treasures, including painted sliding doors, portraits of the Date clan, teacups, scrolls, calligraphy, and woodblock prints, many of Matsushima as it looked in former times, shown on a rotating basis. In all, you'll probably spend an hour at Zuiganji Temple.

Under the supervision of Zuiganji Temple is **Godaido,** a small wooden worship hall on a tiny island not far from the pier. Connected to the mainland by a short bridge, its grounds are open night and day and are free, but there's not much to see other than the bay. Nevertheless, Godaido is often featured in brochures of Matsushima, making this delicate wooden temple one of the town's best-known landmarks.

91 Aza-chonai. ✆ 022/354-2023. Admission for both Seiryuden and Zuiganji Temple ¥700 ($6.65) adults, ¥400 ($3.80) children. Daily 8am–between 3:30 and 5pm, depending on the month.

(241) **Entsuin** 🎯🎯 *Finds*   This lesser-known temple was also built in the early Edo Period, more than 340 years ago, by the Date clan. It features a small rock garden (with seven rocks representing the Seven Deities of Good Fortune), a moss garden with six different types of moss, a lovely rose garden, an Edo-Period garden with a pond and "borrowed landscaping," and a small temple housing an elaborate statue of Lord Date Mitsumune, grandson of Lord Date Masamune, who founded the Sendai fief. Depicted here on a white steed, Mitsumune was reportedly poisoned by the Tokugawa shogunate and died at the tender age of 19 in Edo Castle. The seven statues surrounding him represent retainers who committed ritual suicide to follow their master into death. The interior walls are all covered with an overlay of gold. The painting of an occidental rose on the right-hand door is thought to be the first in Japan (hence the rose garden); other Western flowers include narcissus and corona. Be on the lookout for "hidden" crosses above the door that are slanted; because Christianity was banned in Edo Japan, the Date clan used crosses as a symbol for silent revolt. Expect to spend about 45 minutes here.

67 Aza-chonai. ✆ 022/354-3206. Admission ¥300 ($2.85) adults, ¥150 ($1.40) high-school students, ¥100 (95¢) children. Daily 8am–5pm. Next to Zuiganji Temple (to the left as you face it).

**Kanrantei**   Another famous structure is Kanrantei, the "Water-Viewing Pavilion," just a 1-minute walk from the boat pier. A simple wooden teahouse, it was used by generations of the Date family for such aesthetic pursuits as viewing the moon and watching the ripples on the tide. Originally it belonged to warlord Toyotomi Hideyoshi as part of his estate at Fushimi Castle near Kyoto, but he presented it to the

Date family at the end of the 16th century; it was moved here in 1645, where it remains one of the largest teahouses in Japan.

For an additional ¥300 ($2.85), you can drink ceremonial green tea while sitting on the teahouse tatami and contemplating the bay, its islands, and the boats carving ribbons through the water. After tea, wander through the small museum containing samurai armor, ceramics, lacquerware, and tea-ceremony utensils belonging to the Date family.

56–1 Aza-chonai. ✆ 022/353-3355. Admission ¥200 ($1.90) adults, ¥150 ($1.40) university and high-school students, ¥100 (95¢) children. Daily 8:30am–5pm (to 4:30pm in winter).

## MUSEUMS

242 **Michinoku Date Masamune Historical Museum (Michinoku Date Masamune Rekishikan)** ✿ This wax museum details the life and times of Masamune (1567–1636) through 25 life-size, audiovisual diorama displays. Showing everything from how Masamune lost sight in one of his eyes at age 5, to his marriage at age 13, to his victories in battle, the dioramas bring to life what might otherwise be dull history. At the very least, you get to see how people dressed back then and learn why Masamune was nicknamed the One-Eyed Dragon. Of less interest are some wax figures of early-19th- and 20th-century personalities of northern Japan; be sure to ask for the English-language pamphlet, since otherwise you won't know who the heck they are. Plan on about 30 minutes here.

Matsushima Kaigan. ✆ 022/354-4131. Admission ¥1,000 ($9.50) adults, ¥600 ($5.70) junior-high and high-school students, ¥500 ($4.75) children. Daily 8:30am–5pm (9am–4:30pm in winter). Across from the Godaido Temple and set back from the main street.

**Matsushima Orgel Museum** ✿✿ This is a museum within a museum: It displays the entire Belgium National Music Box Museum, which was bought and shipped lock, stock, and barrel from Bruges, Belgium. The 100 or so music boxes, dating from 1860 to 1950, are priceless. Some were owned by kings; others were designed for theaters, exhibitions, dance halls, cafes, or train stations and are quite huge and elaborate. The largest in the collection (and one of the largest in the world) boasts 619 wooden pipes, drums, trumpets, and xylophones. There are also phonographs, player pianos, harmoniums dating from 1905, and other early inventions (including a 1900 Ediphone). Best of all, some of the music boxes are played on request. You can easily spend 45 minutes here.

33–3 Funendo. ✆ 022/353-3600. Admission ¥1,000 ($9.50) adults, ¥700 ($6.65) junior-high and high-school students, ¥500 ($4.75) children. Daily 9am–5:30pm, to 5pm in winter. Station: Matsushima Kaigan (15 min.). On the main road, an 8-min. walk from the pier.

## ISLANDS

On the southern edge of Matsushima, about an 8-minute walk from Matsushima Kaigan Station, is **Oshima** (also spelled Ojima), a small island once used as a retreat by priests. Long ago there were more than 100 hand-dug caves carved with scriptures, Buddhist images, and sutras, but today the island and its remaining 50 caves and stone images are rather neglected. There's no fee, there's no gate, and the island never closes. Connected to the mainland by bridge, it's a nice quiet spot in which to sit and view the harbor; you can walk around the entire island in about 20 minutes. Because it was a Buddhist retreat, women were forbidden on the island until after the Meiji Restoration in 1868.

At the other end of Matsushima, about a 10-minute walk from the boat pier, is **Fukuurajima,** another island connected to the mainland, this time by a long red concrete bridge with orange-colored railings. It's a botanical garden of sorts, with several hundred labeled plants and trees, but mostly it's unkempt and overgrown—which comes as a surprise in cultivated Japan. It will take you less than an hour to walk completely around the island, and there are many resting spots along the way, including a snack shop selling ice cream and drinks. The island gate is open 8am to 5pm (4:30pm in winter) and admission is ¥200 ($1.90) for adults, half price for children.

## WHERE TO STAY

Because this is a popular tourist destination, accommodations in Matsushima are not cheap, especially during the peak months of May through November. For the Tanabata Festival (Aug 6–8 in Sendai) and the Toronagashi Festival (Aug 15–16 in Matsushima), rooms may be fully booked 6 months in advance and rates are at their highest. Rates are generally lower during the off-season months (Dec–Apr).

Directions are given from the boat pier or train station, whichever is closer. The pier and station are about a 6-minute walk apart.

### EXPENSIVE

⟨243⟩ **Hotel Ichinobo** 🐦🐦   Despite its large size, modern facilities, and the word "hotel" in its name, this property has the atmosphere of a traditional ryokan and offers mostly Japanese-style rooms. It's surrounded by pine trees and boasts lovely landscaped grounds and ponds, with views of the sea and islands from all its rooms and the wonderful public baths. It also offers 26 esthetically furnished Matsushima Club twin rooms that include use of a private lounge; some of these boast glassed-in, private whirlpool baths off private balconies. Kaiseki dinners are served in your room or in one of two restaurants, one featuring a pond where hapless fish await their fate and the other offering Italian cuisine. Glass buffs should not miss the hotel's Kyohei Fujita Museum of Glass, dedicated to Kyohei Fujita, the only glass artist designated a National Living Treasure. Although Ichinobo's location on the northern edge of Matsushima—about a 20-minute walk from the pier—is inconvenient, staff will fetch you upon arrival, and the Loop Line Bus also stops here.

Matsushima Kaigan, Matsushima-cho, Miyagi-gun 981-0215. ✆ 022/353-3333. Fax 022/353-3339. m_yoyaku@ ichinobo.com. 126 units. ¥20,000 ($190) per person; ¥26,000–¥28,000 ($248–$266) Club twin room per person. ¥2,000 ($19) extra per person Sat and holidays. Rates include 2 meals and service charge. AE, DC, MC, V. Free shuttle bus from pier or train station. Loop Line Bus: Hotel Ichinobo stop. **Amenities:** 2 restaurants (kaiseki, Italian); 1 bar; 1 tea lounge; outdoor pool (free for hotel guests); public indoor and outdoor baths; in-room massage; same-day laundry/dry-cleaning service; glass museum. *In room:* A/C, TV, minibar, hot-water pot w/tea, hair dryer, safe, Washlet toilet.

**Matsushima Century Hotel** 🐦   This white hotel, near Fukuurajima island, is popular with families. I recommend taking a Japanese-style room or a combination room with both tatami area and beds, as these all face the bay with a balcony and chairs. Otherwise, if you're on a budget, the cheapest Western-style rooms, though sunny and cheerful, face inland and have no balconies. Meals are served in a restaurant; breakfast is an all-you-can-eat buffet.

8 Aza Senzui, Matsushima-cho, Miyagi-gun 981-0213. ✆ 022/354-4111. Fax 022/354-4191. 135 units. ¥14,000– ¥20,000 ($133–$190) per person in summer; ¥13,000–¥19,000 ($124–$181) per person in winter. Rates include 2 meals and service charge. AE, DC, MC, V. A 5-min. walk east of the pier. Call for a pickup from the station or pier. Loop Line: Century Hotel stop. **Amenities:** 2 restaurants (both Japanese); 1 coffee shop; outdoor pool (free for hotel

guests); public baths (w/sauna) overlooking the bay; in-room massage; same-day laundry/dry-cleaning service. *In room:* A/C, TV, minibar, hot-water pot w/tea, hair dryer, safe (in Japanese-style rooms only).

(244) **Taikanso** 🌸🌸 Able to accommodate 1,100 guests, Matsushima's largest hotel sprawls atop a plateau surrounded by pine-covered hills and offers the best view in town. To compensate for its isolation, a shuttle bus will pick you up from the station if you call; the Loop Line bus also stops. Both Western- and Japanese-style rooms are available, though the cheapest rooms (singles and twins) face inland. All the Japanese-style rooms face the sea, including wonderful combination rooms (the most expensive) which offer the best of both worlds with tatami areas and beds, and offer bedside controls for curtains and lights, showers and deep tubs, wet bars, and wall-to-wall windows with great views. A plus here is that you can choose from six restaurants to dine in, with rates dependent on the meal and restaurant. One of the least expensive is one of my favorites: Shiosai (p. 561), which has the best view in town of both Matsushima Bay and the surrounding hills. The front desk is very helpful with English-language sightseeing information.

10–76 Aza Inuta, Matsushima-cho, Miyagi-gun 981-0213. ☎ **022/354-2161.** Fax 022/353-3431. www.taikanso. co.jp. 256 units. ¥9,800–¥21,000 ($93–$200) per person. ¥1,000 ($9.50) extra in peak season. Rates include 2 meals and service charge. AE, DC, MC, V. Station: Matsushima Kaigan (15 min.). Loop Line Bus: Taikanso stop. **Amenities:** 9 restaurants; 3 bars; 1 coffee shop; outdoor pool (free for hotel guests); indoor and outdoor public baths overlooking the island-studded bay; game room; souvenir and amenities shop; room service (8pm–midnight); in-room massage; same-day laundry/dry-cleaning service. *In room:* A/C, TV, minibar, hot-water pot w/tea, hair dryer, safe.

## MODERATE

**Folkloro Matsushima** *Value* Opened in 1999, this modern, simple budget hotel with Western-style rooms is located on a steep hill above the train station and has a nice outdoor terrace where you can have breakfast (dinner is not available). Catering mostly to couples and families, it offers only twins and larger units (though solo travelers can stay in a twin room); some family rooms, with two twin beds and two sofa beds, have views of the sea. Rail pass holders get a 10% discount. Higher rates below are for peak season.

17 Sanjukari, Matsushima Aza, Matsushima-cho, Miyagi-gun 981-0213. ☎ **022/353-3535.** Fax 022/353-3588. 29 units. ¥7,350–¥8,610 ($70–$82) single; ¥12,600–¥17,220 ($120–$164) twin; ¥17,850–¥20,580 ($170–$196) triple; ¥21,000–¥23,940 ($200–$228) quad. Rates include breakfast and service charge. AE, DC, MC, V. Station: Matsushima Kaigan (10 min.). Take a right out of the station, then another right under the tracks, and continue straight up the hill; the hotel will be on your left. Free shuttle from the station 3–5pm. *In room:* A/C, TV, fridge, hot-water pot w/tea.

**Hotel Daimatsuso** An older, slightly worn hotel, with a lobby crowded by a souvenir shop and vending machines, it's homey nonetheless and close to the train station. It has Japanese-style rooms, facing the sea with balconies. Best are those on the fifth floor, some of which are combination rooms with beds and tatami areas. The cheapest rooms (both Japanese and Western style) have no bathrooms and look unceremoniously onto another building; this is where you'll probably end up if you opt for a room without meals. Rooms come with the basics, though some of the built-in bathroom units are so small you have to wonder how some people fit into them. Dinner is served in your room, while breakfast is served communally in the ground-floor dining room.

25 Azachonai, Matsushima-cho, Miyagi-gun 981-0213. ☎ **022/354-3601.** Fax 022/354-6154. 41 units (4 with toilet only, 29 with bathroom). ¥7,000–¥8,000 ($67–$76) per person without meals; ¥9,000–¥15,000 ($86–$142) per person with 2 meals. AE, DC, MC, V. Station: Matsushima Kaigan (1 min). Walk straight out of the station; the hotel will be on your left. *In room:* A/C, TV, minibar, hot-water pot w/tea, safe.

**INEXPENSIVE**

(245) **Ryokan Kozakura**  An inexpensive, 30-year-old ryokan, Kozakura is very simple but serves delicious and generous Japanese meals in your tatami room. Friendly owners don't speak much English. One drawback is that it's on the main truck route; if you're a light sleeper, request a room at the back.

13–7 Aza Fugendo, Matsushima-cho, Miyagi-gun 981-0213. ✆ 022/354-2518. Fax 022/354-5353. 12 units (4 with bathroom). ¥3,150–¥6,300 ($30–$60) per person without meals; ¥6,300–¥15,750 ($60–$150) per person with 2 meals. No credit cards. A 5-min. walk from the pier. Take a right onto the main street and continue past the 3rd signal; the ryokan is just past a sake shop, on the left. In room: A/C, TV, minibar, hot-water pot w/tea.

## WHERE TO DINE

In summer, stalls up and down the main street of Matsushima sell grilled octopus, corn on the cob, and crab.

(246) **Donjiki Chaya** NOODLES/ODANGO  This rustic noodle shop is a convenient place for an inexpensive lunch if you're visiting Zuiganji and Entsuin temples. Built about 400 years ago, it's easy to spot because of its thatched roof, with sliding doors pushed wide open in summer and tatami seating. In addition to buckwheat noodles, it also serves *odango*—pounded rice balls covered with sesame, red-bean, or soy sauce for ¥480 ($4.55). There's an English-language menu.

Entsuin-mae, Matsushima. ✆ 022/354-5855. Noodles ¥380–¥550 ($3.60–$5.25). No credit cards. Apr–Nov daily 9am–5pm; Dec–Mar Sat–Sun and holidays 9am–4pm. In front of Entsuin Temple, a 5-min. walk from Matsushima Kaigan Station or the pier.

**Shiosai** ✿✿ Value FRENCH  Located atop a hill, this restaurant has the best view in town. Book a table at sunset close to the floor-to-ceiling windows overlooking Matsushima, where you can watch the day fade and lights in the town below begin to glimmer. Only set meals are available, but they're very good and surprisingly inexpensive. My ¥2,300 ($22) dinner consisted of pumpkin soup, seafood cocktail and steak, salad, bread, dessert, and coffee or tea. It's a good place for a romantic meal. Or, from 2:30 to 4pm, come for dessert and coffee or local Matsushima Brewing Company beer and enjoy the view.

Taikanso Hotel, 7th floor, 10–76 Aza Inuta. ✆ 022/354-2161. Set lunches ¥1,600–¥5,000 ($15–$48); set dinners ¥2,300–¥5,000 ($22–$48). AE, DC, MC, V. Daily 11:30am–2:30pm and 5:30–8:30pm (last order). For directions, see "Where to Stay," above.

**Ungai** ✿ Finds BUDDHIST VEGETARIAN  Located on the grounds of Entsuin Temple (dining here gets you free admission to the temple), this is a great place for a peaceful meal, as you dine in a modern tatami room and look out over a garden. It serves three set meals typical of Buddhist vegetarian cuisine (which features many small dishes with vegetables and tofu that change with the seasons); let your budget be your guide. Although reservations should be made 1 day in advance, your hotel may be able to reserve on the same day.

Entsuin Temple, 67 Aza-chonai. ✆ 022/353-2626. Reservations required. Set meal ¥3,500 ($33), ¥5,000 ($48), and ¥7,000 ($67). No credit cards. Daily 11am–2pm. Next to Zuiganji Temple (Entsuin Temple is to the left when facing Zuiganji Temple; the restaurant entrance is just past Entsuin's entrance).

## 2 Kakunodate, Town of Samurai Homes ✿

**Kakunodate** was founded in 1620 by feudal lord Ashina Yoshikatsu, who chose the site for its river and easily defended mountain. His samurai retainers settled just south of his hilltop castle, in modest thatched-roof homes behind wooden fences along

wide, fine streets, which they lined with weeping cherry trees imported from Kyoto. To help support themselves, the samurai engaged in cottage industry, crafting beautiful products made from cherry bark. Meanwhile, merchants settled in their own district, in narrow, cramped quarters. Many of the town's 14,600 residents are direct descendants of the town's original samurai and merchants.

Although the castle is long gone, Kakunodate's castle-town architectural layout remains remarkably intact, with one of the country's best-preserved (though regrettably small) samurai districts in Japan. It's also famous for its cherry trees, not only in the samurai district, but also along the banks of the Hinokinai River, and crafts produced from local cherry bark are still famous throughout Japan. Yet Kakunodate is an unpretentious village, with only a few of the souvenir and tourist shops that plague other picturesque towns.

## ESSENTIALS

**GETTING THERE**    From Tokyo, take the **Tohoku Shinkansen train** from Ueno or Tokyo Station to Morioka and then the **Akita Shinkansen** to Kakunodate. (You can travel via some Shinkansen the entire distance without having to transfer in Morioka.) The trip takes about 3½ hours and costs ¥15,850 ($151) for an unreserved seat. Kakunodate is just one stop after Tazawako. (See "Towada-Hachimantai National Park: For the Active Traveler," below.)

**VISITOR INFORMATION**    After you exit Kakunodate Station, look for the **Kakunodate Tourist Information Center** to the right, housed in a replica of a traditional warehouse (© **0187/52-1170;** open daily 9am–6pm). There you can pick up an English-language map from the helpful, English-speaking staff.

**ORIENTATION & GETTING AROUND**    You can walk to all the sights and lodging and dining recommendations below (though you might opt for a short taxi ride to your accommodations if you're weighed down by luggage). To reach the samurai district, about a 15- to 20-minute walk from the station, walk straight out of the station and continue until it ends at a T-intersection (you'll see a post office across the street; this is the former merchant district and the heart of the city). Here, you turn right.

**CAR RENTALS**    If you've rented a car through **JR Eki Rent-A-Car** (© **0187/53-2070**), you can pick it up at Folkloro Kakunodate, a JR-owned hotel beside the train station to the left. For **Toyota Rent-A-Car** in Kakunodate, call © **0187/55-2100.**

## SEEING THE SIGHTS

Kakunodate is at its most glorious (and crowded) in late April, when its hundreds of cherry trees are in full bloom. The most popular viewing spot is along the Hinokinai River, where two rows of some 400 cherry trees form a shimmering tunnel of blossoms for 2km (1¼ miles). They were planted in 1933 to commemorate the birth of the present emperor, Akihito.

**THE SAMURAI DISTRICT (BUKEYASHIKI)** 👣👣    Of Kakunodate's 80-some samurai mansions built during the Edo Period, only six remain. Still, the district retains its feudal atmosphere to an amazing degree, thanks to its wide streets flanked by weeping cherry trees and dark wooden fences. These fences and traditional entry gates are employed even today to conceal more modern homes, giving a clean, crisp line of vision throughout the district. It's a strong contrast to the jumble of most Japanese cities, and even to the merchant district just a short walk away.

If you're walking from the station, the first place of interest will be the ㉔⑦ **Aoyagi Samurai Manor (Kakunodate Rekishi-mura Aoyagi)** ✿✿✿, Higashi Katurakucho 26 (📞 **0187/54-3257**), to the right through an impressive entry gate. Its English-language name is misleading, since it's actually a compound of several traditional buildings spread throughout a garden, each filled with a wealth of eclectic treasures from the 17th to 20th centuries; all of them were collected through the ages by the Aoyagi family. As you wander through the buildings, you'll see samurai armor, rifles, swords, dolls, kimono, sake cups, Ukiyo-e (woodblock prints), scrolls and screens, Meiji-Era uniforms and medals, farm tools, antique phonographs, and cameras. One building serves as a fascinating antiques store (with high prices), while others hold a gift shop and a restaurant. You'll want to spend at least an hour exploring here. Open daily 9am to 5pm (to 4pm in winter). Admission is ¥500 ($4.75) for adults, ¥300 ($2.85) for junior-high and high-school students, and ¥200 ($1.90) for children.

Next door is the **Ishiguro Samurai House** ✿✿, Omotemachi (📞 **0187/55-1496**). In contrast to the Aoyagi Samurai Manor, this thatched-roof home remains almost exactly as it might have looked when it was constructed 200 years ago by the Ishiguro samurai family. After the Meiji Restoration, the family became landlords and collected rice as rent. Today, English-speaking, 12th-generation Ishiguro Naotsugi continues to live here; he has opened five simple but elegant rooms to the public in the main house. Family heirlooms, including samurai gear, winter *geta* (fur-lined and with spikes), scales for weighing rice, and old maps of Kakunodate are on display in a former warehouse. The medical illustrations (copies), by the way, are from Japan's first book on anatomy, copied from a Dutch book in 1774 by Kakunodate samurai Odano Naotake. You can see everything in less than 30 minutes, though if Ishiguro-san is on hand to answer questions, you might linger longer. Open daily 9am to 5pm. Admission is ¥300 ($2.85) for adults and ¥150 ($1.40) for children.

## SHOPPING

Kakunodate has been famous for its cherry-bark crafts since the Edo Period. You can observe this painstaking craft by watching artisans at work at the ㉔⑧ **Kakunodatemachi Denshokan,** Omotemachi Shimocho 10–1 (📞 **0187/54-1700**), just a couple minutes' walk from the samurai houses, above. In addition to seeing how strips of cherry bark are applied to tea canisters, boxes, vases, and other crafts, you can tour a museum devoted to the craft and shop for cherry-bark products in its large shop. Admission to the denshokan is ¥300 ($2.85) for adults and ¥150 ($1.40) for children. It's open daily 9am to 5pm (to 4:30pm in winter).

## WHERE TO STAY

Although you can easily tour Kakunodate's sights in a day, I've included a few accommodations in case you're arriving from Tokyo or seeking respite in a small town. Keep in mind that you should book well ahead if you hope to stay here during peak seasons: cherry-blossom season (roughly end of Apr through beginning of May) and summer holidays (mid-July through Aug).

**Folkloro Kakunodate**    No English is spoken at this JR-affiliated hotel, but its location next to Kakunodate Station and its simple but clean, modern, and inexpensive Western-style rooms make it a logical choice for a 1-night stopover. Only two types of rooms are available: 11 twins and 15 family rooms that sleep up to four. Note, however,

that the family rooms seem cramped for four but are roomy for two. Your rail pass entitles you to a 10% discount. Higher rates below are for peak season. A breakfast buffet is served in a pleasant coffee shop.

Iwase Nakasuga-sawa 14, Kakunodate, Senboku-shi, Akita. © **0187/53-2070.** Fax 0187/53-2118. 26 units. ¥7,350–¥9,030 ($70–$86) single; ¥12,600–¥18,900 ($120–$180) twin; ¥17,850–¥22,050 ($170–$210) triple; ¥21,000–¥25,200 ($200–$240) quad. Rates include breakfast and service charge. AE, MC, V. To the left after you exit the train station. **Amenities:** Restaurant (Japanese/Western food); car-rental agency; nonsmoking rooms. *In room:* TV, fridge, hot-water pot w/tea, hair dryer.

(249) **Ishikawa Ryokan**    One of Kakunodate's oldest ryokan, open since the Edo Period and now in its fifth generation of innkeepers, it now occupies a dated building constructed in 1920. Although corridors suggest the ordinary, the Japanese-style rooms are fine, simple but with nice wood details. And the elderly owners are every bit as self-effacing and hospitable to guests as their ancestors must have been to traveling samurai and other high officials. Though they don't speak English, they make your stay here a real treat. Meals are served in your room.

Iwasemachi 32, Kakunodate, Senboku-shi, Akita. © **0187/54-2030.** Fax 0187/54-2031. 11 units (2 with bathroom, 1 with toilet only). ¥9,000–¥17,000 ($86–$162) per person. Rates include 2 meals. No credit cards. A 12-min. walk from the station. Walk straight out of the train station and turn left at the 4th street (1 block before the T intersection); the ryokan will be on your right. *In room:* A/C, TV, hot-water pot w/tea.

(250) **Tamachi Bukeyashiki Hotel** 🎔🎔 *(Finds)*    This delightful hotel is deceiving—it looks as though it has been here since the Edo Period, with its whitewashed walls, open wooden beams, and rustic ambience, but it was built in 1999. It combines tradition with modern comfort, with gleaming wood floors, contemporary Japanese art, and Japanese- and Western-style rooms that exude class, from sensuously curving paper lampshades to ceramic tissue holders. Breakfast is served in a dark-wood-tabled restaurant overlooking a garden. In short, this small, intimate establishment is a perfect choice for experiencing Kakunodate's relaxed, small-town charm.

Tamachi Shimocho 23, Kakunodate, Akita. © **0187/52-1700.** Fax 0187/52-1701. 12 units. ¥13,000–¥19,000 ($124–$181) per person with 2 meals. ¥10,500 ($100) per person with breakfast only. Winter discounts available. AE, DC, MC, V. A 12-min. walk from the station. Walk straight out of the train station and turn left at the 3rd street; the hotel will be 2 blocks down, on your right. **Amenities:** Restaurant (Japanese). *In room:* A/C, fridge, hot-water pot w/tea, hair dryer, Washlet toilet.

## WHERE TO DINE

In addition to the choices here, a simple dining room at the Aoyagi Samurai Manor, called **Inaniwa Korai Udon** (© **0187/52-8015**), offers inexpensive noodle dishes, including tempura soba (¥1,260/$12) and *sansai udon* (noodles with mountain vegetables, ¥840/$8). Open daily 10am to 4pm (but only on weekends in winter), it has an English-language menu.

(251) **Nishinomiyake** 🎔 VARIED JAPANESE    This pleasant and inexpensive restaurant is located in the family compound of the Nishinomiya clan, a samurai family that later became merchants and built the main house and five warehouses that are on display today. The restaurant is in a warehouse dating from 1919 and offers a limited menu of fried seafood, noodles, beef hash with rice, and other dishes. Best, perhaps, is to order one of the obento lunch boxes. After your meal, be sure to wander through the other warehouses, including a small museum housing family treasures and a crafts shop.

Tamachi Kami-cho 11–1. ✆ 0187/52-2438. Obento ¥1,500–¥2,000 ($14–$19). No credit cards. Daily 10am–6pm (5 in winter). Station: Kakunodate (8 min.). Walk straight out of the train station and turn left at the 3rd street; the restaurant will be almost immediately on your right.

252 **Sakura Tei** ⚔ LOCAL SPECIALTIES    You'll sit on tatami mats next to a koi pond and small garden while you dine on local dishes, including *kiritampo nabe* (a one-pot stew consisting of newly harvested rice pounded into a paste and then charcoal grilled before simmering in chicken broth with vegetables) cooked at your table, *inaniwa udon* (handmade noodles), and the best *oyakodon* (rice topped with chicken and egg) I've ever had, made with free-range Hinai chicken.

Yokomachi 18. ✆ 0187/53-2970. Set lunches ¥1,575–¥1,890 ($15–$18); noodles ¥1,050–¥1,155 ($10–$11). No credit cards. Daily 9am–5pm. Station: Kakunodate (9 min.). Just before the Samurai District, across from the Town Office marked on the map.

## 3 Towada-Hachimantai National Park: For the Active Traveler

Towada-Hachimantai National Park, spreading 862 sq. km (333 sq. miles) through north-central Tohoku and shared by three prefectures, is blessed with mountain ranges, lakes, streams, and hot-spring spas. It's perfect for the outdoor enthusiast, offering hiking in summer and skiing in winter. Most easily accessible from Tokyo is **Lake Tazawa** at the southern end of the park, with its nearby ski lifts, hot-springs, and biking and hiking opportunities. Far to the north, and a good choice if you're heading onward to Hokkaido, are the pristine **Lake Towada** and delightful **Oirase Stream** with its riverbank hiking trail.

Unfortunately, bus service through Towada-Hachimantai National Park is either infrequent or nonexistent. There is, for example, no bus that connects lakes Tazawa and Towada, so you either have to choose one to visit, or make a long, circuitous journey by bus and train. If you want to see both, your best bet is to rent a car.

### LAKE TAZAWA, NYUTO ONSEN & MOUNT KOMAGATAKE

Lake Tazawa (Tazawako) has the distinction of being the deepest lake in Japan, 423m (1,387 ft.) deep. Crystal clear, it offers swimming as well as cycling along its rim. Nearby are several ski resorts, as well as the Nyuto Onsen rustic hot-spring spas at the base of Mount Nyuto which make good bases for exploring the area. Mount Komagatake is a popular destination for trekkers.

### ESSENTIALS

**GETTING THERE**    From Tokyo, take the **Tohoku Shinkansen train** from Ueno or Tokyo Station to Morioka and then the **Akita Shinkansen** to Tazawako Station. (You can travel via some Shinkansen the entire distance without having to transfer in Morioka.) The trip takes about 3 hours and costs ¥15,240 ($147) for an unreserved seat. Tazawako is one stop before Kakunodate (see the "Kakunodate, Town of Samurai Homes" section above). In Tazawako you can board a bus to all the recommendations below, including Nyuto Onsen.

**VISITOR INFORMATION**    For information on Lake Tazawa and vicinity, including skiing and bus schedules throughout the region, stop by the **Tazawako Tourist Information Center** inside Tazawako Station (✆ 0187/43-2111; open daily 8:30am–6:30pm). They also offer Internet use and a topographical model of the area.

**ORIENTATION & GETTING AROUND**    The town of Tazawako, in Akita Prefecture, is the transportation launching pad for visiting the southern region of

Towada-Hachimantai National Park. **Buses** depart from the Tazawako Bus Terminal across from Tazawako Station for Lake Tazawa, area ski resorts, Mount Komagatake, and Nyuto Onsen hot-spring spas. Ask for bus schedules at the Tazawako Tourist Information Center.

Lake Tazawa is just a 15-minute bus ride from Tazawako Station; note that some buses stopping here go onward to Tazawako Skijo ski resort, Kogen Onsen, and Nyuto Onsen, all of which lie northeast of the lake. Otherwise, a bus departs Tazawako Station approximately every hour for Tazawako Skijo (a 30-min. ride), Kogen Onsen (37 min.), and Nyuto Onsen (45 min.)

**CAR RENTALS**   Tazawako is a good starting point for driving excursions through Towado-Hachimantai National Park. **JR Eki Rent-A-Car** (𝄞 **0187/43-1081**) is located beside Tazawako Station. For **Toyota Rent-A-Car** in Tazawako, call 𝄞 **0187/43-2100.**

## WHAT TO SEE & DO
**SWIMMING & CYCLING AT LAKE TAZAWA**   Just 20km (13 miles) in circumference, Lake Tazawa is popular for its small swimming beach a couple minutes' walk from Tazawako Kohan bus stop. Outside the swimming season—mid-July through August—you'll find nary a soul there. You can rent bicycles here for ¥400 ($3.80) for the first hour and ¥300 ($2.85) for every additional hour; mountain bikes run ¥600 ($5.70) per hour. It takes about 2 hours to ride around the lake; unfortunately, you have to share the road with vehicular traffic, but because this is a popular cycling route, motorists know to keep a lookout. (Still, it may be prudent to avoid weekends and the mid-July-through-August vacation crunch.) Except for one small stretch, the road is mostly flat (it may be easier to circle the lake counterclockwise); it is pleasantly wooded and relatively unspoiled. Along the way you'll pass a golden statue of the legendary Princess Tatsuko, a nymphlike beauty just off the shoreline. According to myth, the princess drank from Lake Tazawa hoping for eternal beauty; instead, she was turned into a dragonlike serpent as punishment for her vanity.

Sightseeing boats, some of which make stops to explore the surrounding woods, operate on Lake Tazawa from late April to early November; a 40-minute trip costs ¥1,170 ($11).

Laka Tazawa is a 15-minute bus ride from Tazawako Station. Many buses travel the route—the name of the bus stop at the Lake is called Tazawako Han—and the fare is ¥350 ($3.35).

**SKIING**   Of several area ski resorts, largest is **Tazawako Skijo** (𝄞 **0187/46-2011**), with nine lifts. A 1-day lift ticket costs ¥3,200 ($30). Ski-equipment rental costs ¥7,000 ($67) for everything; snowboarding is also available. Buses from Tazawako Station (traveling in the direction of Nyuto Onsen) reach Tazawako Skijo in about 30 minutes and cost ¥510 ($4.85).

Smaller, with four lifts and no black (expert) slopes, is nearby **Tazawakokougen Assl Skijo** (𝄞 **0187/46-2723**).

**CLIMBING MOUNT KOMAGATAKE**   Visible from Lake Tazawa, Akita Prefecture's tallest mountain is actually a 1,611m-high (5,370-ft.) dormant volcano. It's a popular destination for hikers, though a bus that deposits hikers at the 8th Station makes it a fairly quick hike—you can reach the top in about 1½ hours. At the peak, you're rewarded with grand vistas of the surrounding mountains, as well as more hiking trails. Since the path is steep at times, wear nonslip soles. (All Japanese will be outfitted in

regulation hiking regalia.) From Tazawako Station, six buses a day make the 1-hour trip directly to Mount Komagatake's 8th Station (¥810/$7.70). Or take a bus 37 minutes to Kogen Onsen (¥580/$5.50) and transfer there for a 25-minute ride to the 8th station ¥410/$3.90).

## WHERE TO STAY

253 **Kuroyu** 🌸🌸    Although I'm partial to Tsuru-no-yu (see below), some consider this Nyuto Onsen's best place to stay. A little more than 1km (½ mile or a 20-min. walk) from the main Nyuto Onsen road, this rustic inn has a secluded location and one of the area's best outdoor baths, separated for men and women and with good views of the surrounding mountainside. The ryokan first opened more than 60 years ago; some of the original thatched-roof buildings remain. Most of the accommodations, however, are in two-story buildings offering small, very simple tatami rooms; meals are served in a communal tatami dining room. Or, you can opt to stay in a very rustic relocated farmhouse and cook for yourself on the open-hearthed fireplace (irori), but you must pack in all your gear (If you plan to picnic or cook for yourself, do your shopping beforehand, as there are no convenience stores within the park). Clearly, what draws most here are the baths, discovered in 1674.

2–1 Kuroyu, Tazawako-machi, Senboku-shi, Akita 014-1201. ☎ **0187/46-2214.** Fax 0187/46-2280. 22 units (1 with toilet only). ¥11,700 ($111) per person, including 2 meals. ¥3,000 ($29) per person rustic room, no meals. Closed mid-Nov to Apr. No credit cards. Bus: From Tazawako Station, 50 min. to Kuroyu bus stop and then a 20-min. walk. Limited morning and evening shuttle service from Qkamura-mae bus stop. **Amenities:** Indoor/outdoor hot-spring baths. *In room:* Hot-water pot w/tea, no phone.

254 **Qkamura National Park Resort Village (Kyukamura Tazawako-Kogen)** This government-owned public lodging offers the convenience of being on Nyuto Onsen's main road (buses from Tazawako Station stop right outside). While it lacks the wonderful ambience of the other rustic inns in the area and has about as much charm as a dormitory, it was recently renovated and offers both indoor and outdoor hot-spring baths. In addition, it's the only place to stay if you prefer Western-style rooms, though Japanese tatami rooms are also available. Rooms are simple but pleasant, with sinks and toilets (three Western-style rooms have bathrooms). If you stay here, you can still sample the other ryokans' hot-spring baths for a modest fee. Buffet-style meals are served in a communal dining room; your Northern Tohoku Welcome Card gets you a free drink.

Komagatake 2–1, Tazawako-machi, Senboku-shi, Akita 014-1201. ☎ **0187/46-2244.** Fax 0187/46-2700. Info@ qkamura-s.com. 38 units (all with toilet, 3 with bathroom). ¥10,800 ($103) single with toilet only, ¥11,300 ($108) single with bathroom; ¥9,800 ($93) per person double with toilet only, ¥10,300 ($98) per person double with bathroom. Rates include 2 meals. AE, MC, V. Bus: From Tazawako Station, 50 min. to Qkamura-mae stop. **Amenities:** Indoor/outdoor hot-spring baths; coin-op washer/dryer. *In room:* TV, hot-water pot w/tea, safe.

255 **Tsuru-no-yu Onsen** 🌸🌸🌸 (finds    By far, this is the best place to stay in Nyuto Onsen, if not in all of Tohoku. Contrary to what you might think, however, it's not refined or elegant; it's not even expensive. Rather, nestled in a wooded valley more than 2.5km (1½ miles) off the already isolated main Nyuto Onsen road, this is about as remote as you can get in Japan. And with its thatched-roof row house of tiny tatami rooms lit by oil lamps, complemented by the sound of rushing water and steam rising from the outdoor baths, it seems positively ancient. I've never seen anything like it.

Tsuru-no-yu opened as an onsen 350 years ago; its oldest building—the row house of connected rooms—is 100 years old; your dinner will be cooked on your open-hearth fireplace (irori); breakfast is served in a tatami dining hall, with all the guests

dressed in *yukata* (cotton kimonos). Additions that ramble along the hillside were constructed over the years, along a rushing stream that serenades you to sleep. If you're on a budget, however, you can stay in the self-cooking wing, which offers simple tatami rooms and allows you to cook your own meals in a communal kitchen. Outdoor sulfurous baths are separated for men and women, but there is one mixed bath. Unfortunately, day-trippers spoil some of the fun of staying here. Evenings, however, are magical. Another plus: This is one of the few onsen open all year, with great cross-country skiing. *Caveat:* Avoid the modern annex Yama no Yado about 10 minutes down the road. Its indoor baths are unspectacular (and its outdoor bath is for both sexes); if you've come this far, stay in the real thing.

Kokuyurin 50, Tazawako-machi, Senboku-shi, Akita 014-1204. © **0187/46-2139.** Fax 0187/46-2761. 35 units (14 with toilet, none with bathroom). ¥8,000–¥15,000 ($76–$143) per person including 2 meals. ¥2,500 ($24) per person in the self-cooking wing, plus ¥500 ($4.75) for kitchen use. MC, V. Pickup available from Kogen Onsen bus station. **Amenities:** Indoor/outdoor hot-spring baths. *In room:* Hot-water pot w/tea, no phone in most rooms.

## LAKE TOWADA & OIRASE STREAM 🍁🍁

Located at the northern end of Towada-Hachimantai National Park on the border between Aomori and Akita prefectures, **Lake Towada** (Towadako in Japanese) is considered one of the park's top scenic gems. It's certainly one of Japan's least spoiled lakes, with only two small villages on its perimeter and encircled by wooded cliffs and mountains. Best, however, is **Oirase Stream,** the only river flowing out of Lake Towada. A shaded mountain stream that courses over boulders and down waterfalls, it is flanked by a hiking trail offering one of the prettiest walks in Tohoku. In autumn, leaves of gold and red render the scenery truly spectacular.

### ESSENTIALS

**GETTING THERE**   Since Lake Towada does not lie close to a train station, your final journey to the lake must be by **bus** to Yasumiya, a small village on Lake Towada with a tourist office and a few accommodations. The name of the bus stop in Yasumiya is Towadako.

From Tokyo, take the 3-hour **Shinkansen train** to Hachinohe, then board a bus to Yasumiya, which takes about 2¼ hours and costs ¥2,420 ($23). Or to get as close as possible to Towada Lake by train, take the Shinkansen from Tokyo 2 hours 20 minutes to Morioka Station, then transfer for the local JR Hanawa Line 2 hours to Towada-Minami Station, where Chuhoku Bus has three runs daily (Apr–Oct only) to Yasumiya, costing ¥1,130 ($11) for the 1-hour trip.

If you are arriving from Hokkaido, take the train to Aomori. Outside Aomori Station, to the left, you can board a **JR bus** bound for Lake Towada, with the last stop at Yasumiya 3 hours later. If you have a JR Rail Pass, you can ride for free; or, your Northern Tohoku Welcome Card gives you a 50% discount off the ¥3,000 ($29) fare. Note that this bus travels the same road as the hiking trail along Oirase Stream (see below) and makes several stops there, with about six runs daily. Also be aware that bus service to Lake Towada is available only from April to early November; for a JR bus, you can make reservations in advance at a major JR train station or travel agency. For more information, contact the **JR Bus** company in Aomori at © **017/723-1621.**

**CAR RENTALS**   JR Eki Rent-A-Car has offices at Aomori Station (© **017/722-3930**) and Morioka Station (© **019/624-5212**). **Toyota Rent-A-Car** also has offices near Aomori Station (© **017/734-0100**) and Morioka Station (© **019/622-0100**).

**VISITOR INFORMATION**    Before leaving Tokyo or the Narita or Kansai airports, pick up the "Towada-Hachimantai National Park" leaflet at the Tourist Information Center, or download it JNTO's website at www.jnto.go.jp by looking under "Regional Tourist Guides."

In Yasumiya, the **Lake Towada Information Center** (© **0176/75-2425;** open daily 8am–5pm) is located next to the JR Bus Center (to the right after you exit the bus terminal's main door).

**ORIENTATION & GETTING AROUND**    Yasumiya, a village on the southwestern shore of Lake Towada, has a bus terminal, a tourist office, and a handful of accommodations and restaurants. On the eastern side of the lake is Nenokuchi, trail head for hikes along Oirase Stream. The **JR bus** that runs between Aomori and Yasumiya also stops at Nenokuchi and several locations along the Oirase hiking trail, making approximately six runs a day from April to early November. Otherwise, your best bet for travel between Yasumiya and Nenokuchi is via **sightseeing boat** (see below).

## SEEING THE SIGHTS

In Yasumiya, the major point of interest is **Towada Jinja Shrine,** surrounded by giant cedars and boasting marvelous woodcarvings of animals. A curious custom here is to buy a fortune, write your wish on the paper inside, twist it into the shape of missile, and then hike 20 minutes to a specific spot near the lake (the last part of the hike is down metal ladders—only for the adventurous on a rainy day) where you then throw your missile into the lake. If it sinks, your wish will come true. Near Towada Jinja Shrine look for the sculpture of two young women. Unlike the golden nymph at Lake Tazawa, these broad shouldered, wide hipped young ladies were sculpted just after the war, when such proportions were thought necessary to rebuild the nation.

**SIGHTSEEING BOATS ON LAKE TOWADA**    The best way to enjoy the pristine beauty of crystal-clear **Lake Towada (Towadako),** a double caldera formed some 20,000 years ago by a volcanic eruption, is aboard excursion boats that cruise the waters April to mid-November. About 44km (27 miles) of undulating coastline marked by capes, inlets, cliffs, and trees that put on a spectacular autumn show make this one of Towada-Hachimantai National Park's major draws. Two cruises are available: a 50-minute cruise that travels between Yasumiya and Nenokuchi, and a 45-minute cruise that begins and ends at Yasumiya. Many visitors take the boat to Nenokuchi (Oirase Stream trail head), send their luggage onward (see below), and begin hiking. The cost of either cruise is ¥1,300 ($12) for adults, but with your Northern Tohoku Welcome Card you'll pay only ¥1,100 ($10); in winter rates drop to ¥1,000 ($9.50). Children pay half fares. A surcharge of ¥500 ($4.75) for adults and ¥250 ($2.40) is levied if you wish to sit in the top lounge.

**HIKING OIRASE STREAM** 𝕽𝕽    To my mind, hiking along the Oirase Stream is the major draw for a trip to Lake Towada. A clear-running, gurgling stream that runs 67km (42 miles) on its way from the lake to the Pacific Ocean, it's at its picture-perfect best in **Oirase Gorge,** where hikers are treated to a myriad of waterfalls, rapids coursing over moss-covered boulders, and a dense wood of Japanese beech, oaks, and other broad-leaved trees. A trail runs beside the stream from Nenokuchi on the lakeshore 14km (8.8 miles) to Yakeyama. Most hikers, however, go only as far as Ishigedo, hiking the 9km (5.5 miles) in about 2 hours. Disappointingly, a road runs through the gorge beside the stream, but the pathway often diverges from the road, and the roar of the swift-running river and the 13 waterfalls masks the sound of vehicles.

The hike upstream (toward Nenokuchi) is considered the most picturesque, since it affords a full view of the cascading rapids.

There are nine bus stops on the road beside Oirase Stream, including Nenokuchi, Ishigedo, and Yakeyama. Since buses run only once an hour or so, you might consider taking a bus first and then hiking back. The Oirase Keiryu Grand Hotel has a **luggage transfer** and **cycle rental** service (call ✆ **0176/76-1111** for information). You can leave your luggage at the JR bus station at Nenokuchi, hike, and then pick it up at the JR bus stop next to the Grand Hotel in Yakeyama or vice versa. There are transfers in both directions four times a day from Golden Week (end of Apr) to early November; the cost is ¥400 ($3.80) per bag. You can rent a cycle for ¥630 ($5.70) for 2 hours at either end of the trail (in the same places as the luggage transfers) and drop it off at the opposite end. Your Northern Tohoku Welcome Card gives 20% discount on baggage transfers and cycle rental.

## WHERE TO STAY

Minshuku Himemasu Sanso and Oirase Keiryu Grand Hotel offer a 10% discount for holders of the Northern Tohoku Welcome Card (be sure to mention the card when making reservations and show it when you check in). Peak season is August and October; book far in advance for these months.

(256) **Himemasu Sanso** *(Value)*   Completely remodeled in 2005, this *minshuku* has a convenient location near the JR bus terminal and offers clean tatami rooms, with views of the surrounding wooded hills. Meals are served communally and usually feature trout from Lake Towada and local wild mountain vegetables; Western-style breakfasts are available on request.

16 Aza Towada, Oaza Okuse, Towada-shi, Kamikita-gun, Aomori 018-5501. ✆ 0176/75-2717. Fax 0176/75-2717. 8 units (none with bathroom). ¥6,300 ($60) per person, including 2 meals. No credit cards. A 5-min. walk inland from the JR bus station. **Amenities:** Hot-spring bath. *In room:* TV, hot-water pot w/tea, no phone.

**Oirase Keiryu Grand Hotel**   The main reason for staying in this large, rather ordinary hotel is its location on Oirase Stream, making it an easy base for hiking the Oirase Gorge trail. It also offers a free bus shuttle from Aomori Station (inquire about departure times when making reservations). The hotel is divided into two sections: the older Daiichi (first) Wing with 105 rooms, and the newer Daini (second) Wing with 85 rooms. I prefer the Daini with its lobby overlooking the stream and maple trees and its hard-to-overlook giant fireplace sculpture by eccentric Okamoto Taro. It offers both Japanese tatami and twin rooms, about half with views of Oirase Stream (which cost an extra ¥2,000/$19). Public hot-spring baths also take advantage of river views.

Oirase Keiryu Onsen, Towada-shi, Aomori 034-0300. ✆ 0176/74-1111. Fax 0176/74-1118. 190 units. ¥13,000– ¥17,000 ($123–$162) per person, including 2 meals. AE, DC, MC, V. Bus: Yakeyama (1 min.). **Amenities:** 6 restaurants; 5 bars and lounges; indoor and outdoor hot-spring baths; rental bikes; game room; souvenir shops; in-room massage. *In room:* A/C, TV, fridge, hot-water pot w/tea, hair dryer, safe.

**Towada Hotel** *(★★★)*   This imposing, elegant hotel is my top choice for a splurge on Lake Towada. Secluded on a wooded hill overlooking the lake (and practical only if you have your own car), it was built in 1938 using huge cedar logs in a mix of Western-lodge-meets-Japanese-temple style, with a modern addition built years later. Former U.S. ambassador Edwin Reischauer and Emperor Showa have stayed here; nowadays most American guests are high-ranking officers from a nearby U.S. military base. Although all rooms face the lake, best are the Japanese rooms, all in the older

part of the hotel and elegant with great views. Western-style rooms, though spacious and beautifully designed, do not have as good a view; be sure to ask for a room on the top floor and be sure, too, to wander over to the older wing for a look at its beautiful wood details in the old lobby (crafted by temple carpenters). Unfortunately, the public baths do not have hot-spring waters, but they do have lakeside views and outdoor tubs. Meals, served in a communal dining room with a mix of Japanese and Western dishes, are substantial. Western-style breakfasts are available.

Kosaka-machi, Towadako Nishi-kohan, Akita 018-5511. © **0176/75-1122.** Fax 0176/75-1313. 50 units (46 with bathroom). Peak season ¥18,000 ($171) per person; regular season ¥15,000 ($143) weekends and ¥12,000 ($114) weekdays per person. Rates include 2 meals. AE, DC, MC, V. Pickup service available from JR bus terminal in Yasumiya. **Amenities:** Restaurant and lounge; indoor/outdoor public baths; Jacuzzi; sauna; in-room massage. *In room:* A/C, TV, minibar, hot-water pot w/tea, hair dryer, safe, Washlet toilet.

**Tsuta Onsen** ✿ This classic, north-country inn dates to 1909 and is one of Tohoku's most famous traditional ryokan. *Tsuta* means ivy in Japanese, a theme carried out not only in pillars, transoms, and other architectural details but also in the dense, surrounding beech forest. Rooms in the oldest wooden structure (built in 1918), up a long flight of stairs, have beautiful wood-carved details and good views but are without bathrooms (they're also cheaper). An annex was built in 1960, while the west wing 1989 addition has an elevator and the convenience of toilets (a few have bathrooms), but its rooms lack the character of the older rooms. For the best views, be sure to request a room facing away from the street. For those who don't like sleeping on futons, three combination units offer both tatami rooms and beds. The hot-spring baths are new but preserve traditional bathhouse architecture, with high ceilings and cypress walls; they're considered beneficial for healing scars and other skin problems. Breakfast is served in a communal dining room, dinner is served your room. Although not as conveniently located as, say, the Oirase Keiryu Grand Hotel (see above), the Tsuta is served by the same JR bus that travels between Aomori and Lake Towada (it's about a 15-min. bus ride to Yakeyama). It also has its own 1-hour hiking trail to a nearby lake.

Okuse, Aza Tsutanoyu, Towada-shi, Kamikita-gun, Aomori 034-0301. © **0176/74-2311.** Fax 0176/74-2244. info@thuta.co.jp. 50 units (4 with bathroom, 20 with toilet only). ¥10,000–¥18,000 ($95–$171) per person, including 2 meals. AE, DC, MC, V. Bus: From Aomori Station, a 2-hr. JR bus ride to Tsuta Onsen stop (1 min.). **Amenities:** Hot-spring indoor bath; in-room massage. *In room:* TV, hot-water pot w/tea.

## WHERE TO DINE

Most accommodations serve breakfast and dinner. For an inexpensive meal on the Oirase Gorge trail, a small snack bar at Ishigedo sells ramen noodles, tempura soba, ice cream, and drinks.

**Komorebi** WESTERN A convenient place for lunch in Yakeyama if you're hiking the Oirase Gorge trail, this simple hotel restaurant offers set lunches that include beef or fish as their main dishes, as well as simpler choices like spaghetti or soup from an English-language menu. There are several other restaurants in the hotel, including those serving Japanese and Chinese food.

Oirase Keiryu Grand Hotel (Daini Wing), Oirase Keiryu Onsen. © **0176/74-1111.** Set meals ¥1,260–¥3,150 ($12–$30). AE, DC, MC, V. Daily 11am–2pm and 6–9pm. Bus: Yakeyama (1 min.).

# 13

# Northern Japan—Hokkaido

**H**okkaido, the northernmost of Japan's four main islands, has a landscape strikingly different from that of any other place in Japan. With more than 77,700 sq. km (30,000 sq. miles) and accounting for 22% of Japan's total landmass, it has only 5% of its population. In other words, Hokkaido has what the rest of Japan doesn't—space. The least developed of Japan's four islands, it's your best bet for avoiding the crowds that plague Japan's more well-known playgrounds during peak travel season.

Considered the country's last frontier, Hokkaido didn't open up to development until after the Meiji Restoration in 1868, when the government began encouraging Japanese to migrate to the island. Even today, Hokkaido has a frontier feel to it, and many young Japanese come here to backpack, ski, camp, and tour the countryside on motorcycles or bicycles. There are dairy farms, silos, and broad, flat fields of wheat, corn, and potatoes. Where the fields end the land puckers up, becoming craggy with bare volcanoes, deep gorges, and hills densely covered with virgin forests and dotted with clear spring lakes, mountains, rugged wilderness, wild animals, bubbling hot springs, and rare plants. The people of Hokkaido are as open and hearty as the wide expanses of land around them.

Much of Hokkaido's wilderness has been set aside as national and prefectural parkland. Of these areas, Shikotsu-Toya, Daisetsuzan, and Akan national parks are the best known, offering a wide range of activities from hiking and skiing to bathing at *onsen,* or hot-spring spas.

Hokkaido's main tourist season is in August, when days are cool and pleasant with an average temperature of 70°F (21°C). While the rest of the nation is afflicted by the rainy season, Hokkaido's summers are usually bright and clear. Winters are long and severe; still, ski enthusiasts flock to slopes near Sapporo and to resorts such as Daisetsuzan National Park. February marks the annual Sapporo Snow Festival, featuring huge ice and snow sculptures.

With its New Chitose Airport, the city of Sapporo—Japan's largest city north of Tokyo—serves as a springboard to Hokkaido's national parks and lakes. Yet despite all the island has to offer, and despite its size and importance, I've seen few foreigners in Sapporo, even in August. To most visitors to Japan, Hokkaido remains virtually undiscovered.

## 1 Hokkaido Essentials

**INFORMATION**   Information on Hokkaido is available online at **www.visit-hokkaido.jp**.

**GETTING THERE & GETTING AROUND**   The fastest way to reach Hokkaido is to **fly.** Flights from Tokyo's Haneda Airport to Sapporo's **New Chitose Airport** take about 1½ hours. Although traditional airfare to Sapporo from Tokyo costs ¥28,600

# Hokkaido

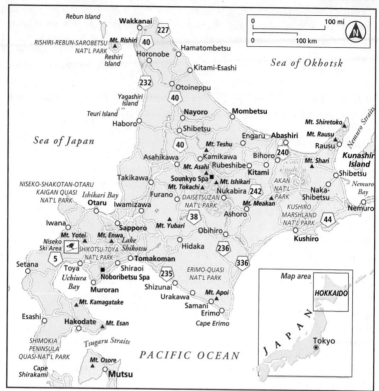

($272), renegade airline **Air Do** (© **0120-057-333**) offers tickets from Tokyo for ¥23,400 ($223) or less. For other destinations, **JAL** flies from Tokyo to **Hakodate** for ¥27,200 ($259) on the western side of the island and from Tokyo to **Kushiro** for ¥33,600 ($320) on the eastern side of the island. **JAL** also flies from Osaka's KIX to **Sapporo** for ¥35,600 ($339). All airfares go up by about ¥2,000 ($19) in peak season, but there are discounts for advance purchase and the off season. From North America or Europe, you might consider flying JAL to Sapporo with a stopover in Tokyo or Osaka.

Travel to Hokkaido by land is generally via the **Tohoku Shinkansen** bullet train from Ueno or Tokyo Station in Tokyo to Hachinohe in Tohoku, followed by the **limited express Hakucho train** from Hachinohe all the way to Hakodate on Hokkaido. For centuries, the only way to travel between Honshu and Hokkaido was via a 4-hour ferry ride, but the opening of the Seikan Tunnel in 1988 allowed the entire trip between the islands to be made by train in little more than 2 hours—more than a fourth of which is in the 55km (34-mile) tunnel. The entire trip from Tokyo to Hakodate (on Hokkaido) via train should take about 6 hours and costs ¥19,950 ($190) for a reserved seat one-way. The trip from Tokyo to Sapporo takes about 9 hours (not including transfers) and costs ¥23,980 ($228) for reserved seating. Your **JR Rail Pass** is good for all trains.

**Public transportation** around Hokkaido is by train and bus. In addition to regular bus lines, sightseeing buses link the national parks and major attractions. Although they're more expensive than trains and regular buses, and although commentaries are in Japanese only, they offer unparalleled views of the countryside and usually stop at scenic wonders. Keep in mind that bus schedules fluctuate with the seasons, and some lines don't run during snowy winter months.

**JR Hokkaido Passes**    If you plan to do a lot of traveling in Hokkaido and you're not traveling with a Japan Rail Pass, you should consider purchasing one of several special passes issued by Japan Railways that allows unlimited travel on JR trains and buses in Hokkaido. The **Hokkaido Rail Pass,** for example, works just like the Japan Rail Pass (you must be a foreign tourist visiting Japan) and is valid for travel throughout Hokkaido. The ordinary pass, which can be purchased abroad (at JTB and other authorized travel agencies) or at train stations in Hakodate, Sapporo, and a few other cities in Hokkaido, costs ¥14,000 ($133) for 3 days and ¥18,000 ($171) for 5 days. Alternatively, the **JR Hokkaido Free Kippu** can be used by anyone (including Japanese and foreigners living in Japan) and can be purchased at any JR rail station. Allowing unlimited travel in Hokkaido, the 7-day pass costs ¥23,750 ($226) for one person or ¥43,220 ($412) for a couple traveling together, but it is not valid April 27 to May 6, August 11 to August 20, or December 28 to January 6. You can also purchase a 5-day **Gururi Hokkaido Free Kippu,** which includes train fare to and from Hokkaido as well as travel around Hokkaido; one that includes transportation from Tokyo and back, for example, costs ¥45,200 ($430) July to September and ¥37,500 ($357) the rest of the year.

**Renting a Car**    Because distances are long and traffic is rather light, Hokkaido is one of the few places in Japan where driving your own car is actually recommended. Because it's expensive, however, it's economical only if there are several of you. Rates for a 1-day rental of a compact car with unlimited mileage begin at ¥6,825 ($65) per day, with each additional day costing ¥5,775 ($55). Insurance runs another ¥1,050 ($10) per day. Car-rental agencies are found throughout Hokkaido, often near train stations as well as at Chitose Airport outside Sapporo and at Kushiro Airport in Kushiro. In Sapporo, **Toyota Rent-A-Car** (© 011/281-0100) is located east of Sapporo Station. **JR Eki Rent-A-Car Hokkaido** (© 011/241-0931), near the south exit of Sapporo Station (their offices are always near a JR station), offers 20% discounts for train fares booked in conjunction with car rentals. For routes and road conditions, go to www.northern-road.jp/navi/eng/index.htm.

**A GOOD STRATEGY FOR SEEING HOKKAIDO**    If you're traveling from Tokyo, your first destination in Hokkaido should be **Hakodate,** a convenient 1-night stopover. From there you can board a local train bound for **Sapporo,** stopping off at **Shikotsu-Toya National Park** along the way. From Sapporo, two worthwhile destinations include **Sounkyo Onsen** in **Daisetsuzan National Park** and **Akan National Park.** To follow this plan, you'll need at least a week. See chapter 2 for information on rail passes and discounts just for Hokkaido.

## 2 Hakodate, Southern Gateway to Hokkaido ⧉

888km (549 miles) NE of Tokyo; 283km (177 miles) SW of Sapporo

**Hakodate,** the southern gateway to Hokkaido, is about as far as you may care to get in a day if you arrive in Hokkaido from Tokyo by train. Hakodate makes a good

1-night stopover because it has one nighttime attraction and one early morning attraction, which means you can easily see a little of the city before setting out for your next destination.

Founded during the Feudal Era, Hakodate was one of Japan's first ports opened to international trade following the Meiji Restoration. Today it has a population of about 290,000, making it Hokkaido's third-largest city. Yet it feels provincial in atmosphere—it's still an outpost despite the renovation of its former warehouse district into shops and restaurants and its wealth of century-old Western-style buildings. That's part of its charm.

## ESSENTIALS

**GETTING THERE   By JR Train**   From Tokyo, take the **Shinkansen** bullet train to Hachinohe (3 hr.), then transfer to a direct train for Hakodate (about 3 hr.). The total fare for a reserved seat is ¥15,350 ($146). There's also a night train that departs Ueno Station in Tokyo around 7pm, arriving in Hakodate the next morning at 6:30am and costing ¥23,180 ($221); if you have a JR Rail Pass, you pay only the ¥12,150 ($116) sleeping-car surcharge. Hakodate is about 3½ hours from Sapporo, Hokkaido's largest city.

**By Plane   JAL** flies from Tokyo's Haneda Airport to Hakodate in 1¼ hours for ¥26,800 ($255). Flights from Osaka's KIX cost ¥33,000 ($314) for the 1¾-hour trip. Limousine buses travel to JR Hakodate Station in 20 minutes for (¥300/$2.85).

**GETTING AROUND**   With the exception of Mount Hakodate, the most pleasant way to see Hakodate is on foot. The city is easy to navigate, and there are many English-language signs. Otherwise, streetcars are the major form of transportation, with fares starting at ¥250 ($2.40); take a ticket upon entering the back door. The tourist office sells 1-day passes, good for all streetcars and buses, for ¥1,000 ($9.50).

**VISITOR INFORMATION**   The **Tourist Information Centers** located in Tokyo and at Tokyo and Osaka international airports have a leaflet called "Hakodate and Vicinity." (You can also download it from JNTO's website at www.jnto.go.jp by looking under "Regional Tourist Guides.") Otherwise, the **Hakodate Tourist Office** (© **0138/23-5440;** open daily 9am–7pm, to 5pm Nov–Mar) is inside the station to your left as you exit the wicket. It has an excellent English-language map of Hakodate and can help with accommodations. Check www.city.hakodate.hokkaido.jp for more information.

## WHAT TO SEE & DO

In addition to the sights here, you might also want to explore the renovated **warehouse district** with its shops and restaurants. History buffs head for the historic **Motomachi,** a picturesque neighborhood of steep slopes and turn-of-the-20th-century Western-style clapboard homes, buildings (including the first kindergarten in Hokkaido) and churches. In front of the Suehiro-cho streetcar stop, the **Hakodate City Museum of Northern Peoples** (© **0138/22-4128**) displays folk art unique to natives living in harsh northern climates and is open daily 9am to 7pm (5pm in winter). The Hokkaido Prefectural Government's old branch office in Motomachi Park contains a small **tourist office** (© **0138/27-3333**) open daily 9am to 7pm (to 5pm in winter).

**MOUNT HAKODATE AFTER DARK**   Hakodate is probably most famous for its night view from atop Mount Hakodate, which rises 330m (1,100 ft.) just 2.8km

(1¾ miles) southwest of Hakodate Station, so you should time your visit just at sunset (though note that it can be chilly up here, even in Aug). Few vacationing Japanese spend the night in Hakodate without taking the cable car to the top of this lava cone, which was formed by the eruption of an undersea volcano. From the peak, the lights of Hakodate shimmer and glitter like jewels on black velvet. I wouldn't miss it, not only for the view, but for the camaraderie shared by everyone making the pilgrimage. There's an informal restaurant here (where you can indulge in a drink or a snack while admiring the spectacular view) as well as the usual souvenir shops.

You can reach the foot of Mount Hakodate via a 5-minute streetcar ride from Hakodate Station to the Jujigai stop. From there, walk about 6 minutes to the cable car that will take you to the top. The round-trip costs ¥1,160 ($11) for adults and ¥590 ($5.60) for children. Cable-car hours are daily 10am to 10pm April 26 through October (from 9am during Golden Week and in Aug), and 10am to 9pm November through April 25. From April 25 to November (daily during peak season but otherwise only on weekends), you can also reach the top of Mount Hakodate directly by bus from Hakodate Station; the 30-minute trip costs ¥360 ($3.40) for adults and half price for children.

**THE MORNING MARKET**   The other popular thing to do is visit Hakodate's morning market, which is spread out just south of the train station daily from about 5am to noon. Walk around and look at the variety of foods for sale, especially the hairy crabs for which Hokkaido is famous. You can make an unusual breakfast of fruit, raw sea urchin, or grilled crab from the stalls here.

## WHERE TO STAY

Hakodate's peak tourist season is in July and August. Accordingly, some hotels raise their rates during this time.

### EXPENSIVE

**Hotel Sea Borne** 🐦🐦   If you're searching for a small boutique hotel with class, this is a top pick. Its elegant lobby, with reproduction antique furniture, imparts a cozy European atmosphere. Each of its rooms is decorated in a different theme, from modern to frilly European to rustic American. Apparently, some Japanese guests are so enamored of the different styles, they request a change of rooms the second night, just for the experience. Jaded travelers, however, may find it a bit over-the-top. Excellent service from a friendly staff, welcome drinks (tea, coffee, or soft drink the first night; a cocktail the second night), good in-room amenities (including four different kinds of shampoo), and a great location near the warehouse district make Sea Borne infinitely better than your standard hotel.

14–28 Suehiro-cho, Hakodate 040-0053. ✆ **0138/27-4411.** Fax 0138/27-0028. www.seaborne.jp. 18 units. ¥13,860 ($132) single; ¥23,100–¥41,580 ($220–$396) double; ¥26,564–¥43,890 ($253–$418) twin. Rates include service charge. AE, DC, MC, V. Taxi: 5 min. Streetcar: Jujigai (2 min.). Turn right and walk 2 blocks toward the bay; it's across the street on your left. **Amenities:** Restaurant (Western); tearoom; room service (5–9:30pm); same-day laundry/dry-cleaning service. *In room:* A/C, TV, minibar, hot-water pot w/tea, hair dryer, Washlet toilet.

257 **Wakamatsu Ryokan** 🐦🐦   Here's a seaside inn worthy of a splurge. Almost a century old (grainy black-and-white photographs in the lobby memorialize Emperor Showa's 1954 visit) but renovated and with a seven-story wing added in 1994, it's the epitome of an updated but elegant ryokan. Pampering begins as soon as you enter the grand, teahouse-style entrance, where a kimono-clad hostess ushers you to your room

and brings a welcome tea. After soaking in the public hot-spring baths overlooking the sea, you'll be treated to a kaiseki feast in your room (again with views of the sea). The sea is so close you'll fall asleep listening to the gentle sound of waves. Bonuses are the nearby Yunokawa public swimming beach and the night illumination of fishing boats searching for squid. The main disadvantage to staying here is location—near the airport (thank goodness planes don't fly at night) and a long, 30-minute streetcar ride from Hakodate Station (a taxi will set you back about ¥2,500/$24).

1–2–27 Yunokawa-cho, Hakodate 042-0932. © **0138/59-2171.** Fax 0138/59-3316. wakamatsu@hakodate.ne.jp. 26 units. ¥33,750–¥82,080 ($321–$782) per person, including 2 meals. ¥3,150 ($30) extra weekends and holidays. AE, DC, MC, V. Taxi: 15 min. from Hakodate Station, 7 min. from Hakodate Airport. Streetcar: 2 or 5 to Yunokawa Onsen (6 min.). Turn right and walk along a canal until it ends; the inn is across the street, to the right. **Amenities:** Hot-spring indoor/outdoor baths; in-room massage. *In room:* A/C, TV, minibar, hot-water pot w/tea, hair dryer, safe.

## MODERATE

**B&B Hakodatemura**   This immaculate, mostly Western-style Japanese Inn Group member, decorated with whitewashed walls, wood furniture, and fresh and dried flowers, is built around a courtyard where you can choose to eat breakfast. In addition to the Western-style rooms, there are two tatami rooms and one triple with a loft bed; only one double has a bathroom. Rules are similar to a youth hostel's (check-in at 3pm, checkout at 10am, and the door locks at 11pm), but what I like most about this place is its location near the warehouse district and Motomachi, only a 15-minute walk from Hakodate Station.

16–12 Suehiro-cho, Hakodate 040-0053. © **0138/22-8105.** Fax 0138/22-8925. www.bb-hakodatemura.com. 16 units (1 with bathroom). ¥5,580 ($53) single; ¥10,200 ($97) twin without bathroom; ¥11,500 ($110) twin with bathroom; ¥14,640 ($139) triple. Western breakfast ¥700 ($6.65) extra. ¥500 ($4.75) extra mid-July to Aug. Winter discounts available. AE, MC, V. Streetcar: Jujigai (2 min.); follow the streetcar tracks for 1 block, turn right, and then turn left. Closed Dec 1–Jan 15. **Amenities:** Coin-op washer/dryer. *In room:* TV, hot-water pot w/tea.

**JAL City Hakodate**   This JAL property, close to Mount Hakodate, the historic district, and Yachigashira hot springs, has the efficiency of a city hotel but adds warmth with friendly service and displays of local artists' works. Capricciosa, an inexpensive Italian restaurant chain, finds a good home here. Built in 1995, it offers rooms with mountain, sea, port, and city views, with the best panoramas from rooms above the eighth floor at no extra charge. Rooms are spacious enough, with small unit bathrooms, bedside controls, and down quilts. Singles have semi-double beds that can be shared by couples for ¥15,015 ($143).

22–15 Horai-cho, Hakodate 040-0043. © **0120/58-2586** or 0138/24-2580. Fax 0138/27-2581. 130 units. ¥10,972 ($104) single; ¥18,480 ($176) double; ¥20,790 ($198) twin. Off-season discounts available. AE, DC, MC, V. Streetcar: Horai-cho (1 min.). Walk back the way you've come and turn right; its on the corner. **Amenities:** 2 restaurants (French, Italian); 1 coffee shop; business center; souvenir shop; in-room massage; foot-care salon; same-day laundry/dry-cleaning service; nonsmoking rooms. *In room:* A/C, TV, minibar, hot-water pot w/tea, hair dryer, Washlet toilet, trouser press.

## INEXPENSIVE

㉕⑧ **Hotel Route Inn Grantia Hakodate Ekimae** *(Value*   Imagine a hotel right next to the station, with rooms equipped with DVD players, Internet connections, and down comforters, a helpful English-speaking staff, inexpensive rates, and hot-spring baths with a view. Dreaming? No, this little hotel has a lot going for it. Despite a no-flair atmosphere and small rooms, it rises above the ordinary with good views (reserve a room above the fourth floor for the best harbor views), large hot-spring

> ### Tips  A Note on Japanese Symbols
>
> Many establishments and attractions in Japan do not have signs in Roman (English-language) letters. Those that don't are indicated in this guide with an oval with a number that corresponds to a number in the appendix showing the Japanese symbols. Thus, to find the Japanese symbol for, say, **Hotel Route Inn Grantia Hakodate Ekimae** (above), refer to no. 258 in appendix C.

baths on the 13th floor with great views, and free lobby computers. Family rooms have one king-size bed (and not much else) that you are welcome to put the whole family in. Kids love the fact that vending machines dispense ice cream in addition to the usual cup noodles and soft drinks.

21–3 Wakamatsu-cho, Hakodate 040-0063. ✆ **0138/21-4100.** Fax 0138/21-4101. 286 units. ¥6,200–¥6,500 ($59–$62) single; ¥12,000 ($114) twin; ¥14,000 ($133) family room. Off-season discounts available. AE, DC, MC, V. A 1-min. walk from Hakodate Station's main exit, to the left. **Amenities:** Restaurant (Japanese); coffee shop; massage/reflexology room; lobby computers w/free Internet access; coin-op washer/dryer; same-day laundry/dry-cleaning service; nonsmoking rooms. *In room:* A/C, TV/DVD player (rentals ¥1,000/$9.50), minibar, hot-water pot w/tea, hair dryer, Washlet toilet.

**Niceday Inn** *Value*    Mrs. Saito, the kind and generous woman who runs this inn, carries on the tradition that her husband started years ago and gives a warm welcome. You'll feel right at home, as staying here is like living with Japanese family. Although Mrs. Saito's English is limited, she offers tourist information and a map, and tries to help with whatever you need. The inn is very simple but offers clean Japanese- and Western-style rooms. No meals are served, but free instant coffee, a refrigerator, a TV, and a public phone are available in the small communal entry room.

9–11 Otemachi, Hakodate 040-0064. ✆ **0138/22-5919.** 6 units (none with bathroom). ¥3,000 ($29) per person for foreigners. No credit cards. Station: Hakodate (8 min.). Take the west exit out of the station and walk straight on past the morning market; after crossing the wide, tree-lined avenue, take the 3rd left (across from the Kokusai Hotel entrance). The inn is a white, 2-story building on your right. *In room:* A/C or fan, no phone.

## WHERE TO DINE

Several of Hakodate's harborfront warehouses have been renovated into smart-looking shopping and dining complexes. They're about a 10-minute walk from Hakodate Station; you can reach the complexes by walking past the Morning Market and continuing along the seaside promenade.

**Hakodate Beer** BAR FOOD    In a brick building near the warehouse district, this eatery has five kinds of beer brewed in the large copper vats you can see as you dine on such fare as fish and chips, the day's pasta, Japanese-style fried chicken, or a "steamboat"—seafood, sliced meat, vegetables, and dumplings cooked in boiling broth at your table and dipped in chile sauce (¥3,130/$30 for three or four people). Set lunches, available only weekdays, are a good deal.

5–22 Ohtemachi. ✆ **0138/23-8000.** Main dishes ¥600–¥1,580 ($5.70–$15); set lunch ¥700 ($6.65). AE, DC, MC, V. Daily 11am–10pm. Streetcar: Uoichiba-dori, then walk 3 blocks toward the bay; it's on the corner. Station: Hakodate (9 min.).

**Hakodate Kaisen Club** SEAFOOD    On the waterfront, this seafood restaurant with a harbor view serves crab dishes and other seafood. It's ensconced above an enormous

seafood market and has a lively atmosphere with seating at wooden tables. Donburi, a bowl of rice topped with raw seafood *(sashimi)* or cooked seafood, is a favorite dish here.

Hakodate Nishi Hatoba 2F, 22–6 Suehirocho. © **0138/24-8107**. Crab dishes ¥2,000–¥5,800 ($19–$55); set meals ¥880–¥1,050 ($8.40–$10); donburi ¥950–¥1,580 ($9.05–$15). AE, DC, MC, V. Daily 11am–10pm. Streetcar: Jujigai (5 min.). Walk toward the harbor and turn left at the waterfront.

259 **Shinmura** SUSHI    Two things make this conveyor-belt sushi bar in the Morning Market unusual—the sushi chefs are all women (women's hands are said to be too hot to make sushi), and you can choose your fish or seafood from tanks out front and have it cut into sashimi right before your eyes. Otherwise, prices are determined by the color of the plate on the belt.

22–2 Ohtemachi. © **0138/27-7885**. 2 pieces of sushi ¥126–¥525 ($1.20–$5). No credit cards. Daily 9:30am–9pm. Hakodate Station (3 min.). From the west exit, walk past the Morning Market; Shinmura is across the next corner on the right-hand side (look for the tanks out front).

**Tao Tao** ASIAN CROSSOVER    This eclectic cafe in a bright yellow building in the Motomachi District offers interesting Asian food, including *obachahan* (Manila-style pork fried rice), tacos with rice, and *phad Thai* (rice noodles Thai-style). The tofu salad is very good, with lots of greens and a spicy dressing. There's an outdoor patio in summer.

15–19 Motomachi. © **0138/22-0002**. Main dishes ¥800–¥980 ($7.60–$9.35). No credit cards. Tues–Sat 6–11pm; Sun noon–11pm. Streetcar: Suehiro-cho (3 min); walk 2 blocks up Hachimanzaka and turn left.

## 3 Sapporo

1,200km (746 miles) NE of Tokyo; 283km (177 miles) NE of Hakodate

Sapporo is one of Japan's newest cities. About 135 years ago, it was nothing more than a scattering of huts belonging to Ainu and Japanese families. With the dawning of the Meiji Period, however, the government decided to colonize the island, and in 1869 it established the Colonization Commission. The area of Sapporo (the name comes from the Ainu word meaning "big, dry river") was chosen as the new capital site, and in 1871, construction of the city began.

During the Meiji Period, Japan looked eagerly toward the West for technology, ideas, and education, and Hokkaido was no exception. Between 1871 and 1884, 76 foreign technicians and experts (including 46 Americans) who had colonization experience were brought to this Japanese wilderness to aid in the island's development.

Sapporo was laid out in a grid pattern of uniform blocks similar to that of an American city. In 1875, the Sapporo Agricultural College was founded to train youth in skills useful to Hokkaido's colonization and development.

The Sapporo of today, capital of Hokkaido Prefecture, has grown to 1.8 million residents, making it the largest city north of Tokyo (and the fifth largest in Japan). In 1972, it was introduced to the world when the Winter Olympics were held here, and its many fine ski slopes continue to attract winter vacationers, as does the Sapporo Snow Festival held every February (see the "Japan Calendar of Events" in chapter 2). In August, when the rest of Japan is sweltering under uncomfortably high temperatures and humidity, Sapporo stays pleasantly cool.

## ESSENTIALS

**GETTING THERE    By Plane**    Flights take 1½ hours from Tokyo's Haneda Airport, 2 hours from Hiroshima, and 2¼ hours from Fukuoka. See "Getting There &

Getting Around," under "Hokkaido Essentials," earlier in this chapter, for flight details from Tokyo. Sapporo's **New Chitose Airport** (© **0123/23-0111**), located about 43km (27 miles) southeast of the capital, is connected to downtown by either **Airport Limousine Bus,** which delivers passengers to a few major hotels in about 70 minutes for ¥1,000 ($9.50); or by **JR trains** that operate every 15 minutes between Chitose Airport Station and Sapporo Station, with the 36-minute trip costing ¥1,040 ($9.90).

**By JR Train**   Trains from Tohoku and other regions on Honshu arrive in Hakodate, where you'll transfer to a train departing every hour or so for Sapporo. The fare from Tokyo to Sapporo costs ¥23,980 ($228), with trips averaging 10 hours including transfers. Trains from Hakodate take about 3½ hours and cost ¥8,590 ($82). Otherwise, three overnight trains also depart from Ueno Station in Tokyo and arrive in Sapporo the next morning, taking about 16 hours and costing ¥25,270 ($241). In addition, an overnight train from Osaka departs at noon and arrives in Sapporo the next day at 9:07am, costing ¥25,620 ($244).

**VISITOR INFORMATION**   Be sure to pick up the useful leaflet "Sapporo and Shikotsu-Toya National Park" at a **Tourist Information Center** in Tokyo or international airports in Tokyo or Osaka (or download at www.jnto.go.jp). In JR Sapporo Station, the **Visitors Information Corner** (© **011/209-5030;** open daily 9am–5:30pm) is in the station's Stella Place (turn left out of the west ticket wicket), where multilingual volunteers provide general hotel, sightseeing, and transportation information. Pick up **Xene**, a bilingual, free magazine with information about Sapporo, including concert and event news. **Plaza I Information Counter** is on the third floor in the MN Building across from the Clock Tower (see "A Stroll Around Sapporo," below) at N1 W3, Chuo-ku (© **011/211-3670;** open daily 9am–5:30pm); it provides information on tourist attractions, daily life, and transportation, and offers guidebooks and maps. Online, you can check www.welcome.city.sapporo.jp or www.sta.or.jp.

**INTERNET ACCESS**   You can get online at **Bon de Bon** (© **011/213-5726;** daily 10am–9pm), a cafe in the basement of the Paseo Mall in Sapporo Station (opposite the east ticket wicket). It charges ¥200 ($1.90) for 30 minutes, and you're expected to order a drink. On the first floor of the Century Royal Hotel (1 min. west of Sapporo station's south exit), **i-café** (© **011/221-3440**) charges ¥200 ($1.90) for 30 minutes.

**POST OFFICE**   **Sapporo Central Post Office,** N6, E1 (© **011/748-2345**), 2 blocks east of Sapporo Station, has a 24-hour window for stamps and mail and ATMs for international credit cards (weekdays 7am–11pm; Sat 9am–9pm; Sun and holidays 9am–7pm).

**ORIENTATION & GETTING AROUND**   After the jumble of most Japanese cities with their incomprehensible address systems, Sapporo will come as a welcome surprise. Its streets are laid out in a grid pattern, making the city easy to navigate. Addresses in Sapporo refer to blocks that follow one another in logical, numerical order.

   **Sapporo Station** lies at the north end of the city, with downtown and many of its attractions, hotels, and restaurants spreading to the south. The center of Sapporo is **Odori (Main St.),** a tree-lined avenue south of Sapporo Station that runs east and west and bisects the city into north and south sections. **North 1st Street,** therefore,

# Sapporo

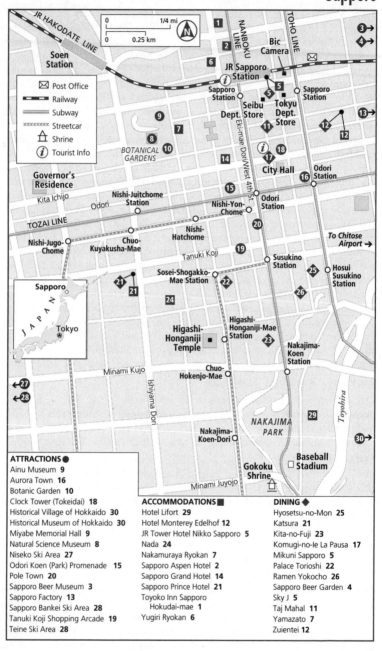

refers to the street 1 block north of Odori. The other determinant landmark is the **Soseigawa River,** which marks addresses east and west. **West 1st Street** runs along the west bank of the Soseigawa River, while **East 1st Street** runs along the east bank.

**Addresses** in Sapporo are generally given by block. **N1 W4,** for example, the address for the Sapporo Grand Hotel, means it's located in the first block north of Odori and 4 blocks west of West 1st Street. If you want to be more technical about it, the entire, formal address of the hotel would read N1-jo W4-chome. "Jo" refers to blocks north and south of Odori, while "chome" refers to blocks east and west of the river. Better yet, street signs in Sapporo are in English.

Central Sapporo is easy to cover on foot. You can walk south from Sapporo Station to **Odori Park** in less than 10 minutes and on to **Susukino,** Sapporo's nightlife district, in another 7 or 8 minutes. For longer distances, transportation in Sapporo is via **bus,** three **subway** lines (which interchange at **Odori Station**), and one **streetcar** line. Fares begin at ¥200 ($1.90) for buses and subways and ¥170 ($1.60) for streetcars, but easier is the **With You Card,** available in denominations beginning at ¥500 ($4.75) and valid for all conveyances. **One-day Cards,** allowing unlimited rides on all modes of transport in 1 day, are also available, costing ¥1,000 ($9.50) for all modes of transport. A 1-day card for subways only costs ¥800 ($7.60), except on weekends and holidays when they're discounted to ¥500 ($4.75). Children pay half fare. Cards can be purchased at subway stations and on buses and streetcars.

Finally, the **Sapporo Stroll Bus** and **Sapporo Walk** are **tourist buses** that travel in a loop to tourist sites around the city April to late October (unfortunately, neither goes go to Nopporo Forest Park). Single fares are ¥200 ($1.90) for adults and ¥100 (95¢) for children. A 1-day pass, ¥750 ($7.15) for adults and ¥380 ($3.60) for children, allows you to get on and off as many times as you want between 9am and 7pm. Buses depart from the south side of Seibu Department Store, and stops are clearly marked.

## A STROLL AROUND SAPPORO

One of the first things you should do in Sapporo is walk around. Starting from **Sapporo Station** (which contains a chic shopping and restaurant complex) take the road leading directly south called **Eki-mae Dori** (which is also West 4th). This is one of Sapporo's main thoroughfares, taking you south through the heart of the city.

**YOUR FIRST STOP**    Four blocks south of the station, turn left on N1; after a block, you'll find Sapporo's most famous landmark, **Clock Tower (Tokeidai),** N1 W2, Chuo-ku (© **011/231-0838**). This Western-style wooden building was built in 1878 as a drill hall for the Sapporo Agricultural College (now Hokkaido University). The large clock at the top was made in Boston and was installed in 1881. In summer, it attracts tourists even at night; they hang around the outside gates just to listen to the clock strike the hour. Inside the tower is a local-history museum, not worth the price of admission. By the way, across the street is Plaza i, where you can obtain information on Sapporo.

**ON TO ODORI PARK**    If you continue walking 1 block south of the Clock Tower, you'll reach **Odori Koen Promenade,** a 103m-wide (344-ft.) boulevard stretching almost a mile from east to west. In the middle of the boulevard is a wide median strip that has been turned into a park with trees, flowerbeds, and fountains. This is where much of the **Sapporo Snow Festival** is held in early February, when ice and packed snow are carved to form statues, palaces, and fantasies. Begun in 1950 to add a bit of

spice and life to the cold winter days, the Snow Festival now features about 220 snow statues and 120 ice sculptures and draws about 2.2 million visitors a year. One snow structure may require as much as 300 6-ton truckloads of snow, brought in from the surrounding mountains. The snow and ice carvings are done with so much attention to detail that it seems a crime they're doomed to melt (see "Japan Calendar of Events" in chapter 2).

Odori Park is also the scene of the **Sapporo Summer Festival,** celebrated with beer gardens set up the length of the park from late July to mid-August and open every day from noon. Various Japanese beer companies set up their own booths and tables under the trees, while vendors put up stalls selling fried noodles, corn on the cob, and other goodies. Live bands serenade the beer drinkers under the stars. It all resembles the cheerful confusion of a German beer garden, which isn't surprising considering Munich is one of Sapporo's sister cities (Portland, Oregon, is another one). Some of the other festivals held in Odori Park are the **Lilac Festival** in late May heralding the arrival of summer, and **Bon-Odori** in mid-August with traditional dances to appease the souls of the dead.

**THE UNDERGROUND SHOPPING ARCADES**    From Odori Park, you can continue your walk either above or below ground. Appreciated especially during inclement weather and during Hokkaido's long, cold winters are two underground shopping arcades. Underneath Odori Park, from the Odori Station all the way to the TV tower in the east, is **Aurora Town,** with boutiques and restaurants. Even longer is **Pole Town,** with 390m (1,300 ft.) of shops, almost 100 in all. Pole Town extends from the Odori Station south all the way to **Susukino,** Sapporo's nightlife amusement center, where you'll find many restaurants and pubs (see "Where to Dine," later in this chapter). Before reaching Susukino, however, you may want to emerge at **Sanchome** (you'll see escalators going up), where you'll find more shopping at the kilometer-long **Tanuki-koji** covered shopping arcade's 300 boutiques and stores.

**THE BOTANIC GARDEN** ✿    Backtracking now toward the station, you should stop at the 13-hectare (32-acre) **Shokubutsu-en;** its entrance is at N3 W8 (✆ **011/ 221-0066**). It contains some virgin forest and more than 4,000 varieties of plants gathered from all over Hokkaido and arranged in marshland, herb, alpine, and other gardens. Of greater interest, perhaps, is the section devoted to plants used by the Ainu, whose extensive knowledge of plants covered not only edible ones but also those with medicinal use and other properties, including organic poison used for arrows to kill bears and other game. Unfortunately, there are no English-language explanations of plant usage. Still, with lots of trees and grassy lawns, it's a good place for a summer afternoon picnic.

Worth visiting on garden grounds is Japan's oldest **natural science museum,** founded in 1882 to document the wildlife of Hokkaido and housed in a turn-of-the-20th-century, Western-style building. Be sure, too, to visit the small, one-room **Ainu Museum,** which displays some fine examples of Ainu artifacts, including traditional costumes, jewelry, farming tools, hunting traps, harpoons, a canoe, and bamboo mouth harps (played by women and children). In any case, you'll probably want to spend an hour touring the garden and its museums.

The Botanic Garden and its museums are open April 29 to September 30, Tuesday through Sunday 9am to 4pm (Oct–Nov 3, 9am–3pm). Admission, including museums, is ¥400 ($3.80) for adults, ¥280 ($2.65) for children. From November 4 to

April 28, only the greenhouse is open (Mon–Fri 10am–3pm; Sat 10am–noon); admission then is ¥110 ($1.05) for everyone.

## MORE TO SEE & DO

**Sapporo Beer Museum** 🐟🐟 Although it's not within easy walking distance of Sapporo Station, if you think of beer when you hear the word "Sapporo," then you should visit the Sapporo Beer Museum. Famous throughout the world, Sapporo beer was brewed in this handsome brick factory from 1890 to 2003; today, the Sapporo Beer Company is the third-largest beer producer in Japan. You can learn all about Sapporo beer at this museum, which explains the history of the company and the brewing process, and shows off company memorabilia (my favorite is the exhibit of advertising posters). Many displays are self-explanatory, but ask for a printed English-language leaflet or join a free 30-minute tour given four times daily, at 10am and 1, 2, and 3pm. For an English-speaking guide, reserve in advance by phone or e-mail (museum@sapporobeer.jp), specifying the time, date, and number of persons.

You might want to cap your tour with a meal or a mug of beer in the adjoining Sapporo Beer Garden (see "Where to Dine," below). Also, about a 12-minute walk from the Beer Museum is **Sapporo Factory**, N2 E4, Chuo-ku (© 011/207-5000), a shopping complex housing a microbrewery, restaurants, 140 shops, and movie theaters.

N7 E9, Chuo-ku. © 011/731-4368. www.sapporobeer.jp. Daily 9am–5:30pm (to 4:30pm Nov–Apr). Bus: Higashi 63 from Sapporo Station to Kita 8 Higashi 7 stop (5 min.); or Sapporo Walk from south side of Seibu Department Store to Sapporo Beer Museum.

## NOPPORO FOREST PARK (NOPPORO SHINRIN KOEN)

If you have an extra half-day or more, I recommend this park on the outskirts for its two very worthwhile attractions. To reach the park, take a **JR train** 10 minutes to Shin-Sapporo Station (¥260/$2.50); go straight out the wicket, then go left. No. 10 platform for a 10-minute ride on **JR bus** No. 22 to the last stop, Kaitaku-no Mura (¥200/$1.90). You can also take the **Tozai subway line** 20 minutes to Shin-Sapporo Station, then get on the same bus. Or, take one of three **JR buses** a day from Sapporo Station (50 min.) directly to the park (¥230/$2.20; ask the tourist office for a schedule.) All buses stop first at the Historical Museum of Hokkaido (Kinenkan Iriguchi) before stopping at the Kaitaku-no Mura. It's about a 15-minute walk between the two attractions.

**Historical Village of Hokkaido (Kaitaku-no Mura)** 🐟🐟 (Kids) This open-air museum of more than 60 historical Japanese- and Western-style buildings, dating mostly from the Meiji and Taisho eras and brought here from around Hokkaido, includes homes, farmhouses, a shrine, a church, a newspaper office, a post office (from which you can mail a letter), a police box (manned by a sword-wielding police officer), and many small businesses, including a blacksmith, brewery, barbershop, grocery, inn, and sleigh factory—all how they would have looked in the past. In summer, staff dressed in Meiji-Era clothing are on hand to answer questions, and there are horse-drawn carriage rides. You can easily spend 2 hours here, wandering through buildings of the fishing village, farm village, mountain village, and town. Kids like being able to run and explore; there's even an old-fashioned playground with stilts, a seesaw, and other traditional play equipment.

Konopporo 50–1, Atsubetsu-cho. © 011/898-2692. Admission Apr–Nov ¥830 ($7.90) adults, ¥610 ($5.80) university and high-school students; Dec–Mar ¥680 ($6.50) adults, ¥550 ($5.25) university and high-school students. Free

for children and seniors; free also for high-school students every Sat. June–Sept Tues–Sun 9am–5pm; Oct–May Tues–Sun 9:30am–4:30pm. Bus: Kaitaku-no-Mura (1 min.).

**Historical Museum of Hokkaido (Kaitaku Kinenkan)**  This museum does a great job detailing Hokkaido's development from prehistoric to modern times, with lots of information in English, including an audio guide (¥120/$1.15 extra). The section on the Ainu displays clothing, a house, and other artifacts, and describes their forced assimilation into Japanese culture. You'll also learn about Hokkaido's early contacts with Russia, the lives of 19th-century Japanese pioneers, the opening of Hakodate Port, the establishment of Sapporo Agricultural College, and more. The Living Experience Room provides hands-on experience with tools, including a handloom, and interactive displays. If history's your thing, you can easily spend 2 hours here.

Konoppuro, Atsubetsu-cho. ✆ **011/898-0456.** Admission ¥450 ($4.30) adults, ¥150 ($1.40) university and high-school students, free for seniors and children. Tues–Sun 9:30am–4:30pm. Closed some national holidays.

## HITTING THE SLOPES

Skiing is big in Sapporo, site of the 1972 Winter Olympics and easily accessible by plane from many cities in Japan—there are slopes within city limits and more than a dozen skiing areas less than 2 hours away, most open from early December to late April. On the west edge of town are Okurayama Jump Hill and Miyanomori Jump Hill, both sites of the 1972 Winter Olympics. Here, too, is the **Sapporo Bankei Ski Area,** just 20 minutes from downtown Sapporo and popular for after-work skiing. You can reach them by subway to Maruyama Koen Station and then by bus.

Farther afield, the **Teine Highland** and **Olympia Ski** areas (✆ **011/681-3191**) are about an hour's bus ride from Sapporo Station. This was the site of the alpine, bobsled, and toboggan events for the Olympics. A new lift joins the two areas, creating Hokkaido's longest run (6km/3¾ miles). A 4-hour, 6-hour, or 8-hour lift pass costs ¥3,500 ($33), ¥3,980 ($38), or ¥4,450 ($42) respectively; ski-rental equipment is available from ¥4,410 ($42) in the day and ¥2,940 ($28) at night. Snowboarding gear costs ¥3,780 ($36) per day. Keep in mind that gear sizes are generally smaller than in the West (ski boots up to 30cm, size 12 in U.S., and snowboard boots up to 28.5cm, size 10½ in U.S.).

**Niseko** (www.niseko.ne.jp), a 3-hour bus ride west of Sapporo, is considered by our skiing friends as the best ski resort in Hokkaido. Three skiing regions, joined by lifts and shuttle buses that provide easy exploration of the different areas, offer variety for skiers of all levels. A day pass here costs ¥4,800 ($46), with rental prices comparable to those at Teine. To get there, reserve a seat with Chuo (✆ **011/231-0500**) or Dohnan (✆ **011/865-5511**) bus company; both go to Niseko from either Chitose Airport or Sapporo Station and cost ¥3,850 ($37) round-trip. For more information on skiing around Sapporo, stop by the Sapporo tourist office or go to www.snowjapan.com.

## WHERE TO STAY

Sapporo has a large selection of fine hotels in various price categories. The busiest tourist seasons are summer and early February during the annual Snow Festival. If you plan to attend the Snow Festival, book your room at least 6 months in advance. At other times you should have no problem finding a room, but it's always wise to make a reservation in advance. In winter (excluding festival time), some upper- and medium-priced hotels lower their room rates, sometimes by as much as 40%—be sure to ask for a discount.

## EXPENSIVE

**Hotel Monterey Edelhof** 🎀🎀 Although opened in 2000, this elegant hotel embraces the architectural exuberance of early 1900s Vienna, with lots of marble, stained-glass windows, Art Deco embellishments, and Otto Wagner–inspired designs. Even the elevators have old-fashioned floor dials, classical music plays in public spaces, and function rooms carry names like Schönbrunn. Forgive me a sudden craving for Sachertorte. Located in downtown Sapporo, on the upper floors of an office building, the hotel offers small but smartly decorated rooms with a slight Art Deco motif. The hotel spa, which uses hot springs tapped deep below ground and has the good Austro-Hungarian Empire name Karlovy Vary, is a huge (though pricey) plus.

N2 W1, Chuo-ku, Sapporo 060-0002. ✆ 011/242-7111. Fax 011/232-1212. 181 units. ¥18,191 ($173) single; ¥33,957–¥46,084 ($323–$439) twin. AE, DC, MC, V. Station: Sapporo (8 min.). **Amenities:** 3 restaurants (2 Japanese, 1 Chinese); 2 lounges; 1 bar; hot-spring spa with sauna and Jacuzzi (fee: ¥1,890/$18); room service (9pm–11pm); in-room massage; same-day laundry/dry-cleaning service; nonsmoking rooms. *In room:* A/C, cable TV, minibar, hot-water pot w/tea, hair dryer, Washlet toilet.

**JR Tower Hotel Nikko Sapporo** 🎀🎀🎀 Elegance and convenience—not to mention top-class restaurants, a deluxe spa (offering everything from reflexology to indoor/outdoor hot-spring baths), and spectacular views from all rooms—make this the best place to stay in Sapporo. Located in Sapporo Station and presided over by a walkie-talkie-toting staff who makes sure everything runs smoothly, it offers rooms (23rd–34th floors) with all the latest in hotel design, including desks with flip tops so they can double as mirrored vanities, LCD swivel TVs, separate tub/shower areas, and towels embroidered with different-colored insignia to take out the guessing game of which towel belongs to whom. A caveat: Because of JR restrictions on signs in its stations, directions to the hotel are minimal; you know the hotel is there—you just can't find it!

JR Tower, W2 N5, Chuo-ku, Sapporo 060-0005. ✆ 011/251-2222. Fax 011/251-6370. www.jalhotels.com. 350 units. ¥16,170–¥18,480 ($154–$176) single; ¥24,255–¥43,890 ($231–$418) double; ¥31,185–¥41,580 ($297–$396) twin. Rates include service charge. AE, DC, MC, V. In the Sapporo Station complex. Turn right after exiting the east wicket and go straight until you exit the building; turn left immediately through glass doors and walk to the end of the end of the long hallway. **Amenities:** 4 restaurants (Japanese, international, French, coffee shop); 1 bar; hot-spring spa with sauna, Jacuzzi (¥1,500/$14); salon; room service (7am–11pm); in-room massage; same-day laundry/dry-cleaning service; in-room massage; nonsmoking rooms. *In room:* A/C, satellite TV, dataport, minibar, hot-water pot w/tea, hair dryer, Washlet toilet.

**Sapporo Grand Hotel** 🎀 This dignified hotel, open since 1934 and one of Sapporo's old-timers, has a good downtown location near the Botanic Garden and Odori Park. An appealing choice of dining and drinking outlets (including Fine French food at Grand Chef) and a helpful English-speaking staff help make your stay enjoyable. The hotel occupies three buildings constructed at various times: Company executives generally stay in the main building, groups and families usually opt for less expensive rooms in the east building, and business travelers take advantage of the mostly singles in the annex. Most rooms are fairly large and nicely furnished but—a sign of the hotel's age—have small windows and small bathrooms. Note, too, that some of the cheapest rooms face another building.

N1 W4, Chuo-ku, Sapporo 060-0001. ✆ 011/261-3311. Fax 011/231-0388. www.grand1934.com. 562 units. ¥18,480 ($176) single; ¥27,720–¥28,875 ($264–$275) double; ¥27,143–¥57,750 ($258–$550) twin. AE, DC, MC, V. Station: Sapporo (8 min.). **Amenities:** 5 restaurants; 3 noodle shops; 2 bars; 2 coffee shops; 1 lounge; business

center; shopping arcade; salon; room service (7am–10am and 5pm–1am); in-room massage; same-day laundry/dry-cleaning service; nonsmoking rooms. *In room:* A/C, cable TV, dataport, minibar, hot-water pot w/tea, hair dryer, Washlet toilet.

## MODERATE

**Hotel Lifort** *(K) (Value)*   Built as a getaway for schoolteachers and owned by a teachers' association, this well-designed hotel looks more expensive than it is and offers comfortable rooms that are open to the public when there's space (Sat is usually fully booked). Located across from Nakajima-koen Park, it offers mostly single rooms, which are small but nicely decorated. Deluxe twins are especially spacious, separated into living and sleeping areas, though don't expect to hang more than one suit in the shallow closet. There are also five Japanese-style rooms, without bathrooms. The best views are of the park. Unfortunately, not much English is spoken.

S10 W1, Chuo-ku, Sapporo 064-0810. ✆ **011/521-5211.** Fax 011/521-5215. 195 units (190 with bathroom). June–Oct ¥7,507 – ¥9,240 ($71–$88) single, ¥13,744 – ¥17,325 ($131–$165) twin. Nov–May ¥6,352 – ¥7,507 ($60–$71) single, ¥11,434–¥13,860 ($109–$132) twin. AE, MC, V. Subway: Nakajima-koen (3 min.). Take exit 1, turn right, cross the big street, and turn right again. **Amenities:** Restaurant (Japanese/Western/Chinese); same-day laundry/dry-cleaning service; nonsmoking rooms. *In room:* A/C, TV, fridge, hot-water pot, hair dryer, Washlet toilets (except Japanese rooms).

(260) **Nakamuraya Ryokan** *(K)*   If you want to stay in a ryokan, this modern and comfortable Japanese inn, just a stone's throw from the Botanic Garden, is a good choice. First opened more than a 100 years ago but now occupying a nondescript 25-year-old building, it offers pleasant Japanese-style tatami rooms, some with a sitting area near the window. The hallways with eaves and slatted wooden doors to each room are a nice touch. Although rooms have their own tub, you might want to take advantage of the public baths here. To receive the low rates listed below, you must book in advance and mention the Japanese Inn Group.

N3 W7, Chuo-ku, Sapporo 060-0003. ✆ **011/241-2111.** Fax 011/241-2118. www.nakamura-ya.com. 27 units. Rates for foreign guests ¥7,350 ($70) single; ¥13,650 ($130) double. Snow Festival rates ¥8,925 ($85) single, ¥16,800 ($160) double. Breakfast ¥1,575 ($15) extra; dinner ¥3,150 ($30) extra. AE, V. Located between the entrance of the Botanic Garden and the Old Government Building. Station: Sapporo (10 min.). **Amenities:** Restaurant (Japanese); in-room massage. *In room:* A/C, TV, fridge, hot-water pot w/tea.

**Sapporo Aspen Hotel**   Built in 1996, this hotel has an English-speaking staff and a convenient location just north of Sapporo Station (its brochure says 100 steps, but I didn't count them). Otherwise, rooms are rather small for the price but are comfortable enough, with windows that open, heavy curtains to block light, sitting areas and desks, and plenty of counter space in bathrooms. The best views are from the west side overlooking Hokkaido University and a distant forest.

N8 W4, Kita-ku, Sapporo 060-0808. ✆ **011/700-2111.** Fax 011/700-2002. info@aspen-hotel.co.jp. 302 units. ¥7,200 – ¥8,700 ($69–$83) single; ¥13,600 – ¥16,600 ($130–$158) twin. June–Sept and Snow Festival ¥9,900 – ¥13,500 ($94–$129) single, ¥18,000 – ¥24,000 ($171–$229) twin. AE, DC, MC, V. Station: Sapporo (a 2-min. walk straight north of the station, on the left). **Amenities:** Coffee shop; rental bicycles (fee: ¥1,570/$15 per day); concierge; in-room massage; same-day laundry service; nonsmoking rooms (reserve in advance). *In room:* A/C, TV, fridge, hot-water pot w/tea, hair dryer, Washlet toilet.

## INEXPENSIVE

**Nada** *(Value)*   A bit of a hike from the station (a 30-min. walk southwest), this little family inn is clean and has friendly hosts who offer Japanese-style rooms, all nonsmoking and including dormitory-style rooms with futons at cheaper prices if you're

willing to share with strangers. The communal kitchen has a cozy, wooden dining area. There is no curfew.

S5 W9 Chuo-ku, Sapporo 064-0805. © **011/551-5882.** Fax 011/551-0303. sapporoinnnada@jcom.home.ne.jp. 10 units (none with bathroom). ¥4,000 ($38) per person; ¥3,500 ($33) per person in dormitory. Winter heating charge ¥200 ($1.90) extra. Breakfast ¥500 ($4.75) extra. MC, V (5% extra if you pay by credit card). Taxi: ¥1,000 ($9.50). Subway: Susukino (10 min.). Walk west on South 4 (Rte. 36) 3 blocks to West 9 (there's a gas station here on the corner), turn left, and then right on the 4th street. **Amenities:** Communal kitchen, coin-op washer/dryer; nonsmoking rooms; rental bikes (fee: ¥500/$4.75 per day). *In room:* No phone.

(261) **Toyoko Inn Sapporo Hokudai-mae** ⭐ *Finds* The motto of this inexpensive business-hotel chain translates roughly as "Eliminate unnecessary luxury but attend to guests' needs." It does so by offering free TV movies, a VCR (there's a video-rental shop next door), free use of lobby computers with Internet access (and free high-speed connections in rooms), special bathroom amenities for women, and little extras like semi-double or double-size beds in the mostly single rooms. The twins are great for friends traveling together (or couples who wish they weren't)—the bathroom splits the room in halves, each containing its own bed, TV, mirror, hair dryer, and more. And true to its motto, the staff is friendly. Since the hotel is located across from Hokkaido University, rooms are understandably hard to come by during February entrance exams.

4-22-7, N8, Kita-ku, Sapporo 060-0808. © **011/717-1045.** Fax 011/717-1046. www.toyoko-inn.com. 180 units. June–Sept and Snow Festival ¥6,510–¥7,140 ($62–$68) single; ¥9,240 ($88) double or twin. Oct–May ¥4,410– ¥5,040 ($42–$48) single, ¥7,140 ($68) double or twin. Rates include free breakfast. AE, DC, MC, V. Station: Sapporo (3 min.). Walk straight north, turn left at the gas station, and then turn right; the hotel will be on the right. **Amenities:** Lobby computer w/free Internet access; coin-op washer/dryer; nonsmoking rooms. *In room:* A/C, TV w/free movies and VCR, dataport, fridge, hot-water pot w/tea, hair dryer, trouser press.

## WHERE TO DINE

Hokkaido's specialties include crab, corn on the cob, potatoes, **Genghis Khan** (a dish of mutton and vegetables that you grill yourself, also spelled "Jingisukan"), salmon, and **Ishikari Nabe** (a stew of salmon and other Hokkaido vegetables, also cooked at your table).

Sapporo is also famous for its Chinese noodles *(ramen),* and the most popular place to eat them is on a tiny, narrow street in Susukino popularly known as **Ramen Yokocho.** Located just 1 short block east of the Susukino Station, it's an alleyway of noodle shop after noodle shop. It doesn't matter which one you choose—just look for an empty seat. Each very small shop consists of a counter and some chairs, with photos of various dishes outside the front door. Most are open daily from 11:30am to 3am. Noodles generally begin at ¥750 ($7.15) for a steaming bowlful.

### EXPENSIVE

**Mikuni Sapporo** ⭐⭐ FRENCH Kiyomi Mikuni has a reputation as *the* Japanese authority on French food. Hokkaido-born and the proprietor/chef of several Mikuni restaurants in Tokyo and elsewhere, Mikuni has brought his expertise home to triumphant reviews. Located on the ninth floor of Stellar Place in Sapporo Station in a setting that is less than stellar, the restaurant overcomes its disappointing decor with great cuisine, available only as set meals. A seasonal, autumn lunch, for example, includes cappuccino-style autumn mushrooms and chestnuts, either pan-fried codfish with potatoes and lentils or braised pork garnished with French beans and sweet-potato purée, plus dessert and coffee. There is an extensive wine list, with knowledgeable sommeliers to advise.

Stellar Place 9F, W2 N5. ✆ **011/251-0392**. Reservations strongly suggested. Set dinner ¥8,000 ($76); set lunch ¥3,800 ($36). AE, DC, MC, V. Daily 11:30am–2:30pm and 5:30–9pm (last order). In Sapporo Station.

**Sky J** ✿✿✿ INTERNATIONAL   Breathtaking views, reasonable prices, and a wide array of tempting dishes make this sleek restaurant a popular place to dine. The lunch buffet gets top ratings, with 30 dishes that run the gamut from Indonesian to Italian and may include such delectable choices as red-bean and olive-paste pasta, coconut milk and Kaffir lime *okara* (a soybean product), and black sesame and squid ink curry. In addition, there are nine kinds of bread and a huge dessert table with make-your-own sundaes. An example of a set dinner, which changes monthly and is served from 5:30 to 9pm, is sea bass and salmon carpaccio, cream of leek and eggplant soup, flat fish in crab sauce with Italian herbs, roast lamb, and cream cheese parfait. From 9pm, the Sky J metamorphoses into a classy cocktail lounge, with live music (and a ¥735/$7 cover charge unless you dine before 9pm), plus a la carte dishes, including steaks.

35th floor, JR Tower Hotel Nikko Sapporo, W2 N5. ✆ **011/251-2222**. Lunch buffet ¥2,000 ($19); set dinner ¥4,500 ($43); main dishes (after 9pm) ¥950–¥3,500 ($9.05–$33). AE, DC, MC, V. Daily 11:30am–2pm and 5:30–midnight. Station: Sapporo.

**Zuientei** ✿✿ KAISEKI   Although the Hotel Monterey Edelhof prides itself on its turn-of-the-20th-century decor, my favorite restaurant here is this 13th-floor escape, a soothing respite with its tall ceiling, bamboo screens, and small inner garden. The handwritten menu is in Japanese, but ordering is easy: Choose one of the kaiseki dinners that change with the seasons or, for lunch, an obento or set meal.

Hotel Monterey Edelhof, N2 W1. ✆ **011/242-7111**. Set dinners ¥4,000–¥7,000 ($38–$67); set lunches ¥1,300–¥3,500 ($12–$33). AE, DC, MC, V. Daily 11am–2pm and 5–9pm (last order). Station: Sapporo (8 min.).

## MODERATE

**Hyosetsu-no-Mon** KING CRAB   A well-known restaurant that specializes in giant king crab caught in the Japan Sea north of Hokkaido, Hyosetsu-no-Mon is in Sapporo's Susukino nightlife district. Its menu (in English-language with photos) is easy enough—it consists almost entirely of king crab dishes. Set courses include a cooked crab, sashimi, crab soup, crab tempura, and vegetables. You can also order a la carte fried king crab claws, deep-fried king crab, tempura king crab, grilled king crab, and crabmeat chowder. Each floor has different seating arrangements, from tables to tatami; the best is the sixth floor where you sit on tatami in a dining hall reminiscent of an old Kabuki theater (you must reserve to sit here). Lunch set meals, served from 11am to 3pm, are a good value.

S5 W2 (next to Sluggers Batting Stadium). ✆ **011/521-3046**. Reservations required for 6th floor. Set dinners ¥2,500–¥12,600 ($24–$120); set lunches ¥2,000–¥2,300 ($19–$22). AE, DC, MC, V. Daily 11am–10pm (last order). Subway: Susukino (2 min.).

(262) **Kita-no-fuji** *Finds* CHANKO NABE   Located in the heart of the Susukino nightlife district, this restaurant specializes in the famous hearty stews favored by sumo wrestlers, *chanko nabe*. After putting your shoes in one of the lockers with famous wrestlers' names on them, you'll be led to your table, tatami room, or counter. The center of the restaurant is dominated by a sumo ring, and sumo memorabilia decorate the walls. As for the nabe, which you'll cook at your table, there's a picture menu but you can also tell them how much you want to spend per person. The more expensive nabe features crab. Unfortunately, the staff in this busy nightspot has no time for cordiality, but this is definitely a unique place to dine.

S7 W4. 🕻 011/512-5484, or 011/512-1339 for reservations. Reservations suggested. Chanko nabe ¥2,300–¥2,700 ($22–$26); nabe with crab from ¥2,900 ($28). AE, DC, MC, V. Daily 4–11pm. Subway: Susukino (7 min.). Beside a disco with a Maya-like facade; look for a free-standing menu and a wooden wall with sumo handprints.

263 **Palace Toriyoshi** 🕭 *Finds* YAKITORI/VARIED   In a building filled with restaurants (you'll notice Asian Café Hoang Tam on the ground floor) and bars in the Susukino nightlife district, this tiny restaurant serves yakitori with a twist, including many original creations by owner/chef Mr. Okuyama. How about cherry tomatoes covered in cheese; lotus root; a small onion filled with minced chicken; tofu salad; or eggplant with minced meat? Since the menu is in Japanese, the best strategy is to tell the waiter what you like to eat and how much you want to spend; Mr. Okuyama will fix a meal to suit your budget. For ¥2,625 ($25), I had sashimi, seven yakitori and original skewers, salad, one of the best savory custards I've ever eaten, and soba.

Japanland Building, 2F (2nd floor). S5 W5. 🕻 011/521-2002. Reservations recommended. Yakitori ¥157–¥273 ($1.50–$2.60); set meals ¥2,625–¥6,300 ($25–$60). AE, MC, V. Mon–Sat 5–11pm (to 10pm national holidays). Subway: Susukino (3 min.).

## INEXPENSIVE

**Komugi-no-ie La Pausa** *Value* ITALIAN   Right across the street from the Clock Tower, this light and airy restaurant serves Neapolitan pizza baked in a stone kiln, as well as homemade pasta and cakes. The "today's pasta" (choose from three) available for lunch with a soft drink is a great deal for ¥780 ($7.45), and my delicious Caesar salad was only ¥680 ($6.50).

N1 W3. 🕻 011/252-2231. Pasta ¥580–¥1,280 ($5.50–$12); set dinners ¥1,680–¥3,280 ($16–$31); set lunches ¥780–¥1,480 ($7.45–$14). AE, DC, MC, V. Daily 11am–11:30pm. Subway: Odori (1 min.). In the same building as i Plaza.

**Sapporo Beer Garden** 🕭 GENGHIS KHAN/BAR FOOD   I can't imagine going to Sapporo without dropping by the Sapporo Beer Garden beside the historic Sapporo Beer Museum. Go late to the museum and then stay for dinner; or, if it's winter or early in the day when the beer garden is closed, dine in the Sapporo Beer Hall, an old ivy-covered brick building built in 1890 as the Sapporo brewery. I personally prefer the second floor's Kessel Hall, where you dine underneath a huge old mash tub once used in brewing beer. For snacks, you can order sausage or potato dishes, but the specialty of the house is Genghis Khan, which you cook yourself on a hot skillet at your table. The best deal in the house is the appropriately named King Viking, which for ¥3,570 ($34) gives you as much Genghis Khan and draft beer as you can consume in 100 minutes. Otherwise, for all you timid drinkers, draft beer starts at ¥515 ($4.90).

Sapporo Beer Museum, N7 E9. 🕻 011/742-1531. All-you-can-eat Genghis Khan ¥2,400 ($23). AE, DC, MC, V. Garden July–Aug Mon–Sat 5–9pm, Sun noon–3pm and 4–9pm. Beer Hall daily 11:30am–10pm. Taxi: 5 min. from Sapporo Station. Bus: See "Sapporo Beer Museum," on p. 584.

**Taj Mahal** *Value* INDIAN   This very good, second-floor Indian restaurant tries too hard with its Indian mirrored fabrics, brass lamps, Indian music, and Japanese staff in Indian dress (the cooks are Indian), as the food alone is reason enough to come here. The service is friendly and the choices are varied—in addition to tandoori and kabobs, they serve chicken, lamb, fish, seafood, and vegetable curries (but no pork or beef). Tasty lunch specials are served until 3pm, but not on Sundays or holidays.

N2 W3. 🕻 011/231-8850. Curries ¥1,180–¥1,650 ($11–$16); set dinners ¥1,200–¥2,450 ($11–$23); set lunches ¥580–¥1,400 ($5.50–$13). AE, DC, V. Mon–Fri 11am–3pm and 5–10pm (last order); Sat–Sun 11am–10pm. Station:

Sapporo (6 min.). Walk south on Eki-mae Dori and turn left when you see JAL and JTB to the right; it's catty-corner from the post office.

## 4 Noboribetsu Spa & Shikotsu-Toya National Park

If you have only a couple days to spare to visit one of Hokkaido's national parks, head to **Shikotsu-Toya National Park** 𝕲𝕲, the closest to Sapporo and the first national park you'll reach if you enter Hokkaido via train to Hakodate. This 987-sq.-km (381-sq.-mile) national park encompasses lakes, volcanoes, and the famous hot-spring resort of **Noboribetsu Onsen** 𝕲𝕲, home to 1,000 people.

Famous for the variety of its hot-water springs ever since the first public bathhouse opened here in 1858, Noboribetsu Spa is one of Japan's best-known spa resorts and is the most popular of Hokkaido's many spa towns. It boasts 11 different types of hot water (each with a different mineral content) and gushes 10,000 tons a day. With temperatures ranging between 113°F (45°C) and 197°F (92°C), the waters contain all kinds of minerals, including sulfur, salt, iron, and gypsum, and are thought to help relieve such disorders as high blood pressure, poor blood circulation, rheumatism, arthritis, eczema, and even constipation.

Also known for its seasonal beauty, Noboribetsu is an impressive sight in spring, when 2,000 cherry trees lining the road into the onsen are in full bloom. In autumn, thousands of Japanese maples burst into flame. In the nearby village of **Shiraoi** on Lake Poroto, a museum and village commemorate the native Ainu and their culture.

### ESSENTIALS

**GETTING THERE**    Noboribetsu Onsen is about a 15-minute **bus** ride (¥330/$3.15; departures three or more times an hour) from the town of Noboribetsu and **Noboribetsu Station,** which is where you'll arrive if you come by train. Noboribetsu Station lies on the main **JR train** line that runs between Hakodate and Sapporo, a little more than 2 hours from Hakodate and 1 hour and 10 minutes from Sapporo. Fares for an unreserved seat are ¥3,850 ($37) from Sapporo, ¥6,190 ($59) from Hakodate.

There are also **direct buses** from Sapporo Station to Noboribetsu Onsen (eight a day) costing ¥1,900 ($18) for the 2½-hour trip. Contact **Chuo Bus** (© 011/231-0500) or **Dohnan Bus** (© 0143/45-2131) for more information.

**VISITOR INFORMATION & GETTING AROUND**    The **Noboribetsu Tourist Association** (© 0143/84-3311; open daily 9am–6pm) is on Noboribetsu Onsen's main street, just a minute's walk north of the bus depot (continue up the hill; it will be on your left side with a clock above the door). Ask for the pamphlet "The Land of Hot Springs" with its map and hot-springs information. You may not encounter anyone who speaks English, but luckily the town is so small you shouldn't have any problem getting around.

### WHAT TO SEE & DO

#### ENJOYING NOBORIBETSU'S NATURAL WONDERS

**TAKING THE LOCAL WATERS**    Although all the spa hotels and ryokan have their own taps into the spring water, almost everyone who comes to Noboribetsu Onsen makes a point of going to the most famous hotel bath in town, **Daiichi Takimotokan** 𝕲𝕲 (© 0143/84-2111), one of the first bathhouses to open at the hot springs. Now a huge, modern bathing hall with some 30 pools containing different

---

*Tips* **Un-Bearable Park**

As you wander around Noboribetsu Onsen, you'll see advertisements for a bear park and an Ainu village attraction. The best thing about this place is the trip via ropeway—the bear park occupies one of the tallest hills around. The 160 or so bears, however, are crowded together in concrete pens in one of the saddest sights I've ever seen, and the Ainu "village" is mainly for souvenirs. Although the bears, many of them rescued from extermination or brought here as orphaned cubs, are luckier than some of their peers (government policy advocated the extermination of Hokkaido brown bears in the 1950s and still allows 300 of the estimated 2,000 remaining wild bears to be hunted and culled annually), the admission (including ropeway) of ¥2,520 ($24) is too high a price for this joyless place. Skip it—you're better off spending your money elsewhere. Or donate money for a cause: Dedicated employees bent on saving brown bears here have begun a nonprofit organization in hopes of moving the bears off the mountain to a place where there's more room.

---

mineral contents at various temperatures, it's an elaborate affair with hot-spring baths both indoors and out, indoor and outdoor Jacuzzis, saunas, steam rooms, and waterfall massage (this is one of my favorites—you sit under the shooting water and let it pummel your neck and shoulders). Although the baths are separate for men and women, there's an indoor swimming pool for families with a slide and play area for children, so be sure to bring your swimsuit. If you're staying at the Daiichi Takimotokan hotel (see "Where to Stay," below), you can use the baths for free at any time—in the evenings, don't miss bathing in the outdoor baths, where you can order beer, soft drinks, or sake and enjoy the nice mountain scenery. Otherwise, Daiichi Takimotokan is open to the public daily from 9am to 6pm (you must enter by 5pm); the charge is ¥2,000 ($19) for adults, half price for children 3 to 12.

264 **Sagiriyu** (*©* **0143/84-2050**) is Noboribetsu Onsen's public bathhouse. Located on the main street next to the Tourist Information Office, it offers two types of hot-spring waters, a whirlpool bath, and a sauna (but unfortunately no outdoor bath). Taking the waters and sauna here costs ¥390 ($3.70) for adults and ¥170 ($1.60) for children. It's open daily from 7am to 10pm.

**HELL VALLEY (Jigokudani)** ✿ To get an idea of what all this hot water looks like, visit Hell Valley at the north edge of town past the Daiichi Takimotokan hotel (see "Where to Stay," below). A volcanic crater 446m (1,485 ft.) in diameter, the huge depression is full of bubbling, boiling water and rock formations of orange and brown. As you walk the concrete path that winds along the left side of the crater (called Hell Valley Promenade), keep an eye down below to the right for a tiny shrine dedicated to the deity that protects eyes (those most in need are apt to miss it); local lore says that if you rub some of the protective water over ailing eyes, they'll be cured. Farther along, you'll soon reach a sign for OYUNAMA and a path leading uphill to the left through lush woods; if you follow it for about 10 minutes, you'll come to a lookout point over a large pond of hot bubbling water called Oyunama (the lookout is across the highway; it's another 5-min. walk to the pond). If you want to take a different route back, follow the path to the right just as you recross the highway. This pathway,

called Funamiya (or Mount Funami) Promenade, traces the backbone of several ridges all the way back into town, passing a number of small stone guardians. If you follow it for 25 minutes to the end (where it's a bit overgrown and neglected), you'll end up in front of Oyado Kiyomizu-ya ryokan (see "Where to Stay," below). But the path diverges at several points, and if you take the wrong path you'll end up at—Hell Valley.

## ESPECIALLY FOR KIDS

In addition to the two theme parks listed below, there's a Bear Park with 160 brown bears crowded into a cement enclosure: It's very sad; skip it.

**Edo Wonderland Noboribetsu (Jidai-mura)** 🐾🐾 *Kids*    A visit to this reproduction of a Feudal-Era village is the closest you can get to taking a time machine back to the last days of the Edo Period. Shops, restaurants, theaters, the downtown, and a samurai district are built as they were of yore, staffed by people dressed in period clothing. See Ninja warriors fighting in a trick mansion, local merchants hawking their wares, Edo-Era tenements with life-size models, and courtesans performing in this Disney-esque re-creation of how Japan might have looked when the shogun reigned. Although shows are in Japanese (the Ninja show is probably the only one that would interest children), the various attractions are fun for the whole family, and if you haven't seen another historical theme village elsewhere in Japan, this rather small one is worth a 2-hour visit. To commemorate the day forever, you can don a kimono, samurai, or Ninja outfit and have your photo taken in front of a traditional backdrop for ¥2,100 ($20)

53–1 Nakanoboribetsu, Noboribetsu-shi. ✆ 0143/83-3311. Admission ¥3,500 ($33) adults, ¥1,800 ($17) children. Apr–Oct daily 9am–5pm; Nov–Mar Thurs–Tues 10am–4pm. Bus: From Noboribetsu Onsen or JR Noboribetsu Station to Edo Wonderland/Jidai-mura.

**Noboribetsu Marine Park Nixe** 🐾 *Kids*    Small children love this combination Danish theme park and aquarium, located near Noboribetsu Station. (If you're traveling with luggage, lockers are available both here and at the station.) The aquarium, one of the largest in northern Japan, is in Castle Nixe, modeled after a Danish castle (and visible from the station), where you'll see sharks, rays, salmon, sturgeon, king crab, frogs, turtles, and other sea creatures. More attractions include a dolphin show, a king penguin parade, a sea lion show, a game arcade, the ubiquitous souvenir shops (selling Danish and aquarium-related gifts), and a handful of kiddie rides (which cost ¥200–¥300/$1.90–$2.85 extra). You can see everything in about 2 hours.

1–22 Noboribetsu Higashi-machi, Noboribetsu-shi. ✆ 0143/83-3800. Admission ¥2,300 ($22) adults, ¥1,150 ($11) children. Daily 9am–5pm. Station: Noboribetsu (a 7-min. walk from the station; walk straight out the exit and turn right after 1 block).

## LEARNING ABOUT THE AINU IN NEARBY SHIRAOI

**Poroto Kotan and the Ainu Museum** 🐾🐾    Shiraoi (an Ainu word meaning "Place of Many Horseflies") was settled by the Ainu long before Japanese arrived; today, it's a small town of some 22,000 inhabitants, including Ainu. Poroto Kotan ("Big Lake Village" in Ainu), nestled on the shores of Lake Poroto, is a mock village of native houses made entirely from wood and reeds, a native plant garden, a dance area, probably the most important Ainu museum anywhere, and a research center dedicated to preserving Ainu culture. If you're lucky, your visit will coincide with two annual festivals: one, in the spring, to pray for life's necessities; the other in the fall to give thanks for the harvests (call for festival dates).

After passing, regrettably, through a huge souvenir hall, you'll find yourself surrounded by traditionally built houses, where there are demonstrations of Ainu weaving techniques, woodworking, and other crafts, and where native dances are performed by Ainu in traditional costume. Unfortunately, bears (and dogs) are kept in captivity here in filthy metal cages, but even this is an Ainu tradition—in spring, when the mother bear left her cave in search of food, Ainu fetched the cubs to keep in a wooden cage in the village until they were old enough for slaughter. Bears were revered as gifts from the gods. The most important thing to see, however, is the museum, with English-language descriptions of Ainu history, culture, society, and traditions, a video (Japanese-language only) and displays of utensils, clothing, jewelry, and other everyday artifacts.

You can try your hand at several different Ainu crafts, which cost ¥500 ($4.75) per craft (¥400/$3.80 for children). If you wish, you can lunch on dried salmon, potato cakes, and herb tea bought from one of the stalls. Although the village is small and can be toured in about an hour, it's an important stop for those wishing to learn about Ainu culture and the indigenous people who have little left of what was once a rich heritage.

2–3–4 Wakakusa-cho, Shiraoi-cho, Hokkaido 059-0902. ⓒ 0144/82-3914. www.ainu-museum.or.jp. Admission ¥750 ($7.15) adults, ¥550 ($5.25) high-school students, ¥450 ($4.30) junior-high students, ¥300 ($2.85) children. Apr–Oct daily 8:45am–5pm; Nov–Mar daily 9am–4:30pm. Closed 1 week for New Year's. Train: JR train 25 min. from JR Noboribetsu Station to JR Shiraoi Station, then a 15-min. walk; walk out to the traffic signal, turn left, and then turn left again at the next light. Cross the tracks; it's on your right. **Note:** Not all trains running between Hakodate and Sapporo (with stops at Noboribetsu Station) stop at Shiraoi, so make sure yours does.

## WHERE TO STAY

The busiest tourist seasons are July through September and during New Year's, which are when hotel rates are at their highest, particularly on weekends. October, when the leaves are changing, is also popular. All the places below charge a daily ¥150 ($1.45) hot-springs tax.

### EXPENSIVE

㉕ **Oyado Kiyomizu-ya** 🐟🐟   You'll be royally welcome at this elegantly modern ryokan with traditional touches, one of our favorites in Hokkaido. After entering the front gate, you'll be ushered down a long corridor decorated with plants, stones, and paper lanterns to the elevator that will whisk you up to your room. Cheapest are average-looking Western-style rooms, making the simple but pleasant Japanese tatami rooms a better choice. For a splurge, combination rooms are actually two-room suites with a tatami room where you'll dine and a separate bedroom. The ryokan is beside a roaring river, the sounds of which will sing you to sleep as you snuggle against fur-lined futons (which cost an astounding $1,000 each!) and down covers. But it's the delicious and abundant seasonal kaiseki meals served in your room that assure the ryokan many repeat guests; the parade of beautifully prepared dishes includes local specialties. Service, as can be expected, is impeccable, and the second-generation owner, Mr. Iwai, speaks excellent English; he can answer your questions regarding Noboribetsu and the surrounding area. (A sake connoisseur, he can also recommend which of the 14 different kinds of sake he keeps on hand might go best with your meal.) If you're looking for a place far from tour groups, souvenir shops, and impersonal service, you'll be happy here.

173 Noboribetsu Onsen-machi, Noboribetsu-shi, Hokkaido 059-0551. ⓒ 0143/84-2145. Fax 0143/84-2146. 43 units. ¥10,000 ($95) single; ¥16,000 ($152) double; ¥24,000 ($229) triple. Breakfast ¥2,000 ($19) extra;

dinner ¥5,000–¥10,000 ($48–$95) extra. AE, DC, MC, V. The staff will pick you up at the station if you tell them your arrival time in advance; otherwise, it's above Noboribetsu Onsen's main street, a 10-min. walk from the bus terminal. **Amenities:** Coffee shop; karaoke bar; indoor/outdoor hot-spring baths (the outdoor bath alternates days for men and women); in-room massage. *In room:* TV, hot-water pot w/tea.

## MODERATE

**Daiichi Takimotokan** ⌖  Thanks to its long history and gigantic public baths with various pools, this is Noboribetsu Onsen's best-known ryokan. Opened in 1858 as the area's first inn and now in its fifth generation of innkeepers (a 30-something woman and probably Japan's youngest female general manager), it remains Noboribetsu's oldest accommodations, though now it's a large, modern facility with little personality and lots of noisy tour groups. Still, the most compelling reasons to stay here are its location near Hell Valley and its hot-spring baths, which hotel guests are entitled to use free anytime, night or day. Another plus: free shuttle bus service November through March from Chitose Airport in Sapporo and throughout the year from downtown Sapporo (call the hotel for reservations). As for rooms, most are simple tatami (only eight are Western-style), with repeat guests usually preferring the west wing (though glazed windows make them a bit dark and in-room meals are not available). Meals are served in a large dining room offering a Japanese, Chinese, and Western buffet or, at slightly higher prices, they are served in some of the Japanese-style rooms.

55 Noboribetsu Onsen-machi, Noboribetsu-shi, Hokkaido 059-0595. ✆ **0143/84-2111.** Fax 0143/84-2202. www. takimotokan.co.jp. 399 units (342 with bathroom, 57 with toilet only). ¥10,000–¥25,000 ($95–$238) per person; peak season, Sat, and holidays ¥2,000 ($19) extra. Rates include 2 meals. AE, DC, MC, V. A 5-min. walk uphill from the bus station, beside Hell Valley. **Amenities:** 3 restaurants (coffee shop; Japanese; Chinese); 2 bars; indoor swimming pool (free for hotel guests); indoor/outdoor hot-spring baths; shopping arcade; in-room massage; laundry/dry-cleaning service. *In room:* TV, fridge, hot-water pot w/tea, safe.

㉖ **Kashotei Hanaya** ⌖  This is one of the most refined members of the Japanese Inn Group ryokan, modern but with such traditional touches as a small Japanese garden off the lobby, flower arrangements, bamboo, decorative floors, and Japanese music playing softly in public areas. Most rooms are Japanese style, with or without bathroom, while the three Western-style rooms are without bathroom (all rooms, however, have toilet and sink). Meals are served in your room. The owner speaks English. The ryokan is on the edge of town, about a 5-minute walk from the bus terminal.

134 Noboribetsu Onsen-machi, Noboribetsu-shi, Hokkaido 059-0551. ✆ **0143/84-2521.** Fax 0143/84-2240. 22 units (5 with bathroom, 17 with toilet only). ¥8,025–¥8,550 ($76–$81) single with toilet only; ¥12,900 ($123) double with toilet only; ¥21,300 ($203) double with bathroom. Japanese or Western breakfast ¥1,050 ($10) extra; dinner ¥2,625–¥7,875 ($25–$75) extra. AE, MC, V. Bus: From Noboribetsu Station to Byoin-mae/Kashotei Hanaya-mae (if you're arriving by bus, you'll get off before reaching the terminal—ask the bus driver to let you know where—the ryokan will be close behind you, across the road). Pickup service also available from Noboribetsu Onsen bus terminal. **Amenities:** Coffee shop; indoor/outdoor hot-spring baths (open round-the-clock); in-room massage. *In room:* A/C, TV, minibar, hot-water pot w/tea.

## INEXPENSIVE

**Takimoto Inn**  If you prefer a hotel with beds to a ryokan with futons, this quiet and moderately priced hotel has the additional advantage of allowing guests to use Daiichi Takimotokan's airport shuttle and famous baths across the street for free. All the rooms are twins (but can be used as singles or triples) and are fairly basic, with small bathrooms. There's no view, but windows do open. Buffet breakfasts and dinners offer a mix of Japanese and Western food.

76 Noboribetsu Onsen-machi, Noboribetsu-shi 059-0551. ✆ **0143/84-2205.** Fax 0143/84-2645. www.takimotoinn. co.jp. 47 units. ¥6,500–¥9,000 ($62–$86) per person, including 2 meals. Sat and peak season ¥2,000 ($19) extra; New Year's, Golden Week ¥3,000–¥4,000 ($29–$38) extra. AE, DC, V. A 5-min. walk uphill from the bus station, across the street from Daiichi Takimotokan. **Amenities:** Restaurant; hot-spring bath (guests can use Daiichi Takimotokan's baths for free); in-room massage. *In room:* TV, fridge, hot-water pot w/tea.

## WHERE TO DINE

㉖⑦ **Fukuan** SOBA   This small, traditional soba shop serves its own buckwheat noodles. Since the menu is in Japanese only, I recommend ordering the *Tenseiro,* a tempura soba meal with shrimp and vegetables; or the *Ebi-tenzaroshi* soba, a summer-time meal of cold soba, shrimp tempura, seaweed, dried fish flakes, and Japanese daikon radish. Or look around at what others are eating. The leg wells are saviors for those errant legs that just won't fit under low Japanese tables.

30 Noboribetsu Onsen-machi. ✆ **0143/84/2758.** Soba ¥680–¥1,400 ($6.50–$13). MC, V. Daily 11:30am–2pm and 6–11pm (closed irregularly 1 day a month). A 1-min. walk from the bus terminal, on the main street across from the tourist information office.

**Poplar Restaurant** WESTERN   If you find yourself looking for a place to stop for lunch, a draft beer, or coffee, try this restaurant, which serves inexpensive Western dishes from a Japanese-language menu with pictures. While they may not win any culi-nary awards, items include beefsteak, hamburger steak, fried shrimp, grilled salmon, grilled pork with ginger sauce, chicken stew, curry rice, shrimp gratin, and spaghetti.

Takimoto Inn. ✆ **0143/84-2205.** Main dishes ¥650–¥900 ($6.20–$8.55); set meals ¥1,100–¥2,500 ($10–$24). AE, DC, MC, V. Daily 11am–2pm (last order). A 5-min. walk from the bus terminal, near Hell Valley and across from Dai-ichi Takimotokan.

㉖⑧ **Tokumitsu** ⚘ SUSHI   This is a friendly, local hangout where you'll be served good, reasonably priced dishes while sitting at the long sushi counter or on tatami. A plastic-food display will help you order dishes like *Chiraishi sushi* (raw fish served over a bed of seasoned rice), eel *(unagi),* or *kani-nabe* (a crab stew you cook yourself), all priced at ¥1,575 ($15). Tokumitsu stays open late as a nightcap spot for locals and tourists alike.

29 Chuo-dori. ✆ **0143/84-2079.** Sushi and sashimi platters ¥900–¥2,500 ($8.55–$24); set meal ¥1,200 ($11). No credit cards. Daily 11am–2:30pm and 4:30pm–midnight. A 1-min. walk from the bus terminal, on the main street across from the tourist office.

## 5 Sounkyo Spa & Daisetsuzan National Park

Although I find it difficult to rank nature in terms of beauty, there are some who maintain that **Daisetsuzan National Park** ⚘⚘⚘ is the most spectacular of Hokkaido's parks. With its tall mountains covered with fir and birch trees and sprin-kled with wildflowers, and its river gorge laced with waterfalls and hiking trails, Daisetsuzan National Park is the perfect place to come if you've been itching to get some exercise in relatively unspoiled countryside. Lying in the center of Hokkaido (east of Sapporo), this national park—Japan's largest—contains three volcanic moun-tain groups, including the highest mountain in Hokkaido, Mount Asahi, 2,254m (7,513 ft.) high. Hiking in summer and skiing in winter are the primary pursuits of the park's visitors.

Nestled at the very edge of Sounkyo Gorge, Daisetsuzan's most famous natural attraction, is **Sounkyo Onsen** ⚘ (*onsen* means "spa" in Japanese), the perfect base for

exploring the national park. Once rather unattractive with a hodgepodge of ugly cement buildings, Sounkyo has reinvented itself with attractive and compatible alpine-style buildings and stone and wood paths that do justice to the magnificent scenic backdrop and its soothing hot springs. Yet it remains a mountain village, home to 600 residents and only a dozen or so accommodations, most of them small affairs. More important, Sounkyo Spa serves as the starting point for bicycle trips along Sounkyo Gorge and for the cable-car trip to the top of a neighboring peak with its hiking trails. From late January through mid-March, it's the scene of the Ice Falls Festival, a winter fantasyland with giant ice castles, frozen waterfalls lit with colored lights, and weekend fireworks. Need I add that Sounkyo is one of my favorite places in all of Hokkaido?

## ESSENTIALS

**GETTING THERE**  The only way to reach Sounkyo Onsen by public transportation is by **bus.** If you're coming from Sapporo, take the **JR train** 2½ hours to Kamikawa (¥6,180/$59 one-way), transferring there for the 30-minute bus ride (¥770/$7.35 one-way) directly to Sounkyo Onsen. Buses depart about 14 times a day and generally connect with train arrivals, but it's always wise to check ahead with the Tourist Information Center in Sapporo.

There are two buses a day—called the Sunrise Asahikawa-Kushiro-go—connecting Sounkyo Onsen with Akanko Onsen in Akan National Park (see the next section for more on Akan), with the one-way fare costing ¥3,260 ($31) for the 3½-hour trip. (Reservations are required; call ✆ **01658/5-3321** in Sounkyo, or 0154/67-2205 in Akan; or drop by the bus terminal in either town.) All bus fares are half price for children.

**VISITOR INFORMATION & ORIENTATION**  The **tourist information office** (✆ **01658/5-3350;** open daily 10:30am–5pm, closed Wed Nov–Apr except during Ice Festival) is located inside the Community Center in front of the Kurodake-no-yu (public bath). There are no signs, so look for the Kurodake-no-yu sign in the center of the village. The staff's English is limited but they can point you in the direction of your lodging or even make reservations for you. They also have a map, an English-language brochure describing the national park and its attractions, and a brochure about Mount Kurodake and its hiking paths. In any case, the village is so tiny that you won't have any difficulty getting around; it's basically two streets leading up to the ropeway, and a pedestrian lane called Canyon Mall Street that wanders through the center of town.

## EXPLORING SOUNKYO ONSEN

Before exploring the environs, you might want to pop into Sounkyo's **Daisetsuzan National Park Visitor Center,** located next to the ropeway (✆ **01658/9-4400;** open June–Oct daily 8am–6pm, Nov–May Tues–Sun 9am–5pm), with displays on the park's animals, plants, and geological wonders. Unfortunately, displays are in Japanese, though an English-language handout offers rudimentary explanations, and a video shows the park's changes through the seasons. If you plan on hiking, you might ask the staff at the information counter for more details on the "Guide to Mountain Climbing" exhibit, as it alerts hikers to places brown bears are often spotted. Entrance to the center is free.

**BICYCLING THE SOUNKYO GORGE** ⚛  The Sounkyo Gorge is a river valley hemmed in on both sides by rock walls rising almost 150m (500 ft.). Almost perpendicular in places, the gorge extends for about 19km (12 miles), offering spectacular

views with each bending curve. The best way to see part of the gorge is to **bicycle** (unfortunately, a permanent rock slide prohibits cyclists from seeing the whole gorge), which you can do in about an hour or so. From Sounkyo, the first part of the trip is along a sidewalk next to a highway strung with cars. The highway winds along a rushing river past a couple of waterfalls until it finally disappears into a dark tunnel (where it belongs). From this point, the gorge belongs to cyclists and hikers and becomes quite narrow. I find this a glorious ride, especially on fine days, and look forward to it every time I come to Sounkyo Onsen. I only wish the ride were longer, especially since bikes, available for rent from Golden Week (end of Apr) to October at Northern Lodge daily from 8am to 6pm (see "Where to Stay," below), cost ¥1,000 ($9.50) regardless of whether you keep them for 1 hour or a whole day.

**GOING TO THE TOP OF MOUNT KURODAKE** ⟪ If you're interested in hiking, or even if you're not, take the **cable car** directly from Sounkyo Onsen to the lofty peak of Mount Kurodake. The trip takes 7 minutes, and round-trip tickets cost ¥1,750 ($17) for adults and ¥900 ($8.55) for children. From the cable-car station, walk a few minutes farther up the mountain, where you'll come to a chairlift. The chairlift ride (my favorite part) takes 15 minutes, swinging you past lush forests of fir and birch. Round-trip fare is ¥600 ($5.70) for adults and ¥400 ($3.80) for children. Ropeway and lift operating hours vary; in summer it's 6am to 7pm, in winter it's 9am to 4pm (call ⟪ **01658/5-3031** for more information).

**DAY HIKES** At the end of the lift, where the hiking paths begin, there's a hut to the left where you sign your name and give your route so that tabs can be kept on people who are on the mountain. You can also rent rubber boots here for ¥500 ($4.75), a must if you don't have hiking boots, since trails are slippery and wet (small streams from winter snows cascade down the trail even in July). Note that rental sizes only go up to 28 centimeters (12 in.). If you're not feeling overly ambitious but are prepared to exert yourself climbing over boulders, you can reach the peak of **Kurodake,** 1,950m (6,500 ft.) high, in about 1½ hours. There, if the weather is clear, you'll be rewarded with views of the surrounding mountain ranges. If you feel like taking a day hike, there's a circular path along the top of mountain ridges that you can hike in about 8 hours. (Be sure to get a map at the tourist information office and note lift operating hours.) The tops of the mountains are really beautiful here, covered with wildflowers and alpine plant life. It would be a shame to come to Sounkyo and not spend a few hours amid its lofty peaks.

**SKIING** From November to May, the mountain becomes a skier's haven, with beginner to advanced slopes. Although you can rent skis up on the mountain at the cable-car station, keep in mind that your feet may be too big (at last check, boots went up to 27cm/11 in.). Skis and boots (for adults) rent for ¥3,150 ($30), while a 1-day cable-car and chairlift ticket goes for ¥3,600 ($34) for adults and ¥2,100 ($20) for children.

**TAKING THE WATERS** In the village Community Center, you'll find **Kurodake-no-yu** (⟪ **01658/5-3333**), a public hot-spring bath with large, spotless, and attractive indoor and outdoor baths plus a sauna. The spa charges ¥600 ($5.70) for adults (half price for children) and is open daily 10am to 9pm (closed Wed Nov–Apr, except during Ice Festival). Buy your tickets at the entrance's vending machine.

## WHERE TO STAY

There are plenty of inexpensive pensions and hotels in Sounkyo. The army of college-age Japanese you see working in the area comes from other parts of Japan to work for

the summer. They may not know a lot about the area, but most of them speak some English. If you want to stay here in July, August, or September, be sure to make advance reservations. Rates below include the ¥150 ($1.45) onsen tax.

## MODERATE

269 **Ginsenkaku** ⋒    Opened in 1998, this modern, functional ryokan offers convenience and rather ordinary Japanese-style rooms with small bathrooms. Except during busy peak periods, Japanese meals are served in your room; buffet breakfasts in a communal dining room offer Japanese and Western choices. The highest prices below include very elaborate meals.

Sounkyo Onsen, Kamikawacho, Kamikawa-gun 078-1701. ⓒ 01658/5-3003. Fax 01658/5-3121. 36 units. Summer ¥10,650–¥30,000 ($101–$286) per person; off season ¥8,500–¥30,000 ($81–$286) per person. Rates include 2 meals and service charge. MC, V. A 4-min. walk from the bus terminal. **Amenities:** Restaurant (Western); bar; lounge; indoor/outdoor hot-spring baths; in-room massage. *In room:* TV, fridge, hot-water pot w/tea, hair dryer, safe, Washlet toilet.

**Taisetsu Hotel** ⋒⋒ *(Value*    Although it's the farthest walk from the bus terminal, this hotel's ridge-top location above town gives it good views of the surrounding gorge and mountains. What makes this a top pick, however, are its gorgeous baths, of which there are three (open 24 hr.). Best are the seventh-floor indoor and outdoor baths with great views and the newer outdoor baths overlooking expansive greenery. As for rooms, most are Japanese-style, and prices are based on meals; ask for a room on a top floor facing the gorge. Six rooms have balconies with private outdoor baths, but if you stay here you're expected to dine in your room at a higher charge. Otherwise, you have your choice of dining in Top of Canyon or paying more to dine in your room. Breakfasts are served buffet style with both Western and Japanese food. A big plus to staying here October 10 to the end of April is that there's a free daily bus service between the hotel (departure at 10am) and Ashikawa Station (departure at 2pm for the hotel).

Sounkyo Onsen, Kamikawacho, Kamikawa-gun 078-1701. ⓒ 01658/5-3211. Fax 01658/5-3420. www.taisetsu.g.com/english. 232 units. ¥9,000–¥15,000 ($86–$143) per person dining in Top of Canyon; ¥12,000–¥18,000 ($114–$171) per person with in-room dining; from ¥30,000 (from $286) per person for rooms with private outdoor baths. Peak season ¥4,000–¥6,000 ($38–$57) extra. Rates include 2 meals and service charge. AE, DC, MC, V. An 8-min. walk from the bus terminal. **Amenities:** 3 restaurants (Japanese, combination Japanese/Western, coffee shop); 1 Japanese-style pub; indoor/outdoor hot-spring baths; sauna; whirlpool baths; in-room massage. *In room:* TV, fridge, hot-water pot w/tea, hair dryer, safe, Washlet toilet.

## INEXPENSIVE

**Northern Lodge** ⋒    This small and personable European-style lodge invites you into its cozy living room complete with fireplace, English-speaking staff, and spotless, mostly Japanese-style rooms, though there are a few twins with down quilts and sofas. The bathrooms are small but you'll probably want to go to the lodge's public hot-spring baths anyway, which use fences for privacy, above which are views of soaring mountains. The communal dining room, decorated with natural wood, offers both European (Swiss fondue) and Japanese cuisine for dinner, and you can choose either Western or Japanese for breakfast. If you're here for the winter Ice Falls Festival, be sure to ask for a room on the fourth or fifth floor facing the river.

Sounkyo Onsen, Kamikawacho, Kamikawa-gun 078-1701. ⓒ 01658/5-3231. Fax 01658/5-3021. 36 units. Summer ¥11,700 ($111) per person; off season ¥9,600 ($91) per person. Rates include 2 meals. MC, V. A 1-min. walk from the bus terminal, across the footbridge over the river and up the hill. **Amenities:** Indoor/outdoor hot-spring baths; rental bikes (¥1,000/$9.50 per day); gift shop; coin-op washer and dryer. *In room:* TV, fridge, hot-water pot w/tea, safe.

**Onsen Pension Ginga** ★ 𝒱𝑎𝑙𝑢𝑒    Opened in 2001, this cute lodge is bright and airy, with a glass-enclosed communal dining room decorated in European drawing-room style and both Japanese- and Western-style rooms, most with large windows providing great panoramic views (best are the corner rooms, and room no. 208). Rooms without bathrooms do have sinks. Japanese meals, served in the dining room, feature local fish and other ingredients. Unfortunately, the hot-spring bath here is small.

Sounkyo Onsen, Kamikawacho, Kamikawa-gun 078-1701. ☎ **01658/5-3775.** 17 units (5 with bathroom). ¥4,875 ($46) per person without bathroom, ¥6,240 ($59) per person with bathroom. Breakfast ¥1,050 ($10) extra. Dinner ¥1,050 ($10) extra. No credit cards. A 2-min. walk from the bus terminal. **Amenities:** Small indoor hot-spring bath; coin-op washer dryer. *In room:* TV, hot-water pot w/tea, no phone.

⑵⑺⑼ **Resort Pension Yama-no-ue**    This pension offers simple tatami rooms with just the basics. There are communal toilets, sinks, and showers; but for a real hot-spring bath, guests staying here are entitled to use the Spa Kurodake in the adjoining building for free. In summer, the small dining room serves ample meals of Hokkaido cuisine. If you stay more than 1 night or in winter, you'll dine at Beergrill Canyon (see "Where to Dine," below). Breakfast is Western style. Since the owner is an avid photographer and butterfly collector, you'll see gorgeous shots of the area and captured butterflies on the walls.

Sounkyo Onsen, Kamikawacho, Kamikawa-gun 078-1701. ☎ **01658/5-3206.** Fax 01658/5-3207. www.p-yamanoue. com 14 units (none with bathroom, 1 with toilet). ¥5,800 ($55) per person. Breakfast ¥1,000 ($9.50) extra; dinner ¥2,000 ($17) extra. No credit cards. A 2-min. walk from the bus terminal. *In room:* TV, hot-water pot w/tea, no phone.

## WHERE TO DINE

**Beergrill Canyon** PIZZA/PASTA    Located in the same building as Spa Kurodake (identified as "Community Center" on the English-language map), this casual restaurant serves various pizzas and pastas from its Japanese-language menu. Choices include pizza with mushrooms and bacon, spaghetti in a white-cream sauce with egg and bacon, spicy curry chicken, and sirloin steak (local beef). For a complete meal, add a minisalad, bread, or rice to your entree by paying ¥250 ($2.40) extra. Wash it all down with beer.

Sounkyo. ☎ **01658/5-3361.** Main dishes ¥650–¥2,500 ($6.20–$24); set meals ¥1,100–¥3,000 ($10–$29). No credit cards. Mon–Fri 11:30am–3:30pm and 5:30–9pm; Sat–Sun 9:30am–9pm (last order). Closed Wed in winter.

## 6 Akanko Spa & Akan National Park

Spreading through the eastern end of Hokkaido, **Akan National Park** ★★ features volcanic mountains, dense forests of subarctic primeval trees, and three caldera lakes, including Lake Akan.

The best place to stay in the park is **Akanko Onsen,** a small hot-spring resort on the edge of Lake Akan and home to 1,900 residents. It makes a good base for active vacations ranging from fishing to hiking and from which to explore both Akan National Park and nearby Kushiro Marshland National Park, famous for its red-crested cranes. It also has a re-created Ainu village, with one of the best music and dance performances I've seen.

### ESSENTIALS

**GETTING THERE    By JR Train & Bus**    Since there's no train station at Akanko Onsen itself, transportation to the resort town is by train to Kushiro or Kitami and then by bus to Akanko. Kushiro is about 4 hours from Sapporo by JR train; Kitami is

4½ hours away. From **JR Kushiro Station,** buses depart four or five times a day for Akanko; the 2-hour trip costs ¥2,650 ($25) one-way. From **Kitami,** buses depart twice a day (at last check at 9:30am and 3pm), and the 70-minute trip costs ¥1,800 ($17). You must make a reservation for this bus by calling © **0157/23-2181** in Kitami or © **0154/67-2205** in Akanko.

If you're coming from Sounkyo Onsen, two buses a day connect Sounkyo Onsen with Akanko Onsen, with the one-way fare costing ¥3,260 ($31) for the 3½-hour trip. (Reservations required; call © **01658/5-3321** in Sounkyo, or 0154/67-2205 in Akan, or drop by the bus terminal in either town.)

All bus fares are half price for children.

In addition to regular buses, there are also sightseeing buses that take in the most important sights in both Akan and Kushiro Marshland national parks along the way. This is the best way to see the national park if you don't have your own car; for details, read "Seeing the Sights," below.

**By Plane**    Because Akan National Park lies at the eastern extremity of Hokkaido, you may wish to fly at least one-way between here and Tokyo. The closest airport to Akanko Onsen is **Kushiro Airport,** with the flight from Tokyo taking about 1½ hours. A one-way ticket costs ¥33,700 ($321). From Kushiro Airport, buses travel to Akanko in about 1 hour and 20 minutes for ¥2,090 ($20).

**VISITOR INFORMATION    Akanko Onsen's Tourist Association** (© **0154/67-2254;** fax 0154/67-3024; open daily 9am–6pm) is located just a minute's walk from the Akanko Onsen bus terminal in the direction of the lake. (Turn right out of the bus terminal and take the first left; it will soon be on your right, just past the police box.) Occasionally there's an English-speaker here, and in any case you can pick up an English-language pamphlet about Akan National Park with a map of the town and two foldouts on hiking. The staff will also make reservations for hotels and ryokan. For information on the park and its natural wonders, drop by the **Akankohan Eco Museum Center** (© **0154/67-2785;** open 9am–5pm, to 7pm late June to Aug; located beside the lake, about a 7-min. walk from the bus terminal), which has free admission.

**ORIENTATION & GETTING AROUND**    Akanko Onsen is small, and walking is the best way to get around. It consists primarily of one main street that snakes along the lake, with ryokan and souvenir shops lining both sides.

## WHAT TO SEE & DO
### SEEING THE SIGHTS
**SIGHTSEEING BUS TOURS OF AKAN NATIONAL PARK**    If you're not renting a car, the best way to see Akan National Park is aboard a sightseeing bus departing from **Bihoro,** which is north of the park and can be reached by JR train from other parts of Hokkaido. That way, you'll travel all the way through the park and see the most important natural wonders en route, ending up at Akanko Onsen.

The bus trip takes 5 hours, making stops at several scenic spots along the way, including **Bihoro Pass** (a scenic overlook) and Kussharo and Mashu lakes. **Kussharo** is one of Japan's largest mountain lakes, but what makes it particularly interesting is its hot-spring waters right on the beach; in summer, you can see people digging holes to sit in the hot springs. **Mashu,** a crater lake that is considered one of Japan's most beautiful lakes, was called "lake of the devil" by the Ainu because no water flows either

into it or out of it. Surely Mashu is one of Japan's least-spoiled lakes: Because of the steep, 198m-high (660-ft.) rock walls ringing it, the lake has remained inaccessible to humans (the bus stops at an observation platform high above the water). The bus also stops at the foot of Mount Iou, with its sulfurous caldrons. *Beware:* Frequent fog often eliminates scenic views, there are tacky souvenir shops at every stop, and tours are in Japanese.

The bus trip, called the **Kuroyuri-gou (Black Lily Tour),** costs ¥3,760 ($36) for adults, half price for children. Buses depart from Bihoro once daily. Be sure to check departures ahead of time, since bus schedules change. For more information, call the **Bihoro bus center** at ✆ **01527/3-4181** (Japanese only) or fax the Tourist Information Center in Akan (fax 0154/67-3024).

**RED-CRESTED CRANES & BUS TOURS OF KUSHIRO MARSHLAND NATIONAL PARK**    Red-crested cranes, the official birds of Hokkaido, are traditionally regarded as both a good omen and a national symbol of Japan. Once threatened with extinction, these graceful and beautiful creatures now lead protected lives in and around **Kushiro Marshland National Park (Kushiro Shitsugen),** Japan's largest marshland and designated a national park in 1987. If you don't have a car, the best way to see the marshlands and catch a glimpse of the cranes in their natural habitat is via sightseeing bus. Tours are conducted in Japanese only but traverse the marshland and make stops at observatories and Tancho-Tsuru Koen (see below). The **Akan Bus Company** (✆ **0154/37-2221**) offers tours that begin and end at Kushiro Station twice a day from May 1 to July 19 and August 21 through October; the 4¾-hour tours cost ¥2,870 ($27) for adults and ¥1,330 ($13) for children. From July 20 to August 20, there's a 7½-hour bus and train tour daily, costing ¥3,500 ($33) for adults and ¥1,750 ($17) for children. Finally a 3-hour winter tour (Feb–Mar 21) costs ¥2,160 ($21) for adults and ¥980 ($9) for children.

If you prefer sightseeing on your own, the best place to learn about cranes is at the excellent **Akan Kokusai Tsuru Center (Akan International Crane Center)** ⚑, 23–40 Akan (✆ **0154/66-4011;** open daily 9am–5pm, closed Mon Apr–Oct). In addition to a film showing their beautiful courtship dance and nesting habits, it has fun, interactive displays with lots of English-language explanations. You'll learn just about everything you'd ever want to know about red-crested cranes here, from why they fly to how much an egg weighs. Best of all, however, is adjacent **Tancho-no-Sato,** an excellent observatory on private land where 200 red-crested cranes live, court, and mate November through March. This is a great place to photograph the birds in action, and you'll be surprised at how large they actually are. Admission to both the International Crane Center and Tancho-no-Sato is ¥400 ($3.80) for adults, half price for children. Plan on staying at least an hour in winter, less in summer when the birds have returned to their native marshlands. The International Crane Center is some 40 minutes from Akanko Onsen by bus; get off at the Tancho-no-sato stop (fare: ¥1,570/$15). Incidentally, the bus that stops here is the same one that goes from Akanko Onsen to Kushiro Airport, so it's possible to stop here, visit, and then catch the next bus to the airport.

In summer, your best bet for observing cranes outside the marshland is **Tancho-Tsuru Koen (Red-crested Crane Reserve),** Kushiro-cho (✆ **0154/56-2219;** open daily 9am–6pm, to 4pm in winter), a marshy area set aside in 1958 for breeding and raising cranes. It now has 24 cranes, some of them second and third generation, living in natural habitats behind high mesh fences. Admission is ¥310 ($2.95) for

adults and ¥100 (95¢) for children. Also on the way to the airport, it's located 57 minutes by bus from the Akanko Onsen bus terminal; get off at the Tsuru-koen stop. If all you want is a quick look, note that one bus a day en route to the airport makes a 15-minute stop at this park, which is enough time to see some of the birds before you continue on.

**ATTRACTIONS IN AKANKO ONSEN**    Although the Ainu originally lived near Kushiro, not Akan, they have built the **Ainu Kotan Village** in Akanko Onsen (© **0154/67-2727**). Although the Ainu Kotan Village itself is just a souvenir shop–lined street, it leads to a thatched-roof lodge where you can see Ainu performing traditional dances and playing bamboo mouth harps. This is the most professional Ainu production I've seen, and since the dances aren't the same as those performed at Poroto Kotan in Shiraoi (see "Noboribetsu Spa & Shikotsu-Toya National Park," earlier in this chapter), these are highly recommended even if you've already been to Poroto Kotan. Thirty-minute shows are performed six times a day in summer (including evenings), less frequently in winter. Admission is ¥1,000 ($9.50) for adults and half price for children. Alongside the performance lodge is the **Seikatsu Kinen Kan** (open May–Oct, daily 10am–10pm), an Ainu home and outbuildings with displays of various Ainu utensils and crafts. Admission here is ¥300 ($2.85) for adults and ¥100 (95¢) for children (skip it if you've been to Poroto Kotan).

## ENJOYING THE OUTDOORS

**BOATING**    For Japanese visitors, one of the most popular activities in Akanko Onsen is a **boat cruise of Lake Akan,** which provides a close-up view of the mountains, islands, and shoreline, all stunningly beautiful. Lake Akan is famous for its very rare spherical green algae, a spongelike ball of duckweed called *marimo* that's been designated a Special Natural Monument. Found in only a few places in the world, marimo is formed when many separate and stringy pieces of algae at the bottom of the 43m-deep (144-ft.) lake roll around and eventually come together to form a ball, gradually growing larger and larger. It takes 150 to 200 years for marimo to grow to the size of a baseball; some in Lake Akan are as much as 29 centimeters (12 in.) in diameter—meaning they are very old indeed. Supposedly, when the sun shines, the marimo rise to the surface of the water, giving Lake Akan a wonderful green shimmer. On your boat cruise you'll make a 15-minute stop at Churui Islet to see the **Marimo Exhibition Center** with a few tanks of marimo, but my favorite part of the tour is when the boat travels through narrow passages between islands and into inlets. One-hour cruises, with English-language explanations, operate from May to mid-November and cost ¥1,620 ($15) for adults and ¥850 ($8.10) for children, including the exhibition center. Boats depart every 30 minutes (every hour May and Nov), with the last boat departing at 5:30pm in summer.

I hope you'll boycott the self-drive speed boats, which disturb the peace and quiet of this nature's wonderland—but maybe the price alone will deter you: ¥1,000 ($9.50) for 5 minutes.

**CANOEING**    To get a real feel for Akan Lake at duck and goose level, take a canoe trip in a two-person Canadian canoe, available May to October. For beginners, a 1-hour trip costs ¥2,100 ($20) for adults and ¥1,100 ($10) for children. There's also a 90-minute Adventure Course for ¥5,300 ($50) for adults and ¥3,700 ($35) for children that goes farther afield, while the 2½-hour Yaitai island course includes a trip to

uninhabited Yaitai island in the lake. You may see carp spawning, deer, or—if you are really lucky—bear. Make canoe reservations at the **Akan Nature Center** (© **0154/67-2081**).

**FISHING** 🐟🐟  Lake Akan is one of Japan's most famous fishing lakes. In addition to kokanee salmon, said to have originated in the lake, sport fish include rainbow trout, steelhead trout, and white spotted char, a native fish. If you want to fish, contact **Fishing Land** (© **0154/67-2057**). A fishing permit costs ¥1,500 ($14) per day and includes fishing in Akan River and Hiotan Pond, as well as the lake. A rental rod and lures cost ¥1,000 ($9.50). Add ¥3,000 if you want to be dropped off at a fishing spot by boat. Fly-fishing season is from May to the end of November, except from mid-July to mid-August when it's too hot. From January to March, you can ice-fish; fishing gear for the day plus having a hole cut in the ice for you costs ¥1,500 ($14).

**HIKING**  Akanko Onsen's easiest walk begins and ends right in town. Start at the **Akankohan Eco Museum Center** at the east end of town, where you'll find an easy, 30-minute footpath leading through a primeval forest of pines and ferns, past *bokke* (volcanic, bubbling mud), and along the lakeshore. It ends at the boat dock with cruises of Lake Akan (see above).

For more serious hiking, while out on your boat trip you'll see two cone-shaped volcanoes: **Oakandake (Mount Oakan)** to the east and **Meakandake (Mount Meakan)** to the south. Both are popular daylong destinations for hikers. **Mount Oakan** (called "male mountain" by the Ainu for its supposed manly features) is dormant, with a summit about a 4½-hour hike from Akanko Onsen. You can reach the trail entrance, Takiguchi, in 5 minutes by bus (going in the direction of Kushiro, get off at the Takiguchi stop). **Mount Meakan** (which the Ainu called "female mountain"), the highest mountain in the Akan area, is active (so check before you go) and is covered with primeval forests of spruce and fir. There are three hiking trails up Mount Meakan. The trail access closest to Akanko is located at the west end of town, where you can follow the Furebetsu Woodland Road, a former transport road, to an old sulfur mine for 3 hours to get to the trail entrance (or take a bus for 35 min. to the Onneto stop). From the trail entrance, it's another 3 hours to the peak, from which you'll have panoramic views of the surrounding area. Pick up English-language alpine guides to Mount Oakan and Mount Meakan at the tourist association.

A shorter hike follows a trail to **Mount Hakuto-zan,** from which you also have a good view of the town and lake. It takes about 20 minutes to reach Akan's skiing area and another 50 minutes to reach Mount Hakuto-zan observatory, a grassy and moss-covered knobby hill that remains slightly warm throughout the year because of thermal activity just below the surface. The woods of birch and pine here are beautiful, and what's more, you'll probably find yourself all alone. Stop at the local tourist office for directions to the trail head and a map in Japanese.

**WINTER ACTIVITIES**  In winter, Lake Akan freezes over and becomes a playland for winter sports. International marathon ice-skating races—200km (124 miles)—held in February have brought attention to the area's natural riches. **Cross-country skiing** (rental equipment ¥1,000/$9.50 for 2 hr.), **ice skating** (¥1,000/$9.50 for 1 hr.), and **ice fishing** (¥1,500/$14 a day) are popular sports. For downhill skiers, the **Kokusetsu Akan-kohan ski ground** (© **0154/67-2881**) is blessed with a magnificent view of Mount Oakan rising behind Lake Akan. The F.I.S.-certified slalom course attracts ski teams and individuals in training, while the intermediate and beginner

slopes are popular with less demanding skiers. A day pass for lifts costs ¥2,500 ($24); ski-rental equipment costs ¥3,000 ($29) per day.

In February, illuminated ice sculptures, traditional dance, nightly fireworks over the frozen lake, and stalls selling food make for a fun midwinter festival. Contact the tourist office for more details.

## WHERE TO STAY
### EXPENSIVE

271 **Yuku-no-Sato Tsuruga** ✿✿✿ *Finds*    Extravagance is the word that comes to mind when describing Yuku-no-Sato Tsuruga, which translates loosely as "Village of eternally playing graceful cranes." Unsurprisingly, cranes are the main motif throughout, but what makes this hotel a standout are its hot-spring baths, among the most beautiful and fantasy provoking I've ever seen. One is designed as a village, spread on several levels and including a cavelike room and an outdoor bath beautifully landscaped with stones and pines overlooking the lake. The other, on the eighth floor, has the usual whirlpool, hot and dry saunas, and baths, as well as a rooftop hot-spring bath with 360-degree panoramic views. The baths, separated for men and women, are switched alternative days so guests may enjoy both. The rest of the hotel, with natural woods throughout, well-designed restaurants (the hotel's massive main dining hall is divided into four buffet stations serving Italian, Japanese, Chinese, and Hawaiian food), and well-appointed guest rooms, do not disappoint. Most rooms are Japanese style, the best of which have lakeside views, large bathrooms, bar areas for entertaining, and seating around an indoor hearth. There are also more than 50 combination rooms with tatami area and beds; five of these have great views of the lake from their own verandas boasting hot-spring baths.

4–6–10 Akanko Onsen, Akancho, Akan-gun 085-0467. ✆ **0154/67-2531.** Fax 0154/67-2754. 243 units. April 30–May 4, July 1–Aug 20 ¥19,950–¥36,750 ($190–$350); Aug 21–Oct 9, June 4–30 ¥17,850–¥34,650 ($170–$330); Oct 10–Nov 2, May 5–June 3 ¥16,800–¥31,500 ($160–$300); Nov 3–Dec 30, Jan 3–Apr 29 ¥14,700–¥29,400 ($140–$280). Rates are per person and include 2 meals and service charge. AE, DC, MC, V. A 10-min. walk from the bus terminal; turn left out of the terminal, take the 1st right to the main street, and turn left. There are also free shuttle buses operating from Kushiro and Kitami stations (reservations required). **Amenities:** 2 restaurants (Japanese and international); 1 coffee shop; 2 bars; 1 lounge; beautiful indoor/outdoor hot-spring baths; game room; shopping arcade. *In room:* A/C, TV, minibar, hot-water pot w/tea, hair dryer, Washlet toilet.

### MODERATE

**Akan View Hotel** *Kids*    Despite its name, this nearly 30-year-old hotel is one of the few around with no lake view. Most of its rooms are Western-style twins, narrow and with tiny bathrooms but with everything else you need; 32 Japanese-style rooms are also available. One of the best things about this hotel are the large indoor thermal pools (you wear your bathing suit here), one for swimming laps and another with slides for children, as well as the usual hot-spring baths (open 24 hr. except during cleaning) with a large, outdoor bathing area. I also like the glass-enclosed barbecue restaurant, open all year, where you can order Genghis Khan (lamb and vegetables), seafood, or beef meals you grill yourself (make reservations to dine here a day in advance). Otherwise, you dine buffet style in the communal dining room.

4–1–7 Akanko Onsen, Akancho, Akan-gun 085-0467. ✆ **0154/67-3131.** Fax 0154/67-3139. 188 units. Summer ¥8,500–¥12,000 ($81–$114) per person; winter ¥5,400–¥10,000 ($51–$95) per person. Rates include 2 meals and service charge. AE, DC, MC, V. A 7-min. walk from the bus terminal. Turn left out of the bus terminal, cross the bridge, and turn right at the stoplight. **Amenities:** 2 restaurants (Japanese/Chinese/Western buffet, Genghis Khan), 1 bar; 1 lobby lounge; indoor swimming pool (free for hotel guests); tennis courts; indoor/outdoor hot-spring baths; rental

bikes (¥500/$4.15 per hour); game room; in-room massage; coin-op washers and dryers. *In room:* TV, minibar, hot-water pot w/tea, safe.

**Lake Spa Takada** 🌟🌟 *Finds* SINCE 2004 reads the sign on this small, welcoming, lakefront inn. The date is a bit of an insider's joke, however, as owner Dameon Takada is a third-generation Akan innkeeper, who (together with his wife and parents) gave up the stress of managing a large hotel and opened this home away from home. The location, food, and service make this a great value, even more so because Frommer's readers enjoy a 10% discount. Meals, created by a chef who goes to the coast daily to shop for the freshest seafood and vegetables, are served in your room or in the restaurant, complete with a cozy fireplace in winter and a lakeside wooden deck in summer. If you've gone fishing, Dameon will grill your catch on the deck barbecue. The rooftop outdoor bath, made of cypress, has a splendid view of the lake. Rooms are mostly Japanese style, though there are also three rooms with beds. Since some of the rooms do not face the lake, specify a lakeside room when making your reservation. Dameon (who, with his wife, Delia speaks flawless English), can also offer insider advice on fishing, hunting, canoeing, hiking, skiing, and (time permitting) will even take you fishing. No wonder 85% of his business is from repeat clients.

1–6–11 Akan Onsen, Akancho, Akan-gun 085-0467. ✆ **0154/67-4157**. Fax 0154/67-4158. www.lakespa-takada. com. 10 units. ¥15,000–¥20,000 ($143–$190) per person. ¥5,000 ($48) off-season discount available. 10% discount to readers of *Frommer's Japan*. Rates include 2 meals and service charge. AE, DC, MC, V. A 5-min. walk from the bus terminal; turn right out of the terminal, take the 1st left, pass the tourist office, veer to the right at the main street, then left to the lake. **Amenities:** Restaurant; outdoor/indoor hot-spring baths; in-room massage. *In room:* TV, hot-water pot w/tea.

### INEXPENSIVE

㉒ **Onsen Minshuku Kiri** Located above a souvenir shop on the main street (look for a wooden, roofed sign with black lettering on white), these simple accommodations include clean Japanese-style rooms and a small cypress hot-spring bath.

4–3–26 Akanko Onsen, Akancho, Akan-gun 085-0467. ✆ **0154/67-2755**. Fax 0154/67-2755. 9 units (none with bathroom). ¥3,500 ($33) per person. Breakfast ¥500 ($4.75) extra. Dinner ¥3,500 ($33) extra. MC, V. A 9-min. walk from the bus terminal; turn left out of the terminal, take the 1st right to the main street, and turn left on the main street. **Amenities:** Indoor hot-spring bath; coin-op washer and dryer. *In room:* TV, hot-water pot w/tea.

## WHERE TO DINE

**Porono** AINU For a different kind of lunch, head to the Ainu Kotan Village and look on the right-hand side for a souvenir shop called Mingei Kissa with a sign reading HANDMADE FOLKCRAFT AND AINU TRADITIONAL FOOD. In the back you'll find two tables, a counter, and funky ethnic decor and music. The menu lists *rataskepu,* a cold vegetable dish with beans, corn, and pumpkin; *pochimo,* a fried potato cake (a bit hard); pumpkin cakes; and drinks like bark tea *(shikerebe).* Or order the Ainu teishoku set meal (rice with red beans and deer soup last time I was there). It's definitely not your usual meal: I did not love the food, but I found it interesting to eat food gleaned from the natural surroundings.

Ainu Kotan Village, Akanko Onsen. ✆ **0154/67-2159**. Dishes ¥350–¥650 ($3.35–$6.20); Ainu teishoku ¥850 ($8.10). No credit cards. Daily noon–11pm (noon–10pm winter).

# Appendix A: Japan in Depth

**W**ith a population of about 127 million, a history stretching back thousands of years, the world's longest-reigning monarchy, and unique forms of culture, art, food, etiquette, and religion, Japan merits more than this short chapter can deliver. Be sure to check "Recommended Books" in chapter 2 for other sources of information.

## 1 History 101

**ANCIENT HISTORY (ca. 30,000 B.C.– A.D. 710)** According to mythology, Japan's history began when the sun goddess, Amaterasu, sent one of her descendants down to the island of Kyushu to unify the people of Japan. Unification, however, was not realized until a few generations later when Jimmu, the great-grandson of the goddess's emissary, succeeded in bringing all of the country under his rule. Because of his divine descent, Jimmu became emperor in 660 B.C. (the date is mythical), thus establishing the line from which all of Japan's emperors are said to derive. However mysterious the origin of this imperial dynasty, it is acknowledged as the longest-reigning such family in the world.

Legend begins to give way to fact only in the 4th century A.D., when a family by the name of Yamato succeeded in expanding its kingdom throughout much of the country. At the core of the unification achieved by the Yamato family was the Shinto religion. Indigenous to Japan, **Shintoism** is marked by the worship of natural things—mountains, trees, the moon, stars, rivers, seas, fire, animals, rocks, even vegetables—as the embodiment of gods (called *kami*) and of the spirits of ancestors. It is also marked by belief in the emperor's divinity. Along with Buddhism (see below), Shintoism is still a driving belief in Japanese life.

Although the exact origin of Japanese people is unknown, we know Japan was once connected to the Asian mainland by a land bridge, and the territory of Japan was occupied as early as 30,000 B.C. From about 10,000 B.C. to 400 B.C., hunter-gatherers, called Jomon, thrived in small communities primarily in central Honshu; they're best known for their hand-formed pottery decorated with cord patterns. The Jomon Period was followed by the Yayoi Period, which was marked by metalworking, the pottery wheel, and the mastering of irrigated rice cultivation. The Yayoi Period lasted until about A.D. 300, after which the Yamato family unified the state for the first time and set up their court in what is now Nara Prefecture. Yamato (present-day Japan) began turning cultural feelers toward its great neighbor to the west, China.

In the 6th century, **Buddhism,** which originated in India, was brought to Japan via China and Korea, and the large-scale Chinese cultural and scholarly influence—including art, architecture, and the use of Chinese written characters—began. In 604, the prince regent Shotoku, greatly influenced by the teachings of Buddhism and Confucianism and still a beloved figure today, drafted a document calling for political reforms and a constitutional government. By 607 he was sending multitudes of Japanese scholars

to China to study Buddhism, and he started building Buddhist temples. The most famous is **Horyuji Temple** near Nara, said to be the oldest existing wooden structure in the world. He also built **Shitennoji Temple** in what is now Osaka.

## THE NARA PERIOD (710–784)

Before the 700s, the site of Japan's capital changed every time a new emperor came to the throne. In 710, however, a permanent capital was established at Nara. Although it remained the capital for only 74 years, seven successive emperors ruled from Nara. The period was graced with the expansion of Buddhism and flourishing temple construction throughout the country. Buddhism also inspired the arts, including Buddhist sculpture, metal casting, painting, and lacquerware. It was during this time that Emperor Shomu, the most devout Buddhist among the Nara emperors, ordered the casting of a huge bronze statue of Buddha to be erected in Nara. Known as the Daibutsu, it remains Nara's biggest attraction.

## THE HEIAN PERIOD (794–1192)

In 794, the capital was moved to Heiankyo (present-day Kyoto), and following the example of cities in China, Kyoto was laid out in a grid pattern with broad roads and canals. Heiankyo means "capital of peace and tranquillity," and the Heian Period was a glorious time for aristocratic families, a time of luxury and prosperity during which court life reached new artistic heights. Moon viewing became popular. Chinese characters were blended with a new Japanese writing system, allowing for the first time the flowering of Japanese literature and poetry. The life of the times was captured in the works of two women: Sei Shonagon, who wrote a collection of impressions of her life at court known as the *Pillow Book;* and Murasaki Shikibu, who wrote the world's first major novel, *The Tale of Genji.*

Because the nobles were completely engrossed in their luxurious lifestyles, however, they failed to notice the growth of military clans in the provinces. The two most powerful warrior clans were the Taira (also called Heike) and the Minamoto (also called Genji), whose fierce civil wars tore the nation apart until a young warrior, Minamoto Yoritomo, established supremacy. (In Japan, a person's family name—here, Minamoto—comes first, followed by the given name; I have followed this order throughout this book.)

## THE KAMAKURA PERIOD (1192–1333)

Wishing to set up rule far away from Kyoto, Minamoto Yoritomo established his capital in a remote and easily defended fishing village called Kamakura, not far from today's Tokyo. In becoming the nation's first *shogun,* or military dictator, Yoritomo laid the groundwork for 700 years of military governments—in which the power of the country passed from the aristocratic court into the hands of the warrior class—until the imperial court was restored in 1868.

The Kamakura Period is perhaps best known for the unrivaled ascendancy of the warrior caste, or **samurai.** Ruled by a rigid honor code, samurai were bound in loyalty to their feudal lord, and they became the only caste allowed to carry two swords. They were supposed to give up their lives for their lord without hesitation, and if they failed in their duty, they could regain their honor only by committing ritualistic suicide, or *seppuku.* Spurning the sort of life led by court nobles, samurai embraced a spartan lifestyle. When **Zen Buddhism,** with its tenets of mental and physical discipline, was introduced into Japan from China in the 1190s, it appealed greatly to the samurai. Weapons and armor achieved new heights in artistry, while *Bushido,* the way of the warrior, contributed to the spirit of national unity.

## Here & Zazen: Buddhism in Japan

Founded in India in the 6th to 5th centuries B.C., Buddhism came to Japan in the 6th century A.D. via China and Korea, bringing with it the concept of eternal life. By the end of the 6th century, Buddhism had gained such popularity that the prince regent Shotoku, one of Japan's most remarkable historical figures, declared Buddhism the state religion and based many of his governmental policies on its tenets. Another important Buddhist leader to emerge was a priest called Kukai, known posthumously as Kobo Daishi. After studying Buddhism in China in the early 800s, he returned and built temples throughout Japan, including the famous 88 temples on Shikoku island and those on Mount Koya, which continue to attract millions of pilgrims today.

Probably the Buddhist sect best known to the West is Zen Buddhism. Considered the most Japanese form of Buddhism, Zen is the practice of meditation and a strictly disciplined lifestyle to rid oneself of desire so that one can achieve enlightenment. There are no rites in Zen Buddhism, no dogmas, no theological conceptions of divinity; you do not analyze rationally but are supposed to know things intuitively. The strict and simple lifestyle of Zen appealed greatly to Japan's samurai warrior class, and many of Japan's arts, including the tea ceremony, arose from the practice of Zen.

Zazen, or meditation, is practiced as a form of mental or spiritual training; laypeople meditate to relieve stress and clear their minds. You achieve zazen in a cross-legged lotus position with your neck and back straight and your eyes slightly open. Usually done in a group—in a semidark room with cushions, facing the wall—meditation is helped along by a monk, who stalks noiselessly behind the meditators. If someone squirms or moves, the offender is whacked on the shoulders with a stick to help him or her get back to meditating. There are several Zen temples where foreigners can join in zazen (see chapter 5); if you'd like to try it, contact the Tourist Information Center in Tokyo or Kyoto, or check the *Japan Times* to see whether a session of zazen is being organized with English-language instruction.

In 1274, Mongolian forces under Kublai Khan made an unsuccessful attempt to invade Japan. They returned in 1281 with a larger fleet, but a typhoon destroyed it. Regarding the cyclone as a gift from the gods, Japanese called it *kamikaze,* meaning "divine wind," which took on a different significance at the end of World War II when Japanese pilots flew suicide missions in an attempt to turn the tide of war.

## THE MUROMACHI & AZUCHI-MOMOYAMA PERIODS (1336–1603)

After the fall of the Kamakura shogunate, a new feudal government was set up at Muromachi in Kyoto. The next 200 years, however, were marred by bloody civil wars as **feudal lords** *(daimyo)* staked out their fiefdoms. Similar to the barons of Europe, the daimyo owned tracts of land and had complete rule over the people who lived on them. Each lord had his retainers, the samurai, who fought his

enemies. This period of civil wars is called Sengoku-Jidai, or **Age of the Warring States.**

Yet these centuries of strife also saw a blossoming of art and culture. Kyoto witnessed the construction of the extravagant Golden and Silver pavilions as well as the artistic arrangement of Ryoanji Temple's famous rock garden. Noh drama, the tea ceremony, flower arranging, and landscape gardening became the passions of the upper class. At the end of the 16th century, a number of castles were built on mountaintops to demonstrate the daimyos' strength, guard their fiefdoms, and defend themselves against the firearms introduced by the Portuguese.

In the second half of the 16th century, a brilliant military strategist by the name of Oda Nobunaga almost succeeded in ending the civil wars. Upon Nobunaga's assassination (by one of his own retainers), one of his best generals, Toyotomi Hideyoshi, took up the campaign, built magnificent Osaka Castle, and crushed rebellion to unify Japan. Nobunaga and Hideyoshi's successive rules are known as the **Azuchi-Momoyama Period,** after the names of their castles.

## THE EDO PERIOD (1603–1867)
Upon Hideyoshi's death (1598), power was seized by Tokugawa Ieyasu, a statesman so shrewd and skillful in eliminating enemies that his heirs would continue to rule Japan for the next 250 years. After defeating his greatest rival in the famous battle of Sekigahara, Tokugawa set up a shogunate government in 1603 in Edo (present-day Tokyo), leaving the emperor intact but virtually powerless in Kyoto. In 1615, he assured his supremacy by getting rid of Hideyoshi's descendants in a fierce battle at Osaka Castle that destroyed the castle and annihilated the Toyotomi clan.

Meanwhile, European influence in Japan was spreading. The first contact with the Western world had occurred in 1543, when Portuguese merchants (with firearms) arrived, followed by Christian missionaries. St. Francis Xavier landed in Kyushu in 1549, remaining for 2 years and converting thousands of Japanese; by 1580, there were perhaps as many as 150,000 Japanese Christians. Although Japan's rulers at first welcomed foreigners and trade (three Kyushu daimyo even went so far as to send emissaries to Rome, where they were received by the pope), they gradually became alarmed by the Christian missionary influence. Hearing of the Catholic church's power in Rome and fearing the expansionist policies of European nations, Hideyoshi banned Christianity in the late 1500s. In 1597, 26 Japanese and European Christians were crucified in Nagasaki.

The Tokugawa shogunate intensified the campaign against Christians in 1639 when it closed all ports to foreign trade. Adopting a policy of **total isolation,** the shogunate forbade foreigners from landing in Japan and Japanese from leaving; even those Japanese who had been living abroad in overseas trading posts were never allowed to return. The only exception was in Nagasaki, where a colony of tightly controlled Chinese merchants and a handful of Dutch were confined to a trading post on a tiny island.

Thus began an amazing 200-year period in Japanese history during which Japan was closed to the rest of the world. It was a time of political stability at the expense of personal freedom, as all aspects of life were strictly controlled by the Tokugawa government. Japanese society was divided into four distinct **classes:** samurai, farmers, craftspeople, and merchants. Class determined everything in daily life, from where a person lived to what he was allowed to wear. Samurai led the most exalted social position, and it was probably during the Tokugawa Period that the samurai class reached the

zenith of its glory. At the bottom of the social ladder were the merchants, but peace and prosperity led to the development of new entertainment forms to occupy their time: Kabuki drama and woodblock prints became the rage, while stoneware and porcelain, silk brocade for kimono, and lacquerware improved in quality. In fact, it was probably the shogunate's rigid policies that actually fostered the arts, since anything new was considered dangerous and quickly suppressed. Japanese were forced to retreat inward, and they focused their energies in the arts, perfecting handicrafts down to the most minute detail whether it was swords, *inro* (small containers for medicine), kimono, or lacquered boxes. Only Japan's many festivals offered relief from harsh and restrictive social mores.

To ensure that no daimyo in the distant provinces would overrun the shogun's power, the Tokugawa government ordered each daimyo to leave his family in Edo as permanent residents (effectively as hostages) and required the lord to spend a prescribed number of months in Edo every other year. In expending so much time and money traveling back and forth and maintaining elaborate residences both in the provinces and in Edo, the daimyo had no resources left with which to wage a rebellion. This is also when inns and townships sprang up along Japan's major highways to accommodate the elaborate processions of palanquins, samurai, and footmen traveling back and forth between Edo and the provinces.

Even though the Tokugawa government took such measures to ensure its supremacy, by the mid–19th century it was clear that the feudal system was outdated and economic power was in the hands of the merchants. Many samurai families were impoverished, and discontent with the shogunate became widespread.

In 1853, American Commodore Matthew C. Perry sailed to Japan, seeking to gain trading rights. But Japanese were unwilling, so Perry departed, his mission unaccomplished. Returning a year later, he forced the shogun to sign an agreement despite the disapproval of the emperor, thus ending Japan's 2 centuries of isolation. In 1867, powerful families toppled the Tokugawa regime and restored the emperor as ruler, thus bringing the Feudal Era to a close.

## MEIJI PERIOD THROUGH WORLD WAR II (1868–1945)

In 1868, Emperor Meiji moved his imperial government from Kyoto to Edo, renamed it Tokyo (Eastern Capital), and designated it the official national capital. During the next few decades, known as the **Meiji Restoration,** Japan rapidly progressed from a feudal agricultural society of samurai and peasants to an industrial nation. The samurai were stripped of their power and no longer were allowed to carry swords, thus ending a privileged way of life begun almost 700 years earlier in Kamakura. A prime minister and a cabinet were appointed, a constitution was drafted, and a parliament (called the Diet) was elected. With the enthusiastic support of Emperor Meiji, the latest in Western technological know-how was imported, including railway and postal systems, along with specialists and advisers: Between 1881 and 1898, about 10,000 Westerners were retained by the Japanese government to help modernize the country.

Meanwhile, Japan made incursions into neighboring lands. In 1894 to 1895, it fought and won a war against China; in 1904 to 1905, it attacked and defeated Russia; and in 1910, it annexed Korea. After militarists gained control of the government in the 1930s, these expansionist policies continued; Manchuria was annexed, and Japan went to war with

China again in 1937. On the other side of the world, as **World War II** flared in Europe, Japan formed a military (Axis) alliance with Germany and Italy and attacked French Indochina.

On December 7, 1941, Japan attacked Pearl Harbor, entering World War II against the United States. Although Japan went on to conquer Hong Kong, Singapore, Burma, Malaysia, the Philippines, the Dutch East Indies, and Guam, the tide eventually turned, and American bombers reduced every major Japanese city to rubble with the exception of historic Kyoto. On August 6, 1945, the United States dropped the world's first atomic bomb over Hiroshima, followed on August 9 by a second over Nagasaki. Japan submitted to unconditional surrender on August 14, with Emperor Hirohito's radio broadcast telling his people the time had come for "enduring the unendurable and suffering what is insufferable." American and other **Allied occupation** forces arrived and remained until 1952. For the first time in history, Japan had suffered defeat by a foreign power; the country had never before been invaded or occupied by a foreign nation.

## MODERN JAPAN (1946–PRESENT)

The experience of World War II had a profound effect on the Japanese people, yet they emerged from their defeat and began to rebuild. In 1946, under the guidance of the Allied military authority headed by U.S. Gen. Douglas MacArthur, they adopted a democratic constitution renouncing war and the use of force to settle international disputes and divesting the emperor of divinity, giving power to the people instead. A parliamentary system of government was set up, and 1947 witnessed the first general elections for the National Diet, the government's legislative body. After its founding in 1955, the **Liberal Democratic Party (LDP)** remained the undisputed majority party for decades, giving Japan the kind of political stability it needed to grow economically and compete in world markets.

To the younger generation, the occupation was less a painful burden to be suffered than an opportunity to remake their country, with American encouragement, into a modern, peace-loving, and democratic state. A special relationship developed between Japanese and their American occupiers. In the early 1950s, as the Cold War between the United States and the Communist world erupted in hostilities in Korea, that relationship grew into a firm alliance, strengthened by a security treaty. In 1952, the occupation ended, and Japan joined the United Nations as an independent country.

Avoiding involvement in foreign conflicts, Japanese concentrated on economic recovery. Through a series of policies favoring domestic industries and shielding Japan from foreign competition, they achieved **rapid economic growth.** In 1964, Tokyo hosted the Summer Olympic Games, showing the world that the nation had transformed itself into a formidable industrialized power. Incomes doubled during the 1960s, and a 1967 government study found that 90% of Japanese considered themselves middle class. By the 1980s, Japan was by far the richest industrialized nation in Asia and the envy of its neighbors, who strove to emulate Japan's success. Sony was a household word around the globe; books flooded the international market touting the economic secrets of Japan, Inc. After all, Japan seemed to have it all: a good economy, political stability, safe streets, and great schools. As the yen soared, Japanese traveled abroad as never before, and Japanese businessmen gained national attention as they gobbled up real estate in foreign lands and purchased works of art at unheard-of prices.

Meanwhile, a snowballing trade surplus had created friction between Japan

and the United States, its chief trading partner. In the 1980s, as Japanese auto sales in the United States soared and foreign sales in Japan continued to be restricted, disagreements between Tokyo and Washington heated up. In 1989, Emperor Hirohito died of cancer at age 87, bringing the 63-year Showa Era to an end and ushering in the **Heisei Period** under Akihito, the 125th emperor, who proclaimed the new "Era of Peace" (Heisei).

In the early 1990s, shadows of financial doubt began to spread over the land of the rising sun, with alarming reports of bad bank loans, inflated stock prices, and overextended corporate investment abroad. In 1992, **recession** hit Japan, bursting the economic bubble and plunging the country into its worst recession since World War II. The Nikkei (the Japanese version of the American Dow) fell a gut-churning 63% from its 1989 peak, and, over the next decade, bankruptcies reached an all-time high and unemployment climbed to its highest level since World War II. Meanwhile, the LDP, which had held power uninterruptedly for nearly 4 decades, suffered a huge loss of public confidence after its top officials were accused of participating in a series of political and financial scandals. But a revolving door of prime ministers (many of whom also became implicated in scandals) throughout the 1990s failed to revive the economy or alleviate voters' growing fears of financial doom.

Public confidence was further eroded in 1995, first by a major earthquake in Kobe that killed more than 6,000 people and proved that Japan's cities were not as safe as the government had maintained, and then by an attack by an obscure religious sect that released the deadly nerve gas sarin on Tokyo's subway system during rush hour, killing 12 people and sickening thousands. But the worst blow came in 2001, when a knife-wielding man stormed into an elementary school in Osaka Prefecture, fatally stabbing 8 children and wounding 15 others. For many Japanese, it seemed that the very core of their society had begun to crumble.

In April 2001, after yet another prime minister resigned due to scandal, Koizumi Junichiro took the political helm. Although a member of the LPD, the long-haired, 59-year-old Koizumi had long been considered something of a maverick, battling against the long-established power brokers of the LPD and vowing to overturn the LPD's long-standing pork-barrel politics by slashing public spending on bridges, dams, and roads; forcing Japanese banks to write off bad loans; and dismantling regulations that protected large sectors of the economy. His cries for reform, coupled by media attention that gave him the revered status of a rock star, won Koizumi more voter support than any prime minister since the bubble economy. Following the September 2001 terrorist attacks in the U.S., Koizumi quickly showed allegiance by pushing through an antiterrorism bill that enabled Japan's military to ship supplies and provide medical and other noncombative support in Afghanistan. In 2003, Japan pledged $1.5 billion in foreign aid to American reconstruction efforts in Iraq.

But Japan's most immediate international worry was its neighbor, North Korea, which lobbed its first missile over Japan in 1998 and declared in 2002 that it had never halted its nuclear-weapons program despite a 1994 nuclear accord. In response, Japan launched two spy satellites in 2003 to monitor North Korea's missile and suspected nuclear-weapons programs. Meanwhile, in 2002 North Korea admitted for the first time that it had abducted 13 young Japanese in the '70s and '80s to teach Japanese language and customs to North Korean spies. Five of the abductees were subsequently repatriated back to

Japan; North Korea maintains the others died of natural causes.

In 1999, Japan adopted a World War II hymn, *Kimigayo,* as its national anthem and declared the traditional Japanese sun flag, a red disk in a field of white, its official flag (until then, the country did not have a legally recognized national flag or anthem). But any overt displays of Japanese nationalism have always spurred criticism from Asian neighbors, who maintain that Japan has never truly apologized or shown remorse for invading and occupying its neighbors. Relations became especially strained in 2005, when Japan's Education Ministry approved revised history textbooks that glossed over Japan's war crimes, sparking outrage in China and South Korea, including anti-Japanese street riots in Beijing, Shanghai, and Seoul.

## 2 Japan Today

Today, after more than a dozen years of financial quagmire, Japan's economy seems to be on the mend. Koizumi, who has said he'll step down as prime minister when his term expires in September 2006, can claim some of the credit for Japan's slow climb out of recession. Since 2003, when the Nikkei plunged to a 20-year low at 7,608 and unemployment stood at 5.1%, the Nikkei has edged over 16,000 while unemployment hovers around 4.1%, the lowest it's been since 1998. Tokyo real estate prices, which had fallen as much as 70% from their 1991 peak, rose for the first time in 2004, spurring investors to return. Among Koizumi's greatest achievements are policies that have helped cut the amount of bad bank loans in half and the privatization of Japan's post office, which does far more than sell stamps and deliver mail. In addition, the projected privatization of a state-owned savings bank (with about a quarter of all financial assets held by Japanese individuals) will create the world's largest bank. The bank, which is also the country's largest provider of life insurance, is due for a complete change in ownership by 2017. A harder sell is the LDP's push to revise Japan's constitution outlawing war, thereby giving the nation's military a greater role in international security. Opponents argue that changing the constitution would raise fears tied to Japan's militaristic past, especially in China and South Korea where Japanese wartime aggression and occupation remain fresh. Other issues that continue to color Japan's diplomatic relations with its neighbors include disputes over island territorial claims and the prime minister's repeated visits to Tokyo's Yasukuni Shrine, which honors the nation's war dead but is viewed by critics as a symbol of Japanese militarism. These and many other issues face Japan as it strives for a permanent seat on the United Nations Security Council.

On the home front, a new set of problems faces today's generation. Homelessness is now so common that it no longer draws stares, even in the swank Ginza District. Crime, once almost unheard of, is on the rise, especially for theft. My former Tokyo landlady fears burglary so much that she refuses to open her doors to strangers. My friend's boyfriend's car was stolen from a parking lot, one of 119 luxury cars reported stolen in Tokyo in 2000. Lurid murders, though rare, garner media attention. In 2005, a spate of grisly crimes targeting schoolchildren horrified the nation. Certainly one of Japan's biggest concerns is its declining birth rate coupled with one of the fastest-aging populations in the world. About 17% of its population is 65 and older; by 2020, that number is expected to hit 25%.

## *Fun Fact*  The Magical World of Vending Machines

One of the things that usually surprises visitors to Japan is the number of vending machines in the country. They're virtually everywhere—in train stations, in front of shops, on the back streets of residential neighborhoods. Most will take bills and give back change. Many have almost nonsensical English-language promotional lines on them, like ENJOY REFRESHING TIME. Some will even talk to you.

And what can you buy in these vending machines? First, there are the obvious items—drinks and snacks, including hot or cold coffee in a can. But if you're on your way to someone's house, you might be able to pick up a bouquet of flowers from a machine. Your CD player is out of batteries? You may be able to find those, too, along with CDs, film, and disposable cameras. Vending machines outside post offices sell stamps and postcards, while those in business hotels may sell razors, cup noodles, and even underwear.

But there are also things sold from sidewalk vending machines that would meet with instant protest in other countries around the world. Cigarettes are sold on almost every corner, where even children can buy them if they want to (from 2008, however, anyone who wants to buy a pack of cigarettes from a vending machine will first have to insert a computer-readable card certifying he's at least 20 years old). Until recently, beer was also readily available, though in an effort to curb alcoholism and underage drinking, access is now more limited.

I remember a vending machine in my Tokyo neighborhood. By day, it was blank, with no clue as to what was inside. Come night, however, the thing would light up, and on display would be pornographic comics.

If it's available in Japan, it's probably in a vending machine somewhere.

Meanwhile, the birth rate in Japan is at an all-time low of 1.29 per woman (the birth-control pill was legalized in 1999), prompting the Japanese Health and Welfare Ministry to announce that a predicted shortage of future workers will severely strain the country's resources for pensions and healthcare.

For the short-term visitor to Japan, however, life in Japan appears much as it always has—humming with energy, crowded beyond belief in its major cities, and filled with acts of human kindness. Crime, though undeniably on the increase, is still negligible when compared to levels in the United States, and Japan remains one of the safest countries in the world. Although it's true I am more careful than I was 15 years ago—I guard my purse in crowded subways, I avoid parks after dark—for Americans such precautions seem merely self-evident. But while I'm cautious about theft and purse-snatching, I never worry about personal safety when I'm in Japan. In fact, it never even crosses my mind. Violent crime—especially against strangers—remains virtually unheard of in Japan.

Certainly one unintended benefit of the recession is that Japan now offers something that would have been unthinkable during the spending-happy 1980s: bargains. The recession has spawned tony French restaurants serving

value-conscious fixed-price lunches, secondhand clothing stores selling last year's designer wear, and 100-Yen discount shops conducting a brisk business. Whereas in the 1980s Japan was best known as an economic powerhouse, today it's known not only for Sony and Toyota but also as an exporter of cool pop culture, from anime and Hello Kitty to fashion and food.

## 3 Minding Your Ps & Qs

As an island nation with few natural resources, Japan's 127 million people are its greatest asset. Hardworking, honest, and proud about performing every task well no matter how insignificant it may seem, Japanese are well known for their politeness and helpfulness to strangers. Indeed, hardly anyone returns from a trip to Japan without stories of extraordinary kindnesses extended by Japanese.

With almost 99% of its population consisting of ethnic Japanese, Japan is one of the most homogeneous nations in the world. That, coupled with Japan's actual physical isolation as an island nation, has more than anything else led to a feeling among Japanese that they belong to a single huge tribe different from any other people on earth—that all people can basically be divided into two categories: Japanese and non-Japanese. You'll often hear a Japanese preface a statement or opinion with the words "We Japanese," implying that all Japanese think alike.

Indeed, one characteristic of the Japanese people that has received much publicity—and is seen (at least by some) as a reason Japan became so economically powerful so quickly—is this **group mentality.** Whereas in the West the attainment of "happiness" is the elusive goal for a full and rewarding life, in Japan it's satisfactory performance of **duty.** From the time they are born, Japanese are instilled with a sense of duty that extends toward parents, spouses, bosses, coworkers, neighbors, and society as a whole. In a nation as crowded as Japan, consideration of others is essential, and consideration of the group always wins out over the desire of the individual.

In fact, I have had Japanese tell me they consider individuality synonymous with selfishness and a complete disregard for the feelings of others.

## MEETING THE JAPANESE PEOPLE

On a personal level, Japanese are among the most likable people in the world. They are kind, thoughtful, and adept in perceiving another person's needs. Japanese have an unerring eye for pure beauty, whether it be in food, architecture, or landscaped gardens; it's impossible to visit Japan and not have some of the Japanese appreciation of beauty rub off.

If you're invited to Japan by an organization or business, you'll receive the royal treatment and will most likely be wined and dined so wonderfully and thoroughly that you'll never want to leave. If you go to Japan on your own as an ordinary tourist, however, chances are that your experiences will be much different. Except for those who have lived or traveled abroad, few Japanese have had much contact with foreigners. In fact, even in Tokyo there are some Japanese who have never spoken to a foreigner and would be quite embarrassed and uncomfortable if they were confronted with the possibility. And even though most of them have studied English, few Japanese have had the opportunity to use the language and cannot (or are too shy to) communicate in it. So don't be surprised if you find the empty seat beside you on the subway the last one to be occupied—most Japanese are deathly afraid you'll ask them a question they won't understand.

## Tips   The Home-Visit System

Recognizing the difficulty foreigners may face in meeting Japanese people, a dozen or so cities offer a **Home Visit,** allowing overseas visitors the chance to visit an English-speaking Japanese family in their home for a few hours. Not only does such an encounter bring you in direct contact with Japanese, it also offers a glimpse into their lifestyle. You can even request that a family member share your occupation, though such requests are, of course, sometimes impossible to fulfill. The program doesn't cost anything, but it does take some advance preparation. You must make arrangements in advance, which differs from city to city and can range from 1 day in advance to 2 weeks in advance, by calling or applying in person at the local administrative authority or private organization (which is sometimes the local tourist office) that handles the city's home-visit program. After contacting a local family, the office will inform you of the family and the time to visit. Most visits take place for a few hours in the evening (dinner is not served). It's a good idea to bring a small gift such as flowers, fruit, or a souvenir of some kind from your hometown. Before your visit, you may be asked to appear in person at the application office to obtain detailed directions; or the office may call with the directions. Note that application offices may be closed on weekends and holidays. Here are a few contact numbers for cities participating in the Home-Visit System: **Narita** (© 0476/34-6251 or 0476/24-3198), **Yokohama** (© 045/221-1203), **Nagoya** (© 052/581-5689), **Kyoto** (© 075/752-3511), **Osaka** (© 06/6345-2189), **Kobe** (© 078/303-1010), **Kurashiki** (© 086/475-0543), **Hiroshima** (© 082/247-9715), **Fukuoka** (© 092/733-2220), **Kumamoto** (© 096/359-2121), and **Miyazaki** (© 0985/32-8457). For more information, contact local tourist information offices.

In many respects, therefore, it's much harder to meet the locals in Japan than in many other countries. Japanese are simply much more shy than Americans. Although they will sometimes approach you to ask whether they might practice English with you, for the most part you're left pretty much on your own unless you make the first move.

Probably the easiest way to meet Japanese is to go where they play—namely, the country's countless **bars,** including those that serve *yakitori* (skewered chicken). Usually small affairs, each with perhaps just a counter and some tables, they're often filled with both younger and older Japanese, many of

whom are regulars. As the evening wears on, you'll encounter Japanese who will want to speak to you if they understand English, and slightly inebriated Japanese who will speak to you even if they don't. If you're open to them, such chance encounters may prove to be the highlight of your trip or, at the very least, an evening of just plain fun.

Janie, who traveled around Japan with her then-3-year-old daughter, found that **traveling with children** opened up opportunities like a magic key. Other children talked freely to her child (they never seemed to have a language barrier), while Janie was able to talk to parents about their children. Complete strangers

she met on a train even invited her and her daughter home; in contrast, some Japanese people she has known for years have never invited her home, preferring instead to meet at coffee shops or restaurants.

Another good way to meet Japanese people is to stay in a *minshuku,* an inexpensive lodging in a private home (see "Tips on Accommodations" in chapter 2). Also, national newspapers and local English-language newsletters list **international club activities;** you may be able to hook up with, say, a hiking or skiing group composed of both Japanese and international members.

Finally, you can meet locals and learn about destinations at the same time through **Goodwill Guides,** a national organization of volunteers (mostly retirees, housewives, and students) who donate their time to guide you around their city free of charge (you pay their travel expenses, admission fees to sights, and meals). There are Goodwill Guides in cities throughout Japan, including Fukuoka, Kumamoto, Beppu, Miyazaki, Kagoshima, Takamatsu, Matsuyama, Hiroshima, Himeji, Kurashiki, Matsue, Kobe, Osaka, Kyoto, Nara, Kanzawa, Matsumoto, Nagoya, Tokyo, Narita, Yokohama, Kamakura, Atami, Ito, Nikko, and Matsushima. Reservations for a guide must be made in advance—usually a week or more. For more information, including contact information, ask for the pamphlet "Goodwill Guide Groups of Japan Welcome You" at Tourist Information Centers in Tokyo or Narita and Kansai international airports; or go to JNTO's website, www.jnto.go.jp, and click "Guide to Japan" and then "Guide Service."

## ETIQUETTE

Much of Japan's system of etiquette and manners stems from its feudal days, when the social hierarchy dictated how a person spoke, sat, bowed, ate, walked, and lived. Failure to comply with the rules would bring severe punishment, even death. More than one Japanese literally lost his head for committing a social blunder.

Of course, nowadays it's quite different, although Japanese still attach much importance to proper behavior. As a foreigner, however, you can get away with a lot. After all, you're just a "barbarian" and, as such, can be forgiven for not knowing the rules. There are two cardinal sins, however, you should never commit: One is you should **never wear your shoes into a Japanese home, traditional inn, temple, or any room with tatami;** the other is that you should **never wash with soap inside a communal Japanese bathtub.** Except for these two horrors, you will probably be forgiven any other social blunders (such as standing with your arms folded or your hands in your pockets).

As a sensitive traveler, however, you should try to familiarize yourself with the basics of Japanese social etiquette. Japanese are very appreciative of foreigners who take the time to learn about their country and are quite patient in helping you. Remember, if you do commit a faux pas, apologize profusely and smile. They don't chop off heads anymore.

Most forms of behavior and etiquette in Japan developed to allow relationships to be as frictionless as possible—a pretty good idea in a country as crowded as Japan. Japanese don't like confrontations, and fights are extremely rare. Japanese are very good at covering almost all unpleasantness with a smile. Foreigners find the smile hard to read—a smiling Japanese face can mean happiness, sadness, embarrassment, or even anger. My first lesson in such physiognomic inscrutability happened on a subway in Tokyo, where I saw a middle-aged Japanese woman who was about to board the subway brutally knocked out of the way by a Japanese man rushing off the train. She almost lost

her balance, but she gave a little laugh, smiled, and got on the train. A few minutes later, as the train was speeding through a tunnel, I stole a look at her and was able to read her true feelings on her face. Lost in her thoughts, she knitted her brow in consternation and looked most upset and unhappy. The smile had been a put-on.

Another aspect of Japanese behavior that sometimes causes difficulty for foreigners, especially in business negotiations, is **the reluctance of Japanese to say no when they mean no.** Many consider such directness poor manners. As a result, they're much more apt to say your request is very difficult, or they'll simply beat around the bush without giving a definite answer. At this point, you're expected to let the subject drop. Showing impatience, anger, or aggressiveness rarely gets you anywhere. Apologizing sometimes does. And if someone does give in to your request, you can't thank them enough.

If you're invited to a Japanese home, you should know that it's both a rarity and an honor. Most Japanese consider their homes too small and humble for entertaining guests, which is why there are so many restaurants, coffee shops, and bars. **If you're invited to a home, don't show up empty-handed.** Bring a small gift such as candy, fruit, flowers, or perhaps a souvenir from your hometown. Alcohol is also appreciated. And if someone does extend you a favor, be sure to thank him again the next time you see him—even if it's a year later.

**Don't blow your nose in public** if you can help it, and never at the dinner table. It's considered most disgusting. On the other hand, even though Japanese are very hygienic, they're not at all averse to spitting on the sidewalk. And, even more peculiar, the men urinate when and where they want, usually against a tree or a wall and most often after a night of carousing in the bars.

This being a man's society, men will walk in and out of doors and elevators before women, and in subways, they will sit down while women stand. Some Japanese men who have had contact with the Western world (particularly hotel staff) will make a gallant show of allowing a Western woman to step out of the elevator first. For the sake of women living in Japan, thank them warmly.

**BOWING**   The main form of greeting in Japan is the bow rather than the handshake. Although at first glance it may seem simple enough, the bow—together with its implications—is actually quite complicated. The depth of the bow and the number of seconds devoted to performing it, as well as the total number of bows, depend on who you are, to whom you're bowing, and how they're bowing back. In addition to bowing in greeting, Japanese also bow upon departing and to express gratitude. The proper form for a bow is to bend from the waist with a straight back and to keep your arms at your sides, but if you're a foreigner, a simple nod of the head is enough. Knowing foreigners shake hands, a Japanese may extend his hand, although he probably won't be able to stop himself from giving a little bow as well. (I've even seen Japanese bow when talking on the telephone.) Although I've occasionally witnessed Japanese businessmen shake hands among themselves, the practice is still quite rare. Kimono-clad hostesses of a high-end traditional Japanese inn will often kneel on tatami and bow to the ground as they send you off on your journey.

**VISITING CARDS**   You're a nonentity in Japan if you don't have a visiting card, called a *meishi.* Everyone—from housewives to bank presidents—carries meishi to give out during introductions. If you're trying to conduct business in Japan,

you'll be regarded suspiciously—even as a phony—if you don't have business cards. Meishi are very useful business tools for Japanese. Likewise, a meishi can be used as an introduction to a third party—a Japanese may give you his meishi, scribble something on it, and tell you to present it to his cousin who owns a restaurant in Fukuoka. *Voilà*—the cousin will treat you like a royal guest.

As a tourist, you don't have to have business cards, but it certainly doesn't hurt, and Japanese people will be greatly impressed by your preparedness. The card should have your address and occupation on it; you might even consider having your meishi made in Japan, with the Japanese syllabic script *(katakana)* written on the reverse side.

Needless to say, there's a proper way to present a meishi. Turn it so that the other person can read it (that is, upside-down to you) and present it with both hands and a slight bow. If you can, try to deliver your card underneath the card you are receiving, to show deference. Afterward, it's customary for both of you to study the meishi for a moment and, if possible, to comment on it (such as, "You're from Kyoto? My brother lived in Kyoto!" or "Sony! What a famous company!"). If you're at a business meeting, place the card in front of you on the table; it's considered impolite to put the card away.

**DINING** Several dining customs in Japan differ from those in the West, many of them involving chopsticks or drinking. For information on dining etiquette and customs, refer to "Tips on Dining, Japanese Style" in chapter 2.

**SHOES** Nothing is so distasteful to Japanese as the soles of shoes. Therefore, you should take off your shoes before entering a home, a Japanese-style inn, a temple, and even some museums and restaurants. Usually, there will be plastic slippers at the entryway for you to slip on, but whenever you encounter tatami, you should take off even these slippers—only bare feet or socks are allowed to tread upon tatami.

Restrooms present another whole set of slippers. If you're in a home or a Japanese inn, you'll notice another pair of slippers—again plastic or rubber—sitting right inside the restroom door. Step out of the hallway plastic shoes and into the bathroom slippers, and wear these the whole time you're in the restroom. When you're finished, change back into the hallway slippers. If you forget this last changeover, you'll regret it—nothing is as embarrassing as walking into a room wearing toilet slippers and not realizing what you've done until you see the mixed looks of horror and mirth on the faces of Japanese people.

**BATHING** On my very first trip to Japan, I was certain I would never enter a Japanese bath. I was under the misconception that men and women bathed together, and I couldn't imagine getting into a tub with a group of smiling and bowing Japanese men. I needn't have worried—in almost all circumstances, bathing is gender segregated. There are some exceptions, primarily at outdoor hot-spring spas in the countryside, but the women who go to these are usually grandmothers who couldn't care less. Young Japanese women wouldn't dream of jumping into a tub with a group of male strangers.

Japanese baths are delightful. You find them at Japanese-style inns (ryokan and minshuku), at hot-spring spas *(onsen)*, and at neighborhood baths *(sento)*; not everyone has his or her own bath in Japan. Sometimes they're elaborate affairs with indoor and outdoor tubs, whirlpools, plants, and statues; sometimes they're nothing more than a tiny tub. Public baths have long been regarded as social centers for Japanese—friends

and coworkers will visit hot-spring resorts together; neighbors exchange gossip at the neighborhood bath. Sadly, however, the neighborhood bath has been in great decline over the past decades, as more and more Japanese acquire private baths. Hot-spring spas, however, remain hugely popular.

In any case, whether large or small, the procedure at all Japanese baths is the same. After completely disrobing in the changing room and putting your clothes in either a locker or a basket, hold a washcloth in front of you so that it covers your vital parts and walk into the bathing area. There, you'll find basins, stools (they used to be wood but are now mostly plastic), and faucets along the wall. Sit on the stool in front of a faucet and repeatedly fill your basin with water (or use the hand-held faucet if available), splashing water all over you. If there's no hot water from the faucet, it's acceptable to dip your basin into the hot bath. Rinsing yourself thoroughly is not only proper onsen manners; it also acclimates your body to the bath's hot temperature so you don't suffer a heart attack. While some Japanese just throw a bit of water over themselves, others soap down completely—and I mean completely—and then rinse away all traces of soap before getting into the tub. At any rate, only when you feel squeaky-clean should you enter the tub. Your first attempt at a Japanese bath may be painful—simply too scalding for comfort. It helps if you ease in gently and then sit perfectly still. You'll notice all tension and stiffness ebbing away.

When you've finished bathing, do not pull the plug, even if you're staying in a private home, since the same bath water is used by everyone. At an onsen, where the hot-spring waters are considered curative, Japanese will often make several trips between the faucet and the baths, being careful not to rinse off the curative waters when they're done. At any rate, I have never seen a group of people wash themselves so thoroughly as Japanese, from their ears to their toes. Japanese are so fond of baths that many take them nightly, especially in winter, when a hot bath keeps them warm for hours afterward. If they're staying at a hot-spring spa, they'll use the baths both at night and again in the morning. Note that some public baths have signs forbidding entrance to anyone with tattoos—tattoos are associated with the Japanese mafia.

## 4 Dealing with the Language Barrier

Without a doubt, the hardest part of traveling in Japan is the language barrier. Suddenly you find yourself transported to a crowded land of 127 million people where you can neither speak nor read the language. To make matters worse, few Japanese speak English. And outside big cities and the major tourist sites, the menus, signs at train stations, and shop names are often in Japanese only.

However, millions of foreign visitors before you who didn't speak a word of Japanese have traveled throughout Japan on their own with great success. Much of the anxiety travelers experience elsewhere is eliminated in Japan because the country is safe and the people are kind and helpful to foreigners. In addition, the **Japan National Tourist Organization (JNTO)** does a super job of publishing helpful brochures, leaflets, and maps; and there are local tourist offices in almost all cities and towns, usually at train stations. The country has done a mammoth job during the past decade updating street signs, subway directions, and addresses in Roman letters, especially in Tokyo, Osaka, Kyoto, and other major cities.

If you need to ask directions of strangers in Japan, your best bet is to **ask younger people.** They have all studied English in school and are most likely to be able to help you. Japanese businessmen often know some English also. And as strange as it sounds, if you're having problems communicating with someone, **write it down** so he or she can read it. The emphasis in schools is on written rather than oral English (many English teachers can't speak English themselves), so Japanese who can't understand a word you say may know all the subtleties of syntax and English grammar. If you still have problems communicating, you can always call the **Tourist Information Center** (© 03/3201-3331) to help with translation. It also doesn't hurt to arm yourself with a small pocket dictionary.

If you're heading out for a particular restaurant, shop, or sight, have your destination written down in Japanese by someone at your hotel. If you get lost along the way, look for one of the police boxes, called *koban,* found in virtually every neighborhood. They have maps of particular districts and can pinpoint exactly where you want to go if you have the address with you. Remember, too, that main train stations in major cities and tourist-resort areas have **tourist information offices** *(kanko annaijo)* that can help you with everything from directions to hotel reservations. The staff may not speak any English, but you shouldn't have trouble communicating your needs.

A glossary of simple phrases and words appears in appendix B of this book. In addition, realizing the difficulties that foreigners have with the language barrier in Japan, the JNTO has put out a nifty booklet called the *Tourist's Language Handbook.* It contains basic sentences in English, with their Japanese equivalents, for almost every activity, from asking for directions, to shopping, to ordering in a restaurant, to staying in a Japanese inn. It also has a short list of useful Japanese phrases to help you get around on your own. Pick up a copy at a Tourist Information Center in Tokyo or at Narita or Kansai airports.

**THE WRITTEN LANGUAGE** No one knows the exact origins of the Japanese language, but we do know it existed only in spoken form until the 6th century. It was then that Japanese borrowed the Chinese pictorial characters, called *kanji,* and used them to develop their own form of written language. Later, two phonetic alphabet systems, *hiragana* and *katakana,* were added to kanji to form the existing Japanese writing system. Thus, Chinese and Japanese use some of the same pictographs, but otherwise there's no similarity between the languages; while they may be able to recognize parts of each other's written language, the Chinese and Japanese cannot communicate verbally.

The Japanese written language—a combination of kanji, hiragana, and katakana—is probably one of the most difficult in the modern world. As for the spoken language, there are many levels of speech and forms of expression relating to a person's social status and sex. Even nonverbal communication is a vital part of understanding Japanese, because what isn't said is often more important than what is. It's little wonder that St. Francis Xavier, a Jesuit missionary who came to Japan in the 16th century, wrote that Japanese was an invention of the devil designed to thwart the spread of Christianity. And yet, astoundingly, adult literacy in Japan is estimated to be 99%.

*A note on establishment names:* Many hotels and restaurants in Japan now have signs in *romaji* (Roman, or English-language, characters) in addition to their Japanese-character signs. For those that don't, take heart—appendix C contains the Japanese-character names of establishments recommended in this

book that have signs in Japanese only; the appendix should help you recognize them.

**OTHER HELPFUL TIPS**  It's worth noting that Japanese nouns do not have plural forms; thus, for example, ryokan, a Japanese-style inn, can be both singular and plural, as can kimono. Plural sense is indicated by context.

In addition, the Japanese custom is to list the family name first followed by the given name. That is the format I have followed in this book, but note that many things printed in English—business cards, city brochures, and so on—may follow the Western custom of listing the family name last.

And finally, you may find yourself confused because of suffixes attached to Japanese place names. For example, *dori* can mean street, avenue, or road; and sometimes it's attached to a street name with a hyphen, while at other times it stands alone. Thus, you may see Chuo-dori, Chuo Dori, or even Chuo-dori Avenue on English-language maps and street signs, but they're all one and the same street. Likewise, *dera* means "temple" and is often included at the end of the name, as in Kiyomizudera, which may be translated into English as Kiyomizu Temple; *jo* means castle and may appear at the end of a castle's name, as in Nijojo, or it may be left off and appear as Nijo Castle.

**WRITTEN ENGLISH IN JAPAN**
English words are quite fashionable in Japanese advertising, with the result that you'll often see them on shop signs, posters, shopping bags, and T-shirts. However, the words are often wonderfully misspelled or are used in such unusual contexts that you can only guess at the original intent. What, for example, can possibly be the meaning behind TODAY BIRDS, TOMORROW MEN, which appeared below a picture of birds on a shopping bag? I have treasured ashtrays that read THE YOUNG BOY GRASPED HER HEART FIRMLY AND LET'S TRIP IN HOKKAIDO. In Okayama, I saw a shop whose name was a stern admonition to customers to GROW UP, while in Kyoto I saw the SELFISH coffee shop and the PITIFUL PUB. A staff member of the Hokkaido Tourist Association whose business card identified him working for the PROPAGANDA SECTION was probably more truthful than most. And imagine my consternation upon stepping onto a bathroom scale that called itself the BEAUTY-CHECKER. But the best sign I've seen was at the Narita Airport, where each check-in counter displayed a notice advising passengers they would have to pay a service-facility charge at THE TIME OF CHECK-IN FOR YOUR FRIGHT. I was unable to control my giggles as I explained to the perplexed man behind one counter what was wrong with the sign. Two weeks later, when I went back through the airport, I was almost disappointed to find that all signs had been corrected. But that's Japanese efficiency.

## 5  Cultural Snapshots: Japanese Arts in a Nutshell

### TRADITIONAL THEATER

**KABUKI**  Probably Japan's best-known traditional theater art, Kabuki is also one of the country's most popular forms of entertainment. Visit a performance and it's easy to see why—in a word, Kabuki is fun! The plays are dramatic, the costumes are gorgeous, the stage settings are often fantastic, and the themes are universal—love, revenge, and the conflict between duty and personal feelings. Probably one of the reasons Kabuki is so popular even today is that it developed centuries ago as a form of entertainment for the common

people in feudal Japan, particularly the merchants. And one of Kabuki's interesting aspects is that all roles—even those depicting women—are portrayed by men.

Kabuki has changed little in the past 100-some years. Altogether there are more than 300 Kabuki plays, all written before the 20th century. Kabuki stages almost always revolve and have an aisle that extends from the stage to the back of the spectator theater. For a Westerner, one of the more arresting things about a Kabuki performance is the audience itself. Because this has always been entertainment for the masses, the audience can get quite lively with yells, guffaws, shouts of approval, and laughter. In fact, old woodcuts of cross-eyed men apparently stemmed from Kabuki—when things got a little too rowdy, actors would stamp their feet and strike a cross-eyed pose in an attempt to gain the audience's attention.

Of course, you won't be able to understand what's being said. Indeed, because much of Kabuki drama dates from the 18th century, even Japanese sometimes have difficulty understanding the language. But it doesn't matter. Many theaters have programs and earphones that describe the plots in minute detail, often in the English language as well. Thus, you can follow the story and enjoy Kabuki just as much as everyone around you. The best place to enjoy Kabuki is Tokyo, where performances are held throughout much of the year.

**NOH** Whereas Kabuki developed as a form of entertainment for the masses, Noh was a much more traditional and aristocratic form of theater. Most of Japan's shogun were patrons of Noh; during the Edo Period, it became the exclusive entertainment of the samurai class. In contrast to Kabuki's extroverted liveliness, Noh is very calculated, slow, and restrained. The oldest form of theater in Japan, it has changed very little in the past 600 years, making it the oldest theater art in the world. The language is so archaic that Japanese cannot understand it at all, which explains in part why Noh does not have the popularity that Kabuki does.

As in Kabuki, all the performers are men, with the principal characters consisting mostly of ghosts or spirits, who illuminate foibles of human nature or tragic-heroic events. Performers often wear masks. Spoken parts are chanted by a chorus of about eight; music is provided by a Noh orchestra that consists of several drums and a flute.

Because the action is slow, watching an entire evening can be quite tedious unless you are particularly interested in Noh dance and music. In addition, most Noh plays do not have English translations. You may want to drop in for just a short while. In between Noh plays, short comic reliefs called *kyogen* usually make fun of life in the 1600s, depicting the lives of lazy husbands, conniving servants, and other characters with universal appeal.

**BUNRAKU** Bunraku is traditional Japanese puppet theater. But contrary to what you might expect, Bunraku is for adults, and themes center on love and revenge, sacrifice and suicide. Many dramas now adapted for Kabuki were first written for the Bunraku stage.

Popular in Japan since the 17th century—at times even more popular than Kabuki—Bunraku is fascinating to watch because the puppeteers are right onstage with their puppets. Dressed in black, they're wonderfully skilled in making puppets seem like living beings. Usually, there are three puppeteers for each puppet, which is about three-fourths human size: One puppeteer is responsible for movement of the puppet's head, as well as for the expression on its face, and for the movement of the right arm and hand; another puppeteer operates the puppet's

## Fun Fact Sumo

The Japanese form of wrestling known as *sumo* began perhaps as long as 1,500 years ago and became immensely popular by the 6th century. Today, it's still popular, and the best wrestlers are revered as national heroes, much as baseball or basketball players are in the United States. Often taller than 1.8m (6 ft.) and weighing well over 300 pounds, sumo wrestlers follow a rigorous training period, which usually begins when they're in their teens and includes eating special foods to gain weight. Unmarried wrestlers even live together at their training schools, called sumo stables.

A sumo match takes place on a sandy-floored ring less than 4.5m (15 ft.) in diameter. Wrestlers dress much as they did during the Edo Period—their hair in a samurai-style topknot, an ornamental belt-loincloth around their huge girths. Before each bout, the two contestants scatter salt in the ring to purify it from the last bout's loss; they also squat and then raise each leg, stamping it into the ground to crush, symbolically, any evil spirits. They then squat down and face each other, glaring to psych each other out. Once they rush each other, each wrestler's object is to either eject his opponent from the ring or cause him to touch the ground with any part of his body other than his feet. This is accomplished by shoving, slapping, tripping, throwing, and even carrying the opponent, but punching with a closed fist and kicking are not allowed. Altogether, there are 48 holds and throws, and sumo fans know all of them.

Most bouts are very short, lasting only 30 seconds or so. The highest-ranking players are called *yokozuna,* or grand champions; in 1993, a Hawaiian named Akebono was promoted to the highest rank, the first non-Japanese ever to be so honored.

There are six 15-day sumo tournaments in Japan every year: Three are held in Tokyo (Jan, May, and Sept); the others are held in Osaka (Mar), Nagoya (July), and Fukuoka (Nov). Each wrestler in the tournament faces a new opponent every day; the winner of the tournament is the wrestler who maintains the best overall record.

If you'd like to attend a sumo match while you're in Tokyo, see the "Spectator Sports" section of chapter 5. Tournament matches are also widely covered on television.

left arm and hand; while the third moves the legs. Although at first the puppeteers are somewhat distracting, after a while you forget they're there as the puppets assume personalities of their own. The narrator, who tells the story and speaks the various parts, is an important figure in the drama. The narrator is accompanied by a traditional three-stringed Japanese instrument called a *shamisen.* By all means, try to see Bunraku. The most famous presentations are at the Osaka Bunraku Theater, but there are performances in Tokyo and other major cities as well.

## THE TEA CEREMONY

Tea was brought to Japan from China more than 1,000 years ago. It first became

popular among Buddhist priests as a means of staying awake during long hours of meditation; gradually, its use filtered down among the upper classes, and in the 16th century, the tea ceremony was perfected by a merchant named Sen-no-Rikyu. Using the principles of Zen and the spiritual discipline of the samurai, the tea ceremony became a highly stylized ritual, with detailed rules on how tea should be prepared, served, and drunk. The simplicity of movement and tranquillity of setting are meant to free the mind from the banality of everyday life and to allow the spirit to enjoy peace. In a way, it is a form of spiritual therapy.

The tea ceremony, *cha-no-yu*, is still practiced in Japan today and is regarded as a form of disciplinary training for mental composure and for etiquette and manners. In Kyoto, I once met a fellow guest in an inexpensive Japanese inn who asked whether she could serve me Japanese tea and a sweet after breakfast. She apologized for her ineptitude, saying she was only a mere apprentice of tea. When I asked how long she'd been studying cha-no-yu, she replied 7 years. That may seem like a long time, but the study of the tea ceremony includes related subjects, including the craftsmanship of tea vessels and implements, the design and construction of the teahouse, the landscaping of gardens, and literature related to the tea ceremony.

Several of Japan's more famous landscape gardens have teahouses on their grounds where you can sit on tatami, drink the frothy green tea (called *maccha*), eat sweets (meant to counteract the bitter taste of the tea), and contemplate the view. Teahouses are traditionally quite small and have room for five or fewer people. There's one entrance for the host and another for guests, so small that guests must crawl through it to enter. In the center of the room is a small brazier for the teapot along with utensils needed

for the making of tea—tea bowl, tea caddy, bamboo whisk, and bamboo spoon. After hot water is added to powdered tea in the bowl and beaten with the whisk, the bowl is passed from guest to guest. Tea etiquette requires that guests compliment the host on the excellent flavor of the tea and on the beauty of the tea implements, which of course change with the seasons and are often valuable art objects.

Several first-class hotels in Tokyo hold tea ceremonies in special tea-ceremony rooms; see chapter 5 for more information.

## FLORAL & LANDSCAPE ARTS

**IKEBANA** Whereas a Westerner is likely to put a bunch of flowers into a vase and be done with it, Japanese consider the arrangement of flowers an art in itself. Most young girls have at least some training in flower arranging, known as *ikebana*. First popularized among aristocrats during the Heian Period (A.D. 794–1192) and spreading to the common people in the 14th to 16th centuries, traditional ikebana, in its simplest form, is supposed to represent heaven, man, and earth; it's considered a truly Japanese art without outside influences. As important as the arrangement itself is the vase chosen to display it. Department store galleries sometimes have ikebana exhibitions, as do shrines; otherwise, check with the local tourist office.

**GARDENS** Nothing is left to chance in a Japanese landscape garden: The shapes of hills and trees, the placement of rocks and waterfalls—everything is skillfully arranged in a faithful reproduction of nature. To Westerners, it may seem a bit strange to arrange nature to look like nature; but to Japanese, even nature can be improved upon to make it more pleasing through the best possible use of limited space. Japanese are masters at this, as a visit to any of their famous gardens will testify.

In fact, Japanese have been sculpting gardens for more than 1,000 years. At first, the gardens were designed for walking and boating, with ponds, artificial islands, and pavilions. As with almost everything else in Japanese life, however, Zen Buddhism exerted an influence, making gardens simpler and attempting to create the illusion of boundless space within a small area. To the Buddhist, a garden was not for merriment but for contemplation—an uncluttered and simple landscape on which to rest the eyes. Japanese gardens often use the principle of "borrowed landscape"—that is, the incorporation of surrounding mountains and landscape into the overall design and impact of the garden.

Basically, there are three styles of Japanese gardens. One style, called **tsukiyama,** uses ponds, hills, and streams to depict nature in miniature. Another style, known as the **karesansui,** uses stones and raked sand in place of water and is often seen at Zen Buddhist temples; it was developed during the Muromachi Period as a representation of Zen spiritualism. The third style, called **chaniwa,** emerged with the tea ceremony and is built around a teahouse with an eye toward simplicity and tranquillity; such a garden will often feature stone lanterns, a stone basin filled with water, or water flowing through a bamboo pipe.

Famous gardens in Japan include Kenrokuen Park in Kanazawa, Korakuen Park in Okayama, Ritsurin Park in Takamatsu, and the grounds of the Adachi Museum. Kyoto alone has about 50 gardens, including the famous Zen rock gardens at Daitokuji and Ryoanji temples, the gardens at both the Golden and Silver pavilions, and those at Heian Shrine, Nijo Castle, and the Katsura Imperial Villa.

# Appendix B:
# A Glossary of Useful Japanese Terms

**N**eedless to say, it takes years to become fluent in Japanese, particularly in written Japanese, with its thousands of *kanji,* or Chinese characters, and its many hiragana and katakana characters. If you know even a few words of Japanese, however, they will not only be useful but will delight Japanese people you meet in the course of your trip.

## PRONUNCIATION

In pronouncing the following vocabulary, keep in mind that there's very little stress on individual syllables (pronunciation of Japanese is often compared to Italian). Here's an approximation of some of the sounds of Japanese:

**a**  *as in* father

**e**  *as in* pen

**i**  *as in* see

**o**  *as in* oh

**oo**  *as in* oooh

**u**  *as in* boo

**g**  *as in* gift at the beginning of words; like "ng" in "sing" in the middle or at the end of words

Vowel sounds are almost always short unless they are pronounced doubled, in which case you hold the vowel a bit longer. *Okashi,* for example, means "a sweet," whereas *okashii* means "strange." As you can see, even slight mispronunciation of a word can result in confusion or hilarity. (Incidentally, jokes in Japanese are nearly always plays on words.) Similarly, double consonants are given more emphasis than only one consonant by itself.

## USEFUL WORDS & PHRASES
### BASIC TERMS

Yes  **Hai**

No  **Iie**

Good morning  **Ohayo gozaimasu**

Good afternoon  **Konnichiwa**

Good evening  **Konbanwa**

Good night  **Oyasuminasai**

Hello  **Haro** (or **Konnichiwa**)

How are you?  **Ogenki desu ka?**

How do you do?  **Hajimemashite?**

Goodbye  **Sayonara (or Bye-bye!)**

Excuse me/Pardon me/I'm sorry  **Sumimasen**

Please (when offering something)    **Dozo**

Please (when requesting something)    **Kudasai**

Thank you    **Domo arigatoo**

You're welcome    **Doo-itashimashite**

## BASIC QUESTIONS & EXPRESSIONS

I'm American    **Amerikajin desu**

I'm Canadian    **Canadajin desu**

I'm English    **Eikokujin desu**

Sorry, I don't speak Japanese    **Sumimasen, Nihongo was wakarimasen**

Do you understand English?    **Eigo wa wakarimasu ka?**

Do you understand?    **Wakarimasu ka?**

I understand    **Wakarimasu**

I don't understand    **Wakarimasen**

Can I ask you a question?    **Otazune shitaino desu ka?**

Just a minute, please    **Chotto matte kudasai**

How much is it?    **Ikura desu ka?**

It's expensive    **Takai desu**

It's cheap    **Yasui desu**

Where is it?    **Doko desu ka?**

When is it?    **Itsu desu ka?**

What is it?    **Kore-wa, nan-desu-ka?**

I like it    **Suki desu** (pronounced "ski")

Where is the toilet?    **Toire wa, doko desu ka?**

My name is . . .    [Your name] **to mo shimasu**

What is your name?    **O-namae wa, nan desu ka?**

What time do you open/close?    **Nanji ni akimasuka? Nanjini shimarimasuka?**

Credit card    **Kurejitto kaado**

Too expensive    **Takasugimasu**

This one    **Kore**

That one    **Are**

## TRAVEL EXPRESSIONS & DIRECTIONALS

Where is . . . ?    **Doko desu ka . . . ?**

Where is the train station?    **Eki wa, doko desu ka?**

Train station    **Eki**

Airport    **Kuukoo**

Subway    **Chika-tetsu**

Bus    **Bus-u**

Taxi    **Takushi**

Airplane    **Hikooki**

Train    **Densha**

Bullet train  **Shinkansen**

Limited express train (long distance)  **Tokkyu**

Ordinary express train (doesn't stop at every station)  **Kyuko**

Rapid train  **Kaisoku densha**

Local train (one that stops at every station)  **Kakueki teisha** (or **futsu**)

I would like a reserved seat, please.  **Shiteiseki o kudasai.**

I would like a seat in the nonsmoking car, please.  **Kinensha no shiteiski o kudasai.**

Where should I transfer?  **Norikae wa doko desu ka?**

Unreserved seat  **Jiyuseki**

Platform  **Platt-homu**

Ticket  **Kippu**

Destination  **Ikisaki**

One-way ticket  **Katamichi-kippu** (or **katamichiken**)

Round-trip ticket  **Ofuku-kippu** (or **ofukuken**)

I would like to buy a ticket.  **Kippu ichimai o kaitai no desu kedo.**

I would like to buy two tickets.  **Kippu nimai o kaitai no desu kedo.**

Exit  **Deguchi**

Entrance  **Iriguchi**

North  **Kita**

South  **Minami**

East  **Higashi**

West  **Nishi**

Left  **Hidari**

Right  **Migi**

Straight ahead  **Massugu** (or **zutto**)

Is it far?  **Toi desu ka?**

Is it near?  **Chikai desu ka?**

I'm lost  **Maigoni narimashita.**

Can I walk there?  **Aruite ikemasu ka?**

Street  **Dori** (or **michi**)

Tourist Information Office  **Kanko annaijo** (or **kanko kyokai**)

Where is the tourist office?  **Kanko annaijo, doko desu ka?**

May I have a map, please?  **Chizu o kudasai?**

Police  **Keisatsu**

Police box  **Koban**

Post office  **Yubin-kyoku**

I'd like to buy a stamp.  **Kitte o kaitai no desu kedo.**

Bank  **Ginko**

Hospital  **Byooin**

Drugstore  **Yakkyoku**

Convenience store   **Konbiniensu stoa**

Embassy   **Taishkan**

Department store   **Depaato**

Downtown area   **Hanka-gai**

Passport   **Pasupooto**

I want to go to . . .   **. . . e ikitai desu.**

I want to go to the station.   **Eki e ikitai desu.**

What time does . . . leave   **. . . nanjini shuppatsu desu ka?**

Train   **Densha**

Subway   **Chikatetsu**

Bus   **Basu**

Ferry   **Ferii**

## LODGING TERMS

Hotel   **Hoteru**

Japanese-style inn   **Ryokan**

Youth hostel   **Yusu hosuteru**

Cotton kimono   **Yukata**

Room   **Heya**

Do you have a room available?   **Heya ga arimasu ka?**

Does that include meals?   **Shokuji wa tsuite imasu ka?**

Tax   **Zei**

Service charge   **Saavice**

Key   **Kagi**

Balcony   **Baranda**

Hot-spring spa   **Onsen**

Outdoor hot-spring bath   **Rotenburo**

Bath   **Ofuro**

Public bath   **Sento**

Where is the nearest public bath?   **Ichiban chikai sento wa, doko desu ka?**

I would like a room with one bed, two beds.   **Singeru** (single bed), **Duberu** (double-size bed), **Tsuin** (twin beds) **no heya o onegaishimasu**.

Does it have a private bathroom?   **Heya ni wa ofuro (tub) toile (toilett) ga tsuitemasuka?**

I'd like a private bathroom.   **Basu toile tsuki no heya o onegaishimasu.**

Does the window open?   **Kono mado wa akimasuka?**

## DINING TERMS & PHRASES

Restaurant   **Resutoran** (serves Western-style food)

Dining hall   **Shokudo** (usually serves Japanese food)

Coffee shop   **Kissaten**

Japanese pub   **Izakaya** or **Nomiya**

Western food   **Yoshoku**

Japanese food   **Washoku**

Breakfast   **Chosoku**

Lunch   **Ohiru/Ianchi**

Dinner   **Yushoku**

I'd like to make a reservation.   **Yoyaku oneigai shimasu.**

I'd like to pay the bill.   **Okanjo o oneigai shimasu.**

Menu   **Menyu**

Japanese green tea   **Ocha**

Black (Indian) tea   **Kocha**

Coffee   **Koohi**

Water   **Mizu**

Lunch or daily special, set menu   **Teishoku** (Japanese food)

Lunch or daily special, set menu   **Cosu,** or **seto** (usually Western food)

What do you recommend to eat?   **Nani ga osusume desu ka?**

This is delicious.   **Oishii desu.**

Thank you for the meal.   **Gochisoo-sama deshita.**

I would like a fork, please.   **Foku o kudasai.**

I would like a spoon, please.   **Saji o kudasai.**

I would like a knife, please.   **Naifu o kudasai.**

May I have some more, please? (if you're asking for liquid, such as more coffee, or
food)   **Mo skoshi o kudasai?**

May I have some more, please? (if you're asking for another bottle—say, of soda or
sake)   **Mo ipon o kudasai?**

May I have some more, please? (if you're asking for another cup—say, of coffee or tea)
**Mo ippai o kudasai?**

I would like sake, please.   **Osake o kudasai.**

I would like a cup of coffee, please.   **Koohii o ippai o kudasai.**

I would like the set meal, please.   **Seto o kudasai** or **Teishoku o kudasai.**

Soda   **Tansan**

Salt   **Shio**

Pepper   **Koshoo**

Baked   **Yaku**

Fried   **Ageru/furai**

Not fried   **Agemonode nai**

Broiled   **Yaku**

Steamed   **Musu**

Grilled   **Yaki**

Well done   **Yoku yaku**

Rare   **Nama**

I'm a vegetarian   **Saishokushugisha desu**

I can't eat meat/pork   **Oniku/butaniku ga taberemasen**

I'm allergic to . . .   **. . . no alelugii desu**

Nuts   **Nattsu/kinomi**

Peanuts   **Piinuttsu**

Milk   **Gyuunyuu/miruku**

Shellfish   **Kai**

## FOOD

**Ayu**   A small river fish; a delicacy of western Japan.

**Anago**   Conger eel.

**Chu-hai Shochu**   Shochu (see below) mixed with soda water and flavored with syrup and lemon.

**Dengaku**   Lightly grilled tofu (see below) coated with a bean paste.

**Dojo**   Small, eel-like river fish.

**Fugu**   Pufferfish (also known as blowfish or globefish).

**"Genghis Khan"**   Mutton and vegetables grilled at your table.

**Gohan**   Rice.

**Gyoza**   Chinese fried pork dumplings.

**Kaiseki**   Formal Japanese meal consisting of many courses and served originally during the tea ceremony.

**Kamameshi**   Rice casserole topped with seafood, meat, or vegetables.

**Kushiage** (also **kushikatsu** or **kushiyaki**)   Deep-fried skewers of chicken, beef, seafood, and vegetables.

**Maguro**   Tuna.

**Makizushi**   Sushi (see below), vegetables, and rice rolled inside dried seaweed.

**Miso**   Soybean paste, used as a seasoning in soups and sauces.

**Miso-shiru**   Miso soup.

**Mochi**   Japanese rice cake.

**Nabemono**   Single-pot dish of chicken, beef, pork, or seafood, stewed with vegetables.

**Natto**   Fermented soybeans.

**Nikujaga**   Stew of beef, potato, and carrot, flavored with sake (see below) and soy sauce; popular in winter.

**Oden**   Fish cakes, hard-boiled eggs, and vegetables, simmered in a light broth.

**Okonomiyaki**   Thick pancake filled with meat, fish, shredded cabbage, and vegetables or noodles, often cooked by diners at their table.

**Ramen**   Thick, yellow Chinese noodles, served in a hot soup.

**Sake** (also **Nihon-shu**)   Rice wine.

**Sansai**   Mountain vegetables, including bracken and flowering fern.

**Sashimi**   Raw seafood.

**Shabu-shabu**   Thinly sliced beef quickly dipped in boiling water and then dipped in a sauce.

**Shochu**   Japanese whiskey, made from rice, wheat, or potatoes.

**Shojin-ryori**   Japanese vegetarian food, served at Buddhist temples.

**Shoyu**   Soy sauce.

**Shumai**   Steamed Chinese pork dumplings.

**Soba**   Buckwheat noodles.

**Somen**   Fine white wheat vermicelli, eaten cold in summer.

**Sukiyaki**   Japanese fondue of thinly sliced beef cooked in a sweetened soy sauce with vegetables.

**Sushi** (also **nigiri-zushi**)   Raw seafood placed on top of vinegared rice.

**Tempura**   Deep-fried food coated in a batter of egg, water, and wheat flour.

**Teppanyaki**   Japanese-style steak, seafood, and vegetables cooked by a chef on a smooth, hot, tableside grill.

**Tofu**   Soft bean curd.

**Tonkatsu**   Deep-fried pork cutlets.

**Tonkotsu**   Pork that has been boiled for several hours in miso, shochu, and brown sugar.

**Udon**   Thick white wheat noodles.

**Unagi**   Grilled eel.

**Wasabi**   Japanese horseradish, served with sushi.

**Yakisoba**   Chinese fried noodles, served with sautéed vegetables.

**Yakitori**   Charcoal-grilled chicken, vegetables, and other specialties, served on bamboo skewers.

**Yudofu**   Tofu simmered in a pot at your table.

## MATTERS OF TIME

| | | | |
|---|---|---|---|
| Now | **Ima** | Morning | **Asa** |
| Later | **Sto de** | Night | **Yoru** |
| Today | **Kyoo** | Afternoon | **Gogo** |
| Tomorrow | **Ashita** | Holiday | **Yasumi** (or **kyujitsu**) |
| Day after tomorrow | **Asatte** | Weekdays | **Heijitsu** |
| Yesterday | **Kinoo** | 1 hour | **Ichijikan** |
| Which day? | **Nan-nichi desu ka?** | 2 hours | **Nijikan** |
| What time is it? | **Nan-ji desu ka?** | 8 hours | **Hachijikan** |
| Daytime | **Hiruma** | | |

## DAYS OF THE WEEK

| | | | |
|---|---|---|---|
| Sunday | **Nichiyoobi** | Thursday | **Mokuyoobi** |
| Monday | **Getsuyoobi** | Friday | **Kinyoobi** |
| Tuesday | **Kayoobi** | Saturday | **Doyoobi** |
| Wednesday | **Suiyoobi** | | |

## MONTHS OF THE YEAR

January **Ichi-gatsu**
February **Ni-gatsu**
March **San-gatsu**
April **Shi-gatsu**
May **Go-gatsu**
June **Roku-gatsu**

July **Shichi-gatsu**
August **Hachi-gatsu**
September **Kyuu-gatsu**
October **Juu-gatsu**
November **Juuichi-gatsu**
December **Juuni-gatsu**

## NUMBERS

1 **Ichi**
2 **Ni**
3 **San**
4 **Shi**
5 **Go**
6 **Roku**
7 **Shichi** (or **nana**)
8 **Hachi**
9 **Kyuu**
10 **Juu**
11 **Juuichi**
12 **Juuni**

20 **Nijuu**
30 **Sanjuu**
40 **Shijuu** (or **yonjuu**)
50 **Gojuu**
60 **Rokujuu**
70 **Nanajuu**
80 **Hachijuu**
90 **Kyuuju**
100 **Hyaku**
1,000 **Sen**
10,000 **Ichiman**

## OTHER GENERAL NOUNS

**Fusuma**   Sliding paper doors.

**Gaijin**   Foreigner.

**Geta**   Wooden sandals.

**Haori**   Short kimono-like jackets (sometimes worn over a kimono), traditionally worn by men.

**Irori**   Open-hearth fireplace.

**Izakaya** (or **Nomiya**)   A Japanese-style bar or pub, with beer, sake, and Japanese food, generally open only from 5 or 6pm.

**Jinja**   Shinto shrine.

**Kotatsu**   Heating element placed under a low table (which is covered with a blanket) for keeping your legs warm; used in place of a heater in traditional Japanese homes.

**Minshuku**   Inexpensive lodging in a private home; the Japanese equivalent of a European pension.

**Nihonjin**   Japanese person.

**Noren**   Short curtains hung outside shops and restaurants to signify they are open.

**Rotenburo**   Outdoor hot-spring bath.

**Shoji**   White paper sliding windows.

**Tatami**   Rice mats.

**Tera** (or **dera**)   Temple.

**Tokonoma**   Small, recessed alcove in a Japanese room used to display a flower arrangement, scroll, or art object.

**Torii**  Entrance gate of a Shinto shrine, consisting usually of two poles topped with one or two crossbeams.

**Washlet**  Bidet toilet.

**Yukata**  Cotton kimono worn for sleeping.

**Zabuton**  Floor cushions.

# Appendix C:
# A Japanese-Character Index of Establishment Names

## TSUMAGO & MAGOME

59  Tsumago
妻籠

60  Magome
馬籠

61  Ryokan Fujioto
旅館　藤乙

## TAKAYAMA

62  Hida Takayama
Museum of Art
飛騨高山春慶会館

63  Lion Dance Ceremony
Exhibition Hall
獅子會館

64  Nagase
長瀬

65  Antique Inn Sumiyoshi
寿美よし

66  Kakusho
角正

67  Suzuya
寿々や

68  Myogaya
茗荷舍

## SHIRAKAWAGO & OGIMACHI

69  Doburoku Matsuri no Yakata
どぶろく祭りの館

70  Gasshozukuri Seikatsu
Shiryokan
合掌造生活資料館

71  Wada Ke
和田家

72  Jyuemon
十右ェ門

73  Koemon
幸エ門

74  Nodaniya
のだにや

75  Irori
いろり

## CHAPTER 8
## KYOTO & NARA

## KYOTO

76  Kinoe
き乃え

77  Myorenji Temple
妙蓮寺

78  Izusen
泉仙

79  Ichiba Coji
市場小路

80  Misogi-gawa
禊川

81  Kushi Kura
串くら

82  Tagoto
田ごと

83  Tofujaya
豆腐茶屋

84  Bio-Tei
びお亭

85  Ganko Sushi
がんこ寿司

86  Gontaro
権太呂

87  Musashi
むさし

88  Omen
おめん

89  Hyotei
瓢亭

90  Mikaku
みかく

121 Sakuda
さくだ

122 Shamisen no Fukushima
三味線の福嶋

123 Tawaraya Ame
俵屋あめ

124 Miyoshian
三芳庵

125 Hamacho
浜長

126 Kitama
きたま

127 To Mu
兎夢

128 Kotobuki-Ya
壽屋

## OSAKA

129 Okonomiyaki Madonna
お好み焼きまどんな

130 Kani Doraku
かに道楽

131 Bar Tachibana
たちばな

132 Fugetsu
風月

## KOBE

133 Kin-no-Yu
金の湯

134 Gin-no-Yu
銀の湯

135 Steakland Kobe
ステーキランド KOBE

136 Hyotan
瓢たん

## MT. KOYA

137 Kongobuji Temple
金剛峯寺

138 Reihokan Museum
霊宝館

139 Ekoin
恵光院

140 Fudoin Temple
不動院

141 Muryokoin Temple
無量光院

142 Rengejoin Temple
蓮華定院

143 Shojoshinin
清浄心院

144 Tentokuin
天徳院

## HIMEJI

145 Koko-en
好古園

146 Asaka Sushi
あさ香すし

147 Kassui-ken
活水軒

## OKAYAMA

148 Yumeji Art Museum
夢二郷土美術館

149 Okayama Prefectural
Product Center
岡山県観光物産センター

150 Abis Inn
アビス イン

151 Matsunoki Ryokan
まつのき旅館

152 Matsunoki-Tei
まつのき亭

153 Okabe
おかべ

154 Shikisai
四季彩

155 Yamadome
山留

## KURASHIKI

156 Ohashi House
大橋家住宅

157 Orgel Musée
オルゴールミュゼ

158 Ryokan Kurashiki
旅館くらしき

159 Tsurugata
鶴形

160 Kamoi
カモ井

161 Kanaizumi
かな泉

## MATSUE

162 Teahouse Meimei-an
明々庵

163 Buke Yashiki
武家屋敷

164 Gesshoji Temple
月照寺

165 Minami-Kan
皆美館

166 Horaiso
蓬莱荘

167 Ryokan Terazuya
旅館寺津屋

168 Kyoragi
京らぎ

169 Daikichi
大吉

170 Kaneyasu
かねやす

171 Yakumoan
八雲庵

## HIROSHIMA

172 Dolce
ドルチェ

173 Onomichi Ekimae
Kowan Chushajo
尾道駅前港湾駐車場

174 Kanawa
かなわ

175 Kushinobo
串の坊

176 No-no-Budou
野の葡萄

177 Okonomi-Mura
お好み村

178 Chii-chan
ちいちゃん

179 Sushi Tei
すし亭

## MIYAJIMA

180 Guest House Kikugawa
菊がわ

181 Iwaso Ryokan
岩惣旅館

182 Miyajima Morinoyado
みやじま杜の宿

183 Fujitaya
ふじたや

# Index

# FROMMER'S® COMPLETE TRAVEL GUIDES

Alaska
Amalfi Coast
American Southwest
Amsterdam
Argentina & Chile
Arizona
Atlanta
Australia
Austria
Bahamas
Barcelona
Beijing
Belgium, Holland & Luxembourg
Belize
Bermuda
Boston
Brazil
British Columbia & the Canadian
  Rockies
Brussels & Bruges
Budapest & the Best of Hungary
Buenos Aires
Calgary
California
Canada
Cancún, Cozumel & the Yucatán
Cape Cod, Nantucket & Martha's
  Vineyard
Caribbean
Caribbean Ports of Call
Carolinas & Georgia
Chicago
China
Colorado
Costa Rica
Croatia
Cuba
Denmark
Denver, Boulder & Colorado Springs
Edinburgh & Glasgow
England
Europe
Europe by Rail

Florence, Tuscany & Umbria
Florida
France
Germany
Greece
Greek Islands
Hawaii
Hong Kong
Honolulu, Waikiki & Oahu
India
Ireland
Italy
Jamaica
Japan
Kauai
Las Vegas
London
Los Angeles
Los Cabos & Baja
Madrid
Maine Coast
Maryland & Delaware
Maui
Mexico
Montana & Wyoming
Montréal & Québec City
Moscow & St. Petersburg
Munich & the Bavarian Alps
Nashville & Memphis
New England
Newfoundland & Labrador
New Mexico
New Orleans
New York City
New York State
New Zealand
Northern Italy
Norway
Nova Scotia, New Brunswick &
  Prince Edward Island
Oregon
Paris
Peru

Philadelphia & the Amish Country
Portugal
Prague & the Best of the Czech
  Republic
Provence & the Riviera
Puerto Rico
Rome
San Antonio & Austin
San Diego
San Francisco
Santa Fe, Taos & Albuquerque
Scandinavia
Scotland
Seattle
Seville, Granada & the Best of
  Andalusia
Shanghai
Sicily
Singapore & Malaysia
South Africa
South America
South Florida
South Pacific
Southeast Asia
Spain
Sweden
Switzerland
Texas
Thailand
Tokyo
Toronto
Turkey
USA
Utah
Vancouver & Victoria
Vermont, New Hampshire & Maine
Vienna & the Danube Valley
Vietnam
Virgin Islands
Virginia
Walt Disney World® & Orlando
Washington, D.C.
Washington State

# FROMMER'S® DOLLAR-A-DAY GUIDES

Australia from $60 a Day
California from $70 a Day
England from $75 a Day
Europe from $85 a Day
Florida from $70 a Day

Hawaii from $80 a Day
Ireland from $90 a Day
Italy from $90 a Day
London from $95 a Day

New York City from $90 a Day
Paris from $95 a Day
San Francisco from $70 a Day
Washington, D.C. from $80 a Day

# FROMMER'S® PORTABLE GUIDES

Acapulco, Ixtapa & Zihuatanejo
Amsterdam
Aruba
Australia's Great Barrier Reef
Bahamas
Berlin
Big Island of Hawaii
Boston
California Wine Country
Cancún
Cayman Islands
Charleston
Chicago

Disneyland®
Dominican Republic
Dublin
Florence
Las Vegas
Las Vegas for Non-Gamblers
London
Los Angeles
Maui
Nantucket & Martha's Vineyard
New Orleans
New York City
Paris

Portland
Puerto Rico
Puerto Vallarta, Manzanillo &
  Guadalajara
Rio de Janeiro
San Diego
San Francisco
Savannah
Vancouver
Venice
Virgin Islands
Washington, D.C.
Whistler

# FROMMER'S® CRUISE GUIDES

Alaska Cruises & Ports of Call

Cruises & Ports of Call

European Cruises & Ports of Call

## Frommer's® Day by Day Guides

Amsterdam
Chicago
Florence & Tuscany

London
New York City
Paris

Rome
San Francisco
Venice

## Frommer's® National Park Guides

Algonquin Provincial Park
Banff & Jasper
Grand Canyon

National Parks of the American West
Rocky Mountain
Yellowstone & Grand Teton

Yosemite and Sequoia & Kings
   Canyon
Zion & Bryce Canyon

## Frommer's® Memorable Walks

Chicago
London

New York
Paris

Rome
San Francisco

## Frommer's® With Kids Guides

Chicago
Hawaii
Las Vegas
London

National Parks
New York City
San Francisco

Toronto
Walt Disney World® & Orlando
Washington, D.C.

## Suzy Gershman's Born to Shop Guides

Born to Shop: France
Born to Shop: Hong Kong, Shanghai
   & Beijing

Born to Shop: Italy
Born to Shop: London

Born to Shop: New York
Born to Shop: Paris

## Frommer's® Irreverent Guides

Amsterdam
Boston
Chicago
Las Vegas
London

Los Angeles
Manhattan
New Orleans
Paris

Rome
San Francisco
Walt Disney World®
Washington, D.C.

## Frommer's® Best-Loved Driving Tours

Austria
Britain
California
France

Germany
Ireland
Italy
New England

Northern Italy
Scotland
Spain
Tuscany & Umbria

## The Unofficial Guides®

Adventure Travel in Alaska
Beyond Disney
California with Kids
Central Italy
Chicago
Cruises
Disneyland®
England
Florida
Florida with Kids

Hawaii
Ireland
Las Vegas
London
Maui
Mexico's Best Beach Resorts
Mini Las Vegas
Mini Mickey
New Orleans
New York City

Paris
San Francisco
South Florida including Miami &
   the Keys
Walt Disney World®
Walt Disney World® for
   Grown-ups
Walt Disney World® with Kids
Washington, D.C.

## Special-Interest Titles

Athens Past & Present
Cities Ranked & Rated
Frommer's Best Day Trips from London
Frommer's Best RV & Tent Campgrounds
   in the U.S.A.

Frommer's Exploring America by RV
Frommer's NYC Free & Dirt Cheap
Frommer's Road Atlas Europe
Frommer's Road Atlas Ireland
Retirement Places Rated

## Frommer's® PhraseFinder Dictionary Guides

French

Italian

Spanish

# THE NEW TRAVELOCITY GUARANTEE

**EVERYTHING YOU BOOK WILL BE RIGHT, OR WE'LL WORK WITH OUR TRAVEL PARTNERS TO MAKE IT RIGHT, RIGHT AWAY.**

*To drive home the point, we're going to use the word "right" in every single sentence.*

Let's get right to it. Right to the meat! Only Travelocity guarantees everything about your booking will be right, or we'll work with our travel partners to make it right, right away. Right on!

*Here's a picture taken smack dab right in the middle of Antigua, where the guarantee also covers you.*

*The guarantee covers all but one of the items pictured to the right.*

For example, what if the ocean view you booked actually looks out at a downright ugly parking lot? You'd be right to call – we're there for you. And no one in their right mind would be pleased to learn the rental car place has closed and left them stranded. Call Travelocity and we'll help get you back on the right track.

Now, you may be thinking, "Yeah, right, I'm so sure." That's OK; you have the right to remain skeptical. That is until we mention help is always right around the corner. Call us right off the bat, knowing that our customer service reps are there for you 24/7. Righting wrongs. Left and right.

Now if you're guessing there are some things we can't control, like the weather, well you're right. But we can help you with most things – to get all the details in righting,* visit **travelocity.com/guarantee**.

*Sorry, spelling things right is one of the few things not covered under the guarantee.

*I'd give my right arm for a guarantee like this, although I'm glad I don't have to.*

*You'll never roam alone.*